AIRWAR

Also by Edward Jablonski

THE GERSHWIN YEARS, *with Lawrence D. Stewart*
HAROLD ARLEN: HAPPY WITH THE BLUES
GEORGE GERSHWIN
THE KNIGHTED SKIES
THE GREAT WAR
FLYING FORTRESS
WARRIORS WITH WINGS: THE STORY OF THE LAFAYETTE ESCADRILLE
LADYBIRDS: WOMEN IN AVIATION
MASTERS OF MODERN MUSIC: SCHOENBERG/BARTÓK/STRAVINSKY
DOOLITTLE: A BIOGRAPHY *with Lowell Thomas*
DOUBLE STRIKE
A PICTORIAL HISTORY OF THE WORLD WAR II YEARS
ATLANTIC FEVER
SEAWINGS

AIRWAR

EDWARD JABLONSKI

DOUBLEDAY & COMPANY, INC., GARDEN CITY, NEW YORK   1979

For my friends,
CLAIRE and PETER CLAY
once of the hospitable "George II,"
Luton, Bedfordshire, and now
of the "Coach and Horses," Rickmansworth,
Hertfordshire, England.

ISBN: 0-385-14279-x
Library of Congress Catalog Card Number 78–8213
Copyright © 1971, 1972, 1979 by Edward Jablonski

Preface

Sometime during the late sixties a friend and editor at Doubleday came up with an idea for a book. We had had some good luck collaborating on *Flying Fortress;* there were many untouched stories, and there were numerous sources for materials, not the least being a great number of former wartime airmen with ideas, recollections, and photographs.

The idea was to produce a book tentatively entitled *Great*—later *Famous Air Battles of World War II.* It was to be a one-volume work that would touch on those battles of the war—the Battle of Britain, the Tokyo Raid, Schweinfurt, Ploesti, etc.—that were decisive to a greater or lesser degree; we planned to trace the evolution of the battle planes of the time and, of course, the stories of those remarkable men who flew them. Without pilot and crew, an airplane, no matter how beautifully designed and formidably armed, is just a lot of hardware. Aircraft may spurt oil and burn, but they do not bleed or feel pain.

The work was begun and research soon revealed that there was much more to the Second World War in the air besides the "big name" battles—and big name aces. It was all rather overwhelming, for the subject seemed too large for a single volume and, even in a multivolumed work, required painful omissions and compromises. Research at home and abroad, face to face and by mail, accumulated an enormous amount of data, information, fact, a few fictions (many of our recollections improve with age), making it obvious that the original concept and title no longer held. Not every battle was famous, nor even great. We chose to drop the idea of recapitulating the war's top ten and to concentrate on the evolution of the twentieth century's deadliest form of warfare.

The result was finally published as four oversized, rather slender volumes; a single volume, at the time, appeared to be impracticable. As economic conditions improved, a two-volume book club edition proved to be reasonably easy to handle, encouraging the return to the original idea of a single-volume *Airwar.*

Meanwhile, letters from readers began to arrive. Most were encouraging, some complimentary, and others pointed out errors (which have been corrected) and omissions. A great number of these communications came from airmen who had fought in the war and their compliments were especially warming, since the author did not serve with the Air Force during the war. There were some complaints because certain units were not mentioned or a certain phase of a battle glossed over; one quite irate former P-47 pilot dipped his pen in poison and suggested that the old Thunderbolt had been slandered when he read that early models of the plane had serious structural problems. Since I had obtained my information from Republic Aviation and had checked my information with one of the P-47's test pilots, Herb Fisher, I felt I was on solid ground. I do hope the upset ex-Jug pilot did not carry out his threat to have all my books removed from certain libraries over which he had control!

Letters from youngsters were interesting. One was compelled to emphasize in replying to them that reading about war and looking at dramatic photographs of battles were not even remotely similar to the experience itself. The sounds, the terror, the stench, the pain, the misery, and that most mysterious experience of all, death, can merely be suggested in words and pictures. There is pride and patriotic satisfaction in studying strike photos with thick black smoke curling upward from an enemy-held city or stronghold or from a stricken battleship —or a disintegrating bomber. But enemy or not, the burning, maimed, and dying were human, as even you and I.

The World War II hobbyist, young as well as old, tends to overlook this fact in his pursuit of numbers, data, precise dates, and correct colors.

The major theme of *Airwar* is to underscore the courage and sacrifice of airmen of the Second World War, not to glorify their derring-do and fun and games. Since the narrative in general moves from highlight to highlight, there is one missing element so characteristic to war: boredom. So is cowardice, since the stories of those who cracked or shirked—or even ran—get swallowed up in the mass of day-to-day detail. Even a war such as that fought in 1939–45, a war fought by the United Nations for good reasons, inevitably produced its darker side. War profiteering, the production of inferior materials for money (at the cost of lives to those who used the planes and ships), military waste, civilian cupidity, and injustices of every description.

When we think of the Battle of Britain we think of courage, unity, sacrifice, but not of the young women of the Women's Auxiliary Air Force who returned to their bomb-wrecked bases in tears. They had gone into nearby towns and villages seeking sleeping facilities for RAF pilots whose living quarters had been destroyed by German bombers. In some places the WAAFs met with cold refusal; the townspeople blamed their own discomforts from bomb spillage on the proximity of the RAF bases, not on the Germans. And we won't go into the pub brawls that often as not resulted from the British view that the Yanks were "Over-paid, over-sexed—and over here." Despite remarkable British-American co-operation there were frictions and bickering. While these little-known incidents had little effect on the outcome of the war, they do underscore the fact that human failings did not disappear in the drama of great events and deeds.

And so it was with the fighting airmen of the war. While they shared the attributes, generally, of youth and good health, they were not supermen—not even Göring's Luftwaffe pilots. They fought in the war's most romantic—and romanticized—setting, which set them apart from the rest of us. Still, anyone who has seen the wreckage of a bomber and its mangled crew loses his appetite for the romance of aerial warfare. Even more compelling is the close study of what bombers had done to their objectives, or a strafing fighter plane to, say, a trainload of troops. And in wartime enemy trains also carried enemy civilians leaving beleaguered cities.

Motives, worthy causes, and patriotism aside for a

moment: consider the bomber crews. Weather permitting, they would have set out regularly as any airline pilot, or factory worker, as to a daily job. Only the job was to drop high explosives on people and property. And while accomplishing their "work," other pilots would come meet them high above the earth and shoot at them. Considered in the light of cold logic, this is not fit work for a human being.

Unfortunately, at the time it was a necessity and almost casually taken for granted. There were questions raised: Why bomb these cities? What is actually being accomplished? Why am I risking my neck? The Allies had very substantial reasons for fighting the Second World War and most such questions went unarticulated; and brave men, day after day, risked their necks and some lost.

The question of whether or not "strategic bombardment" contributed to the quicker ending of the war is not directly answered in *Airwar*; it is implied. Certainly air power decided the Battle of Britain and the Battle of Midway, among others—including the Battle of Japan. The control of air power did not always lay in the hands of airmen. Ground commanders had little conception of where air power should be and where it should not be applied to be effective. Civilian oracles were even more unrealistic.

While strategic bombardment did not accomplish all that its advocates promised and claimed, it did smash the German war machine, making it possible for Allied troops to occupy Germany and eventually its sacred city, Berlin. Had the Luftwaffe had the pilots, aircraft, and fuel—all having been decimated by strategic bombardment—that occupation would have come at a higher cost than it finally did. It was the same in the Pacific: Air power ruled the waves and bombardment wasted the industrial cities of Japan, and the tragic atomic bombings of Hiroshima and Nagasaki unquestionably shortened that phase of the war by at least a year.

This is not to claim all the credit of winning the war for the air forces, for the ground troops, as before, bore the brunt of the battles. This was as it was planned by their commanders; but without their flying brothers-in-arms, it would have been much worse.

The great lesson, if anyone is studying it, of the Second World War—especially as it relates to air power—is that of civilian participation and victimization. No longer can the civilian remain on the sidelines and profit from war and enjoy its dangers and thrills vicariously. When entire nations go to war there are no "innocent" civilians. That is even more true in 1977 than it was in 1945. Those men who fought in these *Airwar* narratives and photographs, fought (most of them) so that this theory might never again be tested. And those who lived, however nostalgic they may be for those exciting youthful days, continue to realize that it had not been a great adventure.

What they accomplished, and their sacrifices, should never be forgotten. Perhaps that is the purpose of *Airwar*, which has now come full circle. In this new one-volume edition—complete and, we hope, fully corrected—we like to think we may bring their stories to a wider, and understanding, readership.

E.J.

Contents

PREFACE   v

VOLUME ONE   TERROR FROM THE SKY

Prologue   Pax Germanica   3
  1. A Nation of Fliers   3

Book I   Blitzkrieg   19
  2. *Schrecklichkeit*   21
  3. "Sitzkrieg"   33
  4. *Was Nun?*   47

Book II   The Battle of Britain   79
  5. *Adlerangriff*   81
  6. Target: RAF   96
  7. Hell's Corner   107
  8. "The Greatest Day"   121
  9. The Blitz   137
 10. "Give it 'em back!"   149

VOLUME TWO   TRAGIC VICTORIES

Book I   Greater East Asia Co-Prosperity Sphere   3
  1. "Hark! The Voice of the Moment of Death"   3
  2. American Renegades   26
  3. First Special Aviation Project   49
  4. Midway: Tragic Victory   73

Book II   The Big League   109
  5. Millennium   111
  6. X-Squadron   132
  7. Tidal Wave   151
  8. Schweinfurt   173

VOLUME THREE   OUTRAGED SKIES

Book I   Kenney's Kids   3
   1. Buccaneer   3
   2. "Clearing the Air"   23

Book II   Some Sailors—And a Few Marines   51
   3. The Island   53
   4. Derailing the Tokyo Express   82
   5. Turkey Shoot   104

VOLUME FOUR   WINGS OF FIRE

Book I   Target Germany   3
   1. Blue Mediterranean Skies   3
   2. Reap the Whirlwind   36
   3. Kites over Berlin   47
   4. *Der Grosse Schlag*   74

Book II   The Divine Wind   125
   5. "Tyger! Tyger! burning bright"   127
   6. Whistling Death   160

ACKNOWLEDGMENTS   219

BIBLIOGRAPHY   223

INDEX   229

AIRWAR

VOLUME ONE

TERROR FROM THE SKY

Prologue
Pax Germanica

I

A NATION OF FLIERS

THE BATTLE OF BRITAIN, and perhaps the outcome of the European phase of the Second World War, was predetermined on June 3, 1936, in the smoldering wreckage of a single aircraft near Dresden, Germany. In later years Dresden would acquire immortality as the site of a more dreadful tragedy than the deaths of one German general and his sergeant-mechanic. But the smaller tragedy and the greater one would one- day be linked by the inexorable, blind dynamics of history.

The accident that summer day in a world relatively at peace was not impressive enough to make world headlines. The New York *Times* reported it deep inside the paper, on page fifteen. It noted briefly that, during an inspection tour of military bases, Generalleutnant Walther Wever, Chief of Staff of the Luftwaffe, had crashed in a takeoff while piloting his personal plane, a Heinkel He-70, the sleek *Blitz* ("Lightning"). With Wever perished his concept of air power, a concept which, four years later, might have spelled victory for his Luftwaffe in its struggle with the Royal Air Force.

To many an American reader wrapped up in postwar isolation, involved with his own Depression-inspired anxieties and eager to shun Europe's cyclic paroxysms, it came as a surprising revelation that Germany had an air force at all.

The *Times* noted that when "the German Air Ministry was created under the Hitler regime he [Wever] was transferred to that branch of the Army with the rank of major general. He became chief of Section 2 in the Ministry in charge of statistics, with the special task of studying the air forces of foreign powers. It was on his latest assignment as Chief of Air Staff that he was promoted to the rank of lieutenant general."

In 1936 the name of Adolf Hitler meant little to most Americans and the name of Walther Wever even less. Wever had served in the infantry during the First World War and in the Reichswehr (German Armed Forces) until Hitler had come into power. Youthful, dynamic, Wever was an advocate of very modern application of air power.

Had the American scanned the page on which the death of Wever was reported, he would have found little there to disconcert him, although the eventual impact of those events were to alter his life greatly within a few years. Two full columns were devoted to a study of "war rumors" in China which the leaders of that country stigmatized as "a plot." A subhead was terse: "Tokyo Doubtful of War." Another more compact article announced: "Peace Aims Snag on Reich Arming." An attempt to frame an air pact between Germany and Britain had failed. With one wary eye focused upon Moscow, Hitler boasted that his Luftwaffe was superior in quality as well as quantity to the Royal Air Force.

He referred to aircraft and numbers, not men; he was unaware of the fact that with the loss of Wever, much of the quality had already been lost.

II

In 1936 not even Hitler, for all his saber rattling, would have predicted another great war within three years. A master of the big bluff, he was fated, like the Kaiser before him, to blunder into catastrophe, taking millions of victims with him.

There are not any simple causes for war, but the summation of countless variables. But if one single element was required to ignite the Second World War that element was Adolf Hitler. In 1936 Imperial Japan was already on the march in the Far East, but without Hitler's Germany it is unlikely that Japan would have attacked Pearl Harbor. Without its Nazi ally Japan would not have been able to challenge the United States and Great Britain in the Pacific. A Second World War without Hitlerian Germany, therefore, is inconceivable.

An easy rationalization for what occurred in Germany during the two fateful decades 1919–39 has been the hard peace imposed upon Germany by the Treaty of Versailles. The terms of the treaty, however malevolent, did not create the mood and setting for the war to come, they merely supplied the later justifications. The implementation for the next war was set in motion on November 9, 1918—two days before the Armistice was signed, ending four of the most wasteful years in man's history.

This implementation was a secret mutual protection agreement between the newly proclaimed German Republic and the newly discredited German General Staff. It was brought about by a simple telephone call. On that November 9 the call came to Berlin over the secret wire which connected it with the Supreme Headquarters at the Hôtel Britannique at Spa in southeast Belgium adjacent to the German border. The new President, Friedrich Ebert, found himself speaking with Lieutenant General Wilhelm Groener (not the wily Hindenburg, who wished to disown any responsibility for dealing with either the enemy or the new Republic). The general, speaking for the High Command, offered a proposition.

Obviously the new Republic needed help and with the aid of the Army it might have a chance of survival. Ebert, who had known Groener during the war and trusted him despite his military credentials, was moved to tears by this generously offered hand from an unexpected quarter. The Republic, in turn, Groener then stipulated, must shelter the Army from the Allies. It was agreed, secretly of course.

It was an anomalous *mariage de convenance,* for the democratic Republic was avowedly anti-military and the Army, especially the General Staff, was equally anti-democratic. But they would need each other, they agreed, in the parlous days ahead —the virulent specter of Bolshevism rose like a grimy cloud in the east and vengeance-bent Allies rolled in from the west. This binding of the German government to the military doomed the Reich to a second dance of death—and the old dance was not yet over.

The Allies, hoping to maim Germany's ability to make war again, made the German General Staff one of its chief victims at Versailles. As the repository of Teutonic military philosophy the General Staff was dissolved, along with its fountainhead, the Kriegsakademie (War College). The Army was reduced to a mere hundred thousand men and its instruments of war were seized by the Allies or destroyed. All military aircraft were confiscated and the German Air Force disbanded. How, with all such restrictions, was Hitler in 1936 able to boast of an air force second to none?

The chief architect, the guiding genius, behind the military resurgence of Germany despite the restrictions of the Versailles Treaty and the supervision of the Inter-Allied Commission of Control was the all but unknown Generaloberst Hans von Seeckt. His very anonymity made him acceptable to the Allies to head Germany's token military force; his reputation as a brilliant military thinker delighted the remnants of the General Staff which still remained in the German Army.

What the Allies did not know then hurt them later. Seeckt regarded the so-called Great War as merely the first of a series which Germany might lose. But Germany would rise again, fight again, and ultimately win. Within the limitations of his small army Seeckt began resuscitating the discredited General Staff and building a new, elite,

Hans von Seeckt (1866–1936), brilliant architect of the resurgence of Germany's war machine. Despite the strictures of the Versailles treaty, and with the co-operation of the Soviet Union in the early 1920s, Seeckt created the antecedents of the panzers and the Luftwaffe even before Hitler came to power.

(NATIONAL ARCHIVES)

more modern Reichswehr under the very noses of the Allies. New, unwarlike names were devised for certain departments of the Reichswehr. The "Ministry of Pensions," for example, ostensibly under civilian control, was actually under the direction of "retired" Army officers. The function of the Ministry was in fact the collection of data on Germany's manpower potential for the next war. In the guise of "historical research," Seeckt's staff officers (although not designated as such) kept abreast of the latest military developments in the world.

Seeckt was no conservative; he fully appreciated the importance of mobility in warfare (as opposed to the attritional trench war of 1914–18). As for aircraft, nearly everyone in the previous war had been blind to its potential. Seeckt brought several airmen into the Reichswehr. Beginning with only three officers, the air branch of the Reichswehr quickly expanded to fifteen. Among the younger officers were Hugo Sperrle, Albert Kesselring, Hans-Jürgen Stumpf, and Wolfram von Richthofen, a former civil engineer and cousin of the celebrated "Red Knight of Germany." It was a good name for Seeckt's growing circle; in a few years all the names would stand for something.

But names only meant little in 1920, when Seeckt sought to improvise a German military renaissance. With a monocled eye on the greater objective, he managed to keep himself and his burgeoning little army out of the internal strife that erupted in Germany. His military elite was thus nurtured even while Germany's government and economy boiled and festered. Thanks to the agreement between the government and the Army, Seeckt was able to side-step those official inconveniences that might have interfered with his plans.

If he was able to dominate or hoodwink his own Minister of Defense, Seeckt was even more ingenious in solving the problem of how to revive the German Air Force and replenish the supply of aircraft which Allies so wastefully destroyed. If he could co-operate with his own government, which he detested, then why not take aid from a government he truly hated—the Bolshevik Soviet Russia?

Soviet Russia from about the summer of 1922, when an organization called Gesellschaft zur Förderung gewerblicher Unternehmungen (Company for the Advancement of Industrial Enterprises) was formed, contributed immeasurably to the rise of a newly militarized Germany. Known more familiarly as GEFU, the company was formed by a joint German-Russian group, the German members being trusted friends of Seeckt. The existence and function of GEFU was known also to Reich Chancellor Dr. Joseph Wirth and Foreign Minister Walter Rathenau. Wirth was especially essential to the project, for he was at the same time Reich Finance Minister, and Seeckt required additional financing which was not forthcoming from his stringent military budget.

Among the "industrial enterprises" established by GEFU was a Junkers aircraft factory at Fili, not far from Moscow (for Germans were forbidden to manufacture aircraft—in Germany). Another enterprise was named Bersol-Aktien-Gesellschaft, a Soviet-German operation at Trotsk, in the province of Samara. Bersol was to produce poison gas. Several factories for producing artillery shells were projected, and some built, in other sections of Russia. Finally, in the same spirit of dedication to the welfare of the proletariat, the Russians granted to Krupp, the German industrial empire, a large tract of land on the Manych River, a tributary of the Don, for use as an "experimental farm." This was ostensibly for the testing and demonstration of tractors and other farm equipment. A "large-size tractor," it might be noted, produced at this "farm" mounted a 7.5-centimeter gun.

At the same time training schools were established in Soviet Russia—all of this with the blessing of the saintly Lenin—where Germans and Russians could exchange the latest developments in the "art of war."

By 1923 an excellent training ground and tank school was established at Kazan on the Volga; there tactics were devised, vehicles developed, and leaders trained for Seeckt's new army. The seeds of Kazan reached full flower when German panzers smashed across the Polish frontier to open the Second World War and, later, Lenin's legacy to his workers came home too as Hitler's Operation Barbarossa.

The "air weapon," the other element essential to Seeckt's mobility concept, was reforged at the German Air Force Center at Vivupal, near Lipesk about 250 miles southeast of Moscow. The so-called "4th Squadron" stationed there was supplied from Germany through the free port of Stettin, where German customs officials winked when necessary. Military materials of embarrassing bulk were slipped across the Baltic under cover of night. German officers sent to Russia for training were first discharged from the Army. Should anything happen to them while in training, it would happen to a civilian, not a German soldier.

Among the early trainees graduated from the aviation school at Lipesk was Hans Jeschonnek, who would one day serve as Chief of Staff of the future Luftwaffe. Thus were hundreds of airmen trained in Russia during the late twenties—the nucleus of an incipient air weapon. At the same time new—and, according to the treaty, prohibited—aircraft were developed and tested in Russia and other countries.

Inevitable training accidents posed special problems, for there was no simple explanation for the shipment of German bodies from Soviet Russia. The Inter-Allied Commission of Control could not be blind to everything. But the solution was efficiently simple. The bodies of young airmen killed while training at Lipesk were returned to their families in Germany in crates stamped: "Machinery—Spare Parts."

To Seeckt none of this sub rosa activity appeared illicit, nor did it cross his mind that he was disloyal to Germany. He did, of course, scorn the so-called Weimar Republic with all its democratic, anti-military avowals. It was merely the instrument —a temporary one he was certain—for his own ambition to fashion a truly formidable German Army. "The Army," he said, "should become a state within a state . . ." which, under his administration, it certainly was, with its own laws and aims free of internal and international law. "But," Seeckt added, the Army "should be merged in the state through service; in fact it should become the purest image of the state." Thus a state dedicated to the art of war. To Seeckt the excuse of the Versailles Treaty was not necessary; he had begun making his plans long before there was such a treaty. All he needed was a lost war.

"We must become powerful," he declared, "and, as soon as we have power, we will naturally take back everything we have lost."

Meanwhile, civil Germany had become a political cesspool—also attributed to the Treaty of Versailles. Political factions, some of them quasi-military, proliferated as Germany itself sank into economic depression. The central hotbed of German reactionary movements was Bavaria, where the disgruntled gathered to voice their disgust with their government and to curse the treaty. It was in Bavaria's capital, Munich, that Seeckt met with the young leader of one of the more clamorous political groups, the German National Socialist Workers' Party. Seeckt was at the time hoping to put the party's own private army, the Sturmabteilungen, to his own use should he require additional hands to rid the Ruhr of the occupying armies of the Allies.

Seeckt was most impressed with the party's fanatical, ranting leader, who seemed capable of haranguing for hours on a subject dear to the general's heart: the criminality of the Versailles Treaty, the ineptitude of the Weimar Republic, and the eventual emergence of a mighty Reich. The party leader was, of course, Adolf Hitler. "We were one in our aims," Seeckt later said of Hitler, "only our paths were different."

Hitler had no intention of placing his Storm Troopers at Seeckt's disposal—as Seeckt had been misled to believe—for he had other plans for his bully boys. This was revealed in the abortive Bürgerbrau Keller fiasco in a Munich beer hall the following November when Hitler unleashed his elite ruffian band prematurely in a misguided Putsch. Among them was no less than war hero Field Marshal Erich Ludendorff, with dreams of glory of his own. Hoping to ride into the role of military dictator of Germany on Hitler's coattails, Ludendorff merely strode through the police firing line— miraculously unhurt—and out of history forever. Sixteen party members lay dead in the street; one party member, second only to Hitler, the ex-fighter ace Hermann Göring, was seriously wounded, and Hitler fled the scene in a thoroughly unmilitary style.

With his rivals out of the way—for Hitler was imprisoned for a while: long enough to dictate Mein Kampf—Seeckt could turn his attention to his own plans for a Putsch and his own dream of a military dictatorship. But within three years Seeckt himself would fall. Not, ironically, for his remarkable building up of a new German military structure or his all but inexplicable dealings with Soviet Russia—instead Seeckt provided comparatively trivial indiscretions which served as well.

For example, he issued an order entitled "The Proper Conduct of Duels Between Officers," which resulted in a small flurry in the press. Such arrant Prussianism at a time when the Germans were concerned with diminishing that wart in the profile of the national stereotype. With characteristic disdain, Seeckt chose to ignore the criticisms. Whereupon he committed another *gaffe*. During the autumn 1926 maneuvers of the 9th Infantry Regiment Seeckt gave permission to Prince Wilhelm, son of the former Crown Prince, to participate in the exercises. The Prince, as one of the deposed Hohenzollerns, was anathema to the sincere democrats and especially to the vociferous Left. The Socialist paper, *Vorwärts,* declared that Prince Wilhelm's presence, in full resplendent uniform, was "not simply a question of whether parliament or the military shall be the predominant factor in Germany; it is a question of democracy or militarism!"

With the world only recently made safe for democracy, it was obvious that Seeckt would have to go. But what few realized at the time was that by then Seeckt had already succeeded in making Germany safe for militarism. And to some extent his accomplishments were known to insiders. His "military genius," as historian John Wheeler-Bennett has written, was a unique combination: "the precision and accuracy of the soldier" and "the vision and imagination of the creative artist. For such he was, an artist in making bricks without straw, in beating ploughshares into swords, in fashioning a military machine which, though nominally within the restrictions of the Peace Treaty, struck admiration and awe into every General Staff in Europe."

By the time Seeckt made his exit, in October 1926, the presidency of the Republic had been filled by the great hero of the First World War, Field Marshal Paul von Beneckendorff und Hindenburg. Bitter because Hindenburg had not lifted a finger to help him, Seeckt permitted the formation of yet another political party around him, the Deutsche Volkspartei. When he realized, after little success, that his future did not lay in politics, Seeckt diverted whatever power his party had to the party he believed had the most promising future: Hitler's resuscitated Nazis. Seeckt died in 1936, never to know what he had done for that party's ultimate destiny.

Hitler, who had in 1923 appeared to be little more than a loudmouthed incompetent revolution-

ary, had within a decade worked his way into the Hindenburg government as Chancellor. Although the senilescent Hindenburg detested the lowly "Bohemian corporal," he was forced eventually to recognize the power of the Nazis. Hitler—by virtue of verbose spellbinding, blackmail, threat, cajolery, murder, and the aid from German big business, bankers, political conservatives, industrialists, Junkers landowners, and an enormous majority of the German people (who found Hitler's anti-Semitism, anti-communism, and anti-Versailles spoutings very good listening)—had made himself politically inevitable.

So it was that when Adolf Hitler became Chancellor of Germany on Monday, January 30, 1933, he was placed in a position to take over the government of Germany, thanks to Field Marshal Hindenburg. And thanks to General Seeckt he had the superb beginnings of a great war machine. Never before had a mere corporal owed so much to a field marshal and a general, particularly to the latter with his dream of the next war.

"The whole future of warfare," Seeckt had observed, "appears to me to be in the employment of mobile armies, relatively small but of high quality, and rendered distinctly more effective by the addition of aircraft. . . ." Although the term had not yet been coined, Seeckt in the early twenties had already visualized the concept of blitzkrieg.

III

There was no Luftwaffe as such when Hitler became Chancellor of the Reich. Significantly, his first important address, made on the very next day, January 31, 1933, was to the troops of the Berlin garrison. He charmed them all.

As for the Air Force, Seeckt and others had done well by Hitler. In 1926—when Seeckt was forced to resign—the German Air Force consisted of two fighter squadrons, a single bomber squadron, and an auxiliary bomber squadron. By 1931 there were four fighter squadrons, three bombardment squadrons, and eight observation squadrons. While the figures might not have been impressive—and they were not supposed to be—they contained within them hundreds of future air leaders, most of them trained in Soviet Russia.

There were other even less obvious developments. In 1926 also the Deutsche Lufthansa Aktiengesellschaft was created as a joint private and governmental enterprise. Lufthansa combined two of Germany's successful though financially unstable airlines, Deutsche Aero-Lloyd and Junkers Luftverkehr. This consolidation came about under pressure from the German Ministry of Air Transport, supposedly a civil agency, headed by a trusted Seecktian, Captain Ernst von Brandenburg. The captain had attained wartime immortality as the leader of the famed Bomber Squadron No. 3, the *Englandgeschwader,* which had flown the giant Gotha bombers to attack London from the air. One of Brandenburg's functions was to arrange for the training of future military (obviously bomber) pilots in special sections of Lufthansa's Deutsche Luftverkehrschule. In time there were four of these flying schools turning out civil pilots who could double as bomber pilots.

Board chairman of Lufthansa was Erhard Milch, an ex-German Air Force pilot who had been a salesman for Junkers. Milch was an astute, sharp-dealing, well-organized administrator. As an ex-World War aviator he naturally came into the sphere of Hermann Göring, who had found politics more profitable than postwar aviation in Germany. The gregarious, bluff, gross, and well-liked Göring loved to meet with other ex-war fliers and relive the beautiful days of the war. Those were the best years of their lives, when men were men and they fought like knights in single combat in the clean air miles above the trenches.

But when Milch sought out Göring in 1928 it was not to talk about the splendid days of the Great War. No romantic, Milch was concerned with more practical matters. Lufthansa was in trouble and needed government backing to survive. Göring with his reputation as an air advocate was the most likely representative in the Reichstag to approach on this matter. The two old fliers struck up a warm friendship and Göring, though he represented a minor party, did all he could to advance the fortunes of Lufthansa. He boasted to Milch that one day the little Nazi party would run Germany and when it did, Milch would have an important

role to play in the new German Air Force. Milch with his shrewd practical mind could hardly take *der Dicke* ("the Fat One") very seriously; and he did not make any effort to join the party.

When the Nazis did come into power Milch was asked by Hitler himself to serve as Göring's deputy Air Reichskommissar. Milch accepted on the condition that he remain Lufthansa's chairman. By April 1933 Göring was Air Minister and Milch Secretary of State for Air; in effect this signified the convergence of German civil and military aviation. Milch was efficient, ruthless, and ambitious; he obviously would fit into the scheme of things very well. There was, however, one slight hitch. His father had the taint of "Jewish blood" and an important platform of the Nazi party was a virulent anti-Semitism. This was easily remedied considering Milch's aspirations and abilities: his mother simply signed a statement in which she swore she had committed adultery. Milch was, it turned out, a pure Aryan bastard.

The advent of Hitler began to entwine the various strands of German society which had been unraveling since the Armistice. The masses as well as big business were behind him. Seeckt had prepared a military machine for him and Hindenburg put him in power. In truth, however, when Hitler became Chancellor, he had no real social program for Germany beyond a determination to "call to account the November Criminals of 1918" and his own ill-defined power lust. Nor, unlike Seeckt, did he have a military program.

In fact, Hitler, the eternal enlisted man, had little respect for the Officer Corps. On its part, the Officer Corps remained aloof from politics as Seeckt had insisted, smugly content with its privileged lot. Their only concern with Hitler was how they might use him to further their fortunes. Militarily Hitler, the leader of a rabble and such roisterers as the Storm Troopers and his private protective guard, the Schutzstaffel, was an amateur; he would be no great war lord. An intuitionist, Hitler was no practitioner of classic strategies.

But he proved more than the match of the Officer Corps as a tactician. He wooed them with respectful references to their honored traditions and to their important role in the state. He bided his time, as the officers preened, and then he ravaged all of

Adolf Hitler, leader of the New Germany, and Hermann Göring, leader of the newly spawned Luftwaffe, in an early happy hour greeting their admirers, the German people. Two men less capable of planning and *executing an aerial war could not be imagined: Hitler neither trusted nor liked aircraft and Göring did not understand them as a weapon of military strategy. This was their major combined contribution to the outcome of the Second World War.* (NATIONAL ARCHIVES)

them: Hitler transformed the famed German General Staff into an ensemble of lackeys. They were masters of nothing.

IV

The Luftwaffe was Hitler's pet; its leader was Hermann Göring, a good friend and number two Nazi. Beyond the Open Cockpit and Flames in the Sky mystique which Göring advocated, there was no long history, no accumulation of tradition and

privilege for Hitler to contend with, as with the Army. And there too was the proficient Milch, to set a new air force on a sound organizational and administrative basis.

The new Air Ministry, under Milch's direction, was formed from the old Commissariat for Air and the Transport Ministry. This last would naturally include Captain Brandenburg's flying schools for bomber pilots. Among those holding high office in the new Ministry were Oberst Walther Wever, who had been transferred from the Defense Ministry, Albert Kesselring, and Hans-Jürgen Stumpf. Göring, faithful to old comrades and to the glorious days of the Great War, saw to it that posts were found for two of his friends of the old days: Bruno Loerzer and Karl Bodenschatz. Youthful flying personnel were available in limited numbers from the school in Russia and in greater numbers from Deutscher Luftsportsverband, where flying enthusiasts learned the art of gliding under Kurt Student, a member of the Reichswehr Air Technical Branch. The most promising of these sporting pilots were sent to Lufthansa's schools for training on powered aircraft. Among those trained in the schools was Adolf Galland. Although ostensibly prepared for civil aviation Galland and other young German pilots received training also in combat flying, aerobatics, and gunnery.

By the beginning of 1934 Milch had projected an expansion of the aircraft industry and the German Air Force which would require more than four thousand planes. During 1933 the prototypes of the Heinkel 111 and the Dornier 17 were in the planning stage; though little known then these aircraft were to become notorious during the Battle of Britain. Milch's plans called for six bomber, six fighter, and six reconnaissance *Geschwader*. The *Geschwader* was comprised of from ninety to a hundred aircraft as compared to the *Staffel*'s nine. In 1931 the German Air Force was reckoned in *Staffels* (roughly equivalent to squadrons in the American Air Force); three years later Milch quite realistically thought in terms of *Geschwader*. Because Hitler was not yet ready to show his hand, such work was of necessity accomplished in secret.

Not so secret was the growth, under governmental encouragement, of "air-mindedness" among Germany's youth of both sexes. Göring fostered this enthusiasm by initiating annual competitions for civil pilots. On March 8, 1934, following a cross-country contest, he made the awards with characteristic verve. He was aware of Milch's planning and Hitler's dreams for the future, but he could not resist invoking the past in speaking of "the spirit of German aviation." It was a curious point to make: that the individual should become subservient to the state, considering that the fighter pilot of the First World War was an archindividualist.

Göring spoke glowingly of "the spirit that in four years of heroic life proved so successful and singled

out German aviation during the war—the team spirit among the crews.

"My comrades! We must admit that after the dissolution of the old German air service it was impossible to carry on the old spirit of comradeship in disciplined form. Most of us were uprooted from our work and the air service remained only a dream. The terrible longing for flying nevertheless remained in all of you." His next statement revealed a hint of the future. "The new Reich," Göring shouted, "has ordained that flying—even in forms other than sport and civil flying—shall rise again!"

This stirred the audience and Göring told them how they, the youth of the new Reich—one year having passed in Hitler's projected Thousand Year Reich—would contribute. "The young Germany," Göring promised them, "shall be brought up in a passion for flying in order that the German nation shall become a nation of fliers!"

He returned to the subject of the spirit of German aviation. "It is your duty to keep this spirit alive," he told them. "You have this duty to the sacrifices that your comrades have made in the greatest struggle of all times. We have the right to honor our heroes and to hold them up as models to our German youth. In no treaty is there a clause demanding the destruction of this spirit, but the cowards who have made our people unhappy for the last decade and a half have tried to break this spirit."

Göring could not close without a tribute to the Führer, from whom all these blessings came. The young aviators had dropped roses on Hitler's retreat, Haus Wachenfeld, near Berchtesgaden, at the close of the competition. In this luxurious villa Hitler too was able to enjoy some of his blessings among the magnificent vistas of the Bavarian Alps. From his terrace he could observe the young German fliers dropping roses, of which Göring said, "This compliment is the natural thanks. . . .

"For without Adolf Hitler, where would German pilots and German air transport be today? Where would have gone our dream—our longing—if he had not created the new Germany? Therefore, comrades," Göring concluded on a hushed note, "before I award the prizes, we will stand and think a moment in silent respect for our leader—our beloved leader—our people's chancellor!"

A year later, almost to the day that Göring summoned a "nation of fliers," the Führer officially announced to the world—on March 9, 1935—the existence of the Luftwaffe. Hermann Göring was named Commander in Chief, Erhard Milch was Secretary of State for Air, and Walther Wever was Chief of Staff. Within a week Hitler repudiated the Versailles Treaty with the declaration of a German Army of no less than thirty-six divisions (this would require some 550,000 men) and the reintroduction of conscription. The Reichswehr, the Officer Corps, and the underground General Staff were elated. At last they could operate in the open, Germany would once again take her place in the sun.

v

The "Bohemian corporal" was not such a bad fellow, after all. He had, in fact, behaved himself commendably so far as the military was concerned. Even the grisly Blood Purge of June 30, 1934 had certain points to the Army's advantage. The slaughter of Ernst Röhm and some of his unwholesome associates eradicated a serious threat to Army authority by curbing the Storm Troopers. If the Army lost two of its own in the contrived conspiracy, it was but the fortunes of war. But neither General von Schleicher, who had been Hitler's immediate predecessor as Chancellor, nor Kurt von Bredow was involved seriously with Röhm. The power of the Storm Troopers was smashed, however, and the military could make allowance for zeal. Hindenburg even sent congratulatory telegrams to Hitler and Göring, commending them for having "saved the German nation from serious danger." Even so, the Storm Troopers were merely superseded by the SS and Göring's private Geheime Staatspolizei (the "Gestapo"). Estimates of the murders, many of them settling intraparty feuds, ran as high as a thousand, although Hitler admitted to only seventy-seven.

That he and Göring succeeded in such mass slaughter without Army interference attested to the internal impotence of the Reichswehr. Irresolute, self-centered, and indifferent to all except their own small world, the Army had already been trapped by Hitler. This snare was further strengthened when he required them to take the new oath he had devised. It contained no pledge to sustain the German Constitution, nor to protect the German government. It did not even swear allegiance to the Reich. Instead, it was a personal oath of loyalty to the corporal himself:

I swear before God to give my unconditional obedience to Adolf Hitler, Führer of the Reich and of the German People, Supreme Commander of the Wehrmacht, and I pledge my word as a brave soldier to observe this oath always, even at peril of my life.

The Reichswehr was no more, supplanted by the Wehrmacht, of which Hitler assumed command. That the oath neglected both patriotism and legality did not concern the German generals; they were too preoccupied building up a thirty-six-division Army.

Even the Luftwaffe had grown considerably. Toward the end of March 1935 Hitler boasted to Sir John Simon, the English Foreign Minister, and Anthony Eden that his Air Force had already reached parity with the Royal Air Force. This was not true, but it had its effect. It was a diplomatic victory for Hitler in dealing with England and France. It also confirmed the fears of Winston Churchill, whose lone voice had been raised in warning against the rise of the Luftwaffe. Hitler's vain boast roused the British government enough to begin expansion of the Royal Air Force and to concentrate upon the single-seater fighter aircraft as outlined in Air Ministry Specification F5/34. Among the aircraft this inspired were the Hawker Hurricane and the Supermarine Spitfire.

Having come out into the open with his military plans, Hitler could proudly announce the opening of the Air Warfare Academy at Berlin-Gatow on November 1, 1935. The principal address of the day was given by the Chief of Staff, Generalleutnant Walther Wever, already widely respected and recognized as a leading exponent of the strategic concept of aerial warfare and a disciple of the Italian military theorist General Giulio Douhet. Greatly influenced, as were other military thinkers in Europe, England, and the United States, by Douhet's ideas, especially as expounded in *The Command of the Air* (1921), Wever was a proponent of the independent air force and of the heavy bomber. As such he was not in tune with Göring's Open Cockpit romanticism. Wever was a realist and a powerful, highly regarded officer whose impact upon the growing German air weapon was bound to be an important one.

He opened his remarks with an allusion to 1918 and the Versailles Treaty when "a leaderless nation collapsed internally and dashed the weapons from the hands of the gallant Army." It was the old refrain, The Legend of the German Defeat, still alive late in 1935.

"How will it be in the future now that a new weapon—the Luftwaffe—has appeared?" Wever asked. "Only in a war of the future will it reach full development. The Air Force, which came into existence hardly twenty-five years ago, found its great military origin in the Great War, from which glorious traditions have been handed down to the Air Force of today. Its greatest heroes are shining examples for us; Manfred von Richthofen—its proudest name. . . ."

Popular First World War ace and between-the-wars stunt flier, Ernst Udet. A dashing, ebullient personality, Udet was a superb pilot but had little conception of the meaning of air power in war. He was the advocate in Germany of the dive bomber (an idea picked up in the United States), which resulted in the Stuka concept. (NATIONAL ARCHIVES)

But, Wever emphasized, the air heroes of the Great War strove for something which only Hitler's National Socialism was making possible: ". . . a strong Air Force with independent status in the services." Wever, however, not wanting to slight the Army, was quick to indicate that an independent Air Force could co-operate with the ground forces where necessary, but he visualized a time when it would be possible to avoid "the positional warfare of massed armies," meaning, of course, the wasteful trench warfare of the Great War.

Wever then made his major point: "Never forget that the bomber is the decisive factor in aerial warfare. Only the nation with strong bomber forces at its disposal can expect decisive action by its Air Force."

Under Wever's direction specifications were drawn up for long-range, four-engined bombers. The result was the Dornier 19 and the Junkers 89, prototypes of which were ready for flight trials late in 1936.

Before this took place, however, Walther Wever died at Dresden in the summer of 1936. With him died the development of the heavy bombers. His successor, Albert Kesselring, canceled the Do-19 and Ju-89 to concentrate on medium bombers and the dive bomber, such aircraft as the Heinkel 111, the Dornier 17, and the Junkers 88 in the former category, and in the latter, the Junkers 87, the "Stuka."

In the reshuffling of the Luftwaffe's command following Wever's death another old Great War fighter pilot, Ernst Udet, was placed at the head of the Air Ministry's Technical Branch. The likable, good-humored, dashing Udet was a fine flier but not gifted with organizational or political skills. With his sunny personality Udet was too wholesome for the company he kept. As Germany's number one living Great War ace (with sixty-two "kills" to his credit), Udet's voice meant something to the amateurs in charge of the Luftwaffe after the death of Wever. Unwittingly Udet did them a disservice with his enthusiastic expertise.

In 1933 Udet visited the United States, one of his stops being the Cleveland Air Races. He was most impressed with the performance of the Curtiss-Wright BFC-2, the "Hawk." As the Curtiss Hawk II, the dive bomber was released for export and Udet, with Göring's help, was able to purchase two

The Junkers 52, all-metal commercial transport which was converted into a troop transport and bomber. As a military plane it first was used in the Spanish Civil War in 1936. (LUFTHANSA PHOTO)

A Junkers 87B Stuka of the Condor Legion over Spain. The Ju-87 proved most effective against ill-defended Spanish installations and received more credit than it actually deserved. (NATIONAL ARCHIVES)

of them in October 1933. The German government authorized payment of $11,500 each. In December Udet demonstrated the Hawk at the Luftwaffe's test center at Rechlin. He delighted in kicking the plane into a screaming dive and pointing it vertically at a pin-point target and then whipping it out of the trajectory dangerously close to the ground. Even so, the High Command was not awed by the performance. Major Wolfram Freiherr von Richthofen was especially unimpressed and resisted Udet's proposals for the development of such a plane (a curious sidelight, for Richthofen later commanded a Stuka unit).

Udet did not advance his cause any when in the summer of 1934 he lost the tail of one of the Hawks while stunting over Tempelhof and had to take to his parachute. But despite Richthofen's objections, by January 1935 development contracts for dive bombers were placed with Arado, Blohm and Voss, Heinkel, and Junkers. The designation for this class of aircraft was "Sturzkampfflugzeug," from which the popular term "Stuka" was derived. Although this referred to all dive bombers, it was the Junkers 87 which became widely known as the Stuka. The Ju-87 was selected over its competitor, the Heinkel 118, which Udet had managed to crash during a test because of his unfamiliarity with a small technical detail. Now head of the Technical Branch, Udet was able to proceed with his Stuka campaign.

Around this same time a new fighter, the Messerschmitt Bf-109, was undergoing tests at Rechlin. The Heinkel 111 had already been displayed at Tempelhof as a "commercial" aircraft with ten seats for passengers and a smoking compartment in the bomb bay. Less susceptible of simulation was the Dornier 17, which was rejected as a mail carrier and taken over by the Air Ministry as a bomber and nicknamed "the Flying Pencil." The first Junkers 88 took off on its test flight on December 21, 1936; it too was a medium bomber. Thus was the character of the Luftwaffe established by the close of 1936—a character much different from that envisioned by Wever in his speech at the Air Warfare Academy.

VI

In the summer of 1936 the new Luftwaffe and its young pilots and aircraft were supplied with a testing arena for their theories in Spain. That hapless country soon became an ideological battleground for the forces of the Left and the Right. Russia sent advisers, technicians, and equipment to the "Loyalists," the Popular Front Republican Government of President Manuel Azaña y Diaz. When the "Insurgents," led by General José Sanjurjo Sacanell (who was killed in the early fighting) and General Francisco Franco, sent out a call for aid from the fascist nations, both Mussolini and Hitler responded in his favor. Göring urged Hitler to intervene "firstly, to prevent the further spread of communism; secondly, to test my young Luftwaffe in this or that technical aspect."

Within a week men and equipment were en route to Morocco, where the fighting had begun, and to Cádiz. Among the aircraft were the Junkers 52, the Lufthansa transport converted to a bomber transport, and Heinkel 52s, obsolescent biplane fighters. By November 1936 the "Condor Legion" under command of Hugo Sperrle and with Wolfram von Richthofen as his Chief of Staff was formed. One of the fighter *Staffels* was commanded by the young "civil" pilot Adolf Galland.

Under Richthofen's direction the technique of close support was developed. Thus was Germany's supposedly independent Air Force wedded to the ground forces. That this was a violation of Wever's early plans went unnoticed in the success of the tactics in Spain. By the summer of 1937 more modern aircraft were dispatched to the Condor Legion.

The Messerschmitt 109B-2 began to replace the He-51s. It marked the end of the biplane fighter era. New tactics, particularly as developed by the youthful Werner Mölders (who replaced Galland as *Staffel* leader in the Jasta 88), proved most effective. The old Great War V-formations were abandoned in favor of the *Rotte,* a two-plane unit of great flexibility. (Two *Rotte* made up a *Schwarm* and three *Schwarms* a *Staffel.*) It was learned that in the old close formations the pilots spent a good deal of time avoiding collision and not enough scanning the sky. The lack of radio communications between aircraft, too, was found to be a serious handicap. The *Rotte* technique was eventually used by most air forces during the Second World War in the leader and wingman combination.

Richthofen, in time commander of the Condor Legion, found that the Stuka Ju-87, of which he had not approved originally, was a most terrifying and useful weapon in his close-support tactics. The ugly, bent-winged dive bomber, with the shrieking sirens attached to the landing gear, was hailed as a scourge of the battlefield. Only a few Stukas were sent to Spain, but these were widely used by alternating

Heinkel 111s approaching a Spanish town. When the He-111 was first introduced in 1936 it was passed off as a ten-passenger commercial aircraft. By late 1937 it was functioning as a bomber in Kampfgruppe 88 in Spain. (NATIONAL ARCHIVES)

A Condor Legion He-111 releasing bombs upon a Spanish town. The success of the missions without escort convinced the Germans that the bomber was impervious to fighter opposition. As with the Stuka, this misconception would come to roost during the Battle of Britain. (NATIONAL ARCHIVES)

Guernica: April 26, 1937. The bells in this burning church rang out to warn of the approach of bombers, a warning which was ignored by the people in the village, unaccustomed to air raids. By nightfall more than sixteen hundred lay dead in Guernica's burning streets. (NATIONAL ARCHIVES)

crews and proved most effective in attacks on such port cities as Valencia, Barcelona, and Tarragona. The Stukas also disrupted communications, destroyed bridges, bombed roads, and harassed troops with frightening invulnerability. Franco's Nationalists had by late 1937 achieved air superiority—thanks to the Germans and Italians—which enabled the Stukas to perform most successfully. It was the same also with the medium bombers which had preceded the Stuka to Spain, the He-111s and the Do-17s. Because they were superior to most of the aircraft of the Republican forces, the German planes gained a reputation beyond reality. The most formidable opponent encountered by the Condor Legion was the Russian Polikarpov I-16, the stubby, rugged little fighter—the fastest of its time. The early Condor Legion fighters, the Heinkel 51s, were no match for the I-16; not until the Messerschmitts

arrived in Spain did the *Ratas* ("Rats") meet a better contender.

The Spanish experience taught the Luftwaffe advanced fighter tactics, as well as the use of radio communications in combat, but the seeming invincibility of the bomber formations encouraged overconfidence, for which a dear price would be paid over England. Also the tradition of ground support as the major Luftwaffe function would take its toll in the future.

Still another tradition was established in Spain. On Monday—market day—April 26, 1937, at four-thirty in the afternoon church bells rang out a warning of approaching aircraft in the vicinity of the Basque village of Guernica. Nestling among the gentle hills of the Vizcaya province nearly twenty miles behind the front lines, Guernica had never been bombed although there had been raids in the area

*Guernica burns after bombing by German aircraft.
History's first senseless terror bombing.*
(NATIONAL ARCHIVES)

before. The alarm conveyed by the church bells meant little to the villagers and the farmers gathered in the market place. Ten minutes after the peal of the bells a formation of Heinkel 111s appeared over Guernica. Small, longish objects began to drop from the bellies of the aircraft; within seconds explosions erupted in the crowded streets of Guernica. Their bombs disgorged, the planes descended to low level and strafed the streets. In another twenty minutes Junkers 52s flew over to pour incendiaries upon the smoking terror of Guernica. These lumbering planes too came down to machine-gun the refugees attempting to flee the village. And so it continued, in flaming, dust-embroiled waves, for three hours until Guernica lay shattered and scorched. In the streets, in the broken cottages and houses, there were 1654 dead and 889 wounded—of a population of 7000.

Guernica was only the first name in history to stand for the fiery desolation from the air; others would follow: Warsaw, Rotterdam, Coventry, London. A nation of fliers had found its wings. Guernica symbolized its potent invincibility.

Only history, in the phrase of John Wheeler-Bennett in its "incalculable variations in the tempo of events," would endow it with fuller tragic significance.

BOOK **I**
Blitzkrieg

2

SCHRECKLICHKEIT

Hardly thirty feet above the fog-enshrouded ground the *Kette* of three Junkers 87B Stukas roared through the slumbrous countryside. Their engines resonating through the river valley, they looked like three ugly predatory birds with gaping jawlike radiators, contorted, splayed wings, and taloned undercarriages. Dangerously close to the earth because of the fog, the *Kette,* led by Oberleutnant Bruno Dilley of Stuka Geschwader 1, sought out its target.

Only minutes before they had taken off from their advance base at Elbing to find the bridges over the Vistula River at Dirschau. They were not, as they had in Spain, to destroy the bridges. Instead they were to keep them open to enable the German Third Army in East Prussia to join with the Fourth Army moving in from the west through the Polish Corridor. The bridges were a crucial supply and transportation link and, it was known, they had been mined by the Poles in the event of a German attack. Once the alarm was given the bridges would be blown and the fine timetable of conquest would be upset.

Dilley's problem was to sever the wires which lay in the left embankment of the Vistula at Dirschau. The fog and the darkness, for it was barely dawn of Friday, September 1, 1939, did not make the mission an easy one. There were trees to skirt and landmarks to seek which disconcertingly slipped past or disappeared in a patch of fog before they could be properly identified. At least the river was in the right place. For an instant Dilley saw the indistinct forms of the bridges emerging from the mist. Snapping his head from left to right, he noted that the others had seen the bridges also. He kicked the rudder and leveled at the left embankment. It would be a low-level attack, not the classic Stuka peel-off and screeching dive, as Dilley, followed by the other two pilots, plunged at the riverbank, released his bombs, and pulled up in as steep a climb as possible. The engine whined in near protest and that sound was coupled with the explosions. The rear gunners in the Stukas watched as the earth shook and erupted in a gush of smoke and dust.

Dilley glanced at his wristwatch: four thirty-four.

They had begun the Second World War eleven minutes ahead of schedule. It was a portent of things to come. Further: although they had hit their target and had, indeed, snapped the wires leading to the explosive charges on the bridges, the Poles had succeeded, by six-thirty, in blowing one of the spans which sagged into the Vistula. By then the war had officially begun.

The "incident" which had justified the unleashing of *Fall Weiss* ("Case White," the code term for the attack on Poland) had already been staged. On August 31 Hitler issued his "Directive No. 1 for the Conduct of War." Classified as "Most Secret," it read (in part):

1. Now that all political possibilities of disposing by peaceful means of a situation on the Eastern Frontier which is intolerable for Germany are exhausted, I have determined on a solution by force.

2. The attack on Poland is to be carried out in accordance with the preparations made for *Fall Weiss,* with the alterations which result, where the Army is concerned, from the fact that it has, in the meantime, almost completed its dispositions.

   Allotment of tasks and the operational target remain unchanged.

   The date of attack: 1 September 1939.
   Time of attack: 04:45 [written in red pencil]. This time also applies to the operation at Gdynia, Bay of Danzig, and the Dirschau Bridge.

3. In the west it is important that the responsibility for the opening of hostilities should rest unequivocally with England and France. At first, purely local action should be taken against insignificant frontier violations.

—Adolf Hitler

Harbinger of war: three—a Kette—Stukas such as began the Second World War in the early morning of September 1, 1939. (U. S. AIR FORCE)

Terror of the battlefield: with engine whining and propeller screeching, the very sound of the Stuka was frightening as it dived to release its bombs.

(U. S. AIR FORCE)

In his proclamation to the Armed Forces issued on the following day, Hitler stated that "Several acts of frontier violation, which cannot be tolerated by a great power, show that Poland is no longer prepared to respect the Reich's frontiers. To put an end to this madness, I can see no other way but from now on to meet force with force."

He was right about the madness. At the German city of Gleiwitz, for example, Polish troops attacked the radio station in the early evening of August 31. An excited voice interrupted the broadcast and shouted over the air that the time had come for war between Poland and Germany. The sound of shots could be heard also. When the foreign press members were taken to Gleiwitz the next morning they saw about a dozen bodies strewn about the area of the radio station—all in Polish Army uniforms.

They were, of course, dead Germans, condemned criminals who had been promised freedom if they participated in the "incident" and escaped. But even that possibility had been considered: all of the Germans had been fatally injected before the attack on the radio station. The SS leader of the operation, Alfred Naujocks, saw to it that those men who fell unconscious from the lethal drug rather than to gunfire were properly inflicted with gunshot wounds for the visiting newsmen. The entire operation had been planned under the direction of Hitler and Heinrich Himmler, leader of the SS. Polish uniforms and small arms had been supplied through the efforts of General Wilhelm Keitel, Chief of the Armed Forces, and Admiral Wilhelm Canaris, head of German Intelligence. While neither approved, neither did they object to Hitler's plans—which were known to them early in August.

II

Hitler's chief military aide, Field Marshal Wilhelm Keitel, whose major function was to agree with Hitler's contributions to the military art. His own final contribution to the war was being present at the surrender ceremonies when the war was over; later he was hanged for his role in the war.

(U. S. OFFICE OF WAR INFORMATION)

It was not to the professional minds of Keitel and Canaris an honorable means of making war, but all this was overlooked in the spectacular thrust of the German blitzkrieg into Poland. It was a kind of war which neither understood—just as neither understood Hitler. Canaris, however, was not the toady that Keitel was (a subservient sycophancy earned him the nickname among his fellow officers of *Lakaitel,* "Lackey"). In fact, Canaris was one of the earliest of the German conspirators who hoped to rid the Reich of Hitler. His conspiracies eventually cost him his life; but on the morning of September 1 Canaris visualized an even greater price when, with tears in his eyes, he said, "This means the end of Germany."

It was a characteristic exclamation, for the professional soldiers had little faith in the war that Hitler had unleashed against their better military judgment. But when Hitler ignited "the torch of war in Europe" the stunning advance of the Wehrmacht behind the Panzer divisions and the Luftwaffe's seemingly ubiquitous Stukas heartened the German generals as much as they shocked a breathless world. All along the German-Polish frontier the wheels of the German juggernaut ground into action. Laughing young, blond soldiers snapped the wooden frontier barrier gates—or smashed through in tanks. The Luftwaffe struck at Polish airfields, railroads, and communications lines, crippling aerial defenses from the beginning and rendering troop movements all but impossible.

In Berlin, Hitler watched the blitzkrieg on a massive battle map: the plan, he knew, was foolproof. Two Army Groups were smashing across the Polish plains toward Warsaw. Army Group North, composed of two armies—the Fourth, which flowed eastward from Pomerania across the Polish Corridor and then would turn south for Warsaw; and the Third, which struck westward from East Prussia toward the Polish Corridor, where, it was hoped, on meeting with the Fourth Army, it would race southward to the Polish capital. Attached to Army Group North, under command of General Feder von Bock, was Luftflotte 1, (Air Fleet 1) under Albert Kesselring, who had served as Luftwaffe Chief of Staff immediately after the death of Walther Wever.

Army Group South (Gerd von Rundstedt) was also to push toward Warsaw in a northwesterly direction through Slovakia and Silesia with its three

Hans Jeschonnek, Chief of Staff of the Luftwaffe when the Second World War began. Like many of the Luftwaffe's top echelon, Jeschonnek had been trained at the secret German Air Force center in Russia. A devoted admirer of Hitler, Jeschonnek (who once even begged Hitler to assume command of the Luftwaffe) was unpopular with his immediate chief, Göring.
(NATIONAL ARCHIVES)

Albert Kesselring, commander of Luftflotte 1 during the Polish blitzkrieg. (H. J. NOWARRA)

armies, the Eighth, Tenth, and Fourteenth. These units were supported by Luftflotte 4 under Alexander Loehr, former commander of the Austrian Air Force, which had been absorbed into the Luftwaffe via Hitler's infamous *Anschluss* in 1938. Chief of Staff of the Luftwaffe was the youthful—forty years old—able Hans Jeschonnek, "graduate" of the school at Lipesk in Soviet Russia, an ardent admirer of Göring, a devotee of Hitler, and an advocate of the high-speed medium bomber and the Stuka.

The two Air Fleets (Luftflotten) were virtually self-sufficient air forces whose components were made up of assorted aircraft types for various assignments as well as antiaircraft batteries (*Flugabwehrkanone*=air defense gun, or more simply *Flak*). The *Geschwader,* the basic tactical unit of the Luftwaffe, took its name from the type of aircraft which

The Polish fighter, PZL-11 (for Panstwowe Zaklady Lotnicze-*State Aircraft Factory). Designed by Zyg-* *munt Pulawski in the early 1930s, the PZL-11 represented Poland's first line fighter against the Luftwaffe in 1939.* (NATIONAL ARCHIVES)

comprised it. The level bombers, mainly Heinkel 111s and Dornier 17s, and later Junkers 88s, were designated *Kampfflugzeug;* the fighters, the Messerschmitt 109 (later the Focke-Wulf 190s), were assigned to *Jagdflugzeug Geschwader (JG)*; the so-called "destroyer" aircraft, the twin-engined Messerschmitt 110 fighter, were termed *Zerstörerflugzeug*. The Junkers 87, and other dive bombers, which included, in the initial days of the war, the Henschel 123, were assigned to *Sturzkampfflugzeug Geschwader (StG)*.

When the war erupted Kesselring's Air Fleet 1 had roughly 800 aircraft with which to support Army Group North (500 level bombers, 180 dive bombers, and 120 fighters). In the south Loehr's Air Fleet 4 had slightly less than 600 planes (310 bombers, 160 dive bombers, and 120 fighters). The Luftflotten total in the east was about 1390 planes (excluding reconnaissance and transport aircraft), which is considerably less than the number generally given as the Luftwaffe strength at the time. In brief, the Luftwaffe was a good close-support air force for the short war Hitler had in mind; he was hoping too that the French and English would permit him to settle "the Polish question" as they had all the other demands since the *Anschluss,* with little interference.

Compared to the less than second-rate Polish Air Force, the Luftwaffe was indeed a powerful Goliath. The total number of planes in the entire Polish Air Force was slightly over five hundred, of which less than half could be called modern. Even that figure tended toward excessive optimism. There were only thirty-six first-rank bombers, the PZL-37, the *Los* ("Elk"), available to combat squadrons on September 1, 1939. These were used to bomb advancing German armored divisions. The Elk was effective, and the Poles attacked with ferocious courage, but the small band was easily overwhelmed by both numbers and the superior performance of the German fighters.

The backbone of the Polish aerial defense force was the attractive gull-winged PZL-11c—the *Jedenastka* (the "Eleventh"). A product of the State

The Messerschmitt 109E, formidable opponent of the Polish Air Force in 1939. This plane was that of Adolf Galland, one of Germany's outstanding fighter pilots and air commanders. (H. J. NOWARRA)

Contrary to legend, the Polish Air Force was not destroyed on the ground in the opening days of the war. PZLs were dispersed to emergency airfields and camouflaged; Polish pilots succeeded in destroying about sixty German aircraft before the Polish Air Force was wiped out, most of it in air fighting with the superior Me-109s.

(EMBASSY OF THE POLISH PEOPLE'S REPUBLIC)

A Polish road after the Stukas had finished with it. (EMBASSY OF THE POLISH PEOPLE'S REPUBLIC)

Aircraft Factory (Panstwowe Zaklady Lotnicze, whence the PZL), the P-11, with its fixed landing gear, high wing, struts, and inferior top speed (about 240 miles per hour as compared with the Me-109's 300), was all but obsolete when the war began. Nor could the little fighters climb to the German bomber altitudes to intercept. In all there were about 158 first-line fighter planes in the Polish Air Force when the Germans struck. Of these there were 128 P-11s and 30 of the more outdated P-7s. Even if the Luftwaffe did not contain multitudes, it did easily outnumber the Polish Air Force around ten to one.

Contrary to the widely held belief, the Polish Air Force was not wiped out on the ground. Long before the tanks began to roll and the Stukas began swooping down on the airfields, the Polish planes were moved to well-camouflaged emergency airstrips. While serious damage was done to the runways, hangars, and the planes left behind, what there was of the Polish Air Force was generally untouched by the strafing attacks and dive-bombing.

The first German plane to fall in the Second World War was a Ju-87 Stuka brought down by Lieutenant W. Gnys (who would later serve in the Royal Air Force's No. 302, "Polish," Squadron in the Battle of Britain) piloting a P-11 of the Second Air Regiment, based at Krakow. Despite the victories it was a hopeless battle and typical of the Polish defense. On the ground Polish horse cavalry charged German tanks and armored cars with sword and lances. The cavalry was decimated from the air also when the Stukas attacked men and horses in the vicinity of Wielun, leaving behind an unreal devastation of dead and dying, smoke, flame, and futility. These were delaying tactics—for the blitzkrieg did not always plunge ahead inexorably—and they were disturbing. Heinz Guderian, commanding a Panzer corps, tells of how a section of his advance was held up by a Polish bicycle company. But these were fugitive and tragic efforts. On Hitler's large-scale map, safe in Berlin, the blitzkrieg moved ahead with breath-taking speed.

As the Poles were pushed back from the frontier they retreated inward toward Warsaw, creating pockets of potential resistance in the vicinity of Posen, Lodz, Krakow, and Przemysl. The roads were choked with retreating soldiers and fleeing refugees. Swarms of Stukas screamed down to bomb

Stuka fodder: a Polish girl weeps over her dead sister after the Ju-87s have swept by.

and strafe the highways in another Teutonic contribution to "the art of war," *Schrecklichkeit* (frightfulness). The roads disintegrated into a massive chaos of terror. The great Nazi steam roller crushed all before it, Polish mobilization was stopped before it had really begun, and resistance was dissipated haphazardly along the frontier or in encircled pockets. With no reserves to call upon the Polish Army was overrun by the panzers, motorized infantry, and the booted German Wehrmacht.

All roads led to Warsaw, which was the last stronghold and the prime target. Göring had had to cancel Operation Seaside, the full-scale attack on Warsaw scheduled for September 1, because of the fog which interfered with the aerial operations in the Army Group North area. The Warsaw-Okiecie airfield, home of PZL factories, was bombed by a few He-111s despite the early morning mist. By the late afternoon the weather had cleared enough for more intensive attacks by He-111s and Stukas. *Kampfgeschwader* 27, named for the World War I hero Oswald Boelcke, flew nearly five hundred miles from northern German bases for the first really heavy bombardment of Warsaw. Escorting the bombers were the *Zerstörer*, the Messerschmitt 110, the so-called "strategic fighter" or "destroyer." It was

Veteran of the Spanish Civil War and erstwhile passenger plane, the He-111 looses bombs on Warsaw.

Destruction on the Bzura River. Luftwaffe bombers spared Warsaw momentarily to smash a counteroffensive by the Polish Posen Army, delaying the blitz- *krieg. Luftwaffe close support broke the Polish offensive, with the Stukas wreaking the havoc in this photograph.*

(EMBASSY OF THE POLISH PEOPLE'S REPUBLIC)

Warsaw, September 25, 1939, bombed out of the war by the Luftwaffe. An He-111 sweeps in to add its *bombs to the already burning city.*

(EMBASSY OF THE POLISH PEOPLE'S REPUBLIC)

during these attacks on Warsaw that the first air battles of any size occurred between the Luftwaffe and the Polish Air Force. The Polish P-11s climbed in vain to reach the bombers; the Me-110s dived to intercept, the Polish fighters darted away. In a matter of minutes five of the P-11s had tumbled to the ground. In the few short weeks of fighting a total of 116 Polish fighters were destroyed in combat (of these 11 fell to antiaircraft fire, German as well as Polish). Some PZLs were lost when their pilots, in desperation, rammed the German aircraft to bring them down.

But nothing held up the German advance. Within a week the panzers of Walther von Reichenau's Tenth Army (of Army Group South) approached the outskirts of Warsaw. By this time the Polish Air Force had been all but completely expended; most of the first-line aircraft had been lost in the savage, one-sided dogfights. Almost as devastating was the supply problem, for without replacement parts and fuel the planes could not fly; communications, too, had been so disrupted that all military command broke down. Only a few of the Elk bombers continued to operate for a few days and then those remaining and the operational PZLs were ordered to Rumania. By September 17, 1939, the air war in Poland was over.

On that day the Soviet Army marched from the east to seal the fate of Poland. The Red Army met even weaker resistance than the Germans had; the Poles that had escaped the German envelopments were pushed back into the Nazi pincers or were captured by the Russians. With neither an army nor an air force, Poland was finished as a fighting power. "The German Luftwaffe," the Wehrmacht report stated, "has won undisputed mastery over the whole of Poland."

But Warsaw remained, crowded with refugees and fleeing soldiers whose officers rallied to a last-ditch defense. The encircled city became a honeycomb of trenches and improvised barricades as civilians and troops alike prepared for the German attack. The government had already fled to Lublin, and then into Rumania—and internment. By September 13 Operation Seaside, the aerial devastation of Warsaw, was reinstated. In the train of the onrushing German troops, the Luftwaffe had set up temporary airstrips within easy striking distance of the capital.

The first sizable air raid occurred on September 13 when Wolfram von Richthofen ordered an attack on military targets—rail centers, public utilities, military establishments—within the city. Later Richthofen was to say that the "chaos over the target was indescribable." The first major aerial attack of the Second World War was not, by German standards, very worthy of those high standards which they had been demonstrating for the past two weeks to a stunned and frightened world. The bombing timetable went awry and various units came in over Warsaw haphazardly. With more than 180 aircraft converging on the target area there were collisions and confusion. But to the terrorized Poles below it was not confusion of command and timing, but a sky filled with aircraft dropping bombs.

Following this attack, Warsaw was given some respite from the air when the bombers were called off to assist the German Eighth and Tenth Armies under pressure of an offensive suddenly launched by the Polish Posen Army, which had been bypassed during the first week of the war. While the Stukas and He-111s and Me-110s were dealing with the Poles in the Bzura River fighting, the dropping of leaflets pleading for the Poles to surrender began fluttering down upon Nazi-encircled Warsaw. Posters soon appeared upon buildings and trees in Warsaw's outskirts promising those who surrendered food and good treatment. But the pleas went unheeded and all attempts by the Germans to propagandize the Poles into surrendering Warsaw "to prevent useless bloodshed and the destruction of the city" failed. The Poles had already witnessed sufficient German frightfulness along their highways, in the villages and towns, and in some Warsaw suburbs to realize the propaganda promises were delusion. They chose to fight to the end. Those who survived had worse than death in store for them. Behind the Wehrmacht into Poland came Dr. Robert Ley, ex-chemist, alcoholic, and chief of the German Labor Front, who believed that "Germans can never live in the same condition as Poles and Jews." And as he conscripted slaves for German industry, he was as good as his word.

On the day that the Russians began moving upon Poland, September 17, the first real mass attack on Warsaw was canceled when it appeared that the Poles were willing to negotiate for the evacuation of civilians and foreigners. The Polish representative did not appear to negotiate. With the Russians

Warsaw after the air blitzkrieg by Richthofen's bombers. ". . . everything was quiet. Warsaw was a dead city."

swarming in from the east, it was even more important to the Germans that Warsaw fall. For the next several days, until September 24, millions of leaflets rained down upon the beleaguered city promising honorable surrender terms—officers would even be permitted to keep their swords!

At eight o'clock in the morning, September 25, Richthofen unleashed the Luftwaffe upon Warsaw. At his disposal were 8 *Gruppen* (240 aircraft) of the Ju-87 Stukas, some He-111s, and a *Gruppe* of the clumsy Junkers 52 transports. In all Richthofen had about 400 aircraft to deal with Warsaw (the usual accepted number has been 800), not an im-

pressive number once again. But never before in the world's history had 400 planes attacked a single city. Here was the sequel to Guernica modernized, refined, and revised according to the concept of *Schrecklichkeit*. Flying two or three sorties through the day, Richthofen's forces were magnified into a massive destructive weapon.

The Stukas began with their familiar shriek, unleashing their bomb loads into the city. Thirty Ju-52s flew low over Warsaw to deliver the incendiaries into the churning clouds of flame, debris, mortar dust, and smoke. These clumsy craft were not ideally suited for their assignment; the incendiary bombs

General Wolfram von Richthofen (center foreground), cousin of the intrepid Red Baron of the First World War and Stuka specialist of the Second. Although originally cool to the idea of dive bombers, Richthofen learned to use them in Spain and then employed the Stukas with devastating skill in Poland. To his left is General Richard Ruoff, whose V Corps troops Richthofen's dive bombers supported in the conquest of France which came later. (HEINZ J. NOWARRA)

were literally shoveled out of their large side entrances (these were specifically for paratrooper use). The lumbering trimotored aircraft were slow and at least two fell to Polish antiaircraft fire. Also, the method of delivering the bombs did not make for accuracy, for thanks to a strong eastern wind, some of the incendiaries fell among German troops. An

immediate demand was made by Eighth Army headquarters for the cessation of the bombing, but Hitler, who had flown to the battle zone in his own Ju-52, instructed Richthofen to continue over the protests of Brauchitsch.

By late morning Warsaw lay under a pillar of smoke that coiled up thousands of feet into the air. And still the bombers came, although it was practically impossible to find specific targets because of the smoke and destruction. By nightfall five hundred tons of high-explosive bombs and seventy-two tons of incendiaries had been dropped into Warsaw. To this was added the massed artillery which encircled the city. After the planes had left the artillery continued.

The red glare of Warsaw's flames could be seen for miles around, as German and Pole alike stood in awe of what the bloody glow in the sky signified. On the next day Warsaw agreed to surrender; food had all but run out, the water supply was ruptured, and ammunition had been expended. The defenders of Warsaw officially capitulated on September 27, 1939. In less than a month Hitler's blitzkrieg had erased Poland, with the help of the accommodating Soviet Army, from the map.

Walter Schellenberg, a young SS intelligence officer, entered what remained of Warsaw and "was shocked at what had become of the beautiful city I had known—ruined and burnt-out houses, starving and grieving people. The nights were already unpleasantly chilly and a pall of dust and smoke hung over the city, and everywhere there was the sweetish smell of burnt flesh. There was no running water anywhere. In one or two streets isolated resistance was being continued. Elsewhere everything was quiet. Warsaw was a dead city."

Tomorrow the world.

3

"SITZKRIEG"

Forty-eight hours after Hitler had launched his blitzkrieg, Great Britain and France submitted their ultimatums to Berlin. Hitler still had hopes for a swift, tidy German-Polish war to be followed by a breathing spell before he made his next move. But the determined British and the reluctant French had decided to honor their promise to fight if Germany violated the independence of Poland. The policy of appeasement had come to an end and on Sunday afternoon, September 3, 1939, the tired voice of Neville Chamberlain informed the world that Britain had declared war upon Germany to fight against "brute force, bad faith, injustice, oppression and persecution."

When Göring learned of the British ultimatum, delivered at nine in the morning by Nevile Henderson, he exclaimed (echoing the view of Canaris), "If we lose this war, then God help us!"

Hitler's solution to "the Polish question" had now become the Second World War. His partner in the "Pact of Steel," Mussolini, backed down at the last moment and informed Hitler that he could not take part in military operations "in view of the *present* state of Italian war preparations."

If Hitler was unable to count upon Mussolini, he had found a worthy ally in Stalin, with whom he had had the audacious foresight to make a Treaty of Non-Aggression (Nazi-Soviet Pact) before embarking upon the Polish adventure. Thus had Hitler spared his nervous High Command the terrors of

Zweifrontenkrieg (war on two fronts). Thanks to his prescience Hitler had turned this double-front war upon the Poles and the campaign had gone smoothly and at a reasonably small cost. This may have been small comfort to the families of the 13,-981 Germans killed in the Polish invasion and of little strategic import to the 30,322 maimed and wounded. The Polish casualty figures because of the savage fighting, confusion, and destruction may never be known. As for the Luftwaffe, it had lost 734 men and 285 aircraft, over a hundred of which were bombers.

After the partition of Poland by Germany and Russia the period followed which Neville Chamberlain called fittingly a "twlight war" and which many Americans referred to cruelly as the "phony war" (a phrase attributed to the isolationist Senator William E. Borah). Following the devastation of Poland there came a strange pause in the blitzkrieg, a sitting war, or "sitzkrieg," in the press. Along the Western Front it was quiet indeed. Neither the Germans nor the Allies seemed anxious to make the first move. The mood in a still invulnerable America was observed, sadly, by Undersecretary of State Sumner Welles, who found that "many people appeared to feel, like Senator Borah, that the failure of Great Britain and France to undertake the offensive was somehow reprehensible. This feeling was almost sadistic."

Nor were the Germans eager to go on the of-

Hitler and Luftwaffe chief Göring in Poland, September 1939, to survey the results of the blitzkrieg. It was a high moment for both, for Hitler's Fall Weiss *had succeeded in answering "the Polish question" and the Luftwaffe had contributed to the bloody solution.*
(H. J. NOWARRA)

fensive. Just two days before he unleashed *Fall Weiss* Hitler had said, "In two months Poland will be finished and then we shall have a great peace conference with the Western powers." But it had not turned out that way—and besides, the High Command did not feel ready to launch a western offensive. Most seemed to agree with the Commander in Chief of Army Group C (which faced the French opposite the Rhine and the Maginot Line), Wilhelm Ritter von Leeb, who wrote, "The sword does not have the edge which the Führer seems to assume." Leeb had in mind the great number of less than first-rate (older men, ill trained) troops under his command, some of whom were already muttering, "It is the generals who push the war."

But the generals were not pushing the war; even Hitler, speaking is Berlin on October 6, 1939—the day after he had entered a wasted Warsaw—appeared to be pushing peace. "Every German soldier," he told the Reichstag and the world, "has the greatest respect for the feats of the French

Army. At no time and in no place have I ever acted contrary to British interests." He continued with a statement of his aims by saying that his "chief endeavor has been to rid our relations with France of all trace of ill will . . ." and that he fervently believed "even today that there can only be real peace in Europe and throughout the world if Germany came to an understanding . . ."

But when he came to the crux of their misunderstanding, Hitler took another stance. "Why should this war in the west be fought?" he asked. "For the restoration of Poland? Poland of the Versailles Treaty will never rise again." He reminded his listeners that this was assured by Nazi Germany and Soviet Russia. Despite what German newspapers called "Hitler's Peace Offer," the speech contained nothing upon which negotiations could be initiated. Hitler closed with a veiled warning. "And let those who consider war to be the better solution reject my outstretched hand."

It was, as usual, the iron fist in the velvet glove, for ten days previously he had already instructed

A French poilu in the spring of 1940, dug in on the Western Front, during the period described as the "phony war." Writing home, the soldier evokes the stagnation of trench warfare of the First World War. That he does not bother to wear a steel helmet is an indication of the general air of non-belligerence of the time. (U. S. INFORMATION AGENCY)

the Wehrmacht High Command to formulate plans for an early attack in the west, an attack that would strike through neutral Belgium and Holland. The generals were thrown into alarmed opposition. They argued that the steel shortage would seriously affect the outcome of a prolonged war—especially as it concerned the production of aircraft—and that the approaching winter, with its short days and certain fog, would interfere with air support. This argument went on for months between the Army High Command on one side and the Führer on the other during the so-called phony war.

II

During this period, however, there was no phony war at sea, where the German U-boats sank British merchant ships, or where the German pocket battleship *Graf Spee,* after a successful career as the scourge of the south Atlantic, was found by the British Navy and driven into the port of Montevideo, Uruguay, where the German captain scuttled his ship and committed suicide.

Also during the period of Hitler's "command crisis," his partner in war Stalin began activities in the Baltic regions to close off the northern approaches to the Soviet Union. "Treaties" were forced upon Estonia, Latvia, and Lithuania which agreed to the establishment of Russian garrisons, as well as naval and air bases in the Baltic states. Finland, however, refused to be bullied into a treaty. The Russians demanded a strip of the Karelian Isthmus, connecting Finland and the Soviet Union, from which it would be possible to shell Leningrad. In addition, there was the port of Hangö, which the Russians had wanted for thirty years as a naval base. In exchange the Russians would happily cede more than two thousand square miles to Finland along their common frontier. Finland found such demands incompatible with their definition of national sovereignty and neutrality. The predictable ensued: attacks in *Pravda,* broken-off negotiations, and border incidents in which the Finns were cast as villains. On November 30, 1939, Russian bombers attacked Viipuri and Helsinki.

The Winter War of 1939–40 was no blitzkrieg. Although greatly outnumbered, the Finns fought

The Graf Spee, *one of the most formidable of Germany's small battleships which operated in the south Atlantic in the winter of 1939. A float plane is in readiness on a catapult aft of the stack. Damaged in a battle* *with British cruisers off South America and unable to escape, the ship was scuttled by its own crew. The captain, Hans Langsdorff, after writing a letter of explanation, committed suicide.* (NATIONAL ARCHIVES)

grimly and imaginatively in the cold, heavily forested terrain. Entire Russian divisions were wiped out in the ghostly, white landscapes. But the Russian masses, tanks, and aircraft, and in time, better leadership, made the difference. The Treaty of Moscow was signed on March 12, 1940. The northern approaches to the Soviet Union were secured at great cost: at least 200,000 Russian dead and nearly 25,000 Finnish dead. It was another deadly move in the massive chess game between the two master dictators. Hitler, despite German sympathies for Finland and Mussolini's outspoken criticism of the German-Soviet Pact, needed Russian aid to circumvent the British blockade. It was still a one-front war—even though Russian naval and air bases in the Baltic could only have an eventual, and obvious, function. Stalin trusted Hitler no more than Hitler trusted Stalin.

Hitler, in fact, during these uncertain months of the "twilight war," could hardly have felt much trust in anyone whether ally, friend, or foe. Using the bad weather as justification he continued to postpone the attack in the west while goading his generals to prepare a blueprint for such an attack and to agree to carry it out. By early January it seemed that he would have his way. With clear weather forecast by midmonth, the day of attack was set (for at least the sixth time) for January 17. But then, for even the gods of war have been known to laugh, another hitch in plans came about.

Luftwaffe Major Helmut Reinberger, commander of the paratrooper school at Stendal, was summoned to assist in the planning of air-borne operations in Holland and Belgium. He was on his way to meet with Kurt Student's staff in Cologne but was held up by the congestion in the Ruhr area railways. In Münster he met a Luftwaffe major, Erich Hoenmanns, in the officers' club and explained his problem. Hoenmanns, eager to visit his wife in Cologne, offered to fly Reinberger to his conference the next morning—January 10. Although he was not supposed to fly while carrying highly secret documents, Reinberger was anxious to be on his way.

They took off the next morning in a Messerschmitt 108, the *Taifun* ("Typhoon"), a prewar sportplane converted into a courier and personal transport. The major was familiar with neither the craft nor, apparently, the route. For in the clouds the little monoplane with the two passengers became lost and off course. In attempting to find his way Hoenmanns inadvertently flicked the wrong switch and turned off the engine.

There was nothing to do but crash-land the *Taifun* near the Rhine River, which Hoenmanns found below the clouds. Except that it was the Meuse, not the Rhine, and they were not in Germany, but in neutral Belgium near Mechelen-sur-Meuse.

When Belgian soldiers arrived at the crash scene they found Reinberger attempting to burn the contents of his briefcase. The fire was stamped out and Reinberger and the hapless Hoenmanns, as well as what remained of the papers, were taken to a nearby army camp. There, too, Reinberger attempted to destroy the papers, which had been placed upon a convenient table, by tossing them into an equally convenient stove. But again the incriminating documents were retrieved from total destruction. Reinberger was certain, as he later reported to Göring, that all that remained were "insignificant fragments, the size of the palm of my hand." He would, naturally, have been most anxious to make that point.

But how much of the papers actually remained? One thing was certain: copies of the fragments which escaped Reinberger's frenetic pyromania were sent to the British and French. There was consternation in all camps. The Germans could not be sure that Reinberger had really succeeded in destroying enough of the evidence. On the other hand, had the Germans, wise war makers that they were, deliberately let the papers fall into the hands of the Belgians? The Allies tended to overestimate the German penchant for adroit skulduggery and leaned toward the latter interpretation. Even the Belgians, who would be among the first to suffer if the plans materialized, did not take the papers seriously enough. Mobilization of the Belgian Army was accelerated, but there was no attempt to unite with the British and French, however, to face the inevitable.

The conferences in Berlin meanwhile were desperate, clouded with doubt and clamorous. Hitler affected an icy calm, always a dangerous sign. Göring, embarrassed by his Luftwaffe, ranted and swore dire retribution. However, it devolved upon Colonel General Alfred Jodl, Chief of the Wehrmacht's Operations Staff, and Hitler's military "adviser" Keitel to determine the next move depending upon how much they thought the Belgians—and the French and British—had learned. The situation was characteristically manic-depressive. One moment all agreed that Reinberger had burned the plans and the next moment they were not so certain. Word had reached Berlin of Belgian troop movements along the frontier. Three days after the incident Jodl noted that a decision had been made: "Order to General Halder [Chief of the Army General Staff] by telephone—All movements to stop."

The Führer was unperturbed (he now had an excuse for another postponement which he could blame on others) as Göring unleashed his vendetta. General Helmuth Felmy, commander of Luftflotte 2, to which Reinberger belonged, and Oberst Josef Kammhuber, his Chief of Staff, were immediately relieved. Felmy, never a Göring favorite, was retired to civil life (though he would later be recalled to serve in Russia) and Kammhuber was sent to Bavaria to command a bomber unit. Kesselring, at the time commanding Luftflotte 1, replaced Felmy.

III

With the attack in the west postponed until the spring (for the weather, too, had turned against the Germans), Hitler turned his eyes northward. The Russians had moved into Finland; it seemed that inevitably the Allies would also invade Scandinavia to cut off that line of approach. Hitler resolved to "save" Norway and Denmark from such a drastic fate. There was the matter, too, of Sweden's supply of iron ore, upon which the German war economy depended so heavily. Equally consequential was the point raised by that stepchild of the Wehrmacht the German Navy. Grossadmiral Erich Raeder insisted that the Imperial Navy could make something of itself if it could operate from bases in Norway, say at Trondheim and Narvik, instead of being bottled up in the North Sea by the Royal Navy.

When Raeder brought up the proposal for a Scandinavian campaign Hitler was in a receptive mood. If he had any fleeting doubts, these were quickly resolved by the doughty and resourceful British.

The auxiliary supply ship *Altmark*, which had been attached to the scuttled *Graf Spee*, had made its way up from the south Atlantic and had slipped through the British blockade into Norwegian waters.

Grand Admiral Erich Raeder, in a prewar portrait. Anxious to make a name for the German Navy, Raeder pressed for an invasion of Norway and Denmark—a move which nearly cost him his fleet. He was later succeeded by Karl Dönitz. (U. S. INFORMATION AGENCY)

The British knew that the *Altmark* carried captured British seamen, survivors of the encounters with the *Graf Spee*. Agents in Norway reported the presence of the *Altmark* and a Lockheed *Hudson* of the RAF's Coastal Command Squadron No. 220 was dispatched to confirm. The *Altmark* was located and soon a British destroyer flotilla converged on the German ship. A Norwegian boarding party inspected the *Altmark* and assured the skeptical British that the German ship was unarmed and carried no prisoners. Winston Churchill, First Lord of the Admiralty, ordered Captain Philip Vian of H.M.S. *Cossack* and commander of the British flotilla, to board the German vessel.

It was night, February 16, 1940, and the *Altmark* had taken refuge in Josing Fiord. With searchlights blazing, the *Cossack,* with Vian aboard, lanced into the narrow inlet. The Norwegian gunboat *Kjell* was first encountered and, with a nod to international law, Captain Vian invited its captain to join him in a search of the *Altmark;* pointedly the British captain made it clear that he intended to board the German ship and release the prisoners he knew were aboard but which the Norwegians apparently could not find. There was no further intervention on the part of the Norwegians.

The *Cossack* then pulled alongside the *Altmark*, which had grounded itself in an escape attempt, the ships were grappled, and a boarding party swarmed over the side. It was like a page out of the career of Francis Drake. There were hand-to-hand combats in which four Germans were killed, several wounded, and a number fled over the side. To the cries of "The Navy's here!" the 299 "non-existent" British seamen were released from locked storerooms and empty oil tanks. In addition to the prisoners Vian also noted several guns, overlooked by

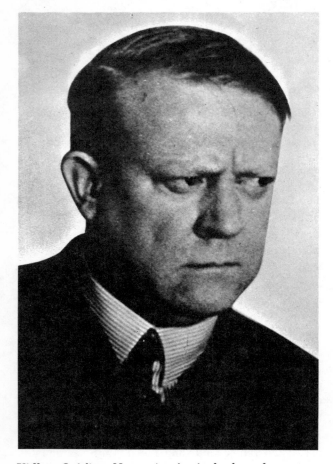

Vidkun Quisling, Norwegian fascist leader, whose name became a synonym for traitor. Quisling assisted the Germans in their invasion of Norway in 1940. Under Nazi occupation Quisling served as premier; after the war he was tried, convicted, and executed for high treason. (NATIONAL ARCHIVES)

the Norwegians, who remained, in the words of Churchill, "passive observers throughout."

Three days later Hitler, who could not remain passive in view of the British resolution, ordered final plans for the "occupation" of Denmark and Norway. "This operation," he stated in a directive dated March 1, 1940, "should prevent British encroachment in Scandinavia and the Baltic. Further it should guarantee our ore bases in Sweden and give our Navy and Air Force a wider starting line against Britain."

Meanwhile the Allies had also been giving serious thought to the strategic importance of Norway and its northern port, Narvik. It was there that Swedish ore was sent via rail for shipment through the North Sea when the Baltic was closed by winter ice. There had even been a plan during the Russo-Finnish War to send troops to help the Finns through Narvik and across Sweden. This raised the question of transit rights across these two neutral countries which the Allies did not actually need to face; the surrender of Finland in March of 1940 made it all academic. Rumors of Allied intentions had already reached Hitler, some through the Norwegian Nazi Vidkun Quisling. Clearly aid to Finland would cut off the Swedish ore, for the English and French would occupy Narvik and the railroad from Narvik to Luleå, Sweden. But the collapse of Finland spoiled Hitler's rationale as well as that of the Allies.

Each side, however, continued with some course of action. Finally, on the morning of April 8, the English began laying mines in Norwegian waters used by German ore ships. What they did not know was that already German warships were under way up the Norwegian coast and troops were ready to move across the border of Denmark. On April 9 Denmark had become a German province and the Luftwaffe had, as Göring insisted, sites for advance fighter bases and air-warning systems. Because the Scandinavian occupation had been prepared in secrecy Göring for possibly the first time had not been informed of *Weserübung* (the code name for the operation) until it had been all but in final form. Göring, whose relations with the other Wehrmacht services had never been good, did not endear himself further by dominating the first meeting he attended on *Weserübung*. The Field Marshal spent most of his time criticizing the already formulated plans, venting "his spleen" as one attendant noted,

A German soldier examines the wreckage of a Norwegian plane, destroyed by Luftwaffe attacks, at Sola. Bombed, strafed, invaded by German paratroops followed by air-borne infantry, the great air base fell into German hands the first day of Hitler's invasion of Scandinavia, April 9, 1940. (NATIONAL ARCHIVES)

Hans-Jürgen Stumpf, whose Luftflotte 5, operating from Norwegian bases, effectively harassed the British fleet in the North Sea and British ground and air forces that attempted to aid the Norwegians.

(NATIONAL ARCHIVES)

Erhard Milch, former board chairman of Lufthansa Airlines, and one of the architects of the Luftwaffe. A shrewd administrator, Milch was a greater asset to the German Air Force than Göring. He was also ruthless in dealing with his rivals; at the close of the war he was a field marshal. (NATIONAL ARCHIVES)

and generally disrupting the conference. As a result some changes were made in the plans, putting heavier responsibilitites on the Army and Navy, as well as ascertaining the bases. All of Denmark was conquered in about five hours. The determinant was the vaunted Luftwaffe, although most of the country was overrun by ground troops. The threatened bombardment in the style of Guernica and Warsaw of Copenhagen ended all Danish resistance.

Norway, also invaded on April 9, was not so readily overcome. The tiny Norwegian Army fought gallantly, but the Germans in a carefully prepared operation succeeded in landing troops in a half-dozen important coastal cities, from Narvik in the north to Christiansand in the south. Within hours the great airfield at Sola, a few miles to the east of the fishing village Stavanger on the southwest

The Focke-Wulf 200 "Condor" as a Lufthansa airliner in the late 1930s and as converted into a Luftwaffe reconnaissance bomber. The Condor was the only long-range aircraft available to the Luftwaffe when war came, and although not designed as a warplane, it was made into one by adding various gun positions and a ventral gondola under the fuselage, which served as a gun position, and eventually a bombardier's position. Though ill suited to its wartime role, with structural weaknesses, and vulnerable to fighter attack, the Condor proved to be surprisingly effective and earned the name of the "Scourge of the Atlantic" after its introduction in the Norwegian campaign.
(LUFTHANSA PHOTO-IMPERIAL WAR MUSEUM, LONDON)

coast of Norway, was in the hands of the Luftwaffe. Early in the morning a half-dozen Me-110s bombed the machine-gun emplacements at Sola (there were no antiaircraft guns). Paratroopers were then dropped to invest the field to be followed by transports (Ju-52s) carrying infantry battalions and a regimental staff. Meanwhile ships disembarked more troops and supplies in the harbor nearby. By the afternoon Sola was a German airfield.

To assure Luftwaffe prestige Göring sent Milch to command the newly formed Luftflotte 5, a temporary command which Milch held for three weeks when he returned to Germany to turn again to administrative details. Milch was succeeded by General Hans-Jürgen Stumpf. From bases established near Oslo, Christiansand, and Stavanger (Sola), the Luftwaffe operated most effectively against Norwegian and Allied troops as well as Allied shipping. The Focke-Wulf 200, the Condor, once the pride of Lufthansa's fleet, was pressed into active service

Junkers 88, the Luftwaffe's all-purpose aircraft. Its functions ranged from that of its original conception as a fast medium bomber through reconnaissance and *fighter plane. Designed in 1936 by a German, W. H. Evers, and an American, Alfred Gassner, the Ju-88 served in the Luftwaffe through the entire war.*

(U. S. AIR FORCE)

as an armed long-range reconnaissance aircraft. The first important use of the Junkers 88, flown by Kampfgeschwader 30, occurred during the Scandinavian campaign. The He-111 also was employed as was the now infamous Stuka.

The Allies sent small, ill-equipped reinforcements to engage in courageous but doomed ventures. Landings were made at Namsos, in central Norway, under command of Major General Carton de Wiart. The British forces soon came under heavy Luftwaffe attack and within days after the landings Namsos was bombed into an "unforgettable spectacle" of flame. General de Wiart informed London that he "could see little chance of carrying out decisive, or indeed, any operations unless enemy air activity is considerably restricted." The Luftwaffe continued to command the skies, just as their propaganda vaunted.

The aircraft carriers *Glorious* and *Ark Royal* were called in from the Mediterranean to assist in the delivery of aircraft, particularly fighters whose range would not permit their being flown directly from Britain. Since most of the best airfields were in German hands, the Allies were forced to construct their own airdromes under less than ideal conditions. The snow in one Norwegian airfield was packed down by a herd of several thousand reindeer. Bribed by the

The crew of an He-111 about to set off on a bombing mission. The Heinkel 111, a descendant of the single-engined He-70, was designed by Walter and Siegfried Gunther and first saw service in Spain and continued to be operational beyond its time. (NATIONAL ARCHIVES)

medical officer's pure alcohol, the keeper of the herd, a Laplander, drove the herd over the snow a few times to produce a perfect landing ground.

The British field was located on Lake Lesjaskog, near Aandalsnes in central Norway, where two hundred Norwegian civilians appeared to assist in scraping a runway under two feet of snow. Once prepared, the field was ready for the RAF: No. 263 Squadron dispatched eighteen Gloster Gladiators, the last of the biplane fighters, which took off from the deck of the *Glorious*. Led by a Blackburn Skua, an early Fleet dive bomber, the Gladiators flew through a snow flurry for nearly two hundred miles over unknown terrain and actually found the little icy strip on Lake Lesjaskog. Not long after, the ubiquitous Luftwaffe—Ju-88s and He-111s—appeared. Before the day ended ten of the eighteen Gladiators were out of operation. The planes had landed on April 24; by April 27 their effort was over, the Gladiators burned, and the pilots evacuated. The wreckage of some of the Gladiators may be found in the vicinity of Lake Lesjaskog even today.

In the north, at critical Narvik, the Allies were able to hold out longer because they were, temporarily at least, out of the Luftwaffe's effective range. A few airdromes were hacked out of the ice and forests, the most impressive of which was located at Bardufoss, about fifty miles northeast of Narvik. Once again the runways were created by civilians under the direction of British and Norwegian engineers and Royal Air Force technicians. Under the snow lay a six-inch coating of ice—and under that frozen soil, some of which turned to mud under the direct rays of the feeble sun. Work began on May 4 and by May 21 a great hand-carved network of landing strips, taxiways, and shelters was ready for occupancy. Once again No. 263 Squadron with its new Gladiators alighted in Norway. They were later joined by No. 46 Squadron, equipped with the modern Hawker Hurricane, based at another field near Skaanland, which lay closer to Narvik.

The Allied forces were, by this time, under double stress. Not only had the Germans enlarged their holdings in Norway, which included bases closer to Narvik, but Hitler had brought the "twilight war" on the Western Front to an end. Was holding Norway at great cost worth the risk of losing France?

Two Gladiators of No. 263 Squadron, RAF, camouflaged against German air attack at Aandalsnes, Norway, in the spring of 1940.
(IMPERIAL WAR MUSEUM, LONDON)

Flight Lieutenant Caesar B. Hull of the ill-fated No. 263 Squadron, which lost all of its Gladiators in and around Norway—although only two in combat; the rest were destroyed in operational mishaps, to German attack while on the ground, or, finally, when the aircraft carrier Glorious, *evacuating them from Norway, was sunk by the German Navy. Hull, wounded in the fighting in Norway, had not been aboard the* Glorious. *He returned to England and was killed while serving with No. 43 Squadron during the Battle of Britain.* (IMPERIAL WAR MUSEUM, LONDON)

Besides which, the tide of battle had turned severely against the Allies—British, French, and Polish troops. The air war was characterized by a quality of epic tragedy with overtones of the romance of air fighting in the First World War. In objective fact it was a clash of the past and the present with the outcome preordained.

On May 26 three Gladiators of No. 263 Squadron took off from the airfield at Bardufoss and flew south to a temporary field at Bodø. The three biplanes, led by Flight Lieutenant Caesar Hull, came upon a couple of He-111s which fired shots at the English planes but without inflicting damage. The Gladiators put down in the muddy strip at Bodø. While refueling was going on another He-111 appeared over the field. Lieutenant Anthony Lydekker immediately took off and engaged the Heinkel while Hull and the other pilot, Pilot Officer Jack Falkson, were briefed on their mission.

The Allies were retreating northward up a valley to the east of Bodø in an attempt to get to the sea and back to England. As Hull explained, the troops "were being strafed by the Huns all day." The three Gladiators were to interfere with the strafing.

The Heinkel having been chased off, Lydekker landed to refuel and the three British planes prepared to take off. This in itself was a major chore, for mud gripped at the wheels of the planes the instant they touched down. The stickier spots were covered with flat boards. In his report later Hull did not say that they took off; instead they "came unstuck about fifty yards from the end and just staggered over the trees." Falkson was not so fortunate and his plane crashed in the takeoff. Feeling certain theirs was a doomed mission, Hull ordered Lydekker to land and continued on alone.

"Saw some smoke rising," he reported, "so investigated, and found a Heinkel 111 at about 600 feet. Attacked it three times, and it turned south with smoke pouring from fuselage and engines. Broke off attack to engage a Junkers 52, which crashed in flames. Saw Heinkel 111 flying south, tried to intercept, and failed. Returned and attacked two Junkers 52s in formation. Number one went into clouds, number two crashed in flames after six people had baled out."

After attacking another Heinkel which raced south (toward the German lines) with smoke in its wake, Hull returned to Bodø to rearm. "The troops

Norway 1940: Norwegian skiers watch a Luftwaffe crew bomb-up a Stuka. The pilot waits upon one of the wheel pants. (NATIONAL ARCHIVES)

were cheered by the report," Hull wrote, "and I thought another patrol might produce more fun." It took a good deal of persuasion to convince the officer in charge of the strip to permit another takeoff from the viscous field. But Hull was most convincing, more planks were laid down, and he took off again. "This time the valley was deserted, and the only thing I could do was amuse the troops by doing some aerobatics. They all cheered and waved madly every time I went down low—I think they imagined that at last we had air control and their worries were over. Vain hope!"

That night, alternating in the remaining two Gladiators, the three pilots furnished air cover for the ships carrying the troops out of Norway. Fortunately there were no enemy aircraft aloft at midnight so Hull once again amused the troops by "beating up" the vessels as they left. By morning, however, it was agreed that the Bodø runway could no longer be safely used even with planks covering practically all of it. Also, at eight in the morning a jetty near the airdrome came under attack by Messerschmitt 110s and the Stukas. Only Lydekker succeeded in taking off immediately to save the Gladiator, but by the time he arrived at Bardufoss he was wounded and the plane a write-off.

Hull meanwhile had taken shelter in a barn and

Messerschmitt 109E-3 of Jagdgeschwader 77, based at Nordholz, near Cuxhaven, in northern Germany. JG 77 *played an active role in the Scandinavian campaign, during which it was moved northward to Westerland at Sylt on the North Sea.* (H. J. NOWARRA)

watched the dive-bombing for a while before noting that the field itself was not being attacked. He climbed into his plane and took off, climbed and attacked a Stuka at the bottom of its dive. He may have hit it, for the Ju-87 made off slowly over the sea. At that instant Hull was attacked by another Stuka, the shots shattering his windscreen. The force of impact had stunned Hull and he was "thanking my lucky stars" as he came to—only to hear the sound of guns from behind and the thudding of hits in his aircraft. The Gladiator turned into a right-hand dive, which Hull felt he would not be able to get out of, when at about two hundred feet the plane pulled itself out. Hull quickly gunned the engine to clear an outcropping of rocks in his path. This achieved, he was "discouraged to hear the sound of machine guns from the rear again . . . so gave up hope and decided to get her down."

The glutinous mud of Bodø would have been welcome as the screaming, strained engine pulled the Gladiator into the ground. The landing legs snapped and with a crashing roar and a ripping of fabric Hull's plane bounced along the frozen rocky ground in a spray of snow, crunching of trees, and a trail of oily smoke. With an injured head and knee, Hull crawled away from the wreck. The Tom-

mies, whom he had served so well in the hours before, sent him to the nearest British aid station, from which he was later evacuated by air to England. Within hours nothing remained of Bodø: jetty, airstrip, town, and forest blazed after a concentrated Luftwaffe attack.

As Hull had observed, it had all been a vain hope. By June 3 evacuation from Narvik was under way. A merciful stratum of mist and low cloud screened the frantic movement to the seaport from the Luftwaffe, whose planes thronged over the entire area at will, dive-bombing and strafing the troops, destroying communications and generally creating havoc.

The few surviving Gladiators of No. 263 Squadron were flown back to the *Glorious*. The ten remaining Hurricanes of No. 46 Squadron would have to be burned because the planes were not supposed to be capable of landing on a carrier deck. Unable to bring himself to destroy the Hurricanes, Squadron Leader K. B. Cross literally pleaded for permission to attempt the impossible. At this crucial moment every aircraft was priceless and the risk, it was finally decided, was worth it. At midnight, June 7, Cross led a formation of ten Hurricanes out of beleaguered Bardufoss and, after an hour's flight, all ten landed safely on the *Glorious*. Tragically this, too, was a vain hope.

The German Imperial Navy, which had inspired Hitler's Scandinavian adventure, had a final blow to deliver. The two battle cruisers *Scharnhorst* and *Gneisenau,* in Norwegian waters and cruising northward, learned from air reconnaissance and intercepted radio messages of much shipping activity between northern Norway and Scotland. The plane had also spotted a British carrier. On the afternoon of June 8 the German warships sighted the *Glorious* and its two escort destroyers, the *Acasta* and the *Ardent*. Outgunned by the German cruisers, all three British ships were sent to the bottom within two hours. Over fifteen hundred British seamen and airmen were lost in the icy sea—as were the twenty planes, ten Gladiators and ten Hurricanes, so splendidly evacuated from Bardufoss. There were only forty-three survivors, among them Squadron Leader Cross and one other member of his Hurricane squadron. For hours, as they waited for rescue, they saw twenty-five of their countrymen, even

some of their squadron mates, die in the Arctic cold.

It was a triumph for the German surface fleet—but with portentous qualifications not apparent at the time. In the battle with the *Glorious,* the *Scharnhorst* took a torpedo from one of the British destroyers. Within two weeks the *Gneisenau* was hit by a torpedo from the British submarine *Clyde*. Both German ships were under repair, and therefore out of action, for close to six months, a critical half year. In addition the cruisers *Königsberg* and *Karlsruhe* were destroyed in Norwegian waters, the former by Fleet Air Arm bombers and the latter by a British submarine. And during the battles of April 10 and 13 Royal Navy ships accounted for no less than ten of the destroyers which had brought German troops to Narvik. One half of the German Imperial Navy's destroyer strength, therefore, was eliminated within four days, and about a third of its cruisers. As a force at sea the German surface fleet counted for little after the Scandinavian campaign.

It was true, in the short view, Hitler had once

The British carrier Glorious, *which served in the Norwegian campaign, delivering aircraft and evacuating the* *wounded. It was sunk on June 8, 1940, during the withdrawal from Narvik with heavy loss of life.*

(NAVY DEPT., NATIONAL ARCHIVES)

again proved himself the supreme war lord, the blitzkrieg concept had proved insuperable, the Luftwaffe incomparable, but at what a price. In order to invade Britain Hitler would need all those ships which lay in dry dock or rusting in the fiords and coastal waters of Norway.

Many missed the full significance of the Scandinavian adventure: that the Luftwaffe had succeeded in disrupting the movement and operations of the most powerful Navy on earth. It was a lesson that would have to be painfully relearned before its implications were fully understood. Even so confirmed

a ground soldier as Jodl had glimpsed this truth. His final report to the Führer on the Scandinavian campaign must have been the ultimate shock to Raeder, happy in his moment of hollow victory. "The Luftwaffe," Jodl submitted, "proved to be the decisive factor in the success of the operation."

Foreign Minister Joachim von Ribbentrop, however, spoke the ultimate in cant when he said, "Germany by its action has saved the countries and the peoples of Scandinavia from annihilation, and will now guarantee true neutrality in the north until the war's end."

4

WAS NUN?

"LIVE and let live was still the policy in the Saar," Bernard Fergusson reported from the Western Front, "and anybody who loosed off a rifle was thought to be thoroughly anti-social." In the positions where the British and French faced the Germans in the Siegfried Line the Germans twice in April "went through the motions of an attack, and the second time overran some French posts on our flank; this was considered to be extremely bad form, and not to be imitated."

This idyllic warfare abruptly ended on May 10, 1940, when the Nazi legions struck the Netherlands, Belgium, and Luxembourg. *Fall Gelb* ("Case Yellow"), the assault along the Western Front, erupted at dawn in Holland as the Wehrmacht smashed across the borders, parachutists dropped from the skies on airfields and other vital defense points, and the cry of the Stuka again shattered the peace of the countryside.

This had been preceded by a curious series of tentative and inconclusive actions during the "twilight war." As word of the attack on Poland flashed around the world, President Franklin D. Roosevelt appealed to all belligerents to refrain from unrestricted aerial warfare; in short, the bombing of cities. The British accepted on the same day, September 1, 1939; the French followed on the next day, and the Germans, having already devastated Polish towns and villages and with plans for the

bombardment of Warsaw in the offing, accepted Roosevelt's request on September 18. So it was that both sides confined bombing attacks only to absolute military targets: no bombs were to fall upon land lest civilians be placed in danger. Only ships at sea, therefore, were legitimate targets.

The RAF was devoted also to dropping propaganda leaflets, beginning with the first night of the war, when ten Armstrong Whitworth Whitley twin-engined bombers of Nos. 51 and 58 Squadrons delivered "Nickles," as the leaflets were called in code, to Hamburg, Bremen, and the industrial Ruhr. Although there was no interception by German fighter planes, the Whitleys did encounter bad weather, severe electrical storms, and icing. One plane crashed in France.

Nickle raids were not popular with crews, a view shared with them by Arthur Harris, commanding No. 5 Group of Bomber Command when the war began (by war's end he would command the bomber forces of Britain), who felt "that the only thing achieved was largely to supply the Continent's requirements of toilet paper for the five long years of war." By virtue of the irrational sapience rampant in the early weeks of the war, and of which there was little dearth throughout the war, the leaflets were marked "Secret" and carefully watched lest any of the British pilots read them. They were for the eyes of the enemy only, it seems. Harris, who

The Armstrong Whitworth "Whitley"—the "Flying Barn Door" to its crews—was one of Bomber Command's first modern bombers. Employed during the "phony war" in dropping propaganda leaflets, the Whitley accumulated impressive "firsts" during its tenure: it was the first British aircraft to drop bombs on German and Italian soil and the first to fly over Berlin to drop leaflets in what the crews called "bumphlet" raids on October 1, 1939. Earlier "marks" were powered by radial engines; beginning with the Mark IV the Whitley's performance was improved with the installation of in-line Merlin engines. By the spring of 1942 the Whitley was retired from Bomber Command; its day was over.

(IMPERIAL WAR MUSEUM, LONDON)

resented the additional complexity of handling the leaflets as secret documents, regarded them with typical acuity. "Many of the pamphlets," he said, "were patently so idiotic and childish that it was perhaps just as well to keep them from the knowledge of the British public, even if we did risk and waste crews and aircraft dropping them on the enemy."

While hazardous, the propaganda raids were useful in that they provided the air crews with training and reconnaissance flights over enemy territory—all of which would serve a more destructive purpose once the gloves came off. Also it became obvious that, against the "gloves off" day, new operational techniques were required particularly as applied to navigation; the conditions under which the crews were expected to operate required attention.

A typical raid of this type and period took place late in October 1939, when four Whitleys (originally five but one turned back) of No. 51 Squadron took off around dusk from a forward base at Villeneuve, France. The weather forecast was deadly: "rain, hail, and sleet showers, risk of thunder; cloud 7 to 9/10, low base 1000 feet, but 500 feet in showers; freezing level 1500 feet; heavy icing anticipated in shower clouds up to 12,000 feet." Except for the single turnback because of the weather, all planes proceeded to their assigned target areas in the Düsseldorf-Frankfurt region and dropped their Nickles under truly impossible conditions.

The Whitley, at best, could reach about seventeen thousand feet—and through most of the route snow clouds jutted up to eighteen thousand feet. While dropping the leaflets from the "dustbin," (a flare chute in the underside of the fuselage), it was not possible to use oxygen. The "droppers" were forced to walk around, cut the strings binding the bundles, and force them through the dustbin, all without oxygen and with little protection against the freezing temperatures. In one of the Whitleys the droppers—otherwise the navigator and radio operator—collapsed from anoxia. They revived on the way home, however, when the plane began icing up heavily and lost altitude. Controls became all but useless and great lumps of ice were flung back from the propellers and thudded alarmingly against the sides of the plane. Despite these problems and others, the pilot brought the plane safely back to Villeneuve.

Another Whitley had similar troubles, even before reaching Düsseldorf-Frankfurt. On the way to the drop zone the front gun turret and the trim tabs on the controls froze. And as the dustbin was being lowered, that too froze. The leaflets had to be transferred from one side of the plane to the other because of the jammed turret. During this painful operation, the crew discovered that it had taken along only a single charged oxygen bottle—all others were empty. As the Whitley lumbered toward the target, the front gunner passed out from the cold and lack of oxygen. The navigator and copilot relieved the pain of the cold by voluntarily butting their heads against convenient hard surfaces. When they descended to a lower altitude their aircraft came under antiaircraft fire. But they pressed on, despite the pilot's sickness from the cold, anoxia and bucking of the plane. More freezing afflicted the rear gun turret as well as the air-speed indicator. But the radio operator tripling also as navigator somehow managed to find his way back to base.

As with the other two aircraft, the third Whitley experienced trouble with frozen dustbins, but with variations and augmentation. The leaflets were scattered but only the combined efforts of the crew raised the dustbin out of the slipstream. The navigator passed out from the exertion. The pilot, after five and a half hours of exhausting flight, turned the controls over to the copilot and then joined the navigator in a loss of consciousness. When the pilot recovered it was to the sight of flames shooting out of his starboard engine. A six-inch coating of ice had formed on the wing. In a cloud, the distressed Whitley staggered into a dive. With the tail controls frozen solid, it took the strength of both pilot and copilot to pull the plane out of the plunge. Though leveled out, the Whitley continued dropping; the port engine, the one which wasn't burning, simply stopped under a thick coating of ice.

"The order was given to abandon ship by parachute," one of the crew later related; "as no reply was forthcoming from the front and rear gunners, the order was immediately cancelled. It was afterwards ascertained that the front gunner was unconscious due to a blow on the head from an ammunition magazine, and the rear gunner was unconscious from a blow on the head from the turret due to the dive and subsequent recovery.

"The aircraft then assumed a shallow high-speed dive. We opened the top hatch [all windows were solidly frozen over] to see where we were going, and the second pilot, who was at the controls, opened the side window. The aircraft emerged from the clouds in heavy rain at about 200 feet above the ground. All we could see was a black forest with a grey patch in the middle, for which we were heading; the second pilot pulled the aircraft over the trees brushing through their tops, and the aircraft dropped flat into a field, travelled through a wire fence, skidded broadside on and came to rest with the port wing against the trees on the further side of the clearing."

All climbed safely out of the Whitley and attempted, with little success, to extinguish the burning engine. The pilot climbed into the cabin to get an extinguisher, only to find that the crash had caused it to discharge. Finally the radio operator found another extinguisher and mounting the wing put out the flames. All were safe and unhurt and even managed a laugh when, the next morning, one of the local farmers asked, in French, "What time are you taking off?"

The fourth Whitley had little trouble on the way to the drop area, which was Munich, despite the blanket of hoary ice on the windows and snow underfoot in the front gunner's compartment. It was a cheerful crew, singing on the way to Germany —"Roll Out the Barrel" was an especial favorite —with particular and brilliant solo efforts praised over the intercom system. It was a noisy if frigid Whitley. Over Munich the Nickling was properly accomplished (with the usual freezing of the dustbin, the raising of which eventually exhausted most of the crew). As the plane neared the French border a cylinder head in the starboard engine blew off. With the loss of power the Whitley descended lower and lower into the thick clouds, after which the other engine began to sputter.

"Abandon aircraft," the pilot announced as the plane, flying at two thousand feet, bore down on some hills in the near distance.

First to jump was the front gunner, who entangled himself in the intercom wiring and dangled outside the aircraft, unable to get free, until the navigator gave him a push. The opening of his parachute knocked him out and when he next awakened he was startled at being ringed in by enormous brown eyes. He had dropped into a pasture and became the center of curiosity of a herd of cows.

The radio operator, who had been forced to jump with an oxygen bottle in his hand because his fingers had frozen to the metal, apparently landed in an adjoining field. He also proved that it was possible to cover a hundred yards in record time while encumbered by full flying regalia, complete to boots, and to hurtle a four-foot hedge while being pursued by a bull.

The navigator jumped, with a resultant sprained ankle; the pilot, after setting the plane in a flat trajectory, also jumped and landed gently in a meadow. The Whitley, ostensibly crewless, remained in flight for a few more minutes, plowed into the ground, and burst into flames. In the rear turret Sergeant A. Griffin, whose intercom had gone defective and who had not heard the order to jump, snatched a fire extinguisher and dashed into the front of the plane to save his fellow crew members. Extremely puzzled to find the crew gone, Sergeant Griffin limped to the nearest village, where he found the rest of the crew and learned that he had actually walked away from the crash of the Whitley. They were taken from the cafe in which they met, after being presented with bouquets, to a French hospital for treatment. By the evening all had returned to No. 51 Squadron.

Bomber Command was, however, engaged in more hostile operations during the period of the war's first days and through the twilight war. These incipient efforts were confined primarily to the North Sea approaches to Germany where the German fleet was concentrated. As with the Germans, the British began with good intentions: "The greatest care is to be taken not to injure the civilian population [the original order stated explicitly]. The intention is to destroy the German fleet. There is no alternative target."

Forty-eight minutes after the official declaration of war a Blenheim, with Flying Officer A. McPherson piloting and carrying a naval observer, took off on the first British aerial mission of the war. According to the Operations Record Book of No. 139 Squadron, the duty was "Photo. Reco." and the Time Up 1200 and Time Down 1650. The Remarks read tersely: "Duty successful. 75 photos taken of German fleet. The first Royal Air Force aircraft to cross the German frontier." The last sentence was a small concession to merited pride. It hardly suggested any of the hardships of the four-and-a-half-hour mission.

The Blenheim (a Mark IV, serial number 6215) came in from the North Sea over Wilhelmshaven at twenty-four thousand feet. The men aboard saw several German ships coming out of Wilhelmshaven and entering the Schillig Roads, among them the *Admiral Scheer* and the *Emden*. But they were unable to wire back the information, for, as with the leaflet-dropping aircraft, they were afflicted with the cold. Their radio frozen, McPherson and the naval observer (a Commander Thompson) could relay the intelligence only after they had returned to England. Thus was the first RAF target of the Second World War decided upon.

The major enemy was the weather, with minor contributions from High Command uncertainty. "The war was only 24 hours old," deplored Flight Lieutenant K. C. Doran, "but already the bombload had been changed four times. Lunch-time on 4th September found us standing by at an hour's readiness, the Blenheims bombed up with 500-pound S.A.P." McPherson's flight having located some German shipping in the region of the Heligoland Bight, it now devolved upon Doran to lead the bombers carrying Semi Armor Piercing bombs. But these too were changed for five-hundred-pound General Purpose (GP) with eleven-second delay fuses. This was a concession to the weather, which, as Doran noted, was reported as "bloody, and the only attack possible would be a low-level one."

With Doran in the lead aircraft, ten Blenheims (five from No. 107 Squadron and five of 110 Squadron) took off for Wilhelmshaven. Another five from No. 139 Squadron were also dispatched but because of the weather never located their target and returned to base without bombing.

Bristol Blenheims of No. 139 Squadron over France, 1940. Although hailed in the summer of 1936 as the last word in modern fast bomber design, the Blenheim proved vulnerable to the Messerschmitt 109 in France; it was also lacking in armament and protective armor for its crew. "XD" was the code for No. 139 Squadron, whose Flying Officer A. McPherson, in a Blenheim, was the first Briton to cross the German frontier when he photographed the German fleet at Wilhelmshaven on September 3, 1939. The following day, Blenheims of No. 110 Squadron made the first bombing raid of the war on Wilhelmshaven.

(IMPERIAL WAR MUSEUM, LONDON)

"Soon after crossing out over the North Sea," Doran of No. 110 Squadron noted, "we ran into bad weather . . . a solid wall of cloud seemed to extend from sea-level to about 17,000 feet." The formation thereupon dropped down to nearly sea level and flew through the clouds. They flew on instruments and dead reckoning. When they estimated they were over Heligoland, they turned and headed for what should have been Wilhelmshaven. They were barely fifty feet over the water when suddenly "a couple of barges appeared out of the murk and vanished." A dim suggestion of a coastline also emerged from the fog. "After a bit of feverish map-reading, we decided we were in the approach to the Schillig Roads. By an incredible combination and judgement we were bang on our track."

The Germans were not expecting any action in such dismal weather, and if anyone heard approaching aircraft no alarms were given. As Doran led the flights of No. 110 Squadron into the attack, now divided into two sections of two and three planes each, the cloud base lifted to around five hundred feet. Doran saw a large merchant ship—and just beyond it, the Admiral Scheer. The Scheer lay in

anchor, away from the shore, protected from the landward side by barrage balloons. Gaining as much altitude as possible—about five hundred feet —without losing sight of the target, Doran led the attack against the Scheer. Once the bombs went it would be necessary to make a sharp turn to the left to avoid hitting the cables of the barrage balloons.

Doran recalled seeing the laundry of the German seamen fluttering on the stern as he approached. The sailors seemed to be idling about, watching with little concern the approach of the Blenheims. Not until the first British bomber flashed over the Scheer, dropping its bomb, did the Germans realize what was happening. From then on the Blenheims were under heavy antiaircraft fire from both the ships and shore-based batteries. The bombs dropped by the first Blenheim struck the Scheer and —thanks to the delayed fusing—bounced off the deck and fell harmlessly into the water. The second plane, its crew under heavy fire, dropped short and the bombs exploded in the water. One Blenheim, its pilot misjudging his height or hit by flak, crashed into the forecastle of the Emden. It was the only serious damage done to any German ship in the attack and also killed some Germans and injured several more. No. 107 Squadron lost four aircraft in the attack and No. 110 Squadron one; it was a costly raid for small results. One half of the attacking force was lost in this first bombing attack by the Royal Air Force in the Second World War.

Later in the same day, September 4, 1939, fourteen Vickers Wellingtons, six from No. 9 Squadron and eight from No. 149 Squadron, made an attempt upon the *Scharnhorst* and the *Gneisenau.* Their presence at Brunsbüttel had been noted by the enterprising McPherson on his historic reconnaissance flight the day before. Bad weather and antiaircraft fire again took their toll and two of No. 9 Squadron's planes did not return. One of the bombers lost was attacked by Sergeant Alfred Held in a Messerschmitt 109 of Jagdgeschwader 77. It was the first British bomber of the Second World War credited to a German fighter pilot. Unlike the attack at Wilhelmshaven by Doran and the Blenheims, the Brunsbüttel attack, which was at a greater distance from the United Kingdom, afforded more time for an alarm to be given and a few aircraft to be dispatched to intercept.

In all, seven bombers were lost on the first day of offensive aerial warfare. It had not been a "wizard" day for the RAF—although it did mean much in terms of civilian morale and it did show what British aircrews could do under extremely difficult conditions. The "restricted bombing" policy naturally kept them from attacking the more likely target: the factories in the Ruhr. The Air Staff, however, waited, feeling that "this delicate and difficult problem may well be solved for us by the Germans, who are perhaps unlikely to refrain for more than a limited period at most, from actions that would force the Allies from all legal restrictions." The expression in vogue in the Air Ministry was that all were waiting for the hated "Hun to take off the gloves." When this occurred Bomber Command, too, would remove the gloves and unleash its force against more important targets than the ships of the German Imperial Fleet. But, in truth, the Bomber Command's bared fist consisted of less than five hundred aircraft, many of which were the out-of-date Battles and the hardly better Wellingtons, Whitleys, and Hampdens. The most effective bomber was the Blenheim, and its early

operations, as already described, were hardly comforting. Against the five hundred British bombers, the Germans, when ready to discard the gauntlet, could muster three times the number.

Nor were the Germans, certainly not the Luftwaffe at least, anxious to violate the restricted-bombing agreement. The Germans, like the British, were most active mining their respective coastal waters or bombing enemy warships.

This policy was in force when the first German bombers, Heinkel 111s and Junkers 88s of Kampfgeschwader 30, appeared over Britain. The bombers had been dispatched to attack the *Hood,* supposedly in the neighborhood of Rosyth in the Firth of Forth. On the morning of October 16, 1939, German reconnaissance aircraft had passed over Rosyth and the possibility of a raid on the port was noted. No. 607 Squadron was sent north from its home base closer to Rosyth. But the early-warning system broke down and No. 607 Squadron was not alerted to the approach of the German bombers until late. On the other hand, the Germans suffered some surprise, for they had been informed by intelligence that there were no fighters in the vicinity of Rosyth. There were two additional units, No. 602 (City of Glasgow) and No. 603 (City of Edinburgh), within striking range of the Firth of Forth.

Kampfgeschwader 30 found the *Hood* docked at Rosyth, therefore too close to land, and consequently civilians, to serve as a target. The small force of nine bombers was forced to select other targets as they approached Rosyth at twelve thousand feet. Captain Helmut Pohle, piloting a Ju-88, picked the *Southampton* for his attack. There was some tardiness in the reactions from antiaircraft gunners in the area, so that the bomb run was reasonably unmolested. One British gun battery was engaged in a practice drill when they saw German planes coming over. The gun crew hurriedly changed dummy ammunition for live, and began firing at the bombers.

By this time bombs had begun raining down on the ships. One bomb cut through three decks of the *Southampton* and careened out the side before exploding against an admiral's barge, sinking it. Damage was done to the *Edinburgh* and the *Mohawk.* Pohle, leading the attack on the *Southampton,* found himself in a good deal of trouble. His Ju-88 was struck by flak and the top housing of the pilot's compartment blew away in the dive. Worse, as he headed out to sea in a race for home he came under attack by a trio of Spitfires—the first he had ever seen. The German aircraft, crippled and yawing, staggered under the heavy gunning of the British fighters, which swarmed in three times. Pouring smoke and carrying two dead crewmen, the Junkers splashed into the sea near Dalkeith, Scotland—the first German aircraft brought down over Britain since the First World War. Captain Pohle survived and was taken prisoner. Another German plane, reported as a Heinkel, also fell into the sea. The credit for bringing down the first German plane was given to No. 603 Squadron, led by Squadron Leader E. E. Stevens.

Like the British raids on German naval ports, the German attacks on Rosyth and other havens for the Home Fleet were tentative, meager, almost haphazard skirmishes. They did not lead to great aerial battles, as had been visualized in the pulp magazines the young fliers had read in school. But they took their toll and the losses were bitter if not spectacular. The missing element of drama was finally provided on December 18, 1939, when two dozen British Wellingtons, of Nos. 9, 37, and 149 Squadrons, set out on an "armed reconnaissance" of the Heligoland Bight, specifically the vicinity of the Schillig Roads and Wilhelmshaven. (Armed reconnaissance eliminated the process of sending out one plane to spot targets and then sending out the bombers to strike them. The Wellingtons were bombed up and ready in the event that worthwhile targets were found.)

It was a perfect day, cloudless and sunny, with superb visibility. Two of the Wellingtons turned back because of mechanical trouble and the remaining twenty-two approached from the north, having kept away from the flak guns stationed on ships along the way. The four formations, at twelve thousand feet, then came in over Heligoland. It was about at this moment that the Messerschmitt 109s of Jagdgeschwader 77 intercepted the British bombers. Doggedly pressing on, the Wellingtons continued their reconnaissance, unable to drop their bombs upon the warships below because they were docked or in harbors and thus not to be attacked. The gunners in the Wellingtons did the best they could to fight off the darting Me-109s, which seemed to be coming in from all directions. The tail guns

of the Wellingtons gave the Germans the most trouble, but the bomb-laden Wellingtons, slow compared to the Me-109s, were terribly mauled. For about eighty miles from Heligoland until they were well out to sea the Wellingtons suffered the attacks of the Me-109s, as well as those of Me-110s which had also joined the battle. Taking advantage of the blind spots in the Wellington's defense, that is, where the guns were unable to traverse, the Messerschmitts accounted for no less than twelve of the British bombers (the claim was, however, for thirty-four) at a cost of two Me-109s (British gunners claimed twelve). Worst hit of the British units was No. 37 Squadron, which lost five of its six aircraft dispatched.

The surviving crews reported that many of the Wellingtons had crashed, burning and with fuel streaming from their tanks; it was a memorable argument in favor of self-sealing tanks. In time these would become standard equipment on all aircraft, but the lessons were always tragic and costly. It was learned also that bombers were susceptible to aggressive fighter attacks. If "the bomber always got through," so did the modern fighter get through the bomber's defenses. It was after this battle over the Heligoland Bight that the British High Command gave serious consideration to switching to night operations, when fighter attacks could be expected to be almost negligible.

Bomber Command's crews endured the worst of the Luftwaffe's effectiveness; but the fighter pilots, too, were subjected to the lessons to be learned in a new kind of warfare.

II

Contemporaneously with the attack on Poland, the northern invasions, the halfhearted bombings and Nickling raids, RAF units were sent to France to fight the Germans.

As in 1914, British aircraft crossed the English Channel shortly after the official declaration of hostilities. Ten squadrons of Fairey Battles of what was termed the Advanced Air Striking Force left for France in the afternoon of September 2. One of the Battles fell into the Channel because of engine trouble; it was the only incident of the crossing. The crew was saved and so the transfer was unremarkable and uncontested. The bomber squadrons were reinforced by four Hurricane squadrons of the Air Component attached to the British Expeditionary Force.

The Air Component, as its name implied, was to work with the BEF, as had, in a sense, the Royal Flying Corps a quarter of a century before, as cover for the troops and protective element for the reconnaissance and photo squadrons (Blenheims and Lysanders), also a part of the Air Component.

The Advanced Air Striking Force was to be employed in the more or less strategic bombardment of targets inside Germany with its Battles and Blenheims; the French, it had been agreed, would supply the fighter protection. The facts of war in its new form hindered the mission of the AASF. The

the French Air Force. Before the war regarded as one of the greatest air forces in the world, the Armée de l'Air was in reality antiquated, afflicted with an effete, defeatist command—in short, ineffectual. The young pilots were able and eager, but they had been betrayed. Neither their aircraft nor the policy under which they were expected to operate was anywhere equal to the task before them.

Burdensome also were the kid-glove bombing rules, observed equally by the Germans and the Allies. Neither side wished to unleash a bomber war on the cities. The French were particularly sensitive to the possibilities of an aroused Luftwaffe and did little to encourage strategic bombardment. It was a policy of kill and let kill just so long as

Fairey "Battles" of No. 218 Squadron, Advanced Air Striking Force in France, 1939–40. The Battle, although obsolete by 1939, was used in front-line service as a reconnaissance bomber during the "phony war" (when this photograph was taken), and as a bomber when the war in the west erupted in May 1940. It was shortly after used as a trainer.

(IMPERIAL WAR MUSEUM, LONDON)

Westland "Lysander," five squadrons of which operated as tactical reconnaissance and photo-survey aircraft for the British Expeditionary Forces in France. Slow, with a top speed of barely two hundred miles an hour (the Me-109 could do well over three hundred), the Lysander was maneuverable but vulnerable and not suited to modern air combat.

(IMPERIAL WAR MUSEUM, LONDON)

impact of the blitzkrieg, especially after the twilight war expired, necessitated the diverting of the bombers to attack the advancing German troops and armored vehicles rather than "strategic" targets behind the lines. The Battles proved less than suitable for modern war.

Late in September 1939, for example, five Battles of No. 150 Squadron were dispatched to reconnoiter ten miles inside the German frontier. They encountered a flight of Messerschmitts and in the battle that followed four of the Battles were destroyed and the surviving aircraft was a write-off on returning to base.

Another handicap was France's Armée de l'Air,

the war remained remotely "civilized." It was also a war of boredom. While the Germans reduced and decimated Poland and then instituted a new order, the French and the British dug in, hoping for the best.

These were tragic, equivocal days which stretched into the months of the twilight war.

The first British fighter squadrons to land in France, and which endured both the boredom of the "phony war" and the frantic humiliation of being pushed out of France, were Nos. 85 and 87 Squadrons of the Air Component and Nos. 1 and 73 Squadrons of the AASF. These Hurricane squadrons were among the first to engage the Luftwaffe, the first British airmen to face the German fliers since 1918. Thanks in part to the press, the opening of the Second World War, at least in the air, was but a sequel to the earlier war. Some of the traditions of that more romantic epic were revived as newsmen sought out aces, colorful characters, human interest stories. The lone fighter pilot engaged in aerial combat high in the heavens furnished good copy—this despite the official negative British attitude toward the glorification of the individual.

Among the first celebrities of the war was a husky, tall, young New Zealander, Flying Officer Edgar J. Kain, of No. 73 Squadron. The friendly, sportive twenty-one-year-old was best known by his

into the equally "impassable" Ardennes Forest. A mere four- or five-minute flight carried the British pilots over Germany. Despite the proximity of "Jerry" (a term which served the British for either the Germans or a chamber pot), the eager fighter pilots found little action in their sector. This was true also of No. 1 Squadron, nesting some thirty miles to the south of Verdun at Vassincourt airdrome near Bar-le-Duc.

At both bases, primitive by RAF standards, the Hurricanes proved their sturdiness, thanks to their rugged construction. Also the wide-track landing gear of the plane was capable of coping with the hazardous, often muddy condition of the landing strips. As for action, apparently the Luftwaffe de-

Among the first to arrive in France were the Hurricane pilots of No. 1 Squadron (left) and No. 73 Squadron. Although they endured the boredom of the

"phony war" they fought furiously after May 1940. Among the No. 73 Squadron members grouped around the antique vehicle is Cobber Kain (on right without hat). (IMPERIAL WAR MUSEUM, LONDON)

nickname "Cobber," an Australian-New Zealand term for "pal" or "chum." With his ready grin, his tousled hair, his crumpled uniform, and his fearless, almost madcap flair for fighting and flying, Cobber Kain seemed a reincarnation of the spirit of Albert Ball or Billy Bishop of the Great War and was the squadron's star performer.

By October No. 73 Squadron was stationed at Etain-Rouvres airdrome near Verdun. The base lay just behind the famed "impregnable" complex of fortresses, the Maginot Line, facing Germany's West Wall. The Maginot Line at this point petered out

voted itself chiefly to reconnaissance and dived into cloud cover and ran for home before the British could intercept.

Not until October 30—the war was nearly two months old—did an RAF fighter bring down its first German plane. Almost directly over No. 1 Squadron's field three German aircraft, Dornier 17s, were seen at high altitude. The airdrome defense section took off immediately in pursuit and Pilot Officer P. W. O. Mould (in Hurricane L1842) overtook the Dornier. The twenty-year-old pilot, the squadron's youngest—a distinction which

King George VI on a visit to an Air Component base in France. The three Hurricanes in foreground belong to No. 85 Squadron (VY), the others to No. 87 Squadron (LK), which like Nos. 1 and 73 Squadrons were the first of the fighter units to serve in France. In the left background are a Blenheim and two Gladiators. (IMPERIAL WAR MUSEUM, LONDON)

Destroyed German bomber in France. At left is the tail section (possibly of an He-111). French soldiers have begun to gather souvenirs from the scattered wreckage. (FRENCH EMBASSY)

A Hurricane 1 landing at Vassincourt, France. The aircraft, belonging to No. 1 Squadron, was then equipped with a wooden propeller. Pilot Officer Mould of this squadron, flying one of these early Hurricanes, scored the first RAF victory when he destroyed a Dornier on October 30, 1939.

(IMPERIAL WAR MUSEUM, LONDON)

earned him the nickname "Boy"—surprised the Germans and shot the Dornier down without a fight.

Two days later, November 2, 1939, Cobber Kain scored the first victory for No. 73 Squadron. The young giant had been lying sprawled on the ground scanning the skies through field glasses when he suddenly leaped up shouting, "I've spotted a Jerry!"

He ran for his Hurricane, which was in readiness, leaped in, and gunned the fighter down the field. Within nine minutes he had climbed to about twenty-seven thousand feet, above a lone Dornier 17, the "Flying Pencil," on a reconnaissance mission. As Kain closed in upon the German plane the rear gunner began firing at him. A few tracers flashed past the Hurricane's cockpit before Kain "squeezed the teat." One sudden flash of fear came into his mind: he hoped that his armorer had not forgotten to arm the eight machine guns in the Hurricane's wings.

The entire plane jolted as the eight guns burst into action—and it was over. Kain dipped onto one wing to watch the Dornier plunge to earth and strike near a small village not far from Rouvres. The German plane had, as described by Charles Gardner of the BBC, "dug a trench four feet deep across a village street, and all that was left of it was a flaming heap of rubble. Gruesome bits of the crew dangled from nearby trees, and the French children were running round with bits of fingers and hands which they had found lying around."

Kain, meanwhile, dived for home and jumped into a vehicle as soon as he had landed to cheers and back-pattings. On arriving at the crash site Kain had to be reassured that no one in the village had been injured by the Dornier. Kain walked over to the twisted, smoking tangle of metal. Three fellow humans had been horribly mangled in the wreckage. It was difficult for Kain to determine which was worse: the sight of the French children playing with bits of Boche or the head of one of the crew, lying at his feet, intact in the helmet and eyes wide open. Kain stood at the edge of the smoldering trench, his face drawn and grimy. Turning away he was heard to say softly, "Well, it was either them or me."

It was not to be a cinematic, pulp-fiction war after all. And it would become grimmer. This was apparent in the build-up of the German fighter squadrons along the Western Front in preparation for Hitler's frequently postponed and permutated *Fall Gelb*. The Messerschmitt 109 squadrons, free of the Polish campaign, and soon outnumbering the French and British squadrons, proved to be more aggressive than they had once been. By the first of the new year 1940, despite the fact that the invasion of France for which the Allies thought they were ready had not yet come off, there was clearly something in the wind. Up to the end of 1939 the RAF had succeeded in destroying about twenty German aircraft—not an impressive number.

The tenor of the air war was, however, imperceptibly, changing. Among the first to experience this was the doughty Cobber Kain. While leading a three-Hurricane flight on patrol, Kain spotted a dozen Messerschmitts. With characteristic dash, he announced to the other two pilots, "Get going, chaps," and dived into the middle of the German formation.

In the first minute or so of the attack, Kain blasted one of the Messerschmitts out of the melee. But he also watched one of the by then crippled Hurricanes racing for the ground and a forced landing. The other Hurricane, Kain noted, was the center of attention of five Messerschmitts. He pulled back on the control stick and came up under one of the German planes, squeezing the gun button. Another Messerschmitt fell out of the battle, streaming black smoke.

It was now Cobber Kain's turn: rushing toward him was a Messerschmitt with guns twinkling. In his rear-view mirror, Kain saw another German plane pouring shells into the Hurricane. Ignoring the rear plane for an instant, Kain activated the eight guns against the oncoming fighter. Nothing happened—Kain had used up his ammunition supply. Luckily his companion knocked the Messerschmitt off Kain's tail—but not before a shell rammed into the engine of Kain's aircraft. There was a burst of flame and thick black smoke filled the cockpit—the air filled with colorful New Zealand profanities. In desperation Kain attempted to ram a German fighter which loomed ahead of him in the thick smoke. But his engine was rapidly dying and the Messerschmitt whisked away.

Cobber Kain was at twenty thousand feet, his plane aflame and he himself choking in the oily smoke. He jerked the stick forward and pushed the nose down. The flames spread and Kain rammed

Squadron scramble by No. 87 Squadron, France 1940. Second plane in the foreground is a Hurricane fitted *with the de Havilland three-bladed propeller, an improvement over the old wooden prop.*

the cockpit hood open and was about to bail out. Then he remembered, when he had taken off he hadn't bothered to fasten his chute properly. He sank back into the smoky cockpit hoping to correct the oversight. He then noted that the dive had smothered the flames, although the cockpit leaked oil and effused smoke. And then the engine came back to life. Hoping to save the precious Hurricane, Kain sought out a place to land and quickly found a spot just at the edge of an airdrome near Metz. He brought the plane down and then hopped out of the tattered Hurricane and, as he himself said, "I fell flat on my bloody face. Passed right out, like a sissy boy."

Kain's cavalier attitude toward regulations (he should have properly adjusted his parachute before ever leaving the ground) had nearly cost him his life. He might easily have been court-martialed for his breach of discipline. As it was, Squadron Leader

Brian Knox would from time to time vent his Dublin Irish on the young New Zealander—this was known as "tearing off a strip" (presumably, and metaphorically, of flesh).

The strip tearing might be earned for some slighting of military courtesy or bearing—the RAF pilots had already begun to fashion curious variations in dress. Kain affected uncreased trousers stuffed into flying boots. Around his neck he generally wore a scarf; a small chain dangled outside his jacket— this carried his identification disks and a small green tiki, the image of a Maori god, as a good luck charm. Like other pilots, Kain liked to wear turtle-neck sweaters. Another shared characteristic was the dashingly wind-blown mop of hair. Members of the Senior Service, the Royal Navy, frowned upon this unkempt noncomformity with some disdain, referring to the bulk of pilots as "the Brylcreem boys." The raffish, tradition-free fighter pilots further dis-

A trio of Hurricanes in attack formation—German-eye view. These aircraft are in a neater formation, however, than was possible in combat. But several German fighter and bomber pilots undoubtedly had a glimpse of Cobber Kain leading a couple of his chaps into a fight in a formation that for an instant may have looked as it does here.

(IMPERIAL WAR MUSEUM, LONDON)

turbed the "naval types" when aboard ship by referring to the bow as "the pointy end of the boat."

Drinking became an off-duty pastime, as it had during the First World War, for the young fighter pilots. Every squadron had its favorite "boozer" in nearby French villages. It was quite unlike their local pubs, back home, with the traditional dart board and the pints of bitters. Champagne was easily obtained in the boozers and it was a reasonable substitute for the delectable English beers. It was, of course, dubbed "giggle water."

Victories were celebrated either in the local boozer or in the squadron mess. And, since victories were few in the early weeks, the officer pilots were frequently invited to the sergeant's mess for a blow. Or else a group of men from one squadron visited another squadron. After much imbibing of giggle water such blows became rather destructive and lacking in decorum. Visiting dignitaries were requested to stand on their heads, as a kind of squadron initiation. Or a playful wrestling match resulted in a battle royal and the eradication of the supply of chinaware, chairs, and even tables.

It was following one of these parties that four members of No. 1 Squadron poured themselves into their car to return to their squadron. Two, in the rear seat, were completely out. The other two, the squadron leader—whose car it was—and a pilot, Paul Richey, manned the forward seat.

Soon they were racing through the darkened French countryside. The following (authentic) conversation took place:

"Not so fast, Paul," cautioned the squadron leader.

Edgar J. "Cobber" Kain of Christchurch, New Zealand, and No. 73 Squadron, RAF. The first official British ace of the Second World War with seventeen victories, Kain was killed while "beating up" his airdome in France just before he was to have returned to England to become a flying instructor.

(IMPERIAL WAR MUSEUM, LONDON)

"OK."

A few minutes later the squadron leader spoke again, "Ease off a bit, old boy."

"OK," Richey hazily agreed.

Three minutes later Richey addressed the squadron leader.

"Hey, I'm not driving, you bloody fool, you are!"

"Am I?" said the squadron leader. "Oh, so I am."

The Brylcreem boys were forming their own traditions and Cobber Kain represented them in the first months of the war. The subject of discipline was not taken too seriously. He smiled (if only inwardly) when Squadron Leader Knox tore off a strip, but rebelled when Knox went a step beyond and grounded him. A really drastic punishment was to put Kain in charge of the operations tent, where

he heard the sounds of the battle over the radio to his discomfiture and frustration.

On March 26, 1940, after completing a full day in the operations tent, Kain had reached the limit. On hearing of much enemy activity over the frontier, he sprinted out of the tent and pulled away in his Hurricane in company with two other No. 73 Squadron men.

"In the Luxembourg corner," Kain later reported, "I saw a number of enemy aircraft and proceeded to investigate at 2:30 p.m. I gave a message on R/T [radio telephone] to Flying Officer Perry and Sgt. Pilot Pyne, who were with me—'Enemy aircraft ahead'—and proceeded to attack. I turned into the enemy which had started to climb and gave a burst at the leader who pulled up, turned on his back and spun away in flames. I then noticed 5 more M.E. 109's working round behind me, so I turned hard right and took a sight on the near machine. I fired a burst at him, he dived away and I took three deflection shots at another M.E. 109 which was slowly turning ahead of me. I got behind this aircraft and gave it a burst. He turned on his starboard side and dived right down towards earth."

Suddenly the sky was clear of aircraft, except for Kain's, so he searched for the other Hurricanes. Seeing nothing, he turned south just as his Hurricane was struck by two shells, one hitting the cockpit and the other the fuel tank.

"The explosion of the hood of my cockpit rendered me unconscious," Kain reported, "but I came to diving steeply. After a while I managed to pull out of the dive and tried to bend down and turn off the petrol, but the flames burnt my face. I headed towards France to gain as much ground as possible and when the flames got too intense I decided to abandon my aircraft."

Heaving himself out of the burning plane, Kain pulled the ripcord at twelve thousand feet. At ten thousand feet he emerged from the clouds where he found that it "was all very still and I thought I was in heaven." Afraid that he would land in Germany, Kain yanked at the strings of the parachute, slipping the air and hastening the descent. He painfully struck the ground near Ritzing in the vicinity of a woods. He gathered up his chute, ran for the woods, hid the chute, and set out in a southerly direction hoping he would find himself in France. He was soon challenged by a French captain and after being properly identified, Kain was sent to Evendorff for first aid. He had been burned and was limping badly. The captain informed Kain that he had dropped into No Man's Land, between the French and German positions.

A French staff car returned Kain to Rouves where the squadron medic, Flight Lieutenant R. M. Outfin, spent two hours cleaning up the burns. Kain's uniform was in tatters and had to be abandoned. As he stood up to leave, Kain winced.

"What's wrong with your leg, Cobber?" Outfin asked.

"I don't know, doc," Kain replied. "Some things went in and I don't think they came out." Whereupon Cobber Kain collapsed. The doctor proceeded to remove over twenty pieces of shrapnel from his leg.

Two hours later, when the officers prepared to go to the sergeant's mess as guests for an evening of "fun and games," Cobber Kain's shouts echoed through the village. He would not be muzzled until he was taken in a stretcher by the doctor and a medical orderly to the sergeant's mess. Kain drank to his comrades' good health. They returned the compliment and the happy Kain was carried back to his billet through the village.

Upon recovery Kain was given a ten days' leave in London, where he was awarded the Distinguished Flying Cross, the first bestowed upon a British airman in France. On rejoining his squadron on April 11, Kain seemed to have changed slightly. He was as good-humored and as eager to fly as ever, but he was more businesslike, even neater. Cobber Kain had become engaged while in London and was to be married in June. Soon he was back in action and had scored about twelve official victories. Even so, the days were short on combat despite the improvement in the weather. What was Jerry up to?

III

At dawn, May 10, 1940, they found out. Massive Nazi columns surged over Dutch, Belgian, and Luxembourg's frontiers as Luftwaffe assaults smashed and scorched the airfields behind the lines. It was the third, and to date the most effective, demonstration of blitzkrieg. The twilight war erupted into a nightmare of panzer and Stuka: *Fall Gelb* had finally come.

The extent of this nightmare was soon obvious in air battles such as were not experienced during the first eight months of the war. Typical was the tragic epic of the Maastricht bridges, which furnished the Germans crossing over the Albert Canal in Belgium. Once secured these would serve as bridgeheads for pouring German troops into northern France.

The desperate Belgians had failed to blow the bridges and appealed to the Allies for aid. Counterattacks by ground troops did not drive the Germans away from the bridges, which by May 11 carried streams of armored vehicles, troops, supplies, and ammunition across the Albert Canal. On this same day the Germans carried out one of the brilliant coups of the war: the capture of Fort Eben Emael, reputed to be the most modern, strongest fort in Europe. It was situated a few miles south of Maastricht overlooking the juncture of the Meuse River and the canal. This formidable position was taken from above, by air-borne troops flown in silently by glider. These were towed by Ju-52s from Cologne and released over Aachen, about twenty miles from the fortress. Nine gliders gracefully landed atop the fort and specially trained troops proceeded to put the fort out of action with explosives, grenades, and flame throwers. Reinforcements arrived by parachute and by the afternoon of May 11, with additional help from the Stukas and ground troops, the Germans had taken Fort Eben Emael. Simultaneously with this, air-borne troops also dropped upon the bridge sites to the north of the fort. One, at Canne, was destroyed by the Belgians, but two, at Veldwezelt and Vroenhoven, fell into German hands.

The task of denying the use of these two bridges to the Germans fell to No. 12 Squadron, known as the "Dirty Dozen." Air Vice-Marshal P. H. L. Playfair, commanding the Advanced Air Striking Force, although realizing the mission was undoubtedly foredoomed, asked for volunteers. Characteristically, the entire squadron stepped forward, but only six Fairey Battles were scheduled for the attack, three for each bridge. Leading one section, Flying Officer Norman M. Thomas was to strike at the concrete bridge at Vroenhoven while Flying Officer Donald E. Garland led the other section against the metal bridge at Veldwezelt. That their four 250-pound bombs could do much damage, especially to the concrete bridge, was questionable. So was their breaking through a Luftwaffe-infested sky, let alone the flak. But they would try.

"You British are mad," a German officer later told one of the Battle pilots, I. A. McIntosh. "We capture the bridge [in this instance the one at Veldwezelt] early Friday morning. You give us all Friday and Saturday to get our flak guns up in circles all around the bridge and then on Sunday, when all is ready, you come along with three aircraft and try and blow the thing up."

But they did try, although "at all costs," as the orders had read.

Early on Sunday morning six Battles warmed up on the tarmac at Amifontaine. Then it was discovered that one of the planes in Thomas's section had a defective radio; the crew switched to another Battle, which, it developed, had a malfunction in the hydraulic system. Only five aircraft took off for the bridges. Thomas led his section, consisting only of one other Battle, piloted by Flying Officer T. D. H. Davy. Garland led his full section, the other two planes of which were flown by Pilot Officer I. A. McIntosh and Sergeant F. Marland.

Thomas and Garland had disagreed upon the tactics of the mission. Thomas believed that the approach should be from a high level while "Garland was determined," as Thomas explained, "to carry out a low-level attack, thinking it not only the best form, but the safest.

"My parting words to him were 'it will be interesting to see the result, and may we both be lucky enough to return.'"

An escort of six Hurricanes from No. 1 Squadron had been supplied to clear the air of German fighters. Thomas and Davy flew at six thousand feet—at a thousand feet seven-tenths cloud cover obscured the ground and afforded some protection from flak batteries. While the Hurricanes tackled the Messerschmitts Thomas led the attack on the Vroenhoven bridge. Enemy fighters bore in upon Davy's plane, however, and a brief exchange of fire ensued in which the gunner of the Battle shot down one Messerschmitt. Other German planes went down in the battle, but five of the six Hurricanes were lost.

Over Vroenhoven the two Battles ran into a wall of flak and machine-gun fire. Diving through this murderous barrage, through the clouds, the two Battles raced for the concrete bridge. Fragments of both planes whipped back into the slipstream as the flak hammered at them. The determined British dropped their bombs on the bridge, some of them from so low that the Battles were endangered by their own bomb blasts. Almost negligible damage resulted to the bridge.

When Thomas pulled his Battle out of the dive he realized the plane was too battered to remain in the air. The engine quickly sputtered out and he had to land. Thomas found an open field and brought the Battle in for a wheels-up landing. Within minutes Thomas and his crew were taken prisoner.

Davy too had engine trouble and a badly sieved aircraft. But he hoped to return to base. When it appeared that the Battle might drop out of the air at any moment, he ordered the other two men to jump. This was in the vicinity of Liége, where one of the crew was captured (mistakenly as a German) and manhandled by Belgian civilians until the police arrived. Davy, even with the lighter load, could not keep the Battle air-borne all the way to Amifontaine. He crash-landed inside Belgium.

Garland's section, meanwhile, had proceeded to the Veldwezelt bridge. Determined to carry out a surprise attack from low level, Garland ordered the fuses on the bombs to be set at eleven-second delay. Thus Garland planned to swoop down, drop the bombs, and just have time to get away. As the three Battles approached the bridge the screen of flak fire roared into a frightful crescendo. McIntosh's plane was the first to be hit and the Battle burst into flame. The pilot kept it on its bomb run as long as possible until the observer released the bombs (although with scant if any accuracy). The burning plane crashed shortly after and the crew pulled the near-unconscious McIntosh from the wreck. The three men found refuge, momentarily, in a ditch.

The air over the bridge was an inferno. The twenty-one-year-old Garland, just newly commissioned a flying officer, was resolute. He led his section, now consisting only of his plane and Sergeant Marland's, into the fury over Veldwezelt. He carefully lined up the Battle on a suicide run and accelerated the slender bomber into the barrage. Just as coolly, his observer, Sergeant Thomas Gray, took meticulous aim before releasing the small bomb load. Whether or not these men saw that their bombs scored direct hits upon their target is not known. The terrific flak onslaught ripped the Battle to pieces. Marland also may have scored hits on the bridge but possibly neither he nor anyone else ever knew.

From the ditch in which he was sheltered, McIntosh saw one Battle still in the air, the focus of the relentless flak guns. "We saw this Battle trying to get away," he said. "Then it suddenly stood on its tail, climbed vertically for about a hundred feet, stalled, and nose-dived to earth." They did not know whose plane it was. It hardly mattered, for all three Battles had been knocked out of the sky and only

McIntosh and his crew survived. For their efforts in the attack Garland and Gray received the Victoria Cross, posthumously, Britain's supreme award and the first given to RAF personnel. But the third crew member, Leading Aircraftman L. R. Reynolds, radio-gunner, inexplicably received no award at all. Davy, who tried to bring his plane back to base, was given a Distinguished Flying Cross.

All five aircraft had been lost, two crews of three men each had been killed, two crews had been captured, and one had made it back to Allied lines. This expensive, almost quixotic, show of valor had achieved only slight damage to the bridge and cratering of the approaches at Vroenhoven. The Veld-

A camouflaged Battle of No. 218 Squadron, Advanced Air Striking Force, in France, 1940. The ground crew prepares the aircraft for combat which, during the "Phony War" never materialized but which, following the unleashing of Fall Gelb (Plan Yellow) *on May 10, 1940, became devastatingly sufficient. Ten out of the eleven Battles of No. 218 Squadron which had been*

sent to help hold up the German advance at Sedan were destroyed on May 14 in a futile attempt. Despite losses of more than half the RAF bombers which participated in the attack at Sedan and despite the concerted effort by both French and British Air Forces, the Germans rolled on into France.

wezelt Bridge suffered serious damage to its western truss and was out of use—temporarily.

The Maastricht carnage was but a prelude. As the seemingly invincible German armored forces overran the Netherlands and Belgium, the French—to the south—were shocked by the unexpected materialization of a German vanguard in the form of Ewald von Kleist's Panzer group thrusting through the "impassable" Ardennes Forest. Soon German armored cars and tanks had crossed the Meuse at Sedan. Even earlier, on May 13, General Erwin

Now, on the morning of May 14, 1940, an attempt was made to stop the flood of Hitler's troops passing over pontoon bridges at Sedan. Ten Battles were dispatched from Nos. 103 and 150 Squadrons of the Advanced Air Striking Force. They attacked their targets and, encountering no fighters or flak, all planes returned safely. Air Marshal A. S. Barratt, in command of all British air forces in France, then planned to send bomber forces to deal with Rommel's panzers at Dinant. He was requested by the French to lend all-out effort to a counterattack at Sedan. Because of the command situation in

A Battle of No. 150 Squadron shot down during the Battle of Sedan, during which forty (mostly obsolete) aircraft vainly attempted to stop the Wehrmacht from crossing the Meuse. (H. J. NOWARRA)

A Ju-52 drops men of Fallschirmjäger-Regiment 1— paratroopers—upon Waalhaven, near Rotterdam, as Hitler began the blitzkrieg into the Low Countries. (H. J. NOWARRA)

Rommel, leading his 7th Panzer Division (attached to Günther Hans von Kluge's Fourth Army), had breached the Meuse at Dinant. The stunned French called for aerial interference of the establishment of German bridgeheads at Monthermé and Sedan.

The latter town had particularly tragic overtones in French history. It had been at Sedan, in 1870, where the Germans defeated Marshal Patrice MacMahon's army, captured Napoleon III, and brought an end to the Second Empire. During the First World War, Sedan, a town of about thirteen thousand people, situated on the north bank of the Meuse on the edge of the Ardennes Forest about five miles from the Belgian frontier, had been occupied by the Germans.

France, Barratt was forced to comply. Instead of Dinant, they would attack at Sedan.

His bomber force had dwindled in just the few days since the blitzkrieg had reignited. On May 10 there had been 135 operational AASF bombers on hand; by the evening of May 12 only 72 remained.

But the early morning bombing of Sedan boded well. Around noon the second wave of Allied bombers was sent in; this consisted of a few French aircraft, which were so badly mauled that the French air effort for the day was ended. Then, beginning at three in the afternoon, all available RAF medium bombers—Battles and Blenheims— were hurled at Sedan.

By this time of the day, which the Germans at

the time called "the day of the fighters," the air over Sedan was alive with German fighters (Messerschmitt Bf-109Es), which were superior in speed to the Hurricane. The Battles and Blenheims were so many sitting ducks. Among the elite units the ill-fated British planes encountered were Jagdgeschwader 2, the "Richthofen" unit named for the First

of the eight planes sent on the mission). More than half the Battles did not return to their bases: No. 12 Squadron lost four out of five planes; No. 88 one out of ten; No. 103 three out of eight; No. 105 six out of eleven; No. 142 four out of eight; No. 150 all four of its planes; No. 218 Squadron ten out of eleven; and No. 226 three out of six. A total of

Flood tide: Ernst Udet, Adolf Galland, and Werner Mölders. During the Battle of France Udet was head of the Luftwaffe's Technical Office, Galland the op- *erations officer of Jagdgeschwader 27, and Mölders the top-scoring ace of Jagdgeschwader 53 ("Richthofen").* (NATIONAL ARCHIVES)

World War ace, and Jagdgeschwader 53, in whose third *Gruppe* (i.e., III/JG 53) was the famed Hauptmann Werner Mölders. On May 14 Mölders added another victory mark to the tail of his Me-109: it was his tenth.

As relentlessly as the British came in to attack Sedan, just so relentlessly did the Luftwaffe take its toll. In all, eight Battle squadrons were dispatched along with two Blenheim squadrons (which lost five

thirty-five Battles were destroyed of the sixty-three sent. Counting the Blenheims, the British lost forty aircraft out of the seventy-one they had been able to muster for the attack on Sedan.

There was but a momentary pause in the German thrust across the Meuse; by nightfall Heinz Guderian's panzers crossed the bridgehead and seized the bridges over the Ardennes Canal. The way was open for a drive toward the north and the English Channel; it would outflank the British Expeditionary Forces and the French armies backing up the Dutch and the Belgians. The beaten, demoralized French Ninth Army fell back from an ever widening German front.

By this same morning of May 14 the fate of the Netherlands had already been decided and reached a grim climax in the bombing of Rotterdam. Within four days after the German attack it was clear that the Dutch were beaten. Queen Wilhelmina and the government had fled to England. Some pockets of resistance held, and they were troublesome, but obviously the small, "neutral" country was no military match for the Germans. Still their stubborn fight interfered with the rapid German advance toward France through Belgium, also neutral.

Orders had come from General Georg von Küchler, commanding the small but potent Eighteenth Army, that resistance in and around Rotterdam must be broken "by every means." By eight o'clock in the morning of May 14 surrender negotiations had begun although not without hairsplitting demands on the part of the Dutch commander in Rotterdam, Colonel P. Scharroo. He refused to deal with Dutch civilians sent by Oberstleutnant Dietrich von Choltitz, whose forces were attempting to cross the bridges into Rotterdam. A stickler for form, Scharroo rejected another, this time more official, capitulation proposal from General Rudolf Schmidt (commanding the XXXIX Corps) because it did not carry the proper "rank, name, and signature."

This same ultimatum, however, carried the threat of an aerial attack upon Rotterdam unless Scharroo surrendered. The plans for this attack had already been formulated: one hundred Heinkel 111s of Kampfgeschwader 54 would bomb the center of Rotterdam. The first bombs fell at around three o'clock in the afternoon even while surrender negotiations were under way.

Immediately before the German bombers took off they had been informed of the possibility of a Dutch surrender. If this came about before they reached the target in Rotterdam red Very pistols were to be fired from the ground and the bombers were to return without dropping their high-explosive bombs. While this may seem a humane precaution on the part of the Germans, it is difficult to understand how it was expected that the bomber crews might discern from bombing altitude the red lights in the haze and flame of the battle below. At best, it was a halfhearted precaution.

The crucial question of time reveals the split-second development of the calamity. It had been around noon that General Kurt Student, leading the air-borne troops in Holland, radioed Schmidt's XXXIX Corps headquarters that "bombing attack Rotterdam postponed owing to surrender negotiations." The attack was set for 3 P.M. Just five minutes before, at 2:55 P.M., General Schmidt sent yet another communiqué to Scharroo outlining surrender terms, giving the Dutch commander three hours in which to come to a decision—that is, until six o'clock.

Obviously communications between the German ground and air forces had become inefficient. The Dutch courier hastened across the Willems Bridge. He had barely reached the other side when a hundred Heinkels appeared over the city.

Recall orders had obviously been sent from Luftflotte 2, but as the planes were on their bombing run, and their receiving antennas having been retracted, the messages were not heard by the bomber radio operators. According to German accounts, desperate attempts were made to divert the bombers by discharging Very pistols into the air, but either the crews did not see them or mistook the signals for Dutch antiaircraft fire. Bombs began falling into the heart of Rotterdam.

Just as his plane's bomb load was dropped, Oberstleutnant Otto Hohne, commander of III/KG 54, spotted two red flares ascending through the smoke below. He shouted the recall order code word to his radio operator, who wired to the rest of the formation and prevented the dropping of all but a few bomb loads. It did not matter a great deal to the Dutch by this time, however.

Just over half of the hundred Heinkels had dropped hundred-pound and five-hundred pound bombs into the center of the old city: a total of ninety-seven tons. Within hours Rotterdam was in

---

Rotterdam after the May 14, 1940, "error" bombing by the Luftwaffe. Although the bombing mission had been called off because surrender negotiations were in progress, more than fifty aircraft dropped ninety-seven tons of explosives into the city, which burned uncontrollably.

(PRESS & INFORMATION SERVICES, ROTTERDAM)

flames: the small fire department was all but help-less because a bomb had hit a margarine factory. Burning oil spread to the timbered buildings and the heart of Rotterdam disintegrated in smoke. A twelve-year-old boy wrote that "There is a funny smell in the air like burned meat and a funny yellow light all over the country from the incendiary bombs. [This is an error. No incendiaries were used.] . . . I went out for a while and they were taking dead people out of the bombed houses. . . . It is awful to watch the people standing by their bombed houses. They don't do much. They just walk around and look at them and look sad and tired."

Rotterdam on that May 14, 1940, became a sym-bol of German *Kultur* like Guernica and Warsaw. The casualties, turned to propaganda uses by the Allies, were exaggerated. The official Dutch figure at the time—and it may have been an honest er-ror—reached thirty thousand dead.

The actual figure would be closer to a thousand men, women, and children—killed in the seven and a half minutes the Heinkels remained over Rotter-dam. In all, twenty thousand buildings were de-stroyed by bombs and the ensuing fires; seventy-eight thousand people were rendered homeless. A square mile of the city smoldered for days. By six o'clock in the evening the Dutch had capitulated. The blitzkrieg had crushed the Netherlands in five days.

Belgium was next on the Nazi timetable. The Belgians, led by King Leopold and reinforced by French and British troops, fought bitterly. The pat-tern was repeated and within eighteen days—on May 27, 1940—Leopold asked for a German peace. This action, however inevitable, was taken without proper consultation with his allies, and placed the French and British forces in serious jeopardy and possible annihilation. Already under pressure by the German forces which had broken through at Sedan, the beleaguered Allies, falling back into France, were left with their left flank exposed. The exhausted armies were rapidly encircled in steel, the panzers, the Stukas, and the Wehrmacht, drawing them closer to the sea at their backs, until the entire British Expeditionary Force, the French First Army as well as units of the Seventh and Ninth Armies, along with Belgian and Polish troops converged upon the French port of Dunkirk.

IV

There were two miracles at Dunkirk, one British, the other German.

The German "miracle" came to pass in the eve-ning of May 24 when from the headquarters of Von Rundstedt's Army Group A an order was issued halting the armored thrust from the south and the west. Panzer Group Kleist and Guderian's 19th Corps pulled up roughly on the line of canals run-ning from Gravelines on the Channel coast and southeasterly through Saint-Omer to Bethune. Rund-stedt had convinced the Führer that the tanks, after the surprising swing through France from the breakthrough at Sedan, should be rested for the major battle of France to come. With the Führer's backing there was no questioning the stop order, despite the objections of Commander in Chief Wal-ther von Brauchitsch. Hitler, who waxed manic-depressive, was one moment decisive and the next cautious. The success of the Lowlands campaign and the breach in the Ardennes was difficult to as-similate. And then Göring promised to destroy the fleeing allies on the Channel with his Luftwaffe. Why exhaust and deplete the Panzer forces if the Air Force could do the job? It was this con-sideration, not the fatuous one that Hitler had elected to spare the British, which resulted in the stop order.

Göring's vanity prompted him to offer more than the Luftwaffe could deliver. Many of the bomber *Geschwader* were still based far from the Dunkirk area, which fact would require long-distance flying and little time over the target. But the Wehrmacht and the panzers had been snatching most of the glory in the Lowlands, while the Luftwaffe con-tinued in a subservient role. Göring longed for a Luftwaffe coup, pure and simple, with no portion of the credit to the Army or Navy.

That the British had already begun to plan Opera-tion Dynamo, the evacuation, was not known to the Germans. That the British would attempt to evacu-ate from such ports as Calais, La Panne, and Dun-kirk seemed likely, but to the land-loving Ger-mans and to Hitler especially, for he had no sea sense at all, any large-scale withdrawal was un-thinkable.

The beach at Dunkirk: troops of the British Expeditionary Forces awaiting deliverance by "the little boats" and the Royal Navy after being driven into a pocket by the Wehrmacht. During the nine days of Dunkirk more than 300,000 men were rescued from the beaches of Dunkirk despite the efforts of the Luftwaffe. (NATIONAL ARCHIVES)

An RAF Coastal Command Lockheed Hudson flies over the beaches of Dunkirk. Oil storage tanks have been set aflame by Luftwaffe bombers.

(LOCKHEED PHOTO)

The British miracle (without qualifying quotation marks) was a stunning accomplishment of flexible planning, courage, civilian participation, imaginative improvisation, and sheer British doggedness. History's most heterogeneous armada gathered along the southeast coast of England. At Dover Vice-Admiral Sir Bertram Ramsay took charge of Operation Dynamo. Besides the craft of the Royal Navy, the Admiralty had pressed civilian motorboats into service. "At the same time," Winston Churchill has written, "lifeboats from liners in the London docks, tugs from the Thames, yachts, fishing-craft, lighters, barges, and pleasure-boats—anything that could be of use along the beaches—were called into service. By the night of the 27th a great tide of small vessels began to flow towards the sea, first to our Channel ports, and thence to the beaches of Dun-

kirk and the beloved Army." A total of 860 vessels of every description took part in the "Dunkirk deliverance," as Churchill called it. Seven hundred were British ships, the rest were French, Polish, Belgian, and Dutch. Nearly 250 ships of the armada were sunk, most of them by the Luftwaffe.

As the men of the British Expeditionary Force limped or were carried ashore, their eyes revealed the harrowing experience they had undergone. Their hollow-cheeked faces were begrimed by the smoke of oil fire, burning vehicles, and shells. These wearied men, returned with only what they wore—for their weapons were abandoned on the beaches at Dunkirk—grateful for their deliverance, brought a bitter question with them.

"Where was the bloody RAF?"

The infantryman, whose concern is generally confined to the few feet of ground he occupies, has little conception of the airman's war. On the Dunkirk beaches the infantryman was only aware of the bombing and strafing of the Luftwaffe. Rarely did he see or recognize a British aircraft overhead. He did not see the Blenheims of No. 107 Squadron bombing the advancing German columns on May 27—the day the evacuation officially began. Coincidentally, it was also the day on which the Rundstedt-Hitler stop order was withdrawn, after a two-and-a-half-day pause.

At dawn on Monday, May 27, the Heinkels began the bombardment of the defense perimeter around Dunkirk; then came Richthofen's Stukas to pin-point the targets. The Dorniers followed. These last were surprised on being attacked by Spitfires of No. 74 Squadron—the first major encounter with this new fighter. Hurricanes of No. 145 Squadron also joined the battle, but the British were always outnumbered by the Messerschmitt 109s and 110s. However, it was soon obvious that the Spitfire was a match for the Me-109 and superior to the Hurricane as a high-altitude fighter.

Even so, great numbers of German bombers broke through the Spitfire and Hurricane formations and bombed the beaches and the ships in the Channel. Oil storage tanks on the western outskirts of Dunkirk were set afire and the black smoke rose as a thick, curling beacon to friend and foe alike. But when the weather turned damp and the ceiling descended this same oily smoke combined with the smoke from the fires in the town and mist to afford cover for the evacuation.

A pilot of No. 43 Squadron described the scene as he saw it from above: "All the harbour at Dunkirk seemed to be on fire with the black smoke from the oil dumps," he said. "The destroyers moved out of the pall of smoke in a most uncanny way, deep in the water and heavily laden with troops. I was flying at about 1000 feet above the beach and the sea. And there I could see the *Brighton Belle*, and the paddle steamers, and the sort of cheerful little boats you see calling at coastal towns on Sunday. Hundreds of boats! Fishing boats and motor boats, and Thames river craft and strings of dinghies, being towed by bigger boats. All packed with troops, and people standing in the water and awful bomb craters in the beach, and lines of men and groups of people sitting down. Waiting, I suppose. And I could see rifles—stacked in threes. And destroyers going back into the black smoke. And wrecked ships on the beach: wrecked ships of all sizes, sticking out of the water. And a destroyer cut in halves by a bomb. I saw it!"

On the beach itself all was a horror. A British gunnery officer sensed "a deadly evil atmosphere . . . a lurid study in red and black. . . . A horrible stench of blood and mutilated flesh pervaded the place. There was no escape from it. Not a breath of air was blowing to dissipate the appalling odour that arose from the dead bodies that had been lying on the sand, in some cases for several days. We might have been walking through a slaughterhouse on a hot day. The darkness, which hid some of the sights of horror from our eyes, seemed to thicken this dreadful stench. It created the impression that death was hovering around, very near at hand. . . ."

The aerial battles generally occurred out of sight of the besieged ground troops. Although German planes did attack mercilessly, the Luftwaffe did not gain mastery of the air over Dunkirk because of the defense afforded by the Hurricane and Spitfire squadrons of No. 11 Group under the command of Air Vice-Marshal Keith R. Park. To contend with the massive formations of German fighters and bombers Park had only sixteen squadrons available —that is, about two hundred fighters. From their bases in southern England the fighters would have to be flown at least fifty miles to the battle area— without the advantage of radar to pin-point the

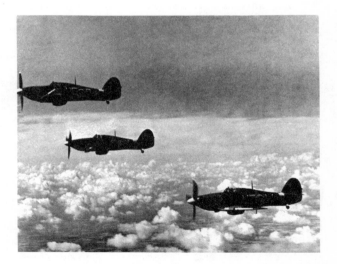

"Where was the bloody RAF?" The Hurricanes (and the Spitfires) operated above the clouds in fighting the Luftwaffe and so were rarely seen by the beleaguered ground troops at Dunkirk. Although RAF fighters intercepted German bombers, some broke through to bomb the beaches. (U. S. AIR FORCE)

German attacks. This meant that fuel limitations enforced about a forty-minute stay over Dunkirk for the Hurricanes and Spitfires.

To send all sixteen squadrons to cover the entire evacuation area was impossible (it was attempted on the first day, May 27, but the wasteful fuel consumption rendered such tactics infeasible; it also left England open to air attack, and the defense of the home islands was the major function of Fighter Command). Beginning on May 29, Park devised a patrol system over Dunkirk, using four squadrons at a time. Consequently there were stretches of time when no RAF fighters patrolled directly over Dunkirk. Also, while attempting to attack the bombers, they were in turn attacked by the Messerschmitts. Two very large formations of German bombers, including the vulnerable Stuka and the vaunted Junkers 88, assaulted the beaches while no British fighters were present. Three other formations, however, had been mauled by the British fighters.

In the turmoil as much, possibly more, shipping was lost through collision as to German bombs. Also owing to the confusion of battle—and faulty aircraft recognition, especially on the part of the Royal Navy—the men in the Dunkirk perimeter fired indiscriminately at friend and foe alike. All aircraft were taken to be hostile by the harassed troops crowding into the sea. Rear Admiral William Wake-Walker recalled several such incidents on June 1, the sixth day of the evacuation. Spitfires flying low over the beaches received the same attention from the British guns as did a Messerschmitt—even after Wake-Walker hoisted the cease fire flag. Later he witnessed a similar piece of action as he stood talking with Captain W. G. Tennant, the senior naval officer in charge of shore operations, when "a Lysander Army Co-op plane came over very low and flew over the pier. It was fired at by several Bofors guns and Tennant said, 'I'm sure that damn fellow is a Hun—he has been flying over here all day.' I then realized," Wake-Walker reported, "it was the plane flying over at my request to see if the pier was being shelled, and I felt sorry for the poor chap; though he seemed none the worse."

Not all the errors were made on the ground, for Spitfires and Hurricanes attacked each other above the clouds also.

The Luftwaffe attacks on June 1 had been so vicious—Stukas by the dozen not only attacked the ships but also came in low to strafe the struggling figures in the water—that Ramsay realized that the evacuation could be continued only at night. The German ground forces had also begun to press in on the perimeter and the sands of Dunkirk erupted with the shelling from German artillery.

The fighting in the air too had become desperate; the initiative belonged to the Luftwaffe, which could muster great numbers of bombers with escorts. As the battle progressed, and as the German infantry closed in, the Luftwaffe gained airdromes closer to battle site. Only the weather and the RAF interfered. But from time to time, such as on May 29 and June 1, the sun broke through and cleared the mist, and the Germans concentrated with fury on Dunkirk. And so it went, intermittently for the nine days.

"Well, another day is gone," wrote Flight Lieutenant R. D. G. Wight of No. 213 Squadron to his mother, "and with it a lot of grand blokes. Got another brace of 109's today, but the whole Luftwaffe seems to leap on us—we were hopelessly outnumbered. I was caught napping by a 109 in the middle of a dog fight and got a couple of holes in the aircraft, one of them filled the office with smoke, but the Jerry overshot and *he's* dead. If anyone says anything to you in the future about the inefficiency of the R.A.F.—I believe the B.E.F. troops were booing the R.A.F. in Dover the other day—tell them from me we only wish we could do more. But without aircraft we can do no more than we have done— that is, our best, and that's fifty times better than the German best, though they are fighting under the most advantageous conditions."

On the morning of June 4, with the Germans within two miles of the beaches, Operation Dynamo was officially closed. About forty thousand French troops remained behind to hold off the Germans —just as they had during the nine days at Calais and Cassel. Theirs had been an enormous contribution to the miracle of Dunkirk—a contribution frequently slighted in view of the performance of the "little boats" and their own political and military leaders subsequently.

Dunkirk was no military victory. The Germans had permitted practically the entire British Army to escape. True, they were weaponless and most of their equipment lay abandoned along the beaches

German troops haul in a trophy from the English Channel, the tail section of an RAF Hurricane shot down during the desperate fighting of the last weeks of the Battle of France. (NATIONAL ARCHIVES)

at Dunkirk, but it was a tough, experienced army. The Luftwaffe had not been able to achieve—if, indeed, they were achievements—a Warsaw or a Rotterdam. This despite the ease with which the smoking, water-outlined target could be found even in bad weather.

The cost of Dunkirk in shipping was high: 6 destroyers were sunk, 8 personnel ships, 5 minesweepers, 17 trawlers, a hospital ship, a sloop, 3 tugboats, 3 yachts, and 182 other assorted craft. The RAF lost over 100 aircraft and 80 pilots in the Dunkirk battles. The Luftwaffe lost about 150 planes, although claims were made for twice that number.

Churchill reminded the British that "Wars are not won by evacuations. But there was a victory inside this deliverance, which should be noted. It was gained by the Air Force. . . ."

If it was not a spectacular victory, even an almost negligible one, it was, on a small scale, a prologue to the coming battle over Britain. It might have served as portent to the Luftwaffe of things to come.

Dunkirk had not been a victory for the British, although 338,000 men had been snatched out of the jaws of the devouring blitzkrieg. But it was a triumph of the British spirit, best expressed by Churchill during the nine days when he said, "Of course, whatever happens at Dunkirk, we shall fight on."

Churchill had been handed the reins of govern-

ment, taking over from the ailing and tottering Chamberlain, in the early evening of May 10, 1940 —that morning the Germans had struck in the Low Countries. Reveling in crisis, defying adversity, and spoiling for a fight, the once discredited Churchill, whose warnings of a burgeoning military Nazi Germany had not contributed to his popularity, was the embodiment of the British spirit. He watched the fighting in France with concern, but never with the loss of hope so evident in the French government and High Command.

When the Germans attacked there were eight Hurricane squadrons in France, the Air Component's Nos. 3, 85, 87, 607, and 615 Squadrons and the AASF's Nos. 1, 73, and 501 Squadrons. By May 12 these were joined by Nos. 79 and 504 Squadrons sent to the dwindling Air Component taxed with the support of the BEF. Under the onslaught of the blitzkrieg in the north of France the seven squadrons of the Air Component had been reduced to about three on May 17; four days later the remnants were ordered back to England.

The fighter pilots who had complained about the "phony war" and the scanty air activity had little cause for gripes after May 10. Their fields were bombed and strafed and they were air-borne from dawn till dusk. The bombers of AASF were spent in bombing the advancing Nazi columns while the Hurricanes furnished fighter cover. There was plenty of action for eager fighter pilots, German as well as British and French.

On May 12 Adolf Galland, one of Germany's outstanding airmen, scored his first "kill," a Belgian Hurricane. Flying with a wingman in an Me-109E, Galland had stolen some time away from his desk job. The two Germans spotted a formation of eight Hurricanes flying at nine thousand feet near Liége. Diving from above, Galland opened on an unsuspecting Belgian. The first burst from Galland's guns startled the Hurricane pilots and the formation scattered. The German concentrated on his victim, now clumsily trying to evade the guns of the Messerschmitt. The poorly trained pilot in the antiquated Hurricane had no chance. Galland's second burst shot away the Hurricane's rudder and the plane spun away. Before striking the ground the aircraft shed parts of its wings. Galland then turned to the remaining Belgian planes. Finding one Hurricane attempting to dive away from the battle, Galland in his superior Me-109 pulled up to within a hundred yards of it. The plane whipped away in a half roll and through an opening in the clouds. But the experienced Galland remained locked to the Hurricane's tail. A burst of gunfire and the Belgian plane pulled up for a moment, stalled, and dived straight into the ground. In the afternoon of the same day, while on a routine patrol flight, Galland accounted for another Hurricane—his third victory of the day.

On the day after the Dunkirk evacuation, June 5, Werner Mölders, the leading German ace with twenty-five "kills" to his credit, joined a battle in the vicinity of Amiens. The contenders were French Dewoitine 520s, the best—and rarest, because of the inefficiency of the Production Office—fighter the Armée de l'Air could muster. Only one group had been supplied with the D-520s before the Germans opened their attack on France. It was the group's planes which Mölders came upon fighting off the Messerschmitts. He fired at one of the French planes and lost it in the general melee: there were nine French aircraft standing off more than two dozen Messerschmitts. Mölders turned back to the center of battle. Suddenly his cockpit burst into flame and smoke, his throttle was shot out of his hand, and the Me-109 flipped into a vertical dive. Struggling inside the smoky cockpit, Mölders found the release catch and sent the cockpit hood off into the slipstream. Unexpectedly the Messerschmitt leveled for a second from its dive, which had pressed Mölders into the cockpit, and he jumped. Mölders, floating down into France, watched his plane crash into the ground. Thus it was that Germany's hero-ace was taken prisoner of war. When the French surrendered subsequently, however, Mölders and all the other German pilots taken prisoner in France were released.

On June 5 also the Germans opened their new offensive, *Fall Rot* ("Case Red"), across the Somme and the Seine. Before long their armor had crossed the Marne—the familiar names of an earlier war echoed the sound of disaster. Refugees filled the roads, fleeing from northern France to the south: these too were familiar scenes. The Luftwaffe contributed innovations by strafing and dive-bombing the clogged highways. By this time there were too few targets to keep them occupied.

The British pilots remaining in France, the rem-

Werner Mölders, who was shot down over France after the Dunkirk evacuation and taken prisoner; with the fall of France he was released and served later in the war as commander of Jagdgeschwader 51 on the Eastern Front. Mölder's official victory score for the Second World War was sixty-eight (and fourteen in Spain); he was killed in an air crash later in the war. (H. J. NOWARRA)

The French Dewoitine 520, the best of the few French fighters operational during the Battle of France. The German ace Mölders was shot down by a French pilot in a D-520. (MUSÉE DE L'AIR)

nants of Nos. 1, 73, and 501 Squadrons, later joined by Nos. 17 and 242 Squadrons, fell back to emergency landing strips southwest of Paris. The constant nervous strain, exhaustion, and high-altitude flying took its toll along with the German fighters. Individual pilots flew patrol after patrol until fatigue caused them to fall asleep in their cockpits while they were refueling and being rearmed. When their Hurricanes were ready, the ground crew had to punch the pilots awake. One pilot reported that he had fallen asleep three times while flying over German-occupied territory. Another pilot landed and fell asleep in the cockpit. He was lifted from the plane and when all attempts to awaken him failed, he was shipped to England. He awakened forty-eight hours later wondering how he had ever got back home.

Meanwhile, France lay broken and without hope in the path of the overwhelming German armies, now being lent close support by the Luftwaffe. Even small pockets of resistance were crushed under the Stukas working with the panzers. The French demanded more British fighter squadrons to deal with the Stukas. But the outcome of the battle was obvious and Churchill, after sending additional Hurricanes, relented and sent no more. Of the necessity of this decision he had been forcefully convinced by Fighter Command leader Air Marshal Hugh Dowding. The latter had estimated that fifty-two fighter squadrons would be required to defend Britain from the attack that must come once France was defeated. On hand were a mere twenty-five; if an additional ten squadrons were sent to France, only to be destroyed in the French holocaust, Britain too must fall. As early as May 15, 1940, Dowding had warned the Air Ministry that "if the Home Defense Force is drained away in desperate attempts to remedy the situation in France, defeat in France will involve the final, complete and irremediable defeat of this country."

Churchill, who was romantically inclined and could not leave a friend or an ally in trouble, was seriously tempted to send an additional ten Hurricane squadrons to France. The French were calling for no less than twenty. The dispatch of ten squadrons was being seriously considered when Chief of the Air Staff Air Chief Marshal Cyril Newall learned from Air Marshal A. S. Barratt, commanding the two British air forces in France,

that even if ten squadrons were sent there would be bases for no more than three.

Instead, at Newall's suggestion, six squadrons based in the south of England rotated to France: three each morning and three to relieve them in the afternoon. Soon after, upon witnessing the chaos and hopeless, desperation in France himself, Churchill concurred and no further fighter squadrons were sent to France.

The extent of the disorder and near paralysis of the French High Command was revealed when Benito Mussolini, concerned that his German colleague had so brilliantly outdistanced him in the race for conquest, declared war upon France and Great Britain. With the German Army within thirty miles of Paris it was safe no doubt for the Duce's legions to attack the Riviera. On May 10, 1940, Hitler had himself a partner in war: it would, in time, cost them both dearly.

It had been agreed in the French and British Supreme War Council that in the event of a declaration of war by Italy British aircraft were to be bombed-up to attack industrial targets in northern Italy.

So it was that in the early afternoon of May 11 No. 99 Squadron (Wellingtons) landed in France, near Salon, to refuel on the way to bomb Genoa. The longer-ranged Armstrong Whitworth Whitleys of Nos. 10, 51, 58, and 102 Squadrons accompanying the Wellingtons were to refuel in advance bases in the Channel Islands (instead of France) and proceed to targets in Genoa and Turin.

The Wellingtons had barely landed when Group Captain R. M. Field, in charge of the bomber force at Salon, was informed by the French that the planes were not to take off for Italy. Still wondering what this was about, Field received an order from the Air Ministry to send the bombers to Italy. The phone rang; it was the French commander again reiterating that bombing operations against Italian targets were forbidden.

From three-thirty in the afternoon till almost midnight Field was involved in a whirl of order and counterorder; it seemed his phone never stopped ringing. The French High Command had even gone to Barratt, at British Air Forces in France headquarters. Barratt called London attempting to get Churchill. He learned that the Prime Minister was in France. Churchill was, in fact, just sitting down

to dinner with French Premier Paul Reynaud, Supreme Allied Commander General Maxime Weygand, General Charles de Gaulle, and members of Churchill's party including Anthony Eden and Chief of the Imperial Staff Sir John Dill.

Churchill was reached through General Hastings Ismay, at Weygand's headquarters, and the Churchillian view was constant: "All our [that is, English] minds ran much more on bombing Milan and Turin the moment Mussolini declared war, and seeing how he liked that."

Insofar as he was able to judge, after sifting the various orders, views, and opinions, Captain Field must dispatch the Wellingtons to bomb Italy. The Whitleys in the meantime had already taken off from the Channel Islands.

As the Wellingtons taxied for the takeoff at Salon, the distracted French added the final touch. French trucks, lorries, and carts were driven onto the airfield and stalled strategically in the path of the British bombers. Thus effectively blocked, and not wanting to fight it out with his allies, Field canceled the mission to Italy. The Whitleys, however, continued on and of the thirty-six sent only thirteen bombed their targets. Bad icing conditions and storms over the Alps greatly curtailed the mission.

It required four additional days of discussion before the field at Salon was cleared of the French obstructions. Eight Wellingtons took off to bomb Genoa but again storms interfered and only one plane found the target.

The situation in France had deteriorated so thoroughly by this time that such missions seemed without point. On June 14 the triumphant Germans marched into Paris. On June 17, 1940, Marshal Henri Pétain, succeeding Reynaud as Premier, asked for an armistice. On the afternoon of June 21 Hitler appeared for less than a half hour in the Forest of Compiègne, some forty-five miles north of Paris, the site of the hated German surrender of 1918. Hitler literally danced at Compiègne and then left the technicalities of the signing of the new treaty to others. France was finished and the British were driven off the Continent again. Cobber Kain's No. 73 Squadron, after covering the final evacuations from Nantes and Saint-Nazaire, was the last to leave. On June 18, as the surviving six Hurricanes thundered down the runway, all non-operational

Where do we go from here? Göring (fifth from right) and his staff gazing from the coast of France across the English Channel at Dover, England. Having won a quick victory the Luftwaffe—and the Wehrmacht—had made no real plans to cross that Channel. (NATIONAL ARCHIVES)

aircraft, supplies, and equipment were set ablaze. France had become a vast funeral pyre.

Looking down upon his stricken country from six miles up, author-pilot Antoine de Saint-Exupéry saw the devastation and the futile burning. "But how many villages have we seen burnt down," he speculated, "only that war may be made to look like war? Burnt down exactly as trees are cut down, crews flung into the holocaust, infantry sent against tanks, merely to make war look like war. Small wonder that an unutterable disquiet hangs over the land. For nothing does any good."

Hitler was jubilant; Versailles was truly avenged. In an outburst of largess he created a flowering of field marshals: Brauchitsch, Bock, Kluge, Leeb, Rundstedt, Reichenau, Witzleben, and Keitel. The Luftwaffe too was honored as Kesselring, Sperrle, and Milch were given their batons.

But there was an unutterable disquiet in the German camp too. The forces of National Socialism, the great German Reich, the Wehrmacht, the immortal Führer himself had achieved incredible heights.

Was nun? "What now?" was the question all the conquerers asked as they stood peering through their glasses across the English Channel. *Was nun?* they wondered as they studied the stark chalk cliffs of Dover.

Was nun? Victory had come so quickly. Poland: twenty-six days; Norway: twenty-eight days; Denmark: twenty-four hours; the Netherlands: five days; Belgium: eighteen days; and France, with its Maginot Line, its great Army and Air Force: thirty-five days.

As they stood arrogantly, assured but questioning the next move, the invincible victors had no idea that, in truth, not even the Führer knew. The tottering British must be added to the victory time-table. All agreed to that.

But how?

BOOK II
The Battle of Britain

Men like these saved England.

AN AIR MINISTRY ACCOUNT OF THE
GREAT DAYS FROM AUGUST 8–OCTOBER 31, 1940

5

ADLERANGRIFF

THINKING now of those days," an English flight lieutenant said in recollection of July–October 1940, "I find that what remains most clearly in my memory is not the sweating strain of the actual fighting, not the hurried meals, the creeping from bed at dawn, not even the loss of one's friends; but rather those odd stolen moments of peace in the middle of all the pandemonium—the heat haze lying lazily over the airfield while we sat munching a piece of grass, waiting to take off; that curiously lovely moment of twilight after the last Spitfire had landed, after the last engine had been switched off, and before the first night fighter took the air, the first searchlight split the darkness and the first wail of the siren was heard again—that moment when the evening lay spread out against the sky, giving for an instant a mocking glimpse of stillness and peace before night fell suddenly like a curtain and the whole hideous cacophony of war broke out afresh.

"But, above all, the thing that remains most clearly imprinted on my memory is the spirit which then existed—the same spirit which inspired everybody from the Station Commander to the lowest aircraft-hand. . . . For that was the first trial, the first flush of battle, and it was a great hour."

Another pilot remembers: "We always had a devil-may-care sort of happiness. Lying in the sun waiting at readiness, there were moments of great beauty; the colours in the fields seemed brightest and the sky the deepest blue just before taking off for a big blitz. At dusk everything became peaceful. We were all happy at the thought of another day accomplished, our Hurricanes standing silhouetted against the sky, looking strong and confident, the darkness hiding their patched-up paintwork. In the morning whilst it was still dark, the roar of engines being tested woke us for another day's work."

"They were wonderful, weird, exciting days," a squadron leader recalled. "Days when aircraft left beautiful curving vapour trails high in the sky, days when some of our friends took off and never came back, when others came back maimed and burnt, never to fight again."

It was, despite the pervading ubiquity of death, an exhilarating time. The warriors were young—the average age was twenty—they were vigorous, and they felt they would never die, at least, perhaps, not today. They were a small band of men, Winston Churchill's "few," who must hold back Hitler's conquerers. They were the despised "soft English," the comic "weekend pilots," the unprofessionals, and surely they must soon be overwhelmed by the unbeatable Luftwaffe. In their Hurricanes and Spitfires they took off from airfields in Kent and Sussex. And here lay some of the root of the spirit: the gentle, trim English countryside—home for so many —was the last thing they saw before climbing five miles up to do battle.

The people of Britain too exhibited a spirit of mordant defiance, a quality of tough fatalism, of

Fighter types: typical RAF men of the Battle of Britain. Standing (right), wearing a "Mae West," is Peter Townsend, who on February 3, 1940, shot down the first German aircraft that fell on England—long before the Battle began. Later Townsend went to France to command No. 85 Squadron and returned to fly in the Battle of Britain, during which he became an ace. (IMPERIAL WAR MUSEUM, LONDON)

Command, Members of Parliament. The subjects ranged from wicked—often impractical—devices of war to the defense of London. The common refrain was one of challenging preparation. To Mr. Josiah Wedgwood, M.P., Churchill wrote that "You must rest assured that we should fight every street of London and its suburbs. It would *devour* an invading army, assuming one ever got that far. We hope, however, to drown the bulk of them in the salt sea."

Finally in the German camp on July 2, 1940— eleven days after the signing of the armistice with

recognizing that they would soon be fighting for their very survival—and finding a fearful elation in the thought. In their small island—*their* small island and they intended to keep it—arose a mood of Shakespearean poetry-drama. Winston Churchill gave voice to this mood and was the living paragon of the Briton whom Hitler must defeat before he could win the war in the west.

With the defeat of France came an easy temper of complete victory in the German Army; plans were made for a victory parade in Paris and lists were drawn up of divisions to be dispersed home.

But the final days of June slipped away and there was no indication that London was seriously considering the peace feelers Hitler had sent through neutrals. This was puzzling, for surely, Hitler thought, the British were beaten. The ex-corporal, now the greatest living field marshal, looked with a wistful corporal's heart at the cold, treacherous English Channel. Certainly the British must come to terms.

Instead the contentious Prime Minister dictated reams of warlike minutes, pithy bits of advice, questions, assurances, demands, criticisms, and suggestive comments to his War Cabinet, the High

Waiting: pilots of No. 611 Squadron, with a ready Spitfire (note parachute on wingtip), enduring one of war's characteristic experiences, tedium. During the Battle No. 611 Squadron, then based at Digby, suffered numerous casualties.

(IMPERIAL WAR MUSEUM, LONDON)

The Ditch, the English Channel from thirty-five thousand feet. Calais is at lower left and Dover's white cliffs above. Only the Ditch—and the RAF—stood be- *tween Hitler and, in the phrase of Wehrmacht Chief of Staff Jodl, "The final German victory over England . . ." which he believed to be "only a question of time."* (ROBERT C. CHAPIN)

France—Keitel issued instructions to all three services to prepare for an invasion of Britain. Hitler did not make his own directive No. 16 for the Conduct of the War, official with his signature until two weeks later. Directive No. 16 opened with these words: "As England, in spite of the hopelessness of her military position, has so far not shown herself willing to come to any compromise, I have decided to begin to prepare for, and if necessary to carry out, an invasion of England.

"This operation is dictated by the necessity of eliminating Great Britain as a base from which the war against Germany can be fought, and if necessary the island will be occupied." This was to be

Operation *Seelöwe* ("Sealion"), and Hitler's own equivocal posture is revealed in the conditional phrases closing each paragraph.

Colonel General Alfred Jodl, Chief of Staff of the Wehrmacht, was more definite when he wrote that "The final German victory over England is now only a question of time. Enemy offensive operations on a large scale are no longer possible." He was correct in the last sentence, but in the first he raised "the question of time." And it was time which the Germans were all but deliberately bestowing upon the British. Jodl too could wax happy, for he knew his army would be spared the initial phases of dealing with the British. The major burden must fall upon the Imperial Navy and the Luftwaffe. Admiral Raeder, as early as November 15, 1939, had instructed the Naval War Staff to look into the chances of invading England. At that time he had not expected to pay so heavily for the conquest of Norway. The loss of half his cruisers and destroyers placed Raeder in no position to deal with the British in the Channel—the German Navy had not even been able to interfere very effectively with the Dunkirk evacuation. Operation Sealion would be spread over a sea front of more than two hundred miles, from Lyme Bay to Ramsgate. How the German Navy could clear, protect, and convoy over so large an area was a serious and, Raeder knew inwardly, an impossible question.

On July 19, 1940—a full month after the last Hurricane took off from France and three days after he had signed the *Seelöwe* directive—Hitler appeared before the Reichstag. The German press was to hail the speech made that day as a "peace offer," Britain's last chance before the blow fell.

"In this hour," Hitler said, "I feel it to be my duty before my own conscience to appeal once more to reason and common sense in Great Britain as much as elsewhere. I consider myself in a position to make this appeal since I am not the vanquished begging favors, but the victor speaking in the name of reason. I can see no reason why this war must go on.

"It almost causes me pain to think that I should have been selected by Fate to deal the final blow to the structure which these men have already set tottering. . . . Mr. Churchill ought perhaps, for once, to believe me when I prophesy that a great Empire will be destroyed—an Empire which it was never my intention to destroy or even to harm. . . .

"Possibly Mr. Churchill will brush aside this statement of mine by saying it is merely born of fear and doubt of final victory. In that case I shall have relieved my conscience in regard to the things to come."

Göring, who had drawn up an ambitious plan for dealing with the British "by attacking the enemy air force, its ground organizations, and its own industry" on June 30, hoped too that the stubborn British would realize the precariousness of their position. He took little interest in the invasion studies being made by the Army staffs. He found little comfort, as the days passed and no word of surrender came from Britain, in watching the emphasis of "the things to come" devolving upon the Luftwaffe. But then his bravado prevailed and he was certain, after the successes of the Luftwaffe since the beginning of the war, that England could very well be blasted out of the war by air power alone.

From the Führer's headquarters on August 1, 1940, was issued the "Top Secret" Directive No. 17 for the Conduct of Air and Naval Warfare Against England:

In order to establish the conditions necessary for the final conquest of England I intend to continue the air and sea war against the English homeland more intensively than before.

Therefore, I order the following:

1. The German Air Force is to overcome the English air forces with all means at its disposal and as soon as possible. The attacks must at first be directed at flying formations, their ground organizations, and their supply organizations; secondly, against the aircraft production industry and the industries engaged in production of antiaircraft equipment.

2. After we gain local temporary air superiority the air war is to be directed against harbors, especially those important to the food supplies, and also against inland food storage facilities. Attacks carried out against the south coast harbors must bear in mind future operations we may wish to carry out and must therefore be restricted to the minimum.

3. The war against enemy warships and merchant ships must, however, take secondary position in the air war unless such ships present attractive opportunity targets, or is an additional bonus to attacks carried out under paragraph 2 above, or where it may be used for training of crews for specialized tasks.

4. The increased air war is to be carried out so that the Air Force can support naval operations on satisfactory opportunity targets with sufficient forces

as and when necessary. In addition, the Air Force must remain battleworthy for Operation Sealion.

5. Terror raids as reprisal I reserve the right to order myself.

6. The intensified air war may begin on August 5. The opening date may be selected by the Air Force itself upon completion of preparations and taking weather conditions into account. The Navy is authorized to begin intensified operations on the same date.

—*Adolf Hitler*

On the following day an order alerting Luftflotten 2, 3, and 5 was issued. They were to begin preparations for *Adlerangriff*—"Eagle Attack." No date

land would surely bring out the RAF and then, perhaps, the legend would fade.

Finally, with the help of Milch, also present at Karinhall, it was decided that *Adler Tag* would take place on August 10, weather permitting. But the weather turned for the worse and *Adler Tag* was postponed until August 13.

The main burden of the attack fell upon Luftflotte 2, with headquarters in Brussels and whose units were deployed in northern Germany, Holland, Belgium, and France north of the Seine, and Luftflotte 3, with headquarters in Paris and units based in western France. Luftflotte 5 would make its

The armourers . . . Give dreadful note of preparation: *while Hitler offered Britain his truculent "peace offer" and Göring wished that Britain might sink into the sea,* *the Luftwaffe got ready for its next objective. Lehrge-* *schwader 1 (left) ground crews check their Ju-88s and* *armorers of Jagdgeschwader 51 load the guns of the* *Me-109.* (H. J. NOWARRA)

was set for the first day of the intensified attack. High-level, and argumentative, meetings were held at Göring's Karinhall to determine general policy and set an *Adler Tag* ("Eagle Day"). There was disagreement between Sperrle (Luftflotte 3) and Kesselring (Luftflotte 2), the former advocating the operations against the RAF, the ports, and supply centers, as Hitler had outlined. Kesselring leaned toward a concentration on a few targets (he had earlier suggested attacking Gibraltar rather than take on the RAF over England). He was soon shown the light and reluctantly agreed, though he had wanted to maintain the legend of the Luftwaffe's invincibility. A direct attack upon the British home-

thrusts from bases in Norway and Denmark. Two *Fliegerkorps* (air corps), 2 and 8, were assigned to establish air superiority over the English Channel and to disrupt, if possible to stop, all shipping into Britain. Fliegerkorps 2 (more correctly designated with Roman numeral), based on the Pas de Calais within Stuka strike of the Straits of Dover, was under command of General Bruno Loerzer, Göring's old First World War best friend. Loerzer's units would operate within the boundaries assigned to Luftflotte 2—an imaginary line, not always observed, which ran across the Channel northerly from Le Havre, cut the English coast near Portsmouth, and continued upward passing slightly to the west of Oxford and, farther north, to the west of Birmingham up through Manchester. All targets to the left of this line, theoretically, were the responsibility of Luftflotte 2; those to the right belonged to Luftflotte 3.

The other *Fliegerkorps*, number 8, based just south of the *Luftflotten* boundary at Deauville, was commanded by Generalmajor Wolfram von Richthofen. Once the chief critic of the Stuka, Richthofen was celebrated as the master of close support and a Stuka virtuoso. His *Fliegerkorps* consisted mainly of Ju-87s.

Ringing the British Isles and poised for *Adler Tag,* therefore, were three massive German air fleets —bombers, dive bombers, single-engined and twin-engined fighters, reconnaissance craft—about 3500 aircraft. Normally about two thirds of the total strength might be serviceable for any given day, however. As of August 10, 1940, for example, Luftflotten 2 and 3, the major units participating in *Adlerangriff,* had at their disposal 1232 long-range bombers (875 serviceable), 406 dive bombers (316 serviceable), 813 single-engined fighters (702 serviceable), 282 twin-engined fighters and fighter-bombers (227 serviceable), as well as about 50 long-range reconnaissance planes.

Across the Channel Air Marshal Sir Hugh Dowding prepared his Fighter Command for the onslaught he knew was coming. The presence of Dowding, like that of Churchill, at this time and at this place, was providential. A brilliant administrator, a sound strategist, and a shrewd tactician, Dowding was, in personality as well as a leader, the opposite of his opponent Göring. For that matter, the aloof Air Officer Commander in Chief, Fighter Command (to use his correct title), shared little in common with his own fighter pilots, who called him "Stuffy," a term of rakish affection rather than scorn.

The words of Churchill must have spurred Dowding, as he took full advantage of the seven weeks between the end of the Battle of France and the opening of the Battle of Britain. "The whole fury and might of the enemy must very soon be turned on us," Churchill had said. "Hitler knows that he will have to break us in this island or lose the war. If we can stand up to him, all Europe may be free and the life of the world may move forward into broad, sunlit uplands. But if we fail, then the

Air Chief Marshal Sir Hugh C. T. Dowding—"Stuffy" to his irreverent but affectionate pilots. For all his diffidence Dowding was a brilliant strategist and proved it as leader of Fighter Command during the Battle.
(IMPERIAL WAR MUSEUM, LONDON)

whole world, including the United States, including all that we have known and cared for, will sink into the abyss of a new Dark Age, made more sinister, and perhaps more protracted, by the lights of perverted science.

"Let us therefore brace ourselves to our duties," Churchill concluded, "and so bear ourselves that, if the British Empire and its Commonwealth last for a thousand years, men will say, 'This was their finest hour.' "

Dowding had sixty squadrons on hand in time for *Adler Tag* with 704 operational aircraft at their disposal (and 289 in reserve). Of these aircraft 620 were Hurricanes and Spitfires (about 400 of the former and 200 of the latter). The rest were Bristol Blenheims, two-engined light bombers em-

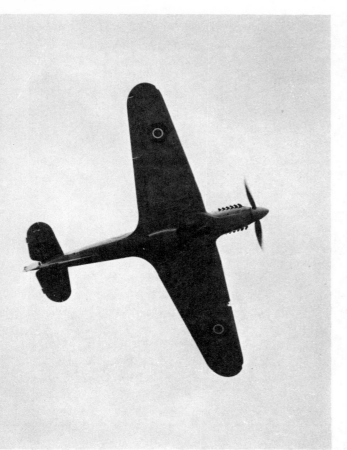

The backbone of Fighter Command during the Battle of Britain: the Hurricane. The Hurricane's performance was limited and was no match for the Me-109 at high altitudes. (HAWKER SIDDELEY AVIATION, LTD.)

ployed as fighters, and the Boulton Paul Defiant, a two-seat fighter which resembled the Hurricane. Over Dunkirk, where the Defiant went into action for the first time, it had proved most successful. German pilots, mistaking it for the Hurricane and not realizing a second crew member manned the rear-firing machine guns, attacked from the rear and were shot down. This advantage lasted briefly, for soon the Germans realized the Defiant was a different plane and dealt with it harshly, for it was no match for the Me-109. Nor was the Blenheim; even less the Gladiator, of which a single flight (six planes) remained operational in one squadron.

The Hurricane was obsolescent by August 1940, though a sturdy fighter and a good aircraft. It was Dowding's plan to have the Hurricanes attack the

German bombers, which were slower and less maneuverable than the fighters, and leave the Messerschmitts, the 109s and the twin-engined 110s, to the faster, more nimble Spitfires. The Spitfire was a better high-altitude performer than the Hurricane— and the German fighters too fought well above twenty thousand feet.

Dowding's major concern at the Battle's inception was not aircraft, but pilots. Churchill had appointed newspaper publisher Lord Beaverbrook (William Maxwell Aitken) to head the Ministry of Aircraft Production in May 1940. Beaverbrook's disdain for red tape, his dynamism and highly charged personality contributed to the rise in aircraft production. In this he was, of course, helped by the urgency of the time, the robust defiance that vitalized all Britons after Dunkirk. Beaverbrook's son, John William Aitken, had served in France with No. 601 Squadron and was flying a Hurricane with the same unit based in Tangmere near the coast of southern England.

The air fighting in France had taken a heavy toll —320 RAF pilots killed or missing and 115 taken prisoners of war. Of the 959 planes lost in France, 229 had been fighters. British workers could replace the planes. The young men, "the effete, pleasure-mad youth of Britain," as Hitler called them, had to be trained, and this took time.

A fraction of the deficiency was alleviated by the "loan" of fifty-eight pilots from the Fleet Air Arm. In time No. 1 Squadron Royal Canadian Air Force joined in the battle and refugee pilots from Poland and Czechoslovakia were formed into squadrons. The latter two proved especially savage fighters.

II

When *Adler Tag* finally dawned Dowding could call upon 1253 pilots—almost 200 short of his authorized establishment. These pilots were deployed throughout the main island of the British Isles, in England, Wales, and Scotland. The greater concentration of squadrons were based in south England —in the counties of Sussex, Surrey, and Kent. To reach London from the bases in northern France the Luftwaffe fighters and bombers would have to cross this area, most of which lay in the province of No. 11 Group, Air Vice-Marshal Keith Park, Air

Lord Beaverbrook, William M. Aitken, who as head of the Ministry of Aircraft Production during the Battle of Britain slashed through red tape and made certain that Fighter Command did not lack Hurricanes or

Spitfires. With him is his son, John ("Max") Aitken, a fighter pilot with No. 601 Squadron. At war's end Aitken's victory score stood at sixteen.

(*Daily Express*, LONDON)

Officer Commanding. To the west of this area lay No. 10 Group's domain, Air Vice-Marshal Sir Christopher Brand, AOC. To the north, into Essex and Suffolk counties, Air Vice-Marshal Trafford Leigh-Mallory commanded No. 12 Group. Scotland and the northern tip of England were the responsibility of No. 13 Group under Air Vice-Marshal Richard Saul.

The bulk of the heavy air fighting was to take place over the domains of Nos. 11 and 12 Groups. No. 11 Group consisted of twenty-two squadrons (fifteen Hurricane, six Spitfire, and one Blenheim) and No. 12 Group of fifteen squadrons (seven Hurricane, five Spitfire, two Blenheim, and one Defiant).

To contend with the attack the Air Ministry also established antiaircraft divisions, a Balloon Command with its barrage balloons (a throwback to the First World War), an Observer Corps, and, of the greatest import to Fighter Command, a network of so-called Chain Home Stations operating Radio Direction Finding equipment. In time this RDF came to be called *"radio detecting and ranging,"* which by mid-war the Americans had abbreviated to "radar." The brain child of Robert Watson-Watt, radar was a decisive factor in the outcome of the Battle of Britain.

In the summer of 1940 a system of radar stations stood along the northern, eastern, and southern coasts of the main island. The spindly masts of the

Radar towers on the English coast, an early detection system that contributed greatly to the outcome of the Battle of Britain.

(IMPERIAL WAR MUSEUM, LONDON)

transmitting and receiving towers were concentrated in the southeastern counties opposite France. Additional stations were erected inland. At the time of the Battle's opening there were twenty-one operational CH stations and thirty CHL (Chain Home Low) stations. The former were capable of picking up objects at a distance of 120 miles but missed low-flying aircraft; the CHL stations supplemented the CH stations on low-flying aircraft up to fifty miles distant. By no means absolutely perfect or foolproof, the English radar system was superior to anything the Germans had developed. And because they had not been able to devise a good system the Germans characteristically assumed the British had also been as unsuccessful.

With radar detecting the Luftwaffe forming up while it was still over France, the RAF was able to send its fighters to meet the German formations. Radar would locate the German formations and enabled the British to ignore diversionary sweeps and concentrate on the main point of attack. It also saved the RAF from wasteful patrols. Pilots were scrambled only when necessary—at least in the ideal situation. Pilots could also keep informed of the rapidly shifting air situation by radio from the ground radar stations tracking and plotting the oncoming Germans. Furthermore, pilots could talk with each other in the air. The German communications system was not as well developed. There was no ground control with radar and while pilots could talk with each other within their own units there was no intercommunication in formations except by signal: the fighters had no radio connection with the bombers. In general this meant operations were dependent upon the orders issued before they had taken off; there was little leeway for the unexpected.

Thus the situation stood when the Germans impatiently girded for *Adler Tag.* Göring, warming up to what was to be the world's first great air battle, expected that the defenses of southern England would be shattered in four days and that the Luftwaffe would take four weeks to eliminate the Royal Air Force. After this, Operation Sealion could be launched and a triumphant Third Reich would be free for more important conquests (especially that of the Soviet Union, which Hitler now seriously considered).

Although the all-out assault was set for the August "Eagle Day," the Luftwaffe ventured over the English Channel before this. On the night of June 5/6 about thirty German bombers flew over the east coast dropping bombs on airfields and upon the vicinity of airfields. Nighttime accuracy, even with the help of a radio beam (code-named *Knickebein,* and quickly jammed by the British), left much to be desired. Such harassment raids were of little military value except to provide the crews with night-flying practice. Also, the raids kept the British on their toes, although they interfered somewhat with production as the workers sought shelter upon the sounding of air raid sirens.

The scattered raids of June were of no great consequence, although some damage was done, and there were a number of casualties, as well as small

Before the curtain rose on the Battle of Britain the Luftwaffe began scattered raids against various port cities on the southeast coast of England and upon vital British shipping in the English Channel. On the left

German bombs fall on Portland, which was attacked for the first time on July 11, 1940. On the right, a view from the nose of an He-111 of English ships under attack in the Channel. (NATIONAL ARCHIVES)

German losses. July saw the beginning of more intensified daylight attacks, particularly upon the port cities—Portland, Falmouth, Plymouth, Dover—and upon shipping in the Channel. By the end of July daylight passage through the English Channel, even for convoys, became hazardous under the attacks of the Stukas, the Messerschmitt 110s, the Dornier 17s, and escorting Me-109s.

Loerzer had selected Johannes Fink as Kanalkampfführer (Channel Battle Leader) to lead a small battle group, Kampfgeschwader 2, to attend to shipping through the Straits of Dover; Richthofen's Stukas did the same to the west. In addition to his own *Geschwader*'s Dorniers, Fink could call upon two *Gruppen* of Stukas (Ju-87s) and two fighter *Geschwader*, JG 26, led by Adolf Galland, and JG 51, led by Werner Mölders. The two

Jagdgeschwader, commanded by the stars of the Luftwaffe, were equipped with the latest Messerschmitt 109Es. Mölders, a great tactician and teacher, was then the high-scoring Luftwaffe ace. He was, interestingly, an ardent anti-Nazi, an aberration for which he was tolerated because of his achievements as a fighter pilot.

If the early July Channel encounters were not conclusive, they were no less deadly for the participants. Flight Lieutenant Alan Deere, leading B Flight of No. 54 Squadron on a convoy patrol— the fourth scramble of the day—crossed the English coast at Deal. At this point the English Channel, that is, at the Straits of Dover, is barely twenty miles wide. Deere, a New Zealander, had been flying since he was nineteen and was a confirmed ace with five official victories to his credit. Shot down over Dunkirk, Deere had joined the "brown jobs" (Army men) and was evacuated by ship back to England.

Leading his flight of six Spitfires, Deere had spotted a silvery plane flying low, escorted by a dozen Me-109s at about a thousand feet and another five serving as top cover. The silver seaplane was a Heinkel 59 decorated not only with the traditional black crosses of the Luftwaffe, but also with a red cross identifying it as an Air-Sea rescue plane. Obviously it was searching for German pilots who had crash-landed in the Channel in the day's early fighting. The RAF had orders to attack the He-59s, red cross or not, for while they rescued the pilots they also reported the British convoys in the Channel.

Ordering half of his flight to attack the seaplane, Deere led two Spitfires to deal with the top-cover Messerschmitts. The German fighters immediately formed into a defensive circle. Diving through the circle Deere shot down one of the German planes and then, as he tells it himself, "straightening out from my favorite defensive maneuver of a tight turn, I found my self head-on to another [Me-109].

"As we sped towards each other at a combined speed of over 500 mph there was little time to think. For my part, the thought of a collision did not enter my head—had it done so I have no doubt I would have tried to avoid it—and when I realized it was to be the inevitable outcome it was too late for evasion action. At one moment the Me-109 was a blurred outline filling my reflector sight and the next it was on top of me blotting out the sky ahead as it passed marginally above, avoiding a direct collision perhaps by a last-minute alteration of course by the German pilot.

"But collide we did; propeller hit propeller, the shock of the impact throwing me forward in my seat, saved only from being crushed on the dashboard by the restraining cockpit harness which bit cruelly into my shoulders.

"The next few moments I recall as a panic-stricken blur as I fought to regain some control over my now vibrating, pitching Spitfire already gushing ominous black smoke into the cockpit. Gain control I did, but sufficient only to keep the aircraft in a too-fast-for-comfort dive towards the English coast, with throttle jammed open but a happily unresponsive engine seized solid by a propeller which under the impact had bent double and dug itself progressively into the engine housing before finally ceasing to turn."

But now fire had begun licking out of the smoke in Deere's cockpit and he knew he had to jump.

The Heinkel 59, which, despite the red crosses painted on its sides (not on this one, however) because of its function as an Air-Sea Rescue plane, was consistently shot down by the RAF. Churchill believed they were used also to make reconnaissance observations during rescue operations. (H. J. NOWARRA)

The Messerschmitt 109, the standard single-seater Luftwaffe fighter during the Battle of Britain. Superior to the Hurricane, it was an even match for the Spitfire. Air battles between the Me-109 and the Spitfire were decided either by pilot skill or luck.

(U. S. AIR FORCE)

Heaving at the cockpit hood he was dismayed to learn that the collision had jammed it shut. Nor could he jettison it mechanically. There was no choice; Deere had to stay with the burning Spitfire, bring it down, and hope to get out somehow on the ground.

"Half-choked by the smoke, licked at by flames I somehow kept the Spitfire heading inland and under a measure of control. I could see nothing directly ahead and only a little to the side as my now burning fighter plunged towards a resting place in the Kentish fields, barely discernible through the smoke and flame. . . .

"I must have prayed, but I don't remember. What I do remember is the crunching sensation as the aircraft hit the ground, fortunately in open country, launched itself in the air again, returned to earth and ploughed a skidding and erratic passage through a field studded with wooden posts, put there as a deterrent to an enemy airborne glider force, shedding bits of fuselage en route."

When the shuddering, bouncing Spitfire finally came to a stop Deere desperately hammered at the perspex of the canopy, broke it open, dived over the side, and ran from the burning wreckage. The Spitfire had come to rest in a cornfield now resounding to the firing of the plane's guns, which had become heated by the flames.

By some miracle, except for slightly burned hands, singed eyebrows, bruised knees, and the cuts from the shoulder harness, Deere was not seriously injured and was back in the battle the next day. His plane, named *Kiwi,* was a total loss, however.

The Me-109 with which he collided had not shared Deere's luck. The tail of the German fighter had been sheared off and, trailing bits of fuselage, the plane fell into the Channel.

August brought a quickening of the tempo of Luftwaffe attacks; by the end of the first week the bombing became heavier and more fierce. Göring waited for an improvement in the weather, however, to launch the all-out attack, set for August 10. Dowding, meanwhile, held his fighters in check, not wishing to waste pilots and aircraft in the preliminary phases of the big battle that must inevitably come. Fighting over the Channel was a risky business; wait for the Luftwaffe to come farther inland to the limit of their range, Dowding wisely cau-

The Messerschmitt 110, the ill-fated Zerstörer (*destroyer*), *which was supposed to operate in the dual role of fighter and bomber and proved to be neither.*
(H. J. NOWARRA)

tioned. Avoid combat as much as possible with fighters—get the bombers; they carried the lethal burden.

But the English weather proved to be characteristically unreasonable. On the evening of August 9, with the Channel socked in with cloud and with Britain under cloud and rain, Göring canceled the large-scale attack of the following day. *Adler Tag,* weather permitting, then was set for August 13.

On the twelfth the prelude to *Adler Tag* took place. While continuing to harass shipping in the Channel and the ports, the Luftwaffe attacked airfields and radar installations. The expanding battle was moving inland.

Spearheading the assault was an *Erprobungsgruppe* (Experimental Group) 210, a mixed unit of fighters, Messerschmitt 109s and 110s, converted to fighter-bombers. The formation, led by Hauptmann Walter Rubensdörffer, consisted of eight Me-109s, some carrying five-hundred- or thousand-pound bombs under their bellies, and a dozen Me-110s, similarly armed. Their targets were the radar antennas along the Kent and Sussex coast. The steel structures, 350 feet tall, rose up out of the marshes and apple orchards of Kent like strange devices from another world.

These spindly antennas were Fighter Command's ace in the hole. Their existence eliminated the Luftwaffe's element of surprise.

On this day the Messerschmitts split up and sped

Me-110s in flight. According to the original conception, these planes were supposed to be able to fight off attackers while on bombing missions, or to serve as escort for heavier bombers. They proved to be sitting ducks for the guns of the RAF. (MUSÉE DE L'AIR)

toward their individual targets upon reaching the English coast. Except for patches of mist the weather was good and the Messerschmitts dropped down out of the sun and raced toward the masts at Pevensey, Rye, Dover, and Dunkirk (the latter on the south bank of the Thames near Canterbury). Although the radar stations had picked up the approaching bombers, the formations appeared small enough to require little more than watching. Almost at the same moment all of the radar stations came under attack and all bombers loosed their bombs on target. The earth shook, buildings collapsed, smoke rose into the air—but, as the Messerschmitts wheeled around for home, the men saw that the masts remained standing.

At Dunkirk two huts had been destroyed but the station continued operating. At Rye all the huts had gone up in the explosions, but by noon the station was back in action. Bombs cut the main electric cable at Pevensey, putting it out for two hours. At Dover the aerials took slight damage and the working quarters were smashed to bits—but Dover continued to operate. These stations were "manned," so to speak, by young women of the Women's Auxiliary Air Force who endured the bombings with exemplary calm.

Though triumphant on returning to their base at Denain, the pilots and crews of Experimental Group 210 found their jubilance premature. Luftwaffe

Communications Chief General Wolfgang Martini learned through detection devices that the radar stations continued to operate despite the on-target attacks by the fighter-bombers.

There was an exception. Just before noon, while more than sixty Ju-88s attacked Portsmouth Harbor, fifteen aircraft veered off and dived toward the radar installation at Ventnor on the Isle of Wight. The heavy bomb concentration destroyed most of the buildings, caused fires which could not be put out because of a lack of water, and seriously damaged the site. Ventnor was out of action for eleven days.

While the radar stations were recovering from the morning attacks the afternoon opened with assaults upon British airfields. Even as the pilots of No. 65 Squadron ran for their Spitfires, the bombs from the Dorniers fell upon Manston, an advance base near the coast. Another airfield, Hawkinge, was also bombed. The fleeing Ju-88s left two hangars destroyed, the workshops afire, and the landing strips cratered. Five people had been killed and four aircraft damaged. For the second time in the day, the airfield at Lympne (actually an unimportant emergency landing field) was bombed. Manston was hardest hit, although like the other stations it was back in operation by the following day. *Adler Tag* eve had cost the RAF 22 fighters and the Luftwaffe 31 aircraft. The toll from July 10 through this August 12 was 150 RAF fighters and 286 German aircraft, including fighters and bombers. And the Battle proper had not yet begun.

Kanalkampfführer Johannes Fink—whose friends lightly called him *Kanalarbeiter* ("Sewer worker") —did not take his position lightly. By seven in the morning of August 13—*Adler Tag,* at last—his Dornier 17s of Kampfgeschwader 2 were air-borne. Fifty-five aircraft roared toward the airdrome at Eastchurch on the south bank of the Thames estuary. All along the coasts of France, Belgium, Holland, and Norway aircraft of the three great *Luftflotten* would converge upon the stubborn British for the Attack of the Eagles.

As was its wont, the weather had turned bad overnight—there were clouds over the Channel and mist and drizzling over the target. Eastchurch, Fink did not know, was a Coastal Command station— not a fighter field. The target of the Luftwaffe was RAF Fighter Command. This was not the only slip of the morning.

When he arrived at the rendezvous point with the fighter escort, the Messerschmitt 110s of Oberstleutnant Joachim Huth's Zerstörergeschwader 26, Fink was annoyed with the behavior of the fighters. Huth's Messerschmitt bore down upon Fink's Dornier, dived, turned, and came back at him. Fink good-naturedly attributed it to the typical fighter pilot's high spirits in celebration of *Adler Tag*. The performance of the Destroyers was ridiculous but understandable. Fink proceeded toward Eastchurch. After cutting through a cloud bank, Fink was further piqued to note that no Messerschmitts were visible anywhere. They had lost one another in the clouds. There was nothing before him except the forbidding coast of England and scattered clouds.

In their stations the radar operators had begun tracking Fink as soon as his planes formed up over Calais. The still inexperienced operators could not predict the Dorniers' destination.

The cloud had thickened so Fink ordered the planes to loosen the formation in order to lessen the chance of collision. When the Dorniers broke through the mist Fink was delighted to see Eastchurch about three miles ahead—and ten thousand feet below. Anxiously peering out of the cockpit, Fink ascertained an unfortunate truth: no fighter escort. The cautious, fifty-year-old leader found some consolation in the sight of the aircraft on the field below neatly lined up, wingtip to wingtip, waiting for them.

Fink led the Dorniers to the attack. At about the same moment some Spitfires of No. 74 Squadron, the only unit dispatched to deal with "a few aircraft," pounced upon the rear of the formation. Oberleutnant Heinz Schlegel's Dornier bucked under the scattered fire from the Spitfire's eight guns. The right engine ground to a stop and began smoking, and Schlegel had trouble keeping the plane from pulling to the left. Another burst from a diving Spitfire solved that problem: the other engine was damaged and, because two of his crew were wounded, Schlegel crash-landed the Dornier in an English meadow. Schlegel and his crew were taken prisoner.

Fink, unaware of the attack going on behind him, dropped his bombs upon Eastchurch. The men on the base below reacted with astonishment as explosions erupted in the early morning. Five Blenheims of No. 35 Squadron went up in smoke. Twelve

men died in the rubble and fire and forty were injured. A direct hit destroyed the operations building. When Fink ducked his plane into the clouds and raced for France, great black clouds of smoke rose up from Eastchurch.

But some of the smoke may have been that of his own planes, for during the fighting Fink lost four aircraft.

Furious because he had had no fighter protection, Fink called Kesselring at Luftflotte 2 headquarters as soon as he had landed. The tone and language of the usually mild Fink prompted a visit from Kesselring, who brought a personal explanation.

A Spitfire harries a Dornier-17, the "Flying Pencil," over England. (NATIONAL ARCHIVES)

Adler Tag had been postponed because of the poor weather. Fink's mission had been canceled although word had come only after he had taken off. The fighters had been informed, which explained not only their absence, but also the odd behavior of Huth's Messerschmitt 110. Fink learned that as he was attacking Eastchurch other uninformed aircraft, the Ju-88s of Kampfgeschwader 54, with Me-110 escort, attempted to bomb the Royal Aircraft Establishment at Farnborough. Fighter interception from No. 11 Group prevented the attack and at least five of the Me-110s, Göring's pet Destroyer, went down under the Spitfire guns. The rest fled for home. The same occurred with a formation of more than eighty Stukas—only they fled before attacking and thus were spared, temporarily, a full-scale encounter with the British fighters. Only Fink's resolute, and vulnerable, formation had succeeded in the morning of Eagle Day.

An attempt to save the glory of the day was made in the afternoon despite the worsening weather. A fighter formation (Me-110s) was sent to the vicinity of Portland to draw off the English fighters. While these engaged the Hurricanes and Spitfires it was expected that the Ju-88s might break through the defenses and bomb the docks and warehouses at Southampton. Most of the bombers got through, causing serious damage while the Me-110s, possibly

Channel near Cherbourg, hoped to find airfields in the Portland area. But cloud cover again interfered —and so did No. 609 Squadron. Diving through the Me-109 escort formation, scattering them, the Spitfires pounded at the "dreaded" Stuka. The slow, clumsy craft was no match for the Spitfire and within minutes five of them lay smashed on the countryside below.

In the same encounter Pilot Officer D. M. Crook of No. 609 Squadron fired at an Me-109, which burst into flame and joined the hapless Stukas in a fiery dive to the ground. The fleeing Stukas spread their bombs over three counties.

The Ju-87 Stuka, once the scourge of the air, reached the end of the road over England in the summer of 1940. (U. S. AIR FORCE)

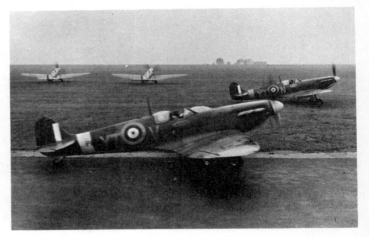

Aroused Spitfires of No. 65 Squadron take off to confront the Luftwaffe. On "Eagle Day" this squadron drove off an attack by the Stukas.
(IMPERIAL WAR MUSEUM, LONDON)

mistaken for bombers, engaged the fighters. The more sprightly Spitfires dived and twisted through the defensive circle which the Messerschmitts had formed under attack. In the savage fighting, five Me-110s fell. Clearly, the escort required an escort.

During the afternoon attacks also Richthofen's Ju-87s had succeeded in bombing the airfield at Detling, while its fighter escort dueled with the British fighters. Another formation of Ju-87s, aimed at a fighter base at Rochford, could not find it because of cloud cover. When attacked by the Spitfires of No. 65 Squadron, the Germans jettisoned their bombs across Canterbury and fled.

Farther west and south, more Stukas, crossing the

As evening fell the Attack of the Eagles subsided into the scattered detonations of wasted bombs and the desperate scream of the Stuka, the onetime Scourge of the Blitzkrieg, running for home. Small night attacks by bombers did not add to the accomplishment of the day. The eagle's wings had been clipped. The German pilots had not lacked courage, only that required efficiency in the High Command which makes sense of complex, large-scale operations.

When *Adler Tag* officially closed, the Luftwaffe had lost forty-five aircraft—thirty-nine to the British fighters—and the RAF Fighter Command had lost thirteen planes, but only seven pilots in combat.

It was not an auspicious beginning.

6

TARGET: RAF

THE FAT ONE was in a sour mood. His Eagle Day had not gone off as planned, what with the breakdown in command which set it off piecemeal. It was that damned English weather, unpredictable, obstinate, capricious—now bright and sunny, then moody and threatening: like the English themselves. Göring was not at all pleased with the course of the battle. The weather on the day following Eagle Day, August 14, had proved too poor for large-scale operations, although the Luftwaffe flew 489 sorties with the concentration upon the airdromes in southeastern England.

On that morning Göring called a conference at Karinhall with his staff and the *Luftflotten* commanders for the next day, August 15. He was obviously not in a joyous temper. He was concerned with the vulnerability of the Stuka and ordered increased fighter escorts for the dive bombers: as many as three *Gruppen* of fighters per *Gruppe* of Stukas.

As for the heavy bombers, he sarcastically invoked one of his pet comments of the period. Göring suggested that they attend to the British aircraft industries and "not the lightship off Dover."

He waxed serious: "We must concentrate our efforts on the destruction of the enemy air forces . . . including the targets of the enemy aircraft industry allocated to the different *Luftflotten*. . . .

"For the moment other targets should be ignored. . . .

"Our night attacks are essentially dislocation raids, made so that enemy defenses and population

shall be allowed no respite; even these, however, should wherever possible be directed against air force targets. . . ." That was the heart of Göring's master plan: the great German Air Force would erase the British Air Force.

Having committed his air force to the extinction of the RAF, Göring then proceeded to do the same to the Luftwaffe with a series of blunders in High Command. "It is doubtful," he concluded, "whether there is any point in continuing the attacks on radar sites, in view of the fact that not one of those attacked has so far been put out of action." Even as he said this repairmen were working against time to put the Ventnor station back into operation and not succeeding very rapidly. Göring, however, had no comprehension of radar's significance. It was yet another one of his decisions which would cost others their lives.

At almost the same moment Göring spoke and decreed, once again the order to postpone the day's missions because of weather had gone astray. In the absence of Loerzer, who was with Göring and the others at Karinhall, his chief of staff, Oberst Paul Deichmann, upon personally viewing the weather conditions—bright, sunny, with some cloud over the Channel—initiated the day's operations. Picking up the field phone, he dispatched the Stukas for England.

For the first time all three *Luftflotten,* based from Norway in the north to Brittany in the south, engaged in co-ordinated daylight attacks. In terms of

Göring with two aides who unconsciously let him down. On the left is the Chief of Air Intelligence, Josef "Beppo" Schmid, whose appraisal of the enemy's air power was frequently inaccurate; in the center, Chief of the Technical Branch of the Luftwaffe, Ernst Udet, who preferred flying airplanes to theorizing about them. Göring, however, betrayed both of them and the Luftwaffe as well by virtue of simple incompetence.

(H. J. NOWARRA)

numbers it was a more impressive German showing than Eagle Day itself.

The day began serenely enough with a few reconnaissance patrols by the RAF. Air Vice-Marshal Park dispatched a squadron from No. 11 Group to keep an eye upon two convoys just off the Thames estuary, but without incident.

That something big was to be expected was noted on the radar screens when just before eleven o'clock large formations were detected. These were the Stukas, with Me-109 escort, meeting over Calais for the twenty-minute flight across the Straits of Dover to attack the RAF airfields in Kent. When the German formations reached the English coast at eleven-thirty, they were met by a squadron each of Hurricanes and Spitfires. Of the nearly fifty Stukas participating in the attack, only four fell to the British fighters. The rest pushed through the defenses to bomb the airfields at Lympne and Hawkinge. The latter, a fighter base, was not seriously damaged, but Lympne, actually a secondary field, was knocked out for two days. Clearly the Luftwaffe was out to get the Royal Air Force Fighter Command.

While this fighting continued, and radar screens blipped with German air activity in the Channel

Stukas en route to their targets—and, more often than not, their doom.

(EMBASSY OF THE POLISH PEOPLE'S REPUBLIC)

area, another development to the north was unfolding on the screens in the Operations Room of No. 13 Group. Shortly after noon "twenty or more aircraft" were reported approaching from the North Sea. This estimate was increased soon after to three distinct formations aimed at Northumberland: "thirty plus," was the new figure. In reality, the radar operators were plotting a *Gruppe* of seaplanes on a diversionary flight toward the Firth of Forth, to the north of the true path of the other aircraft groups.

Unfortunately for the attacking Luftwaffe, the second group, the bombers of Kampfgeschwader 26,

cort planes with adequate range for the flight from the Luftwaffe base, four-hundred miles distant, at Stavanger, Norway. In his high-flying Messerschmitt, Restemeyer planned to direct the battle against the British fighters.

The forewarned Spitfires of No. 72 Squadron had climbed above the approaching Germans. From out of the sun they pounced upon the German formations. Among the first planes to come under attack was Restemeyer's Messerschmitt. With its eight guns firing, the mottled, graceful Spitfire struck the German fighter. The Messerschmitt staggered momentarily in mid-flight, shedding bits of metal, and then

Spitfire takeoff with wheels beginning to tuck into the wing. Early Spitfires required the pilot to crank the wheels up (and down) manually; later models were equipped with automatic wheel gear.

(IMPERIAL WAR MUSEUM, LONDON)

sixty-three He-111s with an escort of twenty-one Me-110s of Zerstörergeschwader 76, were off course. Instead of approaching their targets, British Bomber Command bases at Dishforth and Linton-on-Ouse, the German bombers converged upon the English coast at almost the same point as the seaplane feint.

Having been stirred up by the seaplanes, No. 72 Squadron's Spitfires intercepted the formation of Heinkels and Messerschmitts about thirty miles off the English coast. The bombers droned along at about fifteen thousand feet. A thousand feet above them flew the Me-110s, led by Hauptmann Werner Restemeyer. The heavy fighters were the only es-

with an orange flash exploded. The mangled aircraft spun burning into the North Sea.

While some of the Spitfires engaged the Me-110s, which quickly formed into their customary defensive circle, the others flitted through the bomber formation. The suddenness of the attack, and perhaps the sight of Restemeyer's stricken plane descending, unnerved many of the crews in the Heinkels. Bombs were jettisoned harmlessly into the sea as the Heinkels lightened the loads for evasive action. Many ducked into cloud bank over which they had been safely flying just moments before.

After the first shock of the Spitfire attack had

worn off, the German planes pushed on toward their assigned targets. The fighters had to contend with yet another squadron (No. 79) of Spitfires which had been vectored to the heaving, lofty battleground. The Germans were outnumbered and fought with courage, although handicapped by their aircraft, none of which equaled the Spitfire in maneuverability. Once again the Zerstörer proved itself no match for the darting Spitfire. Although hits were scored by the German fighters and many claims made for "kills," British records do not reveal any losses of any of No. 13 Group's aircraft in the day's battle. Besides Restemeyer's plane, another eighteen

some homes in Portland, destroyed by the loosed bombs.

The surviving German planes turned and scuttled for home. Eight bombers did not return. The "surprise" flank attack by Luftflotte 5 cost twenty-seven aircraft and their crews. The expenditure was high for little return.

The other formation contributed by Luftflotte 5, unescorted Junkers 88s from Aalborg, Denmark, had been detected almost simultaneously with the Heinkels and Messerschmitts farther north. This flight made landfall at Flamborough Head, north of the Humber River. These were fifty aircraft of

He-111s over a German base. (NATIONAL ARCHIVES)

Me-110s were shot down and others returned to their bases in Norway badly shot up, with wounded aboard and crews demoralized.

Meanwhile, also under attack, the Heinkels pressed on for England. Spitfires now harassing the bombers were joined by Hurricanes of No. 605 Squadron. More bombs fell into the sea, joined by smoking Heinkels. Those that passed over the beaches and flew inland were then put upon by antiaircraft guns, further adding to the Heinkel's 'torment. Bombs scattered willy-nilly across the coastal villages—Seaham Harbour, Portland—but to no military point. The most serious damage was to

Kampfgeschwader 30—their target: the airfield at Driffield, home of No. 4 Group of Bomber Command.

This attack fell into the province of Leigh-Mallory's No. 12 Group. Around one o'clock—while the battle raged to the north—No. 12 Group's Spitfires, Defiants, and Hurricanes were ordered up. No. 13 Groups, though heavily engaged, dispatched a squadron of Blenheims to this battle also. It might be noted that the Defiants were specifically dispatched to patrol a convoy in the Humber River. Neither the Defiants nor the Blenheims could have been expected to fight on equal terms with German

Heinkel bombers heading out for targets in Britain.
(H. J. NOWARRA)

An He-111 disintegrates under the eight-gun assault of an RAF fighter attack.

(IMPERIAL WAR MUSEUM, LONDON)

Ju-88, the Luftwaffe's best bomber of the Battle of Britain. (U. S. AIR FORCE)

fighters; however, if, as it was hoped, the German formation contained only bombers the obsolescent aircraft might fare reasonably well. Even so, the Ju-88s were more capable of dealing with Blenheims.

The Spitfires of No. 616 Squadron intercepted the Ju-88s just offshore at Flamborough Head. Instead of breaking up for combat, the German formations dived into the clouds and eluded the British planes—at least temporarily. Then a flight of Hurricanes joined the battle as the Junkers crossed the coast line. The air over Flamborough Head was crisscrossed with machine-gun fire and from time to time the sky became smudged with oily smoke and flame as a Junkers fell under the eight-gun fighters.

Despite the heavy opposition about thirty German bombers broke through and found their targets. With amazing accuracy, considering the harassment, their bombs fell upon Driffield. Four hangars erupted under the onslaught, three blocks of buildings burst open and fell burning, and ten Whitley heavy bombers were destroyed under the heavy bomb concentration.

One of the Junkers was shot down by antiaircraft. But the formation had split up and while the larger one bombed Driffield another dropped its bombs on Bridlington, destroying some houses, and hitting also a nearby ammunition dump.

Then the Junkers turned and ran for Denmark, pursued by the Hurricanes and Spitfires a hundred miles out to sea. The Blenheims joined the pursuit but could not catch up to the swifter Junkers. Ten of the Ju-88s, however, remained smoking and tangled on the Yorkshire countryside or at the bottom of the sea.

Luftflotte 5 had lost, in its first—and last—full-scale daylight attack almost one eighth of its bomber force and one fifth of its heavy fighters. Nor had the feint succeeded in drawing the British fighters away from southeast England. Dowding had not permitted that and as the German bombers of Luftflotten 2 and 3 launched their attacks upon Kent, Essex, and Suffolk, the Spitfires and Hurricanes of No. 11 and No. 10 Groups rose up to meet them.

Even so, Me-110s of Erprobungsgruppe 210, accompanied by swarms of Me-109s and Stukas—about a hundred aircraft in all—slipped across the Channel northeast of London to strike the airfield at Martlesham Heath in Suffolk. While the Messerschmitt 109s held off those few British fighters which

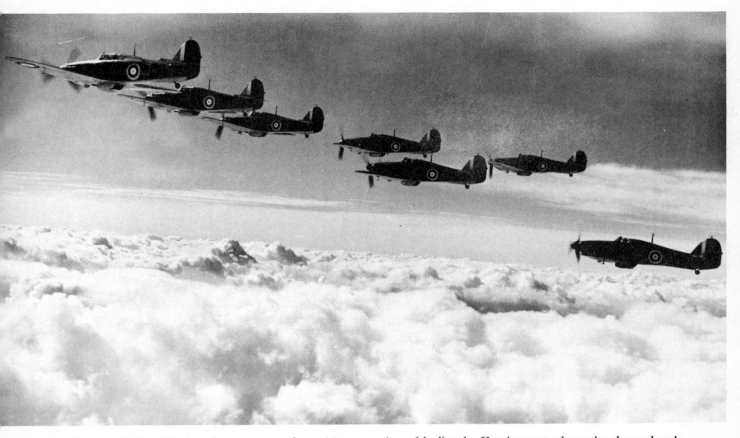

Hurricanes of No. 85 Squadron on patrol awaiting the word to vector in on approaching Luftwaffe forma- *tions. Ideally, the Hurricanes took on the slower bomb-ers while the Spitfires mixed with the Me-109s.*
(IMPERIAL WAR MUSEUM, LONDON)

had come upon them, the Stukas dive-bombed a radio installation and the Me-110s concentrated upon the airfield itself. No. 17 Squadron, part of which was based at Martlesham, had been sent off to intercept a formation of attackers and then suddenly vectored back to their station. The Hurricanes arrived only in time to see columns of smoke rising from Martlesham. It was too late; the German planes had already left for their bases in France.

The Operations Rooms in the sector stations were swamped with German activity in the vicinity of Calais and the Channel. Hundreds of Me-109s swept across the Straits of Dover, contributing to the confusion on the radar screens. And then, around the same time the Me-110s and Stukas freely dealt with Martlesham, the Dornier 17s of Kampfge-schwader 3, with Me-109 escort, had made landfall and were speeding westward over Kent. Almost a hundred bombers made up this formation, plus even

more fighters. Four British squadrons (forty-eight aircraft at best), then patrolling in the general area of penetration, were sent to deal with the Germans. They were easily held off by the high-flying Me-109s. Even the added strength of three more British squadrons did not improve the odds, and the Dorniers continued on to their selected targets. One was the Coastal Command station at Eastchurch; others were radar stations along the southeast coast.

A formation of more than thirty Dorniers pushed on to Rochester, where the most serious strike was successfully made. Bombs—fragmentation, incendiary, and delayed-action—literally rained down, cutting across hangars, workshops, and runways. Rochester, like Eastchurch, was not a Fighter Command station—but it was the home of aircraft factories, among them the important Short Brothers works. It was here that the first of the four-engined heavy bombers, the Stirling, was being built. The destruction to the facility delayed the heavy-bomber time-table several months. It was a crucial blow to the long-range plans of the British.

The British fighters attacked the Germans savagely, but outnumbered, nine Hurricanes and Spitfires were lost. The Germans lost only four planes in the fighting. Still, not all of the British pilots were lost. Flying Officer John Gibson, a New Zealander of No. 501 Squadron, contemplated his sad condition. He had made a pass at a German plane and found himself the victim of the enemy. Over Folkstone, at the edge of the sea, he gingerly sat in his blazing Hurricane planning his next action.

Gibson did not want the burning aircraft to crash on land with the possibility of striking a town, a village, or a farm cottage. He pointed the blistering nose of the Hurricane toward the Channel. Then he had another thought. Gibson wore, as was the wont of many an RAF pilot, new beautiful, hand-made boots. The thought of what the sea would do to such fine craftsmanship gave him pause. Gibson worked off the shoes and tossed them over the side, watched them drop for a second toward the earth below. Once over the water and down now to about a thousand feet, he flipped the Hurricane over and dropped out himself. His chute opened and, shoe-less, Gibson wafted down into the waters of the English Channel. The blazing Hurricane dived smol-dering into the sea.

For his action John Gibson was awarded the Distinguished Flying Cross. More: a Kentish native, upon finding the handsome boots, mailed them off to a nearby airfield and soon after Gibson was as dashingly booted as before his encounter with a Messerschmitt. It had been an action-packed hour.

Then, inexplicably, at the height of the battle there came a pause. Having, to a great extent, thrown Fighter Command off balance by its massive raids, feints, and fighter sweeps, the Luftwaffe permitted the English nearly two hours in which to refuel and rearm. The activity, up to this point, had fallen primarily upon Kesselring's Luftflotte 2. As soon as his forces had completed their missions, Sperrle's Luftflotte 3 should have taken over. Such timing is not always possible under actual operating conditions. Only in retrospect, in the warm security of their armchairs and with the even greater security of time (and the warranty of history), can those who were never there sit in judgment of What

German pilots recounting their experiences during the Battle of Britain. Hauptmann Georg-Peter Eder of Jagdgeschwader 26 (right) carries signal flare cartridges in his flight boots. (H. J. NOWARRA)

Pilots of Jagdgeschwader 27 prepare to take off on an escort mission to England. (H. J. NOWARRA)

Might Have Been. At any rate, the British were granted a breathing spell instead of having to contend with Sperrle's bombers and fighters immediately following Kesselring's quite effective attacks. It should also be remembered that even as these attacks were in progress both Kesselring and Sperrle were at Karinhall listening to their intrepid leader, no mean armchair strategist himself, on how to win the Battle of Britain in just a few days.

By five in the afternoon the radar screens again picked up large formations of German aircraft, perhaps two hundred or more, moving from Luftflotte 3 bases in northwestern France. As the fighter escorts, Me-109s, milled around waiting for the bombers and consuming fuel, No. 10 and No. 11 Groups prepared for the attack. The bombers, Ju-88s, were twenty minutes late: this not only gave the British time to prepare but also limited the time the Me-109s might afford protection for the bombers over England. Also in the German formations were Stukas and Me-110s. Even before the first group of German planes crossed the south coast (roughly in the area of the Isle of Wight) eight fighter squadrons—Hurricanes and Spitfires—were air-borne and waiting.

The evening sky erupted with battling aircraft. The Ju-88s of Hauptmann Jochen Helbig's 4th Staffel (of Lehrgeschwader 1) came under severe attack by swarms of Spitfires which had dropped down out of the setting sun. In seconds Helbig's bomber was punched full of holes by the swift British planes—the Spitfire was nearly a hundred miles an hour faster than the Ju-88. The eight guns of the Spitfire converged upon the German bomber with smashing force. Helbig's gunner managed to wing one of the attackers, which fell smoking out of the fight.

Helbig himself sought the safety of lower altitudes, where the Spitfires could not torment him in diving attacks. With his plane in poor condition he could only continue south for home—the Orléans field in France. But of his seven planes, only two returned. It had been a disaster for Helbig's *Staffel.*

The fighting at this point was a great confusion of tumbling aircraft, of hammering noise, of planes shedding fragments, of silent guns and dead gunners, of great burning veins across the sky—of screaming plunges and the abrupt, bursting crashes of a stricken aircraft. Their scorched, obscene resting places were marked by great scars in the earth. Small cottages burst open to admit precipitate, uninvited death. Orchards were left a burning waste —a village street a litter of scorching brick, glass, wood, and innocent, twisted dead. These were all reminders that the war in the air must finally come to earth.

In the melee of the attack which had decimated Helbig's *Staffel,* although many of the Ju-88s jettisoned their bombs, two formations fought through the British fighters. Three Junkers succeeded in bombing the naval air station at Worthy Down at Southampton. Another formation of a dozen Ju-88s pressed on farther to the north and struck the important sector station of Fighter Command at Middle Wallop. Even as the bombs shattered across the airfield, striking two hangars and runways, Spitfires of No. 609 Squadron were taking off. The German survivors of this attack reported they had hit Andover airfield (not a fighter base), not realizing the importance of Middle Wallop as a sector station which housed the radar equipment for operational control of the fighters in that sector.

A total of twenty-five German aircraft were lost in this phase of the day's fighting: eight Ju-88s, four Stukas, and thirteen Me-110s. This was at a cost of sixteen Hurricanes and Spitfires.

The scarred, crippled, smoking remnants of the once massive formations had hardly dashed for Cherbourg when another formation was plotted forming over Calais. This was an attack on the left flank after the attack on the south. Sixty or seventy aircraft were coming in over the Straits of Dover and many of No. 11 Group's planes were in need of fuel and landing. No. 501 Squadron's Hurricanes were still air-borne, although after two encounters they were low on fuel and ammunition. Air Vice-Marshal Park could do nothing else but dispatch the Hurricanes to Dover. He quickly added an additional four squadrons from Kent and, later, four and a half others.

At six-thirty Test Group 210, which had bombed the airfield at Martlesham Heath earlier in the day, was returning to bomb two sector stations, one at Kenley and the other at Biggin Hill. Hauptmann Walter Rübensdörffer's test group had enjoyed unusual success: it had also put out the Ventnor radar station on the Isle of Wight three days earlier— and its morning had been fruitful. Now it was returning in freshly bombed-up Messerschmitts (both 109s and 110s) as well as Dornier 17s. Jagdge-schwader 52 was to furnish the escort of Me-109s.

Leading his formation of twenty-three aircraft, Rübensdörffer wondered where the fighter escort was. His bomb-laden Messerschmitts, his fighter-bombers, would not be effective bombers until they had reached their targets and dropped the bombs. Another formation of his test group, twenty-seven Dornier 17s, made up the rest of the attacking force. But where were the fighters?

If he had lost the fighters in the darkening sky, now misting up in the early evening, Rübensdörffer had also lost his way. The Dorniers which were assigned Biggin Hill as their target bombed West Malling instead. Although no sector station, West Malling was put out of operation for several days.

Rübensdörffer made an even more serious error. On descending through the mist he spotted an airfield which he believed to be Kenley. He was only four miles off target, but the field he saw was Croydon, ten miles from London. Hitler's standing order was that Greater London, London itself, was not·to be bombed. He still hoped for a negotiated peace and to keep the English reprisal bombers away from German cities.

It was almost seven o'clock in the evening when the Me-110s began dropping bombs on Croydon from an altitude of two thousand feet. The Hurricanes of No. 111 Squadron, patrolling at ten thousand feet, plunged down to the attack. The alarming sudden appearance of the Hurricanes resulted in an almost random spilling of bombs. Although the airfield was struck, causing much destruction to hangars, workshops, and runways, bombs fell haphazardly across the Croydon area. Small war production factories were hit, but so was the Bourjois perfume factory. Sixty-two people died as a result of the bombardment, more than a hundred were injured, many seriously. Once again Rübensdörffer's unit had proved effective, even if in error.

But he himself was in trouble. As he tried to get away from the scene of the attack, a Hurricane caught up with his Messerschmitt. Try as he might he could not shake the British fighter, flown by pilot J. M. Thompson of No. 111 Squadron, as he attempted to speed over Kent and return to France. The Me-110 burst into flame, and still the Hurricane harried them.

Alan Christopher Deere, the indestructible New Zealander who, though shot down more than a half-dozen times, survived the war with a victory score of twenty-two. (IMPERIAL WAR MUSEUM, LONDON)

They had to land. He sought for a likely place in the fields of Kent. He jerked the plane over a small cottage that suddenly came into view, then over a gentle hill and toward a valley beyond. The Messerschmitt trailed sheets of flame and molten metal dripped in its path. And then it was finished for the commander of Erprobungsgruppe 210 as his blazing aircraft struck the earth. Five other Me-110s had also not returned after No. 111 Squadron's Hurricanes attacked them over Croydon. An Me-109 also was lost. The other aircraft of Test Group 210 raced for Calais.

In the twilight moments of the day's battles the smaller skirmishes scattered across the skies of Kent. On his second patrol of the day Flight Lieutenant Alan Deere in a Spitfire (No. 54 Squadron) had in headlong frustration pursued an Me-109 all the way across the English Channel to the Calais-Marck nest of the German fighters. When he sud-

A Spitfire, victim of an Me-109, goes down burning.
(H. J. NOWARRA)

denly realized what he had done, he was himself being stalked by Messerschmitts. Faster than the Spitfire, the German fighters swept into range.

"Bullets seemed to be coming from everywhere and pieces were flying off my aircraft," Deere told the story later. "My instrument panel was shattered, my eye was bleeding from a splinter, my watch had been shot clean off my wrist by an incendiary bullet which left a nice diagonal burn across my wrist and it seemed only a matter of moments before the end."

With his Merlin engine full out Deere raced for England, feeling that never had thirty miles of water seemed so expansive, nor had his Spitfire seemed so slow. But still the hunted, he reached the coast near Folkestone. The German Me-109s, unwilling to repeat his mistake, turned off and returned to Calais-Marck.

Deere was now only eight hundred feet above the ground, and within a minute or so after the enemy planes turned back his straining Merlin engine burst into flame.

"Desperately I tore my straps off, pulled back the hood and prepared to bail out. I was still doing about 300 miles an hour, so I pulled my stick back to get a bit more height. At about 1,500 feet I turned on my back and pushed the stick hard forward. I shot out a few feet and somehow became caught up by the bottom of my parachute. I twisted and turned, but wasn't able to get either in or out. The nose had now dropped below the horizontal and was pointing at the ground which appeared to be rushing up at a terrific speed."

The twisting, plunging Spitfire, now burning fiercely, carried Deere for some minutes when his parachute unsnagged from the seat and the pilot was blown backward along the fuselage. The tail struck his wrist and then he was clear of the plane. He pulled the ripcord.

"None too soon. I hadn't time to breathe a sigh of relief before I landed with a mighty thud in a plantation of thick shrubs." Deere's luck truly held, for his parachute had opened dangerously close to the ground—the shrubs broke the impact of his fall. In a nearby field his Spitfire demolished itself in flame and dust.

After his injuries had been attended to in the hospital, the chief surgeon called Deere's station commander to inform him that the pilot was safe.

In his relief Wing Commander Cecil Bouchier could only say, "Keep him there, he's costing us too many Spitfires!" On that August 15, 1940, Alan Deere—who had shot down his thirteenth German aircraft earlier in the day—had "bent" his fourth Spitfire.

The great air battles of the day ended, a day of very heavy fighting, like a summer storm with the fury spent and small flashes and distant thunder. For the Germans it had been the true Eagle Day, with all three *Luftflotten* taking part in 1786 sorties (to RAF Fighter Command's 974). It was not until much later that the participants realized that August 15, 1940, had been the most active day of the Battle of Britain. It had also been a decisive day. It finished Luftflotte 5 as a daylight threat to England and underscored the vulnerability of the Stuka and the Messerschmitt 110.

The battle had raged over a five-hundred-mile

The remains of an Me-109 brought down on August 15, 1940. Winston Churchill observed the battle in which this fighter participated.

(IMPERIAL WAR MUSEUM, LONDON)

front, from near Tynemouth in the north to Southampton in the southeast. This battle front, however, was three-dimensional and moved inland as well as vertically in a continually shifting pattern. The radar screens, in most instances, were capable of tracing this pattern for the sector stations, from which the sector controller could direct the individual squadrons. It was on this day that Göring ordered the attacks upon the radar stations to stop.

The excited, exhausted pilots of Fighter Command claimed 182 aircraft in the day's fighting. The five massive assaults had come so swiftly that in the confusion of battle several pilots claimed the same plane. The true figure was 89—though not as spectacular it is nonetheless a formidable figure, for many of the aircraft carried multiple crews. The Luftwaffe claimed 82 Spitfires and Hurricanes, plus 5 Curtiss Hawks (which were non-existent in the

RAF) and 14 additional aircraft: a total of 101 British planes. The RAF in fact lost 42 fighters (not counting those destroyed on the ground); but 17 pilots, like the indestructible Alan Deere, walked away from their crashed planes.

The bombing of Croydon, so near to central London, infuriated Hitler, who wanted to court-martial the hapless Oberst Paul Deichmann, who had initiated the savage fighting of the day with the Stukas. But this rage was forgotten in the rush of other, bigger matters. Hitler had the Eastern Front on his mind, although he continued discussing Sealion, the invasion of England. Preparations for the invasion must be ready by the end of August; the landings must be made by September 15. At the conference on July 21, 1940, Hitler had pointed out that among the important prerequisites was "complete mastery of the air."

On August 15, only two days after Eagle Day, the Luftwaffe may not have lost the Battle of Britain; but neither could it win it.

7

HELL'S CORNER

FOR ALL their vaunted Teutonic efficiency, the Germans were not very well served by their intelligence services, Abteilung 5, under the command of Major Josef Schmid, a non-flying friend of Jeschonnek. Ambitious, hard-working, and convivial, Schmid, who liked being called "Beppo," brought some organization to his not very efficient department with the introduction of new members, most of them men he could trust and who would not menace his position. But he fell into the usual trap of underestimating the British air potential and supplied his superiors with the kind of information they liked to hear. In July 1940 Schmid composed an intelligence paper, "Comparative Survey of Royal Air Force and Luftwaffe Striking Power." The gist of the paper was revealed in the third section, "Conclusion," which opened with the very words Göring wished to see: "The Luftwaffe is clearly superior to the RAF as regards strength, equipment, training, command, and location of bases."

Following the great engagements of August 15, the Luftwaffe High Command estimated, basing this figure on Schmid's reports and upon the reports of fighter "kills," that the Royal Air Force had only three hundred fighters on hand. There were, in fact, more than double that number of operational Hurricanes and Spitfires. As the battle became progressively attritional the Luftwaffe pilots grimly joked about those "last fifty Spitfires." Their High Command had assured them that the RAF was all but depleted, though frequently many more than the last fifty met the German formations near the Channel day after day.

Schmid did not so much as mention the radar system (a subject which wouldn't have interested Göring in any case) and he oversold the German aircraft as compared with the British planes. For example, he noted in his "Comparative Survey," referring to the Hurricane and Spitfire, that "In view of their combat performance and the fact that they are not yet equipped with cannon guns both types are inferior to the Me-109, and particularly the Me-109F, while the individual Me-110 is inferior to *skillfully* handled Spitfires." The emphasis is Schmid's. So is the ignorance of the fact that the Me-109F was not in use by the operational units engaged in the Battle of Britain. The tale of the Stuka came to a sad ending over Britain. This aircraft too was overvalued by the Germans. It was a good close-support plane and capable of precision bombing, but was a deathtrap in aerial combat.

On Sunday, August 18, following a relatively quiet day, the pressure upon Fighter Command was resumed in the morning with heavy attacks upon airfields and some strikes upon radar stations. Kenley and Biggin Hill were severely hit with considerable damage especially at the former. Its being knocked out of operations for two days crippled Fighter Command in the Kenley sector.

In the afternoon there was a concentration of

attacks upon Coastal Command and Fleet Air Arm Stations off the south coast at Gosport, Thorney Island, and Ford. The formations were from Luftflotte 3, consisting of Ju-88s, Ju-87s, and great swarms of Me-109s. The Stukas dive-bombed Thorney Island. At the same time, to the northwest nearby Poling, with its radar installations, was attacked by Stukas of Stuka Geschwader 77. The radar station was knocked out for the rest of the month—and the Stuka was knocked out of the Battle of Britain. Tangling with Spitfires of No. 152 Squadron and Hurricanes of No. 43 Squadron, the Stukas paid for their success. Twelve of the twenty-eight Ju-87s dispatched by *StG* 77's first *Staffel* were destroyed, some falling to earth and others

A Spitfire goes down under Luftwaffe guns; although the plane was replaceable, the pilot, if injured or killed, was not. The Battle of Britain reached a critical phase during the daylight raids because of pilot shortage.
(NATIONAL ARCHIVES)

into the sea. Of the sixteen that managed to return to France, six were so badly shot up that they were of little further use. Another thirty were either lost or so severely damaged that they had to be junked. Over a period of just a few days the losses in Stukas all but wiped out an entire *Gruppe*. Richthofen withdrew his *Fliegerkorps* VIII from Cherbourg to the Pas de Calais area, awaiting the day when Sealion would be launched and there would no longer be an RAF. The Stukas could then be employed against the Royal Navy in the forthcoming invasion. Except for an aborted flurry at the end of the month, the Stuka appeared for the last time over England on August 18, 1940. Its legend was dead.

Mercifully bad flying weather closed in on the next day and for nearly a week only sporadic activity was possible. Both camps had time to consider their positions. The most serious problem confronting Air Chief Marshal Dowding was the shortage of experienced pilots. He was reluctantly given some from Bomber Command by the Air Ministry and the training period for new pilots was continued at two weeks instead of the customary four. It had been hoped that the four weeks' course would be reinstated, but the cost of the battle canceled that. Pilots were posted to front-line squadrons with merely ten or at best twenty hours of solo flying.

The strain on experienced pilots took its toll also and replacements were hard to find. For example, in the period from August 8–18 Fighter Command lost 154 pilots, either killed or wounded seriously enough to be out of action. In the same ten-day period only 63 new fighter pilots were graduated from the training schools. And it was Fighter Command that Göring had selected as the primary target of the Luftwaffe.

On the day following the Stuka slaughter the German Air Force High Command again assembled at Karinhall on August 19. Göring's temper had not improved since the last conference. His four-day timetable for the destruction of the defenses of south England was definitely off. Obviously someone was at fault; losses were too high. He listened to the complaints of the bomber commanders—the fighters, they argued, did not fly close enough to the bombers to give proper protection. By the time they arrived upon the scene, the British had swooped in and shot up the bomber formations.

The fighter commanders argued for the "free hunt" technique, which placed the fighters high above and around the bombers. This made it possible for them to achieve flexibility, important to a fighter, and not be chained to the slower bombers. This close-support tactic, it was argued by the German fighter commanders, sacrificed both fuel and the fighter's ability to move about the sky to trouble points.

But the bombers had been suffering terribly under Spitfire and Hurricane attacks. The fighter protection must be doubled, tripled, Göring insisted.

"We have reached the decisive period of the air war against England," Göring told them. "Our first aim is the destruction of the enemy's fighters. If they no longer take the air, we shall force them into battle by directing bomber attacks against targets within range of our fighters." The lesson of Luftflotte 5's misadventure had not been lost on Göring and the ravaged Stuka *Gruppen* of the day before had impressed him also.

"At the same time," Göring decreed further, "and on a growing scale, we must continue our activities against the ground organization of the enemy bomber units. Surprise attacks on the enemy aircraft industry must be made by day and by night. Once the enemy air force has been annihilated, our attacks will be directed as ordered against other vital targets."

This was a passing reference to Sealion, in which Göring had scant interest—and, though they would not have cared to inform him, in which his Luftwaffe High Command had little hope. Time was running out for Sealion, for the autumn days were fast approaching and the Channel would be impossible to cross even without RAF interference. The Royal Navy, still intact, would chop the invaders to bits—those who survived the treacherous Channel waters.

Coincidentally, on that same August 19, 1940, from his No. 11 Group headquarters at Uxbridge, Kent, Air Vice-Marshal Keith Park also issued orders. Having noted that the German attacks had been moving closer inland and with greater concentration upon airfields, Park instructed his controllers in the sector stations upon several points. The main gist was the preservation of pilots.

"Despatch fighters to engage large enemy formations over land or within gliding distance of the coast," Park emphasized. "During the next two or three weeks we cannot afford to lose pilots through forced landings in the sea." The enemy bombers were the major threat. Little was gained by clashing with the Me-109s. "Against mass attacks coming inland despatch a minimum number of squadrons to engage enemy fighters. Our main object is to engage enemy bombers, particularly those approaching under the lowest cloud layer." These, of course, were frequently missed by radar and bombed with devastating accuracy.

When the weather finally cleared enough for full-scale operations on August 24, and continuing through September 6 (when Göring or Hitler issued another fatal decision), the airfields of No. 11 Group came under concentrated attack. The full

Air Vice-Marshal Sir Keith Park, commanding officer of No. 11 Group, whose squadrons were stationed in Kent, in southeast England, and over which most of the fierce fighting of the Battle of Britain occurred.
(IMPERIAL WAR MUSEUM, LONDON)

impact and ferocity of it almost succeeded in realizing Göring's dream of destroying Dowding's shaken Fighter Command.

Kentish skies became an expansive battleground, the setting for desperate encounters between the RAF and the Luftwaffe. In accordance with Park's order to keep the British pilots inland, whenever possible, the fighting occurred over the hop fields and apple orchards of Kent, which to the Germans in this period became known as "Hell's Corner." If the contending pilots suffered in the vicious battles, so did the people below upon whom the de-

Kentish skies became an expansive battleground: *a formation of He-111s approach their bomb run.*
(H. J. NOWARRA)

tritus of battle fell—shell casings, spent bullets, burning pieces of aircraft: the aircraft themselves and jettisoned bombs.

The Luftwaffe's primary targets for the next two weeks were Park's airfields, with emphasis upon the inner fields ringing London. Under Park's command were seven sector stations—Tangmere, Debden, Kenley, Biggin Hill, Hornchurch, North Weald, and Northolt—in southeast England. Twenty-one fighter squadrons were based on these airfields and the Hurricanes, the Spitfires, and the few Blenheims were flown by about four hundred pilots. Although in a pinch Park could request help from the other groups, it would have to be a tight pinch. Dowding did not want to leave his other sectors open to attack while their fighters were engaged in "Hell's Corner." Although the main blow was struck at

No. 11 Group, the Germans at the same time confused the picture by diversionary feints, attacks upon ports, minelaying, as well as night raids upon various industrial targets. Nor were No. 11 Group's airfields the only ones attacked during the period August 24–September 6. They were, however, the worst hit. And its stations lay within range of the Messerschmitt 109s escorting the bombers.

That there was a new tactic was obvious to the British pilots when they met the German formations head on. The Me-109s outnumbered the German bombers about three to one—and the fighters all but clung to their charges. Breaking through such defenses was costly for the Hurricane and Spitfire pilots, if not impossible. Sheer courage was not enough and despite nearly superhuman effort and sacrifice, the bombers frequently managed to get through.

Of the sector stations, Biggin Hill, just to the south of London, sustained the worst attacks. The sector station had been hit heavily on Friday, August 30—which opened what became known as "the Bad Weekend" at Biggin Hill. The new German tactics of mass formations—few bombers and many fighters—of feints along a broad front, confused the tracking of the radar stations as well as the ground observers. It was difficult to determine, once the plots began coming in, just where the main effort would be.

It was around this time that Park instituted the now famed "Tally Ho!" procedure, which he hoped might clarify the situation. Formation leaders were to sing out this cry upon spotting German formations, along with the approximate number and type of aircraft, the altitude, course, and position of the formation when sighted. This actual visual information would help to prevent the dispatch of a single squadron of twelve Spitfires to intercept a hundred enemy aircraft, most of them fighters.

In the battles with such formations, the point of attrition became critical for Dowding. This was aggravated by the onslaught on the fighter bases and especially so in the case of the sector stations. Biggin Hill's Bad Weekend illustrates what might have been had the attacks continued systematically. Friday's raid was followed by an even heavier one on Saturday. Late in the afternoon low-flying Dorniers—only eight in number, but carrying thousand-pound bombs—slipped by the Observer Corps, radar, and the "Tally Ho!" Biggin Hill, which lay on the route to London, was attacked from the north, an approach which misled the defenses, which generally looked for the German planes to come from either the south or the east. The Dorniers flew up the Thames toward London, then turned sharply to approach Biggin Hill, still under repair from the previous day's attack as well as the morning's raid.

This afternoon raid was devastatingly effective. The bombs from the Dorniers cut across the main part of the installation, cutting power lines and gas and water mains, demolishing workshops, gutting hangars and storage facilities. The worst was a direct hit upon the crowded Operations Room; the projectile ripped through the hutment's roof, struck a steel safe, and deflected into the adjoining room before shattering with fulminating shock.

The building plunged into darkness and the air filled with debris, pulverized plaster and shards of eviscerating glass and steel. Instinctively, perhaps, Group Captain Richard Grice had ordered everyone in the Operations Room to get under tables as soon as he heard the approaching whistle of the bomb. Otherwise casualties would have been higher. As

An RAF Operations Room, from which fighters in the air could be controlled from the ground by radar and radio. WAAFs (Women's Auxiliary Air Force) keep track of oncoming German raiders on the mapboard.
(IMPERIAL WAR MUSEUM, LONDON)

it was, more than sixty died or were seriously wounded in the attack. The women of the WAAF inside the Operations Room acquitted themselves admirably, without panic and with a good deal of courage. They continued to carry on with their duties even though services were seriously curtailed. Sergeant Helen Turner and Corporal Elspeth Henderson remained at their phones despite the damage of the direct hit.

Other sector stations were hit on the same day—Duxford of No. 12 Group and two others of Park's No. 11 Group: Debden and Hornchurch. During the raid on the latter Alan Deere experienced another of his incredible adventures. Around the same time that Biggin Hill was being attacked, more Dorniers swung in over Hornchurch. All the aircraft had been hastily scrambled when it became clear that the sector station would be the target. Just as the Dorniers appeared over the field, No. 54 Squadron was taking off. Two sections raced into the air before the bombs began falling. The last section of three planes, led by Alan Deere, was not so fortunate.

The three Spitfires were under way when the first detonations ripped the runway. With the shouting of the controller in their ears and the sound of bomb bursts around them the Spitfires swung into the wind. Deere had the nose of his plane pointed in the right direction, only to find that one of the planes in his section blocked his way.

"Get the hell out of the way, Red Two," he shouted and gunned the engine. Red Two jinked aside and he too had his tail up and the engine roaring. Then all three Spitfires sprinted into the wind: they were air-borne. In seconds they were off the ground and their wheels began retracting into the aircraft. It was at this moment that the bomb hit.

"One moment they were about twenty feet up in close formation," wrote pilot Richard Hillary, who saw the incident, "the next catapulted apart as though on elastic." A bomb had erupted directly under the three planes. Deere's aircraft was thrown up and over on its back before crashing to earth upside down. For a hundred yards the Spitfire crunched and screeched along the runway before jolting to a stop, reeking of highly flammable fuel.

The number three man, Pilot Officer Eric Edsall, had fallen to earth right side up, but with such

force that leg injuries made it impossible for him to walk. He crawled toward Deere's Spitfire, which showed no sign of life. The number two man of Red Section, Sergeant J. Davies, was simply blown out of the airfield, across the boundary fence, where he landed without injury although the Spitfire's tail snapped off. He was missing for a long time that day, for in order to get back onto the airfield he had to walk for miles along the fence.

When Edsall reached Deere's overturned Spitfire he was amazed to find his flight leader still alive,

Prime Minister Winston Churchill on a visit to the Vauxhall Motors plant in Luton, Bedfordshire. Appropriately, the tank was known as the "Churchill."
(HOME COUNTIES NEWSPAPERS, LTD.)

although trapped inside the plane. Deere's most serious injury—which looked worse than it was—was a badly gouged head and the loss of some hair. With Deere pushing from inside and the crippled Edsall pulling from outside, they succeeded in forcing the cockpit door of the Spitfire. Fearing fire, they got away from the plane as quickly as they could hobble. Deere helped Edsall to Station Sick

Quarters. By the next day all three pilots were ready for action again.

The long day came to a close with a night bombing of Liverpool. The technique of night fighting (with the use of radar) was but a primitive idea and there was little that could be done at night, except with searchlight and antiaircraft guns. It was yet another pressure upon Fighter Command. August ended with the heaviest losses for Fighter Command on any single day of the Battle of Britain: thirty-nine fighter planes were destroyed by the Luft-

Luton after a visit from the Luftwaffe; although an aircraft factory had been the target, bombs fell on the city itself and upon the Vauxhall factory, setting some oil barrels aflame.

(HOME COUNTIES NEWSPAPERS, LTD.)

waffe. Fourteen pilots were killed, in addition to those injured or killed in the bombings themselves. The cost to the Luftwaffe, night and day, was forty-one aircraft. The loss ratios were less disproportionate, however than in July, a bad sign for Dowding's Fighter Command. Within days a serious crisis must develop, the tired Air Chief Marshal realized. The "few" were becoming too few.

II

There were no front lines in the sense that they had existed in France. And despite the aerial aspects of the Battle of Britain, the fighting and bombing took their toll on the ground also. On the day that the Bad Weekend at Biggin Hill began, Friday, August 30, 1940, the German raiders pushed through the interceptors and reached the city of Luton, some thirty miles northwest of London. Although some of the bombers jettisoned their bombs while under British fighter attack, the others found Luton at around four in the afternoon.

Luton was a manufacturing town, its main staple being the hat industry. It was also the site of Vauxhall Motors, Ltd., which turned out trucks and the so-called "Churchill" tank. Percival Aircraft, Ltd., manufactured training aircraft (the Oxford and the Proctor) as well as the de Havilland Mosquito. Also located in Luton were the Skefko Ball Bearing Company and Hayward-Tyler & Co., Ltd., which built engines for Admiralty barges.

War had come to Luton on the first day of the war when the city was designated a reception area (defined as "not immune to danger but an improbable target") for evacuees, mainly children, expectant mothers, and the blind from London. Besides the refugees from London (who eventually became homesick and returned) other signs of the war were seen in the narrow streets of Luton. These were smoke screen generators in which sawdust and tar blocks were burned to obscure Luton from possible German bombers. The generators succeeded primarily in coating the hills and homes of Luton with a black oily deposit. Later oil burners were installed for the purpose and were not as dirt-depositing.

But except for such inconveniences, and the alarums of the air raid alarms for raids that never materialized, Luton remained out of the front line until August 30.

Sometimes after, a German communiqué was issued which read: "A squadron of our bombers in daylight on August 23 [sic] raided a plane parts factory in Luton, northwest of London. The first aircraft initiated a great fire, and subsequent aircraft were thus guided to the target, which they completely destroyed."

This is not quite what happened. The bombs fell

A lone German bomber swooped down and dropped its bomb upon a factory in Luton—a factory devoted *to Luton's major industry, the manufacturing of women's hats.* (HOME COUNTIES NEWSPAPERS, LTD.)

first upon the airport, but did not focus there. The explosions ripped across Vauxhall, moving ever closer into the city itself; the bus depot was struck, killing one employee, and a double-decker bus was flung up into the roof of the garage, where it dangled over the rubble. The string of bombs "walked across" Luton, making shambles of the little brick dwellings (most of them belonging to the poor). Bombs even fell upon Vauxhall's cricket ground; the duds gave the bomb disposal crews much work to do.

It was a shocking new experience for everyone. A six-year-old boy ran into his grandmother's house

to tell her of his adventure. The very earth had opened up and lifted him right into the air! When he took her to show her the place, another boy was found there dead. In all, 53 people were killed in Luton that day and 140 injured.

Vauxhall, not a plane parts factory, as the German communiqué claimed, was worst hit. As for the "great fire," while it served admirably as a guide, it was merely some oil barrels at Vauxhall. It did little damage, nor was it a great loss. The damage to the truck assembly factory was more serious, but within a short time even this was cleared away.

Throughout the rest of the war Luton was treated

A not unusual pastoral scene in Kent during the summer of 1940. A Spitfire has just destroyed a German plane, which has come to rest in a sheep meadow.
(SYNDICATION INTERNATIONAL)

to such harsh though not very decisive raids (including some with V-2 bombs toward the close of the war). On October 15, 1940, as the Battle of Britain itself was coming to an end (at least in its intensive phases), the Luton sirens sounded. Shortly after, a lone German bomber appeared high in the sky and dropped a bomb. What its target could have been must remain one of the mysteries of the Second World War. The bomb struck a factory, true, but it was the W. O. Scales and Co., Ltd., a hat factory.

The sportive face of war is no less tragic than its grimmer visage. The explosion of the bomb blasted sewing machines in every direction: some sharp fragments even went into the factory adjoining and killed a young bride who had just come to work that morning. Ribbons, hats, brick, wood, and mortar intermingled in a colorful outburst of swirling death. New Bedford Road brightened when its trees were

suddenly festooned with gaily colored ribbons. But out of this ludicrous gaiety came thirteen dead, most of these dead being young women or girls employed by Scales. There were in addition thirty-five wounded. It took two and a half hours to dig young Tommy Walker out of the debris. The fourteen-year-old boy kept up the spirits of his rescuers by singing all the while.

But Luton was not in Hell's Corner and the people of Kent, who were subjected to much more of such accidental bombings, crashes, and shootings, remained generally in good spirits also. The continual air raid warnings took their toll in loss of sleep as well as loss of production. Watching dogfights even became an interesting pastime, once the initial fears were overcome. This came to be known as "goofing," that is, instead of taking shelter, you goofed.

Few people who watched the fight contrails realized that the spent shells, the lead that went astray, and parts of aircraft came down around them. This was one of the reasons for the tin hats issued to civilians. Jettisoned bombs or out-of-control aircraft, German or British, caused the most frightful, because of its unexpectedness, havoc. Death literally, and senselessly, dropped out of the skies.

But the nature of war had changed so much in a few months and if the sky over your home became a battleground, then your back garden became a graveyard. There was always the chance of a sudden, haphazard, violent end. There were also thousands of close calls which filled the papers with human interest stories. For example, the mother at 4 Hardy Street, Maidstone, Kent, almost every day put her baby out into the garden behind the house to get the sun. On this one Thursday morning she just hadn't gotten around to it. Meanwhile the air had begun to boil over Hell's Corner. The German raiders were heading for Croydon, Biggin Hill, and Eastchurch, among other airfields. It was over Kent that most were intercepted.

Maidstone, where the main office of the *Kent Messenger* is located, afforded many a fine view of the battles. Members of the paper's staff watched from the rooftop of their building. A Spitfire had got onto the tail of a Messerschmitt 110. The battle began high and gyrated and twisted until it was barely a thousand feet over the ground. The Messerschmitt spurted smoke and fire. It lurched and,

War souvenirs in your back yard. These natives of Kent examine what remained of a German bomber after it *came to earth. The "thumbs up" sign was as character-istic as Churchill's V (for Victory) sign.*

(FOX PHOTOS, LTD.)

obviously in serious trouble, began to fall. As the Spitfire pulled away, a single parachute blossomed under the burning German plane. It was then only about four hundred feet up. The German landed on a rooftop in Hope Street, breaking both legs.

The burning plane continued on to Hardy Street, crashed against the corner of the house at number 4, taking a gable of one room with it, and then smashed into the garden. The baby was not there but in the kitchen and escaped injury. Many staff members of the *Messenger* ran to the scene of the crash to find the Me-110 burning fiercely in the garden. But there was an additional danger: the heat of the flames caused the machine-gun bullets still in the plane to explode, spewing them in all directions. Despite this the fire department was soon on the job to put out the fire.

III

Meanwhile, as German invasion barges began to accumulate along the coast, Fighter Command was in a seriously depleted state. And it was Park's No. 11 Group in Kent which had taken the brunt of the German attack.

"I was worried daily from July to September by a chronic shortage of trained fighter pilots and it was not until the battle was nearly lost that the Air Staff of the Air Ministry assisted by borrowing pilots from Bomber Command and from the Royal Navy," Park later recalled, not without some bitterness.

The Air Ministry, Park felt, was not attuned to the demands of a full-scale war in the air. Later, when he was relieved of his command in the post-Battle of Britain shake-up, Park learned that the

The fortunes of air war; an Me-110 has crashed into Hardy Street, Kent, after a losing battle with a Spitfire. (KENT MESSENGER)

training schools were operating only at two thirds of capacity and "following peace-time routines, being quite unaware of the grave shortage of pilots in Fighter Command." Why this should have been true is difficult to determine today. The Air Ministry viewed the Battle of Britain in long-range terms and may have been inclined to see the problems of Dowding and Park as merely parts of the total problem. It was, too, guided by political considerations which would hardly have interested the hard-pressed Park. It was not a simple situation and was crosscut by personalities and the desperation of the times.

Park recalled another difficulty: ". . . when the German Air Force concentrated on bombing my fighter aerodromes, I could get such little help from Air Ministry to repair the bomb damage that I had to borrow some thousands of troops from the British Army to fill in the bomb craters to keep the aerodromes serviceable. For doing so I was severely criticised by the Air Ministry at the time for accepting Army assistance. Had my fighter aerodromes been put out of action, the German Air Force would have won the battle by the 15th September 1940."

The pressures upon Park mounted daily—and each day, several times a day, he was summoned from his office to No. 11 Group's Operations Room

Cottages in a Kentish village after a German bombing raid. This frequently occurred when Luftwaffe crews jettisoned their bombs to escape RAF fighters.
(KENT MESSENGER)

as soon as unidentified aircraft were detected assembling over France.

"On entering the underground operations room," Park relates, "I would examine the plotting table which showed [the] enemy dispositions and [British] fighter squadrons dispatched. Before dispatching further squadrons I would have to decide whether the German aircraft were on a training flight or a reconnaissance flight or gathering for a feint attack by fighter sweep to draw my squadrons into the air and away from the direction of a coming bomb attack.

"Having decided that the radar indicated the beginning of a bomb attack I would dispatch more squadrons and bring others to a high state of readiness in preparation for takeoff." The standard daily state of readiness was: five squadrons (of No. 11 Group) were at "Stand-by," meaning that their planes could be air-borne within two minutes; ten squadrons were in "Readiness" (takeoff time five minutes); five squadrons were ready for takeoff in from ten to fifteen minutes and declared "Available." Another five squadrons were "Released," free for the day to rest the pilots and carry on maintenance on the aircraft.

As for the battle itself: "My plan was to make 'Forward Interception' as near as possible to the coast. My aim was always to intercept the German main attack with the maximum number of fighter squadrons that were available. My Spitfire squadrons were directed against the German fighter escort and the Hurricane squadrons were directed against the enemy bombers."

But Park encountered yet another trial, a theoretical disagreement as well as, perhaps, a personality clash. This was with the commander of No. 12

Air Vice-Marshal Trafford Leigh-Mallory, commander of No. 12 Group, which shared the defense of Kent and London with Park's No. 11 Group.
(IMPERIAL WAR MUSEUM, LONDON)

Group, Air Vice-Marshal Trafford Leigh-Mallory, whose command lay to the north of Park's. "Number 12 Group," Park has written, ". . . was frequently called upon to cover my fighter aerodromes around London which were quite defenceless when I had sent all my squadrons to intercept near the coast. Number 12 Group, however, always delayed dispatching its reinforcements in order to assemble wings of four to six squadrons which went off on roving sweeps from the South East of England, and on several occasions allowed my fighter aerodromes to be heavily bombed."

This disagreement between Park and Leigh-Mallory was to have its repercussions after the height of the Battle had passed. Dowding characteristically remained aloof from the argument, feeling that each group leader must be permitted to act without interference from him. Members of the Air Staff, however, upon visiting some of the fighter stations, listened to the pilots and junior officers of No. 12 Group complaining about not being permitted to take part in the battles over Kent because they were not given sufficient time in which to form. Park saw no point in calling upon No. 12

Group (although he did, of course) only to have it form into wings—"Balbos" they were called, after Italo Balbo, the Italian aviator who had led a mass flight from Italy to Chicago in 1933. By the time the wing had formed up the enemy had attacked and left. But when one of the wings, especially the Duxford wing led by Douglas Bader, did succeed in engaging the German formations, Park admitted (although not without a small barb), "that had already been attacked by 11 Group forward squadrons, they were successful." But there was a sentiment in the Air Ministry that the fighter operations over Kent were not efficiently co-ordinated (rather humanly impossible at the time) and that something must be done as soon as it was politic. The result was that in November Dowding was shunted off to an innocuous job as a British representative visiting aircraft factories in the United States. His position at the helm of Fighter Command was taken over by Sholto Douglas, who had served as a fighter pilot in the First World War and was, during the Battle of Britain, deputy Chief of the Air Staff.

Park, after only eight months, was "posted" to Flying Training Command and command of No. 11 Group was taken over by Leigh-Mallory. Evidently the latter's "big wing" theories had impressed Douglas and Archibald Sinclair, Secretary of State for Air. These changes, of which very little was made at the time, did not come about until late in November 1940. Few Britons realized that Dowding and Park had in fact won them the Battle of Britain.

IV

Sealion could not take place unless air superiority over the Channel was secured, and that was possible only by the destruction of the Royal Air Force— and by early September that seemed feasible. Not, however, to the Germans, who, though noting the claims of the Luftwaffe, were puzzled by the appearance of Spitfires and Hurricanes supposedly no longer existent according to the intelligence of Beppo Schmid. On September 3 German Intelligence Chief Schmid estimated, under pressure from Kesselring and Sperrle, that perhaps Fighter Command had only 100 fighters left—or maybe they had 350. Meanwhile hundreds of invasion barges lay in

Kent was "Hell's Corner" as much for the Luftwaffe as for the RAF. A Do-17 burns on the beach in Kent, *like the Luftwaffe its back broken in an attempt to destroy the RAF.* (FOX PHOTOS, LTD.)

French and Belgian ports in readiness for Sealion—and these were suffering under the attacks of British Bomber Command. The earliest date for the sailing of the invasion fleet, Hitler had informed them on the same day, "has been fixed for September 20, and that of the landing for September 21." The German High Command was also informed that the launching of the attack upon the British Isles (through Kent) would occur "on D-Day minus 10," presumably therefore on September 11.

But the Luftwaffe was faced with eliminating the RAF, which theoretically should have been all but wiped out. Schmid did not know that the attacks upon the forward airfields had done extensive damage to five of them and knocked out two, Manston and Lympne, so effectively that they were unusable by fighter aircraft for several days. Six out of Park's seven sector stations had also been hit, with Biggin Hill forced to evacuate two of its three squadrons. In the period from August 24 through September 6 Fighter Command had lost 295 Spitfires and Hurricanes, with 171 severely damaged. In the same period replacements (new and repaired aircraft) numbered 269. But the most serious factor was the loss of pilots: in this same two-week period 103 pilots were dead or missing and 128 were wounded

seriously enough to be taken out of the Battle. At this rate of loss—an average of 120 pilots a week—Dowding would shortly have no Fighter Command.

Inexperienced pilots were too often lost on their first patrols; veteran pilots were exhausted, jumpy, and vulnerable. The gay young fighter pilot was no more. They were raw-nerved, gray-faced, listless, filled with that hatred that Bader described: "We hated those aeroplanes with their iron crosses and their crooked swastikas flying into our English sky. . . ." Only now it was goaded by desperation. The younger pilots were shocked upon seeing their seniors shooting at Germans in parachutes. This was considered a "Hunnish trick" and not cricket. But it was done.

For all their fatigue, despite the shortage of pilots, Fighter Command continued to intercept the German formations—much to the Luftwaffe's consternation. They were being assured that there was no RAF left. They had no idea, however, how close Schmid was to the truth.

The Luftwaffe High Command then on September 3, 1940, in their conference at The Hague, came to a grand decision. They were certain it would wipe out Fighter Command completely. And as with so many of the Nazi Grand Decisions, it saved the enemy.

8

"THE GREATEST DAY"

ON SEPTEMBER 4, 1940, the day following Göring's meeting with his High Command at The Hague when he had resolved upon a change in Luftwaffe tactics, Hitler spoke on the occasion of the opening of the *Winterhilfe* ("Winter Relief") campaign at the Sportpalast. The majority of his audience consisted of nurses and social workers concerned with *Winterhilfe*.

Hitler was in a rare sardonic, threatening mood—and his audience, including the angels of mercy, responded accordingly to his outbursts.

"In England," he told them, "they're filled with curiosity and keep asking, 'Why doesn't he come?'"

"Be calm," Hitler confided, mockery in his voice; the audience tittered. "He's coming! He's coming!"

Hitler's audience responded thrillingly, encouraging him to speak with his customary mastery bordering on hysteria. When his listeners, most of them women, became quiet again Hitler waxed solemn. Winston Churchill, "that noted war correspondent," was "demonstrating his new brain child, the night air raid. Mr. Churchill is carrying out these raids not because they promise to be highly effective, but because his Air Force cannot fly over Germany in daylight."

German planes flew over England every day, Hitler told them. "Whenever the Englishman sees a light, he drops a bomb . . . on residential districts, farms, and villages."

The very air was charged in the Sportpalast as Hitler came to the point of his speech. "When the British Air Force drops two or three or four thousand kilograms of bombs, then we will in one night drop a hundred and fifty, two hundred and thirty, two hundred, or four hundred thousand kilograms—"

Great waves of applause interrupted Hitler at this point.

"When they declare," he shrieked, "that they will increase their attacks on our cities, then we will raze their cities to the ground!"

The audience rose to its feet, screaming, applauding. Their dedication to mankind did not include the British, the French, the Dutch, the Poles.

"The hour will come," Hitler promised in conclusion, "when one of us will break—and it will not be National Socialist Germany!"

"Never! Never!" screamed the nurses, leaping to their feet again, shouting, nearly hysterical, approving and adoring.

Hitler was in his own way approving of the Luftwaffe's decision of the previous day. The major target of the German Air Force would be London. The fiction of "only purely military targets" was ended. The war between the soldiers was over, it would now become a war between peoples. The civilian no longer enjoyed bystander status: modern war had "officially" taken on a new, deadly posture. Perhaps it had always been there but finally no one pretended. The simple "art of war" was revealed for what it was—and is—the technology of slaughter. This great truth may very well be Hitler's contribution to mankind; he had little else to offer.

II

The fateful decision to bomb London came about by accident. On the night of August 24 (this was the day on which the British airfields first came under heavy attack also) German aircraft dispatched to bomb an aircraft factory at Rochester and oil storage tanks at Thames Haven made a slight error in navigation. As a result bombs fell upon London for the first time since 1918, when the Gotha bombers had flown over the city. Great fires were kindled in London Wall and Fore Street; other sections of the city and its outskirts received isolated bombs. In Bethnal Green about a hundred dwellings were destroyed. Militarily practically nothing was accomplished, except that the old warrior, Churchill, demanded a reprisal raid on Berlin.

Bomber Command did not view this request with equanimity. The Luftwaffe could reach London from just across the Channel, but it was a six-hundred-mile trip—one way—to Berlin. Except for psychological effect, Bomber Command saw little of value in striking the German capital. The long distance precluded heavy bomb loads, for a good deal of the weight carried by the bombers would have to include fuel. But Churchill persisted—as did public sentiment—and on the night of August 25/26 eighty-one British bombers took off for Berlin. These were the Wellingtons, Whitleys, and Hampdens of Nos. 3, 4, and 5 Groups respectively. Of these, twenty-nine aircraft (of Nos. 44, 49, 50, 58, 61, 83, and 99 Squadrons) claimed to have bombed Berlin. The operation was greatly hampered by a thick cloud down to two thousand feet. Twenty-seven other aircraft reached Berlin but, unable to identify their targets, did not bomb; of these, twenty-one returned to England with their bombs and six jettisoned them into the sea. Eighteen bombers struck at alternative targets. Seven were forced to turn back because of mechanical troubles. Five aircraft were lost—three of which were ditched in the sea and their crews rescued.

According to German sources only ten bombers actually dropped bombs in what might have been considered industrial target areas. The rest of the bombs scattered through the city. If it had proved a not very successful mission, this first attack on the German capital came as a distinct shock to Berliners. They had been promised by Göring himself that no British aircraft would ever appear over Germany. The effect was minimal, but the implications were appalling.

Three nights later the British bombers came again and for the first time in history German civilians were killed in Berlin. Ten were dead and twenty-nine injured in the very heart of the Reich. The headlines of Berlin's newspapers read: COWARDLY BRITISH ATTACK! A popular epithet for the crews of Bomber Command was "British Air Pirates." It was a curiously unrealistic reaction to the facts of war—as if Germany could rightfully anticipate half a war.

So it was with these bombings of the very heart of the Reich in mind that Hitler promised, threatened, and exhorted. When he pledged, "He's coming!" Hitler alluded to Sealion, for even as he spoke the barges and other invasion craft converged upon ports along the coast from the Netherlands to northern France.

The stimuli for the Luftwaffe's shift from the airfields to London were not simple. It would be an overstatement to say that the plain and simple motive was Hitler's mad desire (though he was capable of it) to retaliate to Churchill's retaliation. Even Hitler from time to time harkened to professional military counsel. It was goading to have the British bombers over the Reich, but they were in truth doing little real damage to the war machine. Göring believed that with Fighter Command all but finished an attack upon London and all it symbolized to the British would bring out the few remaining fighters which he was assured Dowding had pulled back out of Kent. With London just within range of the Me-109s it would be possible to lure the last Spitfires and Hurricanes into the battle and finish them off. Göring was reasonably certain—and Beppo Schmid had concurred—that most of the airfields of Kent were finished. They required no further attention.

This was the first of two misconceptions. True, Park's No. 11 Group was in poor shape, but it was still deployed throughout Kent. Another two weeks of the kind of pounding it had taken might very well have finished it off. But when the decision was made to make London the major target of the Luftwaffe Park still had his squadrons—they were under strength, they were at nerves' end, they were battle-wearied, but they were there.

The other misconception concerned the Londoners themselves. If the attack were mounted upon the densely populated capital and if it were razed, as Hitler had promised the nurses in the Sportpalast, then the "warmonger" Churchill would be forced

had ordered Paris stripped of all its finest statuary. Among these was an especially fine one of Moses which he had placed in his home. One day, so the tale went, Hitler was found on his knees before the statue of Moses saying, "Oh, Moses, tell me, tell me how you got your people over that little bit of water."

The British had no illusions—they knew that if Hitler could possibly cross, he would. Grim preparations were under way, including a fiendish de-

Lockheed Hudsons on patrol over the English Channel. The first American aircraft to go into RAF service, the Hudson was a versatile plane of all work: photog-

raphy and reconnaissance plane, fighter and bomber. British crews called it "Old Boomerang."

(IMPERIAL WAR MUSEUM, LONDON)

by his own people to sue for a *Pax Germanica*. There would be no need for Sealion, a roseate, though nagging, consideration that Hitler nurtured. It was an idea which Admiral Raeder greatly admired. He had come to detest that English Channel, as did the pilots of the Luftwaffe, who referred to it as the *Shite Kanal*. The concept of a large-scale amphibious operation was regarded with suspicion by the landlocked Germans.

It was around this time that a revealing story was making the rounds of the English pubs, where the natives gathered to enjoy their bitters and bore each other with their bomb stories. This story, however, had to do with Hitler and his problem. He

vice which Churchill found good. Along the southern coast of England, from Beachy Head to Weymouth —the finest landing grounds—a method had been devised to pump oil and petrol into the water. As the first wave of German invasion barges approached this area a single Blackburn Skua dive bomber, piloted by one "Nobby" Clarke, was to flash over the treated waters and drop incendiaries. The invading Germans would be met by a wall of flame. Smaller aircraft, including de Havilland Tiger Moths (ordinarily used as primary trainers), would further harass the invaders with anti-personnel bombs.

It was a grand, if rather horrifying, conception

although never actually put to use—except in one practice session and in various rumors. There were other arrangements awaiting the invaders. The sea approaches were mined, the beaches bristled with barbed wire, the Home Guard was armed with everything from breech-loading rifles of First World War vintage sent by the United States to simple clubs. The doughty Islanders awaited Hitler's coming. Churchill had even prepared a slogan which, like the burning seas device, was never implemented: "You can always take one with you."

For weeks the Photographic Reconnaissance Unit, using the American-built Lockheed Hudson as well as Spitfires, kept a wary camera eye on the Channel coast. The count of invasion barges rose from day to day; to these were added motorboats and other vessels moving from the North Sea toward the Channel ports. At Ostend, for example, there were eighteen barges on August 31. By September 6 the photographs revealed no less than two hundred. The Combined Intelligence Committee in London, after assessing the portents, issued an invasion alert. GHQ, Home Forces alerted its units with the code word "Cromwell," indicating that invasion was expected imminently. In some parts of England Home Guard commanders summoned their members by ringing church bells, thus giving rise to the rumors that parachutists had begun descending upon Britain and that German invasion boats were already approaching the English coast.

That was the mood on Saturday, September 7, 1940, in Britain: some confusion but all in readiness. To Park in No. 11 Group headquarters it promised to be a day like all of the others, with his afflicted airfields heavily attacked and his pilots further taxed. Across the Channel—though Park did not know this until it was released via a radio news broadcast—Göring had arrived at the Pas de Calais. Setting up his headquarters at Cap Blanc-Nez he announced that he had "taken over personal command of the Luftwaffe in its war against England." In his private train Göring brought his personal cooks, a stock of wines, his doctor, his valet, and his nurse.

As Park braced himself for the next round of blows at his sector stations, a massive raid began forming up over Calais. But it was London which was the target and it caught Fighter Command off guard. The first full-scale bombing attack on London began shortly after five in the afternoon: more than three hundred bombers (Ju-88s, He-111s, and Do-17s), escorted by six hundred fighters (Me-109s and 110s), almost a thousand aircraft, converged on the city.

Although there were interceptions, the change in target did confuse the controllers and the heavy fighter protection interfered with the British attack on the bombers. London's inadequate antiaircraft guns could not stop the bombers either, flying as

An He-111 hovers over the Thames, London, September 7, 1940—the day the Luftwaffe diverted its attentions from the RAF fighter stations to London.
(IMPERIAL WAR MUSEUM, LONDON)

they were at altitudes between seventeen thousand and twenty thousand feet. Tons of bombs rained down upon London—the docks, the Woolwich arsenal, the oil tanks, and other military targets were hit and raged into flame. Bombs fell also on the streets of East End, with its clutter of dwellings —now hardly better than slums—dating from the early Victorian period. The heavily populated streets filled with pitiable rubble, dazed refugees, and the dead.

The fires ignited in the first attack blazed well into the night, lighting the way for the night bombers. While the fire brigades, comprised of great numbers of auxiliaries who had never fought a fire, attempted to contend with the out-of-control conflagrations, the German bombers returned to drop additional bombs into the burning areas.

By midnight London was ablaze with nine "hundred-pump" fires (a thirty-pump fire was considered a very big fire). In the Surrey Docks there were two large fires (one 300- and the other 130-pump); there were a half-dozen hundred-pump fires at Bishopsgate Goods Yard and other points along the docks. The heat from the Quebec Yard of the Surrey Docks became so intense it set the wooden

London burns after a Luftwaffe bombing.
(NATIONAL ARCHIVES)

blocks in the roadways ablaze. Paint blistered off the fireboats three hundred yards distant in the Thames.

At the Woolwich arsenal (200-pump) the firemen fought the fires among boxes of ammunition and crates of nitroglycerin. But the docks storing more conventional stock gave the most trouble. Tea, it was soon learned, produced a blaze which was "sweet, sickly and intense"; one fireman thought it ludicrous to be pouring *cold* water on *hot* tea. Liquefied sugar burned fiercely on the surface of the water. Burning rubber released dense black smoke and asphyxiated the firemen. Cans of paint burst, spraying white-hot flame into the air, coating the fire pumps with varnish—which took weeks to clean off. From a spice storage dock fires carried

pepper into the air, making it almost impossible to breathe. To the firemen, inhaling the peppered air was almost like breathing flame itself. And great stores of rum too created difficulties: the casks themselves burst with bomblike intensity and blazing streams of grog poured out of the warehouses into the streets. Grain warehouses burned violently and filled the air with swarms of black flies; hundreds of rats ran in the street. The burned wheat left a residue—"a sticky mess that pulls your boots off."

"The fire was so huge," one of the fire fighters later recalled, "that we could do little more than make a feeble attempt to put it out. The whole of that warehouse was a raging inferno, against which were silhouetted groups of pigmy firemen directing their futile jets at the wall of flame. . . ."

A stretcher-bearer stationed at the Redriff School in the dock area (portions of which were poor residential sections) thought "it looked one flaming mass and the flames were terrifically high. To us it seemed a remarkable thing that people could get out of that area, and when we saw—when we saw the people come streaming down from dockland we were absolutely amazed. They seemed to come like an army marching and running from the area. The people coming from down town [Bermondsey, an inhabited strip between the Surrey Docks and the Thames River] looked in a very, very bad condition, they were dirty, dishevelled and hurrying to get away."

Not all got away, however, and in the attacks of September 7/8 about three hundred Londoners died and over a thousand were seriously injured. But these impressive figures, and the even more impressive fires in eastern London, were not acquired without cost to the Luftwaffe. Although Dowding's Fighter Command had been prepared for a continuation of the attacks on the airfields, it had sent fighters to intercept the mass German formations. Among the most effective was the hard-fighting No. 303 Squadron (Polish), which ripped into the German swarms with cavalrylike ferocity to get at the Dorniers. Corporal S. Wojtowicz, although he succeeded in shooting down a Dornier, found little to exult over. "I turned back from the chase but I was returning with a heavy heart, in spite of my victories, for the whole eastern suburb of London seemed to be burning." It recalled his homeland to Wojtowicz when he had left it a year before.

The switch to London brought a greater burden of responsibility to the German fighters. They were expected to furnish close escort for the bombers, but the RAF pilots avoided the German fighters to slaughter the bombers. Here the Me-109s are readied for the trip across the Channel: arming up, strapping the pilot's boots, and, finally, closing the canopy and pulling the chock from under the wheel. The "arched cat" insignia belonged to 8/JG 51. (H. J. NOWARRA)

General Wladislaw Sikorski, head of the Polish government-in-exile, visiting No. 303 Squadron (Polish). Greeting him is Squadron Commander Witold Urbanowicz, highest-scoring Polish ace of the RAF (seventeen victories); Urbanowicz later served in the U. S. Fourteenth Air Force, brought his score up to twenty when (1944) he destroyed three Zeros.

(EMBASSY OF THE POLISH PEOPLE'S REPUBLIC)

Douglas Bader's Duxford wing also intercepted a large formation of Dorniers with Me-110 and Me-109 escort to the east of London. Bader's No. 242 Squadron succeeded in mixing with the Germans and, though his own plane was damaged, Bader accounted for two enemy fighters. The other two squadrons of Bader's Duxford wing, Nos. 19 and 310, had not caught up with the Germans in time. They had been too low when the order to attack had come. Fighter Command lost forty-two aircraft on September 7, 1940, and fourteen pilots.

All during the day and into the night the German radio reported the progress of the battle to the Reich. In the evening a triumphant, vaunting Göring spoke of the "heavy sacrifices" of the Luftwaffe, but he crowed, "This is the historic hour when for the first time our Air Force delivered its thrust right into the enemy's heart!" The thrust had cost fifty-three aircraft, most of them fighters. It was a heavy toll, but, Göring reasoned, worth it. Even so seasoned a leader as Major Hannes Traut-

loft, of Kampfgeschwader 54, noted that they had been met only by single British fighters "which could do nothing. . . ." Perhaps Fighter Command was down to its last Spitfires.

But in turning to London the Germans afforded Fighter Command the time to put its stations back into efficient operational status. Repairs could be made to the ground installations; communications systems could be restored to normal. The Germans had, by their switch to London, unwittingly granted Fighter Command a sorely needed period of grace. The question was: Could London take it—or would London go the way of Guernica, Warsaw, and Rotterdam? Hitler and Göring were confident it would—with twinges of perplexing doubt which found expression in the vacillation with respect to Sealion.

The canny Dowding, however, had no such qualifications. In June, when he knew that the Luftwaffe had moved into the forward bases in the Low Countries and France, Dowding said, "The nearness

Arming up a Spitfire for the next round with the Luftwaffe. The advantage of fighting over one's own grounds was that during the lull in the battle, or if ammunition was expended, it was possible to land and rearm quickly. (IMPERIAL WAR MUSEUM, LONDON)

The strain of battle fatigued pilots. Sergeant G. B. Booth catches a few moments of that precious commodity sleep while awaiting the call to intercept. Booth was killed during the Battle of Britain.

(KENT MESSENGER)

of London to German airfields will lose them the war." Not that the German shift in target concentration took all the weight off Dowding's shoulders. The daylight attacks continued, some even striking at the airfields and the radar installations. As for the night bombings, they went nearly unchallenged, for the night fighters were not yet operating with radar and had missed the German planes in the dark. The antiaircraft guns did little more than fill the air with projectiles and succeeded only in annoying the bombers a little.

On September 8, the day following the first large-scale daylight bombing of London, only minor raids ensued. On the ninth, however, Fighter Command was ready for the raids which developed in force late in the afternoon. But of the two hundred bombers dispatched against London, only ninety managed to break through the fighters sent up by Park as well as fighters from Nos. 10 and 12 Groups. Perhaps seventy bombers were diverted from their main objective and bombed secondary targets while nearly sixty German bombers were turned back and did not bomb at all or jettisoned their bombs. Some of the latter fell upon Canterbury in Kent. Thirty-seven German planes crashed to earth or into the sea and an additional seven were lost either during the Channel crossing or in landing in France. Fighter Command lost nineteen aircraft and fourteen pilots.

The fighting of September 9 gave the Luftwaffe pause. Yet there remained the hope that a few more days of heavy fighting would wipe out Fighter Command once and for all. By September 13 Hitler wistfully implied that if all went as they hoped he might never have to give the order for the launching of Sealion. He had, on September 11, postponed it once again and promised another, perhaps on the fourteenth: this would set the actual invasion date for September 24. This depended upon air superiority over southeast England and the internal collapse of England hopefully because of the London bombings. On September 14, with disconcerting regularity, Hitler postponed Sealion once again, setting the new warning date for September 17 (and D-Day, as planned, for ten days after, September 27). The unco-ordinated interceptions by Fighter Command on that day all but confirmed the German hopes. The critical moment was at hand: the moment for the Luftwaffe's *coup de grâce* to Fighter Command.

Some of Churchill's "few": a handful of pilots who took part in the Battle of Britain—Pilot Officer John L. Allen, Flight Lieutenant Robert S. Tuck (No. 92 Squadron), Flight Lieutenant Alan C. Deere, Flight Lieutenant Adolf G. Malan (No. 74 Squadron), and Squadron Leader James A. Leathart—and a bugler. *Allen, Deere, and Leathart were all members of No. 54 Squadron (of which the latter was commanding officer) and frequently flew together as a section. Allen died during the Battle. This quintet scored nearly a hundred victories against the Luftwaffe during the course of the war.* (IMPERIAL WAR MUSEUM, LONDON)

III

On the morning of Sunday, September 15, 1940, Winston Churchill, accompanied by his wife, Clementine, drove from his home at Chequers (the official country seat of Prime Ministers) to nearby Uxbridge. It was but another in Churchill's countless visits to the scenes of action. Here, at the headquarters of No. 11 Group, Churchill and his wife were taken by Keith Park down into the Operations Room, about fifty feet below ground beneath Hillingdon Golf Course. "The Group Operations Room was like a small theater," Churchill has written, "about sixty feet across, and with two storeys. We took our seats in the dress circle. Below

Spitfires in attack formation.
(IMPERIAL WAR MUSEUM, LONDON)

us was the large-scale map-table, around which per-haps twenty highly trained young men and women, with their telephone assistants, were assembled."

Opposite the Churchills, Park, and others essential to the operations was a giant blackboard covering an entire wall. This was the "tote board" on which, in a glance, Park was able to ascertain the status of each squadron in each sector of No. 11 Group. This was graphically depicted by vertical subdivisions on the tote board; colored lights indicated the state of readiness of each squadron. Those squadrons in action were indicated by red lights. Correlated with the board was a great map spread across the room, over which the plotters worked, showing the disposition of the squadrons and the plots of the incoming Germans. Officers slightly offstage, so to

speak, in a glass enclosure kept track of British antiaircraft guns. Thus the tote board reduced the three-dimensional battle in the skies to little more than a two-dimensional graph.

The atmosphere was charged with tension, al-though Park, drawn and tired, said to the Churchills, "I don't know whether anything will happen today."

Through the previous night the ground crews had worked on the Hurricanes and Spitfires, patching those which had been damaged in the day's action. Fourteen British fighters had been lost; the Germans too had lost fourteen aircraft, but some of them had been bombers.

By dawn of Sunday the airdromes of Kent rever-berated to the sound of Merlin engines catching and the roar of their warming up. Armorers threaded ammunition belts into the wings of the fighters and petrol bowsers darted here and there among the poised aircraft, fueling them up. The tension increased with the coming light—it promised to be a fine day with some cloud patches possible.

The Churchills had barely settled themselves into "the Hole" at Uxbridge when the radar posts along the Channel reported German aircraft activity forming up over Dieppe. "Forty plus," was the estimate; the bulbs along the bottom of the tote board flashed on and Park's squadrons came to "Stand-by" status. It was now eleven o'clock in the morning and as the minutes ticked by radar stations reported more and more enemy aircraft building up: "Forty plus, sixty plus, eighty plus . . ." Within moments Park ordered eleven of his squadrons into the air; a single squadron from No. 10 Group was requested to cover 11 Group's western boundary. To the north the five squadrons comprising the so-called Duxford wing of No. 12 Group led by Douglas Bader leaped into the air.

Park's Spitfires and Hurricanes intercepted the bomber formations—over two hundred strong with hundreds of fighters escorting—over eastern Kent. The odds, except in numbers, lay with the defenders. For a half hour the radar operators had plotted the massing of the German formations and Park, with uncanny certainty, judged the target to be London. He knew where to place his squadrons for effect. Churchill's cigar had gone dead as he concentrated upon the action unfolding before him.

The Spitfires of No. 72 and No. 92 Squadrons, meeting the Germans over Canterbury, knifed through the formations with guns hammering. It was the first blood of the day. Engines of Dorniers flickered and smoked; some fell from the formation, others broke and turned for the coast. The Me-109s whipped into the melee to protect the bombers. The battle, moving westward across Kent, swarmed in clusters and darting individual combats toward London, leaving in its wake burning aircraft, parachutes drifting through the smoke, and the dead.

The Dorniers of Kampfgeschwader 3, now decimated and with dead men at some of the gun positions, pressed on to London. The shaken crews, who had taken off certain that Fighter Command no longer existed, bombed with no accuracy. Very little of military value was hit: a number of dwellings, a couple of bridges, a suburban electrical plant; a sin-

gle bomb even fell into the grounds of Buckingham Palace, although it proved to be a dud. Sergeant Ray T. Holmes, Hurricane pilot of No. 504 Squadron, which had met the Dorniers on the outskirts of London, was certain he had brought down the plane which had bombed the palace.

Holmes was acting as rear guard for the squadron on patrol; his job was to weave around behind and above the other planes keeping an eye out for German fighters. The squadron had just met the Dornier formation and had broken it up with an attack. "By then," Holmes relates, "the Dornier formation had become ragged and was turning for home, and 504 had broken away to reform and I spotted three Dorniers blazing a lone trail toward London. No one seemed to have noticed them, so I decided to give them a little attention."

Throttling the Hurricane to speed, Holmes overtook the three German planes and then attacked from the flank. The first Dornier spurted oil just as Holmes passed underneath, blotting out his vision when the windscreen was covered. The slipstream cleared the oil away in time for Holmes to get a quick glimpse of the Dornier's tail, just inches from his Hurricane's nose. One of the German's propellers had stopped. Holmes came up from under the plane to attack the other flanking Dornier. The root of the wing caught fire and a parachute ejected from the Dornier. For a few moments the hapless German chutist draped across the wing of Holmes's Hurricane. He then was dragged off into nothingness by the twisted parachute.

Holmes then turned to the lead plane, attacking it from behind. This had little effect and Holmes found himself with only fifteen seconds of firing time left. "I thought a head-on attack might cool his ardor, and climbed up past him to his left from my last breakaway." As he readied for this attack, Holmes noted that his engine sounded rough and that oil (his own) had begun to bubble into his cockpit. As he tore in head-on, eight guns firing, Holmes ran out of ammunition. Frustrated, he simply kept going over the Dornier and "clipped one side of his fragile-looking twin tail with my port wing." The only sensation was a slight bump, and Holmes was certain that little harm could have come to his Hurricane. Then his wing dropped—the tip had been torn off—the nose dropped too, and the controls would not respond. The Hurricane snapped

Douglas Bader (center) with two members of his No. 242 Squadron, George Eric Ball (left) and William L. McKnight. Active through the Battle and the blitz,

Ball and McKnight were killed during fighter sweeps after the RAF went over to the offensive.
(IMPERIAL WAR MUSEUM, LONDON)

into a vertical spin. Holmes fought his way out of the plane and joined his opponents in floating down toward London.

He had afforded Londoners with quite an exciting spectacle, for the German bomber crashed spectacularly into Victoria Station. The surviving German crewmen landed across the Thames in the Kennington cricket oval. Holmes fared not so well: after bouncing off a rooftop in the Chelsea section of London, he came to rest in a Londoner's back-yard trash can.

Although they continued their thrust to London, the tormented German bomber crews wondered where all the Spitfires and Hurricanes had come from. The German fighters—those not tied closely to the bombers—swept in to clear the way, but not all of the British planes could be stopped. These careened through and chopped up the formations.

Adolf Galland, leading his Jagdgeschwader 26 on a forward free hunt, charged into the attacking British fighters but without, even after ten minutes of savage fighting, stopping them. Twisting in his cockpit he saw, nearly two thousand feet below him, a pair of Hurricanes. He flipped into a dive and sent one flaming into the Thames. But after the time spent in France forming up, crossing the Channel, fighting across Kent, and a few minutes of combat, it was time for Galland to streak for home unless he wanted to end up in the *Shite Kanal.*

It was over London on this Sunday, September 15, 1940, that the German bomber formations, having dropped their bombs, and after having traversed miles of smoking sky to do it, received a further shock. Where had all the Spitfires and Hurricanes—which Beppo Schmid had claimed had dwindled to the last fifty—where had they all come from? And

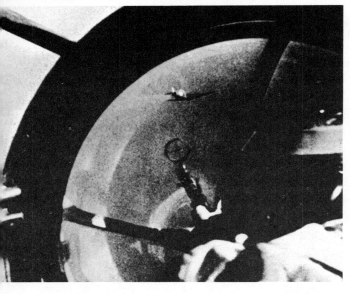

then from the north, like a biblical plague, screamed a full sixty fresh fighters led by Douglas Bader. He had led his squadrons—his own No. 224, the Czech No. 310, and the Polish No. 302 (all in Hurricanes), and the two Spitfire squadrons, Nos. 19 and 611—as high as possible to get above the Germans and into the sun. When he saw the Germans—forty or more Ju-88s and Dorniers—Bader swiftly studied the air around them for a glimpse of the escort. Then alerting the others to the telltale specks in the distance, Bader nosed into the German bomber formation, shouting, "Break 'em up!"

With his eight guns firing Bader swept into the vanguard of the German planes. He kicked the Hurricane around, pulled up and onto the tail of a Dornier. The guns shook the Hurricane as holes and sparks appeared behind the Dornier's right engine. Then a flash, black smoke—and Bader had to jerk the stick to avoid ramming the stricken German bomber. As he pulled off he saw another Dornier slipping into a cloud bank for sanctuary. Above it a lone Spitfire dived into the same cloud. The British pilot had not seen the German bomber. There was a billow of orange flame, black smoke, and with the wings of the Dornier twisted around the Spitfire, the two aircraft fell churning through the air into London.

Bader, twisting his neck, sought more targets and saw only one other plane, a Do-17 spinning and burning. A crewman managed to get out of the gyrating plane, but opened his chute too soon. The silk brushed through the flame and seared away into the clouds. The hapless German, trailing useless shrouds, plummeted straight down. Bitterly, almost without pity, Bader thought, "Now you've got a little time to think about it and there isn't any answer."

And now, except for wisps of black smoke, the curls of evaporating tracers, the sky was empty. Emotionally tired, his fuel low, Bader turned the Hurricane for Duxford.

By twelve-thirty peace had come again to the Sunday skies of England. But the day was only half

---

A Spitfire makes a fighter pass on an He-111 over the Channel. In these (probably in a staged action with a captured Spitfire) photographs the British fighter has come under the tail and the starboard wing, flashes by the nose gunner's position, and begins to turn for another attack. (H. J. NOWARRA)

over. The second, and heavier, round of Luftwaffe attacks began just before two-thirty in the afternoon. There had been less time to scramble the Fighter Command squadrons than in the morning. Bader, again leading the Duxford wing, was critical of this short notice, feeling that his unit could have done much better had it been given ample time to assemble and to meet the Germans head on before they reached London. When they finally met the Germans Bader's aircraft intercepted them from below—not an advantage at all. The Me-109s could bounce them before they got at the bombers.

The Germans came over in three large formations, crossing the English coast between Dungeness and Dover. Park had dispatched twelve of his squadrons in pairs to meet the Germans as they came in over Kent; soon another seven and a half squadrons took to the air. The leading German formation was intercepted over Canterbury by two squadrons from the Hornchurch sector station; soon these were joined by more Hurricanes which had been patrolling over Maidstone. The heavens, as they had two hours earlier, were racked with the sound of guns, the trail of battle and defeat: the reek of cordite and burning metal.

The radios crackled in the Operations Rooms as the controllers sent the fighters to meet the attackers. The Churchills listened as the tension mounted even more at Uxbridge. The language did not always make sense to the layman, but the urgency in the young voices conveyed the drama of the battle.

"Bullfinch patrol Maidstone, Angels twenty," the controller ordered. "Bullfinch" was the day's code name for one of the squadrons; "angels" was an altitude indication: angels twenty was twenty thousand feet.

Then the radio might come to life as the fighter pilots closed with the enemy (these are authentic transcriptions):

"109s at four o'clock above."

"Keep in, Blue 2" (elements in the squadrons were coded by color and number. Blue 2 was the second plane in blue section; Blue 1 led this section; a third plane completed the section.)

"Watch your tail, Red 3!"

"Break right, Red 3, break right!"

The people in No. 11 Group's Operations Room could hear but not see any of this, of course.

"Got the bastard!" the radio crackled. A squadron mate had come to the aid of Red 3.

"Typan [the code name for a controller] to Ferret leader. Fifty plus near Gravesend. One hundred plus approaching you from southeast. One hundred and twenty plus. Angels eighteen. North of Base 2."

"Ferret leader to Typan. Don't tell me any more, you're making me nervous."

A bomber formation is seen and the "Tally Ho!" is given.

"Black 2 to Black leader. Dorniers at twelve o'clock, just below."

"OK. Head-on attack. Break right and left, I'll break upward."

A brief silence, and an unknown voice crackles, "God, that was dangerous!"

It was dangerous for the Germans too. Again, as in the morning's confused terror, the gnawing question was: What was the source, seemingly inexhaustible, of all those British fighters? How confidently, even disdainfully, had they checked off the British airfields, the aircraft factories, as destroyed in the weeks before. That Park had committed all of his squadrons to the battle, as well as the great Duxford wing and a single squadron from No. 10 Group, might not have assured the harried Germans. To them it seemed that the British fighters materialized out of nowhere.

At the battle's climax Churchill, his eye upon the line of lighted electric bulbs on the tote board, asked, "What other reserves have we?"

"There are none," Park told him. All the squadrons of No. 11 Group were in the air and Park had drawn upon the neighboring Groups for reinforcements. Complications arose when, during the great air battles over London and its suburbs, a small bomber and fighter force slipped across the Channel in the south to bomb shipping at Portland—and perhaps to draw off some of the British fighters from the main attack upon London. A single British fighter squadron, of a possible five of the Middle Wallop sector, intercepted—but only after the German bombs had dropped. Even so, the bombing was inaccurate and little harm was done to Portland.

The day's last attack, again in the south, came shortly after six o'clock when about twenty bomb-laden Me-110s came in over the Hampshire coast.

Shot down while on a raid against London, a German crew is taken prisoner while, in the background, their Heinkel burns. (FOX PHOTOS, LTD.)

The target of Test Group 210 was the Supermarine (Spitfire) factory at Woolston. With only twenty minutes' warning, it was almost impossible for Park to get the squadrons up in time, but he did send some of his and some from No. 10 Group to intercept. Again the British fighters did not find the enemy aircraft until after they had dropped their bombs. Once again the bombing was inaccurate, thanks in this attack to the Southampton antiaircraft guns, which trained on the Me-110s on their bombing run, upsetting the aim of the bombardiers and the flying of the pilots. The bombs missed the Spitfire factory but fell into residential areas. Thus ended the last flicker, a whimper, of the daylight battles.

Churchill by this time had returned to Chequers for his afternoon nap. He had been fatigued by the strain in the Operations Room at Uxbridge. It had been a close one. Just one more sizable German attacking force and they would have had nothing with which to meet it. Having slept Churchill immediately called his secretary, John Martin, to learn the very latest news. Martin had a little good to report from Italy or the Atlantic. "However," he concluded, "all is redeemed by the air. We have shot down a hundred and eighty-three for a loss of under forty."

The evening's BBC broadcast, and the newspapers, added a couple more and proclaimed to a jubilant Britain that 185 German aircraft had been destroyed. The official Air Ministry account called it "the Greatest Day." Churchill dispatched a congratulatory message to Dowding on Monday. "Yesterday eclipsed all previous records of Fighter Command," he wrote. "Aided by squadrons of their

Battle's end: a Hurricane pilot of No. 85 Squadron wearily leaves his cockpit as the sun sets after a hard day of combat. (IMPERIAL WAR MUSEUM, LONDON)

Czech and Polish comrades, using only a small proportion of their total strength [not true, but this message was for public consumption] and under cloud conditions of some difficulty, they cut to rags and tatters three separate waves of murderous assaults upon the civil population of their native land. . . . These results exceeded all expectations and give just and sober confidence in the approaching struggle."

But in the light of postwar truth was September 15, 1940, actually "the Greatest Day"? Not if its greatness is measured by the number of enemy aircraft destroyed. The British lost 35 planes that day and 11 pilots. The Luftwaffe lost 30 Do-17s, 15 He-111s, 3 Ju-88s, 3 Me-110s, and 23 Me-109s, plus four others, a total of 78—not 185—aircraft. But of this total the greater number was bombers—fully one quarter of the total sent against England on September 15 during the daylight attacks (a force of 181 bombers came in over London that night). These were lost despite the heavy fighter protection of nearly five fighters for every bomber. But the order which tied most of the fighters tightly to the bombers, excepting the free-hunt units which generally preceded the bomber streams, crippled their fighting abilities.

The tired airmen on both sides of the Channel, hollow-eyed, nerves tingling, muscles tight, were unimpressed with "the Greatest Day" designation. They were too depleted to care. The RAF crews, however, could delight in the news of a great victory despite their exhaustion. The Luftwaffe pilots were shaken and demoralized: their High Command had, in fact, failed them. First, it had misinformed them about the strength of Fighter Command, and second, it had further handicapped the fighters with unrealistic tactics. Even so, the Luftwaffe did not consider the Battle decided, let alone lost.

Nor, in truth, did the RAF High Command, whose members were more realistic than their German counterparts, consider the Battle won. The Battle was won, however, though neither side was aware of it at the time.

The effort of RAF's Fighter Command on "the Greatest Day" contributed heavily to a decision revealed in an entry in the war diary of the German Naval Staff dated September 17, 1940:

The enemy Air Force is still by no means defeated; on the contrary, it shows increasing activity. The weather situation on the whole does not permit us to expect a period of calm. The Führer therefore decides to postpone Sealion indefinitely.

He was not coming after all; he would never come.

9

THE BLITz

THE REPULSE of the Luftwaffe—which Göring promptly blamed on the fighters—on "the Greatest Day" neither closed the Battle of Britain nor ended the planning, however dispirited, for Sealion, despite the Führer's deferment. To remove the vessels and troops from the various ports would be an admission of defeat—and that would not do. This was neatly side-stepped by the propaganda machine. On September 18 the German-controlled Paris Radio informed the British, and the world, that "the legend of British self-control and phlegm is being destroyed. All reports from London concur in stating that the population is seized by fear—hair-raising fear. The seven million Londoners have completely lost their self-control. They run aimlessly about in the streets and are victims of bombs and bursting shells."

London, indeed, had become the target—but after the fighting of September 15 the daylight attacks dwindled significantly. On the eighteenth there was a large flurry—about seventy German bombers appeared over London and were fought off ferociously. The final weeks of September were devoted to relatively minor daylight raids upon aircraft factories. Göring's High Command recognized the urgency of denying the RAF a supply of aircraft. The end of October was characterized by a decided lack of mass raids and the introduction of wider use of fighter-bombers (Me-109s carrying thousand-pound bombs). Although these high-flying aircraft could evade the British fighters and made positive identi-

fication difficult—radar and direct observation could not discern whether the Messerschmitts were merely fighters and therefore not worth scrambling after or fighters carrying bombs—they accomplished little.

In short, though he was unaware of it at the time, Dowding had won the Battle of Britain.

But then began a new terror. For fifty-seven nights, from September 7 through November 2, not a night went by without the drone of German bombers overhead, the crash of bombs and fire in the streets of London. "None of it seems real," wrote Anthony Guthrie to Vivien Leigh and Laurence Olivier. "One can't believe that one isn't living in some highly superior Wagnerian production. The night of the big fires was utterly amazing. . . . We came out [of Sadler's Wells Theatre, London] to find the entire sky crimson from the reflected glare of the fires—you could easily read small print in the street—and on every window reflected back the dancing, terrifying glare."

It was unreal, but the rubble, the burned-out streets, and the dead and injured were undeniable fact. So were the barrage balloons which swayed dumpily over London Bridge; Londoners called these balloons, which were not especially effective except against low-flying aircraft, "our dumb friends." Although not of much use, their floating presence was comforting. The air raid warning signals—"sireens" or "Wailing Winnies"—cried out nightly for those fifty-seven nights. The average

Luftwaffe target map. The circled A locates a South-wark power station on the south bank of the Thames.

Almost directly north, across the river, may be seen St. Paul's Cathedral.

nightly raiding party consisted of about 160 bombers during this period—ranging from 7 on the night of October 6, when bad weather interfered, to more than 400 on October 15. There was little the defenses could do to counter these attacks. The night fighter, equipped with radar, was but a crude idea in the early days of the blitz; antiaircraft defenses were weak and inaccurate. Like the dumb friends

the sound and flash of the guns were more inspiring than effectual. By September 10 the number of heavy antiaircraft guns protecting central London was increased from 92 to 199; restrictions forbidding gunners from firing at aircraft they could see or which were officially detected led to a massive barrage over London when next the Germans came. This, while rarely if ever accounting for downed

He-111s cross the English Channel during the winter of the blitz. (IMPERIAL WAR MUSEUM, LONDON)

An incendiary bomb burns in a London street; once burning an incendiary was difficult to control and was *most responsible for the damage to London during the blitz.* (IMPERIAL WAR MUSEUM, LONDON)

A German bomber after a raid on England, lucky to have made the return trip. The pilot, slightly dazed, sits atop the fuselage while others (including cameraman) study what appears to be antiaircraft shell hole behind the port engine. (H. J. NOWARRA)

German bombers, was disconcerting and did force the Luftwaffe formations to fly higher—and it did make a joyful noise for the beleaguered Londoner.

Although the Luftwaffe's objectives were primarily the docks, the railways, public utilities, as well as governmental and financial centers, the chief victims were the ordinary Londoners, generally of the poorer classes. They lost sleep, were improperly fed, lost their pitiable possessions, their homes, and their loved ones. The panic predicted by the Germans, however, did not occur. Instead a grim resolution set in, a tough, bitter humor, a deep sense of fellowship (as class lines, temporarily at least, broke down), and a determination not to be defeated by "'Itler." But they died by the hundreds on each of the fifty-seven nights as well as other nights throughout the remainder of the Second World War.

On the big night of October 15, when 410 bombers dropped 528 tons of high explosives and 177 canisters of incendiaries, 400 civilians died and 900 were seriously injured. Rail traffic between London and the cities to the north and south was disrupted or stopped. Where once fifty trains ran per day, only four were running after the raid. Hundreds of fires broke out and water mains burst, some filling the underground tube stations. While all of this was disrupting, damaging to property, and took a heavy toll of life (although never as high as had been predicted before the war), little of military import was

achieved. Neither did the railroads, docks, factories, or utilities close down, nor did the Londoner petition his government for an early armistice.

There was reason enough for fear and panic. The Germans sowed vicious fires with their incendiaries, more destructive than the high-explosive bombs. They also dropped delayed-action bombs, thus rendering streets and buildings hazardous until the bomb exploded or was dealt with by the UXB (Unexploded Bomb) Disposal Squads. Churchill, in his memoirs, recalled one of these remarkable groups, "the Holy Trinity," consisting of the Earl of Suffolk, his lady private secretary, and "his rather aged chauffeur." This unique, gallant trinity, working at a trade for which none of their previous experience had prepared them, had actually learned how to disarm the UXBs. This was a most delicate operation, calling for courage as well as skill. All the proper mechanisms inside the bomb had to be taken apart without disturbing the detonation device. "Thirty-four unexploded bombs did they tackle with urbane and smiling efficiency," Churchill reported. "But the thirty-fifth claimed its forfeit. Up went the Earl of Suffolk in his Holy Trinity. But we may be sure that, as for Greatheart [a character in *Pilgrim's Progress*], 'all the trumpets sounded for them on the other side.'"

Churchill admired such eccentric valour and while he appeared to make light of their tragic end he mordantly expressed the mood of the time, of people he termed "the grim and the gay," the unbeatable British courage which "'Itler" found so unfathomable.

II

By December 8, 1940, London was no longer the prime target of the Luftwaffe night war. On November 14 Göring had decided, since the bombing of London seemed to accomplish so little, that attention should be given the smaller industrial cities. These presented less sprawling targets than London, if more difficult to find. But with Kampfgeschwader 100 leading the way with incendiaries which were planted with the help of an electronic navigation device they called *X-Gerät* ("X-Device"), there was no problem finding the target for the 450 bombers that night. *X-Gerät* was operated on a complex system of radio beams, a main beam plus beams which intersected it.

A Luton *News* historian noted that on November 14, "just after tea German bombers flew over Luton for hour after hour on the way to the Midland city of Coventry." The Luton hat factories were spared that night, but for about ten hours wave after wave of Heinkels and Junkers dropped five hundred tons of high explosives and about nine hundred incendiaries upon the old cathedral town, which had achieved notoriety with the legend of Lady Godiva and Peeping Tom, dating from the eleventh century.

Coventry housed, besides the legend and a beautiful medieval cathedral, factories devoted to the manufacture of machine tools and parts for aircraft industries. The main target was the facilities of the Standard Motor Company; in short, Coventry, according to the "civilized rules of warfare," was a "legitimate" military target. When the last German bomber left at around six-thirty in the morning Coventry, its cathedral included, was a flaming ruin. By 3:30 A.M. at least two hundred major fires were reported in the center of the city, but hydrants were buried under the debris and many water mains were destroyed. The main railroads were blocked so that rescue teams coming from other towns could come only to Coventry's outskirts and then were forced to make their way through the rubble, flame, and danger of unexploded bombs. The once maligned Civil

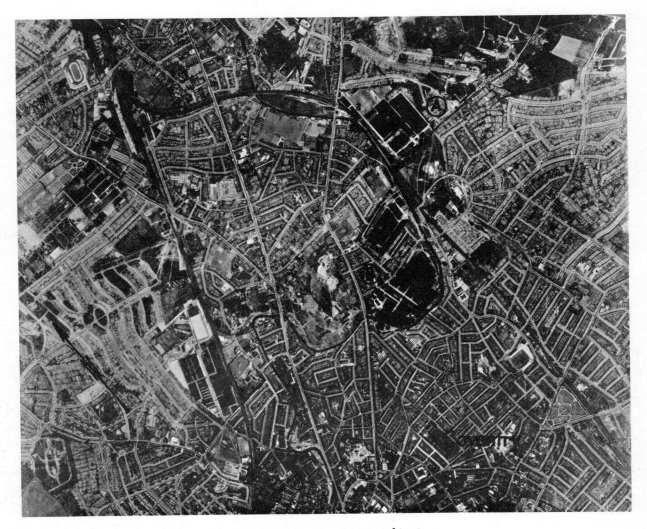

Target map, Coventry. Dark areas A and B mark the two factory objectives.

(IMPERIAL WAR MUSEUM, LONDON)

No. 23 Victoria Street, London, falls to earth after a German bombing raid.

Defence workers, who had become unpopular because of their insistence upon no lights showing and who seemed to spend most of their time, with nothing to do, in the local pubs, came into their own. These anonymous heroes, who went about their work quietly and matter-of-factly, saved the lives of countless men, women, and children at the risk and at times the cost of their own lives. Ordinary citizens transformed by emergency dashed into blazing, crumbling buildings to save a life. Or they worked for hours to rescue someone trapped in the wreckage of what was once a home.

The Germans boasted later of what they had done to Coventry; they even coined a word to describe what would happen to other towns devoted to the making of arms: "Coventrated." But because of the widespread havoc, impossible to confine to the purely military targets, Coventry joined Guernica, Warsaw, and Rotterdam as a symbol of German frightfulness and thoroughness.

No less than five hundred shops in the city's shopping center were put out of business; only the spire of the cathedral remained standing; twenty-one factories essential to the aircraft industry were hit. The destroyed water and gas mains halted work in other factories not as severely hit. The death toll reached at least 554 and 865 people were seriously wounded. But despite the shattering damage and the casualties there was no panic and comparatively

London burning following a bad night blitz.
(NATIONAL ARCHIVES)

minimal work stoppage. The fires were under control by the evening of November 15. Three days later all the rail lines, except one which took an additional three days, were cleared and running.

Work was resumed at the Standard Motor Company on November 16 by half of its usual staff. Factories which suffered more severe destruction were longer in resuming production, but despite Coventration, Coventry was not knocked out of the war as Göring presumed. Other "arms towns" including Birmingham, Sheffield, Manchester, and Bristol were treated to the same near-saturation bombing during the winter weeks of November and December. So were the ports, Liverpool, Portsmouth, Southampton, but with the same inconclusive results. There were the same casualties, the same fires and rubble, and the same stiffening of the British spirit.

"Have you ever spent the night in a hole in the garden?" asked a young woman schoolteacher from Norwich. "Well, you're too damn tired to bother about the bombs. Luckily our soil is gravel so it's not as bad as it might be but dirt is dirty and full of ants . . . lift up your tin hat, as you grovel in the entrails of the earth, and see the Milky Way above you and the searchlights finding the bomber which you can hear, directly above you. Would you think you'd be scared or wonder what was going to happen—I should have thought so—but you simply try to see if you can see it and it never enters your head that you might be here, there, and everywhere in about two seconds."

In Clydebank (a shipbuilding center in Scotland) a woman made a comment that deserves preservation. She had just finished sweeping debris from her walk when she said to her neighbor, "Well, there's one thing about these raids, they do make you forget about the war."

Be grim and be gay, Churchill had asked of them. They could be practical too, as witness the statement of a lord mayor of one of the port cities which had been noted for its slums. "At least we can say that the Luftwaffe did for us in twenty seconds what we have been trying to do for twenty years," he said. "It removed the slum dwellings. . . ."

The switch to the arms towns and the ports did not mean that London had ceased to be a target completely. In fact, on the night after the Coventry attack London was the major target and Coventry received only a token visit. Had it been reversed the rapid recovery of Coventry might have been seriously cut short. But Göring was certain he had finished it. So the raids continued on through November and December, weather permitting—for the season of rain, snow, ice, and fog came to interfere with German operations. During December Britain enjoyed fifteen bomb-free nights, thanks to the weather.

On December 29, 1940, a Sunday evening at the end of Christmas week, just before seven o'clock the bombers came. They were led to their objective by ten Heinkels of the pathfinder Kampfgeschwader 100, which, in turn, was turned into the *X-Gerät* beam which was laid directly across London. It was a dark night and the winds, from the west and southwest, ranged to as high as fifty miles an hour at an altitude of six thousand feet. So it was that the incendiaries sown by the ten Heinkels drifted slightly eastward from the beam into the section of London known as The City, London's financial center, as well as Westminster, site of Buckingham Palace, No. 10 Downing Street, and other government buildings. In the center of all this stood St. Paul's Cathedral, the masterpiece of Sir Christopher Wren, which had been built 1675–1710.

The attacking force was not very large: 136 bombers, but they dropped 127 tons of high explosives and more than 600 canisters of incendiar-

ies. The HE, with some scattering, fell mainly into the riverside boroughs of London. The incendiaries, which scattered also, very quickly ignited nearly fifteen hundred fires. Six were classified as "conflagrations," twenty-eight were "major," and fifty-two were "serious." Because it was a Sunday evening many of the buildings, even the churches, were locked, making it impossible to deal with the incendiaries which fell onto the roofs. Also, on this night the Thames was at its lowest ebb, a problem further complicated when bombs ruptured an emergency main pipe used in fighting fires. Hose pressures waxed and waned throughout the blazing nightmare.

For about three hours the German aircraft droned over London and then returned to France to reload. But luckily the bases had become weathered-in and the bombers did not return, affording the hard-pressed Londoners the time to try to save their city undisturbed by further bombing. Some fires even by then were so out of control that nothing could be done. Water evaporated in mid-air even before reaching the flames. Sections of The City were merely abandoned and cordoned off to burn out.

"For miles around the sky was a bright orange-red," one Londoner recalled; "the balloons in the barrage stood as clearly as on a sunny day. St. Paul's Cathedral was the pivot of the main fire. All around it the flames were leaping up into the sky. And there the Cathedral stood, magnificently firm, untouched in the very center of all this destruction."

Not quite untouched, for at least two dozen incendiaries struck the dome and only some bounced off into the street. The men of the St. Paul's Cathedral Watch and volunteers (many of them architects) joined forces to fight the fires. Although the water supply failed early, emergency containers of reserve water placed around the cathedral by the leaders of the watch were put to use. Those incendiaries which blazed against the structure threatening to incinerate the old, dry beams were put out with minimal damage.

But one incendiary had struck the dome and had become lodged in the outer lead shell. It protruded hundreds of feet off the ground, sputtering, melting the lead of the outer dome. Fearfully the men of the watch observed helplessly as the single in-

A Hurricane I night fighter takes off to engage the Luftwaffe during the blitz. In this period the single-engined fighters did not prove very effective against the German bomber forces.
(IMPERIAL WAR MUSEUM, LONDON)

cendiary seemed about to fall inside the inner dome into the dry timbers. "We knew," the dean of the cathedral said, "that once the fire got hold of the Dome timbers it would, at that high altitude, quickly be fanned into a roaring furnace."

Across London, a woman in Bethnal Green, wearing her tin hat, stood with some firemen on a roof and gazed toward The City. "And I've always remembered how I was choked," she said; "I think I was crying a little. I could see St. Paul's standing there, and the fire all around, and I just said: 'Please God, don't let it go!'"

The incendiary in the dome, now burning fiercely, moved as the lead flowed in the intense heat. Then the bomb fell away from the dome—no one knows quite how—and into the stone gallery of the cathedral, where the relieved men of the watch disposed of it.

St. Paul's was saved and became the symbol of British strength during the Battle of Britain. But other historic buildings did not escape what became known as the Second London Fire. The first, in 1666, resulted in the rebuilding of the city

Not all raids on England during the blitz were made at night. This Me-109 had made a day sortie over the London area, attacked two British trainers, misjudged their speed, and came to grief in Windsor Great Park.
(FOX PHOTOS, LTD.)

by Christopher Wren. Eight of Wren's churches were consumed in the Second London Fire; so were the Guildhall, the County Hall, and portions of the Tower of London. Nine hospitals, although not targets, were hit; so were five railway stations and sixteen underground stations. The dead numbered 163 with more than 500 seriously injured. Sixteen firemen died, some of them in the crew which had successfully fought off the flames threatening the house of Dr. Samuel Johnson, just off Fleet Street, not far from St. Paul's. The small crew had just left the historic house and had lost their way in the narrow, smoke-filled streets. They had just emerged near a burning building when a member of the pump crew fighting that fire saw them.

"I thought when I saw them that they were too near," he said. "Just at that moment a wall, which looked as if it was bulging dangerously, crashed down on them. As we looked around all we could see was a heap of debris with a hose leading towards it."

Although the Sunday night raid was the last of the year, it was not the last of the fire raids of the blitz. Bad weather interfered with operations during the first two months of 1941, London and several port cities received major attacks. By March, with the coming of somewhat better weather, the raids were resumed with greater ferocity if not in number. In April some of the German bomber strength had been drawn off to assist in the Balkans. Then an even more critical withdrawal came in May as Hitler prepared for his Russian offensive.

Despite the wholesale withdrawals of the Luftwaffe, or perhaps because of them, the effort of the remaining forces was intensified. The effort devolved upon Sperrle's Luftflotte 3, which had to cover for the units which had slipped away. Between the first great fire raid in December and those later in the winter of 1941 much had been learned, at no little cost, about dealing with the night bombers. Roof watchers were stationed throughout London (and other target cities) to keep an eye out for incendiaries, and techniques were developed to deal with them most efficiently. Also, means had been developed to confute the *X-Gerät* beam, as, for example, on the night of May 8/9, when the target was the Rolls-Royce factory at Derby. The beam was detected early and deflected

electronically so that the great German bomber force dropped most of its bombs in the moors northeast of Derby. At the same time "Starfish" were lighted —these were decoy fires which appeared to be pathfinder markers. On this same night Starfish beckoned the German bombers away from Nottingham, which the German pilots mistook for a burning Derby. Consequently, the bomber stream "corrected" and bombed the Vale of Belvoir (mistaking it for Nottingham) with high explosives, an oil bomb, and incendiaries. This effort netted them a casualty toll of two cows and two chickens.

London was easier to find and during the second half of April it received two of its worst raids, so memorable that Londoners ever after referred to them by name, "the Wednesday" (April 16/17) and "the Saturday" (April 19/20). On the first 890 tons of high explosives and 4200 canisters of incendiary bombs fell; on the Saturday the weight increased: 1026 tons of HE and 4252 canisters of incendiaries rained on London.

Then on May 10/11 came another heavy blow, the last of the night offensive. On that same night deputy Führer Rudolf Hess, having stolen a Messerschmitt, flew alone from Germany and parachuted to earth near Glasgow. He was looking for Lord Steward, the Duke of Hamilton, whom Hess had met at the Olympics in Germany in 1936. Hess insisted that he had come on a peace mission; he was certain that he could convince the British with Lord Steward's help of the Führer's kindly intentions toward Britain and bring the war to an end.

Meanwhile London burned. More than 400,000 civilians were to die in the blitz, and 46,000 suffered serious injuries. A million homes were destroyed. The average Londoner was thoroughly familiar with Hitler's intentions. Out of the ruins of one of the buildings a woman emerged covered with blood and powdered brick and plaster. Her eyes were dull, her face drawn, she said nothing to her rescuers except the phrase she repeated, like a litany, over and over again: "Man's inhumanity

The main shelter during the blitz was the London Underground, the subway. Deep under the streets of the city, Londoners sought refuge from Hitler's bombers and proved, in the phrase at the time, "London can take it." (IMPERIAL WAR MUSEUM, LONDON)

to man, man's inhumanity to man, man's inhumanity to man . . ."

By the late spring of 1941 the blitz was over. So in fact was all planning for Sealion. But the future of the Third Reich, and its leaders, its cities, its people—innocent and guilty—was assured.

"Man's inhumanity to man . . ."

On that December night when St. Paul's stood out of the smoke and flame with an almost human British show of defiance and dignity, the newly appointed Deputy Chief of the Air Staff stood on the roof of the Air Ministry building watching the fulminating desolation. He was Arthur Harris. Moved by the fiery spectacle, he spoke to the old sentry on the roof, reminding the man that they were looking directly upon history. The old man, however, who called himself "an observer of nature," seemed more interested in the sex life of the cats on the rooftops of Whitehall.

"The last time London was burnt," Harris tried again, "if my history is right, was in 1666." But the sentry was not impressed. The conflagration was to Harris such a "fantastic sight" that he went downstairs and brought up his chief, Air Chief Marshal Sir Charles Portal, from his office to see it.

The two airmen, one of whom would in time be Chief of Bomber Command, watched the sea of flame in bitter silence. As they turned away from the awesome sight, so unreal in its magnitude, Harris said to Portal, "Well, they are sowing the wind."

For they have sown the wind, and they shall reap the whirlwind.

"Man's inhumanity to man . . ."

10

"GIVE IT 'EM BACK!"

THE pattern of modern war was unmistakably defined: Everyman had become a legitimate military target. The war of the peoples had begun.

The Germans were ill advised to expect the Londoners to panic in the street. Instead, there was fear, dread, grief, and loss, but no panic. And there was a hard mood of retribution. During the blitz the King and Churchill made visits to the hard-hit areas; the King, for example, visited Coventry immediately after its devastating attack. Churchill recalled one of his experiences at the site in the south of London where a large land mine had exploded. He was terribly moved, walking through the ruins of what had been two dozen homes of the poor in the district. As if in defiance of the Germans, the people had stuck tiny British flags in the ruins. The people crowded around the old warrior, cheering, happy just to touch him, and saw tears in Churchill's eyes.

They showed him a great crater, perhaps twenty feet deep and forty yards across, at the edge of which teetered an Anderson shelter. (This was the uncomfortable and not always effective government-issued air raid shelter widely used by the poor.) Still alive, though dazed by the miracle of their escape, were the inhabitants, a young man, his wife, and their three children. All were smiling, enjoying their celebrity. As Churchill turned to go, he sensed "a harsher mood" which animated the tattered crowd, then someone shouted, "Give it 'em back!"

"Let *them* have it too!" another shouted, and the cries followed Churchill as he left the scene. "Give it 'em back!" became a battle cry of the non-combatants who suffered under the new mode of the "art of war." And Churchill did all he could to comply with the mood of his people. "Certainly the enemy got it all back," he wrote later, "in good measure, pressed down and running over. Alas for poor humanity!"

II

The members of the Air Staff, viewing the situation more professionally, did not regard the principle of "Give it 'em back!" as militarily sound. With London as a target, it followed in popular logic that Berlin must also be a target. When the towns and cities suffered, then it was expected that the lesser German cities and towns should suffer also. Berlin, especially, as far as the average Londoner—and Winston Churchill—was concerned was a most enticing objective. Bomber Command would have preferred targets of more strategic value. In the long months of the Battle of France, the Battle of Britain, and the blitz, during which the Luftwaffe pretty much dictated the turn of events, Bomber Command operated defensively as much as offensively. Instead of concentrating upon the oil installations in Germany, as it would have wished, Bomber Command had to contend with invasion

A Coastal Command B-17 coming in over an English cottage after an over-water patrol.
(IMPERIAL WAR MUSEUM, LONDON)

barges on the coast of the North Sea and across their own Channel.

When it became reasonably obvious that the Germans had abandoned their daylight attacks and postponed their Sealion plans—toward the end of September 1940—Bomber Command hoped to resume strategic operations upon German industry crucial to the supply of the war machine. But the blitz, with its heavy London toll, plus the temper of London's population (as well as of others with even greater political influence) split the effort. Under pressure it was resolved by Bomber Command to resume the strategic offensive against the industrial complex in the Ruhr and to "Give it 'em back" in Berlin. The German capital was one of a dozen German cities (originally twenty or more) which could be attacked "to affect the morale of the German people." Among the other "morale" targets were Hamburg, Cologne, Munich, Leipzig, Essen, Dresden, Breslau, Frankfurt, Düsseldorf, and Stuttgart.

The primary objectives, now that the invasion threat had receded, were to be oil and morale. The desired emphasis would be upon the oil targets, but with the rather hazy "morale" now accepted as an objective, purely military definition of targets became academic.

Reports from inside Germany encouraged the "area bombings," that is, attacks not aimed at precise military pin points but at the general vicinity of known targets. Fire would do the rest, as successive waves of bombers disrupted the work of the fire fighters. Neutral visitors in Berlin reported that German morale had indeed suffered under the unexpected bombings of their city. Germans were shaken, but like the Londoner, the Berliner proved he could take it. In truth, the effect upon morale never approached the effect expected.

The concession to area attacks upon populated areas was not an admission of wanton British brutality. It was a recognition of a fact: not all bomber crews were so skilled that they were able to find the target area, let alone bomb it. Weather, flak, poor navigation, fear: all interfered with the performance of air crews. There were great distances to cover—the flight to Berlin traversed nearly six hundred miles, part of it over the North Sea and the rest over Germany itself. And then, there was the return trip.

Meanwhile, the Battle of the Atlantic also shunted Bomber Command from strategic targets. As it had during the First World War, the U-boat danger became critical, menacing the food supply and essential war materials, the bulk of which Britain had to import. Also there were the German battle cruisers, particularly the *Scharnhorst* and the *Gneisenau*, which aircrews readily nicknamed the "Salmon" and the "Gluckstein." The *Bismarck*, the great German battleship which had taken a terrible toll of British shipping, was sunk in a combined sea and air battle late in May 1941. But Hitler continued to promise

RAF Coastal Command "Fortress I" (the B-17C) over a British Atlantic convoy on watch for German submarines. (IMPERIAL WAR MUSEUM, LONDON)

to starve the British in their island and to cut off war supplies by sinking their ships from under the sea, on the surface, and from the air.

To fight this Battle the aircraft of both Bomber Command and Coastal Command were confronted with an area of roughly ten and a half million square miles of sea. Not only the U-boat and the battleship must be found in this great expanse but also the Luftwaffe reconnaissance planes and bombers. The British employed not only their own aircraft, such as the Short Sunderland, a giant flying boat, but also American-made Lockheed Hudsons and Consolidated Catalinas. In time, by 1942, the Boeing B-17 Flying Fortress, which Bomber Command had not been able to use effectively for various reasons, was employed by Coastal Command in sea reconnaissance and long-range convoy patrol. Later another heavy American bomber, the Consolidated

The U-boat's friend, the Focke-Wulf Condor, the Luftwaffe's only long-range four-engined aircraft during the Battle of the Atlantic.

(IMPERIAL WAR MUSEUM, LONDON)

The U-boat's chief enemy: the Short "Sunderland." This wide-ranging flying boat was capable of long overwater flights on antisubmarine patrols. The "Flying *Porcupine," as it was called because of its armament (eight guns in various positions) by German pilots, also took part in sea rescues.*

(IMPERIAL WAR MUSEUM, LONDON)

B-24 Liberator, joined the B-17 as a reconnaissance aircraft.

Long over-water flights, beset by sudden Atlantic squalls, fog, and the perils of icing, were as hazardous as they were boring, with an occasional spurt of action to relieve the monotony. The quarry was the U-boat or German aircraft which were capable of bombing British convoys or spying them out and radioing their positions to U-boat packs. Thanks to the Luftwaffe's dedication to the close-support concept, no long-range heavy bomber was available for such missions. Pressed into service was the Focke-Wulf 200 Condor, a four-engined transport, late of Lufthansa. Modified, the Condor, despite an impressive range, was still not a true bomber; even the addition of guns—a 20-mm. cannon in a top turret, plus twin machine guns in a forward firing position and another covering the tail—did not complete the conversion. The added weight and protuberances served to decrease the speed of the Condor, rendering it vulnerable to fighter attack. With all its deficiencies as a battle plane, the Condor was the best the Luftwaffe could muster in the Battle of the Atlantic.

With its range of nearly fourteen hundred miles (remaining air-borne for sixteen hours) the Condors, mainly of Gruppe I of Kampfgeschwader 40, harassed the Atlantic convoy routes from bases near Bordeaux in France and Trondheim in central Norway. The old war horses, the Ju-88s and He-111s, were assigned the shorter flights closer in to the British Isles and, from northern Norway, to the run to Murmansk over which the Allies supplied Russia after Hitler chose to abandon Sealion, lessen the air pressure on Britain, and attack his ally, Soviet Russia, in June of 1941.

It was during the winter and spring months of 1940–41 that the Battle of the Atlantic raged most critically; shipping losses to U-boats and German bombers rose alarmingly. In March of 1941 532,000 tons of shipping sank to the bottom of the Atlantic; in April the losses rose to 644,000 tons (of which 296,000 tons was accounted for by the Ju-88s, He-111s, and Condors).

The solution to the problem lay in increasing the efforts of Coastal Command over the Atlantic, stepping up Bomber Command's bombing of U-boat bases and construction yards, and stiffening the anti-submarine convoys which accompanied the mer-

chant ships beyond the range of protecting aircraft. The greater part of the fighting was a matter of ship against U-boat, or U-boat against aircraft—rarely did the classic dogfight occur over the Atlantic. The larger reconnaissance-bomber aircraft were not suited to such actions—and fighter aircraft did not have the range to venture far out to sea.

The work was monotonous and grueling for both German and British crews, what with the erratic weather and the tedium. The pilot of a Lockheed Hudson, one Pilot Officer Down, described how he and his crew longed "for some real liveliness" following a typical escort patrol.

"We did our usual stuff over them for more than a couple of hours, circling round and round in wide sweeps looking for possible danger. There wasn't a sign of anything in the air or on the sea. . . ."

Knowing that his relief was flying out and that his fuel was getting low, Down signaled "Goodbye and good luck" to the convoys and turned for home. But just for good measure he decided to make another circuit of the convoy. Half through the maneuver, Down spotted one of the escort ships signaling "Suspicious aircraft to starboard."

Down was all but certain that the plane was in fact a Coastal Command Wellington also on convoy patrol. "I flew over to have a look at her, pulling up my front gun sights just for practice. In fact, I was just remarking to Ernie [Ernest Corken, co-pilot and navigator] that we were in a lovely position, and that I had the Wellington beautifully in the sights, when he suddenly let out a wild Irish oath—Ernie is from Ulster—and shouted, 'It's a Condor!'"

The two planes, the large Condor and the smaller Hudson, began exchanging gunfire. The faster, more maneuverable Hudson overtook the Condor, pumped shots into it, then swept away. Down came back alongside the big transport until it looked "like the side of a house." From a range of forty feet the Hudson crew again poured machine-gun fire into the Condor. The German plane turned away, exposing its underside, into which the profane Ernie and the Hudson's rear gunner streamed bullets. "There was a wisp of smoke, a sudden belching of smoke, and then flames shot out from beneath his two port engines."

Slowly the Condor, close to the water, seemed to be pulling away. But with distance the big air-

A German U-boat under attack by a Sunderland in the Atlantic. (IMPERIAL WAR MUSEUM, LONDON)

craft also lost altitude until Down and his crew saw the German plane splash into the sea. As he flew over the Condor, Down saw that "its wing tips were just awash—and Ernie photographed [it]. Four of the crew were in the water, hanging on to their rubber dinghy. . . . A fifth man was scrambling along the fuselage. We learned afterwards that a Met. man [weather observer] who had been aboard had been shot through the heart. The others were all right."

II

Sinking a submarine or shooting down a German plane was gratifying to air crews, but it was not quite giving it 'em back. Keeping the supply lines open was essential, but that could be left to the convoys themselves with their depth charges and massive antiaircraft gun concentrations. But striking at Germany and at the Luftwaffe: that, it was believed, should be the main concern of the Royal Air Force and especially Bomber Command.

Gradually, as the force of Bomber Command increased and as its units were released from the Battle of the Atlantic, it could be brought to bear di-

Night attack on a German submarine by a Coastal Command plane. Three flares illuminate the scene as a depth bomb explodes to the right of the U-boat.

(U. S. AIR FORCE)

A Condor down in the Atlantic after an encounter with a Coastal Command Hudson.

(IMPERIAL WAR MUSEUM, LONDON)

rectly upon Germany. But with a difference, for as had been learned during the Battle of Britain by the Luftwaffe and by Bomber Command in its initial operations, bombing heavily defended targets by day was suicidal. Bomber Command would bring the war to Germany and to the occupied countries primarily at night. The concept of pin-point precision upon absolute military targets, subsequently, diminished in favor of "area" attacks.

By the summer of 1941 a change came into the policy of Bomber Command. Bombing accuracy had not been good (after the war it was learned that of the total number of bombs dropped on southwestern Germany from May 1940 to May 1941 nearly half fell in open country). Hitting factories in the Ruhr, heavily ringed with flak, was extremely difficult and costly. On July 9, 1941, Air Marshal Sir Richard Peirse, Commander in Chief, Bomber Command, was instructed by the Air Staff to "direct the main effort of the bomber force, until further instructions, towards dislocating the German transportation system, and to destroying the morale of the civil population as a whole, and of the industrial workers in particular."

In effect, this was a concession to the "Give it 'em back" advocates, but it was also an admission of the failure of the daylight missions and the night missions against small targets, such as factories or

oil installations. It was, at the same time, a turn in the direction of taking the offensive; it boded ill for the German civilian.

Nor was it "a piece of cake" (or what the Americans were to call "milk runs") for bomber crews. Missions were long and tiring, formations were small —so were bomb loads consequently—as individual aircraft carried their lonely crews to the target and, if lucky, back. The same determination, courage, and defiant invincibility that characterized the civilian of the blitz was exhibited by the bomber crews. Weather made the flights to and from the German targets a nightmare of navigation, and flak, if not always accurate, did fill the night sky with bursting shells. And there was always the chance that on the return home, as light began to break, German fighters based in France might intercept the strays and the crippled.

This occurred in the early morning of July 7, 1941, in the early phase of the "area bombings," when a Wellington bomber of No. 75 (New Zealand) Squadron was intercepted by a Me-110. The Wellington had just successfully dropped its bombs on Münster, a comparatively small city but an important traffic junction in the Ruhr. Except for the distraction of searchlights and light flak over the city, the Wellington ran into no trouble until after it had left Germany and headed for home over the Zuider Zee in Holland.

Before it could be driven off by the Wellington's tail gunner, Sergeant A. J. R. Box, the Messerschmitt had succeeded in hitting the British bomber with cannon fire and incendiaries. The pilot, Squadron Leader R. P. Widdowson, nosed the Wellington into a dive in an attempt to elude the attacker. As the Messerschmitt dropped out of the fight, apparently hit by Box's guns, Sergeant James Ward, ex-schoolmaster and the plane's copilot, was thrust into the cockpit by the Wellington's dive. Ward had been in the astrodome on lookout for German interceptors, and after seeing the Me-110, learned that radio communications inside the plane were out. As he approached the cockpit to inform Widdowson of the problem, Ward was thrown forward by the dive.

The two men, relieved to see the Messerschmitt leave, soon found much to concern them. Ward peered out of the cockpit toward the right wing. "The starboard engine had been hit and the hydraulic system had been put out of action, with the

Wellingtons of No. 75 Squadron (New Zealand) setting out on mission to Germany.
(IMPERIAL WAR MUSEUM, LONDON)

result that the undercarriage fell half down, which meant, of course, that it would be useless for landing. . . . The bomb doors fell open, too, the wireless sets were not working and the front gunner was wounded in the foot.

"Worst of all, fire was burning up through the upper surface of the starboard wing where the petrol feed pipe had been split open."

Attempts to reach the fire with fire extinguishers, even coffee from flasks, were useless, for the flame was too far from the fuselage. The prospect of taking to their parachutes seemed equally hopeless.

The burning Wellington approached the Dutch coast. Before attempting to cross the North Sea Widdowson flew parallel with the shore while he and the crew discussed their next move. "I think," he said, "we'd prefer a night in the dinghy in the North Sea to ending up in a German prison camp." All agreed—they should attempt to get as close to England as possible. The flame was now steady on the wing and did not seem to be spreading. The lattice-like structure of the aircraft (technically known as geodetic) stood out in skeletal relief where the fabric had been burned away. The geodetic method of structure of the Wellington, a kind of loose basket weave, afforded it great strength without adding weight. But to copilot Ward it suggested a kind of askew ladder. It was his idea to get out of the

Sergeant James Allen Ward, V.C.
(IMPERIAL WAR MUSEUM, LONDON)

plane through the astrodome, crawl along the wing (wearing a parachute, of course, and tied to the Wellington by a rope), and put out the fire.

To Ward it seemed to be a better alternative to the possibility of freezing in the North Sea. After a brief argument the crew agreed to participate in the attempt. As the fire grew hotter, the crazy scheme of Ward's seemed less impossible. Widdowson throttled down the Wellington as much as possible and still keep it air-borne, so that the rush of air against Ward would be at a minimum. Ward then crawled through the astrodome. "Then I reached out with one foot and kicked a hole in the fabric so that I could get my foot into the framework of the plane, and then I punched another hole through the fabric in front of me to get a hand-hold, after which I made further holes and went down the side of the fuselage on to the wing. Joe [the navigator] was holding on to the rope so that I wouldn't sort of drop straight off."

Inching along, Ward moved along the wing, on which he gouged and kicked holes for his hands and feet. "Once I could not get enough hold and the wind lifted me partly off the wing and sent me against the fuselage again . . . it was like a terrific gale, only worse than any gale I've ever known."

Ward persisted until he reached the burning area. He had brought along a canvas cockpit cover to stuff into the hole, hoping to smother the fire with it. The cockpit cover, catching the wind, nearly took Ward with it. But he continued to stuff it into the wing—and, before the cover blew into the slipstream, the fire went out. Ward had cut off the

supply of fuel long enough to extinguish the flames. It flared up again after Ward returned to the plane so exhausted that he could not remember how he got back. Seeing the flames he could only think, "This is pretty hard, after having got as far as this."

But it was a mere flare-up of fuel which had collected in the fabric and had been ignited by the heat of the exhaust. The fire went out and Widdowson brought the Wellington down "beautifully," as Ward described it, after the crew pumped the wheels down by hand. The only mishap was that the Wellington ended up in a barbed-wire entanglement. "Fortunately nobody was hurt though, and that was the end of the trip."

For his exploit over the North Sea Ward was given the Victoria Cross; Widdowson received the Distinguished Flying Cross and rear gunner Box the Distinguished Flying Medal. Ward died in action within two months of receiving his decoration.

If the British could bomb Germany by night, so could the Germans bomb Britain. Early attempts to deal with the German night raiders were not very successful. Defiants and Blenheims, which were no match for German fighters, were pressed into service as night fighters. Spitfires and Hurricanes were also

The Boulton Paul "Defiant," showing its rear gun turret, which deceived the Luftwaffe briefly (mistaking it for a Hurricane), but which proved to be inferior as a fighter. Mauled during the Battle of Britain, it was converted to a night fighter by the end of the summer of 1940. (U. S. AIR FORCE)

The Bristol "Beaufighter," deadliest of the two-man night fighters introduced into the blitz in the winter of 1940. (U. S. AIR FORCE)

used, but pilots were not properly trained for night fighting nor were fighter bases equipped for night flights. And air-borne radar was crude and inefficient. Consequently, interceptions by British night fighters were rare; claims for enemy aircraft destroyed were even rarer.

By late 1940, as the blitz diminished, certain advances were made in technology and aircraft. The former was the Mark IV AI (Air Interception) set and the latter the twin-engined Bristol Beaufighter. The plane was the first designed which was capable of carrying the added weight of the radar equipment without sacrifice of performance and firepower. With a two-man crew (one to operate the AI set) and generally in co-operation with a ground-controlled radar (GCI, Ground Controlled Interception), the Beaufighter proved a scourge to German night bombers.

The Mark IV AI had a range of about four miles so that the Beaufighter was guided to an enemy plane by ground control. The set also cut off at six hundred feet; by the time the Beaufighter was within that range, the enemy aircraft was generally under visual observation by the pilot. With the enemy plane in his sights, the Beaufighter pilot

One of Britain's outstanding night fighter teams: Wing Commander John Cunningham (left) and Flight Lieu-

tenant C. F. Rawnsley; the former was the Beaufighter pilot and gunner, the latter radar operator.
(IMPERIAL WAR MUSEUM, LONDON)

was capable of bringing it under massive fire: four 20-mm. cannons were mounted in the nose and six .30-caliber machine guns were set in the leading edges of the wings.

The first squadrons began receiving the Mark IV-equipped Beaufighters in September of 1940. One of these was No. 29 Squadron, to which a young Bomber Command pilot, Guy Gibson, had been assigned as a flight commander. This assignment was regarded as a rest tour at the time, the action in night fighter units till then having proved rather tepid. While "resting" with No. 29 Squadron, however, young Gibson accounted for three enemy aircraft. Obviously the new system worked.

Number 604 Squadron was issued its first Beaufighter in October. Originally flying Blenheims in convoy protection and escort patrols, the squadron's pilots complained of never seeing one enemy aircraft. And then, with the switch to night fighting it was, apparently, more of the same: they rarely saw the German raiders and, if they did, the slow Blenheims were unable to overtake them.

Then came the Beaufighter; within a month No. 604 Squadron had scored its first victory. This had been accomplished by ex-test pilot John Cunningham and radar operator Warrant Officer J. R. Phillipson. By war's end Cunningham was the second highest-scoring night fighter pilot, with twenty victories. (Bransome Burbridge, a conscientious objector when the war began, had the highest score, twenty-one.)

In April 1941 Cunningham formed a deadly partnership with Sergeant C. F. "Jimmy" Rawnsley (as radar operator). One of their early missions, that of the night of April 12, 1941, is typical of a night fighter action. Already air-borne in their Beaufighter they were ordered by GCI to intercept a northbound raid at thirteen thousand feet. Cunningham throttled the Beaufighter to "buster" (full speed), flying due north into the dark night. Rawnsley was ordered after a short while to "flash" his AI set, but he did not pick up the enemy plane.

Ground control then suggested that Cunningham bring the plane down 2000 feet on a course of 350 degrees. During the descent Rawnsley flashed again, picked up a "blip" on the set. Whatever it was was four miles away. With Rawnsley guiding, Cunningham closed in on the blip source. Suddenly out of the misty night, above and about 2500 feet away,

Cunningham recognized the familiar outline of an He-111. Apparently unaware of the approaching Beaufighter, the pilot of the German plane continued in steady flight.

Cunningham brought the Beaufighter within eighty yards of the German bomber before opening fire. "Immediately there was a big white flash in the fuselage centre section and black pieces flew off the fuselage," Cunningham wrote in his report. "E/A went into a vertical dive to the right and about half a minute later the sky all around me was lit up by an enormous orange flash and glow. Bits of E/A were seen to be burning on the ground."

Three nights later, Cunningham and Rawnsley destroyed three Heinkels—the first time a night fighter team had scored a triple victory. (The entire night fighter toll for the month of the previous January had totaled three.) Obviously the Beaufighter and Mark IV, plus the pilot-radar operator teams (Cunningham and Rawnsley, Burbridge and F. S. Skelton, J. R. D. Braham and W. J. Gregory, and others), had proved most formidable against the German night bombers; when the Beaufighter was joined by the de Havilland Mosquito night-bombing became an extremely hazardous undertaking for the Luftwaffe.

Not all effective night fighters were teams. An extraordinary pilot was Richard Playne Stevens, who had been a civil pilot before the war. Stevens enlisted in the RAF at a rather "advanced" age—thirty-two, the maximum limit for enlistment. Stevens, who had not participated in the Battle of Britain, enlisted in the RAF with an especially poignant compulsion to give it 'em back. His wife and children had been killed in a German night raid on Manchester.

Stevens was an exceptionally well-equipped pilot with hundreds of hours of night flying (between London and Paris) to his credit. Using a non-radar-equipped Hurricane Stevens flew with a legendary abandon. Some even hinted that when he attacked a German bomber formation he screamed like a man gone mad. Without ground radar control Stevens found the enemy aircraft by flying into British antiaircraft bursts. He was certain he would find his quarry there.

During the year in which he was active Stevens shot down fourteen German bombers. His score for some time exceeded that of the two-man, radar-

Opponents in the phase of the war that followed the blitz when the RAF turned to offensive "sweeps": the

Me-109E (top left), the newer 109F (top right), the Hurricane Mark II-B (armed with bombs), and the Spitfire Mark V-B. (H. J. NOWARRA/U. S. AIR FORCE)

equipped Beaufighters. Finally, one night in December 1941, Stevens took off to harass an enemy airfield across the Channel in France and never returned. The demon which had driven him had ultimately brought him peace.

III

Stevens had been killed while on an early intruder mission—sudden night attacks on enemy airfields. The tide was changing by the end of 1940: even Fighter Command was operating offensively. Intruder missions and their daytime counterpart, the fighter sweep, were designed to keep the Luftwaffe busy in the west, thus affecting the campaigns in the east, to which Hitler had ordered the bulk of the air forces for his Russian gamble. To contend with the growing RAF forces, the Germans mustered only two *Geschwader,* JG 2 and JG 26, consisting of about two hundred fighters, most of them

RAF armorers belting ammunition in preparation for a Spitfire fighter sweep.

(IMPERIAL WAR MUSEUM, LONDON)

Me-109Es with a sprinkling of the newer Me-109Fs. The Spitfire Mark V was a decided match for the Messerschmitt.

The secondary objective of the sweeps and intrusions was to destroy enemy equipment, aircraft, and installations. The initial "rhubarb," as the smaller (generally two aircraft) fighter assaults were called, occurred on December 20, 1940. Two pilots, G. P. Christie and C. A. Brodie of No. 66 Squadron, took off from Biggin Hill and, after crossing the French coast at Dieppe, pounced upon a German field at Le Touquet, strafed it, and returned to England without opposition.

About two weeks later, weather permitting, two formations of fighters—five squadrons in all—crossed the Channel and wheeled over the German-occupied coast of France. As before, there was no challenge from the Luftwaffe. The next day, January 10, 1941, the first "circus" took place: this was a large aggregation of aircraft, a squadron of Blen-

Spitfire Vs of No. 122 Squadron in various stages of multiple takeoff. Formed after the Battle of Britain, the squadron was very active during the fighter sweep phase. (IMPERIAL WAR MUSEUM, LONDON)

Group Captain Adolf Gysbert "Sailor" Malan of Wellington, South Africa. An exceptional commander, Malan's final victory score totaled thirty-five. He survived the war but died of sclerosis in 1964.
(IMPERIAL WAR MUSEUM, LONDON)

Merchant Navy before he enlisted in the RAF in 1935. Malan's nickname, "Sailor," was a reminder of his nautical days. At Dunkirk Malan scored his first two victories and by the time the evacuation was over was unofficially an ace.

At thirty Malan was just about a decade older than the average fighter pilot. He seemed aloof to the younger men, matter-of-fact, blunt in speech, and not given over to the usual boyish high jinks. In the air Malan was methodical and ruthless. Killing in the air to Malan was simply that: killing and not a sport. He was the author of the RAF's *Ten Rules for Air Fighting,* in which he expounded his

Wing Commander Douglas Bader. Bader best summed up the mood of the British fighter pilot during the Battle of Britain when he said, "We hated those aeroplanes with their iron crosses and their crooked swastikas flying into our English sky and dropping bombs indiscriminately on our English towns."
(IMPERIAL WAR MUSEUM, LONDON)

heims with a six-squadron escort of fighters. The objective was a Luftwaffe airfield near Calais. This time there was a flurry of opposition, costing Fighter Command a Hurricane and two Spitfires, the latter two crashing while landing in England. One pilot died in one of the crashes.

The rhubarbs and circuses were not in fact very decisive as far as "getting on with the war" went, but were good for the morale of pilots, who had for so long been on the defensive. The sweeps were also good preparation for operating in large formations (for future escort missions when the air war would become predominantly a matter of heavy bombardment); at the same time great leaders to lead such formations were developed.

Perhaps the greatest of these new leaders, some of them survivors of "the Battle," was Adolf Gysbert Malan, a South African who had served in the

method of survival for the benefit of others. Malan survived the war, a living exemplification of his own theories, ending his combat tour with a score of thirty-two (some sources credit him with thirty-five), before being taken out of battle to instruct and command.

Malan was a superb commander, fearing neither friend nor foe. During the height of the Battle of Britain Churchill visited No. 74 Squadron, then commanded by Malan. The inquiring Churchill asked Malan what might be done to improve operations.

"Send me more bloody petrol bowsers," Malan blurted. These were the little trucks which darted across airdromes to refuel fighters during combat. It is said that within the hour Malan had his bowsers. Churchill greatly admired Malan for his directness and ability and later became the godfather of Malan's son.

By May of 1941 Malan was commander of the Biggin Hill wing. To the north, based at Tangmere, was another wing commander, Douglas Bader, who also led his squadrons over the Channel on sweeps. The long-time advocate of the "big wing" tactic, so controversial during the Battle of Britain, had also evolved another technique, which was called "finger four" formation. The larger formation broke up into units of four planes, rather loosely formed (like the fingertips of one's hand, thus the name). This supplanted the old World War I "vic" or V-formation which had proved so ineffective in the early months of the war. The loose finger four formation permitted the mutual protection of the vulnerable tails of one's squadron mates. The day of the "Hun in the sun" was just about finished.

Wing commanders, almost by virtue of their administrative position, did not always accumulate spectacular victory scores. By the summer of 1941 Bader had taken a toll of more than twenty German aircraft when his colorful fighting career came to an end. Leading a large formation in a sweep over France, Bader, in company with three other Spitfires, bounced a formation of Messerschmitt 109s. In the melee, after accounting for two 109s, Bader collided with another enemy plane. The collision tore the aft half of the Spitfire's fuselage away. Pinned into the wreckage by centrifugal force, Bader fell twenty thousand feet before he was able to tear himself out of the cockpit. And he nearly did

Pilot Officers Eugene Tobin, Vernon Keogh, and Andrew Mamedoff, three of the seven Americans who took part in the Battle of Britain. Following the Battle they transferred into the all-American "Eagle" squadron, No. 71. (IMPERIAL WAR MUSEUM, LONDON)

not make that, for as he attempted to jump from the plane his artificial leg caught in the cockpit.

All but resigned to death, Bader continued to struggle half in and half out of the cockpit when a strong lunge snapped the leg away and he fell free of the shattered Spitfire. As Bader floated earthward an Me-109 approached head on. Whether the German had intended to fire upon the British pilot dangling helplessly under his parachute or not, Bader could never say. The plane loomed closer as Bader stared, wondering what would happen. Then the German pilot flipped away and was soon out of sight. It must have been unnerving to see a fellow airman—even an enemy—falling out of the sky with only one leg.

No. 71 Squadron, February 1941 (from left): William Nichols, Ed Bateman, Stanley Kolendorski (Polish), W. E. G. Taylor, Andrew Mamedoff, Eugene Tobin, Nat Maranz, Luke Allen, Peter Provenzano, K. S. Taylor, R. Tongue (British), Gregory Daymond, and Samuel Muriello. By the time this photograph was taken Keogh had been killed in an accident; Mamedoff and Tobin, also of the original Battle of Britain trio, were later killed in action.

(IMPERIAL WAR MUSEUM, LONDON)

Flight Lieutenant Chesley Peterson and Flight Officer Gregory Augustus Daymond, Americans who served with distinction in No. 71 "Eagle" Squadron.

(IMPERIAL WAR MUSEUM, LONDON)

Eagle Squadron (No. 71) Hurricanes "beat up" the field in traditional RAF style.

(IMPERIAL WAR MUSEUM, LONDON)

Genesis of a "sweep": pilots of No. 340 Squadron ("Ile de France"), composed of Free French personnel, leave an RAF briefing (upper left), study their maps—of their own homeland generally—while waiting for the

order to take off (upper right). The word comes through to man their Spitfires in cockpit readiness (lower left); and finally, "En l'air!"

(FRENCH EMBASSY)

Bader was taken prisoner, treated with respect by Adolf Galland, who also arranged for the delivery by the British for a replacement of the broken artificial limb. (The British complied although to the Germans the delivery lacked somewhat in sportsmanship: a box containing the artificial leg was dropped immediately after a regular bombing raid.) Meanwhile, also, the leg which had been abandoned in the Spitfire was recovered and carefully repaired by the Germans and presented to Bader. From then on he never gave his captors a moment's peace, for true to form Bader spent the rest of the war attempting to escape. He became so difficult that he was finally shipped to the practically escapeproof prison at Colditz Castle, from which he was freed after the end of the war.

Better known in the United States than even the redoubtable Bader during those days of the sweeps were the so-called "Eagle Squadrons," whose members consisted of Americans. These were, initially, No. 71 Squadron, followed by No. 133 Squadron and finally by No. 121 Squadron.

The Eagle Squadrons were the brain children of a soldier of fortune, Charles Sweeny, who originally had hoped to form a kind of Lafayette Escadrille to fight the Russians in Finland. Among Sweeny's first recruits were Eugene Tobin, Andrew Mamedoff, and Vernon Keogh (who eventually ended up in the RAF and participated in the Battle of Britain). Sweeny had about thirty young men willing to fight in the air, but the fall of Finland closed that avenue of adventure. Sweeny then got them into France, from which they were driven by the victorious Germans. Most of the pilots landed in England, where for various reasons—the most important of which was the pilot shortage—they were permitted, along with other aliens, to enlist in the RAF.

Another American, artist Clayton Knight, assisted in enlisting Americans for the RAF, although he was not associated with Sweeny. In time enough Americans had gathered in England, despite official American declarations of neutrality, to warrant the formation of an all-American unit. Thus did Tobin, Mamedoff, and Keogh transfer from No. 609 Squadron to No. 71 Squadron in September 1940.

The Yanks did not get off to a very good beginning. The squadron by the following spring, although in constant training, had seen no action. The Americans did not take too gracefully to the British conception of discipline; Sholto Douglas complained to Henry Arnold that No. 71 Squadron in his opinion suffered from "too many prima donnas." Two months later, when No. 71 Squadron participated in one of its first sweeps over Calais (May 15, 1941), Section Leader John Alexander shot up the Hurricane of his wingman while attempting to get a Messerschmitt which had jumped the wingman. With disconcerting impartiality Alexander fired into both aircraft and succeeded in driving off the Messerschmitt. His wingman barely made it back to England.

In the nine months of the squadron's existence its only score was one scrapped Hurricane. In addition, it had lost pilots in training accidents, among them the veteran Keogh. And when No. 121 Squadron was formed, the day after the shooting up of Alexander's wingman, the situation worsened because of the rivalry between the two units and jealousy over publicity.

It appeared that the Eagle Squadrons were more trouble than they were worth, but again, leadership made the difference. Under the command of Walter Churchill (not related to the Prime Minister) and later H. de C. A. Woodhouse the American units became fine combat units. From among their own members too came such outstanding pilot-leaders as Gregory Augustus Daymond, late of Hollywood and only twenty when he became a full-fledged fighter pilot; another great Eagle leader was Chesley Peterson, who had been rejected by the U. S. Army Air Force because of an "inherent lack of flying ability." Both men in time won the Distinguished Flying Cross and in turn commanded No. 71 Squadron.

The Eagles proved themselves during the period of the fighter sweeps and received credit for destroying more than seventy German aircraft—enough planes to outfit six German squadrons. Besides the sweeps, the Eagles participated in less exciting, but no less essential, convoy patrols—this duty generally fell to No. 133 Squadron.

With the entry of the United States into the war the survivors of all three Eagle Squadrons were absorbed into the U. S. Air Force as the 4th Fighter Group. They would be heard from again.

Brenden "Paddy" Finucane, Irish poet of the air, leader of fighter sweeps, whose final words when he fell into *the Channel were, "This is it, chaps."*
(IMPERIAL WAR MUSEUM, LONDON)

IV

But until England could depend upon massive aid from America the Channel sweeps continued. No longer did anyone speak of the Battle of Britain, nor even the blitz; the fight was being taken back to the enemy, by the bombers at night and the fighters by day. A new spirit of hope had begun to glimmer. The mood was once again more gay than grim.

This was expressed by Brenden Finucane, better known as "Paddy," an outstanding pilot and wing commander by the summer of 1942. "It's a grand life," he said, "and I know I'm lucky to be among the squadrons that are carrying out the sweeps."

Finucane loved flying and the sky. "Sure," he once said, "the queen of heaven tonight has more stars than she knows what to do with. Often and often I'm put to it not to collide with the stars up there, and me dodging in and out the clouds. Stars now, have a great hold over me."

It was Finucane's dream that he might destroy twenty-one enemy aircraft by October 14, 1941, his twenty-first birthday. Poet he may have been, and a dreamer, but by that date he had shot down two dozen German planes and had been awarded the Distinguished Service Order. Finucane had one great hatred—the English Channel, which he called "demented."

The Channel persisted as a formidable ditch and mercilessly swallowed up Bomber Command planes returning from German raids and fighter pilots after sweeps, despite the brilliant rescue work of the RAF's Sea Rescue launches and planes.

The frightful Channel weather was greatly responsible for the success of the famous Channel Dash (February 11–13, 1942), when the battle cruisers *Scharnhorst* and *Gneisenau,* plus the cruiser *Prinz Eugen,* broke out of the French port of Brest, slipped through the English Channel, and returned to ports in the fatherland. The success of the operation was also due to unusually close cooperation between German naval and air forces. Adolf Galland's units, some flying the new Focke-Wulf 190 fighters, participated in the action. Despite heroic attempts by British fighters and bombers under poor weather conditions the German ships actually made it through "their" Channel to the shocked dismay of England.

That the German ships had had to flee French waters was an indication of the turn of battle, the true and conclusive end of the Battle of Britain.

It was in the summer of 1942, long after the German ships had fled, that Paddy Finucane took his last flight. Having completed a sweep, Finucane, accompanied by his wingman, a Canadian, Pilot Officer Alan Aikman, had swooped down for some strafing on the way home. Hidden among the sand dunes near Le Touquet was a machine-gun nest which opened fire on the lead Spitfire as it passed over. Finucane's plane shuddered momentarily and then continued toward England. Aikman, meanwhile, dropped down, strafed the gun position, then swung out over the Channel to overtake Finucane.

Pulling up alongside the Spitfire, Aikman radioed, "You've had it, sir, in your radiator."

"I thought so," Finucane replied; "my engine's running a temperature. I shall have to get out of this." The Spitfire had lost altitude and was too low for Finucane to parachute; he would have to ditch in the "demented" Channel. As his plane splashed into the water Finucane said, "This is it, chaps." The Spitfire fell tail first and sank immediately. Aikman circled the spot in vain, for Finucane never came to the surface. The twenty-two-year-old wing commander drowned in the waters he never loved.

The ascendancy of such leaders as Malan, Bader, and Finucane marked the official close of the Battle of Britain, of the transition from the dogfighting, exciting days of the Battle to the more deadly, businesslike making of war. Although Britain was hard pressed by a lack of supplies and men, this lack was inadvertently to be provided for by a handful of warlike men in Tokyo.

VOLUME TWO

TRAGIC VICTORIES

BOOK I
Greater East Asia Co-Prosperity Sphere

I

"HARK! THE VOICE OF THE MOMENT OF DEATH"

THE huge aircraft carrier pitched in the dark, heavy sea and great lashing waves saturated the small groups of men struggling on the vast, perilous deck. Ropes had been strung between open spaces to give them something to which to cling. Alongside, dangerously close, a fuel tanker bobbed and tossed, threatening to snap the hoses coupling it to the carrier. The howling wind drowned out all communication, even shouting, so that refueling the carrier was dependent upon hand signals. Their previous training for such a contingency had not prepared the men for this. Even the massive carrier seemed an insignificant cork in the turbulent seas.

The two ships pitched eccentrically, a hose ripped apart, whiplashing across the carrier deck. Seamen were swept overboard screaming into the icy Pacific. Their shipmates stared in helpless stupefaction, but only for a moment, for their officers, prodding and gesticulating, made it clear that the refueling must continue. No attempt was made to recover the men from the water. There was too little time and time was more precious than life in their grand enterprise. Certainly it was more precious than the lives of a few nameless seamen, perhaps even more precious than the life of the admiral himself. He stood on the upper bridge, a squat, heavy old man,

his face a wet, impassive mask. He had been opposed to this operation from the beginning.

The date was November 28, 1941; and he was Vice-Admiral Chuichi Nagumo. Aristocratic, conservative, a samurai, he was, with misgivings, leading a massive Japanese task force upon the "Hawaii Operation." Nagumo's flagship, the *Akagi,* originally designed as a cruiser, had been converted into a heavy carrier to subvert the restrictions upon battleships as result of the Washington Conference (1921–22). Under Nagumo's command were no less than six carriers: besides the *Akagi* there were the other heavy carriers *Kaga, Soryu,* and *Hiryu* and two light carriers, *Zuikaku* and *Shokaku.* To these had been added two battleships and two heavy cruisers in the support force (under Vice-Admiral Gunichi Mikawa); the scouting force, under Rear Admiral Sentaro Omori, consisted of a light cruiser and nine destroyers. Three submarines patrolled in advance and along the flanks of the armada. A supply force of eight tankers would attend to the necessary, and hazardous, chore of refueling the task force in its three-thousand-mile passage from Tankan Bay in the Kurile Islands to a point in the Pacific Ocean about two hundred miles north of Oahu, Hawaiian Islands.

Vice-Admiral Chuichi Nagumo, Japanese Imperial Navy, who commanded the Japanese Task Force in the Hawaii Operation. A traditionalist, Nagumo had little faith in aircraft in a sea war. (U. S. NAVY)

Hideki Tojo, a general in the Japanese Army, whose rise to political power culminated in his appointment as premier of Japan in October 1941, and led to war with the United States and Great Britain.

(NATIONAL ARCHIVES)

Despite the imposing forces at his command, Nagumo was tormented by doubts. He was, after all, a traditionalist, a torpedo expert, and the heavy reliance upon aircraft for the success of the operation impressed him very little. Sea battles were decided by the great battleships trading volleys, not by a few flimsy aircraft.

The Hawaii Operation had been the brain child of Admiral Isoroku Yamamoto, Commander in Chief of the Combined Japanese Fleet. Called "the father of Japanese naval aviation," the fifty-six-year-old Yamamoto possessed the sharpest mind in the Japanese Navy. Harvard-educated, he had served

in Washington in the Japanese embassy during 1925–27. Yamamoto liked Americans and their ways and had become a devoted baseball fan, an excellent bridge player, and quite deadly at poker. It was during his stay at Harvard, where he majored in the study of the oil industry, that Yamamoto became interested in aviation. This was around the close of the First World War. Japan, allied in that war with Great Britain, France, and the United States, though not very active, was rewarded after the war with the German possessions in the Pacific north of the equator: the Marshall and Caroline islands and the Marianas (excepting Guam, which was a possession of the United States). These islands, little known to Americans in the twenties, would become household terms in the forties.

Yamamoto, like most of the leaders of the Imperial Japanese Navy, did not want to go to war with the United States. However, the United States had traditionally been the major, if hypothetical, adversary of the Japanese Navy in the Pacific. The Japanese Army regarded Russia as its foe, although China was its earliest real victim. For his stand against war with the United States Yamamoto had risked assassination by the zealots promulgating the "Greater East Asia Co-Prosperity Sphere." Among these were General Hideki Tojo, who in October 1941 became Premier of Japan—a triumph for the Japanese war party.

Tojo, a veteran of Japanese aggression in China, in progress since 1931, was head of the Kodo (Army) party. He had served as commander of police security forces in Manchuria (established as the puppet state Manchukuo in 1932). Tough, aggressive, authoritarian, Tojo was an admirer of Hitler and his methods. The concept of the Greater East Asia Co-Prosperity Sphere was an Army inspiration that originated with General Hachiro Arita while he served as Minister of Foreign Affairs. He had also engineered a pact with the Axis powers against Russia.

Arita's Greater East Asia Co-Prosperity Sphere called for recognition of the economic and political interdependence of the Japanese Empire and the so-called Southern Regions—the raw-material-laden East Indies, Malaya, the Philippines, Java, Sumatra, Thailand, and Burma. On the surface, the scheme appeared to be a plea of "Asia for Asians" (the Chinese, apparently, excepted), but its ultimate and true aim was the acquisition of oil, primarily, for the Army and Navy of Japan. Tojo and his followers in the cabinet realized that such a course would inevitably lead to dealing with Russia on land and with Britain, the Dutch, and the United States on the sea.

However, with both Russia and Britain embroiled with Germany and with Holland under domination, only the United States remained as the major obstacle to the dream of a Japanese Empire in the East. By September 1940 Japan had signed a Tripartite Pact with Italy and Germany, stipulating that the signatories would assist each other should any one of them be attacked by a nation not then at war when the pact was signed. Obviously this could have been only the United States. A year later, at an Imperial Conference, Japan resolved to go to war with the United States "when necessary."

Yamamoto opposed the pact with the Axis; so did Premier Prince Fumimaro Konoye. But the war party was gaining power rapidly and Japanese expansion in the Pacific had begun to arouse the British, Dutch, and Americans. Steps were taken to curb Japanese designs. President Franklin D. Roosevelt placed an embargo on scrap iron and steel "to all nations outside the Western Hemisphere except Britain." On October 8, 1940, the Japanese Ambassador to the United States, Admiral Kichisaburo Nomura, referred to the embargo as "an unfriendly act."

In Tokyo the Army party was less euphemistic and Premier Konoye, fearing a collision course in international relations leading to war with the United States, summoned Yamamoto. The Prince anxiously inquired about the chances of victory in the event of war. Yamamoto's reply was characteristically outspoken and terse. "I can raise havoc with them," he said, referring to the United States, "for one year or at most eighteen months. After that I can give no one any guarantees."

Yamamoto, as usual, spoke from facts with which he was completely familiar. He knew the status of the Japanese fleet and the naval air forces; he realized at the same time how long the limited supply of oil would hold out in the event of war, "when necessary."

Prince Konoye, weak, vacillating, but hoping for peace, tried to curb Tojo, then serving as Minister of War. The Army and the industrial trusts, the *Zaibatsu* controlling factories, mines, trading firms, banks, and newspapers, had too firm a grip on the government. Even the exalted Emperor could not restrain the jingoistic surge to war.

The Konoye cabinet fell on October 18, 1941; Tojo then became Premier and formed a new cabinet around his war party. War was now inevitable. The implement would be the plan, conceived by Yamamoto in May 1940, called "the Hawaii Operation." If war they must, Yamamoto contended, then the United States fleet must be eliminated from that war at the outset. While the stunned Americans picked up the pieces from this single, sharp blow, the Japanese would be free to swoop down upon

Target of the Hawaii Operation: Pearl Harbor; Ford Island lies inside the harbor, most of its area devoted to airstrips. Pearl City is to the right; above left:

U. S. Navy Yard. This photograph was taken some weeks before the attack; the ships are not situated as they were on December 7, 1941.

(NAVY DEPT., NATIONAL ARCHIVES)

the rich islands to the south. A defense perimeter running from Japan through the Pacific around the Marshalls and Gilberts, New Guinea, and the East Indies up into Burma would be established. The military forces, it was assumed, of Britain and the United States would then be battered against the strong perimeter until they cried for a negotiated peace.

But all depended upon the Hawaii Operation, Yamamoto said. For all its audacity and now admired brilliance, it was not an original idea. As early as 1909 the American Homer Lea, who had served as a general in the Chinese Army, had

warned of such an attack. This he put forward in his book *Valor of Ignorance.* But this was theory. In 1938, however, it was proved in practice by Admiral H. E. Yarnell, U. S. Navy. This occurred during a naval practice maneuver, Fleet Problem XIX, in which Yarnell led what he called a "task force" (a new term at the time) from the carrier *Saratoga.* Yarnell staged a successful surprise attack upon Pearl Harbor by launching aircraft just before dawn on a Sunday. No aircraft rose to meet the "attackers," which executed mock bombings upon the Ford Island Naval Air Station, the Army's Hickam and Wheeler fields, and the Wailupe radio station. All "enemy" aircraft returned to the *Saratoga* after theoretically sinking the ships in Pearl Harbor. The portent of Fleet Problem XIX was lost neither upon Admiral Yarnell, who failed to get a sympathetic ear, nor upon Admiral Yamamoto, who did not lack for bellicose ears in Tokyo.

All minds, however, were not attuned to Yamamoto's. When it became obvious that there would be war with the United States, Yamamoto set in motion studies predicated upon an attack on the U. S. Pacific Fleet, then based as a deterrent to Japanese expansion, at Pearl Harbor. It had been there since April 1940; Yamamoto began considering his Hawaii Operation the following month. By the beginning of the next year the secret explorations for Hawaii Operation had begun in earnest.

Yamamoto's chief of staff, Admiral Shigeru Fukudome, first learned of the plan when he was ordered to find an air officer "whose past career has not influenced him in favor of conventional operations." Fukudome was expected to accomplish this quietly, without admitting even other members of the Naval High Command into the planning.

His choice was Rear Admiral Takijuro Ohnishi, then serving as chief of staff to the commander of the Imperial Navy's land-based air force. One of Ohnishi's major problems was to devise a means of launching aerial torpedoes into the shallow waters of Pearl Harbor. This was critical, for either the torpedoes, as now used, would bury themselves into the mud in the harbor bottom, or else they would bounce over the decks of ships without result. To assist him, Ohnishi called in another naval aviator, Commander Minoru Genda. Only recently returned from London, Genda was quite excited over a recent feat of Britain's Fleet Air Arm. His own intelligence reports had revealed how in November 1940 torpedo-laden Fairey Swordfish bombers took off from the carrier *Illustrious* on a nighttime mission against the Italian fleet based at Taranto and succeeded in sinking three of Italy's six battleships. A mere eleven torpedoes launched from the obsolescent Swordfish had, in a single attack, completely transformed the naval situation in the central Mediterranean. Italy's battleship strength had been cut in half, leaving the remaining half at the mercy of the Royal Navy. Both Genda and Yamamoto had noted this exploit with considerable interest, especially since the depth of the Taranto harbor was about eighty feet (Pearl

Harbor was just a bit more than half that). The torpedoes had been specially prepared by the British with the simple addition of wooden fins. If the British had succeeded, why not the Japanese? It was a matter of devising a torpedo which could work in a depth of about forty feet.

But Genda and Yamamoto were not alone in recognizing the fuller significance of the Taranto attack. American Secretary of the Navy Frank Knox informed Secretary of War Henry L. Stimson in a memorandum that the "success of the British aerial torpedo attack against ships at anchor suggests that precautionary measures be taken immediately to protect Pearl Harbor against a surprise attack in the event of war between the United States and Japan. The greatest danger will come from the aerial torpedo. . . ."

Stimson agreed and so informed the Hawaiian Command. But Admiral Husband E. Kimmel, Commander in Chief, Pacific Fleet, objected to the placement of torpedo nets in the harbor because of the resulting interference with the movement of ships in so confined an area. He was, of course, right in his judgment, but it would prove to be an exorbitant rectitude. It was all but unthinkable that Japan, though launched on a campaign of conquest, would venture so far from home waters. Then too there was the problem of the torpedoes. True, the British had cut the required depth for launching in half; nothing pointed to the possibility of Japanese technicians cutting it in half again. Besides, it was widely known that the Japanese had inferior aircraft and that their equally inferior pilots would never master the technique of dive-bombing. It was an audacious conceit indeed.

After completing preliminary studies Ohnishi estimated a 60 per cent chance of success for the Hawaii Operation, provided absolute secrecy was maintained—and along with it complete surprise. His superior, Fukudome, was less optimistic; he gave the plan about a 40 per cent possibility. Yamamoto, however, upon analyzing Ohnishi's conclusions, was more than ever convinced that the plan could succeed. Though still opposed to war with the United States, Yamamoto firmly believed that if his government wanted war his Hawaii Operation was the only assurance of short-range success.

The General Staff of the Imperial Japanese Navy, which was responsible for operations, did not con-

Frank Knox (center), although opposed to Roosevelt's New Deal, was appointed by him as Secretary of the Navy (1940–44). Roosevelt hoped that this appointment would contribute to national unity in a time of crisis. It did and Knox would, before his death, become secretary of one of the world's largest navies. To his right is William Halsey; on his left is Chester Nimitz. Both of these men were to play important roles in the rebuilding of American naval power in the Pacific following the Pearl Harbor disaster.

(NAVY DEPT., NATIONAL ARCHIVES)

Husband E. Kimmel, commander of the U. S. Pacific Fleet at the time of the attack on Pearl Harbor. Relieved of his command subsequently for "errors of judgment," Kimmel believed to the end of his life that Roosevelt was responsible for Pearl Harbor.

(NAVY DEPT., NATIONAL ARCHIVES)

Roosevelt's Secretary of War Henry L. Stimson (left) in conversation with Major General James Doolittle (this photograph was taken somewhat later in the war, after Doolittle's famous raid on Tokyo).

(NATIONAL ARCHIVES)

cur. The consensus was that it was too risky. When war games were held in Tokyo during August the General Staff was further convinced of the risks when, on paper, two carriers were lost when the plan was tried out. While they argued, the Imperial Conference on September 6, 1941, decided that, "when necessary," Japan would go to war with the United States.

This did not settle the arguments between the General Staff and Yamamoto, but it did precipitate the need for definite planning. Some members of the Naval General Staff believed that Japan should strike to the south and attack America only in self-defense should the American fleet venture out of Pearl Harbor—which, of course, it would do as soon as Japan attempted to move into the Philippines.

In the face of opposition Yamamoto stood adamantly. Upon receiving a detailed paper from the General Staff in which five major objections to the Hawaii Operation were enumerated (the major one being that any loss of surprise would prove costly in casualties), Yamamoto sent a blunt message to the Staff. Unless his plan was accepted Yamamoto "must resign from his position and retire into civilian life." The date was now November 3, 1941— and this was quite a blow. The crisis was resolved quickly. Rather than lose their respected commander in chief, all argument over the feasibility of his plan ended. The Hawaii Operation was on.

Within two days Yamamoto issued Operation Order Number 1, of which the critical sentences were: "In the East the American fleet will be destroyed. The American lines of operation and supply lines to the Orient will be cut. Enemy forces will be intercepted and annihilated. Victories will be exploited to break the enemy's will to fight." This was followed shortly by Yamamoto's setting "X-Day" for Sunday, December 7, 1941. This day was selected because of the well-known American propensity for relaxing on weekends; it was likely, too, that a good proportion of the fleet would be in Pearl Harbor, in keeping with that propensity.

The fervid Army war party was anxious to open the war on December 1, but Yamamoto held out for the additional week in order to have a little more time for preparations. The Army Command, which was to lead a simultaneous attack southward into the Philippines and Malaya, acceded. On this same date, exactly one month before X-Day, Yamamoto appointed Admiral Nagumo, head of the First Air Fleet, commander of the Pearl Harbor striking force.

Surreptitiously, in twos and threes and singly, the carriers and ships of the striking force slipped out of their various ports and made for the assembly area, Tankan Bay in the cold and fog-enshrouded Kurile Islands to the north of Japan. By November 22 the thirty-one-ship armada, including the three screening submarines, had anchored in Tankan Bay for refueling and final orders. Only then did the pilots of the six carriers learn the reason for the many weeks they had spent in practicing shallow-water torpedo bombardment. The news that they were to attack the United States fleet was received with exultant acclamation. Healthy young men excitedly screeched out their banzais ("Ten thousand years!") to the Emperor and to Japan. Their joy was tinctured by their realization of the great risk of their mission and of the possibility that they would all die in such a venture. To die for the Emperor in glorious battle was the dearest wish of every pilot in the striking force.

They were to be led by Commander Mitsuo Fuchida, an experienced naval aviator of some twenty-five years' service, who had trained them for their "divine mission." Fuchida had, aboard the 6 carriers, 423 aircraft, of which 353 were to be used in the attack; the rest of the planes were held in reserve or patrolled over the ships of the striking force. Fuchida's planes were the Nakajima B5N (later named "Kate" by the Americans), the Aichi D3A ("Val"), and the Mitsubishi A6M ("Zero"). The Kates had a dual function: some would operate as high-altitude level bombers and others as low-level torpedo bombers. The Val, with its fixed landing gear, obviously German-inspired, was to function as a dive bomber. The Zero was a fighter aircraft, completely unknown in the West, and would serve as escort for the bombardment aircraft. The Zero was superior to any fighter planes the Americans then had in the Pacific.

While Nagumo contemplated the wretchedness of his lot and Fuchida's young pilots glorified theirs, hundreds of miles to the south of the main task force the advance force of twenty-seven submarines refueled at Kwajalein in the Marshalls and bore down upon Hawaii. Five of the submarines were

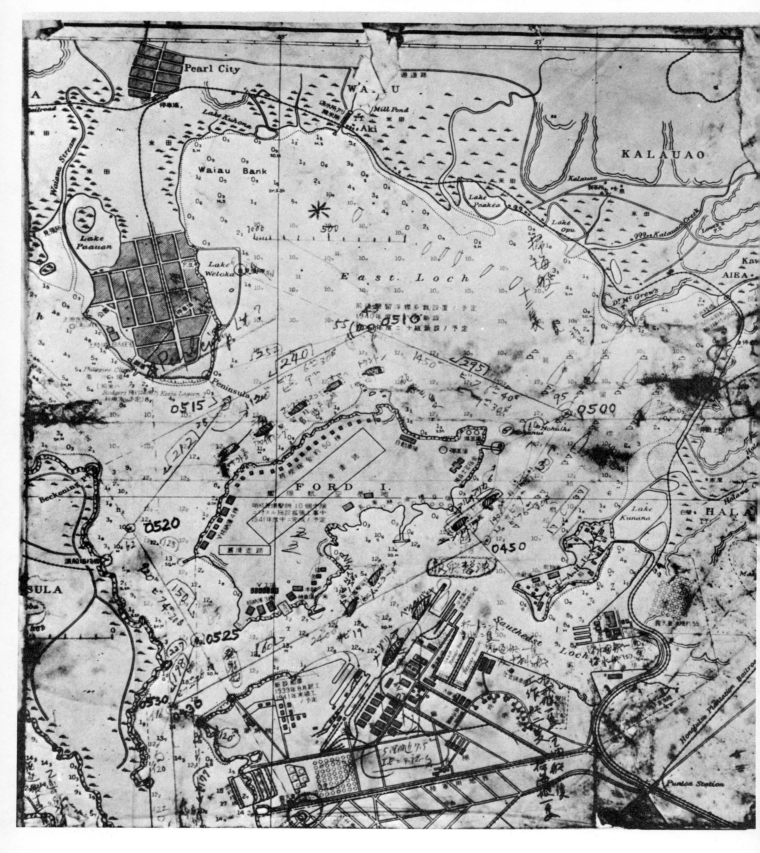

Zero fighters on a carrier deck ready to take off for Pearl Harbor. (NAVY DEPT., NATIONAL ARCHIVES)

assigned to the "Special Attack Unit" and carried midget, two-man submarines on their decks in a large tube. The conventional submarines were to encircle Oahu to sink any American warships that might escape Nagumo's planes and cut off any reinforcements and supplies that might be sent to Hawaii from the American mainland. The midget submarines were expected to penetrate into Pearl Harbor itself, after the aerial attack had begun, to contribute to the havoc. The air leaders, and Yamamoto himself, did not approve of the submarines' participation in the attack, but were overruled. The submarine service wished to take part in the divine mission also. The men in the midget submarines, certain they were going to death, gloried in the sentimentality of such lovely doom. Most, as it eventuated, found that very destiny.

That not one of Nagumo's thirty-odd ships was

Map of Pearl Harbor carried by Japanese pilot indicating positions of ships (not always accurate) and depth markings. (NAVY DEPT., NATIONAL ARCHIVES)

spotted during the eleven-day voyage from Tankan Bay to the point about two hundred miles north of Oahu where the planes were to be launched, must be one of history's most curious accidents. Nor were the submarines discovered until early in the morning of December 7, about five hours before the actual air attack had begun. Absolute radio silence was maintained by all ships. To cover up this blackout, ships remaining in the home waters supplied the missing signals of the absent ships.

The course of Nagumo's armada lay pretty much out of the usual shipping lanes, which is one good reason he was not discovered. If he had been discovered before December 5 the whole operation would have been canceled. The weather, too, proved an ally, although costing the lives of a few crewman. As the striking force veered southward on December 4, it approached improved if not ideal weather conditions. No word had come, as Nagumo hoped, to call off the attack. Instead, on December 2 Yamamoto radioed from his flagship *Nagato*, anchored in Hiroshima Bay, *Niitaka Yama nabore* ("Climb Mount Niitaka"), which philosophically meant "Climb the highest mountain." Niitaka is the highest peak in Formosa. This was the order to carry out the Hawaii Operation.

The ships with the beautiful names, "Flying Crane," "Haze," "Summer Cloud," "Wind on the River," "Blue Dragon," proceeded as planned. On December 6 the course shaped due south. In an emotion-packed ceremony the tattered, history-imbued flag flown by the immortal Admiral Heihachiro Togo at the Battle of Tsushima Strait (where he wiped out the Russian fleet in 1905) was run up the mast of the *Akagi.* All hands who could be spared were permitted on deck, where they joined in singing the national anthem. Impassioned cries of banzai pierced the night air and ascended to a cloud-dimmed moon. The ships in Nagumo's task force surged ahead at twenty-four knots, leaving the tankers behind.

There was one frustrating note that night. Reporting from Honolulu, Ensign Takeo Yoshikawa, posing as "Vice-Consul Morimura" in the Japanese embassy while keeping an expert eye on the American fleet in Pearl Harbor since August (1941), reported that as of 1800 (6 P.M.), December 7 (actually December 6 in Hawaii), Pearl Harbor, although a paradise of targets (more than ninety ships), harbored not one American carrier.

This was bitter news for Yamamoto, who hoped to cripple the American's chances of retaliation from the air. To Nagumo the absence of the carriers made little difference. Yoshikawa had reported nine battleships in the harbor (actually there were eight); this was target enough. Still Nagumo was made additionally uneasy when he considered that the American carrier planes could wreak havoc with the carefully laid plans of the Hawaii Operation if they caught the task force at the launching point.

Unknown to the Japanese only two of the expected four carriers were in the Pacific. The *Hornet* and the *Yorktown* had been transferred to the Atlantic; the *Saratoga,* it was known, had left long before for the West Coast for general overhaul. That left the *Enterprise* and the *Lexington.* Where were they? Yamamoto, aboard the *Nagato* three thousand miles away, was concerned. Aboard the *Akagi,* Admiral Nagumo did not sleep.

The elusive American carriers had, in fact, slipped out of Pearl Harbor days before. On November 28, just two days after the Nagumo task force left Tankan Bay—in fact, on the day that Nagumo had lost seamen during the first refueling—the *Enterprise,* under Rear Admiral William F. Halsey, had set out for Wake Island accompanied by three cruisers and nine destroyers. Aboard the *Enterprise* were the men and planes of Marine Fighter Squadron 211 (VMF-211), led by Major Paul A. Putnam. The squadron took off from the flight deck of the *Enterprise* in their dozen Grumman F4F-3s (Wildcats) on December 4 to bolster the garrison at Wake. On December 7 Halsey was well on his way back to Oahu—about two hundred miles to the west—when the attack came.

As for the *Lexington,* it too had left Pearl Harbor, under Rear Admiral J. H. Newton, in the company of three heavy cruisers and five destroyers. The *Lexington* was bound for Midway Island to deliver there Major C. J. Chappell, Jr.'s VMSB-231 (a scout-bomber squadron) and eighteen Vought SB2U-3s (Vindicators). Newton had not arrived at Midway on December 7, and when he learned of the attack, he turned around and returned, with the Vindicators, on December 10.

On Sunday morning, December 7 (December 8 in Tokyo, across the International Date Line), at six o'clock, Nagumo reached latitude 26° north, longitude 158° west—about 275 miles due north of Pearl Harbor. This was the launching point. Already two float planes, one each from the heavy cruisers *Tone* and *Chikuma,* had been catapulted into the dawn's darkness to scout ahead and for one final look at Pearl Harbor for signs of unusual activity.

The flight decks of the Japanese carriers erupted into feverish preparation. Planes were manhandled and pushed around, engines snarled, figures darted here and there. In the pilots' briefing room Fuchida reviewed the plan of attack. He would lead the first wave in one of the high-altitude Kates. If certain that surprise had been achieved, he would fire a single flare, in which case the attack was to open with the torpedo attacks upon the ships in the harbor by the Kates. This would be followed by the other Kates with conventional bombing after which the dive-bombing Vals would swoop down. The Zeros would contend with any American attempt at defense and could strafe the installations also.

Pearl Harbor bound: December 7, 1941. The Americans are about to be introduced to the Mitsubishi "Zero," an aircraft superior to any then in the Pacific.
(NAVY DEPT., NATIONAL ARCHIVES)

The spearhead of the Japanese attack on Pearl Harbor: the Nakajima "Kate" (Type 97) attack bomber/torpedo bomber. These Kates are armed with torpedoes.
(NAVY DEPT., NATIONAL ARCHIVES)

If surprise had been lost, Fuchida would fire two flares. The attack then would begin with the Vals, dive-bombing to create confusion to enable the Kates above to concentrate on their bomb runs, particularly on the harbor defenses. Then the torpedo bombers could deal with the ships.

As he spoke Fuchida referred to a blackboard on which the disposition of the American fleet in Pearl Harbor was chalked. Pilots made last-minute notations. Fuchida then left the briefing room and hurried up to the bridge, saluted, and told Nagumo, "I am ready to carry out my mission."

The old man replied, "I have confidence in you." It was a solemn moment, grim, simple, and gloriously infused with ineffable *amor patriae*. Neither man realized, in the exhilaration of the moment, the fuller implications of what they were about to do. Only Yamamoto, tense though impassive in

Hiroshima Bay, understood—for he had grasped the significance of the absence of the American carriers. Neither Yamamoto nor Nagumo was to live to see the devastation the Hawaii Operation would bring upon their beloved Japan. The seed of tragedy, as Yamamoto knew, was implanted in the blossom of victory.

Aircraft engines throbbed, then roared, on the pitching carriers whipped with salt spray. The early morning darkness was alleviated only by two parallel lines of soft blue lights along the flight deck, designating the runway. The carriers almost in unison turned into the wind—northward, opposite to the direction in which they had been moving—so that the planes could take off into the wind. In the uneasy seas the aircraft would need all the lift possible.

Fuchida sprinted to his waiting Kate. He wore a

white silk *hashimaki* (the traditional warrior's head-band, symbol of his willingness to die), a gift from the maintenance crews. The ends of the band fluttered in the slipstream as Fuchida clambered into the cockpit. At the opposite end of the flight deck a faint green light described a circle in the murky darkness; the pilot throttled the engine into full power. The Kate bounded along the wet deck, which lurched in the swelling sea. Blue lights winked past each wingtip as the Kate thundered down the flight deck. When it had almost reached the end, the carrier itself seemed to heave the Kate into the air. Cries of banzai celebrated the airmanship of the take-off.

While Fuchida circled above, the other planes of the first attack wave rose from the carriers to join him—183 aircraft in all, and all were air-borne without an accident. Fuchida had taken off the *Akagi* at 6 A.M. By six-fifteen all planes were ready to form up for the flight south. Cloud layers had formed from about three thousand feet to ten thousand. Leading his formation, Fuchida climbed into the clear air above the clouds. From that height he could not see the ocean, and no one on the ocean could see him. Fuchida's Kate was followed by forty-eight others—the level bombers. To his right, and slightly below, Lieutenant Commander Shigeharu Murata, of the *Akagi*, led forty torpedo-bearing Kates; to Fuchida's left, and above, Lieutenant Commander Kakuichi Takahashi of the *Shokaku* spearheaded the Vals, fifty-one in all, to serve as dive bombers. Lieutenant Commander Shigeru Itaya's forty-three Zeros appeared to dart nervously over the bomber formations, ready to pounce at the first sign of enemy activity.

But there was no activity. An Army radar station on the northern tip of Oahu, manned by two privates, George Elliot and Joseph Lockard, had earlier picked up the blip of one of the float planes scouting ahead of the attack force. They noted it, but because it was a Sunday they could assume that it was a private pilot out for an early morning flight. It was a fine morning for it. If the weather just north of Hawaii was a bit murky, it was fine over the islands: the clouds had begun to break, a dazzling sun came through. It promised to be a glorious day.

When Elliot and Lockard reported their plot, nothing was made of it. One officer, perhaps not

An Aichi "Val" dive bomber, its dive brakes down, plunges on "Battleship Row," Pearl Harbor.
(NAVY DEPT., NATIONAL ARCHIVES)

quite recovered from Saturday night's festivities, cracked, "Hell, it's probably just a pigeon with a metal band around its leg."

A couple of minutes after seven o'clock the two men were startled to see one of the most massive blips they had ever seen on the radar screen. Had the green Elliot caused the set to go haywire? Lockard checked it over and it seemed all right; sure enough, there was a big plot about 140 miles to the north and just about 3 degrees east. They immediately reported this—for they had never seen such a plot before—to the plotting center at Fort Shafter near Honolulu. They failed to arouse any official reaction. The duty officer, Lieutenant Kermit Tyler, was quite certain that they had spotted the Boeing B-17s due in that morning from California; or else the *Enterprise,* returning from Wake, had launched some planes.

The Japanese planes had been air-borne for an hour and a half; the sun had begun to break through the cloud which had hidden the formations from observation from below. Fuchida "strained [his] eyes for the first sight of land. Suddenly a long white line of breaking surf appeared directly beneath [his] plane. It was the northern shore of Oahu."

The Kate banked to the left, swinging toward the western shore of Oahu as the great formation followed. The sky over Pearl Harbor appeared to be clear—of cloud as well as aircraft. "I peered through my binoculars at the ships riding peacefully at anchor. One by one I counted them. Yes, the battleships were there all right, eight of them! But our last lingering hope of finding any carriers present was now gone. Not one was to be seen." But "below me lay the whole U. S. Pacific Fleet in a formation I would not have dared to dream of in my most optimistic dreams."

As his radio operator sent the signal to attack, "To . . . to . . . to . . . ," Fuchida fired the flare. In the Sunday-sleepy harbor below it was obvious that they had carried off the surprise. The dive bombers climbed out of harm's way to fifteen thousand feet as the level bombers swooped down to about three thousand and the torpedo bombers knifed down to sea level. They would initiate the attack. But something was obviously wrong. The Zeros had not taken their "Surprise Achieved" positions. Fuchida, realizing that the fighters may not have seen the signal, fired another flare. As far as

the bombers were concerned, surprise had been lost, and the plan became confused. The dive bombers, along with the now alerted Zeros, plunged into action. Worse, the torpedo planes too were screaming in upon Pearl Harbor from the sea. Fuchida looked at his watch: seven forty-nine, Pearl Harbor time.

Despite the last-minute blunder with the two signal flares, Fuchida was certain that they had caught the Americans completely off guard. More off guard than he imagined, for the delivery of the official ultimatum in Washington, delayed while the lengthy message was being decoded in the Japanese embassy, was delivered an hour and twenty minutes after the attack had begun. Instead of giving the Americans a half hour advance notice, as Yamamoto had anticipated, the other blunders of the day had plunged Japan into a Pacific war with a "sneak attack."

"Tora . . . tora . . . tora . . ." ("Tiger, tiger, tiger"), Fuchida's radio operator signaled to the anxious Nagumo on the *Akagi,* informing him that the surprise attack was successful. Because of some freakishness in the atmospheric conditions, the message was distinctly picked up in distant Tokyo and by Yamamoto's flagship in Hiroshima Bay.

The Army's Wheeler Field, a fighter base, was the first objective. Neat rows of Curtiss P-40s were lined, wingtip to wingtip—as a precaution against sabotage—on the field. Twenty-five Vals, led by Lieutenant Akira Sakamoto, proceeded to erase all fighter opposition they might have expected from Wheeler Field. At the same time Lieutenant Commander Takahashi, who led the dive bomber units, pounced with twenty-six Vals upon Hickam Field, the Army bomber base, just south of Pearl Harbor. The formation diverged as some of the Vals broke off to attack the various installations on Ford Island, in the center of Pearl Harbor. It was around the island that most of the important ships, singly and in pairs, were berthed.

The languid Sunday tranquillity was shattered by the scream of diving aircraft, the whine of falling bombs, explosions—followed by the characteristic blossom of thick, black smoke of flaming metal. This same smoke, as he feared, complicated the mission of Lieutenant Commander Murata's Kates, which were to torpedo the ships grouped around Ford Island.

A Japanese photograph records the first strikes around Ford Island. Outer row of ships are (left to right): Vestal, West Virginia, and Oklahoma; inner row: Nevada, Tennessee, and Maryland. Of these the Okla- homa *was sunk, the West Virginia* sunk but later repaired, the repair ship Vestal *and battleships* Nevada, Tennessee, *and Maryland* damaged and later repaired.

(NAVY DEPT., NATIONAL ARCHIVES)

A Val has just dropped a bomb near the Oklahoma *and* Maryland *on the far side of Ford Island. On the near side, the* Utah *(a target ship the Japanese thought was the carrier* Saratoga*)—the third ship from the* left*—lists to port. In the upper right of the photograph another Val sweeps over the Navy Yard.*

(NAVY DEPT., NATIONAL ARCHIVES)

One of Murata's pilots, his second-in-command, Lieutenant Inichi Goto, was infuriated when, just as he was leveling off for the run on the battleships at anchor, the Vals flashed by him. Goto was then flying in the vanguard of one column of Kates, while Murata led the other. Not realizing that Fuchida had fired the second flare which precipitated the attack by the Vals, Goto was angrily certain that the dive bombers had jumped the gun to steal the glory of making the first attack on the Americans.

There was nothing else to do but proceed, despite the confusion and now the smoke. Goto concentrated on his run: speed, height, and then the correct release point. The battleship—the *Arizona*—grew larger in his sight; there seemed to be no one on the decks of any of the ships. Oblivious to everything else, Goto timed the moment of release, and the torpedo, with its odd wooden fins, dropped from the Kate's belly. The weight gone, the Kate vaulted as Goto pulled back on the stick and kicked the rudder bar to get up and away. For a fleet moment he twisted his head to see over the tail: a foaming white wake churned the water, leaving a momentary track which terminated at the side of the *Arizona*.

Antiaircraft fire from American ships, once the impact of the surprise attack had worn off, begins to seek out Japanese Vals. (NAVY DEPT., NATIONAL ARCHIVES)

Panorama of Pearl Harbor minutes after the opening of the attack: ships burn in the harbor and the sky fills with antiaircraft bursts.

(NAVY DEPT., NATIONAL ARCHIVES)

Struck by the heavy concentration of fire from the American ships, a Val begins a fiery plunge into Pearl Harbor. (NAVY DEPT., NATIONAL ARCHIVES)

A broiling geyser of flame, smoke, and water shot high into the air.

"We hit her!" Goto shouted and circled round to view the damage.

But the "Americans were better prepared and reacted much faster after the shock than I would ever have thought possible." Machine-gun tracers were fanning and curving up at the Kate; Goto decided to pull away from the heated air over Ford Island. It was true, within minutes after the first bombs fell some of the men on some of the ships had begun firing at the Japanese planes. But the sudden impact of the realization that there were real aircraft, with orange-red circles on their wings, dropping real bombs and shooting real bullets created uncertainty and confusion on the ships as well as ashore. Army personnel were sure that some crazy Navy pilots were having sport with them—and vice versa. That this could be real war took time to penetrate. Men who once regarded themselves as professionally military wandered about not quite knowing what to do.

Those who might have gone into immediate action were handicapped for other reasons: many guns were simply not ready to be fired, or there was no ammunition available—and if it was, perhaps it was

locked away and no one seemed to have the key. For many there were simply no weapons at all. One sailor, in impotent despair, threw wrenches and other handy objects at the low-flying Japanese planes. Adult males burst into blubbering tears of helpless frustration. The abrupt reality of what was happening was difficult to grasp: one minute it had been a typical, peaceful Sunday; the next it had become an incredible concatenation of hundreds of swirling, flashing airplanes, explosions, acrid smoke, shouting, the sound of bugles, alarms, waterspouts, and little, moving, parallel scallopings of water caused by the twinkling guns in the planes strafing them. Suddenly someone you had known for years was inexplicably dead. Or the ship on which you had served for a decade had become a shattered, smoking hulk sinking into the mud of Pearl Harbor.

The battleships clustered around Ford Island were sumptuous objectives. The Kates hammered them from the side in torpedo attacks and from above with level attacks. Within minutes, so-called Battleship Row and American naval power in the Pacific were a shambles. Simultaneously the same destiny was allotted to the Naval Air Station at Kaneohe, on the eastern side of Oahu, where twenty-seven of thirty-six Consolidated PBYs (Catalinas) were destroyed. The Marine Corps Air Base at Ewa, ten miles west of Pearl Harbor, lost almost all of its fighter planes (forty-seven out of forty-eight), belonging to Marine Aircraft Group 21 (MAG-21), to strafing Zeros.

At Hickam Field, just south of Pearl, gouts of oily smoke ascended from mangled old Douglas B-18s, as well as from the more recent Douglas A-20s (Havocs) and Boeing B-17s. Several of the factory-fresh, unarmed B-17s, just flown in from California, were caught up in the attack as they came in to land. Many of them were shot up by Zeros as they attempted to land and if they landed, were strafed along with their hapless crews. As at Wheeler, the Army fighters at Bellows Field, almost directly east of Honolulu, were rent and flared where they rested on the ground. Very few American fighters, in fact, got off the ground.

Several pilots of the 47th Pursuit Squadron succeeded in reaching Haleiwa, a small, relatively insignificant training field in northwestern Oahu, by automobile. The field had not been as diligently worked over by the Zeros as the major airfields and

U. S. Naval Air Station, Pearl Harbor. The Chance Vought OS2U "Kingfisher" has been hit by a bomb. *It is one of eighty U. S. Navy aircraft destroyed in the attack.* (U. S. NAVY)

A rescue party searches for survivors from the burning West Virginia. One seaman is being assisted out of the water; two more may be seen on the bridge. (NAVY DEPT., NATIONAL ARCHIVES)

Hickam Field, the Army Air Force bomber base near Pearl Harbor; more than twenty bombers were destroyed at Hickam. (U. S. AIR FORCE)

As the Pearl Harbor attack opened, twelve new B-17s were approaching Hickam Field after a flight from the United States. Early radar detection of the Japanese attack were mistaken for the approaching B-17s, many of which arrived over Pearl Harbor during the attack. This was one of the new B-17s. Piloted by Captain Raymond Swenson, it was attacked by Zeros. A bullet ignited flares in the radio compartment and upon landing the burning plane broke in half. All of the occupants escaped except Flight Surgeon William Schick, who was killed by a strafing Zero as he ran from the wreck. (NAVY DEPT., NATIONAL ARCHIVES)

a few of its planes were still flyable. Taking off, without orders, by the way, a fact which would have later consequences, in P-40s as well as obsolescent P-36s, they attempted to intercept the attackers. Neither of the American planes was any match for the Zero. Even so, Lieutenant George S. Welch claimed four enemy planes before the Japanese finished with Pearl Harbor; although Welch received the Distinguished Flying Cross for his actions that day, a request that he be awarded the Congressional Medal of Honor was turned down because he had taken off without orders. Other pilots who managed to take off were Lieutenants John J. Webster, Harry M. Brown, Kenneth A. Taylor, and John L. Dains. On his third time up the last-named was shot down over the Army's Schofield Barracks by antiaircraft fire. Other pilots of the 44th and 46th Pursuit Squadrons attempting to get into the battle were shot down by the fast, amazingly adroit Zeros; many American pilots were killed on the ground as they ran for their planes.

Ten thousand feet above the writhing shambles, Fuchida prepared for the run by the level bombers upon the battleships moored around Ford Island. A few, berthed inland and adjacent to another ship, were difficult for the torpedoes to hit. Antiaircraft bursts from both the ships and the land batteries burst around the Kate formation. Fuchida's Kate recoiled as the firing became uncomfortably accurate. The plane bounced from a close one which punctured the fuselage and damaged a rudder control wire. But the plane remained in flight so Fuchida, with his eye on the lead plane, continued on the bomb run. Just then they flew into cloud, missing the release point—they would have to do it again. The air around the Kates was pocked with the gray-black puffs of shellbursts.

Fuchida's pilot banked the Kate, circled around Honolulu, and returned to Battleship Row. Other planes, meanwhile, had succeeded in dropping their bombs. Just as he was about to make a second attempt, Fuchida witnessed a "colossal explosion in Battleship Row," the violence of which tossed the Kate about seven miles away from Ford Island. The battleship *Arizona,* anchored at the northeastern tip of the island, adjacent to the repair ship *Vestal,* had gone up in one massive explosion. Bomb hits from above (for the ship was moored inland from the *Vestal* and was barely hit by torpe-

does) on the powder magazines and boilers tore the old battleship apart. A fireball shot five hundred feet into the air, a shock wave flared out, blowing men off the decks of nearby ships into the oily waters of Pearl Harbor. A complete loss, the *Arizona* sank into the offshore mud, taking 1103 lives with it of the total of 1400 men aboard. Among those lost were Captain Franklin Van Falkenburgh and Rear Admiral Isaac C. Kidd, who died instantly as they stood on the bridge of the *Arizona.*

Antiaircraft smudges continued to harass Fuchida but he proceeded with the bomb run. This time the lead plane dropped its bombs and the other Kates dropped in unison. Fuchida then fell to the floor where he lay, eye to peephole, to observe the results. The size of the bombs diminished as they plunged downward. He saw concentric ripples in the water where some missed, but as he watched two of them fell directly to the left of two ships moored side by side. The *Maryland* and *Oklahoma* shuddered under the detonations.

Upon completing their runs, the bombers fled to the north and the safety of the carriers. No attempt was made to screen the direction—there wasn't enough fuel left for that. By 8:30 A.M. almost all aircraft of the first attack wave, excepting Fuchida's Kate and a few strays, had left for the carriers. An unreal quiet suffused the air over Pearl Harbor, seemingly clear of Japanese aircraft. But the harbor itself and the area around it were choked with the effluvium of flaming ships, aircraft, harbor installations, and men. The living, now wrathful, made preparations for what might come next. Makeshift gun installations of wreckage and debris were erected; guns were ripped off ruined planes and set up in odd places. Guns were even issued to the weaponless (some, it is true, without firing pins and many without ammunition). Rescue operations were under way immediately in Pearl Harbor itself.

The second wave came in around 8:54 A.M. Lieutenant Commander Shegekazu Shimazaki of the *Zuikaku* led the formation of 170 planes. Shimazaki personally led the 54 Kates assigned the level bombing; Lieutenant Commander Takashige Egusa (*Soryu*) led the 80 Val dive bombers and Lieutenant Saburo Shindo (*Akagi*) commanded the 36 Zero fighter covers.

Fuchida, as over-all commander of the aerial attack, had remained behind to observe and direct

One of the spectacular explosions witnessed by Mitsuo Fuchida as he lay in the belly of a Kate: the Shaw *blowing up in a dry dock in the Navy Yard.*

the second wave. As he watched, the Zeros darted in to strafe Battleship Row and the airfields. The Vals hurtled in from the east to maul further the ships at and around Ford Island. Most of the level bombers concentrated on Hickam Field as others bombed Ford Island and the Kaneohe Naval Air Station. Smoke and flame of the early attack interfered with bombing accuracy—and antiaircraft was fiercely thick. Despite this not one bomber of the second wave was lost, although several were holed by gunfire. Six Zeros and fourteen Vals of the second wave did not return to the carriers. The first wave had lost only three Zeroes, one Val, and five Kates. The total losses of both waves were twenty-nine aircraft and their crews (fifty-five men).

In terms of "the values of war" it was a small price to pay. In roughly two hours at a "reasonable" expenditure of a handful of men and a few planes (plus one submarine and all five of the midget submarines), the Japanese had achieved precisely that which Yamamoto had promised them with the Hawaii Operation. The nearly total crippling of the American Pacific Fleet at Pearl Harbor cleared the way for the conquest of the Philippines, Malaya —and for the other objectives of the Southern Operation.

American losses were appalling: 2403 killed, 1178 wounded. Of the 68 civilian dead, many died in or near military installations. Those killed in Honolulu were undoubtedly the victims of American shells incorrectly fused in the chaos of activity. At Pearl Harbor, of the battleships, the *Arizona* and *Oklahoma* were destroyed beyond recovery; the *California* and *West Virginia,* also sunk, were

Seamen salvage a Kate from the waters of Pearl Harbor; only five were lost in the attack.
(NAVY DEPT., NATIONAL ARCHIVES)

eventually put back into service; the *Maryland, Tennessee, Pennsylvania,* and *Nevada* had all suffered damage but could—given time—be salvaged. Of the cruisers, the *Helena, Raleigh,* and *Honolulu* were damaged but repairable. Destroyers *Cassin* and *Downs* were lost; the *Shaw,* though hit and spectacularly exploded, was later restored to service. Both the *Utah,* a radio-controlled target ship, and the *Oglala,* a minelayer, were completely out of action. The repair ship *Vestal,* which had been next to the *Arizona,* was restored to service. So was the seaplane tender *Curtiss,* which lay smoldering under the wreckage of Lieutenant Mimori Suzuki's Zero, which had crashed into the deck during the attack.

Not a single battleship which lay in Pearl Harbor that day escaped the attack, which had been most thoroughly planned and efficiently executed. Although the damage was not absolute, it would be a long time before the salvageable ships would be ready for action.

Almost half of all the aircraft—Army, Navy, Marine—on Oahu were destroyed, a total of 188 of the pre-attack strength of 394, not all of which were truly operational. But the carriers had been spared and so had the repair shops at Pearl Harbor. And so had the fuel depots, rich with oil. Instead, the Japanese had bombed a baseball diamond in the belief that it was a cleverly camouflaged fuel tank farm.

Upon reporting to Nagumo aboard the *Akagi,* Fuchida—as well as other air commanders—suggested an additional strike at Pearl to deal with targets that might have been obscured by smoke

The first Zero to go down under American guns: it is the aircraft of pilot Takeshi Hirano of the Akagi's *first wave.* (U. S. NAVY)

or simply overlooked in the excitement of the moment. Besides, he hoped it might give them the opportunity to deal with the still untouched carriers, wherever they might be. But Nagumo, with his chief of staff, Rear Admiral Ryunosuke Kusaka, concurring, maintained that the attack had accomplished its strategic objective—excepting those hauntingly missing carriers. The task force, therefore, before the Americans completely recovered, would set course north-northwest and withdraw. No amount of respectful debate could force Nagumo to change his mind. At one-thirty that vivid Sunday afternoon the *Akagi* raised a signal flag: all ships were to head for home waters. Swiftly and silently the ships slipped into the heavy mist.

Back at Pearl Harbor frenetic preparations were under way for the invasion which seemed the inevitable next phase in Japanese operations. Wild rumors swept Oahu; nervous sentries became a greater menace than the new enemy. The least unexpected noise or light ignited a chain of frenzied shooting.

Everything that flew was fair game. The planes of the *Enterprise* suffered from friend and foe alike. Early in the morning Commander Howard L. Young with Lieutenant Commander Bromfield B. Nichol as his passenger took off from the carrier and headed for Pearl Harbor. Nichol was a member of

Admiral Halsey's staff and was being sent ahead to report the delivery of the men and planes to Wake Island; the information was considered highly secret and therefore could not be sent by radio, even in code. The two men were accompanied by another plane, also a Douglas SBD (the Dauntless). Other SBDs were launched later to scout the seas. The *Enterprise*'s crew was envious, for the planes would be in Oahu within two hours—the carrier would require an additional six.

But by the time Young arrived over Ford Island, conditions of the island prompted him to think that all safety precautions were being violated by the Army. Then one of the "Army" planes pulled away from the island and hurtled at them. Nichol was rather surprised to note that "a lot of burning cigarette butts" came flashing by. Some, flicking against the wing, ripped pieces of aluminum into the slipstream. Then the plane turned and the red-orange circles became visible.

Young and his wingman dived their Dauntlesses for Ford Island, escaping the Japanese planes but running into shattering fire from "friendly" guns on the ground. As Young braked the Dauntless, a sailor stood up with a machine gun; he hated all aircraft. He was prevented from firing at Young's Dauntless by a pilot who recognized the plane—but this only by threatening the sailor with a tremendous rock.

The other planes from the *Enterprise* were not so fortunate, especially those of Scouting Squadron 6. Swarms of Zeros pounced on them as they came in for landings. The death of one young pilot was heard at the *Enterprise,* which then learned that Pearl Harbor was under attack. Ensign Manuel Gonzales was heard over the radio, "Do not attack me! This is 6-Baker-3, an American plane!"

Then Gonzales' voice again, "We're on fire. Bail out!"

Soon after, flags were run up the yardarm of the *Enterprise.* There was something unreal about their message: *Prepare for battle.* Scout planes, torpedo planes, and fighters were launched to search for the attackers. Grumman Wildcats hovered overhead on combat air patrol (CAP). The Wildcats also escorted the torpedo-carrying Devastators, but although there were many alarums, there were no enemy carriers or planes about. That night the Devastators returned to the *Enterprise,* but the Wildcats because of less fuel capacity were ordered to

A homemade propaganda leaflet dropped by a Japanese pilot over Pearl Harbor. Japanese inscription on left reads: "Hark! The Voice of the Moment of Death. Wake up, you fools." Japanese wishful thinking is evident in the bursting aircraft carrier, not one of which was in Pearl Harbor the Sunday of the attack. That the carriers escaped would have its later effect in the Pacific war; but "the fools" had been rudely awakened that morning. (NAVY DEPT., NATIONAL ARCHIVES)

return to Pearl Harbor. The six planes with landing lights full on and with wheels down wheeled in over Ford Island after clearing with the tower. A single machine gun opened up on them across the channel from Ford Island, another joined in, then others, and all of Ford Island flashed as tracers converged on the Wildcats. One merely continued its glide across the channel into Pearl City, where it crashed and burned, killing pilot Herbert Menge. Two others were shot down, one crashing and burning in a cane field. Three of the pilots flicked off their lights and jammed their throttles and headed out to sea until things quieted down. Two managed to land, but pilot David Flynn's engine gave out and he was forced to parachute. It had proved a costly and fruitless search for the Japanese carriers.

But they had vanished into the spacious Pacific. Yamamoto had proved that the airplane was more than a match for the immobile battleship, but it was an infamous victory.

2

AMERICAN RENEGADES

MEI-LING SOONG, exquisite, formal, and hard as nails, best known to the world as Madame Chiang Kai-shek of China, referred to a small band of American youngsters as her "angels—with or without wings." It was a neatly turned phrase, much used during the early months of the Pacific war, even if few could explain its precise meaning. Another winsome phrase, also widely quoted, was "the Lady and the Tigers," with all its curious ambiguity Not to the "angels," however. If the genteel Madame had to make the choice, for all her endearing phrases, they would be angels indeed. There was no sacrifice too great, in terms of the lives of others, for her beloved China.

Within weeks after Japan went to war in the Pacific, Madame Chiang's "angels" were renowned as the "Flying Tigers"; no one knows the derivation of the name. The Japanese preferred calling them "American renegades," partly because they had become, as the American Volunteer Group, members of the Chinese Air Force and partly because of their unorthodox fighting style. In fact, during those grim

early months of the Pacific war, only the Flying Tigers spoiled the succession of Japanese aerial victories—and this while flying inferior aircraft.

Credit for the Flying Tigers' tactics and for their ability to meet the Japanese in battle with a type of aircraft which, in other areas, the Japanese destroyed readily, must go to the man who led them, an ex-U. S. Army Air Corps captain, Claire Lee Chennault. Hard-bitten, tough, and self-sufficient, Chennault had been in China since 1937, when he was retired from the Air Corps because of chronic bronchitis and partial deafness. He had been hired by Generalissimo Chiang Kai-shek to serve as his adviser in military aviation; Madame Chiang, it might be noted, was the National Secretary of Aviation. Chennault, then forty-seven, was given the rank of colonel in the Chinese Air Force.

He found, however, that he had little effective air force to command. The Japanese were well established in Manchuria and bombing Chinese cities at will. The Chinese armies, those under Chiang's command, fell back before the better-equipped and disciplined Japanese. The Generalissimo abandoned Nanking, then Hankow, until the seat of his Kuomintang government was temporarily established inland at Chungking. The Japanese, however, were not Chiang's only foes. He was either at odds or made deals with various provincial governors, war lords and the Communists under Mao Tse-tung. Consequently during the war in China there were in fact several wars as these factions fought together and then fought each other.

Into this typical oriental political situation descended Claire Chennault, who was fated to an extraordinary education in duplicity, graft, cupidity, nepotism, equivocation, and the old-fashioned double cross. While these themes are not directly germane to the development of the air weapon, they were to vex Chennault considerably during his service in China. The cost in goods, time, money, and lives would not be trivial.

Chennault's was not the first attempt at patterning the Chinese Air Force along foreign lines. As

early as 1932 an "unofficial" air mission led by Colonel John H. Jouett gave it a try. Bringing nine American pilots—including one Harvey Greenlaw, who would in time become Chennault's chief of staff—Jouett found the Chinese Air Force ineffectually graft-ridden. With Chiang Kai-shek's blessing Jouett generally shook up the organization, set up a proper training school, and arranged for the purchase of modern foreign planes. But diplomatic pressures from Japan, as well as differences with Chiang, forced Jouett out of China in 1934. In desperation Chiang turned to other nations for assistance in building a modern air force; he found the Russians and the Italians most willing. However, the occidental soldier-of-fortune *laissez faire* outlook (this was especially true of the Italians) did little to improve the efficiency of Chiang's air force. Very soon the planes Jouett had purchased piled up around the Chinese countryside.

Madame Chiang attempted to remedy the woeful situation by hiring a couple of ex-U. S. Army Air Corps stunt fliers, William C. McDonald and John H. Williamson, to organize a flying school in 1936. The two men had been members of a trio known as "Three Men on a Flying Trapeze," which had thrilled the crowds at air shows and races. Their most celebrated stunt was flying through complex aerobatics while their planes were attached, wing to wing, by a twenty-foot length of rope. The leader and third member of the group was Claire Lee Chennault. McDonald and Williamson suggested that Madame Chiang approach Chennault to do something about the hapless Chinese Air Force. Chennault, by then retired, was known for his textbook *The Role of Defensive Pursuit*, the doctrine of which had made a deeper impression upon the younger pilots than Chennault's superiors.

Chennault's first exposure to the internationally manned air force was disheartening. Many an aircraft was wiped out merely in the process of landing; half of his small force of American and British fighters (eleven out of twenty-two) was destroyed in this way; likewise four out of five Martin bombers. The last bomber was lost during a surprise Japanese air raid. The polyglot air force took off in every possible direction, crashing into the bomber on the ground and further erasing fifteen fighters from the operational inventory.

One of Chennault's first moves was to institute

Claire Lee Chennault, master tactician and pilot who created the "Flying Tigers." This photograph was taken *after the Flying Tiger phase—when Chennault commanded the Fourteenth Air Force later in the war.*

(U. S. AIR FORCE)

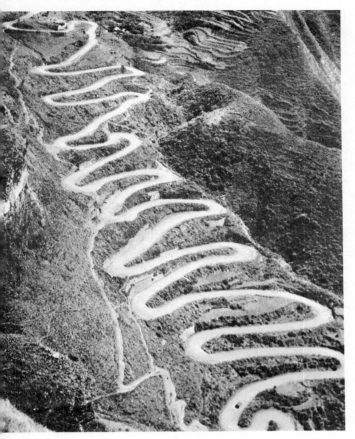

Back door to China: the Burma Road, more than seven hundred miles of hazardous driving—and corrupt Chinese officials. (U. S. OFFICE OF WAR INFORMATION)

was an almost insuperable effort. The Russians, who had been supplying the Chinese with money, planes, guns, and even aircrews, had, by the summer of 1941, a Nazi invasion to contend with—which closed that avenue of aid. The Japanese controlled the eastern seaports of China, as well as Indo-China (thanks to Vichy France), leaving the one major life line into China via the port of Rangoon, Burma. Materials delivered to Rangoon were sent by rail to Lashio, in the north; this was the western terminus of the Burma Road, a curling ribbon of more than seven hundred miles, a tortuous drive by truck, which had been all but clawed out of the mountains by hand during 1937–38. At the eastern end of the road lay Kunming, China.

By March of 1941 the United States, awakening to the Japanese threat in the Pacific, was committed to full lend-lease aid to China. The Burma Road thus became more crucial than ever. Only two obstacles intervened in the full exploitation of the Burma Road: the Japanese bombers based at Hanoi and the Chinese officials responsible for the Burma Road. Graft, featherbedding, and sheer inefficiency prevented the delivery to China of much of the materials that arrived in Rangoon. Even despite the official commitment to China and the widespread sympathy in the United States for the Chinese, there was no overwhelming aid on the way, in fact. Both military and government officials in the United

an early warning system with lookout stations, linked by radio, strewn across China. Whenever the Japanese bombers left their base at Hanoi, Indo-China (after the fall of France), it took but a few minutes before Chennault knew about it in Kunming. In the beginning (before the Flying Tiger era) the main job was to get the few surviving Chinese aircraft dispersed or evacuated to escape bomb damage. Later, of course, the early warning system could be employed for interception. Proof of Chennault's capabilities as a teacher was demonstrated late in the summer of 1937. Chinese pilots, taught by Chennault, intercepted Japanese bombers over the battered city of Nanking and shot them out of the skies.

But the teaching of tactical potency was Chennault's minor problem. He required more men and more aircraft. Merely getting materials into China

Curtiss P-40 "Tomahawk" with Flying Tiger shark's mouth, Rangoon. (U. S. AIR FORCE)

States, with wary eyes upon Europe and recent developments in north Africa, viewed Hitler and not Tojo as the major threat.

Prompted by the seriousness of the China situation, Chennault returned to the United States in the spring of 1941 accompanied by General P. T. Mow of the Chinese Air Force. Chennault by this time was a brigadier general. With the co-operation of T. V. Soong, Chinese Foreign Minister and brother of Madame Chiang, Chennault eventually reached the sympathetic ear of President Roosevelt. Basing his plea for aid to China on the importance of keeping the Burma Road open, Chennault asked for aircraft—and a voluntary force of experienced American pilots to fly them. This was a delicate proposition politically, for such open aid would be in violation of American-Japanese neutrality, such as that was. Besides, Hitler continued to engage American attention.

The aircraft were forthcoming, thanks to the intervention of Secretary of the Treasury Henry Morgenthau, Jr., who had Roosevelt's backing. Although all first-class aircraft were high-priority items for the burgeoning U.S. national defense program, or for shipment to Britain and Russia, Chennault was able to obtain the release of a hundred Curtiss Wright P-40Bs ("Tomahawk"), originally allocated to Sweden—and which had already been rejected by the RAF as obsolescent. Despite this rejection, the P-40s were better planes than those Chennault already had. And the RAF continued to use them until the later D and E models ("Kittyhawk") appeared.

Assured of his aircraft, Chennault broached the subject of trained pilots. Predicting a general outbreak of war in the Pacific, he succeeded in arousing the sentiments of Roosevelt as well as officials in the War and State departments. So it was that from May through July of 1941, various Army and Navy air bases were visited by Chennault or by Captain Harry C. Claiborne, C. B. Adair (both ex-U. S. Army Air Corps men), and Richard T. Aldworth, a former World War I pilot and a vice-president in an organization known as CAMCO, Central Aircraft Manufacturing Corporation.

This was an interesting firm. It was, in fact, the contracting agent between the American volunteers and the Chinese government. According to the contract signed by the pilots and ground crew volun-

teers, they were to serve for one year in China "to manufacture, service and operate aircraft" as members of the American Volunteer Group. There was no mention, not even in fine print, of fighting the Japanese. Minimum salary for flying personnel was $600 per month in American money (lend-lease, of course). Flight leaders received $675 and squadron commanders $750. A bonus of $500 was promised for every confirmed Japanese plane destroyed— this point was verbal and also not included in the CAMCO contract. Ground crew salaries ranged from $150 to $350 a month; for this time—the summer of 1941—these could be regarded as very good salaries.

The attractive fiscal promises were not the sole reasons for volunteering. Some pilots, in training for years, longed for a little action. Others sensed that, in time, the United States would have to go to war and hoped to gain combat experience (this was especially true of the Navy pilots). Some volunteers were driven by the simple spirit of adventure and others by a dedication to the cause of China. This was before they learned that the cause of China and the cause of the Chiang Kai-sheks were not necessarily identical. Others admitted that they were out for the money—so there was a complexity of reasons for the forming of the American Volunteer Group. Some may even have succumbed to the rather exaggerated blandishments of the recruiting staff—who were rewarded for their efforts in bounty, so much per head. As Gregory Boyington, an ex-Marine pilot who had volunteered to escape serious financial problems, observed, "The two ingredients necessary to accomplish this human sale were greedy pilots and a few idealists."

Whatever their motivations, 90 pilots (over half of whom came from the ranks of the Navy and Marines) and 150 non-flying personnel assembled in July in San Francisco. Among the ground people were radio operators, mechanics—even a flight surgeon and two nurses. Supplies, too, had been purchased with lend-lease funds by Soong and Chennault, who had gone on ahead to arrange for a training base in Burma. The first contingent of the American Volunteer Group slipped out of San Francisco aboard a Dutch ship on July 11, 1941, more or less secretly. The furtiveness encompassed some quite blatant passport falsification. When he left on a subsequent ship, Boyington was, according to his passport, "a member of the clergy." It could hardly be considered inventive typecasting.

It was September, after a meandering voyage of many stops, before the first of the American Volunteer Group arrived at Rangoon, some twenty miles up the Rangoon River from the Gulf of Martaban. A subsequent trip by rail took them deeper into the jungle to an RAF base at Toungoo, where they were to receive their schooling from Chennault. Burma, it turned out, was not quite the tropical paradise painted by the recruitment staff. Getting off the toy train at Toungoo, many a young pilot felt foolishly country-clubbish as he carried tennis rackets and a set of golf clubs. There were no golf courses or tennis courts at the Kyedaw airdrome, about ten miles out of Toungoo. There were only moldering troop barracks, oppressive heat, an incredible proliferation of insect life, giant rats, poor food.

Some of the P-40s, however, had arrived at Rangoon, and were assembled and flown up to Toungoo. "The runway," Chennault wrote in describing the place, "was surrounded by quagmire and pestilential jungle. Matted masses of rotting vegetation carpeted the jungle and filled the air with a sour, sickening smell." Even before training got under way, Chennault was handed the resignations of five pilots who "were eager to return to the United States and air-line jobs."

Chennault drew upon his past experiences with the Japanese and as a teacher, "ranging from the one-room schools of rural Louisiana to director of one of the largest Air Corps schools," to prepare the new pilots for what would come. He stressed the excellent flying qualities of the Japanese pilots, although emphasizing their tendency to fly mechanically and employ a set tactical routine. Chennault also introduced the Americans to the Zero fighter, indicating its strong points as compared with the P-40: higher ceiling, superior maneuverability, and better climbing ability. But, Chennault also pointed out, the P-40 was a more rugged aircraft, could take more punishment, and, thanks to the self-sealing fuel tank, was not so readily combustible. The P-40 was also equipped with armor plate, which the Zero lacked, thanks to the Japanese pilots' insistence on high maneuverability. Also, the heavier P-40 could outdive (that is to say, outrun) the Zero. "Use your speed and diving power to make a pass, shoot and break away," Chennault told them.

Another dictum: "Fight in pairs." These tactics were quite unorthodox to pilots who had been trained along the romantic dogfight concepts of the First World War. The "hit and run" principle was particularly upsetting (but exceptionally wise, as they would learn). When this idea filtered around, the RAF issued an order that any British pilot seen diving away from a combat would be subject to court-martial. The Chinese Air Force had a more direct solution: a firing squad.

But Chennault prevailed, although his lecture on the Zero seems to have led to a few more pilot resignations. Those who remained then had to contend with the P-40, for which few had little regard. Many longed to use the Brewster Buffalo, which the RAF had, instead. Chennault, no admirer of the P-40 himself and particularly not of its liquid-cooled Allison engine, realized that for all its imperfections, the P-40 could be used to beat the Japanese, if properly handled.

The transition to the P-40 by pilots who had been trained in other aircraft (some had even piloted B-17s) was not simple. The narrow-tread landing gear of the P-40 made landing upon hard, earthen runways a hazard. Even experienced pilots washed out precious planes. And there were other accidents. Former Navy pilot John D. Armstrong (Hutchinson, Kansas) collided in a mock dogfight in mid-air with Fighter Leader John G. Bright. The latter managed to take to his chute, but Armstrong did not and died in the crash. A few days later Maax Hammer (Cairo, Illinois), caught in a sudden monsoon, crashed while attempting to land and was killed. On another training flight, Peter W. Atkinson (Martinsburg, West Virginia) suffered a malfunction of his propeller governor; the propeller ran wild and the P-40 all but fell apart in a screaming power dive, taking Atkinson with it.

There being no spare parts for the P-40s, the wrecks were salvaged for replacement parts. There were no replacements for the men. As training progressed, both men and aircraft, especially the latter, were consumed. The military grapevine began to transmit the libelous rumor that Chennault's volunteers would not, as worded in a wire from T. V. Soong, "be ready before February 1942 and will not last two weeks in combat. Your comment requested."

Chennault's printable comment was that the group

would be ready by November 1941. He was correct, although by this time he had only forty-three operational P-40s and eighty-four pilots. Of these "survivors," Erikson E. Shilling (who doubled also as Group Photo Officer) conceived the idea of decorating the remaining P-40s with a blood-red mouth, shark teeth, and an evil eye in the radiator area. The Japanese, Shilling was certain, would be superstitious about the shark and the evil eye. This was not original with Shilling, of course, for the British had so decorated their P-40s and the Germans had used similar designs on their Ju-87 Stuka and the Me-110. At the same time someone with Hollywood connections had approached the Walt Disney studios for an idea of an identifying insignia. A Disney artist came up with a cunning leaping tiger, with tiny wings, jumping through a V, the V for Victory sign popularized by Churchill. It was from this insignia that the popular name Flying Tiger came into currency, although the group was already called that before the design had been drawn, possibly because of the tiger shark connotation.

Chennault divided the remaining men and planes into three squadrons. The first, called "Adam and Eve," was commanded by Robert J. Sandell, an ex-Army pilot from San Antonio, Texas; the second, "Panda Bear," was led by John Van Kuren Newkirk, formerly of the Navy and Scarsdale, New York; "Hell's Angels" was the popular name of the third squadron, which was under the leadership of Arvid Olson, a Californian and onetime Army pilot.

Despite this paper readiness, the Flying Tigers had not yet tangled with the Japanese in November, as Chennault had predicted; nor, for that matter, did they join in battle immediately after the Pearl Harbor attack. Wisely, Chennault did not wish to send his pilots into combat until they had the fullest possible preparation. There were other considerations: a promised delivery of supplies had not materialized in November and there was an acute shortage of aircraft, ammunition, and parts.

II

Curiously, the popular belief continues that the Flying Tigers fought against the Japanese before the Pearl Harbor debacle. In fact, nearly two weeks passed—during which the Americans who fought back, especially in the Philippines, suffered badly—before the Flying Tigers encountered Japanese planes for the first time.

On December 10 Chennault initiated the evacuation of the Kyedaw airdrome. Arvid Olson led the Hell's Angels (i.e., the 3rd Squadron), consisting of twenty-four pilots and twenty-one Tomahawks, south to Mingaladon, near Rangoon, to co-operate with the RAF in protecting the port from Japanese aerial attacks. This handful of men and planes were added to another handful in No. 67 Squadron, a British fighter squadron equipped mainly with the Brewster Buffalo (later they were to receive Hurricanes). The remaining two AVG squadrons left for the main base at Kunming, China, on December 18, some flying their operational aircraft and others, mainly ground personnel, taking to the Burma Road in trucks and other vehicles. "The departing travelers," observed Russell Whelan in his story of the group, "shed no tears as they looked their last on Toungoo, that suburb of Gehenna."

Kunming was no Garden of Eden either, although the AVG base had been rather sumptuously appointed with fine living quarters, a library, a good hospital, tennis courts, and a baseball diamond (Chennault was an ardent proponent of physical conditioning). But Kunming, capital of the Yunnan province, had been bombed by the Japanese just prior to the arrival of the Americans. With a population of more than 500,000, Kunming was an enticing target for Japanese Army air units based in French Indo-China. From former French air bases formations of Kates, escorted either by Claudes or Zeros, came over to bomb Kunming, and like most oriental cities, it burned with a lovely light, or so it appeared to those flying safely above the shambles. It was this destruction, rather than a quaint Chinese city, that the Flying Tigers first saw when they came to the Yunnan province.

The following day, December 19, 1941, was uneventful while the 1st Squadron waited impatiently in the ready shack. The next morning the Adam and Eves took the morning patrol—five P-40s and Squadron Leader Robert Sandell in his plane. But the sky remained clear of the enemy. The six men, tense, almost disgusted by the inaction, landed to refuel. It was then that the radio crackled and word came through that a formation of Mitsubishis (Sallys) appeared to be headed for Kunming and were then about sixty miles away. Chennault immediately ordered Newkirk and three others of his Panda Bear squadron up to protect the field. As soon as Newkirk sighted the enemy formation, he radioed Chennault, who then dispatched Sandell and thirteen others to intercept.

Within moments the Flying Tigers and the Japanese met in battle for the first time. The bombers, confident after so many uncontested months, had no fighter escort. The Tigers approached the Sallys from above—the Japanese planes unconcernedly flying in a beautiful flat-V formation. Sandell had spotted "ten enemy two-engined bombers, single tail, aluminum construction—and that red sun on the wing tips." The Tigers, as per Chennault's teaching, attacked in pairs, leaving a "weaver" above to look out for the unexpected appearance of fighters.

At Sandell's signal the dozen P-40s pounced upon the neat Japanese formation. Fritz E. Wolf (Shawano, Wisconsin) "attacked the outside bomber of the V. Diving down below him, I came up underneath, guns ready for the minute I could get in range. At 500 yards I let go with a quick burst from all my guns [four .30 caliber in the wings and two .50s in the upper nose]. I could see my bullets rip into the rear gunner. My plane bore in closer. At 100 yards I let go with a burst into the bomber's gas tanks and engine. A wing folded and a motor tore loose. Then the bomber exploded. I yanked back on the stick to get out of the way and went upstairs. . . ."

Selecting another bomber, Wolf dived down again. Pulling up behind he watched the Japanese rear gunner frantically firing, but felt no hits. He closed in to within fifty yards before letting loose with his full battery of guns, concentrating on one of the Mitsubishi's engines. Flame and smoke wisped into the slipstream, followed by a blossom of fire, and the Japanese bomber was ripped to pieces in a violent orange-red explosion. Wolf kicked rudder and dived away from the massive zone of flame and debris.

The Tigers swooped into the bomber formation from all directions, confusing the gunners but not disrupting the symmetry of the formation itself. Chennault had been right, the Japanese flew almost mechanically. When a bomber fell burning, another plane gracefully moved in to tighten the formation.

In an attack on the formation Edward Rector

Edward Rector of Marshall, North Carolina (in a post-Flying Tiger portrait), flight leader of the 2nd ("Panda Bears") Pursuit Squadron. Rector remained with the Flying Tigers even after it was officially disbanded in 1942.

(U. S. OFFICE OF WAR INFORMATION)

(Marshall, North Carolina) sliced under the Mitsubishis, got one, and took a burst of fire himself. His smoking Tomahawk was last seen by other Tigers under control; obviously Rector was seeking an emergency landing place. There were few of these in the thick jungle below.

Finally, after perhaps twenty minutes or so, with ammunition gone, or guns jammed, the Tigers, excepting Rector, returned to the Kunming base. They had lost one, but the Japanese had lost six, and even some of the remaining four Mitsubishis limped back toward Hanoi trailing smoke. It was a very good score, but Chennault's laconic comment was, "It was a good job . . . next time get them all."

A search party went out to look for Rector but had to return empty-handed when darkness enveloped the jungle. The next morning Rector himself phoned from a nearby town. He had crash-landed the P-40 in the jungle, had somehow managed to

Arvid E. Olson, Jr., Los Angeles, California, squadron leader of the 3rd ("Hell's Angels") Pursuit Squadron, AVG. (U. S. OFFICE OF WAR INFORMATION)

find his way to the town, and was on his way back to Kunming with only minor injuries. The first Tiger encounter with the Japanese had proved an almost total victory. But Chennault cautioned them; the next time there would be fighter escort. But they had learned, too, of the Japanese aircraft's susceptibility to fire because of the lack of self-sealing fuel tanks.

Meanwhile, a thousand miles away in Rangoon, the men of the Hell's Angels fretted, anxious about the presence of the Japanese. Certainly Burma lay in the path of the conquering juggernaut of Japan. The victories at Kunming only galled them more. Finally, on the morning of December 23, 1941, the not very efficient air raid sirens of Rangoon sounded, but after the exciting scramble no bombers appeared in the sky. Before noon the sirens wailed again. Antiaircraft fire was seen bursting irregularly in the sky over Rangoon, and the distant *chunk* of bombs bursting on the ground signaled that the Japanese planes had truly arrived.

At Mingaladon airdrome the Tigers and the RAF roared into action: about twenty-seven Allied aircraft, P-40s and Buffalos, swept up to meet the bombers. The first wave consisted of eighteen bombers and the second of about thirty. The latter was escorted by a large swarm of twenty Zeros.

The Tigers leaped upon the second formation, concentrating upon the bombers, hoping to disrupt their formations before they could release their bomb loads. The British pilots, in their Buffalos, gallantly went for the Zeros. First blood of the bomber formation went to Kenneth Jernstedt (Yamhill, Oregon), who destroyed one of the bombers in his first diving attack. His wingman was Henry Gilbert (Lovell, Wyoming), at twenty-one the youngest of the Flying Tigers. As he dived Gilbert shot out bursts at a couple of bombers, striking them but without hitting vital spots. In the attack, his P-40 was hit by a cannon shell and screamed out of the battle to crash into the jungle below. There had been no parachute and Henry Gilbert was the first Flying Tiger to die in combat.

The second fatality came soon after. Charles Older (Los Angeles) had flared one of the bombers, which burst into an inferno of detonating ammunition and bombs. Neil Martin's (Texarkana, Arkansas) P-40 flew into the spewing mass and followed the wreckage of the bomber to the ground.

Older by then had whirled about to shoot another bomber out of the air, which had become turbulent, fiery, and confused as fighter attacked bomber and fighter attacked fighter. The Zeros joined in the tumbling and soon Tiger Paul Greene (Glendale, California) found himself beset by Zeros. The nimble craft danced around him, firing into the P-40 until the plane took fire. Greene swooped the P-40 onto its back and dropped out of the cockpit. But once his chute had opened, one of the Zeros had flipped around to deal with Greene, dangling helplessly in the chute. Frantically grabbing at the chute risers, Greene managed to avoid the bullets, but the chute itself was holed. As a result Greene landed so forcefully that he injured his spine.

Greene's plane, of course, was lost, as were those of Gilbert and Martin. Another, piloted by George McMillan, was wiped out when he came in for a landing, although he escaped injury. The Tigers, therefore, had lost two men and four aircraft in their first air battle over Rangoon. Five RAF Buffalos, with pilots, had fallen to Japanese guns. The Japanese lost six bombers (probably with five-man crews) and four fighters. It was, then, a victory for the Tigers and the RAF. But Rangoon had been heavily bombed by the first wave of bombers. Fires raged and the toll was high—at least two thousand killed. The looting of corpses and sacking of dwellings in the bombed-out sections of the city somehow seemed more horrifying than the merciless bombing itself. The Burmese harbored little fidelity to the English and loved the Indians and Chinese only a little more.

Two days later, Christmas Day 1941, the Japanese returned. There was scant advance warning, for the single radar unit then operating in Burma was hardly sufficient (to say the least) and was further burdened by out-of-date equipment and an inefficient telephone service.

To circumvent this handicap, Squadron Leader Arvid Olson had put up a trio of P-40s for aerial reconnaissance. George McMillan, who had lost a plane in the battle two days before, sighted a large bomber force approaching Rangoon. About sixty miles from the city, there were about eighty bombers and twenty fighters. McMillan immediately radioed the base; at about the same moment the RAF received its report.

Thirteen P-40s and fifteen Buffalos were rushed aloft in an attempt to gain altitude before the bombers reached the city. About ten miles from Rangoon, the Japanese force divided—about half proceeding on to Rangoon and the rest heading for Mingaladon airdrome. The Tigers dived at the stream heading for the city, leaving the RAF's Buffalos the thirty or so bombers aiming for Mingaladon.

The Tigers, employing Chennault's hit-and-run technique, knifed through the bomber formation at top speed, snapping bursts into the Japanese aircraft and avoiding entanglement with the Zeros as much as possible. Within minutes of their first assault, five Japanese bombers blazed into the rice paddies below. But almost immediately another formation hove into view, this time twenty bombers with eight fighters. There was no lack of targets: a total of 28 Allied planes opposed 108 Japanese bombers and fighters.

Robert Smith (Los Angeles), having dived through the initial formation, had no time to gain altitude, so he attacked the new wave from below. The Nakajima practically blew up in Smith's face, pockmarking his P-40 with bits of engine. The Tomahawk staggered momentarily but Smith got it under control and dived into the battle again. Edmund Overend (Coronado, California) was not as fortunate. Although he had succeeded in ripping the

wing off one of the bombers, he had run into gunfire which jammed his controls and interfered with his maneuverability. A Zero darted onto his tail and Overend had good reason to be grateful for the armor plating which lined the back of the cockpit. Exploiting this safety factor, plus the P-40's diving speed, he left his attacker behind. But then he realized he did not have enough fuel for the return flight to Mingaladon. Rather than abandon the plane, Overend set the P-40, wheels up, into a swamp. Within hours he was back at the airdrome to learn of the battle's outcome.

Of the thirteen Tomahawks which had taken off, eleven had returned to Mingaladon, including one piloted by Parker Dupouy (Farmingdale, New York) with four feet of wing gone. When his guns jammed, Dupouy had a Zero on his tail. Kicking the P-40 around abruptly, Dupouy rid himself of the harassing fighter by colliding with it. The Zero collapsed and fell, but Dupouy made it back to the base.

Like Overend, George McMillan had been knocked out of the battle but had crashed into the jungle and returned on the following day, nursing an injured ankle, in an oxcart. In exchange for the two P-40s, the Tigers were officially credited with destroying thirteen bombers and ten fighters. Other Japanese aircraft had also been destroyed but fell into the Gulf of Martaban and could not be confirmed. The RAF pilots were credited with six bombers and the thwarting of serious damage to the base. The cost to No. 67 Squadron was five pilots and their Buffalos. The total Japanese loss was at least twenty-nine aircraft, most of them bombers, or about a third of the attacking force. It was a most disproportionate exchange.

However, the Christmas Day bombing of Rangoon proved even more vicious than that of December 23, the casualty toll reaching as high as five thousand dead. But Japanese losses impressed the enemy and large bomber formations stayed away from Rangoon for a while. During this uneasy period thousands fled the city, causing near paralysis of its functions and vital services—including the movement of supplies up to the Burma Road. But in time a local paper could announce a return to near normality with: "Daylight robberies have started again."

During the lull Olson's 3rd Squadron was relieved

Pilots race for their P-40s. (These are not, of course, Flying Tigers, but the base is in China and re-creates the action of a Tiger interception.) (U. S. AIR FORCE)

by Newkirk's 2nd (Panda Bear) Squadron, which arrived at Mingaladon by December 29, 1941. The Japanese bombers and fighters came back in force on the same day. Again a handful of Tigers in their P-40s and the British in their lumbering Buffalos rose to meet the formations, which as on Christmas Day split in two to strike at both Rangoon and Mingaladon. The bombers this trip, however, succeeded in getting to the air base in addition to contributing to the panic and waste in Rangoon. But again the losses for the Japanese were off balance, the Tigers claiming eighteen and the British seven. One P-40 flown by Allen Christman (Fort Collins, Colorado) was lost in the encounter, but Christman parachuted to safety. The RAF lost six pilots with their planes. By this time the Americans had begun to appreciate the ruggedness of the P-40s and no longer envied the British in their Buffalos.

Burma had become an aerial thorn in the side to the Japanese. All other aerial battlefields—over the Philippines, Malaya, Hong Kong—were dominated by Japanese bombers and the superb Zero fighters. Only the "American renegades" and a squadron of the RAF Buffalos (rapidly depleting) seemed capable of spoiling the succession of Japanese victories.

The Japanese closed the year with a change in tactics. First a small formation came over to lure off the Tigers and the RAF, and then a larger formation would follow at about the time the defenders would have to return to the ground to refuel and rearm. There was more concentration also on Mingaladon. On the first attempt seventeen Allied planes were dispatched to fend off about sixty Japanese attackers. Fifteen of these, officially, did not return to their base at Hanoi.

By January 1, 1942, the Flying Tigers had sixty confirmed victories to their credit. It prompted a tribute to them, and to Chennault, via Radio Tokyo: "We warn the American aviators at Rangoon that they must cease their unorthodox tactics immediately, or they will be treated like guerrillas and shown no mercy whatsoever." Radio Tokyo also inflated the forces of the AVG—man and planes; the victory claims over them, if true, would have wiped out Chennault's small band three or four times over.

But they were not supermen. At besieged Rangoon hunger was added to their other discomforts, among which were fatigue and illness. And they contributed further to their fame as "no angels" in the bars of Rangoon, which seemed more impervious to the ill fortunes of war than most other businesses. It became a tiresome war, almost without purpose and without hope of victory. To the men in Burma it seemed obvious that their fate was but a secondary consideration in the larger strategies. Supplies, tools, materials of all kinds only trickled in. Their P-40s before long had become a patchwork of scraps. Engines, rejects to begin with, wheezed and smoked and maintenance became a heroic epic in itself.

The truth was that the China-Burma-India theater of operations did rank low on the priorities lists. Churchill and Roosevelt had met and resolved that the major enemy was Nazi Germany and that first considerations in terms of strategic thinking, men, and supplies would be devoted to that philosophy. The Pacific, meanwhile, was subsidiary, with the beleaguered China-Burma-India area at the bottom of the list. Even those supplies that were eked out for delivery on the Burma Road often were intercepted en route and "requisitioned" by other services and areas.

It was then with a feeling of being neglected stepchildren that the Flying Tigers took to the air day after day to fight overwhelming numbers of Japanese. Though they fought remarkably, miraculously well, the end, so far as Burma was concerned, was inevitable. Unknown to the Tigers, the political situation would affect them. Churchill had hoped to reinforce the British garrisons in Burma but to his

David L. "Tex" Hill of Hunt, Texas, squadron leader of the "Panda Bears" (2nd). Hill's score was more than a dozen Japanese aircraft.
(U. S. OFFICE OF WAR INFORMATION)

bitterness he was refused an Australian division which he had wanted to send to Burma. This left a Burmese army to confront the surging Japanese.

Late in December, Chiang Kai-shek, realizing what a Japanese invasion of Burma would mean to the Burma Road, offered to send Chinese troops to help in its defense. But Sir Archibald Wavell, the commander in Burma, demurred. He had no love for Chiang and little confidence in Chinese troops. He had other complexities, for the Burmese resented and detested the British as well as the Chinese, believing that such allies were a greater threat than the bringers of the Greater East Asia Co-Prosperity Sphere.

The Tigers, too, with the New Year, changed their tactics: they went over to the offensive. On January 3, 1942, John Newkirk led Noel Bacon (Randalia, Iowa) and David Hill (Hunt, Texas; Hill was, naturally, called "Tex") on a strafing mission. Leaving Mingaladon while it was still dark, the three Tigers swept in upon the Japanese base at Tak, Thailand (about two hundred miles east and slightly north of Rangoon). But as Newkirk gunned the Japanese planes parked along the runways, about a half-dozen enemy fighters, already air-borne, tumbled out of the clouds upon the attacking Tigers. One of the Japanese fighters attached itself to Newkirk's tail as he, unaware of it, hammered at the grounded aircraft. Bacon came to his leader's aid and began shooting at the plane shooting at Newkirk. In turn, Bacon was attacked and Tex Hill swooped in to his aid. Another Japanese fighter joined the train as Newkirk, leading a formation of shooting aircraft, gave his full attention to strafing the men and planes on the ground. So intent was he on his "work" that he was still unconscious of the drama unfolding in his wake. Bacon shot the fighter off Newkirk's tail and Hill cleared Bacon's tail and whipped around to destroy another Japanese fighter. Hill, however, had his share of problems, for a fuel tank had been punctured in such a manner that it did not seal and he was losing gas; in addition he was out of ammunition. Hill had to streak for home while Newkirk and Bacon continued strafing Tak. Soon they too pulled away and flew westward.

Upon landing at Mingaladon, they were greeted by Hill, who congratulated Newkirk upon his flying skill, which had so frustrated the Japanese fighter

James H. Howard, St. Louis, Missouri, squadron leader at one time of the "Panda Bears"; Howard later transferred to the Ninth Air Force in Europe (when this photograph was taken). (U. S. AIR FORCE)

on his tail over Tak. Newkirk found this unbelievable until he checked the tail section of the Tomahawk and found more than twenty bullet punctures in it.

While the three Tigers had been strafing Tak, others had intercepted a large formation of Japanese fighters near Rangoon. Two had gone down in an early attack, but five of them concentrated on Allen Christman's P-40. The deadly cross fire shredded the plane's rudder and ripped out an aileron. The plane lurched out of control so that Christman was for the second time forced to jump. But the Japanese, who so heartily condemned the "unorthodox tactics of the American renegades," were not finished with Christman. They bore down on him as he floated under his chute, gunning him as they flashed by. Seeing this, George Paxton (Abilene, Texas) rushed in to aid the helpless Christman. Although he succeeded in driving off the Japanese fighter, in the encounter Paxton was wounded in the arms and legs and had to leave for the base.

The other Tigers, infuriated by the attack upon Christman, attacked the remaining Japanese so ferociously that they drove them off. But this was only a temporary reprieve for Christman. Twenty days later—January 23, 1942—he was once again forced to leave his seriously damaged Tomahawk during an air battle and was later discovered dead in a rice paddy. He and his parachute were riddled.

Early in January, probably because of the mauling their formations took, the Japanese introduced another innovation: night bombing. None of the aircraft at Mingaladon were equipped for night flying, so the Japanese bombers came over, took careful aim, enjoyed a fine bomb run, and generally ranged over Rangoon unmolested. The only antiaircraft fire of any consequence came from the warships in the river—and these guns were of little use above three thousand feet. On January 8 an attempt was made to intercept the bombers, but it was a vain attempt. Also, in trying to land in the dark, Peter Wright, blinded by gushing hydraulic fluid from a damaged landing gear, lost control of the Tomahawk. The plane veered off the runway and skidded into a parked car. Wright was not seriously injured but Kenneth Merritt, who had been asleep in the vehicle, died in the flaming wreckage.

It was the day's second loss, for during a strafing attack upon Meshot airdrome, Charles Mott's Tomahawk, evidently hit by ground fire, streaked flame. Mott parachuted to safety—and imprisonment for the duration.

The next day's strafe proved more successful. Newkirk and four other Tigers, accompanied by six RAF Buffalos, paid a return visit to Tak. When all planes pulled away safely they left behind at least two dozen burned Japanese aircraft, three burned-out trucks, and a pocked, windowless administration building.

In mid-January Chennault sent reinforcements from Kunming. Robert Sandell flew down with five others of the 1st Squadron; among these was Gregory Boyington. Shortly after, an additional eight men flew in to bring relief to the exhausted men of 2nd Squadron.

Boyington was happy to be away from Kunming, where he had not endeared himself to Chennault's second-in-command, Harvey Greenlaw. Greenlaw's experiences in China, begun in 1932 with the arrival of the unofficial Jouett air mission, no doubt

*P-40s over the unfriendly, mountainous terrain of China,
the "theater of operations" of the Flying Tigers.*
(U. S. AIR FORCE)

made him useful to Chennault. Greenlaw's wife, Olga, was listed on the AVG roster as "War Diary Statistician." According to Boyington, her husband was not very popular with the pilots. He had acquired the rank of lieutenant colonel, in the Chinese Air Force, and had a penchant for threatening one and all with immediate court-martial for minor as well as major breaches in discipline. The Flying Tigers found discipline, except in the air, a most unimportant commodity in their forgotten theater of operations. Boyington could not bring himself to take Greenlaw and his threats seriously either. From time to time he found himself snarling at Greenlaw, "Get lost, Greenlaw, or I'll bend your teeth."

That there were personality problems among the Flying Tigers was of course normal, if not in keeping with the legend of dedication and self-sacrifice to the Cause as propounded in the semifictional newspaper accounts of the time. Considering their living and fighting conditions, it is surprising that they managed to fight at all—let alone not clash from time to time with one another. The Flying Tigers, they themselves would have conceded, had more than

their fair share of mavericks—it was the very nature of the unit. They even, though rarely, had a coward or two. Boyington must be included among the more colorful mavericks.

In his first encounter with the enemy, however, Boyington came away profoundly disappointed with himself. He had taken off as part of a ten-plane formation. Two of the planes, led by veteran Louis Hoffman (San Diego, California), at forty-three the oldest member of the Flying Tigers, served as top cover. The other eight, presumably led by another veteran, were to deal with any Japanese planes. It was too late when Boyington realized they were being led into combat for the first time by one of their own inexperienced number. They then stumbled upon a large formation, perhaps forty or fifty Japanese fighters with fixed landing gears (either Nates or Claudes), within minutes after taking off.

Their formation "leader" blindly led them directly beneath the Japanese planes flying about two thousand feet above them. Between the misled Tigers and the Japanese flew Hoffman and the other pilot, both oblivious to the danger overhead, assuming that the "leader" knew what he was doing.

Boyington, twisting his head, looked up in time to see the Japanese planes begin to peel off to dive

A helping hand: Chinese warn American pilots of the presence of Japanese aircraft in the vicinity. An elaborate if primitive but most effective warning system was devised by Chennault. If he received desultory co-operation from Chinese officials, Chennault was graciously treated by the Chinese people.

(U. S. AIR FORCE)

upon the P-40s. Hoffman's plane took a heavy pounding and fell straight down. The remaining Tigers scattered in all directions, like startled minnows. Suddenly Boyington found himself all alone in a wide, empty sky—except for Japanese fighter planes determined to shoot him out of it. Smarting under the ignominy of it, Boyington put the P-40's diving ability to full use: he ran for his life. Then he relearned something he forgot in the confusion of the moment: never try to outturn a lighter aircraft, or attempt to dogfight with a more maneuverable aircraft. Also, that day Boyington learned something they were not telling the folks back home. The Japanese were very skilled pilots who obviously did not suffer from myopia and could shoot.

Boyington fired at the darting little planes, but did not succeed in knocking one down. The rattle of return fire sounded ominously funereal. The P-40

tossed under the strike of an incendiary shell which came into the cockpit, pinking Boyington's arm— although he was not aware of it at the time. When he landed the shell stuck into his sleeve and had burned his arm slightly. Boyington was so upset by his performance that he hardly found the wound worth mentioning.

Hoffman had crashed near the field and was buried the next day; he had left a wife and two children. The day after that, January 28, 1942, Boyington, having been introduced to the facts of war, went into battle again. He was a member of the same formation, excepting Hoffman of course, that had been in the earlier battle. But this time he came in from above. Still terribly affected by the death of Hoffman, the Tigers fought savagely. Boyington destroyed two planes himself. During the battle he heard a voice over his radio shouting, "This is for

Cokey [Hoffman], you son of a bitch!" Sixteen Japanese aircraft never left the vicinity of Rangoon on that day.

To the residents of Rangoon, particularly the English colony, it was, as Boyington put it bitterly, "a bloody good show." But they lived in a vacuum and on borrowed time. Certain that the Empire would win the last round as it had always, according to tradition, they merely waited for that final day. They were unaware, or seemed to be, that the only battle being won was the small one in the air over Rangoon. On the ground the invading Japanese approached inexorably.

The last bastion of the Burra Sahib was the Mingaladon Golf Club, but even that fell to the invasion of boisterous young pilots, British and American. This was most disturbing, for the youngsters laughed loudly, shouted vulgarly, drank the whisky, and bought up the cigarettes. The managing member was approached by a delegation ordering him to see that the sale of cold beer and cigarettes to "the young roughnecks" be stopped. After all, he was reminded, "the members' needs must be considered first. If we sell our stocks to all these young fellows there'll be nothing left for the members."

The members were in fact running out of everything, including time.

On January 20, 1942, two divisions of the Japanese Fifteenth Army had crossed the Thai frontier at Moulmein; within ten days they had flanked the Indian division defending the area and had taken the city. The Japanese now had a firm foothold in Burma. The handwriting was on the clubhouse wall and the roof about to fall in.

Not until mid-February was it deemed crucial enough to accept Generalissimo Chiang Kai-shek's offer of aid, which took the form of two crack units, the Chinese Fifth and Sixth Armies. But it was already too late, even as they moved southward toward Rangoon. Also arriving too late was Lieutenant General Joseph W. Stilwell, who had been appointed chief of staff to Chiang Kai-shek. The outspoken, fifty-nine-year-old, gruff Stilwell, an expert in Chinese affairs (he spoke and wrote the language), was descending into a political-military miasma. There was little love lost between Chiang Kai-shek (and of course the Madame) and the British, who were, in fact, doing most of the fighting in the theater.

III

High-level decisions also spelled trouble for Chennault. Plans had already been made to establish a Tenth U. S. Air Force in the China-Burma-India theater with Brigadier General Clayton Bissell in command. The Flying Tigers would, it was proposed, be absorbed into this command as the 23rd Fighter Group. Chennault would then be subordinate to Bissell. Neither Chennault nor Chiang found this ideal. Quickly a feud between Bissell and Chennault developed. Stilwell, soon enough, found himself entangled in it besides developing an antipathy to Chiang and feuding, in turn, with Chennault also.

On February 14, 1942, Stilwell left the United States for this prickly assignment. There being yet no efficient Air Transport Command, his long voyage was confused, miserable, and meandering. On the day his plane took off from Miami for Africa, Singapore, the impregnable, fell to the Japanese. In his diary Stilwell had written, "Events are forcing all concerned to see the vital importance of Burma." By the time Stilwell landed in India, on February 25, the fall of Rangoon—and of Burma—was only days away. Perhaps Burma was of vital importance, but Stilwell had neglected to consider other elements besides Japanese terrorism—namely a crumbling colonialism, feudalism, and the infinite capacity for pettiness among the great.

The state of the tattered Flying Tigers at Rangoon was low too. "Where, oh where is the U. S. Army?" one Tiger noted in his diary. "Where, oh where is General Wavell? Does the First Squadron of the A.V.G. and a few R.A.F. kids have to handle the whole Japanese invasion?" Men as well as machines had begun to wear dangerously. Robert J. Sandell, commander of the 1st Squadron, was killed testing his newly repaired Tomahawk. Robert H. Neale (Seattle, Washington) succeeded Sandell as leader of the Adam and Eves, and now commanded the AVG effort in Burma. His command, in late February, consisted of ten weary pilots, nine overworked ground crew men, and seven wearier P-40s. The British had three Buffalos, four P-40s, and twenty Hurricanes.

The evacuation of Rangoon began in earnest around February 20, 1942, although it had initiated with the first bombings. Now the road to the north and the river were choked with refugees and every description of vehicle. The dacoits (professional thieves) preyed upon the refugees, Burmese as well as British, killing them for their few possessions and money. Rangoon itself was shambles.

O. D. Gallagher described the final blistering days: "With few exceptions the normal civilian population had gone, including the fire-brigade and all municipal employees. The empty streets were patrolled by troops carrying tommy-guns and rifles. The only other inhabitants were criminals, criminal lunatics and lepers."

One civil service officer, having misread his instructions pertaining to the evacuation of Rangoon, had inadvertently released five thousand convicts upon the already afflicted city. "At night," Gallagher recalled, "they made Rangoon a city of the damned. They prowled the deserted streets in search of loot. When they were seen looting they were shot by the soldiers." As for the diseased— "Lepers and lunatics wandered about aimlessly in search of food some sharing pickings of the refuse-heaps with the many mongrel dogs." Fires, set by looters or by the owners of property themselves who did not want the Japanese to take over their homes, raged through the city. Military demolition contributed to the holocaust. Ammunition, fuel, and other supplies which might be put to use by the Japanese went up in smoke. Looters destroyed medical supplies on the docks. It seemed to them there was no possible use for the small bottles except to throw them against walls of buildings. The more volatile liquids exploded and burned wastefully, chokingly, to the gleeful laughter of the now maddened Burmese.

This was the final deranged scene that the few remaining Tigers, the last defenders of Rangoon— for the British had pulled out three days before —witnessed before they scrambled away to a new base at Magwe, farther north. Neale led a formation of the few operational Tomahawks; the rest, pilots and ground crew under crew chief Harry Fox, piled themselves and their equipment into whatever trucks they could commandeer and took to the north road. In one of the last air battles over Rangoon Edward J. Liebolt's plane had been shot up so that he had to take to his parachute. He floated down into captivity, for by then Japanese troops had all but encircled Rangoon.

Rangoon fell on March 7, 1942; at Magwe the Tigers and the RAF dug in. The remnants of the Burma Army escaped up the Irrawaddy River toward Prome. The Chinese armies coming south were still of no help. Chiang and Stilwell had an early disagreement over the disposition of these troops: Chiang believed they should attempt to hold Mandalay; Stilwell thought it would be better to reinforce the British farther south and to keep, if possible, the Japanese from ever getting to Mandalay.

By March 20 reconnaissance planes reported that Japanese planes were already based at Mingaladon. The British quickly dispatched ten old Hurricanes and nine Blenheims to bomb their former base. Arriving unexpectedly the small force succeeded in destroying sixteen planes on the ground and, in the ensuing air battle, a further eleven in the air. Of these, two were knocked down by the Blenheims. It was a blow in the face to the conquering Japanese.

Retaliation came the following day and continued into the next. On the morning of March 21, with but little advance warning, the first wave of ten Japanese bombers, with an escort of twenty fighters, came over Magwe. Five planes rose to meet them, three Tigers (William Reed, Kenneth Jernstedt, and Parker Dupouy) and two Hurricanes. Even as their engines labored to get the five aircraft high enough to meet the attackers, more enemy bombers and fighters came in from the northeast. Bomb bursts erupted on the airdrome as the Tigers dived into the Japanese formations.

Dupouy, on his first pass, slashed a Zero out of a seven-plane formation, only to find himself besieged by the remaining six. These whirred and darted about his P-40 until Dupouy himself was struck. He dived for Magwe. Reed had already suffered the same fate and had returned to the field also. Jernstedt careened into a formation of ten bombers, the guns of which focused on his plane and rapidly sieved it, wounding the pilot. Jernstedt too was forced to return to the doubtful "safety" of besieged Magwe.

Soon, also, one of the Hurricanes came scurrying in, attempted to set down on the bomb-pocked runway, struck a hole, overturned, and came to a grinding crash near a slit trench occupied by some of the Tigers. Frank N. Swartz (Dunmore, Pennsylvania), John Fauth (Red Lion, Pennsylvania), and a ground crew man, William Seiple, scrambled from the trench to pull the British pilot out of the Hurricane. As they ran a bomb explosion caught them and all three went down. Dr. Lewis Richards, surgeon of the Tigers, left the trench to administer to Swartz, who appeared to be injured most seriously. Richards then had Fauth and Seiple pulled into the trench and he, despite the bursting bombs and strafing Zeros, placed Swartz into a jeep and raced to the base hospital. Fauth died the next morning and Swartz and Seiple were evacuated to Calcutta, but Swartz later died of his wounds. Magwe itself was a ruin—besides damage to the buildings and runways, six P-40s, eight Hurricanes and three Blenheims had gone up in smoke.

The next day brought more of the same; remaining at Magwe was pointless. Some of the Tigers flew their flyable aircraft farther north to Loiwing. The RAF remained longer in a vain attempt to hold off the Japanese but they too were quickly overwhelmed. More planes were damaged and five of the surviving P-40s had to be evacuated to Loiwing by truck. The British fled to the west, to Akyab on the Bay of Bengal and eventually to India, out of harm's way, to attempt a recovery. Except for the few impoverished Tigers at Loiwing, it was the end of air power in Burma.

Driven out of Burma, the RAF flew to India and the Tigers returned to Kunming. Chennault then planned a surprise raid on the major Japanese air base at Chiengmai in central Thailand. To accomplish this, Chennault mustered a handful of men and aircraft of the 1st Squadron, led by Robert Neale, and the 2nd Squadron, led by John Van Kuren Newkirk: a total of ten P-40s.

Chiengmai lay beyond the range of the P-40 so the Tigers flew to a nearly deserted advance field at Nam Sang on March 23, and slept that night under the wings of their planes. They had gassed up for a long flight and took off in two sections before daybreak of the twenty-fourth. The plan was to rendezvous near Chiengmai (rather than approach it en masse, which would alert the Japanese) and then swoop down upon the base while it was still dark. The ground would be discernible from the air, though the Tigers' P-40s would be difficult to see from the ground.

For some reason the two groups missed the rendezvous. Neale's small unit of six planes arrived first, but there was no sign of Newkirk and his men. They were unable to wait: both the covering dark-

ness and surprise would be lost. Neale ordered William D. McGarry and Edward Rector up to twenty thousand feet to provide high cover and then, leading Boyington, William Bartling, and Charles Bond, dived on a fine concentration of Japanese aircraft below.

At twelve thousand feet they were met with vicious antiaircraft fire. Plunging through, luckily unhit, the four P-40s, their engines howling and guns chattering, spread fire among the planes and running figures. Flames shot up in their wake as they pulled up, banked, and came in for another pass. Now the field was alight with the fire of burning planes and they could better see their targets. But with more light also came more intense ground fire. Rifle and machine-gun slugs nicked and ripped at the Tomahawks.

To McGarry and Rector, observing the inferno from above, the excitement was too much to ignore. When the original quartet dived in for a third pass, the top-cover men plummeted down to contribute also. With all six guns hammering, the two extra Tomahawks intensified the flaming havoc as they ran the gamut of heavy ground fire. At least twenty fires were burning on the field and Neale knew it was time to get away. As they did the sky puffed with random bursts of antiaircraft.

McGarry obviously was in trouble, for his P-40 trailed smoke as they left Chiengmai. Though he tried desperately to keep the plane in flight, McGarry realized that with rapidly failing oil pressure he had no chance. But they were still fifty miles from the Salween River, inside Thailand. On the other side of the river lay the safety of the Chinese troops, but the oil pressure went completely and McGarry inverted the plane and parachuted into the jungle. (He was captured by the Siamese and turned over to the Japanese and remained a prisoner until the war ended.)

Meanwhile Newkirk, realizing that he and the Panda Bears had missed the rendezvous with the Adam and Eves, decided that they could attack another, nearby field while the 1st Squadron attended to Chiengmai. But they found no aircraft on the satellite airdrome so Newkirk pulled away and headed for Chiengmai also. On the way they strafed a railroad station, setting some warehouses afire. Newkirk then spotted two armored cars on a road. They were tempting targets and so, followed by Henry Geselbracht and Frank Lawlor, Newkirk dived upon the cars with all guns shuddering the P-40. As he shot over the cars, Newkirk's plane suddenly gushed flame. The stricken Tomahawk hurtled into the ground at full speed, trailing fire and molten metal, scorching a trail through the jungle before it came to rest, a blazing mass of crumpled metal. His wingmen found it hard to accept the death of "Scarsdale Jack" Newkirk, who had led the 2nd Squadron from the inception of the Flying Tigers. For miles, as they returned to China, they could see his black funeral pyre curling out of the green jungle of Thailand.

Newkirk's successor as commander of the 2nd

Kweilin, China, the last—and best—major base of the Flying Tigers. It had a mile-long runway, revetments for the protection of parked aircraft, and caves in the hills for men and machines. (U. S. AIR FORCE)

Somewhere in China: Lieutenant General Henry H. Arnold, Brigadier General Claire Chennault, his antagonist Lieutenant General Joseph Stilwell, British Field Marshal Sir John Dill, and Brigadier General Clayton L. Bissell. The latter's position in the China-Burma-India theater was a delicate one since he was placed in command over the veteran, and favorite of Chiang Kai-shek, Chennault. Bissell's careful attention to details in his planning earned him the nickname of "Old Woman" among the Chinese, accustomed to Chennault's more hell-for-leather approach. (U. S. AIR FORCE)

Squadron was James H. Howard (St. Louis, Missouri), an ex-Navy pilot of remarkable courage. Soft-spoken, undemonstrative, Howard had made an early impression upon the RAF pilots one day when he singlehandedly plowed into a large formation of Japanese fighters. Howard took his service in the Flying Tigers seriously; he had been born in China.

But they were locked obviously in a losing battle and, despite the Tiger victories, still remarkably disproportionate, the battle had come to seem so aimless. For every Japanese plane destroyed, another ten appeared to take its place. But there were no replacements for the Tigers—and new planes were hard to come by. A few P-40Es (Kittyhawks) had trickled in, but that was all. Exhausted, ill, or depressed, or just simply sickened by conditions, pilots and ground crew men resigned or were "dismissed."

Boyington was one of those who had his fill of fighting for Madame Chiang's China. A six-victory ace, he decided to get out and to have his commission in the Marine Corps reinstated—as had been secretly agreed upon when he signed up for the AVG. Chennault did not take an enlightened view of Boyington's wish to return to his old branch of the service. Boyington left, nonetheless, and worked his way homeward. He found, upon arriving at Karachi, India, requesting transportation by air, that Chennault, instead of authorizing air travel to the United States for Boyington, suggested that the black sheep be drafted into the Tenth Air Force as a second lieutenant. Boyington, steaming, booked passage on a ship bound for New York. His subsequent career in the Marine Corps speaks for itself, though he may have gone on the rolls of the Flying Tigers as a "deserter."

Chennault had other, more serious burdens as

well. The Burma Road was closed (necessitating the flying of supplies over "the Hump" of the Himalaya Mountains between India and China); Chiang Kai-shek and Stilwell detested each other; Madame Chiang demanded more help from the United States, broadly hinting from time to time of making a separate peace with Japan; and then there was Bissell, who would command the Tenth Air Force and Chennault along with it.

Bissell had appeared at Kunming to give a recruiting lecture which proved ill-timed and badly worded. Resentful, morale at low ebb, some of the Tigers trained a young Chinese boy to greet the ever growing number of Air Corps planes carrying brass with the phrase "Piss on Bissell, piss on Bissell." It did not impress Very Important Persons on the arriving aircraft with the state of American military discipline in China.

Chennault and Stilwell too had their disagreements, partly a question of rank (Stilwell being Chennault's superior), as well as the traditional hostility between the ground-oriented soldier and the air expert. Chennault had certainly proved himself, but Stilwell had little faith in the piecemeal air force at his disposal in Burma and China. Crusty and stubborn, he even refused to be evacuated by air from Burma with the Japanese hard on his trail. "The Air Force didn't bring me here," he declared, "and it doesn't have to fly me out. I'll walk." And he did.

"It's the ground soldier," he snapped at Chennault one day, "slogging through the mud and fighting in the trenches who will win the war!"

"But God damn it, Stilwell," Chennault rasped in cogent reply, "there aren't any men in the trenches!"

The men of the Flying Tigers, also, found conditions more and more difficult to take. Dispirited, wearied, repelled by Chinese corruption and indifference to loss of life, they became more disgruntled and found their sacrifices difficult to reconcile with their achievements.

Their relationship with Chennault even deteriorated and at one point, in a disagreement with an order from Chennault (to make a flight over Chinese troops to improve their morale), twenty-eight out of thirty-four Tigers resigned. Whereupon Chennault threatened to have anyone who attempted to leave Loiwing shot. Chennault later reconsidered and the

U. S. Air Force General Henry Arnold visits Chennault in China, shortly after the Flying Tigers had been disbanded. (U. S. AIR FORCE)

resignations were withdrawn, but the mood of the Tigers remained dismal.

It was the irascible Stilwell who summed up the Burma experience: "I claim we got a hell of a beating. We got run out of Burma and it was humiliating as hell. I think we ought to find out what caused it, go back and retake it."

The Tigers, withdrawn to Kunming, existed in military limbo. Their planes were barely operational and some pilots refused to fly them. They speculated upon their future—if any, in the Tenth Air Force. Many only wanted to return to their homes for a while before considering their military future. By May 1942 it seemed that they could contribute so little, with their few planes and exhausted men, to the war in China.

Meanwhile, U. S. Army Air Force brass had also invaded China. Some, men newly from civilian ranks, assumed that the "famous" Flying Tigers were bound to be a "bunch of prima donnas." As the day of contract expirations approached pressure was applied on both pilots and ground crews to transfer over to the U.S. air forces. One particularly arrogant recruitment speech, the gist of which was roughly: "join up now or be drafted a private as soon as your contracts expire," caused a small incident. Many Tigers simply got up and walked out on the high ranker with his mouth open. Such men, fresh from the States, eager to avenge Pearl Harbor, anxious to get on with the war, and undoubtedly a bit envious of the reputation and the actual achievements of the Flying Tigers, could not comprehend the weariness of the Tigers, or their anxiety to get home just once again before "getting on with the war," to recover from nagging illnesses caused by overwork, various tropical diseases, and malnutrition. When disbandment time came they simply wanted to go home for a while.

Radio Tokyo jubilated over the approaching end of the Tigers. A quick dispatch of their replacements in the green Tenth Air Force was joyously predicted by Tokyo Rose. But a transition had been in progress for a long time and the interim would not prove to be as vulnerable a period as Tokyo believed. Chennault was to remain in command of what would be called the China Air Task Force (under Bissell's Tenth Air Force), which would consist of the 23rd Fighter Group and the 11th Bombardment Squadron (M). Chennault had already selected his commander for the 23rd Fighter Group: Colonel Robert Scott. Scott, a Transport Command pilot who had been stranded in China and who had attached himself to the Tigers. Although at thirty-four he was considered overaged for a fighter pilot, Scott had proved himself in fact a "one-man air force" while on missions with the Tigers and on solo hunts.

The bomber squadron was equipped with North American B-25s, the famed Mitchells of the Doolittle Tokyo raid. (Eventually, in March 1943, though not without acrimony and torment, the China Air Task Force evolved into the Fourteenth Air Force, Major General Claire Lee Chennault commanding; the Tenth Air Force then confined its responsibilities to Burma and India.)

The official day of deactivation of the American Volunteer Group was July 4, 1942. By this time it was known that very few of the original Tigers had decided to remain in the China Air Task Force —just five pilots, David Hill, Edward Rector, Charles Sawyer, John G. Bright, and Frank Schiel, Jr., plus a few of the ground crew—that was all. Several pilots, rather than transfer into the U. S. Army, found jobs in China with China National Airways and with aviation industries. Others returned to their homes to rest and then, if they passed their physicals—which many did not—returned to their old branch of service.

Twenty pilots, to confute Radio Tokyo, offered to remain on duty with the 23rd Fighter Group under Scott during the transitional period. During this time one of the veteran pilots, John E. Petach (Perth Amboy, New Jersey), was killed in a dive-bombing attack upon gunboats in a lake near Nanchang. Petach had married Emma Jane Foster (State College, Pennsylvania), who had served, along with Josephine Stewart (Dallas, Texas), as a nurse in the American Volunteer Group.

The 23rd Fighter Group, known also as the Flying Tigers, continued in the tradition of their predecessors in defense of the air route over the Hump (as once the original Tigers had defended the Burma

Robert Scott, ex-transport pilot turned Flying Tiger. During the final days of the AVG Scott roamed the skies with the Tigers or alone and left a pile of Japanese planes in his wake. Scott remained with Chennault to command the 23rd Fighter Group.

(U. S. AIR FORCE)

Men of the 23rd Fighter Group, heirs to the traditions of the Flying Tigers: Colonel C. D. Vincent, Major Albert J. Baumler, Colonel H. E. Strickland, and

Brigadier General Claire L. Chennault, commander of the China Air Task Force (later to form the nucleus of the Fourteenth Air Force). (U. S. AIR FORCE)

Road) and chopped away at Japanese air strength in the China-Burma-India theater. After Scott left for other duties other commanders took over, among them Colonel David Hill, and later, Colonel Edward Rector, of the original AVG.

In the brief span of its operational existence, officially from December 18, 1941, to July 4, 1942, the Flying Tigers had destroyed 286 (confirmed) Japanese aircraft. The true toll would probably be closer to double that number, for many "kills" were not officially accepted when enemy aircraft plunged into thick jungle or water and could not be found. But even the officially accepted figure represents a great loss in terms of planes and men—for most were bombers with multiple crews. The cost to the

AVG was nine pilots (not counting Petach, who was lost after the dissolution of the AVG) and less than fifty P-40s. An additional nine pilots were killed in flying accidents and four were listed as missing in action.

The major contribution of the Flying Tigers, besides proving Chennault's tactical genius, was in the revelation that Japanese aerial invincibility was an illusion. During the early months of the Pacific war, while British and American defenses crumbled, the Flying Tigers, outnumbered, ill equipped, even ill used, but resilient, fought the Japanese and won. That they had done this may have been, in time, even more important than their accredited 286 Japanese aircraft at $500 per head.

3

FIRST SPECIAL AVIATION PROJECT

Mᴀɴ's ᴄᴀᴘᴀᴄɪᴛʏ for "the bold undertaking" is infinite; the romanticism, not the risk, is all. The challenge of unfavorable odds merely increases incentive and, once initiated, the venture is confronted as if success must be the only possible outcome. Risk, motivation, questioning uncertainty—all are submerged in what appears to be the logic of preparation.

So it was with the unique Doolittle raid on Tokyo and other Japanese cities in the spring of 1942, a dismal spring in the wake of a series of Japanese victories in the Pacific. As an expression of human ingenuity, courage, audacity, and daring the Doolittle mission was an immortal feat; as military strategy it was evanescent—but of extensive impact.

Lieutenant Colonel James H. Doolittle, however, on the day after the raid sat dejectedly in the wreckage of the plane that he had had to abandon, certain he would be tried by a military court. All sixteen aircraft which had participated in the attack had been lost; of the eighty men he had led, Doolittle could account for only five. And one of them was himself.

II

To strike back at Japan was all but an obsession in high governmental and military circles in the weeks and months following the Pearl Harbor attack. President Franklin D. Roosevelt rarely missed an opportunity to bring it up during his sessions with the Chiefs of Staff. It was, however, simpler to dwell upon than to execute. There were no land-based bombers near enough to Japan to bomb it. Carriers could not venture near enough to the Japanese home islands to launch their fighters and scout bombers without risking the loss of carriers—as well as the aircraft. However alluring the conception, it appeared to remain impracticable until bases could be established in China, or even Russia. Obviously the Philippines were already lost.

But with all the talk of vengeance in the air, someone was bound to offer some kind of suggestion. This came from the U. S. Navy's Captain Francis S. Low, an operations officer on the staff of Admiral Ernest J. King, Chief of Naval Operations. Low's

Architect of the "First Special Aviation Project," Captain Francis S. Low, operations officer on the staff of Admiral Ernest J. King. Low was the first to offer practical suggestions for activating an idea which a nation shared after the attack on Pearl Harbor: a bombing raid on Tokyo.

(NAVY DEPT., NATIONAL ARCHIVES)

Implementer of the Low concept: Captain Donald W. Duncan, Admiral King's air officer. Duncan proved, on paper and within certain limitations, it was possible to send bombers to bomb Japan.

(NAVY DEPT., NATIONAL ARCHIVES)

idea hinged upon the possibility of finding a long-range medium Army bomber which could take off from the deck of a carrier. Thus could a striking force be launched beyond the danger zone around Japan, keeping the vulnerable carrier out of the reach of bombers. This was an impetuous, perhaps quixotic, but appealing conception—even to the hardheaded King. He sent Low to see his air officer, Captain Donald W. Duncan, on the following day, a Sunday, to explore the probabilities further. King also cautioned Low to speak to no one else of the idea.

The two men met on January 11, 1942. Duncan immediately rejected one aspect of the idea. No bomber, not even a medium, could possibly land on a carrier deck. They required a long runway

and did not come equipped with arrester hooks for carrier landings. But it was possible that such a bomber, fueled and bombed-up, could take off from a carrier, complete its mission, and (thanks to its range) continue on to bases on land.

The plane Duncan had in mind was the North American B-25 (Mitchell), and the carrier, the recently commissioned *Hornet*. He would, however, need to work out the details before offering any real suggestions. Five days later Duncan emerged with thirty handwritten pages (the subject matter being too sensitive to entrust to a secretary for typing) of closely reasoned computations. Weather, winds, range, bomb loads, fuel, number of aircraft, minimum take-off run, and a dozen other complexities had been carefully worked out by Duncan.

Admiral King, who was not easily impressed, *was* impressed with Duncan's work. He then ordered Low and Duncan to approach Lieutenant General Henry H. Arnold, Commanding General of the Army Air Forces, with the idea. He saw them on the next day, January 17, and the subject of their visit must have proved a bit startling to Arnold. On January 4, 1942, for example, he had composed a memorandum upon returning from a White House meeting, part of which read: "We will have to try bomber take-offs from carriers. It has never been done before but we must try out and check on how long it takes." (This was relative to the coming invasion of north Africa and not to an attack upon Japan, however.) The memo went to the War Plans Division of the Army Air Forces for study, but before Arnold had heard from his staff, here were two Navy men confronting him with the idea and assuring him it could be done.

Arnold was most enthusiastic over the idea and promptly called King to settle the division of responsibility and to get things under way. King selected Captain Duncan as the Navy co-ordinator and Arnold agreed to provide a man to undertake the Air Force's end of the project. This was not difficult —the one man who had the flying skill, the technical background, and a love of derring-do was James H. Doolittle of Arnold's staff. One of the great aviation pioneers, Doolittle combined aerial swashbuckling with scholarship. He had received several trophies for breaking records in speed flights, for aerobatics, and for more scientific contributions such as taking off, flying, and landing a plane without ever seeing out of the plane's cockpit. He had served in the Army Air Corps and had a Doctor of Science degree from the Massachusetts Institute of Technology. Resigning from the Air Corps in 1930 (he had enlisted in 1917), Doolittle became manager of the aviation department of the Shell Oil Company. He was recalled to active duty, with the commission of major, in July 1940. Doolittle's job was to work with the auto industries then converting to defense industries. Early in 1942 he was called to Washington to serve on Arnold's staff as a special trouble shooter. One of his first problems was the myth of the "Widow Maker," the pilot's name for the Martin B-26 (Marauder). Doolittle proved that this fast, effective medium bomber was no killer and that pilots properly trained could handle it. He had just about

completed this assignment when Arnold called him into his office to ask an odd question.

"Just what airplane," he began, "have we got that will get off in five hundred feet with a two thousand bomb load and fly two thousand miles?"

No maker of snap judgments, Doolittle informed his chief he would have to give the problem some consideration. Upon returning the following day he told Arnold that either one of two planes just might do it. The Douglas B-23 or the North American B-25 with modifications seemed the most likely.

Arnold offered one more condition. "The plane must take off from a narrow area not more than seventy-five feet wide."

"Well," Doolittle told him, "then the only answer is the B-25. It has a sixty-seven-foot wing span."

The man selected by General Arnold to lead the raid on Tokyo: James H. Doolittle, here standing beneath the nose of a Martin "Marauder," which he had proved was an outstanding aircraft. (U. S. AIR FORCE)

The span of the B-23 spread to ninety-three feet, much too wide for a carrier deck.

Only then did Arnold tell Doolittle what it was all about. He and King had agreed that a Navy task force would move out with the bombers around the first of April. Doolittle was to train the crews and supervise whatever modifications might be required which could enable the B-25s to take off a carrier deck, say within four or five hundred miles off Japan, bomb various military targets, and continue on to land bases in China or Russia.

Doolittle, characteristically, went into immediate action. He flew to Wright Field, near Dayton, Ohio, to confer with Brigadier General George C. Kenney, commander of the Air Corps Experimental Division and Engineering School. Kenney and his staff were given the task of preparing the B-25B aircraft for a mission about which they knew absolutely nothing. However, they too attacked the problem of designing new fuel tanks, bomb shackles, and other innovations for the planes. Soon after Doolittle wrote

a memo to Arnold: "The work of installing the required additional tankage is being done by Mid-Continent Airlines in Minneapolis. All production and installation is progressing according to schedule and the 24 airplanes (6 spares) should be completely converted by March 15th."

At the same time other work progressed. By the end of January Brigadier General Carl Spaatz, then serving as Arnold's deputy for intelligence, had furnished a list of ten likely target cities, among which were Tokyo, Yokohama, Kobe, and Nagoya. As for the Navy's role Captain Duncan had arranged for the *Hornet* to be in San Francisco by April 1. Near Norfolk, on February 2, Duncan had stood with Captain Marc A. Mitscher, commander of the *Hornet,* to observe an experiment. The day before, two Army B-25s were hoisted aboard and after being taken out to sea the two Mitchells, piloted by Lieutenants John E. Fitzgerald and James F. McCarthy, proved that a two-engined medium bomber could indeed be flown off the deck of an aircraft carrier.

Admiral Chester A. Nimitz, Commander in Chief, Pacific Fleet (left), who approved of the Special Avia- *tion Project and assigned Vice-Admiral William Halsey (right) and the carrier* Enterprise *to the mission.*
(NATIONAL ARCHIVES)

Upon accomplishing this epochal feat, the two young pilots, mystified, returned to their landlocked base wondering why they had done what they had done.

Duncan later flew out to Hawaii to meet with Admiral Chester W. Nimitz, Commander in Chief, Pacific Fleet, and to arrange for more hands. Nimitz, who approved of the project, assigned Vice-Admiral William Halsey to it, thus adding a second carrier, the *Enterprise,* to the armada. Before he left for San Francisco to confer with Mitscher (and finally to tell him what it was all about), Duncan wired Arnold: *Tell Jimmy to Get on His Horse.* It was the signal for Doolittle and his crews to head for California.

Doolittle had begun assembling his crews immediately after initiating the modification program on the B-25s. All crews came from the three squadrons of the 17th Bombardment Group and its cognate, the 89th Reconnaissance Squadron. These units were not special, hand-picked combat veterans (although some had had experience with dealing with submarine patrols); they were simply the most experienced with the relatively new Mitchell bomber. In other words, they were not an elite unit, but a typical Air Force assemblage of men. However, upon being informed that volunteers were needed for a very hazardous but most important mission, the response was overwhelming. From these volunteers twenty-four crews were mustered and, under Major John A. Hilger (who was C.O. of the 89th Squadron and selected by Doolittle as his second-in-command), reported in at Eglin Field, Florida, by the first of March.

The B-25s to which these crews were assigned were not the planes they had known before. The fueslage interior looked like a Rube Goldberg invention and was crowded with extra fuel tanks in the bomb bay, in the crawlway between sections of the plane, and later even in the position where a belly turret had been originally installed. This lower turret gave so much trouble that Doolittle remarked, "A man could learn to play the violin good enough for Carnegie Hall before he could learn to fire that thing." The malfunctioning, jamming lower turret was pulled out to make room for a sixty-gallon collapsible rubber fuel tank. The one remaining turret, however, would plague the mission with its vagaries, and the added fuel tanks and fittings with theirs.

To save weight the large radios were removed; with radio silence essential the heavy radios would be of no use. For protective firepower the B-25 now had only the twin .50 machine guns in the upper turret and a single .30 in the nose. There had been no tail guns, an oversight attended to by Captain Charles Ross Greening, the mission's gunnery and bombing officer, who fashioned fake twin .50s from broomsticks, painted black and protruding menacingly from the tail. It was hoped these would be enough to discourage attack from the vulnerable rear.

Greening also contrived an ingenious bombsight. The famed Norden sight would not be of any use at the low altitude at which the attack was to be carried out; besides, the Air Force had little desire to risk so valuable an instrument upon so risky a mission. One at least would have been bound to have fallen into enemy hands. Therefore Greening devised a simple gadget, which he called the "Mark Twain," from about twenty cents worth (in 1942) of metal, which proved to be more accurate at the proposed fifteen-hundred-foot bombing altitude than the Norden.

On March 3 Doolittle arrived at Eglin and to an assembly of puzzled airmen said, "My name is Doolittle. I've been put in charge of the project you men have volunteered for. It's a tough one and it will be the most dangerous thing any of you have ever been on. Any man can drop out and nothing will ever be said about it."

Stressing the need for complete secrecy, Doolittle would not reveal to them the nature of their mission or their targets. They would have to follow him blindly and hope for the best—or drop out, as he had offered.

Then their special training began. This was characterized by another rather curious touch, the crews thought. Lieutenant Henry L. Miller, USN, an instructor from the Pensacola Naval Air Station, had come to teach them how to lift a heavily loaded B-25 off the ground within an impossibly short distance. This would require pulling the B-25 up in a dangerously near-stall attitude after a take-off run of about five hundred feet, about one tenth the distance they had been originally trained to use. But with few exceptions, under Miller's tutelage, they learned. Soon twenty-four pilots could yank the B-25 into the air, its tail wheel all but scraping the

Henry L. Miller, an instructor at Pensacola Naval Air Station who was given the job of teaching U. S. Army Air Force pilots how to take off from a carrier deck with a heavily laden bomber. (U. S. NAVY)

ground, some within less than four hundred feet.

While the pilots learned short-run take-offs, other crew members practiced their specialties. It became appallingly obvious that most gunners had never fired a weapon before, nor had any ever operated a power turret. The turrets proved to be consistently troublesome and required so much repair and adjustment that the crews had very little time for actual gunnery practice in flight. Another source of trouble was the auxiliary fuel tanks, which developed leaks. Engines and carburetors were finely adjusted for the most economic fuel consumption— this could mean the difference between landing in the sea or on land.

Simulated bomb runs were practiced over the Florida coast. The B-25s came in from the ocean at low level, skimming housetops, dodging trees, and sweeping under telephone wires. In dropping prac-

tice bombs, they found that Greening's "Mark Twain" sight worked very well.

About mid-March Doolittle became concerned with his part in the mission. Would Arnold pull him out once he had completed the modifications and the crew training? Having come so far, Doolittle wished to go all the way. He flew to Washington hoping to get Arnold's permission to lead the attack. This might not prove to be easy. Doolittle was forty-five, twice the age of most of the pilots on the mission, and he was an irreplaceable member of Arnold's staff. Still Doolittle, applying what he later called "my sales pitch," gave it a vigorous try. He produced every possible reason for leading the mission, all but swamping Arnold with words. In self-defense, Arnold simply passed the buck.

"OK, Jimmy," he managed to wedge in a word, "it's all right with me provided it is all right with Miff Harmon" (Major General Millard F. Harmon, Arnold's Chief of Staff).

Whereupon Doolittle shot into Harmon's office, where he pulled off an ancient ploy in the repertory of every boy whoever talked his parents into giving him something neither really wanted him to have.

"Miff," Doolittle began as soon as his foot was in the door, "I've just been to see Hap and gave him my report on this project I've been working on. I told him I wanted to lead the mission and he said it was OK with him if it's OK with you." Arnold had, of course, counted upon Harmon to say no. But "Miff was caught flat-footed, which is what I intended," Doolittle recalls. Harmon could only answer, "Sure, Jimmy, whatever is all right with Hap is all right with me. Go ahead."

Doolittle went, pausing only long enough outside Harmon's door to hear him explaining to Arnold why *he* had given Doolittle permission to lead the Tokyo raid. Before Arnold caught him to countermand the consent, Doolittle hurried back to Eglin. Not until the *Hornet* had put out to sea was Doolittle absolutely certain that he would lead the mission.

Shortly after Duncan's suggestion that he get on his horse came through, on March 23 twenty-two B-25s took off the landing strip at Eglin for the last time; two others, training casualties, remained behind. Three days later all aircraft arrived safely at McClellan Field, near Sacramento. It was here that the final inspections and adjustments were to be made before the final fifteen planes would put out to sea aboard the *Hornet*.

Doolittle ran the gamut of annoyances at McClellan. The Sacramento Air Depot employed a number of civilians, along with the Army men, as maintenance personnel. None were aware of the pressures upon Doolittle—nor were the civilians particularly impressed with military demands. Suddenly, literally out of the clear blue sky, they had received twenty-two tampered-with B-25s with a little man in charge demanding immediate attention. The crews made a point of sticking together and remaining aloof from the people on the base (a security measure, though mistaken as snobbishness by base personnel). When it became apparent that things were moving too slowly despite his admonitions, Doolittle called Arnold, who managed to stir up some action from Washington. It did not add to Doolittle's popularity.

New propellers, painted black for protection from salt air and water, were to be installed. The crazy tubing of the auxiliary fuel tanks was to be checked. But, Doolittle cautioned, nothing was to be removed

Marc A. Mitscher, captain of the Hornet *and host to Doolittle's Tokyo raiders.*
(U. S. OFFICE OF WAR INFORMATION)

from the planes, nor were any mechanical settings to be changed. In spite of this there was still margin for well-intended error. One day Doolittle caught a mechanic revving up an engine and backfiring it. That was bad enough, but then the mechanic explained that the carburetors had been "checked, found way out of adjustment and fixed up." Some, as those on the plane he was revving up, had even been changed. The hairline adjustments on the engines made at Eglin now amounted to nothing.

Doolittle stormed and raged, but it was too late to begin a new series of adjustments at McClellan. Doolittle had his own crews try to put the engines back into shape. By this time the men of the "First Special Aviation Project" were quite unpopular around McClellan Field, with Doolittle, otherwise a most genial and friendly type, leading the list. The consensus was that they were all a bunch of "jokers," had odd ideas on how a B-25 should be maintained, and were not quite right in the head.

On April 1 Doolittle was ordered to fly the planes to the Alameda Air Station, not far from McClellan Field. As he was about to climb into his plane he was given a form to sign, a typical Army paper necessary to the clearance of his aircraft. The form invited comment upon the work done at McClellan.

Doolittle took the form and wrote a single word across the face of it: "Lousy."

"Just a minute, sir," the base operations officer stammered. "You must fill in a detailed report. This won't do."

"I haven't got time," Doolittle answered, jumped into the plane, and took off.

John Hilger, his executive officer, stood nearby grinning. The disgruntled base officer came over to him saying, "He has no clearance to leave this base and I won't sign it. . . . Who does he think he is? . . . I'll tell you one thing: your colonel is heading for a lot of trouble."

"He sure is," Hilger concurred. Doolittle invariably found trouble.

III

At Alameda the Navy took over the B-25s, attached them to "donkeys," and towed them to the pier to be hoisted by crane to the flight deck of the *Hornet*. Their crews, all of them graduates—including Doolittle himself—of Captain Henry Miller's special training course, had been selected as the top of their class of the twenty-two flight teams. Doolittle took over the plane of Captain Vernon L. Stinzi, who had become sick. Ultimate selection of the crews was left by Doolittle to his staff and to Miller.

All fifteen Mitchells, as had been originally planned, were aboard when Doolittle scanned the deck and thought perhaps there was room for one more. He suggested to Mitscher that an extra bomber be brought aboard. Once they were out to sea it could be flown off and sent back. It seemed a good idea, even if only to demonstrate to the crews that it could be done. None of them, including Doolittle, had actually done it. "It would give them a lot of confidence," Doolittle offered. Mitscher ordered a sixteenth B-25 lifted aboard. Their Navy instructor, Lieutenant Henry Miller, was then all but kidnapped in order to serve as copilot for the extra Mitchell. Besides Miller, there were also seventy officers and sixty-four enlisted men of the Army Air Forces as guests of the Navy. The *Hornet* pulled out of the harbor at ten-eighteen in the morning (in broad daylight) on Thursday, April 2, 1942. Still no one aboard, except Doolittle, Mitscher, and Miller, knew where they were heading.

There was no little uneasiness among the espionage-conscious aircrews as Task Group 16.2 steamed under the Golden Gate and Oakland bridges in full view of motorists above. It would take little military intelligence to gather that something was afoot: a carrier, three cruisers, four destroyers, and a tanker. The carrier was the oddest sight, with a number of large planes (not carrier planes obviously) lashed to the aft end of the flight deck.

Later that afternoon Mitscher announced over the ship's loudspeaker: "This force is bound for Tokyo." At the same instant the word was flashed to the other ships in the group. Great cheers resounded over the waters as the ships plowed ahead. Morale could not have been better, nor could the relationship—co-operative and considerate—which developed between airmen and seamen. To avenge Pearl Harbor, whatever the risks, was exhilarating and above all the most desirable objective of the war at that moment.

Soon after, the deadly business of preparation got under way. Target folders were distributed and vari-

The flight deck of the Hornet *with an unusual cargo, U. S. Army Air Force B-25Bs on the way to bomb Tokyo. Two of the escorting destroyers bring up the rear.* (U. S. AIR FORCE)

ous targets were assigned to the five three-plane elements. It was decided to keep the extra B-25. Doolittle would open the attack with his single plane approaching Tokyo at around dusk to bomb the Shiba Ward, an industrial section, about three hours before the other bombers followed. The fires laid by Doolittle's bombs would serve as beacons for the others. Lieutenant Travis Hoover would follow with the first element to bomb factories, warehouses, and gas and chemical installations in northern Tokyo; Captain David M. Jones's second element would concentrate on oil storage tanks, power stations, and several factories in an area to the north of the Temple of Heaven, the Emperor's palace (which was declared off limits as a target). Captain Edward J. York's element was to hit factories and power stations in the southern Tokyo area bordering on Yokohama. Captain Charles Ross Greening's element was given targets in Yokohama proper, with concentration on the dock areas and the Navy Yard. The fifth element, Major John A. Hilger leading, would fan out over the coast and hit targets assigned in Nagoya, Kobe, and Osaka.

Such a distribution would in a sense diffuse the effectiveness of the attack; they could hardly hope to erase an important industry from Japan's war-making potential. They would do some damage, but

The sixteenth, and last, B-25 with its aft section jutting over the Hornet's *fantail. It was this aircraft's propeller that during the takeoffs injured Navy man Robert Wall.*
(U. S. AIR FORCE)

most of that would be to the morale of the people of Japan, who had been assured that their home islands would never be touched by the enemy.

The task group steamed toward the scheduled rendezvous with Task Group 16.1, Halsey's group with the *Enterprise,* on Sunday, April 12. Halsey's return to Pearl Harbor, however, was held up by storms so that the rendezvous was delayed by one day. The days at sea were devoted to sessions with Doolittle on procedure. The crews checked and rechecked their planes. The Navy furnished an intelligence officer, Lieutenant Commander Stephen Jurika, who lectured the crews on the Orient and Orientals. Commander Apollo Soucek, air officer of the *Hornet,* reviewed the subject of carrier takeoff and carrier operations. Until the actual takeoff, therefore, none of the crews would have ever taken off a carrier, nor would they have ever seen a B-25 lifted off a carrier. This did not seem to worry the crews, particularly the pilots.

Commander Frank Akers found the pilots ". . . a carefree, happy group [who] seemed little concerned as to the danger of their mission or what might happen to them if they were shot down over Japan." They were, Akers found in lecturing them on navigation, quite inattentive. Their major prob-

lem was getting the plane off the deck—the rest of the mission would follow in due course.

The still inexperienced gunners managed to get in some practice from the *Hornet*'s deck by shooting at kites, the closest they were to come to shooting at an air-borne target until they would be in combat.

Each plane was to carry four five-hundred-pound bombs, in most cases three demolition and one incendiary. In the discussions on bombing Doolittle told them, "You are to look for and aim at military targets only, such as war industries, shipbuilding facilities, power plants and the like." He stressed again that the Emperor's Imperial Palace was to be untouched and that they should keep their bombs out of residential areas.

There still remained the question of where they would land after they had completed their missions. Doolittle had left the United States believing that this problem had been solved, but in truth it was not; also, because of the strict radio silence, it was not possible to inform him of this hitch. In the early stages of the mission's planning negotiations had got under way with both China and Russia. The reaction from both was not encouraging. Russia, despite the tantalizing offer of fifteen only slightly used B-25s on lend-lease, refused upon learning that they were to bomb Japan first. Still at peace with Japan, Russia did not want to become involved with such a project.

Chiang Kai-shek was hardly more co-operative. He was given the merest gist of the First Special Aviation Project, just the fact that Japan was to be bombed. Nothing about how or when. This was for a very good reason: military information in China, including that of Chiang's staff, became Japanese property with disconcerting speed. Chiang offered two objections, suggesting that the mission be delayed. First, he reasoned that the bases being requested for use for American bombers were too close to Japanese-held territory. Second, he feared reprisals upon the Chinese if Japan were attacked. It was a curious point of view, considering the years of "reprisals" which had already been inflicted upon the Chinese. However, his fears were not without foundation, as the aftermath of the mission would prove.

Unknown to Doolittle and his men, therefore, no actual preparations were being made for their arrival as they pored over their target folders at sea.

Aircrews, Doolittle, and Mitscher (left foreground) assemble on the deck of the Hornet *in mid-Pacific.*
(U. S. NAVY)

The verbiage between Chungking and Washington became increasingly frigid. Chiang strongly believed that the aircraft could be better employed against Japanese bases in Burma. But by this time, Washington informed him, it was too late to cancel the mission. By mid-April, Chiang, after frequent changes of mind, gave halfhearted permission for arrangements to be made to receive the B-25s in China. A number of forward bases would be furnished with radios to send out a beam to guide the planes to land; there they would be refueled and flown deeper into China—to Chungking.

IV

Halsey's delay in returning to Pearl Harbor had no effect upon the mission. He left Hawaii, flying his flag on the *Enterprise,* commanded by Captain George D. Murray, on April 8. Halsey's group consisted of a carrier, two cruisers, four destroyers, and a tanker. In addition, two submarines patrolled the areas in advance of and to the flanks of the two groups, which on April 13 merged as Task Force 16 under the command of Halsey.

By this time the Japanese had been aware of an impending action for five days. They had monitored

radio signals between Mitscher, Halsey, and Pearl Harbor and could conjecture that a fairly large-scale operation was in the making. It was even surmised that an attack upon Japan itself would take place, the guess being that it would occur around April 14. The radio silence which then descended upon TF 16 threw off that prediction and the Japanese relaxed somewhat, although never completely.

Combined Fleet Headquarters in Tokyo ordered a concentration of naval aircraft from the 26th Air Flotilla into the Tokyo area. The vast network of picket boats, most of them onetime fishing boats, ringing the eastern approach to Japan were alerted. These picket boats, equipped with radios, operated about 650 to 700 miles offshore, beyond the range of carrier-borne aircraft. They could warn of the approach of enemy carriers long before the planes might be launched. Although expecting some form of early warning system, the Americans were not aware of the extent of this floating picket line. Meanwhile, in Tokyo, certain of its efforts, Combined Fleet Headquarters sensed no need for alarm.

Task Force 16 surged due west at sixteen knots for five days (losing Tuesday, April 14, on crossing the International Date Line) without incident. The *Enterprise* maintained a screen of fighters and scout-bombers on combat air patrol, weather permitting—and the weather turned foul. It was as if the theme of the Pearl Harbor attack had returned. Ships tossed and rolled and refueling became a dangerous essential operation. One man was thrown overboard but was pulled from the sea by one of the destroyers. (To this extent the theme varied from the Nagumo operation.) As the bad weather persisted the hope was that the bombers could be launched within five hundred miles of Japan.

Constant vigil was maintained and tension mounted as the launch date, set for April 19, approached. On the fifteenth an English broadcast was picked up from Tokyo:

Reuter's British News Agency has announced that three American bombers have dropped bombs on Tokyo. This is a most laughable story. They know it is absolutely impossible for enemy bombers to get within five hundred miles of Tokyo. Instead of worrying about such foolish things, the Japanese

*people are enjoying the fine spring sunshine and
the fragrance of cherry blossoms.*

This was a stunning bit of news, even if not true.
Had the Japanese somehow learned of the First
Special Aviation Project? Had they been spotted
and was the Japanese fleet, plus its formidable
armada of aircraft, waiting for them to finish what
had been left undone at Pearl Harbor?

Whatever the individual trepidations the broadcast produced, the preparations on the *Hornet* continued. The air patrols spotted no Japanese activity,
which was a good sign. There was more than enough
to keep the crews busy, with tricky fuel systems,
the power turrets, and small mechanical problems
with plugs, generators, and the hydraulic systems.

After the tankers and destroyers left the task force,
on April 17, the carriers with four cruisers as escort
increased speed to twenty knots. The weather continued to be blustery and winds approached gale
force. The B-25s were positioned on the flight deck;
Doolittle's, which was first in line for take-off, had
but 467 feet of runway. White guidelines were
painted on the deck, one for the left wheel and the
other for the nosewheel. Lining up on these, the
pilot would manage to keep his plane's right wing
tip about six feet away from the *Hornet*'s island.
The sixteenth plane, assigned to Lieutenant William
Farrow, was parked at the stern with its tail section protruding. All, with minor mechanical reservations, was ready for the April 19 launchings.

But then, unexpectedly, the tension was released
with the expectation of action. At three in the early
morning of April 18, the *Enterprise* reported a radar
sighting of two enemy surface craft. "General Quarters" reverberated through the entire task force as
all ships veered sharply to avoid the enemy craft
and all hands peered into the gloom. For a single
instant a light flashed in the distance and then nothing. Forty-one minutes later the "All Clear" was
sounded and all who could returned to their bunks
and the tension returned intensified.

At dawn, despite the squalls, the *Enterprise* dispatched its search flights and fighter patrols—
Douglas SBDs (Dauntlesses) and Grumman F4Fs
(Wildcats)—which fanned out in advance of the
force. At 5:58 A.M. Lieutenant O. B. Wiseman, in
an SBD, sighted a Japanese patrol craft. Ducking
into cloud he attempted to hide, but was reasonably
sure he had been seen. Returning to the task force,

*Mission leader Doolittle affixes Japanese medals
(which had, in peaceful times, been awarded to Navy
men H. Vornstein, J. B. Laurey, D. J. Quigley, and S.
Jurika) to a five-hundred-pound bomb which was then
loaded into* The Ruptured Duck, *piloted by Major
Ted W. Lawson.* (U. S. NAVY)

Wiseman flew low in order to enable his gunner to
drop a message on the deck in a "beanbag." Again
Halsey ordered a shift in the task force's bearing.
But by seven thirty-eight, with winds buffeting and
waves sweeping across the decks, it was obvious to
Halsey that he must do something about the Army
bombers. At this time lookouts on the *Hornet* had
spotted a Japanese vessel—it was Patrol Boat No.
23—the *Nitto Maru*. If they saw the little boat in
the swelling seas, obviously the Japanese could
see a great carrier. This was confirmed moments
later when the *Hornet* intercepted a signal which
had originated nearby. The picket boat had wired,
*"Three enemy aircraft carriers sighted our position
650 nautical miles east of Inubo Saki at 0630
[Tokyo time]."*

Aboard the task force ships it was 7:30 A.M.
The *Nitto Maru* had seen both the *Hornet* and
Enterprise (obviously mistaking one of the cruisers
for a third carrier). Halsey ordered the *Nashville*
to deal with the *Nitto Maru*.

As for the bombers, Halsey realized, there was
nothing to do but get them off. This was a real
risk (though a lesser one than exposing the men

Japanese fishing boat sighted by American search planes and which was sunk by a Navy ship. The ap- *pearance of the* Nitto Maru *forced the Tokyo raid to get under way sooner than had been hoped.*

(U. S. AIR FORCE)

and ships of the task force to a full-scale attack) for they were more than six hundred miles offshore —and two hundred miles from a point at which it was hoped they could have launched the bombers. Also, it was a day earlier than Chiang had been informed the attack would occur; perhaps the airfields would not be ready to receive the bombers after the raid. This was assuming they would have enough fuel to reach them. Halsey at this time had no idea that the preparation of Chinese bases had crumbled in a series of disagreements and plane crashes.

At eight o'clock Halsey flashed a message to the *Hornet*:

Launch Planes To Colonel Doolittle and his gallant command Good Luck and God bless you

v

The *Hornet* exploded with activity; signal horns blared and men raced for their action stations. Doolittle, who had been on the bridge with Mitscher, hurtled down the ladder shouting, "This is it! Let's go!" The ship's klaxon boomed, "Now hear this: Army pilots, man your planes!"

The deck swarmed with men rushing about their various businesses. The airmen clambered into their planes, tossing in their baggage, equipment, map folders, and odd personal possessions (one officer carried a small record collection and a wind-up phonograph). The Navy deck-handlers, called "airedales," scurried over the wet, wind-spumed flight deck, taking their positions for the launch. The rough seas would not make the already complex operation any simpler. Soon the deck boomed and roared to the sound of thirty-two engines.

Lieutenant Edgar G. Osborn poised at the end of the tossing bow, checkered flag in hand, eyes on Doolittle's plane, his feet gauging the pitch of the deck and the feel of the sea. The *Hornet* had rolled into a trough and began to rise; Osborne rotated the flag, faster and faster. At the right moment, he hoped, Doolittle would gun the engines, the airedales pull the wheel chocks and drop to the slippery deck. Osborn gave the signal to go. The engines of the B-25, full power on, thundered and the plane moved—all too slowly it seemed. The flaps were down for more lift and the aircraft moved faster and faster, trundling clumsily toward the end of the deck, now being lifted by the swelling sea. The two Wright Cyclones grew louder and the Mitchell picked up speed; even before he ran out of the short span of deck, Doolittle eased the heavily loaded plane off, all but hanging on his propellers, and pulled up and away from the *Hornet,* whose decks resounded with cheers, shouts, whistles, and the merriment of capering men. Doolittle circled, swooped low, and swept over the deck to check his plane's compass—the weeks aboard ship would have undoubtedly thrown the compasses of the B-25s off. Satisfied, Doolittle pointed the aircraft at Tokyo and was quickly enshrouded in the distant mist and out of sight. The next plane, Travis Hoover's, pulled off the deck five minutes later, described the same circle as had Doolittle's, and it too disappeared in the morning haze.

The original plan, of course, had been abandoned; there would now be no three-hour wait for the rest of the planes. The *Nitto Maru* had decided that.

One after the other the B-25s took off from the flight deck, almost without incident. The water spray and unsteady decks, even the powerful gusts of wind, made for anxious moments as men slipped on the deck or staggered dangerously close to the whirling propellers. In the last section of planes, Lieutenant Donald Smith's B-25 nosed into the tail of Hilger's, which preceded his in the take-off line. Smith took off with a gaping hole in the plexiglass nose of his plane.

The last plane (William G. Farrow, pilot) was caught in the roll of the ship and seemed destined for a watery doom. It poised momentarily on the crest of a wave, then began to skid in reverse. Airedales ran to stop its movement, lest it fall into the sea. They succeeded, but as Farrow gunned the plane forward again Seaman Robert W. Wall slipped and fell into the path of one of the propellers. A blade struck him and Wall went down; he lay stunned under the spinning blades for a moment, then oblivious to the danger tried to rise. His crewmates moved in quickly and dragged him away. Farrow, sickened by the implications of the accident, had no recourse but to proceed with the takeoff. (Wall had been struck in the left arm; it was subsequently amputated and he recovered).

The time was 9:20 A.M., exactly one hour from the moment that Doolittle had taken off—Doolittle would have 620 miles to fly to his target, Farrow faced 600 miles of over-water navigation. Now all B-25s were air-borne and bound for Japan. The instant Farrow slipped into the fog, Halsey ordered all ships to turn about and head full speed away from the dangerous waters before they met more potent vessels than picket boats. Like the Nagumo force at Pearl Harbor, Task Force 16 vanished into the Pacific.

Not without some moments of fury. Three Japa-

The order has come from Halsey to "Launch planes," and the deck of the Hornet *becomes alive with the sound of engines. Deck handlers lie on the deck to avoid propeller blades. The day is dark and damp, visibility is poor.* (NAVY DEPT., NATIONAL ARCHIVES)

Doolittle, in the lead Mitchell, begins the take-off run along the wet—and short—deck of the Hornet.
(U. S. AIR FORCE)

Doolittle lifts the B-25 off the Hornet. *White lines painted along left of carrier deck are there to guide the pilots in the alignment of their left undercarriage* *and nosewheels to keep the right wing of the plane from striking the carrier's island.* (U. S. AIR FORCE)

nese patrol boats were sunk, five prisoners were taken, and three American aircraft were lost. The crews of two were rescued, but one, based on the *Hornet*, went down taking its pilots, Lieutenants G. D. Randall and T. A. Gallagher, with it. They were victims of the weather, not enemy gunfire.

Three minutes after Doolittle's plane left the *Hornet*'s deck the *Nashville* succeeded in sinking the *Nitto Maru*. The tiny, bobbing craft proved an elusive target and it required "938 rounds of 6″ ammunition" to sink it. Even dive bombers could not get at it "due to difficulty of hitting the small target with the heavy swells . . ." as the gunnery officer of the *Nashville* later reported. Finally the *Nitto Maru* did sink, and although a search was made, no survivors were found.

It was a small victory, for already Tokyo had put "Tactical Method No. 3 against the United States Fleet" into operation. Vice-Admiral Nobutake Kondo's Second Fleet, just returned from actions in the southern seas, was ordered to confront the U.S. fleet. Kondo's force was to be supported by Vice-Admiral Shiro Takasu's First Fleet out of Hiroshima Bay. Even Vice-Admiral Nagumo's carrier force, at the moment of alarm passing through the Bashi Strait near the southern tip of Formosa upon completion of its operations in the Indian Ocean, was ordered to rush homeward to engage the enemy. More immediately, however, the bombers and fighters from the Kisarazu Air Base near Tokyo were dispatched to begin the search for the American ships.

At Combined Fleet Headquarters in Tokyo, where the bulk of the preparations was under way, all was anxiety and tension. There had been no second message from the *Nitto Maru* to confirm its sighting. The patrol planes had not reported anything (thanks to the covering of bad weather under which Task Force 16 lay). One of the regular patrol planes, however, on its morning patrol had reported seeing a twin-engined landplane about six hundred miles at sea. Such a report could not be taken seriously in Tokyo—no American plane could have reached that point from any American base and, certainly, there were no such carrier-borne aircraft extant. Meanwhile, the weather in the search area deteriorated and the Japanese search planes were forced to return to Kisarazu after a fruitless quest.

If the weather at sea was harsh, the sky over Tokyo was bright and clear. Along the waterfront a few barrage balloons drifted in the brilliant sun. Its rays flashed from the wings of several aircraft also, aloft practicing for a demonstration a week hence celebrating the Emperor's birthday and the dedication of a shrine to the war dead. By coin-

cidence that morning at nine o'clock a practice air raid drill took place. The public did not participate, but firemen and air raid wardens did. By noon the drill drew to a close; most of the barrage balloons had been pulled down. The only planes still flying were a few trainers and three Army Defense fighter planes; at this point in the alarums and excursions at Combined Fleet Headquarters the Army was not regarded as particularly essential. The threat to the Empire, as far as the Navy officials were concerned, still lay far out at sea. There was no air of foreboding in Tokyo as its people went about their customary Saturday bustle. It was as if there were no war at all—their great military leaders had assured them of their immunity from enemy attack.

At twelve-thirty that Saturday afternoon the illusion was shattered. The dream drew to an end the moment that James Doolittle raised his B-25 off the deck of the *Hornet.* "Took off at 8:20 A.M. ship time," he was to write in his report later. "Take-off was easy. Night take-off would have been possible and practicable.

"Circled carrier to get exact heading and check compass. Wind was from around 300°.

"About a half hour after take-off, was joined by A/C 40-2292, Lt. Hoover pilot, the second plane to take off. About an hour out passed a Japanese

A Mitchell leaves the Hornet *as the others await their turns. Note the choppiness of the water in the foreground.* (U. S. AIR FORCE)

Yokosuka Naval Base from the right-hand cockpit of No. 40-2247 (Crew No. 13), Lieutenant Edgar E. McElroy, pilot, and Lieutenant Richard A. Knobloch, copilot and photographer. (U. S. AIR FORCE)

camouflaged naval surface vessel of about 6000 tons. Took it to be light cruiser. About two hours out passed a multi-motored land plane headed directly for our flotilla and flying at about 3,000 ft.—2 miles away. Passed and endeavored to avoid various civil and naval craft until landfall was made north of Inubo Shuma.

"Was somewhat north of desired course but decided to take advantage of error and approach from a northerly direction, thus avoiding anticipated strong opposition to the west. Many flying fields and the air full of planes north of Tokyo. Mostly small biplanes apparently primary or basic trainers.

"Encountered nine fighters in three flights of three. This was about ten miles north of the outskirts of Tokyo proper. All this time had been flying as low as terrain would permit. Continued low flying due south over the outskirts of and toward the east center of Tokyo.

"Pulled up to 1,200 ft., changed course to the southwest and incendiary-bombed highly inflammable section. Dropped first bomb at 1:30 (ship time).

[It was twelve-thirty in Tokyo when the first bombs fell.]

"Anti-aircraft very active but only one near hit,"

Having released its bombs, McElroy's Mitchell pulls away from Yokosuka as machine shops burn from a bomb hit. (U. S. AIR FORCE)

Doolittle noted. "Lowered away to housetops and slid over western outskirts into low haze and smoke. Turned south and out to sea. Fewer airports on west side but many army posts. Passed over small aircraft factory with a dozen or more newly completed planes on the line. No bombs left. Decided not to machine gun for reasons of personal security. Had seen five barrage balloons over east central Tokyo and what appeared to be more in the distance.

"Passed on out to sea flying low. Was soon joined by Hoover who followed us to the Chinese coast. Navigator plotted perfect course to pass north of Yaki Shima. Saw three large naval vessels just before passing west end of Japan. One was flatter than the others and may have been converted carrier. Passed innumerable fishing and small patrol boats.

"Made landfall somewhat north of course on China coast. Tried to reach Chuchow on 4495 [kilocycles] but could not raise.

"It had been clear over Tokyo but became overcast before reaching Yaki Shima. Ceiling lowered on coast until low islands and hills were in it at about 600'. Just getting dark and couldn't live under overcast so pulled up to 6000' and then 8000' in it. On instruments from then on though occasionally saw dim lights on ground through almost solid overcast. These lights seemed more often on our right and pulled us still further off course.

"Directed rear gunner to go aft and secure films from camera. [Unfortunately, they were jerked out of his shirt front where he had put them when his chute opened.]

"Decided to abandon ship. Sgt. [Fred A.] Breamer, Lt. [Henry A.] Potter, Sgt. [Paul J.] Leonard and Lt. [Richard E.] Cole jumped in order. Left ship on AFCE (automatic pilot), shut off both gas cocks and I left. Should have put flaps down. This would have slowed down landing speed, reduced impact and shortened glide.

"Left airplane about 9:30 P.M. [ship time] after about 13 hours in the air. Still had enough gas for half hour flight but right front tank was showing empty. Had transferred once as right engine used more fuel. Had covered about 2,250 miles, mostly at low speed which more than doubled the consumption for this time.

"All hands collected and ship located by late afternoon of 19th. Requested General Ho Yang Ling, Director of the Branch Government of Western Chekieng Province to have a lookout kept along seacoast from Hang Chow Bay to Wen Chow Bay and also to have all sampans and junks along the coast to keep a lookout for planes that went down at sea, or just reached shore.

"Early morning of 20th, four planes and crews, in addition to ours, had been located and I wired General Arnold, through the Embassy at Chungking: *Tokyo successfully bombed. Due bad weather on China coast believe all airplanes wrecked. Five crews found safe in China so far.* Wired again on the 27th giving more details.

"Discussed possibility of purchasing three prisoners on the seacoast from Puppet Government and endeavoring to take out the three in lake area by force. Believe this desire was made clear to General Ku Cho-tung (who spoke little English) and know it was made clear to English-speaking members of his staff. This was at Shangjao. They agreed to try to purchase of three [American prisoners] but recommended against . . . due to large Japanese concentration.

"Bad luck:

"(1) Early take-off due to naval contact with surface and air craft.

"(2) Clear over Tokyo.

"(3) Foul over China.

"Good luck:

"(1) A 25 mph tail wind over most of the last 1,200 miles.

"Take-off should have been made three hours before daylight, but we didn't know how easy it would be and the Navy didn't want to light up. Dawn take-off, closer in, would have been better as things turned out. However, due to the bad weather it was questionable if even daylight landing could have been made at Chuchow without radio aid.

"Still feel that original plan of having one plane take off three hours before dusk and others just at dusk was best all-around plan for average conditions."

When he dropped out of the B-25, Doolittle, like the others in the crew, fell into the unknown. There was no certainty that they had been over Chinese-held territory, nor even that they were over inhabited country. Prepared for anything in the deep blackness, Doolittle remembered, once his chute had jerked open, to come down in a knees-up attitude. He had broken both his ankles in a youthful accident and did not want to chance it again. His landing, however, was "soft" in the extreme, for he landed in a rice paddy, up to his neck in fertilizing night soil. Reeking and cold from the dampness, Doolittle set out to find refuge from the night winds. He soon learned that the phrase they had been taught aboard the *Hornet, "Lushu hoo megwa fugi"* ("I am an American"), did not exactly open doors (he later learned that it was the wrong dialect for the section in which he had come down). He found refuge finally in an old water mill, although sleep was an impossibility because of the cold.

In the morning he found a farmer who led him to a military outpost and trouble. The Chinese major in charge, who understood some English, found it difficult to believe Doolittle's story. He had not heard of the mission because the word had not been transmitted because of the breakdown in the preparations. Doolittle then led a group of soldiers to the farmhouse whose door had been bolted to him the night before, and the frightened people inside denied the whole tale. Hoping to furnish his parachute as evidence Doolittle led the major and three soldiers to the rice paddy in which he had come down in the night. It was gone. The soldiers began muttering among themselves and the major looked more doubtful than ever. But at this moment two of the other soldiers emerged from the farmhouse carrying the parachute; the farmer would have willingly exchanged Doolittle's life for such a great quantity of high-grade silk.

Finally convinced, the major smiled, shook Doolittle's hand, ordered food, and sent word back to the outpost to send out search parties for the rest of the crew. All by this time had experienced their own little dramas. Crew chief Paul Leonard had been fired upon by a small patrol and took to the woods; navigator Henry Potter and bombardier Fred A. Breamer were taken prisoner by a band of guerrillas and robbed. They were aided by an

Disheartened, Doolittle sits beside the wing of his B-25 the morning after the Tokyo raid.

(U. S. AIR FORCE)

English-speaking Chinese boy. The guerrilla chieftain returned their valuables and arranged for them to be taken to the outpost. The search went on until all of the crew had been found, all luckily unhurt except for bumps and bruises.

Doolittle, accompanied by Leonard, clambered up the mountain on which the B-25 had crashed. It was a depressing sight, for it was nothing now but a mangled pile of junk. Silently the two men picked through the debris. Doolittle found his oil-soaked Army blouse—someone had already clipped off the brass buttons. It then all caught up with him; dejected, he sat down.

Leonard spoke gently. "What do you think will happen when you go home, Colonel?"

"Well," Doolittle replied, "I guess they'll send me to Leavenworth."

"No, sir," Leonard offered. "I'll tell you what will happen. They're going to make you a general."

Doolittle managed a weak smile at Leonard's obvious attempt to cheer him up. He had lost sixteen planes and at this gray instant, he had no idea where seventy-five men could be.

". . . and," Leonard persisted, "they're going to give you the Congressional Medal of Honor."

Doolittle worked up another smile at the extravagance. Even Leonard recognized that and added, "I know they're going to give you another airplane and when they do, I'd like to be your crew chief."

Tears, a rare Doolittle commodity, filled his eyes. This was the highest tribute of all, from one professional to another. He was never to forget Leonard's request on that mountaintop. (All of Leonard's predictions came true: Doolittle was awarded the Medal of Honor and promoted to brigadier general—skipping a colonelcy—and when he returned to active duty in north Africa flying a Martin B-26, Master Sergeant Paul Leonard served as his crew chief. Leonard was killed on January 5, 1943, during an air raid on an Allied base near Youks les Bains, Algeria.)

Within hours after Doolittle had wired Arnold of the completion of their mission, the news of the bombing of Tokyo and the other cities was flashed across the nation. Affecting an air of mystery President Roosevelt announced that the B-25s had taken off from Shangri-La, a Tibetan never-never land in the popular novel *Lost Horizon* by James Hilton. A full year went by before it was revealed that the Mitchells had been launched from the deck of the *Hornet*. Meanwhile, a wave of jubilant excitement swept the country with a resultant quickening of morale.

Morale in Japan sank, despite the fact that the military damage inflicted by Doolittle's crews was light. The Japanese war leaders had lied to their people about their invulnerability to American attack. This introduced an uneasy air of doubt where once all had been optimistic. Hoping to regain this optimism, the Japanese leaders quickly flooded the media with further deceits.

The official voice of the militarists was the Tokyo

Asahi Shimbun, which, in part, printed of the Doolittle raiders that "While fleeing helter-skelter to avoid the curtain of shells which burst forth from our antiaircraft batteries, the enemy planes chose innocent people and city streets as their targets. They did not go near military installations. They carried out an inhuman, insatiable, indiscriminate bombing attack on the sly, and the fact that they schemed to strafe civilians and non-combatants demonstrates their fiendish behavior."

Radio Tokyo added its permutations: "The cowardly raiders purposefully avoided industrial centers and the important military establishments and blindly dumped their incendiaries in a few suburban districts, especially on schools and hospitals." The motif of the bombardment of schools and hospitals was developed into a major theme in the propaganda following the raid. Claims were also made for nine American planes shot down.

VI

Of the sixteen aircraft participating in the First Special Aviation Project only one made a safe, intact, wheels-down landing, the one piloted by Captain Edward J. York. During their flight to Tokyo York had noted that fuel consumption had been alarmingly high. Upon bombing a factory in the Tokyo area, York asked navigator Lieutenant Nolan A. Herndon for a heading to Russia instead of China. Thanks to the carburetor switch made at Sacramento they could hardly anticipate better than ditching in the sea three hundred miles off the China coast. Russia remained their only chance, even if they had been told (not ordered) to stay away.

After an uneventful flight York brought the B-25 down onto an airfield about forty miles north of Vladivostok in a perfect landing. Perhaps, York hoped, since they and the Russians were allies they might be permitted to refuel and get out of Russia in the morning to rejoin the others in China. Instead, the five men were interned and the plane confiscated. Although the Americans were reasonably well treated, they remained virtual prisoners until they escaped (by arranging bribes) into Iran about a year later.

Eleven crews, including Doolittle's, bailed out and four attempted crash landings. The crews which bailed out generally fared best. Corporal Leland Faktor, engineer-gunner in Lieutenant Robert M. Gray's plane, however, died of injuries sustained when he landed in mountainous country in his parachute. His burial was attended to by an American missionary, the Reverend John M. Birch. Most of the others who bailed out, and who were injured, suffered sprained ankles, leg and back injuries. Faktor was the only fatality.

Lieutenant Dean Hallmark attempted to ditch his plane in the water near Hanchang, on the China coast. The impact threw Hallmark through the windshield and injured the others. Hallmark, however, in company with Robert J. Meder and Chase J. Nielsen, despite their injuries, set out for the beach. Meder turned back when he saw William J. Dieter and Donald Fitzmaurice floundering in the surf. He pulled Fitzmaurice onto shore and, though injured and exhausted, returned to the ocean to look for Dieter. He found the bombardier on the beach, face down in the water. Both Fitzmaurice and Dieter were dead of injuries and possibly drowning. But the three surviving officers were fated for worse: all three fell into the hands of the Japanese.

Ted Lawson also attempted to bring his plane down in the coastal waters and, like Hallmark, was flung through the windshield, along with navigator Charles L. McClure and copilot Dean Davenport. Robert Clever, the bombardier, smashed through the plexiglass and metal nose of the aircraft. Of the five-man crew only engineer-gunner David J. Thatcher was not seriously injured, or rather, was the least injured. Lawson, whose left leg was ripped open terribly, was in the worst state. Limping and in pain himself, Thatcher attended to the injuries of the others. With the aid of Chinese he had the men moved inside a nearby hut (though not without hideous pain to all), for once the news of the Tokyo raid was known and the B-25s came crashing down, Japanese patrol activity became intense.

By various means, ranging from junk to improvised stretcher, the men were spirited into unoccupied China, to a small hospital in the village of Linhai. By this time Lawson was so far gone with infection that he could neither eat nor speak. Thatcher informed Chungking of their state and

The Chinese, civilians as well as soldiers, rallied to the aid of the Tokyo raider crews. Those Chinese who were suspected of helping the Americans suffered terribly at the hands of the Japanese soldiers.

(U. S. AIR FORCE)

was joined in a few days by Lieutenant Thomas R. White.

White was the unique member of the mission; he was not an airman at all but a doctor who had volunteered for the raid. He was permitted to go as a gunner member of the crew of Lieutenant Donald Smith. The latter had crash-landed his plane in the same vicinity, so White, once informed of the fate of Lawson's crew, made his way to Linhai. To keep out of the path of the Japanese, Smith, his crew, and the remarkable Thatcher of Lawson's crew moved on to Chungking. White remained with Lawson, McClure, and Davenport, treating them skillfully with the primitive means at hand. He also doubled as a dentist for the Chinese villagers. In time, White was forced to amputate Lawson's left leg, which saved the pilot's life. When some recovery was made, White had the three men evacuated out of the path of the vindictive Japanese.

Lieutenant William Farrow's crew, of the ill-fated

After the mission: Madame Chiang awards the Tokyo raiders decorations in appreciation for their feat. With her are Doolittle (now a brigadier general; he had been a lieutenant colonel when he took off from the Hornet), *Colonel John A. Hilger (pilot of the fourteenth plane), and Lieutenant Richard E. Cole, who had been Doolittle's copilot.* (U. S. AIR FORCE)

sixteenth plane (the propeller of which had gashed Seaman Wall's arm), bailed out near the China coast at Shipu, in Japanese-occupied territory, and fell into the waiting arms of the Japanese. Along with the survivors of Hallmark's crew these men were "tried," after a long period of hideous treatment, by a Japanese military court. This mockery, held on August 28, 1942, in Shanghai, decreed that all eight prisoners were to be executed because they had "suddenly exhibited cowardice when confronted with opposition in the air and on the ground, and with intent of cowing, killing, and wounding innocent civilians, and wreaking havoc on residences and other living quarters of no military significance whatsoever" and further "did carry out indiscriminate bombing and strafing." The early themes of press and radio were worked up in the "trial" as a full-fledged symphony.

The eight prisoners, who had been tortured and starved and were in poor health (Hallmark, for example, was unable to sit up and attended the proceedings in a cot), had no conception of what it was all about. They were made to sign blank papers which were subsequently filled in in Japanese. They even signed "confessions," also in Japanese, without the slightest conception of content. All men were in a state of befuddlement as well as physically weak.

Ultimately the death sentence was applied to only three of the eight—Hallmark, Farrow (both pilots) and Harold Spatz (engineer-gunner), all three having unwittingly signed their own death warrants; their portions of the "confessions" admitted to bombings of civilians and strafing. The remaining five, George Barr, Robert Hite, Jacob DeShazer (all of Farrow's crew), Nielsen, and Meder, were "spared" through the alleged god-given leniency of the Emperor. Their sentence was life imprisonment as "war criminals."

This meant forty months of solitary confinement for the five men. During this tortuous period Meder died of maltreatment, disease, and sheer neglect. Nielsen, Barr, Hite, and DeShazer were rescued by an American parachute team on August 20, 1945, at Peiping. Of the survivors, DeShazer eventually returned to Japan—as a missionary, an exemplification of compassion in the highest degree.

Substantial, if not definitive, damage was done by the Doolittle mission. Possibly the greatest injury

was to the self-esteem of the Japanese Samurai. Although it had not been hit, the very fact that the air over and around the Emperor's Imperial Palace had been violated by enemy aircraft was a gross affront to those who had sworn their very lives to keep this from happening. The militarists, with a keen professional eye, tended to denigrate the raid—English-speaking members referred to it as the "Do Nothing Raid"—but they knew better. It was a harbinger of things to come.

The reaction to the raid was savagery unleashed. The mistreatment of the eight prisoners was reprehensible, but the slaughter of the Chinese which followed the raid was manic barbarism without military justification. Fifty-three battalions of Japanese troops moved inland, ravaging the land, and in about three months they had killed 250,000 Chinese—soldiers as well as civilians—in the rampage. Villages in which the American airmen had hidden or were cared for were all but deracinated. Chinese who had taken small token gifts—coins, gloves, a scarf—or who had taken parts from the planes were tortured and killed. Wang Poo-fang, a village schoolteacher from Ihwang, near which the plane of Lieutenant Harold Watson had crashed, related a single incident which could be multiplied a thousand times over.

"We fed the Americans," Wang said, "and carried them to safety so that they could bomb Tokyo again. Then the dwarf-invaders came. They killed my three sons; they killed my wife, Angsing; they set fire to my school; they burned my books; they drowned my grandchildren in the well." The schoolmaster, too, had been flung into the well, but managed to climb out after the Japanese had moved on. There was little of his village left to him.

All airfields, which might have served as landing spots for possible future raids, were destroyed, ridged with trenches (all work being done by Chinese), and rendered unusable. And then the Japanese troops moved back from a wasteland of twenty thousand square miles.

Another unreasonable means of vengeance was the so-called "balloon bombs," the Japanese equivalent to the German V-weapons of the later months of the European war. The balloon bombs, however, were much less sophisticated though equally senseless. They were constructed of rice paper and potato paste by Japanese civilians in their homes. Carrying

Made in Japan: vengeance balloons released over the Pacific to drift on the winds to the United States. At top left is one of the balloons in flight over the northwest United States. Below it is a close-up demonstrating the workings, theoretically, of the balloon. Balloons did not always work and, in the lower photograph, woodmen chop a tree in which one had become lodged. Others worked, however, and killed several people, haphazardly and senselessly.

(U. S. AIR FORCE)

booby-trap bombs, about ten thousand of these giant balloons were released near Tokyo to be carried across the Pacific at high altitudes by prevailing winds. Many actually completed the voyage—about 280 were found in the American Northwest, Canada, and Alaska. Six picnickers were killed in a forest near Lakeview, Oregon, when they came upon one of these homemade balloon bombs. As late as 1955, a decade after the last of the balloons had been released, one was discovered in Alaska and tested by the Department of Defense, which found the device "still highly explosive and dangerous."

The Doolittle raid had not been, as Imperial General Headquarters in Tokyo implied, a "Do Nothing Raid." Perhaps its most strategic consequence was that it settled a bitter controversy. This argument had been under way for weeks between Combined Fleet and the Imperial Naval General Staff. Yamamoto had been pressing for an early, full-scale, decisive battle with the U. S. Pacific Fleet.

That the carriers had escaped the Pearl Harbor attack never ceased to vex him. The truth was emerging that aircraft, not battleships, would decide the Pacific war, but the Imperial Naval General Staff did not wish to rush into a major fleet engagement.

The coming of Doolittle decided the issue. Yamamoto sensed that the bombers had come from an American carrier—and he reminded his critics that the failure to keep Doolittle from Tokyo was a reflection upon the General Staff as well as Combined Fleet. Consequently by the end of April Yamamoto's controversial plan was completed and approved by the General Staff. On May 5, 1942, Admiral Osami Nagano issued, in the name of the Emperor, Imperial General Headquarters Navy Order No. 18, directing Yamamoto "to carry out the occupation of Midway Island and key points in the western Aleutians in co-operation with the Army."

4

MIDWAY: TRAGIC VICTORY

By THE SPRING of 1942 the virus that came to be called the "Victory Disease" infected the Japanese. Few were immune, from the man in the street on up into the honored and seemingly invincible purlieus of Combined Fleet and the Naval General Staff.

Invincible indeed—from Pearl Harbor through the fall of Wake Island, the destruction of the British ships *Prince of Wales* and *Repulse,* the surrender of Hong Kong and Singapore—the uncoiling of the Greater East Asia Co-Prosperity Sphere into the southern Pacific had gone unchecked for nearly six months. Then came news of the fall of the Philippines with the surrender of Corregidor on May 6, 1942. Yamamoto had truly "run wild." His leadership had been as good as his word, but the question was, in early 1942, what were the long-range plans to be? Even the most optimistic among his admirers had not expected so unremitting a succession of victories.

Should they consolidate their cheaply won holdings, or should they extend their "security perimeter"? In Yamamoto's mind there was little question of the next move. He knew they could not dig in and wait for the American industrial machine to grind into action and take it all away. Several plans had been under consideration by the middle of January. One favored an all-out attack upon Hawaii, another pointed toward India and

Ceylon, and a third advocated an Australian offensive. This last originated from the Naval General Staff, the argument being that Australia must be cut off as a future springboard for an Allied counteroffensive against Japan. The attack upon Hawaii had originated from the Chief of Staff, Combined Fleet, Rear Admiral Matome Ugaki, who based his thinking upon the possibility of such an attack luring the American fleet to its destruction by the Imperial Navy.

The Navy's plan to take Ceylon was rejected by the Army, which did not have the troops to back up the amphibious landings proposed. Ugaki's Hawaii plan was shot full of holes by his own staff because of the impossibility of achieving another surprise attack. Also, there was the formidable job it would pose for carrier-borne aircraft to maintain air superiority over so large an area as the Hawaiian Islands. The Australian plan was scuttled also by the Army High Command, which insisted it would be unable to supply the required ten divisions. However, there was obvious merit in isolating Australia.

Yamamoto, however, favored another plan—related to Ugaki's Hawaii proposal, but not so formidable in terms of area. In early April he introduced his Operation MI, the major point of which appeared to be the occupation of the Midway atoll. In truth, the occupation of the atoll was secondary in

Yamamoto's mind; his wish, his dream, was to lure the American fleet, and especially its carriers, into one massive decisive battle with the Imperial fleet. Once over—with a Japanese victory, inevitably—the reeling Americans must ask for peace before they had properly geared for war.

Yamamoto's proposal set off another round of debate. The Naval General Staff rose in opposition to the plan. One of the most serious objections was: Even if the atoll were taken, how would it be kept supplied, if, for some reason, the U.S. fleet had

Before the storm: flight deck of the U.S.S. Enterprise, *Pacific 1942.* (NAVY DEPT., NATIONAL ARCHIVES)

not been destroyed? Could Midway truly function as an advance base for Japanese air patrols, considering the range (six to seven hundred miles) of patrol planes? Would the United States actually sue for peace merely because Midway had fallen? Finally, Midway was within bombing range of Hawaii; would not the long-range U.S. bombers menace the occupation force as well as attempts to supply it?

But these arguments were beside the point, for Yamamoto's dream, incited by the fever of the Victory Disease, visualized the mass sinking of American carriers. Despite the objections, Yamamoto—as he had before the Hawaii Operation—made it clear what he desired. The Naval General

Staff, bludgeoned, halfheartedly assented to the operation. Arguments, even opposition, continued on into April until the Doolittle raiders appeared over the sacred soil of Nippon. Debate was ended and Operation MI went into active preparation.

II

If the Doolittle raid was a portent, during the planning of the Midway operation another occurred of even greater immediate significance to Yamamoto, the Battle of the Coral Sea. This was the first naval battle in history in which the ships themselves did not exchange a shot. All the fighting was done by aircraft and in this battle, though ostensibly "won" by the Japanese, Japan suffered its first setback of the war.

This crucial engagement was ignited by Japanese operations aimed at the dual-pronged invasions of Tulagi, in the Solomons, and Port Moresby, in strategic proximity to Australia, in southern Papua, New Guinea. From the first of February the American carriers *Enterprise* and *Lexington* had been making hit-and-run raids upon Japanese-held positions in the Marshalls, the Solomons, and northern New Guinea. Yamamoto recognized the importance both of clearing this area of the American carriers and of the establishment of bases for future operations.

What Yamamoto did not know was that, thanks to Army cryptographers, the Japanese codes were no secret to the enemy and his plans, in turn, were no secret to Admiral Nimitz. By mid-April Nimitz was aware of the impending operations; by the twentieth he even knew the date: May 3. Whereupon he sent Task Force 17, built around the *Yorktown* and *Lexington* and under the command of Rear Admiral Frank Jack Fletcher, to counter the Japanese move.

To accomplish this Fletcher had only about half the force that was at the disposal of Vice-Admiral Shigeyoshi Inouye, Commander in Chief, Imperial Fourth Fleet. This massive force was, it is true, divided into three parts, each of which was assigned its special task in the Port Moresby-Tulagi invasions. The Tulagi Invasion Group (twelve assorted ships) was to occupy that base, which was defended by a few Australian troops, and establish an air base there for future operations. The Port Moresby Invasion Group consisted of eleven troop transports covered by several heavy cruisers, light cruisers, and the light carrier *Shoho*. Also covering the two invasions was the main Carrier Striking Force (carriers *Zuikaku, Shokaku*) with its protective heavy cruisers and screen of destroyers. The plan envisioned was that the invasions would bring out the American carriers, which, when they ventured into the Coral Sea, would be destroyed by the Japanese forces.

The already alerted Nimitz was ready with Task Force 17, to which had been added a support group (two heavy cruisers, a light cruiser, and two destroyers) of what was then called "MacArthur's Navy" under Rear Admiral Crace, Royal Navy.

On May 3 the Japanese opened the battle by taking Tulagi; on the following day planes from the *Yorktown* bombed the Japanese positions at Tulagi. This revealed that an American carrier was indeed somewhere in the area. The *Zuikaku* and *Shokaku* were headed south from Rabaul (where they had gone to deliver fighter planes) to engage the enemy task force. Meanwhile, the Port Moresby Invasion Group continued on its course.

Not until dawn of May 7 did search planes make contact—in the Coral Sea. Japanese scouts reported sighting the American task force, specifically "a carrier and a cruiser." Rear Admiral Chuichi Hara, commander of air operations, under orders from Vice-Admiral Takeo Takagi, commander of the Carrier Striking Force, sent out the entire bombing strength of the two Japanese carriers (a total of seventy-eight bombers, torpedo planes, and fighters) to make an all-out attack. The "task force" turned out to be the destroyer *Sims* and the oiler *Neosho,* neither really worth the wholesale effort. Both were sunk, the *Sims* first (almost within minutes); the *Neosho,* which had been spared at Pearl Harbor, was scuttled a few days later, after smoking and drifting helplessly. But the loss of these ships had pulled the Japanese planes away from the *Lexington* and *Yorktown,* whose planes had been launched. While the Americans were off on their own wild-goose chase ("two carriers and four heavy cruisers"—actually two outdated light cruisers, three gunboats, and a seaplane tender) they unexpectedly came upon the light carrier *Shoho*. The *Lexington*'s Scouting Squadron 2 led the assault, followed by a torpedo squadron and a bombing squadron. All

three had scored hits, but the *Shoho* had turned into the wind to launch its planes. The *Yorktown* planes arrived at this moment, catching the *Shoho* in a position where evasive action was impossible, and soon the word went out in the excited voice of Lieutenant Commander Robert Dixon, commander of the *Lexington*'s scout bomber squadron: "Scratch one flattop!"

Within minutes the *Shoho,* a burning shambles, sank into the sea, taking five hundred crewmen to

Below decks of a carrier, the hangar deck, where engineers work on a fighter, the Grumman F4F "Wildcat." (NAVY DEPT., NATIONAL ARCHIVES)

the bottom. This development unnerved Vice-Admiral Inouye so much that he called off the Port Moresby invasion and recalled the transports to Rabaul. Until he was certain the American carriers had been cleared out of the Coral Sea, Inouye felt that he could not expose the invasion forces to aerial attack. This was a decision that later greatly displeased Yamamoto, for Inouye could not exploit the advantages that came his way later in the battle.

On May 8, finally, the Japanese spotted the American carriers and launched another full-scale attack. The Japanese had the advantage of heavy weather cover, but the *Lexington* and *Yorktown*

Prelude to Midway: the Battle of the Coral Sea, the first major sea battle in which surface ships did not exchange a shot. Fought by aircraft in the vicinity of the Solomon Islands, the Coral Sea battle blocked the Japanese in their drive toward Australia and New Zealand. One of the American losses was the carrier Lexington. *Wildcats on the flight deck following bomb hits by Japanese planes.*

(NAVY DEPT., NATIONAL ARCHIVES)

A destroyer moves in to pick up Lexington *crew men after the order to abandon ship has been given. Japanese torpedo planes and dive bombers caused fires and internal explosions; the "Lady Lex" was finally sunk by the American destroyer* Phelps.

(NAVY DEPT., NATIONAL ARCHIVES)

lay in bright day. The Americans missed finding the *Zuikaku* but did locate the *Shokaku* and succeeded in hitting it with two bombs. Seventy Japanese aircraft, meanwhile, attacked the American carriers savagely. The *Yorktown,* struck by a single bomb, lost sixty-six men, but the *Lexington,* torpedoed and bombed, was left burning and listing after the encounter. Damage-control parties seemed to bring the three fires which blazed under control, but internal explosions doomed the "Lady Lex." New fires spread as gasoline poured into the flames. Captain Frederick Sherman ordered "Abandon Ship," the wounded were evacuated, and the *Lexington,* rather than be abandoned to the Japanese, was sunk by American destroyers.

Trading the *Lexington* for the *Shoho* was no true victory, but the invasion of Port Moresby was canceled. Also, both the *Shokaku,* which would be out of commission for two months being repaired, and the *Zuikaku,* which had lost many of its pilots, were to be denied to Yamamoto for his Midway operation. This fact did not trouble him, for his pilots had sunk the *Lexington* and claimed to have sunk the *Yorktown.*

Nimitz, however, was concerned over the temporary loss of the *Yorktown* in his planning to counter Yamamoto's Midway assault. It was estimated that three months would be required to return the carrier to fighting trim. However, at the Pearl Harbor dry dock a miracle occurred. An army of workmen swarmed over the carrier, working night and day, and within two days the patched-up, scarred *Yorktown* was ready for action.

Despite his losses, Yamamoto was ready, afflicted as he was by then with singleness of purpose and the Victory Disease. He wanted those other American carriers.

III

Midway atoll lies about 1150 miles to the northwest of Hawaii. Its two major islets, Sand and Eastern, were not impressive land masses—Sand Island, the largest, was barely two miles long. In 1859 one Captain N. C. Brooks claimed the two islands for the United States; Secretary of the Navy Gideon Welles placed it under informal U. S. Navy jurisdiction in 1867. Two years later the Congress author-

ized channel dredging between the two islands. In 1900 the Japanese arrived for the first time to prey on the islands' bird population, killing the terns, gannets, and goonies for their feathers. In 1903, fearing that Japan would claim the atoll, President Theodore Roosevelt again placed it under naval jurisdiction and the Japanese poachers were driven off. Midway became a link in the trans-Pacific cable between the Philippines and Hawaii in the same year.

Americans recalled Midway best before the war as one of the way stations for Pan American Airways' *China Clipper* in 1935. Four years later the Navy's Hepburn Board, along with other recommendations, found that Midway was "second in importance only to Pearl Harbor." By August 18, 1941, Midway was commissioned as a Naval Air Station with a complement of around eight hundred men. Dock facilities and airstrips were built and gun positions installed. Although shelled on December 7, 1941, Midway had escaped serious damage and invasion. The planned air strike was canceled

Frank J. Fletcher, Task Force 17 commander—and victor—in the Battle of Midway.
(NAVY DEPT., NATIONAL ARCHIVES)

because of bad weather. While the Japanese concentrated on Wake Island, which proved no easy objective (although overrun by the Japanese on December 23), Midway was granted a period of grace, except for an occasional shelling by submarine.

The strategic position of Midway, relative to the Hawaiian Islands, would bring out the American fleet, which was Yamamoto's most feverish dream. It was no fantasy, however, for his Hawaii Operation, having put most of the U.S. battleship strength out of consideration, placed the Americans in the position of the underdog. Even though the Coral Sea Battle had "scratched" one light carrier and sent the *Shokaku* and the *Zuikaku* into temporary retirement, Yamamoto was capable of amassing a large number of ships for his Midway Operation—nearly two hundred. Among these were eight carriers (four heavies), eleven battleships, twenty-two cruisers, sixty-five destroyers, and twenty-one submarines. About seven hundred aircraft, dive bombers, torpedo bombers, and fighters, were at Yamamoto's disposal.

Rear Admiral Frank J. Fletcher had to counter this force with 3 carriers (including the hastily repaired *Yorktown*), 7 heavy cruisers and 1 light cruiser, and 15 destroyers. Aboard his carriers, Fletcher carried about 230 aircraft; in addition, there were a number of Midway-based planes, Marine fighters and scout bombers, Navy torpedo bombers and patrol bombers, totaling 98. The Army Seventh Air Force, too, had moved 17 B-17s up from Hawaii and 4 B-26s, converted into torpedo bombers. Although handicapped in terms of sheer weight, Fletcher enjoyed certain advantages: he knew Yamamoto was coming, he knew where Yamamoto would strike and when, so that he could concentrate his meager forces at the point at which they would prove most effective.

Yamamoto, on the other hand, split his forces in a characteristic attempt at a diversionary feint. This took the form of what was called the Northern, or Aleutians, Force under Vice-Admiral Moshiiro Hosogaya, who was to spearhead the Midway Operation by an attack upon American installations at Dutch Harbor and the invasion and occupation of Attu and Kiska. Two carriers, *Ryujo* and *Junyo*, whose air commander was Rear Admiral Kakuji Kakuta, accompanied the Northern Force. It was

hoped that this attack, so close to the American homeland, would bring out the American fleet, send it scurrying off into the northern Pacific, and leave Midway more or less unguarded for the main attack.

If not, Yamamoto planned to meet the American fleet and planes, after Midway itself had been struck, when they came out of Pearl Harbor to meet the surprise Japanese thrust. Yamamoto's forces consisted of the 1st Carrier Force, under command of Admiral Chuichi Nagumo, who had led the Hawaii strike upon Pearl Harbor. Nagumo had, in addition to screening and support groups of battleships, cruisers, and destroyers, four great carriers, *Akagi* (his own flagship), *Kaga, Hiryu,* and *Soryu.* That the temporary loss of the *Shokaku* and *Zuikaku* denied him one third of his air power did not disquiet Nagumo. He was certain, after six months of victory, that he and his carriers were invincible.

Yamamoto, aboard his flagship, the giant battleship *Yamato,* would command all the Midway-Aleutians forces, from what was named the "Main Body of the Main Force." This force, consisting of three large battleships, the light carrier *Hosho,* cruisers, destroyers, and seaplane carriers, would be situated about six hundred miles northwest of Midway, ready to come to the aid of Nagumo and the Midway Invasion Force or the Aleutian Invasion Force, as the course of the battle demanded.

Before the strikes were made various submarines of the Advance Submarine Force were to be dispersed northwest of Hawaii to spot the American ships as soon as they left Pearl Harbor to meet Nagumo's challenge at Midway. That, at least, was the plan—on paper. In practice, it did not work out quite as Yamamoto had expected.

The submarines were to have been in position by June 1, but because of delays in overhauling some of them and poor weather, the sub cordon was not established until June 4. By this time the great armada of Combined Fleet had been steaming toward its several objectives for ten days, ten days of nearly complete ignorance of the movements of the U.S. fleet.

The elaborate preparations required for the Midway-Aleutians Operation filled the airwaves with messages, most of which U. S. Intelligence intercepted, decoded, and flashed to Pearl Harbor. Thus two of the favorite Japanese techniques, surprise and feint, were rendered pointless from the beginning.

Task Force at sea, spring 1942: a view from the aft flight deck of the Enterprise *bearing TBFs; bringing* up the rear are a destroyer, a tanker, and, in the distance, the Hornet *and a tanker.*

(NAVY DEPT., NATIONAL ARCHIVES)

Not that every step of the proposed operation was lucidly outlined for Nimitz. His guess was that, in view of the massive preparations which were under way, the objective must be Midway. But there was no absolute certainty that the "AF" to which the Japanese referred so frequently in their messages was, indeed, Midway. Admiral King, in fact, was equally certain that it was Oahu, Hawaii.

Naval Intelligence then tricked the Japanese into the identification of AF. Dutifully, as ordered, Midway sent a message in the clear to Pearl Harbor reporting that its water distillation apparatus had broken down. Within days a Japanese radio message was intercepted reporting that AF was low on water. Midway it was!

This was only the first in a series of unanticipated errors which would beset Yamamoto. Another occurred when the submarine squadrons were delayed in taking up their positions to the north and northwest of Hawaii. By the time they had arrived, the

The lost Zero of the Aleutians; Tadayoshi Koga's Reisen *on its back in the tundra of Akutan Island. The Americans now had a nearly intact, once mysterious, Zero.* (NAVY DEPT., NATIONAL ARCHIVES)

two American task forces had already crossed the assigned cordon lines. When the time came for opening the Midway-Aleutians Operation, Yamamoto had no idea of the whereabouts of the American fleet, nor of its composition, however disproportionate compared to his.

Even while the several Japanese task forces approached their targets the American task forces lay in wait at "Point Luck," about 350 miles northeast of Midway. On May 28, the day the last Japanese ship left port, Rear Admiral Raymond A. Spruance's Task Force 16 (the *Enterprise* and *Hornet*) left Pearl Harbor for Point Luck. Two days later Rear Admiral Frank J. Fletcher, aboard the expeditiously rejuvenated *Yorktown,* left for Point Luck to join forces with Spruance and to take tactical command of the task forces. Nimitz would oversee the battle from his headquarters at Pearl Harbor. Thus he would be able to watch the progress of the battle from a central point. Yamamoto, on the other hand, would be aboard the *Yamato,* and thanks to the need for radio silence, would frequently be completely out of touch with the progress of the battle.

Nimitz was taking one risk in assuming that the main force was aimed at Midway and not the Aleutians. He concentrated his main striking force, therefore, in the vicinity of Midway, leaving the defense of the Aleutians to a small token force, mainly cruisers, under the command of Rear Admiral Robert A. Theobald. Fortunately for Nimitz his guess had been right, and although the Japanese succeeded in landing troops on Attu and Kiska, they neither gained strategic ground nor succeeded in luring the main American forces away from Midway. In fact, they suffered one serious loss in the Aleutians. This occurred on May 3, 1942, with an inconclusive attack by a formation of Kates, escorted by a half-dozen Zeros, upon Dutch Harbor. After leaving the carrier *Ryujo,* the Japanese planes encountered no opposition but heavy rain and thick fog. Over Dutch Harbor it was clear enough for the Kates to bomb and the Zeros to strafe the harbor installations and moored flying boats. There was some return fire from the few Americans based there, but Dutch Harbor was left a smoking shambles as the Japanese formation completed its attack and pulled away to reassemble for the return flight to the *Ryujo.*

It was then that Flight Petty Officer Tadayoshi

The crew of the Navy Catalina that spotted the Japanese fleet approaching Midway. Back row (*left to right*): *R. J. Derouin, Francis Musser, Ensign Hardeman, Jewell H. Reid* (*pilot*), *R. A. Swan. Front row: J. F. Grammell, J. Goovers,* and *P. A. Fitzpatrick.*
(NAVY DEPT., NATIONAL ARCHIVES)

Koga, flying an A6M2 *Reisen,* noticed that his aircraft trailed fuel in his wake. By radio he informed the bomber leader, Lieutenant Michio Kobayashi, that he did not have enough fuel to return to the *Ryujo* and would attempt to land at one of the designated emergency landing sites in the area. He would then await a pickup by Japanese submarine, according to the plans made for such emergencies.

Koga came in upon Akutan Island, a small island to the east of Dutch Harbor. Choosing a smooth, clear area, Koga lowered the wheels, opened his canopy, and cranked up his seat for the landing approach. Kobayashi, meanwhile, had scouted the landing area, which he later described as perfect. Koga skillfully brought the Zero lower, touched his wheels down, and with a great splash the Zero whipped over onto its back. The "flat and clear" landing spot was actually spongy tundra. Kobayashi circled over the wrecked Zero and assumed that Koga was either dead or seriously injured. He also assumed that, because of the marshy terrain, it would be impossible, or extremely difficult, to retrieve the "heavily damaged" plane. Five weeks

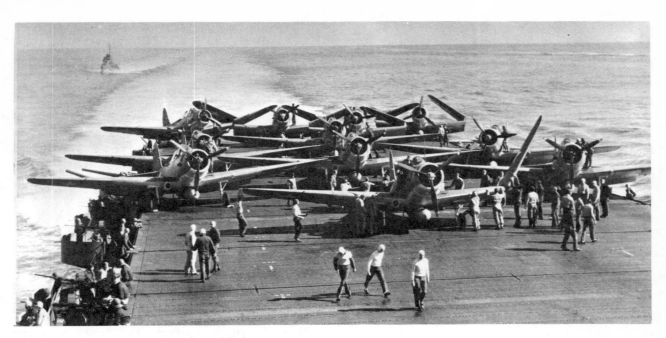

The Enterprise, *with the Douglas TBD-1s ("Devastator") of VT-6 on deck, races from "Point Luck" toward Midway.* (U. S. OFFICE OF WAR INFORMATION)

later, however, after the Zero was spotted by a Navy reconnaissance plane, the U. S. Navy sent a party to Akutan Island. There they found Koga hanging from his seat straps in the cockpit. He had evidently struck his head when the plane turned over and was killed. But the Zero was not as damaged as Kobayashi had supposed. It was in fact virtually intact, the first Zero to fall into American hands in so good a condition. Koga's plane was salvaged and shipped to the Naval Air Station, North Island, San Diego, and restored to flying condition. Tested by American pilots, the Zero revealed all of its secrets, good points as well as bad. It also led to the production of a plane specifically designed to deal with the Zero, the Grumman F6F ("Hellcat"). The loss of the single plane in the Dutch Harbor attack, the hoped-for diversion opening the Battle of Midway, was to cost the Japanese dear and ended the reign of the Zero over the skies in the Pacific.

Assuming that the Aleutian attacks were feints, the Americans awaited the main thrust at Point Luck. From Midway itself scouting planes were sent out to search for the oncoming Japanese fleet. It was around nine in the morning of June 3 that Ensign Jewell H. Reid, pilot of a Midway-based Catalina, flying about seven hundred miles to the west of Midway, spotted a large number of Japanese ships. He had found the transports of the Midway Invasion Force. Reid tracked the ships, dodging in and out of clouds, counting, checking direction and speed. For nearly two hours Reid and his crew observed what they believed was the main Japanese fleet headed for Midway at nineteen knots; the eleven ships were pointed east. As Reid reported his find to Midway and Pearl Harbor, Rear Admiral Raizo Tanaka, commanding the transport group, informed Yamamoto that all hopes for surprise were over. Yamamoto had counted upon unleashing an aerial attack upon Midway before the Americans ever realized the battle had begun. The initiative had now fallen into enemy hands. A heavy antiaircraft barrage forced Reid away from the Japanese surface force, but he had seen enough.

Midway, so long under the tension of waiting, came alive with preparation. Nine B-17s, led by Lieutenant Colonel Walter Sweeney, took off shortly after noon and reported that "Late in the afternoon, at a distance of 570 miles south of west of Midway, interception of the Japanese force was effected."

Sweeney's reaction upon seeing the vast Japanese fleet was less phlegmatic. "Good God," he said to his copilot Everett Wessman, "look at 'em!" It seemed that as far as the eye could see the waters below were dotted with ships trailing thin white wakes, like skates on a frozen pond. Smaller escort ships circled around the armada describing less regular patterns, like nervous water insects. It was an awe-inspiring sight; Sweeney estimated (erroneously) no less a force than forty-five ships.

The B-17s attacked in elements of three, Sweeney leading the first, dropping his six-hundred-pound bombs at the gyrating ships from an altitude of eight thousand feet. Antiaircraft fire flashed up at them furiously, appearing to one crewman "like a Times Square electric sign gone haywire." The next three Flying Fortresses followed, dropping their bombs from ten thousand feet; the last three dropped theirs from an altitude of twelve thousand feet. All three elements claimed either direct hits or near misses, and as all nine B-17s wheeled away from the antiaircraft fire, Sweeney looked back to see a battleship and a transport, seemingly still in the water, with "huge clouds of dark smoke mushroomed above them."

Although a total of thirty-six bombs were dropped by the B-17s, not one struck the dodging Japanese ships. The claims, plus others to follow, as well as the newspaper headlines attributing great feats to the Air Force bombers, would lead to much wartime feuding between the U. S. Navy and the Air Force.

Vice-Admiral Nagumo, meanwhile, was literally in a fog. His huge carrier striking force lay under a blanket of heavy weather, screening him from enemy search planes. At the same time it rendered navigation hazardous and also prevented Nagumo's search planes from being launched. One nagging question haunted him, one which he blurted out finally to his by now apprehensive staff; "But where is the enemy fleet?"

Some of the fog under which Nagumo proceeded was man-made. Yamamoto's staff, aboard the *Yamato,* had picked up radio transmissions in the Hawaii area which led them to suspect unusual enemy activity and the possibility of an American sortie. But Yamamoto did not inform Nagumo of this activity. He assumed that Nagumo was aware of it, which he was not, because Nagumo's ships were hundreds of miles closer to the enemy. Yamamoto was also all but fanatical upon maintaining radio silence. Meanwhile Nagumo glared into the swirling fog, hoping that the American carriers were still in the vicinity of the Solomon Islands, where Japanese intelligence had last placed them. The 1st Carrier Striking Force plunged through the fog toward Midway. Tomorrow, June 4, would re-

solve all things when Nagumo sent his planes off to bomb Midway.

Admiral Fletcher, in the area of Point Luck, had considered Ensign Reid's report of the sighting of the main force of the Japanese fleet. If Reid was right, then Fletcher's task forces were ill situated to challenge the invasion attempt. But Fletcher, judging from Reid's report of the location of the Japanese ships, concluded that they must be part of the invasion fleet and not the main attack force at all. There had been no carrier detected. And Fletcher's sixth sense told him that the air strike would materialize out of the area of murky weather to the northwest of Midway; further: the Japanese would, according to previous practice, launch their planes at dawn. So far, there was no sighting of Japanese carriers, however. But Fletcher's carriers would be in place, about two hundred miles north and slightly east of Midway, when morning came.

Dawn began to break at around four that morning. Though still under cloud, Nagumo's carriers came into a clearing. Despite the broken clouds and intermittent showers, stars were visible for the first time in days. A light wind blew from the southeast, which would aid the launch of the first attack wave. Nagumo could find some comfort in that. They would be precisely on schedule and Nagumo was aware of Yamamoto's addiction to timetables.

A Dauntless is given the signal to take off on a search mission. (DOUGLAS AIRCRAFT)

At almost the same moment that attack preparations were under way on the Japanese carriers, Midway too resounded to the roar of engines. Eleven Navy Catalinas were about to take off on search missions; streaks of light fanned into the dark eastern sky—it was 4:30 A.M. when the Catalinas, already fifteen minutes air-borne, prodded the western darkness in search of the Japanese ships. The PBYs were followed shortly after by bomb-laden planes from the Seventh Air Force's 5th and 11th Bombardment Groups, ready to attack the oncoming ships of the invasion force, which had been attacked the day before. Obviously, Nagumo was not aware of the attack, for before he ordered the first attack wave launched, he issued an estimate of the situation which revealed an unwonted optimism in Nagumo's generally conservative outlook. Two items, in retrospect, were tragically ironic: "The enemy is not yet aware of our plan, and he has not yet detected our task force," Nagumo had observed. And "There is no evidence of an enemy task force in our vicinity." According to all of the intelligence at his command, Nagumo could send his airmen off to bomb Midway believing that which he hoped was true was, indeed, true.

At a point about 240 miles northwest of Midway the 108 planes of the first attack wave took off from the four Japanese carriers. Thirty-six Zeros served as escort for the 36 Vals (dive bombers) and 36 Kates (torpedo bombers). The first wave was led by Lieutenant Joichi Tomonaga, on his first mission in the Pacific war. By 4:45 A.M. the formation had taken off and headed for Midway. The Vals and Kates flew in V-shaped echelons and the faster Zeros darted here and there over the formations to stay with them. As soon as the first wave was under way, Nagumo ordered the second wave, also 108 aircraft, to be readied. These would attack an enemy task force if it should appear, or if a second strike upon Midway were necessary, they would be ready. Eighteen Zeros circled over the striking force on air combat patrol.

Although not expecting American carriers or warships until after the Midway attack had begun, Nagumo, as an extra precautionary measure, dispatched several search planes to scour the seas to the south and east of his four carriers. Even so, the measure was much less systematic than usual. Of the seven planes, two took off on schedule; one developed engine trouble and returned before completing its search pattern and others returned early upon flying into the squally weather which clung to

Marine SB2Us (Vought-Sikorsky "Vindicator") leave Midway in search of the Japanese fleet, June 4, 1942.
(U. S. NAVY)

Nagumo's ships. The critical planes, as it turned out, those which were to be launched from the cruiser *Tone,* were delayed a half hour because of a malfunctioning catapult. The search pattern of one of the planes would have carried it over the American carriers—had it been launched.

Fletcher, too, was sending off search planes, ten Dauntlesses from the *Yorktown,* but they also missed the enemy carriers, still hidden under heavy weather. But the pilots of PBY Flight 58, Lieutenants Howard Ady and William Chase, churning through patches of clear and cloudy sky, spied a thin feather on the water to the north. It was a ship's wake; then another, another—and more. They dipped down and saw Japanese carriers below. They immediately radioed a maddeningly laconic message to Midway, intercepted by Fletcher waiting in the dark, "Enemy carriers." That was all. This answered very few of the questions racing through Fletcher's mind. Where were the carriers? How many were there?

These questions were not immediately forthcoming, for the Catalina had been spotted and anti-aircraft fire rose up from the ships. Zeros, too, began climbing to intercept the American plane. Ady and Chase dipped into a cloud bank and were lost to the Japanese gunners, as well as to the fighter pilots. After some moments, they selected another break in the clouds and circled back for another look. Almost directly below them they saw Tomonaga's bombers and fighters, halfway to Midway. Their radio crackled, "Many planes heading Midway, bearing 320°, distance 150." And then Fletcher began accumulating his answers when a third message came in, "Two carriers and battleship bearing 320°, distance 180, course 135, speed 25." Because he had to wait for the search planes, Fletcher ordered Spruance to "proceed southwesterly and attack enemy carriers when definitely located. I will follow as soon as planes recovered."

At Midway too all hands prepared for action. Shortly after the message "Many planes heading Midway," the radar picked up the Japanese formation. Air raid sirens blared, aircraft lifted into the air, and men rushed to gun positions and shelters. The B-17s headed for the transports were reached by radio and directed to strike at the carriers. The four B-26s armed with torpedoes and six Grumman TBFs ("Avengers"), making their first combat sortie,

The Brewster F2A ("Buffalo"), no match for the Zero, made its single U.S. combat effort at the Battle of Midway and was hopelessly outperformed—to the tragic cost of Marine pilots. (NAVY DEPT., NATIONAL ARCHIVES)

were vectored toward the Japanese carriers. In addition Marine dive bombers, sixteen SBD-2s (Dauntlesses) led by Major Lofton B. Henderson, and eleven SB2U-3s (Vindicators) led by Major Benjamin Morris, all of VMSB-241, were also sent to deal with the carriers.

As for the oncoming Japanese bombers and fighters, within ten minutes of their first sighting Marine fighters of VMF-221 were air-borne for interception. There were twenty-five fighters, nineteen of which unfortunately were the hopelessly inferior Brewster F2A Buffalos; the remaining six were Grumman F4F Wildcats. Major Floyd B. Parks led the first attack upon the Japanese formation with a dozen planes. Thirty miles out at fourteen thousand feet Parks sighted a Japanese formation twenty thousand feet below him. The Zeros, evidently assigned to strafe Midway and not expecting interception, flew beneath the dive bombers. Parks led a diving attack upon the unsuspecting bombers. Within minutes he was joined by Captain Kirk Armistead with the other thirteen Marine fighters and a general melee ensued. The Zeros swarmed over the Buffalos and Wildcats and of the twenty-five which had gone into the battle, only ten Marine fighters returned. In exchange for five or six Japanese planes the Marines lost thirteen Buffalos and two Wildcats,

Midway following the Japanese air attack by Tomonaga's first wave of Vals and Kates. Two of the island's *indigenous inhabitants, gooney birds, nest in the foreground.* (NAVY DEPT., NATIONAL ARCHIVES)

and of the ten planes which returned only two were operational.

Tomonaga pressed on to Midway and at six-thirty the first bomb fell; bombs continued falling, despite the heavy antiaircraft fire, for the next twenty minutes. Hundreds of bombs tumbled down upon both Sand and Eastern islands. Several buildings were left burning on both islands; the powerhouse on Eastern was struck, so was the post exchange; a bomb crashed into the command post of Major William W. Benson, killing him and several other men. Bombs fell along the northeastern edge of Sand also, demolishing barracks, setting a seaplane hangar aflame, and detonating fuel storage tanks. Very little damage was done to the airstrip and, of course, since most of the Midway-based aircraft were out searching for Nagumo's carriers, very few planes went up in smoke. Thirteen Americans lay dead and eighteen were wounded. Although unaware of the small casualty toll, Tomonaga saw that not enough damage had been done to Midway—and that

Midway flag raising. The Japanese attack came simultaneously with the raising of the colors, which proceeded as scheduled despite the "bombs bursting in air." (Note: this was not a posed photograph.)

(U. S. NAVY)

Grumman TBF ("Avenger"), which made its battle debut at Midway. (NAVY DEPT., NATIONAL ARCHIVES)

Of the six new Avengers that had been dispatched from Midway, only one returned; this is it.

(U. S. NAVY)

antiaircraft fire was savagely profuse as he led the formation away from Midway, now marked by curling columns of black smoke and fire. He radioed to Nagumo on the *Akagi,* "There is need for a second attack. Time: 0700."

When this message was received Nagumo was in a state of passive perturbation; the Catalina piloted by Ady and Chase had been seen and clearly it had seen them. The Americans must now be aware of the presence of Japanese carriers. What to do? Should he send another strike against Midway, or should he hold his planes in readiness for a possible attack from enemy carriers, if they were around?

A bugle blared announcing "Air Raid!" At this time the Japanese had no radar system. It was just five minutes after Tomonaga's request for a second Midway attack. A flag whipped up the mast of one of the destroyers: "Enemy planes in sight." Shortly after, a bridge lookout on the *Akagi* shouted, "Six medium land-based planes approaching! Twenty degrees to starboard. On the horizon." Nearly ten miles away were the four Army Marauders, "their bellies cut and sutured to carry torpedoes," a detachment from the 22nd Bombardment Group (Medium) and the 38th Bombardment Group (M). Leading the four B-26s was Captain James F. Collins. As he sighted the Japanese ships he saw also six Navy Avengers, low on the water, swarming with Zeros.

The Avengers were a detachment of Torpedo

Squadron 8, the main body of which was based on the *Hornet* at Point Luck. Caught by the impending battle at Midway en route to join the rest of the squadron, they had to operate from the islands rather than from the *Hornet*. The six TBFs were led into the battle by Lieutenant Langdon K. Fieberling. He and Collins had sighted the Japanese carriers at about the same time.

Leading the attack, Fieberling bore down upon the carriers through a virtual curtain of antiaircraft fire and a trio of Zeros, the pilots of which took the chance of being struck by their own shellfire. Within moments three of the Avengers were aflame and cartwheeled into the water. But the survivors pushed onward, through the all but impenetrable gunfire. By this time the Marauders, too, had joined in the attack, flying through the barrage of gunfire. Even the big guns on the larger ships were depressed to fire into the onrushing planes, raising great waterspouts in their flight paths as dangerous as the fire itself. It was near suicide, as the planes and crews were chopped to bits in the unescorted attempt at the carriers.

When the torpedo bombers came within range only three planes of the original six remained. One of the Marauders was shot down, then another. The last, which had managed to release its torpedo, flashed over the deck of the *Akagi,* burst into flame, and plunged into the sea. When the attack was over, only two B-26s and one TBF returned to Midway. Not one of the torpedoes had hit its target. The ferocity of the Japanese defense had forced the Americans to release the torpedoes from too great a distance, which enabled the ships to maneuver out of their paths. Nagumo watched one of the torpedoes pass harmlessly by the *Akagi* in a curling white wake.

As soon as it was clear that the Americans had either been driven off or had crashed into the sea, Nagumo made his decision. As Tomonaga had suggested, there would be a second attack upon Midway itself. Evidently the land-based torpedo bombers would give them no further trouble.

This decision entailed complications for the deck crews of the *Akagi* and *Kaga,* for the planes then ready on their flight decks were armed with torpedoes in readiness for an attack upon American carriers. But to this moment none had been sighted. So the planes were brought below decks and the torpedoes removed and replaced with conventional bombs. The aircraft of the *Hiryu* and *Soryu* were not affected by Nagumo's decision, for they were already armed for dive-bombing. The torpedo bombers from these carriers were part of Tomonaga's first attack wave; the dive bombers for this wave had come from the *Akagi* and *Kaga.*

As this changeover was being feverishly made, the carriers came under another attack, this time from Sweeney's Flying Fortresses. From the *Akagi* great water geysers could be seen rising around the *Hiryu* and *Soryu* as the fourteen B-17s, untroubled by the Zeros, whose pilots seemed wary of the big bombers, dropped their full load of bombs. Again, upon their safe return to Midway, claims for hits upon the carriers were made, but actually no bomb from the B-17s hit any of the carriers.

Nagumo could take pride in the effective manner in which the men in his force dodged the American missiles or destroyed their planes. But to his surprise, the delayed *Tone* search plane had wired back a report of "Ten ships, apparently enemy. . . ." But what kind of ships? Nagumo wished to know. This was an unexpected turn, for American surface ships, hundreds of miles from Midway, were not anticipated for another day or two. Nagumo sent orders below and to the *Kaga:* Stop rearming the bombers with conventional bombs and begin arming with torpedoes.

There was another interruption in the rapidly developing battle. The Marine Dauntlesses and Vindicators from Midway, led by Henderson and Morris, arrived to make glide-bombing attacks upon the carriers. Henderson led, with his sixteen Dauntlesses, an attack upon the *Hiryu*. Because of his pilots' unfamiliarity with the Dauntless, Henderson decided upon a glide attack rather than a dive-bombing. At eight hundred feet he was met by a swarm of Zeros and within minutes eight of the Dauntlesses, including Henderson's, went down in flames. There were no hits made on any enemy ships.

Major Morris's slower Vindicators came upon the Japanese ships shortly after Henderson but not in a position for an attack on any of the carriers. They attacked battleships instead and although claiming to have hit the *Haruna* or *Kirishima,* may have only succeeded in a near miss. Two of the Vindicators were lost in the attack and a third crashed in the sea five miles from Midway. The pilot was alive,

Enterprise *Wildcats prepare for takeoff to escort the bombers and torpedo planes of the U.S. fleet.*
(NAVY DEPT., NATIONAL ARCHIVES)

but the gunner, Private Henry I. Starks, was dead; he had never fired a machine gun before in his life until the Battle of Midway. Major Morris later took over the command of VMSB-241, upon the loss of Henderson, but was himself lost later in the day during a search flight for "a burning enemy carrier," which was never found.

Once again the Japanese carriers had fought off heroic but ineffectual American attacks, and Nagumo could take some consolation in that. But then the *Tone* search plane wired another report on the American surface fleet it had found: "Enemy ships are five cruisers and five destroyers."

There was a break in the tension on the *Akagi's* bridge.

"Just as I thought," said intelligence officer Lieutenant Commander Ono, expressing everyone's sense of deliverance; "there are no carriers."

Eleven minutes later the *Tone* plane reported, "Enemy force accompanied by what appears to be aircraft carrier bringing up the rear." The imprecision—"what appears to be aircraft carrier"—was hopeful, but maddening. Ten minutes later the plane reported, "Two additional ships, apparently cruis-

ers. . . ." Nagumo realized he must face reality; so great a number of ships must contain at least one carrier. If so, however, where were the carrier aircraft?

Nagumo now decided that he must launch his torpedo-armed aircraft against the American surface fleet, whatever its composition. The Japanese would then however, be without proper fighter escort, for all of the Zeros from the projected second wave had been sent aloft to fight the several waves of attackers which had come from Midway. The Zeros would need to land to refuel. And any moment would bring the return of the first attack wave; Tomonaga's bombers and fighters would need the deck space for landing—and they too would require refueling and rearming. While Nagumo pondered his next move, he received a message from Rear-Admiral Tamon Yamaguchi, whom many regarded as the heir of Yamamoto and who led the 2nd Carrier Division (the *Hiryu* and *Soryu*). "Consider it advisable," Yamaguchi radioed, "to launch attack force immediately." Yamaguchi, having successfully dodged the B-17s, was concerned with the *Tone's* search plane's reports of the American surface fleet and the probable carrier. The enemy task force must be attacked immediately.

But Nagumo continued to vacillate. He was aware of the importance of attacking the American ships, but he could not send off the torpedo planes without escorting Zeros—or with Zeros on the verge of running out of fuel. He had himself witnessed the virtual butchery of the American attackers without escort. Then he made up his mind: they would recover the Midway returnees, rearm, and be ready for the enemy surface fleet. Another order went to the hangar decks below as the readied planes were cleared from the flight decks to receive the incoming aircraft. The bombs were to be changed to torpedoes—again. As this proceeded Nagumo sighted the first of the returning planes. He signaled the *Kaga, Soryu,* and *Hiryu:* "After completing recovery operations, force will temporarily head northward. We plan to contact and destroy enemy task force." He then radioed Yamamoto, hundreds of miles away aboard the *Yamato,* and Vice-Admiral Nobutake Kondo, with his Midway Invasion Force, of his decision. Finally, after nearly forty minutes, all of the first attack wave planes had been recovered

and were being feverishly refueled and rearmed. Nagumo ordered the carrier force to steam away from Midway to a position from which the second attack wave could be sent against the American fleet. Meanwhile, his carriers were in their most vulnerable state: decks and hangar decks crowded with planes, bombs, and fuel hoses. But this nagging thought was overlooked in the excitement of preparing to finish off the American fleet.

Spruance, in the *Enterprise,* with the *Hornet* as company, had steamed toward the Japanese carrier force as soon as word had come of its location. Spruance, like Nagumo, had difficult decisions to make. He had planned to launch planes about a hundred miles from the Japanese carriers, but his chief of staff, Captain Miles Browning, described by Samuel Eliot Morison as "one of the most irascible and unstable officers ever to earn a fourth stripe, but a man with a slide-rule brain," suggested an earlier launch. Browning's thinking told him that Nagumo would attempt to launch a second attack upon Midway. Why not catch him while he was refueling his

John Waldron, dedicated commander of VT-8, "Torpedo 8" of the Hornet, *which was wiped out at Midway; right: Clarence W. McClusky, air group com-*

mander of the Enterprise *who led the attack on the Japanese carrier* Kaga.

(NAVY DEPT., NATIONAL ARCHIVES)

planes? Decisive, brilliant, even enigmatic, Spruance took the advice, and further, he decided to launch a full-scale attack (knowing that Fletcher would follow later with reinforcements from the *Yorktown*).

About 7 A.M. the *Hornet* and *Enterprise* turned into the wind; they were nearly two hundred miles away from the expected position of the enemy carriers, but Spruance believed the risk of the long distance would be worth it, indeed, if Browning were proved correct. At this same moment, Tomonaga's planes had begun their return flight from Midway and Nagumo's carriers had come under the attack of the Army B-26s and the Navy Avengers.

Among the first aircraft off the *Hornet*'s flight deck were the torpedo bombers of the main section of Torpedo 8, fifteen ancient Douglas Devastators. Leading this squadron was a Navy career pilot, tough, aggressive, sharp-eyed, proud of his Sioux Indian forebears, Lieutenant Commander John C. Waldron. A devoted Navy man, Waldron had welded his men into a well-disciplined unit without ever losing their devotion. Along with the Torpedo 8 (VT-8) planes, the *Hornet* launched thirty-five bombers and ten fighters. The total of sixty *Hornet* aircraft were led by the carrier's Air Group Commander, Commander Stanhope C. Ring.

Lieutenant Commander Clarence W. McClusky led an equal number of aircraft (actually thirty-seven bombers, fourteen torpedo bombers, and ten fighters) off the *Enterprise*. The air reverberated to the roar of more than a hundred planes, which formed into units and headed for the expected point of interception with the Japanese carriers. Fletcher too followed these planes up with a dozen torpedo bombers, seventeen dive bombers, and six Wildcats—these last under the leadership of Lieutenant Commander John S. Thatch. The dive bombers were under the command of Lieutenant Commander Maxwell F. Leslie, who suffered an ironic mishap early in the flight. When the planes had climbed to an altitude of ten thousand feet, he signaled the squadron to arm their bombs. Leslie himself pushed the newly installed electrical device and, to his dismay, experienced the unmistakable lurch of a suddenly lightened aircraft. He soon learned through hand signals from his number two man on the left (whose rear gunner joined in the frantic wigwagging) that the squadron commander had lost his thousand-pound bomb. From the right another

Dauntless veered over, pilot and gunner signaling. Obviously a short or some other mechanical quirk had caused the bomb to fall instead of merely arming it. There was nothing for Leslie to do but to lead his squadron into the battle without a bomb. Within minutes, to his further dismay, he learned that three other planes had suffered the same accident. All seventeen planes pushed on, though only thirteen were properly armed. Lieutenant Paul Holmberg, Leslie's number two man, laconically commented, "When this bad news was confirmed, the skipper made many frustrating motions with his hands and lips. . . ."

Meanwhile, the *Hornet* and *Enterprise* planes neared the point of interception. Nagumo's decision to turn north, away from Midway, while his planes refueled actually took the carriers out of the line of interception. Intermittent cloud cover, too, played its role. For as Ring led the *Hornet* planes along the line, he saw none of the Japanese carriers, then hidden under cloud. He continued farther, along the line, followed by the bombers and fighters, until he saw nothing but ocean or clouds. Perhaps Nagumo had turned southward, toward Midway, Ring thought, and turned toward the atoll. But he found nothing there but the smoking reminders of the Japanese bombings. He had made a wrong guess. Although some of his planes managed to return to the *Hornet,* some, dangerously low on fuel, had to put down at Midway; some did not make it and splashed into the waters around Midway.

Waldron, leading Torpedo 8, on the other hand, sensed that Nagumo would change course. To Waldron's left, a few miles to the south, flew Lieutenant Commander Eugene F. Lindsey's fourteen Devastators of Torpedo Squadron 6. Above him, at twenty thousand feet, zigzagged the ten Wildcats led by Lieutenant James S. Gray as fighter escort of the *Enterprise* bombers. The agreement between Gray and Lindsey was that when the torpedo bombers found the Japanese carriers, Lindsey would signal Gray for fighter protection during the attack. However, in flying through cloud Gray's fighters attached themselves inadvertently to Waldron's Devastators. There was no agreed signal, of course, between the *Hornet*'s Waldron and the *Enterprise*'s Gray.

Thus, because of a series of small twists and turns of fate, Waldron's slow-moving Devastators were the first of the carrier planes to find the Japanese car-

Ensign George H. Gay (recuperating in the U.S. naval hospital at Pearl Harbor), the lone survivor of Waldron's Torpedo 8.

(NAVY DEPT., NATIONAL ARCHIVES)

riers. Certainly one of the reasons was Waldron's mystical determination. When his men received their attack plan that day, attached to it was a letter from Waldron:

Just a word to let you know that I feel we are ready. We have had a very short time to train and we have worked under the most severe difficulties. But we have truly done the best humanly possible. I actually believe that under these conditions we are the best in the world. My greatest hope is that we encounter a favorable tactical situation, but if we don't, and the worst comes to worst, I want each of us to do his utmost to destroy our enemies. If there is only one plane left to make a final run in, I want that man to go in and get a hit. May God be with all of us. Good luck, happy landings and give 'em hell.

Waldron led the Devastators to the point of interception, and when he found nothing, some sixth sense told him to turn north. This brought them around the edge of the large bank of cloud through which they had passed. And there—about eight miles distant, off his starboard wing—lay Nagumo's carrier striking force. Ordering Torpedo 8 into bat-

tle formation, Waldron descended to within a few yards above the Pacific, assigning targets to the various elements, barking commands in a dry, emotionless voice. The fifteen Devastators lined up on their targets, Waldron selecting the nearest carrier.

Fifty Zeros which had been circling over the Japanese fleet dropped down to intercept the intruders. Without fighter protection they should be relatively simple to deal with. The Devastator was slow, underarmed (one .50-caliber and one .30-caliber machine gun: the pilot controlled the forward firing gun and the radio-gunner manned a flexible gun); the Douglas TBD-1 was obsolete by 1942. It could barely manage two hundred miles an hour top speed, and when on its torpedo run, the plane lumbered along, a moving target.

Even before Waldron reached anywhere near a torpedo release point, the swift Zeros thronged around the hapless Devastators. In seconds, the Pacific erupted with the blazing splashes of fiery Devastators. The Zeros closed in from all sides and shot the torpedo bombers literally to pieces. Ensign George Gay, the squadron's navigator, piloted the fifteenth Devastator and watched the decimation of Torpedo 8 with horror. One after the other the burning planes careened into the water, crumbling in the impact, spurting foam, smoke, and flame. Gay saw Waldron still pressing on although both his wingmen had been shot down. A Zero flashed across the Devastator's path, spraying it with machine-gun fire, and Gay saw flame licking from a ruptured fuel tank; then the tank burst into an orange-red blossom. Waldron, evidently trying to get away from the scorching flames, clawed the canopy open and stood up. At full speed, with torpedo still slung under the fuselage, the blazing Devastator slammed into the Pacific.

Gay continued on his run. The skipper was gone, he realized; as he darted his eyes over the water, he realized too everyone was gone but him. His was, in Waldron's tragically prophetic phrase, the "only one plane left." The Zeros whirred in to attack the fifteenth Devastator. Gay tried to ignore them as he centered his sight on a carrier, even then maneuvering out of his line of sight. He sensed the thud of Japanese machine-gun fire striking the plane; there was stinging pain in his left arm. A spent slug had dug into the flesh of the arm; another fragment of steel, possibly a piece of the cockpit torn away, cut his hand. His gunner, Robert Huntington, shouted, "Mr. Gay, I'm hit!" Through the frenzied, unremitting attack of the Zeros, Gay prodded the Devastator toward his target.

The single aircraft became the center of attention of the ship's antiaircraft guns as well as of the converging Zeros. Bits of cockpit burst in around Gay's feet, control cables severed, and he had trouble keeping the Devastator under control. He had to release that final "pickle," as Waldron called the torpedoes. Gay, of the thirty men who had begun the attack, was the only man alive. Huntington sprawled lifelessly in the rear cockpit.

Gay had further trouble with his torpedo release mechanism, undoubtedly shot up by the Zeros. Unable to use his left hand, Gay gripped the control column between his knees and with his right hand pulled the emergency release lever. The torpedo dropped and the lightened plane leaped up into the air and within minutes skimmed barely ten feet over the bow of the carrier. Gay kicked the rudder, turning south, now barely above the waves. It was over for Ensign Gay, so he flattened out the Devastator and stalled into the sea. He splashed in with great force, tearing away the right wing, which bounced along the surface like a flat rock. Gay tore open the canopy as water poured in on him. He glanced again at the rear cockpit. There was nothing to do for Huntington. Quickly Gay swam away from the sinking plane, concerned over what would happen when the Zeros came around to investigate.

Inflating his life jacket, Gay bobbed around the waters strewn with the debris of battle. He found a boat bag, which contained an inflatable rubber raft, holding onto it for future use. It would not be healthy to use it now, with the Zeros whipping over now and then. Then he found a floating cushion which had been knocked free of the Devastator. Placing the cushion over his head, Gay found refuge from the searching Zeros and for the next few hours watched the unfolding drama of the Battle of Midway. (After dark Gay inflated his rubber boat and was found the next day, the sole survivor of Torpedo 8's attack, by a Navy PBY. Upon being taken to Pearl Harbor for medical attention, Gay was asked by a doctor how he had treated his wounds. In his Texas-inflected speech Gay replied that he had soaked his wounds in "salt water for several hours.")

A Dauntless, dive brakes down, drops a bomb.
(DOUGLAS AIRCRAFT)

It was a jubilant Zero leader who could report to Nagumo that all fifteen American torpedo bombers had been sent burning into the sea. Not one torpedo strike had been made. The war gods smiled, indeed, upon Nagumo.

But Nagumo hardly had time for an impassive smile, for a lookout shouted, "Enemy torpedo bombers, thirty degrees to starboard, coming in low!" This was followed by another exclamation, from the opposite lookout, "Enemy torpedo bombers approaching forty degrees to port!" The tempo was accelerating. The starboard attackers were Lindsey's fourteen Devastators of VT-6 (the *Enterprise*), which had flown parallel to Waldron's squadron, but some miles to the south. Like Waldron, Lindsey sensed that the carriers lay to the north instead of closer to Midway, as Ring had thought. Also like Waldron, Lindsey swooped in to attack (his major target being the *Kaga*) without fighter escort. For some reason Lindsey never called Gray, still circling over the the scene of the battle at twenty thousand feet. Instead, he plunged into the attack and was cut to

Dauntlesses at Midway: as a Japanese ship burns following an earlier attack, another wave of SBDs close in for the kill. (NAVY DEPT., NATIONAL ARCHIVES)

ribbons by antiaircraft and the swarms of Zeros. In minutes, ten of Lindsey's fourteen planes (including his own) were sent spinning and flaming into the sea. The four remaining planes released their torpedoes, but again not one struck home.

Almost stimultaneously the *Yorktown*'s VT-3, commanded by Lieutenant Commander Lance E. Massey, a dozen Devastators in all, in company with Thatch's six Wildcats, arrived upon the scene. As they hurtled toward the Japanese carriers, some of the Zeros could be seen landing. Obviously the earlier fighting had depleted the fuel and ammunition of the Japanese fighters. But this did not prevent others from swamping Thatch's little band and also Massey's Devastators on their torpedo run-ins. The air once again filled with puffs of smoke and machine-gun fire crisscrossed above the water, breaking the surface with evenly spaced, vicious geysers. Like Waldron and Lindsey before him, Massey raced headlong into certain devastation. His and six other planes were quickly shot into the sea. The five remaining planes continued on the run-in and

splashed their torpedoes into the churning water. Three planes were flamed by the Zeros just moments after. Of the twelve TBDs Massey took into the attack, only two returned to the *Yorktown*.

In about a half hour, roughly from 9:28, when Waldron's VT-8 had attacked, until 10 A.M., when the last of Massey's torpedoes went astray, Nagumo's carriers had been attacked by forty-one American aircraft and had destroyed thirty-five. Not one torpedo struck any Japanese ship. Now at last the battle-churned skies were free of enemy aircraft and the sea, here and there, emitted rising smoke. But the destroyed planes did not stay afloat long and all that remained was oil-soaked, scorched flotsam. Under one of the insignificant dots floated Ensign Gay.

Now Nagumo could give his full attention to launching the counterstrike. All during the attack by the doomed torpedo bombers preparations had gone on to get the planes ready to strike at the carriers, the source of the thirty-five planes they had just annihilated. Soon after, the planes were bombed-up and ready for take-off. The four carriers turned into the wind. Within five minutes their bombers would be air-borne and racing for the American carriers. The gods continued to smile. At ten-twenty Nagumo gave the order to begin launching the attack.

At ten twenty-four the air officer on the *Akagi* signaled, and a Zero gathered speed and roared off the deck. A lookout screamed, "Hell-divers!"

Plummeting out of a nearly cloudless sky were several Dauntlesses. The men on the deck of the *Akagi* watched this sudden materialization with stunned horror. The dive bombers plunged toward the *Kaga,* almost unopposed except for sporadic machine-gun fire from a few alert crews and some splotches of antiaircraft fire. The Zeros had been pulled down to the water by the attack of the torpedo bombers, whose sacrifices now would begin to assume implications beyond blind heroism.

The Dauntlesses were the *Yorktown* dive bombers led by Maxwell Leslie, whose own bomb had been accidentally dropped into the sea. He and the sixteen others arrived not long after the Japanese carriers had scurried out of the way of Massey's torpedo attack. Leslie had his eye on the nearest two, the *Soryu* and the *Kaga.* The latter, with more than twice the tonnage of the *Soryu,* impressed Leslie as the more tempting target. Signaling his wingmen, he led the bombers into a seventy-degree dive. Although bombless, Leslie contributed to the general destruction by firing his .50-caliber machine gun, beginning at ten thousand feet and pulling out at four thousand because the gun had jammed. On the decks of the *Kaga* he saw many planes apparently ready for take-off.

Leslie was followed by Lieutenant Paul Holmberg, who like his commander aimed the Dauntless at the great red circle painted on the *Kaga*'s flight deck. The wind screamed over the Dauntless as Holmberg dived down to twenty-five hundred feet. He pushed the electric bomb release and, just to make certain, also snatched at the manual release. Holmberg's thousand-pound bomb burst near the *Kaga*'s superstructure, spilling flame, flinging shattered metal, ripping and tearing across the deck, leaving a screaming, red trail of horror in its wake. More planes dived, some achieving only near misses, but three other bombs followed across the flight deck. Planes were flung over the side into the sea by the force of the explosions. Fuel tanks burst and poured flame into the holocaust, fires enveloped the flight deck and poured onto the men and planes below. Within minutes, the *Kaga* was a hopeless flaming pyre, despite the efforts of damage-control crews.

As Leslie and his men attacked the *Kaga* McClusky and his thirty-seven Dauntlesses from the *Enterprise* came upon the scene. McClusky had followed the wake of a destroyer which had left the main carrier group to deal with an American submarine, the *Nautilus,* which had been harassing it. The destroyer, moving at a fast clip would head, McClusky was certain, for the carriers—and he was right. McClusky's planes came in from the southwest, almost at right angles to Leslie's. The *Akagi,* which had been fleeing northwestward, was nearest to McClusky's formation; the giant carrier made a sharp turn to the south. The smaller *Soryu,* which had been passed over by Leslie in favor of the *Kaga,* was also in McClusky's view. The first bomb had already burst on the *Kaga*'s deck, billowing black smoke. McClusky felt certain it would need no further attention. The remaining two carriers (the *Hiryu* was farther to the north and out of sight) had turned into the wind to launch aircraft.

Two minutes after Leslie dropped down upon the *Kaga,* the *Enterprise* Dauntlesses, divided into two formations, dived on the *Soryu* and the *Akagi.* Mc-

Clusky led the *Soryu* attack and Lieutenant Wilmer E. Gallagher led the attack upon the *Akagi,* Nagumo's flagship. Unopposed by the Zeros, the Dauntlesses whipped through the air toward their targets, dropped their bombs, and pulled away. Two direct hits smashed onto the *Akagi*'s deck—neither of which would have normally seriously stopped the carrier. But the detonations flared the fuel in the waiting planes; the intense heat, in turn, detonated the bombs and torpedoes the Japanese planes carried. The air became deadly with metal splinters and flame. Pilots died in their cockpits, or were blown overboard burning into the sea. Deck hands became screaming torches. The helpless wounded were literally roasted to death on the twisted, scorching decks.

Three direct hits transformed the nearby *Soryu* into a similar inferno; within twenty minutes Captain Ryusaku Yanagimoto ordered the carrier abandoned. Men leaped into the water away from the searing heat and explosions. Because of the several order changes of the bombers' bomb loads, many bombs and torpedoes had been left lying about the decks, which added further hazard. The *Soryu* was obviously doomed. His men tried to force Yanagimoto, who was an extremely popular officer, to leave the bridge, but the captain refused. A burly petty officer, a Navy wrestling champion, was sent to take Yanagimoto by force if necessary. He was prevented by the determined look in his captain's eyes—he left without touching the officer. The last known act of Yanagimoto was his singing of *"Kimigayo"* the national anthem, as he remained on the smoke-obscured bridge. Shortly after 7 P.M., following nine hours of drifting and blazing, the *Soryu* sank steaming under the sea. It was the first of the Japanese carriers to be lost.

The *Kaga* followed within twelve minutes—at 7:25 P.M. During its fiery death throes the carrier came under a submarine attack. Three projectiles streaked for the stricken carrier; two missed and one struck a glancing blow. It was a dud which broke in two; the warhead sank harmlessly into the depths but the buoyant rear portion of the torpedo remained afloat to serve as an improvised floatboard for several of the *Kaga*'s crew. But eight hundred others went to the bottom when the burning hulk, torn by severe explosions, sank to the bottom.

Nagumo found the realities difficult to grasp.

Japanese torpedo bombers race through heavy anti-aircraft fire for the American ships. Shrapnel splashes in the foreground. A cruiser (left) and a destroyer (right) fire at three approaching enemy planes.
(U. S. NAVY)

From the *Akagi*'s bridge he could see the smoke of the *Kaga* and *Soryu* staining the distant skies. Around him there were confusion, shouting, the acrid stench of burning metal; Rear Admiral Ryunosuke Kusaka, Nagumo's chief of staff, was shouting something to him. In the noise of explosion, the confusion, the smoke, Nagumo stared at him. Kusaka said something about leaving the *Akagi*. Nagumo seemed oblivious to the sense of Kusaka's statement; he nodded and turned away from his chief of staff. The *Akagi*'s deck was a flaming shambles, but Nagumo did not wish to leave.

"Sir," Kusaka pleaded, "most of our ships are still intact. You must command them." The old man, ashen, found it all very difficult to believe: in two minutes a handful of planes had wiped out three quarters of his carrier force. Captain Taijiro Aoki joined the men, added his voice gently to the argument. The *Nagara,* a light cruiser, had pulled up alongside and the two men convinced Nagumo that he should retire to the *Nagara*. Aoki assured Nagumo, "I will take care of the ship. Please, we all implore you, shift your flag to the *Nagara* and resume command of the force."

Aoki also argued that since there were no communications systems working, Nagumo must leave the ship in order to carry on. The old admiral realized the sense of this statement and consented to leave. By this time the fires had spread so heavily that Nagumo could leave the bridge only by sliding down a rope to the deck. He was then led along an outboard passage to the anchor deck, where he stiffly climbed down a rope ladder into a waiting boat, which took him to the *Nagara*.

Yamamoto, who had positioned the ships of the main force too far away from Nagumo's carriers to be of any help to him, found it difficult also to comprehend the meaning of what was happening. When Captain Aoki, still aboard the doomed *Akagi,* wired for permission to sink the carrier after ordering the survivors off, Yamamoto, upon intercepting the message, ordered the scuttling delayed. Aoki then lashed himself to the anchor, on the only fire-free portion of the ship, and waited. Eventually, Yamamoto sensed the inevitable and gave the order to sink the carrier. A rescue party went aboard and convinced Aoki he should not go down with the ship. Rather than permit the ship to fall into enemy hands, even

The Yorktown *under attack by torpedo bombers led by Tomonaga, whose plane was destroyed by American* guns *after it had released its torpedo. The* Yorktown *lists, the result of earlier strikes.*

in derelict form, Japanese destroyers sent torpedoes into its sides. At 4:55 A.M. in the morning of June 4, Nagumo's flagship sank bursting into the sea, carrying 263 dead with it. That was the third carrier to go.

Aboard the *Hiryu,* the fourth and last carrier of Nagumo's striking force, Admiral Yamaguchi prepared to attack the American ships. Because of his position to the north of the other three carriers, he had escaped attack from the dive bombers. Gazing around the horizon, Yamaguchi was readily aware of his responsibilities: his planes only could strike at the American fleet.

Just four minutes before a reluctant Nagumo abandoned the *Akagi,* the resolute Yamaguchi launched eighteen dive bombers and six Zeros against the now known position of an American carrier. The small force was led by Lieutenant Michio Kobayashi, a veteran of Pearl Harbor. On the flight Kobayashi lost two of his escorting fighters, whose overzealous pilots darted away to attack a

formation of American Dauntlesses returning from the battle scene. These may have been Leslie's planes triumphantly finished with the *Kaga.* Kobayashi lost further to an American Wildcat attack, so that by the time he came within the vicinity of the carrier, only eight of the original eighteen bombers continued to follow him.

Meanwhile, just before noon of that June 4, the radar aboard the *Yorktown* detected the approach of Japanese aircraft, and all preparations were made to meet an enemy attack: refueling of aircraft was stopped, watertight doors were slammed closed, an auxiliary tank on the stern holding eight hundred gallons of aviation fuel was pushed over the side, fuel lines were drained and filled with carbon dioxide. Fighters were sent out to meet the attack, and returning planes, including Leslie's flight, already low on fuel, were waved off and ordered out of antiaircraft fire zones.

Kobayashi swept in for the attack with his decimated forces; two of the eight planes went down before the guns from the ships and the remaining six swept through the murderous wall of fire. Three bombs struck the *Yorktown,* the second of which caused the most serious damage because it had pierced the side of the carrier and detonated within the ship. A rag stowage compartment burst into flames, sending harsh black smoke out of the *Yorktown.* The other two bombs also caused intense fires, but working quickly and efficiently, the damage-control parties soon checked the most serious blazes. However, by twelve-twenty the *Yorktown* stood dead in the water, the engines stopped. Fletcher knew he would be out of communication with his other ships if he remained aboard the stricken, burning *Yorktown.* He transferred with his staff to the cruiser *Astoria.* Meanwhile, damage-control work continued on the *Yorktown.*

While Kobayashi led the attack upon the *Yorktown,* Yamaguchi finally learned the full measure of the American carrier strength. A *Soryu* scout plane had returned to the Japanese fleet and, finding its home carrier ablaze, landed upon the *Hiryu.* The pilot's radio had gone out on him and he was unable to report that he had seen three carriers, naming them—the *Enterprise,* the *Hornet,* and the *Yorktown!* which was supposed to have been sunk at the Coral Sea.

Only five bombers of the original eighteen and three fighters of six returned to the *Hiryu.* Among the missing was attack leader Kobayashi. From the surviving pilots Yamaguchi ascertained that the elusive *Yorktown* was dead in the water and spouting smoke. With two more carriers in the vicinity Yamaguchi ordered an immediate attack. All available aircraft must seek out and strike the two remaining carriers. It was not a very impressive array of air power: ten bombers (one of them an orphan from the *Akagi,* burning in the distance) and six Zeros (two of them strays from the *Kaga,* also smoldering), sixteen planes altogether to be led by Joichi Tomonaga, who had led the morning's attack upon Midway. In that attack the left-wing fuel tank had been punctured, but Tomonaga ordered his plane readied despite this. When he took off he knew he was on a one-way flight. Even if not struck down by the enemy, he would not have enough fuel in the single intact tank to bring him back to the *Hiryu.*

All sixteen planes had cleared the *Hiryu's* decks by twelve forty-five. During this period between attacks, the fires on the *Yorktown* were brought completely under control. The decks were cleared of wreckage, holes patched up, and four boilers warmed to life. Within two hours, no longer smoking, the *Yorktown* moved under its own steam. The planes circling overhead were signaled to land, although some, with fuel too far gone, splashed into the waters near other ships. Among these were the aircraft flown by Leslie and Holmberg. Their two Dauntlesses stalled into the water near Fletcher's new flagship, the *Astoria,* and the pilots and gunners were taken from the sea.

About an hour later—at 2:42 P.M.—Tomonaga's small force swarmed in upon the *Yorktown* from all sides. The air boomed and cracked to the sound of gunfire, antiaircraft bursts, and the engines of planes. American fighters attempted to intercept the bombers and tangled with the Zeros. Japanese torpedo bombers were blasted out of the air, but some broke through once again. Tomonaga weathered the storm of fire, dropped his torpedo, and disintegrated under a direct hit. The Japanese force was cut precisely in half: of the ten bombers which took off from the *Hiryu* only five returned; of the six Zeros, three returned. But they claimed two hits upon "a carrier of the *Yorktown* class." Having found the newly restored *Yorktown* moving through the Pacific, apparently unharmed, Tomonaga mistook it for another carrier.

But of the five bombers which had survived the attack, two had indeed sunk a torpedo each deep in the port side of the *Yorktown.* Within minutes the great carrier listed dangerously. The power had gone off and counterflooding, to correct the list, was impossible. There was nothing for Captain Elliott Buckmaster to say but "Pass the word along to abandon ship."

Back at the untouched *Hiryu,* Yamaguchi learned that a second carrier—as his by now exhausted pilots believed—lay dead and smoldering in the water. To Yamaguchi it meant that only one more carrier remained; there was still the chance to snatch some fraction of victory out of their frightful losses. He still had five dive bombers, four torpedo bombers, and six Zeros—with these Yamaguchi would launch a twilight attack upon the "last" American carrier.

But the surviving pilots, many of whom had been active since the morning Midway strike, must rest.

Around five o'clock in the afternoon, during a lull, they were served sweet rice balls (for many the first meal since dawn). A search plane was made ready to find the last carrier for the twilight attack.

Fletcher, meanwhile, realizing he was cut off from on-the-scene reports from pilots, placed Spruance in command of the carrier activities. At almost the exact moment that Tomonaga's bombers came in to attack the *Yorktown* for the second time, a *Yorktown* search pilot, Lieutenant Samuel Adams, spotted the *Hiryu*. He radioed its position back to the carriers and Spruance prepared for an attack on Yamaguchi's ship. Twenty-four Dauntlesses warmed up on the *Enterprise;* they were armed with thousand-pound and five-hundred-pound bombs. Some of the aircraft were from the listing *Yorktown;* all were led by Lieutenant Wilmer E. Gallagher, who had taken part in the earlier attack upon the *Akagi* and *Soryu* with McClusky. On the *Hornet* Captain Marc Mitscher watched sixteen Dauntlesses ready to take off in search of the *Hiryu*. The first planes began taking off around three-thirty in the afternoon.

Gallagher's force found the *Hiryu* at five o'clock, just as the weary pilots wolfed down their sweet rice balls. The scout plane was about to leave the deck when the dread cry rang out, "Enemy dive bombers overhead!" Gallagher's Dauntlesses hurtled down upon the carrier. Antiaircraft fire was pumped up at them as the carrier's captain, Tomeo Kaku, ordered full right rudder in an evasive turn. Three bombs fell into the sea, but there were more and four of them crashed explosively along the flight deck. Flame and gouts of smoke heaved into the air. As on the other three carriers, gassed-up and bombed-up planes burst into flame, spreading the fiery, consuming havoc.

When the *Hornet*'s planes arrived they found the *Hiryu* burning and turned to attack the other ships in the area. But their attacks upon the *Haruna, Tone,* and *Chikuma* were fruitless. Likewise, once again, some of the B-17s from Midway arrived and dropped bombs without making any hits. The *Hiryu,* however, was, like all of the other Nagumo carriers—the *Akagi,* the *Kaga,* the *Soryu*—doomed. The entire carrier force was erased from the Pacific. Attempts were made to bring the fires under control, to get into the engine rooms—but to no avail. Before dawn on June 5 Yamaguchi ordered all the survivors—about eight hundred men—to

Raymond A. Spruance, commander of Task Force 16 at Midway. (NAVY DEPT., NATIONAL ARCHIVES)

come on deck. He had decided to order abandonment of the *Hiryu*.

"As commanding officer of this carrier division," he told them, "I am fully and solely responsible for the loss of the *Hiryu* and *Soryu*. I shall remain on board to the end. I command all of you to leave the ship and continue your loyal service to His Majesty the Emperor." Characteristically, his staff pleaded to be allowed to share his fate, but Yamaguchi ordered them to leave the ship also. Captain Kaku, the ship's skipper, was also determined to remain and begged Yamaguchi to leave; it was the captain's place to go down with the ship. But Yamaguchi was firm, saying merely, "The moon is so bright in the sky."

Kaku, taking his place beside Yamaguchi, said, "We shall watch the moon together." Thus, poetically, did they face the end. Yamaguchi had ordered the final scuttling of the *Hiryu,* which occurred around dawn of the next day, June 5, when four torpedoes were shot into the carrier's sides. However, a search plane which Yamamoto had sent off from the carrier *Hosho* (the single light carrier which had been attached to the main force) to find Nagumo's force located the *Hiryu* still afloat an hour and a half later. The pilot also saw several men still alive on the derelict. Immediate orders went off to Nagumo to send a rescue ship, but when it arrived after daylight no trace of the *Hiryu* remained. (The survivors, members of the engine-room crew who had been trapped below decks, were freed when the Japanese torpedoes blasted open a passage for them. When the *Hiryu* sank they floated around in an abandoned lifeboat they had found until rescued by an American ship. None of these men saw either Yamaguchi or Kaku, who may have already committed suicide.) More than four hundred crewmen went down with the *Hiryu,* along with Yamaguchi and Kaku.

The last of Nagumo's impressive carrier force was gone; the few surviving aircraft, those Zeros which had been in the air when the dive bombers struck, fluttered helplessly over the burning ships, unable to land. As the fuel ran out, the planes fell into the sea.

The fate of the *Hiryu,* if it totally depressed Nagumo, did not take the fight out of Yamamoto, miles from the battle arena aboard the *Yamato.* He had no real idea of what ensued hundreds of miles east. Battle reports were all but incoherent, but one fact was clear: Nagumo's carriers were suffering at the hands of the American airmen. Reacting forcefully, Yamamoto, shortly after noon on June 4, ordered the carriers of the Aleutians Force to race down to Midway; he ordered the heavy cruisers, which were to cover the Midway invasion, to close with the American fleet—and he too would move in to engage the enemy in a last-ditch surface battle. Yamamoto hoped that the cruisers of the Kondo force might meet the Americans in a night action.

But the wary Spruance did not wish to press his luck. Instead of pursuing the Japanese fleet, and risking a night engagement, he reversed course. "I did not feel justified," he reported, "in risking a night encounter with possibly superior enemy forces,

but on the other hand, I did not want to be too far away from Midway the next morning [June 5]. I wished to have a position from which either to follow up retreating enemy forces or to break up a landing attack on Midway."

Yamamoto continued to receive grim news from the scene of action. Even after he had heard that the *Hiryu* had been stricken, he transmitted orders of unbelievable optimism:

(1) *The enemy fleet has been practically destroyed and is retiring eastward.*

(2) *Combined Fleet units in the vicinity are preparing to pursue remnants of the enemy force and, at the same time, to occupy Midway.*

But Nagumo persisted in afflicting him with oppressive information. At each successive report the American forces seemed to increase until Nagumo reported on the evening of June 4 that "Total enemy strength is five carriers, six heavy cruisers, and fifteen destroyers. They are steaming westward. We are retiring to the northwest escorting *Hiryu.* Speed, eighteen knots."

"The Nagumo force," Chief of Staff Rear Admiral Matome Ugaki bitterly and wearily said, "has no stomach for a night engagement!" But Yamamoto, whose stomach literally churned and pained, did and he continued to plan for such an engagement. He relieved Nagumo of his command, except for the still floating but burning *Akagi* and *Hiryu,* and turned the surface fleet command over to Vice-Admiral Nobutake Kondo, who commanded the ships of the Midway Invasion Force (Second Fleet). Kondo managed to instill some of the lost aggressiveness to the fleet and made plans for the night action. But soon, what with Spruance's evasive move to the east, it became obvious that the action could not possibly take place until dawn. Once again in daylight their ships would be at the mercy of the American carrier planes. Various alternative plans were discussed by Yamamoto's staff, each one more impractical than the previous one. One suggestion was that all possible large Japanese ships approach Midway on the following day, June 5, and shell it, a suicidal and therefore attractive solution to the problem of defeat. It would have placed most of the Japanese Navy within the reach of shore-based batteries and shore-based aircraft as well as of the remaining carrier planes. Admiral Ugaki disabused the staff of this idea. He suggested that they wait

The Japanese heavy cruiser Mikuma, *its eight-inch guns useless after attacks by Marine and Navy Vindicators and Dauntlesses, lies helpless in the water. The Vindicator of Richard Fleming smolders on the aft turret (right). The* Mikuma *was sunk soon after by Navy carrier Dauntlesses.*

(NAVY DEPT., NATIONAL ARCHIVES)

for the Aleutian carriers and then perhaps launch another attack. "But even if this proves impossible," he asserted, "and we must accept defeat in this operation, we will not have lost the war."

There was a gloomy silence following this statement, for Ugaki had voiced the unspeakable. Who among them could face the prospect of defeat? "But how can we apologize to His Majesty for this defeat?" someone inquired.

"Leave that to me," Yamamoto interjected sharply. "I am the only one who must apologize to His Majesty." He recognized the fruitlessness of

attempting to engage the Americans at night. The *Kaga* and *Soryu* were gone; he then had to turn to the scuttling of the *Akagi*. It would be the first time in history that a Japanese warship was scuttled. It was a difficult decision; at 2:50 A.M. on June 5, Yamamoto gave the order. Within five minutes he issued another, the first sentence of which read:

"THE MIDWAY OPERATION IS CANCELED."

But the drama was not ended simply because its author so decreed; events and characters had taken on their own dynamisms. Within an hour after Yamamoto had canceled the Midway Operation an American submarine, *Tambor,* under the command of Lieutenant Commander John W. Murphy, Jr., patrolling about ninety miles west of Midway, spotted several Japanese ships. They appeared to be heading away from Midway at high speed; they were, in fact, four heavy cruisers, in company with two destroyers, which had been dispatched to carry out a night bombardment upon Midway. When the cancellation order came, the ships, under the command of Rear Admiral Takeo Kurita, turned around and steamed northwest. Upon sighting them, Murphy, still uncertain of the ships' nationality, began to stalk them. In the dark, it was all but impossible to identify the cruisers, so Murphy stalked them until dawn. He then identified the ships as Japanese, but almost simultaneously the Japanese spotted the *Tambor* and the alarm went out. Murphy ordered a dive and the Japanese ships began emergency maneuvers. The first two cruisers, the *Kumano* and *Suzuya,* turned hard to port as ordered. So did the *Mikuma,* next in line, but the *Mogami,* the last ship in line failed to read the emergency turn signal and plowed into the *Mikuma.* The *Mogami,* in ramming into the *Mikuma,* suffered a serious slicing away of a portion of the bow and was forced to stop. The *Mikuma,* although not as seriously damaged, left a telltale trail of oil in its wake. Eventually both ships continued under way, but at reduced speed.

When the morning's searches began on June 5, the oil slick of the *Mikuma* was picked up by Midway-based dive bombers of Marine Aircraft Group 22, six Dauntlesses under Captain Marshall A. Tyler and six Vindicators under Captain Richard E. Fleming. Tyler led the Dauntlesses in a diving attack upon the *Mogami,* but scored only near misses. Almost simultaneously B-17s dropped bombs from high altitudes but without success.

Fleming brought his flight in upon the *Mikuma* in a glide attack. As he headed for the target his Vindicator burst into flame from heavy antiaircraft fire. Fleming managed to drop his bomb, but could not pull away, for the old plane was blazing furiously. It crashed at full speed into a turret just aft of the bridge. Flames from the fiery wreck were sucked into an air-intake system and detonated fumes in the starboard engine room, killing all the men inside. Fleming's crash, mistaken for a suicide attack by the Japanese, caused more damage to the

Mikuma than the near misses (two men were killed on the *Mogami*) and its collision with the *Mogami.* Now both cruisers limped away from the fury of the avenging Americans.

At dawn the following day, June 6, Spruance dispatched the last air strikes of the Battle of Midway. Around eight in the morning Mitscher's *Hornet* dispatched twenty-six dive bombers with fighter escort; at ten forty-five the *Enterprise* sent off thirty-one dive bombers, three torpedo bombers, and a dozen escorting Wildcats. The final sortie was launched at one-thirty, after some of the earlier planes had returned to relate the successes of the initial strikes. The *Hornet*'s twenty-six dive bombers, upon returning to the scene of battle, found little to do. The first wave from the *Hornet* attacked both cripples, with the heaviest casualties being suffered by the bow-less *Mogami.* The *Hornet* and *Enterprise* Dauntlesses finished off the *Mikuma* with five direct hits. Spreading fires set off internal explosions, which sent the ship to the ocean bottom. The *Mogami,* despite its rent bow and the six hits which rendered it a floating vessel of anguish, eventually reached Truk, although it was to be out of operation for a year. The *Mikuma* (discounting the four lost carriers) was the heaviest warship lost by Japan since the war's opening. In addition, there were many dead and wounded aboard the destroyers, the *Arashio* and *Asashio,* assigned by Yamamoto to stand by the damaged cruisers. These too came under bombing and fighter attacks. With no Zeros to oppose them the Wildcats strafed at will.

The *Yorktown,* which the Japanese had claimed three times to have destroyed, had not sunk after being abandoned on June 4. Fletcher directed that the *Hughes,* a destroyer captained by Lieutenant Commander Donald J. Ramsey, "stand by *Yorktown.* Do not permit anyone to board her. Sink her if necessary to prevent capture or if serious fire develops."

By the morning of the fifth Ramsey saw that the *Yorktown* was not sinking; the list was stabilized at twenty-five degrees. He suggested that salvage operations be attempted and several ships were dispatched to assist. A burst of machine-gun fire from the tilting deck of the *Yorktown* revealed that two crewmen, left for dead, had recovered slightly from their wounds; they were taken off the *Yorktown.* A further search revealed that in the abandon-

The Yorktown *in distress at Midway with destroyer* Hughes *at "Stand by." Although badly hit, the York-* town *seemed capable of being saved and taken under tow.* (NAVY DEPT., NATIONAL ARCHIVES)

Men of the Yorktown *walk the slanting deck of their carrier; Japanese torpedoes from submarine I-168* ended all hope of saving the Yorktown.

(NAVY DEPT., NATIONAL ARCHIVES)

Hit in the same torpedo attack as the Yorktown, *the* Hammann *sinks into the Pacific.* (U. S. NAVY)

Midway secured; it belongs again to the goonies, the Marines, the Navy, and the Seventh Air Force, whose B-24 approaches for a landing. (U. S. AIR FORCE)

ment a number of secret papers and decoding devices had been left aboard. The minesweeper *Vireo* arrived around noon and took the *Yorktown* in tow. It was a great burden for the little ship and little speed was made, but the wounded ship moved slowly toward Pearl Harbor.

Buckmaster, the *Yorktown*'s skipper, asked for a volunteer salvage crew to board the carrier. Soon, with 141 enlisted men and 29 officers, he boarded the destroyer *Hammann,* which in company with destroyers *Benham* and *Balch,* pushed off for the crippled *Yorktown.* They arrived at daybreak on June 6 and immediately began working according to the plan drafted by Buckmaster. The various parties were hard at work; cooks prepared lunches, gunners were on duty at their antiaircraft guns, a medical group attended to the identification and assembling of the dead. Electrical power was drawn off the *Hammann,* directly alongside, to run the pumps to drain the flooded engine rooms. Water was pumped aboard to quench the fire in the rag-stowage room. By midafternoon the list had decreased by two degrees. Destroyers circled around the *Yorktown* and *Hammann.*

Suddenly a hoarse cry went out: "Torpedoes!" Men aboard the *Hammann* opened up with their

Isoroku Yamamoto, who, as he had promised, "ran wild" in the Pacific "the first six months" after the initiation of the Hawaii Operation. His time began running out at Midway and ended over the jungles of the Solomon Islands. (U. S. NAVY)

guns on the four white streaks in the water rapidly closing from the starboard side. One streak missed completely and continued on harmlessly, but one detonated into the side of the *Hammann* and the other two, passing underneath the destroyer, smashed violently into the *Yorktown.*

The torpedoes had come from the Japanese submarine I-168, commanded by Lieutenant Commander Yahachi Tanabe. Originally sent by Yamamoto to "shell and destroy enemy air base on Eastern Island" in the vain attempt to deal with Midway with surface ships, Tanabe had attempted that but with little success. Later, when the drifting *Yorktown* was found by a float plane, Yamamoto ordered Tanabe to attack the carrier. Having found it, Tanabe delivered his torpedo attack. The I-168 soon came under attack also, but despite the heavy depth charging (Tanabe counted sixty near misses),

the submarine escaped. His was the only decisive Japanese naval action of the Battle of Midway.

Within five minutes the *Hammann,* all but broken in half, sank to the bottom. The *Yorktown,* which had been listing to port, lost a good deal of the list because of the hits in the starboard side, but the carrier now lay deep in the water. Buckmaster continued to hope to salvage the ship, but during the night the *Yorktown* again listed to port. At dawn, June 7, 1942, it could be seen that the *Yorktown* was finally doomed. The ships flew their colors at half-mast; men, many in tears, removed their hats. The death rattle from the *Yorktown*— the sound of loose gear that slipped along the decks, the other equipment and furniture below—echoed over the still waters. The flight deck rolled under the oil-slicked waters, then the gallant *Yorktown,* heaving and shuddering, vanished into the Pacific.

The Battle of Midway was over.

EPILOGUE

A great mantle of secrecy descended upon the outcome of the Battle of Midway in Japan. Only the mildly successful, though inconsequential, Aleutian Operation was mentioned in the newspapers. Nothing was said of the Midway encounter itself and all references to it were deleted from diaries and official reports. The wounded were even held incommunicado and brought into naval hospitals after nightfall. Captain Mitsuo Fuchida, who had led the aerial attack upon Pearl Harbor and was prevented from leading the attack upon Midway by illness, was taken wounded from the *Akagi,* and tells of his stealthy evacuation from a hospital ship ". . . after dark . . . on a covered stretcher and carried through the rear entrance [of the hospital at the Yokosuka Naval Base]. My room was in complete isolation. No nurses or medical corps men were allowed in and I could not communicate with the world outside. All the wounded from Midway were treated like this. It was like being a prisoner of war among your own people."

Yamamoto too went into isolation. He had led the Imperial fleet of Japan into its first major naval defeat in three hundred years. Four of Japan's finest carriers had been sent to the bottom of the Pacific —3500 Japanese seamen (among them about 100 first-line, irreplaceable pilots) died, ten times the number (307) of Americans lost. More than 300 aircraft were lost (the total number based on the carriers, plus some which were being ferried to be based on Midway as soon as it was under Japanese domination); American aircraft losses numbered 147. The course of the Pacific war was completely changed at Midway.

As the Japanese fleet sped out of the range of Spruance's planes, the latter called for a halt of the pursuit. After several days of intense fighting he knew the pilots must be near nervous and physical exhaustion; his ships were running dangerously low on fuel and they were approaching dangerous waters. They had destroyed about half of Japan's carrier strength, but little of the remainder of the surface fleet. Wisely Spruance ordered a return to port.

Yamamoto, ill with severe stomach cramps, remained in his cabin unable to eat anything except gruel for several days. In the wake of the retreating *Yamato*, the *Nagara* too sped toward safer waters. Aboard the cruiser was Admiral Nagumo, dispirited, broken, a man without a ship—the man who had led the Pearl Harbor attack had failed at Midway. Though he returned to sea, Nagumo was a depleted man and did not find peace until July 6, 1944, when he committed suicide on an island named Saipan. His body was never found.

Yamamoto recovered from his mysterious illness and regained his powers sufficiently to press for the occupation of Guadalcanal in the Solomon Islands. This was Japan's southernmost conquest. After hard and painful fighting it was taken back by the Americans—the Greater East Asia Co-Prosperity Sphere was gradually, and bloodily, shrinking. But despite these setbacks, the Japanese continued to revere Yamamoto and to respect his leadership. The very presence of the man in a distant outpost —and no matter how primitive the outpost, the man was invariably immaculate, composed, dedicated— inspired all who saw him.

So it was that following the fall of Guadalcanal Yamamoto planned to fly to Rabaul, New Britain, headquarters of the Seventeenth Army—which had fought at Guadalcanal—and then to proceed eastward to inspect naval bases near Bougainville in the Solomon Islands. Bougainville was the northernmost of the Solomon group and still held by the

Japanese; Guadalcanal, the southernmost island, lay about four hundred miles away. According to the planned schedule, Yamamoto, in company with several officers including his chief of staff, Vice-Admiral Matome Ugaki, would leave the main naval base at Truk, spend an evening at Rabaul, and then leave for Kahili airdrome, on the southern tip of Bougainville, arriving at precisely 9:45 A.M.

As before, all preparations for this "secret" move were known by American cryptologists within hours after the coded messages were sent to the Japanese forward bases alerting them of Yamamoto's impending inspection. Word was flashed to Washington; Secretary of the Navy Frank Knox immediately issued orders to intercept Yamamoto's party and "destroy it at all costs." The loss of Yamamoto would tell heavily upon the Japanese and upon the future development of the war. Along with the order arrived a most meticulous itinerary indicating Yamamoto's exact position during his entire tour. Admiral William Halsey, commanding the southern Pacific, assigned the mission to Rear Admiral Marc A. Mitscher, COMAIRSOLS (Commander Air Solomons), who turned it over to Major John W. Mitchell of the Air Force's 339th Fighter Squadron.

A total of eighteen Lockheed P-38s (Lightnings) were to take part in the mission. Mitchell would lead the sixteen-plane cover section and Captain Thomas G. Lanphier the four-plane attack unit. It was decided that the best means of carrying out the mission was to intercept Yamamoto as he came into the Kahili airdrome. It was not without hazards, for the Kahili-Buin area swarmed with Zeros (or Zekes, as the newer models were called). Only the P-38 had the range—a round trip of nearly a thousand miles—taking into consideration the circuitous route which would be necessary to escape detection. Navigational as well as flying skill was essential to the mission.

Mitchell's timetable was carefully geared into that of the punctual Yamamoto's. At exactly seven twenty-five in the morning of April 18, 1943, Mitchell led his planes off the runway of Henderson Field, Guadalcanal. The field was named for Major Lofton R. Henderson, who had died in the Battle of Midway. Two of the eighteen P-38s were forced to turn back almost immediately; one had malfunctioning auxiliary fuel tanks and the other blew a tire during the take-off run. These two planes cut Lanphier's attack section in half, leaving himself and Lieutenant Rex T. Barber (of the 70th Fighter Squadron) to carry out the attack. Mitchell then assigned Captain Besby Holmes and Lieutenant Raymond Hine to the attack section.

The sixteen P-38s flew for two hours and nine minutes, about 30 feet above the Pacific, a distance of 435 miles, dodging small islands which might be harboring enemy coast watchers. At 9:35 A.M., if all had gone well, they would meet Yamamoto about 35 miles west of Kahili. All through the flight absolute radio silence was observed; Mitchell's navigation was superlative. As the time drew near

the hazy mountains of Bougainville appeared out of the sea. The P-38s swung inland. It was nine thirty-three.

Suddenly the silence was broken by the voice of Captain Douglas S. Canning in the cover section. "Bogey. Ten o'clock high!" About five miles distant Lanphier made out a flight of two Mitsubishi (Betty) bombers, escorted by six Zekes. This was one hitch: they had hoped to have gained altitude before attacking. Now they had to climb, which

The Lockheed P-38 "Lightning," selected as the instrument of Yamamoto's destruction.

(LOCKHEED-CALIFORNIA)

Thomas G. Lanphier, "credited" with shooting down Yamamoto's plane. (U. S. AIR FORCE)

placed them at a disadvantage. All aircraft released their belly tanks in preparation for the attack. Besby Holmes of the attack section, however, could not drop his tank. Raymond Hine stayed with him for protection—with auxiliary tanks the P-38 lost speed and could not maneuver properly in an air battle. Lanphier and Barber, at full throttle, roared in on the Japanese formation. Mitchell's top cover climbed to be on the lookout for possible Zero reinforcements.

The Japanese suddenly became aware of the P-38s; the two Bettys dived for the jungle and three of the Zeros turned upon Lanphier's plane. The Lightning was by this time on a level with the lead Betty and met the assault of the lead Zero head on. Both pilots exchanged wasted shots and then, more calmly, Lanphier took careful aim and the Zero spun into the jungle burning and minus a wing. The other two Zeros flashed by the P-38 as Lanphier made a sharp turn away. He was next aware of the shadow of one of the Bettys moving rapidly over the treetops.

Lanphier lunged the P-38 into a full power dive, then realized he would overshoot the bomber. By this time the duo of Zeros had whipped around to attack him again. To Lanphier it seemed that all were on a collision course, with all four aircraft des-

Lieutenant Besby Holmes, center, is congratulated by Brigadier General Dean G. Strother, commander of

Thirteenth Air Force Fighter Command, after the Yamamoto mission. (U. S. AIR FORCE)

tined to meet at an imaginary point over the jungle. He maintained his course, however, eyes upon the Mitsubishi, racing in almost at right angles to the Betty's flight path. When it came into his sights he pushed the gun release button. In an instant the right engine of the Betty burst into flame; seconds later the entire wing was ablaze. The two Zero pilots, seeing that the Betty was doomed, no longer considered suicide. They pulled up sharply and away from Lanphier's Lightning.

The stricken Betty, dripping flame, suddenly lost its wing and crashed into the jungle. The ball of fire erupted into a savage explosion and only thick black smoke and red flame remained of the Betty.

The other Mitsubishi, carrying Ugaki, was attacked by Barber, who pursued it over the jungle toward the sea. Ugaki had observed the crash of his chief's Betty and knew that within minutes he too must share Yamamoto's fate. Barber's gun's decimated the crew, spattered the interior of the plane with bits and pieces of metal, killing the passengers also. A cannon hit in the right wing crippled the Betty so that the pilot brought it into the water at full speed. Only three men, one of them the injured Ugaki, survived the attack. With the aid of Mitchell's top cover, the Zeros, which attempted to avenge the attack, were driven off. Holmes, having finally dropped his tanks, shot a Zero off Barber's tail.

Lanphier and Barber raced from the vicinity of the crashed bombers by hedgehopping, dodging, and skidding. Of the sixteen aircraft which participated in the mission, only one, Lieutenant Raymond K. Hine's, failed to return. He had assisted Holmes in driving the Zeros away from Barber's P-38. (Although Lanphier was credited at the time with the victory over the Betty carrying Yamamoto, this victory was questioned by Barber, who thought he had shot down the critical Betty. Holmes also claimed a Betty, the one which fell into the sea, and thought that the bomber which fell into the jungle had been shot down by Barber. Lanphier, however, also claimed a Betty which fell into the

jungle. Unless there was a third Betty, which the Japanese claim there was not, the victory claims cannot be clarified.)

Whatever the dispute over the honors of having assassinated Admiral Yamamoto—honors which should be shared by all pilots who participated in the remarkably executed raid—there is no doubting that his loss was grievous to the Japanese. Their most gifted strategist was gone—and there was no one of equal stature to replace him. The one man who might have, Yamaguchi, had, in an excess of vainglory, chosen to go down with the *Hiryu* at Midway.

Yamamoto was succeeded by Admiral Mineichi Koga (who died within a year in an air accident), but the Japanese fleet had long since stopped "running wild." After Midway, a battle in which not one surface ship exchanged a shot with another, and yet which was the most decisive naval battle of the Second World War, the doom which Yamamoto had predicted for Japan should the war be prolonged was inevitable. After Midway, also, Yamamoto spoke of his own death, which he predicted with a curious wistfulness. Shortly before the interception near Kahili, Yamamoto composed a poem, a sequel to one he had written on the day of the Pearl Harbor attack. In the earlier quatrain he expressed contempt for the world's opinion of the brilliant attack he had engineered; even his own life was insignificant except as "the sword of my Emperor." In his final poem, translated by John Deane Potter, Yamamoto rhapsodized

> *I am still the sword*
> *Of my Emperor*
> *I will not be sheathed*
> *Until I die.*

The sword of the Emperor had been sheathed at Midway by a small band of courageous men in their Buffalos, Vindicators, Marauders, Wildcats, and Dauntlesses. No one knew that better than the wise Yamamoto.

BOOK II
The Big League

Hitler built a fortress around Europe but he forgot to put a roof on it.

—FRANKLIN DELANO ROOSEVELT

5

MILLENNIUM

WINSTON CHURCHILL arrived in Washington within two weeks of the Pearl Harbor attack for the "Arcadia" conferences with President Franklin D. Roosevelt and other political and military chiefs. On the day of Churchill's arrival—December 22, 1941 —Japanese troops landed on Luzon in the Philippines to begin the inexorable crushing of Mac-Arthur's outnumbered and ill-equipped Filipino and American troops. By New Year's Day 1942, when Arcadia ended, the Allies agreed that, despite the Japanese conquests, Nazi Germany prevailed as the prime enemy.

But until the United States was capable of joining the British in the offensive, it would be necessary for the Empire to carry on alone as before. True, the situation had brightened somewhat: the Battle of Britain had proved abortive and now the Germans had embarked upon Barbarossa, the attack upon Russia which Hitler, with a love for coining phrases, termed the "eight-week war." The nightly terror which had fallen upon Britain was pretty much over by 1942. Hitler's neat little time-table was off a bit in the east so that he was forced to drain off much of the Luftwaffe strength from France and the Low Countries to pour it into the Balkans, north Africa, and the capacious Russian maw. Nearly half of the Luftwaffe was in Russia by the spring of 1942. A quarter of the Luftwaffe's strength remained on the Western Front and in Ger-

many. Although the bombers of Luftflotte 3 were few and aging, the fighters were modern and formidable. Among these were the late-model Messerschmitt 109 and the new Focke-Wulf 190. Some of the latter were converted eventually into fighter-bombers which made harassing "tip and run" raids upon Channel shipping and English seaside towns. These raids were not decisive, merely bothersome and deadly on a small scale. It was, in effect, a kind of stalemate.

Although the Russians clamored for a "Second Front," the only means by which the Allies could possibly bring the war directly to Germany in the spring of 1942 was via British Bomber Command. In February 1942 a new commander in chief, Air Marshal Arthur T. Harris, was appointed to replace Sir Richard Peirse, who had endured a hard and frustrating year as Chief of Bomber Command. Bomber crew losses had increased; bombing accuracy, primarily because of inadequately trained crews, had decreased. During the same period Bomber Command's forces were diverted to the Middle East and effective bombing missions into Germany became more academic than real. Without men and aircraft equal to the task such missions were hardly better than the German tip and run raids—and wasteful in terms of men and machines. So although he was not responsible for the situation, Peirse as commander in chief must serve as scapegoat. But it by no means improved the state of Bomber Command simply because Peirse was dispatched to the Pacific to head the all but non-existent Allied Air Forces there.

Harris had been absent from the battle scene since May of 1941, when he had been placed at the head of an RAF delegation and was sent off to Washington. It was the function of the delegation to acquire American aircraft for the RAF, but the attack on Pearl Harbor, for some time at least, quickly placed the American Air Force high on the priority list, and Harris had little to do.

When he was recalled to command the bomber offensive, Harris had inherited not only the afflictions of the depleted Bomber Command, but also an outstanding senior air staff officer, Air Vice-Marshal Robert H. M. S. Saundby, an old friend from early flying days. Both men were advocates of the "strategic bombardment" concept—the direct attack upon the enemy's warmaking facilities. In less guarded language: an attack upon Germany's industrial cities. If such assaults could be made regularly and in force, both Harris and Saundby believed, they would have a serious effect upon the future of the war.

The job facing Harris was a tough one indeed. He had been handed the task of dealing with several of Germany's greatest industrial concentrations at a time when his forces were being drained away to fight in the critical Battle of the Atlantic and to be used by the Army for close support in north Africa. In brief, while Bomber Command was expected to operate with greater impact than before, almost at the same time this was made difficult, or even impossible, by denying its expansion. Just three days after Harris had taken over, Sir Stafford Cripps, then Lord Privy Seal, spoke in the House of Commons touching upon the subject of whether or not "the building up of this bombing force is the best use that we can make of our resources." It being wartime, Cripps refrained from encouraging a public debate on the subject; he hinted, however, that if "the circumstances warrant a change, a change will be made."

While the semipolitical arguments proceeded and reams of paper were consumed for memos and minutes, Air Marshal Harris went on with his own plans undisturbed. He realized that only decisive accomplishment could save Bomber Command from

High Command conference at Bomber Command: Air Vice-Marshal R. Graham, Air Vice-Marshal Robert Saundby, and, seated, Air Marshal Arthur T. Harris, Commander in Chief. Harris and Saundby planned the Bomber Command attacks on Germany's war industries from 1942 until the end of the war.

(IMPERIAL WAR MUSEUM, LONDON)

complete dispersal and, in his view, waste. He believed too that unless a target was saturated with a series of concentrated blows, there would be little result from several scattered missions. Saturation could be achieved only if a target were correctly identified and bomb loads concentrated within a reasonably small area. By using "Gee," a new electronic navigational device, and by employing both advance aircraft to drop flares to mark the target and other early-wave planes to follow with incendiaries, the area would be clearly, even accurately marked for the succeeding waves of the main force bombers carrying high-explosive and incendiary bombs. It was a page torn from the book of the Luftwaffe, but the system was applied with greater intensity.

By early March Harris had initiated his campaign, although the first targets were not primary ones necessarily. The Renault works near Paris, which supplied war materials to the Germans, was struck by 235 bombers using Gee, which succeeded in knocking it out for about four months. A few days later Essen, home of a giant Krupp arms complex, was bombed using Gee for navigation and the flare system (later to be known as "pathfinder"); in all, 211 bombers were dispatched, but Harris found, upon studying the post-raid photographs, that the mission was not a success. The Krupp works was barely touched (many incendiaries were not dropped until after the flares had burned out; the resulting fires, scattered as they were, misled the succeeding waves of bombers). One bomber, struck by flak, had jettisoned its bomb load, which fell upon Hamborn, not Essen, causing fires which appeared to following bomber crews as signals for a target area. By pure accident many of the bombs intended for Krupp fell instead upon the Thyssen steelworks.

But Harris could not operate on such luck and he soon learned that Gee was not a foolproof device. Within limitations it was fine, but in order to work properly a good clear moonlit night was essential. It could bring a bomber force within reasonable proximity to a target, but the rest of the mission depended upon the human eye.

It was not until the end of March 1942 that Bomber Command could claim a truly successful raid. This was the March 28/29 strike upon the city of Lübeck, a Baltic port of great importance to the German supply system. The dwellings in Lübeck were predominantly wood and Air Staff pressed Harris upon the use of incendiaries. In the resulting attack nearly half of Lübeck was destroyed. Bad weather interfered with subsequent missions dispatched to Essen, Dortmund, Cologne, and Hamburg.

Hitler, meanwhile, issued his Baedeker order on April 14, in which the term *Terrorangriffe* ("terror attacks") appears. These, the Führer pointed out, were to be made upon targets which might "have the greatest possible effect on civilian life." Thus such raids were aimed at undefended, or lightly defended, cathedral cities such as Bath, Norwich, and York, beginning late in April. As Goebbels confided to his diary, Hitler "shares my opinion absolutely that cultural centers, health resorts and civilian centers must be attacked now. . . ." So much for philosophy and morality.

Harris contributed to Hitler's fury with a series of attacks upon Rostock beginning on the night of April 23/24 and continuing through the following three nights. Rostock was, like Lübeck, a port city on the Baltic and also the site of a Heinkel aircraft factory. Over the four nights a total of 521 aircraft were sent to bomb (468 claimed they had succeeded; twelve aircraft were lost) and severely crippled the city, besides damaging the Heinkel works and devastating nearly three quarters of Rostock.

Throughout these tentative, almost experimental early weeks of his tenure, Harris pondered a daring plan. What with the "successes" obtained upon Lübeck and Rostock, which greatly improved the morale of the bomber crews besides giving Hitler a jolt, what might be accomplished by a truly massive force concentrating upon a major target? Say a thousand bombers over a city like Hamburg or Cologne. He spoke of this fancy to Saundby, who immediately and quietly undertook the research to learn if it was not so much a fancy after all.

The next time Harris broached the subject, Saundby informed him that it was indeed feasible at that time, in May 1942. Harris was skeptical, though he continued to listen to Saundby's statistics. If they put up all of their first-line operational units plus training units and borrowed a few aircraft and crews from Coastal Command and perhaps from the Army, a total of a thousand bombers could be dispatched against a single target. Thus assured of at least one aspect of the plan, Harris turned to the others.

These would include target selection, weather, the use of Gee, the risk of collision, and, of course, the inevitable political backing. Harris was quite aware of the implications of failure; but if successful, the "result of using an adequate bomber force against Germany would be there for all the world to see, and I should be able to press for the aircraft, crews and equipment we needed with far more effect than by putting forward theoretical arguments, however convincing, in favour of hitting the enemy where it would hurt him most. . . ." In addition, "from such an operation we should also learn a number of tactical lessons of the greatest possible value, lessons which could not be learned any other way and without which we could not prepare for the main offensive."

By a main offensive Harris visualized hundreds of such massive raids upon the industrial cities of

Germany, which might possibly eliminate the need for an invasion of Europe.

However much exhilarated by the concept, Harris (who was no dreamer) realized also that "if anything went seriously wrong . . . then I should be committing not only the whole of my front-line strength but absolutely all of my reserves in a single battle." Using instructors and trainees from the Operational Training Units further risked, if the losses were great, the crippling of the training program for years to come. But then, since Bomber Command was being picked to pieces and dwindling away anyway, the dramatic conception of a thousand planes over a single target in one raid might make the impression that could save the Command.

To obtain official backing Harris approached his chief, Sir Charles Portal, who guardedly approved, although cautioning that Air Staff also must recognize its "usefulness" and that proper political backing was important. Harris immediately found his backer: Winston Churchill. The Prime Minister's home, Chequers, was but a ten-minute drive (at the high speed at which Harris generally drove his battered old Bentley) from Harris's home, Springfield. This was a handsome Victorian mansion situated near High Wycombe, headquarters of Bomber Command, about twenty miles directly west of London.

The two men, the flamboyant Churchill and the reserved but tough Harris, got along very well. After dinner on a Sunday evening in mid-May 1942, Harris broached the subject of a thousand-bomber raid. The very grandeur of the conception impressed Churchill. For all the romanticism, however, Churchill pressed for concrete details. The target? Hamburg or Cologne. Why not Essen (then regarded as the most important target in Germany)? Because of the limitations of Gee, it was necessary to strike at an easily identified city, Hamburg because it lay on the estuary of the Elbe River (although out of Gee range), and Cologne because of its location on the Rhine River.

There was the delicate point: How many aircraft did Harris expect to lose? Even this eventuality was taken into consideration. Fifty aircraft, or about 5 per cent of the force.

"I am prepared for the loss of a hundred," Churchill told Harris.

The Thousand Plan (Operation Millennium) was on.

II

On May 19 Harris received a letter from Portal informing him that the Prime Minister "warmly approved" of the plan and that it seemed that there was all likelihood of "the co-operation of Coastal Command unless they have special operations on hand." Within two days Harris had a letter from Sir Philip Joubert, Chief of Coastal Command, telling him that "I can go your 250 . . ." in answer to Harris's request for 250 aircraft. Thus Coastal Command would supply one quarter of the total force.

Rapid planning and preparation became essential, for the raid had to take place within the next period of full moon (May 26–30), a week away. Counting Coastal Command's promised 250 planes, Harris had by this time accumulated via his four operational groups, two bomber training groups, and Flying Training Command (with 21 aircraft) a total of 1081 planes and crews. With a force of this size, consisting of a large number of inexperienced crews, a serious possibility of many collisions over the target had to be faced. Although much was to be gained by concentrating a large force over a small space in a short time, there was still this nagging problem.

He asked Dr. B. G. Dickins, head of Bomber Command's Operational Research Section, to work out the probabilities scientifically. He quickly learned that with a single aiming point the risk of collision was very high, but that with three, which divided the forces into three parallel streams, the risk came down to just a little more than one an hour. There were chances also of aircraft being hit by the bombs of other aircraft because the different waves would come in at staggered altitudes, which to some extent lessened the chance of collision. But, theoretically at least, even these possibilities were less than those of being hit by flak or being shot down by night fighters.

With so great a concentration over the target in so short a time—if Cologne, which Harris had already decided would be the target, it would be for ninety minutes—it was hoped that the defenses would be saturated. Radar plots would pile up, gun crews would become confused, and the entire defense system in the area of Cologne would be swamped.

The night of May 27/28 was set for the attack, a night which promised a good moon. But it was just before this that Harris suffered his first blow. Coastal Command was forced to defect from the raid on orders from the Admiralty. A quarter of the total force was gone. Clearly the Admiralty did not wish to place so large a proportion of their planes in jeopardy. If Harris failed, they too would fail; if Harris carried off his scheme, the Admiralty would lose also. Harris would have proved his point and the Admiralty, which clamored for a diminished Bomber Command, would lose their appeal for bombers in the Battle of the Atlantic. There was little that Harris could do but curse the Admiralty. The Bomber Command planes, by May 26, stood ready at fifty-three airfields; training had ceased and the mission must go on.

The weather next turned on Harris. Thunderstorms and clouds over northern Germany made the mission impossible. The next night it was the same. Meanwhile hundreds of bombers and thousands of men waited for something to happen. The mission was postponed for a third time. In order not to make the Germans suspicious of an impending large mission, Harris sent a force to bomb targets in France and another to lay mines. As each wasted day went by, the chance of a security leak became greater.

The extra days, however, gave the ground crews the opportunity to put more aircraft on the Operational Forms. By the morning of Saturday, May 30, thanks to the hard work of these men, Harris actually had his thousand aircraft; more, in fact. On that morning, with good weather promised on home bases, there were 1046 bombers awaiting the signal to take off. Other planes, from Army Co-operation Command and Fighter Command, although not participating directly in the raid, would provide diversionary attacks along the way.

But the full moon period was drawing to a close, and unless the force took off that night, it would have to wait another month before the Thousand Plan could be attempted again. The continental forecast—again thunder and cloud, with chance of clearing—was less than ideal. Hamburg was curdled over with cloud. However, Harris's weather expert,

Magnus Spence, predicted that Cologne might clear around midnight. Also, by the time the bombers returned to England some of their bases would undoubtedly be fogged in. But planes from those bases could be diverted to the still clear fields. It was the weather over Germany which most troubled Harris. With cloud over the target, the mission might very well prove fruitless, and with fog over England, with hundreds of milling aircraft, the mission could be disastrous. Still, to Harris, who had but that night and the next before the favorable moon period ended, Spence's prediction sounded better than any they had had so far.

Harris was alone now. It was up to him, however much Saundby sympathized, and he did, for Harris had seen it in an instant in which their eyes met as he lit a cigarette, stalling for time perhaps. He placed the cigarette into a holder, which he clenched in his teeth, and then leaned over the map that lay on his desk. Harris said, "Thousand Plan tonight. Target Cologne."

The word was flashed out immediately to the fifty-three bases scattered northward from London along the east coast of England, with a few farther inland and west of the capital. Unless the weather changed considerably during the remainder of the day, Operation Millennium would take place. With incredible efficiency the more than a thousand aircraft were readied for the mission—the English countryside, especially in East Anglia, resonated to the "dreadful note of preparation." There were shouts and curses; engines shuddering into life barked, snorted, and died, inspiring more curses and activity. Bomb loads ranged from 4-pound and 30-pound incendiaries to be used by the advance force marking the target area (nearly 500,000 incendiaries would fall on Cologne that night) through 4000-pound high-explosive bombs. In between were 2000-pound, 1000-pound, 500-pound, and 250-pound high explosives —about 1300 of these assorted bombs to sow destruction in the marked areas and to disrupt firefighting attempts by German Civil Defense units.

Nearly half of the force consisted of the Vickers Wellington, the "Wimpy" to crews (named for the "Popeye" cartoon character J. Wellington Wimpy). The Wellington was a favorite among aircrews because of its rugged ability to absorb battle damage and remain airworthy. It was reliable, tough, and a good plane to fly. The Wimpy, though designated

Vickers "Wellington," the "Wimpy," favorite of Bomber Command pilots. Its remarkable geodetic construction, the conception of Barnes N. Wallis of Vickers, made it a rugged aircraft capable of withstanding battle damage. Nearly six hundred Wellingtons participated in the thousand-plane raid on Cologne (although not these pictured: Wellington 1s of No. 311 [Czechoslovakian] Squadron).

(IMPERIAL WAR MUSEUM, LONDON)

as a heavy bomber, was powered by two engines rather than four. So was the Avro Manchester, a few of which also participated in the raid. Also a heavy bomber, the Manchester proved to be underpowered, and when two additional engines were later added, it was transformed into the four-engined Lancaster, one of the best bombers of the Second World War. A few of the early Lancasters, fitted with their four engines (Rolls-Royce Merlin), also went to Cologne that night.

The Short Stirling, Bomber Command's first four-engined heavy bomber, delivered the 2000-pound bombs, hundreds of the 500-pounders, and thousands of the incendiaries. By 1942 the Stirling, not a very popular aircraft among pilots, was gradually being retired to such less hazardous operations as minelaying and glider towing. Bomber Command's second four-engined heavy, the Handley Page Halifax, was second in weight of numbers to the Wellington of the participating aircraft. The Halifax was assigned mainly to the incendiary force which initiated the raid.

The two-engined bombers, besides the Wellington and the Manchester, were the Armstrong Whitworth Whitley and the Handley Page Hampden, both early designs which had formed the backbone of Bomber Command during the early months of the war. Both took part in the target-marking phase of the operation. Both aircraft soon after Millennium were gradually withdrawn from heavy bombing operations. Training aircraft, such as the de Havilland Tiger Moth and the Avro Anson did not take part

"Short Stirling," the RAF's first four-engined heavy bomber. Designed in the late 1930s according to curious specifications (the wing span was determined by the width of RAF hangar doors: a hundred feet; the span of the Stirling was ninety-nine). The performance of the plane was affected by the wing design, restricting its operational ceiling. On missions to Italy, Stirlings were forced to fly through the Alps, rather than over them.

(IMPERIAL WAR MUSEUM, LONDON)

in the Thousand Plan, although popular legend has long contended so.

All through the morning and afternoon of Saturday, May 30, the 1046 Wellingtons, Stirlings, Whitleys, Hampdens, Manchesters, Halifaxes, and Lancasters—each with its own special bomb load—were serviced, armed, and standing ready for the signal to take off.

The aircrews, totaling about six thousand men, came from all corners of the Empire, from Australia and New Zealand to Canada, and even from the United States. The Americans ranged from the inevitable boy from Brooklyn (Charles Honeychurch; although he was not a boy, being then in his thirties) to the equally inevitable representatives of the "Royal Texas Air Force," Bud Cardinal of Fort Worth and Howard L. Tate, Jr., of Dallas. Gunner-radio operator R. J. Campbell came from Pawling, New York. One American, Flying Officer Frank Roper, piloted a Lancaster of No. 207 Squadron.

The British crewmen characteristically ranged across the spectrum of personalities, ranks, attitudes, and ages. For example, flying in one of the leading waves was a fifty-year-old air vice-marshal, J. E. A. Baldwin, Air Officer Commanding, No. 3 Group. During the First World War Baldwin had bombed Cologne; he could not let the opportunity slip by in Millennium, for obvious reasons. "I'm going to see for myself," he announced simply. As AOC, No. 3 Group, he was not supposed to take part in operations, but since he received no definite order to that effect (possibly because he had never both-

H. M. King George VI, in RAF air marshal uniform, visits a Bomber Command base and inspects a typical Lancaster crew. (IMPERIAL WAR MUSEUM, LONDON)

ered to mention it at HQ), Baldwin flew as second pilot in a Stirling of No. 218 Squadron. The pilot was Wing Commander Paul Holder, a South African, who commanded the squadron.

Alongside such veterans as Baldwin and Holder, there were also young men still in their teens, some of them pilots, some gunners, others navigators. Many first pilots had only been promoted from second (in U.S. usage, copilot). By the curious workings of the British system, several pilots in command of aircraft were non-commissioned officers, technically outranked by navigators and bombardiers. Inevitably, most pilots were called "Skipper," a reminder of Britain's seafaring traditions. The pilot was in complete charge of the plane, whatever his rank.

Leslie Manser, with the rank of flying officer, was skipper of a Manchester. A gentle, sensitive young man of twenty, his appearance was deceiving. When first encountered by one of his crew, Manser

quickly came under suspicion: he was too pretty to be the skipper of a bomber. At the controls of his plane, however, the youthful Hertfordshire man was as tough as any man in his crew. A superb pilot, extremely cool, competent and at the same time fully dedicated to the safety of the other five in the crew, Manser left no doubt in their minds as to his authority and competence. His copilot was Sergeant Leslie Baveystock, older than Manser, married and the father of an infant daughter. The navigator was Flying Officer Richard Barnes, the radio operator Pilot Officer Norman Horsley. The latter had finished his tour of duty, but was ordered to make one more operation before being posted to a training unit as an instructor. Barnes was a pilot, but was also a skilled navigator (his nickname was "Bang On" because of his reputation for directing his aircraft bang on the target). Neither man had any misgivings about flying with Manser, although Horsley sensed that "making one more ops" might be stretching his luck a bit far.

The rest of Manser's crew was made up of the two gunners: in the Manchester's tail was B. W. Naylor and in the nose, A. M. Mills. Horsley, in addition to operating the radio, also manned the top-turret guns of the plane.

All five men would, by Sunday morning, owe their lives to Manser.

Rumor had spread early throughout Bomber Command that on that Saturday night the "Big Show" would be on. So long as Bomber Command's chief meteorologist Magnus Spence could promise a reasonably stable weather situation, Harris permitted the preparations to continue through the day. By six in the evening the formal briefings on the various stations could officially begin. The scene was similar in all fifty-three stations. The men jammed into the briefing rooms, some diffident, some boisterous, some silent, all apprehensive. At one station the briefing room was furnished with folding seats which had been salvaged from a bombed London movie theater. The station commander entered with what appeared to be a smile on his face. After quiet had settled upon the room, he told the men, "You may have guessed there's something special on tonight. Well, this is what it is. We're bombing Germany tonight with over a thousand aircraft."

The men sprang to their feet, cheering, pounding each other on the back, and danced about. The tension of the past few days was over—and all believed that they would take part in a worthwhile operation. When calm had been restored, the station commander read them a message from Harris.

The force of which you form a part tonight is at least twice the size and has more than four times the carrying capacity of the largest air force ever before concentrated on one objective. You have an opportunity, therefore, to strike a blow at the enemy which will resound not only throughout Germany, but throughout the world. In your hands lie the means of destroying a major part of the resources by which the enemy's war effort is maintained. It depends, however, on each individual crew whether full concentration is achieved. Press home your attack to your precise objective with the utmost determination and resolution in the foreknowledge that, if you individually succeed, the most shattering and devastating blow will have been delivered against the very vitals of the enemy. Let him have it—right on the chin!

While the incendiary vanguard, primarily consisting of Gee-equipped Wellingtons and Stirlings from several squadrons of No. 3 Group, began taking off for Cologne, aircraft of the intruder forces also took off. These were the Blenheims of No. 2 Group and of Army Co-operation Command as well as Bostons,

Havocs (American-built Douglas A-20s), and Hurricanes of Fighter Command. Altogether these totaled eighty-eight aircraft, which were to "intrude" along the route to Cologne, bombing night fighter airfields, hopefully to draw the night fighters away from the main bomber stream. The Luftwaffe fields in northern France, Belgium, and Holland lay adjacent to the route of the thousand bombers. During this phase of the operation the weather proved to be a formidable hindrance. Coming in low over the Continent the men in the intruder aircraft found the German airfields hidden under heavy cloud and all but impossible to find. In some instances the bombers were unable to find the airfields at all, and if they did, the small bombs they dropped (250- and 40-pounders) had little permanent effect upon the targets.

All through the hours of the mission, from the time the first bomber took off for Cologne until the final bomb fell upon Cologne (theoretically at 2:25 A.M. Sunday morning), the intruders did all they could to harass the Luftwaffe, but with no great success. Of the eighty-eight aircraft which took part, however, only three were lost.

Nor did the major part of the operation proceed

Avro "Manchester," the predecessor of the four-engined Lancaster. The Manchester was regarded as a failure and plagued with engine problems until powered by four Merlins, which led to the highly successful Lancaster, Britain's most potent bomber. The Man- *chester pictured has not had an upper gun turret installed; this was done at about the point where the letter "E" is painted. "EM" is the code for No. 207 Squadron; an American, Frank Roper, was a pilot in this unit on the thousand-plane raid.*

(IMPERIAL WAR MUSEUM, LONDON)

Handley Page "Hampden," an advanced aircraft for its time—it first flew in 1936—but afflicted with shortcomings by 1942. A few Hampdens carried bombs in the Cologne mission, as well as other succeeding thousand raids, but it was not retained as a night bomber and went into Coastal Command operation as a tor- *pedo bomber. These aircraft, of No. 185 Squadron (which by the night of the raid had been converted into an operational training unit and did not participate), illustrate why the Hampden was frequently called "the Frying Pan."*

(IMPERIAL WAR MUSEUM, LONDON)

according to plan. Many heavily laden bombers struggled to achieve altitude and their pilots found themselves all but blind in the cloud. Icing too became a serious problem, rendering the planes sluggish and straining the already laboring engines even more. Some planes were forced to turn back before getting away from England because of straining engines, inability to gain altitude, or other mechanical problems. The first planes of the incendiary force, the Wellingtons and Stirlings of No. 3 Group, began lumbering down the flare paths of their runways around 10 P.M. Within a half hour all aircraft were ready to begin the flight to Cologne. Very soon it was clear that there would never, in actuality, be a thousand bombers over the target. Boomerangs, the planes with various mechanical problems, began to return with crestfallen and genuinely disappointed crews. About a hundred planes were thus forced to return.

Others were stopped by other mishaps. A Wellington of No. 12 Squadron, obviously suffering engine trouble, simply burst into flame and crashed in Norfolk, killing all aboard. Others, unable to gain the altitude and the safety of the larger formations, ran

into German night fighters and were shot down over Holland. Or, despite overheating engines, pilots continued on, hoping for the best—such a pilot was Pilot Officer Reece Reed of No. 101 Squadron—only to lose an engine and be forced to bail out.

Flying on Gee, the leading Wellingtons pushed on through the disconcerting overcast toward Co-

Wellingtons, which flew in the vanguard of the thousand-plane attack on Cologne.

(IMPERIAL WAR MUSEUM, LONDON)

logne. The conditions promised little success. The air was bumpy and with so many planes in the air, pilots became especially sensitive to the chance of collision. Around midnight the leading bombers were within less than an hour's flying time from Cologne and the cloud was still dense and rough.

In Cologne, veteran of 106 bombings, the routine Yellow Alert had been sounded; minutes later, one minute before midnight in fact, the Red Alert was flashed. It was still too early to tell where the British bombers were heading, but the efficient Warning Control of Cologne was on the job as usual. There was still no reason to sound the sirens.

When the vanguard Wellingtons approached within sixty miles west and slightly north of Cologne, the weather miraculously began to clear. In minutes the night sky flooded with moonlight and below the force glistened the Rhine. Germany lay in darkness, except for the glimmer of a lake and the bright curling Rhine pointing toward Cologne. The river, running generally north and south, intercepted the flight path of the bombers, coming from almost due west now, at right angles. The two lines crossed at the Hindenburg Bridge. About a mile to the west of the bridge lay that quarter of the city known as the Neumarkt, in the center of the Old City on the left bank of the Rhine. The Neumarkt was the aiming point for the first of the incendiaries.

At seventeen minutes after midnight the sirens

Night Mission to Germany: Lancasters await the signal to start engines. (IMPERIAL WAR MUSEUM, LONDON)

keened in Cologne. The dutiful, the experienced, the expectant, and the cynical moved into shelters. They had done it before—so many times, it was becoming a bore. And Göring had promised them that there would be no English bombers. . . .

Two Stirlings of No. 15 Squadron, one piloted by Wing Commander J. C. Macdonald and the other by Squadron Leader R. S. Gilmour, approached Cologne at an altitude of fifteen thousand feet. They had first skirted the city, turning north, in order to make the bombing run on the Neumarkt from the north. Off their starboard wing the Rhine glittered in the bright moonlight, the river gracefully arching eastward above the Hindenburg Bridge. The moonlight and intense shadows brought out the city's details. Less than a half mile northeast of the Neumarkt lay the famous cathedral of Cologne, begun in the thirteenth century and completed six hundred years later. The cathedral was not a target. However, just above it lay the main station on the rail line which crossed the Rhine over the Hohenzollern Bridge. The other two aiming points lay a mile to the north and a mile to the south of the Neumarkt.

As the two Stirlings settled on their bomb runs the first burst of flak came up. They were neither accurate nor numerous. Precisely, one half hour after the air raid sirens sounded in Cologne—at 12:47 A.M.—the first incendiary bombs fell from the two Stirlings and spattered across the Neumarkt. The fires these 4-pound and 20-pound bombs ignited would serve as aiming points for the bombers of the main force. During the next hour and a half Cologne would suffer bombing attacks by no less than nine hundred bombers—not the spectacular thousand perhaps, but tragically sufficient.

When the bombers in the train of Macdonald and Gilmour started on their bombing runs, the Germans had already lit dummy fires away from the critical centers of Cologne, hoping to confuse the attackers. In addition, the midnight sky was sliced with heavy flak and blindingly vivid with searchlights. If there was a beginning of terror on the ground, it was as terrifying at eighteen thousand feet. Within minutes after the initial bomb drop, even before the first conflagrations erupted in the Old City, the bombers had begun to take antiaircraft hits; some flared and fell out of the crisscross of the searchlights. The atmosphere bounced with flak, tossing the planes around as pilots, flying on instru-

Night Mission II: A Handley Page "Halifax" (105 attacked Cologne in the night of May 30/31, 1942) gets the signal to begin its takeoff.
(IMPERIAL WAR MUSEUM, LONDON)

ments to keep from being blinded by the lights, weaved to distract the flak-directing instruments, dodged lights, and worried about collision. Quite soon pilots discarded the carefully laid plans for the operation and proceeded under the desperation of the moment. Bombers struck by flak jettisoned bombs as quickly as possible; others, awed by the lights, the flak, and the sight of Cologne burning, bombed directly rather than proceeding according to the briefings on definite bomb runs. Some pilots, even after bombing, circled Cologne to watch in horrified fascination the great sheets of flame which appeared to engulf the city.

Aircraft, therefore, converged over the target area from many directions at different altitudes, some assigned and some enforced by the bomb loads and overtaxed engines. The first collision occurred during the incendiary phase. As one pilot approached the aiming point in a confusion of light, noise, and concussion, he saw one bomber nearby suddenly dissolve in one burst of flame, a great orange ball which remained in place for a moment as small pieces of dripping metal scattered away from it. Keeping directly on his run to give his bombardier the highest chance of accuracy, the pilot found him-

self dangerously close to a Stirling just above and ahead. There were about four hundred yards between him and the Stirling, so he kept a wary eye on his airspeed as well as the Stirling. From below, almost directly under the Stirling, loomed the form of a Wellington.

Night Mission III: Halifax lifts off the runway. Later "Marks" (Halifax III et seq.) were powered with air-cooled Rolls-Royce "Merlins" in place of liquid-cooled "Vultures." (IMPERIAL WAR MUSEUM, LONDON)

Night Mission IV: Lancaster I of No. 61 Squadron; sixty-seven Lancasters bombed Cologne the night of the raid. The only known collision over the target involved a 61 Squadron Lancaster and a Halifax. (IMPERIAL WAR MUSEUM, LONDON)

"There were aircraft everywhere," one bombardier later reported. "The sky over Cologne was as busy as Piccadilly Circus. I could identify every type of bomber in our force by the light of the moon and fires."

The Stirling and the Wellington flew on toward

Night Mission V: A No. 50 Squadron Lancaster, barely off the ground, has already retracted its undercarriage. (U. S. AIR FORCE)

the center of the fires, their crews oblivious to the hazardous proximity of their aircraft. Besides "jinking" (taking evasive action) they were also being bounced by the slipstreams of the planes which had preceded them. The Stirling dropped down and the Wellington rose, but nothing happened and they continued flying with only a few yards separating them. And then they came together again. The Stirling had gained a fraction in speed so that, with a dazzling shower of sparks, the Wellington's propellers cut off its tail section. For a moment the two great planes hovered in unreal suspension; the next moment the Wellington blew out of existence; the four-engined Stirling gyrated down into the holocaust of Cologne, taking its crew with it.

When the incendiary force concluded its job of seeding with flame, there was no doubt as to the location of the target. The stricken city could be seen as far as two hundred miles away. "It was almost too gigantic to be real," one pilot observed. "But it was real enough when we got there. Below us in every part of the city buildings were ablaze. Here and there you could see their outlines, but mostly it was just one big stretch of fire. It was strange to see the flames reflected on our aircraft.

Night Mission VI: A Stirling heads for Germany—
seventy-one bombed Cologne.
(IMPERIAL WAR MUSEUM, LONDON)

It looked at times as though we were on fire ourselves, with a red glow dancing up and down the
wings."

The airspace over Cologne churned with the heat
of the fires, aircraft slipstreams, and the sporadic
burst of antiaircraft fires. Under the unremitting onslaught—about eleven planes crossed over the city
every minute—the defenses had indeed been saturated. The guns ringing Cologne could not keep up
with the great numbers of aircraft. Night fighters
operating on the edge of the flak areas could deal
with but a few of the bombers—and these frequently only after the bomb load had been dropped
into Cologne's inferno. Halfway through the attack
crews noticed a decided confusion and debilitation
on the part of Cologne's flak guns—of which there
were around five hundred.

The bombers of the main force, scheduled to follow the incendiary force, came over and bombed
for an hour. The first plane to arrive was a Wellington of No. 103 Squadron (of No. 1 Group), whose
pilot, a giant New Zealander, Clive Saxelby, brought
it in along the Rhine and without opposition re-

leased the bombs into the marked area. Saxelby
then pulled away and headed for England. It had
been an easy drop and the engines of the Wellington sang beautifully as it cruised over Holland. Out
of the dark came strange flashes which punctured
the fuselage, shattered bits of equipment, and
erupted into a fire in the plane's midsection. The
oxygen system went out immediately, controls went
out of order, and the fire spread.

Saxelby pulled off his oxygen mask, opened the
side window of the cockpit, and for a fleeting moment saw a Messerschmitt 110 in the gloom. They
had been found by a night fighter. With the hydraulic system shot up, the wheels of the Wellington
had come down and the bomb bay doors had
opened, making control of the plane difficult in
addition to slowing it up. Saxelby dived away from
the German fighter while the navigator attempted
to beat out the midsection fire with his bare hands.
Fabric shriveled and pulled away; the tail too caught
fire and lost much of its fabric. The radio operator joined the navigator in fighting the fire, which
in time was extinguished, leaving wide patches of
exposed framework showing. But the controls were
almost too much for Saxelby (his copilot, a man unknown to him before that night, had been killed in

Night Mission VII: A Whitley of No. 10 Squadron air-
borne. Employing the obsolescent Whitley was an op-
erational barrel scraping; only twenty-three bombed
the target during Millennium. (U. S. AIR FORCE)

the attack by the Me-110). By lashing the control column with rope, Saxelby managed to maintain a near-level flight across the rest of Holland and the North Sea and to the first base they found in England—Honington.

Leslie Manser's Manchester was one of the main force bombers. Like so many of the heavily loaded two-engined bombers, the Manchester could not climb to a safer altitude without dangerously overheating the engines. Manser was forced to bring the plane in under the other bombers at around seven thousand feet. Although he could take some comfort in assuming that the flak would be concentrating on the greater number of aircraft, in truth the overladen radar operators found it simpler to select strays.

On the approach to the drop point the Manchester seemed poised upon the fingers of several searchlights. Just as flak accuracy decreased with altitude, it inversely improved the lower a plane dropped. With the main force up at least twice the height of Manser's Manchester, the stray was quickly boxed in by flak bursts. Manser, the pilot

so many had regarded as "too pretty" to be a pilot, selected an area within the target zone still untouched by fire. Bang On Barnes peered through the bombsight and centered on the area as Manser guided the Manchester across Cologne in even flight.

"Bombs gone," Barnes announced. The Manchester elevated upon losing its burden and, almost instantaneously, recoiled under a direct flak hit. The controls threatened to tear out of Manser's hands as he fought to keep the tumbling and rocking plane under control. But he realized, too, that they must get away from the searchlights—for the flak had plotted their range. Manser heaved forward on the control column and dived away from the lights. When they entered blackness he eased the plane out of the dive. It responded beautifully and came out at less than a thousand feet. They could not remain at that height either, for even ground machine-gun fire could reach them. Pulling back on the controls Manser guided the plane up to two thousand feet; should they have to jump it was a safer altitude also. The plane had taken a hit in the bomb bay, luckily after the bombs had been dropped. The fire had gone out, but that proved only a temporary blessing. The strain on the left engine had been too much. The instruments flickered strangely and then a flash of fire shot out of the engine.

Manser coolly ordered copilot Baveystock to feather the left engine and to activate the fire extinguisher. The rest of the crew, including rear gunner Naylor, who had been wounded by the flak, began to make ready to jump. As Manser and Baveystock watched, the flames from the engine swept back along the wing. The question was: How long before the fire reached the fuel tank in the wing and blew them all over the sky?

But Manser only said, "Let's wait." And they did, for like their skipper the men in the aircraft wanted most of all to get back to England. The eerie flames consumed the fabric of the wing, burned the engine mount, and then, after about ten minutes, the fire went out. Manser had been right. He turned the Manchester toward home as the crew attended to other important details. Naylor lay in a rest bed in the rear of the plane, attended to by radio operator Norman Horsley. But the plane continued to lose altitude and it seemed unlikely that they could ever reach England. All possible equipment which could be spared and torn loose was flung from the plane to lighten it—even guns. The Manchester, despite this, continued to lose air speed. The engine must soon give up—or blow up. Manser found it more and more difficult to keep the plane under control.

Reluctantly he ordered the crew to jump. Mills, the nose gunner, left through the front exit, followed by Barnes, the navigator. Horsley helped the wounded Naylor through a side exit and followed soon after. The plane by this time shuddered and wheezed and was dangerously near stalling point.

Baveystock returned to the cockpit to make certain that Manser had his parachute. He attempted to clip it on the pilot. But he was stopped by Manser, who ordered him to jump immediately. Baveystock went forward to the forward hatch and jumped. But the plane at this time was scarcely a hundred feet above the hedgerow- and dike-crossed countryside of Belgium. In remaining behind to check Manser's parachute Baveystock had all but canceled his chances of survival. He leaped into the darkness, pulled his chute ring—and plunged into the water of a drainage ditch. Although the

parachute had not opened completely, it had decelerated Baveystock's falling speed and the water in the dike did the rest.

The Manchester continued on for only a few hundred feet before striking the ground with a terrific explosion. When he climbed out of the dike Baveystock tried to get to the burning wreck, but the heat of the flames—and the ammunition still aboard detonating—made it impossible. Manser had died in the aircraft; he had kept it aloft long enough to save his entire crew. Baveystock, Horsley, Naylor, and Mills, with the aid of the Belgian underground, finally returned to England. Navigator Barnes, injured in his parachute jump, was captured by the Germans. When the others eventually returned to England and told their story, Manser was posthumously awarded the Victoria Cross—the only participant in the Thousand Plane raid to receive it.

The final fifteen minutes of the raid involved the heavies, the Halifaxes and Lancasters of Nos. 4 and 5 Groups, which followed the main force to which Manser's Manchester belonged. Their function was to drop the 1000- and 4000-pound bombs into the furious chaos. These last two hundred planes would deliver the finishing touches to the destruction besides hindering whatever fire fighting was still possible in Cologne. By 2:25 A.M., Sunday morning, May 31, 1942, Cologne was a man-made hell. To the mystical Leonard Cheshire, who had completed a tour of duty and was then commanding a conversion unit (i.e., a training unit which prepared pilots accustomed to two-engined planes to operate four-engined craft), the hundreds of aircraft pointing toward the crimson glow which was Cologne was "the most monstrous sight in all the history of bombing." As he brought his Halifax in on the bomb run and the city came into view "there was a sudden silence in the aeroplane. If what we saw below was true,

---

Night Mission VIII: A typical German flak and searchlight concentration over a German city (not Cologne). Flak was responsible for most losses over the target. Of the twenty-two British bombers lost over Cologne, sixteen fell to antiaircraft fire, four to night fighters, and two to a collision.

(ALIEN PROPERTY CUSTODIAN, NATIONAL ARCHIVES)

Cologne was destroyed. We looked hastily at the Rhine, but there was no mistake; what we saw below was true."

The orders had been that all bombing was to cease at two twenty-five precisely; all planes which had not bombed were to turn back. This was to ensure the returning planes as much darkness as possible. The German night fighters were problem enough without having to contend with the day fighters also.

When he took off at 1:15 A.M., Flight Lieutenant George Gilpin had scant hopes of reaching Cologne by two twenty-five. The other aircraft of No. 61 Squadron had left an hour ago. His Lancaster, of the squadron's conversion flight, had been ignored while the rest of the squadron's Lancasters—sixteen altogether—were made ready. Though he pleaded, Gilpin had little luck until the regular planes had been bombed-up and armed. Then all joined in, including himself and his crew, to get the plane ready. The bombing had been progressing for nearly an hour before Gilpin trundled the Lancaster to the runway, half expecting not to get the takeoff light. But it came and he gunned the engines and got away before anyone changed his mind.

Gilpin put the Lancaster into a climb and pulled away over England. They should have little trouble finding Cologne, for there were two navigators aboard the Lancaster. When Gilpin had been granted permission to go on the raid it was with the proviso he could scratch together a crew, for most of the men at his station were assigned to the regular squadron bombers. Gilpin had all positions

filled, having assigned the role of navigator-bombardier to an old school friend, John Beach. But there was still need of a nose gunner. It was while he was out seeking a gunner that Gilpin found Flight Officer D. H. Brewer, who, having never flown in a Lancaster, jumped at the chance to go. But Brewer was not a gunner in fact, but a navigator.

They crossed the North Sea at about seventeen thousand feet and below them saw streams of returning bombers of the first wave. Their Lancaster was the only plane flying toward Germany. Gilpin consulted with Beach, asking for an estimated time of arrival over the target.

"0305."

"Forty minutes late?"

This would be counter to orders and Gilpin was not anxious to break rules. Nor was he anxious to waste the effort. He asked Beach for a heading toward another target. But it never came; there was a curious silence on the intercom, an eloquent testimonial to the wishes of the crew. Gilpin let it go at that, for as they crossed over Holland the glow of Cologne lit up the eastern horizon like a premature sunrise.

The Lancaster, then, at three in the morning, was the only plane in the air over Cologne, shimmering below. A pillar of smoke reached up to fifteen thousand feet. It seemed ludicrous for a single bomber to drop its load into the carnage which hundreds of bombers had wreaked. But Beach, lying in the nose, guided Gilpin assiduously on the bomb run. Although there were no fighters now over Cologne, the searchlights stabbed into the air, holding the Lancaster in their blinding light. Then the flak came hurtling up, leaving drifting puffs in the sky. Carefully Beach centered on the aiming point in the center of the burning mass.

Since he was in the nose serving as a scratch "bomb aimer," Beach was not seated in his regular position in the navigator's seat behind Gilpin. On the bomb run a piece of flak tore through the cabin and ripped out the navigator's seat—luckily unoccupied. The impact shook up Gilpin a little but he continued with the run until he heard Beach's quiet "Bombs gone." Gilpin immediately dived the Lancaster out of the beams of light, and although the flak continued to track them, they left Cologne and made for the sea.

When they reached the Dutch coast for the flight over the North Sea and home, the Lancaster was flying on three engines, one having given up on the way. Day had come as they approached England —luckily there had been no fighters. Gilpin brought them all home safely. Millennium was over.

Perhaps with the landing of Gilpin's Lancaster, it could be said that the operation was concluded, but in fact it was not. Even before the great bomber, coming in on three engines and with one propeller feathered, touched down gently at the base at Syerston, a single twin-engined aircraft raced into the air before dawn from its base at Horsham Saint Faith in Norfolk. This was a de Havilland Mosquito of No. 105 Squadron, one of the units which had served with the Advance Air Striking Force in France during the early weeks of the war. Called the "Wooden Wonder" or the "Termite's Delight," the Mosquito was of practically all-wood construction, which eluded radar detection. It was also faster than the German fighters of the period.

On the mission to Cologne, the Mosquito was dispatched to drop bombs (for this highly versatile plane could be used as a bomber as well as fighter, among other functions) and to photograph the destruction of the Millennium bombing. The pilot brought the Mosquito over Cologne at twenty-three thousand feet during the early morning, but although his bombardier could release their bombs, the smoke made it impossible to photograph the damage. Three additional Mosquitos left Horsham Saint Faith at later intervals, and of the two which returned, it was with the same result: too much smoke—for a vast fire cloud rose up to fifteen thousand feet—to take photographs. Only the survivors in the city below realized the extent of the effect of Millennium.

III

German propaganda quickly sneered at British claims of a thousand bombers over Cologne, claiming that the figure was closer to seventy and that the defenses had accounted for nearly half that number. Early British estimates of the impact of the raid were naturally exaggerated. Upon viewing the devastation, however, five days after the attack when

Night Mission IX: de Havilland "Mosquito," which flew a reconnaissance mission to Cologne the morning *after the thousand-plane raid and found smoke rising fifteen thousand feet into the air over the city.*

(DE HAVILLAND PHOTOGRAPH)

Night Mission X: A Stirling coming in for a landing in England. (IMPERIAL WAR MUSEUM, LONDON)

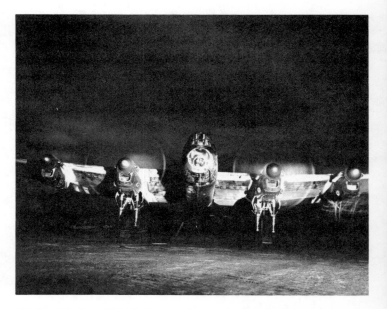

Night Mission XI: A Lancaster, engines warming up and wheels chocked, ready for the next mission.
(IMPERIAL WAR MUSEUM, LONDON)

reconnaissance photographs could be taken, it was clear that more than six hundred acres of the city had been eradicated.

Dismay was the mood in Cologne. Although the official Luftwaffe view was that a few English bombers had broken through the defenses, the city's police president reported that the "number of enemy aircraft over the city could not be estimated." Hitler's toady, Gauleiter Joseph Grohé, supplied his leader with his estimate of a "thousand or more," which Hitler used in a screaming attack upon the Luftwaffe.

The raid had killed 469 people and wounded 5027; more than 45,000 were bombed out of their homes. The incendiaries accounted for the most terrible aspects of the raid, spreading wildly and burning buildings and destroying life and property. This single attack caused the death of more people than all previous attacks upon Cologne combined.

Other than some spectacular figures, had the Thousand Plan accomplished what Harris had wished for? What had been the cost? And what would the future of this kind of warfare be?

The Millennium losses, considering the ambitiousness of the undertaking and the fact that so many inexperienced crews participated, were reasonably low. Forty-one aircraft were listed as missing on the morning after the raid; 3 planes of the intruder force were also missing. Thus it was officially noted that of the total aircraft involved in Millennium, 44 out of 1134 (combined bombing force and intruders) were missing.

And yet Churchill would have been prepared to defend the loss of a hundred aircraft and crews, if necessary, on the floor of the Parliament. Harris had predicted a loss of forty planes; he was a realistic professional. The casualty rate had been 3.8 per cent—a not unacceptable proportion. It was Harris's belief that "we should never have had a real bomber offensive if it had not been for the thousand-bomber attack on Cologne, an irrefutable demonstration of the power of what was to all intents and purposes a new and untried weapon." Another professional, Herr Goebbels, although no soldier, took his own realistic view of the raid when he noted in his diary that he could not "believe that the English have the power to continue such bombing attacks. . . ." Still he was nagged by the possibility of a number of such large-scale attacks, which

he admitted (to himself at least) "can damage us considerably." It was true that Harris would not be able to continue such attacks, risking his regular squadrons, his reserves, instructors, and trainees night after night. In fact, only one more raid of such scale took place in 1942 (June 25/26; the target was Bremen); an earlier attack upon Essen did not achieve the magical magnitude of a thousand. Not until the full weight of the U. S. Eighth and Fifteenth Air Forces came to operate over Europe could thousand-bomber raids become a daily and nightly procedure.

But Harris had made his point—the Thousand Plan had not failed. Cologne had suffered and, if not knocked out of the war, was thrown into confusion and industrial inaction for several weeks. The price of war, too, was brought home to the hapless civil population. The importance of morale under fire is always a questionable point—the human spirit endures under incredible adversity—but before the thousands of evacuees left Cologne they were compelled to sign a statement promising not to discuss the situation in Cologne. Though not readily measurable, the impact upon the German spirit was no less real. Harris had saved his command from the depletion it had suffered during the weeks before he was given its leadership. He had not "destroyed Cologne," as he had asserted, but he had saved Bomber Command and its continued existence and growth would have its effect upon the German war machine.

There were eventual changes in the Luftwaffe brought about by the Cologne attack; it was clear that aircraft would have to be siphoned away from the Russian front. There would be a greater need for more fighter protection over the cities of the Fatherland. Consequently, the German Army would lose some of its air cover. These were subtle yet far-reaching consequences.

There was an even more subtle, sublime might even be the word, sequel, the effect of which was pernicious to the Luftwaffe. This may have been the most important of all the "fruits" of Cologne. While the raid developed in all its fury, Hitler fumed at his headquarters at Rastenberg. His mind was saturated with the conquest of Russia and this sudden, full-scale onslaught from the west exasperated him. Göring was at that moment living the good life in his castle at Veldenstein. When the noon conferences took place on the Sunday following the attack, it devolved upon Jeschonnek and Bodenschatz (Göring's personal aide) to represent the Luftwaffe before the Führer.

Having heard reports from a representative of the Navy and the Army, Hitler turned to the young chief of staff. Jeschonnek did not begin immediately and was prodded by the Führer. "General Jeschonnek, I am waiting. . . ." Clearly Hitler was in a mood, although the devoted, naïve Jeschonnek appeared to be unaware of it.

"There was an RAF attack on Cologne," Jeschonnek began hesitantly, "a pretty heavy attack."

"How heavy?"

Jeschonnek shuffled some papers. "According to preliminary reports," he answered, "we estimate that two hundred aircraft penetrated our defenses. The damage is heavy . . . we are still waiting for final estimates."

"You are still waiting for final estimates . . ." Hitler mocked and shouted, "and the Luftwaffe thinks there were two hundred enemy aircraft!" His voice cracked and rose shrilly. "The Luftwaffe was probably asleep last night! But I was not asleep—not when one of my cities is under fire!"

The Luftwaffe, Hitler intimated, deceived him as usual. Thank God he could depend upon such reliable men as Gauleiter Grohé in Cologne.

"Let me tell you what Gauleiter Grohé has to say! Listen—I ask you to listen carefully—[shouting] there were a thousand or more English aircraft—you hear!—a thousand, twelve hundred, maybe more!" Hitler stopped, his face a livid, apoplectic study in wrath. Composed, but no less furious, Hitler then spoke in a cold tone. "Herr [not Reichsmarschall] Göring, of course, is not here; of course not. . . ."

Bodenschatz had slipped out of the room during the speech, upon assessing the situation. He reached Göring at Veldenstein by phone. "Chief," he said, "you had better come at once. There is trouble."

That he was *persona non grata* was obvious to Göring as soon as he entered the Führer's headquarters later that day. He had gone into the room briskly, but wearing an appropriate air of earnest sobriety. Göring was visibly shaken when Hitler disregarded his outstretched hand. The former corporal had never actually trusted flying men and he had been proved right. If he had failed to appreciate the potential of air power, from that moment on he would refuse even to attempt to understand it. The inner deterioration of the Luftwaffe was assured. Suspicion, vilification, abuse of function, and, even more damaging, the estrangement of Göring and Hitler, sealed the fate of the "Air Weapon."

Harris had not only won the battle; philosophically and morally at least, he had won the war.

6

X-SQUADRON

Lookouts in the small convoy of ships plying the night-shrouded North Sea quickened to the thick rumble of several aircraft engines bearing down from the direction of England. Immediately gunners brought their gun barrels around and waited; a challenge signal vaulted from the convoy commander's ship. Three dark, massive forms came hurtling toward the ships; the planes were barely fifty feet over the water and must have been doing better than two hundred miles an hour.

A Very pistol was fired from a side window in the lead plane and all the men in the convoy relaxed. The signal color was correct for the night, May 16, 1943; the aircraft were British. As was the custom, the convoy's skipper acknowledged recognition with the message "Good hunting" by Aldis lamp. From the lead plane another Aldis flashed as the plane grew smaller in the night. The seamen read the message as the light became a pin point:

We are going to get damn drunk tomorrow night.

As they pondered this curious intelligence two more groups of the same aircraft (Lancasters, they appeared to be) swept over the convoy toward Holland, probably on the way to Germany.

The pilot in the lead Lancaster was the young, stocky veteran of three tours of duty (bombers, night fighters, and bombers again) who was frequently referred to by his men as "the baby skipper," Guy Penrose Gibson. Not many weeks before

—in mid-March—he had returned from his 173rd sortie—a mission to Stuttgart—bringing his Lancaster back on three engines, expecting to take a much needed rest. Gibson hoped to have a few days' leave, the first in about a year, which he would spend with his wife in Cornwall relaxing. He would smoke a pipe, take walks with his dog, and forget about the war for a while. Instead he found himself leading a fantastic night mission.

At twenty-four, Gibson had served as squadron commander of No. 106 Squadron, had been awarded the Distinguished Service Order (with bar) and the Distinguished Flying Cross, and had acquired the reputation in Bomber Command as one of the finest minds in the service. Gibson had been born in 1918 in Simla, India, where his father had served as Conservator of Forests. He grew up in Kent, however, in the area which would serve as the setting for the Battle of Britain, and went to St. Edward's School, Oxford. Though powerfully built, Gibson never grew much taller than slightly over five feet. Whether or not this accounted for his physical drive is beside the point, for as recollected by the warden at St. Edward's, he "was one of the most thorough and determined boys I have ever known. . . ."

By the time he was well into his teens, Gibson had become air-minded and hoped to seek work as a test pilot. When he approached Vickers-Armstrong

Guy Gibson, who led one of the most daring bombing missions of the war during the Battle of the Ruhr. A born pilot and leader, Gibson earned a Victoria Cross for his part in the Dam Busters raid.
(IMPERIAL WAR MUSEUM, LONDON)

(who would later manufacture the Wellington), Gibson was told to join the RAF "to get all the flying time you can." However, upon applying Gibson was informed that his "legs were too short." But the determined Gibson had made up his mind and after exercising and stretching, he returned to the RAF and apparently, by sheer dint of will power, passed the physical requirements. In 1935 Guy Gibson began training with the RAF, hoping that when he had completed his courses, he might return to Vickers for a job as test pilot. The stocky youngster fell into the routine very well—he had a taste for pretty girls and drink and a love of animals. He also revealed a flair for flying and a mind which absorbed, classified, and retained details.

The political situation kept Gibson in the RAF after his enlistment expired and when war finally came he was a pilot of a Hampden in No. 83 Squadron based at Scampton in Lincolnshire. Gibson took part in the frustrating operations during the "Phony War," as well as more profitable strikes upon targets in the occupied countries and the Sealion barges during the Battle of Britain. Upon completing his tour with the bombers, Gibson was stationed—for "a rest"—with No. 29 Squadron, Fighter Command. While serving with this night fighter unit, Gibson succeeded in shooting down three enemy aircraft. Following his "rest" tour Gibson was sent to an Operational Training Unit, which did not please him at all. But it was a good post, for Gibson had married Evelyn Mary Moore, a young and pretty actress, and he spent much time at home. Even so, Gibson did not like the role of flying instructor and made it fairly obvious. Not long after Arthur Harris took over Bomber Command Gibson managed to get an interview with him and within days (two, in fact) was posted, in February 1942, to No. 106 Squadron as Wing Commander (Acting). Upon completing his tour with the squadron, its "baby skipper" looked forward with longing to the easy days with Eve at Cornwall.

But he had barely unwound from the Stuttgart mission when he was informed the following day that he would not go on leave; he was to be posted at Headquarters, No. 5 Group instead.

Air Officer Commanding of No. 5 Group was Air Vice-Marshal the Honorable Sir Ralph Cochrane, like Saundby an old prewar squadron mate of Harris. Cochrane, scion of a noble Scots family, was a lean, no-nonsense, crisply decisive man whose aviation experience dated back to the First World War. When Gibson reported to him at group headquarters at Grantham, it was with the gloomy expectation of being assigned to write a textbook on bombing. Having barely finished congratulating Gibson on the bar to his DSO, Cochrane immediately came to the point.

"How would you like the idea of doing one more trip?"

Visions of fighters and flak came into Gibson's mind. He had hoped all of that was over, at least for a while. But all he could do was ask, "What kind of trip, sir?"

"A pretty important one, perhaps one of the most

devastating of all time," Cochrane replied. "I can't tell you any more now. Do you want to do it?"

The urgency seemed so pressing that Gibson had begun trying to remember where he had left his flying kit. Certainly the trip of which the AOC spoke was scheduled for that very night. His answer reflected the state of his mind: "I think so, sir." Gibson was then sent away mystified.

But the trip was not scheduled for that night, or the next. On the third day after the first interview Gibson was once again ordered to Grantham's main office. Seated in Cochrane's office was a man Gibson knew, stocky, thirtyish, experienced Group Captain Charles Whitworth. Cochrane was cordial, even offered Gibson a cigarette before he broached the subject of "the trip." He began by warning Gibson that it would not be an "ordinary sortie. In fact, it can't be done for at least two months."

"Hell," Gibson thought, "it's the *Tirpitz*. What on earth did I say yes for?" The great 45,000-ton battleship, launched just six months before the war began, was a major source of anxiety to the British at this time (the *Tirpitz* did not prove as formidable in action as it promised, but this was not apparent in 1943). The battleship was then lying in Trondheim Fiord in Norway, all but impossible to reach by air and a threat to convoys to Russia.

Cochrane went on, without slipping Gibson the least hint of the nature of the target or of the mission itself beyond telling him that Harris regarded the training for the raid so important "that a special squadron is to be formed for the job. I want you to form that squadron. . . ."

Stressing the importance of the training and the little time in which it must be done, Cochrane suggested that Gibson go immediately to the personnel section to begin assembling his crews and arranging for aircraft and other equipment as well as ground crews. All Gibson knew actually was that he was to undertake some important mission or other and that his special squadron was to be based at Scampton, where Group Captain Whitworth was commander and where Gibson had begun his active career with No. 83 Squadron less than four years before.

When he left Cochrane's office for the personnel section Gibson's head swam and his ears rang with the order, "I want to see your aircraft flying in four days' time."

What aircraft, with what crews? Gibson wondered as he climbed the stairs to begin selecting pilots and crews and to start all the other gears meshing for the mysterious trip. Whatever it all ultimately would lead to, the trip was obviously of highest priority, for within two days a squadron of seven hundred men was formed and ordered to report to Scampton. In fact, its formation had come so quickly that the Air Ministry was itself not prepared for it and called it temporarily X-Squadron. Finally it was assigned the number 617.

II

That it was an elite unit was patent in the beribboned crews that began arriving at Scampton on March 21, 1942. "These were the aces of Bomber Command," Gibson noted. He had selected pilots he knew personally or by reputation; the rest were suggested by Bomber Command. It was a standing order, another tribute to X-Squadron's uniqueness, that the other squadrons must surrender requested crews on demand. This did not always work out to perfection. "Some of the squadrons which had been told by the SASO [Senior Air Staff Officer] to supply us with tip-top men had taken the opportunity to get rid of some of their duds. . . . Then another squadron supplied me, rather unkindly, with two pregnant WAAFs [Women's Auxiliary Air Force]. They were married, of course, but they weren't any use to me because they had to leave the service, anyway. There were other little games played on us which I won't mention." Gibson, however, managed to assemble twenty-one crews, some of them from his own No. 106 Squadron—all of them veterans with thousands of sorties to their credit.

When he called the 147 men of the aircrews together for their first official meeting, Gibson was still at a disadvantage. There was little of a solid nature which he could tell these 147 knowledgeable men. "You're here," he told them, "to do a special job, you're here as a crack squadron, you're here to carry out a raid on Germany which, I am told, will have startling results. Some say it may even cut short the duration of the war. What the target is I can't tell you. Nor can I tell you where it is. All I can tell you is that you will have to practice low flying all day and all night until you know how to do it with your eyes shut. . . ."

It would be some days before Gibson was to meet the gentle, white-haired man—a civilian—who had initiated all of this inexplicable activity. He was Dr. Barnes N. Wallis, an outstanding designer and aeronautical engineer employed by Vickers-Armstrong. Wallis, who had designed the structure of the airship R-100, had contributed also to the design of the Wellington bomber (in which work he had teamed up with Vickers' chief designer, Rex K. Pierson). Wallis's major conception was the geodetic system of construction, which made the Wimpy a rugged though comparatively lightweight aircraft.

A brilliant mathematician, the fifty-year-old engineer began to consider the problem of bombs as

Dr. Barnes Wallis, inventor-engineer-designer, who made many contributions to Britain's war effort as well as to aviation. (VICKERS LIMITED)

soon as the war started. Wallis, in his own way, was a proponent of strategic bombardment. When war came he believed that the standard bombs then available to Bomber Command lacked the power to destroy important industrial targets: the five-hundred-pounders then in use would not do. Also, unless targets were selected with care, what bombs were dropped would accomplish little more than temporary damage. Wallis, in short, began to visualize a superbomb to be dropped upon a super target. It followed that his mind would consider the Ruhr, the great center of Germany's heavy industry. Within this highly defended area lay a complex of great dams, targets which could not be dispersed like a factory, nor even very easily camouflaged.

Wallis studied the situation closely and selected three of the dams as primary targets: the Möhne, the Sorpe, and the Eder. The first two, as Wallis later explained to Gibson when finally the young wing commander was permitted to know what he was about to attempt, held back "about 76 per cent of the total water available in the Ruhr Valley. If they were to be breached, the consequent shortage of water for both drinking and industrial purposes might be disastrous. Of course, the damage done by floods if they were breached quickly would result in more damage to everything than has ever happened in this war." The Möhne Dam alone, holding back a lake about twelve miles in length, would release about 140 million tons of water, if breached, into the Möhne Valley.

The Eder Dam was not a water supply dam as were the other two, but a source of hydroelectric power. It was somewhat larger than the Möhne, with a capacity of about 200 million tons of water.

Such were the targets, but there were no bombs then existing that could burst them. An object which could hold back 200 million tons of water would not breach under the impact of a mere five-hundred-pound high-explosive bomb. It was to this problem that Wallis applied himself next, studying the structure of dams and of the nature of explosion: shock, tension, and dozens of other variables. When he felt he had the answers to all of the problems, Wallis took his idea to the Air Ministry. He was not greeted with open arms and cries of recognition. Although Wallis's idea had been conceived early in the war, it was not until Harris took over Bomber

Command that it trickled down to him. Nor did the astute Harris seize upon the Wallis plan with joy and expectation.

The various ministries had come to be all but besieged by hundreds of inventors, idea men, armchair generals, and just plain screwballs with thousands of schemes and gadgets for winning the war. Wallis's device for a big bomb (an "earthquake bomb," he sometimes called it) would require a large aircraft to carry it (he called that a "victory bomber"). Neither bomb nor aircraft existed when he submitted his plan. Because of his reputation in the industry, Wallis's idea was not completely dismissed, as were so many others at the time. But, depite that, it took a long time before anyone in the Ministry of Aircraft Production read his paper with any understanding. This was Sir Henry Tizard, who had championed Watson-Watt's radar. A committee was formed to study Wallis's formulations (among which the dams project was but one) and soon after, another committee was formed known as "The Air Attack on Dams Committee." It took months before the idea took on any definite form, depending not only upon the accuracy and validity of Wallis's computations, but also upon the advent of a bomber which could lift and deliver a bomb of tremendous weight. Meanwhile, new very high explosives were being developed. So it was that when the high-capacity bombs became feasible—according to Wallis's figures it would have to be about ten thousand pounds in weight, explosive as well as casing—the Lancaster was on hand to carry it.

Months of experimentation followed, with Wallis practicing on small models of dams and bombs and filling pages with computations. Quite simply, it was Wallis's idea that in order to breach so sturdy an object as the Möhne Dam, the special bomb would have to be released at low altitude, with the aircraft traveling at a specific speed. Before the bomb—which was shaped like an oil drum—was dropped, it must be made to revolve. Upon release it was supposed to skip and jump along the water's surface until it struck the dam. Then it would, because of the spin, roll down the face of the dam to the proper depth and only then explode. The tremendous forces, magnified by water pressure, would have the force of an earthquake and would, theoretically, burst the dam. That is what Wallis's figures said and that is what he believed.

Eventually, with models and with test bombs Wallis proved that it could be done. However, when he finally took his idea to Harris, the latter was skeptical. He had heard of the little man with the dams idea. Another crackpot with what Harris termed a "panacea target," single targets that everyone—except the Germans—would assume might end the war in a single blow. These targets, often as not, were difficult to hit, well defended, and, even if hit, might very well prove not so conclusive after all. They were costly in terms of crew losses, spectacular, even dramatic—but wasteful. Harris had his own plan for ending the war—a city by city erasure of German industries with large forces of heavy bombers. Wars were not decided with single panacea blows. Harris regarded Wallis with misgiving and doubt.

He told Wallis he found the idea a bit beyond belief and, further, he was not ready to risk a squadron of Lancasters on it. One of Wallis's champions was Joseph "Mutt" Summers, chief test pilot at Vickers, who had been assisting Wallis in testing the dummy bombs in a converted Wellington off the coast of England. At the point where the two stubborn men, Wallis and Harris, were about to clash, Summers interceded and promised Harris that they could prove that the bomb worked.

"Prove it," Harris snapped, "and you'll get your squadron."

The two men brought out the film that Wallis had been shooting over the past half year and with Saundby operating the projector, the four men observed the results of Wallis's experiments.

When the film ended all Harris would say was, "Very interesting. I'll think it over."

This was not very encouraging. Wallis found that others also were less than enthused and he had even been asked to stop "making a nuisance of yourself at the Ministry." Exhausted, depressed, and fed up, Wallis offered to resign from all war work. This only aroused an outcry of "Mutiny!" Wallis seemed to have come to a dead end. But other forces had been at work, for approval of the idea had come down from the Chief of the Air Staff, Sir Charles Portal; Churchill had voiced his approval and others had chimed in. The date was February 26, 1943; the operation must take place sometime in May, when the water level of the dams was at maximum. That left three months in which to select and train

The objective: the Ruhr dams, in this instance the Möhne, holding back more than a million tons of water. (IMPERIAL WAR MUSEUM, LONDON)

crews, make and test the bomb, and modify the Lancasters to carry it.

It was Mutt Summers who brought Gibson finally to meet Wallis after No. 617 Squadron had begun training at Scampton. By coincidence, it had been Summers who had advised Gibson, so many years before, to enlist in the RAF. The trip from Scampton had been exceedingly cloak and dagger. Gibson was driven south, past London, and left at a small country railway station. He took a train for Weybridge, where he was supposed to meet someone. The someone turned out to be Summers, who then drove Gibson to Wallis's home in the peaceful southern countryside. Gibson found Wallis "neither young nor old, but just a quiet, earnest man who worked very hard. He was one of the real back-room boys of whom little can be told until after the war. . . ."

An awkward situation arose immediately, for Gibson admitted that to date he had not been informed of the target or of the "Wallis bomb." Wallis checked a list of names of persons with whom he could discuss the project and did not find Gibson's there.

"This is damned silly," Summers said. But Wallis would not discuss the plan except in general terms. He did run a film he and Summers had made which revealed something to Gibson. He saw a Wimpy come in within two hundred feet of the sea and drop a strange cylindrical object. Gibson was certain that if that were a bomb, the detonation would blow the plane sky-high, but instead the cylinder bounced along as the Wellington pulled out of the way of danger.

Clearly, they were to come in low over a target situated on or near the water. Was it the *Tirpitz,* Gibson wondered, or was it the U-boat pens?

Wallis explained that the cylinder was, indeed, his special bomb, the placement of which would require exceptional skill. However, the test bomb was but a quarter of the size of the real thing, so that further testing would be necessary. Gibson asked if any full-scale bombs existed.

"No, not yet," Wallis admitted, "the first will be ready in about a week's time with a modified Lancaster to carry it. Avro's is doing a great rush job to get the special fittings put on; I believe they're working twenty-four hours a day. Now what I want to know from you is this. Can you fly to the limits

I want? These are roughly a speed of two hundred and forty miles an hour at a hundred and fifty feet above smooth water, having pulled out of a dive from two thousand feet, and then be able to drop a bomb accurately within a few yards."

Although still mystified, Gibson left Wallis knowing just a bit more about their proposed mission. He promised to see if it would be possible to meet the requirements for the bomb drop, but that was all. So it was that the two men worked, in their separate spheres, concurrently toward a date in the middle of May, the younger man without concrete information and the older one still uncertain that the weapon he had invented would actually work.

Gibson assigned his crews the unpleasant task of flying low over lakes, rivers, and reservoirs. Within days the complaints began coming in—reports of low-flying aircraft. Even Gibson's own maintenance crews complained of leaves and branches jammed into the radiators.

"This means you are flying too low," Gibson told his flight leaders "You've got to stop this or else someone will kill himself. And I might also tell you that the provost marshals have already been up to see me about reported dangerous low flying. We all know we've got to fly low, and we've got to get some practice in, but for God's sake, tell your boys to try and avoid going over towns and aerodromes and not to beat up policemen or lovers in a field, because they'll get the rocket if they do."

The following day Gibson was summoned to Cochrane's office. On the floor stood three large packing cases. Cochrane handed Gibson a screwdriver and promised he would show him the targets—although he would not tell him either what they were or where they were located. Gibson removed the lids and peered into the boxes—there perfectly scaled were models of three dams, obviously very large and sturdy. But Gibson's first reaction upon seeing them was a fleeting thought: "Thank God, it's not the *Tirpitz*."

Without revealing much more, Cochrane told him to take a plane and fly down to see Wallis in Weybridge. At least now the men could discuss the problem intelligently. It was Wallis who informed Gibson that the three dams lay in the Ruhr Valley—"Happy Valley" to the bomber crews because of the deadly flak barrages they never failed to encounter there.

Gibson wondered why the special bombs, and why the stringent conditions—altitude, speed—for the attack. Wouldn't any large bomb hitting the dams knock them out?

Wallis explained the difference between a vault dam—the curved type which held back water by its configuration "much the same as the arch of a bridge"—and the dams they were after, which were called gravity dams and which retained water by their own weight. "As these are a hundred and forty feet thick, of solid concrete and masonry, a hundred and fifty feet high, you can see that there is a colossal amount of masonry to shift." Wallis further explained that the attack would have to take place when the water level was at its highest. At that moment it was twelve feet from the top of each dam; they would attack when the level reached four. This would give them the proper water capacity and also leave the four-foot space against which the bomb would strike after its last bounce carrying it over the floating torpedo nets which protected the dam, and then permitting it to roll down the dam toward the base before detonating. This was precision at its most precise. Gibson looked doubtful. They were to do this at night in addition to all the other contingencies.

"I have calculated," Wallis continued, "that the water level will be suitable during the week May 13–19, that is, in about six weeks' time. This, as it happens, is a moon period—I think you will have to do it at night or dawn—you couldn't get into the Ruhr by day, could you?"

"God, no!"

That was settled. There was another point. In order that the bomb could make the correct number of skips before striking the lip of the dam, it must be released at just the right point. Otherwise it might bounce over the dam (which might prove fatal to the Lancaster which had dropped it) or might fall short of the dam and merely sink into the water and detonate without effect. It was just one more detail which needed attention. There was a sense of urgency about the entire project which Gibson found unsettling, but he returned to Scampton to continue the training. He promised to see Wallis in two weeks, on April 16, to observe the test drops of the first two full-scale prototypes of the Wallis bombs.

Early in April Wing Commander C. L. Dann from the Ministry of Aircraft Production casually dropped in on Gibson at Scampton. With breath-taking abruptness Dann broached the subject of getting the correct sighting of the Möhne and Eder dams. Considering the few people in on the project —Gibson was the only man in the squadron who knew of the targets—it came as a shock that a man could walk in off the street, so to speak, and begin talking about a most ticklish subject.

"How the hell do you know all this?" Gibson demanded. Dann explained that he was a bombsight expert and had been asked to help solve the problem in connection with the dams. A mathematician, Dann had studied the aerial photos of the Möhne and Eder dams and found that each dam had towers at either end two hundred yards apart. Using these as the base of a triangle, Dann very quickly devised a simple bombsight which could be made of a few pieces of wood. The bombardier simply lined up two nails with the towers through a peephole. When all came in line, it was—provided the speed of the plane was correct—the drop point. Within hours the device was tested and found to be remarkably accurate.

Dann's little gadget solved that problem, a skilled pilot could manage the problem of air speed, but neither man nor instrument could make certain that the plane was flying at the correct height. Flying over water was especially deceiving. Also, they would be down low in a darkened valley, surrounded by hills. It was a serious problem indeed.

III

While Wallis worried over the casing of his bomb, which did not stand up to the strain of the test drops, Gibson continued with the training of No. 617 Squadron. They had progressed beautifully in all areas but the sticky one of height—how to find 150 feet and how to stay there? One solution seemed to be trailing a weight from a wire. The weight would be placed at the 150-foot mark. When it struck the surface of the water they would be at the proper height. Upon testing it was found that the wire and weight trailed almost directly behind the plane. Judging by eye was completely useless. There seemed to be no solution to the problem.

One day another "back-room boy" appeared out of the depths of the Ministry of Aircraft Production.

He was Sir Ben Lockspeiser, KCB, FRS, and he had a suggestion—an old one really, which had been employed in the Great War. Altimeters then were even more primitive than those of 1943, so it might be possible to employ classic trigonometry instead. Place spotlights in either wingtip so angled that when they converged on the surface of the water the distance from the aircraft to the water would be exactly 150 feet. This made sense and was almost as simple as the little wooden bombsight that Dann had conceived.

Gibson dispatched a Lancaster to Farnborough (Royal Aircraft Establishment), where Aldis lamps were fitted into the nose and near the tail (this was Gibson's slight variation on the idea). This task Gibson had assigned to Squadron Leader Henry Maudslay, who commanded B Flight of the special unit. Upon his return the following day, Maudslay took the Lancaster up at dusk and demonstrated the device for Gibson. When the beams of light merged beneath the low-flying plane Maudslay found that he could maintain the correct height with a little help from the navigator. Within days all the Lancasters were fitted with fore and aft Aldis lamps and practiced using the "spotlight altimeter calibrator" under observation of ground instruments. It was found to work with amazing accuracy. As Gibson watched the demonstrations he could not help but wonder about how much flying around with Aldis lamps on would aid the German gunners.

Late in April Gibson had an urgent summons to meet with Wallis. The little man's face was lined and he was visibly tired when he told Gibson, "The whole thing is going to be a failure unless we jiggle around with our heights and speed."

What could this possibly mean?

Wallis explained that he had continued experimenting with the bombs, shattering most of them. Upon studying the films and graphing the results Wallis had come up with one more set of conditions: Could they approach the dams at 60 feet and at a speed of 232 miles an hour? "If you can't," Wallis added, "the whole thing will have to be called off."

Dire thoughts raced through Gibson's mind. If 150 feet was low, 60 feet was very low. At that height you would only have to hiccup and you would be in the drink.

He promised, however, to try that night. The deflection of the Aldis lamps was changed and although the big aircraft seemed to be moving along awfully close to the ground, accuracy was excellent. It could be done and on May 1 Gibson called Wallis to reassure him. When another test was run at the new height and speed the bomb worked. But the time drew nigh, for from April 17 through May 1 the water level in the Möhne had risen five feet, within ten feet of the lip. The high-level period would soon be upon them; all the modified aircraft would be required and the bombs were yet to be manufactured.

The first special Lancaster had been flown into Scampton on April 18, another nineteen following at intervals—the last arrived on May 13. Around the same time lorries delivered the Wallis bombs to Scampton; the bombs were factory-fresh and still warm. The odd devices, weighing 9250 pounds, carried a charge of RDX, a very high explosive, weighing 6600 pounds. The cylinder itself was five feet long and fifty inches in diameter. The bombs were not cranked into the aircraft as was normal, but the Lancasters were lifted at the tail by a crane and lowered onto the bombs. These were fitted into the special cutout in the fuselage with the axis of the bomb at right angles to the centerline of the Lancaster's fuselage. The effect, since the bomb bay doors had been removed, was as if a garden roller had been installed into the aircraft. When the bomb was about ready to be dropped a hydraulically operated motor attached to pulley by a belt drive was activated and the bomb would begin to spin (backward toward the tail). At the point of release the spin would reach five hundred revolutions per minute. It was this rotation which carried the bomb skipping over the surface of the water and then, with the remaining momentum, rolled it down the face of the dam to explode at the correct depth. At least, that was the plan.

Gibson delegated the job of checking the modified aircraft to his engineering officer, the "plumber," Flight Lieutenant C. C. "Capable" Caple, and the handling of the bombs to his armament officer, Flight Lieutenant "Doc" Watson. There were still the routes to plot—coming and going to the dams—which would best avoid flak concentrations and night fighter fields; there was the question of communications. This last problem was solved when it

was decided that in addition to the standard radios, all of the Lancasters were to be equipped with Very High Frequency Radio Telephones. This enabled the men to communicate with each other directly and would make it possible for Gibson to direct the operation in the target area. Such intercommunications had never been used before on bombers.

As the middle of May approached the pressures increased and Gibson himself showed the strain. He was irritable, impatient, and quickly lost his temper. A large carbuncle blossomed on his face; when he saw the base doctor (who knew nothing of the impending mission), Gibson was informed that he was "overworked. You will have to take two weeks off." Gibson burst out laughing and left. In two weeks it would all be over.

On May 15 Cochrane dropped by and told Gibson that, weather permitting, the squadron would take off the next night. After two and a half months, it seemed almost like good news.

During this period of training Gibson had divided the squadron into two flights, but for the raid itself there were to be three waves. The first, led by Gibson, consisted of nine Lancasters, which were to attack the Möhne Dam first; if successful, and if any bombs remained, they would continue on to the Eder Dam. These two dams were to be attacked from 60 feet and at 232 miles an hour, as had been calculated by Wallis. A second wave—which in fact would take off first—was made up of five bombers and would attack the Sorpe Dam (which was of a different construction from the other two) from the lowest possible height and at 180 miles an hour. The third wave, five Lancasters, was to be a mobile reserve and under control of No. 5 Group headquarters (Cochrane) and not Gibson. Since all reports of the success or failure would come into Group HQ, the mobile reserve aircraft could be sent by Cochrane to any unbreached dam or to other dams in the area. It was hoped that, in addition to the Möhne, Eder, and Sorpe dams, Gibson's crews might also deal with such smaller dams as the Lister, Schwelm, and Ennepe.

Of the original twenty-one crews, nineteen therefore would carry out the raid. One of the special Lancasters had been damaged five days before the raid during a training mission (spray had shot up against the low-flying aircraft and damaged the underside badly enough to put the plane out of action).

The other eliminated plane was forced to stand down because of an illness among the crew. In all, the nineteen Lancasters carried 133 men.

IV

The first Lancaster to take off from Scampton was piloted by Flight Lieutenant R. N. G. Barlow of the second wave (which took off first because of the greater distance to its target); it was nine twenty-eight in the evening of May 16, 1943. Within two minutes the second plane took off, Sergeant V. A. Byers, pilot; then, one minute after him, Pilot Officer G. Rice in the third aircraft; within eight minutes Flight Lieutenant K. L. Munro lifted his heavy Lancaster off the runway and vanished into the east. (At this moment—9:39 P.M.—Gibson's first wave (Möhne) began taking off.) The fifth and last plane of the second-wave force (Sorpe), piloted by a blond giant from Brooklyn, Flight Lieutenant Joseph C. McCarthy, did not get away on schedule. In fact, there was a delay, infuriating to McCarthy, of more than a half hour.

"Our favourite Yank, F. L. McCarthy, caused quite a disturbance," the squadron diary [written by squadron adjutant Flight Lieutenant H. R. Humphries] noted. "He arrived at his aircraft and after finding she had hydraulic trouble came dashing back to our only reserve aircraft. When inside he noticed he had no compass card and came rushing back to Flights frantically screaming for one. He had also pulled his parachute by mistake and the white silk was streaming all over the ground, trailing behind him. With perspiration dropping off his face, good old Mac ran back to his aircraft with everyone behind him trying to fix him up with what he wanted."

Of the five aircraft of the second wave only McCarthy's actually dropped its bomb on the target. The first two planes, Barlow and Byers, were lost. The latter was hit by flak at Texel as he crossed over the Dutch coast, and Barlow fell (whether by accident or by flak is unknown) into the Zuider Zee. Rice too had trouble at the Zuider Zee, for the Lancaster was down too low and the plane struck the water; two engines fluttered out and the Wallis bomb ripped off the plane. Rice could do nothing else but return to Scampton on the remaining two engines. The fourth plane, Munro, was hit by flak also, just as it crossed into Holland at Vlieland,

knocking out the intercommunications systems. It was pointless to continue on the mission, so Munro also returned to Scampton.

By the time McCarthy finally took off, so "browned off" (as the current expression went) that he was ready to leave without a parachute, all of Gibson's first wave had already left. McCarthy continued on alone, unaware of the fate of Byers and Barlow and that Munro and Rice had been forced to return to base. His navigator, Flight Sergeant D. A. McLean, plotted a dog-leg course, across the North Sea almost due east to Vlieland, then south across the Zuider Zee, an eastward turn where the course intercepted the Rhine. Slightly north of the Möhne, McLean set them on a southerly leg; the Sorpe lay just a few miles southwest of the Möhne.

McCarthy eased the Lancaster into the misty valley, hoping to get as low as possible. He had to be especially wary of the hills at each end of their run; it would mean dive in, slow up to the prescribed 180 miles an hour, drop bomb, and pull out before piling up against the farther hill. Warily, McCarthy circled the target—which looked just like the model they had studied during the final briefings. There was no flak at least. Coming down low through the mist, however, almost put them in the water. They were low enough. The bombardier, Sergeant G. L. Johnson, zeroed in on the aiming points as McCarthy held the Lancaster in a steady run.

"Bomb gone," he called out; almost at the same instant, McCarthy pulled back on the throttles and the control column to get away from the target and to avoid the looming black hills. He was leveling out over the hills when the bomb shattered against the dam wall. Circling back, the crew saw that the bomb had hit the parapet and had caused damage. But the dam had not burst. They wired the message back to No. 5 Group—where Wallis, Harris, and Cochrane awaited all scraps of information about the raid. McCarthy then turned "T for Tommy" for home.

Gibson took off at nine thirty-nine (the same time as the hapless Munro) in company with the aircraft of pilots Flight Lieutenants John V. Hopgood and H. B. Martin. Just as they were about to leave Gibson had said to Hopgood, "Hoppy, tonight's the night; tomorrow we will get drunk." It had been a long-standing tradition to say this just before a mis-

Crew of G George, special Lancaster ED 932/G (the G suffix denoting that the aircraft carried special equipment and must be constantly under guard): Flight Lieutenant R. D. Trevor-Roper, the squadron gunnery leader and mid-upper gunner of G George; Sergeant J. Pulford, flight engineer; Flight Sergeant G. A. Deering, rear gunner; Pilot Officer F. M. Spafford, bombardier —"bomb aimer" in RAF terminology; Flight Lieutenant R. G. Hutchinson, the squadron's signals leader and radio operator of George; Wing Commander Guy Gibson; and Pilot Officer H. T. Taerum, navigator.

sion, dating to their days together in No. 106 Squadron. Earlier Squadron Leader Melvyn Young (known as "Dinghy" because he had been twice saved from the sea) had also contributed another standing "joke." As they enjoyed the traditional luxury before takeoff (repeated after a mission) of bacon and eggs, Young asked Gibson, "Can I have your egg if you don't come back?"

"Sugar off," Gibson replied banteringly and then "told him to do something very difficult to himself."

Young led the second three-plane element (the other pilots: William Astell and David Maltby) and Squadron Leader Henry E. Maudslay led the third, consisting of his plane and those flown by David Shannon and L. G. Knight. The latter's plane was air-borne by ten o'clock.

The first-wave aircraft took a different course from that of the second wave; it was a more southerly route crossing over the Dutch coast south of Rotterdam, almost skirting the northern boundary of Belgium. They had crossed over the North Sea without incident, except for a brief meeting and an exchange of messages with a small British convoy. As they approached the coast, all gunners took their positions and Gibson, still holding the Lancaster to an altitude of less than a hundred feet, zigzagged around the known flak positions. He was assisted in this delicate operation with directions from the navigator, Canadian H. T. "Terry" Taerum. Gibson's plane, *G George,* followed by the eight others in the first wave, thus threaded its way across Holland and Germany. The route twisted and turned at irregular intervals to confuse the German defenses, which were having a difficult time of it also because the bombers flew too low to be picked up by radar.

The frequent shifts in route were complex and required concentration. Over Holland an airfield not on their maps suddenly sprang out of the night. It was heavily defended, although no fighters rose to challenge them. Near it was a check point for another turn in the route. Gibson radioed the two formations following closely behind him to look out for the nest of guns near Gilze-Rijen. The others made their turns, but Flight Lieutenant William B. Astell's Lancaster, in the second element, came within flak range of the airfield. The Lancaster lifted away for a moment, then flew into the ground, burned for a few seconds, and shattered when the Wallis bomb detonated.

After crossing the Rhine the eight remaining planes of Gibson's force passed into the Ruhr—Happy Valley. Flak barges along the river opened up with gunfire and followed the aircraft with searchlights, but lost the British planes among the trees. Gunners in the planes exchanged fire with the German gunners, disrupting their aim and at times even putting out the blinding lights. But all eight Lancasters flew past Dortmund, Hamm, Soest—all known flak centers. Just beyond Soest were the Ruhr hills over which lay Möhne Lake, at the end of which squatted their first target. Gibson studied it and found that the dam "looked grey and solid in the moonlight as though it were part of the countryside itself and just as immovable. A structure like a battle-ship was showering out flak all along its length, but some came from the powerhouse below it and nearby. There were no searchlights."

The effect of the flak over the water was curious, for the varicolored reflections on the smooth black surface doubled the actual number of shells spurting out at them. Gibson estimated the number of guns as twelve firing from five different positions on and around the dam. The shells were either 20 or 37 millimeter—"nasty little things."

Pulling away from "those bloody-minded flak gunners" Gibson circled the area, orienting himself and planning the next move. Over the intercom he heard the crew chattering.

"Bit aggressive, aren't they?"

"Too right they are."

"God, this flak gives me the creeps," Gibson interjected.

"Me too."

Gibson called in the other planes and found all answered but Astell. *Had Bill got the hammer?* "Well, boys," Gibson said with no enthusiasm whatsoever, "we had better start the ball rolling. Hello, all Cooler aircraft. I am going to attack. Stand by to come in to attack in your order when I tell you."

As the others dispersed out of range of the flak, Gibson circled to get into position for a run on the dam. He called John Hopgood: "Hello, *M Mother.* Stand by to take over if anything happens."

"OK, Leader. Good luck."

Gibson, now two miles from the dam, put the plane into a flat dive. The features of the Möhne stood out clearly in the light of the moon. In sharp relief stood the two towers on which the bombardier would set his little wooden sight. He was an Australian, Pilot Officer F. M. "Spam" Spafford, who reacted to the setting with professional interest. "Good show," he said. "This is wizard!"

But as they came down toward the surface of the lake, Spafford, in the "bomb-aimer" position in the nose, said excitedly, "You're going to hit them. You're going to hit those trees!"

"That's all right, Spam," Gibson told him, "I'm just getting my height."

Then to navigator Taerum, "Check height, Terry."

Flight Engineer Sergeant J. Pulford managed the throttles and flaps to maintain the precise air speed. Spafford lined up the sight with the two towers at either end of the dam and flicked on the fusing switches. The Wallis bomb began to revolve. Taerum gave directions for height, the searchlights in the fuselage having been turned on. When the two beams met he called out "Steady," and they were

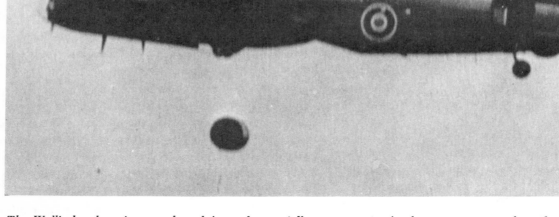

The Wallis bomb as it was released from the specially converted Lancaster. The cradle that held the bomb actuated the bomb's backward revolution, which caused the bomb to skip over the surface of the water. The cut-out fuselage to accommodate the bomb and the gear may also be seen. The Lancasters thus equipped were called the "Steamrollers of Scampton."

(IMPERIAL WAR MUSEUM, LONDON)

at sixty feet. The gunners at the dam opened up on the illuminated target. The flak came twisting through the darkness as Gibson raced for the dam. The two gunners in the plane returned the fire as Gibson, almost certain they were flying into oblivion, bore down upon the target taking directions from both Taerum (height) and Spafford (distance and line).

The air reeked with cordite and the plane shuddered under the vibration of the guns firing. The sky was crisscrossed with spent tracers. A Very light popped out of the Lancaster in the hope of blinding the flak gunners. Suddenly Spafford's voice came over the intercom: "Mine gone."

Someone said, "Good show, Leader. Nice work." Gibson gunned the Lancaster up and away from the flak and from the explosion. There was a thunderous booming behind them and when Gibson turned the Lancaster, a thousand-foot water column hung in the air. Spafford had placed the bomb exactly right, but except for churning water, there seemed to be no real damage. Gibson studied the effect and waited until the surface calmed down before ordering the next attack. The spotlights would not work unless the surface was smooth. The eight planes circled as far from the guns as they could,

waiting. Gibson spoke to Hopgood. "Hello, *M Mother*. You may attack now. Good luck."

Hopgood brought his plane in from the same direction as had Gibson. The gunners were now alert to the direction of the attack and concentrated heavily on the approaching plane. Hopgood speared into the flak. About a hundred yards from the dam a flash of fire shot behind an inboard engine. The bomb did not drop until too late (possibly because the bombardier had been hit), so it fell onto the powerhouse, overshooting the dam. Hopgood's Lancaster staggered on as if the pilot were attempting to gain altitude. At around five hundred feet *M Mother* flared and crashed into the ground.

"Poor old Hoppy," a voice said over the intercom. Although the plane burned furiously, two men actually escaped, the bombardier, Flight Sergeant J. W. Fraser, and the rear gunner, Pilot Officer A. F. Burcher. The other five men, including Gibson's old friend Hopgood, died in the crash.

Still the Möhne Dam stood intact. Gibson ordered the third attack, by Squadron Leader H. B. "Mickey" Martin in *P Popsie*. The run was repeated, again with heavy flak fire. Gibson had drawn off some of the flak by bringing *G George* into range and shooting at the German gun positions. Martin's bomb fell a few yards short and had little effect upon the dam. The Lancaster itself was rather badly shot up; a fuel tank in the right wing—luckily empty—was punctured and the aileron shredded. But Martin brought the Lancaster away without further damage.

He added his plane to Gibson's as a decoy when the fourth plane, Squadron Leader Melvyn Young's *A Apple*, attacked. The bomb seemed to fall exactly right but the dam continued to stand. The next plane was piloted by Flight Lieutenant D. J. H. Maltby; this was number five. Again the area lit up with flak and machine-gun fire as the great bomber, seemingly held to the surface of the lake by two streams of light, bore down on the dam. The bombardier, Pilot Officer J. Fort, placed the bomb with uncanny accuracy. The squat barrel-like object bounced along the surface of the water, struck the wall, and then rolled down. A great geyser of water shot up and again the water roiled and churned.

Waiting for the disturbance to subside, Gibson swung around to get another view. He alerted the next pilot, Flight Lieutenant David Shannon, to prepare for his run. As Gibson came down he saw unusual eddies in the water and it appeared that the dam had moved. He heard someone shouting, "I think she has gone!" when the dam gave way. It was a massive rent of a hundred yards through which a mountain of water spilled into the valley below. Gibson's radio operator wired the news to Group headquarters at Grantham that the Möhne Dam had been successfully breached. The time was just four minutes before one o'clock in the morning of May 17, 1943.

Wallis had listened to the report of each released bomb with increasing misgiving. He had hoped one good strike would do the job, but on and on the raid went: *G George, M Mother, P Popsie, A Apple,* and then *J Johnny*—Maltby's plane—and the signal that the Möhne had burst. Wallis stood still for but a moment before throwing his arms over his head and literally danced around the room. Harris and Cochrane stopped him long enough to shake his hand in congratulations. At the same time the men in the seven Lancasters orbiting the Möhne burst into cheers, "to shout and scream and act like madmen. . . ."

From where he circled the frightful scene, Gibson saw not only the wall of water ramming through the valley, destroying everything in its path and overtaking fleeing automobiles, but also the still burning wreckage of Hopgood's plane just beyond the dam. *Hoppy has been avenged,* Gibson thought and then, after ordering Mickey Martin and Dave Maltby to return to base, led the way south- and eastward to the Eder. Only three aircraft still carried bombs—Henry Maudslay's, David Shannon's and L. G. Knight's. Melvyn Young as deputy leader made up the fifth plane, though his bomb had been expended on the Möhne.

The five aircraft encountered much fog as they flew through the valley leading to the Eder Dam. Although there were no antiaircraft defenses at the Eder, the hills surrounding it, plus the fog, made it an exceptionally difficult target to find. Gibson had arrived first and succeeded in locating the fog-enshrouded target, but until he had fired a Very light over the dam, the others had not been able to pick it out.

Shannon began moving in for the attack, which would be the same as those upon the Möhne. But there were complications. The Eder was more inaccessible than the Möhne. A castle stood in the bomb run. The plane would have to dive in over the castle, from about a thousand feet to the required sixty, zero in on the target, drop the bomb, and pull up before crashing against the cliffs of a mountain just about a mile beyond the dam. Shannon made at least five attempts but always something happened and he zoomed away without dropping the bomb. Finally, giving up for the moment, Shannon decided to circle the area to become better acquainted with it.

While Shannon studied the terrain, Gibson sent in *Z Zebra*, Henry Maudslay's Lancaster. Maudslay too found it a difficult run and made two attempts without dropping the bomb. On the third all eyes watched as the big Lancaster slipped down over the castle, leveled out on the lake. The spotlights converged under the plane on the water and soon a red Very light arced out above *Z Zebra*. The bomb had been dropped. But something had gone wrong; the bomb had been released too late. It fell, struck the parapet, and caught Maudslay's plane in the blast. The whole valley erupted in a glaring flash. Gibson was stunned. *Henry had disappeared.* There was no burning wreck on the ground. Desperately Gibson called, "Henry—*Z Zebra*—are you OK?"

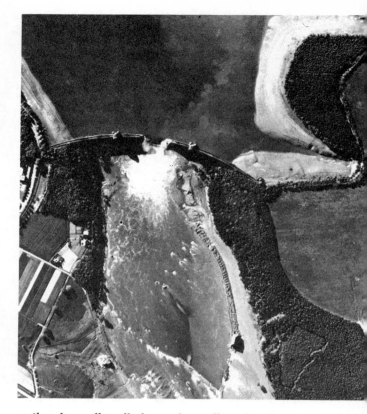

The Möhne Dam before and after: an aerial reconnaissance photograph taken before the mission (left)
shows the dam wall and, faintly, the protective torpedo
nets. The bombs had to be dropped at the correct
speed and altitude to be able to bounce over the net,

strike the wall, roll down the wall under the water,
and burst against the face of the wall. The effects of
the blast may be seen in a photograph taken the day
after the raid—the Möhne breached; lower water
level exposes sand of the banks.

(IMPERIAL WAR MUSEUM, LONDON)

Although no plane was in sight, all were certain
they heard Maudslay's voice faintly: "I think so,
stand by." And then there was nothing.

Shannon returned again and, after a test run,
came in for the second time (on his second round
of attempts). The plane dropped the bomb perfectly
as Flight Sergeant L. J. Sumpter, the bombardier,
brought the towers into line and pressed the release.
The bomb detonated against the face of the dam,
but it continued to stand.

There was only one more left; unless it worked
Gibson would have to ask for aid from the mobile
reserve planes. Lester Knight, an Australian, brought
his Lancaster in for a practice run. It went wrong
and he pulled away and circled, with Gibson giving
him advice over the radio telephone, and came in
for another try. Carefully Knight brought the Lancaster in, down to sixty feet and straight for the
dam; bombardier Flying Officer E. C. Johnson
guided Knight toward the drop point and the bomb

fell when all imaginary lines of the mathematical
problem converged. The bomb struck the wall, rolled
down, and then from out of the depths a terrific
boom erupted, shooting water a thousand feet into
the air. As if shaken by a great earthquake the
Eder Dam cracked, spouting tons of water into the
sleeping valley below. To Gibson the rushing waters
seemed more destructive than those of the Möhne,
ripping through the countryside, uprooting everything in their path, and even as he watched he
"saw them extinguish all the lights in the neighborhood as though a great black shadow had been
drawn across the earth."

With no bombs remaining, Gibson ordered the
four surviving Lancasters to return to base. The
Eder had been breached at one fifty-four in the
morning. Dawn was on the way and they would do
well to get away before the fighters came out in
droves. They had been air-borne for more than
four hours, fuel would be low, and with the coming

light, the fighters would be thick. On the homeward flight they again passed over the Möhne. The geography of the valley had been completely changed. They continued flying down low to confute fighter passes.

The Lancasters droned over Germany and Holland and strove for home. But over Holland, just as he passed over the coast, Young's plane was hit by flak. He could not nurse it all the way to Scampton, and for the third—and last—time Dinghy Young ditched. No one survived the crash into the sea. So it was, then, that of the nine planes which Gibson had led into Germany that night, he returned leading only Shannon and Knight—to join those of Martin and Maltby, which had come back earlier.

When Gibson had radioed that he had no additional bombs, the five aircraft of the mobile reserve, the third wave, were directed to their targets by Group headquarters. These Lancasters had taken off shortly after midnight and by the time Gibson had turned for home the bombers were being dispatched to their targets. The first plane off was *C Charlie,* guided by Pilot Officer W. H. T. Ottley, who was ordered to attack the Lister Dam; the radio operator, Sergeant J. Guterman, acknowledged the message. That was the last heard from Ottley's crew. It may have been his plane that Gibson, then on his flight home, saw flying at five hundred feet in the vicinity of Hamm. "He got the chop," Gibson noted, wondering who it had been. He and his crew believed that it might have been a German night fighter which had been tracking them, hit by its own antiaircraft fire. But it was probably Ottley's *C Charlie,* for the wreckage of his plane was found near Hamm the next day.

Three planes were dispatched to the Sorpe Dam to add to the destruction which McCarthy, of the ill-fated second wave, had accomplished. These were *S Sugar* (Pilot Officer L. J. Burpee), *F Freddie* (Flight Sergeant K. W. Brown), and *Y Yorker* (Flight Sergeant L. T. Anderson).

S Sugar never got beyond Bergen op Zoom, Holland, where it fell to flak or a fighter. *F Freddie* had trouble finding the Sorpe because of the thickening mist, but Brown dropped down low and released some incendiaries which illuminated the area. Bombardier Sergeant S. Oncia was then able to place the bomb precisely on the target, although

this second strike did not add to the damage—the Sorpe remained standing. When *Y Yorker,* which had taken off one minute behind *F Freddie,* came upon the target area pilot Anderson found the valley completely filled with mist. Neither Sergeant L. Nugent, the navigator, nor Sergeant S. Green, the bombardier, could find any landmark upon which to base a bomb run. *Y Yorker,* crewed with disappointed men, was forced to make the return trip to Scampton still carrying the Wallis bomb.

O Orange (Flight Sergeant W. C. Townsend) was sent to the Schwelm Dam, which was found despite the early morning mist. Townsend made three runs on the target before bombardier Sergeant C. E. Franklin released the bomb. It was a perfect drop, but the single bomb had little effect upon the dam. The time was then 3:37 A.M., and when *O Orange* crossed the Dutch coast for the final leg of the flight daylight was breaking over the North Sea. When Townsend set his plane down at Scampton his was the last of the Lancasters which would return from the dams mission. Eight would never return; of the fifty-six men aboard these aircraft only two survived. Nearly half of the superb crew which had made up No. 617 Squadron was lost. It was, in the phrase of historians Charles Webster and Noble Frankland, "a costly success."

v

The "Dam Busters," as the squadron was popularly called, had furnished bomber chief Arthur Harris with a demonstration of the fallacy of attacking panacea targets, but on the other hand proved him wrong when he insisted that the Wallis bomb (or any bomb then available) could actually breach a well-built dam. Wallis had been proved correct in his theoretical conceptions of bomb design and the effects of certain bombs upon dams —but his strategic thinking had been optimistic. The major catastrophe he had expected—which was also expected by those more militarily oriented than he—did not result. The havoc was serious enough and for many it was total tragedy, but despite the inundation, the rupture of the Möhne and Eder dams had no long-range or even long-lasting effects upon the German war effort.

Goebbels admitted that the "attacks of the British bombers on the dams in our valleys were very successful. The Führer is exceedingly impatient and angry about the lack of preparedness on the part of the Luftwaffe." It was true—a single blow by so few aircraft had had a decided impact. Nearly a thousand people drowned (many caught in air raid shelters) and more than two hundred were listed as missing. About half of the casualties, however, were slave laborers from the east—they were easily replaced from Germany's store of prisoners from Poland and Russia. Livestock too perished in the flood and thousands of acres of agricultural land were despoiled. Seventy per cent of the harvest in the Ruhr and Möhne valleys was ruined, as was all of the root crops, such as potatoes.

Industrial stoppages resulted with the washing out of railroads, the blacking out of electrical power, and, most of all—as a result of the Möhne breach —because of the shortage of water. A critical lack of water for drinking purposes afflicted about four and a half million people in the area; also industries requiring water, such as the coking plants in Dortmund, were forced to operate at a loss in production for two months.

The effects were extensive but not decisive. Within weeks, or at most within two or three months, the Germans had cleared away much of the dam-

Post-mission debriefing: Bomber Command Chief Harris and Air Officer Commanding, No. 5 Group, Air Vice-Marshal Sir Ralph Cochrane (standing) get a first-hand report of the dams raid while members of G George talk with a Bomber Command intelligence officer (left seated); bombardier Spafford speaks as navigator Taerum and gunnery officer Trevor-Roper listen. These three men of Gibson's crew, like their leader, were later killed in other missions.

(IMPERIAL WAR MUSEUM, LONDON)

age and the Ruhr remained the major industrial center of the Third Reich for the rest of the war. Had all dams been breached that night of the Dam Busters' raid (a physical impossibility, of course, in terms of men and bombs), the tale would have been different and much sadder for Germany. If the Sorpe (which was in fact immune to the Wallis bomb because of the dam's structure) had gone, the effects would have been more serious. Following the night of May 16/17, 1943, all important German dams were allotted heavier defenses. Further attempts upon them would have meant simple suicide—and none were made.

As he had promised the now dead Hopgood,

Gibson and the survivors got drunk. Gibson, however, left early to begin writing to the next of kin of the fifty-six men who had not returned. Wallis, though elated by the success of his bomb, was depressed at the thought of the loss of the young men. He stood around with the survivors that early morning, an untouched drink in his hand and tears in his eyes, saying, "If I had known, I wouldn't have started this."

In wartime, however, the exchange of fifty-four young lives for victorious headlines, for a setback for the enemy, seemed worth it. No one would question the attack, its costs, or the result: not when the very spirit of the moment seemed permeated

The Queen and King visit No. 617 Squadron after the mission to award decorations. In the background the Queen speaks with an airman. In the foreground the King exchanges views with "Our favourite Yank,"

Flight Lieutenant Joseph C. McCarthy of Brooklyn. Gibson is to the King's left, back to camera.

(IMPERIAL WAR MUSEUM, LONDON)

with destruction, sacrifice, death, and "good show." It was as normal as being alive.

Eve Gibson, who had assumed that her husband had been, as she had been informed, having an easy time of it at a training school, learned from the newspapers that he was an international hero. Gibson joined her for a rest after he had completed writing his letters. When he joined Eve, Gibson was a very old young man.

No less than thirty-three decorations were awarded for the dams raid. This was unusual, for the British are parsimonious with their decorations. Gibson was given the Victoria Cross. Among those who received the Distinguished Service Order was the Brooklynite Joseph McCarthy. The squadron was the most celebrated in Britain by then. Harris, despite his distaste for special units, decided to keep No. 617 Squadron together as a unit, and to employ it upon highly specialized targets demanding high precision. Although it was all but impossible to replace the lost crews immediately, No. 617 Squadron did operate as a precision night unit during the rest of the war. In fact, among other amazing feats—such as blasting a railroad tunnel in northern France with another Wallis bomb, the "Tallboy"—it was No. 617 Squadron which eventually finished the *Tirpitz,* which had so haunted Gibson.

But by this time the brilliant young commander was dead. After the raid he was sent to the United States, accompanying Churchill, on a kind of goodwill tour. When he returned in the spring of 1944 Gibson, who it was thought had already done his bit, was offered work as an executive with commercial firms—which he readily turned down. He was even asked to run for Parliament, an idea with which he toyed for a while, but he withdrew from that also. He grew restless, for he had been a year "off Ops." and he was unhappy. Finally he went directly to Harris and bullied his way back into active duty with No. 627 Squadron.

Gibson was base operations officer of the squadron, which like No. 617 was in No. 5 Group. The squadron began operations as a Pathfinder force (with No. 8 Group), marking targets with the Mosquito. Attached to No. 5 Group, the squadron took part in various special operations—bombing, target marking, dropping of "window"—the metallic ribbon which disrupted German radar—and minelaying.

On the night of September 19/20, 1944, Guy Gibson voluntarily assigned himself the task of master bomber on a raid to the Ruhr. He would fly around the target, a factory at Rheydt, directing the operations of the attacking Lancasters. When the attack was over, Gibson radioed the bombers. "OK, chaps. Now beat it for home." It was the last time his voice was heard, for over Holland something occurred and the Mosquito smashed into a hill. The men were buried by the Germans in a common unmarked grave near Bergen op Zoom. It was there that Burpee in *S Sugar* had "got the hammer" too a year before when Gibson and his X-Squadron had made history.

7

TIDAL WAVE

At Casablanca, French Morocco, Winston Churchill and Franklin Roosevelt met in January 1943 to outline the future Grand Strategy of the war. In this beautiful setting facing on the sea, following the successful launching of Operation Torch, the invasion of north Africa under Lieutenant General Dwight D. Eisenhower, the Allied leaders and their Combined Chiefs of Staff came to several key decisions. Uppermost in their minds, though they did not always agree upon details, were aid to Soviet Russia, sustained pressures on the Mediterranean flank, a future cross-Channel invasion of Europe, and the question of the Pacific war.

Among the objectives to be gained before the larger strategies could be achieved, at least in Europe, was control of the German submarines so effectively menacing Allied shipping. Another was the Luftwaffe, which stood in the way of strategic bombardment and any hopes for an invasion of Europe in 1944. Both these obstacles could be dealt with by air power. When he came to the Casblanca conference it had been Churchill's intention to persuade Roosevelt to get the American Air Force to give up its devotion to strategic bombardment by day and join the Bomber Command nighttime area assault. After five months of bombing, the U. S. Eighth Air Force had not yet dropped a single bomb on Germany proper. The first mission of the Eighth Air Force's Bomber Command was a modest—only

a dozen B-17s participated—strike upon the marshaling yards at Rouen-Sotteville, France, on August 17, 1942. All twelve bombers returned safely and it was at least a sign that bombers in formation could bomb pin-point targets in daylight and make it back to their bases. Such high-altitude attacks, it was believed, would make it difficult for flak-gun accuracy, and the combined gun strength of the formation itself would make fighter opposition costly.

The British had found in their experience that daylight operations were deadly; and the Germans had learned this also. But the Americans persisted in clinging to the concept of precision daylight bombardment. This was not mere bullheadedness, although it was believed that a heavy bomber with its massive firepower (the Flying Fortress was armed with a dozen .50-caliber machine guns and the Consolidated B-24 Liberator with ten) and protective armor could withstand attack by fighters. The best argument in favor of American daylight precision bombardment was simply that the aircraft were designed for it and the Americans were trained for it. A change in operational technique would entail a prolonged retraining of crews, modifications in the aircraft, and a consequent delay. Even under "normal" wartime conditions, it had taken long enough to mount the Rouen-Sotteville attack, small as that was. Assembling men and equipment was a complex matter, considering the demand for both.

Casablanca: Franklin D. Roosevelt and Winston Churchill meet to plan the future strategy of the war with their chief military advisers. Standing behind them are (from left) Lieutenant General Henry H. Arnold, Ad- *miral Ernest J. King, General George C. Marshall, Admiral Sir Dudley Pound, General Sir Alan Brooke, and Air Chief Marshal Sir Charles Portal.*

(U. S. AIR FORCE)

Until the United States could contribute its full share to the offensive the operations of the Eighth Air Force from the United Kingdom were, of necessity, circumscribed. Up until the Casablanca conference, the heavy-bomber missions were, in a sense, experimental pinpricks, experimental because there was a good deal to learn under combat conditions and pinpricks because Major General Ira C. Eaker, who commanded Eighth AF Bomber Command, did not have sufficient numbers of planes and crews to do anything else. An effective attack force which could strike deep inside Germany and still be able to fight its way in, bomb, and return must contain about three hundred heavy bombers. The largest force Eaker had been able to muster in the half year from August 1942 to the January 1943 Casablanca meetings was but a third of that number.

In that half year one of the major lessons learned was that if German fighter pilots proved aggressive enough, there really was no such thing as a true "Flying Fortress." Although Eighth Air Force losses

had not been excessive in the half year of operations, there had been losses and interferences with bombing runs. These were not spectacular, but planes and crews were lost and targets could not be eliminated because they had not been accurately bombed. What was needed, then, was an Allied fighter plane which could escort the bombers to and from target areas to engage the German fighters. At the time of Casablanca no such fighter with the range say to go to Berlin and back was in action. The P-40 could not do it, nor could the Hurricane or Spitfire. Thus the British preferred their major bombing raids to take place at night and the Americans went out during the day. The advent of the Thunderbolt (Republic P-47) and the Mustang (North American P-51) was yet almost a whole year away. In the interim the skies over Europe would be lacerated in the most monstrous air battles in history.

At Casablanca Eaker convinced Churchill of the efficacy of the American plan and the Prime Minis-

The Boeing B-17 "Flying Fortress," on which the U. S. Army Air Force based its "precision daylight bombardment" concept—and which British Bomber Command rejected as inviting the disastrous possibility of high casualties and aircraft losses. Because of the bristling heavy armament of the B-17 it was believed it could stand off German fighter attacks. This did not prove to be true in combat; Luftwaffe pilots developed a hazardous technique of head-on attack that was most effective. The B-17F (left), the first Lockheed-built B-17, though an improvement on the earlier models still lacked firepower in the nose. This was later resolved with the addition of twin guns in the "G" model. The other photo, a view from the port waist-gun position, shows one of the nine .50-caliber machine guns (plus one .30) carried by the Flying Fortress. (ERIK MILLER; LOCKHEED/U. S. AIR FORCE)

The Consolidated B-24 "Liberator," which came after the B-17 and which would join it in bombing Germany. The B-24 was not as easily flown as the B-17, nor could it achieve the altitude of the Boeing. It did, however, have a greater range and could carry a heavier bomb load. The prototype (left), the XB-24 was initially flown in 1939 (the first B-17 flew in 1935) and had no gun turrets. Top view of a B-24D clearly shows the high-aspect ratio wing designed around the low-drag Davis airfoil as well as the nose-gun position (before the nose turret was installed in the B-24G), top and tail turrets.

(CONVAIR/GENERAL DYNAMICS; U. S. AIR FORCE)

Standing in the way of the American daylight attacks upon German industry were the German fighters such as this Messerschmitt Bf-109G; engine-mounted 20-mm. cannon could rip a wing off an enemy bomber. Though formidable, the cannon had a tendency to jam; as did the wing-mounted cannon of the Bf-109F.
(ALIEN PROPERTY CUSTODIAN, NATIONAL ARCHIVES)

In effect, therefore, the Directive left the interpretation of how this was to be accomplished up to General Eaker and Air Chief Marshal Harris. Although the Directive implied precision attack, it did not deny the area attack. Harris, with his experience, had little respect for plans on paper and continued to go his way. "The subject of morale had been dropped," Harris noted, "and I was now required to proceed with the general 'disorganisation' of German industry, giving priority to certain aspects of it such as U-boat building, aircraft production, oil production, transportation and so forth, which gave me a very wide range of choice and allowed me to attack pretty well any German industrial city of 100,000 inhabitants and above. But the Ruhr remained a principal objective because it was the most important industrial area in the whole of Germany, which was why it had been originally chosen for morale-breaking attacks; the new instructions therefore made no difference."

Eaker by April 1943 had formulated what the British refer to as the Eaker Plan, but which was more officially known as "The Combined Bomber

ter, though reluctantly, dismissed his own plan of suggesting to Roosevelt that the American daylight approach be abandoned. Out of this came what was called the Casablanca Directive, outlining in effect the joint future operations of British and American Bomber Commands. Operating as before, British by night and Americans by day—thus giving Churchill his cue for the phrase "bombing around the clock"—the bombing offensive was to be based upon a system of target priorities. These were agreed upon by the Combined Chiefs of Staff, advised by industrial analysts such as Britain's Ministry of Economic Warfare. The targets, in order of priority, were the German submarine construction yards, the aircraft industry, transportation, oil installations, and other targets in enemy war industry.

The most potent adversary of the American daylight bomber streams, the Focke-Wulf 190 (in this instance the FW-190A of JG 26). Nicknamed the Würger ("Butcher-bird"), the 190 was heavily armed—two machine guns on upper cowling, two cannons in the wing roots, and two more machine guns farther out on the wings. The major weakness of the FW-190 was that its performance fell off above twenty thousand feet (the B-17s operated above this altitude). It was still a tough fighter when dealing with enemy escort planes as well as bombers. Although superior to the Me-109, the Focke-Wulf was not built in the quantities the Messerschmitt was.

(IMPERIAL WAR MUSEUM, LONDON)

Offensive. from the United Kingdom" (April 12, 1943). A month later a modified version of the plan, code word "Pointblank," was approved by the Combined Chiefs of Staff. This defined the mission of the U. S.-British Air offensive, which, in general terms, was aimed at weakening German resistance so "as to permit initiation of final combined operations on the Continent." It called for an expansion of the American bombing forces in Europe, pointing out that "at least 800 airplanes must be in the theater to dispatch 300 bombers on operations." Until such a force existed, there would be little point in attempting precision attacks upon the German aircraft industry, which remained second on the priorities list.

Lest there be misunderstandings and consequent resistance from certain strong-minded air marshals, it was emphasized that "This plan does not attempt to prescribe the major effort of the R.A.F. Bomber Command. It simply recognizes the fact that when precision targets are bombed by the Eighth Air Force in daylight, the effort should be complemented and completed by R.A.F. bombing attacks against the surrounding industrial area at night."

Under the section entitled "Intermediate Objective" another important point was made: "The Germans, recognizing the vulnerability of their vital industries, are rapidly increasing the strength of their fighter defenses. The German fighter strength in western Europe is being augmented. *If the growth of the German fighter strength is not arrested quickly, it may become literally impossible to carry out the destruction planned and thus to create the conditions necessary for ultimate decisive action by our combined forces on the continent.*" In other words, the invasion of Europe would be stalled unless the Luftwaffe could be "neutralized."

Eaker, however, almost immediately had to give up some of his planes to the Mediterranean when the Northwest African Air Force was formed to assist Eisenhower's ground troops in the invasion of north Africa; more would go when "Husky," the invasion of Sicily which had been decided upon during the Casablanca meetings, went into effect. It would be extremely difficult for the Eighth Air Force to mount the Pointblank operations if its forces continued to be drained off to other theaters. At the moment when Eaker hoped for "at least 800 airplanes" in order to mount raids of three-hundred-bomber

strength, he was aware of the fact that in the three months since Casablanca the average American bomber attack force consisted of a mere eighty-six planes.

II

Sometime between the end of June and the Fourth of July, Eaker lost his two veteran B-24 groups, the 44th and the 93rd. These were soon joined by the newly formed, inexperienced 389 Bombardment Group—also equipped with Liberators. They combined with two units already in the Mediterranean's Ninth Air Force: the 98th and 376th Bombardment Groups (B-24s). All units began operations against various Husky targets, including, on July 19, Rome. On the following day all were ordered off operations to begin intensive training near Benghazi in Libya.

The curious feature of this training, besides the heavy security precautions, was the fact that the airmen were being trained to fly the Liberator at an extremely low level. This was a worrisome feature considering the flying characteristics of the Liberator and the danger of passing through prop wash near the ground. Also mystifying was that very few knew what the assignment was all about. The answer lay in that parenthetical phrase (referring to "attacks upon Ploesti") which had appeared following "Oil" in the Combined Bomber Offensive paper.

This Rumanian city was situated in the south central section of the country known as the Wallachian plain, in the heart of the oil-producing regions. Ploesti lay in the center of vast fields, refineries, cracking plants, great complexes which supplied Nazi Germany—thanks to dictator Ion Antonescu—with more than half of its crude oil supply. A full third of Germany's petroleum needs came from Ploesti; the other two thirds came from other sources including its own synthetic plants, which extracted petroleum products from coal. Without oil Germany could not function militarily, a fact of which Hitler was acutely aware even before Pearl Harbor. There were pitiable outcries from the Navy, the Luftwaffe, and the panzer-dependent Wehrmacht. Even with Germany's synthetic plants increasingly productive, Ploesti remained the major source of oil. And oil, if the Combined Chiefs and their Committee of Operations analysts had been aware of the critical situation

Liberators practicing for a low-level mission over the Libyan Desert near Benghazi, north Africa.
(U. S. AIR FORCE)

in Germany, would have been placed first on the priorities list, not fourth.

To Harris Ploesti represented another despised panacea target. Besides, it was not within reach of Bomber Command in England. He continued to concentrate upon the Ruhr. Eaker complied with the spirit of the Combined Bomber Offensive whenever he could muster enough planes to strike at the sub pens or other high-priority targets within reach of the Eighth Air Force. But his resources had dwindled so much because of the diversion of several of his heavy-bomber groups to Africa.

These purloined groups came into the province of Major General Lewis H. Brereton, a cocky bantam of a man who commanded the Ninth Air Force. Brereton, who had been in command of the Far East Air Force in the Philippines when the Japanese struck, had moved out of the Philippines into Java. When Java fell Brereton worked his way across Burma and India until he arrived in Egypt late in June 1942. His nine battered Flying Fortresses became the United States Army Middle East Air Force. In close co-operation with the RAF, the Middle East Air Force assisted in the war upon Rommel by bombing Mediterranean supply ports and convoys at sea. Prior to the breakthrough at El Alamein, the force attacked the harbors of Tobruk and Benghazi, among others, and when Rommel was driven out of Africa, it set up bases around Benghazi—although by this time the unit was called the Ninth Air Force. Brereton's forces by then had been joined by the Northwest African Air Forces

Lewis H. Brereton (here a lieutenant general), commander of the Ninth Air Force at the time it made its attack on Ploesti. (U. S. AIR FORCE)

(Major General Carl Spaatz) to work with RAF, Middle East. The missions of all these air forces were co-ordinated by Mediterranean Air Command under Air Chief Marshal Sir Arthur W. Tedder. It was a complex international co-operative effort which, despite differences, worked very well.

This was because ultimate command of all units actually continued under normal national division. Americans served under American leaders and British under British; no attempt was made to intermix the units. At the high levels of command there was a good deal of give-and-take, a willingness to co-operate, and mutual respect, so that despite the command complexities—a concession to political needs—operations came off remarkably well.

So it was that on June 11, 1943, Brereton received a message from Tedder "concerning Operation SOAPSUDS. It will be mounted from the Middle East, and three more heavy groups are en route to join the Ninth Air Force." Soapsuds was the initial code name for the Ploesti bombing, later changed to "Tidal Wave." Coincidentally, exactly one year before to the day of Brereton's diary entry American bombers had taken off to bomb Ploesti. This was done by the "Halverson Detachment," led by Colonel Harry A. Halverson. Originally equipped with twenty-three B-24Ds, the Halverson Detachment was to have been sent to Chinese bases for bombing missions against Japan. However, delays en route found Halverson in north Africa at a critical moment, and his Liberators were pressed into service there. Taking off on June 11, 1942, Halverson led thirteen Liberators toward the oil fields of Ploesti. One plane was forced to turn back and a dozen succeeded in reaching the target after a long over-water flight, crossing over neutral Turkey. Although accomplishing little damage, the Halverson Detachment planes had struck the first American blow against the Axis. No American life was lost, although one aircraft crash-landed and four, short of fuel, landed in Turkey, where their crews were interned. But the implications of the remarkable mission were lost in the excitement of the news from Midway, which still dominated newspaper space. Those planes which returned from Ploesti remained in the Middle East and were absorbed into Brereton's Ninth Air Force.

Colonel Jacob E. Smart, of Arnold's staff, had conceived the idea of a low-level mission against Ploesti. Surprise, it was hoped, would thus be achieved despite the fact that the Liberator was not designed for low-level performance. A large force, it was assumed, coming in low could deal much damage to the oil complexes. There was another assumption: that except for sporadic Russian attacks upon Ploesti, no large-scale attempt had been made since the Halverson mission, and therefore the German defenders might be caught off guard and unprepared.

Although it was soon proved by aircrews that the Liberator could indeed operate at zero altitude, the assumption that the Luftwaffe was unprepared at Ploesti was ill founded. It was, in fact, one of the best defended targets in all of Europe. The heavy antiaircraft concentrations ringing the city were under the efficient control of Oberst Alfred Gerstenberg, a former faculty member of the Russian-based Luftwaffe air center at Lipesk. In addition to Gerstenberg's guns, several Luftwaffe units were within calling distance of the oil fields—three fighter groups equipped with the Me-109 and a night fighter group with the Me-110. The Rumanians too could supply fighters, but the Germans did not count upon them. Although some were given Messerschmitts, most Rumanian pilots were saddled with inferior Rumanian and Bulgarian fighters.

As commander of 9th Bomber Command, Brigadier General Uzal G. Ent was entrusted with the detailed planning of the mission. Like Brereton, Ent had his serious reservations about a low-level attack; likewise, so did the group commanders leading the mission. But when a conference was held by Brereton in Benghazi on July 6, he "invited no discussion whatsoever among the commanders" and "stressed the necessity for absolute ruthlessness in the immediate relief of any Commander who at any time during the training period showed lack of

Colonel Jacob E. Smart, who believed that Ploesti could be hit by a surprise low-level bombing to throw off what was also believed to be weak defenses.

(U. S. AIR FORCE)

Brigadier General Uzal G. Ent, chief of 9th Bomber Command, and upon whom the planning of the Ploesti mission devolved. Ent did not care for Smart's concept of the low-level mission. (U. S. AIR FORCE)

caught up in the grandeur of the conception. Perhaps he was conscious of the historic impact of such an undertaking when he told the crews, "You should consider yourself lucky to be on this mission." More than three hundred of his auditors would not have agreed; they were dead the following day.

III

The cast for this historical drama included a number of iron men. The leading one was undoubtedly the unpopular, but tough, Colonel John R. Kane, leading the 98th Bomb Group ("Pyramiders"). A hard-driving professional warrior out of Texas, Kane carried the nickname of "Killer." Whether this applied to his attitude toward the Germans or his own men—or himself—is disputable. That he was obsessed with making war upon the Germans could not be denied. When the mission to Ploesti was activated Kane rescinded the orders which would have enabled men in the 98th who had completed their tour of duty to return to the United States. This did not endear him further to his men, who had

leadership, of aggressiveness, or of complete confidence."

It had been Brereton's decision, selected from two suggested plans, a high-level attack launched from Syria or the low-level attack from Benghazi, to attempt the low attack. Once he had decided he adhered to the decision whatever his personal feelings and those of the men actually given the job of carrying it out. Even a petition signed by the group commanders and by Ent made no difference. Late in July Tedder had suggested postponing the attack or canceling it in favor of attacks upon aircraft factories at Wiener Neustadt near Vienna. But now Brereton opposed Tedder on the grounds that "the Ploesti refineries are more important to the Axis war effort than the Messerschmitt factory and because training had almost been completed for Tidal Wave and to call it off now would seriously impair the morale of the entire Bomber Command." Would a cancellation have been as bad for morale as much as knowing your commander (Ent) believed the mission would be a success "even if none returned"?

Despite his misgivings Brereton was certainly

John R. "Killer" Kane (here seen as an air cadet), who would lead his "Pyramiders" (98th Bomb Group) to Ploesti despite a number of hitches. (U. S. AIR FORCE)

never loved him. Kane was as courageous as he was coldly ruthless. He was one commander Brereton would have never replaced. It was also unlikely that Kane would have fulfilled the requirements of "officer and gentleman," but he was an amazing war leader.

Another fine leader was Colonel Leon Johnson, leading the 44th Bomb Group (nicknamed the "Eight Balls"), a businesslike, quietly efficient veteran; Lieutenant Colonel Addison Baker led the 93rd Bomb Group, known as the "Traveling Circus," originally "Ted's Traveling Circus." This was in honor of the commander, Colonel Edward J. Timberlake, who had preceded Baker as group leader. Timberlake was involved with the Ploesti raid as an operational planner because of his experience with B-24 operations, most of it earned in the north African campaign. In turning over his Traveling Circus to Baker, Timberlake was acknowledging Baker's capabilities as a superb leader.

Colonel Keith K. Compton ("K.K."), a Missourian, led the 376th Bomb Group ("Liberandos"). Described by a former squadron mate as "a real gung ho type," Compton had served with Timber-

Keith K. Compton, "a real gung ho type," commander of the "Liberandos" (376th Bomb Group); mission leader Ent would fly in Compton's aircraft to Ploesti —and back. (U. S. AIR FORCE)

lake and was placed by the latter in command of the Liberandos. This group would lead the mission and General Ent would fly in Compton's plane.

The fifth group, the recently activated 389th Bomb Group, was led by Colonel Jack Wood. These unseasoned men had taken the name of "Sky Scorpions." Although a detachment of the 389th had arrived in Libya as early as July, most men participating in the raid would not have had any combat experience.

Major Ramsay D. Potts, Jr., a Tennessean, who "wanted to fly and wanted to fight Hitler," was a twenty-six-year-old deputy commander in Addison Baker's 93rd. A brilliant young leader, Potts had guessed long before he was told that the target for which they trained would be Ploesti. During this period, Potts recalls that the weather at Benghazi "was absolutely frightful." The air was so filled with fine sand (which ruined engines and other parts of aircraft) that at times it was impossible to see five feet ahead. Aircraft became so hot that touching them resulted in serious burns. Dysentery afflicted one and all, from colonel to sergeant.

Leon Johnson, commanding officer of the "Eight Balls" (44th Bomb Group), a superb battle leader.
(U. S. AIR FORCE)

Scale map (1:5000) of Ploesti built for the Air Force by RAF technicians in England in a week and flown to Africa. It was transported from group to group for study in a truck. Top (just left of center line) is Concordia Vega, largest production unit at Ploesti; counterclockwise, in wedge-shaped area, is Xenia, one of the smaller installations; almost directly below, near bottom, Columbia Aquila; to immediate right below is Astra Romana; to far right near center (i.e., directly east of Ploesti) is Romana Americana, owned by American Standard Oil; although a target, it would not be hit during the mission. (U. S. AIR FORCE)

But training continued despite the hardships. A dummy target area, duplicating in full scale the dispersed installations at Ploesti, was built by engineers. Practice missions at zero altitude were made upon the target. One mission, on July 28, wiped out the desert Ploesti in two minutes. The RAF provided a beautifully made table-top, three-dimen-

sional map of Ploesti which was studied by pilots, navigators, and bombardiers. Special films were made based upon the most recent, though outdated, intelligence. The smooth, confident voice of John "Tex" McCrary, an ex-newspaperman turned Air Force public relations expert, assured the crews of the weaknesses of Ploesti's defenses. "The fighter defenses are not strong and the majority of the fighters will be flown by Rumanian pilots who are thoroughly bored with the war." As for antiaircraft, it was estimated that there were a mere "eighty heavy AA guns and 160 light AA guns," but these were "largely disposed for a night attack" and the "heavy ack-ack should not trouble you at low altitude." Besides, all "the antiaircraft guns are manned by Rumanians, so there is a pretty good chance there might be incidents like there were in Italy at the beginning of the war—when civilians could not get into shelters because they were filled with antiaircraft gunners."

But there were forty batteries of the wicked 88s (88-mm. rifles which were employed against tanks and ships as well as aircraft)—240 guns in all, besides the smaller 37-mm. and 20-mm. guns: hun-

Edward Timberlake, former commander of the "Traveling Circus" (93rd Bomb Group), assisted in the planning of the Ploesti mission. The photograph was taken while the group was still stationed in England.

(U. S. AIR FORCE)

dreds of guns ringing Ploesti and many of them manned by Luftwaffe gun crews, not Rumanians. It was not deception, merely wishful thinking based on the best and latest intelligence reports. But it was the basis for one of the more horrible realizations to be met in the target area by the men in the five groups of Liberators.

At dawn on Sunday, August 1, the first of 178 Liberators, *Wingo-Wango,* piloted by First Lieutenant Brian Flavelle and carrying the mission navigator Lieutenant Robert Wilson, lifted out of the Libyan dust and pointed for the island of Corfu, a three-hour flight across the Mediterranean. At this point the mission would bear northeast across the mountains of Albania and Yugoslavia and eventually the Danube River. This led into the Wallachian plain and Ploesti. The trip would cover, for those who made it both ways, a distance of roughly twenty-seven hundred miles.

The cumbrous, slab-sided "pregnant cows," swollen with fuel for the long trip (additional tanks were installed in the bomb bay of each plane), seemed to struggle to rise off the ground. Although the extra fuel meant sacrificing pay load—1000-

Aircrew: men who would fly the mission to Ploesti; 93rd Bomb Group. (RAYMOND C. WIER)

pound and 500-pound bombs as well as incendiaries —each Liberator carried more than 4000 pounds of explosives: a total of 311 tons of destruction in the entire striking force. All planes were overloaded, some of them made heavier by extra nose guns (in formation lead planes which were to attack flak-gun installations on their bomb runs) and armored crew stations protecting the men from ground fire.

The bombs carried delayed fuzes; the first two waves would thus drop bombs timed to detonate after a period of from one to six hours. This would make it safe for the planes which followed to drop their bombs, theoretically, without flying into the bursts of the preceding aircraft or through the fires the early bombs might have set. There were seven major target areas. Five were situated at Ploesti; another was at Brazi, which was almost adjacent to Ploesti and just to the south; the seventh target was at Campina, about eight miles northwest of Ploesti.

Aboard the 178 Liberators were 1725 Americans and one stowaway, an Englishman. RAF Flight Lieutenant George C. Barwell, a gunnery expert, had been given unofficial permission to fly as topturret gunner in the plane of Major Norman C. Appold, leading B Section of the leading group, the Liberandos (376th). Led by Compton, the

Pre-mission pep talk: General Brereton addresses the 376th Bomb Group before its men boarded their Liberators for Ploesti. Curious portent: as he spoke a sudden wind came up and Brereton was blown off the platform. (U. S. AIR FORCE)

376th Bomb Group put up twenty-nine B-24s; at the head of the formation flew Flavelle's *Wingo-Wango,* leading the bombers to Ploesti. Tucked into the 376th formation was Compton's plane, *Teggie Ann,* carrying the mission command pilot, General Ent.

Following the Liberandos came Baker's Traveling Circus (93rd) with thirty-nine aircraft and Killer Kane's Pyramiders (98th) with forty-seven tawny (almost moth-eaten in appearance) B-24s; the Eight Balls, Johnson's 44th Bomb Group, came up with thirty-seven bombers; behind Johnson were the Sky Scorpions (389th), led by Wood, with twenty-six Liberators. Each group, some divided into two forces, had its assigned targets; all were scheduled to approach their targets in the order in which they had taken off. A strict radio silence was maintained in order not to alert German detection stations. Unknown to the men aboard the Liberators, the Germans were aware of a large force taking off from Libya, although the destination was not known.

"The very first news of the Ploesti operation was bad," Brereton noted in his diary. *Kickapoo,* which had taken off with Kane's Pyramiders, developed trouble shortly after pilot First Lieutenant Robert Nespor had it air-borne. With flame shooting out of an engine, Nespor turned around and headed back for the field. In coming in he was forced to attempt a landing upon a runway still obscured by clouds of red desert dust. *Kickapoo* came in, settled onto the runway, roughly bounced along, and rammed into a concrete telephone pole. Only two men survived the burning wreck.

But the armada, led by *Wingo-Wango,* continued on its way. From time to time over the Mediterranean a Liberator here and there feathered a propeller—a sign of engine malfunction—wheeled out of the formation, jettisoned bombs and fuel into the sea, and headed back for Africa. Before they came within sight of Corfu, ten Liberators had gone; six of these came from Kane's Pyramiders.

The remaining 167 planes were bearing down on Corfu when the lead plane began to behave peculiarly. As the other craft in A Section scattered out of harm's way, *Wingo-Wango* swooped and dived, climbed and dived directly into the sea. Even during these shocking moments radio silence was not violated and no one could know what had oc-

Wingo-Wango, *Brian Flavelle's Liberator, has silently fallen into the Mediterranean, taking "Tidal Wave's" lead navigator Robert Wilson with it.*

(RAYMOND C. WIER)

rurred in the lost plane. Only a tall column of smoke rose from the Mediterranean marking the spot where the aircraft had plunged. The formation was supposed to continue on its way—and it did, except for Flavelle's wingman, First Lieutenant Guy Iovine. Unable to leave the stricken ship, he dipped his B-24 down and circled over the spot hoping to find survivors to whom he might drop rafts. But there was no one, and then to his dismay Iovine found that he was unable to get the heavy plane back up to formation altitude. There was nothing to do but head back to Benghazi.

The mission navigator was lost in Flavelle's plane; the deputy navigator was in Iovine's. John Palm, in *Brewery Wagon,* moved into the lead spot; his navigator, young William Wright, was now chief navigator of the mission to Ploesti.

Now 165 of the original 178 planes turned northeast over Corfu. Spotters, still uncertain of the formation's destination, kept close watch on the B-24s and telephoned various Luftwaffe stations in the area. But there was some suspicion in Bucharest that the target might be Ploesti.

The formation had hugged the sea for the first leg, but as it approached Albania the Pindus Mountains would necessitate a climb. The mountains peaked to nine thousand feet, but a build-up of cloud massed up to seventeen thousand feet. Compton led the 376th through at sixteen thousand feet, followed by Baker's 93rd. Kane elected to go through at twelve thousand feet leading his 98th, which had spread out according to procedure for passing through cloud, and was followed by Johnson's 44th and Wood's 389th Groups. At sixteen thousand feet a tail wind hurried the two lead groups toward Ploesti while at twelve thousand the three other groups bucked winds through the soup. Thus when the five groups finally emerged from the cumulus, Compton's and Baker's formations were out of sight of Kane, Johnson, and Wood's Liberators. Radio silence made it impossible for the force to reassemble for the final attack. By this time also men in the American bombers had seen enemy planes hovering below them, unable to climb to the height at which the bombers flew without proper oxygen equipment. These were Bulgarian pilots in antiquated fighters. Leon Johnson then realized that all hopes for surprise had come to nothing. And with the three groups trailing the two lead groups, all chances of making a concerted attack upon the seven target areas were likewise lost.

About sixty-five miles west of Ploesti lay the first IP (Initial Point), the city of Pitesti. It was here that the formations were to assume attack altitude, about five hundred feet, and the 389th would leave the other groups to attack the Campina targets. The final IP was the town of Floresti, about thirteen miles northwest of Ploesti. Turning southeast at Floresti would bring the four remaining groups in over Ploesti for their low-level bombing runs.

Brewery Wagon, the lead plane of the 376th Group, carrying William Wright, the new mission navigator, continued on past Pitesti. Slightly behind was *Teggie Ann,* flown by Captain Ralph Thompson, as copilot to Compton and carrying mission leader Ent as a passenger. *Brewery Wagon* passed over Targoviste on the way to the final IP, Floresti; here the most fatal incident of the mission occurred. Mistaking Targoviste for Floresti, Compton ordered Thompson to make the southeast turn for the final run on the target. Palm's *Brewery Wagon* continued on the correct flight path, but all planes following saw the command ship turn and turned in train. *Brewery Wagon* wavered, seemed about to join in the wrong turn, but convinced that Wright was correct, Palm continued directly on to the target alone. But *Teggie Ann,* meanwhile, pointed both the 376th and 93rd at Bucharest instead of Ploesti.

Ramsay Potts, among the first to realize that the lead plane with Compton and Ent had made a wrong turn, broke radio silence to warn of the error. But too late; Potts was forced to turn also because of being boxed in by the formation. (U. S. AIR FORCE)

Major Ramsay Potts, leading B Section of the 93rd, realized instantly that the turn had come too soon. So did Major Norman Appold of the 376th. It was too much for both men and they broke radio silence—it no longer mattered—shouting, "Not here!" (Appold) and "Mistake!" (Potts). The latter hoped to break away from the formation, but was "boxed in and had no choice but to turn."

The two lead groups were now heading into Gerstenberg's most potent flak-gun concentration—and for the capital city of Rumania, a city of no military consequence. Within minutes the spires and steeples of Bucharest came into view. To the men in the racing Liberators, now around fifty feet above the ground, it did not at all look like the target for which they had been briefed. Alerted gun crews ran to their 88s and alarms rang in fighter bases for miles around. Why the Americans should attack Bucharest was a total mystery, but Rumanian and German alike ran to his gun station or to waiting fighter aircraft. The Battle of Ploesti had been prematurely ignited.

Addison Baker, leading the 93rd, which had followed the 376th on the wrong course, was aware also of the wrong turn. So was, by then, Ent and Compton in *Teggie Ann.* But it was Baker who reacted first. Seeing the church spires of Bucharest ahead instead of the stacks of Ploesti, which stood to his left, without breaking radio silence Baker executed an almost right-angle turn toward the target. With near miraculous skill and remarkable discipline the rest of the Traveling Circus followed: Lieutenant Colonel George S. Brown leading A Section swinging to Baker's right, and Ramsay Potts, with B Section, wheeling to Brown's right. Now in a broad frontal formation the 93rd approached Ploesti from the south instead of from the west as it had been briefed. Ploesti looked strange to the navigators and bombardiers as its stacks loomed up out of the ground.

IV

The one plane on the correct course, John Palm's *Brewery Wagon,* all but embraced the earth as it charged for the target. Almost on Ploesti *Brewery Wagon* took a direct .88 hit in the nose, killing young William Wright, who had led the formations

The payment for Ploesti begins: the antiaircraft guns, having been forewarned by the wrong turn, are ready for Brewery Wagon, *which had not made the error— thanks to the navigation of William Wright, whom Ent overruled—and which continued "as briefed" for Ploesti until struck in the nose by a German .88 shell.* (RAYMOND C. WIER)

The 93rd, having swung back on course because of Potts's realization of the navigational error of Teggie Ann, *passes by a burning Liberator.*

(RAYMOND C. WIER)

A view from the cockpit of Kenneth O. Dessert's Liberator; flame billows up from an oil tank. To the right, in the lower left-hand corner of the windscreen may be seen Hell's Wench, *carrying Group Commander Addison Baker and mission planning assistant John J. Jerstad. Struck by an .88 shell and burning, the plane continued on its run over the target and crashed; no one survived, not even the two men who parachuted from the burning plane.* (RAYMOND C. WIER)

Lieutenant Colonel Addison Baker, commander of the 93rd Group, here photographed in his office using the public address system, while the group was still stationed in England. Baker died in the crash of Hell's Wench *and was awarded a Medal of Honor for his role in the mission to Ploesti.* (U. S. AIR FORCE)

so brilliantly, and bombardier Second Lieutenant Robert W. Merrell. Palm too had been hit; his right leg was all but blown away. With three engines gone—two of them gushing flame—there was nothing to do but salvo the bombs and try to land. Half in shock upon learning that his leg remained attached to him by the merest shred, Palm had been unaware of the attack of a Messerschmitt on *Brewery Wagon* as it came crunching into the ground. Copilot William F. Love foamed the engines and the distressed plane came in without further burning. Palm, who later had his right leg amputated below the knee, and the seven other survivors were taken prisoner by the Rumanians and Germans.

Having turned for Ploesti, leaving the 376th still on the wrong course to Bucharest, Baker's 93rd ran into the muzzles of flak guns awaiting them. The alarms which had alerted the capital's defenses also quickened the rings of guns around the true target area. Baker flew directly into an inferno: the planes were so low that gun crews simply boresighted and used instantaneous fuzes. So it was that *Hell's Wench,* Baker's plane, with young Major John J. Jerstad, one of the important assistants to Timberlake in the planning of the mission, as copilot, bore down upon the target area. One of the first obstacles was the balloon barrage. *Hell's Wench* flew into a cable, which luckily snapped, freeing the balloon. But then an .88 shell smashed into the nose of the Liberator and more hits followed, into the wings and the cockpit. Aflame, *Hell's Wench* proceeded toward the target; but Baker knew it would not remain aloft with the bomb load and he jettisoned the explosives. The plane continued leading the rest of the 93rd toward the target. A chute or two blossomed out of *Hell's Wench,* and it appeared that Baker had attempted to bring it up high enough to enable the men to have sufficient altitude from which to drop.

Hell's Wench, still burning, continued to lead the force into the target area, attempting to clear the stacks which spiked up into its path. To observers it appeared to be completely afire in the cockpit area although still seemingly under control. About three hundred feet above the ground *Hell's Wench* suddenly veered into the earth with a splashing flame. Baker had succeeded in bringing his group over the target, but everyone—including the few men who had been able to leave the doomed plane —died.

Those who followed placed the first bombs into the Ploesti target area. The first bomb fell from Walter Stewart's *Utah Man,* only survivor of Baker's three-plane wave. However, the bombs rained down upon targets assigned not to the 93rd, but to the 44th (still coming up, though late, but, as briefed, in company with Kane's 98th). Liberators had begun dropping out of the force before Ploesti was reached as point-blank antiaircraft fire smashed into the low-flying aircraft. Black funeral pyres dotted the route to the target. Gunners in the aircraft engaged in duels with the enemy machine gunners and antiaircraft crews. Some of the machine-gun fire from the planes ignited the unimportant tank farms, smudging the area with leaping flames and dense, black smoke, introducing just one more hazard into the affrighted air.

It was an unimaginable scene as the thirty-four (of the original thirty-nine) 93rd Bomb Group planes swept through at more than two hundred miles an hour and barely off the ground. Their attack could only have taken minutes, but lifetimes ended and complex actions occurred in those few minutes. More than half of the attacking planes did not come out of the fiery target area. Some struck balloon cables; some were hit by flak or other gunfire; some, flying through the turbulence of earlier planes, simply slammed into the ground. Hidden guns popped out of fake haystacks or special mobile flak nests on railway cars with drop sides. Liberators trailed sheets of flame and crashed into fields of wheat or corn even before arriving at the target.

Ramsay Potts, in *Duchess,* led the final 93rd element, Target Force 3, into fumid Ploesti. Deeply fearful that the wrong turn had "wiped out our chance for a successful mission," Potts knew his small force would not be able to hit its target. Having weathered a murderous sequence of flak guns, it would be difficult enough to find an alternate target. Potts and his wingmen turned to find their assigned target but with Astro Romana directly in their line of flight began dropping bombs; this target in the original planning had been assigned to Kane's 98th. The planes behind and around *Duchess* began shredding parts of fuselage or wing,

some continuing on but others smashing to earth in fiery, gashing crashes. One of Potts's wingmen, *Jersey Bounce,* with nose shot away, engine trailing flame, painfully rose over various obstacles until pilot Worthy Long managed to skid it into a clearing, where it burst into flame. Half the crew managed to get out of the plane.

Rumanian fighters, which had vaulted into the air from near Bucharest, initiated attacks on the harassed 93rd Liberators. As one of Potts's B-24s emerged out of the target area, a low-winged monoplane clung to the big aircraft. Apparently in distress, the Liberator roared above the streets of Ploesti with the little Rumanian fighter underneath (all but scraping the street) firing into its belly. With a massive boom the American bomber crashed into the women's prison, in which not only the crew of the plane but around sixty prisoners died trapped in the flames.

As Potts led the remnants of the 93rd away from Ploesti, he was on a near-collision course with planes of the 376th, now coming in to bomb. Ent and Compton had faced the frightful truth: they had led the force into a wrong turn. During the run from Targoviste to the outskirts of Bucharest they had, indeed, "served their time in hell." And there was more to come. Ent spoke into the command channel and ordered the 376th away from Bucharest, turning north and following a railroad linking the capital with Ploesti. The question now was: Should they circle to come in from the briefed course or should they bomb from a completely unfamiliar approach?

This vexing question was answered when Ent, observing the savagery of the antiaircraft fire, ordered the men to hit "targets of opportunity." The B-24s had been flying north, directly into heavy flak, and most then swerved away to the east, to strike at whatever targets they could find. According to the original plan the target of Compton's planes was the Romana Americana refinery—deliberately selected because of its onetime (i.e., before the Germans took over) American ownership. There must be no favoritism displayed in the Ploesti attack. Because of the confusion, as well as the heavy flak reception, the Romana Americana complex was not hit at all that day.

Major Norman Appold led his five Liberators of

Norman C. Appold, who had like Ramsay Potts realized Teggie Ann *had made a wrong turn, but who pressed on toward Ploesti and saw a mass confusion over the target. Despite this, Appold bombed his target of opportunity, Concordia Vega.* (U. S. AIR FORCE)

the 376th directly into Ploesti instead of spreading out as did the other planes. Appold had selected what appeared to be an untouched target of importance (it was: Concordia Vega, which had been assigned to Baker's 93rd). But even as he approached on the bomb run, Appold was disconcerted to see other B-24s flying through the smoke directly toward him; these were the survivors of Potts's force leaving the target. But there was more for Appold to see: as he bore down on Concordia Vega more B-24s appeared to be converging upon him. These were Killer Kane's Pyramiders, somewhat late after joining up upon emerging from the cloud mass, and now on the proper target run.

If ever there was a demonstration of just how a carefully planned military operation could go awry thanks to the simple introduction of human error, Ploesti became a classic.

There is a classic Army axiom: when in doubt

do everything. Appold, however, was not in doubt. He had selected his target and went for it; blind good fortune would have to see to the rest. His five bombers groped through the hail of fire and smoke and dropped their bombs directly into the target area. Only then did he lead his planes up and over Potts's planes rushing away from Ploesti. Appold turned also and, while Barwell in the top turret engaged in duels with various low-lying gun positions, pulled away from the nightmare in noontime Ploesti.

The other 376th aircraft, seeking targets of opportunity, scattered in sweeping turns to the west of Ploesti. Compton's *Teggie Ann* salvoed into a small complex of buildings, not one of the briefed targets. Other planes followed suit, dropping their loads to the north and west of Ploesti before veering south near Floresti—where they converged with Jack Wood's Sky Scorpions, which had bombed at Campina.

v

It was at Floresti, the third IP and correct turning point for the run into Ploesti, that Kane's 98th and Johnson's 44th began their massed approach. The dividing line between the two forces was a railroad track running from Floresti to Ploesti. A heavily armed flak train ran along this track, firing at Kane's Pyramiders to the north and Johnson's Eight Balls to the south as the two forces, flying abreast, came upon Ploesti.

While Kane's Pyramiders and sixteen of Johnson's Eight Balls bore down upon their Ploesti targets, Colonel James Posey, also of the 44th, led an additional twenty-one Eight Ball Liberators toward his target, Brazi, about five miles southwest of Ploesti. Here was located the Creditul Minier refinery, production center for high-octane aviation fuel.

Leading in *V for Victory,* piloted by veteran John H. Diehl, Posey swept into Brazi in the first wave. Diehl had to pull the plane up to avoid chimneys, but the bombs fell precisely into the target area. Brazi had not been struck by any of the earlier planes which had scattered over Ploesti seeking targets. This part of the mission occurred exactly as planned—and the Brazi refinery was totally destroyed at a cost of two Liberators.

Kane's Pyramiders come in over Ploesti to find that their targets have already been hit by Baker's Traveling Circus. (JERRY JOSWICK: U. S. AIR FORCE)

But the fate of the remaining Eight Balls and the Pyramiders was totally different. As they approached Ploesti, it seemed that they would be further hindered by murky rain clouds low over the target area. Several Liberators in both Kane's and Johnson's forces had been damaged by the flak train, and the dark cloud was but one more unforeseen hitch. But as they charged down upon Ploesti it became clear that the "rain" was in fact smoke, the effusion of the bombings by the 93rd Group. This smoke, now rising above bombing height, not only added turbulence, but also secreted chimneys, barrage balloon cables, and bracing wires of the chimneys. Intense flame, too, shot into the air intermittently throughout the entire target area.

It was at this point that both Johnson and Kane could have swerved off course and fled. Their targets, obscured by smoke and livid with flame, had already been struck. They could turn back and no one would question their decision. It is unlikely that the thought so much as flickered through the minds of these two quite opposite men. Johnson expressed their attitudes when he said that "we had all agreed ahead of time that we weren't going

that far without trying to get our targets. . . ." Kane had come to bomb Ploesti and he would not leave until he had. So he led his decimated Pyramiders into the inferno. One of his crew, Raymond B. Hubbard, recalled that the "fire wrapped us up. I looked out of the side windows and saw the others flying through smoke and flame. It was [like] flying through hell. I guess we'll go straight to heaven when we die. We've had our purgatory."

"It was more like an artist's conception of an air battle than anything I have ever experienced," Johnson later told Brereton. "We flew through sheets of flame, and airplanes were everywhere, some of them on fire and others exploding. It's indescribable to anyone who wasn't there."

Kane, at the controls of *Hail Columbia,* churned up the target area with his fixed front guns and led the way into Ploesti. The heat was so intense at his attack altitude that his left arm was singed; *Hail Columbia* also received a hit in an engine and when the smoke- and flame-blacked B-24 escaped from the inferno it was flying on three engines. Of the forty-one planes which had begun the target run at Floresti, only nineteen followed Kane out of the smoke. But their bombs lay in the assigned target zone, compounding the destruc-

The 98th Bomb Group flies over an already burning Astra Romana. Stacks in the heavy smoke were as much a danger as German flak.
(JERRY JOSWICK: U. S. AIR FORCE)

tion laid on by the distracted 93rd. There had been, however, just one more hazard—the explosions of the delayed-action bombs.

Johnson's "White Five" target force of sixteen Liberators flew directly into a curtain of black smoke, evidence of the earlier visit of Baker's Traveling Circus. The great B-24s, twisting and turning to avoid balloon cables and chimneys, wallowed like so many winged whales in a fiery sea. With shocking regularity the leviathans foundered to the bottom of the murky ocean, spurting red, bloodlike flame. Of the sixteen planes which entered the "White Five" (Colombia Aquila refinery) target area only seven, with Johnson's *Suzy-Q* in the lead, came out.

But leaving the area of the target did not conclude the nightmare, for both Kane's and Johnson's survivors came under severe fighter attack—mainly Luftwaffe men in Me-109s. As he raced away with all the power his three straining engines could muster, Kane's *Hail Columbia* was laced by fighter fire, with punctures in the wing (with a resultant buckled wing spar), the tip of a propeller shot away, and a holed blade on another. Knowing he could never make it back over the planned with-

Leon Johnson's 44th approaches Columbia Aquila, only to find it burning; of the sixteen planes that flew in, only seven came out.
(JERRY JOSWICK: U. S. AIR FORCE)

drawal route to Benghazi, Kane set course for Cyprus, throwing out all excess weight on the way.

The Sky Scorpions (389th) were led with only the slightest hitch by Jack Wood to their target at Campina ("Red Target"). Wood too had inadvertently led his formation into a wrong turn; he corrected it by a smoothly executed turnabout and a vault over a small ridge. The Scorpions came in in two forces, Wood leading a dozen B-24s and Major John A. Brooks, his deputy, leading seventeen. With forward firing guns chattering, Wood led the forces into the until then untouched Steaua Romana complex. Like Posey's attack upon Brazi, Jack Wood's attack upon Campina was "as briefed." His group had the least losses of all involved. Of the twenty-nine attacking planes, six were lost, one of them flown by Second Lieutenant Lloyd Hughes, the only man of the Ploesti mission below the rank of major to receive the Medal of Honor.

Hughes's Liberator had been struck by flak as it approached the drop point. A wide stream of fuel poured out of a ruptured bomb bay tank, twist-

One of the targets hit "as briefed," Steaua Romana, the objective of the green "Sky Scorpions" (389th Group) led by Jack Wood.
(JERRY JOSWICK: U. S. AIR FORCE)

Lieutenant Lloyd Hughes (as an air cadet), one of the Sky Scorpions who did not leave the target area; Hughes was awarded the Medal of Honor for the mission. (U. S. AIR FORCE)

dos (376th), they came under fighter attack. From the dropping of the first bomb by *Utah Man* just before noon, until the last—placed by the 389th's *Vagabond King,* piloted by John B. McCormick— less than a half hour had elapsed. But for the survivors, most of them spread across the skies of Rumania with damaged planes, wounded, dying, and dead aboard, there were still the fighters to contend with until the German and Rumanian planes ran out of fuel. Keeping the tattered, scorched Liberators air-borne was an epic in itself.

The plan, having gone so completely astray, no longer held. On paper it had been intended that all targets would be hit simultaneously and that all survivors of the attack should return to the Libyan bases together. Thus would they be able to defend each other in formation with massed guns. The withdrawal from Ploesti was not orderly as different groups in various stages of distress left the target areas. Some planes were badly damaged and could not keep up with a formation, others came away under fighter attack.

An attempt was made to form ragged groupings

ing and flashing under the big plane like a liquid ribbon of fuze. Now on his bomb run, Hughes did not attempt to land or to evade the wall of flame which stood in the path. In an instant Hughes's Liberator was set afire. The bombs fell into the target, but the stricken plane, a white sheet of pure fire streaming from the left wing, had no chance. Obviously still under control, Hughes seemed headed for a stream bed for an emergency landing. A bridge loomed in the path of the burning plane, but the plane rose above the obstruction, lowered again—and then a wing tip brushed the riverbank. The blazing Liberator whirled across the earth, spattering molten wreckage and scarring the meadow in its scorching death throes; all but two men in the plane died in the crash.

The Sky Scorpions were the last to bomb in the Ploesti area, and in addition to dodging the target-of-opportunity seekers of Compton's Liberan-

"Getting the hell out": a Liberator at treetop level rushes away from burning Ploesti. Some bombers nearly scraped the earth and returned with cornstalks in their bomb bays.

(JERRY JOSWICK: U. S. AIR FORCE)

for the sake of survival. Some aircraft, not badly damaged, throttled down to remain with others which could not keep up and thus became easy targets for fighters. A trail of ammunition belts, radios, guns, seats—anything no longer required and which added weight to a struggling plane—followed the Liberators from Ploesti to the sea. The least hurt groups, the 376th (Liberandos) and the 389th (Sky Scorpions), managed to form up and head for home over the planned route, although not as a single unit. Some of the 44th and 98th (the worst hit Eight Balls and Pyramiders) joined together for the flight back, but the Pyramiders' leader, John Kane, with other planes in tow, made for Cyprus. It was a shorter flight than to Africa, although not without its Bulgarian mountain barrier. Planes which could not make it even that far landed in neutral Turkey, where crews were interned. In all, seven Liberators came down in Turkey, and one ditched into the sea off the Turkish coast; twenty-three came down at Allied bases in Malta, Sicily, or Cyprus.

It was nighttime before Kane brought *Hail Columbia* into the RAF base at Nicosia, Cyprus. Although the flare path was lighted, the exhausted

In the wake of "Tidal Wave," Rumanians fighting the fires at Ploesti. Although smoke and flame were impressive, the attack did not knock out the target. (U. S. AIR FORCE)

Journey's end: a Liberator sets down in north Africa after the Ploesti mission. (U. S. AIR FORCE)

iron man brought the wheezing Liberator in a little short, snagging the landing gear in a ditch which the British, with characteristic perversity, placed at either end of runways. The main wheels snapped and the Liberator came in on its nose and with tail threatening to rise and upend them. Kane and copilot John S. Young pulled on the controls to prevent flipping onto their back. The tail came down as the battered aircraft bellied screechingly along the runway. Bumping along, Kane was surprised to see two wheels and a propeller racing ahead. The plane twisted to a halt, and for the first time in more than twelve hours, Killer Kane left his seat.

On the return flight to Benghazi more planes were lost to the last fighter attacks and fell into the sea; two aircraft flying in formation entered a cloud and never came out—they had collided. Finally, after nearly twelve hours of waiting, the men at Benghazi heard the first of the survivors approaching. Brereton awaited the arrival of Compton and Ent, from whom he had had no word since around noon, when the simple message "Mission Successful" had been radioed from Ploesti.

In the deepening African twilight the giant bombers fluttered back, their engines whining from strain, the planes themselves whistling because of bullet- and flak-riddled surfaces. Planes came in without brakes, without proper control, some crash-landed with dead and wounded aboard. When the dispirited Ent revealed to Brereton the story of the mission, the latter realized that he had no triumph on his hands. The extent of damage to Ploesti would not be known until reconnaissance photographs were taken. From eyewitnesses it was clear that Ploesti had been hard hit, so that Ent's curiously premature and wildly optimistic "Mission Successful" message seemed less ironic.

But the ravages of the toll began to come in, intimated by the condition of men and aircraft as they landed at Benghazi. Ramsay Potts brought *Duchess* down and his feet had barely touched the ground before he was telling Timberlake of a military nightmare.

Of the 164 Liberators which had gained the target area, 41 had been lost to enemy action. An additional 14 (including the 8 interned in Turkey) were lost through other causes, such as the takeoff accident of *Kickapoo,* the inexplicable dive into the sea of Flavelle's plane near Corfu and the collision in the clouds over Bulgaria. Thus the total plane loss added up to 54. (And of those which had returned to Benghazi, barely 30 were still flyable.) This would mean too the loss of 540 men.

The final death toll of the Ploesti raid, according to Air Force files, came to 310. The number of wounded was initially given as 54 (3 of whom were in Turkey), but that number plus 20 lay in hospitals in Rumania. More than 100 prisoners, also, spent the rest of the war in Rumania.

The cost to the Ninth Air Force for less than a half hour's work was, indeed, high. This was implicit in the awarding of no less than five Medals of Honor (the highest number for any single air action) to Ploesti raiders, to the quick—Leon Johnson and John Kane—and the dead—Addison Baker, John Jerstad, and Lloyd Hughes.

On August 4, 1943, following the preliminary estimates, Brereton noted in his diary, "While the TIDAL WAVE operation was extremely successful, I was somewhat disappointed because we failed to hit White No. 1 and 2 at all." White No. 1 was Romana Americana, the American-leased section of Ploesti; No. 2 was Concordia Vega, which had, in fact, been hit by the determined Appold with his five planes that had not swerved away, as had the others of the 376th, to seek targets of opportunity. Brereton assigned his discomfiture to the fact that the 65 to 75 per cent destruction he had hoped for had not been achieved. Still, he believed that a 60 per cent figure had been reached and had "put a serious dent in Germany's oil supply." As reported centuries before by Plutarch, it had been another victorious warrior, Pyrrhus, who had said, "Another such victory . . . and we are finished."

In truth, the extent of damage was closer to 40 per cent, and while bombs and fire (as well as crashing aircraft) did knock out some facilities for four to six months, no "serious dent" was put in Germany's oil supply. In fact, Ploesti had never produced to full capacity, so that other units could be activated to make up the loss. With slave labor in plentiful supply, the Germans very quickly restored the damaged facilities, and Ploesti, instead of being knocked out of the war, was as potent as ever. It was not until late in the spring of 1944 that any more attempts could be made upon the heavily defended target. When the U. S. Fifteenth Air Force, based at Foggia, Italy, was formed and powerfully armed with B-17s and B-24s, Ploesti could be struck en masse from high level. By that time, too, long-range American fighter planes could escort the bombers to and from the target.

But Ploesti was never to be an easy target, with its heavy flak concentration, and many men died attempting to put a stopper to Hitler's oil supply. By the end of August 1944, a little over a year after Tidal Wave, the oil fields did stop functioning. In September the Russians moved in and occupied the ruin. It had taken thousands of bombers (and a further expenditure of more than 350 bombers lost). In short, the men who undertook and carried through Tidal Wave had attempted the impossible. Their true achievement could be measured only in courage and not decisive results. For the tragedy of Ploesti is that there were no decisive results.

8

SCHWEINFURT

Over another panacea target, ball bearings," Air Chief Marshal Sir Arthur Harris exclaimed with undisguised scorn, "the target experts went completely mad." The outspoken Briton, it is true, was speaking from the vantage point of hindsight, but he was no less critical and skeptical at the time. He resisted all pleas, suggestions, and even demands which had initiated with the "panacea mongers" despite their quite accurate information that about half of Germany's supply of ball bearings, so essential to the machines and instruments of war, was produced in the Bavarian city of Schweinfurt.

Harris rejected the claims for Schweinfurt's importance (in which rejection he was not correct), stating that even if Schweinfurt were entirely destroyed the effect upon German war production would not be as disastrous as was "so confidently prophesied." The fiery Bomber Command leader, standing firm against his own chiefs of the Air Staff, argued that Schweinfurt was a relatively small city and would therefore be difficult to find at night, that it was heavily defended, and that even several full-scale attacks would achieve, in his firm but considered opinion, only dubious results.

For months the doughty Harris endured the pressures of his chiefs, who in general agreed with the American policy of concentration upon selected targets. They argued that massive destruction in a few key industries would naturally be more effective than widespread small destruction in many. Harris preferred the larger population centers, for such cities were easier to locate—and they housed many, many Germans. These were the cities to destroy, not little Schweinfurt with its population of sixty thousand. While the crisis boiled in Bomber Command, the American Eighth Air Force, committed to the spirit and letter of the Combined Bomber Offensive, a major objective of which was the crippling of the German aircraft industry, prepared to spring upon Schweinfurt.

Eighth Air Force Bomber Command (more correctly VIII Bomber Command) had, since its initial modest mission to the Rouen-Sotteville marshaling yards (August 17, 1942), concentrated its slowly expanding forces upon such ungrateful targets as submarine pens, besides various industrial targets in the occupied countries and Germany and Luftwaffe airfields. By the beginning of 1943 it was grievously clear that the German Air Force was indeed a formidable enemy. As German pilots gained experience against the American bomber formations, composed mainly of the Flying Fortress and the more recent Liberators, tactics were devised to interfere seriously with bombing missions. The early Fortresses and Liberators were weak on frontal armament, so German pilots learned eventually to attack in small formations, ranging from single aircraft to a half dozen, from the front. The head-on

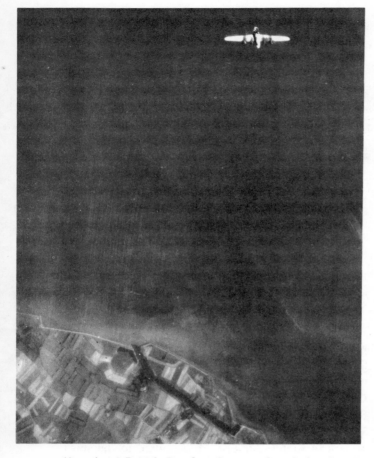

Aircraft of British Bomber Command and the American Eighth Air Force, by night and by day, shared the menace of German flak guns in occupied Holland. Flying Fortress Lady Liberty *falls toward Flushing after being cut in half by a direct hit.* (U. S. AIR FORCE)

must be eliminated. This did not preclude attention to other targets. Weather, the number of operational aircraft, the range limit of escort planes also played a part in the planning.

The force that Eaker was capable of dispatching in the year which separated Mission No. 1, when a dozen B-17s flew to Rouen-Sotteville, and Mission No. 83, when 237 bombers struck various German operated airfields in France, had grown. But post-holing runways, wrecking operations buildings and barracks, and destroying parked aircraft could only be defined as tactical—warmaking with an immediate, short-range objective. The more strategic aspect was notable in missions toward the end of July 1943—Missions 78, 79, 80, for example—when the Fiesler aircraft components factory at Kassel, the Focke-Wulf plant at Oschersleben, and the Heinkel works at Warnemünde (all of which

Colonel Curtis E. LeMay, commander of the 3rd Air Division (right), *who led the first shuttle bombing mission from England to Regensburg to north Africa. To LeMay's right: Brigadier General Haywood S. Hansell, commander of the 1st Bombardment Wing (units of which later comprised the 1st Air Division). When this photograph was taken LeMay was commander of the 305th Bomb Group. Later in the war both Hansell and LeMay were to play important roles in the development of the B-29 as an air weapon.*

(U. S. AIR FORCE)

attack, considering the double closing speed of the two aircraft, the always present danger of collision, and the sight of twinkling wing guns and cannon, was unnerving, to say the least. Although aggressive Luftwaffe fighter attacks did not succeed in turning back any of the American bomber forces, they did succeed in knocking aircraft down and, with the head-on attack, in interfering with the accuracy of bombing. Flak was another problem, but a more impersonal one, and one which depended to some extent upon chance. A German pilot in an Me-109 or an FW-190 was out to get you, specifically, and this was rattling.

It was true, then, as noted in the Combined Bomber Offensive document, that before the major target systems could be dealt with, the Luftwaffe

belonged to the complex which turned out the formidable FW-190) were heavily hit. They were also zealously defended; the three days' missions cost forty-four heavy bombers. And, if the Eighth had not succeeded in erasing the factories from Germany's war economy, it did initiate serious thought among the German High Command about dispersing such factory complexes, which dispersal promised to disrupt production as critically as damage.

The first anniversary of the Eighth's first mission from Britain was to be celebrated with Mission No. 84, the most impressive up to that moment. It sparkled with superlatives: more aircraft than ever before, more bomb tonnage than ever before; the deepest penetration into Germany ever attempted and a strike against the then two most critical targets: the Messerschmitt factories at Regensburg and the ball-bearing plant at Schweinfurt.

"It was a bold strategic concept," Lieutenant General Ira C. Eaker has written of the Regensburg-Schweinfurt mission. "It was the first shuttle bombing mission of the war. The 3rd Air Division, the

Aircrew quarters, Grafton-Underwood, England. Men of the 384th Bomb Group hug the stove between missions. Galoshes are a concession to England's muddy airfields. The steel helmet was not an affectation; it was worn by aircrews in combat. (ROBERT CHAPIN)

force attacking the Messerschmitt fighter factory at Regensburg, took off from English bases and landed in fields in North Africa. The decisions by the VIII Bomber Commander, Major General Frederick L. Anderson [who replaced Eaker, now head of the Eighth Air Force], and the 3rd Air Division Commander, Colonel Curtis E. LeMay, to proceed to Regensburg with but part of the force, when the 1st Air Division [led by Brigadier General Robert Williams] was delayed in take-off due to weather, were *two* of the most dramatic and courageous command decisions of the air war in Europe. This battlefield was a thousand miles long and five miles above the earth. It was fought in sub-zero temperatures and the gladiators, friend and foe, wore oxygen masks."

Brereton's Ninth had bled at Ploesti; now, less than a month later, it would be the turn of Eaker's Eighth.

II

Major General Frederick L. Anderson, commander of the Eighth Air Force's Bomber Command during the Schweinfurt missions. (U. S. AIR FORCE)

By June of 1943 about ten heavy bombardment groups had arrived in England, taking over ex-RAF

With a jack raising the wing, 384th Group ground crew men prepare to remove a wheel from a B-17.
(ROBERT CHAPIN)

fighter bases dotted the routes to and from the targets. Allied fighter planes could not venture beyond a certain point because of limited range. From that point on, it was a running battle of unexampled destructiveness and terror.

Obviously one solution, until the advent of the fighter capable of escorting the bombers round-trip, was to rid the sky of the Luftwaffe. So it was that the Regensburg-Schweinfurt mission was visualized as a double blow: directly upon the Messerschmitt factory itself and indirectly by striking at Schweinfurt's anti-friction-bearing complex which supplied ball bearings for several war industries.

"The plan of attack," Eaker has written, "called for the 3rd Air Division with 150 Flying Fortresses to cross the Channel at 8 A.M., fly to Regensburg, more than three hours away from English bases, attack the fighter factory there, and proceed to landing fields in Africa, fuel being insufficient for return to England.

"The 1st Air Division with 150 heavy bombers would follow 30 minutes later and bomb the ball-bearing complex at Schweinfurt, returning to English bases. It was visualized the 3rd Air Division would bear the brunt of German fighter reaction on the way in, and the 1st Air Division would have to fight its way out. Such long-range U.S. fighters as were then available would escort the 3rd Division in and the 1st Division out."

The 384th was one of the groups belonging to

stations in East Anglia and the Midlands. One of the most recent arrivals was the 384th Bombardment Group (H) based at Grafton-Underwood, from which the first heavy bomber strike had been made the previous August. In time the 384th adopted the slogan "Keep the Show on the Road," the contribution of Major S. L. McMillan, deputy group commander, who went down on the group's second mission—a strike upon the docks at Hamburg. Writing from a German prisoner of war camp, McMillan provided the heartening phrase, the philosophy of which the men in the group might have found ironic. In its first four days in combat the 384th lost ten aircraft on the wrong side of the Channel.

These losses, as well as the others decimating 8th Bomber Command, were more a tribute to the Luftwaffe's assertiveness than a reproach to the capabilities of the 384th Group. Even if bomber formations had grown larger during the critical first year of 8th Bomber Command's operations (thus massing defensive firepower), numerous German

B-17F of 384th Bomb Group; triangle on tail signifies that the group belonged to the 1st Air Division; "P" was the group's code letter. (ROBERT CHAPIN)

The airman's English enemy: the weather. Sudden changes made takeoff and assembly difficult and frequently led to collision over bomber bases. After a mission bad weather added to the toll when distressed aircraft attempted to land. (U. S. AIR FORCE)

the 1st Air Division and was alerted by a field order the evening before the mission was scheduled. Speculations about the nature and location of the target for what was rumored to be a "big one" had begun six weeks before. Would it be Berlin, or Hitler's private fortress in Berchtesgaden? Berlin seemed likely, for the Eighth had not yet struck at the capital of the Third Reich. Each group was ordered to pick their best navigator-bombardier team and to detach them to headquarters for special training. "We didn't know where the target was," Malvern Sweet, navigator of *The Ex-Virgin,* admitted, "but we could draw pictures of what it looked like."

During this same period of waiting, partly to recuperate from previous mission losses and partly to await a good turn in the weather, LeMay, commander of the 4th Combat Bombardment Wing (later the 3rd Air Division) placed his crews on bad-weather practice. The foresighted commander's reasoning was characteristically clear-cut: it was unlikely that they would have clear weather over both the bases and the target. Practicing blind takeoffs would take care of the poor visibility over England, LeMay calculated. Once above the clouds—and provided target visibility was good—all would be

as well as could be. LeMay planned to lead the force to Regensburg and then to Africa. But his foresightedness, as it eventuated, led to an ominous twist in the outcome of the mission.

The 1st Bombardment Wing (later the 1st Air Division) was preparing for the mission in its special training of navigator-bombardier teams. It was not, however, unlike LeMay, giving due consideration to the weather contingencies.

After several scrubbings, the mission was finally "laid on" for August 17, 1943. As was its capricious wont, English weather contributed its set of unknown factors. "It was so foggy," Curtis LeMay recalls, "that we had to lead the airplanes out with flashlights and lanterns, in order to get them onto the runway." The weeks of instrument takeoff paid off; LeMay managed to get all 146 B-17s of the 3rd Division off the ground and above the clouds. As division leader, LeMay flew in the lead aircraft of the 96th Bombardment Group and found to his consternation that there were no escort fighters to be found in the sky. Then there was a further hitch: the 1st Division too was socked in by fog but could not get off the ground as scheduled (this was timed for ten minutes after LeMay's force had crossed the enemy coast). With the approach of the Schweinfurt force, some of the German fighter attack, it had been hoped, would be drawn off the Regensburg force; and friendly fighters—eighteen squadrons of American P-47s and sixteen squadrons of Spitfires—could take on the Luftwaffe as planned.

Because he had to arrive at the African bases before dark, LeMay could not wait for the fog-bound 1st Division, nor could he spend time hoping for the arrival of the fighters. So he proceeded on to Regensburg. "Our fighter escort," LeMay has written, "had black crosses on their wings." In truth, American and British fighters did arrive to protect some of the other groups, although not the 96th with which LeMay flew—for the bombers stretched across miles of air—but had to turn back when fuel ran low. They returned to their bases to refuel and rearm in order to take off again to escort the Schweinfurt bombers.

LeMay meanwhile hurtled through a ferocious air battle. Flak had begun coming up at Woensdrecht, within minutes after the B-17s had crossed the North Sea. Eight minutes later German fighters ripped through the formations and the battle was on. For almost two hours, until Regensburg was reached, the violent battle ensued and both German and American aircraft fell. LeMay and his surviving men placed the bombs neatly into the Messerschmitt factories, hitting every important building besides destroying a number of finished aircraft awaiting delivery to the Luftwaffe.

"I lost twenty-four out of my hundred and twenty-seven planes which attacked the target at Regensburg," LeMay has noted. His battered formations, however, pushed onward from Regensburg for North Africa. This confused the German fighters, who expected the B-17s to return over the same route flown on the way in. It was on this final leg of the mission that six of the Regensburg force's twenty-four losses occurred, some falling over Italy and others splashing into the Mediterranean. LeMay landed at the base at Telergma in Africa and found facilities more than primitive. His losses had been the second highest (the first: the June 13 attack on Bremen, which cost twenty-six planes) sustained by the Eighth Air Force in its year of operations. There had not been any fighter protection, so far as he could see, and upon arriving at Telergma he found that no arrangements has been made to house his men or to service the B-17s. Though he had gone to Africa himself a month before to arrange for the shuttle mission, the war had moved on in North Africa, taking LeMay's arrangements with it. LeMay was not in a good mood when he reported on the first, historic shuttle mission from England to Africa: and he was not shy about letting this be known.

LeMay's Regensburg groups had gotten away around 9:35 A.M. But the Schweinfurt force, unable to take off in the heavy fog, was "stood down." This was a hopeful development for the waiting men; perhaps, like all the others, this mission too would be scrubbed.

During the early morning briefing, when the cover was removed from the large wall map and the men had a chance to see their route and target, there was an audible reaction. That it would be a long mission had already been gleaned by many from the bomb load and the fuel they carried. Berlin remained the favorite of the rumor mongers. Whistles, indrawn sighs, and several "Wows!" greeted the map unveiling in the briefing room of the 546th Squadron of the 384th Bombardment Group. There was a seemingly interminable ribbon

running from the base at Grafton-Underwood across the North Sea, over occupied Holland, and deep into Germany. There had never been so long a ribbon before.

Considering the probabilities which the crews must face, a special effort was made by the briefing officers to stress the importance of Schweinfurt as a target; why they carried a mixed bomb load of five-hundred-pound general-purpose bombs and incendiaries: the ball-bearing factories at Schweinfurt were floored with wood. This was, they were informed, so that if a bearing dropped to the floor it would not be damaged. No detail was too minute, apparently. The GPs would open up the factories and the incendiaries would set them ablaze. A thorough job must be done, for "we don't want to have to go back there."

Lieutenant Frank A. Celentano, ex-Cornell law student, and a navigator in the 546th Squadron, sat through the briefing in a state of unease. He had been assigned to a strange ship, *Lucky Thirteen,* because his regular plane, *Battle Wagon,* was under repair. But that was not the worst of it. The squadron had been assigned the low position in the 384th Group's formation—low and at the rear: "Coffin Corner." In this most vulnerable position in the formation, German fighters generally struck with most telling effect.

And then the waiting followed. "If you didn't get off right away," Celentano recalls laconically, "you lost enthusiasm." The longer the wait, the more apprehensive the crews became; tension set in. The longer they waited, the more likely the Germans would guess the target. "Word had gone out that the mission was bound to be called off. We were hoping it would be, particularly because of the weather. The danger of collision was ever-present. There was nothing quite so chilling as pulling up above the clouds into the clear air and seeing a column of black smoke rising up from the clouds. It was always a sign that two planes had come together in the overcast."

For more than three hours Celentano and the other crews of 230 Flying Fortresses had a good deal to think about: from the soupy English weather to the long ribbon on the map. And then, unexpectedly, about one in the afternoon, a green flare shot up from the control tower and it was time to crank engines. Celentano settled in his position in

Lieutenant Frank Celentano, navigator of the 546th Squadron, 384th Group, who went to Schweinfurt for the first time in Lucky Thirteen *in the low rear position in the bomber stream—"Coffin Corner" to airmen.*

(FRANK CELENTANO)

the nose of *Lucky Thirteen* as pilot Lieutenant Philip M. Algar gracefully lifted the heavy B-17 off the runway and climbed, without incident, through the clouds. He tucked the plane into Coffin Corner at the end of the 384th's bomber stream, the eighteenth plane in the formation. Major Thomas P. Beckett, leading the group that day, brought them into the wing formation, which then joined the division, led by Brigadier General Robert Williams.

Even before they arrived over Germany, *Lucky Thirteen*'s luck had gone bad. Over Holland the formation had come under 20-mm. attack and *Lucky Thirteen* rocked to the blast of a hit in the plane's center section. Both waist gunners, Loring C. Miller and John Schimenek, were hit. Miller, unaware of his own injury—a sliver of shell had punctured his lung—called in to inform Algar that Schimenek had been hit. He said nothing about himself. But soon Miller was too busy to think about the pain in his chest.

"There were at least 200 enemy fighters attacking us," Celentano was later quoted in the London *Daily Herald*. "F.W. 190's, some with the old yellow noses, some painted black and some half black and white. Some were painted just like our P.47s and maneuvered like them but they did not fool us.

"It's a lot of ballyhoo to say that Germany's first-line fighters have all been shot down. They came at us four abreast and fought like hell."

"When we got over the enemy coast we had to lose altitude because of the lowering overcast," Beckett in the lead plane related later. "That's where the fighters got to us. Although we had fighter support, enemy fighters kept hitting us anyhow."

During the fighter attack, mainly by FW-190s, Miller manned his waist gun, but the seriousness of his wound began to show. He remained, however, at his gun, firing at the countless attackers. Algar ordered radio operator Francis Gerow to take over Miller's gun and Miller was forced to lie down. Even then he indicated to Schimenek that he was all right and need no attention and that Schimenek must remain at his own gun.

"After the fighters left," Beckett continued, "we climbed back to altitude. When we got to the target there were no fighters there." But by this time there were a number of 384th planes gone too. Celentano found that *Lucky Thirteen* had graduated from Coffin Corner during the battle to squadron lead— and that there remained only two or three planes to lead.

Lead navigator of the 384th was Lieutenant Edward J. Knowling, who brought the survivors of the

A Flying Fortress neatly tucked into formation—in "Coffin Corner."

(ERIK MILLER/LOCKHEED-CALIFORNIA)

The 384th encounters flak over the target; bombs have begun to descend through the overcast and the flak comes up. German fighters generally pulled away at this point to let the radar-directed antiaircraft guns do their work. (ROBERT CHAPIN)

A B-17 falls over Schweinfurt after a fighter attack.
(U. S. AIR FORCE)

hour-long fighter assault over Schweinfurt. A squadron commander of one of the other groups, the 305th, formerly commanded by LeMay, observed bitterly, "Our navigator has an easy job today. All he has to do is follow the trail of burning Fortresses and parachutes from the task forces ahead of us."

The 384th's lead bombardier was Second Lieutenant Joseph W. Baggs, who found the target area partially obscured by a smoke screen. As he came in, eye peering through the bombsight, he picked what appeared to be the target. "At that time it was about the only thing I could see that resembled the target as described," he said at the debriefing later. "But as we got closer I could see our target at the right. I saw the race track and knew where I was. . . ." Correcting and adjusting his sight, Baggs led the 384th to the target. "As we got over the target we noticed that the first building on the target was on fire," Baggs said.

In *Lucky Thirteen* it was obvious that if Loring Miller was to have any chance for life, the plane would have to get below an altitude at which an oxygen mask was required. As soon as the bombs were dropped into the ball-bearing factory area, Celentano plotted the shortest course for Grafton-Underwood. Algar then began an immediate but gradual descent to a lower altitude; he also throttled to maximum speed. From time to time, until normal breathing could be resumed, the now unconscious Miller had to have his oxygen mask removed to empty it of blood. Otherwise he might have drowned in his own blood.

Celentano had plotted their route so skillfully that *Lucky Thirteen* skirted most of the heavy flak areas, and, as luck would have it, there were no further fighter attacks. By this time, perhaps, the German fighter pilots were exhausted, after fighting LeMay's Regensburg force earlier and the Schweinfurt aircraft coming and going. *Lucky Thirteen* thundered in over Grafton-Underwood shooting red flares from the side windows, indicating wounded aboard, and as Algar touched the runway an ambulance trailed the bomber until it stopped. Schimenek and the grievously wounded Miller were rushed to the hospital. The shell fragment was removed from Miller's lung and he recovered. For his "gallantry and devotion to duty," Sergeant Loring Corwin Miller of Stockton, California, was awarded the Silver Star.

The Focke-Wulfs and flak were not the only weapons employed by the Germans that day over Schweinfurt. Teutonic genius for destruction seemed unlimited to the point of creativity. Some of the fighter bombers, Ju-88s and Me-110s, were equipped with rocket launchers and spread terror through the bomber formations when their smoking missiles pierced them. A direct rocket hit snapped a B-17 in half and trapped the entire crew in the gyrating pieces of the falling aircraft.

The sky was transformed into swiftly moving, soaring debris- and smoke-glutted battleground: tracers interlaced in beautifully intricate but mad patterns, smoke of various shadings floated among the clouds, pieces of exploded or collision-shredded aircraft fell to earth, and the sky was dotted with white (American) and yellow (German) parachutes.

Observing the battle from his perch in the nose of *Lucky Thirteen,* Frank Celentano had found it difficult to fathom; as he watched in fascinated helplessness a crewman leaped from a badly burning Fortress. The figure fell away from the distressed plane toward the safety of the earth; but when the chute opened it too was aflame. In an instant the airman's brief refuge had ended and he had a 25,000-foot fall in which to consider the fortunes of war.

Other German aircraft introduced another innovation. They actually flew over the American bombers and dropped bombs upon them timed to detonate within the bomber formations. While neither accurate nor effective, the tactic was unnerving to the American crews, and now and then a B-17 actually fell to the air-to-air bombing.

There was yet another curiously fiendish device. German fighters, FW-190s, trailing cables from which bombs dangled, approached the American bombers from above—which incidentally brought the fighter under attack from the top-turret guns of the Fortresses. When the German pilot brought his plane with the bomb dangling in the proper position, he electrically detonated it. This method was not very effective either, but during the fighting some

Back at Grafton-Underwood, ground crews anxiously search the sky for returning aircraft.

(ROBERT CHAPIN)

actually worked. As one tail gunner, Sergeant Thomas Murphy of the 381st Bombardment Group, watched, an FW blew the wing off a B-17 with the cable device.

If the German High Command did not understand its own air weapon and if the Luftwaffe High Command was remarkably ineffectual in its strategy, there was no denying the courage of the Luftwaffe's pilots or the imaginativeness of their tactics.

Despite the unrelenting ferocity of that German opposition, however, the bomber formations fought through to Schweinfurt, dropped their bombs, and then fought as tenaciously to get back to England. It was a monotony of terror. But then the German fighters began to withdraw as fuel and ammunition depleted, and the Fortresses, some of them hardly more than a pile of flying wreckage, struggled to get back home.

At Grafton-Underwood the last of the 384th's strays had begun to straggle in. Five of the eighteen planes which had taken off would never return: *Deuces Wild, Snuffy, M'Honey, Vertical Shaft,* and *Powerhouse II.* Fifty men: of these forty were taken prisoner, four escaped and made their way back to England eventually, and six were killed. One plane which circled Grafton-Underwood was *El Rauncho,* piloted by colorful Randolph Jacobs. Like *Lucky Thirteen, El Rauncho* had trouble almost from the start of the mission. Over the enemy coast a 20-mm. shell holed the left wing; that was followed by a flak burst in the wing which interfered with aileron control. The fuselage was struck, the top-turret gun simply stopped operating, and the oxygen supply of the ball turret gunner leaked. There was a gash in the tail. But no one, luckily, was hit, and Jacobs completed the mission and brought the plane home. When he lowered the landing gear and the air spun the wheels, Jacobs saw that a piece of flak had lodged in one of the tires. Suddenly, too, the two port engines sputtered out and the plane fell thousands of feet before Jacobs brought it under control about eight hundred feet over the field. The landing gear came up but there was no time to feather the windmilling propellers as he brought *El Rauncho* in for a wheels-up, belly-scraping landing.

"The *El Rauncho* pointed steeply down, then levelled off at the tree-tops and began feeling for the runway," Walter E. Owens, historian of the 384th, has written. "She must have been going a hundred and fifty miles an hour when the friction of aluminum on concrete began throwing off sparks. The plane slid at a terrific pace the full length of the runway, screeching all the way and leaving a shower of sparks behind. At the far end she whirled abruptly about and careened over an anti-aircraft emplacement, finally coming to a stop only twenty-five yards from a parked aircraft."

With studied calm Jacobs climbed out of the wreckage. After begging a light for his cigar, he turned to look at the pile of junk which had once been a Flying Fortress and said, "I guess they didn't want us to get at their nut and bolt factory."

There were thirty-six 1st Air Division B-17s missing testifying to that fact. The day's total losses, then, added up to a total of sixty Flying Fortresses lost on the Schweinfurt-Regensburg mission, more than twice the toll of any previous mission. And this does not count those planes like *El Rauncho* which, although they had returned to England, would never fly again. Six hundred men too were lost— dead, wounded, and missing—in Germany, France, and Holland. To these could be added the wounded, like Loring Miller, who would be out of action for a long time. Other planes carried severely wounded men who died days or weeks after the battle; some men were dead on arrival. In short, mere numbers of aircraft lost do not fully reveal the full extent of losses.

The bombing at Regensburg had been excellent, but that at Schweinfurt not quite so good. The Germans reported that eighty high-explosive bombs had fallen into the two major bearing plants; in one more than six hundred machines were destroyed or damaged. A drop in production followed, which gave the Germans pause. They must seek out other sources of high-quality bearings, of Swiss or Swedish manufacture if need be, and consideration would have to be given to the dispersal of ball-bearing facilities. While this would make the industry a less neat panacea target, it also produced a loss in production which was almost equally effective.

But two facts were underscored by the hard-fought missions. One was expressed bluntly by the 384th's Frank Celentano, in direct contradiction to popular newspaper reportage, when he said, "It's a lot of ballyhoo to say that Germany's first-line fighters have all been shot down." The other, hanging like a gloomy cloud over the Eighth Air

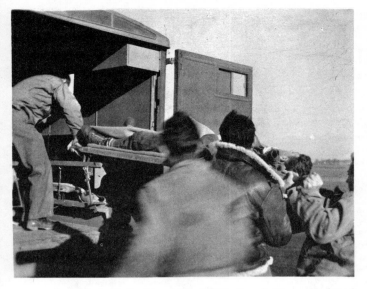

A wounded airman of the 384th Bomb Group is lifted into an ambulance after returning from a mission in a shot-up B-17. (ROBERT CHAPIN)

Force, was that they had not not wiped out Schweinfurt.

They would have to go back.

III

Meanwhile, however, small missions were "laid on" to relatively nearby targets in France and the Low Countries to which the bombers could be escorted by the P-47s. It was not until September 6 that the Eighth had recovered enough to attempt another large-scale mission—this time to bomb aircraft and friction-bearing factories in Stuttgart. The three B-24 groups which had been detached to North Africa for the Ploesti mission had returned to England and what operational strength remained of these groups was added to the B-17 divisions. Replacements made it possible finally on September 6 to dispatch no less than 407 bombers, of which 69 were B-24s. The Liberators were employed in a diversionary sweep over the North Sea while the Fortresses aimed at Stuttgart. Weather once again interfered with the operations and only 262 bombers succeeded in bombing—and most of these targets were targets of opportunity. The day's losses, however, were high: 45 Flying Fortresses.

Most of September 1943 was notable for its poor bombing weather, so experiments were made with blind-bombing equipment in certain lead aircraft. At first there were only twelve radar (H2X) sets available, which were scattered through the bombing divisions. With these few sets in lead planes, the divisions could be led directly, more or less, over a target obscured by cloud. Specially trained operators manned the equipment, and reasonably good, if not excellent, results were obtained in the early attempts. These missions marked the initiation of what would eventually be called "Pathfinder" bombings. The lead plane of each group equipped with H2X found the target, and when this plane dropped its bombs, all other planes in the group did the same. Eventually exceedingly accurate blind bombing by radar became a common practice.

However, if the Allies could find targets electronically through the overcast, so likewise could the Germans find enemy aircraft. In order to confuse gun-directing radar, various devices were used, such as "window," strips of metal-coated paper which when dropped from aircraft made it difficult for antiaircraft radar to distinguish, so to speak, the wheat from the chaff. Another device was called "carpet," a transmitter carried in aircraft for jamming radar receivers.

But in September 1943 these were experimental attempts and did not always contribute much to the Combined Bomber Operation plan. Early in October it was possible, with new planes and crews, to concentrate on industrial targets inside Germany. On October 4 more than 360 heavy bombers took off for assorted targets in the vicinity of Frankfurt, as well as French airfields and marshaling yards in western Germany.

The second week of October 1943 proved to be one of the most critical in the history of the Eighth Air Force. On the eighth a large force (more than 350) bombed Bremen and Vegesack (with a loss of thirty planes). The next day another sizable force (a total of 352) bombed various targets, ranging from naval targets in Poland to the Focke-Wulf factories at Marienburg. This last was a superb demonstration of the efficacy of Eaker's confidence in daylight precision bombardment. The factory area was blanketed by five-hundred-pound general-purpose (GP) bombs plus incendiaries and all but wiped out. The damage was so severe that

THE FLIGHT IS DROPPING "WINDOW," WHICH CREATES THE SO CALLED "WINDOW CLOUD".
THE SCOPE OF THE RADAR ON THE RIGHT SHOWS THE RESULT.

THE PLANES MUST REMAIN IN THE "CLOUD". OTHERWISE THEY WILL REGISTER ON THE RADAR SCOPE.

PLANES A AND B ARE EQUIPPED WITH CARPET. PLANE C WILL ALSO BE "HIDDEN" AS IT IS IN
THE SAME AREA. THE SCOPE AT THE RIGHT SHOWS THE RESULT.

THE PLANES HAVE MOVED CLOSER TO THE RADAR SET. PLANES B & C ARE STILL "HIDDEN"
BUT PLANE A IS TOO CLOSE AND STICKS OUT ALTHOUGH IT IS STILL JAMMING.

The workings of "window" and "carpet" as explained to airmen of the Eighth Air Force. Both devices con-fused German detection and flak-gun-aiming devices.
(ROBERT CHAPIN)

no attempt was made to repair the factory. Losses for the day amounted to twenty-eight planes. The next day, October 10, the bombers attacked rail and waterway targets at Münster. The Luftwaffe swarmed out in full fury that day, concentrating on a single group in the formation, decimating that before going on to another. Of the 236 planes bombing Münster, it was the thirteen of the 100th Bombardment Group, in the lead, which took the worst of the new tactic. Of the day's thirty losses, twelve belonged to the 100th (a turn of fate which gave rise to the legend of the "Bloody Hundredth"), the single exception being Robert Rosenthal's *Rosie's Riveters,* which alone returned to England.

The total losses of those three consecutive days in October were eighty-eight planes. At such a rate, 8th Bomber Command could be eliminated from the war in a week. The Münster mission was officially Number 114; following that a three-day pause permitted the bomber forces to recuperate for the next one.

IV

Colonel Budd Peaslee, who had served as a popular commander of the 384th during its first missions, had been made deputy wing commander of the 40th Wing (the 92nd, 305th, and 306th Bombardment Groups) of the 1st Air Division. When Mission 115 was "laid on" it was Peaslee's turn to act as 1st Division air commander for the mission.

"From the beginning," Peaslee has written, "Mission Number 115 was in doubt. A persistent low overcast had hung over the English bases for three days." To the mission-scarred men, the day broke propitiously. "There was considerable speculation that the mission would be scrubbed and they could return to their sacks till noon. This was a happy thought but it was not to be."

Briefings were held in the dank, bone-chilling darkness as crews assembled to learn of the day's target. A dull silence invariably descended when the map was uncovered showing the black ribbon stretching from England into Germany. *Yank* staff correspondent Walter Peters attended one of these briefings; he was detailed to fly that day in the first combat mission of a B-17 newly named *Yank.* Upon leaving the briefing room he overheard an

erudite though unsophisticated radio-gunner offer the intelligence that the city they were to attack that October 14 was "named afer a very special pig."

Apparently, to the unseasoned airman the name of Schweinfurt had little other significance.

To Budd Peaslee it had more than etymological portent. His old command, the 384th, had bled over Schweinfurt in August. It meant, too, that as air commander of the 40th Wing, he would lead them again along with the rest of the 1st Division deeply into Germany and, he hoped, back. The hope was that the "first" Schweinfurt had proved so rough a mission because of chance; the second might very well prove to be a "milk run" (an easy mission).

As air commander Peaslee was to fly as copilot in the lead aircraft, flown by Captain James K. McLaughlin of the 92nd Bombardment Group. At different points over England the 92nd would be joined by the 305th (Curtis LeMay's old command) and 306th Groups. These three groups constituted

Budd Peaslee, air commander of the 1st Division on Mission 115 (Schweinfurt), October 14, 1943.

(ROBERT CHAPIN)

A B-17 of the 303rd Bomb Group in an East Anglian wheat field near Molesworth before the Schweinfurt mission. (U. S. AIR FORCE)

the 40th Combat Bombardment Wing. Also participating would be the 91st and 381st Groups (under supervision of the 1st Combat Bombardment Wing) and the 41st Wing (303rd, 379th, and 384th Groups). These three wings made up the striking force of the 1st Air Division, which was to contribute 149 Flying Fortresses to the striking force.

The 2nd Air Division, B-24s of the 93rd and 392nd Groups, was also to bomb Schweinfurt. Their sixty Liberators, however, did not get to the target.

The 3rd Air Division was to contribute seven groups (also combined into wings for command purposes): the 94th, 95th, 96th, 100th, 385th, 388th, and 390th. This division would provide a total of 142 Flying Fortresses.

Theoretically, if all went as planned, a total of 291 Fortresses and 60 Liberators were to go to Schweinfurt. But it was not to be. The Liberator bases, for example, were so badly fogged in that only 29 even managed to get off the ground. Unable to form up in the dense, swirling fog, 8 returned to their bases and the remaining 21 made a diversionary sweep toward Emden, hoping thus to draw away some of the German fighters from the B-17s, if they ever got off.

Peaslee sat in the left-hand seat of McLaughlin's Fortress, eyes on the control tower. There was still a question of whether or not Mission 115 would actually take place. But a weather plane, having crossed over Schweinfurt, radioed back that the target area was clear. The green flare went up and

the mission was on. McLaughlin throttled up the great plane and with Peaslee keeping an eye on the runway (to assure that the plane remained on the fog-enshrouded concrete), McLaughlin took off on instruments; at intervals, eighteen other 92nd Group B-17s followed. Above the clouds, in the brilliant sunlight, the planes assembled into combat boxes, proceeded to the assembly point, where the 306th Group joined them.

But where was the 305th? On this mission the group had been assigned the low position in the wing. However, in the confusion of attempting to assemble above the clouds, the 305th was unable to find the planes in the 40th Wing. Rather than scrub the mission, and thus deny the formation its sixteen aircraft, Major G. G. Y. Normand, in the lead B-17 of the 305th, attached to the 1st Wing. This left Peaslee's 40th Wing short an entire group. According to SOP (Standard Operating Procedure), he would have been justified in aborting; instead Peaslee relinquished command of the mission to Colonel Archie J. Olds, Jr. (then commander of the 45th Combat Wing). Peaslee then ordered his two groups to join up with the three groups of the 41st Wing.

One of the components of the 41st Wing was his old group, the 384th. On this Thursday Frank Celentano was acting as lead navigator for the group; he was in his regular plane, *Battle Wagon,* also carrying the 384th's air commander, Major George W. Harris. They lifted carefully through the haze, formed up, and proceeded toward Schweinfurt. Above the clouds it was a welcome sight to see the other B-17s of the group as well as the P-47s of the 56th and 353rd Fighter Groups (about a hundred in all), assigned to escort the bombers part of the way. On the return, also, they were to be waiting to protect the bombers.

Not so welcome, however, was the loss of several B-17s, forced to turn back because of engine trouble or some other mechanical malfunction. Twenty-six Fortresses returned to their bases for such reasons. The combined forces of the two air task forces were reduced from 291 to 265 Flying Fortresses. Once the bombers crossed the enemy coast the German fighters began pouncing on them. The American Thunderbolts swept down to intercept, and although many succeeded, they did not prevent some of the Me-109s and FW-190s from sweeping through the bomber formations. And when the P-47s were forced to turn back near Aachen because of their limited fuel supply, the Luftwaffe smashed down upon the B-17s in the most savage aerial assault of the war.

It was the first Schweinfurt all over again, with deadly interest. The interceptions by German fighters were so finely co-ordinated and timed that a suspicion arose (never actually confirmed, however) that the Luftwaffe had been forewarned of the mission. Whether or not this was true, the Germans were very well prepared for the invaders. Every possible technique employed in the past —unnerving head-on fighter attacks, cannons, rockets lobbed into the formations from the rear, and air-to-air bombing, as well as flak—was unleashed that day. If Ploesti represented a burning, low-level inferno, the second Schweinfurt was a freezing, high-level (above twenty thousand feet) inferno.

Wave after wave of German fighters, their guns winking in the wings, tore at the formations again and again. As at Münster, there was an attempt to concentrate upon a definite portion of the bomber stream. The 1st Division received the brunt of the attacks, with special attention to the lead planes, for the Germans knew that the air commander, lead

Fortresses of the 91st Bomb Group over Schweinfurt.
(U. S. AIR FORCE)

navigator, and lead bombardier flew in this plane. Likewise, the group in Coffin Corner was attacked ferociously. In this spot in the 1st Division it was the 305th Group, which had missed the rendezvous with Peaslee over England and had attached itself to the 1st Combat Wing. The Thunderbolts had barely turned for England when the 305th planes took their first mauling—and it continued all the way to Schweinfurt. Curiously, the battle let up over Schweinfurt itself, partly because the German fighters had to return to their bases to refuel—and to give the flak a chance. About two-forty in the afternoon the first bombs of the 1st Division fell upon Schweinfurt and continued to fall for about six minutes. Six minutes after that, at 2:52 P.M., the first bombs of the 3rd Division began tumbling from the bomb bays. The sky filled with 1000-pound and 500-pound high-explosive as well as 100-pound incendiary bombs, a total of 395 tons of the HE and 88 tons of incendiaries. And despite the ordeal through which the survivors had passed, the bombing was remarkably accurate and, as was later learned, effective.

But of the 291 bombers which in the original plan were to have set out for Schweinfurt, only 228 actually succeeded in placing their bombs on the target. The rest, other than those planes which had aborted, lay burning along the penetration route of the two air divisions. On the return flight, too, German fighter attacks were relentlessly pressed. The fighting was swift, concentrated, and confused; Fortress gunners claimed 186 German planes that day (although the more accurate total may have been closer to 35). Even if the claims had been realistic, it would still have been a costly exchange.

Sixty Flying Fortresses were lost over the Continent and 5 others were abandoned over England, making a total of 65 B-17s totally destroyed. In addition, 140 planes had returned in various stages of damage, 17 beyond possibility of repair. The human toll was even more depressing: 600 men were missing, the fate of many never to be known. Many died in exploding planes, or were trapped in gyrating B-17s, or were killed in fighter attacks or by flak.

The orphan 305th Group lost twelve of its sixteen aircraft before reaching Schweinfurt; three B-17s of the 305th dropped bombs on Schweinfurt—and only two returned to their English base at Chelveston

Bomb run: 91st Bomb Group Flying Fortress Bomb Boogie *now under the control of the bombardier in*

the nose as he zeroes in on the target. The bomb bay doors are open awaiting the moment of "bombs away." (U. S. AIR FORCE)

(one had aborted earlier in the mission). The 306th Group lost ten planes, which made it the second in losses. The 92nd Group, the third component of the 40th Wing, lost six B-17s (plus another which crash-landed in England), so that Peaslee's 40th Wing lost twenty-nine planes over the Continent, about half of the total of the entire mission.

High losses in individual units had a despairing effect on the survivors in those units and rendered them less potent while replacement crews were trained.

Schweinfurt revealed the terrible workings of chance in aerial warfare (always present in the form of flak), for not all units came under strong fighter attack. In part, the fate of an individual aircraft depended on its position in the formation. Although every group in the 1st Air Division lost at least one plane, there were three in the 3rd Division which did not lose a single B-17 (the 100th, 385th, and 388th). Bruce R. Riley, pilot of *Riley and Crew,* flew to Schweinfurt with the 3rd Air Division and found that "from the standpoint of the 390th Bomb Group, [it] was a rather routine mission. . . . During the short times I was

Strike photo of the 100th Bomb Group, Schweinfurt, Thursday, October 14, 1943. (U. S. AIR FORCE)

"Now we have got Schweinfurt," *General Arnold said after Mission 115, and so it had appeared to the crews that left it burning. Schweinfurt was hard hit, but it was* *not finished. But so had the Eighth Air Force been hard hit, if not finished.* (U. S. AIR FORCE)

able to glance away from our formation, I saw at least three Forts blow up ahead over the target, probably due to direct hits by flak. Our one loss was due to a fighter attack that ruptured three out of four fuel tanks on the plane that went down."

If chance, luck, fortune, or whatever that unknown but ever present factor present in every air battle was operative, so was truth. Despite the frightful and wholesale onslaught and the withering sight of blasted, burning, and falling planes, the bomber crews thrust on through the opposing German fighters, despite their various gadgets of destruction. There were no aborts over Germany; aircraft continued over the targets on less than full

engine power, some made bomb runs (the average time was six minutes) while burning, during which time it was likely that a B-17 would explode. Some did.

That truth was the fact of American courage. A second truth was more difficult to face. The losses over Schweinfurt, added to those losses already accumulated during the early weeks of October, proved clearly that such deep penetrations into Germany without fighter escort were self-defeating. The cost in men and aircraft was not worth it, however strategically important the target.

The October 14, 1943, Schweinfurt attack was, in fact, the most effective upon that target made

SCHWEINFURT
K: 1785
Neg. No. 32020

during the entire course of the war. There were fifteen others, however, which would mean fourteen sequels to the mission which Martin Caidin so aptly called "Black Thursday." It would appear, therefore, that when General Arnold announced to the newspapers, "Now we have got Schweinfurt," he was being overoptimistic. He was also being honest, insofar as he knew. Secret reports from inside Germany via neutral Sweden hinted at great devastation at Schweinfurt. Reconnaissance photographs, as well as the strike photos, sustained this belief. The Air Force informed its crews, via the official publication *Impact,* that "All five plants—representing about 65 per cent of the ball- and roller-bearing capacity of Germany—were so heavily damaged that *our bombers may never have to go back.*"

And they did not go back to Schweinfurt, not for another four months. The truth is that they could *not* go back. Air superiority over Germany had reverted to the Luftwaffe. But when they did go back, in the spring of 1944, in conjunction with the RAF's Bomber Command—the British bombed Schweinfurt for the first time on February 24, 1944 —many wondered why it was necessary if such devastation had been wrought in October.

Schweinfurt had suffered heavy destruction, which had interfered with production. But not forever, as intimated in the optimistic reports, but for a month and a half. Since Schweinfurt was granted four months of grace, there was time to repair the damage and to reorganize the anti-friction-bearing industry, which, as reported in the *United States Strategic Bombing Survey* (September 30, 1945), "precipitated, also, the disperal of the industry from Schweinfurt, forced the expansion or construction of old and new plants, and accelerated the program of substitution and redesign in order to reduce the excessive and often luxurious use of bearings in many types of equipment."

Under the organizing genius of Hitler's armament czar Albert Speer and more directly under Speer's special commissioner for ball bearings, Philip Kessler, the co-ordination of the industry was undertaken to disperse the installations as well as to in-

Crew of Battle Wagon *of the 384th Bomb Group assemble for a debriefing after the "rugged" mission to Schweinfurt. The group lost a total of nine B-17s on the mission, six over enemy-held territory and three battle-damaged planes abandoned over Britain.*
(FRANK CELENTANO)

ventory stock. The latter contained surprises for all, including the Germans. It was discovered that large surpluses of anti-friction bearings were stored in Germany by the millions and that, however effective the raid upon Schweinfurt had been, many industries requiring ball bearings continued to operate normally; redistribution of surplus stock made up for any losses.

The RAF and Eighth Air Force bombers joined eventually to eliminate Schweinfurt from the war map, but by then, because of dispersal, Schweinfurt was no longer a vital military target. By October 9, 1944, when the Eighth Air Force dropped more than eight hundred tons of bombs upon Schweinfurt, it was "a city which was less than one-half as important industrially as in August 1943," according to the *United States Strategic Bombing Survey.*

"Now we [had] got Schweinfurt," but it no longer mattered. Bomber crews viewed the Schweinfurt mission with characteristic dark humor but with more realism when they spoke of Black Thursday as the day when "We took out 150% of the ball-bearing industry."

It would be inequitous to assert bluntly that the two Schweinfurt missions accomplished nothing— despite the failure of the second, for all its pre-

Post-mission reconnaissance photo showing the heavily damaged factory areas of Schweinfurt.
(U. S. AIR FORCE)

cision, to "take out" the ball-bearing industry. In purely objective terms, numbers, percentages, the missions were frightfully expensive in loss of life and aircraft, but they were not total failures. The second mission to Schweinfurt, especially, has become a symbol of both courage and failure. That the one was not enough to prevent the other lay in the nature of the target itself and in the fact that long daylight flights without escort were doomed to terrible opposition.

Schweinfurt was not the greatest loss suffered by the U. S. Air Force in the course of the war; later battles over Berlin claimed more bombers. It was the worst to date.

It was, in a word current at the time, "rugged." But any mission whatever the number or percentage of loss, was "rugged" if your plane did not return or did return badly chewed up by the Luftwaffe. Airmen who fought in the two major theaters of operations invariably referred to Europe as "the Big League" because of the potency of Luftwaffe fighters during the waning days of 1943 and the flak. Heavy bombardment during daylight, without massive formations and fighter protection, seemed to be at an impasse.

But inside Germany, unknown to Allied air leaders arguing about the cost of daylight missions and the foolishness of panacea targets, there was serious consternation. The bombing was taking on a serious pattern, no longer the derring-do of knocking out a dam, or a foolhardy low-level attack on an oil field. The bombing was beginning to look more businesslike, less haphazard.

"The Luftwaffe leaders knew that they could not stop our bombers," Eaker has observed, "and save their weapons-making establishments." A subtle, almost sudden twist had come—at great cost perhaps, but it had come.

"For Germany," Eaker concluded, "it marked the beginning of the end."

VOLUME THREE

OUTRAGED SKIES

BOOK I
Kenney's Kids

I

BUCCANEER

THE Pacific theater of operations offered an infinity of vista: great stretches of water and curving horizons, broken only by jungle-gnarled islands, coruscated atolls, and palm-fringed islets. There was more water than land and more sky than either. Clearly it was not a setting for massive land battles, such as Europe was, and distance precluded the strategic bombardment of the Japanese homeland. Instead, until air bases could be established within range of Japan, a series of contained, savage land battles must be fought, along with far-flung naval engagements and air battles. The deeper strategy lay in eliminating Japanese air power, in order to permit Allied naval and ground troops to function.

At Midway it had been revealed, to those receptive to revelation, that the war in the Pacific would be dominated, even resolved, by aircraft and not the battleship. Classic sea-borne warfare by the books was finished in the Pacific no less than land war in Europe. Those who clung to the old concepts were committed to certain defeat. Midway had proved this; but if it had proved that Japan could no longer win the Pacific war, that the end was not immediately in view was equally certain.

The United States Navy coveted all that Pacific water, and with its triumph through carrier aviation at Midway, it had raised its eyes to the heavens also. The Navy was most anxious to avenge Pearl

General Douglas MacArthur, General Sir Thomas Blamey, commander of Australian ground forces in the Southwest Pacific, and MacArthur's Chief of Staff, Lieutenant General Richard K. Sutherland. Before Kenney could feel he rightfully commanded MacArthur's air force, he found he had to come to a proper understanding with Sutherland, who, though he brilliantly served MacArthur, liked having his finger in every pie—including Kenney's air forces. Kenney, putting his cards on the table in characteristic out-in-the-open manner, emerged as the only and full commander of the air forces in the Southwest Pacific—and remained as such for the rest of the war.

(U. S. ARMY)

Curtiss C-46 "Commando" of Air Transport Command flying over "the Hump" between India and China. Not only were the U.S. air forces and the RAF in- *volved in fighting the Japanese in the air, the problem of supplies of the entire China-Burma-India theater was solved by air.* (U. S. AIR FORCE)

Harbor, hoping to assume full strategic control of the Pacific. Therein lay sufficient fuel for interservice argument, with enough remaining for international disagreements as well. The British had their hands full in the China-Burma-India theater, what with personal intrigues and a complex supply problem; in China proper Chennault continued to have to make do with what little he could get from the United States and the even less he received from Chiang Kai-shek. These theaters were preponderantly land masses and the problem of their internal politics interfered only indirectly with the Pacific.

All that stood between the U. S. Navy and full

control of the Pacific was General Douglas MacArthur. After enduring the ignominy of being booted out of the Philippines, the patrician, vain, and egocentric MacArthur found small consolation in being given half command of a second-rate war. MacArthur's share of the theater, called the Southwest Pacific Area, included, running southward, those regions in Japanese hands, the Philippines, Borneo, Celebes, New Guinea (the northern coast of which in time was overrun also), and the great subcontinent of Australia, which lay in the path of the invaders and where MacArthur languished, awaiting definition of his command.

The remainder of the Pacific "belonged" to Admiral Chester W. Nimitz, based at Pearl Harbor. A line running north and south, eventually along the 159th meridian just east of Australia cut through the Solomon Islands, skirting one of the southernmost of the group, Guadalcanal (which placed it technically under naval jurisdiction), while leaving the largest island, Bougainville (in the north) under MacArthur's jurisdiction. The definition of command became at times rather hazy, if not heated. In their respective theaters, MacArthur and Nimitz were absolute monarchs commanding all forces, naval, ground, and air. Where the battle lines merged or overlapped, the question of jurisdiction must be decided by co-operation, which was not always readily forthcoming in the scramble for supplies, men, matériel, and power.

Where MacArthur was motivated by a histrionic sense of his position in history, Nimitz was a cool professional Navy man who aimed for as much co-operation as possible. MacArthur's real naval bête noire was Admiral Ernest J. King, Chief of Naval Operations, Commander in Chief, United States Navy. King, blunt, decisive, brilliant—as was MacArthur—viewed the war from the standpoint of the United States Navy. Not only did this earn him the enmity of such men as Churchill (a navy man himself), but of a host of U. S. Army, Air Force, and Navy men as well.

MacArthur suspected King's Pacific planning was a personal vendetta out of Washington. That Europe was the favored battleground in 1942 was but another unfortunate sting, for the supplies required for MacArthur's avowed return to the Philippines were drained away. Isolated as he was in Australia, MacArthur pondered the defense of that great land mass with few troops, a worn-out and he believed a "disloyal" air force, and little hope of acquiring the means and the men to turn the losing defensive war into the offensive.

MacArthur assumed command of the Southwest Pacific Area on April 18, 1942. "None of the three elements of my command—naval, air or ground— was adequate " he said. He had left more troops in the Philippines than he had at his disposal in Australia, and these were either the remnants of the fighting which had gone before or green troops, illequipped and poorly trained. His small naval detachment had no carriers. His air force, commanded by Lieutenant General George H. Brett, was little more than a ragtag of P-40s, P-400s (an early export model of the Bell P-39, Airacobra), P-39s, and a few worn-out B-17s, the even more worn Douglas A-24s (the Air Force version of the Navy's Dauntless) which were joined later by a trickle of B-25s and B-26s.

Brett was not regarded by MacArthur as one of the loyal ones (primarily because Brett did not get along with MacArthur's Chief of Staff, Major General Richard K. Sutherland). As far as the entire Air Force was concerned, MacArthur was certain it would contribute little to the war. Brett and MacArthur were thoroughly estranged, and Sutherland by no means eased the situation. Sutherland, in fact, enjoyed the position of all but running the show and, as described by an old classmate of his at the Army War College, "rubbed people the wrong way. He was egotistic, like most people, but an unfortunate bit of arrogance combined with his egotism had made him almost universally disliked."

From Australia MacArthur hoped to lunge northward via New Guinea, at the great Japanese base at Rabaul, in New Britain. From Rabaul, Japanese fighters and bombers were positioned to sweep down into New Guinea to attack the major Allied base at Port Moresby, to initiate the assault upon Australia. On the other hand, the Navy had its attention drawn to the Solomons, where great activity on Guadalcanal made it obvious that the Japanese were constructing an air base there. From the Solomons, by bombing Allied bases in the New Hebrides and New Caledonia, the Japanese could eventually cut the supply lines to Australia as well as the South Pacific. From air fields in the Solomons also the Japanese could protect Rabaul, with its concentration of ships and aircraft.

Brett had much to contend with as the commander of the Allied Air Forces in the Southwest Pacific besides Sutherland. His personality, a mingling of hauteur and ego, caused trouble too. Brett could not bring himself to warm up to the Australians, particularly with its governmental representatives, members of a "radical" Labour government and therefore "left wing." The problem of replacement and supply was formidable and the morale of exhausted crews was low. Fatigued men flew long distances, much of it over water (the 49th Fighter Group, with its P-40s, for example, was based at

Darwin in northern Australia), to engage in combat with superior Japanese aircraft, or to drop a small load of bombs without appreciable results. Planes that should have been junked were patched and flown until they fell apart. Some did, and airmen resented serving in a forgotten theater, forgotten because of the "Hitler first" strategy. Deliveries of supplies arrived slowly; and crates when they finally came, were found to have been pilfered by desperate crews en route. Disgruntled by poor food, miserable living conditions, and the methods of the Australian Air Force and its part in the operations, American airmen had grown apathetic and believed that if conditions prevailed, an Allied victory was hopeless.

The sacking of Brett would not solve all of the problems, but according to the workings of the military mind he was "responsible" (momentarily and conveniently excluding the Japanese) and therefore must go. And so it was that on August 4, 1942, stubby, cocky, pugnacious, and anything but aristocratic Major General George C. Kenney succeeded Brett as air commander in the Southwest Pacific. This tough, outspoken, practical, no-nonsense fighter found himself a rather lone figure in a nest of prima donnas and debilitated warriors.

Kenney, upon arriving in Brisbane, seat of MacArthur's command, was established in the air-conditioned Lennon's Hotel and spent some time listening to Sutherland berating the Australians, various American officers, with emphasis upon the consistently unlucky Lewis H. Brereton (who had been MacArthur's air commander in the Philippines), and, of course, the obstinate Brett. The Air Force was especially vile: ". . . none of Brett's staff or senior commanders was any good, the pilots didn't know much about flying, the bombers couldn't hit anything and knew nothing about proper maintenance of their equipment or how to handle their supplies. He also thought there was some question about the kids having much stomach for fighting. . . . In fact, I heard just about everyone hauled over the coals except Douglas MacArthur and Richard K. Sutherland."

Shrewdly the canny ex-World War I fighter pilot, whose experience with aircraft maintenance, production, and manipulation went back more than two decades, said little at this point. But he thought, ". . . Sutherland was inclined to overemphasize his [own] smattering of knowledge of aviation."

George Kenney, who ran the "air show" in Mac-Arthur's section of the Pacific. Down to earth, pragmatic, loyal, Kenney not only won over MacArthur but also his own men, whom he called "kids," because, in the main, that was what they were.

(U. S. AIR FORCE)

It was not until the next morning that Kenney was ushered in to meet with MacArthur, in lonely splendor, on the eighth floor of a nine-story office building in downtown Brisbane. After initial formalities, MacArthur began pacing and speaking, repeating the same criticisms of the Air Force which Sutherland had spouted the evening before. In MacArthur's view, "air personnel had gone beyond just being antagonistic to his headquarters, to the point of disloyalty. He would not stand for disloyalty."

During a pause in the outpouring of words, Kenney rose to full height (he was about a head shorter than MacArthur), deciding "it was time to lay my cards on the table."

He began by reminding MacArthur that he had come out to the Pacific because MacArthur had requested him and that "as long as he had had enough confidence in me to ask for me to be sent out to run his air show for him, I intended to do that very

B-17E, one of the few, based near Mareeba, Australia.
"A formation of five or six B-17s was regarded . . . as
. . . impressive . . ." (U. S. AIR FORCE)

thing." Kenney bluntly told the general that he could
run an "air show" better than or as well as anyone
available. The emphasis was on the fact that he—
Kenney—would run the air show. As for loyalty,
the day that Kenney no longer felt loyal to his chief,
"I would come and tell him so and at that time I
would be packed up and ready for the orders sending me back home."

MacArthur's stormy expression changed; the
fierce glint left his eyes. He studied the small man
before him, appraising him, then walked over, threw
an arm around Kenney's shoulders, and said,
"George, I think we are going to get along together
all right."

George Kenney served as air commander in the
Pacific from that day until the end of the war. If
he could pledge loyalty to MacArthur, whom he
genuinely admired, it was exceeded only by his devotion to his "kids," the young airmen who were
then fighting a great war with so little.

With characteristic promptitude, Kenney applied
himself to finding out what was wrong. He had
arrived on July 28 and would not assume command
until August 4. He found Brett's directorate system,
"with about a dozen people issuing orders in the
commander's name, . . . too complicated for me. I
decided to see how it worked first but I was afraid
I was not smart enough to figure it out. Furthermore, it looked to me as if there were too many
people in the headquarters. . . ."

In the interests of Allied co-operation, Kenney
found a rigid attempt to intermix Australian and
American throughout the organization. Obviously, it
did not always work. Despite the crowded office,
Kenney learned also that the bulk of the Allied
Air Staff, along with all personnel and supply records, was based in Melbourne about eight hundred
miles distant. But not so distant as MacArthur, only
three floors above in the same building. Brett could
never reach the commander and was forced always
to deal through Sutherland. This was not Kenney's
way of running an air show.

That same evening he borrowed Brett's Flying
Fortress, the famed *Swoose*, which enjoyed a better
press than Brett and took off for the forward bases

in Australia and in New Guinea. At Port Moresby, in southern New Guinea, Kenney found little to comfort him. The organization and procedure were "chaotic." Bombing missions, for example, were assigned out of Brett's headquarters in Brisbane. Orders were then sent to Major General Ralph Royce in Townsville to the north; Royce, in turn, notified the 19th Bombardment Group (H), based at Mareeba, about two hundred miles north of Townsville, and "the 19th Group sent the number of airplanes it had in commission to Port Moresby, where they were refueled, given their final 'briefing' on weather conditions along the route to the target and whatever data had been picked up by air reconnaissance.

"The fighter group at Port Moresby [35th Fighter Group] sat around waiting for the Japs to come over and tried to get off the ground in time to intercept them, which they seldom did, as the warning service rarely gave the fighters over five minutes' notice that the Nip planes were on the way." Those aircraft which did get off the ground seemed to operate without leadership, even on bombing missions. A formation of five or six B-17s was regarded as an impressive number then in the Pacific, although what with problems with weather or engines, it was a good mission if three aircraft found the target—Japanese shipping or the bases at Rabaul. But the meager accomplishment rarely made the effort worth it. Kenney found, too, that aircrews frequently abandoned missions when Japanese aircraft intercepted them, fearing that a single bullet would detonate either the auxiliary fuel tanks or the bomb load. No one had thought to inform them that this was not necessarily true.

If MacArthur demanded that a man be loyal, Kenney insisted that he be an "operator." Within days after his arrival and inspection of conditions, quite a number of non-operators were sent back to the States. He found the system of supply especially reprehensible, overladen with an obsession with paper formality. "An average time of one month elapsed from the time the requisition started until it was returned, generally with the notation 'Not available' or 'Improperly filled out.'" When told that desperately needed replacement parts for combat aircraft were denied to the fighting units, Kenney found it difficult to believe, "but the kids made me eat my words when they showed me a whole filing case of returned requisition forms. I

took along a handful for future reference and as evidence that some of the people in the organization were playing on the wrong team."

Immediately, too, Kenney began sending in his own team of operators. He had discussed his views on the air situation in Australia and New Guinea with MacArthur, asking for authority to send anyone home he regarded as "deadwood." MacArthur concurred and Kenney moved quickly. He found men who were genuinely tired from earlier campaigns, or ill from Australian heat or New Guinea jungle; they deserved relief, but those "who were not pulling their weight could go home and the rest would move north to take their turns eating canned food and living in grass huts on the edge of the jungle."

Kenney had been preceded to the area by two competent officers, Brigadier Generals Kenneth N. Walker, a bombardment specialist, and Ennis C. Whitehead, a fighter commander. In time Walker would head Kenny's bomber command and Whitehead, as Kenney's deputy, moved into Port Moresby to command the advanced echelon of what was to become the Fifth Air Force. With him Kenney had brought young Major William Benn, who had served as his aide when Kenney was commander of the Fourth Air Force in San Francisco. Benn, as were Walker and Whitehead, was definitely an operator. Anxious to serve in a combat unit Benn was happy to be given command of the 63rd Squadron of the 43rd Bombardment Group, which at the time of Kenney's advent was depleted—"all they had left was a flag and a couple of guys to hold it up." As soon as the 43rd Group became operational with B-17s, it would take the work load off the much abused 19th Bomb Group, then commanded by Lieutenant Colonel Richard N. Carmichael. The 19th Group had been, in Kenney's words, "kicked out of the Philippines and out of Java and kicked around ever since."

Upon his arrival Kenney had requested an inventory of aircraft strength (when he had asked Brett, the latter told him simply that he did not know). According to the books, Kenney learned in a few days that he had "in the United States part of the show, 245 fighters, 53 light bombers, 70 medium bombers, 62 heavy bombers, 36 transports, and 51 miscellaneous aircraft, or a total of 517. . . . The Australian Royal Air Force listed 22

An Airacobra and a B-17 nestled in revetments near Port Moresby, New Guinea. The P-39 was a disad- *vantaged contender as far as the Zero was concerned; the Fortress, the "E," with a stinger in the tail was respected by Japanese pilots.* (U. S. AIR FORCE)

squadrons, but most of these were equipped with training planes doing anti-submarine patrol off the coasts of Australia itself. Two fighter squadrons in New Guinea had a total of 40 planes, and four reconnaissance squadrons had a total of 30 aircraft."

But out of the 245 American fighters, 170 were awaiting salvage or were being overhauled, none of the light bombers were ready for operations, and "only 37 mediums were in shape or had guns and bomb racks to go to war with." Of the 62 heavy bombers only 43 were more or less fit to fly; less than half of the mixed bag of transports were flyable. As for the "miscellaneous" aircraft, none was fit for combat. A Dutch squadron, equipped with American B-25s, was training but required a good deal of time before it would be ready for combat.

"All told I had about 150 American and 70 Australian aircraft, scattered from Darwin to Port Moresby and back to Mareeba and Townsville, with which to dispute the air with the Jap." Kenney estimated that the Japanese had at least five times the number of planes he could muster, besides being in a position to replace losses within days from their homeland.

The greatest concentration of Japanese air power facing Kenney's forces was based at Rabaul, New Britain. The 25th Koku Sentai (Air Flotilla) consisting of the Tainan Kokutai (Air Corps), the 4th Kokutai, and the Yokohama Kokutai, under Rear Admiral Sadayoshi Yamada, operated from Rabaul chiefly against Port Moresby as well as Guadalcanal in the Solomons. These were land-based units, equipped with the Zero fighters; in addition there were bomber units (mediums: *Nell, Betty*) which attacked Port Moresby regularly and which gave occasional attention to Darwin and other Australian ports. In addition to the land-based planes there were also the planes of the Japanese carrier divisions to consider.

Until he could obtain better and more aircraft as well as replacements for tired crews, Kenney faced a formidable job.

By this time the Joint Chiefs of Staff had decided on a plan of operation giving priority to the Navy's proposal to move into the Solomons as against MacArthur's to move into New Guinea to seize and occupy the Buna area.

The honor, then, of making the first American offensive move in the Pacific fell to the U. S. Navy, not to MacArthur, under Vice-Admiral Robert L. Ghormley, commander of the South Pacific Area. The honor fell, more specifically and traditionally, to the 1st Marine Division, which was to assault the

Solomons. MacArthur's contribution to the offensive was to be a Kenney-mounted bombing mission against Rabaul. This small effort did not please MacArthur, nor did it comply with the image of himself as a major contributor to the offensive.

While these decisions were being made, the Japanese themselves began moving ashore at Buna on July 21, 1942. Having been thwarted in an invasion attempt at Port Moresby in the Battle of the Coral Sea, the Japanese hoped to move in on this chief Allied base by crossing over the Owen Stanley Mountains, through the Kokoda trail, to take Port Moresby from the rear. This would not only place Australia within more convenient striking distance, but would also serve as protection for Rabaul as well as the Solomons in the South Pacific.

The assault in the Solomons was scheduled for August 7, 1942, just about a week after Kenney had begun moving and shaking up his command. For his first official "show" he had promised MacAr-

A Flying Fortress off the coast of New Guinea. About forty were operational when Kenney arrived to assume command of the air forces in the Southwest Pacific.

Zero pilots respected the big bomber, although many had been worn out by constant use.

(U. S. AIR FORCE)

thur that twenty B-17s would be ready for the mission and he guaranteed that sixteen to eighteen would bomb the target. MacArthur appeared skeptical, though hopefully commenting that, if so, it would be the "heaviest bomber concentration flown so far in the Pacific war."

One of Kenney's first moves upon visiting the base of the 19th Bombardment Group at Mareeba was to order all flying suspended until the group's B-17s could be put in some sort of flying condition. On the day of his visit Kenney found that a maximum effort by the group might have gotten about four bombers into the air. Engines were sadly worn and many planes were grounded for lack of tail wheels. Rather than bother with requisition forms, Kenney reached Major General Rush B. Lincoln, in Melbourne eight hundred miles distant, by phone and simply read off a list of the supplies required by Carmichael's group.

When he checked in at Mareeba a few days later, Kenney was gratified to hear that Carmichael hoped to have twenty B-17s ready for the mission to Rabaul. So great a number of aircraft caused some concern among squadron commanders when Kenney impressed them with the importance of holding formation—they had not flown in such large numbers before. Defensive formations were important to the bombers to hold off, with their gun concentrations, attacking Japanese fighters.

On the morning of August 7, 1942, Carmichael had sixteen B-17s at Port Moresby, where they refueled after flying up from Mareeba. While the Marines were heading in for their objectives in the Solomons—Tulagi, Gavutu, Tanambogo, and Guadalcanal—Carmichael led his formation over the treacherous Owen Stanleys to Rabaul. There were now thirteen B-17s; one having crashed on takeoff and two others having been forced back with engine trouble. Proceeding on to Rabaul and the bomber base, Vunakanau, the Fortresses encountered fighters, little dancing Zeros which swarmed in around the bombers. During the attacks one Fortress, piloted by Captain Harl Pease (whose aircraft was not functioning properly) was shot down burning; it was the only B-17 lost in the attack. Bombs pirouetted down upon the parked bombers of Vunakanau, wreaking havoc and leaving smoking bombers to clutter the runway. Kenney thought eleven of the twenty Japanese fighters were de-

stroyed, but another claim amounted to seven. Whatever the claims, Japanese fighters and bombers of Rabaul had been kept busy during the Solomons landings. Kenney was also certain that the bombing had destroyed perhaps seventy-five parked aircraft, although the figure appears rather generous. Some fighters of the Tainan Kokutai had rushed down to Guadalcanal to challenge Marine and Navy fighter planes over the invasion beaches. In this battle Japanese ace Saburo Sakai accounted for four American planes before being seriously wounded himself and his Zero shot up. All but blinded by his wounds, Sakai managed to fly his damaged plane over the nearly six hundred miles from Guadalcanal back to Rabaul.

The success, though limited, of the 19th Group's Rabaul mission was good for the group's morale and for Kenney's reputation as an "operator." He quickly revealed a near-fiendish inventiveness in dealing with the air situation in the Pacific. Soon (by August 9) he could announce the formation of the Fifth Air Force and began injecting spirit into it and developing its personality in his own aggressive image.

II

Kenney, as he explained to MacArthur, visualized his primary mission as the taking out of Japanese air power "until we owned the air over New Guinea. There was no use talking about playing across the street until we got the Nips off of our front lawn."

His methods were far from conventional. During his flight from the United States to Australia, Kenney had discussed with his aide, Major William Benn, the possibilities of low-altitude bombing to knock out ships. This was not, in fact, a new concept. Earlier in the summer Benn had observed demonstrations of the idea at the Eglin Field, Florida, proving ground. Here the hope of bouncing bombs into tanks from fighters was being tested under the direction of Colonel Sargent Huff. The British had also tried minimal-altitude bombing, but had given it up. It remained for Kenney and Benn to give the idea its special significance in the Pacific. High-altitude bombing, such as had been attempted at Midway by the B-17s, proved ineffective. Since the Japanese were dependent upon "open-water defense" (that is, shipping supplies and reinforcements to their outposts in large convoys), thus counting upon the vastness of the Pacific, the ability of ships to maneuver, and their own Navy and aircraft to protect them, dealing with ships at sea presented a challenge. As they flew eastward, Kenney and Benn considered the possibilities of swooping down close to the water, much like a Navy torpedo bomber, to eject the bomb from the plane. Dropped at the correct speed, altitude (about mast-high), and distance from the ship, the bomb with delayed-action fuzes literally skipped along the water until it struck the side of the vessel. It would then, ideally, sink a little and detonate against the side of the ship. Meanwhile, the bomber would have cleared the enemy ship and hurtled away from the scene of the explosion. Shortly after their arrival in Australia, Kenney "fired" Benn as his aide and placed him in command of the 63rd Squadron (43rd Bombardment Group) so that he might test the feasibility of "skip-bombing" with the B-17.

Kenny realized that in order for his skip-bomber to be effective it must be able to overwhelm the deck defenses of Japanese ships. The skip-bomber must have plenty of firepower in the nose, a problem he turned over to a slender, tanned, raffish character, Major Paul I. Gunn. Because he was over forty, Gunn was nicknamed "Pappy" by the younger pilots and was so called even by Kenney, himself then about fifty.

When the war began in 1941, Gunn was an experienced pilot and operations manager of the new Philippine Air Lines. As a captain the second day of the war Gunn began a legendary career flying supplies, evacuating refugees, and accomplishing impossible flying feats under the eyes and guns of the Japanese. He used the Philippine Air Lines civilian Beechcrafts for his missions, frequently hugging the ground and thinking how much harm he could do to the Japanese if only he had had guns installed in the nose of the Beechcraft. This was not, of course, an original conception, for the concept of attack aviation was not in itself new (Kenney, in fact, had taught the subject in the Air Corps Tactical School for a decade). One of the Air Force units Kenney found languishing in Australia when he arrived was the 3rd Bombardment Group (Light), specialists in ground assault and equipped with the Douglas A-24 (Dauntless), the Douglas

A-20 (Havoc), and a third squadron with the North American B-25; the fourth squadron had no planes at all.

The "fortunes of war" brought together Kenney, Benn and his skip-bombing Flying Fortresses, the 3rd Group's assortment of twin-engined attack planes, and the wild-flying, resourceful Pappy Gunn.

If MacArthur had a historic mission to fulfill in his promise to return to the Philippines, Gunn had a deeper, more personal one. When the air forces were scrambled out of the Philippines after the fall of Corregidor in May of 1942, Gunn's wife and four children were imprisoned at the Santo Tomás prison camp near Manila.

Walter D. Edmonds perceptively observed ". . . Pappy Gunn governed himself as though there were two wars against Japan: the one the United States had on its hands, and his own. He fought them both."

Kenney had one other device in mind when he arrived to take over the Allied Air Forces in the Southwest Pacific. "Back in 1928," Kenney has written, "in order to drop bombs in a low-altitude attack without having the fragments hit the airplane I had put parachutes on the bombs; the parachutes opened as the bombs were released from the airplane. . . . With a supersensitive fuze, which kicked the thing off instantaneously on contact with anything—even the leaf of a bush—the bomb was a wicked little weapon. . . ." These so-called "para-frags" were small bombs, weighing about twenty-five pounds, which fragmented in more than a thousand pieces that could "go through a two-inch plank." Kenney's targets were not planks, of course, and he considered "trying them out on some Jap airdrome and wondering if those fragments would tear airplanes apart—as well as Japs, too, if they didn't get out of the way." It was while he was in Washington awaiting transportation to the Pacific and "looking around for anything that was not nailed down" that Kenney found several thousand of his parachute bombs still stored away. He had them shipped to Australia.

Another wicked weapon was named the "Kenney Cocktail"; this was a standard M-47 100-pound bomb loaded with white phosphorus which, when it burst, flung out streamers of burning incendiary material in all directions for 150 feet. Its effect upon man and machine was deadly. By the end of

A Douglas A-20 "Havoc" demonstrating a skip-bombing on a Japanese freighter. Splashes to left of ship mark the spots at which the bombs bounced (two from the photo ship and two from the Havoc in the photograph). One of the dangers of skip-bombing was collision with the target; another was being caught in your own bomb explosion. This type of bombing required great skill. (U. S. AIR FORCE)

1942 Kenney's name was known in Tokyo whose radio referred to him as "the Beast" and one of the "gangster leaders of a gang of gangsters from a gangster-ridden country."

Kenney held no grand strategic illusions. He wished "to own the air over New Guinea" primarily so that MacArthur's ground troops, Australian and later American, could push the Japanese over the Owen Stanley Mountains back to Buna and out of New Guinea. Co-operation with the ground forces would be essential to this design. "Tanks and heavy artillery can be reserved for the battlefields of Europe and Africa," Kenney wrote to his chief, Arnold. "They have no place in jungle warfare. The artillery in this theater flies. . . .

"In the Pacific theater we have a number of islands garrisoned by small forces. These islands are nothing more or less than aerodromes or aerodrome areas from which modern fire-power is launched."

"The Air Force is the spearhead of the Allied attack in the Southwest Pacific," Kenney believed. "Its function is to clear the air, wreck the enemy's land installations, destroy his supply system, and give close support to troops advancing on the ground.

"Clearing the air means more than air superiority; it means air control so supreme that the birds have to wear our Air Force insignia. Wrecking the enemy's ground installations does not mean just softening them up. It means taking out everything he has —aerodromes, guns, bunkers, troops. Destroying his supply system means cutting him off the vine so completely and firmly that he not only cannot undertake offensive action but, due to his inability to replenish his means to wage war, he cannot even maintain a successful defense."

In order to carry out his mission, however, Kenney was forced to improvise and get along as best he could with what little he had. One of the innovations was a converted Havoc (A-20 light bomber), the handiwork of Pappy Gunn, which instead of its meager four .30-caliber machine guns had an additional four .50 calibers in the nose. Its limited range, too, had been increased with the introduction of two 450-gallon fuel tanks in the bomb bay which would give the Havoc the additional fuel to get over the 13,000-foot barrier of the Owen Stanleys. One further modification was a fanciful bomb rack installed in the old bomb bay; this carried the parachute-fragmentation bombs which Kenney wished to try out on a Japanese airfield.

The first opportunity arrived on September 12, 1942. Captain Donald P. Hall led nine Havocs of the 89th Attack Squadron (of the 3rd Bombardment Group) in low over the Buna, New Guinea, airstrip. The first element, with Hall in the van, swooped in over the palm trees and saw to their delight a number of new enemy aircraft neatly lined up on the strip. With their forward firing guns churning up the area before them the Havocs swept over the Buna strip scattering parafrags (forty per plane) in their wake. As the light bombs gently lowered to the ground aroused Japanese guards, apparently assuming paratroopers were being dropped, rushed out to fire at them. Until the first supersensitive fuze touched something, the hapless riflemen did not realize how exposed they were to the vicious effect of the descending silken packages.

The primary objective was, however, aircraft, and Hall's bombers scattered the bombs across the airstrip and pulled away to escape the bomb blasts— as well as Japanese antiaircraft fire. The parafrags, falling about fifty yards apart, began doing their work, wrecking aircraft (claims were made for sev-

enteen of the twenty-two planes on the strip) and very quickly discouraging both the men with rifles and the antiaircraft crews. The second wave strung out its bombs with no interference from the ground. To complete the job, postholing the airstrip itself, Kenney followed the Havoc attack with B-26s and B-17s (five of the former, seven of the latter), which bombed from higher up with thousand-pounders onto the runways. Not one American plane was lost and the first parafrag mission was judged a success, for even if the claims for aircraft destroyed were exaggerated, serious damage had been done at Buna.

By this time the Japanese were dangerously near Port Moresby, pushing the Australian 7th Division before them. Upon seeing the situation firsthand, Kenney flew back to Australia, suggesting that the Australians be reinforced with Americans of the 32nd Division. Although MacArthur felt the 32nd was ill trained, he realized that unless the Japanese were stopped before reaching Moresby, Australia itself would become a battleground. He had decided to send the 32nd Division to New Guinea and put his staff to work arranging for transportation.

Kenney suggested flying the troops to Port Moresby; MacArthur's eyes lit up, but his staff demurred. After all, when a body of water intervened between the place where you wished to send troops and the place where they were at, it followed that you placed these troops on ships for transport. This was the normal way to do it. It would also take two weeks, Kenney argued. Planes would get them there in a day or two. To MacArthur's staff this just didn't seem proper and they wanted the movement to proceed "in an orderly way." But MacArthur elected to let Kenney fly the 126th Regiment of the 32nd into Moresby. By borrowing transport planes from the Australians Kenney transported the first 230 infantrymen to Port Moresby by the evening of September 15, 1942; the rest of the regiment was still waiting at the docks. Disappointed, Kenney asked to be given another regiment (the 128th Infantry), and over the protests of his staff MacArthur said all right.

Soon ground troops were arriving in Port Moresby at a rate of six hundred a day. By this time Kenney was using a dozen Australian civil transports and even had American civilians working for him. Two B-17s had arrived from the United States with ci-

Factory-fresh Lockheed P-38 "Lightning," which re-lieved the P-40 and P-39 in the Pacific. No dogfighter, *it was heavy and sturdy and carried plenty of fire-power. Its twin engines were an added safety device.*
(ERIK MILLER/LOCKHEED-CALIFORNIA)

vilian pilots, employees of the Boeing Company. Kenney pressed them into service and soon the B-17s were ferrying troops out of Australia. The last of the 128th Infantry had been transported to Port Moresby and the remainder of the 126th Infantry was still at sea; they arrived two days later. MacArthur was elated, Kenney was "crowing," and MacArthur's staff was put out. There were dark suggestions voiced within MacArthur's hearing that Kenney was "reckless and irresponsible."

Kenney's job did not conclude with the delivery of the bulk of the 32nd Division to Port Moresby. He would have to see that they were supplied, that various Japanese airfields—Rabaul, Lae in New Guinea—were given attention, besides bombing and strafing Japanese emplacements along the Kokoda trail. Further, there were calls for assistance in the South Pacific from Admiral Ghormley and the Solomons campaign. This generally called for B-17s to bomb Rabaul during the day and Catalinas of the Royal Australian Air Force during the night.

III

The Japanese too had the problem of supply and replacement. Like MacArthur's staff, their thinking favored the "orderly way," which generally meant large convoys of ships, transports with escorts. Supply by air, though not completely ignored, was not seriously considered by the Japanese. Once the air over New Guinea was owned by Kenney, it left the Japanese convoys open to aerial attack. By the end of the year Kenney had acquired some B-24s (this was the 90th Bombardment Group), which were plagued, however, with mechanical problems (cracked nosewheel collars) and out of action for a month. When new collars were specially manufactured and the group made its first missions in mid-November 1942, it demonstrated a need for further training (on the second mission—to Rabaul—the B-24 carrying Group Commander Colonel Arthur Meehan did not return, nor did one other, and the other crews had little idea of where they had been). This was a bitter development for Kenney, who had already relieved the overworked 19th Bombardment Group, which had begun flying their equally overworked B-17s back to the United States. In

time, however, the 90th Bombardment Group's B-24s—and crews—were ready. They would then join up with Kenney's then only active heavy group, the 43rd.

Also arriving in the Pacific by the end of 1942 was the Lockheed P-38 ("Lightning"), a plane which seemed unloved in Europe, but which Kenney favored for the simple reason that it flew. There were other good reasons, of course, once the kinks were ironed out of the plane (initially leakage in the intercooling system); it was a superb fighter for the Pacific theater. Its twin engines was one of its blessings, considering the distances over which it must range. A single-engined craft simply went down and out, but with its two engines, the P-38 could lose one and still return to its base. It was a great, heavy aircraft for a fighter and although it could not match the Zero in dogfighting, it proved to be the scourge of the Japanese fighter in the Pacific. The Lightning was faster than the Zero, achieving a top speed of more than four hundred miles an hour; it could outclimb and outdive the Japanese fighter, performed exceptionally well at high altitude, and carried plenty of firepower (20-mm. cannon and four .50-caliber machine guns). In addition, the P-38 came equipped with features which the Japanese hardly considered (because they added weight): self-sealing fuel tanks and armor plating to protect the pilot.

Twenty-five Lightnings had arrived in Brisbane in September but remained grounded until the various mechanical defects had been cleared up. Newly arrived pilots were forced to wait until the P-38s were ready or use the worn-out P-39s and P-40s for combat. The bugs were not eliminated from the P-38s until December; meanwhile another batch of twenty-five arrived but without feeds for the guns —these too were grounded until the feeds could be installed. Finally, by October Kenney had sixteen P-38s of the 49th Fighter Group flown up to Port Moresby. Further complications set in what with leakages discovered in the cooling system, problems with disintegrating wing tanks—and "borrowing" of the operational P-38s by the South Pacific command for the Solomons campaign.

Eventually, in December 1942, the P-38s began to operate. The first Japanese plane brought down by one was achieved in an unorthodox manner. According to General Kenney "a big good-natured New Orleans Cajun named Faurot" was flying over

Japanese fighter pilots, who "owned the air" over New Guinea when Kenney arrived to take over the aerial operations for MacArthur. These Zero pilots, often victorious over American and Australian pilots in their P-40s and P-39s, would find the arrival of the Lightning in the Pacific a serious challenge to their superiority. (DEFENSE DEPT., U. S. MARINE CORPS)

the Japanese air base at Lae. For days the Americans had radioed insulting messages (Japanese and Americans exchanged such insults over their radios in English), but without inciting the Zeros to come up. Faurot on this day carried, as did the others in the flight, two five-hundred-pound bombs under his plane's wing. The plan was to make holes in the runway at Lae. Finally after the by now traditional exchange of insults the Americans had succeeded in arousing one of the Japanese pilots. His Zero had begun a takeoff run when Faurot noticed him and dived. He was down to two thousand feet when he recalled that he carried a thousand pounds of bomb, which would deter him immeasurably if he and the Zero tangled. Faurot quickly released the two five-hundred-pounders, pulled back on the control column to escape the blast, and pulled around in a turn, ready to pounce on the Zero. As he watched, the two bombs fell into the water at the end of the runway, which ran right to the beach. The resultant splash caught the Japanese plane, at that moment at runway's end and lifting off the ground. The Zero lurched crazily and careened into the water, a total wreck.

"When the kids returned, I asked Faurot if he had nerve enough to claim 'the first Nip brought down in air combat in this theater by a P-38.' He grinned and asked if I was going to give him an Air Medal. I had promised one to anyone that got an official victory. I said, 'Hell, no. I want you to shoot them down, not splash water on them.'" Kenney, whose relationship with his "kids" was marked by an affectionate, bantering humor of the crusty father, awarded Faurot his Air Medal, although warning him that "he'd better keep the whole thing quiet."

With a few airplanes to his credit and some new eager kids to fly them, Kenney felt himself reasonable able to take on the "Nip" in his own back yard. Curiously this was echoed, almost in Kenney's own words, in a Japanese diary found in New Guinea. Early in December 1942 the diarist noted of Kenney's Kids that "they fly above our position as if they owned the skies."

Kenney's first great opportunity to prove himself in a spectacular manner came in March 1943. Buna on the northeast coast of New Guinea was wrested from the Japanese—after a half year of savage ground fighting—in January; Guadalcanal, in the Solomons, had been reluctantly abandoned by the Japanese, also following a half year of sanguinary land, sea, and air battles leading to the first major land defeat by the Japanese. The Nipponese tenta-

Lightning in battle dress showing its armament: a 20-mm. cannon and three of the four .50-caliber machine guns in the nose. (ERIK MILLER/LOCKHEED-CALIFORNIA)

cles into the Solomons and New Guinea constricted bloodily. In the Solomons the focus shifted to the northernmost island, Bougainville; in New Guinea it moved up the coast, about 150 miles from Buna to the Lae-Salamaua area in the Huon Gulf.

Having abandoned Guadalcanal and Buna the Japanese proceeded to reinforce their position at Lae. Late in February 1943 Kenney's intelligence unit had learned that a Japanese convoy, forming at Rabaul, was scheduled to arrive in Lae early in March. This would coincide with a period of bad weather predicted for the area, which would curtail air operations. Although the information was meager, Kenney sensed a large-scale troop movement in the offing. He alerted General Whitehead at Port Moresby and ordered reconnaissance aircraft to cover the area of the Bismarck Sea.

Meanwhile about five thousand troops of the Japanese 51st Infantry Division assigned to reinforce the Lae-Salamaua garrison had begun boarding seven merchant vessels in Rabaul Harbor. Eight destroyers were to serve as escort, along with an air cover of about a hundred fighters (not simultaneously, but on a schedule in order to furnish protection over a period of days, generally in groups of twenty to thirty). Special service vessel *Nojima* rounded out the convoy of sixteen ships; aboard one of the transports, the *Kembu Maru*, besides troops, was a precious cargo of aviation fuel and other supplies.

The convoy set forth under cover of darkness and stormy weather the night of February 28. The weather hindered Kenney's reconnaissance planes and it was not until the afternoon of March 1 that a B-24 crew spotted "fourteen ships with Zero escort" about 150 miles west of Rabaul. The weather closed in again, preventing further spotting as well as an attack by eight B-17s of the 43rd Group which did not locate the convoy.

The weather continued bad on March 2 and it took until midmorning before a 90th Group B-24 found the convoy and radioed its position—about fifty miles north of Cape Gloucester, New Britain, heading south for the Vitiaz Straits. As soon as possible the 43rd Group's B-17s left Port Moresby, climbed the Owen Stanleys, and began dropping thousand-pound bombs from sixty-five hundred feet. This first flight of eight Flying Fortresses made the attack without fighter protection, having missed its

rendezvous with the P-38s. Zeros closed in and in the fighting three were claimed shot down; all B-17s returned to Port Moresby claiming hits on two transports, reporting that one had split in two and sank within minutes of the initiation of the attack. This was the *Kyokusei Maru,* whose survivors, about eight hundred men, were taken aboard two destroyers and rushed to Lae during the night. The destroyers rejoined the convoy early the next morning.

A second flight of B-17s, twenty in all, followed the first to continue the bombing, claiming two hits and several near misses. Crews reported ships dead in the war, burning or sinking as well as the rescue operations of the two Japanese destroyers. Further defensive attacks by Zeros holed the B-17s but did not knock any of the bombers down; one Zero was claimed. In the early evening further bombing attacks by the 43rd Group near the northern entrance to the Vitiaz Straits claimed one vessel "left sinking" and another Zero. Enemy fighters, it was noted, were less persistent than in the earlier phases of the battle. As the sudden tropical night fell, the B-17s returned to Port Moresby while a Royal Australian Air Force PBY Catalina remained over the Japanese convoy during the night; in the morning a B-17 appeared to relieve the Catalina and found the convoy off the Huon Peninsula and within striking range of the medium bombers.

On Wednesday, March 3 at "ten o'clock the big brawl began about 50 miles southeast of Finschhafen, right where we had planned it," Kenney has written. Australian Beauforts of the RAAF 9th Operational Group carrying torpedoes opened the attack but without success; soon after, Australian Beaufighters, armed with nose cannons and machine guns in the wings, swooped in for a low-level attack. Above the Beaufighters B-17s co-ordinated a high-altitude attack and B-25s a medium-level attack with the Beaufighters. The sea churned with the explosion of bombs, the splash of cannon, and machine-gun fire whipping across the dodging Japanese ships. Thousands of feet above the carnage Zeros and P-38s fought their battles. The Battle of the Bismarck Sea had reached a climax.

Following the Beaufighter, B-17, and B-25 attack, twelve B-25Cls, newly converted into powerful strafers by the hand of Pappy Gunn and led by Major Edward Larner of the 90th Squadron (3rd

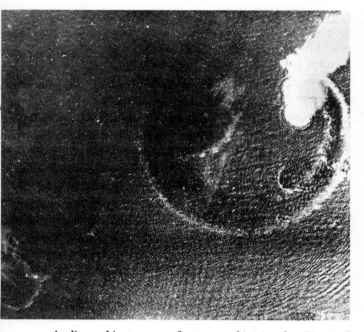

A direct hit upon a Japanese ship in the Bismarck Sea. The wake of the evasive circle of the ship may be seen. (U. S. AIR FORCE)

Bombardment Group), swept down to the water for the most savage attack of the battle.

Larner was one of Kenney's favorites among his kids. When Kenney first met Larner the latter was a lieutenant who had "fire, leadership, and guts." This had been demonstrated during the Buna campaign at least twice, the first time during a strafing run on Japanese artillery and machine-gun positions at Soputa, just inland from Buna. Larner, leading the 90th Squadron, blazed in on the gun positions at a low level. An antiaircraft burst under the tail of his plane, tipping its nose, flung Larner's plane through the treetops for hundreds of yards, battering the plane as well as various trees. As laconically reported by the pilot, "following this accident I was able to make only two more strafing passes before the plane became so unmanageable that I thought it best to return to base where repairs could be made."

As Kenney observed, Larner landed the B-25 at nearly 175 miles an hour because of the damages to the wing surfaces which affected the lift. The underside of the plane was grooved where a palm tree had grazed it; the wing was dented and gouged

Battle of the Bismarck Sea: Japanese destroyer in distress, burning, losing oil, and dead in the water after Kenney's Fifth Air Force bombers hit it.

(U. S. AIR FORCE)

and one engine was stuffed with foliage and bits of branches. The plane was in a condition that would have normally suggested abandonment, but Larner brought it home instead. Kenney gave him a Silver Star and promoted him to captain.

The second incident occurred when Larner brought his B-25 down low to strafe a Japanese machine-gun position—so low that the aircraft's tail bumper had hit the ground and dragged through the sand for several yards. Larner explained that he had been forced to go so low because he had "to look in the windows of the bunker to see what to shoot at."

As he studied the scraped-up plane, Kenney stood with one of Larner's machine gunners. The sergeant sighed audibly and said, "I guess I'll have to quit this pilot of mine. He's gone nuts. He runs into trees and tears 'em down and now he thinks he's a farmer and he's started plowing up the ground with his tail bumper. . . ."

Catching the mood, Kenney replied with the suggestion that he could fix it up. "I've got a chauffeur over at my headquarters who wants to shoot a pair of fifty-caliber guns. How about swapping jobs?"

The gunner hesitated just an instant before answering. "General I'd better stick. You see, Captain Larner is so crazy he really needs me to look after him."

So it was that Major Larner lead his strafers down into the melee that had become the Battle of the Bismarck Sea. The twelve B-25s, each with eight forward-firing .50-caliber machine guns in the nose, plus two in the top turret—ten in all—razed all before them as they came in at five hundred feet. The Japanese ships broke convoy formation and scrambled in an attempt to get out of the way. The B-25s swirled and separated, selecting a target. Waiting in an 89th Squadron Havoc, Pilot Edward Chudoba heard the B-25 pilots arguing over targets as the radio sputtered, "This is my ship—go get yourself a ship!"

The machine-gun fire blasted the decks clear of return fire as Larner's squadron bore down upon the dodging Japanese ships. At the correct point of release, five-hundred-pound bombs were flung from the B-25s and skipped along the water. Of the thirty-seven released the 90th Squadron claimed seventeen as direct hits. The destroyer *Arashio* took three of them, snapped out of control, and smashed into the

already hit *Nojima*. The *Nojima* sank within minutes and the *Arashio* sank several hours later. This meant that its crew was to suffer the further attentions from the planes which followed.

Having caused frightful distress to the convoy (a cruiser and a transport sank, two destroyers and seven other ships were damaged), Larner led his B-25s back to Port Moresby. All twelve of his planes returned, although one, shot up in the attack, crashed during its landing run without serious injury to the crew.

The 89th Squadron, also of the 3rd Bombardment Group, followed the 90th, in their Havocs. "I got my first sight of the battle," Edward Chudoba later recalled, "when a ship ahead and to the left blew up, throwing flames a half mile into the air. I thought it was a destroyer, but the destroyer I had marked in that position slowly pulled away revealing a tanker [this may have been the *Kembu Maru* with its cargo of men, replacement parts, and aviation fuel] beyond it sending up flames and smoke from stem to stern. . . ."

One of "Pappy" Gunn's "commerce destroyers," a B-25 with four .50-caliber machine guns in the nose and two on either side of the fuselage just below the wing. The bombardier's compartment was removed and so was the Mitchell's lower turret. The eight forward-firing guns concentrated a withering fire in the plane's path. (U. S. AIR FORCE)

"We were now about opposite the middle of the convoy on its port [left] side. Our two Vs of six Havocs each wheeled almost at right angles to the left to come in against it broadside. We were sliding down from about 2,000 feet now at an angle that would have us brushing the masts as we went over the enemy ships. . . .

"The time was exactly 10:03. The ships ahead were rapidly growing larger now.

"Young Charles Mayo (just turned twenty-one), my right wingman, and I were flying on the right side of our V of six ships. There was a ship ahead and two to the left. I dived and turned to the left under Captain Clark, our flight leader, and Mayo followed me. But the two planes on the left side of our V formation were going after the nearest ship on the left. I swung back and toward the big ship ahead. In spite of Captain Clark's warning not to pile up on the same ship, things were getting a bit confusing. I looked over my shoulder and there was Clark behind me. Young Mayo on my right said, 'I'm going off and get me a fat one.'

"The ship was rushing broadside at me now. I pulled the trigger on the wheel that started my machine guns spurting. I could see tracers and big stuff coming from the ship. I was pulling the bomb switch when a bullet came through the plexiglass canopy. Thirty caliber, I found later. I couldn't see a man on deck. The gun crews were well hidden. I let my two 500-pound bombs go now, just as I used to release them on calm days to skip against that old wreck at Port Moresby.

"Wham! I got it just as I passed over the ship. Ol' Adam LaZonga shuddered with the blow. (The plane was named for the great lover of the Li'l Abner strip and Adam sure could take it.) There was something wrong with the right wing and the plane wasn't flying right. I thought I had been hit with ack-ack. Captain Clark told me later that I had clipped off the top of the ship's radio mast. There was a dent on the front surface of my wing six inches deep."

The target was one of the troop-carrying transports, the Tamei Maru, which sank. All twelve of the 89th Squadron's Havocs returned to Port Moresby. During the battle Chudoba overheard radio conversations between the bombers and fighters, for the Zeros had begun concentrating on the B-17s in this climactic phase of the battle.

"Hey, Joe," Chudoba heard a Fortress pilot yell, "come on down. I've got three Zeros on my tail."

"Come on up," Joe said. "I have thirty of them."

The thirty or so Zero pilots must have been hard pressed to make any decision as to which planes to attack: the skip-bombing Mitchells and Havocs, the Beaufighters below, the B-25s in between, or the B-17s above. The Fortresses were the largest and appeared therefore to be the deadliest, so many Zeros attempted to get at them. One flown by Lieutenant Woodrow W. Moore was severely hit in the wing, which burst into flame. Moore ordered the bombs salvoed and the crew to jump. Seven managed to get out of the plane before it went into a steep dive and plunged into the Pacific, taking Moore with it.

As the seven chutes floated down the Zeros strafed them. Captain Robert Faurot (he who had splashed down the first Japanese plane with a P-38) left the fighting and with his two wingmen, Lieutenants Hoyt A. Eason and Fred D. Schifflet, all of the 35th Fighter Group, dived down to aid the helpless bomber crewmen. All ten men, the seven in parachutes as well as the fighter pilots, perished in the ensuing fight, although Kenney believed that the P-38 pilots took "five Japs along with them."

These four aircraft, one B-17 and three P-38s, were the only Allied planes lost in the Battle of the Bismarck Sea. Although the weather turned sour by the afternoon of March 3, a few more strikes were made by B-17s, Larner's B-25s again and RAAF Bostons of the 9th Operational Group. It was the final co-ordinated attack, for the battle was over except for such details as mopping up, sinking ships that remained above water but could not move, and picking up survivors, if any.

Five torpedo boats of the U. S. Navy's Seventh Fleet ("MacArthur's Navy") slipped into the battle area after dark that night and sank one of the crippled ships, and on the morning of the next day, Thursday, March 4, bombers dispatched another stray. The battle was as good as over and high jubilation ensued in the Fifth Air Force. Kenney, about to leave for conferences in Washington, wired Whitehead: Congratulations on that stupendous success. Air Power has written some important history in the past three days. Tell the whole gang that I am so proud of them I am about to blow a fuze.

Historian Samuel Eliot Morison, with exceptional grace for a Navy man, called the Battle of the Bismarck Sea "the most devastating air attack on ships of the entire war, excepting only that on Pearl Harbor." At the cost of thirteen men killed, twelve wounded, and four aircraft (plus two which crash-landed), Kenney's forces had sunk every transport (probably eight, although exact figures seem never to have been determined) and four destroyers for a total of twelve of the original eighteen ships which had left Rabaul. An estimated three thousand Japanese troops went down with the transports, about half of those which had boarded the ships; of the six thousand troops intended for Lae only about eight hundred reached there. These were the survivors of the sinking of the *Kyokusei Maru,* which the B-17s had broken in half in the initial attack of the battle on March 2.

For the Japanese it was almost as shocking a defeat as Midway. But in addition to the loss of men, ships, and aircraft (claims were made for twenty), it meant something even more costly: the end of large-scale supply and reinforcement runs to northeastern New Guinea. The beleaguered Japanese troops must subsist from that day on on what little could be brought in by barge, submarine, and other small craft.

The ultimate effect upon the development of the situation in New Guinea was far-reaching indeed. It meant that MacArthur could seriously consider moving up the carapace of the turtle-shaped island and toward the Philippines.

2

"CLEARING THE AIR"

The Battle of the Bismarck Sea had been unique; the Japanese would never again place so many men and ships within the range of land-based aircraft. But if the sea was less a threat, there still remained along the line of MacArthur's projected advance in New Guinea several Japanese air bases at Lae (including those at nearby Salamaua and Nadzab) and at Wewak (a complex of fields including those at But, Dagua, and Boram). At the same time there was also the target at Rabaul, New Britain, with its inviting Simpson Harbour and several air bases: Vunakanau, Keravat, Lakunai, Rapopo, and Tobera. From Rabaul the Japanese were capable of interfering with MacArthur's plans in New Guinea as well as those of Vice-Admiral William F. Halsey (who had relieved Ghormley as commander) in the South Pacific.

Kenney therefore unleashed the devastating fury of his Pappy Gunn gadgetry upon Japanese shipping and air power along the route of the proposed Allied advance. He hoped to "clear the air" with everything he had until the Japanese had nothing.

With the Buna area secured, it was possible to establish airstrips at nearby Dobodura; thus the fighters, especially, were spared the high haul over the Owen Stanleys. MacArthur had his strategic eye next upon the Huon Peninsula, particularly Lae and Salamaua. But these targets lay nearly two hundred miles west of Dobodura, which meant that although

within fighter range, the time possible over the target was so brief for the fighters that they could give little protection to the bombers. Consequently, Kenney sent out Lieutenant Everette E. Frazier, an aviation engineer attached to the Fifth Air Force, to scout out the location for an advance airdrome within flying distance of Lae and the Wewak complex of Japanese airdromes.

Frazier, by air and by foot in the jungle, covered hundreds of square miles of New Guinea until he found a likely spot, all but under the very noses of the Japanese in the vicinity of Marilinan, more specifically at the village of Tsili-Tsili, within sixty miles of the Japanese at Lae. Kenney preferred calling the location Marilinan—"it was a pretty name"—in case "the Nips should take us out, somebody might throw that Tsili-Tsili thing back at me." While the base was being built Kenney decoyed the Japanese to another position, which was made to look like an active installation. The Japanese bombed the decoy spot and somehow did not find the Marilinan base until it was completed and operating. By mid-August more than three thousand troops were based in the area, including the 2nd Air Task Force, commanded by Lieutenant Colonel Malcolm A. Moore and later by Colonel David W. Hutchison.

The Japanese bombed the forward base for the first time on August 15, 1943, when a dozen Sallys escorted by a dozen Zeros swooped down by sur-

A C-47 (the civilian Douglas DC-3) of the 6th Troop Carrier Squadron, with P-39 escort, flying over New Guinea. (U. S. AIR FORCE)

prise and shot down a C-47 carrying men of the ground echelons of the 35th Fighter Group, stationed at Marilinan; another transport crashed into the jungle and was never found. Escorting P-39s tangled with the bombers and fighters while the other C-47s sought refuge in the treetops and flew back to the comparative safety of Port Moresby. Four P-39s (but only one pilot) were lost and claims were made for eleven Japanese bombers and three fighters in the battle.

Realizing now that American planes were based in their back yard, the Japanese followed with a strafing raid on the following day. They were met not only by P-38s but also by the new P-47 Republic Thunderbolt, flown by the 348th Fighter Group led by Colonel Neel Kearby. The Japanese lost nine fighters (of the approximate fifteen dispatched) and five bombers (of sixteen). American losses

amounted to one Thunderbolt. After these two costly attempts, the Japanese chose to leave Marilinan reasonably unmolested.

On the next day, August 17, 1943, Kenney opened up his campaign upon the Wewak airdromes. Reconnaissance photos revealed more than two hundred aircraft distributed among the installations at But, Boram, Dagua, and Wewak. It was after midnight that B-17s and B-24s from Port Moresby began dropping bombs on the various targets. Although Japanese night fighters attempted interception, antiaircraft fire and searchlights proved to be the most formidable, resulting in the loss of three heavy bombers. Early morning photographs accounted for "at least 18 unserviceable" aircraft left on the Japanese airdromes, in addition to the damage to the strips which two hundred tons of bombs could do. But this was only the curtain raiser designed to foul the strips in order to interfere with Japanese aerial efforts during the next act.

At dawn the B-25 "Strafers," with P-38 escort, slashed across the tops of the palm trees in the Wewak area for the climax of "the show." Lieutenant Colonel Donald P. Hall, who had first experimented with the parafrag bomb during the early days of the Buna campaign, led the 8th and 13th Squadrons (3rd Bombardment Group) down upon the strips at Boram. It was, as Kenney observed, a "sight to gladden the heart of a strafer." Japanese bombers, perhaps sixty or more, lined up on both sides of the runway with engines warming up in preparation for

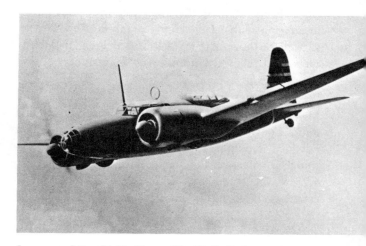

Japanese Mitsubishi, Type 97, "Sally," heavy bomber which occasionally operated as a fighter.

(U. S. AIR FORCE)

A Sally taking off during a Fifth Air Force attack on a Japanese base in New Guinea. Shortly after it was destroyed by another bomber, a B-25 Mitchell.

(U. S. AIR FORCE)

takeoff. No doubt the Japanese planned to avenge the midnight bombings by the B-17s and B-24s. Half a hundred fighters, the escort, also lined up on other runways getting ready to take off. The lead bomber had begun its run down the strip when Hall roared in with his potent Mitchells.

A shattering burst from his nose guns caught the Japanese bomber still on the runway. Enveloped in flame, it crashed to the ground and rendered the runway inoperable for any further takeoffs. The 8th and 13th Squadrons, seventeen planes altogether, led by Hall, in the words of Kenney, "swept over the field like a giant scythe," blasting at the lined-up bombers and fighters with their nose guns and drop-

ping parafrags in their wake. The bombs wafted down among the smoking, burning wreckage, further detonating aircraft and ripping up planes. Fuel drums burst into flame, adding their liquid propulsion to the holocaust. Those antiaircraft positions missed by the strafers were deracinated by the parafrags. In just minutes, the airdrome at Boram was left a burning, wreckage-strewn charnel house. Men of the 8th Squadron believed that they had left fifteen of the sixty or so planes they had counted on the strips totally destroyed and over twenty-five burning. The 13th Squadron was more expansive, claiming that of eighty or so aircraft it had counted all had been destroyed or severely damaged.

Parafrags falling on a Japanese airstrip at Boram, New Guinea. Earlier attacks have already decapitated palm trees and burned up bombers (lower left); at *upper right a fuel truck about to service a Zero will be the victim of the floating bombs.*

(U. S. AIR FORCE)

At the same time, twelve B-25s of the 90th Squadron (3rd Bombardment Group) were attending to Wewak proper. The surprise attack caught a number of Japanese fighters on the ground and left half of them, about fifteen, destroyed or damaged. Those Oscars (the Nakajima Ki.43) which got off the ground were driven off by the gunners in the Mitchells, leaving nothing to be done by the escorting P-38s, of which there were no less than eighty-five hovering around waiting for something to do.

Of the twenty-six B-25s which had taken off from Port Moresby that morning, assigned targets at Dagua and But, only three managed to rendezvous, because of bad weather. These three continued on to Dagua (But was not hit at all) and, despite their small number, created a burning shambles with guns and more than a hundred parafrags. Gunners shot down one intercepting Oscar, but at least seventeen lay in burning junk heaps on the ground when the Mitchells returned to Port Moresby.

Precise damage could not of course be estimated, but following what the Japanese came to call "The Black Day of August 17," there was little of the Japanese Air Force remaining in the Wewak area. But that did not mean it no longer existed, as was revealed on the following day, when similar strikes were made on Wewak. The weather spoiled the efforts of the heavy bombers to some extent; of the

Japanese antiaircraft gunners seek shelter from the bombing-strafing Fifth Air Force Mitchells as a parafrag drifts toward their gun position. (U. S. AIR FORCE)

A "sight to gladden the heart of a strafer": Mitchells seeding the airbase at Dagua, New Guinea; smoke from a burning "Helen" bomber fills the air as three neatly lined-up "Tony" fighters await their turn.

(U. S. AIR FORCE)

forty-nine which took off only twenty-six succeeded in bombing Wewak and Boram. The 3rd Bombardment Group followed with another low-level strafing and parafrag attack. The airdrome appearing to be pretty well taken care of, the 3rd swung out to sea, struck at some cargo vessels anchored off Wewak, and then blazed supply dumps at Boram.

The 38th Bombardment Group had been assigned Dagua. Major Ralph Cheli of the 405th Squadron led the attack, which was intercepted by about a dozen Japanese fighters, Zekes and Oscars, several miles out of Dagua. The fighters furiously attacked the low-flying Mitchells, concentrating on Major Cheli's flight. Within seconds, one of the B-25s was forced to pull away because of damage and fluttered back to base. An Oscar which had attacked this plane swung into Major Cheli's also and sent a burst along the right wing and engine. Flame erupted from the Mitchell as Cheli continued leading the

Though the tide was turning, the air war over Boram, Wewak, and Dagua was not one-sided. Here is a Mitchell down in the water off New Guinea.

(HENRY W. UHLIG/U. S. AIR FORCE)

B-25s toward Dagua, still two miles away. Rather than pull up, Cheli remained in place at the head of the squadron leading the attack. His leaving the formation at this critical point might easily have upset the strike; he chose to remain near the ground (too low to take to parachutes) with himself and his crew in the burning Mitchell.

The plane spouted flame as Cheli swept in over Dagua, strafing and dropping parafrags. This completed, Cheli instructed his wingman to take over the formation for the return flight, saying that he would attempt to bring the burning plane down into the sea. He turned and made for the water, reached it in fact, but it was too late. The flames had reached

a fuel tank and the explosion ripped a wing off the B-25, which crashed into the Pacific. Ralph Cheli was awarded the Medal of Honor for his action that day.

These two days of low-level attacks had succeeded in seriously crippling the Japanese aerial potential in New Guinea. By the end of the month it was estimated that more than two hundred aircraft had been destroyed on the ground alone (the revised, more precise figure was 175, which is still impres-

Troops of the 503rd Parachute Infantry float down upon Nadzab, New Guinea, in MacArthur's move to eliminate the Japanese stronghold at Lae.

(U. S. AIR FORCE)

The death of a Zero over Salamaua south of Nadzab and Lae about a week before the latter fell to MacArthur's forces. (U. S. AIR FORCE)

sive). Claims were made for 126 Japanese aircraft accounted for in combat against the loss of five Mitchells, four B-24s, and thirteen fighters in combat and by accident during the month of August.

Marilinan, from which attacks could be mounted, served also as an emergency field and refueling depot for the fighters. Kenney concluded the field "had already paid for itself."

By late August MacArthur was confident that his forces could strike at another Japanese stronghold up the spine of New Guinea—Lae in the Huon Gulf. Amphibious troops, both Australian and American, went ashore near the village of Hopoi to set up a beachhead about fourteen miles east of Lae on the morning of September 4, 1943. This was preceded by naval and air bombardment of the landing area as well as concentrated bombing of Japanese positions in New Guinea and Rabaul. Even so, some Japanese aerial activity interfered slightly with the Lae landing, although at heavy cost, for Kenney's P-38s and P-47s swarmed around for in-

terceptions. Within four hours of the opening of the operation some 7800 troops had been put ashore along with their weapons and supplies.

The next morning the C-47s of the 54th Troop Carrier Wing lifted off the strips at Port Moresby carrying Australian troops and the men of the U. S. 503rd Paratroop Regiment. The unarmed transports, seventy-nine C-47s carrying about seventeen hundred men, were met by their first escorts over Thirty-Mile airdrome. As the armada proceeded, the escort eventually rose to a hundred fighters. Over Marilinan, just southwest of Lae, the C-47s formed into drop formation and flew to Nadzab, which flanked Lae to the west. What followed was one of the finest, most precise airdrops of the war, as, according to Kenney, MacArthur in his command B-17 observed "the show . . . jumping up and down like a kid." The paratroopers landed without meeting any resistance, and their C-47s returned to Port Moresby without the loss of a single plane. The Americans soon joined with the Australians and the area belonged to the Allies. Almost immediately construction of an air base was begun at Nadzab; Lae itself fell on September 16, 1943, and Kenney became proprietor of yet another major base.

Another way station like that at Marilinan was an airdrome constructed on Kiriwina, one of the Trobriand Islands, which lay almost directly east of Dobodura, New Guinea, and about 325 miles from Rabaul to the north. From the strips on Kiriwina, built by Royal Australian Air Force engineers, it would be possible for the B-25s to "stage" (refuel, etc.) before heading for Rabaul with weighty bomb loads. Fighters, primarily P-38s, were able to escort the bombers to Rabaul and not concern their pilots too much with fuel problems, for even if the Mitchells returned to New Guinea, the fighters could always land at Kiriwina. The heavy bombers could use Dobodura as their staging area. By October Kenney was ready to launch an offensive upon Rabaul similar in intensity to those with which he had been afflicting the Japanese along the northern coast of New Guinea.

Reconnaissance photograph of Vunakanau, one of the major Japanese air bases at Rabaul, New Britain (an island group east of New Guinea). This strip had already been visited by the Fifth Air Force as evidenced by wreckage. (U. S. AIR FORCE)

Rabaul had long been a prime target area, what with its several airdromes (two of which, at Lakunai, had been built by the Australians before the war), its harbor facilities, and warehouses in the city itself. As an important Japanese base, feeding men and matériel into New Guinea and the Solomons, Rabaul was also heavily protected: the estimate by early October 1943 was about 145 fighters, 124 bombers, and over 350 antiaircraft guns. The Japanese Navy had also installed quite efficient early warning radar systems. From Rabaul, too, bombing missions to New Guinea and to the Solomons were dispatched. In co-operation with the forces of Halsey's South Pacific units, and to assist in taking some of the pressure off the Allied Bougainville offensive in the Solomons, Kenney was determined to "take out Rabaul."

II

He had begun this task shortly after his arrival in the Pacific with the August 7, 1942, strike, which had consisted of thirteen 19th Bombardment Group Flying Fortresses. Rabaul had been under intermittent attack and regular reconnaissance since the previous January, in fact. From time to time Kenney would send a force of bombers to hit the shipping

or airfields in the area; but it was a costly target. During the Buna campaign Kenney and his Bomber Command chief, Brigadier General Walker, agreed that striking at Rabaul's shipping would confute Japanese plans to send reinforcements to New Guinea. On one of these strikes, that of January 5, 1943, Walker disobeyed Kenney's orders and flew in one of the dozen bombers sent to bomb Rabaul Harbor. Although Kenney had ordered a dawn attack, Walker believed a noon attack would achieve higher accuracy. While this may have been true— for claims for no less than ten ships sunk or burning were made—the antiaircraft fire was murderous and attacks by defending Japanese fighters profuse, if not expert. However, two American bombers were lost, one of them carrying Walker. Apparently hit by flak, the B-17, with engine burning, lost altitude and attracted two Zeros, which followed the plane away from the main battle. That was the last seen of Walker's B-17 by those ten crews which returned to Port Moresby.

When it came time to intensify the Fifth Air Force's attention on Rabaul, a campaign scheduled to open the middle of October 1943, Kenney was able finally to plan a sizable attack. There were no dozen or so patched up B-17s now, but several squadrons each of Mitchells, P-38s, and B-24s— nearly 350 aircraft. This too was a tribute to the resourcefulness of Kenney, who, by whatever means, had built up his air force. He fought with MacArthur's staff, he fought with Arnold's staff in far-off Washington, he demanded, "squawked," to use his term, and simply took what he could. This affected supplies, matériel of all types from planes to food for his "kids." If Service of Supply, bogged down with red tape, would not issue fresh food to his front-line fliers, Kenney arranged for a fleet of aircraft to smuggle it in from Australia. While this infringed on rules and regulations, it made a great deal of difference to the men who fought in terms of health and morale. Kenney even blinked when refrigerators were flown into New Guinea labeled as aircraft engines; if anything, he no doubt initiated the shipment of contraband.

He regularly had to defend his men. When Service of Supply officers in Sydney complained of the behavior of Kenney's airmen on leave, indicating that it was time "these brats grew up and behaved themselves," Kenney lashed out at the complainants, in-

dicating that he didn't want his kids to get "old, fat, bald-headed and respectable like some people present because I was quite sure that, if they did they would no longer shoot down Nip planes and sink Nip boats."

In so many words, Kenney told the by now red-faced rear echeloners that since leave was granted to men who had been fighting the war, it was just too bad that their cavortings disturbed the slumber of the SOS. So far as he was concerned they could . . .

Just then MacArthur appeared in the doorway.

Kenney stopped talking to say, "Good morning, General."

MacArthur studied the group for just a moment, then said, "Leave Kenney's Kids alone. I don't want to see them grow up either." Chuckling, but with great dignity, he left.

MacArthur enjoyed Kenney's at times gauche style, his bluntness, his unconventional handling of supply and command problems. It was as if the austere, limelighted MacArthur could unbend through Kenney. Soon he came to call Kenney "Buccaneer," in recognition of the airman's freewheeling, productive manner of operating. On the other hand, Kenney was popular also with his men, who admired his informal swashbuckling manner—and the fact that he never failed to go out on a limb for them, if necessary.

They, in turn, willingly went out on a limb for Kenney. Taking out Rabaul was one of those limbs. On the eve of the opening of the intensive campaign, Kenney wrote to Arnold, "This is the beginning of what I believe is the most decisive action initiated so far in this theater. We are out not only to gain control of the air over New Britain and New Ireland but to make Rabaul untenable for Jap shipping and to set up an air blockade of all the Jap forces in that area."

Because of the oncoming monsoon predicted by his weathermen, Kenney unleashed his bombers on October 12, 1943, three days ahead of the agreed-upon date of the official top-level meetings. The early morning phase of the attack was led by Lieutenant Colonel Clinton U. True, commanding officer of the 345th Bombardment Group, at the vanguard of more than a hundred strafer Mitchells. Flying low over the water to elude radar, the Mitchells crossed the Solomon Sea to Kiriwina (where the

The Fifth Air Force delivers parafrags to Vunakanau bomber revetments in Kenney's offensive on Rabaul.
(U. S. AIR FORCE)

P-38 escort was picked up) and swung around to approach Rabaul. As they came in at treetop level, the formations split: the forty Mitchells of the 3rd Group veered sharply to port, streaking for the airdrome at Rapopo, and the sixty-seven aircraft of the 38th and 345th Groups turned slightly, to pounce upon Vunakanau. The attacks followed the pattern of those at Wewak and Lae. The 3rd Group, for example, swept in in a succession of shallow Vs, about a dozen Mitchells across, with the Vs about a mile apart. Spraying the target area with their eight nose guns, the Mitchells roared over the airfields dropping their parafrags into revetments (con-

structed to protect aircraft from horizontal bomb blasts) and over the general dispersal area.

Surprise having apparently been achieved, the Mitchells encountered remarkably little opposition. Antiaircraft fire was neither persistent nor accurate. Fighters, however, attempted interception and in a battle over Vunakanau with Zekes (the more modern Zero) the Mitchell piloted by Lieutenant Sidney W. Crews, with engine aflame, crashed into the waters of St. George Channel. It was the only Mitchell lost in the attack.

As soon as the Mitchells had cleared the area, a dozen Australian Beaufighters of No. 30 Squadron swooped down to work over Rapopo and Tobera. One of these aircraft was knocked down by ground fire.

A Japanese bomber burns after a parafrag has alighted near it. (U. S. AIR FORCE)

Shortly after noon the B-24s of the 90th Bombardment Group came in high over Simpson Harbour to drop thousand-pound bombs on the shipping in the harbor. Zekes quickly rose to challenge the Liberators, and in the ensuing battle, which lasted for more than a half hour, two B-24s were lost, with gunners in the bombers claiming ten of the forty Zekes and Zeros attacking. The Liberators of the 43rd Group followed the 90th Group's planes (which drew off most of the Japanese fighters) and strung their bombs across the harbor. Crewmen reported burning ships and much confusion in Simpson Harbour and heavy but inaccurate antiaircraft fire. Escorting P-38s claimed twenty-six Japanese fighters shot down; the strafer-bombers estimated that no less than a hundred Japanese planes had been destroyed on the ground with another fifty badly damaged. The heavies claimed over a hundred ships of various sizes, function, and tonnages sunk or destroyed—rather optimistic claims, as revealed in later photoreconnaissance. Exact damages could not be known, in fact, because of the speed of the action and the smoke left in the target areas by the Mitchells. But the claims were not as critical as the fact that the big campaign on Rabaul had begun with a decided success and with a reasonably small loss.

Despite intermittent bad weather, which either canceled out strikes or interfered with missions, the Fifth Air Force continued pounding away at Rabaul. Unless Kenney maintained a constant assault the Japanese were able to repair damage and replace lost aircraft. Meanwhile, too, Japanese strikes were mounted upon Allied positions in New Guinea, to upset any plans for what appeared to the Japanese to be a softening-up prelude for an invasion of Rabaul. This clearly near-suicidal effort was never attempted, however. It was the fate of Rabaul to be bypassed, isolated, as were so many other Japanese strong points on the way to Tokyo.

The ships in Simpson Harbour were as important as targets as were the aircraft on the five major airdromes of Rabaul. When the weather grounded planes, the ships continued to bring in supplies and troops. It devolved upon the 8th Photo Squadron, flying converted P-38s (the F-5), to keep an eye on the weather as well as the installations at Rabaul. Reconnaissance had revealed a concentration of ships in Simpson Harbour toward the end of October, making an attack from low level (always more effective than high-altitude bombing against ships) next on the Fifth Air Force agenda.

The weather caused the scrubbing of several missions to Simpson Harbour at the end of October. November came and the bad weather seemed fated to continue; the missions of the first and second were also canceled. But then, P-38s in the Rabaul area reported, after the morning mission of November 2, 1943, had been scrubbed, that not only was the weather over Rabaul promising, but that Simpson Harbour was filled with ships: a destroyer, a tender, and about twenty assorted transports. The mission was on again.

Because of the sudden shift in plans, not many Fifth Air Force aircraft were dispatched from New Guinea and the base at Kiriwina. According to Kenney there were seventy-five (Air Force historians say eighty) B-25 strafers and fifty-seven P-38s (historians claim eighty). The actual numbers assume a certain importance because of the intensity

The attack on Rabaul's Simpson Harbour, November 2, 1943. As shore installations burn in the background, a skip-bombing Mitchell sweeps across the harbor as ship burns. (U. S. AIR FORCE)

Rabaul goes up in smoke after the November 2 mission to Simpson Harbour. (U. S. AIR FORCE)

of the battle which ensued. It is likely that Kenney's are closest to the actual figures because the squadrons participating were not up to full strength.

Nine B-25 squadrons took part in the attack: the 8th, 13th, and 90th (of the 3rd Bombardment Group); the 71st and 405th (38th Bombardment Group); and the 498th, 499th, 500th, and 501st of the 345th Bombardment Group. Furnishing fighter cover for the strafers were six fighter squadrons: the 9th (49th Fighter Group); the 39th (35th Fighter Group); the 80th (8th Fighter Group); and the 431st, 432nd, and 433rd of the 475th Fighter Group.

By 11 A.M. the force was air-borne and headed for Rabaul. The P-38s of the 39th and 80th Squadrons opened the attack by swooping in upon the harbor to shoot up the antiaircraft installations there. Major Benjamin Fridge followed with the four B-25 squadrons of the 345th Group to strafe the gun emplacements around the harbor, drop Kenney Cocktails (the phosphorus bombs), and sweep over to

Lakunai airdrome and do the same there. The Kenney Cocktails laid a screen of smoke over the land-based guns and ignited Rabaul itself.

But unlike the earlier squadrons, the planes of the 345th ran into tough interception and intense anti-aircraft fire. Several Mitchells were shot up during the attack and three were lost. The initial attack, however, prepared the way for the remaining five squadrons of B-25s, led by Major John P. Henebry, which had time to circle over Rabaul (impossible normally because of the harbor guns) for an effective run on the shipping in the harbor.

As Henebry dropped down upon Simpson Harbour, two Japanese destroyers which lay in the mouth of a river opened up on the forty-one Mitchells. This plus the smoke of the already burning ships disturbed, to some degree, the plan of attack. Despite this the strafers, breaking up into small units, poured fire in upon the ships in the harbor. Some of the Japanese ships shot directly into the water in the path of the approaching American planes, geysering water into the very cockpits of the B-25s. At the same time, especially aggressive Zeros pounced upon Henebry's squadrons. These fighters proved more effective than any encountered by the Fifth Air Force in quite some time. They were veteran Japanese Imperial Navy pilots of the 1st Koku Sentai (Carrier Division) from old Admiral Nagumo's carriers *Shokaku, Zuikaku,* and *Zuiho.* It had been a long time since the Fifth Air Force men had seen so many Zeros in the air at one time.

Kenney, who called this battle "the toughest, hardest-fought engagement of the war" for his air force, estimated that the Japanese put up "between 125 and 150 fighters" that day. Their numbers, and skill as pilots, enabled the Japanese to break through the P-38 escort to get at the Mitchells bombing the harbor. Despite the persistent Zeros and the ground fire, the Mitchells slashed at the ships, striking more than forty, of which twenty-four were hit by bombs and seventeen strafed.

In the melee, six B-25s and one P-38 were knocked down into Simpson Harbour. Henebry's plane was so badly shot up that when he left the battle area, his B-25 was full of holes and one engine was gone. With extraordinary airmanship, Henebry skimmed and yawed away from Rabaul until the Mitchell fell into the Pacific just short of Kiriwina. Henebry and his crew were rescued shortly after.

One of Henebry's squadron commanders, Major Raymond H. Wilkins, did not get away from Rabaul. Leading the 8th Squadron, the last to attack, Wilkins flew on the formation's left flank, which brought him under fire from cruisers near the shore. The area by this time, actually only twelve minutes after the initial attack, was a turmoil of smoke, machine-gun tracers, water spray, and concentrated antiaircraft fire.

"Smoke from bombs dropped by preceding aircraft necessitated a last-second revision of tactics on his part," Wilkins' Medal of Honor citation reads, "which still enabled his squadron to strike at vital shipping targets but forced it to approach through concentrated fire, and increased the danger of Major Wilkins' left-flank position.

"His airplane was hit almost immediately, the right wing damaged, and control rendered extremely difficult. Although he could have withdrawn he held fast and led his squadron in to the attack."

Wilkins' forward-firing eight-gun battery roared to life as he "strafed a group of small harbor vessels, and then, at low-level, attacked an enemy destroyer. His thousand-pound bomb struck squarely amidships, causing the vessel to explode. Although antiaircraft fire from this vessel had seriously damaged his left vertical stabilizer, he refused to deviate from his course. From below mast-head height he attacked a transport of some nine thousand tons, scoring a hit which engulfed the ship in flames. Bombs expended he began to withdraw his squadron.

"A heavy cruiser barred the path. Unhesitatingly, to neutralize the cruiser's guns and attract their fire, he went in for a strafing run. His damaged stabilizer was completely shot off." With his directional control all but gone, Wilkins might easily have flown into the path of the Mitchells flying alongside him. He rolled the plane slightly, with what little aileron control he still had, to avoid colliding with his wing mates. In doing this he exposed the belly and full wing surfaces to the heavy fire erupting from "those damned cruisers." In an instant the Mitchell's left wing crumpled and the bomber smashed into the sea.

Wilkins and his crew were among the forty-five men lost in the attack: one of the heaviest tolls suffered by the Fifth Air Force. Eight bombers and nine fighters were lost (although four of the pilots of the latter were found and crews of three bombers, such as that of Henebry, were picked up). A Mitchell and three P-38s, badly damaged in the fighting, cracked up while landing at Dobodura. It had been an expensive "show."

Simpson Harbour had been left a smoking shambles when the last Mitchell of the 8th Squadron passed through its hail of fire. But any accurate assessment of the damage would have been questionable. The first official communiqué claimed fifteen Japanese vessels, of various types, sunk and an additional thirteen damaged (after the war the Japanese admitted to three merchant vessels, a minesweeper, and two small ships sunk and damage to a ten-thousand-ton tanker). Whatever the differences, the attack proved costly to the Japanese also.

Besides the damage to shipping in the harbor (and tankers were an especially precious commodity at the time), the town of Rabaul was also set aflame, which accounted for the destruction of supplies. In

As the fighting progressed all around Rabaul and Simpson Harbour, Kenney Cocktails fanned over Lakunai gun positions (center and right bottom), scourging the hapless gun crews. (U. S. AIR FORCE)

the air fighting, bombers and fighters claimed sixty-eight Japanese planes shot down; the strafers claimed an additional sixteen destroyed on the ground at Lakunai plus ten float planes which were left burning in the harbor. So, if the battle had been hard on the Fifth Air Force, it was also a definite blow to the Japanese.

By the end of November, with Halsey's carriers closing in on Rabaul, Kenney relinquished the further "neutralization of Rabaul" to the South Pacific forces, which included the recently formed Thirteenth Air Force besides the Marine and Navy pilots. Although Rabaul was never invaded, any such attempt would have been costly in the extreme, it was not completely taken out either. But the incessant attacks upon it eventually forced the withdrawal of air units stationed there by February 20, 1944. Left behind were nearly 100,000 ground troops, who waited in 350 miles of tunnels and caves. It was one of the good fortunes of war that the Joint Chiefs did not order an invasion of Rabaul. Had they, "Tarawa, Iwo Jima and Okinawa would have faded to pale pink in comparison with the blood that would have flowed" in an attempted assault on Rabaul, in the opinion of Samuel Eliot Morison. Even so, the blood continued to flow until the end.

Meanwhile, Kenney gave his attention to MacAr-

A low-flying Mitchell, of the 345th Bomb Group, Thirteenth Air Force, catches a Japanese "frigate" (destroyer escort) off the coast of China. In moments the B-25s of the group, known as the "Air Apaches," finish off the ship which capsizes. (U. S. AIR FORCE)

thur's advance up the coast of New Guinea, employing the methods used upon Rabaul as he went.

III

The attacks by strafers, the deliverers of Kenney Cocktails, parafrags, and the heavy bombs, were protected whenever possible by fighters. Kenney's fighter pilots were among the most colorful of the war, and the so-called "Ace of Aces" of all American wars was one of Kenney's Kids. Richard Ira Bong, "a blond, blue-eyed cherub" from Madison, Wisconsin, first came to Kenney's attention in San Francisco. Kenney was then commanding the Fourth Air Force when word came to his office that one of his pilots "had been looping the loop around the center span of the Golden Gate Bridge in a P-38 fighter plane and waving to the stenographic help in the office buildings as he flew along Market Street."

From nearby Oakland a lady complained of having her washing blown off the line by a low-flying aircraft. Though angry and a bit embarrassed over the performance of one of his pilots, Kenney was also delighted. Kenney himself had nearly been dismissed from the Air Service in the summer of 1917 for flying under the bridges of New York's East River.

Kenney laced into the youthful pilot, a "boy about five feet six, with a round, pink baby face and the bluest, most innocent eyes," affecting his harshest voice and sternest expression. He reminded Bong of the trouble he had caused, which would make it necessary for Kenney to talk with everyone, from the governor on down to the lady with the washing.

Then Kenney's curiosity got the better of him. "By the way," he said to Bong, "wasn't the air pretty rough down in the street around the second-story level?"

The innocence vanished from Bong's eyes. "Yes, sir, it was kind of rough, but it was easy to control the plane." He then launched into a speech on the excellent aileron control of the P-38 before realizing that he was in his commanding general's office for an entirely different reason.

Kenney rather dramatically began tearing up the pile of complaints that had accumulated on his desk thanks to this cherubic "airplane jockey." Threatening the by now incredulous Bong with in-

Richard Bong, P-38 fighter pilot, New Guinea, 1943. Bong would become the American "ace of aces" with a total of forty confirmed air-to-air victories.

(U. S. AIR FORCE)

stant dismissal from the Air Force should he ever repeat his performance, Kenney added further reprimand: Bong was ordered to report to the lady near Oakland.

And "if that woman has any washing to be hung out on the line, you do it for her. Then you hang around being useful—mowing a lawn or something —and when the clothes are dry, take them off the line and bring them into the house. And don't drop any of them on the ground or you will have to wash them over again."

Almost immediately after the incident, Kenney was on his way to the Pacific and when he placed a request with Arnold for fifty P-38 pilots, he specifically requested that Bong be among them.

In Kenney's professional eye, Bong (who was then twenty-two) combined those several qualities which add up to a superb fighter pilot. Quick reflexes, good physical condition, a sense of joy in the very idea of flight, an understanding of aircraft and its limitations, as well as his own. Aggressiveness too was an important psychophysiological component. Along with this must be a self-confidence bordering on an overwhelming sense of invincibility. The hesitant, too cerebral fighter pilot did not generally survive. Swooping down for a screaming attack, most often as not upon an unaware enemy—for in reality, for all of the scorekeeping, combat aviation was no clean sport—the fighter was too preoccupied with air speed, angle of attack, getting a bead on the enemy aircraft to consider the outcome of this attack as less than fatal for the enemy.

Like so many other American fighter pilots, Bong was not, in the beginning at least, a very good shot. He actually completed his first tour of missions, with more than twenty "kills" to his credit, before he attended a school for training in aerial gunnery. The bulk of Bong's forty official victories can be attributed to his courage (another term for aggressiveness or self-confidence), his skill with the P-38, and a willingness to work as part of a team.

Early in the Pacific war it became obvious that the dogfighting tactics of the First World War were suicidal with the Zero, which could dance circles around the heavier American fighters. "Defense against Jap fighters is resolved around the superior speed of our fighters," Bong pointed out, and it was that difference between the machines, his and the Japanese, that he exploited, not individual flying abilities. The Japanese were better pilots—and had much sharper vision than early Allied propaganda intimated. So were their aircraft better under certain conditions; because they were less ruggedly constructed, weight and speed were important in battle. As Bong observed, "An indicated airspeed never less than 250 miles per hour in combat is good life insurance."

Even so, there were sudden unknowns confronting even an experienced pilot—and it was these too which often saved him. One of these incidents occurred to Bong even after he had already achieved acedom. He and his wingman intercepted a Japanese bomber formation, escorted by Zeros, over the Buna area of New Guinea. The bombers seemed beautifully set up for a quick, slashing attack. "Any number of Nips," he once wrote, "can be safely attacked from above. Dive on the group, pick a definite plane as your target, and concentrate on him. . . ."

As he concentrated on his bomber, Bong, with the fighter pilot's instinct for searching the air

around him, came to a sudden shocking realization. On his wing was not a twin-boomed P-38, but a Zero with a large red circle on its side. In seconds it could slip behind him and begin firing with its cannon.

Chopping the throttle of one of his engines, Bong suddenly flipped away in a careening dive. Checking his rear-view mirror, and not seeing a Zero, he leveled out at five thousand feet. Suddenly, there it was again, pulling up behind him, but too distant for accurate shooting. Bong flipped the P-38 once again and dived for the water. The Zero could not follow him there—it might plunge into the Pacific if it did, or else pull apart in the high-speed dive.

Japanese bombers ("Sally") in the gun camera of an American pilot. While thus occupied once Richard Bong acquired himself a Zero for a wingman.

(U. S. AIR FORCE)

Bong opened the throttles and raced over the water, glancing again into the mirror. He had left the Zero way behind; maybe now he could deal with the persistent Japanese. He snapped the plane into a tight turn and found himself in the middle of a nine-plane Japanese formation he had not seen until that instant.

There was nothing in the books to cover this situation. Bong relied on instinct as he yanked the great plane's nose into the path of the lead Japanese aircraft. A short burst from Bong's gun blew the Zero out of his way. This apparently had shaken the remaining eight Zeros, for their fire was not accurate. Bong ripped the P-38 through the scattering Japanese formation and shot and detonated another Zero. Ramming his engines at full throttle, he climbed for altitude, loosing another burst at a passing Zero. The Japanese plane paused, emitted smoke, and fluttered away from the battle.

By this time Bong was far from the dispersed Japanese planes and heading for home base.

Despite the preoccupation with keeping score of kills, the true function of the fighters was, of course, protecting the bombers during the attacks upon shipping or such bases as Rabaul, Lae, Wewak, and the other steps toward the Philippines. Lone-eagle fighting generally ended in the death of the eagle.

The system of fighting in pairs may have denied a wingman his share of "credits" (and there were those pilots who resented it), but it did preserve life. But not forever.

Once the American pilots began adding up kills it was inevitable that a certain rivalry would grow among the pilots. It was a good-natured, locker-room kind of competitiveness, this obsession with kills, except that instead of touchdowns men's lives were at stake.

When Bong passed the score of First World War ace Captain Eddie Rickenbacker, the latter sent the young ace a case of scotch with which to celebrate. This resulted in quite a tempest in a scotch glass, for a flood of complaints and criticism deluged Kenney for permitting this (in fact, Bong himself did not drink and was more delighted with a gift of Coca-Cola from Generals Arnold and MacArthur). The back-home do-gooders could not reconcile themselves to the fact of the "boys'" drinking, although they readily accepted the fact that they were out killing their fellow man. Wartime provides

the setting for any number of moral incongruities, with the most pietistic leading the pack.

When Bong arrived in New Guinea to embark upon his legendary career as a fighter pilot, the top-scoring ace of the time was Boyd David Wagner, who was best known as "Buzz," with a score of eight. A veteran of the early Pacific fighting, Wagner returned to the United States only to die in an accidental crash during a takeoff at Eglin Air Force Base.

Bong's rival during his initial tour was another youngster, Captain Thomas J. Lynch of Catasauqua, Pennsylvania. Lynch had led the first P-38 mission (December 27, 1942), twelve in all, from the Laloki airstrip near Port Moresby. Intercepting a Japanese bomber and fighter formation over Dobodura, the P-38 pilots returned from the battle claiming no less than fifteen Japanese planes. Bong, Lynch, and another future ace, Lieutenant Kenneth C. Sparks, claimed two apiece. Although the green fighters committed any number of tactical errors—firing from too great a distance, attempting to dogfight with a Zero—their initiation into battle had been exciting and without loss. Kenney, in reporting the battle debut of the P-38 to Arnold, noted that "morale in that squadron [the 9th of the 49th Fighter Group] is so high it almost scares you."

Another group, the 348th, had arrived in New Guinea around the end of June 1943. The commander, Colonel Neel E. Kearby, looked to Kenney "like money in the bank." The 348th was equipped with the Republic P-47 ("Thunderbolt," or "Jug") and Kearby was anxious to prove what the as yet unpopular aircraft could do. The P-47 was a hulk of an aircraft, the largest single-engine one-man fighter of the war. It did not have the range of the P-38 (until fitted with belly tanks), was difficult to maneuver, had a weak landing gear, and could, in a power dive, freeze the controls so that the pilot could not pull out. Or if he did, the action could tear the tail section away. Despite these drawbacks, the P-47 properly manned became one of the outstanding fighters of the war.

Kearby, one of its earliest exponents, was anxious to show what the plane, his group, and he himself could do. He had barely met Kenney before he asked about "scores," the implication being, Kenney believed, that he "wanted to know who he had to beat." It was not until August that the 348th

Neel E. Kearby, who commanded the 348th Fighter Group, and who proved that the P-47 "Thunderbolt" was a formidable aircraft in the Pacific.

(U. S. AIR FORCE)

Fighter Group's Thunderbolts were ready for action. Then in September, during the air fighting over Lea and the subsequent (September 5, 1943) taking of Nadzab by American paratroopers, Kearby got his chance. With a wingman as company Kearby dived on two Japanese planes, a bomber and a fighter. With his wingman following, Kearby dropped the Thunderbolt upon the enemy planes about four thousand feet below. The two planes were flying along rather close together, the bomber in the lead with the Zero following. Kearby squinted in the sight and shot off a long, exploratory burst as his wingman held his fire and twisted his neck looking for other Japanese fighters.

To the surprise of both wingman and Kearby a wing ripped off the fighter and the bomber ex-

ploded before their eyes. By the end of September Kearby's score had grown to eight, one half of Bong's score at the time.

Multiple victories seemed to be a Kearby specialty, for on October 11 he gave an amazing demonstration which won him the Medal of Honor. During a fighter sweep over the Wewak area in company with three others, Major Raymond K. Gallagher, Captain John T. Moore, and Captain William D. Dunham, Kearby sighted a single Japanese plane below them.

Kearby led his flight down upon the lone Zero and in seconds sent it down burning (the eight .50-caliber guns of the P-47 literally tore the flimsy plane apart). Then as the four Thunderbolts pulled up out of their dive they saw ahead of them a large formation of Japanese fighters and bombers, about forty-five planes in all.

Kearby plunged into the formation in an instant, the three others following. The heavy P-47 lumbered through the astonished Japanese spouting fire: three enemy planes burst into flame within minutes. Then, kicking rudder, Kearby turned to see that two Zeros had got onto the tail of one of his flight. He roared in and with two bursts sent the two Japanese down burning. Instinctively he scanned the air around him and saw that a Zero had begun a dive upon another P-47. Kearby whipped the guns into the enemy plane, which collapsed, falling like a bird with a broken spine.

Realizing that they were getting low on fuel, Kearby called his men in—all were safe. Besides Kearby's seven victories, two more had been accounted for by other members of the flight and another had been seen leaving the battle on fire. Because it had not been seen to crash this was claimed as a "probable." Discounting this one, it meant that the Japanese had lost nine planes to the four Thunderbolts in a single action.

But there was an additional hitch. Kearby's gun camera had run out of film in mid-attack on the seventh plane and there was no "official" evidence, the three other pilots then being occupied themselves, that the seventh plane had been destroyed. So Kearby was credited with an official six victories in a single battle (the record to that date was the Navy's Lieutenant Edward "Butch" O'Hare, who had shot down five Japanese bombers in a single action). For his feat, Kearby received the Medal of

Honor and his score stood at fourteen, only three less than Bong's.

Shortly after, Bong was sent home for a rest (with a score then of twenty-one), and while he was away Kearby's total rose to twenty. At this time Bong's other rival, Thomas Lynch, had a score of sixteen (he too had been sent back home for a rest), so that the rivalry of these three aces now became intense.

When all three were in operation their individual scores were watched daily; by the beginning of March 1944 Bong and Kearby were tied (with twenty-two) and Lynch trailed with nineteen.

Whether or not the desire to be top ace blunted Kearby's customary vigilance, or whether it was a simple matter of running out of luck, would be difficult to ascertain. On March 4, 1944, Kearby was again leading a four-plane flight (Major Samuel Blair, Captain William Dunham, and Captain William Banks), this time over Wewak, New Guinea. Sighting a fifteen-plane Japanese formation, Kearby ordered an attack, the first assault of which sent one enemy plane down under his guns. He had broken the tie.

Thomas J. Lynch, one of Richard Bong's friendly rivals and battle companions. (U. S. AIR FORCE)

Turning, he rammed back into the battle and with a long shot, knocked another Zero down. Kearby was now official Ace of Aces. Then three Zeros converged upon his Thunderbolt. Dunham and Banks swept in with guns firing, each taking one of the Zeros off Kearby's tail. But the third from close up fired a burst of cannon directly into the cockpit of the P-47. It tipped on its nose and fell directly into the jungle; no parachute was seen. Obviously Neel Kearby was dead in the plane.

Ironically, on that same day Bong had destroyed two enemy aircraft; the score was still tied. Lynch with nineteen victories was now Bong's closest rival.

At this stage, Lynch—a lieutenant colonel—and Bong—a captain—had teamed up. They had been taken out of their regular squadrons and placed upon the staff of General Paul Wurtsmith, commander of Kenney's Fighter Command. Lynch was nominally Wurtsmith's operations officer and Bong his assistant. Thus it was hoped to keep the two fighters out of combat as much as possible and preserve their experience, which could be transferred to the new pilots coming into the Pacific.

This worked on paper, but it was difficult to keep the two men out of battle. They either went off together, or attached themselves to other squadrons and continued to add to their scores. They remained, as they did at the time of Kearby's death, Bong: twenty-four, Lynch: nineteen.

Just five days after Kearby's last fight, Bong and Lynch took off on one of their two-man hunts. Over Tadji, New Guinea, they surprised another two-man combat team and each took out one. There being no other Japanese aircraft in the sky, they pointed their P-38s down toward the water, where they spotted a Japanese ship, a corvette obviously headed for Hollandia. It was the best they could find, so they swept down upon the vessel. Raking the deck with .50-caliber bullets, the P-38s dived and pulled away, dived and pulled away as the guns on the ship's deck traded fire with them.

Suddenly Bong noticed that Lynch had turned away and headed for shore; an engine trailed smoke. Even more suddenly one of the propellers tore away, and as Bong watched in horror, he saw Lynch struggling out of the cockpit, ready to jump. Before he and his chute were free of the plane, the P-38 detonated. If Lynch had had a chance, the

Despite the superiority of American air power over New Guinea, attacking Japanese strongholds was not without hazard. In this series of photographs a Fifth

Air Force Havoc attacking Kokas, New Guinea, is hit by antiaircraft fire and plunges into the water.

(U. S. AIR FORCE)

flame of the explosion canceled that—the chute certainly burned and Lynch, if not already dead, fell to his death. Bong circled the area for signs of life (something he realized was futile), but there were no indications that Lynch had survived. He returned to his base and Kenney, concerned with Bong's morale, sent him to Australia, ostensibly to ferry a newly arrived P-38 back to New Guinea. But Kenney saw to it that the depot commander would not have one ready for two weeks.

By early April Bong had returned, and by the twelfth, upon adding two more kills to his credit in a battle over Hollandia, he had passed the score of Rickenbacker, making him the American Ace of Aces of both world wars. Kenney quickly took him out of combat, partly because there was some concern from Washington over the recent deaths of Kearby and Lynch and the loss of their "invaluable

services." Bong was returned to the United States at this point to be reunited with his family, his fiancée, Army public relations officers—and to study gunnery. He was to return to the Pacific as an instructor upon completion of this course.

Meanwhile, a new rival had arisen: Major Thomas Buchanan McGuire, Jr. When he arrived in the Pacific, in the spring of 1943, McGuire was assigned to Bong's own unit, the 49th Fighter Group. Bong's score was then eight. In time McGuire was reassigned to the 475th Fighter Group to serve in the 431st Squadron. A fine pilot, McGuire quickly revealed himself as one of the outstanding air fighters in the Pacific.

But it seemed to be his fate that he always remained eight victories behind Bong. Even when Bong was away from combat, McGuire himself was also out of things with various jungle illnesses. "I'll

*Thomas B. McGuire, Jr. (here an air cadet), one of
Kenney's most aggressive "kids," who risked his life—
and lost it—trying to aid a fellow pilot.*

(U. S. AIR FORCE)

bet," he once told Kenney, "when this war is over,
they'll call me Eight Behind McGuire."

In time McGuire became commander of the 431st
Squadron and his victory score mounted rapidly. "A
fighter pilot must be aggressive," he believed. "The
enemy on the defensive gives you the advantage,
as he is trying to evade you, and not shoot you
down. Never break your formation into less than
two-ship elements. A man by himself is a liability.
. . . On the defensive, keep up your speed.

"Go in close, and then when you think you are
too close, go in closer."

McGuire was an excellent teacher and conscientious in looking after green pilots. All through
Bong's combat career, McGuire trailed his victory
tally, but it was obvious that he might eventually
overtake the top ace, for the word went out that
Bong must be taken out of combat. Following Bong's
return from the United States he was supposed
to instruct, not fight—except in self-defense. By
late December 1944, when MacArthur had indeed
returned to the Philippines, Bong's score had grown
into the thirties. If the Japanese air forces had

petered out over New Guinea, there was still fight
left in them over the Philippines. Bong therefore had
to "defend" himself rather frequently, even if he only
went along to observe how a squadron he had
trained in gunnery performed on a routine patrol.

Within hours of arriving at Tacloban, Bong was
"forced to defend himself," in the words of Kenney's
report to Arnold, and shot down his thirty-first
Japanese plane. The following day, while on a reconnaissance mission to find possible sites for airfields in the Tacloban vicinity, he accounted for
two more Japanese aircraft within view of the Allied
airdrome.

Arnold wired Kenney: "Major Bong's excuses in
matter of shooting down three more Nips noted with
happy skepticism by this headquarters. Subject officer incorrigible. In Judge Advocate's opinion, he
is liable under Articles of War 122." This referred
to willful or negligent damage to enemy equipment
or personnel.

Tacloban was a busy place indeed, for when
McGuire arrived there in early October (1943), it
was just in time for a tangle with a Japanese fighter
formation. The twenty P-38s, warned by radio of
the approaching ten Japanese fighters, shot down
six and drove the rest off. One of the victims was
McGuire's twenty-third victory. Elated upon landing, McGuire said, "This is the kind of place I like,
where you have to shoot 'em down so you can land
on your own airdrome! Say, how many has Bong
got now?"

The slender, little major learned he was now ten
behind. With Bong himself in the area, McGuire
jokingly kept an eye on him, muttering words about
taking off "to protect his interests." The two men
were good friends and teamed up to go "Nip hunting." Now and then McGuire "permitted" Bong to
accompany his squadron on regular patrols during
which each shared in the kills.

When Bong's official score reached forty (his actual score was probably much higher), Kenney decided to take him out of combat. He had flown 146
combat missions and had nearly 400 hours of combat time. He had lived a charmed life and Kenney
felt it was time to stop tempting fate. Bong was reluctant, hoping to bring his score to an even fifty,
but Kenney was unyielding.

Bong would be sent home to rest, to marry the
girl back home, and to get into an entirely new con-

cept in aviation, the jet plane. In order not to spoil his stateside reception, Kenney grounded McGuire, who had finally broken his "eight behind" jinx.

"You look tired to me," Kenney told McGuire.

"General, I never felt better in my life. I've gained five pounds in the last month. Besides, I'm only two behind—"

"That's just it," Kenney told McGuire. "You are tired and you won't be rested enough to fly again until I hear that Bong is back in the United States and has been greeted as the top-scoring ace of the war." Kenney explained that he did not want Bong to arrive in San Francisco to be greeted with "Hello, Number Two, how's the war going?"

McGuire laughed and understood Kenney's point,

saying he certainly did not want to spoil anything for Bong. He promised to take a few days off to rest, although he seemed quite anxious for Bong to be on his way. Kenney promised that he would personally place Bong on a transport in a day or two.

On this last day Bong, perhaps for the first time, learned a fact of war. Bong in his P-38 and Kenney in his B-17 proceeded to an airdrome at San Jose, Mindoro. Just as they landed and taxied to a parking area the sirens sounded. Colonel Gerald Richard Johnson, Bong's old group commander, led some P-38s to the attack.

When the Lightnings intercepted the Japanese formation, Johnson fired at the leader. The plane burst into flame instantly as Johnson turned away

". . . the formation was bounced by a single 'Hamp' . . ." *a later model of the Zero, the so-called clipped-wing variant of the maneuverable fighter. Also called* the "Hap," the name was changed after General Henry "Hap" Arnold learned of this designation.

(U. S. AIR FORCE)

to tackle another enemy aircraft. The action occurred almost directly over the field, so that Kenney and Bong watched in fascination.

As they watched, the Japanese pilot, unable to stand the flames, jumped from his plane. "The Jap pilot hit flat on the steel plank surface of the airdrome about a hundred feet from where Dick and I were standing. It was not a pretty sight. I watched for Bong's reaction. I had predicted a long while ago that if he ever found out that he was not shooting clay pigeons, I would have to take him out of combat. . . . He walked over to some bushes at the edge of the field and for the next five minutes was violently ill."

Kenney was certain more than ever that he was correct in taking Bong out of combat. McGuire, however, returned to the battle as soon as he knew that Bong had received his hero's welcome. Word came in on January 6, 1945; on the seventh McGuire was in the air again.

In the morning he took off in company with another experienced P-38 pilot (a Major Rittmayer of the Thirteenth Air Force) and two new pilots. To familiarize the green pilots, McGuire intended to make a quick sweep over a Japanese field on Negros Island, west of Leyte. The morning promised to be quiet, for as they flew along at about two thousand feet there seemed to be no Japanese air activity.

Unexpectedly the formation was bounced by a single "Hamp" (a late variant, the A6M3, of the Zero), which fastened itself to Rittmayer's tail, pouring fire into the P-38. McGuire reacted immediately and characteristically—he swept in to the rescue of the pilot in distress. To do this, however, he was forced to violate several of his own precepts for air combat. He had to turn the heavy P-38 tightly, and he had to do this at extremely low altitude—and with two heavy auxiliary fuel tanks attached to his wings.

McGuire apparently forgot about the wing tanks in the urgency of the moment, as he tipped the P-38 in a vertical bank to go to Rittmayer's aid. Ordinarily, since he was so skilled a pilot, he might have succeeded, but with the extra weight and resistance of the wing tanks it was not possible. In the tight turn the P-38 shuddered in mid-air for a moment, stalled, and then dropped straight to the ground. A massive explosion ripped out of the jungle. Meanwhile, the Hamp pilot persisted on the

other P-38, and in moments, Rittmayer joined McGuire in death. The Japanese pilot then slipped down among the hills of Los Negros and blended into the jungle and out of sight. The two new pilots returned to Leyte with the grim news.

The courageous Japanese pilot who single-handedly attacked the four-plane formation was, according to recent research, probably Shoichi Sugita. whose own victory tally placed him, by war's end, in the position of Japan's number two ace; he was therefore McGuire's Japanese counterpart. Sugita's score, however, was eighty, just twice that of Bong's.

Japanese aces, unlike those of the Allies and Germany, were not publicized; they were, in fact, as little known to their own countrymen as to the enemy. Partly this was because it was simply expected of them to serve the Emperor and if in so doing they shot down many enemy aircraft, so be it. Another reason for their scanty fame was simply class consciousness. Only the high officer class received due recognition; the non-commissioned officer or the skilled fighter who had come from the lower classes was not mentioned.

Nor were they looked after as in the fatherly manner of Kenney, "buccaneer" though he was supposed to be. Japanese pilots were expected to go until they died or dropped. Many flew in an exhausted, run-down state; many flew although seriously ill with malaria, dysentery, and other tropical diseases, or diseases caused by poor diet and fatigue.

One such remarkable pilot was Hiroyoshi Nishizawa, who, before he was killed while piloting a transport rather late in the war, shot down more than a hundred Allied planes. Nishizawa was Japan's top-scoring fighter pilot, although his name was not known during the war except to fellow pilots, who called him "the Devil." Sugita was second; the famed Saburo Sakai was third, with sixty-four victories. Other outstanding Japanese fighter pilots were Waturo Nakamichi (fifty-five victories), Naoshi Kanno (fifty-two), Yasuhiki Kuroe (fifty-one). Temei Akamatsu was one of the most fascinating airmen, for he was so totally un-Japanese in outlook. Like a throwback to the First World War, Akamatsu was an undisciplined advocate of wine and women and possibly song. His total score was fifty (he survived the war), which he shared with Kinsuke Muto and Toshio Ota.

These men fought under conditions of abuse and

A Japanese Nakajima L2D ("Tabby"), an obvious copy of the Douglas DC-3, such as carried Japanese ace Hiroyoshi Nishizawa to his death in the latter months of the war. (This Tabby was actually destroyed by Sergeant W. Tackett of Los Angeles from the top turret of a B-24 piloted by Captain Augustus V. Connery, East Providence, Rhode Island, while on a bombing mission over the Celebes.)

(U. S. AIR FORCE)

hardship which their commanders expected them to endure, in addition to being overwhelmed by a steady flow of fresh young pilots which the enemy sent against them. And these pilots flew better aircraft than the Japanese did toward the conclusion of the war.

But Bong was safely out of all that and happy in a new life; he had married Marjorie Vattendahl, the girl from Wisconsin, and he was working at the Lockheed plant in California, testing a new jet fighter, the P-80. Bong was still the American Ace of Aces; McGuire's score had been thirty-eight—and these would remain the two highest victory scores of the war.

Bong had made it, he had survived, a rare thing with top-scoring fighter pilots. But he could not elude the irony of endings; on the front page of the New York *Times* dated Tuesday, August 7, 1945, which carried the headline beginning "FIRST ATOMIC BOMB DROPPED ON JAPAN," there was another news item.

Just the day before, August 6, 1945, Richard Bong, aged twenty-five, died when the "Shooting Star" jet he was testing crashed and burned at Lockheed airport at Burbank. The concurrence of the two events, merging the atomic bomb and the jet aircraft, ended forever the kind of war that Richard Bong—and Neel Kearby, and Thomas Lynch, and Thomas McGuire, and, for that matter, George C. Kenney—had fought. History assured Bong his special place: he would be the American Ace of Aces forever and there would be no more rivals.

Approaching Guadalcanal, summer of 1942; in the foreground the Enterprise *and in the distance the* Saratoga. *Above, a Dauntless, with arrester hook down, is about to make a landing on the* Enterprise.
(NAVY DEPT., NATIONAL ARCHIVES)

BOOK II
Some Sailors—and
a Few Marines

3

THE ISLAND

THE military High Thinkers, with their penchant for simple but at the same time grandiloquent catchwords, called it Operation Watchtower. The directive, issued by the Joint Chiefs and dated July 2, 1942, ordered the South Pacific Force (Vice-Admiral Robert L. Ghormley commanding) to seize and occupy the "Santa Cruz Islands, Tulagi and adjacent positions" in the Solomon Islands chain. One of the "adjacent positions," not even mentioned in the directive, was an island named Guadalcanal.

The United States Marines, who took, held, and died on this pestilential island, coined their own word for the operation: Shoestring.

"Shoestring" was less grand than "Watchtower," but closer to the realities of the situation. Partially, the problem lay in the simple fact of inexperience in what was the first real offensive move in the war, and the first American amphibious operation since 1898. And it was made with less than adequate planning and equipment plus mixed emotions at high level. Ghormley was not too certain as to what his objectives were: Were we beginning on the road to Tokyo or merely stopping the Japanese before they became too well entrenched in the Solomons?

The entire operation had been conceived and set under way—inspired by the burgeoning airfield on Guadalcanal—in so great a hurry that Ghormley had little time to prepare for whatever it was he was supposed to accomplish. He was pessimistic, indeed, when he first began working on the project: there were no maps of the area, his amphibious forces had not yet arrived in the Pacific, and there was little intelligence on the disposition of the Japanese in the area. If Ghormley harbored doubts, Vice-Admiral Frank J. Fletcher, to whom he had delegated execution of the operation, did not like it at all—and said so. Fletcher as carrier commander was loath to expose his three precious carriers (the *Enterprise, Saratoga,* and *Wasp*) in an undertaking which he "opposed" and which he felt "sure . . . would be a failure."

He made it clear, in fact, at a meeting (not attended by Ghormley) before the assault, that he would not leave the carriers exposed while the Marines were being put ashore for more than two days. It was estimated that it would take five to complete the job. This would, of course, in turn, expose the Marines to attack by the Japanese. Fletcher's attitude, no doubt, could be attributed to the fact of his not seeing any point to the entire operation, and more subtly, to the fact that two carriers (the *Yorktown* and *Lexington*) had gone down under him; he did not wish to court further disasters.

But King, despite the objections of the Joint Chiefs, had initiated Watchtower, and it would go, as ordered, early in August 1942.

Bridge conference on the Wasp *with Dauntlesses spotted on flight deck. Hatless Commander D. F. Smith and steel-helmeted Captain Forrest Sherman, skipper of the* *carrier, attend while Rear Admiral Leigh Noyes receives report from Lieutenant Commander W. N. Beakley (back to camera). Operation Watchtower is under way.* (NAVY DEPT., NATIONAL ARCHIVES)

II

Guadalcanal stank—literally.

It was the effluvium of green decay that first told the sleepless Marines of the amphibious force in the early morning of August 7, 1942, that they had arrived off Red Beach. The smell of the place was evil and the consensus was best expressed by the Marine who was supposed to have said before the invasion began, "What do we want with a place nobody ever heard of before?" He was not alone,

for Ghormley back in Auckland at South Pacific Force headquarters and Fletcher aboard the *Saratoga,* a hundred miles south of Guadalcanal, struggled with the same question.

The initial aerial operations, following the pre-invasion softening up of the Guadalcanal-Tulagi-Gavutu area by the B-17s of Kenny's 11th Bombardment Group during the last week in July and early August, were the attacks by carrier planes upon the various proposed landing areas. Taking off from the *Enterprise, Wasp,* and *Saratoga* before sunrise, the Wildcats and Dauntlesses assembled in the still darkened sky about thirty miles west of Guadalcanal.

It was delicate, if nerve-racking work. In the darkness, although navigation lights were permitted, the usual mix-ups occurred. Fighters and bombers formed up, or squadrons intermixed as pilots mindful of collision gingerly tried to assemble with their own units. What unity had been achieved was suddenly dispersed when a sudden bright flash and explosion erupted under the rendezvous area. Scattering pilots were certain that two unfortunate planes had come together in the dark. Actually one of the Dauntless pilots had accidently dropped his bomb, which blew up on striking the water. By the time the fighters and scout bombers convened again, the invasion beaches—to the utter surprise of the Japanese—came under heavy fire from American naval big guns.

With the coming of first light, as the Marines clambered out of transports into landing craft offshore, the Wildcats and Dauntlesses swept over Beach Red (Guadalcanal) and Beach Blue (Tulagi, about twenty miles northeast of Florida Island). With very little opposition the carrier planes bombed and strafed the two landing areas, blasting buildings, vehicles, warehouses, gun emplacements, and, near Tulagi, a number of float planes moored offshore.

Shortly after 9 A.M. the Marines of the 1st Division began moving in—the landing at Guadalcanal proceeding "with the precision of a peacetime drill." It was not quite so in the vicinity of Beach Blue, where fifteen hundred Japanese fought, and most died, before the little islands of Tulagi, Gavutu, and Tanambogo could be declared secured.

The major problem on Guadalcanal at first seemed to be the accumulation of supplies on the beach. The Japanese troops (six hundred, not five thousand as Allied intelligence had assumed) fled inland, abandoning much of their own supplies. The laborers, who had been constructing the airstrip, inland and to the west of Beach Red, also faded into the jungle. Brigadier General Alexander A. Vandegrift, commanding the Marines, could not stop unloading troops in order to clear Guadalcanal's beaches of the clutter. By noon he realized that "smoothness" and "precision" were gone.

At twelve-thirty the first bombers from Rabaul arrived. Forty-five planes, bombers with fighter escort, of the 25th Koku Sentai opened up the Japanese counterattack. Navy F4Fs caught the initial wave over Florida Island, after Lieutenant Vincent DePoix of the *Enterprise* spotted them and led three other Wildcats into the attack.

Within minutes smoking Bettys dropped from the neat formations and Zeros whipped into the Wildcats. At the same time on the beaches, all unloading of transports was stopped and ships scurried about to afford as poor targets as possible for the bombers. Antiaircraft too came into action. The guns and the Navy fighters distracted the bombers, so there were no hits on the shipping as bombs dropped uselessly into Sealark Channel—a body of water between Florida and Guadalcanal which would become better known as "Iron Bottom Bay." During the early minutes of the first aerial battle over Guadalcanal Navy pilots deposited the initial metal into the bay in the form of Bettys and Zeros.

The first attack had been expected, thanks to an enterprising Australian coast watcher, the ex-planter Paul Mason, who saw the Bettys and Zeros flying over Buin on Bougainville, three hundred miles to the north of Guadalcanal. HQ radioed the message to Brisbane, which relayed it to Pearl Harbor, from which it was sent to the Solomons. But later in the afternoon another attack, this time by dive bombers, came in without advance warnings, and despite the Navy planes on combat air patrol, managed to strike the destroyer *Mugford*. While the ship did not sink, twenty-two men died in the bombing. *Saratoga* Wildcats all but annihilated the attackers, but the harm had been done.

The Japanese planes were as persistent as gnats, despite losses. (Of the fifty or so planes sent from Rabaul that day, about thirty were lost. It was in this first battle over Guadalcanal that Saburo Sakai was badly wounded and somehow managed to return to Rabaul in his Zero.) Some of the losses were those Vals which ran out of fuel on the way back. But a simple fact had emerged: the Japanese could be expected to fight hard for the "place nobody ever heard of before."

The reason lay in an unfinished airstrip on Guadalcanal. If the Japanese had expected to use it to strike at New Zealand and Australia-bound shipping, the Allies could employ it to hammer away at Rabaul.

D-Day, Guadalcanal, August 7, 1942. Bettys from Ra-baul skim the surface of Sealark Channel (Iron Bot-tom Bay) as antiaircraft bursts attempt to put them into the bay. (DEFENSE DEPT., MARINE CORPS)

While Guadalcanal remained quiet, the heavy fighting progressed across Sealark Channel. It was savage and bitter fighting, which, on land, gave the Americans the first shocking, acrid taste of the Japanese soldiers' lethal fighting style. For the time being, the Marines on Guadalcanal were spared this introduction. They gathered souvenirs abandoned by the Japanese, cursed the heat and the insects, and moved farther inland.

The aerial assault, despite the previous day's losses, continued on August 8. Early warning came via coast watcher Jack E. Read on Bougainville, who counted "Forty bombers heading yours." While the Navy Wildcats sought the expected attackers over Savo Island, in the channel between Guadalcanal and Florida, the Bettys dropped down to the water, skimmed in over Florida, and made for the ships.

As the Wildcats tangled with the Zeros overhead, the Bettys were met by a wall of antiaircraft from the ships in the channel. The bombers bore down upon the American ships, then flared one by one, cartwheeling in a pattern of flame before sinking into Iron Bottom Bay. At least a dozen Bettys

went down in the wall of fire from the ships, but one released a torpedo, which struck the destroyer *Jarvis*. The *Jarvis* was caught by Japanese torpedo planes the following day as it made for Nouméa, New Caledonia, and sunk with all hands.

Another stricken Betty flew directly into the transport *George F. Elliott*. Although the troops had already left the ship, the supplies still in the hold burned and the *Elliott* was beyond salvation. The fire went out of control and the *Elliott* was scuttled at twilight—the first American contribution to the debris of Iron Bottom Bay.

The next morning there was much more. Vice-Admiral Gunichi Mikawa, after hastily assembling ships from Rabaul and Kavieng, raced to the Solomons to deal with the enemy. His orders opened with these words: "We will penetrate south of Savo Island and torpedo the enemy main force at Guadalcanal." And as he led his force of seven cruisers and a destroyer toward the island he wired the ships that "In the finest tradition of the Imperial Navy we shall engage the enemy in night battle. Every man is expected to do his best."

The weather and a series of American blunders

were with Mikawa. Fletcher, fearful lest his carriers be struck by Japanese planes or submarines, but using as an excuse that he was low on fuel (this was not true), withdrew the three carriers from Guadalcanal. This also withdrew Navy reconnaissance planes as well as the bombers and fighters which had been countering the Japanese. Although a search plane had spotted Mikawa's ships near Guadalcanal, its warning was neither properly understood nor distributed.

Early in the morning of August 9, 1942, Mikawa's cruisers began firing their deadly "Long Lance" torpedoes at the unsuspecting Allied ships. No one expected the Japanese, who all Americans were told and believed suffered from poor eyesight and could not see at night, to attack after one-thirty in the morning. Following a terrible night battle, the in-

famous battle of Savo Island, the morning light found four heavy cruisers and a destroyer at the bottom of Iron Bottom Bay. More than a thousand men were dead and seven hundred wounded. Mikawa, unaware of his advantage, had slipped away before he did all the damage he might have done, but he had done enough.

By noon Rear Admiral Richmond Kelly Turner, who was in command of the ships of the amphibious force, withdrew his transports from the danger zone. With Fletcher gone and Turner gone, that left only sixteen thousand of Vandegrift's Marines, with only half their supplies, to wonder what the Japanese would try next. They had been furious in their air attacks, had wreaked havoc in the Battle of Savo Island. What would they try now?

The answer came with the initial run of the

The Ichiki detachment, transported to Guadalcanal by the newly instituted "Tokyo Express," has a rendezvous with death and the U. S. Marines on the Tenaru

River. Their major objective had been the airfield on Guadalcanal, which had fallen into American hands.
(DEFENSE DEPT., MARINE CORPS)

"Tokyo Express." The American ships having left Guadalcanal, the Japanese planes took to bombing the airfield being readied by the Marines. Submarines surfaced during the day to lob shells into it and destroyers stood offshore at night. Almost nightly "Washing Machine Charlie" flew down from Rabaul to keep the Marines from sleeping. The Japanese, certain there were only three thousand Americans on Guadalcanal (the actual number was closer to nineteen thousand), dispatched the Ichiki detachment to "quickly attack and destroy the enemy in the Solomons" in co-operation with the Japanese Imperial Navy.

The Ichiki detachment, commanded by Colonel Kiyanao Ichiki, was brought from Guam, to which it had been taken after the Midway fiasco. Instead of sailing home, as the detachment had been promised, it went instead to Truk, and by August 18, having been brought there by the Tokyo Express, began going ashore on Guadalcanal. Within two days the Ichiki detachment was ripped to pieces in a swift series of horrible battles. As Vandegrift reported, ". . . I have never heard or read of this kind of fighting. These people refuse to surrender. The wounded will wait until men come up to examine them . . . and blow themselves and the other fellow to pieces with a hand grenade."

Reinforcements for the "Cactus Air Force," Marine Wildcats at Henderson Field, Guadalcanal.
(DEFENSE DEPT., MARINE CORPS)

Having lost about eight hundred of his men in heedless slaughter (charging automatic weapons with bayonets), Ichiki had no other recourse but to join the honorable dead. After ripping his regimental colors to shreds, inundating them with oil, and setting them afire, Ichiki blew out his brains.

The pattern was established: if the Marines operated on a shoestring, the Japanese chose to use small rubber bands. From Rabaul the bands stretched dangerously; the Tokyo Express would bring in small, inadequate detachments under cover of night and the Imperial Navy would venture forth from time to time. But although they coveted Guadalcanal—especially its airfield—the Japanese High Command, with eyes elsewhere (New Guinea) was unwilling to pursue its course in the Solomons except fragmentally. In the ensuing hard six months, the Japanese and the Americans would learn a good deal about each other.

III

The day before the Battle of Tenaru River, which wiped out the Ichiki detachment, the first elements of what was called the "Cactus Air Force" landed upon Guadalcanal. On August 17, 1942, the Japanese field, taken over and completed by the Americans, was named Henderson Field, for the Marine

dive bomber commander Major Lofton Henderson, who died at Midway. Cactus was the code name for Guadalcanal.

On August 20 the first Wildcats of Marine Aircraft Group (MAG) 23 began alighting on the strip at Lunga Point. These were nineteen new Grumman F4F-4s of Marine Fighter Squadron (VMF) 223, led by a lean Oklahoman, Captain John L. Smith. Along with the Wildcats came a dozen SBD-3s of Major Richard C. Mangrum's VMSB-232 (Marine Scout Bomber Squadron). The arrival of this tiny air force was greeted by the cheering Marines, who pitched in to change the hard-rubber tail wheels (for carrier deck landing) to pneumatic tires.

The next day Smith of Fighting 23 took four Wildcats out to strafe the remnants of the Ichiki detachment. While on patrol over Savo Island Smith sighted several Zeros and led his men in to the attack. The Zeros had the advantage of perhaps two thousand feet of altitude on the Wildcats, so Smith could do little else but turn the more rugged planes into the aggressors. A Zero flashed by without hitting Smith's plane; then another came in and Smith rolled and found the belly of the Zero in his sights. His mouth went dry, he later remembered, and his heart beat heavily as he squeezed the button. For an instant he watched the stitching of his guns travel along the underside of the Zero, which burst open and flamed. As Smith watched, the Japanese plane fell to the beach of Savo. He had killed his first enemy (the first of nineteen).

Turning back to the battle, Smith unhappily noticed that one Wildcat was missing. Searching, he led the two remaining planes to a formation of strangely gyrating and performing aircraft—but they were all Zeros. Why they insisted upon performing like so many Sunday afternoon pilots at an air show, Smith could not fathom. Perhaps they knew that the Wildcat could not dogfight with the Zero; at the same time they wasted the precious fuel for the long return flight to Rabaul—if they ever got there.

Smith led the two pilots back to Henderson, where they saw the fourth Wildcat. Technical Sergeant John D. Lindley's F4F had been hit in the Zero attack and he made for the landing strip, where he crash-landed. Emerging oil-soaked from the cockpit, Lindley collapsed to the ground. He was not

John L. Smith, USMC, commander of the first squadron of fighters to arrive at Guadalcanal. Smith survived the months of hard fighting over the Solomons (for which he received the Medal of Honor), later became an instructor. (DEFENSE DEPT., MARINE CORPS)

seriously hurt and eventually returned to the battle. But his plane was out for the time being.

Fighting 23 had had its first encounter with the dreaded Zero, and although they lost a plane, they had not lost a man. And Captain Smith had actually scored against a Zero. The myth of the invincible Zero was nearing its bitter end.

But the little Cactus Air Force grew slightly. On August 22 the 67th Fighter Squadron, commanded by Captain Dale Brannon, flew up with five Army P-400s (the inferior export P-39, which pilots called "Klunkers"). Two days later an unexpected increment, eleven SBDs, orphans on the wing, flew from the stricken *Enterprise*. These were the Dauntlesses of "Flight 300" led by Lieutenant Turner Caldwell, which, unable to land on the thrice-hit deck of the *Enterprise* during the Battle of the Eastern Solomons, were forced to seek haven at Henderson Field. Immediately drafted into the

Bell P-39s, which in its export version was designated P-400 (originally intended for Britain but repossessed by the Army after Pearl Harbor). Although disparagingly called "Klunkers" by Air Force pilots, the planes served with distinction in the Cactus Air Force. Here they are mud-mired on Henderson.

(U. S. AIR FORCE)

Cactus Air Force, these strays from the *Enterprise* would spend the next month on Guadalcanal.

Thus the battle for Guadalcanal took on its own peculiar forms: on land, at sea, and in the air, with Henderson Field at the focus of action. Emphasis might shift from one aspect of the fighting to the other when the fighting on land erupted bloodily; and then it might shift to the sea (such as the ill-starred Battle of Savo Island). The aerial fighting was generally on a small scale because both forces operated under their individual handicaps—the Marines and their small units, lack of spare parts, minimal fuel supply, and the problem of the weather and climate.

The Japanese had access to a supply of replacement aircraft (which were brought into Rabaul from the homeland, Tinian, Truk, and other outposts). These planes and the new pilots were then tossed away in piecemeal, wasteful attempts. Both aircraft and men were pressed beyond endurance and both were consumed with abandon.

When both sea and air battle combined, the results were more decisive than the prodigal thrusts from Rabaul. Such was the Battle of the Eastern

Solomons (August 24–25, 1942). In this engagement, primarily a battle of carrier forces, land-based Marine aircraft participated in their first major air battle in the Solomons.

Yamamoto had assigned a formidable armada of carriers, battleships, and cruisers to protect four transports of the Tokyo Express carrying fifteen hundred troops to Guadalcanal. The striking force, under Nagumo, somewhat recovered from Midway, was based upon the heavy carriers *Shokaku* and *Zuikaku;* the light carrier *Ryujo* was assigned to a diversionary group under Rear Admiral Chuichi Hara, whose task it was to draw American attention away from Rear Admiral Raizo Tanaka's transports and the big carriers.

When word came in from coast watchers and reconnaissance planes of the presence of large Japanese naval forces proceeding toward Guadalcanal, Admiral Ghormley ordered Fletcher's three carriers north to cover the sea approaches to Guadalcanal. Ever since Fletcher had pulled away from Guadalcanal he had patrolled in the seas to the south of the Solomons. By dawn of August 23 the *Enterprise, Saratoga,* and *Wasp* lay east of Malaita Island (about 150 miles east of Henderson Field).

August 22 and 23 the two fleets feinted gingerly in unfavorable weather (unfavorable, that is, for search planes), neither actually finding the other although both Japanese and Americans knew of

A Marine Wildcat takes off to meet an oncoming Japanese bomber force. Henderson was either soaked in mud or choked with dust, neither of which was salutary for engines or aircraft.

(DEFENSE DEPT., MARINE CORPS)

one another's presence. Fletcher, misinformed by his intelligence that the Japanese fleet still lay far to the north and thus not expecting action, sent the *Wasp,* with its screen, off to refuel. This left the *Saratoga* and *Enterprise* aircraft plus the tatterdemalions of the Cactus Air Force to take on Yamamoto's forces.

As the *Wasp* pulled away to the south, Yamamoto ordered Vice-Admiral Nobutake Kondo, commanding the Guadalcanal supporting force, to press on with the attack.

Shortly after nine o'clock on the 'morning of August 24 an American Catalina on patrol spotted a Japanese carrier, just about 200 miles north of Malaita—and about 280 miles from Fletcher's remaining carriers. It was the *Ryujo* on its mission of diverting Fletcher away from the other two Japanese carriers and the landing forces approaching Guadalcanal.

While the ruse worked—Fletcher dispatched bombers and torpedo planes from the *Saratoga* and *Enterprise*—the cost was rather excessive for the inconsiderable *Ryujo.* After dodging the *Enterprise* Avengers and Dauntlesses, it was struck by planes from the *Saratoga* and sunk. Meanwhile, the fifteen bombers and dozen fighters which the *Ryujo* had launched earlier had tangled with Smith's Fighting 23 on the way to attack Henderson Field.

Not one of the Japanese planes reached Guadalcanal. The Wildcats intercepted the Japanese formation and destroyed sixteen enemy aircraft—six of which were Zeros. One of Smith's few veterans of VMF-223—a veteran, in fact, of Midway—Captain Marion Carl knocked down two Kates and a Zero himself. Other Fighting 23 members, Lieutenants Zennith A. Pond and Kenneth D. Frazier and Gunner Henry B. Hamilton, each shot down two of the attackers. The surviving Kates and Zeros, driven off by the Wildcats, returned to the *Ryujo,* only to find a crazily listing, careening, and burning carrier. The planes were ordered to fly on to the Japanese field at Buka near Bougainville to the north.

The Marines of Fighting 23 chipped away further at the myth of the Zero in the opening fight of the Battle of the Eastern Solomons. But not without cost to them, for the squadron suffered its first serious losses that day. Fred Gutt, noted for his sardonic humor, was seriously wounded; Roy Corry,

The Zero, specifically the "Zeke 52," the mythical fighter of the early months of the Pacific war, but which the Marines, especially of Smith's "Fighting 23," found vulnerable. A beautifully designed, nimble aircraft, the Zero was susceptible to the heavy-gunned American planes. Its pilots were unprotected by armored cockpits and it burned easily.

(U. S. AIR FORCE)

the gunnery officer—also, like Carl, a Midway veteran and who had given Smith cause for concern on the ship coming over because he brooded about his chances of death in the air—was lost. The last seen of him was when he dived into a swarm of Zeros. The first to go, however, had been a youngster named Bailey who had married just the day before he joined VMF-223. His Wildcat was last seen afire as it splashed into the sea.

The *Ryujo* and its aircraft having been attended to, there still remained the *Shokaku* and *Zuikaku,* whose special targets were the American carriers. Almost simultaneously the two carrier captains, Fletcher and Nagumo, became aware of each other's presence when their respective search planes came upon carriers. This was Nagumo's desired moment; he ordered the aircraft launched, the first wave, consisting of sixty-seven planes led by Lieutenant Commander Mamoru Seki, which raced for the spot where an American carrier had been sighted. A second wave, launched less than an hour later and consisting of forty-eight planes, was led astray by a navigational error and never found the American carriers.

Seki's Kates, Vals, and Zeros, however, found the *Enterprise.* As soon as "bogies" were discovered on the radarscopes of the two American carriers, now about ten miles apart, the air above them filled with more than fifty Wildcats. Lieutenant A. O. Vorse, leading a section of four F4Fs from the *Saratoga,* was the first to sight the Japanese planes —two groups of bombers, shepherded above and below by fighters.

With a shout of "Tally Ho!" Vorse pointed the four Wildcats at the bombers, still about ten thousand feet higher than the American planes. Zeros dropped down to intercept, but the Wildcats, straining at full throttle, continued to climb above the Zero's top altitude. Now with the advantage of altitude, Vorse led a screaming attack upon the Japanese bombers. But again the Zeros darted in to disrupt the run on the bombers, and in the ensuing dogfight three Zeros and what appeared to be an Me-109 fell burning into the sea. Out of ammunition and low on fuel, the four Wildcats returned to the *Saratoga,* except for Vorse, who had to land in the water—he did not have enough fuel to make it all the way. A destroyer swept by to pick him up.

But the bombers continued coming in. Some had dropped very low to avoid radar, but four Wildcats, the section of Ensign G. W. Brooks, had been dispatched by the fighter director of the *Enterprise* to investigate a curious echo on the radarscope. Sixty miles from the carrier Brooks and his section found eleven bombers, Vals and Kates—but without Zeros —heading for the *Enterprise.* Brooks's first burst destroyed a Val, and as he turned away, a Kate came into his sights. Another quick burst and the bomber splashed wing over wing across the water. Within minutes four other bombers, victims of the other members of Brooks's section, fell into the sea, three of them shot down. One Val, its pilot rattled by the attack, simply flew into the water. The five survivors turned tail and fled.

Above the *Enterprise,* too, the battle raged, and burning aircraft—American as well as Japanese— fell into the Pacific. With all its fighters air-borne and its bombers aloft, the *Enterprise* waited. Men on deck squinted into the sunny yet cloud-flecked sky, smeared by the smoke of falling aircraft. Crews at their battle stations manned their 20-millimeters. About twenty-five miles away from the *Enterprise,* Seki fired a signal flare. The Zeros had climbed to

engage the Wildcats, the Kates descended to near water level for torpedo attacks, and the Vals, dividing into small groups, prepared for dive attacks.

Around twelve minutes after five in the afternoon, the first Val tipped on its nose and dropped toward the *Enterprise.* Even while it was still out of range a nervous 20-millimeter gunner indicated its approach with his tracers. In seconds other guns, from the carrier itself and from its escort, the *North Carolina,* joined in on the Val. Soon other bombers followed the Val; the Japanese pilots felt that they were diving into "a wall of fire."

But they came on nonetheless, despite the heavy antiaircraft fire and the Wildcats. Within two minutes of the opening of the attack the *Enterprise* took its first bomb of the war. It struck the aft elevator and cut through three decks before detonating. The explosion whipped the *Enterprise,* throwing men in the forward section to the deck, blasting men from their gun positions, tossing them like rag dolls across the decks. Below, where the bomb had burst, more than thirty men lay dead.

Within seconds a second bomb burst, five yards from where the first had hit. In a searing flash, men suddenly vanished from the earth. The great carrier, spouting black smoke, listed; a quarter of its guns were out of action and more than seventy men dead. But repair parties went to work immediately attending to dozens of injured, and began to clear the damaged area and to contain the fires.

Even while this went on a third bomb fell onto the flight deck. Less effective than the first two bombs, the third, however, ripped a ten-foot hole out of the flight deck and knocked an elevator out of operation.

Suddenly, after about four minutes of concentrated havoc, the last of Seki's bombers, a Val, hugging the water raced for its own carrier.

The listing, burning *Enterprise,* though in serious trouble, was not in danger. Even while the damage-repair crews worked, the great ship continued to make speed and even informed the concerned men aboard the *North Carolina* that it "required no assistance." Within an hour after the last bomb had struck, the *Enterprise* was able to turn into the wind to land its aircraft, all except Turner Caldwell's fuel-depleted Flight 300, which landed at Henderson Field (to join the Cactus Air Force).

The *Saratoga* escaped attack, and although two

The third bomb striking the Enterprise, *putting the elevator out of operation and killing Navy photographer* Robert Frederick Read. *Following the Battle of the Eastern Solomons, the* Enterprise *was under repair for two months.* (NAVY DEPT., NATIONAL ARCHIVES)

heavy Japanese carriers were found, they too escaped serious damage (the *Zuikaku* received one bomb on the flight deck). Returning Japanese pilots gleefully reported sinking the *Hornet,* Doolittle's "Shangri-La," and thus avenging the insult to the Emperor. It was, of course, the *Enterprise,* not the *Hornet,* and it was not sunk, but would be out of battle for two months while being repaired at Pearl Harbor.

The carrier battle was over on the first day; both Fletcher and Nagumo gingerly husbanded their carrier strength. As the day came to a close, five Avengers and two Dauntlesses, led by Lieutenant Harold Larsen of the *Saratoga,* were sent out to do something about Kondo's advance force heading for Guadalcanal. The handful of planes attacked and sent the seaplane carrier *Chitose* back to Truk with a thirty-degree list, the loss of the port engine, a fire aboard, and casualties. Kondo continued looking for Fletcher, but by midnight gave up the search.

But "Tenacious" Tanaka, the brilliant overseer of the Tokyo Express, continued on for Guadalcanal with his troop-laden transports. While the carriers and fighting ships had been battling to the east of the Solomons, Tanaka had been coming in from the north. On the morning of August 25, Tanaka's ships

"You never had it so good"—*Marine camp on Guadalcanal during the rainy season.*

(DEFENSE DEPT., MARINE CORPS)

were discovered and Mangrum's Dauntlesses of VMSB-232 and the mixed bag of strays of the *Enterprise,* Flight 300, took off to stop the Japanese.

Before they had found the ships, however, Smith had to turn back his protective Wildcats, at the end of their fuel for the trip out. The Henderson Field bombers, meanwhile, continued their search. Suddenly, as if they had materialized out of the mist, there were the ships: the cruiser *Jintsu,* Tanaka's flagship, plus eight destroyers and the transports.

The Marine and Navy bombers struck. Lieutenant Lawrence Baldinus, of VMSB-232, neatly placed a bomb on the deck of the *Jintsu,* just forward of the bridge and between the two forward turrets. In a reverberating flash, the ship leaped in the water. Tanaka was knocked unconscious as plates buckled, bulkheads were sprung, communications went out, and the forward ammunition lockers flooded. Tanaka, when he came to, realized his flagship was finished as a warship for the time being. He transferred his flag to the destroyer *Kagero* and ordered the *Jintsu* to return to Truk.

Having barely taken up his new post, Tanaka saw Ensign Christian Fink of Flight 300 place a thousand-pound bomb into the heavily loaded transport *Kinryu Maru.* He immediately ordered the destroyers *Mutsuki* and *Yayoi* to run alongside the stricken transport, glowing with heat, to take off survivors.

The American dive bombers, having expended their bombs, circled the scene of damage—the *Jintsu* limping away and the *Kinryu Maru* (which was later sunk) burning furiously—and returned to Henderson. Tanaka then felt he could apply himself better to the problems at hand. But no sooner had the Dauntlesses become specks in the south than high overhead appeared a formation of eight Flying Fortresses. This was not so distressing to Tanaka; as the antiaircraft batteries opened up on these planes, from Colonel LaVerne Saunder's 11th Bombardment Group based in the New Hebrides, Tanaka took some consolation in the fact that the high-flying heavy bombers had never hit a ship, despite American claims to the contrary.

A pattern of five-hundred-pound bombs tumbled from the open bomb bays and before Tanaka's horrified eyes the *Mutsuki* erupted in a series of three flashes and sank. Shortly after, around noon August 25, 1942, Tanaka was ordered to retire to the Shortland Islands, one of the smaller Solomon groups, south of Bougainville. The first major attempt by the Japanese to reinforce Guadalcanal had failed; it had cost them the *Ryujo,* ninety aircraft, and hundreds of men. American losses amounted to seventeen planes and the services of the injured *Enterprise* for several weeks. If the battle of the carriers had not been truly decisive, at least the full contingent of reinforcements had not been landed on Guadalcanal.

IV

That Marine and Navy morale was high could not be attributed to conditions at Henderson Field. For all its blood-soaked significance, Henderson was no pleasure drome. "Henderson Field," Robert Sherrod wrote, "was a bowl of black dust which fouled airplane engines or it was a quagmire of black mud. . . ." Maintenance of the few aircraft was formidable because of the dust and mud; then too there was the humidity. The oil that prevented gun barrels from rusting on the ground caused them to freeze up at fighting altitude.

Ground crews therefore had as tough a time as the airmen. All shared the miseries of climate and the shortage of fresh food (captured Japanese rice was eaten, but only after the careful removal of worms). Malaria and dysentery were common and

so was nagging fatigue. There was no rest at night thanks to "Washing Machine Charlie" or "Louie the Louse," who either dropped random bombs or lighted up the Marine areas with flares so that Tanaka's ships could shell the field and the Marine positions around it.

Yet there was a dash to the style of the pilots of the Cactus Air Force. They became familiar, when photographs came out of the Solomons, in their informal flight clothes all but invariably topped with a blue baseball cap—popular because the visor protected the eyes from the blinding sun. But living and fighting operations took their toll and the problem of reinforcement and supply became critical.

During the day supplies could be brought in by American ships—provided they eluded Japanese submarines and planes. When night fell the big ships raced away from Guadalcanal and the smaller vessels slipped into Tulagi; the land-based Marines dug in. All awaited the arrival of the Tokyo Express, which arrived to land reinforcements and to bring in supplies while its destroyer escort shelled the American positions. Thus, piecemeal, each side kept the fighting going but neither was able to swing the balance.

But piece by piece the American buildup continued at what seemed a piddling pace to those Marines on Guadalcanal. Clearly the Japanese intended to take back Henderson Field, and so it became essential to hold the island. At the end of August the rest of MAG-23 joined its forward echelons—these were Major Robert E. Galer's VMF-224 (with nineteen Wildcats) and Major Leo R. Smith's VMSB-231 (twelve Dauntlesses). At the same time, however, almost twice as many planes were flown in to reinforce Rabaul. The situation remained generally as before: shoestring and rubber band. But standing resolutely between the proper reinforcement by the Japanese of the Guadalcanal forces were the shoestring Marines, the bombers and fighters of Kenney's Fifth Air Force, and the few B-17s and P-39s of those groups that would one day be unified into the Thirteenth Air Force.

Vice-Admiral John S. McCain, commander of all air operations in the South Pacific, stated the facts when he informed Nimitz that "Guadalcanal can be consolidated, expanded and exploited to the enemy's mortal hurt, the reverse is true if we lose Guadalcanal and if reinforcement required is not available Guadalcanal cannot be supplied and cannot be held."

Plenty of action soon blooded the newly arrived Fighting 24 and squadron commander Galer himself opened his string of victories with a double. The veterans of Fighting 23 joined with the new men on missions in order to give them the benefit of their experience.

John Smith continued as his squadron's leading ace with his closest competitor for that position being Marion Carl. But even the veterans could lose a battle, and on September 14, 1942 (while on land the Marines fought at Bloody Ridge to hold Henderson from a heavy attack) Carl's Wildcat was shot into the sea. Carl checked his parachute and took to the air himself. Landing in the water, he swam to shore, where he met one Corporal Eroni, one of the local scouts in the service of Martin Clemens, the Australian coast watcher.

It took Carl and Eroni five days to return to Henderson Field, during which time the colorful and likable pilot was mourned by his squadron mates. He arrived a gaunt, unshaven tall man in dirty khakis at the headquarters of the commander of the 1st Marine Air Wing (1st MAW), Brigadier General Roy S. Geiger. The latter had only recently arrived in Guadalcanal himself to organize operations. His headquarters had been established only two weeks previously in a wooden shack, called "the Pagoda" by the men, about two hundred yards from the Henderson runway—called "the Bull's-eye."

When Carl reported to Geiger the latter was visibly pleased that the man given up for lost had returned. So was Smith, who happened to be in the Pagoda. After relating his adventures with Eroni and the wheezy little launch that had brought him back, Carl—as had the aces in New Guinea—wondered about his score as compared with Smith's.

"Well," Geiger told him, "Smitty has run his score up to fourteen during the five days you were away. That puts you only three behind. What can we do about it?"

"Goddammit, General," Carl retorted, "ground him for five days!"

Thus did the double-edged sword of attrition oscillate from one crisis to the other. Three days before Marion Carl went temporarily missing Cactus Air Force received an unexpected reinforcement: twenty-four Wildcats of VF-5 (Lieutenant Com-

Robert E. Galer, commander of Marine Fighting 24 of Guadalcanal, thirteenth-scoring ace of the Marine Corps and Medal of Honor recipient.

(DEFENSE DEPT., MARINE CORPS)

mander Leroy C. Simpler commanding), rendered homeless after the torpedoing of the *Saratoga* by Japanese submarine I-26. While the carrier put into Pearl Harbor, joining the *Enterprise*, there also undergoing repair, its airmen spent nearly ten days twiddling their thumbs at Espiritu Santo in the New Hebrides. By September 11, 1942, they had arrived at Henderson in time for the heavy battling around the airfield.

Although Admiral Ghormley had consistently refused to permit carrier-based aircraft to operate from Guadalcanal (except the *Enterprise*'s Flight 300, which had no other place to go), he dispatched Simpler's Wildcats to Henderson's attrition center. Obviously something was brewing—and it was, for the Japanese were determined to seize Henderson Field.

The operational toll at Henderson because of primitive repair facilities and fatigued pilots was

Marion E. Carl of Hubbard, Oregon, and a top-scoring ace of Fighting 23. (DEFENSE DEPT., MARINE CORPS)

high. On one day in September, for example, eight planes crashed during takeoff. Two were put together again but the remaining half dozen were dragged off to the plane bone yard to be cannibalized for parts. One fighter pilot, it was reported, looked at the growing junk heap and said to another, "At this rate we can whip ourselves without any assistance from the Japs."

Bombing attacks were intensified, Japanese destroyers shelled Marine positions, and Major General Kiyotaki Kawaguchi arrived, via the Tokyo Express, in the evening of the same day the *Saratoga* had been hit, to organize the taking of Henderson. These plans were most thorough, for they embraced even the surrender ceremonies in which the Americans were expected to participate in the role of the vanquished.

Meanwhile, with the pickup in the activity of the Tokyo Express, a concentration of naval forces at Truk-Palau, and additional aircraft flown into Rabaul noted, all efforts were made to reinforce the Marines at Guadalcanal. When Kawaguchi struck on September 12 one battalion, led by Lieutenant Colonel Kusukichi Watanabe, was expected "to dash through to the airfield." The Marines, expecting something, took a different view. Like the Ichiki detachment, Kawaguchi's force, which fought furiously, was chopped to pieces by the Marines. Further, Kawaguchi's men came under various air attacks, one of the worst being the noonday (September 12) visit by more than two dozen Bettys with Zero escort, which mistakenly bombed and strafed Kawaguchi's rear echelon at Tasimboko on the north coast.

Even the Klunkers, the three remaining airworthy 67th Squadron P-400s, came in low during the final phase of the Battle of Bloody Ridge to end all Japanese hopes of making the dash to Henderson Field.

The fighting was hard and the Marines suffered 59 dead (to the Japanese toll of 708), but despite the clear-cut victory on land, there was a disaster at sea.

On September 15, the day following the Battle of Bloody Ridge, the *Hornet* and *Wasp,* the two remaining carriers in the Pacific, had been called to escort six transports carrying the 7th Marines to Guadalcanal. While moving into the waters of the Coral Sea known as "Torpedo Junction" (between Espiritu Santo and Guadalcanal), the carriers came under submarine attack. The battleship *North Carolina* was hit by a torpedo; so was the destroyer *O'Brien.* Although the *North Carolina* remained afloat and returned to Espiritu Santo, the *O'Brien,* after making temporary repairs, split in two on its way to the United States.

The *Hornet* eluded the Japanese "fish" but three twenty-one-inch torpedoes ripped into the *Wasp* and it sank, a burning mass of junk. That left only the *Hornet* against Nagumo's large carriers, the *Shokaku* and *Zuikaku,* and the light carriers *Zuiho* and *Junyo.* This was an unhealthy imbalance of naval power in the Pacific and it did not bode well for the Marines and Navy and Army men on Guadalcanal.

The only slight brightness was the additional Navy aircraft that, deckless because of the loss of carriers, bolstered up the always tattered Cactus Air Force. "What saved Guadalcanal," Brigadier General Ross

The Wasp, *torpedoed en route to Guadalçanal, before it sank on September 15, 1942.*

(NAVY DEPT., NATIONAL ARCHIVES)

E. Rowell, commander of the Marine Pacific Air Wings, commented, "was the loss of so many carriers." On October 1, 1942, General Geiger had a total of fifty-eight operational aircraft (Wildcats, Dauntlesses, Avengers, and the usual three Klunkers) on Guadalcanal. But at Rabaul the Japanese had about three times this number.

And the Japanese remained resolute in their plans to take Guadalcanal. Lieutenant General Harukichi Hyakutake, commander of the Seventeenth Army at Rabaul, had his own timetable to keep. His major project was the taking of Port Moresby, but before that he wished to recapture Guadalcanal by October 21. After the disasters of the Ichiki detachment and the Kawaguchi force,

however inexplicable, Hyakutake proposed to lead the recapture himself. As additional insurance he built his force around two tough divisions, veterans of the fighting in the Philippines, Java, and other conquered areas. These units, the 2nd (Sendei) and 38th Divisions, were equipped with heavy artillery and tanks, neither of which Ichiki nor Kawaguchi had had. At the same time the aircraft strength at Rabaul was raised to 180; a bomber base was established at Buka in the northern Solomons and fighters could be accommodated at Buin on Bougainville. Even the generally unsympathetic Imperial Navy co-operated with the promise of such great battleships as the *Haruna, Kongo, Hiei,* and *Kirishima.* The Tokyo Express was in fine shape.

By the time Hyakutake himself arrived by the nightly express he had around twenty thousand (perhaps several thousands more; precise figures were not maintained during these tense days) troops awaiting the word to go. On this October 9 Hyakutake, the soul of efficiency, had a good idea of which spot was to be selected for the surrender of General Vandegrift.

On this same day twenty Wildcats of MAG-14 arrived (making the total forty-six fighters); the planes were led in by Major Leonard K. Davis. These were the aircraft of VMF-121, a squadron whose executive officer was Captain Joseph J. Foss. Smith's veteran VMF-223 had by this time become depleted with six pilots killed and six wounded. Eight, among them Smith himself, survived. Smith, with a score of 19, was the squadron's ace, and Marion Carl was second with a total of 16. But the contribution of Fighting 23 did not lay in numbers (the squadron total was 111½), but in the day-to-day fighting against odds for nearly two months. For his part John L. Smith was awarded the Medal of Honor and returned to the United States to train future Marine fighter pilots.

Richard Mangrum, who led the first of the Dauntless squadrons (VMSB-232), like Smith, survived although the squadron had suffered eleven killed (seven of whom were pilots) and five wounded (four of these being pilots); the rest of the squadron had to be evacuated by air for hospitalization. Only Mangrum was able to leave under his own power.

Flight 300 of the *Enterprise* had been used up in the battling and its last crew members were shipped out to return to their carrier by late September. The weight of the bombing effort out of Henderson devolved upon Major Gordon A. Bell's VMSB-141, which began arriving on September 23 and which by October 6 could muster twenty-one pilots, and upon Leo Smith's depleted VMSB-231 and other strays which had come in from the south.

Joseph Foss got his first Zero on October 13, 1942, during an afternoon raid by Japanese bombers and Zeros. It was this day which the Japanese selected to open their final seizure of Guadalcanal, which Hyakutake told his troops would "truly decided the fate of the entire Pacific."

The first of the Japanese bombers, coming over just after noon, holed the runway at Henderson and a nearby strip, Fighter 1. Even more irreparable

harm was done when five thousand gallons of aviation fuel went up in smoke. More bombers came over about an hour later and again Henderson was worked over. Because both raids had come without advance warning there was little opportunity for interception, except for a couple of Zeros, one of them shot down by Foss.

Just before these raids the first Army troops, the "Americal Division" (164th Infantry Regiment), had debarked to be treated to the typical atmosphere of Guadalcanal. Nighttime brought even more of the same. To the Marines' surprise, just after six o'clock in the evening shells began falling on Henderson. There were no Japanese ships offshore. This was "Pistol Pete," one of the heavy artillery guns which had been brought in on the Tokyo Express only two nights before.

But that was only the preliminary to the evening's diversion. From time to time Pistol Pete would lob one over, just to keep everyone on their toes, and nerves' edge, and then in the middle of the night Louie the Louse flew over and planted three flares across Henderson Field, a red one at one end, white in the middle, and blue at the other end. For the next hour and a half the *Haruna* and the *Kongo*

Marines extinguish a burning Wildcat at Henderson Field after a Japanese bombing raid.
(DEFENSE DEPT., MARINE CORPS)

laid more than nine hundred fourteen-inch shells into the Henderson area, ripping up the steel matting of the runways, damaging planes, and killing men. It was a nightmare, literally, of flame, explosion, and terror. As Tanaka observed he found that "the whole spectacle [made] the Ryogoku fireworks display seem like mere child's play. The night's pitch dark was transformed by fire into the brightness of day. Spontaneous cries and shouts of excitement ran throughout our ships."

This exhilaration was not echoed ashore. When the Marines and soldiers finally crawled from their foxholes, the destruction their bleary eyes took in was disheartening. To begin with, forty-one men were dead, five of them pilots; one of the latter was Major Gordon Bell, only recently arrived with his replacement Dauntlesses. General Geiger, who had dived into shelter knowing he had thirty-nine Dauntlesses to dispatch against the Japanese, found upon emerging that only four were still flyable. Sixteen of his forty Wildcats were wrecks and all of the remaining ones required repairs. Two Flying Fortresses, of eight which had arrived from Espiritu Santo, were destroyed. The surviving six got away from Henderson as soon as possible, some on less than full power.

About the only damage that no one regretted was

a direct hit upon a ration dump which deposited bits and pieces of Spam in every direction for a half mile. And since the airfield was the center of attention, General Geiger's Pagoda was also hit. This structure, which afforded the Japanese a good aiming point, was bulldozed to the ground, and the Marine aviation commander moved his headquarters to the eastern end of Henderson Field.

And so it went on: savage fighting in the jungle around Henderson, bombardment by night and day, as each contender attempted to reinforce their forces on the island. This made for what Samuel Eliot Morison called "a curious tactical situation . . . : a virtual exchange of sea mastery every twelve hours." It was like some mad changing of the guard, with the Japanese in control at night and the Americans by day. But Hyakutake, with the aid of Yamamoto, hoped to change all that once and for all.

The night following "the Night," as the Marines called it, the Japanese ships returned, this time in the form of a couple of cruisers, which laced the Henderson area with nearly eight hundred eight-inch shells to cover the landing of more reinforcements. By dawn of the next day, October 15, the Japanese believed that Henderson had been pretty well taken care of—and they were not far from wrong. In the morning an American search plane came upon five Japanese transports, standing off Tassafaronga (about ten miles west of Henderson on the north coast of Guadalcanal) rather discon-

Bombed-up Dauntlesses over Guadalcanal head for their targets—ships of the Tokyo Express.
(DEFENSE DEPT., MARINE CORPS)

A Consolidated PBY "Catalina," a patrol bomber that Marine Major "Mad Jack" Cram converted (for one battle) into a dive bomber.

(CONVAIR/GENERAL DYNAMICS)

certingly unloading troops and supplies in broad daylight.

Geiger found he had little with which to contest this affront. Only three Dauntlesses were in condition to get off the ground, and only one actually did. The other two cracked up while attempting to get off the pocked Henderson runway. But single attacks could accomplish very little, especially when the Zeros could come down from Bougainville to circle over the transports. But as the day progressed, ground crew men patched up the aircraft and found some long-forgotten supplies of fuel hidden in the swamps around the airfield; they siphoned this fuel

into whatever planes could be mustered for disputing with the Japanese their bold attempt to take over during the American daylight period of sea mastery.

By ten in the morning, three hours after the first single-plane attacks, a dozen Dauntlesses were ready to fly. Wildcats, Klunkers (P-400s), and even a single Catalina went out to raze the transports' rendezvous area. Major Jack Cram, the pilot of the Catalina, *Blue Goose,* General Geiger's personal aircraft, took off with two two-thousand-pound torpedoes slung under the Catalina's wing. He had arrived from Espiritu Santo with the torpedoes, but found there were no Avengers in condition to deliver them. Although no PBY had ever made a daylight torpedo run before, Cram, by dint of vocal power, obtained permission to drop the fish. Cram, who earned the nickname of "Mad Jack" on this mission, took off in company with a mixed flight of Dauntlesses and Wildcats. Counting his slow Catalina, the American formation consisted of twenty-one planes. Over the Japanese transports milled about thirty Zeros.

As the Dauntlesses raced in for their attacks, Cram set the Catalina on its own, near-dawdling bomb run. The big plane soon came under anti-aircraft fire from the ships (one hit sheared off the plane's navigation hatch). Cram bore down on one of the transports and released the torpedoes, both of which tore into the side of one of the transports, ripping it open.

Mad Jack Cram, though successful in his un-orthodox mission, was now in plenty of trouble. Several Zeros, upon realizing what the pilot of the Catalina had been up to, peeled out of the fighting above and began devoting full attention to the *Blue Goose*. Having already dived the Catalina beyond its normal safe speed, Cram tested the groaning airframe and wing even more in attempting to evade the Zeros. Although he managed to keep his crew and himself from being holed with his crazy aerobatics, the Catalina itself was punctured half a hundred times on the way to Henderson Field. Coming in low to pull in to the field, Cram found he still had one angry Zero on his tail. His airspeed was also too high for a landing, so Cram continued on to the satellite field, Fighter 1.

His luck improved over Fighter 1, for as he waddled onto the strip one of the fighter pilots, VMF-121's Lieutenant Roger Haberman, forced out of the fighting with a smoking Wildcat, also came in to the field. Seeing the Catalina under attack, Haberman eased his Wildcat, its wheels already lowered for landing, onto the Zero pilot's tail and shot the Zero out of the air.

When Geiger saw what remained of his command plane he threatened Mad Jack Cram with a court-martial for "deliberate destruction of government property," and then awarded him the Navy Cross.

By the day's end the Japanese had lost three transports, which burned and had to be beached, with much destruction to their cargoes. This included

Major Jack R. Cram, aide and pilot for Marine Major General Roy S. Geiger.

supplies, artillery ammunition, and, of course, troops. Even B-17s had come up from the New Hebrides to sink one of the ships. Fighters, in addition to mixing with the Zeros, also strafed the transports and the beaches, inflicting a terrible toll on the Japanese troops. American losses were three Dauntlesses and four Wildcats, but those Japanese ships which had not been destroyed pulled away from Tassafaronga.

Still, nearly five thousand troops had been landed and the night was again rendered hideous by shelling from cruisers. On October 15 Geiger had only thirty-four aircraft (nine Wildcats) to stand off any Japanese attempt to retake Guadalcanal. The truth was that all was not at all well in the Solomons. While the word was not released to the American public, the words of Admiral Nimitz were arresting:

Harold W. Bauer (in an early photograph), who earned a Medal of Honor on the day he arrived at Henderson Field, and was lost in combat before he could be decorated. (DEFENSE DEPT., MARINE CORPS)

"It now appears that we are unable to control the sea in the Guadalcanal area. Thus our supply of our positions will only be done at great expense to us. The situation is not hopeless, but it is certainly critical."

General Vandegrift was far less reticent when he informed Ghormley that it was "Urgently necessary that this force [i.e., Vandegrift's command on Guadalcanal] receive maximum support of air and surface units."

Ghormley was able to send additional Wildcats of VMF-212 (some of whose pilots were already at Henderson), under Lieutenant Colonel Harold W. Bauer. This put Geiger's fighter strength up to twenty-eight; also arriving with Bauer's flight were seven Dauntlesses which had accompanied them up from Efate (New Hebrides). As the formation set-

tled down for a landing late in the afternoon they found they had arrived in the middle of a dive-bombing attack. Nine Vals were working over the U.S.S. *McFarland*, which had just delivered a cargo of aviation fuel and was preparing to pull out of the Solomons with medical evacuees aboard.

Seeing this, and despite nearly empty fuel tanks after the long flight north, Bauer singlehandedly took after the Vals. He dived into the squadron of Japanese bombers and slashed through with his guns hammering; in minutes four Vals fell away burning. Bauer, now dangerously low on fuel, had to pull away and land at Henderson Field. He was to receive a Medal of Honor for this attack, but he did not survive to accept it.

V

The date of Bauer's Medal of Honor fight was October 16, 1942. On this same day Ghormley received word of great activity by the Japanese fleet in the vicinity of the Santa Cruz Islands, south and east of the Solomons. Ghormley recognized the situation as more than critical, wired Nimitz that his "forces [were] totally inadequate to meet" the impending threat. In two days, on October 18, 1942, Ghormley was out. He was replaced by a "more aggressive commander" (the words are Nimitz's) in the person of Vice-Admiral William F. Halsey. When word was released in the Pacific it was greeted by cheers from the men, who had been discouraged over the stalemate at Guadalcanal.

General Hyakutake, meanwhile, had formulated his plan of attack upon the Henderson perimeter; there would be three simultaneous assaults at widely separated points. The main push would come up from the south under Lieutenant General Masao Maruyama. A keen sense of history motivated the general, for he instructed his engineers to construct a trail through the swamp and jungle leading to Henderson Field, which he, free of false modesty, decided to name "the Maruyama Road." The total plan was elaborate, therefore complex, and like so many grand military enterprises, appeared fine on paper and sounded beautiful in high-level discussion, but proved to be much different when attempted "on the ground" and with live men instead of symbols.

Timed to coincide with Hyakutake's seizure of

Henderson Field, Yamamoto at Truk had impressive plans for the Combined Fleet. He assembled four carriers, five battleships, fourteen cruisers, and forty-four destroyers for an all-out effort which, it was planned, would settle the bothersome Solomons question once and for all. Yamamoto was emboldened by the knowledge that with the *Wasp* sunk and the *Saratoga* undergoing repairs, his only carrier opposition would come from the *Hornet*. He did not know, however, that the *Enterprise* had recovered from the three bomb hits taken in the Battle of the Eastern Solomons and was ready for action.

The land battle opened first, when Hyakutake's three-pronged attack got off to an unco-ordinated start on October 23. Communications being what they were in Guadalcanal's jungles, the neatly laid plans went quite readily awry. To soften up the American positions for Hyakutake's grand blow a large force of Japanese bombers with fighter escort came down from Rabaul and Buin. These were met by two dozen Marine and Navy Wildcats.

Climbing to meet the Japanese, Joseph Foss counted sixteen bombers and perhaps twenty-five Zeros. As he led his flight in an attack upon five Zeros, Foss found himself about to be victimized by twenty, which dived out of the sun. The Wildcats snapped into a fast dive to accumulate the speed to escape the enemy fighters. As he zoomed out of the way Foss caught a glimpse of a Wildcat on the tail of a Zero. Another Zero was attached to the Wildcat. Foss reacted immediately and the second Zero quickly, under his guns, disintegrated in mid-air. Foss, who witnessed several such explosions, described the process: "The motor goes off in a crazy, lopsided whirl. The pilot pops out of his cockpit like a pea that has been pressed from a pod. The air is filled with dust and little pieces, as if someone has emptied a huge vacuum cleaner bag in the sky. The wing section, burning where it had joined the fuselage, takes a long time to fall. It goes down like a leaf—sailing, then almost stopping as it attacks the air, sailing again, and attacking the air again." Foss was forced to turn sharply to avoid "the falling junk" as he whirled into another Zero. Before he was forced out of the fighting with a badly smoking engine, the result of a head-on attack by a Zero, which he also shot out of the sky, Foss had shot down four of the day's tally of twenty Zeros and four bombers.

Joseph J. Foss, USMC, who shot down twenty-six Japanese planes over the Solomons (twenty-three of them over Guadalcanal during the period October 9–November 19, 1942) to earn himself the Medal of Honor and the accolade of America's ace of aces until Richard Bong's score began accumulating over New Guinea. (DEFENSE DEPT., MARINE CORPS)

Rain on the next day discouraged all activity except for the Japanese troops slithering through the jungle over the prematurely named Maruyama Road. The day after, October 25, 1942, went down in Marine history as "Dugout Sunday." Thanks to the mud, most U.S. aircraft were immobilized when the Japanese planes came over in the morning and gave the Marine positions a severe mauling. Japanese land, sea, and air traffic picked up; the big final push was on.

American aircraft were unable to get off the airstrips until later in the day, but once they did they dealt severely with the Japanese. Once again Foss scored copiously, five Zeros in a single combat —bringing his total up to sixteen (his final score would be twenty-six). Dugout Sunday, which had begun so propitiously for the Japanese airmen, closed with a loss of twenty-two aircraft to fighters and four to antiaircraft guns.

Three hundred miles to the east of Guadalcanal, meanwhile, Yamamoto's Guadalcanal support force, the Third Fleet (Nagumo), and the Second Fleet (Kondo) waited. This powerful force was assigned the task of intercepting American attempts to reinforce the Guadalcanal garrison, presumably being torn to ribbons by Hyakutake's troops on the island, and also to prevent the survivors from escaping. Aware of the presence of the large Japanese naval forces to the north of the Santa Cruz Islands, Halsey ordered Task Force 61 (the *Enterprise*) and TF 17 (the *Hornet*), the only carrier forces available, to a rendezvous point north of the New Hebrides. To this was also added TF 64 (built around the battleship *Washington*). These forces were under the tactical command of Rear Admiral Thomas C. Kinkaid of the *Enterprise*.

The odds were far from even. Nagumo with his 4 carriers could count on 212 aircraft; Kinkaid had 171. There was but 1 American battleship to stand against 4 Japanese (as it eventuated, Task Force 64 did not participate in the battle, which left only the *South Dakota* of TF 61). To round out the picture: there were 12 Japanese cruisers versus 6 American, and 24 destroyers against 14. Nagumo exuded confidence for the first time since Midway, even more so, for he was not aware of the fact that the *Enterprise* had returned to active duty.

Still, Nagumo was uneasy. He awaited word of Vandegrift's surrender to Hyakutake, but it did not come. In fact, because of some confusion (and poor communications between the three broad arrows pointing toward Henderson Field on his field map), Hyakutake had been forced to postpone the concerted assault. Nagumo fretted and wired Hyakutake to get on with the American defeat, for the ships were running low on fuel. Then good word came from the island: Kawaguchi, of the ill-fated earlier fighting at Bloody Ridge, in an excess of hope was certain he saw some of his men overrun Henderson Field. A naval liaison officer with the ground troops sent the message, "Airfield taken." It was a premature conclusion, as it turned out, but it was enough for anxious Nagumo. He refueled and turned toward Guadalcanal, not knowing the Marines were blunting the land attack.

After midnight, October 25, 1942—Dugout Sunday on Guadalcanal—a Catalina out of Espiritu Santo found the Japanese fleet. The message sent was laconic: "Sighted enemy task force Lat. 'a' Long. 'b' course 'c' speed 'd' x-ray. Please notify next of kin." The Catalina, after dropping flares upon the Japanese force, shadowed the carriers for a time, attempting to collect more information. Then the big flying boat, low on fuel, turned away.

So did Nagumo, who reversed course. When Dauntlesses, Avengers, and Wildcats, launched from the *Enterprise* later in the day, fanned out searching for Japanese ships, Nagumo had slipped into the darkness and no enemy ships were found. The same frustration attended Nagumo. He was aware of the Americans and the increase of aerial and radio activity, but he had no real idea where their carriers were.

On October 26 all mystery was dispelled when a search plane from the *Shokaku* sighted the American forces bearing northwest. A search mission from the *Enterprise* also spotted Nagumo's carriers. There were no longer any military secrets as men began preparing for attacks upon the carriers in what came to be called the Battle of Santa Cruz.

Two Dauntlesses, one piloted by Lieutenant Stockton B. Strong and the other by Ensign Charles Irvine, came upon the big *Shokaku* and the small *Zuiho;* the *Zuikaku* was hidden under cloud some miles away. Strong signaled to Irvine that they would attack the nearest carrier, the *Zuiho,* so Irvine moved in closer, though behind Strong's Dauntless. So far so good, for they had moved into attack position without antiaircraft or Zero interference.

Strong rolled over, put his flaps in dive position, and with an eye on his aiming scope, plummeted toward the slender yellow deck of the *Zuiho*. Three hundred yards behind, Irvine followed. The Dauntlesses screamed down out of the sun until each reached a point about fifteen hundred feet above the *Zuiho,* which, Strong noted, carried no aircraft on its decks. Evidently a strike had already been launched by Nagumo. Strong released his five-hundred-pound bomb and seconds later Irvine's arched away from the belly of his Dauntless also. Both struck the *Zuiho* in the after section of the flight deck, ripping the deck open, toppling antiaircraft guns, and ending the *Zuiho* as an effective carrier for the rest of the battle. Although it would have been possible to launch aircraft, which he had already done, Captain Sueo Obayashi reported to Nagumo that the *Zuiho* would not be able to land any aircraft. The *Zuiho,* vulnerable and all but helpless, must leave the scene of combat.

Strong and Irvine, meanwhile, had pulled out of their dives, then sought the safety of near-water flight to escape the antiaircraft fire and the attacks by Zeros. While their rear gunners fought off the Zeros that came in too close, Strong radioed the location of the *Zuiho* and the amount of damage he estimated he and Irvine had done to it. Irvine's Dauntless had taken some hits in the wing and tail, which slowed him up a bit, as the two Navy planes strained at full speed for the *Enterprise.* The question was: Where would the *Enterprise* be? If it had come under observation, the ship would have certainly shifted course; if the Japanese planes, absent from the *Zuiho*'s flight deck, had found it, the situation could even be worse.

Finally, after a forty-five-mile chase, close to the waves and then dodging through puffs of cloud,

the Zeros gave up after losing two of their number to the Dauntless gunners. With practically no fuel the two Dauntlesses settled down upon the deck of the *Enterprise.* The time was ten twenty-six; the Dauntlesses had been air-borne since six that morning. They had done a good morning's work—and the *Enterprise,* thanks to a sudden local rain squall, had momentarily escaped attack.

At 5:15 A.M. Nagumo had launched the first attack group, under the command of Lieutenant Commander Mamoru Seki, from the *Shokaku* and the *Zuikaku.* For this strike the *Shokaku* had provided twenty-two Vals and twenty-seven Zeros; the *Zuikaku* put up eighteen Kates. Thus the strike was composed of dive bombers, torpedo bombers, and fighters. As the formation proceeded toward the American carriers they passed another group of aircraft going in the opposite direction. These were Dauntlesses from the *Hornet* on their way hoping to do hurt to the Japanese carriers. For some reason Lieutenant Commander Hideki Shingo, leading the *Shokaku*'s Zeros high above the bombers,

An Avenger of Air Group 10 prepares to take off from the Enterprise *at Santa Cruz. Hand-held signs give aircrews last-minute information; sign directly* *under the cowling reads: "Jap CV [carrier] Speed 25 at 8:30" and, directly over wheel, "Proceed without Hornet."* (NAVY DEPT., NATIONAL ARCHIVES)

A Kate passes over a cruiser, its target a carrier; Battle of Santa Cruz.

(NAVY DEPT., NATIONAL ARCHIVES)

did not see the *Hornet* formation, or did not recognize the planes as those of the enemy, so no attack was ordered. For this oversight Shingo's home ship would suffer. It was a ludicrous fraction of a moment as the bomber pilots, brothers under the skin though enemies, passed each other on similar errands. The good luck of the men of the *Hornet*'s first strike force would last until it found the Japanese ships.

Not so, however, for the men of the first *Enterprise* team. Eight Avengers, three Dauntlesses, and an escort of eight Wildcats took off early and headed for the presumed position of the Japanese carriers. Barely a half hour out from the *Enterprise* the formation suffered a sudden attack from above by Zeros. Almost simultaneously two Avengers, one of them flown by Lieutenant Commander John A. Collet, commander of Torpedo 10, spiraled burning into the ocean four thousand feet down. In the slashing attack by fighters from the already burning *Zuiho,* the *Enterprise* force was cut in half. The Wildcats, at a disadvantage at low altitude, were handicapped; three went down into the ocean and another, smoking, turned back for the *Enterprise,*

only about fifty miles away. When the survivors reassembled only four Avengers remained with the three Dauntlesses to make the attack and there were only four Wildcats to protect them.

But they did not find the carriers and dropped their bombs and torpedoes into what was believed to be "a *Kongo*-type" battleship. While the *Kongo* and the *Haruna* were units in Vice-Admiral Kondo's advance force, they were not hit that day. This was probably the *Chikuma,* a cruiser in Nagumo's striking force. Though struck and damaged rather heavily, the *Chikuma* continued to function despite casualties.

Though deprived of the Zero escort, which turned back after it had attacked the *Enterprise* force (because of fuel consumed in the fighting), Lieutenant Commander Seki led his Vals and Kates toward the *Hornet.* As combat air patrol Wildcats swept in to attack, Seki dived toward the *Hornet.* Heavy antiaircraft fire rose to hammer him and shortly after he had given his command for the attack, Seki was hit several times. His plane rolled over on its back, flame streaming behind, and continued toward the *Hornet.* Bombs were flung into the carrier

The Battle of Santa Cruz, October 26, 1942. The air filled with antiaircraft fire, the sea churning with the movement of heavy ships and plunging aircraft—and the Enterprise (left) dodging a bomb or Japanese plane. (NAVY DEPT., NATIONAL ARCHIVES)

from the Vals. A stricken Val, probably Seki's, came in upon the *Hornet,* careened off the stack, smashed through the flight deck, and burst with the detonation of its own bombs. And then the Kates came in, low on the water, to jab torpedoes into the carrier's sides. Two fish cut into the engineering spaces and the *Hornet,* spouting steam, flame, and gouts of black smoke, lurched to the starboard. During the torpedo attack another suicidal run was made on the *Hornet,* portent of things to come, when a Kate, which may have been that of Lieutenant Jiichiro Imajuku, ran in upon the *Hornet* from dead ahead (seemingly under control), smashed a gun gallery, rolled into a ball of flaming metal, and exploded near the forward elevator shaft.

The U.S.S. *Hornet,* Doolittle's "Shangri-La," was finished and truly could the Japanese at long last claim vengeance for the Tokyo raid. But for those who believe wars can be fought on vengeance, the *Hornet* would, before it sank into the Pacific, have its small share. Led by Lieutenant James E. Vose, the *Hornet*'s dive bombers located the *Shokaku* and broke through the screen of antiaircraft fire and Zeros. Bombs splashed across the deck of the *Shokaku,* Nagumo's flagship, splintering great holes in the deck and producing violent flames, twisting hot gun barrels out of action and starting fierce blazes below decks. Although the *Shokaku* was to escape the final fate of the *Hornet,* it was no longer capable of either taking or launching planes and its communications were out. Nagumo was forced to leave the battle. He turned over the command to Rear Admiral Kakuji Kakuda aboard the unharmed *Zuikaku* and fled northward for Truk. The *Shokaku* would be out of the war for nine months.

But the *Zuikaku* and the *Junyo* (the latter of

Kondo's advance force) were still very much in the battle. Vals and Kates from both these carriers found the *Enterprise,* and though the Japanese planes were badly mauled by fighters and heavy antiaircraft fire, three bombs struck the *Enterprise,* causing terrible fires and damage and resulting in the death of forty-four men. The Kates too added to the misery of the day, but skillful dodging under the cool command of Captain Osborne B. Hardison saved the *Enterprise* from further damage. Gunners of the *South Dakota,* a battleship armed with heavy AA batteries, destroyed Japanese planes attempting to hit the *Enterprise* also. The *South Dakota,* however, suffered a hit from one of the *Junyo* bombers. So did the cruiser *San Juan.* The destroyer *Smith* was crashed by a Kate, which set the ship aflame. And as it drew into the vicinity of the *Hornet* to take men from the burning carrier, the

To reduce the hazard of fire, a damaged Dauntless is pushed off the deck of the Enterprise *into the waters off Santa Cruz.* (NAVY DEPT., NATIONAL ARCHIVES)

destroyer *Porter* was torpedoed by Japanese submarine I-21. The *Porter* sank, taking fifteen men trapped in the firerooms, and later the *Hornet,* "a flaming mass," was sunk by the Japanese destroyers *Makikumo* and *Akigumo.*

The *Hornet* and *Porter* were the only ships, both American, which were lost in the Battle of Santa Cruz. Truly could the Imperial fleet make claims for a great victory in what they called "the Battle of the South Pacific." Despite the damages to the *Shokaku* and *Zuiho,* it could be said that Yamamoto had won the battle, but there was a subtle perplexity to consider. No Japanese ships had gone down, it was true, and the only carrier which sizzled under the sea was American, but under that sea also were sixty-nine Japanese aircraft totally lost, with an additional two dozen forced down into the sea. Some of the pilots from the latter were saved, but all the aircrews of the sixty-nine bombers and fighters, the few remaining veterans of Pearl Harbor, the Indian Ocean, and the Coral Sea, were lost.

Lieutenant Stanley W. "Swede" Vejtasa of VF-10, the Enterprise, *climbing into the cockpit of his Wildcat.* (NAVY DEPT., NATIONAL ARCHIVES)

If the Battle of Santa Cruz was frustrating in its lack of a clean-cut victory it was also obvious that American "carrier strength in the Pacific was now dangerously low," in the words of King. Even so, the Japanese had lost their last major attempt at taking back Guadalcanal. But the loss of so many experienced pilots, who might have trained more "sea eagles" for Nippon, was a heavy price to pay for the *Hornet* and the *Porter* and seventy-four U.S. planes.

Typical of the aerial action which marked the ferocity of the Santa Cruz battle was that engaged in by Lieutenant Stanley W. "Swede" Vejtasa. Leading three other members of VF-10 (the famed Lieutenant Commander James Flatley's "Grim Reapers" of the *Enterprise*) Vejtasa spent more than nine hours in the air on October 26, 1942. Shortly after Captain Hardison all but oscillated his

massive *Enterprise* out of the attack of five torpedo planes, Vejtasa and his four Wildcats were vectored to investigate more unidentified, incoming aircraft.

It had been an active flight, for Vejtasa had already destroyed two dive-bombing Vals, and upon reaching the new point, he saw no less than eleven Kates streaking for the *Enterprise*. If the Kates split up, as was customary, Hardison would have had to make the *Enterprise* dance to elude all of them. With his wingman, Lieutenant Leroy Harris, Vejtasa approached the stepped-up column of three Vs plus two Kates trailing. The other two men in his flight, Lieutenant Stanley E. Ruehlow and Ensign W. H. Leder, teamed up to attack. While Ruehlow and Leder were busy with a pair of Zeros, Vejtasa and Harris came in below and astern of the Kates. As soon as they were within range both men began firing and each took out one Kate, the two trailing the three V-formations. They pushed throttle to overtake the nine remaining Kates and just as they did entered a great cumulus cloud.

Vejtasa no longer saw Harris, but ahead of him, dimly, he could make out some Kates. He moved in, aimed at the left-hand member of the formation, and opened with his six .50-calibers. The Kate exploded and fell away. The next plane lost its rudder and then burst into flame and fell too. Alerted, the third Kate attempted to turn, but the faster Wildcat turned more sharply and Vejtasa opened up on the Japanese bomber. It had exposed its length to the spray of Vejtasa's guns and the last plane of the V splashed into the sea.

Low on ammunition, Vejtasa spotted another Kate, but it had pulled well away from him and he elected to leave it to the antiaircraft fire which awaited it. As he circled the arena of battling ships Vejtasa saw another Kate, obviously free of its torpedo, fleeing the scene. The Wildcat dived upon the bomber, and with his last few rounds Vejtasa knocked down his seventh enemy plane of the day. The four VF-10 Wildcats had so disrupted the Kate attack that three of the survivors jettisoned their torpedoes and fled. Two others did not even drop theirs, although the one Vejtasa had left for the ship's antiaircraft batteries may have been the Kate that crashed into the *Smith*.

The Battle of Santa Cruz ended, a tactical victory for the Japanese. The *Hornet* was gone and the *Enterprise* had been hit and crippled; this left only

". . . and the last plane . . . splashed into the sea."
The Battle of Santa Cruz, though it cost the Ameri- *cans the* Hornet *and crippled the* Enterprise, *cost the Japanese heavily in aircraft and experienced pilots.*
(NAVY DEPT., NATIONAL ARCHIVES)

two carriers in the Pacific, the *Enterprise* and the *Saratoga,* which was also crippled and undergoing repair. Wisely, Kinkaid pulled away to the south out of reach of Kondo's big ships and Kakuda's remaining aircraft. The *Zuikaku* and *Junyo* were still capable of dispatching bombers which might have spelled the end of the *Enterprise.* Nor could

Kinkaid risk the possibility of a night engagement for the simple reason that the Japanese were better at it at the time than the Americans. It was a frustrating engagement all around: the Japanese had won, but they had lost too many experienced pilots. The battle ashore, which the naval battle had been designed to cover, had failed.

4

DERAILING THE TOKYO EXPRESS

GUADALCANAL remained in American hands. General Hyakutake's beautifully reasoned plan of attack and his formal, very proper surrender ceremony never came off. By October 28, with more than three thousand Japanese dead on Guadalcanal and sixty-nine irreplaceable pilots deep in the sea off Santa Cruz, it was obvious that another Japanese attempt to take the miserable island had miscarried. The island took on a significance beyond its strategic importance (which militarists eventually realized was secondary). The Allies were determined to keep it and the Japanese were resolved to take it back. It became for both sides as much a matter of "face" as military consequence.

But to the men garrisoned on "the Canal" it was much less a matter of face than skin. Keeping alive was the major preoccupation, of course—and scrounging simple comforts (like keeping dry). Even these basic pursuits became monotonous in day-after-day operations. But when the fighting came again, monotony was regarded with nostalgia. Between battles the Marines engaged in the art of bitching, their most colorfully profane antipathy being reserved for "Dugout Doug" MacArthur. The average line Marine was sure that only MacArthur's grabbing and holding of equipment, such as the P-38 for example, was responsible for the shoestring operation on Guadalcanal. General Arnold of the Air Force was placed a few degrees above MacArthur, and almost on an equal level was General Marshall. At this time, actually, supplies that might have gone to the Pacific were being sent instead to Europe for the projected invasion of North Africa. But the so-called "Big Picture" was of little concern to the Marine who believed himself all but marooned on 'Canal.

Yamamoto, on Truk, was unhappy also. Despite all his attempts to co-ordinate the operations of the Imperial fleet with those of the Army, the Army had not yet taken back Guadalcanal. And this failure by the Army cost the Imperial Navy heavily in men, ships, and aircraft. The Army, on the other hand, could not understand that the Navy was unable to maintain its ships indefinitely at sea "consuming valuable fuel" while the Army fought out its inconclusive land battles.

As always, the solution must devolve upon the Imperial Navy. Obviously Hyakutake's error lay in attempting to take Henderson Field by land. Just as obviously—at least it appeared so to Yamamoto —Henderson must be taken from the sea by very heavy bombardment. This would ground the planes and keep the men in their foxholes while reinforcements were brought in. With Henderson pulverized, it would be no problem for Hyakutake's starving, ill-equipped, sick, and dying troops (plus reinforcements, of course, not so hungry and better equipped) to end the protracted, embarrassing wretchedness of Guadalcanal.

The plan, as outlined to Hyakutake by Captain Toshikazu Ohmae, Chief of Staff, Southeastern Fleet, seemed to make sense. While Tanaka's Tokyo Express brought reinforcements (the 38th Division) to Guadalcanal in eleven transports down The Slot (the channel between New Georgia and Santa Isabel islands northwest of Guadalcanal), a large force of battleships, a cruiser, and destroyers from Admiral Kondo's Second Fleet would subject Henderson Field and environs to a tremendous shelling. At the same time another force of Kondo's fleet would lay to the north of Savo Island to furnish distant cover. Close in, Vice-Admiral Gunichi Mikawa, with cruisers and destroyers, would provide close support for the landings of the 38th Division.

During the night of November 12/13, 1942, what has come to be known as the Battle of Guadalcanal erupted when the Japanese raiding force, under Vice-Admiral Hiroaki Abe, on its way to open the shelling upon Henderson, ran up against a handful of American ships under the command of Rear Admiral Daniel J. Callaghan. With his five cruisers and eight destroyers Callaghan took on Abe's two battleships (the *Hiei* and *Kirishima*), the cruiser *Nagara,* and fourteen destroyers.

For the next twenty-four deadly, confused minutes "one of the most furious sea battles ever fought," according to Admiral King, illuminated the dark night sky and rocked the air with savage gunfire. At close quarters the two fleets fought to a near standstill, with the heaviest loss on the American side. Four American destroyers and two cruisers were lost. The Japanese lost only two destroyers, but the battleship *Hiei* had been hit many times, which prevented the planned heavy bombardment of Henderson Field (for this failure Abe was relieved of his command). Callaghan paid the full price for this frustration, for he and nearly all of his staff aboard the *San Francisco* were killed when the bridge of the ship was struck. More than seven hundred American lives were lost in the nightmarish battle. But Abe had run and Henderson had been spared.

Also frustrated was "Tenacious" Tanaka, who

An Avenger on a takeoff run from the flight deck of the Enterprise. *Aircraft of this unit (CV-6) sank the first Japanese battleship of the war, the* Hiei (*with the aid of other Navy and Marine planes from Guadalcanal*). (NAVY DEPT., NATIONAL ARCHIVES)

was ordered to turn back from his Express run and await further word. While he fumed on his way back to the Shortland Islands, dawn came to Guadalcanal. Marine pilots in Dauntlesses and Avengers found the crippled *Hiei* just ten miles north of Savo Island. Though in trouble, the Japanese ship, screened by five destroyers, could still put up anti-aircraft fire. But under the attack of the first ten planes, two torpedoes went into the side of the battleship. More Dauntlesses came shortly after and further harassed the stricken ship.

Meanwhile, as the damaged but operational *Enterprise* plowed northward for Guadalcanal, nine Avengers escorted by six Wildcats were dispatched

Dauntless on morning patrol in the Pacific.
(NAVY DEPT., NATIONAL ARCHIVES)

to the island. As they came into Guadalcanal the
Enterprise pilots spotted the *Hiei.* While the Wildcats discouraged the lurking Zeros the Avengers,
led by Lieutenant Albert P. Coffin, swooped down
upon the Japanese battleship and put three more
torpedoes into it. This continued for most of the
day as Marine and Navy aircraft ran a bomb
shuttle between the *Hiei* and Guadalcanal. In the
fighting eight Zeros were destroyed. They too had
failed in this mission, for by night the ship, abandoned and scuttled by its crew, sank into the Pacific
—the first Japanese battleship to be sunk by American forces.

Despite this upset, Yamamoto's plan proceeded.
The following night (November 13/14) was torn
by a thousand eight-inch shells lobbed into Henderson from cruisers sent from Rabaul. No great damage
was done, though two Wildcats were completely destroyed and fifteen others pocked by shell fragments.
These, along with a holed Dauntless, were repaired
and ready to fly by the next day. None of the eight
P-38s sent down by MacArthur only the day before
suffered any damage, however. The holes in Fighter
1 were quickly filled. The Japanese ships had proved

less destructive than previously, partly because they
had been harassed during their bombardment by
little PT boats from Tulagi, which had flitted dis-
tractingly around them.

On November 14, 1942, Tanaka, all but certain
that Henderson Field had really been put out of
commission by the night naval bombardments, raced
his Express down The Slot with the largest number
of reinforcements to date (three thousand men of a
combined naval landing force and eleven thousand
troops of Lieutenant General Tadayoshi Sano's 38th
Division). The eleven transports were screened by
a dozen destroyers and a small umbrella of Zeros
from the light carrier *Hiyo.*

At 9:49 A.M. Lieutenant Doan Carmody, flying a
search Dauntless from the *Enterprise,* now closer
to Guadalcanal, found the transports in The Slot.
The ships were 120 miles from Guadalcanal, making
fourteen knots; the Express was due to arrive at
the island around seven in the evening. After radioing this information to the *Enterprise,* Carmody,
in company with another Dauntless (pilot: Lieutenant W. E. Johnson), dived upon the Japanese ship
formation in The Slot. Both missed with their bombs,
however, because of heavy antiaircraft fire and the
quick action of seven Zeros of Tanaka's air cover.
Johnson's SBD fell into the sea and two Zeros
swooped down to spray the splash point and the
debris. During the next few hours, this depredation
would be heavily avenged.

If ever there was a hell on earth, it was carried
on Tanaka's eleven transports that November 14.
With merciless desperation, fed by the knowledge
that more Japanese reinforcements on Guadalcanal
could be fatal, Marine and Navy aircraft assaulted
the Tokyo Express. All afternoon every flyable plane
on Guadalcanal, plus others from the *Enterprise,*
fully loaded with bombs or torpedoes, raced to The
Slot. Despite the whirring Zeros, of which there
were only a few thanks to the hesitant Kondo 150
miles to the north, who sent small numbers from
time to time from his two carriers, the Dauntlesses
and Avengers ripped into the Japanese ships. Thousand-pound bombs rained onto the decks of the
transports and torpedoes slashed into their sides.
Even the Wildcats, when they ran out of Zeros,
dived to water level to strafe the crowded decks.

The first attack, made by eighteen Marine Dauntlesses led by Major Joseph Sailer, Jr. (VMSB-132)

A beached, burned-out Japanese troop transport the morning after the "Buzzard Patrol," which literally slaughtered the men and ships of the Tokyo Express November 13–14, 1942.

(DEFENSE DEPT., MARINE CORPS)

and Major Robert Richard (VMSB-142), plus seven Avengers led by Lieutenant Albert P. Coffin of the *Enterprise*'s VT-10, scored hits on three transports and a cruiser. More *Enterprise* pilots, under Lieutenant Commander James R. Lee, joined in what became by midday virtual slaughter.

But true to his nickname, Tanaka tenaciously pressed on, leaving a transport here and there en route in his bloody wake. Transports lay dead in the water burning, some split open spilling men, dead and injured into the churning water, as destroyers circled in an attempt to rescue men as well as fight off the attacking American planes. The carnage on the Japanese transports, inhumanly overcrowded to begin with, was ineffably obscene. For the packed though human cargo of the transports the hours, for those who had hours, between about twelve-thirty and nightfall were one shattering crescendo of terror, pain, and death. And there was no place to hide.

Some American fighter pilots, who had come in close enough to see the butchery on the transports as well as the encrimsoned waters around them,

were literally sickened by the sight. Some vomited in their cockpits. But they machine-gunned the thousands of bobbing heads in the water, the helpless near-drowned clinging to debris and wreckage. By 4:45 P.M., when the final strike took off from Henderson—led by Glen Estes of the *Enterprise*'s VS-10: four Dauntlesses (three of which were Marine) and fighter cover—seven Japanese transports had been sunk or were sinking or burning or both. Estes dropped the last bomb of the day, made a direct hit and returned to Henderson.

The four surviving transports were in bad shape also, but Tanaka proceeded to Guadalcanal. Sometime after midnight he arrived, quite depleted, at his destination. There was nothing to do but beach the crippled transports. About 3000 troops were landed with a mere 260 cases of ammunition and 1500 bags of rice. The rest of their supplies and perhaps another 3000 of their comrades lay at the bottom of The Slot, dead or missing. Of those who had escaped the slaughter of what the Americans came to call the "Buzzard Patrol," less than 2000 were picked up out of the water. Exact figures may

The forward deck of one of the beached Japanese transports after attacks by American planes and ships. (DEFENSE DEPT., NATIONAL ARCHIVES)

never be determined, but Tanaka's determination—and the determination of the Buzzard Patrol—had wiped out about half of the largest attempt by the Tokyo Express. Every transport was lost, for the four beached ships were worked over the following day by aircraft, the destroyer *Meade,* and artillery.

The cost to the Americans was comparatively light: six Dauntlesses and two Wildcats. One of the latter was that of Lieutenant Colonel Joseph Bauer (VMF-212), who had gone out to escort the bombers. In company with Joseph Foss, Bauer had strafed a transport, after which both pilots were attacked by Zeros. Bauer shot one out of the air and Foss took off after the other. Antiaircraft fire from a Japanese destroyer spoiled the chase for Foss, who returned to the spot where he had last seen Bauer. Circling low over the water, Foss found pieces of the fallen Zero. About two miles away, swimming near an oil slick, Foss spotted Bauer in the water.

Circling, Foss attempted to eject his rubber boat, but found he was unable to because it was jammed. He circled again, lower, and realized that Bauer, bouncing and gesticulating in the water, was ordering him to return to base. Foss also found he could not radio for assistance, so he throttled back to

Henderson to organize a rescue party. Despite an intensive search Bauer was never found.

II

The closing phase of the Battle of Guadalcanal, which had opened so disastrously for the Americans but which developed into a Japanese tragedy, was another nighttime surface battleship brawl. Vice-Admiral Kondo approached Guadalcanal to shell the airfield to cover the landings of Tanaka's "sorry remnant" (Tanaka's phrase) with the battleship *Kirishima* (sister ship of the *Hiei,* lost the day before), five cruisers, and nine destroyers.

Kondo ran into an American naval group (battleships *Washington* and *South Dakota* and four destroyers), under the capable command of Rear Admiral Willis Augustus Lee, in the vicinity of Iron Bottom Bay. Though in the battle which opened before midnight of November 14 Lee had lost three destroyers and the *South Dakota* was damaged, Kondo lost one destroyer and, most importantly, the *Kirishima* (so badly damaged that it was scuttled). The great battleship sank in waters close to the *Hiei,* and with it went Kondo's brilliant career. He had failed once again to ravage Henderson Field.

The common soldier behind Japanese lines by late December was certain that he had been abandoned. "Have not seen one of our planes in ages," one confided to his diary, "but every day enemy planes dance in the sky. . . ." It was a dance of death, for the strafing, dive-bombing, and bombing cut off supplies, reinforcements, and medical necessities.

While great men, irresolute yet unyielding, grappling with ego rather than conscience, sought a face-saving solution, little men died in mass, faceless numbers. At last, after weeks of acrid argument, two men called at the Imperial Palace on the final day of 1942. They were an admiral, Osami Nagano, Chief of the Naval Staff, and a general, Hajime Sugiyama, the Army's Chief of Staff. They had arrived unsmiling and they left unsmiling, but when they did leave it was with grim permission from Hirohito himself. The Japanese would abandon Guadalcanal.

Sometime during the first week of February 1943 the Tokyo Express was scheduled to run in reverse. This odious operation was a carefully guarded secret; even officers (except of exalted rank) on Guadalcanal had no idea of what was happening. New troops were even brought in to conceal the true plan. All of the activity appeared to the watchful Americans like the beginnings of a real push on Guadalcanal. "Until the last moment it appeared that the Japanese were attempting a major reinforcement effort," Admiral Nimitz wrote in retrospect. "Only skill in keeping their plans disguised and bold celerity in carrying them out enabled the Japanese to withdraw the remnants of the Guadalcanal garrison."

By February 8, 1943, after six months of appalling fighting, Guadalcanal was taken over by the Americans. Like Midway, it marked a turn in the tide from the defensive to the offensive and it was the first defeat on land experienced by the victory-drunk Japanese Army. At the same time, although he fought ferociously and often as not to an existial, sacrificial death, the Japanese soldier had proved not to be a jungle superman. The myth was over for the Japanese soldier just as it was for the Zero, the super fighter plane.

III

Although the Japanese were out of Guadalcanal, it did not mean that the Solomons were entirely abandoned by them. Late in November 1942 preparations for constructing an airfield on Munda Point, New Georgia, were noted by Allied reconnaissance planes; so was construction on some of the smaller islands of the New Georgia group, Kolombangara and Vella Lavella. An airfield on Munda Point, however, meant only a 175-mile flight to Henderson Field, which placed it within easy reach of the Zero. And at the top of the Solomons there was Bougainville, with no less than five airfields, the largest of which was Kahili, near the southern tip of the island. If the Americans had paid heavily for Henderson Field, the Japanese had full intentions of exacting a high and bloody interest on it.

Attempts were made to discourage the building up of the new Japanese positions, now the new terminals for the Tokyo Express. Between the hard days of October, when the Americans might have been pushed out of Guadalcanal, and the nearly

Jefferson J. DeBlanc, one of the "few Marines," with Medal of Honor awarded for leading his flight into a large Japanese fighter formation before it could interfere with American Dauntlesses and Avengers.
(DEFENSE DEPT., MARINE CORPS)

magical spiriting away of the Japanese in February, there were times when the fighting became as intense as in the shoestring days. On one mission, January 31, 1943, a young Marine lieutenant, Jefferson Joseph DeBlanc, a section leader in VMF-112, was assigned to escort Dauntlesses and Avengers to bomb enemy shipping in Vella Gulf. The target area lay less than fifty miles east and slightly north of the Japanese air base on Kolombangara Island.

Upon arriving at Vella Gulf the Marine formation was met by a large number of enemy fighters. DeBlanc led his six Wildcats into the mass of Zeros at fourteen thousand feet, hoping to keep them away from the bombers while they worked over the shipping. As the battle developed, it broke up into single Wildcats against several Zeros. DeBlanc dived down to the altitude at which the dive bombers were trying to operate only to find he had swept into a large formation of float planes (probably the Mitsubishi A6M2-N, an adaptation of the Zero and called the "Rufe" by the Allies). Slashing into the Rufes, DeBlanc quickly sent three of them down burning, thus breaking up their concentration on the Dauntlesses, which proceeded to harass the Japanese surface ships in the gulf.

In the fighting DeBlanc's Wildcat had been hit and he was low on fuel. He realized he would have to return to Guadalcanal, so he climbed to get his bearings and as much height as he could. As he nursed the Wildcat up to the high clouds, DeBlanc, twisting his neck in the traditional fighter pilot fashion, spotted two Zeros closing from behind. He was now alone, for the other Wildcats were spread across the sky in their own private battles and the Dauntlesses and Avengers were engaged in bombing the Japanese ships.

DeBlanc would have to fight it out, though a stricken Wildcat was a poor match for a Zero. Timing his rudder kick for the precise moment, DeBlanc jerked the Wildcat into the path of the attacking Zeros. A good hit sent one rocketing across the sky as the other flashed by, turned, and came back at the Wildcat. DeBlanc felt the Grumman shuddering under the strain of his maneuvers and the impact of enemy slugs. As the Zero raced in, its guns twinkling maliciously, DeBlanc turned sharply again and shattered the frail Japanese plane with all four of his guns. The Zero fluttered down to the sea.

Safe now, DeBlanc found himself in other peril. The Wildcat was now in such poor condition that he knew he would never make it back to Guadalcanal. Smoking and with engine heaving badly, the plane started down for the water. DeBlanc fought with the plane to keep it from plowing into the ocean as he straightened out practically at treetop height over Kolombangara. Clearing the Japanese-held island, DeBlanc steadied the Wildcat out to sea and at a dangerously low altitude took to his chute. Upon landing in the water he found that he had been wounded in the back, arms, and legs. Supported by his lifejacket, DeBlanc spent about six hours making his way back to the beach at Kolombangara. Luckily he was not found by the Japanese but, after subsisting for two days on coconuts, was found instead by friendly islanders, who turned him over to the local coastwatcher. In about two weeks a Catalina arrived off Kolombangara to

pick up DeBlanc as well as Staff Sergeant James A. Feliton, who had parachuted during the same battle as had DeBlanc. The latter was immediately sent to a hospital to recuperate and was awarded the Medal of Honor.

On the same day that Lieutenant DeBlanc and Sergeant Feliton were taken off Kolombangara and only six days after the last living Japanese soldier had been evacuated from Guadalcanal, a curious incident occurred over Bougainville.

Navy PB4Ys (the Army's B-24, Liberator) had taken off to bomb targets on Bougainville—no mean round trip of six hundred miles—with an escort of new fighters.

As the American bombers and fighters approached Bougainville, a lone Zero pilot ignored the war momentarily in order to fly alongside the new fighters to study them with peacetime inquisitiveness. Before he was driven off the Japanese pilot saw a strange-looking plane, half beautiful and half ugly. It was deep blue in color with a pale blue, almost white underside. The pilot sat way back on the fuselage under a bubblelike canopy; a great stretch of nose projected before him, ending in a wide cowling under which roared a massive eighteen-cylinder Pratt and Whitney "Twin Wasp" engine. Its most curious feature was the graceful inverted gull wing which jutted down and then up and away from the fuselage. Once seen, this aircraft was not mistaken for any other: it was the Chance Vought F4U-1, the "Corsair." American ground troops called it "the Bent Winged Bird" in time.

The Corsair, which had arrived at Henderson Field on February 12 flown by VMF-124, had originally been designed as a carrier fighter. Problems developed during carrier landing tests, because of the plane's long nose, which interfered with the pilot's vision. It also had a tendency to bounce upon touching the deck and had other bugs, which discouraged the Navy from stationing the plane on carriers for a time. Meanwhile, it was turned over to the Marines, in whose hands, and later also the Navy's, the Corsair proved to be one of the outstanding fighters of the war. Some Japanese pilots, in fact, regarded it as the most formidable American fighter of the war. It was faster than any Japanese plane, besides which it could climb much faster (about three thousand feet a minute) and had a greater range capability than any single-engined

Newly arrived Corsairs at Guadalcanal being prepared for combat. The plane in the foreground is having its *guns bore-sighted with a homemade device.*
(C. L. SMITH/DEFENSE DEPT., MARINE CORPS)

fighter operating in the Pacific at the time. And it was rugged, which suited the hardened Marines perfectly.

But it would take time to learn how to use the Corsair's capabilities fully. This was demonstrated on the day following the incident with the curious Zero pilot in what became known as "the Saint Valentine's Day Massacre." Navy Liberators, on a bombing mission to Kahili airfield, Bougainville, were escorted by P-40s (low cover), P-38s (high cover), and Corsairs of VMF-124, staggered in between. This became the standard pattern for missions at this time, with the bombers at around twenty thousand feet and the P-38s and Corsairs above them. On this day, however, the system did not function too well, for as the formation approached Kahili it was bounced by perhaps fifty Zeros (almost certainly alerted and waiting). Two Liberators went down, as did two P-40s, two Corsairs, and, worse, the entire top cover of four P-38s. Japanese losses came to three or four Zeros, one as result of a collision with a Corsair.

This action, generally used to reveal how the Corsair nearly failed in its first test of real combat, is actually a better exemplification of the not yet (or ever, for that matter) dampened zeal of the Japanese fighter pilot. And, too, the "Zeke," as the Zero by this time was coming to be called, was still a formidable plane in a melee. But in the Corsair the Zeke had met its nemesis; it would only take a little time, a little experience, and a few Marines to establish this.

Allied fighter pilot's view of a "Zeke," on the tail.
(U. S. AIR FORCE)

But the problem of the inexperienced pilot was becoming even more serious for the Japanese, whose first-line veterans had been lost at Midway and Guadalcanal and whose new pilots were poorly trained for lack of experienced pilots to teach them. The American situation was differently handled, for when it was possible (and if they survived) veteran pilots were taken out of combat and given assignments training young fighter pilots. This is what happened with John Smith, Marion Carl, and Joseph Foss after they had left Guadalcanal. When Smith attempted to return to combat duty he was emphatically told, "Not until you have trained a hundred and fifty John Smiths." When he did return, almost two years later, Smith flew a Corsair.

IV

The Marines and their Corsairs owned the air over the Solomons and Kenney's Kids had begun "to play in the back yard of the Nip" in New Guinea; it was an ignominious situation to stomach in Tokyo. With the loss of Guadalcanal and then,

within a month, the Battle of the Bismarck Sea, Imperial headquarters burned with a hard, brittle flame of revenge. Yamamoto himself took full command of this vengeance operation, called *I-go Sakusen* ("Operation A"), a newly devised plan directly generated by the turn of fortune in the Pacific. *I-go Sakusen* was to wipe out, once and for all, the total American air power from the Solomons and New Guinea.

Planning *I-go Sakusen* for early April 1943, Yamamoto established his headquarters at Rabaul, major target of Kenney's forces in New Guinea and the major goal of Halsey's forces, climbing up the bloody Solomons ladder. Loath to expose his few remaining carriers to American aircraft, Yamamoto nonetheless stripped all carrier planes from their respective ships. Those from the 1st Carrier Division (the *Zuikaku* and *Zuiho*) went to Rabaul under command of Vice-Admiral Jisaburo Ozawa (who since November 16, 1942, had replaced Nagumo as commander of the Third Fleet). The aircraft of the 2nd Carrier Division (the *Junyo* and *Hiyo*) were flown to the base at Ballale, just south of Bougainville. The 21st Koku Sentai was to operate from Kavieng at the northern tip of New Ireland under Rear Admiral Toshinosuka Ichimaru (although the main body was stationed at Rabaul under command of Ozawa). The 26th Koku Sentai (Rear Admiral Kanae Kozaka) would strike from Kahili. In all, Yamamoto amassed about 350 warplanes for his strikes, Zekes, Nells, Bettys, Kates, and a few Vals. He was decidedly out for blood.

The first large assault came shortly after noon on April 7, 1943, when coast watchers and radar operators reported massive formations of enemy aircraft heading for Guadalcanal. There were, in fact, no less than 67 Vals escorted by 110 Zekes. The warning went out to ships in the harbor and to the men at Henderson, "Condition *very* Red."

The attack was met by all possible flyable fighters, seventy-six, Army, Navy, and Marine: P-38s, P-39s, Corsairs, and Wildcats. In the heavy fighting which followed, some of the Vals broke through the American fighter defenses and sank several ships in Tulagi Harbor and off Guadalcanal (the tanker *Kanawha,* the destroyer *Aaron Ward,* and the Australian corvette *Moa*).

First Lieutenant James E. Swett, of Marine VMF-221, on his first combat mission, ran into some of

James E. Swett, USMC, who broke up a Japanese dive bomber attack (for which he received the Medal of Honor) and became an ace on his first combat mission. (DEFENSE DEPT., MARINE CORPS)

the Japanese attackers. Leading a division of four Wildcats toward Tulagi, Swett spotted a large formation of Vals within minutes of arriving. There were between fifteen and twenty Japanese planes headed for Tulagi Harbor; shouting "Tally Ho!" Swett dived into the Vals. But even before he could begin shooting—for the first time in combat—he heard more shouting in his earphones. Someone else in his division had spotted Zekes diving from above. Already in a steep dive aimed at the dive bombers, Swett concentrated on the immediate menace and, as his Medal of Honor citation was to read, "during his dive personally exploded three hostile planes in mid-air with accurate and deadly fire."

Separated from the rest of his division, Swett was forced to do the best he could, what with the heavy concentration of "friendly" antiaircraft fire bursting around him—and six additional Vals, which bore onward toward the ships. One of his guns, too, was inoperative, so he had but five 50s with which to contend with the enemy formations. Racing in behind the Vals, Swett soon learned that the five guns worked well on the Vals, and the fourth plane swept away burning and trailing bits and pieces.

And so it went on until he shot down two more Vals, making his total for the battle seven—he had become an ace in his first combat. But as he closed in on the last of his victims Swett's Wildcat was hit by the fire of the Val's rear gunner. As his canopy shattered, blood covered his face, but Swett continued firing until his guns no longer responded: he had exhausted his ammunition. But before he did, he saw that the gunner in the rear cockpit of the Val had slumped over and smoke had begun to wisp out of the Val.

Swett's own problems were too many for him to worry about making certain that his eighth victim crashed into the waters of Iron Bottom Bay (his official score stood then at seven). He himself was injured by the flying bits of the canopy, and with his engine temperature in the red, Swett realized that the Japanese gunner had hit his Wildcat's lubricating system. The Pratt and Whitney growled and thumped, grew hot, and finally fused, and the propeller froze.

Too low now to take to his chute, Swett prepared to ditch off Florida Island. As he brought the Wildcat down near the water he suffered further consideration from "friendly" AA. Then the Wildcat splashed into Iron Bottom Bay, bounced and smacked into the water again. Swett, though held in his seat by straps, was thrown forward, smashing his nose against the gun sight. It took some time, after this stunning impact, for the pilot to place all things into focus. He knew he must get out of the swiftly sinking Wildcat. But he could not, for with a muddled, pain-racked head, he was not thinking clearly. As the plane sank Swett found that his chute harness had caught on a small handle in the cockpit.

As the Wildcat swirled down to the bottom, Swett continued to struggle until the strap loosened from the handle, which at the same time ejected the life raft stored in the plane. Suffocating, Swett finally surfaced with the help of a hastily inflated "Mae West," although encumbered by parachute, flying clothes, and the uninflated life raft. More struggling freed him and he inflated the raft and crawled, hurting and bleeding, into it. In a short time he was picked up by a small boat, whose passengers carried rifles as a precaution. Japanese pilots had demonstrated a deadly aversion to rescue, often attempting to kill their would-be Samaritans.

Yamamoto's revenge operation I-go Sakusen *was a simultaneous series of fruitless (but not always completely) strikes upon Guadalcanal and New Guinea. On April 12, 1943, more than a hundred Japanese aircraft struck the Fifth Air Force base at Port Moresby,* *New Guinea, setting an oil dump aflame with heavy loss of fuel and lubricants. Yamamoto's "Operation A" was his final contribution to Japan's war effort before he was shot down. He died believing the operation had been successful, which, in fact, it had not been.* (U. S. AIR FORCE)

"Are you an American?" someone shouted from the boat to Swett in his dinghy.

"You're damn right I am," he answered.

"It's OK," the voice was heard to say, according to legend; "he's another one of those loud-mouthed Marines."

Yamamoto's first big blow of *I-go Sakusen* had proved rather expensive, for claims were put in that day for a hundred planes by pilots and AA gunners. The actual number was closer to thirty-nine (twelve Vals and twenty-seven Zekes; Japanese postwar figures admit to the loss of twelve Vals but only nine Zekes). American losses for the day amounted to seven aircraft but only one pilot, Major Walden Williams of the 70th Fighter Squadron.

Yamamoto's other big raids were aimed at New Guinea, and he believed that by April 14, according to the claims of his pilots, Operation A had fulfilled its function. Four days later Yamamoto crashed in a burning Betty after being intercepted

Kenneth Walsh, USMC, first to achieve acedom in a Corsair. (DEFENSE DEPT., MARINE CORPS)

by P-38s over Kahili. Yamamoto's successor, Admiral Mineichi Koga, although not as brilliant a man, continued to practice the great man's philosophy—perhaps with less intensity—and did all he could to bloody the rungs of the Solomons ladder.

By the close of April more Corsairs had come into Guadalcanal, and by May 13, 1943, the first Corsair ace was brought to the fore. He was Lieutenant Kenneth Walsh of VMF-124, born in Brooklyn and who began his military career as a flying private in the Marines. During one of the preliminary phases of Yamamoto's Operation A, on April 1, 1943, Walsh shot down his first three Zekes. On the day of Yamamoto's big blow, Walsh, like Swett, was shot down but was pulled out of the water unhurt and was soon back flying a new Corsair. On May 13 in mixed company of Marine and Army fighters, Walsh encountered twenty-five Zekes escorting a Japanese photo plane. Admiral Koga was bringing more and more planes into Rabaul and he was most anxious to know all about the aviation facilities on Guadalcanal. There were, in fact, four airfields by this time.

During the battle with the Japanese formation, Walsh shot down three Zekes; he was officially an ace. The Japanese lost sixteen fighters, although the photo plane escaped. Three Corsairs were lost in the fighting, one of them flown by Walsh's squadron commander, Major William Gise.

Meanwhile, American troops began taking and occupying other islands in the Solomons, each step bringing them closer to Bougainville, gateway to Rabaul. The Russell Islands were occupied in February; next in line came Munda (New Georgia), the battle for which opened on June 21. Soon it was possible for the Marines to operate from a forward base on Munda for the strike on Vella Lavella, next step up the ladder. In doing this, Halsey elected to bypass Kolombangara (garrisoned by ten thousand Japanese troops), which would place American planes within ninety miles of Kahili on Bougainville.

The Vella Lavella landings took place on August 15; although the action on the beaches was reasonably normal, Japanese aerial activity was furious. Bombers and fighters came down from Kahili, Ballale, and Buin (in spite of American bombings aimed at grounding the Japanese planes during the landings) to harass the ships and troops on the beachhead. That day Kenneth Walsh was leading a division of five Corsairs of VMF-124; his score by this time had risen to ten enemy aircraft.

Fresh from a recreation tour in Sydney, Australia, Walsh was unexpectedly surprised by five Zekes at ten thousand feet. The fight became generally confused and Walsh soon found himself alone chasing a Zeke away from the battle. The powerful Corsair caught up with the Japanese fighter after a five-mile chase and with one quick blast Walsh knocked the plane down. Turning back for the beachhead, Walsh inadvertently flew into a formation of nine Vals, on their way to bomb the beach. Coming from under the Vals, Walsh quickly lessened their number by two. But he was now in a tough spot: Vals, with their rear gunners, below him and Zekes above. His Corsair became the center of destructive attention. Diving Zekes put two large 20-mm. holes through his right wing, more peppering knocked out his hydraulic system, shreds of his horizontal stabilizer flew off into the slipstream, and, still unknown to Walsh, the right tire was holed.

With his superior speed capability, Walsh rapidly pulled away from the shooting gallery. Other pilots took over the fighting (in addition to the three Japanese planes shot down by Walsh, fourteen others

Munda Point airfield, New Georgia. Trees show effects of bombing and artillery fire—American and Japanese.
(DEFENSE DEPT., MARINE CORPS)

fell in the day's fighting) as Walsh guided his tattered Corsair home. He brought it in to Munda Field (which was just one day old) and as anxious Marines observed, landed the Corsair with hardly a bump, even compensating for the flat right tire. When Walsh stood in the cockpit he was cheered by the troops for bringing in so badly mauled an aircraft. The plane, in fact, was junked.

Fifteen days later Walsh returned to Guadalcanal and took part in a bombing mission to Kahili. The plan was to take off from Fighter 2, fly to the Russell Islands air base, take on plenty of fuel for the expected battle over Kahili, and join up with the Liberators. Then the two dozen bombers with two squadrons of Corsairs as well as the usual low-cover P-39s and P-40s would press on to Bougainville. All went well for Walsh until after he had

taken off from the Russells. To his dismay his engine lost power and he could not keep up with the formation. Signaling to his wingman, Lieutenant W. P. Spencer, that he would have to drop out, Walsh, instead of attempting to return to the Russells or Fighter 2, guided his Corsair toward New Georgia with its advance base at Munda. Pushing his Corsair into a dive, Walsh brought the wheezing Corsair down onto the strip at Munda. There he was met by Captain James Neefus, commanding VMF-221, to whom he explained his problem and asked for another plane. Without recourse to red tape, Neefus permitted Walsh to requisition a ready, fueled, and armed Corsair on stand-by. Walsh jumped out of his plane and into the other; within

Corsairs on Munda—the Marine fighters arrived within
a week after the airstrip was taken from the Japanese.
(CHESTER L. SMITH/DEFENSE DEPT., MARINE CORPS)

minutes he raced down the runway and after the large Kahili-bound formation.

Walsh pushed the throttle in order to rejoin the bombers and at the same time he pulled the Corsair up as high as it could go—about thirty thousand feet before he spotted aircraft ahead. Happy that he had caught up, he gunned his engine and found he had caught up, instead, with a formation of from forty to fifty Zekes. Soon after, he also saw the Liberators, some distance beyond the large formation of enemy fighters, under attack by Zekes and antiaircraft. A great air battle developed over Kahili as fighters from Kahili, Ballale, and Buin took to the air. Walsh, still undetected by the Japanese intent upon the bombers, pulled in behind the Zekes. He

was able to knock down only two before the others realized that a lone Corsair was pecking away at their formation.

The battle became a confused melee as Zekes turned on Walsh, who dived through the Liberator formation, shouting warnings on his radio. With the large number of planes in the air it became difficult to sight on any one of them and be certain he was an enemy. The sky became crisscrossed with tracers and, from time to time, a burning Liberator falling, for the Zekes were especially aggressive. The bombing run completed, the bombers turned away for the flight back to Henderson. During this phase of the battle Walsh destroyed two more Zekes, but he had had just about all the luck possible for the day. As he followed his fourth victim down to observe its fiery splash, Walsh, in turn, was trailed by four Zekes. They boxed him in, and with the advantage of altitude (and the fact that Walsh had just about expended his ammunition), they began working him over with cannon and machine-gun fire.

Smoke streamed from under the Corsair's cowling, fuel pressure dropped, the engine churned. The only other sound was that of Japanese lead pounding away at the tough Corsair. Walsh was about ready to resign to fate when a P-40 and a few Corsairs came in to take the Zekes off his back. But, though spared the final blow, Walsh knew he could not make it to any base. He must ditch off Vella Lavella. With consummate grace Walsh bounced the gull-winged craft into the Pacific a mile off Barakoma Point, where American Seabees, working on a new airstrip, observed the smoking plane.

The great plane splashed in, leaving a foamy wake, bumped up, and splashed again, then stopped and began to settle. Walsh had hardly been shaken and quickly left the Corsair and dropped into the water. Within half an hour a Seabee boat came out to pick him up and by the next day Walsh was returned to Guadalcanal. When he was ordered back to the United States in November 1943 Walsh, a Medal of Honor recipient, had destroyed twenty enemy aircraft (his twenty-first was scored during his second tour of duty in 1945).

With Vella Lavella in American hands and Kolombangara all but ignored (the Japanese evacuated the island in September–October), the next prize was to be Bougainville. This was the largest and northernmost island of the Solomons—with Rabaul but 210 miles away. With the experience of Guadalcanal behind them it was decided by the South Pacific planners that to take all of Bougainville, with its garrison of about 40,000 Japanese in the northern tip, near Buka airfield, and the southern tip, near Kahili, would be exceptionally violent and costly. So it was that Halsey elected to send the Marines in near the island's center, at Empress Augusta Bay, beat out a beachhead, and then establish a perimeter inside which airfields could be constructed.

Bougainville, like Guadalcanal, was a tropical pesthole, and the vicious land fighting was as brutal as that on the Island. If anything, the climate—wet—and the mud—glutinous—were worse. And the Japanese soldier fought to the death.

On November 1, 1943, while troops of the 3rd

Under the cover of Marine Avengers, the Marines head for the beaches of Bougainville, Solomon Islands, November 1, 1943. (DEFENSE DEPT., MARINE CORPS)

Marine Division and the 2nd Raider Regiment splashed ashore at Cape Torokina on Empress Augusta Bay, Avengers and Dauntlesses swooped in low to strafe and bomb the beachhead. Navy and Marine planes patrolled over the area in anticipation of the reaction from the several nearby Japanese air bases. This came minutes before the first barge ground upon the beach. About thirty Zekes and bombers converged upon Torokina to be challenged by the P-40s of the New Zealand Royal Air Force's No. 18 Squadron, the P-38s of the U. S. Air Force's 18th Fighter Group, as well as Navy and Marine Wildcats and Corsairs. In the first skirmish Captain James E. Swett, returned to VMF-221 after his dip in the sea, shot down two Vals besides sending a Tony (the Kawasaki Ki. 61 *Hien*), one of the newer Japanese fighters, smoking away from the beachhead and off the tail of one of the New Zealand P-40s.

In this initial encounter with the Japanese opposition to the Bougainville landings, seven of their aircraft were lost, with no losses by the Allies.

In the early afternoon, during the patrol of VMF-215—five Corsairs led by Lieutenant Colonel Her-

Bougainville-based Avenger takes off the island's air-strip on a bombing mission. Avengers were used by *Marines as torpedo and regular bombers.*
(DOUGLAS WHITE/DEFENSE DEPT., MARINE CORPS)

bert H. Williamson—a large formation of Japanese bombers and fighters came in to strike the ships and troops now cluttering up the shore line of the beaches at Torokina. Williamson led his Corsairs down upon the enemy bombers and a confused battle developed.

Flying with VMF-215 was one of the most colorful Marine pilots of the war, Lieutenant Robert M. Hanson, son of Methodist missionaries from Massachusetts. Hanson had been born in India in 1920 and had been a Marine flyer since February 1943. In the battle of the afternoon of the Bougainville landings, Hanson singlehandedly attacked six Kates with such ferocity that several jettisoned their bombs before reaching Torokina. Three others fell in flames under Hanson's guns (two others were knocked down by other men of VMF-215). But a rear gunner in one of the Kates shot down Hanson.

Setting his Corsair down on the water, Hanson broke out his dinghy and sat in it awaiting further developments. For nearly six hours Hanson waited until he saw the destroyer *Sigourney,* on its way back to Vella Lavella to pick up more passengers

for Torokina. Alternately waving and paddling, Hanson set out for the *Sigourney* cheering himself with the Cole Porter song "You'd Be So Nice to Come Home To." The American ship veered slightly from course, picked up the redoubtable Marine, and continued on to Vella Lavella.

Upon returning to VMF-215 Hanson continued with his nonchalant spree of destruction. In one period of seventeen days he shot down twenty enemy aircraft, which earned him the nickname of "Butcher Bob." Four of these victories were achieved on January 30, 1944, during an Avenger strike on Rabaul. Hanson flew with the escort and during the battle over the great Japanese base, now within easy reach of the base at Torokina, shot down four of the twenty-one Japanese planes destroyed during the mission. This brought his total of Japanese planes destroyed up to twenty-five.

Three days later, on February 3, the day before Hanson's twenty-fourth birthday and a week before he was scheduled to return to the United States, Hanson volunteered for a strafing mission in the Rabaul area, upon Cape Saint George, New Ireland. On this point, across the channel from New

Robert M. Hanson, whose way with a Japanese plane earned him the name of "Butcher Bob" at Bougainville. (DOUGLAS WHITE/DEFENSE DEPT., MARINE CORPS)

Gregory "Pappy" Boyington, "AWOL" Flying Tiger and leader of the Marine's raffish "Black Sheep" (VMF-214). (DEFENSE DEPT., MARINE CORPS)

Britain, stood a lighthouse which afforded the Japanese a fine lookout. Though never actually destroyed, it was a bothersome, challenging target. Hanson came in low over the cape and never came out of his run. Apparently hit by antiaircraft guns, Hanson crashed into the sea ending one of the most meteoric fighter pilot careers in the Pacific.

Until he was killed, it appeared that Hanson would equal or even surpass the score of another doughty Marine, Major Gregory Boyington, who had himself been splashed into the Pacific over Rabaul a month before Hanson was lost. Boyington's record (which included his Flying Tiger tally also) stood at twenty-eight (two reported after the war) enemy planes when he went down on January 3, 1944. After an extensive search Boyington was listed as "missing in action."

This, like his "desertion" and subsequent dishonorable discharge from the Flying Tigers, was an exaggeration. Although his wingman, Captain George

M. Ashmun, had been killed during the bitter fighting over Rabaul, Boyington had succeeded in parachuting from his burning Corsair. He dropped into Saint George Channel, off Rabaul, and was worked over for about a quarter of an hour by four strafing Zekes. Although unhit, Boyington was taken prisoner by a submarine which surfaced near him and he spent the rest of the war as a celebrity prisoner, although not an especially well-treated one.

A stanch individualist, Boyington (called "Pappy" by his men because of his advanced age of thirty-one) had returned to the Marines after he had bid a not too fond farewell to the Flying Tigers. While he rankled under discipline and adhering to the book, he was a born flyer and a unique leader. He may not have fitted into the organization of a squadron, but he could lead one. In recognition of this he was given permission to organize his own unit of misfits, appropriately dubbed "the Black Sheep" but more formally Marine Fighter Squadron 214

Tending his flock: Boyington briefs his Black Sheep before a fighter sweep over Rabaul; Boyington was *listed as Missing in Action after one of these sweeps and remained a prisoner of war for the duration.*

(MARINE CORPS)

(VMF-214). This occurred after a couple of fairly uneventful tours by Boyington in the Solomons.

When Bougainville's airstrips were sufficiently secure, Major General Ralph J. Mitchell, Marine commander of the aerial operations in the Solomons, instituted the first harassing fighter sweeps over Rabaul. The first of these—December 17, 1943—in which Boyington participated consisted of no less than seventy-six planes (twenty-three New Zealand P-40s of Nos. 14 and 16 Squadrons, twenty-two of the new Grumman F6F "Hellcat," and thirty-one Corsairs). With this formidable array of air power, the Japanese were not anxious to take off despite Boyington's profane invitations to "come up and fight."

"Come on down, sucker," was the Japanese answer. And the only fighting occurred at the P-40 level, which cost three of these, including that of New Zealand Wing Commander Freeman; however, the New Zealanders got five Japanese planes and

the Americans two. But it was not worth the effort, and upon his return Boyington argued that such a mixed bag of aircraft (all with different performances) and so unwieldy a number simply did not work.

Boyington believed in smaller, more flexible, and better-matched formations—which he got for future fighter sweeps upon Rabaul, as well as for escort missions with bombers. This was found to be more efficient, and Boyington's Black Sheep scored heavily against the Zekes. Between the first strike of December 17 and the first of the New Year, fighter sweeps over Rabaul claimed nearly 150 Japanese planes shot out of the air (after the war the Japanese admitted to 64).

Rabaul by early 1944 was in serious trouble. As new airstrips were completed on Bougainville, even short-range medium bombers could make the round trip to Rabaul. Before long, too, Thirteenth Air Force Mitchells based on Stirling Island (in the

Treasury group south of Bougainville) were reaching the beleaguered base. It was by no means out, as General Kenney rather prematurely claimed in early November 1942, but it was becoming more and more untenable for both shipping and aircraft.

Hoping to hold off the inevitable (which the Japanese believed meant an American invasion of Rabaul), Koga sent the air groups of the 2nd Koku Sentai (Carrier Division), under Rear Admiral Takaji Jojima, to bolster up the 26th Koku Sentai (in this instance, Air Flotilla—that is, land-based Navy planes). Late in January 1944 about 130 aircraft arrived from Truk to bring the total of planes at Rabaul up to the 300 mark. But it was to no avail as the massive American air power grew. Japanese pilots, long stationed at Rabaul, were worn, tired, and dispirited. It seemed that American planes came over almost at will, not only to bomb but to strafe the gun positions.

Just such a mission fell to the Bougainville-based Navy squadron, VF-17, which had arrived on January 24, the day before the planes of the 2nd Koku Sentai landed at Rabaul. On February 19, after several days of grueling operations, VF-17 was scheduled for an early morning strafing attack upon gun positions around Rabaul. Of the twenty Corsairs assigned to the job, sixteen were to concentrate upon the AA installations and the newly arrived Zekes and Tonys at Lakunai airfield. The four other Corsairs were assigned top cover, which was led by Lieutenant Merle Davenport.

The twenty Corsairs rose into a beautifully clear, sunlit sky. Climbing to about seventeen thousand feet, the Navy planes pushed onward toward New Britain. As the outline of the island emerged sharply from the glittering sea, Lieutenant Ira C. Kepford noticed that something appeared to be wrong with the Corsair of his wingman, Ensign Donald McQueen. It flew erratically and spouted puffs of smoke from the cowling. Closing in he saw that McQueen was having engine trouble—a common malady, thanks to the fine coral dust which abounded on Bougainville. McQueen must turn back, and so must Kepford, for without a wingman he could not participate in the raid on Rabaul. But Lieutenant Commander Roger Hedrick, commander of VF-17, ordered McQueen back to base and granted Kepford permission to continue with the formation until they arrived over Rabaul. There

Ira C. Kepford, Corsair pilot of Navy Squadron VF-17, based at Bougainville.

(NAVY DEPT., NATIONAL ARCHIVES)

seemed little possibility of McQueen's being attacked on his flight back to Bougainville.

Scanning the sky and convinced that it was clear, Kepford pulled up alongside Davenport's plane and, dipping the Corsair's gull wings, blew a kiss to Davenport and his wingman and made a wide turn for the flight back to base. Reluctant to leave, Kepford deliberately made a ranging turn as he studied the Japanese positions below. Suddenly he saw a black object in the sky approaching him. As it came closer he recognized it as a float plane (a Rufe) and swept in for the kill. The Rufe pilot, unaware of the presence of the lone Corsair, soon was sent down into the water.

Having followed the Japanese plane to make certain it had crashed, Kepford again climbed to resume his flight back to Bougainville. In the distance, high above and closer to Rabaul, Kepford spotted more dots—as he counted them he realized they were Zekes, more than fifty, waiting to pounce on Davenport and the Corsairs at seventeen thousand feet. Kepford radioed the information to Davenport, hoping that he had not yet been seen by the Japanese planes. He hugged the waves and hoped, but not for long. Four fighters, two Zekes and two of the new Tojos, dived out of the big formation to take care of the lone stray.

When they came within range the enemy fighters opened up on the Corsair. Thinking fast, Kepford suddenly "popped his flaps," which caused the Corsair to slow down abruptly, and the lead Zeke overran him. As it pulled up to turn, Kepford shot away most of its tail surfaces and the Zeke pilot, discouraged, left the battle. The two Tojos (the fast Nakajima Ki. 44 *Shoki*) came in from the right and the remaining Zeke closed in from the left. Apparently the Japanese pilots were trying to force Kepford to head north instead of south. His Corsair had just been equipped with an emergency water-injection system which, when applied, charged the engine with a great surge of power for a limited time.

This, Kepford reasoned, was an emergency: all but boxed in by three enemy fighters far from home base. He rammed in full throttle and activated the water injection and began to outstrip the Zeke and even the faster Tojos. The Corsair ran out of energy over the western shore of New Ireland—the enemy planes had driven Kepford to the north—and he was still far from home. In desperation he eased back on the throttle and injected water again. Once again the Corsair responded and the plane shot ahead. Though the three planes continued to pursue him, they were not putting any holes in him.

The chase continued at close to four hundred miles an hour, very near the surface of the sea. Kepford saw that his fuel was getting low and his emergency spurts had been consumed; the engine complained after the injection. He must move quickly. The Zeke was still close behind him. Kepford suddenly kicked left rudder and the Corsair whipped quickly to the left as Kepford's blood drained in the turn. His vision faded under the pres-

The battle-scarred Corsair of Ira Kepford; "Skull and Crossbones" was squadron insignia.

(NAVY DEPT., NATIONAL ARCHIVES)

A Corsair comes in for a landing on the Bougainville strip, constructed of linked steel matting over sand.

A C-47 is ready for takeoff. In the distance, below Corsair, a barrage balloon floats limply.

(P. SCHEER/DEFENSE DEPT., MARINE CORPS)

sure of the turn, but he managed to keep from blacking out completely.

The Zeke had followed with terrifying persistence and as Kepford's vision returned he saw the guns sparkling in the wing of the enemy plane. But at the same time the Zeke had attempted to turn more sharply, inside the Corsair's turn. As a wing dipped in the turn, the Zeke's wing tip brushed the water. There was a small splash, and then a series of big ones as the Japanese fighter cartwheeled across the surface of the water until its wings ripped off and it sank into the sea.

Anxiously Kepford looked back to see what became of the Tojos, but they had been lost in the turn and no longer continued the chase.

Despite the great consumption of fuel during the emergency use of the water-injection system, Kepford, though shaken, managed to return to Bougainville. He emerged from his shot-up Corsair bathed in perspiration, shaking with shock and with tears streaming down his face. A shot of brandy and nearly twenty-four hours of sleep restored the future Navy ace (with a total of seventeen victories he was the fifth-ranking ace in the U. S. Navy). The water-injection emergency system was widely

adopted and undoubtedly, as it did Kepford's, saved many an American airman's life.

On February 20, the day following Kepford's encounter, Rabaul was all but abandoned by the Imperial Navy. The 2nd Koku Sentai was pulled out and what remained of it returned to Truk, now the main Japanese base in the Pacific. Within days Allied bombers flew over the once hazardous area without escort. Rabaul, the formidable, became a milk run.

By March 6, 1944, the Green Islands, north of Bougainville and only 115 miles east of Rabaul, were occupied U. S. Marines and New Zealand troops. MacArthur's forces had already taken Cape Gloucester on New Britain itself. When Emirau Island, ninety miles north of the chief Japanese air base at Kavieng in New Ireland, was taken in April of 1944, it bottled up Rabaul completely. Invasion of Rabaul was unnecessary. Those Japanese troops stranded there were not going to do anything, nor were they going anywhere. Isolated, the Japanese troops remained there until the war ended, harassed continually by bombardment and the demoralizing realization that they wasted away ineffectually on another worthless island.

The ring closing in around Rabaul; Thirteenth Air Force Mitchells have just bombed a supply dump at Rataval. Simpson Harbour and Rabaul lie in the distance. (U. S. AIR FORCE)

Rabaul checkmate: as surface ships carry troops to occupy Green Island, B-25s head for Rabaul to occupy Japanese air power during the beachhead landings. The taking of Green Island neutralized Rabaul. No invasion was necessary. (U. S. AIR FORCE)

5

TURKEY SHOOT

FAR to the north of the steaming, fevered Solomons lay another island chain of questionable worth. Though still in the Pacific, the string of islands called the Aleutians was in another world. The contrast between the Solomons and the Aleutians could hardly have been more extreme if, indeed, they had been on different planets. Many who served in each frequently wished they were.

The Japanese had invaded the Aleutians, setting troops ashore at two of the westernmost islands, Attu and Kiska, as a subsidiary action of the ill-fated Battle of Midway. They had lost the great naval-aerial battle in exchange for two tiny, inhospitable, wind-swept rocks. They also lost an almost intact Zero on one of the Aleutians close to the American base at Dutch Harbor. The sequel to this single mishap, in the form of the Grumman F6F "Hellcat" fighter in the summer of 1943, rendered the taking of Attu and Kiska extremely costly.

The proximity of these two islands to Alaska, and therefore to the North American mainland, made it imperative that the Japanese be driven off. On the other hand, the Japanese saw the Aleutians "pointing like a dagger at the heart of Japan," so that the islands—on a map in the hands of an armchair strategist, at least—took on great strategic significance. Depending on which side pushed the hardest, it appeared that the islands formed stepping-stones into the back yard of the other. This was

true, of course, provided the terrain and the weather could be nicely disregarded.

But to those who were there it was impossible. Admiral King stated the problem in his report to the Secretary of the Navy: "Since the Aleutian Islands constitute an aerial highway between the North American continent and the Far East, their strategic value is obvious. On the other hand, that chain of islands provides as rugged a theater for warfare as any in the world. Not only are the islands moun-

A snowbound Alaska-based Airacobra; with the Japanese in the Aleutians, the North Pacific became one of the most uncomfortable theaters of war and especially inimical to aerial operations. (U. S. AIR FORCE)

A P-40 based on Umnak Island (Aleutians); "Flying Tiger" markings are a tribute to the father of the pilot, Major John Chennault. (U. S. AIR FORCE)

tainous and rocky, but the weather in the western part of the islands is continually bad. The fogs are almost continuous, and thick. Violent winds (known locally as 'williwaws') with accompanying heavy seas make any kind of operation in that vicinity difficult and uncertain."

This was, as was characteristic of the cool King, true though understated. However, to the men of the Eleventh Air Force and the Navy's Patrol Wing 4 the Aleutians were no "aerial highway."

Nor were they an attractive spot for ships. As wryly put by Major General Simon B. Buckner, Jr., in charge of the Alaska Defense Command (which in turn, actually came under the command of the Navy in the person of Rear Admiral Robert A. Theobold), "the naval officer had an instinctive dread of Alaskan waters, feeling that they were a jumping-off place between Scylla and Charybdis and inhabited by a ferocious monster that was forever breathing fogs and coughing up 'williwaws' that would blow the unfortunate mariner into uncharted rocks and forever destroy his chances of becoming an admiral."

All operations in the Aleutians were circumscribed and dictated by nature, not man. Consequently assignment to the theater was more like being relegated to a frigid purgatory than to war. But operations did take place, whenever possible, as the Navy flew reconnaissance missions and the Air Force bombed the Japanese holdings at Attu and Kiska. "During April and May," an Air Force historian noted, "the weather for air operations is bad, during the rest of the year it is worse." Distance was another factor, for to reach Kiska, for example, the heavy bombers had to make a trip of twelve hundred miles from their base at Umnak. Bomb load would have to be sacrificed to fuel. Weather fore-

Mud, cold, fog—the conditions under which men and machines operated in the Aleutians. These Eleventh

Air Force Liberators have just returned from a bombing mission in the soup. (U. S. AIR FORCE)

casts were meaningless, for in an instant a target was fogged over. The Aleutians war was one primarily of waste and frustration.

The Japanese shared these frustrations with the Americans, for air operations for them were equally difficult. The problem of supply was acute. In time, the Americans had hacked out bases on Adak and Amchitka islands, which were much closer to the Japanese-held islands than Umnak or Dutch Harbor. By March of 1943, although still a forgotten theater, the Japanese found that attempting to supply their garrisons in the Aleutians was hazardous. Naval ships and planes, Army Air Force bombers and fighters (the P-38s of the 54th Fighter Squadron and the P-40s of the 18th Fighter Squadron) made supply runs by Japanese surface ships nearly hopeless. Even so, they remained.

Although not wishing to transform the northern Pacific into a major theater of operations and therefore complicating the priorities for the other theaters, notably North Africa and the warmer reaches of the Pacific, the Joint Chiefs of Staff agreed that the Japanese should be knocked out of Attu. At the same time Kiska, which was more heavily occupied, could be bypassed and cut off from the Japanese bases in the Kurile Islands. This idea, put forward by Admiral Kinkaid, in command of the North Pacific Force, seemed feasible and was put into operation.

The two Japanese garrisons were bombed as frequently as weather permitted, by the Eleventh Air Force B-24s as well as by P-38 and P-40 fighter bombers. Finally, in May 1943, the 7th Infantry Division went in to take Attu from the Japanese. This is a simple statement, but taking Attu was no

Mission's end: after bombing Japanese positions in the Aleutians, this B-24 found its own home base socked in with fog and had to find a soft landing spot nearby in a smooth tundra. (U. S. AIR FORCE)

plus good common sense, eventually decided the issue. Even as American plans were under way to invade Kiska, the Japanese under cover of a period of heavy fog evacuated all of their troops from that unfriendly island. When the landings were finally made, the American and Canadian infantrymen found an eerie welcome: no Japanese; only three yellow dogs.

When troops entered what had been the Japanese command hut at Kiska they found a message scrawled on the wall: "We shall come again and kill out separately Yanki jokers." But they did not come again and the "Yanki jokers" were left with the world's worst weather, tundra, muskeg, and fog.

The new Yorktown *in the Pacific. The great carrier's keel was laid six days before Pearl Harbor and it was launched on January 21, 1943. Commissioned in April, the* Yorktown (*named for the ship that went down at Midway*) *began operations in the Pacific by August. The earliest combat experience was gained by strikes upon Japanese-held islands such as Marcus, Wake, the Gilberts, Kwajalein.*

(NAVY DEPT., NATIONAL ARCHIVES)

II

The Central Pacific, after the Battle of Midway, lay in a deceptive tranquillity for more than a year. While the fighting raged to the south and west (and later in the north), the forces and materials were slowly accumulated for the Central Pacific sweep toward Japan. What resources—men and matériel— could be spared from the European theater, where by the summer of 1943 the Allies had invaded Italy, went into the planning for the Central Pacific offensive.

Thus a great fleet, the Fifth, was organized under command of Vice-Admiral Raymond A. Spruance to spearhead the assault. The steel point of this head was no less than eleven carriers, including the new *Yorktown* and *Lexington,* both heavy carriers, replacing the older carriers. Also recently commissioned were the *Essex* and the *Bunker Hill.* Added to these were the veteran *Saratoga* and *Enterprise.* Five light carriers, all recently launched, were the *Independence, Princeton, Belleau Wood, Monterey,* and *Cowpens.* These were not all. For also to be employed in the operation ahead were eight escort carriers (the CVEs), smaller than the light carriers and designed to participate in close support of amphibious landings. In all, the Fifth Fleet had about nine hundred planes under its control for its assault into the Gilberts, Marshalls, and Marianas.

Preliminary strikes were made upon Tarawa and Makin (in the Gilberts) by carrier planes beginning on November 13, 1943; diversionary attacks were also made upon Wake and Marcus islands to the

simple task. From May 11 through the thirtieth, besides contending with the cold (the division had been trained with typical military wisdom in California) and the weather, the men of the 7th Division fought an outnumbered but ferocious enemy. The fighting came to a horrible close with a shrieking banzai attack, and when that failed, the survivors committed suicide by putting hand grenades to their heads.

From Attu it was possible to bomb Japanese bases in the Kuriles, at the northern extremity of the Japanese home islands. Also it was possible to pound Kiska. The loss of Attu and the bombing of Kiska,

north. That this succeeded in confusing the Japanese as to where the next American assault would come was obvious. Admiral Koga sent Ozawa's Third Air Fleet (Koku Kantai) and Kurita's Second Air Fleet to the Marshalls, expecting the first heavy blow to fall there. When that did not come, he had nothing else to do (besides wonder) but return the planes to Rabaul.

The B-24s of the Seventh Air Force—originally based in Hawaii—began flying long-distance bombing missions to the Gilberts and Marshalls. The Seventh Air Force opened up its chapter in the Central Pacific offensive when on November 13, 1943, nine Liberators of its 431st Squadron (which was based on Funafuti in the Ellice Islands, south of the Gilberts) bombed Tarawa Atoll. Other units of the Seventh were based upon several other islands: Nanomea and Nukufetau (also in the Ellices) and Canton in the Phoenix Islands. Besides two B-24 squadrons at Canton, there were also two fighter squadrons, one of P-40s and the other of P-39s. These were stationed alongside the A-24s of the 531st Fighter Bomber Squadron. Another fighter squadron was stationed at Baker Island, a forward base, east of the Gilberts and north of the Ellices. This was to function as a staging area for fighters and a port in a storm for crippled bombers.

The Seventh Air Force, as can be seen, was dispersed over, in its own phrase, "one damned island after another."

This might very well have summed up the emotions of Admiral Mineichi Koga as he tried to decide, during the spring of 1943, where the next full-scale allied assault would fall. His head must have swirled under the widespread attacks; only strikes to begin with, but an indication of what was in the offing. His predecessor, Yamamoto, had been right. Given time, the great American productive potential would uncoil like a massive spring. Soon it would be reaching for the big base at Truk.

All doubts were cleared up when troops of the American 27th Infantry Division began coming ashore at Makin in the Gilberts on November 20, 1943. The next day Marines of the 2nd Division stormed the beaches of Tarawa. By November 24 the Army commander could claim small literary immortality by announcing "Makin taken"; but the Marines on Tarawa were destined to fight one of their most savage battles over the same period of time. Makin was lightly held, but Tarawa was not. The Air Force and carrier plane bombings had not softened up the Japanese positions. And although the pre-invasion naval bombardment was hoped to finish the job (it was more massive than aerial bombings), it did not penetrate the coconut log, concrete, and coral sand emplacements. The Navy, experiencing its first large-scale amphibious operation, miscalculated the degree of bombardment these Japanese fortifications could withstand. The prize of Tarawa was the airfield on Betio Island.

Rear Admiral Keiji Shibasaki with 4836 picked troops of Imperial Marines under his command, and the knowledge that fifteen months of burrowing and building had gone into the island's defenses, boasted that "a million Americans could never take the island in a thousand years."

He was, of course, wrong, for a considerably lesser number secured the island in about three days. The cost was high: nearly 1000 Marines died (of a total of 3301 casualties) and nearly all of Shibasaki's crack troops were wiped out (4690 killed out of a force of 4836). The admiral himself was buried, possibly still alive, in one of his nearly impregnable bombproof shelters by Marine bulldozers. Gasoline, poured into air vents, and hand grenades did the rest.

Aerial operations during the Gilberts battle were shared among the various groups of Task Force 50, commanded by Rear Admiral Charles A. Pownall. (Land-based aircraft were assigned to Task Force 57, but these too came ultimately under Navy control.) Task Group 50.1 (built around the *Yorktown, Lexington,* and *Cowpens*) operated in the area between the Marshalls and the Gilberts to interfere with any attempt by the Japanese to reinforce the Gilberts during the operations there. Carrier planes were engaged principally in attacks upon Japanese airfields on Mili and Jaluit in the Marshalls.

Task Group 50.2 (the *Enterprise, Belleau Wood,* and *Monterey*) was assigned to the Northern Assault Force, which took Makin. Task Group 50.3 (the *Essex, Bunker Hill,* and *Independence*) supported the Betio landings. Another group, 50.4 (the *Saratoga* and *Princeton*), after attending to the airfield on Nauru Island, west of the Gilberts, operated later to the southwest of Tarawa as a relief group.

At first Japanese air reaction was light. The Solomons campaign had taken a heavy toll of the carrier-

Carrier strike on Wake Island as the Fifth Fleet ranged through the Central Pacific freely, confuting the Japanese. Wake, which had fallen on Christmas Eve 1941, a symbol of American defeat in the Pacific, was struck repeatedly by carrier planes although not invaded.

Isolated, its original strategic importance dwindled. As the Dauntless pilot prepares to make his bomb run, smoke may be seen rising from what had been Camp Two (center, across lagoon) on Wake itself.

(NAVY DEPT., NATIONAL ARCHIVES)

A Seventh Air Force Liberator begins the softening up for the projected Marshalls campaign. The B-24 is about to turn on its bomb run for Wotje. Other islands in the group: Kwajalein and Eniwetok.

(U. S. AIR FORCE)

Deck landing accident aboard the Enterprise *en route to the Marshalls, November 1943. The Hellcat has veered off the flight deck and caught fire. Catapult officer, Lieutenant Walter Chewning, with one foot on the belly tank, climbs onto the wing to assist the pilot.* (NAVY DEPT., NATIONAL ARCHIVES)

based aircraft; so had the battling in the New Guinea area. The Betio airfield was secured before Japanese air attacks materialized on the night of November 25.

That the Japanese were planning counterattacks was demonstrated early in the morning of the twenty-fifth. A submarine had slipped into the ship concentration and put a torpedo into the escort carrier, *Liscombe Bay,* some twenty miles off Makin. The first inkling of this was noted by the men aboard the other ships when they heard an explosion and then "a few seconds after the first explosion, a second explosion which appeared to come from inside the *Liscombe Bay* burst upward, hurling fragments and clearly discernible planes two hundred feet or more in the air [burning bits of metal and other debris fell on the decks of a destroyer five thousand yards away]. The entire ship seemed to explode and almost at the same instant the interior of the ship . . . glowed with flame like a furnace." In twenty minutes the *Liscombe Bay,* the first of its type to be lost, sank, taking 644 of its crew, including Rear Admiral H. M. Mullinnix and Captain I. D. Wiltsie, with it.

Search planes and torpedo planes immediately launched from the *Enterprise* found no trace of submarine I-175 which had sunk the little carrier.

That night the air hummed overhead with the sound of engines as Japanese "snooper" planes sought the American ships. A flare blossomed over the ships as radar-directed guns scanned skyward. It was near daylight on the ships, but the sky, except for the radarscopes, was screened in night. This was a prelude, as it had been at Guadalcanal: snoopers illuminated the target area with flares and the bombers followed. But no bombs came that first night, perhaps because the radar-controlled guns of the *North Carolina* discouraged the bombers, or because no real attack had been planned.

Something was afoot, obviously, for the next day snoopers poked around the edges of radar screens as soon as the sun dipped. Aboard the *Enterprise* counterplans were being discussed to deal with the clearly impending night attack.

Newly arrived aboard the *Enterprise* to command its Air Group 6 fighters was Lieutenant Commander Edward H. O'Hare, Medal of Honor recipient. Butch O'Hare had singlehandedly saved the *Lexing-*

Edward "Butch" O'Hare, Medal of Honor winner, who had singlehandedly saved the Lexington *by destroying or driving off nine Japanese bombers.*

(NAVY DEPT., NATIONAL ARCHIVES)

ton off Bougainville in February 1942 by breaking up an attack by nine Japanese bombers. At that time O'Hare flew the F4F Wildcat; his new aircraft aboard the *Enterprise* was the F6F Hellcat, the plane specifically designed to fight the Zero. It was the plane which the lost Zero of the Aleutians had inspired. The Hellcat was tougher, faster, and a better high-altitude fighter than the Zeke. The lighter Japanese plane continued to be more maneuverable, but it paid for it by flaming all too readily, by lack of armor protection for the pilot, and by a comparatively flimsy construction which under the six 50s of the Hellcat all but disintegrated.

The Hellcat had been in action since August 31, 1943, when VF-5 of the *Yorktown* flew it in a carrier strike on Japanese installations on Marcus Island; VF-9 of the *Essex* was also equipped with the

An F6F "Hellcat," the aircraft specifically designed to vanquish the Zero, taking off from the deck of a carrier. This is one of the hundreds of fine Navy photographs *taken by, or under the supervision of, photographer Edward Steichen (a Navy captain during the war).*

(NAVY DEPT., NATIONAL ARCHIVES)

The toughness of the Hellcat is revealed in this photograph of one which has returned to its carrier after combat. Flames inside the fuselage have shriveled the skin; fire pours out of the flaps. Soon after, the pilot was rescued by shipmates and, though burned, survived the incident. (NAVY DEPT., NATIONAL ARCHIVES)

Poised on the flight deck, this Avenger gets the flag for takeoff. (U. S. NAVY)

A rocket-armed Avenger springs into the air. Rockets were used in the Atlantic against German submarines and in the Pacific against Japanese shipping.
(U. S. NAVY)

Hellcat and participated in this strike. But it was during the Gilbert campaign that the Hellcat saw its first real action.

The planners of the *Enterprise,* however, had something else in mind for the coming night. If a radar-equipped Avenger could lead a Hellcat into the proximity of a Japanese bomber, the Hellcat could do the rest. That evening at dusk O'Hare took off with his wingman, Ensign Warren Skon, in their Hellcats. They were followed by an Avenger piloted by Lieutenant Commander John Phillips, *Enterprise* bomber leader. In the Avenger were also radar operator Lieutenant Hazen Rand and gunner A. B. Kernan. At the same time the large radar set in the Combat Information Center would track both the friendlies and the bogies.

The bogies came and went but little happened until Phillips was directed from the *Enterprise* toward enemy aircraft. O'Hare and Skon could not find the Avenger in the dark, let alone an enemy plane. Phillips meanwhile had the bogie on his own screen and with Rand guiding him came upon a Betty heading for the ships.

Three miles away O'Hare and Skon were startled to see a sudden flare in the sky. It fell burning into the water, forming a burning lake in the blackness. Other Bettys in the Japanese formation, surprised by the unexpected attack, began firing wildly at one another.

If that was where the action was, O'Hare and Skon turned and raced to the scene. Phillips meanwhile had been vectored onto another Betty. As he approached he heard O'Hare request that he turn on the navigation lights of the Avenger so that he and Skon could find him. Reluctantly Phillips flicked on the lights, which, as he had expected, alerted the Betty. But soon that bomber too went burning into the sea. Moments later, Kernan fired at a dark form passing near the Avenger's tail.

Under orders from the *Enterprise* all three American planes turned on their navigation lights to enable them to assemble. If there were enemy aircraft nearby this would of course place the Avenger and Hellcats in jeopardy. The two fighters moved in closer to the Avenger. Soon the two Hellcats overtook the Avenger, to their left. To better cover the larger plane, Skon throttled back, swooped under the tail, and took a position off the left wing of the Avenger. O'Hare slid back toward the right wing.

Suddenly Kernan's ball turret came to life, firing, according to his report, between the two Hellcats at a darkened plane approaching from the stern. The .50-calibers lighted up the night and then again there was darkness. O'Hare's Hellcat, with navigation lights still on, veered to the left and down. Skon, certain that O'Hare was attacking, followed, but the veer became a dive and the Hellcat disappeared into the night. All Skon's attempts to call his leader were fruitless, as were the searches made the next day by other aircraft. Butch O'Hare was gone. Although he may have been hit by a Japanese plane, it was more than likely that Kernan had hit him by mistake. It was a tragedy for Kernan (though not absolute, for there will always be the chance that a Japanese gunner shot O'Hare down) and the men of the *Enterprise*.

But then tragedy and error are the very ingredients of war. Six hundred men had died, too, in the *Liscombe Bay;* a thousand Marines lay dead on Tarawa alongside four times that number of Japanese. The death of one more airman increased the figure by a single digit. But it did not diminish the tragedy.

Tragedy multiplied becomes history, eliminating thus biography; and great numbers simply become symbols which stir the blood but only afflict the heart individually. Whatever the cost, Tarawa, Makin, and Abemama—the Gilberts—belonged to the Americans. The lessons learned there at so great a price would not be wasted.

III

The next step in the Central as well as South Pacific was defined at the so-called Sextant Conference in Cairo on December 3, 1943 (attended by Churchill, Roosevelt, and Chiang Kai-shek). Admiral King opposed the idea of relinquishing the Pacific war to MacArthur, submitting his own plan to the Allied Combined Chiefs of Staff for a dual approach in the Pacific. The Combined Chiefs concurred and issued their directive stating that the "advance along the New Guinea-Netherlands East Indies-Philippine axis will proceed concurrently with operations for the capture of the Mandated Islands. A strategic bombing force will be established in Guam, Tinian, and Saipan for strategic bombing of Japan proper." For this final phase a new bomber, the Boeing B-29 Superfortress, was being delivered to combat-training units in the United States.

The step between the Marianas (Guam, Saipan, and Tinian) was the Marshalls campaign. It proved to be one of the most successfully handled of the early combined operations, "characterized," in the words of Admiral King, "by excellent planning and by almost perfect timing in the execution of those plans." The experience gained in the Gilberts was not lost in the planning of the Marshalls invasions. As soon as the Seventh Air Force could begin launching bombing missions from new bases in the Gilberts the initial softening up of the targets began. With D-Day set for January 31, 1944, the carriers moved in two days before to strike at Majuro, Roi, and Kwajalein (in the Kwajalein Atoll), Taroa and Wotje. In concert with the Navy attacks, the Seventh Air Force sent over its B-24s and B-25s to harass the Japanese and to keep them off balance.

Japanese antiaircraft guns took their toll, but fighter defenses were weak because so many planes had previously been destroyed on the ground. Snoopers seemed even more timid than in the Gilberts. Then around dusk of January 29 the sudden appearance of nine planes low on the water electrified the fleet. The planes were quickly identified as twin-ruddered Nells and became the focus of destroyer antiaircraft guns. Combat air patrol Hellcats dropped down to attack the intruders also.

A trail of smoke came from one of the bombers before it splashed into the water. Loudspeakers on the American ships about then began booming, "Cease firing! Cease firing!" The planes that had been identified as Nells were, in fact, Mitchells of

Flaming Kate *stopped by the gunners of the* Yorktown *off Kwajalein, Marshall Islands, December 3, 1943.*

the 820th Squadron (41st Bomb Group). The Mitchells had been on a mission to Wotje, where they were to have bombed shipping and shore installations. Coming in low over the water to avoid Japanese radar they had approached the unalerted Navy ships looking like torpedo bombers. The error cost the life of one man, injured five, and destroyed one Mitchell. Two others, seriously damaged, managed to return to Tarawa.

One by one, with almost clockwork precision, the islands fell: Majuro on January 31, Roi and Namur on February 2—but Kwajalein, the largest and strongest-held, took longer. Heavy shelling, much heavier than that which preceded the Tarawa landing, pounded the island for two days, almost up to the moment that the troops were put ashore. At nine-thirty in the morning of February 1, 1944, the Army's 7th Division (which had fought on Attu) began moving in. Like Tarawa, Kwajalein was ingeniously fortified and cluttered with tank traps, pillboxes, snarls of barbed wire, and trenches. The survivors of the weeks of bombing and the hours of shelling had to be rooted out, and, as before, the Japanese fought fanatically, almost heedlessly to the death. When the fighting ended all but the 35 Japanese who had surrendered were annihilated—close to 5000 men. The total cost of taking all of the Kwajalein Atoll was 372 soldiers and Marines; the Japanese lost 7870 men of 8675 which had garrisoned that atoll.

Eniwetok, Marshall Islands, under carrier plane attack. U. S. Marines take shelter in a shell hole as others set up machine guns (upper center); a burned out twin-engined Japanese bomber lies at bottom left.

(U. S. NAVY)

Navy Corsairs of the Intrepid *ready for a strike on Truk. Originally not regarded as suitable for carriers, the Corsair proved otherwise. These F4U-2s are* equipped with "radomes" near starboard wingtip for night operations. The Japanese hated this plane and called it "Whistling Death."

(NAVY DEPT., NATIONAL ARCHIVES)

When the taking of Majuro and Kwajalein had come off so smoothly, it was decided that one more of the Marshalls, Eniwetok Atoll, might be taken even earlier than had been originally planned. Set for May 10, D-Day on Eniwetok was moved up to February 17. This atoll lay about 325 miles west and north of Kwajalein and about 1000 miles from the Marianas. The pattern of softening up, bombardment, and assault was repeated, and by February 20 Eniwetok fell to American forces and the Marshall Islands belonged to the United States. Several of them—Jaluit, Mili, Maloelap, and Wotje (as was Nauru in the Gilberts)—were not invaded at all. They harbored Japanese troops, held air bases, but with the other positions in American hands these atolls were isolated from everything but American air and surface attacks.

During the Eniwetok assault, Truk, the vaunted "Gibraltar of the Pacific," Japan's most formidable base outside the home islands, was rendered almost neutral by the carrier planes of Rear Admiral Marc A. Mitscher's Fast Carrier Force. On the morning of February 17, after a surprisingly uneventful trip from Majuro in the Marshalls, a fighter sweep of seventy-two Hellcats pounced upon the air base at Truk. Fighting in the air cost four Navy planes, but the Japanese lost more than fifty in the air and even more on the ground. Avengers followed the fighters, planting incendiaries on the base, leaving behind less than a hundred operational planes with which the Japanese might contend the Eniwetok landings. Dive bombers destroyed the ships in the harbor, so that by February 18 Truk was no longer any kind of Gibraltar—and, in fact, was no longer even

Free riders: several Navy pilots came to grief near Truk during a carrier strike (April 30, 1944) due to Japanese antiaircraft or mechanical failures. This King-fisher was sent to retrieve the dunked pilots and picked up so many—six from the Enterprise *and one from the* Langley—*that pilot John A. Burns could not take off.* (NAVY DEPT., NATIONAL ARCHIVES)

Truk. As "a formidable bastion" it was no more impressive, or potent, than any other bypassed island in the Pacific.

The Marshalls campaign closed with a carrier strike in the Marianas. Not since the fall of Guam (the largest and southernmost of the Marianas) in December 1941 had American planes passed over these islands. The purpose of the carrier raid was double: to cover the Eniwetok landings and to begin reconnaissance photography of Saipan, Tinian, Rota, and Guam for the proposed seizure of these islands for future bases. For the first time since the early Gilberts assaults, the Japanese attempted to fight back vigorously. As the carriers approached the Marianas the evening of February 21 was marked by heavy fighting.

Three attempts by bombers to stop the American ships were made by an estimated forty Japanese ships. Intense antiaircraft fire either shot them down

Last moments of a Japanese "Jill" (Nakajima B6N) torpedo bomber during an attempt at American ships off Truk. (NAVY DEPT., NATIONAL ARCHIVES)

or drove them off, and the armada, undamaged though zigzagging, continued westward to the morning's launch point. As at Truk, Hellcats swept in over the Japanese bases, strafing and burning. Aerial opposition by Japanese fighters, many already burned on the ground, was sporadic, tentative, and lacking in characteristic Japanese fatal determination. At the same time small ships in and around Saipan, Tinian, and Guam were strafed and bombed.

Japan's inner defense line, which ran through the Marianas, had been pierced. There was consternation in Tokyo and Admiral Koga, after ordering the fleet to evacuate Truk, hurried home to confer with the Imperial General Staff. The principal Japanese naval base was moved farther westward to Palau, practically on the doorstep of the Philippines. The defensive line was drawn from the Kuriles in the north, down past the home islands, through the Bonins, southerly through the Marianas, and westward to Palau. This line, Koga stated, must be held to the death. Palau lay across the path of Mac-Arthur's forces hopping up the northern coast of New Guinea, as well as in the seas through which Halsey's ships moved toward Japan. And the Marianas, just to the northeast in the Philippine Sea, were also within reach.

American aircraft carriers became the main objective of Koga's plan, Order 73. He was fated never to know of the failure of this order, for on March 31,

The fighting in the Central Pacific intensifies; the American carriers have moved in close to Saipan, Mariana Islands, for a strike before the coming invasion. (NAVY DEPT., NATIONAL ARCHIVES)

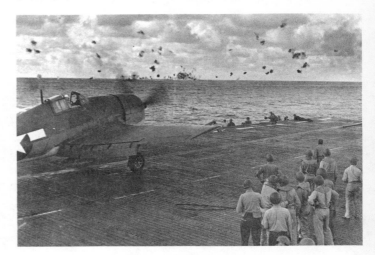

1944, Koga was lost in a storm while flying from Saipan to Davao in the Philippines. He was succeeded by Admiral Soemu Toyoda, who like Yamamoto had opposed Japan's entry into war and was a realist besides, and, in the words of Samuel Eliot Morison, "a much more aggressive character," compared to Koga.

When he became Commander in Chief, Combined Fleet, Toyoda rather bluntly said, "The war is approaching areas vital to our national security. Our situation is one of unprecedented gravity. There is only one way of deciding this struggle in our favor."

The Americans must be stopped, once and for all, in the Marianas.

IV

As the Imperial Navy made preparations for an all-out effort to stop the enemy, Minister of the Army and Prime Minister General Hideki Tojo criticized the Navy's efforts as "hysterical" and refused to permit the use of Army aircraft in the Marianas. Toyoda could do nothing, then, but alert and deploy his naval forces. He would co-ordinate his carrier force, under command of Vice-Admiral Jisaburo Ozawa, with the land-based forces of Vice-Admiral Kakuji Kakuda. Kakuda's headquarters were on Tinian and his planes were deployed through the Marianas, the Carolines, Iwo Jima, and Truk—a total of about a thousand.

The Palau anchorage having been rendered unwholesome by the marauding American carriers, Ozawa awaited developments at Tawitawi, in the Sulu Sea, just west of the southern Philippines. Under Ozawa's command was the largest fleet assembled since the attack on Pearl Harbor: seventy-three ships, including nine carriers, among them the new heavy carrier *Taiho*. Never before in Japanese naval history had such a heavy concentration of battle planes been assembled. There were nearly 450 planes—Zekes, Kates, Vals, and the newer Nakajima *Tenzen* ("Jill") torpedo bomber and the not quite so new Yokosuka *Suisei* ("Judy") dive bomber. The latter two planes were designed to replace the aged Kate and Val.

To meet the rampaging American forces, Ozawa

had divided his aerial forces into three carrier divisions. The 1st, under his command, consisted of the three heavy carriers *Taiho* (the flagship), *Shokaku,* and *Zuikaku* (the two surviving veterans of the Pearl Harbor attack). Stationed aboard these carriers were the pilots of the 601st Kokutai (Air Corps). Rear Admiral Takaji Jojima commanded the 2nd Carrier Division: the light carriers *Hiyo, Junyo,* and *Ryuho,* carrying the 652nd Kokutai. The 3rd Carrier Division (Rear Admiral Sueo Obayashi) was assigned to the main body, which consisted also of battleships and cruisers which were to deal with the American fleet. Obayashi commanded the light carriers *Chiyoda, Chitose,* and *Zuiho* (653rd Kokutai). With so vast an accumulation of air power plus the assistance which might be expected from Kakuda's land-based planes, Japanese naval officers anticipated a great aerial slaughter of the Americans. This was planned to be finished by the battleships of Vice-Admiral Takeo Kurita's force, which included the great *Yamato* and *Musashi,* two of the world's most modern battleships. An exhilarating excitement gripped the young pilots as they waited impatiently for the word to leave Tawitawi.

Even these young, untried, inexperienced, and ill-trained warriors were inclined to a touch of "victory fever."

Only the veterans awaited the coming battle with reservations. The training of the pilots aboard the nine carriers, excepting a handful of experienced leaders, was tragically inadequate, ranging from as little as two months to a maximum of six. But lack of experience began at the top, for Ozawa had never taken part in a carrier battle. He was to oppose Rear Admiral Raymond A. Spruance, who had proved himself at Midway. Directly opposing Ozawa was Vice-Admiral Marc A. Mitscher's formidable Task Force 58. Mitscher not only had quality—better-trained men, better aircraft, his own battle shrewdness—on his side, he also had overwhelming, American-made quantity, as Yamamoto had foreseen.

Early in June 1944 Task Force 58 began its approach upon the southern Marianas. Only clichés could do it justice: "massive array of sea-air power," "the greatest armada ever assembled," for as "far as the eye could see"—and beyond—great, warlike ships churned through the Pacific. There were seven heavy carriers (the *Hornet, Yorktown, Bunker Hill,*

Task Force 58 ". . . the greatest armada ever assembled . . ." in the summer of 1944 poised to move into the Marianas. (NAVY DEPT., NATIONAL ARCHIVES)

Wasp, Enterprise, Lexington, and *Essex*), eight light carriers (the *Bataan, Belleau Wood, Monterey, Cabot, San Jacinto, Princeton, Cowpens,* and *Langley*), seven new battleships, eight heavy cruisers, thirteen light cruisers, and sixty-nine destroyers. This does not include those ships directly assigned to Vice-Admiral Richmond K. Turner's amphibious forces, which would invade Saipan, then Guam, and then Tinian. Among the ships of Turner's force were several old battleships which had been damaged at Pearl Harbor, besides eight of the smaller escort carriers.

But before the landings could be made Mitscher's planes must begin clearing away Japanese aerial potential in and around Saipan. Leaving Majuro anchorage on June 6, 1944 (the same date but because of the International Date Line the day before the Normandy landings in Europe), Mitscher

put to sea. His carriers transported about double the number of aircraft Ozawa had on his carriers—over 890 planes, the bulk being Hellcats, plus Avengers, Dauntlesses, and the new Curtiss SB2-C "Helldiver." Pilots, incidentally, disdained the public relations name of the plane and preferred calling it simply the "2C."

According to plans, the amphibious forces, Marine and Army, would go ashore on Saipan on June 15. Three days before, Mitscher's carrier planes were to sweep over the Marianas airfields, bringing up the curtain on the operation. However, on the tenth Japanese air patrols spotted the approaching carriers; Toyoda, long suspecting, at last knew. Commander in Chief, Combined Fleet, had formulated his own plan: he hoped to lure the American fleet into the waters off the western Carolines (southwest of Guam). There, roughly in the vicinity of the Palau Islands and other Japanese bases (Yap and Woleai), with his vast aerial force he would annihilate the American carriers. Toyoda expected the

Island and flight deck of the Lexington *before Saipan.*
(NAVY DEPT., NATIONAL ARCHIVES)

landings at Palau and tended to regard any Marianas operations as diversions masking MacArthur's New Guinea moves.

But Mitscher's main task was to prepare the way for and cover the landings in the Marianas; it would be difficult, however alluring, to entice him into the western Carolines. In fact, as soon as he realized that Japanese reconnaissance planes had found Task Force 58, Mitscher put on speed and steamed ahead for the Marianas. By the afternoon of June 11, though still about two hundred miles east of the Marianas, Mitscher launched his first fighter sweep —the Hellcats being guided to the targets by the better-equipped (in terms of navigational instruments) Avengers.

Although the Japanese had been aware of TF 58's presence, they were apparently preparing for the customary dawn attack for the next day. Also, undoubtedly, they were preparing for a snooper attack on the carriers that very evening. About two hundred Hellcats swarmed down upon Saipan, Tinian, and Guam, destroying planes on the ground and in the air. About 150 Japanese planes were erased from Kakuda's ground-based air forces in the Marianas, crippling all possible strong air retaliation. The first night off Saipan was free of Japanese attack.

The next day American destruction of airfields and other installations continued, and on the thir-

teenth the battleships started pounding the landing beaches. On this day, also, the Japanese fleet left Tawitawi and proceeded northward. Obviously the Americans intended to invade the Marianas (which had been the prediction of Commander Chikataka Nakajima of the Naval Intelligence Staff) and not Palau (as the Staff, in general, believed). Immediately canceled was Operation *Kon* (a plan to retake the importantly strategic island of Biak, off the northwest coast of New Guinea, which had fallen to MacArthur's forces), and Toyoda ordered Ozawa to proceed at full speed for Saipan—about two thousand miles away. At the same time Kakuda's land-based planes were ordered to hold off the Americans until Ozawa's forces arrived.

By this time about five hundred planes had been destroyed and with the remaining handful there was little resistance forthcoming, at least not from the air. On June 15 Marines and Army infantrymen (2nd and 4th Marine Divisions; 27th Infantry Division) struck the beaches of Saipan. They had been properly cautioned by Navy manuals and talks. The troops were warned to beware of sea life ringing the island: "sharks, barracuda, sea snakes, anemones, razor-sharp coral, polluted waters, poison fish and giant clams that shut on a man like a bear trap."

An officer read off, according to regulations, the joys of life ashore: leprosy, typhus, filariasis, yaws, typhoid, dengue fever, dysentery, saber grass, insects, snakes, and giant lizards.

"Eat nothing growing on the island," he continued reading; "don't drink its waters and don't approach the inhabitants." The End.

"Any questions?"

A hand was raised.

The officer nodded.

"Why don't we let them keep the island?"

Unlike Japanese Naval Intelligence, the young American Marine had never heard of the B-29. On Saipan, northernmost of the islands coveted by the Americans, the Japanese had constructed Aslito Field. At the northern end of the island—that is, opposite to the end on which Aslito lay—another airstrip was being set up. It was because of these air bases, primarily, that the Americans did not want the Japanese to keep the island, and for which the invading troops were expected to risk the nearly countless hazards of life in and around Saipan.

The invasion of Saipan, with carrier plane cover, begins; June 15, 1944. A Japanese ship burns near the shore. (NAVY DEPT., NATIONAL ARCHIVES)

Besides these natural perils there were Lieutenant General Yoshitsugo Saito's thirty thousand troops. Also on Saipan as Commander in Chief, Pacific Fleet, in command of all Japanese Marine and naval units in the area, was Vice-Admiral Chuichi Nagumo, the reluctant hero of Pearl Harbor. Nagumo agreed with others in the Japanese High Command: the Americans were aiming for Palau. Meanwhile Saito, grumbling because the Navy had lost supply ships and troop ships to American submarines, did the best he could to prepare "to destroy the enemy at the water's edge."

The day before the landings began Nagumo, having witnessed the aerial strikes of the previous four days, hedgingly proffered a prediction and a definition. "The Marianas are the first line of defense of our homeland. It is certain that the Americans will land in the Marianas group either this month or the next." They landed, of course, the next day.

During the Saipan invasion carrier sweeps over Guam to the south held down Japanese aerial intervention. On his mission Ensign A. P. Morner, Ironwood, Michigan, encountered six Zekes, shot down three, but was wounded himself and his Hellcat damaged—which resulted in this crash landing on Morner's home carrier. (U. S. NAVY)

Stowaways: Air Force Thunderbolts of the 318th Fighter Group (73rd Squadron) aboard the carrier Manila Bay. *Japanese Vals from Saipan contributed the splashes to port.* (U. S. AIR FORCE)

"Where are our planes?" lamented tank man Tokuzo Matsuya in a characteristic query. "Are they letting us die without making any effort to save us? If it were for the security of the Empire we would not hesitate to lay down our lives, but wouldn't it be a great loss to the Land of the Gods for us all to die on this island? It would be easy for me to die, but for the sake of the future I feel obligated to stay alive."

Marine Lieutenant General Holland M. Smith, in command of the ground troops for the invasion, found that "Saito met us at the beaches at Saipan in approved Japanese fashion, and our hopes of quickly expanding our beachhead were somewhat dampened. . . . The long twenty-five-day continuous attack against strongly entrenched and fiercely resisting troops on Saipan proved the most bitter battle in the Pacific up to that time." Intense mortar and artillery fire, plus suicidal, screaming night attacks by the Japanese, made life ashore dreadful and, for many, short. By June 18, however, Aslito Field fell to the Army's 27th Division. On June 22 Thunderbolts of the 19th and 73rd Squadrons of the 318th Fighter Group, catapulted from the es-

Thunderbolt of 73rd Squadron leaves deck of Manila Bay *for Aslito Field (renamed Isley Field), Saipan.* (U. S. AIR FORCE)

cort carriers *Manila Bay* and *Natoma Bay,* landed at Aslito to join the Navy planes already there. By this time the field was renamed Isley Field, in honor of Commander Robert H. Isley, commander of the *Lexington*'s torpedo planes. Two days before the Saipan landings Isley's Avenger was hit by anti-aircraft fire over Aslito and crashed in flames onto the field itself. From Isley Field the Seventh Air

Aslito Field, Saipan, showing the ravages of American carrier plane attacks. Intact aircraft parked among the wrecks are U. S. Navy and Air Force planes.

(U. S. NAVY)

Force Thunderbolts engaged in close-support operations, a blasting away at Japanese positions in front of Marine and Army troops. Once established in the still beleagured airfield, the P-47s, when not engaged in sporadic air battles, bombed and strafed Japanese positions on Saipan and Tinian. By July, when the fighting on Saipan ended, the Thunderbolts of the 318th Fighter Group were armed with yet

another weapon, at first popularly called the "fire bomb." These were the first of the frightfully effective napalm, diesel oil, and gasoline mixtures (later napalm and gasoline), which when dropped in wing and belly tanks from about fifty feet upon Japanese strong points (particularly caves) created a havoc of flame.

Meanwhile, even as American troops went ashore on Saipan, word was flashed from the submarine *Flying Fish* that a large Japanese carrier force had been sighted in San Bernardino Strait, headed for

Marc Andrew Mitscher, USN, an early Navy air pioneer, canny air leader during Solomons campaign and commander of carrier force in the Central Pacific for the Marianas assault.

(NAVY DEPT., NATIONAL ARCHIVES)

the Marianas. The next day, June 16, *Seahorse,* another submarine, sighted more ships off Surigao Strait. Spruance knew then that the Combined Fleet was coming out in full force. He immediately canceled the proposed June 18 landing on Guam (although not the June 16 air strikes upon Iwo Jima in the Volcano Islands and Chichi Jima in the Bonins, south of the Japanese homeland).

American submarines, which were to play an important role in the impending "decisive battle," tracked the Japanese fleet, waiting for the moment when they might launch their fish. Spruance positioned his carriers by June 18 about 160 miles west of Tinian. On this same day—the day that Aslito Field fell—Ozawa's forces had arrived at a position about 500 miles west of Saipan. The opposing fleets by June 19 were about four hundred miles apart.

Ozawa, therefore, had the advantage. His planes, thanks to the lack of armor plating and the lack of the heavy self-sealing fuel tanks, enjoyed a greater range than the American carrier fighters. Even before his carriers came within range of the American

carriers—Ozawa's major targets—he could launch his planes, which, after combat, could land on the Marianas airfields (excepting, of course, Aslito). Japanese search planes, meanwhile, sought out the American fleet as the Japanese carriers made preparations to hurl total destruction upon Spruance's carriers.

June 19 dawned clear over the American carriers. The night before, the pilots had been disappointed because Spruance would not authorize Mitscher, in tactical command of the carriers, to speed westward to intercept the Japanese. Spruance had in mind that the primary mission of Task Force 58 was to cover the Saipan invasion. If the carriers were too far west, there was always a possibility of Japanese ships coming in to pound the Americans from the sea. Aboard the *Lexington,* his flagship, Mitscher was reported to have stalked into his sea cabin to blow off steam in private. On the *Enterprise* Captain Matthias B. Gardner, complying, said nothing but is reported to have "hurled down his hat and stomped on it." (Spruance was later criticized for holding his carriers near Saipan and not taking the offensive on June 18. Critics, however, ex post facto as usual, possessed certain vital information which at the time the Japanese were not bestowing upon Spruance.)

Mitscher's eager pilots, however, would not lack for action on the nineteenth. An early morning strike on Orote Field on Guam was mounted to keep that base neutralized in the event that the impending battle materialized. About thirty Wildcats pounced on the already beaten-up field; a rather surprising antlike activity seemed in progress as Japanese planes were pushed out of revetments and put into the air with frantic resolution. The Wildcats began the morning's decimation, shattering the Japanese planes, barely air-borne, out of the bright morning sky.

In about an hour and a half of fighting, the American combat air patrol shot down thirty-five of Kakuda's land-based planes, which had up to that morning escaped previous attacks. Meanwhile, tension aboard the carriers mounted as Mitscher wondered about the location of the Japanese carriers.

Ozawa had begun launching his planes at dawn, search planes and bombers (a total of seventy-three), which fanned out into a squally sky to look for the American fleet. The imperfect weather over

Hellcats of VFN-76 on the Lexington *near Saipan; radomes converted these planes into night fighters that* dealt with Japanese night "snoopers," reconnaissance planes and bombers.

(NAVY DEPT., NATIONAL ARCHIVES)

the Japanese ships, stretching nearly to the American dispositions, was a disadvantage to the inexperienced Japanese pilots. Animated with patriotism and little else, they were led like strangely pugnacious sheep to slaughter. Ozawa's first raid, led by Lieutenant Commander Masayuki Yamagami, began taking off at daybreak and vanished into murky eastern sky. Then Ozawa waited. He could afford to, for his ships were still beyond the range of Mitscher's carrier planes.

He was determined to make a thorough job of the Americans, so even as the planes of the first raid were taking off the van carriers of the 3rd Carrier Division, the planes of the 1st Carrier Division began launching also. Forty-eight Zekes, fifty-four Judys, and twenty-seven Jills took off from the *Zuikaku, Shokaku,* and *Taiho.* From the bridge of the latter, Japan's great new carrier, Ozawa observed the air swarming with planes. The *Taiho* was a gigantic vessel of more than sixty-four thousand tons. Launched just three months before (April 4, 1944), the *Taiho* was considered unsinkable.

As the last plane left the deck of the flagship a torpedo track was discovered knifing through the water at the *Taiho.* Warrant Officer Sakio Komatsu, whose plane was in the last wave, saw the churning line in the water and died believing he had saved the flagship by diving into the torpedo, detonating it. But that was not the only "fish" which had been ejected from the torpedo tubes of the *Albacore,* an American submarine in the area (under command of J. W. Blanchard), and despite attempts to turn the *Taiho,* it was struck. The blow jammed an elevator and fuel piping ruptured, filling the hangar space below decks with fumes. A single spark did the rest, for within six hours the *Taiho* was ripped by a splintering explosion. A mass of flames from stem to stern, the *Taiho* turned over and sank.

Admiral Ozawa in the meantime had moved to another ship, the heavy cruiser *Haguro.* He was an unhappy man, for even while the *Taiho* reeked with impending doom yet another carrier was attacked—this time the *Skokaku,* which became the victim of Lieutenant Commander H. J. Kossler's submarine *Cavalla.* The *Shokaku* sank even before the *Taiho.*

Before these misfortunes, however, Ozawa had launched about four hundred planes in four attack waves. The first of these was detected by American

A Japanese plane shot aflame by antiaircraft fire from American ships attempts to crash into flight deck of escort carrier Sangamon, Marianas.
(NAVY DEPT., NATIONAL ARCHIVES)

radar when they were almost 150 miles away, at Guam. When the first blips of aircraft apparently approaching from the open sea appeared on the radar screens, it was Mitscher himself who took the microphone of the TBS (Talk Between Ships) and initiated what would come to be called the "Marianas Turkey Shoot."

"Hey, Rube!" echoed through the fleet, alerting

A twin-engined Japanese bomber goes down near the Kitkun Bay *near Saipan on the eve of the Marianas "Turkey Shoot."* (NAVY DEPT., NATIONAL ARCHIVES)

pilots to scramble and antiaircraft gunners to prepare their guns. Great rings of destroyers and cruisers, guns pointing skyward, had been formed
around the carriers in four large groups spread over
hundreds of square miles to the west of the Marianas.

The old American circus battle cry activated the
carriers, and the Wildcats that had been over Guam
turned about and raced out to sea. They would intercept the oncoming Japanese, but Guam continued
to suffer under bombers and torpedo bombers. At
10:07 A.M. the ticker tape on the *Lexington* read:
"Unidentified planes have been picked up bearing
333°, 45 miles away." Hellcats from the *Essex,
Cowpens, Bunker Hill,* and *Princeton* vectored in
upon the oncoming planes—the scouts and scout
bombers of the Japanese 3rd Carrier Division. In
the first skirmish, well to the west of the American
carriers, about twenty-five Japanese planes (of seventy-three) were splashed into the sea. The survivors continued on resolutely, only to be met head
on by another formation of Hellcats—sixteen more
Japanese planes fell into the sea. Those still flying
(about thirty) broke through the battle line (the
battleships and destroyers that stood fifteen miles
in the vanguard of the carrier formations). One of
the bombers scored a direct hit upon the *South
Dakota,* but not one Japanese plane reached the
carriers. Of the original seventy-three only twenty-
four survived for the time being. Some crash-landed
on Guam and others returned to their own carriers.

The first large attack wave, the 129 fighters,
bombers, and torpedo bombers of the 1st Carrier
Division, were intercepted about an hour after the
battle had begun. The Japanese planes ran head
on into a mass of Hellcats, which shattered the formations—about a hundred planes fell before the
carriers were reached. And the six of these which
actually broke through were destroyed by savage
antiaircraft fire or the combat air patrol planes circling the carriers.

Commander Ernest M. Snowden, of the *Lexington,* recalls how "We could see vapor trails of
planes coming in with tiny black specks at the head.
It was just like the skywriting we all used to see
before the war. The sky was a white overcast and
for some reason the planes were making vapor trails
at a much lower altitude than usual. That made it
easier for our boys to find the incoming Japs."

There were plenty of Japanese to go around, apparently. One young pilot, Ensign Bradford Hagie,
found action even during a simple ferry flight. He
had been forced to land on another carrier the
previous day with engine trouble. Anxious to return
to the *Lexington,* about three thousand yards away,
he took off the next morning during what turned out
to be the attack by the first wave. Hearing the radio
chatter about the approaching unidentified aircraft,
he remained air-borne for a while and on his way to
the *Lexington* shot down three planes.

When the second, larger wave approached another young pilot sat gloomily in his Hellcat off to
one side of the battle, circling out of the way because his engine was giving him trouble. He was
Lieutenant Alexander Vraicu, and with his windscreen smeared with oil and his engine incapable of
pulling at full power, he and five other "orphans"
(planes with assorted problems but still flyable)
orbited over the carriers. The decks had to be kept
clear for takeoffs for the fighters.

Disappointed, Vraicu, who had gained much experience as a wingman of Butch O'Hare's, listened
to the sounds of battle to the west on his radio. He
heard the voice of the fighter director of the *Lexington* calling out vectors of approach.

"Vector 265." Vraicu turned the Hellcat in that
direction, sharply squinting his eyes until he saw
three forms in the sky coming his way. They proved
to be the first of perhaps fifty planes, Zekes, Judys,
and Jills. Other Hellcats began to race for the
formation also. The air armadas met, converged,
and then sprang apart into twisting individual air
battles. Vraicu had forgotten about his engine
trouble; the Japanese planes had ventured too close
to the American carriers. Vraicu dived into the formation of Japanese bombers, opening up on the first
plane in sight—a Judy. Within five seconds his
voice was heard over the radio, "Scratch one Judy!"

Over the next few minutes Vraicu's guns sliced
through one Judy after another, until his score for
the single battle amounted to six. To the youthful
pilot it seemed that there were simply too many
planes to be taken care of, and that some came in
dangerously close to the American ships. To his dismay he saw one lone Judy heading for a battleship,
and he kicked his Hellcat around hoping to head
off the bomber. But antiaircraft bursts came up and
the Judy flew through the puffs for a few moments

*Japanese ships dodging attacks from American carrier
planes, June 19, 1944, the day of the "Turkey Shoot."*
(NAVY DEPT., NATIONAL ARCHIVES)

and then flashed apart a thousand feet in the air.

Low on fuel, Vraicu returned to the *Lexington.*
For some reason the gunners began shooting at him
and Vraicu voiced his views on the ship's gunners
as he circled and came in again for a landing.
When his plane stopped, Vraicu stood up in the
cockpit and held up six fingers. In eight minutes he
had brought his total score up to nineteen.

A third Japanese raid was led astray by a faulty
compass reading and missed most of the fighting.
About a dozen of the forty-seven planes of the 2nd
Carrier Division ran into Hellcats, which shot down
seven. The remaining forty returned to their carriers.

When the fourth raid was launched, some of the
spared pilots of the third raid joined it to make up
a force of about eighty aircraft. This force too was
led astray, but instead of returning to the carriers,
the planes turned north, toward Guam, and ran into
the Hellcats of the *Cabot, Wasp, Monterey,* and
Bunker Hill. The day's slaughter continued in a
whirl of dogfights—Japanese bombers attempting
to get at the carriers were shot out of the air.
Eighteen, met by Hellcats, were soon cut in half.
The scattered survivors of the raid, forty-nine in all,
were jumped over Guam as they attempted to find
haven there. Thirty planes flared and fell; the remaining nineteen that finally landed, in various
stages of distress, either crashed or were strafed into
junk. Of the eighty planes which had left on the
strike, nine returned to their home bases. The last

"Turkey Shoot" victor Alexander Vraicu of the Lexington *indicates his score during one battle in a Hellcat with a bad engine.*

(NAVY DEPT., NATIONAL ARCHIVES)

of the survivors of the day's battle fled for their carriers around six forty-five in the evening. The final battle of the Turkey Shoot occurred over Guam when four Hellcats, led by Lieutenant Commander C. W. Brewer over Orote Field, pounced a limping Jill attempting to land. Brewer's forces were in turn jumped by a large number of land-based Zekes, which had somehow eluded the day's bombings and strafings. Brewer was killed in this last battle of the day as darkness fell on the great battle arena.

The coming of night brought little comfort to Ozawa; he had no decisive victory to report. Two of his largest carriers were deep under the sea and 346 of his planes simply did not return to the carriers. And not one American plane had approached the Japanese carriers during the entire day. Toyoda, at Combined Fleet headquarters at Hiroshima, ordered Ozawa to withdraw before the Americans found his other carriers. Bitterly, Ozawa complied. He planned to refuel his ships and strike back with all he had on the next day.

Spruance then unleashed the straining Mitscher, who set off westward with three carrier groups, leaving one in the vicinity of the Marianas to continue creating a hell on earth on Guam and Rota. At

one o'clock on June 20, 1944, Ozawa transferred to the carrier *Zuikaku* (now the sole surviving veteran of the Hawaii Operation); he planned to strike again on the twenty-first. It appeared that he might have his way, for there was no sign of the American fleet. Search planes launched by Mitscher had not found the Japanese fleet either.

At one-thirty in the afternoon Lieutenant R. S. Nelson had taken off in an Avenger and set off on his search pattern. Two hours and ten minutes later, when he was about at the end of his tether, Nelson found what no one had yet found in the past several days: the Japanese fleet. He began sending a message back to the *Lexington,* but distance and weather garbled it and, although alerted, Mitscher was unable to make a decision. And in less than four hours he knew the sun would go down suddenly, as it did in the Pacific.

As Nelson continued sending messages they were picked up by the Japanese cruiser *Atago* nearby. They could only mean that the Americans had found the Japanese fleet. Ozawa was immediately notified and he ordered all refueling stopped and the ships away at twenty-four knots.

It took nearly fifteen minutes of sending before Nelson's contact report finally made any sense. Mitscher had already begun to make his plans, however. When Nelson's final, corrected position and disposition report came in at 4:05 P.M., Mitscher was prepared to launch his aircraft. But not without risk, for it was already late in the day and the Japanese ships were 275 miles away. It meant a long flight for them, then the battle and a long flight back.

"Taking advantage of this opportunity to destroy the Japanese fleet was going to cost us a great deal in planes and pilots because we were launching at the maximum range of our aircraft at such a time that it would be necessary to recover them after dark," Mitscher realized. "This meant that all carriers would be recovering daylight-trained air groups at night, with consequent loss of some pilots who were not familiar with night landings and who would be fatigued at the end of an extremely hazardous and long mission."

At four forty-one the carriers turned into the wind and ten minutes later no less than 216 planes were air-borne, 85 of them Hellcats. Two hours of flying brought them within sight of the Japanese ships.

Avenger pilot Lieutenant Ronald Gift of Marlette, Michigan, after a successful strike upon Japanese ships that had fled the shambles of the "Turkey Shoot." Gift's was one of the planes that was able to land in the dark when Mitscher canceled blackout regulations. The chalked message over Gift's head was the motto of Navy bomber pilots.

(NAVY DEPT., NATIONAL ARCHIVES)

Six oilers, left astern after Ozawa had ordered the ships away, were the first to come under attack. Dive bombers swept down and disabled two—*Genyo Maru* and *Seiyo Maru*—so thoroughly that they were abandoned and scuttled by evening.

One of the last messages the American pilots had seen as they raced from their ready rooms was chalked on the blackboards, "Get the CARRIERS." Worthy targets, the carriers were the prime objectives so far as most pilots were concerned. Leaving the transports burning and scattered, the carrier pilots continued their search for the Japanese carriers. Soon they came into view.

Lieutenant George B. Brown, Avenger pilot from the *Belleau Wood,* led seven other Avengers (four of them from the *Yorktown*), circled around the Japanese ships, and then selected the *Hiyo* to the port. The *Yorktown* Avengers split away and headed

to the starboard for the larger *Zuikaku* (now Ozawa's flagship), and the four *Belleau Wood* Avengers headed for the *Hiyo*. Antiaircraft fire was desperately heavy and Brown's Avenger was hit as he ran the plane in. He had not yet dropped his torpedo when a fragment of his left wing ripped away and flames filled the cockpit of the Avenger.

The Marianas prizes: in this reconnaissance photograph which spans a distance of twenty-six miles in a southwesterly direction, Saipan lies in the foreground. The airstrip near Marpi Point, Saipan's northernmost tip, is at the bottom of the photo. Aslito airfield is hidden under a cloud near top left of the picture. Across Saipan Channel lies Tinian with one of its two airstrips visible. With the conquest of the Marianas a new phase in the Pacific war would follow: B-29 operations from Saipan, Tinian, and Guam. (U. S. AIR FORCE)

The hazards of landing on a carrier deck under poor lighting conditions after combat. A Wildcat has come in, the pilot has misjudged his speed, or his arresting hook has not caught, and his plane does not stop until it ends up in the Pacific. Nor before it damages all other objects in its path. Mitscher's decision to turn on carrier landing lights helped to diminish the number of such landings. (NAVY DEPT., NATIONAL ARCHIVES)

The radioman and gunner bailed out, but Brown, who had said before taking off that he would get a carrier "at any cost," continued the run. The fire had burned itself out and Brown dropped his torpedo; his wingman, Lieutenant Benjamin Tate, dropped too but did not claim a hit. Lieutenant Warren Omark, however, placed a torpedo into the *Hiyo*.

Tate, harassed by two Zekes and with one gun shot out, ducked into a cloud and lost the Japanese fighters. He then joined up with Brown's badly shot-up Avenger. The plane moved erratically and Brown appeared to be bleeding badly. Then Tate lost sight of Brown. Omark, having eluded a Zeke and a couple of Vals, caught up with Brown and tried to guide him back to the American carrier positions. Brown finally disappeared in a cloud and was never seen again. His two crewmen, who had parachuted, were rescued the following day, safely floating in their life jackets. They had witnessed the death throes of the *Hiyo,* which sank about two hours after Brown and Omark had placed their torpedoes into the carrier.

There was fighting aloft too, for Ozawa had scraped together about seventy-five planes to meet the Hellcats, Avengers, and Helldivers. As the Hellcats fought off the Zekes, the bombers attacked and strafed other ships, among them the *Zuikaku,* which though badly hit was not sunk, the *Junyo, Ryuho,* and *Chiyoda* (all light carriers). In the heavy fighting sixty-five Japanese planes went down; American losses reached twenty, victims of fighters and anti-aircraft.

When the day ended Ozawa's log noted the tragedy of the two days' fighting of what was officially known as the Battle of the Philippine Sea. "Surviving carrier air power," it was written, "35 aircraft operational." Though he wished to continue the battle, Ozawa canceled the order for a surface battle and ordered the ships back to Okinawa.

About 190 American planes turned away from the battle and headed for their home carriers. Many were shot up, most were low on fuel—and night had fallen an hour before the first plane appeared over the American carriers. Task Force 58 turned into the wind and the hard-bitten Mitscher made another vital decision that day. Earlier in the day he had risked his pilots and planes on a long-range strike and now he believed he owed them something. In defiance of all regulations, caution, and possible Japanese snoopers and submarines, he turned to Captain Arleigh Burke, his chief of staff, and said, "Turn on the lights."

"We had almost reached the force when we saw the lights come on," Lieutenant E. J. Lawton of the *Enterprise* recalled in describing the homecoming of the planes. "It is clear that the task force did all in its power to make it easier for us to get home. Lieutenant [V. Van] Eason led us in over the *Enterprise* but her deck was fouled for some time. We circled for a few minutes, watching the lights of the planes below fan out in the pattern of a landing circle. But there had been too much strain in the last five hours to reduce things to a pattern now; and inevitably, landing circles became crowded, intervals were lost and deck crashes occurred. Many planes—too many—announced that their gas was gone and they were going into the water. Others were caught short in the groove."

Japanese air power in the Marianas: a Marine grins down from a "meatball" on a Zeke wingtip at Aslito, Saipan. (U. S. NAVY)

"Seen from above, it was a weird kaleidoscope of fast-moving lights forming intricate trails in the darkness, punctuated now and then by tracers shooting through the night as someone landed with his gun switches on, and again by suddenly brilliant exhaust flames as each plane took a cut, or someone's turtleback light getting lower and lower until blacked out by the waves closing over it."

About 80 planes crashed or splashed into the water during the landing attempts. Rescue ships picked up 59 men; in all, 49 were lost, either in battle or because they sank in their aircraft before they could be rescued. The two days' total loss to the American fleet was 130 planes (compared to Ozawa's 480—this number includes both carrier- and land-base aircraft). Seventy-six American airmen perished in the Battle of the Philippine Sea, a fair trade, in the arithmetic of war, for hundreds of Japanese pilots and planes and three carriers.

The trade for the Marianas as future air bases

Guam secured: an 11th Bomb Group (Seventh Air Force) plane takes off for a mission from the Marianas *for strikes on the Bonins and Carolines.*

(U. S. AIR FORCE)

and harbors for ships and submarines was also worthwhile. Guam and Tinian fell by August 10 and the Marianas were officially declared "secure," although thousands of enemy troops in hiding had to be killed before the islands were completely free of fighting.

Political repercussions in Japan were nearly as drastic as the military defeat. General Tojo, who had scoffed at the thought of a Marianas invasion by the Americans, declared upon the fall of Saipan that "Japan is threatened by a national crisis with-

out precedent." When the fall of Saipan was officially announced to the bewildered people of Japan, so was the fall of Tojo's cabinet. The Emperor, urged on by the *jushin* (elder statesmen without power who advised him), accepted the resignation of Tojo on July 18, 1944.

The Greater East Asia Co-Prosperity Sphere, which had swollen under Tojo's bellicose domination like some bloated balloon, had begun its inexorable collapse. The arrogant samurai had been diminished into just another turkey.

VOLUME FOUR

WINGS OF FIRE

BOOK I
Target Germany

I

BLUE MEDITERRANEAN SKIES

ALL roads theoretically led to Berlin—even those that seemed to lead to Rome.

The low road would run painfully and erratically through north Africa, bridge the Mediterranean into Sicily, and cross the three-mile Strait of Messina onto the toe of Italy. The high road would traverse the hostile sky from Britain's Bomber Command and Eighth Air Force bases in East Anglia. With bases in Italy, the reasoning went, it would be possible to strike at Germany from two directions along the high road. To many, strategists and non-combatants alike, the skirmishing in the Mediterranean appeared to be a roundabout route to Berlin, even by air.

It was the bumbling Mussolini who inadvertently brought attention to the Mediterranean theater with an ill-advised invasion of Greece on October 28, 1940. Three weeks before, Hitler himself revealed an Axis interest in the Balkan-Mediterranean area when he unilaterally moved German troops into Rumanian oil fields to assure the German war machine a source of fuel and lubricants. At the same time he flanked his other ally, Russia, the invasion plans of which were already in progress. This establishment of a *Festung* (fortress) Ploesti was smoothly accomplished because of an "understand-

ing" with Rumanian dictator General Ion Antonescu, a devout Nazi.

Mussolini, envious of Hitler's run of victories, longed for one of his own. With Italian-dominated Albania as a springboard he had hoped to occupy Greece, making a triumphal entry as Hitler had into Czechoslovakia before the war. Also, Mussolini wished to bring off his triumph alone, without any aid from Hitler. With the Rumanian take-over fresh in his mind, Mussolini ordered his troops across the Albanian border into Greece. There was no puppetlike Antonescu to smooth the way, and the Italian legions, met by stiff Greek resistance, barely made it across the border. This was bad enough, but worse followed: Mussolini's bungle had triggered British intervention in Greece. Hitler did not wish to have British bomber bases within range of the Ploesti oil fields. By the turn of the year, with Italian troops pushed back into Albania, Hitler realized he would have to strike. This brought the spotlight to the Balkans and the Mediterranean, diffusing the German forces further.

Italy's belated, rather reluctant entry into the war had also activated a vast, sprawling battleground across north and northeast Africa. The first six months, following Italy's declaration of war upon

General Ion Antonescu, dictator of Rumania and a Hitler puppet, greets General Kurt Pflugbeil, chief of Luftflotte 1. The Luftwaffe had come to Rumania to protect the Ploesti oilfields from the British and Hitler's "ally," Russia. (H. J. NOWARRA)

In the foreground Mussolini beams down upon marching Italian soldiers in Greece in the spring of 1941; in the background is the reason for the smile, Hitler, who had to send German troops into Greece to win the war for Mussolini there. (NATIONAL ARCHIVES)

Britain and the Free French, the fighting in north Africa was sporadic and tentative. But led by Marshal Rodolfo Graziani, Italian forces moved eastward out of the Italian colony of Libya into Egypt on September 13, 1940, clearly with the Suez Canal as the objective. Although Graziani's troops outnumbered Lieutenant General Sir Archibald Wavell's forces by about five to one, the Italians advanced only sixty miles into Egypt, established defensive positions, and waited. The British were sorely disappointed that Graziani had not doubled the thrust, for awaiting him near Mersa Matruh was the Western Desert Force's 7th Armored Force, eager to strike.

While Graziani waited to see what Wavell would do, Mussolini began stirring up the Mediterranean with his vain Grecian misadventure. British troops were sent from Egypt to occupy Crete in the eastern Mediterranean and Lemnos in the Aegean Sea off the Dardanelles, as well as the Greek mainland around Athens. These latter sites served as bases for the Gladiator and Blenheim squadrons (Nos. 30, 80, 84, and 211 Squadrons) also shifted from Africa. Handicapped by weather and terrain, the pilots of these squadrons operated in close co-operation with the Greek forces over the battle lines, besides bombing Italian air bases in Albania.

From Malta, too, came aid to the Greeks and discomfort for the Italians. When war came to the Mediterranean Malta, strategically centered in the sea, could hardly be regarded as a hornet's nest of air power. Its total force consisted of five aged Fairey "Swordfish" (which crews affectionately called "the Stringbag") and even more ancient de Havilland "Queen Bees" (a variant of the Tiger Moth) and four Gladiators. One of the latter was soon damaged beyond repair and the three remaining Gladiators operated against the Regia Aeronautica (Italian Air Force) for several weeks so effectively that their estimated number was thought to be twenty-five. The Gladiators became celebrated on Malta under the names of *Faith, Hope,* and *Charity.*

Also operating out of Malta was the carrier *Illustrious,* equipped with "Stringbags" of Fleet Air Arm. On the night of November 11, 1940, the Swordfish of the *Illustrious* swooped down upon the Italian fleet in anchor at Taranto and dropped their torpedoes despite a high concentration of antiaircraft fire and a balloon barrage. In a few moments the

Fairey "Swordfish" of Fleet Air Arm; Swordfish of the British carrier Illustrious *crippled the Italian fleet at Taranto and demonstrated to the Japanese the possibility of destroying ships in a shallow harbor—Pearl Harbor, to be specific. The "Stringbag" was a lumbering but well-loved aircraft whose pilots harassed Italian and German ships from British bases in Malta.*

(U. S. AIR FORCE)

balance of naval power in the central Mediterranean shifted as half the battleship strength of the Italian fleet was knocked out of action for a half year. (It was this performance by aircraft upon ships in port that inspired the Japanese tactics at Pearl Harbor).

A month later Graziani in Egypt learned what the British planned to do. On December 9 Wavell launched an offensive which drove the Italians out of Egypt, across northern Libya into Bedafomm (south of Benghazi), where by February 7, 1941, the remnants of the Italian Tenth Army were rounded up. More than 130,000 prisoners were taken, along with hundreds of tanks and guns as well as other spoils. With advance outposts established deeper into Libya at El Agheila, the British planned to drive on to the port of Tripoli and perhaps complete the elimination of Italian forces in north Africa, but this was upset when British troops were withdrawn for the fighting in Greece (where Hitler had finally decided to intervene on January 19). Even so, the Italians were in deep trouble in Africa too.

Hitler again provided succor, this time in the person of Lieutenant General Erwin Rommel and the troops of the Afrika Korps. To accomplish his mis-

The popular "Desert Fox," Erwin Rommel, visiting front-line Afrika Korps troops in March 1941, around *the time he began to push the British back across north Africa into Egypt.* (H. J. NOWARRA)

sion Rommel could draw upon Fliegerkorps X, based on Sicily and commanded by General Hans Ferdinand Geisler. Rallying the remnants of the Italian forces, which were bolstered by German panzer troops and motorized divisions, Rommel began pushing the British out of Libya and back toward Cairo and, beyond that, the Suez Canal.

Rommel had arrived in Tripoli on February 12, 1941, and was ready to open his offensive by March 24. Thus began an oscillatory warfare that shifted back and forth across the deserts of Libya and Egypt and in which Rommel impressed the world, and particularly the British, with his wily generalship. The desert war was primarily one of armored vehicles, of tanks and movement. Rommel very quickly proved himself to be a master tactician, skilled in the art of thrust, parry, and surprise; his skill encompassed also the ability to improvise, to

exploit the situation as it developed in the field. He was often seen either in the vanguard of his panzers, which endeared him to his own men as well as to his enemies, or reconnoitering the wasted battleground in his Storch observation plane.

When Rommel sprang into action neither he nor the British were very strong in the air. Mussolini could take the blame for the one and credit for the other: the British stripped much of their air power in north Africa for the diversion in Greece and Fliegerkorps X was expected to assist in the Balkans as well as in Africa. One of its prime functions was to harass the British on Malta in order to keep the supply routes into Tripoli open. So it was that Air Marshal Sir Arthur M. Longmore, Commander, RAF, Middle East, could muster only four squadrons (and two of these of about half strength). Two were fighter squadrons: No. 3 Royal

Australian Air Force Squadron, equipped with Gladiators and later with Hurricanes; No. 73 Squadron (Cobber Kain's old unit), with its Hurricanes. No. 6 Squadron with its Lysanders was to be employed in reconnaissance, and No. 55 Squadron with its Blenheims would double in reconnaissance and bombardment.

Geisler dispatched planes to Africa for Rommel's use; they numbered a little over a hundred, mainly Ju-87 Stukas, with about thirty Me-110s and an equal number of Me-109Es of Jagdgeschwader 27. A few Ju-88s rounded out the force, under the command of Fliegerführer Afrika, Generalmajor Stephan Frölich. Considering the distances and the conditions under which aircraft were operated in the desert, it was a modest force, and Rommel was forced to depend upon his own genius for improvisation.

Beginning with Rommel's attack in late March of 1941, the desert war swayed across north Africa like a giant scythe: striking at Wavell's positions, Rommel pushed to the point at which Graziani had left off in 1940. Then Wavell was relieved by General Sir Claude J. E. Auchinleck. When he was ready for his counteroffensive, the Western Desert Force was redesignated the Eighth Army. Auchinleck, in turn, pushed Rommel back into Libya by December 1941. The pendulum made another swing when the Afrika Korps went over to the offensive

again on January 21, 1942; by the end of June Rommel was positioned at El Alamein, less than a hundred miles from Alexandria. His troops, like the British, were exhausted; supply lines were overextended and reinforcements were not forthcoming because Hitler needed them desperately in Russia, where brutal fighting had been in progress for a year.

Despite the precarious condition of the weakened Afrika Korps, Rommel, now a field marshal, was determined to press on. Mussolini, it was rumored, had already made plans for an entry into Cairo on a white horse. While neither Mussolini nor his white charger concerned him, Rommel believed he had the British "on the run" and he hoped to run them into Cairo in ten more days of fighting. But his own troops had already endured a month of heavy combat without rest and the British, though beaten and weary also, dug in at El Alamein. They took comfort in the proximity of their sources of supply and the RAF bases in Egypt. At this juncture General Sir Harold Alexander replaced Auchinleck as Commander in Chief, Middle East, and Lieutenant General Bernard Law Montgomery assumed command of the Eighth Army.

Summoning up the characteristic magisterial courage of the man who is given life-or-death decisions over the lives of others, Montgomery, self-centered, self-sufficient, and self-assured, announced, "Give

A desert Stuka; the north African campaign gave the Ju-87 another chance after its failure in the Battle of Britain. It proved to be an excellent tank buster if not a worthy opponent of the Spitfire or Hurricane.
(U. S. AIR FORCE)

A desert Messerschmitt 109E. This plane, though fitted with shackles for a drop tank, is not yet equipped with a tropical filter. (H. J. NOWARRA)

Desert life: ground crew plays cards, with the JG 27 Messerschmitt in desert camouflage in the background. The plane has the longer special desert filter attached to the fuselage near the nose. (H. J. NOWARRA)

Prize of the desert war: a captured Hurricane taken when Rommel's Afrika Korps overran a British airdrome. It was, in turn, taken back when the British took back Gambut in Cyrenaica, east of Tobruk. (H. J. NOWARRA)

me three weeks and I can defeat the Boche. Give me a month and I can chase him out of Africa." Whereupon he took two months just getting prepared to drive Rommel out of Africa—and then he would not do it alone.

Stubbornly the British held the Alamein line, and the Germans were halted in their push toward Alexandria. During the stalemate Rommel flew to Germany, where he reported to Hitler. He said that the bombers of the RAF's Western Desert Air Force were ripping up his panzers with 40-mm., American-made shells.

"Impossible," Göring interjected. "Nothing but latrine rumors. All the Americans can make are razor blades and refrigerators."

"I only wish, Herr Reichsmarschall," Rommel answered, "that we were issued similar razor blades."

More substantial than razor blades, although not yet in any real numbers, were the American men and planes which had been arriving piecemeal and at times pell-mell in the Middle East. Following the Japanese attack on Pearl Harbor and Hitler's subsequent declaration of war on the United States, that aid which had been coming into Britain and the Mediterranean through Lend-Lease was, in theory at least, stepped up.

The first Americans to arrive manned the Liberators of Colonel Harry Halverson's "Project No. 63," en route to China bases from which it was planned

they would bomb Tokyo itself. While in Khartoum, the Sudan, Halverson learned that their intended base in China had been overrun by the Japanese, and upon the official declaration of war upon Rumania on June 5, 1942, it was decided to divert Halverson's Liberators to bomb Ploesti. The mission, the first time any American aircraft bombed enemy targets in Europe, took place on June 11-12. A dozen B-24s (of thirteen dispatched) succeeded in bombing the oil fields, although without doing much damage. No men were lost, although four Liberators had landed in Turkey (the crews were interned) and another was crash-landed. Those B-24s which had survived the mission and the desert maintenance problems (about seventeen of the original twenty-three) were pressed into service bombing Italian supply ships in the Mediterranean as well as enemy-held ports.

Additional American units began to trickle into Africa. Major General Lewis H. Brereton arrived on June 28 in Fayid, Egypt, with seven Flying Fortresses (survivors of the 7th Bombardment Group's 9th Squadron and orphans of the Japanese storm in the Pacific). Brereton had been ordered out of India, where he had commanded the Tenth Air Force, and placed in command of the United States Army Middle East Air Force; later it would be designated the Ninth Air Force.

Additional reinforcements arrived: the 98th Bombardment Group (H) with B-24s, the 12th Bombardment Group (M) with B-25s, and the 57th Fighter Group with P-40Fs. Before the green American units went into combat they were given full benefit of the accumulated experience of the men of the Desert Air Force. Fortunately, too, Brereton and the Air Commander in Chief, Middle East (replacing Air Chief Marshal Sir Arthur Longmore), Air Marshal Sir Arthur Tedder, were advocates of inter-Allied co-operation. Reflecting the attitudes of the chiefs, the British and American units blended remarkably.

"The Americans work in very well with our squadrons," Tedder wrote to Chief of Air Staff Sir Charles Portal. "They now [October 21, 1942] have their own fighter wing with two squadrons, [64th and 15th] who have already shown up well in combat. Their third fighter squadron [66th] which has had more experience and which we can make reasonably mobile, is in one of our own fighter wings [No. 239] and will go forward. They are learning from us and we are learning from them. . . ."

When Montgomery was finally ready to pounce, just two days after Tedder had written to Portal— on October 23, 1942—he believed he had the manpower and that his men were trained to use their equipment. His postponement, despite Churchill's goading from time to time, had not been in vain. The Eighth Army enjoyed about a two to one superiority in manpower over Rommel; Montgomery also had more tanks, guns, and aircraft.

That Hitler finally realized that north Africa was more than a side show was revealed when he withdrew Field Marshal Albert Kesselring from the

The war in the desert was characterized by the absence of front lines, by movement and position. An Me-110 crew prepares for a reconnaissance mission over British positions in Cyrenaica. (H. J. NOWARRA)

Night-fighting Hurricanes near Suez. Equipped with 40-mm. cannon the Hurricane proved a formidable enemy of Rommel's tanks.

(IMPERIAL WAR MUSEUM, LONDON)

Russian Front to command the Mediterranean. Kesselring had commanded Luftflotte 2 during the Battle of Britain. Also drained away from Russia were the staff and remnants of Fliegerkorps II (commanded by Göring's old World War I comrade, Bruno Lörzer). By this time Fliegerkorps X had been withdrawn from Sicily and into the Balkans.

Kesselring on paper may have appeared to have an impressive array of air power at his disposal. But as Commander in Chief, South, the about 3000 planes under his command were dispersed quite tenuously throughout the vast Mediterranean and the Balkans. And the new Fliegerführer Afrika, General der Luftwaffe Hoffmann von Waldau, could count on little more than 600 of those rather widely scattered forces. On the eve of Montgomery's offensive he had about 380 fighters, of which most were Italian and only 165 Me-109Fs; he had about 150 bombers, plus 75 Italian attack planes and a few seaplanes and reconnaissance aircraft. But of these only about half were operational, thanks in part to the disruption of Axis supply routes into north Africa by Allied air and sea effort.

Opposing Waldau was Air Marshal Sir Arthur Coningham, commander of the Western Desert Air Force, with some twelve hundred planes in Egypt

and Palestine, predominantly fighters. Of these, more than eight hundred were ready to fly when Montgomery was ready to move. At the same time there was a small force of the USAAF on hand: forty B-24s, six B-17s, thirty-five B-25s, and forty-nine P-40s. Another thirty-five, a sampling of all types, were not operational at the time.

So it was that even before the battle opened the Luftwaffe and Rommel were at a numerical disadvantage. In fact, Montgomery's attack came at a time when Rommel was in Germany on sick leave. His deputy at the head of the Afrika Korps, General Georg von Stumme, died of a heart attack during the opening phase of the offensive and Rommel was rushed back to El Alamein. His appraisal and fear of the power of the RAF, which he had tried to explain to Hitler and a skeptical Göring, was revealed in the shambles of his army, the smashed panzers; El Alamein had been blasted into a graveyard of tanks. Luftwaffe airfields had been bombed and strafed so that Montgomery's troops could move forward unmolested by enemy aircraft. British and American bombers attacked shipping at Tobruk and later Benghazi and Tripoli.

Night-operating RAF Wellingtons bombed German gun positions and troop concentrations, and behind the front the Hurricanes of No. 73 Squadron swooped down upon the German and Italian troops out of the dusk to harry them and to shoot up their vehicles. Specially equipped (with a 40-mm. cannon under the wing) "tank busters," Hurricane IIDs of No. 6 Squadron and No. 7 Squadron (South African Air Force), scourged the Afrika Korps tanks.

The decisive ground fighting, under the air umbrella, was a triumph for Montgomery. Rommel fell back. "British air superiority," he stated, "threw to the winds all our operational and tactical rules. . . . The strength of the Anglo-American Air Force was, in all the battles to come, the deciding factor." But Hitler would not hear of this. "In the situation in which you now find yourself, there can be no other consideration than to hold fast, never retreat, hurl every gun and every man into the fray. . . . You can show your troops no other way than that which leads to victory or death."

With such chilling counsel from his Führer, Rommel, more battlewise, found his own solution to "the situation." He retreated. His forces began withdrawing on November 2 with Montgomery's troops in pursuit; by the fifth it was obvious that a new "desert fox" had come upon the scene. Strewn in the wake of the once invincible Afrika Korps were such expendables as burned-out tanks and other vehicles, victims of the flying tank busters and of British "Crusader" tanks. Left behind also were the Italian infantry (also regarded as expendable by the Germans) and German dead.

As Rommel recoiled toward Tunisia he received further disheartening news: Anglo-American landings had been made on November 8, 1942, in French Morocco and Algeria in northwest Africa. This was Operation Torch, led by Lieutenant General Dwight D. Eisenhower. Despite token resistance by the French the invasion forces were speedily landed and drove eastward for Tunisia.

With the advent of Torch came the introduction of New air units into the Mediterranean. "Borrowing" from the Eighth Air Force's not very considerable strength in England, the Twelfth Air Force was activated for the Torch landings and placed under command of Major General James H. Doolittle. From the Eighth Air Force (still mounting missions upon German-held France despite poor weather and small forces) Doolittle had been given two B-17 groups (the 97th and 301st Bombardment Groups); he also brought two P-38 units (1st and 14th Fighter Groups), the 33rd Fighter Group (P-40s), two groups of Spitfires with American pilots (31st and 52nd Fighter Groups), as well as the 15th Bombardment Squadron (L). The C-47s of Air Transport Command came to replenish the Allies with men, parts, and supplies.

Brereton, meanwhile, commanded the Ninth Air Force (successor to the U. S. Army Middle East Air Force), which moved in from the east with Montgomery while Doolittle's Twelfth came from the west with Eisenhower. Thus were the Afrika Korps and the hapless Luftwaffe strangled from both directions. Even so, the fight did not immedi-

Flying over the pyramids of Egypt, this Air Transport Command C-47 represents one of the aspects of the United States into the war: supply and transportation. Rommel's lack of these decided the war in Africa.
(U. S. AIR FORCE)

Mitchell medium bombers over the north African desert on the way to bomb German positions, supply routes, and harbors. (U. S. AIR FORCE)

Luftwaffe air base at El Aouina, Tunisia, under bombing attack by the Allies. German planes have been *caught on the ground, some of them as they were taking off to defend the base, and burn uselessly.*

(U. S. AIR FORCE)

ately go out of either and until the Allies held air superiority over Tunisia (March 1943) the Messerschmitts and Stukas, and the panzers, took their toll. But it was a lost cause.

As the jaws of the Allied pincers closed on Tunisia, the Anglo-American air units again underwent transmutation with the formation of the Northwest African Air Forces under Major General Carl Spaatz. The NAAF merged both British and American units for a concentrated push on Rommel. Doolittle co-ordinated the heavy bombardment in the theater and Coningham the tactical operations. Tedder remained in over-all command in the Mediterranean. It was the beginning of the end for Rommel.

The Luftwaffe in Africa suffered too. Its bases were bombed and strafed. Its supply routes, whether by sea or air, were torn to bits by Allied

bombers and fighters. One attempt to fly aid to Rommel ended in disaster when on April 18, 1943, a large formation of German transports, about a hundred Ju-52s, escorted by Italian Macchi C-202s, Me-109s, and Me-110s, was intercepted off Cape Bon by Allied fighters. These were forty-six P-40s of the Ninth Air Force's 57th Fighter Group, a dozen P-40s of the 324th Group's 314th Squadron, and twelve Spitfires of the RAF's No. 92 Squadron. The latter were providing top cover for the American P-40s.

The Junkers were skimming the Mediterranean in three perfect V-formations about a hundred feet above the sea. Their mixed escort numbered about thirty fighters. One pilot upon sighting the trimotored transports thought it to be "the most beautiful formation I've ever seen. It seemed like a shame to

the German fighters fared poorly, flying around in "a confused and inferior fashion, possibly due to the low altitude. . . ." As the Warhawks destroyed the Junkers, the Spitfires and the remaining P-40s took on the Me-109s and Macchis.

When the battle was over, all but six of the P-40s and one Spitfire returned to their home bases. The German formations, however, were heavily decimated. Claims were necessarily high (partly because of the confusion of the fighting), ranging from seventy to fifty Ju-52s (the Germans admitted to the loss of fifty-one in addition to sixteen or more fighters of the escort. The massacre was but the climax to a deliberate campaign (Operation Flax) to sever Rommel's supply line into Tunis.

A prelude to that terrible Palm Sunday had occurred only a week before when B-25s, with P-38 escort, on a shipping sweep came upon some thirty-five Axis planes in an air convoy over the Sicilian strait. Both Mitchells and Lightnings bore in for the attack and accounted for twenty-five enemy aircraft, twenty-one of them Ju-52s carrying precious supplies for Rommel in Tunisia.

Scourge of the Afrika Korps and the Luftwaffe: P-38s above the African desert. The heavy Lockheed fighter earned the name der Gabelschwanz Teufel ("Forked-tail Devil") in north Africa. It was an especially devastating tank buster. (ALLIE MOSZYK)

break it up. Reminded me of a beautiful propaganda film."

Captain James Curl, leading the low squadron of P-40s, however, was not moved by the beauty of the formations. Leaving the Spitfires, led by Squadron Leader Neville Duke, and a squadron of P-40s to handle the German fighters, Curl led three squadrons of P-40s in an attack upon the transports. With a wild whooping the Americans dived into the neat formations. The ensuing ten minutes have come to be known as "the Palm Sunday Massacre," as the Warhawks slashed the Ju-52s into flaming ribbons. The slow, clumsy Junkers crashed into the sea or smashed onto the beaches of Cape Bon. Even

Several pilots who had participated in the "Palm Sunday Massacre," members of the 66th Squadron, 57th Fighter Group. Captain James M. Curl, who had led the low squadron in the attack upon the German transports, squats in center with a cigarette and drink in hand. (U. S. AIR FORCE)

Wrecking Rommel's supply line: B-25s, with P-38 escort, come upon Ju-52s in the Sicilian Straits on the way to Tunisia with supplies. In minutes twenty-five of the thirty-five German transports were destroyed. (U. S. AIR FORCE)

By sea and by air the beleaguered Germans in north Africa were denied supplies by air power. A munitions ship blows up in the Mediterranean off Bizerte after being hit by Allied bombers (left). A giant Messerschmitt 323, a six-engined transport with a wing span of 180 feet used for carrying supplies and troops, recoils under an air attack on an ill-fated run for Tunisia. (U. S. AIR FORCE)

Trapped in the massive pinch, his supplies cut off, his troops exhausted, Rommel was incapable of continuing the fight. It was on May 13, 1943, that Colonel General Dietloff Jurgen von Arnim surrendered the surviving Axis forces in Tunisia; it was an inglorious end for the once proud Afrika Korps. About 240,000 troops (of which 125,000 were German) had chosen not to fight to the death according to the Führer's wishes. Rommel, three days before the surrender, had escaped by air to Germany. At the time it was all that the Luftwaffe could do for him.

The Luftwaffe lost much in Africa, not the least of which was one of its brighter stars. He was twenty-two-year-old (in 1942) Hans-Joachim Marseille of Jagdgeschwader 27. His sunny disposition and prankish nature endeared Marseille to his squadron mates, if not always to his commanders. His skill as a pilot (first demonstrated during the Battle of Britain) and amazing marksmanship eventually earned Marseille the rank of *Oberleutnant* (first lieutenant). His Me-109, painted in desert colors with a large yellow 14 on its sides, was known throughout north Africa. If German records can be trusted Marseille destroyed no less than 158 Allied aircraft before he died.

Unlike most fighter pilots he had been a master of the deflection shot. Approaching from the side (most pilots preferred the classic tail attack), Marseille by a feat of mental computation was able to gauge the speed of the enemy plane relative to his own and knew the moment when he must fire his guns. The laws of physics did the rest.

Not even Marseille's youth, however, shielded him from the ravages of daily battle at high altitudes. When his score had reached 101 (he had exceeded the magical 100), Marseille landed and when his ground crew rushed to his plane to assist him out, he waved them away. His drawn face was a pasty white, and when he finally pulled himself from the cockpit, his hands shook and he moved like an old man. Marseille was finished for the time being as a fighter pilot.

After an enforced two-month leave Marseille returned to command his old 3 Staffel of JG 27 as a *Hauptmann* (captain) late in August 1942. It was about this time that Montgomery was preparing the Eighth for his push on Rommel. By September 1, obviously back in fighting trim, Marseille in the course of three sorties had shot down seventeen planes, most of them P-40s. There were plenty of enemy aircraft, for while Montgomery waited to strike at El Alamein, the RAF came over from Egypt.

On September 30 Marseille led his squadron to escort Stukas on a raid. Although no enemy planes were encountered, he ran into trouble. Smoke suddenly was seen belching from his cockpit and his engine burst into flame. Unable to see, Marseille nevertheless stayed with his plane, hoping, no doubt, that before he bailed out he could get as close to base as possible. He counted also on the plane not blowing up in mid-air.

With his wingman Rainer Pöttgen flying alongside radioing instructions, Marseille attempted to direct the 109 toward El Alamein. Before they reached the airfield, Marseille realized he would never make it and would have to get out of the stricken plane. He flipped it over on its back, released the canopy, then dropped out. As he left the cockpit, and as the plane dipped downward and fell away, the tail surfaces struck Marseille in the chest. His parachute never opened as the young ace fell onto the desert below.

II

Hitler left Mussolini to flounder around in the Mediterranean for six months before he ordered the Wehrmacht and the Luftwaffe (specifically Lohr's Luftflotte 4 based in friendly Antonescu's Rumania) to strike. On April 6, 1941, with Rommel again on the offensive in north Africa, German troops invaded Yugoslavia and Greece. The curtain rose on a typical scene: Luftwaffe bombers destroyed the center of Belgrade, killing seventeen thousand people. This was in punishment for otherwise co-operative Yugoslavia's refusal to permit German supplies and troops bound for Turkey use of its railroads. Within two weeks Yugoslavia capitulated to the blitzkrieg.

A week later, on April 23, the Greek government surrendered also. The survivors of the small British force that had been attracted to Greece as Hitler had feared by Mussolini's invasion was withdrawn. The decision was made, however, to establish an

*Hans-Joachim Marseille, the "Star of Africa," whose
final victory score before his death totaled 158.*

(H. J. NOWARRA)

army on the island of Crete, southeast of Greece
and almost directly north of the north African bat-
tlegrounds. Crete was a strategic island, indeed, and
Churchill himself argued for its defense. Under
Major General Bernard Freyberg a force of about
forty-two thousand—British, Australian, New Zealand, and Greek troops—was established on Crete.

Hitler coveted the little island also and wished to
make it "the crowning glory" of the Balkan campaign. He had said, in fact, when writing to Mussolini chiding him "with the warm heart of a friend"
about the Grecian blunder, that he himself would
not have taken that action "without a previous,
lightning occupation of Crete, and to this end I
wanted to bring you practical proposals—namely, to
employ a German paratroop division, and an air-
borne division."

Having been denied the opportunity by his friend's
precipitate invasion the previous October, Hitler ordered the aerial invasion of Crete in May. Curiously,
Lohr himself had suggested such an investment of
Crete once the Balkans were overrun. Göring, then
based in Austria, rather liked the idea, for since the
Battle of Britain, he was eager for a spectacular job
for the Luftwaffe. Hitler, of course, approved, but

German paratroops taking a British gun position, Crete, May 1941. (H. J. NOWARRA)

A stricken Ju-52, having dropped its cargo of German paratroopers into the inferno that is Heraklion aerodrome, falls burning to earth. This is the second wave of the assault on Crete, Hitler's "crowning glory" of the Balkan campaign, Operation Mercury. For the hapless German air-borne troops, Mercury was a winged messenger of death. After Crete—although it was taken by the Germans at great cost—German paratroops would never be capable of participating in any major future operations. Casualties were so high that these units were crippled for the rest of the war.

(IMPERIAL WAR MUSEUM, LONDON)

Ceremonies celebrating the taking of Crete; survivors of the German 1st Parachute Regiment stand at attention to receive honors. The cost of taking Crete from the air all but ended German full-scale paratroop activity for the rest of the war. (H. J. NOWARRA)

not before remarking that *he* had thought of the idea several months before. He visualized Crete as a rampart to the Balkans as well as a base for aerial operations against Britain's African strongholds: Alexandria, Cairo, Suez, among other points in the eastern Mediterranean. Certain other voices, among them Keitel's, were raised suggesting that an air-borne invasion of the British colony of Malta, an island to the west in the central Mediterranean, might be more useful. But Hitler had his heart set on the "crowning glory."

It was code-named Operation Mercury and fell to

Kurt Student's newly formed Fliegerkorps XI, consisting of paratroops and air-borne troops. The first large-scale invasion of the war opened in the morning of May 20, 1941, when after an initial bombardment of the drop areas, nearly five hundred Ju-52s appeared over Crete dropping parachutists and pulling gliders. The plan also called for seaborne convoys with reinforcements from the north, but which, as it eventuated, were driven off by the British Mediterranean Fleet. This was accomplished at great cost, however. The Mediterranean Fleet, operating to the north of Crete, was beyond the range of the RAF and within reach of Luftwaffe bombers and fighters of Richthofen's Fliegerkorps VIII based on the Greek mainland.

Thus did the entire investment of Crete devolve upon the air-borne troops. As with nearly all best-laid plans, a number of things went wrong with Mercury. Dust-laden airfields in Greece disrupted the takeoff of the Ju-52s; the first planes to leave stirred up clouds of dust that prevented subsequent takeoffs until the dust settled (a delay as long as twenty minutes). Another delay was caused by a shortage of fuel, during which the British, prewarned by Intelligence, prepared for the invasion on Crete. Although the 28,000 troops on the island outnumbered the 15,000 air-borne troops committed to Mercury, the island garrison was exhausted after the Greek campaign itself and ill equipped. They could count upon only a dozen aircraft, Hurricanes and Gladiators mainly, while Richthofen commanded 650 aircraft, bombers and fighters, not counting transports and gliders.

The outcome was inevitable when the Ju-52s appeared over Maleme airfield, the major objective on Crete (this field lay at the western end of the island; other objectives, attacked by the second waves, were the airfields at Rethymnon and Heraklion, like Maleme on the north coast of Crete, but located near the center of the island).

After the initial bombardment by the bombers and strafing attacks by fighters, the Ju-52s released their gliders, which swooped down onto Maleme. Not all made good landings as they bounced into the unusually hilly terrain, splintering and tossing out their occupants. Some crashed into hillsides, injuring the troops they carried and killing some. Only the stunning effects of the preinvasion aerial attacks prevented the defenders from finishing the job of wiping out the glider troops. The Germans who had

landed safely began moving in on Maleme airfield.

The glider troops were followed by the parachutists, who jumped from low altitude to join in the fighting on the ground. The defenders fought back savagely and it appeared that taking Crete would be no simple matter. The decision was made to throw in more men. As the Junkers disgorged their cargoes, the island's defenders shot them to bits; one German battalion lost four hundred of its six hundred men. Casualties were inflicted either while the men dangled helplessly from their parachutes or when they were injured while landing in the unfamiliar rocky terrain. Some died as they vainly tried to extricate themselves from trees into which they had drifted; the rest fell in fighting with New Zealand troops.

And still they came on. A third wave of Ju-52s arrived in the afternoon of the second day, May 21, bringing the entire 100th Mountain Regiment. Maleme was by then precariously held by the Germans, but as the transports came in to land British artillery fire began to fall among them. Antiaircraft shot the Junkers out of the sky and the artillery shattered them on the ground—and with them more German troops died.

The runway became a shambles of wrecked and burning aircraft; one divisional commander of the 100th Mountain Regiment said that "Maleme was like the gate of hell." A captured British tank was used to clear the wrecks off the runway to make way for those Junkers which had escaped the guns or were only damaged. By the end of the day there were no less than eighty wrecked Junkers along the edges of the runway.

To the weary defenders it appeared that Germany had an unlimited supply of manpower at Hitler's disposal, for despite the frightful slaughter, troops continued to pour in from the sky. Hitler's profligacy turned the tide; with Maleme taken, even more troops could be flown in. Exhausted, without air protection and supplies, it was obvious that the Crete garrison could not hold out. By May 24 General Freyberg realized the situation was hopeless. Three days later the ships of the Mediterranean Fleet appeared off the southern coast at Sphakia to evacuate the remaining defenders (more than fourteen thousand men, about half of the original number on Crete when the battle began) to Alexandria in Egypt.

Hitler had his "crowning glory." Crete had fallen

in ten days, but at what cost? More than 200 aircraft had been lost (119 of them Ju-52s), not counting the expendable gliders. More than 5000 German troops had died, of which 3600 were highly trained paratroopers. Crete had, in fact, eliminated the German parachute force from the rest of war. It had been a costly victory and an ironic one, especially after the center of the war in the Mediterranean shifted westward with the victories of Montgomery and the Torch landings of Eisenhower in north Africa the next year. Crete's strategic location was not what it once was; much more important was the island of Malta, still held by the British.

After the fall of Crete Hitler crowed, "There are no more unconquerable islands," conveniently and characteristically ignoring that island which lay across the English Channel. He had already become absorbed in his own massive blunder, Barbarossa, the invasion of Russia, which, thanks to Mussolini, had to be postponed while Hitler cleaned up in Greece and generally stabilized the Balkans. What was the Mediterranean to him when he planned to outgeneral Napoleon in a holy crusade against Communist Russia?

III

Even as he denied the existence of "unconquerable islands," Hitler overlooked another: Malta, just to the south of Sicily in the central Mediterranean.

If Hitler chose to disregard Malta, astride the supply routes into north Africa, there were those more

A Beaufighter such as was stationed on beleaguered Malta (an island Hitler chose to ignore) and had an important effect on the outcome of the war in the Mediterranean. (IMPERIAL WAR MUSEUM, LONDON)

directly concerned who did not. Almost as soon as Italy declared war on Britain the Regia Aeronautica began its bombing runs from Sicily, less than sixty miles away, in June of 1940. By the end of the month the redoubtable *Faith, Hope,* and *Charity* were joined by a few Hurricanes, eventually more (some flown off British carriers), and Fleet Air Arm Swordfish, a Hudson, a Skua, as well as a handful of Wellingtons. It was possible then to peck away at Italian targets as the Italians rather half-heartedly bombed Malta.

It was when Hitler was convinced of Africa's importance—militarily nil, he believed, but if lost would have a "strong psychological effect on Italy" —that the strategic role of Malta was recognized. With the coming of the new year and the establishment of Fliegerkorps X in Sicily Malta was fated to suffer the harsher attentions of the Luftwaffe. The island's fortunes were to fluctuate with those of the newly arrived Rommel. By March the residents and troops on Malta could expect nearly daily visits from Luftwaffe bombers. The arrival of new Hurricane IIs in April turned the balance toward the defenders, whose Mark I Hurricanes had been no match for the Me-109Fs. The next month further relief came with the gradual withdrawal of Fliegerkorps X into the Balkans. In the comparative lull additional reinforcements arrived: a few Martin "Marylands" to be used as reconnaissance planes, some Blenheims to replace the Wellingtons, and a squadron of Beaufighters. Malta had not become suddenly a great impregnable armed camp, but it was a formidable hornet's nest of the Mediterranean. And besides the tiny air force, Malta harbored cruisers, destroyers, and submarines.

By November 1941 the effect of Malta was felt even in Berlin, and directly in Russia. Maltese-based ships, submarines, and bombers had ripped at Italian convoys bringing troops, supplies, and fuel to Rommel. Fuel especially was a precious commodity in the mobile desert war. Because of this deficiency Rommel's offensive into Egypt petered out and while he was forced to wait, the British prepared to push him back into Libya whence he had come. Even the exhaustion of his troops would not have deterred Rommel from trying to reach Cairo at the time, flushed with victory as he was. But Malta had.

Hitler turned briefly from his map of Russia and realized what was occurring elsewhere. It was then,

Street scene, Malta 1942. The city of Valetta under Nazi aerial siege. Hitler did not regard tiny Malta with the same strategic romantic respect as he did Crete, consequently Malta was never invaded by the Nazis. It eventually became a most strategic island as the war in the Mediterranean unfolded: it would cost him Africa, Sicily and finally Italy.

(IMPERIAL WAR MUSEUM, LONDON)

late in 1941, that he sent Kesselring and Lörzer to the Mediterranean. As Commander in Chief, South, Kesselring was ordered by Hitler primarily to "obtain air and sea supremacy in the area between southern Italy and north Africa in order to establish safe shipping routes to Libya"; to accomplish this it would be "particularly important to suppress Malta." He was also to co-operate with German and Italian forces in north Africa and put a stop to enemy shipping in the Mediterranean.

Beginning in December 1941 Malta became the chief target of the Luftwaffe in the Mediterranean. The attacks intensified through the first of the year and reached a crescendo in April 1942, when the Luftwaffe bombed the little island as often as two

hundred (and on two occasions more than three hundred) times a day. By April 12 Kesselring informed Hitler that Malta's air and naval bases had been eliminated.

It was a premature appraisal, but even Tedder when he visited Malta a few days later was not heartened by what he saw. Only six serviceable Hurricanes remained and the airfields were pocked and torn; the docks were blown into the sea and the city of Valetta was filled with rubble. With invasion all but imminent the defenders and civilians alike faced starvation. With the Luftwaffe persistently overhead no convoys had been able to break through since February. On April 20 the American carrier *Wasp,* however, arrived to deliver forty-

Pantelleria, Italian island fortress between Tunis, north Africa, and Sicily, is taken out of the war by air power in Operation Corkscrew. (U. S. AIR FORCE)

seven Spitfires. By the next day, after a night and day of bombing, only seventeen remained serviceable. The Spitfire, unlike the Hurricane, was superior to the Me-109F. When they arrived in sufficient numbers, it was hoped, the Luftwaffe's attacks would dwindle. On May 9 the *Wasp* in company with the British carrier *Eagle* dispatched sixty-four Spitfires (of which two were lost at sea en route) and within five minutes of arrival they were ready for action. The Spitfires did not solve Malta's problem, but a subtle change was imminent. "One lives here only to destroy the Hun and hold him at bay," one of the Spitfire pilots observed after a few days on Malta, "everything else, living conditions, sleep, food and all the ordinary standards of life have gone by the board. It all makes the Battle of Britain and fighter-sweeps seem child's play in comparison. . . ."

Air Vice-Marshal Sir Hugh P. Lloyd, RAF commander on Malta, later wrote of that May 1942 that "Our diet was a slice and a half of very poor bread with jam for breakfast, bully beef for lunch with one slice of bread, and except for an additional slice of bread it was the same fare for dinner. . . . Officers and men slept in shelters, in caverns and dugouts, in quarries. . . ." The supply of ammunition and bombs was depleting. "Malta was faced," Lloyd concluded, "with the unpleasant fact of being starved and forced from lack of equipment into surrender. The middle of August was starvation date, and as we should all have been dead before relief arrived, the surrender date was much earlier. . . ."

On June 16, after a fierce air-sea battle, the first

Pantelleria after Corkscrew. Italian and German aircraft destroyed in the bombardment of the island lie scattered in burned-out wreckage, never having got off the ground. (U. S. AIR FORCE)

two merchantmen docked in Malta under a protective cover of Spitfires. Despite the heavy losses, the proof was there that Malta would survive.

Developments in the camp of the enemy also assured the survival of the tiny island. Late in May Rommel, thanks to Kesselring's suppression of Malta, was on his way toward Cairo again. Plans for an invasion of Malta were postponed and units of the Luftwaffe were drawn away from Kesselring in expectation of the summer offensive in Russia.

The Italians, even Mussolini, continued to fret about Malta, but Hitler had lost interest again. He could point to the Afrika Korps and its victories, including the taking of Tobruk, which had held out for so long, and then the pressing on for Egypt. Even Rommel, who once offered to lead an assault upon Malta, was willing to dismiss the island from his mind. Egypt became the prize, but he was stopped at El Alamein, where he would meet with Mont-

gomery, who planned to "knock Rommel for a six" and "tidy up the battlefield."

When that occurred a recovered Malta contributed to the defeat of the Afrika Korps in Tunisia in May 1943. Malta remained Britain's unsinkable aircraft carrier in the Mediterranean.

With north Africa in Allied hands, British and American strategists felt they could turn to Europe for the next assault. Although Stalin clamored for a Second Front, the Anglo-American leaders could not visualize a direct assault upon the coast of France at the time. Churchill believed that the Russians would benefit from, and that the Allies could undertake, a strike at what he called, in one of his less felicitous phrases, "the soft underbelly of Europe": Mussolini's Italy.

Unlike Hitler, the Allies chose not to overlook the islands of the central Mediterranean. To get at the underbelly two islands would have to be taken:

The port of Messina, Sicily, a German stronghold, was heavily bombed by Northwest Africa Air Forces and the Ninth Air Force. Large-scale bombings were car- *ried out before landings were attempted by ground troops. Sicily was the step before Italy itself; Messina was the heaviest hit of Sicilian targets.*

(U. S. AIR FORCE)

Pantelleria and Sicily. Tiny Pantelleria, about half-way between Tunisia and Sicily, the Italians referred to as their Gibraltar. While this was a rather grand conception of the island, it did lay in the path of any invader bound for Sicily. The very nature of Pantelleria—hilly, eroded, few beaches, a soil with a heavy volcanic ash content—made it a poor objective for amphibious troops. Its single airfield could put up aircraft that would spot any

invasion forces far out at sea. Besides being heavily fortified, Pantelleria was garrisoned by ten thousand troops. While the Allies attempted to "neutralize" them, German and Italian forces in Italy could have time to prepare for their coming on the mainland.

After weighing the possibilities it was decided to bomb Pantelleria into submission from the air: Operation Corkscrew, beginning May 18, 1943.

Some fifty medium bombers and the same number of fighter-bombers opened the campaign by striking at the main harbor area and the airfield. By June 11, the date set for the invasion, British and American aircraft had dropped six thousand tons of bombs on Pantelleria. German and Italian fighters attempted to interfere with the assault, but with little success because of escorting Allied fighters.

In the evening before D-Day Mussolini had been informed by Vice-Admiral Gino Pavesi that "the Allied bombing could be endured no longer"; the Italian dictator himself authorized the surrender of Pantelleria.

When the assault troops began landing on the island the next morning a white flag appeared on a hill. The invasion proceeded with minimal resistance —the single Allied casualty being an infantryman who was bitten by a jackass.

For the first time in the history of warfare a sizable military objective had been taken by air power alone. True, it was a small objective (about forty-two square miles), but the significance of the fact was great and parlous.

In July Sicily, the next island steppingstone into Italy, became the setting for the first sizable Allied air-borne operation. The Luftwaffe, already bombed out of Sicily by Allied bombers based in Africa and Malta, did not interfere with this phase of the air and sea invasion. But everything else did: high wind, flak, smoke from preinvasion bombing, trigger-happy seamen, and fate. As the Germans learned at Crete, much could go wrong. In the night of July 9, 1943, gliders towed from Africa by C-47s were released over Sicily. In the near fiasco, because of an unfortunate high wind, only twelve gliders actually came to earth in the designated landing zone; about sixty-five swept into the sea and hundreds of the heavily laden troops of the 1st Airborne Division drowned. The remaining fifty-six gliders scattered widely over Sicily. Fortunately the defenders were more confused than the dispersed air-borne troops, mistaking the dispersal for a truly full-scale invasion. The Italian defenders, disheartened, could not bring themselves to fight with any resolution.

The glider drop, as at Crete, was followed by paratroopers. These, the American 82nd Airborne Division, were also scattered all over the place. Even as this ensued, a great convoy of ships carry-

Sicily, August 1943. General Dwight D. Eisenhower and Air Force General Henry H. Arnold at Castelvetrano airfield after the fall of Sicily.

(U. S. AIR FORCE)

ing the British Seventh Army and the American Eighth Army (under command of two new military stars, Bernard Montgomery and Major General George Patton) sailed forth from widespread ports, but mainly from north Africa, under an umbrella of Pantelleria-based P-40s of the 33rd Fighter Group and Malta Spitfires. The convoy reached Sicily untouched by Axis aircraft.

Co-operative efforts between the Luftwaffe and the Regia Aeronautica had deteriorated to nearly zero, so that no truly concerted attempt was made to interfere with the amphibious assault. The seaborne invasion proceeded more smoothly than had the one from the air, and within twenty-four hours all beachheads had been secured. In Berlin Goeb-

Albert Kesselring (here a prisoner of war), former commander of Luftflotte 1 (Poland), Luftflotte 2 (Battle of Britain and Russia), and commander in chief of all German forces in Italy. (U. S. ARMY)

mans fought tenaciously and brutally—Italian deserters were shot without mercy. But they were overwhelmed by sheer numbers and equipment and pushed into the northeast corner of Sicily around Messina. It was a battle, however ferociously fought, that could have but one outcome: the Germans were squeezed out of Sicily, which fell on August 17. It had not been a total victory, for the Germans had succeeded in evacuating much heavy equipment and troops. Even Hitler was disappointed, hoping as he did to make of Sicily "another Stalingrad."

It had not been that for the Germans, but for Mussolini it had been a Waterloo. He was deposed on July 25, even before Sicily officially fell, when

Italy was "boned with the Apennines," which made fighting different on the ground as well as in the air. Twelfth Air Force Thunderbolts equipped with extra fuel tanks and bombs lift over the mountains to lend a hand to the American Fifth Army.

(ARTHUR F. SCHRAMM/U. S. AIR FORCE)

bels cursed the day Germany had ever become allied with "the macaroni eaters."

By D plus (July 13, 1943) Spitfires from Malta were flown in to begin co-operative air-ground work with advancing Allied troops. Within a week American fighters of the 31st and 33rd Fighter Groups arrived to lend a hand. By the last week of July the hard-pressed Germans had begun to evacuate the island, although by no means without a fight. The tough 1st Parachute Division had been flown in from southern France via Rome to combine with the equally tough "Hermann Göring Division" to give battle where the Italians had all but capitulated. German supplies were flown into Italy and then transported across the narrow Strait of Messina, where Sicily and the Italian toe nearly touched. A heavy flak concentration made bombardment at this point costly to the Allies.

Taking advantage of the rough terrain, the Ger-

Outstanding fighter-interceptor of the Regia Aeronautica was the Macchi-Castoldi 202 Folgore ("Lightning"). Developed from earlier radial engine designs, the Macchi C. 202 was the result of the combination of an Italian airframe, the work primarily of Macchi's chief designer Mario Castoldi, and a German in-line engine, the Daimler-Benz. The clean design resulted in a formidable aircraft, with a top speed of more than three hundred mph, plenty of armament, and, in the hands of a trained pilot, a dangerous adversary. Fortunately for the Allies, the number of Folgores produced was small because of supply problems. A small plane (the wingspan was just under thirty-five feet and length of fuselage a fraction over twenty-nine feet), the Macchi C. 202 might have even proved a match for the Mustang. (AERONAUTICA MACCHI)

King Victor Emmanuel told him, "You are the most hated man in Italy."

IV

Only five days after the first Allied troops (the British Eighth Army) landed on the Italian mainland at Reggio di Calabria, just across the Strait of Messina, Italy surrendered unconditionally, on September 8, 1943. But this surrender by the post-Mussolini regime under Marshal Pietro Badoglio, once celebrated conquerer of Ethiopia, did not end the war in Italy. It had been Mussolini himself who had once said, "If the Germans ever get here they will never go home." Badoglio had hoped to slip out of the war as gracefully as possible and merge with the winning side.

That was not quite how the Germans planned it, however, for Italy became a bitter battleground for the remainder of the war. Kesselring was to command the battle in Italy, with or without Italian co-operation. The "soft underbelly" had turned to stone; it proved, in the words of Samuel Eliot Morison, "to be boned with the Apennines, plated with the hard scales of Kesselring's armor, and shadowed by the wings of the Luftwaffe."

The day following Italy's surrender the U. S. Fifth Army landed on the beaches near Salerno, thirty miles south of Naples, on the west coast of Italy. To the east, at Taranto, the British 1st Airborne Division secured the finest port in southern Italy. Before the landings aircraft of the Northwest African Air Force, a remarkable amalgam of British and American units, cleared the air of the Luftwaffe or grounded it by bombing its bases. Offshore American-British naval gunfire contributed to the landings. When the troops went ashore at Salerno they were covered by Mustangs, Lightnings, Spitfires, and even Seafires of Fleet Air Arm. The wings of the Luftwaffe appeared to have been clipped.

However, on the same day that the British took over Taranto and began moving northward toward Foggia and its complex of airfields, the Italian fleet began putting to sea. According to the surrender terms they were to proceed to Malta. One group of Italian ships was attacked by Ju-88s with bombs and radio-controlled glider bombs. The flagship *Roma* was hit by a glider bomb, caught fire, and in minutes exploded and sank.

Allied ground forces meanwhile moved inexorably up the foot and ankle of Italy. If the Northwest African Air Force fighters and bombers helped to clear the way, there was still a good deal of stiff fighting on the ground. Fighters assisted in air-ground co-operation in missions ranging from strafing to directing artillery fire. The heavy bombers—B-17s and B-24s—of the Twelfth Air Force struck at airfields and rail yards, and the mediums—B-25s and B-26s of the Tactical Air Force—bombed lines of communication and enemy troop concentrations. Co-ordination between ground and air forces was accomplished through the so-called "Rover Joe" system, Rover Joes being controllers who traveled with advancing troops and who, as airmen on the ground, could understand the problem of the infantrymen and could also, by radio, communicate with the men in the air.

By October 1 the Fifth Army had fought its way into Naples from the Salerno beachhead and the Eighth Army, moving up from the south, had com-

bined with the 1st Airborne Division which had occupied Foggia. The Allies by mid-October were solidly established in Italy with a front line running across the peninsula from Naples on the west and Foggia on the east. On October 13, 1943, Italy declared war upon Germany, and if the Army had lost its taste for battle and proved no match for the Wehrmacht, Italian partisans would strike at the Germans with decisive fury.

The road to Rome, low and high, was no easy road. The comparative ease with which the Allies had established the line Naples-Foggia across Italy was no intimation of things to come. If the Luftwaffe in Italy was forced to fight, in the phrase of Kesselring, "a poor man's war" because of the increasing Allied bomber offensive upon the fatherland and the turn of events in Russia, the German ground troops fought ferociously. The war in Italy became predominantly a footslogger's war, the fortunes of which frequently pivoted upon terrain and weather; the landscape was especially advantageous to defense. The venerable travel cliché "Sunny Italy" became a grim joke with the coming of winter. The war in Italy developed into a miserable GI war, but it was air power—Allied air supremacy—that tipped the scales.

The first winter halted the Allied advance at Kesselring's Gustav Line, cutting across Italy at the Volturno and Sangro rivers. It was a night-

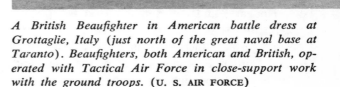

A British Beaufighter in American battle dress at Grottaglie, Italy (just north of the great naval base at Taranto). Beaufighters, both American and British, operated with Tactical Air Force in close-support work with the ground troops. (U. S. AIR FORCE)

Sunny Italy? Fifteenth Air Force Liberators at Foggia contend with the elements of an Italian winter: snow and rain, both of which brought an even more invidious *enemy, mud. Curtailment of air operations multiplied the miseries of the ground fighting.* (U. S. AIR FORCE)

mare of rock, mud, and cold. The race for Rome, for the time being, was stopped. Aerial operations too were crippled by one of the worst winters Italy had suffered in decades. For the Luftwaffe it was, in effect, a time of respite; not comfortable, but an opportunity to recuperate from Allied attacks. The once indomitable, numerous Luftflotte 2 (commanded by Richthofen) had dwindled to a remnant of around 350 aircraft.

Opposing the Luftwaffe was the newly constituted Mediterranean Allied Air Forces, which merged and shifted around the units that had comprised the Northwest African Air Forces and Mediterranean Air Command. General Eisenhower was ordered to England to prepare for the projected Allied landings in France; accompanying him were Tedder, Spaatz, and, eventually, Doolittle. The latter on January 6, 1944, assumed command of the Eighth Air Force. Lieutenant General Ira C. Eaker came from the Eighth Air Force to head the Mediterranean Allied Air Forces. The heavy units of Doolittle's previous command, the Twelfth Air Force, were used to form the nucleus of another strategic striking force, the Fifteenth Air Force, which would be capable of lashing at not only Germany itself, but also the Balkans, occupied Czechoslovakia, Poland, Hungary, and the Rumanian oil fields. Until he left for England, Doolittle commanded the Fifteenth, which then was taken over by Major General Nathan F. Twining, late of the Thirteenth Air Force and the fighting in the Solomons. The

Fifteenth Air Force was based in the airfields of Foggia and was, technically, formed to participate in the strategic bombardment of Germany and its satellites and not in the tactical fighting in Italy.

The Twelfth Air Force medium bombers and fighters remained in the Mediterranean. Brereton's Ninth Air Force, after returning some of its "borrowed" heavy groups to the Eighth Air Force, had its tactical units reassigned to the Twelfth and joined the Eighth in England. There it would be reorganized as a tactical air force for participation in the invasion of the Continent.

Thus was a great ring of steel being drawn around *Festung Europa.*

But while all these changes ensued, the Germans continued to hold the Allies in Italy on the Gustav Line with aid from snow-choked mountains, bitter cold, and muddy lowlands. The latter inspired the observation, credited to Private Elmer Ponks of Gladwin, Michigan, that "The trouble with this mud is that it's too thick to drink and to thin to plow."

The Allies' failure to pierce the Gustav Line gave birth to the idea of going around the right flank by sea and making an assault at Anzio and Nettuno behind the German lines on the west coast. While the expected surprise assault by the U. S. VI Corps was carried off on January 22, 1944, the effect was forfeited, as ten days were spent "consolidating the beachhead" before pushing inland. By then Kesselring had moved in tough panzer units, zeroed in the beachhead with artillery, and trapped the invaders in a small pocket for no less than four months. In Berlin the papers predicted "another Dunkirk." They were nearly right.

Meanwhile, attempts to breach the Gustav Line itself were unsuccessful; the road to Rome was blocked by strong German positions at the town of Cassino and in the heavily fortified mountains rising behind it. The inland road to Rome was dominated by the Benedictine monastery atop one of the peaks. The monastery, built by St. Benedict in the sixth century, was unquestionably one of the shrines of Catholicism, but it was also, as far as the Allied commanders who faced it believed, a German observation post, which surveyed the bogged-down misery of their troops for miles.

Shortly before he left for England, Eisenhower had issued a directive in which he had stated, "If we have to choose between destroying a famous building and killing our men, then our men's lives count infinitely more and the building must go. But the choice is not always so clear-cut as that. In many cases the monuments can be spared without any detriment to operational needs. Nothing can stand against the argument of military necessity. That is an accepted principle. But the phrase 'military necessity' is sometimes used where it would be truthful to speak of military convenience or even of personal convenience. I do not want it to cloak slackness or indifference."

There were divided views in the Allied camp. Eisenhower's successor, General Sir Henry H. Wilson, and his British commanders believed that the Germans were using the abbey as an observation post. American commanders disagreed, among them Fifth Army commander General Mark Clark, General Eaker, and his British deputy, Air Marshal Sir John Slessor. Wilson, however, heeded the demands of his commanders on the ground before the abbey. To assure himself, Eaker flew over the position in a Piper "Cub" and was certain he saw a radio antenna on the abbey itself and troops moving in and out. There were also, below and around the abbey, gun positions from which snipers harassed the Allied troops, artillery observation posts, gun emplacements, and ammunition dumps. Wilson, unaware of Kesselring's strict orders that the abbey was not to be entered by Germans (the German troops seen by Eaker may have been the guards posted at the gates), ordered the bombing of Monte Cassino. (According to Abbot Gregorio Diamare, the monastery was not occupied by German troops.) When leaflets were dropped upon the abbey warning of an impending heavy aerial and artillery assault, the German commander of the paratroopers in the vicinity of the abbey asserted that it was merely a ruse.

At eight-thirty in the morning of February 15, 1944, B-17s, Mitchells, and Marauders dropped five hundred tons of bombs on the historic shrine, reducing it to a pile of rubble. Although the tomb of St. Benedict escaped damage, the church and courtyard were destroyed and hundreds of Italian women and children who had taken refuge in the monastery died.

But the plan had failed. As soon as the bombing stopped, the Germans, who had promised to stay out of the abbey unless the Allies bombed it, moved into the ruins to set up gun emplacements. The position was now more impregnable than before. The Allies, therefore, continued to be stalemated on the Gustav Line and entrapped on the beach at Anzio.

A new plan called for a "mass air operation"

Mitchells of the Twelfth Air Force pass a boiling Mount Vesuvius as they fly for Cassino to bomb a block in the road to Rome. (U. S. AIR FORCE)

The Abbey of Monte Cassino following the Allied bomb-
ings. The possible view—if Germans actually occupied
the abbey—may be noted in the background vista.
(U. S. AIR FORCE)

upon the town of Cassino itself, which, theoretically, would blast a hole in the line through which the Allied troops would pour. Weather interfered until March 15, when, beginning with a B-25 assault at eight-thirty, more than a thousand tons of bombs were dropped by 275 B-17s and B-24s of the Fifteenth Air Force and 200 medium bombers (B-25s and B-26s) of the Twelfth. Like the abbey a month before, the town of Cassino was demolished. But as they had been warned by Eaker, who had not agreed with the plan, the troops entering the town were held up by rubble, craters, debris, and, after the shock had worn off, by the Germans who had sought refuge in shelters and tunnels under the town. That was not all; some of the bombs from the heavies had fallen among Allied troops.

While the use of air power had accomplished at Cassino what was expected of it—it had, indeed, destroyed the abbey and the town—it had not enabled the ground troops to take Cassino. The ground forces, hindered by the rubble, had not been able to move in quickly enough, nor with sufficient number. It had been an error to employ aircraft as artillery.

While the battle at Anzio and Cassino continued, the medium bombers and fighter bombers initiated Operation Strangle, whose objective was "to reduce the enemy's flow of supplies to a level which will make it impracticable for him to maintain and operate his forces in Central Italy." Marshaling yards, railroads, bridges, roads—all systems of communication became the prime targets. When the Allied spring offensive along the Gustav Line opened on May 11, 1944, German troops, short of supplies,

were forced back. Cassino fell on May 19 to Polish troops; French troops broke through the Gustav Line on the Garigliano River and the German retreat was on. On May 23 the Fifth Army broke out of the Anzio beachhead with the aid of heavy air support and took the city on the twenty-fifth. The

Tactical Air Force Mitchells executing Operation Strangle at Terni, north of Rome, cutting the rail *lines over which German troops in Rome might obtain supplies.* (U. S. AIR FORCE)

The cost of Strangle: A Marauder is struck by an .88 flak shell during a mission over Italy.

(U. S. AIR FORCE)

with the statement: "I, Mussolini, resume supreme direction of Fascism in Italy." This was not, as before, true. Supreme command of what remained of Fascist Italy north of Rome belonged to Kesselring.

The Germans were kept on the run by Allied ground troops supported by sorties by the Mediterranean Allied Air Forces. Bombers, fighter-bombers, and fighters harassed the retreating Germans, shattered columns of vehicles, and destroyed bridges in the path of retreat. The Luftwaffe in Italy, now commanded by General E. R. von Pohl, barely showed itself to contend these strikes. By early August the Allies had pushed up to Florence, after which several of their divisions and most of their air support were diverted to the invasion of southern France. This left only the veteran Desert Air Force for close support in Italy. In September the tactical units that had operated in France returned to Italy; but by this time Kesselring had dug in again on the Gothic Line, which ran from the Adriatic, just to the north of Ancona, to the Tyrrhenian at Leghorn, in time for another Italian winter. Although

entire Allied battlefront surged ahead. Kesselring hoped to establish new defensive lines in the path of the Allies but found his forces short of fuel and ammunition following the Strangle operations, and the retreat became a near rout. In the evening of June 4, 1944, troops of the Fifth Army were welcomed with flowers, shouting, tears, kisses, and wine in Rome.

Two days later Eisenhower's forces landed on the beaches of Normandy and for most, except those who were there, Italy became a secondary theater, a "forgotten front," as the combatants called it.

Although history's spotlight had shifted to the newly opened Western Front, and despite the fall of Rome to the Allies, the war continued in the Mediterranean for nearly another year. When Mussolini was, for the last time, delivered by Hitler from captivity, Il Duce from northern Italy postured

Flying Fortresses pass over the ruins of an ancient Roman aqueduct near Rome—the ruins casting long shadows across a modern highway. Objectives of the Fifteenth Air Force bombers were transportation targets in northern Italy. (U. S. AIR FORCE)

Operation Dragoon, the invasion of southern France into which the bulk of Allied air forces formerly employed in the Italian campaign was drawn. Twelfth

Air Force C-47s deposit troops and supplies in an area between Nice and Marseilles, August 15, 1944.

(U. S. AIR FORCE)

the Allies succeeded in breaking through the Gothic Line, the coming of the rains in late September brought a sequel to the previous winter on the Gustav Line.

It was the mixture as before, six months of cold, snow, and mud. While the ground forces were mired down or crouched in foxholes and the weather proved to be not too unreasonable, the air forces of the Mediterranean command, some 280 squadrons strong, pursued their mission: cutting off all Nazi supply routes into Italy and all withdrawal routes out. By this time, late 1944 and early 1945, it was unlikely that the Luftwaffe could have put up 280 aircraft to oppose the Allied assault.

Medium bombers and fighter-bombers ranged over the Apennines, over the plain of the Po River, and even across the Alps. The B-25s and B-26s of the Twelfth Air Force were specifically assigned targets in the Brenner Pass, an escape route directly

into Germany; the Desert Air Force pummeled Tarvisio to the east, the route into Austria. Bridges, railroads, and highways became unsafe for any kind of travel, from tank to bicycle. The strategic forces (Fifteenth Air Force and No. 205 Group, RAF) united with the tactical units in a ruthless interdiction of the battleground. By spring of 1945 only a trickle of supplies was reaching the beleaguered Germans.

If the Luftwaffe in Italy had been rendered all but impotent, the flak remained an ever present danger. A direct hit by the deadly "88" could cut a wing in half, detonate a bomb load, or sever an engine. The weather too was a danger, particularly over the mountains, where ten minutes of flying time might bring an abrupt change in the conditions. "The Apennines," observed Roderic Owen in his history of the Desert Air Force, "produced Jekyll and Hyde conditions. A blue sky to the west could

Marauders cross the Alps in a bombing mission to Germany itself; once the Allies had moved into northern Italy it was possible even for medium bombers to strike at German objectives. Note the effect of the freezing air upon the "skin" of the B-26.

(U. S. AIR FORCE)

Hit by flak on a tactical support mission, this Liberator of the 779th Bombardment Squadron (464th Group, Fifteenth Air Force) falls over northern Italy.

(U. S. AIR FORCE)

With P-38 escort 97th Bomb Group (Fifteenth Air Force) Flying Fortresses from Foggia, Italy, set out to bomb the Linz marshaling yards in Austria. Heavy bombers could now close in upon Hitler from two directions, England and Italy. (U. S. AIR FORCE)

mask scudding clouds to the east." Missions over the Alps were equally hazardous; aircraft which had not been damaged by the enemy simply disappeared in the overcast—frequently because of disorientation and a resultant flight into a mountain —and were never heard from again. The war may have bogged down, but death never took a holiday.

When not diverted to the tactical requirements of the ground war, such as bombing bridges and the Brenner Pass area, the B-17s, B-24s, Wellingtons, and Halifaxes of the Mediterranean Strategic Air Forces began reaching out for targets in occupied countries and even into Germany itself. By day Fifteenth Air Force bombers, escorted by P-38s and P-51s, struck at aircraft factories in Austria, railroad systems in Hungary, even the once dreaded objectives at Ploesti and Schweinfurt. As early as June 1944, using Foggia as a base, the Fifteenth completed the first shuttle mission to Russia, bombing rail targets in Hungary on the way out and a Rumanian airfield on the return trip.

No. 205 Group bombed many of the same targets at night without escort. Another specialty was mining the Danube River at night in low-flying (two hundred feet and lower) Liberators and Wellingtons. These "gardening" missions, as they were called, blocked the river traffic, denying Germany precious oil and coal. Beaufighters frequently accompanied the heavies to attack the vessels in the river and other nearby targets, such as railways.

In mid-April 1945 the Allies began their final drive into the Po Valley after an intensive air offensive by both tactical and strategic aircraft. The technique of "carpet bombing," the laying of a massive, concentrated bomb saturation upon enemy positions directly in front of Allied troops, was employed. First the heavies laid the carpet and were followed by the mediums and fighter-bombers to complete the devastation.

With Allied armor and air power in pursuit, the Germans fell back. By the end of April the polyglot Allied armies—British (including Canadians, English, and New Zealanders), French, Polish, Italian, and American—burst into the Po Valley and fanned westward toward Turin, north toward Milan, and eastward toward Venice. At the same time Italian partisans caught Mussolini trying to flee into Switzerland, shot him and his mistress, Clara Petacci, and brought their bodies to Milan, where they were displayed hanging by their heels like sides of beef.

The Germans were finished too and it devolved upon General Heinrich von Vietinghoff, Kesselring's successor (the latter had been transferred to the Western Front), to surrender the German forces in Italy. On May 2, 1945, the war in Italy ended unconditionally, with the German Army there a demoralized shambles and the Luftwaffe non-existent. It had been a hard war, no "soft underbelly" by any means, but it might have been harsher had not Allied air power paralyzed the ability of the German troops to move freely and had not the system of communications been consistently disrupted. Even the withdrawal, that final, bitter expedient, had been impossible. General Fridolin von Senger und Etterlin, who commanded the XIV Corps of the German Fourteenth Army, summarized the impact of Allied air forces in the final battle as well, in effect, as in the entire Italian air campaign. He said, "The effect of Allied air attacks on the frontier route of Italy made the fuel and ammunition situation very critical. It was the bombing of the Po crossings that finished us. We could have withdrawn successfully with normal rear guard action despite the heavy pressure, but owing to the destruction of the ferries and river crossings we lost all our equipment. North of the river we were no longer an Army."

2

REAP THE WHIRLWIND

THE high road to Berlin left the German land-scape scorched with the ruins of its cities and the graves of hundreds of thousands of civilian dead. North Africa, the Mediterranean, Italy—all were merely collateral to Allied strategic air forces; the prime, the true target was Germany.

This, crudely put, "get Germany," was to be the mission of the strategic air forces—Bomber Command, RAF, the Eighth Air Force, and, once it was established at Foggia in Italy, the Fifteenth Air Force. The plan called for the Americans to bomb with reasonable accuracy by day upon con-

Frustrating and dangerously protected targets were the German sub pens situated around the Bay of Biscay in France. Among the first attacked was Lorient in a long campaign of little result because of the practically bomb-proof installations, which the Germans boasted *were impervious. By June of 1943, when this attack on Lorient occurred, individual bombing was aban-doned in favor of entire groups dropping when the lead plane released its bombs. The result was a heavy target concentration—but even this did not knock out the sub pens.* (U. S. AIR FORCE)

One of the major targets of the Allied Strategic Air Forces: the Luftwaffe, in the air in combat or on the ground in factories where it was replenished. This is an Me-109 assembly line at Wiener Neustadt, Austria. (U. S. AIR FORCE)

the RAF and the Eighth Air Force commanders. There was general agreement upon the priorities, which gave first place to the German aircraft industry, second to the ball-bearings industry, third to oil, and so on. As revised slightly in Britain the list was headed by submarines (the industry, the pens from which they operated, and the vessels themselves) followed by, as in the original, aircraft, ball bearings, oil, synthetic rubber and tires, and military transport vehicles.

As finally emended by the end of April 1943, the list was preceded by what was termed as an "intermediate objective"—"German fighter strength" followed by the primary objectives once again with submarines first, "remainder of the German aircraft industry" second, ball bearings third, and oil fourth. This was not so much a revelation of dissension among the military planners as it was an admission

centrated targets while the British struck, generally at the same targets, by night. The American method was called "precision" bombardment (and there were times when it was, thanks to skillful crews and the Norden bombsight) and the British technique "area" bombing. The British method was less costly to aircrews and hard on German civilians who happened to live in the general area of a selected target. What it meant, in effect, was that German cities which housed German war industries were fair game for Bomber Command's Lancasters. This was not, even at the time, regarded as a "civilized method of waging war," as ironic a sophism as was ever coined by man.

It was reasoned in the higher reaches of the Allied High Command that in order to destroy Germany's war machine certain key industries must be bombed out of existence—just which was open to argument. A Committee of Operations Analysis was formed to study the problem of target selection and to provide priority lists. This American group submitted its recommendations in March 1943 to the British High Command (the Air Ministry and the Ministry of Economic Warfare) as well as to

Bombs for Messerschmitt: Fifteenth Air Force Liberator in one of its first major missions attacks the Me-109 plant at Wiener Neustadt, Austria. (U. S. AIR FORCE)

A stick of bombs falls toward the Focke-Wulf factory in the suburbs of Bremen. Damage was extensive enough after this raid of April 17, 1943, to force the removal of the facilities deeper into Germany, to

Marienburg. Of the 107 bombers that attacked, 16 were lost to flak, bursting short in this photograph, and particularly aggressive fighter attacks.

(U. S. AIR FORCE)

that before any serious consideration could be given to a heavy strategic bombardment of Germany the Luftwaffe would have to be eliminated. The German fighter was the single crucial obstacle to the Allied Combined Bomber Offensive.

The submarine was granted a high priority as a concession to the havoc it wreaked in the Atlantic at the time. It was a worthy though frustrating target, as the Eighth Air Force had learned in its early operations during the previous winter. Striking at the German submarine pens in France around the Bay of Biscay, the Eighth Air Force B-17s encountered heavy flak and aggressive fighters. The cost in crews and aircraft was high and the bombings

accomplished little or nothing, except to kill French civilians: and this was no accomplishment at all.

It was in the valley of the Ruhr that the greatest concentration of German industry lay, great sprawling factories in more than a dozen cities clustered on the banks of the Ruhr, the Rhine, and the Dortmund-Ems Canal. Bomber Command initiated the Battle of the Ruhr in May of 1940 with an inconclusive raid by a mere thirty-six bombers upon München Gladbach, directly southwest of the Ruhr proper. It was not until the spring of 1943 that Air Chief Marshal Harris' Bomber Command was capable of mounting truly sizable attacks upon the Ruhr industries. In these attacks Bomber Command could expect little assistance from the depleted Eighth Air Force, whose heavy-bomber units were being shunted off to north Africa and the Mediterranean. Although the Eighth had flown its first mission in August of 1942, it had not actually dropped any bombs upon German soil until January 27, 1943, when it attacked the U-boat bases at Wilhelmshaven.

Carrying the battle into Germany and into the heart, Berlin, fell to Harris and Bomber Command. "At long last we were ready and equipped," Harris noted when the true Battle of the Ruhr opened on the night of March 5/6, 1943, with an attack upon Essen, home of the Krupps works. By "ready and equipped" Harris meant that he had the Lancasters and the electronic device—Oboe—to make the attack feasible. Oboe was so named because the sound its sending station directed over the target was continuous and low like that of the musical instrument. Because it required ground stations Oboe

had a limited range of about 350 miles (which covered only the central Ruhr area and was of no use for deeper missions into Germany). This limitation was circumvented when it was decided to install the Oboe set in a target-marking Mosquito instead of the bombers themselves. The Mosquitos could fly at an altitude at which the earth's curvature would not interfere with the signal (which was beamed at the aircraft and in turn beamed back to another station). If on proper course the pulse was the continuous note, if off course the signal broke up into dots and dashes. Course and distance were calibrated by Oboe with remarkable accuracy. The pathfinding Mosquitos then marked the target area with flares and the bombers followed to accomplish the mission.

It worked exceedingly well on the Essen raid, when 442 bombers dealt the first major blow to the Krupp factories. This was not the last as the

A "Former Naval Person" (as he signed his messages to President Roosevelt) observes with evident satisfaction as a Lancaster takes off in England for a night mission to Germany.

(IMPERIAL WAR MUSEUM, LONDON)

spring moved into summer. After one heavy raid Essen was left in a blazing ruin; in the center the Krupp plants were hardly more than a mass of smoldering wreckage. When Gustav Krupp von Bohlen viewed the result of Bomber Command's night visit the next morning he suffered a stroke from which he never recovered—and which saved him from prosecution as a war criminal after the war.

Other towns and cities in the Ruhr suffered under the growing power of Bomber Command: Duisburg, Bochum, Dortmund, Düsseldorf, and Wuppertal, among others. It was at Wuppertal on May 29/30, 1943, that the attack took an ominous turn for the Germans. That night more than seven hundred bombers succeeded in saturating Barmen-Wuppertal (scarcely touching the other section, Elberfeld-Wuppertal), causing monstrous fires and great loss of civilian life (2450). What Rotterdam and Coventry had been to the Allies, Wuppertal became to the Germans. Goebbels denounced the attack (which had knocked out five of the six major factories) as a "kind of aerial terrorism . . . the product of the sick minds of the plutocratic world-destroyers."

"A long chain of human suffering," he admonished "in all German cities blitzed by the Allies has borne witness against them and their cruel and cowardly leaders—from the murder of German children in Freiburg on May 10, 1940, right up to the present day." Freiburg, as Goebbels well knew by then, had been bombed by off-course Luftwaffe He-111s. But the death of fifty-seven civilians, among them women and thirteen children, had served him well in his denunciations of Allied bombing ethics.

The bombing of Wuppertal was one of the most effective area attacks up to that time and came near the close of the Battle of the Ruhr, which ended, as far as heavy concentration was concerned, by July 1943. Harris then turned his attention to Hamburg, next step on the road to Berlin.

II

The second largest city in the Reich, Hamburg was an important shipping and shipbuilding center; it housed other, lesser industries too, but the major concern was with the U-boat production factories. That was sufficient reason for a Bomber Command

A Bomber Command Lancaster scatters incendiaries upon Duisburg in the Ruhr.
(IMPERIAL WAR MUSEUM, LONDON)

attack on the city; another was, since it was beyond Oboe range, that it was susceptible to an H2S (also called "Home Sweet Home" for the two H's and the S). This radar device, carried in the pathfinder aircraft, operated much like a primitive television set— it scanned the ground below the attacking force, picking out certain features of the area. It was especially effective over cities situated near or on water. Hamburg was located some fifty miles inland from the North Sea on the Elbe River; its features were revealed remarkably even on the not yet completely perfected H2S.

During the Battle of Hamburg the radar-jamming device called "window" was also used. Tin-foil strips were released from aircraft and completely threw off radar-controlled flak guns as well as German night fighters. The battle was opened by Bomber Command the night of July 24/25, 1943, when nearly eight hundred Lancasters, Halifaxes, and Wellingtons planted the first seeds of a holocaust. Flying Fortresses of the Eighth Air Force followed up with smaller daylight raids on the twenty-fifth

Aerial battleground at night. Starlike clusters are target indicators dropped by "pathfinder" aircraft.
(IMPERIAL WAR MUSEUM, LONDON)

and twenty-sixth, concentrating on the city's dock areas. The climax came on the night of July 27/28, when 787 bombers were dispatched. Fires from the earlier attacks were still burning (fed by coke and coal stored in Hamburg for the coming winter); the succession of attacks had also disrupted attempts by firemen to extinguish the fires.

Hamburg, as a palpable target because of its major industry, had one of the most efficient Air Raid Precaution organizations in Germany; its shelter system was one of the finest. But for what occurred in the wake of the bombing in the early morning of July 28, 1943, stringent precautions and ingeniously constructed shelters meant nothing. The bomb loads combined high explosives with incendiaries, and when the newly made fires combined

with the fires of the preceding attacks the result was what one observer called a "lake of fire."

The first man-made fire storm was unleashed upon Hamburg in that lake. The heat generated a powerful suction that uprooted trees three feet thick and drew them into the fire. The same thing happened to human beings.

A secret German document prepared after the attack described the fire storm with undisguised awe—"beyond all human imagination"—and hopelessness:

Through the union of a number of fires, the air gets so hot that because of its decreasing specific weight, it receives terrific momentum, which in its turn causes the surrounding air to be sucked toward the center. By that suction, combined with the enormous difference in temperature (600–1000 degrees centigrade), tempests are caused which exceed their meteorological counterparts (20–30 centigrade). In a built-up area the suction could not follow its shortest course, but the overheated air stormed through the streets with immense force, taking along not only sparks but burning timber and roof beams, so spreading the fire more and more, developing in a short time into a fire typhoon as was never before witnessed, against which every human resistance was quite useless.

Searing winds of 150 miles an hour swept through Hamburg in a howling fury. Dwellings, trees, people—all incinerated in its path. Bomb shelters proved to be not havens, but deathtraps. The thousand-degree heat produced searing vacuums around them, asphyxiating and cremating the occupants. By August 3, when the Battle of Hamburg was over, half of the city was gone and perhaps 50,000 dead. (The number will never be known and ranges from 31,647 actually counted by December 1943 to the greater number, which is probably closer to the true figure. As a comparison, it might be noted that the most authoritative figure for the number of people killed during all of the bombings of Britain is 51,509.)

The survivors would ever refer to those few days and nights as *Die Katastrophe.* Goebbels reported that Hamburg *Gauleiter* Karl Kaufman called it "a catastrophe the extent of which staggers the imagination . . ." and that "the entire city must be evacuated except for small patches. He spoke of about 800,000 people who are wandering up and down the streets not knowing what to do." But

Goebbels found Kaufman "a bit too lyrical and romantic for so great a catastrophe. . . ."

Minister of Armaments Albert Speer, no romantic but a pragmatic realist, went so far as to inform Hitler himself that if such attacks were made on six other German cities devoted to German war production, it would bring "a rapid end to the war." The attack even galvanized the dilatory Göring, who attempted to rally the Luftwaffe into a real defensive force and to encourage the production of fighters for that force. But Hitler had the last word as usual. "Terror can only be broken by terror!" he ranted. "Everything else is nonsense. I can only win the war by dealing out more destruction to the enemy than he does to us. . . ." Whereupon he ordered Oberst Dietrich Peltz, the youthful *Angriffsführer England,* to plan a series of revenge attacks upon Britain. With the Luftwaffe then dispersed to the Eastern Front and the Allies overrunning Sicily, Peltz had little in the way of air power to attack England. When he did, beginning

around the first of the next year, it resulted in what the British called, somewhat disdainfully, the "baby blitz." The attacks were inconclusive and wasteful and demonstrated little more than the fact that the Luftwaffe was a victim of the inner decay of its own High Command.

III

Hitler had no understanding of the meaning of air power, nor of the change that it had undergone since he had unleashed his Stukas on Poland. He remained ever the corporal with his feet in the mud and delusions of grandeur. Although he had ignited a world war, his vision remained limited by his own megalomania. He fixed his eyes to his battle map, a flat wall map, not a globe, and refused to look up. It simply did not dawn on him that since the Battle of Britain the only attacks upon the Reich itself had come from the air. Nor did he

An Eighth Air Force Liberator is cut in half near Hamburg during a daylight attack upon the city's docks.

Flak stopped the B-24 before it reached the German city. (U. S. AIR FORCE)

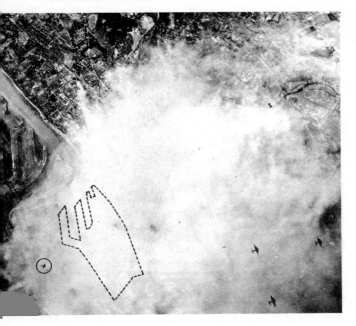

A conception of the Hamburg catastrophe may be realized from the extent of the fires that obscured the city when Eighth Air Force bombers arrived the morning following the initial Bomber Command attacks. The Eighth Air Force target, the dock areas, is covered over with smoke (the target area is indicated by the dotted line). In the circle: a lone FW-190 pursues Fortresses of the 381st Bomb Group leaving the target.

(U. S. AIR FORCE)

At the same time he simply shifted the guilt for his ineptitudes to the shoulders of others.

The first suggestion that all was not well in the Luftwaffe was revealed as early as November 1941. Ernst Udet, chief of the technical office of the Luftwaffe, had become Göring's chief scapegoat as well. Udet was blamed for the failure of the Battle of Britain, he was blamed for the decline in aircraft production that seemed to follow every successful campaign, and he was blamed for the fatal lack of a long-range heavy bomber. During the 1941 summer offensive in Russia a critical decline in aircraft production brought Udet under fire again. Göring placed Udet's functions in the hands of the superefficient Milch. Within five months Udet had become little more than a name in his own office.

In November Udet shot himself, first scrawling over his bed a final message: "Reichsmarschall, why have you deserted me?" The message was discreetly removed and Göring released the news that Udet had been killed "testing a new weapon." Although he seriously considered court-martialing Udet posthumously, Göring consented to an impressive state funeral attended by nearly all of the great German

realize that in the inevitably impending Battle of Germany the Luftwaffe represented his first line of defense. Besides, defense was inconceivable to Hitler; he would listen only to plans for attack or the fight to the death.

When Hamburg was burned late in July 1943 Hitler and Göring were estranged to an embarrassing degree to the *Reichsmarschall*. The Luftwaffe had failed to bring off Sealion, it had permitted a thousand bombers to strike at Cologne and now Hamburg, not to mention the American Flying Fortresses, which flew over the Reich during the day. Insofar as Hitler was concerned, the Luftwaffe was "not doing its job."

Göring, cut to the quick not only by the Führer's tongue-lashings but by his refusal to shake hands, chose to withdraw from the scene of conflict. He would send deputies to Hitler's meetings and cultivate his own comfort and the vast art collection he had gathered in the wake of the German armies.

Victims of Göring: Udet and Jeschonnek both committed suicide because of Göring's practice of using them as scapegoats for his own failures.

(H. J. NOWARRA)

airmen and with Göring himself leading the funeral procession.

The situation inside the German High Command was so bad that when Werner Mölders, an outspoken non-Nazi, was killed in a crash in attempting to fly to Udet's funeral, rumors hinted that he had been assassinated.

Having lost his chief scapegoat, Göring selected another, Jeschonnek, the young Luftwaffe chief of staff. Jeschonnek all but worshiped Hitler and Göring resented that also; but Hitler detested the Luftwaffe, so Jeschonnek's lot was not a happy one. It took a turn for the worse when Harris opened his offensive in the Ruhr, destroyed Hamburg, and appeared to be heading for Berlin itself. Then on the night of August 17/18, 1943, barely two weeks after the Hamburg mission, Bomber Command succeeded in making a surprise raid on Peenemünde, home of Hitler's "secret weapon," of which the world had been hearing so much.

This was the German rocket research center on the Baltic Sea, which was not as secret as Hitler had hoped. While a small force of Mosquitos dropped flares upon Berlin, creating the impression that the capital was to be the night's objective, close to six hundred bombers released their loads on Peenemünde. The mission was remarkably successful, although it did not wipe out the home of Hitler's "vengeance weapons." Two important scientists were killed, there was a delay in the development of the V-weapons, and certain phases of production and testing were moved from Peenemünde.

The shock of the attack and the confusion under which the Luftwaffe, led astray by the Mosquitos over Berlin, had responded to it created further tension in the higher reaches of the Luftwaffe. Unable to face what was inevitably in store for him the next morning, Jeschonnek shot himself. Like Udet he left a message: "I can no longer work with the Reichsmarschall. Long live the Führer." His death, attributed to a stomach hemorrhage, was not announced immediately, so that it might not be associated with the bombing of Peenemünde.

Jeschonnek's successor as Luftwaffe chief of staff was General Gunther Korten, another Hitler toady (and who later died in Hitler's bunker on July 20, 1944, when a bomb intended for his Führer exploded).

If the Luftwaffe High Command degenerated under the pressure of total war, its pilots did not lack courage and determination. Here Major Heinz-Wolfgang Schnaufer, top-scoring (121—most of them four-engined bombers) night fighter ace, studies the tail of his Me-110. The British admired Schnaufer and called him "the Night Ghost of Saint-Trond" (for his base in Belgium).

(H. J. NOWARRA)

Bomber Command lost heavily over Peenemünde to flak and to night fighters. Forty bombers did not return from that mission. Hitler thus could not say that the Luftwaffe was not doing its job. Nor could he have overlooked what the Luftwaffe had done during the same day over Regensburg and Schweinfurt when the Eighth Air Force lost so heavily to its fighters.

Despite Hitler's attitude, attempts were made sub rosa to prepare for the defense of Germany. To counter Harris's bombers a system called the "Kammhuber Line," the brain child of Josef Kammhuber, was devised. This employed an elaborate network of searchlight belts across the western approaches to the Reich and a lesser one to the west of Berlin. The night-flying Ju-88s, Me-110s, and Do-17s, carrying electronic devices, were controlled from the ground by the "Würzburgs," the German version of radar. These ground control stations were called *Himmelbetten,* and despite some disadvantages (for instance, when an enemy plane passed from the zone of control of one station into another, it could escape, for German night fighters were

A "Würzburg" radar installation, or Himmelbett. *The giant radar antennas of the Würzburg proved to be* *remarkably effective, but were rendered all but useless when "window" was dropped during Allied bombing raids.* (U. S. AIR FORCE)

A bombed-out railroad station that Hitler was unable to shun: the Potsdamer Station, Berlin. British and *American heavy bombers had reached the heartland of Nazi Germany.* (U. S. AIR FORCE)

strictly forbidden to operate except in their own zones), the system proved to be fairly effective.

However, when Kammhuber approached Hitler, hoping to expand the *Himmelbetten* through all of Germany, he ran into trouble. Basing his request upon the figures of American aircraft production which had been supplied him by German Intelligence, Kammhuber hoped Hitler would be impressed enough to give his blessing to the project. Instead Hitler refused to believe that the figure—five thousand military planes per month—was accurate (it was in fact quite accurate, if on the conservative side). Kammhuber was clearly exaggerating, Hitler insisted.

"Nonsense!" Hitler shouted. "I will not stand for such nonsense." Kammhuber left with his plan for the defense of the Reich a shambles. On September 15, 1943, he was notified that his Nachtjagdfliegerkorps XII would be disbanded and its units dispersed to various other *Luftflotten*. Kammhuber was demoted and the night-fighter system began to disintegrate. The nighttime protection of Germany continued, though with much less direction, with Kammhuber's twin-engined night fighters and the single-engined fighters of Jagdgeschwader 300, the contribution of Major Hajo Herrmann.

An ex-bomber pilot, Herrmann came forth with the suggestion that FW-190s, without radar, could be used at night to attack British bombers. With the Lancasters silhouetted by *Himmelbett* searchlights, or illuminated by flares, the FWs could readily find them and shoot them down. This simplistic approach appealed to Hitler—it would not require the construction of costly ground stations—and he smiled upon it. The one serious problem was flak. Herrmann, however, reached an agreement with flak commanders about timings and altitudes of the bursts, thus affording his fighters some immunity.

In time Herrmann commanded three *Geschwader,* the original JG 300 plus JG 301 and JG 302, which were nicknamed *Wilde Sau* ("Wild Boars") in honor of their tactic of diving heedlessly into enemy bomber formations at night. It had been the *Wilde Sau* which had accounted for most of the British bomber losses on the Peenemünde attack. The plan was courageous, and it cost Bomber Command dearly, but it was haphazard and unable to cope with the growing power of Bomber Command as well as the Eighth and Fifteenth Air Forces.

Discouraged, Kammhuber resigned in November of 1943; on November 18 Harris opened the first major phase in the Battle of Berlin. More than four hundred aircraft dropped their bombs upon the heart of the Reich. With the specter of Hamburg fresh in mind (and an even more recent burning of Kassel in October) the appearance of enemy bombers was a chilling experience to the inhabitants of Berlin. "Hell itself seems to have broken loose over us," Goebbels commented.

Hitler was not impressed by the portent. The hearts of several German cities lay in smoldering ruin but they served only as an excuse to berate the Luftwaffe or to chide Göring. Hitler could not, however, bear to look upon the devastation of his cities. When his train passed through bombed-out areas the window shades were discreetly drawn; what he did not wish to see he did not behold. But reality was catching up with him and there was an irony in his future: although he could not stomach the sight of ruined cities he would live out the final weeks of his life in the very center of one.

3

KITES OVER BERLIN

Whatever the official conception of Berlin's strategic importance, to the eager pilot in the ETO (European Theater of Operations) it was the ultimate objective. It was, after all, the headquarters of the hated Hun. However little the absolute destruction of the Reich's capital might contribute to the ending of the war was, in truth, immaterial: the "Big B" remained an ever beckoning symbol. That it might contain millions of helpless (even innocent—but who considered that?) civilians was also immaterial, irrelevant, or incidental; this was Total War.

The professional German militarists, of whom Hitler was not one, conceded that Harris's Bomber Command devastated German cities, but that the effect upon German morale was minimal. It stiffened non-combatant attitudes in general (as it had those of the English) and aroused the German's sardonic sense of humor—frequently at the expense even of Hitler and Göring. But there was no great upsurge of civilian pleas for surrender.

But what the German professionals—Minister of Arms and War Production Albert Speer and Milch —feared most was American bombing by day, aimed at specific war industries. If the Americans were permitted to intensify and concentrate their attacks on any single target for any length of time the war would be lost.

By the turn of 1944 the Allied Air Forces ap-

proached that point, but it was a tragic paradox that in spite of it the war was not lost by Germany until another year and a half went by, months of great cost in lives and destruction. The paradox, simply stated, was this: although the Allied heavy-bomber strength by the middle of January 1944 made it possible to strike at Germany several times

The major dread of German war production experts: American bombers attacking specific targets by day.
(CECIL COHEN)

Another source of discomfort to the German planners—American mass production. B-17s roll out of Boeing's plant at Seattle. (THE BOEING COMPANY)

a week with immense bomber formations (ranging from four hundred to eight hundred bombers) and the advent of the P-51 Mustang made escorted missions deep inside Germany possible, German war industries did not crumble even under repeated blows, and Germany, therefore, did not crumble either.

Why?

There were several reasons, not the least of which was the ability of German industries to recover rapidly from the raids. The dispersal which followed the Schweinfurt-Regensburg mission also made it difficult to damage with any finality specific industries that might have clogged the German war machine. Weather was always a factor, of course, preventing or interfering with missions.

The year 1944, for example, opened with bad weather, forcing whatever missions that were mounted to depend upon "blind bombing" (radar) rather than visual tactics. Inexperienced operators of the H2X device (an American adaptation of the British H2S) scattered bombs across target areas and caused little real damage to specific targets. The much vaunted, very secret miracle devices were not miracle workers despite occasional success, such

as the bombing of docks, submarine construction yards, and the city of Kiel on December 13, 1943; and on this mission Oboe was used, not the more recent H2X. The former operated on a beam projected from sending stations in England, the latter was carried in the bombers themselves—the so-called "Pathfinders," and were not limited to the sending power of the stations in Britain.

The main target, in preparation for the forthcoming invasion of Normandy, was the Luftwaffe. Unless the factories could be seen it was not possible to concentrate the bombing pattern on the targets. The first opportunity to strike at the Luftwaffe in 1944 came on January 11, when the weather cleared over central Germany. An attack was mounted consisting of 663 Flying Fortresses and Liberators, with a fighter escort of Spitfires, P-47s, P-38s (allocated to the nearer outgoing and incoming legs of the mission), and P-51s (over the target areas). The targets were the FW-190 plant at Oschersleben, the Ju-88 plant at Halberstadt, and the Me-110 plants at Brunswick. These cities were grouped quite close together; they were also directly in line with Berlin, which lay about ninety miles beyond.

It was an impressive concept, but certain factors as usual intervened. If the weather over central Germany was fine, it was poor over England and complicated takeoffs and assembly over England. Along the way the weather worsened and the B-17s of the 3rd Bombardment Division and the B-24s of the 2nd Division were ordered back to England. Some of the B-17s of the 3rd Division, however, approaching the target, decided to continue on with the 1st Division, which was about fifty miles from Brunswick when the "recall" came. This decimated the force greatly, for only 238 bombers struck at their primary targets (the others bombed targets of opportunity).

Fearing that Berlin was the objective, the Luftwaffe reacted, after what had seemed a quiescent period, savagely. More than two hundred fighters, Me-109s, FW-190s, and Me-110s (armed with rockets) rose up to meet the bombers and their escort. The German pilots, their planes equipped with extra fuel tanks, could wait until the escorts were forced to turn back before dropping their tanks and lancing through the bomber formations. The two-engined fighters merely stayed out of gun range and lobbed rockets into the combat boxes.

HOW THE TARGET IS LOCATED

OVERCAST BOMBING

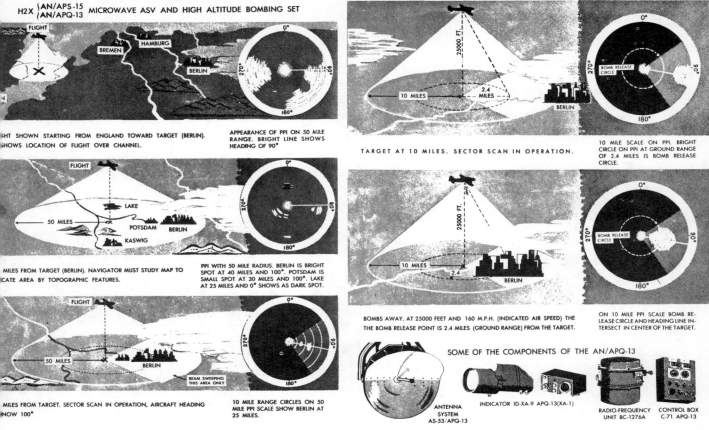

H2X {AN/APS-15 {AN/APQ-13 MICROWAVE ASV AND HIGH ALTITUDE BOMBING SET

[GHT] SHOWN STARTING FROM ENGLAND TOWARD TARGET (BERLIN). [S]HOWS LOCATION OF FLIGHT OVER CHANNEL.

APPEARANCE OF PPI ON 50 MILE RANGE. BRIGHT LINE SHOWS HEADING OF 90°.

[50] MILES FROM TARGET (BERLIN). NAVIGATOR MUST STUDY MAP TO [LO]CATE AREA BY TOPOGRAPHIC FEATURES.

PPI WITH 50 MILE RADIUS. BERLIN IS BRIGHT SPOT AT 40 MILES AND 100°. POTSDAM IS SMALL SPOT AT 30 MILES AND 100°. LAKE AT 25 MILES AND 0° SHOWS AS DARK SPOT.

[50] MILES FROM TARGET. SECTOR SCAN IN OPERATION, AIRCRAFT HEADING [IS N]OW 100°.

10 MILE RANGE CIRCLES ON 50 MILE PPI SCALE SHOW BERLIN AT 25 MILES.

TARGET AT 10 MILES. SECTOR SCAN IN OPERATION.

10 MILE SCALE ON PPI. BRIGHT CIRCLE ON PPI AT GROUND RANGE OF 2.4 MILES IS BOMB RELEASE CIRCLE.

BOMBS AWAY. AT 25000 FEET AND 160 M.P.H. (INDICATED AIR SPEED) THE BOMB RELEASE POINT IS 2.4 MILES (GROUND RANGE) FROM THE TARGET.

ON 10 MILE PPI SCALE BOMB RE-LEASE CIRCLE AND HEADING LINE IN-TERSECT IN CENTER OF THE TARGET.

SOME OF THE COMPONENTS OF THE AN/APQ-13

ANTENNA SYSTEM AS-53/APQ-13

INDICATOR ID-XA-9 APQ-13(XA-1)

RADIO-FREQUENCY UNIT BC-1276A

CONTROL BOX C-71 APQ-13

How H2X located targets and how overcast bombings were accomplished with the aid of newly developed navigational devices. (ROBERT CHAPIN)

The P-51s, of the 354th Fighter Group (the first to be issued the Mustang), raced in to the defense of the bombers that attacked Oschersleben and Halberstadt, which seemed to be taking the brunt of the German attack. But there were only forty-nine Mustangs, which had to be shared between the two forces, and it was impossible to protect the Fortresses with any thoroughness. A further factor had interjected itself: the Mustangs had joined with the bombers earlier than scheduled so that fuel remaining for battling over the target was limited. Still, the pilots gave a good account of themselves. It was on this mission that Major James H. Howard, squadron commander of the 356th Fighter Squadron (of the 354th Fighter Group, Ninth Air Force) and a former Flying Tiger, won the Medal of Honor by taking on what one bomber commander believed was "the entire Luftwaffe."

Howard disclaimed that, saying that he had not even seen the thirty fighters "all at once the way the bomber people tell it." In an interview with *Stars and Stripes* writer Andrew A. Rooney, Howard told of his encounter. The bombers had passed over the target (Oschersleben) when the German fighters struck. The P-51s swept in to the defense of the bombers. In the initial fighting Howard became separated from the rest of his flight.

"The first plane I got was a two-engined German night fighter [Me-110]. I went down after him, gave him several squirts and watched him crash. He stood out very clearly, silhouetted against the snow that covered the ground. He went down in a cloud of black smoke and fire and hit the ground. Shortly after that an FW came cruising along underneath me. He pulled up into the sun when he saw me. I gave him a squirt and I almost ran into his

B-17s of the 384th Bomb Group bombing through the overcast on instruments. (U. S. AIR FORCE)

The North American P-51 "Mustang," the plane that turned the tide in the daylight bombings of Germany. Capable of escorting the bombers all the way to and

from the deep penetration targets, the Mustang was also an outstanding fighter plane. (U. S. AIR FORCE)

canopy when he threw it off to get out. He bailed out.

"Then I circled trying to join up with the other P-51s. I saw an Me-109 just underneath and a few hundred yards ahead of me. He saw me at the same time and chopped his throttle, hoping my speed would carry me on ahead of him. It's an old trick. He started scissoring underneath me but I chopped my throttle and started scissoring at the same time and then we went into a circle dogfight and it was a matter of who could maneuver best and cut the shortest circle. I dumped twenty-degree flaps and began cutting inside him, so he quit and went into a dive, with me after him. I got on his tail and got in some long-distance squirts from three hundred or four hundred yards. I got some strikes on him, but I didn't see him hit the ground.

"I pulled up again and saw an Me-109 and a P-51 running along together. The 51 saw me coming in from behind and he peeled off while the Me started a slow circle. I don't remember whether I shot at him or not. Things happen so fast it's hard to remember things in sequence when you get back.

"Back up with the bombers again, I saw an Me-110. I shot at him and got strikes all over him. He flicked over on his back I could see gas and smoke coming out—white and black smoke. It could be that he had some sort of smoke equipment to make it appear that he was damaged worse than he was."

If he had doubts about his victory (he did not claim this plane in his report), Howard did not waste time in ascertaining it. He climbed back up to the level of the bombers.

"I saw an Me-109 tooling up for an attack on the bombers. They often slip in sideways, the way this one was doing. We were both pretty close to the bombers, and I was close to him. I gave him a squirt and he headed straight down with black smoke pouring out."

Although he had not come under fighter attack up to this point, for the Luftwaffe concentrated primarily on the bombers, Howard's luck was not all good. When he jumped the first plane all four of his guns were operating, but by his third attack only two functioned; finally only one. This was an early problem the Mustang pilots faced. Howard pulled away from the burning Me-109 and climbed again to bomber level, approaching from the left side of the formation.

"I saw an Me-109 over on the starboard side getting into position to attack the bombers," Howard related. "I dived on him from where I was and got strikes all over him with my one gun. He turned over on his back and skidded out. He thought he had lost me with the skid and he pulled out into a forty-five-degree dive. I followed him down and kept on shooting.

"I'd been with the bombers for more than an hour altogether by then and just before I left I saw a Dornier 217—I think it was—coming alongside the bombers, probably to throw rockets. I dived on him and he left, but I never did fire a shot at him." He was officially credited with shooting down four enemy planes, and given the Medal of Honor for singlehandedly standing off an entire *Gruppe* of enemy aircraft. Major Howard returned to his base, leaving when his fuel supply was dangerously low, to find that his Mustang had but a single bullet hole, through the left wing.

The fighting over Oschersleben had been ferocious; of the 174 Fortresses which bombed the A.G.O. Flugzeugwerke A.G. there, 34 were lost, most of them to enemy fighters. The day's total losses with 26 shot down over Halberstadt amounted to 60 bombers. Claims were made for 152 German fighters, although the actual loss was 39. But the bombing had been good, with a high percentage of effective hits within a thousand feet of the aiming point. There was heavy damage to the factory installations at Oschersleben and near Brunswick.

The heavy weather set in again the following day, thus precluding an immediate sequel and giving the Germans time to repair and disperse. And if the Luftwaffe again had proved itself formidable, the implications of the raid were not lost on Speer, who could see that the aircraft industry was under planned assault. Nor were they ignored by fighter general, General der Jagdflieger Adolf Galland, who recognized what the appearance of the Mustang so deep inside Germany meant. But while he called for more fighters, and Speer agreed with him, Hitler called for bombers with which he could avenge the attacks upon Germany by bombing England. The cross-purposes of the two points of view would in time have its effect.

But because the serious attacks upon the German aircraft industry had led to feverish productivity, the number of fighters being produced in the Reich

Dornier 217, a later development of the Do-17, which was used to launch rockets into American bomber streams. (H. J. NOWARRA)

rose instead of lessened. During the last half of 1943, for example, the average monthly fighter production had been about 850 aircraft (the Allies estimated it to be about 640); during the first half of 1944, under Speer's hand, it averaged 1581 (Allied estimate, based on the estimated damage to the industry, was 655). While the Allied air commanders did not underestimate the Luftwaffe, it was, as the year began, a greater threat than they had imagined.

As if to underscore this self-evident fact, a new directive issued by the Combined Chiefs of Staff dated February 13, 1944, called for the "progressive destruction and dislocation of the German military, industrial and economic systems, the disruption of vital elements of lines of communication and the material reduction of German air combat strength, by the successful prosecution of the combined bomber offensive from all convenient bases."

The next day Arthur Harris read the Air Ministry version of the directive. The over-all plan no longer contained any mention of "undermining the morale of the German people." Under Section 3, "Concept," Harris read:

Overall reduction of German air combat strength in its factories, on the ground and in the air through mutually supporting attacks by both strategic air forces pursued with relentless determination against

James Howard, former Flying Tiger pilot, is being congratulated after receiving the Medal of Honor by Robert M. Lovett, U. S. Assistant Secretary of War for Air. (U. S. AIR FORCE)

same target areas or systems so far as tactical conditions allow, in order to create the air situation most propitious for OVERLORD is immediate purpose of Bomber Offensive.

The primary objective was "the German Air Force"; "Other objectives" included "Crossbow" targets—the bombing of flying bomb launching sites, which had begun to burgeon across the English Channel—"Berlin and Other Industrial Areas," as well as targets in "South Eastern Europe," which came into the sphere of the Mediterranean Allied Air Forces and particularly the new Fifteenth Air

Force. The plan, appropriately, was given the code name "Argument." Harris was not convinced that striking such panacea targets would achieve the results hoped for. Among the assigned target cities was Schweinfurt, which was, Harris was hopefully informed, to be destroyed "at as early a date as possible."

This proposed directive, however, was not sent to Bomber Command for fear it could "lead to trouble with Harris." There was trouble anyway, for even a less strongly worded memo aroused Harris, who reiterated his objections to bombing such a distant, well-defended, and unprofitable target. It was not, Harris persisted, "a reasonable operation of war." But his chiefs, Portal and Sinclair, persisted also, and on January 27 Harris was officially ordered by letter from Deputy Chief of the Air Staff Air Marshal Sir Norman Bottomley to strike at Schweinfurt.

Bomber Command was to join the newly redesignated U. S. Strategic Air Forces (commanded by General Carl Spaatz), whose function was to coordinate the strategic operations of the Eighth and Fifteenth Air Forces. These operations, in turn, were co-ordinated with those of Bomber Command. This "Combined Bomber Offensive" was aimed at the

B-17 of the U. S. Strategic Air Forces, whose primary objective was the Luftwaffe, as a prelude to a projected invasion of France. (CECIL COHEN)

Luftwaffe, as per the directive of February 13, and would serve as an overture to Overlord.

Although Harris remained at his post, there were shake-ups in the American camp. Lieutenant General Ira C. Eaker was sent to Italy to take command of the complex Mediterranean Allied Air Forces. His old command, as head of the Eighth Air Force, was taken over by Major General James Doolittle. Major General Frederick L. Anderson, deputy for operations of the U. S. Strategic Air Forces, served as the direct co-ordinator of the bomber forces of the Eighth and the Fifteenth. The latter bomber command was under the direction of Major General Nathan F. Twining.

With this quite complex command structure it was hoped that an equally complex series of heavy attacks could be made upon Germany's airframe factories, aircraft assembly plants, and anti-friction-bearing plants and thus lay low the Luftwaffe.

II

By the night of February 19, 1944, the weather over Germany once again breaking, the time came for putting Argument into operation. Although England lay under a heavy coating of cloud, which would complicate getting away and possibly landing, and the Fifteenth Air Force was caught up in the frenzy of the Anzio beachhead, General Spaatz elected to "Let 'em go."

What was to come to be called the "Big Week" opened ominously with an attack the night of February, 19/20, 1944, by RAF's Bomber Command upon Leipzig. More than eight hundred bombers and fighters proceeded toward their objective upon what was hoped was a diversionary route; to German radar plotters it appeared that Berlin was the target. This brought out the night fighters slashing at the bomber stream. Even before the stream turned south, short of Berlin, for Leipzig, it had suffered heavy attack. Seventy-eight bombers, or nearly 10 per cent of the attacking force which succeeded in bombing Leipzig, never returned to England. It was not a propitious beginning for the intensified Combined Bomber Offensive.

Spaatz's "Let 'em go" still stood on February 20, and the largest force of aircraft up to that time lifted through four to five thousand feet of murk and set off for Germany. England literally shook under the roar of thousands of powerful engines. More than a thousand heavy bombers alone were dispatched. The escort consisted of no less than thirteen P-47 groups and two each of P-38s and P-51s from Eighth Air Force Fighter Command and from the Ninth Air Force. The RAF provided an additional sixteen squadrons of Spitfires and Mustangs.

The major targets lay in an area between Brunswick in the north and Leipzig in the south (with some other objectives to the north in Poland); all were associated with aircraft production. In this same area was Oschersleben, which had cost so dear on January 11. The men in the great air armada of close to two thousand warplanes flew toward their objectives with some trepidation. Again the route appeared to point toward Berlin.

The Luftwaffe came up to meet them and rammed into a wall of "little friends," or "peashooters," as the fighters were called by the bomber crews ("big friends"). Of the 941 Fortresses and Liberators that bombed Leipzig, Bernburg, and Brunswick (besides other targets of opportunity) a total of 21 was lost. Three fighters were listed as missing. A figure closer to 200 was actually expected.

The results of the bombing were good: production of the Ju-88 in Leipzig was knocked out for about a month. The Me-109 suffered too at the city's Erla plant, and so did the workers. About forty completed Messerschmitts were destroyed in the factory's wreckage, and over four hundred workers who had taken shelter in slit trenches and air raid shelters died in the attack.

The next blow fell upon Stuttgart that night when six hundred RAF bombers struck at aircraft factories in that area. The daylight attack was aimed at Brunswick, but cloud interfered with the mission by the Eighth Air Force and the Fifteenth could not participate at all. The next day—February 22, 1944 —proved to be better and the Fifteenth struck at Regensburg from the south while, as had been planned, the Eighth hit several target cities, among them Gotha, Oschersleben, Aschersleben, Bernburg, and Schweinfurt. The mission went awry because of poor weather over English bases, and several bombers of LeMay's 3rd Division collided in mid-air during the attempts to assemble above the clouds. LeMay ordered the mission scrubbed. The B-24s of the 2nd Division became so dispersed during their

assembly that they would have been unable to form into proper combat boxes in time for arrival over their targets; these aircraft were called back also.

This left only the B-17s of the 1st Division to continue with the attack from England, and the Fifteenth Air Force from Italy. Of the 466 bombers the Eighth Air Force dispatched only 255 dropped bombs (and of these only 99 actually hit their primary targets, because of cloud); of the 183 bombers sent by the Fifteenth Air Force 118 bombed the Messerschmitt plant at Regensburg.

The decreased forces ran into the Messerschmitts of Jagdgeschwader 1 and 11, which mauled the bombers even before they reached their targets. Forty-one bombers went down, although some degree of effective bombing was accomplished upon the Ju-88 night-fighter factories at Aschersleben (knocking it out for two months) and Bernburg. The Fifteenth Air Force did well at Regensburg, although at the cost of fourteen aircraft.

Fighter escort, which had proved so formidable on the Sunday opening day of the Big Week, was unable to contend with the Luftwaffe on Tuesday. This was partly because of the scattering of the bomber forces and partly because of the change in German tactics: attacking the bombers *before* they reached the target areas. The P-51s dispatched to furnish fighter cover over the targets found themselves in the wrong place or, because of the change in targets because of cloud, too distant from the bombers to provide effective help.

Wednesday offered only poor weather predictions, so after three successive days of operations, the Eighth Air Force "stood down," a welcome relief. But the Fifteenth Air Force continued from its end with a small force (102 bombers), which struck at the ball-bearing-producing plant at Steyr in Austria.

Thursday's weather brought a return of the massive co-ordinated attacks. The Fifteenth Air Force dispatched 104 bombers for a return visit to Steyr and a strike upon an aircraft component plant there. Eighty-seven actually bombed Steyr (the remaining 27 bombers, which had become separated from the main body, hit an oil refinery at Fiume); the Steyr bombers, despite heavy escort of Thunderbolts and Lightnings, lost 17 of their number.

From England the Eighth sent a force of B-17s to bomb Schweinfurt (the first attempt since the

A 453rd Bomb Group Liberator homeward bound after bombing a Luftwaffe base during the "Big Week," February 21, 1944. (U. S. AIR FORCE)

October 14 disaster), B-24s to hit Gotha's Me-110 works, and another force to the north to strike at targets in northeastern Germany and Poland (aimed at the FW-190 production). Schweinfurt, with its dreaded reputation, proved to be heavily defended, and the fighter escort was heavily engaged, losing 10 (and claiming 37 enemy aircraft). Bomber claims for German fighters were very high and, if not accurate, at least were an indication of the heavy fighting. Of the 234 Fortresses that dropped bombs on Schweinfurt's ball-bearing works, only 11 were lost.

Of the 239 B-24s dispatched to Gotha, 33 were lost, and bombing was very accurate. The Schweinfurt and Gotha attackers drew off the German fighters from the north, which left the force that was to bomb the FW-190 factory practically untouched.

With the coming of night Harris's Bomber Command contributed its share by sending a force of 734 four-engined bombers (most of them Lancasters) to a still burning Schweinfurt. Air Staff had

finally had its way, although Harris, as usual, had the final word. The loss of 33 aircraft was not prohibitive (though serious enough), but as Harris had so long protested, Schweinfurt was too small a target to hit effectively at night (and too worthless by day). Of the first wave of bombers only 7 were plotted over the target—and of the second wave only 15. More than 300 bombers had placed their bombs within three miles of the ball-bearing works and 30 did not even come near it.

But a further truth was that, despite the day's accuracy and the night's additional damages, however inaccurate, it made little difference to Germany's supply of ball bearings, since nearly half of Schweinfurt's capacity for production had been dispersed since the October raid. But this kind of information was not being furnished to the planners of Argument by Speer and company.

Friday, February 25, 1944, dawned "bright and clear" over nearly every target in Germany. Those selected for attention were the Messerschmitt plants at Regensburg (scheduled for attack by both the Eighth and Fifteenth Air Forces), the Messerschmitt main plant at Augsburg, the ball-bearing works at

Stuttgart, and an Me-110 components factory at Fürth.

The Fifteenth Air Force, with the bulk of its bombers that day committed to targets in Italy, contributed 176 heavies to its portion of the Regensburg strike. It was upon this force that the Luftwaffe concentrated its attack. Previous experience had taught the Germans that fighter escort from the south was not as heavily "laid on" as from the west. The Fifteenth Air Force still lacked the long-legged (i.e., Mustang) fighters. So, with little or no cover during the phase of its deepest penetration and with small (comparatively) forces, added to the decision of the commander of the German Flieger-division 7 (a Generalmajor Huth) to concentrate on the southern force, the Fifteenth lost one fifth—a total of thirty-three bombers—of its attacking force. With its heavy escorts, including the Mustangs, which could furnish cover over targets even as distant as Regensburg, plus a total bomber strength of more than seven hundred, the Eighth Air Force lost 31 aircraft.

Those aircraft which fought through to their primary targets bombed them with what must have been disheartening effect to Speer. Regensburg and Augsburg, particularly, suffered under massive tonnages of bombs (five hundred tons on Augsburg alone). Regensburg had suffered so badly that for a time it was considered not worth salvaging. However, initial digging revealed that despite the rubble and heavy damage to buildings, the important machine tools had hardly been damaged at all.

To close the Big Week the RAF returned to Augsburg on the night of February 25/26, 1944, compounding the destruction to a despairing degree. The Big Week, which was of course named after the event, was terminated by the weather, not because the Allies believed that their work was done.

What "work," in fact, had been done? Had it actually been a "big week"? It was a popular, not official, designation (it was also called "Blitz Week" by airmen). The taciturn British called it nothing special—they were merely "getting on with the war." But for the Eighth and Fifteenth Air Forces, coming at last into their own, it had truly been a big week. More than 3300 Eighth and more than 500 Fifteenth Air Force bombers had attacked Luftwaffe targets and deposited close to ten thousand tons of bombs on them. In the six-day campaign

a total of 226 bombers were lost (damaged bombers that returned to their bases were also written off); 28 fighters were lost.

Strategic targets were hit as they had never been before; if the total objective had not been attained (for the aircraft industry was not wiped out), a great deal of serious damage was done. Production was crippled for several months (fewer, however, than was estimated by Allied intelligence) and measures were taken to counter this inside Germany. The result was that, because of the work of Speer's lieutenant in charge of the aircraft industry, Otto Saur, fighter production actually rose following the Big Week instead of falling.

This did not make the Big Week a failure, however. Besides the damage done to factories and the number of aircraft destroyed on the ground, the Luftwaffe suffered in the air. The experienced German fighter pilots lost in the encounters with the peashooters, particularly the Mustang, were irreplaceable.

The Luftwaffe night bombers were active too during the Big Week. While responsible air leaders called for more fighters to meet the aerial offensive, Hitler demanded retaliation upon English cities. A young though veteran officer, Dietrich Peltz, was selected to serve as *Angriffsführer England* and to direct the attack. Furnished with few aircraft and inexperienced crews, Peltz accomplished very little in his initial attempts during the spring and through 1943, when he could barely raise a force of 100 bombers for a mission. By the beginning of 1944 he had more than 500 bombers (Ju-88s, Dornier 217s, Heinkel 177s, Ju-188s, Me-410s, and a handful of FW-190 fighter bombers), of which about 460 were operational. With these, but still with green crews, Peltz carried out what was called "the Baby Blitz" (January–May 1944).

The weather showed no favoritism and the *Angriffsführer England* complained of its interference with the success of his missions. About the time that the Allies were sending nearly a thousand bombers per mission against Germany, Peltz averaged about two hundred, which concentrated upon London during the Big Week. The great number of incendiaries dropped indicated that the Germans hoped to raze the British capital; announcements which followed the raid—"several hundred aircraft" which dropped "hundreds of thousands" of incendiaries—were so exaggerated that the claims seemed ludicrous, perhaps more for the eager ears of the rancorous Führer than anyone else. The Baby Blitz did damage, killed people, destroyed property (a high percentage of which could hardly qualify as military objectives), but achieved little more than a smile from Hitler.

III

After the Big Week came "Big B."

The advent of the peashooters made this possible;

Fighter pilot Don Gentile with his commanding officer, Donald Blakeslee (right). Latter led the first formations of the 4th Fighter Group's Mustangs to Berlin, March 3, 1944. (U. S. AIR FORCE)

the fighting during the Big Week proved that which everyone knew: there was no such thing as a "flying fortress." Without fighter escort to and from the target as well as target support, the bomber toll would be costly.

It was Göring, after it was all over, who said that the day he saw American fighters over Berlin he knew "the jig was up." It was a sign of military perspicacity which had, until that March 4, 1944, not been readily discernible . . . if then.

The fighters over Berlin were the Mustangs of the 4th Fighter Group (Eighth Air Force) and those of the Ninth Air Force's 354th and 363rd Groups. The 4th Group had evolved from the Eagle Squad-

rons, several of whose members continued to fly with the 4th. Early in January 1944 the 4th was commanded by the brilliant, young (about twenty-seven), pugnacious Colonel Donald Blakeslee. He had succeeded Colonel Chesley Peterson (who, at twenty-three, had been the youngest colonel in the U. S. Army), an Eagle veteran, detached for duty to the Ninth Air Force to assist in its planning for Overlord.

Blakeslee's Mustang may have been the first American Mustang over Berlin, but he did not fire a shot. In fact, the arrival of the Americans over the Reich capital, though epochal, was not as impressive as the newspapers would have had it. The International News Service, reporting from London under the March 4 [1944] dateline, reported the operation, "carried out in 56-below zero cold and covering 1,500 mile round trip distances," as if it had been a true success: "Escorted U.S. Flying Fortresses, plowing through clouds nearly six miles high, staged history's first American bombing attack on the Berlin metropolitan district today." The London *Evening Standard* editorialized to the effect that this daylight assault was "a sign of unshakeable comradeship" of the British and Americans (this was in answer to German broad hintings at disagreements between the Allies).

The first American attempt to reach Berlin actually occurred on March 3, but cloud, piled to nearly thirty thousand feet, caused the mission to be scrubbed except for a few bombings of opportunity targets short of Berlin. It was a bitter disappointment, for among the more "intrepid" pilots it had become a matter of pride and rivalry to be the first over Big B.

Blakeslee was without doubt one of the most intrepid and, since he led the fighters which spearheaded the first combat box of Fortresses in the run over Berlin, was probably the first of the fighters over the city. But thick, high clouds again interfered. Most of the Fortress forces returned to their bases, or bombed targets of opportunity, but the 95th and 100th Bombardment Groups stubbornly continued on to Berlin with Blakeslee's Mustangs countering the Luftwaffe.

Over Berlin, when the Eighth Air Force for the day dwindled down to a mere twenty-nine B-17s (eleven 100th Bomb Group, the rest from the 95th) and around twenty Mustangs (many had been forced to abort because of various mechanical troubles), the Luftwaffe struck. Even these forces were not impressive—the estimate was about thirty to thirty-five Me-109s and FW-109s. Green flares arched from the bombers, indicating enemy fighters were attacking.

Blakeslee led his fighters in on the German attackers. He himself jumped an Me-109 and fastened to its tail; when he pressed the gun nothing happened. His guns had jammed. Cursing, Blakeslee throttled the Mustang, overtook the German plane, and, as he flew alongside, waved to the pilot. The German waggled his wings in wondering gratitude and flipped away. Blakeslee climbed to a position over the clouded battle zone and directed the fighters to the spots of contention.

"The P-51s saved the day," one of the 100th's gunners said—the 100th lost one plane that day. The 95th lost four B-17s. The day's target had been the Bosch electrical plant in a suburb of Berlin, which actually showed through a break in the clouds for a moment or two. But then it covered again and most of the bombs were dropped with the help of radar; very little damage was done, in fact. But the German capital had finally been attacked by American bombers (German propaganda that night announced that the bombers had been turned back before they ever reached Berlin). Göring, apparently, had not communicated his perturbing divinations to Herr Goebbels.

Even so, it was the initial blow in a new phase in the Battle of Berlin—the final phase.

On March 6 the first full-scale attack took place, the targets being the Bosch works, the Erkner ball-bearing plant, and the Daimler-Benz factory, where aircraft engines were produced. These were not the only targets, for it was hoped that the Luftwaffe would come out to protect the *sancta civitas* of Germany. On this Monday, when even the weather momentarily seemed co-operative, the Luftwaffe co-operated also in its most deadly fashion. If German interception had not been very zealous since the Big Week, it was absolutely ardent on the first big mission to Berlin.

The Germans had devised a new tactic in an attempt to deal with the serious problem of the Mustangs over the target. Three *Gruppen* were dispatched as a unit, one to attack the bombers and the other two to engage the fighters. The newer, high-

flying Me-109 (equipped with the latest Daimler-Benz engine) bounced down upon the Mustangs and Thunderbolts, which on this day also made the trip to Berlin. Besides the Messerschmitts the Germans had mustered FW-190s, equipped with cannon and machine guns, as well as the twin-engined fighters (many drawn from the night fighter units) with their rockets fired out of bomber machine-gun range. About two hundred German aircraft met the oncoming American force.

The Fortresses and Liberators were covered in relays by Lightnings, Thunderbolts, and Mustangs across the North Sea and Holland and deep into Germany. The bomber formations stretched over a distance of fifteen miles from lead group to "tail-end Charley" of the last. The Lightnings and Thunderbolts weaved around the bombers to keep within striking distance of the slower-flying Fortresses and Liberators.

The bombers had flown only fifty miles into Germany when the German fighters struck. The high squadron of the 100th Bomb Group took the brunt of the first attack before the Thunderbolts could sweep in to their aid. Looking up from the lead bomber Major Albert M. Elton was shocked to see that of the nine ships in the high squadron, six trailed sheets of flame. More shock was in store, for another great formation—it seemed like fifty—of German fighters tore through the bombers again. The air filled with burning debris as the large planes were forced to leave the formation. Pilots attempted to keep the planes flying level so that the still living among the crews could jump. Bombs were jettisoned across the countryside on the way to Berlin.

Robert Koper of Beloit, Wisconsin, ordered the crew out of his burning B-17 and was the only man aboard when the ship blew up in the air. Jack Swartout, of San Francisco, piloting *Nelson King,* the lead aircraft of the 100th's 351st Squadron, watched an FW-190 come in head on as the guns rattled. He felt the ship shudder—and then a swift lurch. Swartout found the plane difficult to control even with the help of his copilot, F. G. Lauro. The Focke-Wulf had torn off the tip of the vertical fin. Another ship, flown by Richard Helmick, who saw the trouble Swartout and Lauro were in, pulled alongside to give some support to the stricken bomber—always a favored Luftwaffe

The first full-scale mission to Berlin: March 6, 1944, when Luftwaffe fighter pilots fought ferociously. A

Flying Fortress with an engine aflame falls toward Berlin. (U. S. AIR FORCE)

Chief challengers of American daylight bombers: the Me-109 and the FW-190, backbone of the Luftwaffe's fighter force. By 1944, when Allied bombers began attacking Berlin in great numbers, the Messer-

schmitt had just about reached the end of its line; the Focke-Wulf (designed by Dr. Kurt Tank) was a dangerous adversary. It operated also as a fighter-bomber (as did the 190 illustrated).

(IMPERIAL WAR MUSEUM, LONDON)

Robert S. Johnson, one of the high-scoring fighter pilots of the 56th Fighter Group who fought over Berlin. Johnson's final score was twenty-eight (making him the fourth-ranking U.S. ace). He is seen here with his crew chief, Ernest D. Gould. (U. S. AIR FORCE)

target. But Helmick had to abandon his position off Swartout's wing when another burning bomber began falling directly toward his plane, which he pulled out of the way.

Unable to join up with any other planes, Swartout turned *Nelson King* around for the long, lonely flight back to England. Before he left, however, the bomb load was dropped "somewhere in Germany."

For forty-five minutes the battle raged—from eleven fifty-nine when the first German fighters had hit until twelve forty-five—and Elton counted no less than seventeen bombers from the 13th Wing (95th, 100th, and 390th Groups) which went down aflame. And Berlin was still a half hour away. In vain, it seemed to the hard-hit groups of Elton's wing, did they look for their own fighters. One lone Thunderbolt flashed through the formation on the tail of an FW-190. The Thunderbolts that had been weaving above them when the Germans arrived were off fighting in another part of the sky.

It was over Berlin that the flak thickened as, for ten seconds, the bombers held a steady course on the bomb run. And on the edge of the flak zone the German fighters waited for the cripples. Mustangs and Thunderbolts tore into the German

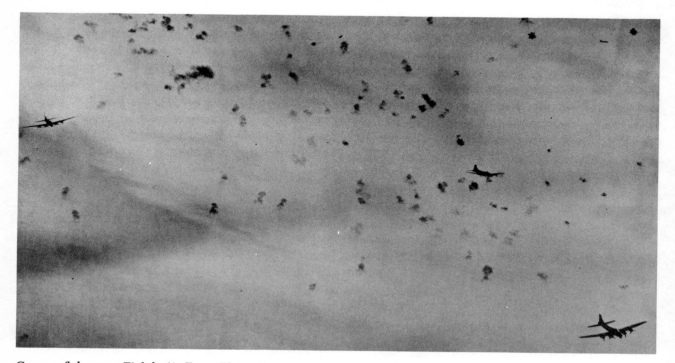

German flak greets Eighth Air Force Flying Fortresses over the target. (U. S. AIR FORCE)

fighters, but there seemed an overwhelming number of them and they fought recklessly, with determination and with seeming desperation. If the men in the bombers did not see the American fighters as often as they would have wished, the Luftwaffe saw them.

The 56th Fighter Group (commanded by Colonel Hubert Zempke) made its first trip to Berlin that day in its Thunderbolts. Leading A Section himself, Zempke assigned B Section to a young Oklahoman, Robert S. Johnson. Each section consisted of thirty-five P-47s. Over Berlin they joined their archrivals, the 4th Fighter Group in their sleeker Mustangs—which the pilots referred to as "kites"—to take on the Luftwaffe.

If the October 14 mission to Schweinfurt could be called "Black Thursday," the March 6 Berlin attack was definitely "Blue Monday" for both sides. Sixty-nine heavy bombers of the 660 which bombed did not return to their bases in England and 11 fighters were lost in the melee. Bomber crews claimed they had shot down no less than 97 German fighters of all descriptions—the fighters claimed a more modest 82. As was inevitable in such a widespread battle, duplications of claims were made, especially by bomber gunners. But postwar evaluations of German records put the German losses for the day at 80, almost half of its attacking force. The loss in pilots was even more serious than the loss of aircraft.

When the bombers returned two days later, the effect of Monday's fighting was obvious. As 462 bombers dropped their loads on the Erkner bearing factory in a nearly clear sky few German fighters ascended to contest the privilege. Over 170 Mustangs, in turn, were on hand to protect the big friends. Consequently, most of the 37 bombers that fell that day had been flak-ed. But the Erkner friction-bearing factory was hit hard and with chilling precision. Berlin Radio was not advertising that, but it did announce that "a large number of enemy planes were destroyed" over Berlin and admitted that "Berlin has become the front line of the air war."

Hitler, however, was not listening.

The Big B had been attacked and rapidly lost its glamour; like Schweinfurt and Ploesti it stood for heavy losses even if from time to time it appeared that the Luftwaffe had gone under. Soon the more defiant bomber crews sang a bitter song:

Don't take my boy to Berlin,
The dying mother said;
Don't take my boy to Berlin,
I'd rather see him dead.

IV

Captain Don S. Gentile, of Piqua, Ohio, one of Blakeslee's 4th Fighter Group hot-shots, was quoted in the *Stars and Stripes* after the March 6 Berlin mission as saying that "There were so many planes up there today that we were choosy about which ones we shot down."

This was considered a characteristic remark to attribute to a spoiling-for-a-fight fighter pilot, although difficult to assign with any certainty to Gentile. He was not given to such quotes. He was not clever and witty as were so many young pilots; Gentile's chief concern was to shoot down more enemy aircraft than any other pilot in the Air Force.

The 4th Group, with its comparatively long history, its Eagle Squadron traditions, and its youthful pride and combativeness, radiated a glow of cockiness, love of battle, competitiveness (among themselves and with the 56th Fighter Group, Zempke's "Wolfpack"). More typical of the general outlook of the 4th was a sentence penned by Captain Allen

A 384th Bomb Group Fortress, its tail sheared by flak, follows the group's bombs into Berlin.

(ROBERT CHAPIN)

Milestone: a special photograph taken of the first airmen of the 384th Bomb Group who bombed Berlin —and returned. (ROBERT CHAPIN)

Bunte, who after a battle had closed his official report with the words: "I claim one Me-109 destroyed and one hell of a lot of intrepidity."

Bunte, originally from Eustis, Florida, though never fated to become one of the aces, was one of the 4th's reliables. His intrepidity never deserted

him. Early in April 1944, while on a sweep deep inside Germany shooting up German airdromes, his Mustang struck a high-tension wire and burst into flame. Spotting a nearby lake, Bunte extinguished the fire by the simple expedient of splashing the Mustang into the water. His squadron (334th) mates assumed that was the end of Bunte. The plane nosed into the lake and sank. The impact knocked Bunte unconscious, but though under water he managed to come to in order to free himself of seat belt and chute harness. In time he surfaced, half inflated his dinghy, floated to a tree in the lake, and eventually staggered ashore.

There he was found by that rare human in those days, the "good" German, who wrapped him in a blanket, gave him a cigarette, and delivered him to the Luftwaffe and captivity.

In a galaxy of stars, it was Gentile who seemed to outshine the rest, even the redoubtable Blakeslee. Blakeslee, in fact, though a fine pilot, was not a marksman (he still managed to shoot fifteen enemy aircraft out of the air and to destroy two on the ground); his forte was that intangible, "aggressive leadership." Blakeslee spent more than three years leading his men into battle and, in his case at least, back. He carefully doctored his flight time,

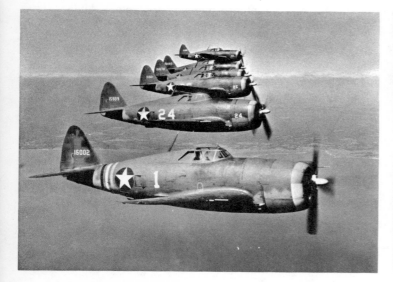

The Republic P-47 "Thunderbolt" (or "Jug" to fighter pilots), one of the toughest and most versatile aircraft of the Second World War. The early model D (left), the so-called "Razorback," arrived in England in the

spring of 1943; the later bubble canopy was introduced in the D models, as were other innovations to increase range and speed of climb. The P-47N (right) was the long-range model (actually designed for Pacific operations). (B. B. GILKES; REPUBLIC AVIATION)

cutting a few hours here and there (or not at all when serving with a unit other than the 4th) so that he survived over a thousand hours of combat time. Blakeslee was a born warrior.

Gentile's chief rival in the 4th Group was the youthful Duane W. Beeson of Boise, Idaho. At nineteen Beeson enlisted in the Royal Canadian Air Force (1940), and later the 71st Eagle Squadron. He transferred into the 4th Fighter Group in September 1942, along with the other Eagle veterans, Gentile, Blakeslee, Howard Hively, Oscar Coen, et al. The 4th took over an RAF base at Debden, where they lived—because it was a permanent station—in comparative luxury.

The major discomfort seems to have been the change from the dainty Spitfire to the bulky Thunderbolt. Accustomed to the lighter British aircraft, the ex-Eagles found the heavy "Jug" not much to their liking. The P-47, like all untried planes, had its share of bugs and the "prima donnas" (as the 4th Group men were thought to be) found all of them. When he knocked down an FW-190 in a diving fight, Blakeslee was congratulated on the fact that he had proved the P-47 could outdive a Focke-Wulf. "It ought to dive," he is supposed to have said; "it certainly won't climb."

Blakeslee, using his persuasive powers, coaxed Major General William Kepner, head of the Eighth Air Force's Fighter Command, into acquiring some Mustangs for the 4th. At this time the P-51s were going to the Ninth Air Force fighter groups in expectation of tactical support for the coming invasion of *Festung Europa*. Blakeslee talked well for his group and acquired the P-51s in time for the initial assaults on Berlin by the Eighth Air Force. Since the Mustang more closely resembled the Spitfire than the P-47, the 4th Group pilots who had flown the English plane had little trouble in making the transition. Blakeslee promised Kepner that he would have his Mustang group in the air twenty-four hours after delivery of the new fighter. To his pilots he merely stated, "You can learn to fly them on the way to the target."

On the other hand, the 4th's friendly enemies, the 56th Group, equipped with the Thunderbolt, did very well with it. Zempke's Wolfpack led all the other fighter groups in Europe in the number of enemy aircraft destroyed. This did not sit well with the 4th Group pilots, who darkly hinted that

North American P-51 "Mustang," the favored aircraft of the 4th Fighter Group. (B. B. GILKES)

while they remained with the bombers as they were supposed to, the 56th went off hunting the "wily Hun" individually. Also, because the 56th was based closer to the English coast than the 4th, the Wolfpack had more time (i.e., more fuel) to spend over the battle area. These were, of course, rationalizations, but they do reveal the curious philosophy which grew out of keeping "kill" scores. When Gentile spoke of being "choosy" about which planes were to be shot down, he may not have been merely tossing off a printable phrase. But woe to the man who had chosen the wrong plane. One fighter pilot, at least, was nearly court-martialed for shooting down his commanding officer's enemy plane. Since the CO was the number one and the fighter pilot was his wingman, or number two in pecking order, the plane they were attacking belonged, according to unwritten law, to number one.

The more zealous pilots were known to remove a fellow squadron member off the tail of an enemy by shouting the warning word "Break!", the signal that an enemy was getting onto your own tail. When you took evasive action, your savior moved in and shot down your victim. It was all in the game.

Beeson and Gentile never, as far as is known, stole from one another, but each followed the other's scores after missions—just as Bong and McGuire had in the Pacific. Beeson was the more volatile personality, more obviously aggressive, while Gentile revealed little emotion or anxiety. Both men raced neck and neck for several months, approaching the magical Rickenbacker number of twenty-six, until the Germans settled the question once and for all. Leading a low-level mission against a German airdrome in April 1944, Beeson was hit by flak, bailed out, and spent the next thirteen months in Stalag Luft I (with some time spent in solitary for having addressed one of his captors as a "Hun").

On the day that Beeson and the intrepid Bunte went down, Gentile had destroyed five German planes on the ground, which officially brought his score to thirty. (In the European theater enemy aircraft destroyed on the ground received official recognition; according to the American Fighter Aces Association, which recognizes only "aerial victories" against "piloted aircraft," Gentile's final score was 19.84—whatever that means.)

What it did mean was that the youthful (he was then twenty-four) pilot received newspaper space not only in his home town, but all across the United States—and even in England (where the official attitude toward aces continued to be aloof). Gentile was wooed by writers (Ira Wolfert literally moved into Gentile's room, there being a vacancy because his former roommate, Lieutenant Spiro Pissanos, had been forced down in France and taken prisoner). Other correspondents arrived to bring Gentile the attention and fame he had never conceived was possible. He found himself a celebrity with people bidding for his story, girls for his favors, and superior officers for his proximity. It was a heady life.

Gentile's combat record, he was the first to admit, was not entirely of his own making. If the PROs (public relations officers) tended to stress the individual achievements, for the simple reason that the public preferred its heroes singly, the pilots realized that, except for unusual incidents, practically every aerial victory was a two-man job. The wingman concept was an effective lifesaver and equally effective as an enemy destroyer.

Gentile had formed an interchangeable wingman team with a peer, John T. Godfrey. That grand phrasemaker, Winston Churchill, called Gentile and Godfrey "the Damon and Pythias of the twentieth century." But their friendship was purely military. It was so effective that legend has it that Göring said he would exchange two squadrons for the capture of Gentile and Godfrey.

While they were rivals, the two men in battle were all business and operated with a unique give-and-take which enabled them to survive for so long (Gentile was taken out of combat and Godfrey also, though the latter returned and was eventually shot down and taken prisoner; he finally escaped near the end of the war).

Working together the two pilots had developed a technique of interchanging the roles of number one and wingman as the situation demanded. During the March 8, 1944, mission to Berlin the two broke up a large attack upon a Flying Fortress combat box and accounted for six enemy aircraft between them. On the way home, all but out of ammunition, the two men attached themselves to a distressed Fortress, escorting it back to England until they broke off to land at Debden.

This was, of course, their primary function, and it was in this special category that these two young men proved formidable. Godfrey, particularly, had his personal reasons. His P-51, *Reggie's Reply,* was named for his brother, who was lost when his U. S. Navy ship had been sunk by a Nazi U-boat. Besides an exceptional personal motivation Godfrey had extraordinary eyesight—always a valuable asset to the fighter pilot. Quick reflexes and an aggressive spirit, supreme self-confidence, plus the will to excel and,

Don Gentile and John T. Godfrey, Winston Churchill's "Damon and Pythias" fighter team of the 4th Fighter Group, after an escort mission to Berlin.

(U. S. AIR FORCE)

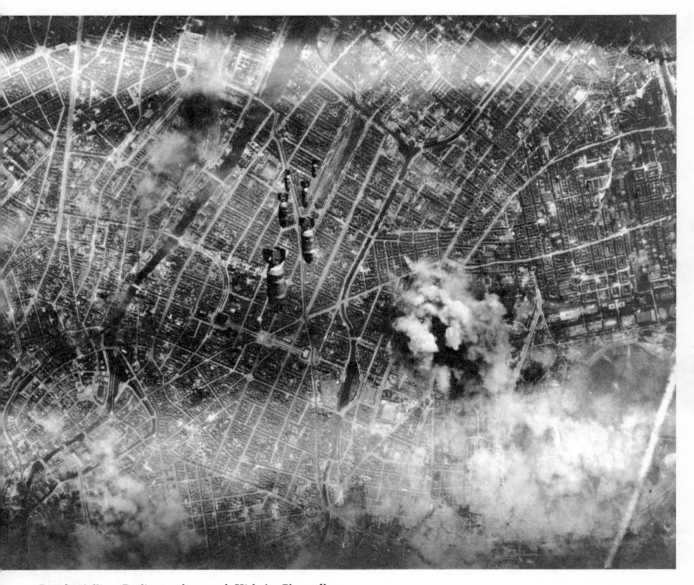

Bombs falling Berlin-ward toward Hitler's Chancellery and Goebbels' Ministry of Propaganda buildings, east of Potsdamer railroad station. (U. S. AIR FORCE)

most of all, to survive combined to produce the kind of pilot both Gentile and Godfrey were.

Youth was an essential because of the physical, mental, and emotional drain of air fighting, not the least of which was sucking on an oxygen mask. The tension immediately preceding a mission as well as the letdown after were debilitating. The blackout which came under the pressures of a fast dive, the recovery (if you recovered), and a sharp skidding turn were never pleasant. The world grew dim around the edges or completely black for a fraction of a moment as the pull of gravity pulled blood away from the brain. Tremendous cold too was a hazard. So was gnawing fear, however much self-confidence the pilot had built up; perhaps he was better than any enemy flier, but there was always the chance that flak would get him. And even the non-superstitious succumbed to the apprehension that at some unknown point luck would run out.

Fighter pilots like Gentile and Godfrey had courage, but they also knew fear—and admitted it. There came the point in their flying careers when even the competition of the "sport" would not sustain them,

Gentile's Shangri-La *sweeping past the photographers —and about to be "pranged," that is, cracked up for no reason at all.* (U. S. AIR FORCE)

when it seemed (especially after a very close call) that surviving one more mission was impossible. Instinct and training and the exhilaration of battle brought the pilot through, but many a very brave man landed at his base and found himself shaking so uncontrollably that he was unable to get out of his plane. There were very few "iron men" like Blakeslee, who seemed impervious to the wear and tear of operations and who fought being taken off combat duty "to fly a desk."

As in the Pacific, star performers in Europe were taken off operations when they acquired a certain notoriety and shipped back to the States for the full treatment—adulation and interviews. Blakeslee had little respect for the celebrity treatment, especially after Gentile, on returning from his last mission, and responding to an audience and a full battery of newsreel cameras, decided to "beat up the field." Near the ground he elected to "fly right into the lens" and succeeded only in "pranging his kite," to Blakeslee the supreme delinquency. After so many missions in his P-51 Gentile managed finally to bounce it into the ground for the benefit of the press. Although he was not seriously injured—still the base doctor saw to it that he was kept out of the reach of Blakeslee for several days—the kite was pranged

indeed, its propeller bent in two directions and its back broken about halfway between cockpit and tail. *Shangri-La* would never fly again.

Blakeslee, who always threatened to throw any man out of the squadron who pranged a kite in a pointless buzz job, was livid. He raged at the newsmen, "You people have just ruined one good man!" Thus ended Don Gentile's last combat mission; since he was scheduled to be taken off operations, it made little difference to his career as a hot-shot combat pilot, although it was an ignominious way to end it. He and Godfrey returned to the United States (just in time to miss out on the "fun" of D-Day). Both were given appropriate greetings by their home towns—Piqua, Ohio (Gentile), and Woonsocket, Rhode Island (Godfrey)—and, to dramatize the efficacy of teamwork in aerial combat, appeared together—both sporting rather dashing mustaches—at War Bond rallies. Gentile was a lion, a role Godfrey did not deny him, but Godfrey soon grew restless and wished to get back to the 4th Fighter Group.

Gentile was denied any chance of returning to

Godfrey and Gentile, back home, doing their War Bond rally circuit. Gentile never returned to combat, but Godfrey was quickly shipped back to Europe after he publicly stated his views about "brass hats."

(U. S. AIR FORCE)

combat; he married and became an Army Air Forces test pilot (like Bong, his Pacific competitor, he was killed while flying a jet). Godfrey may have gotten himself shipped back to Europe because of certain statements he made about the Air Force training system "spoon-feeding" its future combat pilots. The "kid-glove policy by 'brass hats' in this country is endangering the lives of all youngsters now in training camps," he intimated.

"They won't let the kids fly when it's cloudy. They won't let them do this or that—until it makes you ill. They wouldn't let me fly the Ohio River with a two-thousand-foot ceiling. I can remember taking off in England when you jumped straight into overcast and stayed that way up to thirty thousand feet or more. . . ."

This did not sit well with the "brass hats," although taking any truly drastic measures against one of the country's best-known heroes would have been extremely indelicate and risky. So, as phrased by Grover C. Hall, Jr., ". . . his status as outstanding AAF warrior evoked the quality of mercy and it fell as a gentle rain. . . ." Godfrey was told to keep his mouth shut and was permitted to return to combat.

But when he did, early in August of 1944, the Luftwaffe was no longer so much in evidence, and like so many fighter pilots of the Eighth and Ninth Air Force, he took to shooting up trains in lieu of aircraft. Strafing missions were considered more dangerous than escort missions because of the hazards of ground fire and the proximity of the ground itself—not to mention high-tension wires, trees, and other obstacles. While churning up Herzberg airfield in Germany, Godfrey was struck by flak and plowed into the ground. Though he attempted to hide out for a couple of days, he was captured by the Germans. He succeeded in escaping from his Stalag Luft (on his third attempt) and made it back to the Allied lines on April 17, 1945, at Nuremberg. By then the air war was all but over in Europe.

While Gentile and Godfrey were the most celebrated of the 4th Fighter Group's high-spirited crew, there were many others of note also: Duane Beeson, already mentioned; Ralph K. "Kid" Hofer, who liked to hunt on his own and disappeared one day in July 1944 over Hungary; James Goodson, who was known as "the King of the Strafers"; and Howard Hively, Fred W. Glover, Willard Mil-

Gun-camera views of a fighter strafing a German train in the final months of the war, when Luftwaffe planes became scarce. (U. S. AIR FORCE)

"Beware of thin cirrus clouds . . ." *haven of German fighters which pounced upon fighters and bombers. In* *the foreground an H2X ("Mickey")-equipped B-17 accompanies other Fortresses over Germany.*

(CECIL COHEN)

likan, Nicholas Megura, James A. Clark, Kendell E. Carlson, and Pierce W. McKennon, to name but a few more of the dozens of colorful characters of a colorful group.

When the war ended the group was commanded by Colonel Everett W. Stewart. Blakeslee had returned to the States, to other duties and to marriage. When he left the 4th Group, it was with a minimum of emotional display, as befitted the man. But, as a curious sequel to the Gentile incident, the always alert Blakeslee unwittingly revealed his inner feelings during a simple flight after he had been relieved of his command and forbidden to fly in combat. While coming in for a landing, bemused and out of

sorts, he put down but without remembering to lower his landing gear. Blakeslee, the imperturbable, had pranged his own kite.

It was time to go home; and he did.

When the war ended there were fifteen fighter groups in the Eighth Air Force (and eighteen in the Ninth); the entire war effort, obviously, had not fallen on the 4th Fighter Group. It was that this unit closed the war as the highest-scoring group in the ETO (1016 enemy aircraft). Second was its archcompetitor, the 56th Fighter Group, Zempke's famed Wolfpack, with 1006. 5 enemy aircraft destroyed (both in the air and on the ground).

"A fighter pilot must possess an inner urge to do

combat," Zempke once told his men. "The will at all times to be offensive will develop into his own tactics. If your enemy is above, never let your speed drop and don't climb, because you'll lose too much speed. If you're attacked on the same level, just remember you can outclimb him. Beware of thin cirrus clouds—the enemy can look down through them but you can't look up through them. Don't go weaving through valleys of cumulus clouds, either with a squadron or by yourself. The enemy can be on your tail before you know it.

"When popping down out of a cloud, or up, always do a quick turn and look back. You may have jumped out directly in front of a gun barrel. When attacked by large numbers of enemy aircraft, meet them head on. In most cases half of them will break and go down. Handle all those remaining in an all-out fight until you're down to one—then take him on.

"If there are twenty aircraft down below, go screaming down with full force to pick out the most logical target at the point of firing. Then pull up to a good altitude and develop an attack on one of those remaining enemy pilots who had been shaken out of his helmet by your sudden onslaught.

"I stay with the enemy until he is destroyed, I'm out of ammunition, he evades into the clouds, or I'm too low on gas and ammo to continue. When you have your squadron with you and the enemy has so much altitude you never would get up to him, stay below and to the rear of him—he'll be down.

"Learn to break at the proper time to make a head-on attack—the enemy doesn't like it. Don't run. That's just what he wants you to do. When caught by the enemy in large force, the best policy is to fight like hell until you can decide what to do."

Zempke, a forestry major from the University of Montana and a prewar Army Air Corps pilot, happened to be in Russia demonstrating the P-40 to Soviet Air Force pilots when the Japanese attacked Pearl Harbor. During December 1942–January 1943, as commanding officer he brought over the 56th Fighter Group and its massive new Thunderbolt fighter (the P-47B). Zempke's group joined the 78th—which had lost most of its P-38s and pilots to the north African invasion. It too was issued the heavy, ungainly, but powerful P-47.

The Wolfpack went into combat in April of 1943

and by November of that year had exceeded its own goal of a hundred enemy aircraft destroyed by Christmas. It was the first American fighter group in Europe to achieve this score—which was more than mere scorekeeping, for it represented, in the words of fighter commander Major General William Kepner, "an untold number of our bombers . . . saved."

The 56th Fighter Group had its full share of aces, among them Zempke himself. Others included Gerald W. Johnson, Walker Mahurin, David Schilling, Robert S. Johnson, and Francis Gabreski. Zempke, Schilling, and Gabreski were called by the Germans "the Terrible Three," in recognition of their deadliness as fighter pilots.

Gabreski was enrolled as a pre-med student at

Hubert A. Zempke, commanding officer of the 56th Fighter Group—the "Wolfpack." His Thunderbolt is fitted with the new "paddle blade" propeller, which increased the P-47's rate of climb. (JOSEPH ORAVEC)

Notre Dame when he enlisted as an aviation cadet in July 1940; he was commissioned the following March. On December 7, 1941, Second Lieutenant Gabreski was serving with the 45th Fighter Squadron of the 15th Fighter Group and stationed at Wheeler Field, Hawaii. The Japanese bombing and strafing of the field, Gabreski recalls, was "effective." But so was U.S. antiaircraft gunnery later. When he was able to take off some two hours after the attack had begun (and, in fact, was over), Gabreski and the other eleven pilots in their P-40s had their formation broken up over Pearl Harbor by American antiaircraft fire. Gabreski remained with the 15th Group for almost a year (a year of near inactivity) and then was transferred to 8th Fighter Command in England because of "linguistic qualifications." He was able to speak Polish as well as a little Czech.

So for a while Gabreski continued with near inactivity, serving with Intelligence as interpreter. But "I wanted to fly airplanes." That became a clear, rather loud statement after a month, and the Air Force, wishing to keep Captain (as he was by then) Gabreski happy, shipped him to Ferry Command at Prestwick, Scotland, where he flew airplanes, all types, from the B-24 to the P-38.

"It was pretty dull after two months and I started saying 'get me out of Ferry Command!'" Which was easier said than done; Gabreski languished for another month until in November 1942, after a chance meeting with Polish fighter pilots serving with the RAF in London, he got himself transferred to No. 315 Squadron ("Deblin"). Technically Gabreski was assigned as a liaison officer to the Polish Air Force on TDY (temporary duty). Flying the Spitfire, Gabreski participated in twenty combat missions, acquiring good training in aerial combat.

So it was that when the 56th Fighter Group was forming up, Gabreski was ready when asked by Colonel Robert Landry, then lining up "talent" for the group. Gabreski joined the group as the operations officer of the 61st Squadron; in time he commanded this squadron as "Keyworth Blue Leader."

Making the transition from the Spitfire to the Thunderbolt posed no serious problem for Gabreski; he soon learned to love the plane's ruggedness. During an escort mission to Oldenburg, Germany (November 26, 1943), Gabreski was leading a section of the 61st Squadron when he caught sight of a large

formation of Me-110s. These were the rocket-firing fighters which tore up the bomber formations so badly. In turn, the 110s were themselves escorted by single-engined fighters above.

Keyworth Blue Leader immediately swept in to break up the attack. With the squadron behind him, fanning out and selecting their targets, Gabreski made a pass on the Messerschmitts. The Big Thunderbolt tore through the formation and Gabreski kicked it into a turn and looked back to see what the result had been. He spotted a lone Me-110

"Keyworth Blue Leader" Francis Gabreski in his 56th Fighter Group Jug. Gabreski was the third-scoring fighter ace of the war and the number one living ace when the war ended. (U. S. AIR FORCE)

which had broken away from the others and seemed headed for home. Undoubtedly he had made a hit, for the plane had begun a descending spiral.

Gabreski closed in "rapidly, firing on the way. At first I was really wasting ammunition. Then I got a real good burst into the cockpit and the engines. All my guns were bearing on the airplane when—about a hundred yards away—it exploded and instantly decelerated.

"It appeared to me as if I would ram right into him; quickly I pushed forward on the stick. Burned parts of the plane came through the vent system into my cockpit, fragments of the Messerschmitt hit the Thunderbolt, but I managed not to run into an engine."

In seconds Gabreski had swept through the debris and, finding himself still air-borne and his P-47 apparently operational, scanned the battle area. He saw another Me-110 maneuvering into position out of the bomber's gun range in order to begin lobbing rockets. Gabreski throttled the Thunderbolt into position and with a few short bursts sent the second Messerschmitt burning in a steep dive.

Though outnumbered, Gabreski's section had suc-

Gabreski and Steven Garick discussing fighter tactics in England after a fighter sweep over France.

(U. S. AIR FORCE)

ceeded in breaking up the attack by the rocket launchers (for which he was awarded with the Distinguished Service Cross).

It was only after he had returned to his home base at Halesworth that he actually realized what the exploding Messerschmitt had done to his P-47. The wing's leading edges were crushed and the left wing was badly torn. The engine cowling was dented and gouged and the plane was scorched. A 20-mm. shell was lodged in the engine. One cylinder was cracked but not seriously enough to have impaired the engine's efficiency.

Having studied his aircraft, Gabreski walked into

the debriefing session and claimed "two Messerschmitt-110s destroyed and one P-47 half destroyed."

By the summer of 1944 Gabreski had thirty-one aerial victories to his credit—the highest score in the European theater. (His ground-destroyed score was 2.5 officially.) He had accumulated hundreds of hours of combat time and at least a dozen decorations, including those from the Polish, British, and French governments. The air war had changed a great deal in the twenty-one months he had been flying in fighter planes. The war was not over, but it was more difficult to find the Luftwaffe air-borne. Consequently, the fighters went down to the deck to shoot up the Luftwaffe in its own nests, on the ground.

On July 20, 1944, after escorting bombers on a mission, Gabreski led the fighters in an airdrome strafing. This had become customary at this phase of the war. Having spotted the airfield, near Coblenz, Gabreski decided to finish off its parked planes.

If no planes rose to challenge the Thunderbolts, there was plenty of flak. Gabreski dived the big aircraft down to treetop level and began working the field over, leaving a trail of pockmarked concrete in his wake along with burning planes. Racing over the field close to the ground Gabreski found himself "overshooting a plane on the ground. I stuck the nose down a little to get on the target and the propeller hit the ground. Oil sprayed all over my windshield and canopy. . . .

"The engine was obviously failing and this meant I must either belly-land or bail out. But bailing out meant climbing up into the flak. So I found a nearby wheat field and despite excess speed—about one hundred and seventy, two hundred miles an hour—I set the plane on the ground with the wheels up. Just before I struck, I kicked to the side so that the wing crumpled and took much of the shock of the impact.

"Crumpling and crackling, the plane plowed across the field and then stopped. The aircraft was still in one piece—but smoking. That scared me. I tried to open the canopy but couldn't open it more than four or five inches. I removed the parachute but I still couldn't push through the narrow opening. The smoke got thicker and thicker. I was really frightened by that time; my adrenalin was flowing

German fighters burning on their base after American fighter planes strafed the field. (This photo came from the gun-camera of Colonel Ben Rimerman, who destroyed six planes.) (U. S. AIR FORCE)

Thunderbolts "on the deck" (in this photo caught during takeoff). It was at about this height that strafing missions were carried out and during which Gabreski's propeller struck the ground and he ended up in a German POW camp. (U. S. AIR FORCE)

heavily and I managed to pull the canopy open enough so I could jump out and began running from the burning plane. There was a crackle and whistle which I realized was bullets from some troops approaching the plane.

"I outran the troops and moved into a nearby woods, where I found a shelter inside which there was a religious shrine. I hid under the shrine and when the soldiers searched the shelter I was hidden within a foot of the search party.

"After that, for four days, moving only at night, I walked for what I thought was Luxembourg. On the fourth day I became more ambitious and even walked in the daytime. I walked right by a farmer and a little boy with a few cows."

The two immediately set up a hue and cry and within minutes Gabreski was in the hands of the Wehrmacht and on his way to Stalag Luft I at Barth on the Baltic Sea in northern Germany. There he would join the Air Force elite, among them Gerald Johnson of his own 56th Fighter Group, Duane Beeson of the 4th—and, eventually, even Zempke.

Gabreski was turned over to the Luftwaffe and sent to the interrogation center at Dulag Luft. As one of the Terrible Three, his fame had obviously preceded him. He opened the door and walked in to confront the interrogator—"we called him 'Stone Face' Scharrf." The stone face cracked into a smile.

"Well, Colonel, we've been expecting you for a long time."

4

DER GROSSE SCHLAG

WHEN Colonel Hubert Zempke was knocked down at the end of October 1944 he, like Gabreski, was greeted by a Luftwaffe officer with a sense of humor.

"Now," he said beaming, "when we get old Blakeslee, the war will be over."

He was close to the truth; only his reasoning was wrong. The war was over, or should have been, but Hitler refused to concede to the facts. The Germans faithfully fought on, trusting in the intuition of a madman; the slaughter and destruction continued despite the inevitable outcome.

The beginning of the end had finally come with the invasion of Normandy on June 6, 1944—D-Day. Hitler's vaunted Atlantic Wall, despite its various fiendish killing devices, the brain children of that military darling, Rommel, had a hole in it. It was an opening which literally ascended to the skies. On the eve of D-Day the Supreme Commander Dwight D. Eisenhower could say with near certainty to troops about to embark upon what he called a "great crusade," "You needn't worry about the air. If you see a plane it will be ours."

Assaulting the beaches at Normandy, though successful, was no simple walk-in; and had Eisenhower been overly optimistic in his appraisal of the air situation, and had the Luftwaffe been able to lash out in force, the story of the bloody beaches of Normandy would have been tragically bloodier.

Where was the Luftwaffe?

The American GI was pragmatic; he wanted to believe his Supreme Commander, but he would also wait to see how it all turned out. But it was true, except for a few ineffectual fighter sweeps over the landing beaches, there were no German aircraft.

The most persistent inquirer as to the absence of the Luftwaffe was the German soldier, while the beaches churned and seethed under the pounding of Allied naval guns, heavy bombing, medium bombers, and fighter bombers. Sperrle's Luftflotte 3, with headquarters in Paris, could only count on about 320 operational aircraft—and of these only 125 were fighters—to meet the overwhelming sea and air invasion, plus the literally thousands of Allied planes (the American Eighth and Ninth Air Forces alone dispatched 8772 aircraft; to these were added some 5656 by the RAF's Second Tactical Air Force, Air Defence of Great Britain—formerly Fighter Command—Coastal Command, and Bomber Command). Considering the number of aircraft in the air that day, Allied losses were reasonably low—and most could be attributed to flak—reaching a total of 113 (71 American). Only 33 German aircraft were claimed to have been destroyed—an index to the minimal countermeasures attempted by the Luftwaffe.

This was yet another consequence of the Combined Bomber Offensive of the previous winter.

The Normandy beach one month before D-Day. P-38 pilot Albert Lanker of the 10th Photo Reconnaissance Group obtained this "dicing" shot showing the various types of obstacles Rommel had distributed along the coast of France. (U. S. AIR FORCE)

German soldiers scatter as Lanker comes in closer to "dice" the timber ramps, which were mined or armed with saw-toothed blades for dealing with landing craft. (U. S. AIR FORCE)

Lanker photographs gun positions dug into the side of a cliff at Normandy; a pillbox is situated at the bottom of the cliff. (U. S. AIR FORCE)

Before the Normandy landings heavy bombers joined the mediums, and the fighters, in cutting off all arteries —roads and railroads—into the invasion area. A Flying Fortress bombs a rail junction at Versailles two days before D-Day. (U. S. AIR FORCE)

Anxious Luftwaffe chiefs had begun bringing the fighters closer to home to fight off the bombers over Germany. The invasion, which everyone expected any minute, began to take on secondary importance to the protection of the Reich.

On the morning of D-Day Geschwaderkommodore Oberst Josef Priller of Jagdgeschwader 26 commanded three *Gruppen* which had been dispersed all over France. One, I/JG 26, was based at Rheims in northern France; another, III/JG 26, had been flown to Metz, also in northern France, closer to the German border. The third, II/JG 26, had been sent all the way to Gascony in southern France and based near the city of Mont-de-Marsan.

Priller, whose victory score had reached a total of more than ninety "kills," was as outspoken as he was headlong in his fighter tactics. He raged over the dispersal of his units from his base at Lille. With invasion obviously in the air, he bluntly told an officer at Fliegerkorps II that he thought they were all insane; the squadrons they had so stupidly scattered all over France would be needed along the coast. Priller, with a reputation for a hot temper, was permitted to abuse even a general, but was then told that the weather had turned bad on June 5 (the original date set by Eisenhower) and the good days of May had gone by, so there would be no invasion.

At the Lille airdrome Priller, who had remained to oversee the movement of his *Geschwader*'s supplies, records, and ground crews, commanded two aircraft—FW-190As—on the morning of June 6. One of the planes was his; the other belonged to his *Rottenflieger* (wingman), Feldwebel (Flight Sergeant) Heinz Wodarczyk. Angry, disgusted, and certain that something real was brewing, Priller suggested to Wodarczyk that for the moment there was nothing further for them to do except get drunk. Which they did.

He was awakened in the early morning by a

nervous caller from Fliegerkorps II. There was a good deal of air activity and something seemed to be going on in the Channel; perhaps—as a precaution —he should place his *Geschwader* on the alert. Hung over, sleepy, and still disgusted, Priller, once more or less awake, erupted in fine style. Verbally he strafed the Fliegerkorps, then the Luftflotte High Command, on up to Göring himself. Had the fools forgotten that they had ordered all his planes away? His whole damn *Geschwader* at Lille was already on the alert with its total air force of two planes.

"Who the hell am I supposed to alert?" he shouted. "I'm alert. Wodarczyk is alert!" He hung up.

But the phone rang a few moments later. Fliegerkorps again, informing him that all was well, there was no alert, and there would be no invasion. Well, they were wrong again.

The phone rang for the third time just before eight o'clock later that morning. The invasion *was* on. An attempt would be made to get his *Gruppen* back. Meanwhile, could he do something? The two FWs were ready to go, of course—but that readiness was for the trip to join his *Geschwader*. He and Wodarczyk could get down to the invasion area and strafe the beaches. Invading troops would be like sitting ducks to aerial attack. But how many other Luftwaffe planes would be in on the show?

The two men ran to their "Butcher Birds" and before they took off Priller ordered Wodarczyk to stick to him as he had never stuck before. They

might very well be the only German planes over the invasion area—and he did not really expect that they would make it.

The two planes raced southward from Lille and crossed the Somme (near Abbeville they saw great loose formations of Allied fighter planes, but succeeded in skirting them). Near Le Havre, approaching the Normandy beaches, Priller led Wodarczyk into the clouds. Through breaks in the cloud they saw a sight that shook the imagination: thousands of ships dotted the Channel, ships of every description from small, skittering landing craft to great battleships which pounded the beaches with their big guns. The beaches were black with troops, supplies, vehicles, and the debris of battle.

The air was black too: fighters, bombers, supply planes, antiaircraft bursts. But except for their two Focke-Wulfs, there were no German planes. With amazing objectivity, Priller looked upon the impressive sight of Allied endeavor and said, "What a show!"

Their contribution, he knew, would be very small. What with the planes, the ships with their flak, and the barrage balloons, they just might make one pass before they fell.

Coming from the east, the first beaches they came to were those of the British—"Sword," "Juno," and "Gold," a stretch of about fifteen miles.

"We're going in, Wodarczyk," Priller said. "Good luck." He pushed the throttle all the way, eased the control column forward, and hurtled down on Sword beach. Barely a hundred feet over the sand, and racing at more than 350 miles an hour, Priller and Wodarczyk opened up with their machine guns

British-built "Horsa" gliders on June 6, 1944—D-Day —awaiting American air-borne troops to board for France. (NATIONAL ARCHIVES)

Gliders carrying air-borne infantry were towed by C-47s; so-called "snap" takeoff is demonstrated here as the C-47 catches the glider towrope. Glider was then released over the landing areas in France.

radar installations by the RAF had its effect. Then on D-Day itself the heavy onslaught hammered at airfields, destroyed planes on the ground, and furnished close support to the troops on the beachheads. It was not till around eight in the evening —thanks to a breakdown in communications—that the first German reinforcements left Cologne for France. All of twenty-two fighters took off in the twilight with Villacoublay (near Paris) as their destination. The hastily trained pilots got lost in the darkness, ran into Allied fighters, encountered bad weather, and suffered accordingly. Only two of these planes actually arrived at Villacoublay. The rest were shot down, crashed upon landing at advanced bases under Allied attack, or suffered accidents because of pilot error. By the next day—D plus 1—

and cannon. Their unexpected and sudden attack sent men scurrying for cover, but despite the confusion and terror, some fire came back at them. The two planes whipped over the British beaches, the target of countless antiaircraft guns from the ships, and came to the eastern edge of the Americans' "Omaha" beach, where at an altitude of less than fifty feet over the carnage they dodged balloons. Their ammunition spent, Priller and Wodarczyk climbed for the clouds to the south and inland, away from the beaches of Normandy. They had made their pass and were miraculously unscathed. As the two lone aircraft zoomed away from the flak and ground fire, there were men in the British ships who were happy to see them make it after their incredible show of courage.

Priller and Wodarczyk, however, were the only representatives of the once irrepressible Luftwaffe to appear over Normandy on D-Day (a handful of Ju-88s bombed the beachheads during the night). All the "conquests, glories, triumphs, spoils" had "shrunk to this little measure."

There had been plans and promises: when the invasion came the *Oberkommando der Luftwaffe* would dispatch reinforcements to Sperrle for meeting it on the beaches. But preinvasion strafing and bombing of airfields and particularly of German

A Marauder of the Ninth Air Force passes over Allied landing craft headed for the beaches of Normandy. The B-26 is painted in special invasion stripes, making it easier to identify by ship crews and ground troops.

only one of the original twenty-two aircraft was still operational.

Aerial activity on D-Day, and for days following, was one-sided; the Allies had complete air superiority. A German soldier could write home that "the American fliers are chasing us like rabbits." So were British Mustangs and Typhoons pursuing troops as well as paralyzing troop movements by rail and road. Bridges too were destroyed if no vehicles were found. (For weeks in advance of the invasion railroads and bridges over which reinforcements might have come into Normandy were also destroyed. So, of course, were other such targets in other areas, so as not to give away the location of the landing areas. However, on the night before the invasion, leaflets were dropped from Allied planes

Flying arsenal: a Marauder of the 386th Bomb Group moves in on an objective literally bristling with guns. Note the cut-out gun position below the tail; also the forward firing guns just below the wing—and a bomb about to fall from the bomb bay. (U. S. AIR FORCE)

The business end of a Hawker "Typhoon"; a fighter-bomber of considerable impact, particularly in low-altitude operations against trains and troops.
(IMPERIAL WAR MUSEUM, LONDON)

advising the French inhabitants to get out of the general zones of invasion.)

Field Marshal Rommel had hoped to catch the invaders on the beaches and, with sufficient reinforcements, stop them at the water's edge. But when he called for additional Panzer forces, these were denied him. Hitler had ordered that no panzers could be used without his permission. Thus as the Allied bridgehead widened and deepened and the German commanders phoned frantically, Hitler slept. He did not awaken until three in the afternoon, when he did grant permission to Rommel to add the 12th SS Panzer and the Panzer Lehr divisions to his already available 21st Panzer Division, which had begun moving into Normandy from the vicinity of Caen.

But it was too late; reinforcements were harried by Allied aircraft and did not arrive in force until June 9; by this time, in the words of Rommel's chief of staff, Hans Speidel, "the initiative lay with the Allies." And they had come, despite Hitler's wishful thinking, to stay. Within three weeks of landings thirty-one Allied squadrons were operating from airfields in and around the beachheads. Traveling over the roads of France was a hazard. By the end of July seventeen of the Ninth Air Force's eighteen fighter-bomber groups were operating from

Normandy airstrips—gashed through the hedgerows —to join the various tactical aircraft—fighters and medium bombers—of the RAF and the U. S. Air Force.

No one was safe, not even generals. In the afternoon of July 17, 1944, as he raced in an open staff car on a return trip to his headquarters after visiting various trouble spots, Rommel was attacked by Spitfires of No. 602 Squadron. The planes dived on the car, driving it off the road, where it overturned. Rommel, flung from the car, suffered a fractured skull. Although he survived the serious injuries, Rommel later committed suicide as an alternative to standing trial for high treason for his complicity in a plot on Hitler's life which occurred three days later.

On July 10—the day Gabreski went down—an attempt was made to kill Hitler with a bomb. It failed in its primary purpose, although several high officials then in Hitler's bunker were killed, among them Jeschonnek's successor, Luftwaffe General Gunther Korten. He, in turn, was to have been succeeded by Werner Kreipe. The latter, however, because of certain mannerisms was known around Führer headquarters as "Fraulein" Kreipe. Hitler would not hear of his appointment (although Kreipe had proved himself a competent staff officer), dismissing the idea with the remark that he would not "have any woman around the place."

The job fell to General Karl Koller, once a staff officer of Luftflotte 3 (during the Battle of Britain) and then serving as Chief of Operations of the Luftwaffe. Koller was experienced, capable, and all but totally fed up with the Reichsmarschall. He was summoned to Karinhall, Göring's country estate not far from Berlin. The setting was mythical, a sprawling hunting lodge gone baroque beyond the wildest dreams of an extravagant prince. Göring named it for his first wife, a Nordic (Swedish) beauty who had been a particular favorite of Hitler and who, if possible, exceeded him in virulent anti-Semitism. Karinhall thus became a shrine to her (for a time the first lady of the Reich) and a symbol of Göring's position in the government. In time he had Karin's body removed from its grave in Sweden and placed in a magnificent vault at Karinhall. Her macabre proximity seemed not to upset Göring's second wife, a former actress, Emmy Sonnemann.

As the war turned more sour, Göring could be found more frequently in the comfortingly medieval setting, away from the realities of the twentieth century.

The great main hall of Karinhall was dominated by a massive stone fireplace; the log walls prickled with antlers of such stags as were unlucky enough to have run into the Great Hunter (one of Göring's official titles was that of Reich Master of the Hunt). The skins of bear decorated the floor.

Koller, embittered and driven by the realities, found such trophies uninteresting. When Göring told him that he wished to appoint Koller chief of staff of the Luftwaffe, he assumed that Koller's reluctance to accept was attributable to the fact that he had not been asked before. Koller than asked if he could speak frankly. Göring granted permission.

Although he did not use the colorful language Priller employed, Koller was as blunt as Galland in his criticism of his chief. Göring had not shown his face in the Luftwaffe operations headquarters in a year. He kept in touch only by phone, and at that, it was all too frequently through an adjutant and not directly. Also, Koller had a large file of unanswered telegrams sent to Göring, requesting decisions on important matters. As a precaution, these were filed in the official War Diary—a complete record in an official state paper of Göring's abandonment of his authority and duty.

Göring's heavy head was by then buried in his hands. Whimpering and moaning, he finally pleaded, "Koller, you must help me. You must accept. I'll be good, I promise."

Koller accepted, later admitting that when Göring was contrite he was "irresistible." The Luftwaffe had a new, hardheaded chief of staff, but did the *Chef des Generalstabs der Luftwaffe* have an air force? When Koller assumed his duties, he too might very well have asked the one great question of D-Day: "Where is the Luftwaffe?"

II

The Luftwaffe had been frittered away in the Battle of Britain, had been squandered in the Russian offensive, and was being consumed by the Allied air offensive. And when Hitler elected to activate Barbarossa, the Russian sneak attack, he

Wo ist die Luftwaffe? *Lightnings, in invasion stripes, on the prowl. This kind of formation would have been* *near suicide had there been a Luftwaffe to worry about.* (U. S. AIR FORCE)

Henschel 123s in Russia; during the early months of Barbarossa even such obsolete aircraft as these were more than a match for the inferior Russian Air Force. These aircraft, also of the Stuka class, were used for dive-bombing. (H. J. NOWARRA)

Hans von Seeckt at the Kazan tank schools and at Lipesk's aviation center. The wheels of a blind but inexorable justice turned greedily, for if Hitler bestowed, Russia absorbed: men, tanks, and aircraft.

Barbarossa, which erupted on June 22, 1941, marked the final resurgence of the Stuka, that unlovely harbinger of blitzkrieg. By this late date it would have seemed improbable that yet another classic blitzkrieg could be executed successfully. But it was, despite the warnings through British sources in Moscow and the near-pathological suspicion with which Stalin regarded an ally; he trusted his friend Hitler until the Heinkel 111s bombed Russian airfields and three great German army groups moved along a front stretching two thousand miles. With first light the Stukas came to bomb the airfields and to assist the panzers. In the first day an estimated two thousand Russian aircraft were destroyed, most of them on the ground. It was like a repeat of the Polish campaign.

Heinkel 111 bombing up for a mission in Russia.
(H. J. NOWARRA)

Heinkel bomber on the way to its target in Russia.
(H. J. NOWARRA)

placed the German war machine in a precarious position: war on no less than three fronts. The major front, of course, lay in the east, where the objective was "to vanquish Soviet Russia in a swift campaign."

No less than four *Luftflotten,* comprising nearly two thousand operational warplanes—two thirds of Germany's aerial strength at the time—were unleashed by Barbarossa. It was overwhelming, swift, surprising, and ironic. For Hitler now returned, with interest, to the Russians the Stukas and panzers which had been fostered there in the heyday of

The Polikarpov I-16, which first saw combat in the Spanish Civil War, later in the little-known war between Japan and Russia (May 1939–June 1940), and later on the Eastern Front after the launching of Barbarossa. Called Mosca *("Fly") by friend and* Rata *("Rat") by foe, the I-16 was one of the world's first modern fighters. Conceived in 1932 and first flown late in 1933, the I-16 could boast several advanced design ideas for the time, including a retractable landing gear. Though a tough plane to take off with and land, it was good in flight. By 1941, however, it was obsolescent.* (NAVY DEPT., NATIONAL ARCHIVES)

The Russians fought courageously, but poorly led and ill equipped, they fell back under the onslaught. Russian aircraft, most of them obsolete, were no match for the Me-109, particularly the new "F" model. Even the Stuka was capable of dealing with such aircraft as the Polikarpov I-15, a biplane with a fixed landing gear (the I-153 was a variant of the same plane with a retractable undercarriage). The "Rata" (Polikarpov I-16) was a more formidable, though also outdated, fighter plane, and while it could deal with the Stuka, it was no match for the Messerschmitt.

It would have appeared then that the Great Military Thinker had done it again. The German war machine rolled practically unchecked into Russia, averaging as much as ten miles a day. By September the German armies had pushed hundreds of miles into Russia all along its broad front. The Russians had fallen back, were taken prisoner or killed; Russian casualties totaled into the millions. By late September, although German forces were practically at the gates of Moscow, the Russians gained an inestimable ally, "General Winter." By December it was obvious to all but Hitler that the new blitzkrieg had failed. As if to assure the ultimate failure, he appointed himself the Supreme Commander of the German forces on December 16; by this time, thanks to Japan, Russia had yet another ally of which it could be suspicious: the United States.

Both the Luftwaffe and the Russian Air Force were tied down to their armies; but Russia enjoyed one advantage. Its British and American allies, however suspect, employed strategic air forces. Germany had no such advantage. Even though the Russian air forces were virtually destroyed in the first phase of the blitzkrieg, the Germans were not capable of destroying the Urals factories deep inside Russia. The "Urals Bomber" (the four-engined Ju-89 or the

The Russian Yak-9, one of the newly developed Soviet fighters that proved capable of taking on the Luftwaffe. (U. S. AIR FORCE)

Do-19) which Wever had projected simply did not exist when it was needed. Despite Barbarossa Russian aircraft production rose sharply. It took time, but the Russians, particularly with the aid of General Winter, rammed the German war machine right back to Berlin.

Barbarossa was not proving to be the "swift" war Hitler had foreseen. During the spring and summer the Germans would revive the offensive, only to have winter set in again. Operations of aircraft became nearly impossible because of the ferocious cold. Vehicles froze to the ground, engines not kept running did not run again, some burst when the water-cooling system solidified. Planes skidded on icy landing strips, many crashed in the fog, others simply disappeared and were never heard from again. While the Wehrmacht and the Luftwaffe remained frigidly immobile, the factories of the Urals turned out new tanks—the powerful T-34—and new aircraft—the Lavochkin 5, the Yakovlev 9, and the Ilyushin 2 ("Sturmovik")—to which were added Hurricanes, Tomahawks, and Airacobras.

The Luftwaffe suffered further loss of numbers

—again to Hitler's ambitions—when Kesselring was withdrawn from the Russian front and sent to the Mediterranean as Commander in Chief, South and other units were withdrawn to reinforce the defenses of the Reich, under attack by both the RAF and the U. S. Air Force.

When winter came in 1942 it was obvious to all but its author that Barbarossa was a serial, not a short story, and that the ending would be sad. The summer offensive had brought the Sixth Army of General Friedrich Paulus up to the Volga, just north of Stalingrad. But once there, with troops exhausted, supply lines long, and forces thin, Paulus ran out of steam. The Luftwaffe, lacking numbers, was reduced to purely support actions in conjunction with the infantry or artillery. Bombers were employed as transports, carrying supplies to troops. When Paulus suggested that the Stalingrad front be withdrawn so that his flanks would not be exposed, Hitler replied, "I will not leave the Volga!"

He was not, of course, actually there. Paulus was, and with his armies composed of reluctant Rumanian, Italian, and Hungarian troops, besides Germans, he feared the consequence of the Russian winter offensive. In brief, the consequence was that twenty-two German divisions were encircled in and around the rubble of what had been Stalingrad. Hitler, in spirit, stood fast on the Volga.

His pleas for permission to withdraw having been denied, Paulus next had the problem of supplying 250,000 men. This would require some seven hundred tons of material each day: How was he to keep Hitler on the Volga if his troops were starving, freezing, and out of ammunition and fuel?

Hitler solved that too. He cornered Göring at a situation conference at the Führer headquarters and told the Luftwaffe chief that unless the Sixth Army could be supplied by airlift at Stalingrad the army was lost.

Göring, anxious to get back into Hitler's good graces after so many Luftwaffe "failures," answered, "We will do the job!" Göring, so out of touch with any practical operation of the war, had no idea of what he promised. At the time, no air force in the world was capable of airlifting such tonnages every day, even in the best of climates. Over the protests of several men wiser than he, among them Jeschonnek and Von Richthofen (who termed the whole idea as "stark, staring madness"),

Göring ordered the Stalingrad airlift to begin. It was hoped that at least three hundred tons could be taken into the surrounded area every day, but even that, despite heroic efforts on the part of the Luftwaffe, was never realized.

Aircraft fell to the weather, to the resurgent Russian Air Force, especially to such aces as Alexander Pokryshin and Ivan Kojedub, accident—and "madness," for Hitler ordered Paulus to hold Stalingrad to the end. Paulus, who *was* on the Volga, surrendered on February 2, 1943. Hitler never forgave him for not committing suicide. Of his army only ninety thousand men remained—the entire army was lost and with it went enough aircraft for an entire *Fliegerkorps,* close to five hundred—most of them Ju-52s and He-111s. And with these aircraft went more than two thousand men.

After the calamity of Stalingrad the Germans were able to attempt only one more summer offensive (July 1943), with the Luftwaffe replenished—at the cost of the reserve strength in Germany. But by this time the Soviet Army had been welded into a huge, powerful, relentless weapon. By winter a

A German air base in Russia following a bombing attack by the Soviet Air Force, which destroyed Ju-52 *transports sorely needed to airlift supplies to the tottering Wehrmacht.* (H. J. NOWARRA)

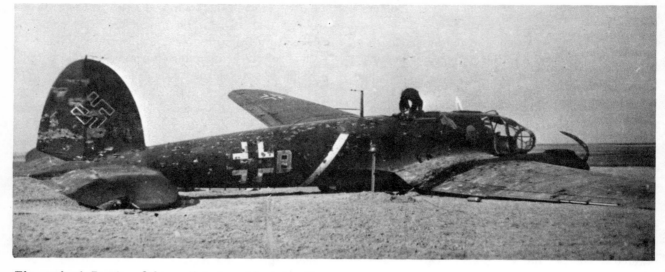

The zeal of Russian fighter pilots is evident in this badly shot-up He-111. (H. J. NOWARRA)

broad wedge had been driven into the German positions across the Dnieper River. The Russian offensive refused to be halted and by the summer of 1944 the Crimea and Leningrad were free of German troops and Soviet forces entered Rumania. The Germans and, more ominously, the Russians pursuing them were on the way to Berlin. By July 12, 1944, the Berlin Radio could warn its people, "The enemy is at the gates of the Reich!"

The Luftwaffe had failed the Führer again, despite the sacrifices of the summer before, when no less than seventeen hundred planes had been scraped away from the defense of the homeland and the broiling Mediterranean. That had been done at a time when the fighters especially might have been put to good use in Sicily or over Hamburg of *Die Katastrophe*. Hitler could not grasp the reasons behind the failure of the Luftwaffe, whose strength he had dissipated over the entire, all but interminable Russian front, where it was at the mercy of German ground commanders from one end of the line to the other, demanding the services of tired aircrews and tired aircraft.

It was also at the mercy of growing numbers of Russian and other Allied fighters. Where, indeed, was the Luftwaffe now that the barbarians menaced the very gates of the fatherland?

It was, by the summer of 1944, outnumbered, outgunned, outmanned, and outdated. The fate of the

Stuka, obsolete since the Battle of Britain, was representative of the entire German Air Force.

The Stukas, like most German aircraft (and Russian, for that matter), were confined to ground-support roles. Despite the improvement in Russian aircraft, the Stuka still operated as an effective tank buster. In the summer of 1944 the Stuka had returned to Poland—and so had the Russians. The indestructible Hans-Ulrich Rudel, veteran of literally thousands of operational flights, was stationed with his Stuka Geschwader 2 near the Polish town of Mielec, about sixty miles east, and slightly north, of Krakow.

Not only did Rudel's Stukas have to contend with Russian tanks and aircraft, they had also begun to run into American Mustangs. This too symbolized the approaching end. On July 25, 1944, Rudel encountered a formation of P-51s and for the first time in his career ordered his Stukas to jettison their bombs, abandon their mission, and return to Mielec.

Rudel's own account of this encounter (in *Stuka Pilot*) is curious. According to his count there were "nearly three hundred of them." He succeeded in bringing his fifteen Stukas back to his base but heard that "a neighboring unit suffered heavy losses from this huge formation of Mustangs."

At this time there was a total of fifty-eight Mustangs operating in Russia, the fighter cover for seventy-six P-38 fighter-bombers that had come from Italy on a shuttle bombing mission. While the heavy bombers bombed Ploesti, the P-38s with their P-51 cover attacked other Rumanian oil fields, after which they continued on to Russian airfields.

Flying top cover for the P-38s delighted the P-51 pilots, who harbored little love for the twin-boom plane. Ernest Shipman, a very young Mustang pilot with the 31st Fighter Group (307th Squadron), was already an ace when he took part in the battle Rudel had witnessed. Like his squadron mates Shipman resented the "condescending attitude" of Lightning pilots. The fact that some P-38 pilots had already shot down Mustangs (apparently mistaking them for Me-109s) added to the natural animosity.

How it felt to be very young and a fighter pilot flying the "fastest in-line fighter in the world" was preserved in a contemporary diary kept by Shipman. He was a typical young American air enthusiast who had avidly read the adventures of *G-8 and His Battle Aces;* at the same time he was a thorough student of tactics.

Hans-Ulrich Rudel, whose specialty was destroying Russian tanks in a Stuka; he is also credited with the destruction of eleven Russian aircraft. (H. J. NOWARRA)

"On this particular day [July 25, 1944]," he wrote, "we [flew] top cover for one of the two P-38 groups while it strafed a German airfield in Poland [this was Mielec]. We stayed around until the 38's left the field after starting a number of fires and then left for home ourselves.

"We were quite close to the front on the German side and the German army was in full retreat. There wasn't a cowpath that wasn't clogged with men and vehicles. Our guns were full of ammunition and the enemy was literally crawling over the ground below us, but we did not attack. This was because of the orders that had come down to us from the top. As you can guess our mission to Russia was to impress the Russians with the power and glory of the American air forces rather than to impress the Germans. We were to go to Russia in one piece, fly pretty formations and come home in one piece."

The mission had not been mounted as a troop-strafing one. The squadron leader, therefore, did little more than acknowledge the comments of his pilots who noted the presence of enemy troops below. He did not order an attack. But, as Shipman phrased it, "popular opinion swung it and we went down after them. After three passes we pulled up and headed for home.

"We were on course for about half an hour when somebody called in Enemy Aircraft. Col. [Yancey] Tarrant, the group C.O., immediately got nasty on the radio and said we were over the Russian lines, the planes we saw were probably Russian, and to stop clowning around. He was apparently more worried about our looking intact for the Russians than putting some of the enemy out of commission. How he knew whether the planes that had been spotted were friendly or not I shall never know for he was leading another squadron that was completely out of sight of us."

The moment Tarrant's voice went off the air, another cut in.

"Russian, hell—those planes are Stukas!"

At the same instant Shipman saw them, "black angular ships swooping low over what appeared to be a mill by the side of a stream. One look convinced me that our squadron, which numbered twelve ships that day, was heavily outnumbered. But on the other hand the enemy ships were Stukas, a flock of sitting ducks.

"The enemy planes were dive bombing in threes,

a stunt I had never seen before. The building they were attacking shuddered with the impact of their bombs as each wave pulled up from its bomb run. We were at 2000 feet and approaching at what was about 10 o'clock to them. Brown [the squadron leader] pulled down in a diving turn to the left and the rest of us followed. What happened in the next five minutes will always be a little confused in my mind."

The Ju-87 Stuka, which enjoyed a temporary resurgence as a battle plane in Russia, but then once again was fated for slaughter by the newer Russian fighters and the American Mustang. (U. S. AIR FORCE)

The Mustangs bounced the Stukas, Shipman estimated, about three or four waves behind the lead bombers hurtling three abreast upon the Russian building (probably a small factory). The American planes had by then been seen by the Germans, for they immediately began jettisoning their bombs. Even with the diminished weight, the Stuka was a poor contender, lacking speed although capable of making abrupt turns. Shipman had dived into the formation and found himself on the tail of a Stuka.

"My first burst went wild but a little correction put my guns on the target. In spite of the hits I was getting on the fuselage, the ship ahead of me showed no ill effects. I fired again. Before I had a chance to see what happened, I saw tracer going by my

canopy and I broke around to the left all in one motion. The ship whose tracer I had seen was a P-51; he was shooting at the same Stuka as I and I had been clumsy enough to get between him and his target. I never found out who that eager beaver was.

"There were plenty of other ships in the neighborhood and I chose the nearest one. He began to smoke almost immediately. It looked as though I almost had one in the bag when tracer began to come over my canopy again. After what had just happened I decided to ignore it. I had found this Stuka and if whoever it was behind me wanted one he could look for his own—the sky was full of them. I took another squirt at the plane ahead of me and then noticed something about the tracer arching over my head. Instead of the usual two lines of tracer that we fired for aiming purposes, there were four or more coming from behind me. I looked over my shoulder into the airscoop of a Stuka. The model we were attacking carried two twenty-millimeter cannons, one under each wing, and this one was no exception. These were blazing away, accompanied by machine guns in the wing roots, down the leading edges of the pants on the non-retractable landing gear and, I think, in the nose. [Besides being used as a dive-bomber the Stuka was also used for strafing and strafing necessitates considerable armament.] I got the hell out of there fast. The only reason I didn't get it on the spot was, I suppose, that the pilot had little experience with aerial gunnery, being in a ship and at a job that called for ground gunnery exclusively.

"Somewhere about here I got into a pass to the right on three of them. I started to fire at ninety degrees and got the lead ship in the engine and the front cockpit (I'm sure of this because the films showed it). Flames started coming out from under his belly and he went out of my sight. Now I'm not sure if it was on a continuation of this pass or on another one to the right that one of them tried to ram me.

"I was after the second ship of a group of three and we were all turning as tight as possible. The Stuka can make a mighty tight turn and I was really wasting ammunition because I didn't have the proper lead. I closed down as close as I could and then began to break away. The third Stuka was in a vertical bank to the left. As I pulled up I looked over at him. Looking down into the canopy I could see the pilot and the rear gunner, both looking up at me. Then the German wrenched his ship into a bank that could only crash his ship into mine. I pulled back on my stick as I had a few times before. The Stuka rolled up at me and disappeared under my plane. The last I saw of it was its left wing, black with a white cross on it, as it arched toward my plane. Fascinated is a poor word, but that's what I was as I stared at my right wing, expecting to see it dissolve as that Stuka went through it. In a second the danger was past, for my wing remained as big and beautiful as ever. . . .

"This episode rattled me but not to the point where a passing Stuka had no appeal. I started after him and then noticed that he was smoking and wobbling badly. I assumed that he was on his way in, which he was. Another was not far from this one and taking off for the big timber. I came down on him from above, not realizing that in doing so I was giving his rear gunner a beautiful shot. I was getting fine hits up and down his fuselage when something hit my ship with a concussive thump—more of a shock wave than a sound. I stopped firing and thought to myself, *I'm hit.*

"However, my controls responded and my engine sounded okay, so I decided that the damage couldn't be too serious. The Stuka was still in front of me and I went back to work on it. The smoke began seeping into my cockpit. I was on fire! I forgot about the Stuka and everything else. The only thing I thought of was getting clear before the tanks went. I pulled up, for at all times during this fight I had not been 2000 feet above the ground and the hills in the neighborhood went up to 800 or so feet. I wanted out, but paused in my stampede not knowing whether to roll over first and then drop out, pulling the canopy, or pull the canopy and then roll over. It may sound silly but that minor point kept me in the plane while the fire burned itself out. I realized suddenly that I wouldn't have to bail out after all for the smoke was subsiding.

"When I realized this I banked over to take a look at the Stuka I had been after. As I watched, it crashed in flames against a hill. Simultaneously the smoking Stuka I had passed up crashed and exploded not fifty yards away. I checked my tail and, seeing that was clear, took a look around. The Stukas had disappeared and so had the squadron."

The valley over which the battle had occurred was, to Shipman, an amazing sight. Besides the two Stukas which he had just seen crash, there were perhaps ten others strewn through it. Great black curls of smoke rose up from the crashes. The Stukas had virtually been slaughtered. (Shipman, however, as he gazed down had no idea that all crashes represented German planes, but the sight of a dozen destroyed aircraft in so small a space was one he had never seen before.)

Shipman then heard the voice of Tarrant on the radio ordering all Mustangs to return to their base. "With my ship in the shape it was in, I decided that he had a point.

"Turning back to the course we had been flying, I began checking ahead for the squadron. I saw several P-51s ahead and headed for them. As I approached a flight of Russian-flown P-39s came over the 51s ahead of me and started into a dive after them. They were making a pass from the rear and this brought them close to me. When I was sure that they could see me I wiggled my wings like hell. The lead 39 wiggled acknowledgment and the Russians swung off to our right and, presently, out of sight.

"I was closing the gap between me and the ships ahead when another 51 came up from the left. By odd coincidence it was my wingman. I was surprised and relieved to see him. We closed up with the other ships and headed for home.

"Then I began checking on my battle damage. My hydraulic pressure was at zero, there were several holes in my wings, and the cracks around the ammunition box cover on my right wing were smoke stained. There was a hole in this cover and from the signs I concluded (wrongly) that a stray slug had set off some rounds in the ammunition boxes, causing the smoke that had given me such a scare."

Although the length of the mission, the impromptu strafing of German troops, and the Stuka slaughter had consumed much fuel, none of the Mustangs were forced to make emergency landings because of a lack of fuel. However, like Shipman's, some planes were shot up.

"With my hydraulic pressure at zero I knew that my gear would not lower in the usual way and that I would have to rock it down. This involves putting the gear handle in the down position and letting gravity pull the gear into place. When the pilot feels the gear hit bottom, he rocks his ship wildly to throw the weight of the oleo struts into a fully down position. This causes the spring loading locking pins to snap into place, locking the gear in the down position. I did not call in for an emergency landing because others were calling in emergencies and with my wingman checking on my wheels from his vantage point, there wasn't much more to be done.

"I told my wingman to keep an eye on my wheels when I put them down. We went into our landing peel-off and went through the procedure described above to lower my gear. I called my wingman and asked him what he thought. He was flying behind and below me, where he could see my wheels, and he called back that they looked down and locked. But as I glided down toward the landing strip a red flare arched up in front of me. I poured on the coal and went around wondering if my wheels *were* down as I rocked the ship all over the sky. On my next try I got another red flare. My gas was getting dangerously low and so when I got a flare again on my next pass, I called the tower asking if my wheels looked down and locked to them. They called back assuring me that they were. I then asked, 'Why all the red flares?' The tower came back with the bland answer that my flaps weren't down.

"The flaps are hydraulically operated as well as the wheels and zero hydraulic pressure means no flaps. I got on the radio and told the tower that my goddam flaps wouldn't come down because my goddam hydraulic system was shot out. (If I recall correctly, this is a watered-down version.)

"On my next pass I landed without any greater mishap than several good bounces. This business about the flaps is an example of how far the asinine regulations of the swivel-chair air force back in the States could go.

"As I sat filling out my Form 1 the crew chief, who had been inspecting my plane, climbed up on the wing root, next to my cockpit, with an excited expression on his face. He wanted me to take a look at the battle damage my ship had received. I complied and was not long in finding out what had excited him so. The smoke that I had mistaken for a hit in my ammunition box had actually come from a burning gas line in my right wing. An incendiary bullet of what would be the equivalent of our .30 caliber had neatly clipped the gas lead from my right wing drop tank installation. The gas in the line had been set on fire and would certainly have

fired the whole ship if the drop tank had been attached. As it was, a fire must have been gayly burning for thirty seconds or so in the wheel well, not more than a few inches from the rubber tire.

"My gun camera films were fairly clear. They revealed the strafing of the enemy vehicles and, along with the films of the others in the squadron, dozens of enemy planes. One of my films came close to giving me heart failure a week or so after we were safely back at our base in Italy [San Severo]. My camera showed a Stuka at fairly close range with one or two others further ahead of it and off to the sides. Toward the end of that particular film, the scene shifted downwards disclosing another Stuka which appeared huge on the screen. That one had been out of sight under my nose, and probably with his rear guns working away like fury, all the while I was firing on the one ahead of it. I had no idea how close he was, nor even that he had been there, until we ran off the films."

Five days later the 31st Fighter Group participated in a more conventional action: escorting Fifteenth Air Force Liberators to targets at Budapest. The strategic forces were concentrating on oil targets (the most important, most effective of all, it was learned after the war). Shipman's squadron that day was led by a man the others called, with minimal affection, "Wild Willie S——, the Village Idiot." But he developed radio trouble and before he peeled off for a return to San Severo, turned the squadron over to Shipman. Flying blightly as a flight leader, Shipman was reasonably happy with his lot—this was to be his final mission for a while and he expected to take some time off for a visit to Cairo. Now, "the Village Idiot" had handed him the responsibility of the entire squadron, despite the fact that the deputy squadron commander was himself on the mission, flying at the head of "Blue Section."

This arrangement did not seem right to Shipman, who discussed it with Blue Section leader (himself not eager to lead the entire squadron). Finally, however, Shipman took over Blue Section and the deputy squadron commander assumed responsibility for the squadron—reluctantly. Their two Mustangs shifted across the sky as the formations joined up with the heavy bombers. "There was usually a certain amount of confusion during the time when contact was made, by radio, between the bombers and

Mustangs of the 31st Fighter Group (Fifteenth Air Force), carrying wing tanks which will be dropped in an instant, peeling off for an attack. (U. S. AIR FORCE)

the fighters," Shipman noted. "This was because of the number of planes involved and the necessity for one small part of these to be distinguished from the others and located in the vastness of the sky.

"Contact was invariably made but rarely without some difficulty. On this particular, and for me unfortunate, mission things surprisingly went like clockwork. While we were making contact with the wing of bombers we were responsible for, we heard other bombers calling in enemy aircraft that were attacking them from above at six o'clock."

Minutes later Shipman saw a P-38 some distance away on the tail of an Me-109. The German plane trailed a long plume of white, glycol from the engine's cooling system, apparently hit by the P-38.

But the Messerschmitt raced away from the battle area as the great armada continued on its way. The battle gave Shipman "some useful information. This was that P-38s, the pilots of which were considered trigger-happy by our pilots, were in the neighborhood. This always meant that we had to be on our guard against the enemy forces as well as our own."

Shipman positioned his section above the Liberators, where the P-51s weaved back and forth to keep as close as possible to the slower bombers. Just as he had led his planes on the outward leg of the course, Shipman looked back at the bombers and saw two or three Me-109s and an FW-190 "diving in a long diagonal slant through the bombers." Ordered to deal with the enemy fighters, Shipman (as did the other pilots in his section) had to prepare for combat. This was not as simple a procedure as the layman believes.

"The sudden turn in events meant that I must drop my [auxiliary fuel] tanks, make a sharp diving turn to the left, keep an eye on the enemy planes and make the usual hasty preparations for a fight: . . . tightening the straps on the oxygen mask, turning on the gun switches, the gun sight, checking the gasoline situation, checking the maneuverability of the flaps and pushing the three components of the throttle quadrant—the prop pitch, mixture, and throttle controls—into full forward position. There is also the necessity, when leading a section . . . of a hasty check on the disposition of the planes moving into battle."

Shipman's luck began to fail when he jettisoned his drop tanks; one tank did not fall. Already in a sharp turn, which even under perfect trim conditions would have brought the Mustang into a stall, Shipman fought to keep the plane from going out of control. The drag of the unjettisoned tank finished the job. "My ship shuddered and mushed down through the air on its left wing. I fought to regain full control before my plane fell into a spin. In this I was successful but I had lost sight of the German planes." The enemy fighters had swept through the formation and disappeared into thick clouds below.

What followed contributed to Shipman's total disenchantment with the P-38 and its "trigger-happy" pilots. One of the twin-boomed fighters, apparently mistaking the P-51 for an Me-109, dropped down on him and shot Shipman out of the sky. His plane was in such condition that he could do nothing but bail out, cursing the P-38 all the way down to enemy territory. Ernest Shipman, ace with seven victories to his credit, became an enforced guest of the Third Reich for the rest of the war.

III

The Normandy invasion preparations had resulted in placing all air forces, tactical and strategic, in England under the direct command of General Eisenhower. The strategic bombardment program was thus temporarily set aside as heavy bombers were employed in more or less direct support of ground troops.

Even after the Allies were firmly established in France heavy bombers were used tactically—bombing enemy airfields or enemy troop concentrations in proximity to Allied troops. This was not how the strategic planners would have wished it. As early as March 1944 General Spaatz in his paper "Plan for the Completion of the Combined Bomber Offensive" outlined the particular American point of view and suggested that oil targets be struck instead of transportation, as was being then put forth as supreme. Advocating transportation targets were Harris (who continued to view the oil industry as a panacea target), Tedder (who was Eisenhower's air operations

Ernest Shipman, 31st Fighter Group, ace with seven victories to his credit before being downed by an overzealous P-38 pilot. (ERNEST SHIPMAN)

Eighth Air Force Liberator bombing German positions at Saint-Malo, Brittany (southwest of the Normandy *beachheads), as heavy bombers were employed in tactical missions shortly after D-Day.* (U. S. AIR FORCE)

supervisor for the invasion), and Brereton, the commander of the Ninth Air Force.

By late March Eisenhower, after listening to the arguments pro and con, himself voted in favor of transportation—railroads, bridges—but reaffirmed his confidence in Spaatz (with whom he had had such fine relations in the African invasion) by leaving the way open for a resumption of the strategic program with a concentration on oil as soon as possible after Normandy fell to the Allies. In making this choice Eisenhower noted that he was certain "there is no other way in which this tremendous air force can help us during the preparatory period, to get ashore and stay there."

Though Spaatz was certain the Luftwaffe would vigorously defend oil targets—and thus be forced into attritional air battles—he doubted that it would be concerned much with rail centers. These were remarkably (and relatively) easy to restore what with the highly efficient German employment of slave labor. Then too, in France there was the certainty of civilian casualties.

However, once Eisenhower had made his decision, Spaatz, while doubting its ultimate effect, believed it was justified. The fact that German units were denied access to the invasion area meant that enemy troops on the beaches would be forced to fight without reinforcements for hours and even days because

Interdiction: isolating the Normandy battlefields in preparation for D-Day. This railroad bridge, which crossed the Seine just south of Rouen, was taken out by British Second Tactical Air Force and U. S. Ninth Air Force medium bombers. By June 12 all seven rail bridges that linked Brittany with Normandy on the Seine were knocked out; so were thirteen road bridges.
(U. S. AIR FORCE)

delicate yet, as it turned out, powerful arrangement and it worked—not without slight international friction: but it worked.

One of the concerns of the British, concurrently, had come about in May of 1943 when a beautiful young WAAF, Constance Babington-Smith, scrutinizing a reconnaissance photo, spotted a curious pilotless aircraft on a launching site on the island of Usedom in the Baltic Sea. The place was Peenemünde, Germany's experimental station for rocketry. Later similar sites were picked up on other aerial photographs in France north of the Seine. Coupled with Hitler's ominous references to secret weapons that would decide the outcome of the war, the discovery of these sites was chilling. The launching sites apparently pointed in the general direction of England. Understandably, to the British the destruction of these sites took precedence over synthetic petroleum plants.

Flight Officer Babington-Smith had spotted the first of the German *Versuchsmuster* weapons—a long-range missile. This was the V-1 (originally designating an experimental type), a flying bomb. By the time the V-2, a rocket, appeared Hitler had a weapon which indeed (had he realized it) might have decided the war. It was no longer "experi-

the area had been cut off. Bridges were down, railroads were disrupted, and roads were a perilous shambles.

The command structure which accomplished this was anything but simple. Both the RAF and the U. S. Air Force were loath to be commanded by a fellow ally. Careful balances of command, therefore, had to be devised which could accomplish the job without injuring national pride. Where an Englishman was commander, it was likely that an American would be his deputy; and vice versa. It was a

A Douglas A-20 "Havoc" on a hunt over France; a former German airfield is scarred with the bombs of earlier missions. (U. S. AIR FORCE)

A Fortress of the 401st Bomb Group bombing the German rocket weapon development center at Peenemünde. It was here that fuel for the V-1 bombs was produced. The campaign against V-weapon sites and centers was code-named "Crossbow." (U. S. AIR FORCE)

mental," but a *Vergeltungswaffe* ("vengeance weapon"). The V-1s and V-2s, however, were not launched until after D-Day, when they did blindly cause death and destruction of little military import beyond contributing to the joy of Hitler. It was an example of science corrupted by the license of war.

The more conventional air weapons were used to assure the success of Overlord. Much of the load of the preparatory missions fell to the U. S. Ninth Air Force, by D-Day the largest tactical air force in the world, composed of medium bomber units (Douglas A-20s, Douglas A-26s, and Martin B-26s), fighters (predominantly P-47s, plus P-38s and a single P-51 group), and troop carriers (Douglas C-47s). The Ninth operated in conjunction with the British Second Tactical Air Force with its assorted aircraft:

Spitfires, Mosquitos, Mustangs, and Typhoons. These forces, along with the so-called Air Defence of Great Britain (formerly Fighter Command), came under the direction of Air Commander in Chief of Allied Expeditionary Air Force, Air Chief Marshal Sir Trafford L. Leigh-Mallory. Harris continued to control Bomber Command and Spaatz controlled the American Strategic Air Forces.

Harris undoubtedly spoke for both men when he pointed out that the "only efficient support which Bomber Command can give to Overlord is the intensification of attacks on suitable industrial centers in Germany as and when opportunity offers. If we attempt to substitute for this process attacks on gun emplacements, beach defenses, communications, or dumps in occupied territory, we shall commit the irremediable error of diverting our best weapon from the military function for which it has been equipped and trained to tasks which it cannot effectively carry out. Though this might give a specious appearance of supporting the army, in reality it would be the greatest disservice we could do to them. It would lead directly to disaster."

After Eisenhower's decision such theory could be violated in practice if the need arose—and it did. Until the heavy—that is, strategic—forces could be drawn away from their primary function, it devolved upon Leigh-Mallory to employ his tactical air forces in preparing the Overlord assault areas for the invasion. The attack began on French rail centers and switched to bridges (which proved most attractive as targets), so that by D-Day every bridge across the Seine below Paris had been destroyed. As for the railroads, suffice it to say that the only German troops which reached Normandy after D-Day walked there. Airfields within 130 miles of Normandy were rendered unusable. Radar stations, ranging from Ostend (Belgium) to the Channel Islands, were knocked out. At the same time tons of bombs were dropped upon the burgeoning V-weapons sites. For every attack upon the actual assault area, two others were made elsewhere, so that the Germans would have no idea of where the invasion would come. By a curious quirk, only Hitler of all the German military "minds" had guessed that the attack would open at Normandy. By the time he had offered this observation his stock as a great military philosopher had fallen among the professional military men in Germany. His errors, in fact,

Dance of death: Coastal Command Beaufighters attacking a German minesweeper in the North Sea.
(IMPERIAL WAR MUSEUM, LONDON)

had given the High Command so bad a name among the professionals (rather than for his crimes against humanity) that a number of them had attempted to assassinate him. In this too they failed.

As Harris had indicated, bombing the coastal defenses was not effective, although the medium bombers and the fighter bombers (the Thunderbolts) performed this function with great dispatch and, frequently, at great cost. Flak was thick and deadly and the medium bombers and fighter-bombers of necessity operated at a vulnerable altitude.

The British Second Tactical Air Force participated in unusual low-level missions in the preinvasion period in Mosquitos. Group Captain P. C. Pickard led nineteen Mosquitos of Nos. 487, 464, and 21 Squadrons on a jailbreak. A large number of French

Resistance leaders were imprisoned at Amiens and it seemed a worthy project to release them. On February 18, 1944, in near-scrubbing weather, Pickard led his planes in the attack. Although the raid was successful—more than 250 prisoners escaped through the bomb-breached walls—Pickard's Mosquito was shot down by two FW-190s and he and his navigator, Flight Lieutenant J. A. Broadley, were killed. So were 102 prisoners, unfortunately. But the main prisoner, a Monseiur Vivant, an important leader in the Resistance movement, went free.

Another Mosquito mission of unique distinction was accomplished by six aircraft of No. 613 Squadron led by Wing Commander R. N. Bateson. The target was a single building, the Kleizkamp Art Galleries, in The Hague. The Gestapo had taken over the building and used it for storage of records and a file on the Dutch. Bateson led his Mosquitos to the town, circled it, and then at a height of fifty feet above the street, flew toward the art gallery. The German guard standing in front of the building looked up and saw six aircraft racing directly for him; he threw down his gun and ran. Seconds later two bombs skipped through the gallery doorway; another two went through windows on either side of the door. The bombs that spilled over detonated in a German barracks, burning it to the ground.

Although Dutch officials were killed by the bombs that struck the art gallery, the official files of the Gestapo were blown to the winds, burned, and otherwise destroyed. The surviving Dutch keepers of the files returned to work, replacing the destroyed cards with fake information, thus thoroughly disrupting the Gestapo's efficient system. All Mosquitos returned safely to England.

Such missions, while not strategic by any definition, were typical of the imaginative daring of the RAF crews. This same daring and imagination, coupled with that of the Ninth Air Force's crews, opened great holes in the German defenses at Normandy and across France into Germany. Typical of the kind of mission that fell to the medium bombers is one gleaned from the history of the 387th Bombardment Group (M). The language is typical in its laconic recital of the salient facts.

"On June 7 it was learned that the 17th German Panzer Division was moving north to the invasion beachhead. The report called for a mission to deny this route to the Germans. Because of bad weather the formation attempting to bomb the rail junction at Rennes was not successful, but it did get good results on a railroad west of Vire and on a choke point of vehicles near Saint-Lô. The next morning a highly successful mission was flown against the railroad junction at Pontabault. The best strike was made by Lieutenant Rudolf Tell, bombardier in Captain Robert E. Will's flight, whose bombs hit the target perfectly.

"The afternoon mission [June 8, 1944; D plus 2] proved to be one of the most remarkable ever flown by the Group. Capt. Rollin D. Childress was to lead eighteen aircraft [Marauders] to a fuel dump in the Forêt Grimbosq, south of Caen. At the take-off at 1958 hours, the ceiling was 900 feet. The formation assembled without difficulty; but on going up through the solid overcast it became widely dispersed. Eleven of the planes returned to the base.

One crash-landed at Gravesend. One, piloted by First Lieutenant Raymond V. Morin, crashed while attempting to land at Friston in ceiling zero weather.

"Captain Childress rallied three aircraft with his own and continued on, sometimes at deck level in quarter of a mile visibility. He managed to find the target, and his bombardier, First Lieut. Wilson J. Cushing, bombed it with great accuracy from 6000 feet. As the formation of four turned off target, moderate extremely accurate flak shot down the fourth airplane, piloted by Capt. Charles W. Schober. The airplane exploded in mid-air and no parachutes were observed. Included in Capt. Schober's crew was Capt. John D. Root, group weather officer.

"The remaining three aircraft, proceeding homeward, braved terrible weather conditions over England and landed at the base at 2230 hours. Captain Childress was congratulated on his tenacity and perseverance by Col. Millard Lewis, commander of the 98th Combat Wing, and by the group commander, Lieut. Col. Thomas H. Seymour.

"The effectiveness of the bombing was attested to by a congratulatory telegram from the ground forces which stated that the important fuel dump, the immediate supply for an entire Panzer division, was destroyed."

Once the beachhead was secure, there remained the problem of moving inland. This "breakout," it was concluded, could be implemented by concentrated air power, employing not only the fighter-bombers and mediums of the Ninth, but also the Fortresses and Liberators of the Eighth Air Force. Where the Germans had managed to stiffen their positions in the face of the advancing Allies the plan was to slash a hole through the German lines with a heavy concentration of aerial bombardment. The official code name for this operation was "Cobra."

Weather, the usual menace, helped to get Cobra off to a poor start. On July 24, 1944, the Ninth Air Force's fighter-bombers took off, but three of its six groups returned to base upon being recalled because of the bad weather. Leigh-Mallory, who was in France and saw the impossibility of effective bombing, postponed the attacks, and later in the day canceled them.

Unfortunately, when this word came down to the Eighth Air Force it's more than fifteen hundred heavy bombers were already on the bombing runs;

only a few of the planes in the last formations received word in time to turn away from the target area. Visibility was so bad over the target that the lead formations did not attempt to drop on the primary targets: German positions directly in front of the Allied troops. Some bombers did drop, but made several runs before identifying the correct drop zone. About three hundred bombers succeeded in dropping on what was hoped to have been the proper targets. But these hopes were not fulfilled.

Accident and error unleashed an envenomed Cobra which did not discriminate between friend and foe. On one bomb run a lead bombardier found his bomb release stiff and in attempting to loosen it dropped some of his bomb load. The other ships in the formation, fifteen in all, seeing the bombs released from their lead ship, dropped their bombs also. The bombs fell two thousand yards inside Allied positions, killing sixteen troops of the Ameri-

A direct flak hit has sheared off this Marauder's engine. This occurred over Toulon Harbor, in southern France, where another invasion was under way. The B-26 was one of the Twelfth Air Force mediums borrowed for the second invasion of the Continent.

(U. S. AIR FORCE)

A Marauder, hit by flak, is enveloped by flame as it falls into France. Despite Allied aerial supremacy flak, as always, took its toll. (U. S. AIR FORCE)

can 30th Infantry Division and wounding about sixty. A single B-24 flew over a Ninth Air Force field in France, at Chippelle, at which instance something struck the B-24's nose turret. The bombardier recoiled from the sudden impact and inadvertently struck a toggle switch. Seconds later two Ninth Air Force medium bombers ready to take off on a mission blew up with their crews and full bomb loads after being struck by the toggled bombs. Other planes were damaged also.

At another point a Thunderbolt swept down, turned, and ran in on an ammunition dump, which blew up with pleasing violence. Except that the pilot had made a wrong turn and had attacked an Allied dump. To complete the day's toll, three heavy bombers were knocked down by flak, presumably German.

Despite the day's misadventures, the second application of Cobra followed the next day, when weather conditions promised better possibilities of success. There were other forces at work also. The previous day's activities revealed to the Germans the point at which the Allied breakout was most likely to occur. Consequently, while the U. S. Army soldiers moved out of the bombing zone, so did those of the Wehrmacht. In some areas this meant retaking ground once held by the Allies because of the evacuations away from the bomb lines. Those Germans who suffered the saturation bombings, however, were in no condition to hold or take any ground for some time after. Although casualties were not excessive, for the Germans had dug in intelligently, the effect upon communications and especially upon morale was "shattering," to employ the word most often used by the Germans.

The very sight of literally thousands of enemy aircraft (1507 Flying Fortresses and Liberators, 380 Marauders and Invaders, and 559 Thunderbolts) was dispiriting, and the cry again was heard, "Where is the Luftwaffe?"

To Generalleutnant Fritz Bayerlein, commander of the Panzer Lehr division, the battlefield looked like the dead and pocked *Mondlandschaft* (moon landscape). His unit was heavily hit, with a good number of his troops "either dead, wounded, crazed, or dazed." The command post of his 902nd Regiment had been in the center of the bomb carpet and that was entirely gone; thirty or more of his tanks lay toppled on their backs or upended in bomb craters. Bayerlein's divisional flak guns were all but useless because of the great number of enemy aircraft; half the guns were knocked out in the opening minutes of the attack.

But, as on the day before, "gross errors" took their toll. In general, the bombing was more accurate than the first Cobra, but human error as ever resulted in bombs falling short and consequently within American lines. The 30th Infantry suffered again as heavy bombers released some of their bombs, killing 120 and injuring 380. Among the dead was Lieutenant General Lesley J. McNair.

In short, the effort did not equal the effect. Even if it were possible to accept Allied casualties as one of the "fortunes of war," the actual accomplishment was less than expected. Allied troops did not "pour through the great gaps" in the enemy lines, although the way was broken for the infantry of the First U. S. Army, followed later by the rampaging tanks of Patton's Third Army in August.

While the Cobra carpet bombings had been effective on a limited scale, they only served to underscore Harris's view on the "irremediable error of diverting our best weapon from the military function for which it had been equipped and trained to tasks which it cannot effectively carry out." The use of heavy bombers in close support of troops was, in effect, a military perversion, although at the time an expedient one. Nor was it abandoned merely because it did not function to perfection. As a substitute for artillery, capable of delivering greater firepower in a given time, the heavy bombers were incomparable, although in theory it was a step backward.

If the ground-support role of the high-altitude heavy bomber proved to be less than successful, the co-ordination between ground troops and the fighter-bombers, particularly the Thunderbolt, was excellent. Thunderbolts frequently teamed up with Allied tanks, with which they communicated with two-way radios as had the "Rover Joes" in Italy.

Liberators assembling over England for a mission to bomb in front of Allied troops in France.

(CECIL COHEN)

Liberators in a "carpet" bombing mission over Tours, France, during the "Cobra" operation to force a break in the German lines for Allied troops. Smoke markers indicate drop point—the entire formation releases the bombs when the lead bomber drops. Such bombings so close to friendly troops were not truly effective and were often fatal to foe and friend alike.

(U. S. AIR FORCE)

Jug pilots could spot enemy gun positions, antitank traps, and German tanks, warn their own forces, and attack the enemy. The fighter-bombers strafed and bombed German troop concentrations and artillery installations, engaged an intermittently emergent Luftwaffe, and played an important part in the interdiction campaign, the isolation of the Germans in the battlefield by cutting off their lines of communications: bridges, railroads, and highways.

After the breakthrough at Saint-Lô the Allies swept across Normandy; another invasion, in southern France, was also successfully launched and the German blitzkrieg machine was squeezed even as it was rammed back toward the Rhine. As winter approached the possibilities for fighter-bomber cooperation with ground troops diminished—and Spaatz could again consider the release of his heavy

bombers for the continuation of the attack upon Germany behind the Rhine. He hoped to strike particularly at oil targets and the Luftwaffe. Berlin too became an important target city by the end of June. With the coming of winter Spaatz could take up the Battle of Berlin again.

Robert Chapin, lead navigator of the 384th Bombardment Group, upon reflection did not regard Berlin as tough a target as the cities related to the oil targets (Brüx, Blechhammer, Merseburg, Ruhland, and, among others, Ploesti). But Berlin, he knew, "was tougher psychologically." The "most frustrating missions," however, were those to the V-weapons sites, for the slightest mist would obscure the heavily camouflaged installations. These sites, too, were not very vulnerable to bombing and never did get knocked out of operation until ground troops overran them. But not before Hitler's indiscriminate "vengeance weapons" (flying bombs and V-2 rockets) took 8938 civilian lives and left nearly 25,000 seriously injured in their blind wake. From the first flying bomb, the "doodle bug," which fell on England on June 12, 1944, until the final V-2, which fell on March 27, 1945, a corner of England with London at its center was even more of a "Hell's Corner" than Kent had been during the Battle of Britain.

The V-weapons, though terroristic, were militarily pointless, however much they supposedly advanced "civilization" toward the Space Age.

The weapon which Chapin recalls that really "shook up the troops" was the jet fighter. As he sat in the nose of a B-17 one day, Chapin heard the pilot announce the approach of a jet fighter. Chapin, as usual busy with his navigational computations, and bombardier Richard Crown, likewise preoccupied with his own work, rarely actually saw enemy fighters even in the height of combat. The dawn of the Jet Age, however, was too important to miss. The two men peered out of the plexiglass nose.

"Where?" Chapin asked.

The pilot called out the "clock" position directly out in front of their plane (as lead team Chapin and Crown flew in the lead aircraft along with the command pilot, at this time Colonel Theodore Ross Milton). At a point that appeared to be miles distant, Chapin saw a tiny dot which suddenly expanded into a strange-looking aircraft that "zoomed out of nowhere" and through the bomber formation.

Although it did no damage, the very appearance and incredible speed of the plane had a disquieting effect upon the men in the bombers. Not even the Mustang could overtake the Messerschmitt 262.

Several factors, luckily for the Allies, inhibited the full employment of the Me-262, an aircraft which could very readily have had a decisive effect upon the air war over Germany. When he saw the Messerschmitt demonstrated for the first time, Hitler, gorged with the virulence of vengeance, glanced at the fighter and snapped, "Can that thing carry bombs?"

Neither Göring nor Messerschmitt wished to say nay to their Great Captain, so they answered with a qualified yes. The qualification lay in the fact that the Me-262 was designed as a fighter-interceptor, to meet the greatest need in Germany at the moment: to stop the Allied heavy bombardment from obliterating German cities and, worse, from destroying the German synthetic oil industry. The jet plane could carry a light bomb load, but that would seriously impair its performance; so would operating at a low level as a fighter-bomber. In short, all the advantages of the fact that it was a jet aircraft would be sacrificed. Hitler's so-called "Blitz Bomber" would not be superior to Allied fighters.

Hitler's meddling from the moment of the Messerschmitt's inception, therefore, canceled it out as any kind of potent weapon. Not until after D-Day did Hitler relent to the degree that he would permit the Me-262 and the word "fighter" be mentioned in the same sentence. He conceded that it just might serve the function for which it was conceived—but not if it interfered with bomber production. Bomber production was in itself an interference, for to meet Hitler's demands the fighter would have to be converted into a bomber—it would need bomb clips installed, it would require a bombsight, all of which took time.

Adolf Galland, then general of the fighters, was

Thunderbolt of 365th Fighter Group seeks out enemy positions for American tanks. In communication with tank commanders by two-way radio, pilot of P-47 would spot targets such as German tanks and anti-tank gun positions, or warn of tank traps. American artillery frequently dealt with these targets in co-operation with tactical pilots or American tanks.

(U. S. AIR FORCE)

A Spitfire pursues a V-1 flying bomb ("doodle bug" to the English) over the English countryside. The Spitfire, the P-47, and the P-51 were capable of overtaking the bomb, and either shot it down or tipped it out of its trajectory by flipping it with the wing of the pursuing plane. (U. S. AIR FORCE)

The V-1, the first of Hitler's "vengeance weapons," known as "doodle bugs" to the English. Pilotless, these were brought down by balloon barrage, antiaircraft fire, and fighters capable of speeds in excess of four hundred miles an hour. These included the Spitfire XIV, the Thunderbolt, the Mustang, and the first of the war's operational jets: the Gloster "Meteor."

(U. S. AIR FORCE)

Antiaircraft fire tracks a doodle bug over London at night. Many were knocked down in this way.

(IMPERIAL WAR MUSEUM, LONDON)

so outspokenly opposed to the perversion of the Me-262 that he argued himself out of his post. Dismissed, Galland was given the opportunity to form a jet fighter unit, Jagdverband 44 (ironically, he ended the war as he began it, as a squadron commander). This, the second jet fighter unit (the earlier one was Jagdgeschwader 7, *Gruppen* of which had gone into combat in October of 1944), like its predecessor had come too late. Even so, the two Me-262 units took a high toll of American bombers while they operated.

Like any new aircraft, the Me-262 had its share of bugs, and with Hitler assuming the role of aircraft expert, it had even more than its fair share. Accidents occurred during testing and training; despite this the first operational unit was hurried into service. One of the first operational jet units was the so-called "Kommando Nowotny," named in honor of its leader, Major Walter Nowotny, a fighter ace with a score of more than two hundred "kills" to his credit. It was Nowotny's jets that first "shook up the troops" of the Eighth Air Force. Prior to that, most of the jet type of fighters encountered were the odd but quite ineffectual Me-163 (*Komet*).

Nowotny died as result of an engine failure after

A V-2 missile on its blind way to England.

(NATIONAL ARCHIVES)

he had taken off to knock down his 258th enemy aircraft. As he came in to land he reported his left jet engine had gone out. Thus crippled, he became an easy target for a swarm of Mustangs which pounced on his tail. When he came within sight of his own home base at Achmer, either Nowotny's Me-262 was hit by the American fighters on his tail or he crashed into the ground. The former is more likely, for via radio Nowotny's voice was heard: ". . . attacked again . . . hit . . ." His fighter then disintegrated in a sudden flash of flame.

As for Galland, he was shot out of the sky while attacking a formation of Marauders of the 17th Bombardment Group over Neuburg on the Danube. Neuburg was a major aviation center, complete with airfield and plant. According to Galland's own account, he was shot down by a Mustang, whose pilot had surprised him while he was attacking the Marauders. According to Air Force files, no claim by a fighter pilot of an Me-262 was made that day (April 26, 1945), although two claims were made by Marauder gunners of the 34th Bombardment Squadron. Since the jet did not go down immediately, perhaps the Mustang pilot did not think he had succeeded in his attack.

But he had. Galland himself was injured and his instrument panel was a shambles. His engine pods

One of Hitler's secret "vengeance weapons" (a V-1)   *begins to fall into Piccadilly, London.* (U. S. AIR FORCE)

A V-2 hits the target: Smithfield Market, London. More than 100 people died, 123 were seriously injured, and Hitler was not one day closer to victory. (NATIONAL ARCHIVES)

Lead navigator Robert Chapin, lead bombardier Richard Crown, and Group Commander Theodore R. Milton of the 384th Bomb Group. Chapin recalls that of all of Hitler's surprises, the introduction of the Messerschmitt 262 jet fighter "shook up the troops" most. (384TH BOMB GROUP)

were tattered and running ragged. Afraid that if he were to bail out he would be shot up in his chute, Galland returned to his base at Riem. Despite his poorly operating engines, Galland brought the plane in for a landing. Unable to control the fuel feed, he could only cut off the engines completely once he was over the field and ready to land. Trailing twin plumes of black smoke, he approached the landing strip—only to find that the field was under attack by Thunderbolts. Because his radio had also been destroyed Galland had not received the warnings of this. With the engines flared out Galland could do nothing else but land.

The Messerschmitt wobbled down to earth and then Galland found he had other problems. His nosewheel had been shot flat, and at a speed of 150 miles an hour his landing was extremely noisy and rough. The Thunderbolts ignored the crippled jet in favor of smashing up the field. When he could, Galland jumped from the plane and into the nearest bomb crater, where he cringed under the bombardment. Finally a mechanic ran to an armored tractor, which he drove through the rubble and the shellbursts to Galland. Hobbling onto the vehicle, Galland said nothing, but in heartfelt gratitude slapped the courageous mechanic on the shoulder. Galland ended up in the hospital at Munich, where it was found he had two shell splinters in his knee. That mission was his last of the war.

Despite the jets, the great formations of bombers continued to bomb Germany. Once the initial shock of their presence was over it was possible—and necessary—to deal with them.

IV

To Hitler, it must have seemed those pagan gods to whom he prayed were not listening. His Atlantic Wall and his most brilliant general had not kept the Allies out of Normandy; his vengeance weapons had failed to bring Churchill to his knees and his Blitz Bomber neither blitzed nor bombed.

Further: the Allied strategic bombardment effort, for all the internal argument, was having its effect. The oil strikes had begun seriously to curtail the training program for new Luftwaffe pilots. Due to the fuel shortage, training flights were carefully rationed. Many young pilots were sent to certain de-

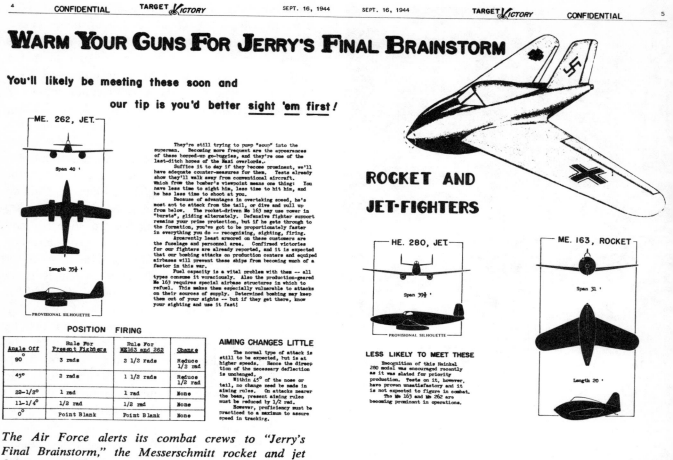

The Air Force alerts its combat crews to "Jerry's Final Brainstorm," the Messerschmitt rocket and jet fighters and the Heinkel 280. (RAYMOND C. WIER)

struction, even in the superior jet fighters, because they were ill trained and lacked experience. And those veterans who might have compensated for some of that inexperience were already dead or being worn out in interminable operations.

The squeeze on oil even cut into operations. While Speer had succeeded in increasing the production of aircraft, the denial of fuel chained them to the ground. Because of this Luftwaffe interception would be sporadic and only very important targets would be defended. Fuel and oil would be hoarded until Berlin, or Vienna or some similar critical target area, was attacked and the Luftwaffe, assumed dead, would rise out of the ashes.

Hitler hated being on the defensive; his was a philosophy of attack. The thought of surrender was inconceivable—even after France had been won back and Allied troops had crossed into Germany.

(This occurred five years and eleven days after Hitler had launched *Fall Weiss* upon Poland.) "As far as I was concerned," Field Marshal Gerd von Rundstedt, Commander in Chief, West, later said, "the war ended in September [1944]." For Rundstedt, perhaps, but not for the German people, not for troops on both sides, and not—especially—for Hitler.

"I think it is pretty obvious," the Führer said in conference one day with some of his staff, "that this war is no pleasure for me." It is unlikely that any more fatuous statement has ever been made. "For five years," he continued in a characteristic outburst of self-pity, "I have been separated from the world. I haven't been to the theater, I haven't heard a concert, and I haven't seen a film. I live only for the purpose of leading this fight, because I know if there is not an iron will behind it this battle cannot be won.

"I accuse the General Staff of weakening combat officers who join its ranks, instead of exuding this

The Messerschmitt Me-262 of Jagdstaffel 77. Had Hit-ler not interfered with the production and design of this aircraft the last months of the war might have proved gloomier and bloodier than they were. This was not, however, the first operational jet; the British Glos-ter Meteor was used against doodle bugs as early as July 1944—the Me-262s of KG 51 went into action a month later. (U. S. AIR FORCE)

A hidden Me-262 plant at Obertraubling, Germany. Final assembly was completed here before the jets were delivered to jet units. (U. S. AIR FORCE)

iron will, and of spreading pessimism when General Staff officers go to the front. . . ." This was the old refrain, for in the twilight of the Third Reich the former corporal harked back to the good old days of the First World War, when the military situation, for him at least, was much simpler than it was in 1944.

"If necessary," he conceded, "we will fight on the Rhine. . . . We'll fight until we get a peace which secures the life of the German nation for the next fifty or hundred years and which, above all, does not besmirch our honor a second time, as hap-pened in 1918. . . ."

By September, when Rundstedt believed the war was over, the Allied advance lost its impetus. The rapid advance across France had stretched the sup-ply lines. Patton's Third Army, for example, came to a halt for five days because of a lack of fuel. All fuel, all ammunition, all essential supplies had to be brought in by truck from the Normandy beaches or the port of Cherbourg to the front lines —distances ranging from four to five hundred miles. Also, along the German West Wall (called the Sieg-fried Line by the Allies) were fortifications which ran from the Netherlands southward to Switzerland. Despite his defeatism, Rundstedt held the West Wall firmly.

Lancasters bombing through the overcast by day; the target is a vengeance weapon base in France.
(IMPERIAL WAR MUSEUM, LONDON)

Hitler called the operation ultimately (for the code name changed biweekly in the interest of supersecrecy) *Die Wacht am Rhein.* Whether this was a bitter allusion to Allied occupation of Germany after the First World War or a flicker of rare sardonic humor it would be impossible to ascertain. But Hitler's plan when he told his military leaders was regarded as a form of madness. Late in November the Allies had taken Antwerp, which served as an important port. Hitler's grand plan had come to life one day when he heard the word "Ardennes" mentioned.

"Stop!" he shouted and raised his hand for silence. "I have made a momentous decision. I am taking the offensive." He then dropped the personal pronouns and brought his hand down upon a map.

"Here," he said with eyes afire and his racked body electric for the first time in years, "out of the Ardennes. Across the Meuse and on to Antwerp!"

This was a stunning decision, and Hitler's military advisers saw little chance of success. It was a plan that might have worked in 1940, when Britain

It had been Eisenhower's plan to invade Germany along a broad front through the West Wall, but the critical problem of supply intervened. Two of his commanders urged Eisenhower to give one of them his own head for the plunge into Germany: Montgomery in the north was certain he could penetrate into the Ruhr (provided he was given priority on supplies and reserve troops intended for other units), and Patton promised with equal certainty that he could reach the Rhine. Eisenhower rejected both ideas and continued to favor his "broad front" concept.

He did, however, approve of an attempt, suggested by Montgomery, to drop troops by air into the Netherlands to assist the British Second Army across river obstacles. Although the drop, the largest air-borne operation of the war and code-named "Market," was executed successfully, it fell short of its intended objective because of unexpected, stiff German resistance. Montgomery had hoped that "Market," plus its ground phase, "Garden," would open up a corridor through the Netherlands which would lead directly into the heart of Germany. To Eisenhower "Market-Garden" had furnished "ample evidence that much bitter campaigning was to come." And when it came, the whim of Hitler's vaunted "iron will," it was with dismaying surprise.

The curse is off Ploesti, although the flak is as thick as ever. Fifteenth Air Force B-24s deal a hard blow to Hitler's major oil source. Without oil neither the Wehrmacht nor the Luftwaffe could operate effectively.
(U. S. AIR FORCE)

and France were on the run and German troops invincible—and there was still a Luftwaffe. (Rundstedt's comment was typical of the general outlook: "If we reached the Meuse we should have got down on our knees and thanked God—let alone try to reach Antwerp.") By driving a wedge between Eisenhower's armies (thus, Hitler predicted, trapping the British on the sea as at Dunkirk) Hitler would prove that, despite Allied victories, Germany was not finished and would not capitulate—"Never! Never!"

To make this impression, Hitler scraped together all possible troops, with the main blow falling to two panzer armies, Josef Dietrich's Sixth SS Panzer Army and Hasso von Manteuffel's Fifth. All possible armor was thrown into the gamble, about eight hundred tanks. Göring promised no less than three thousand fighters for the Luftwaffe's part of "the Watch on the Rhine"—code-named *Der Grosse Schlag* ("the Great Blow").

After waiting for a weather prediction which promised several days of poor flying weather, grounding Allied aircraft, Hitler suddenly unleashed his Ardennes counteroffensive on December 16, 1944. This came as a shock to the Allies, confident that the German capability for another offensive was a thing of the past. The Fifth Panzer Army smashed through the American lines, as consternation in the various Allied capitals evidenced a fear of success and a second Dunkirk. The Germans knew that the American defenses in the Ardennes sector were thinly held, and it was there that the deepest thrust was made; this became popularly known as "the Battle of the Bulge." It was a stunning surprise, and during the period from the sixteenth through the twenty-sixth of December the Americans suffered terrible losses; but the Watch on the Rhine failed and, in fact, never even reached the Meuse. When the weather cleared, Allied aircraft ripped up the panzers and cut off supply lines. The German thrust literally ran out of gas.

Though the gamble was lost, Hitler continued stubbornly to insist that his generals continue with the attack even though it was obvious by the end of December that it had failed. But having sacrificed men and tanks (the totals of casualties exceeded 120,000 troops and about 600 tanks), there still remained the Luftwaffe and *Der Grosse Schlag*.

The Great Blow would answer once and for all

Winter 1944–45: weather such as this on the base of the 92nd Bomb Group in England and over the Continent furnished Hitler with the setting for a surprise blow in the Ardennes. (U. S. AIR FORCE)

that haunting question, "Where is the Luftwaffe?" Göring had promised three thousand fighters. These had been husbanded for what Galland had assumed would be a true great blow, upon the Strategic Air Forces' heavy bombers; instead Hitler diverted them to the land battle in the Ardennes.

When Hitler heard of Göring's promise, he smiled sardonically and told Manteuffel, "Göring has reported that he has three thousand planes available for the operation. You know Göring's reports. Discount one thousand, and that still leaves a thousand for you and a thousand for Sepp Dietrich." The number that actually participated in *Der Grosse Schlag*—which Luftwaffe pilots called Operation Hermann—was closer to 900 (numbers vary from 790 to 1100; after the war Göring claimed 2300). Planes and pilots were even drawn from JG 104, a training unit.

Like the Ardennes offensive itself, Operation Hermann was prepared with the utmost secrecy and unleashed with devastating surprise. In the early morning of New Year's Day 1945 hundreds of Me-109s and FW-190s warmed up on various German airfields behind the lines. Both experienced and inexperienced pilots were to take part in the surprise attack upon Allied airfields in the Netherlands and Belgium and a single base in France, a total of seventeen. Because the formations were a mixed bag, the

"Bulge" weather on the Continent, which grounded the Allied planes while Hitler's panzers smashed through the American lines. (U. S. AIR FORCE)

returning to their base found it under attack by about fifty German fighters. Within minutes eighteen of the attackers had been shot out of the air at the cost of a single Spitfire.

The American base at Asche, near Chièvres, Belgium, was jumped at around ten o'clock in the morning. A dozen Mustangs, led by Lieutenant Colonel John C. Meyer, deputy commander of the 487th Squadron (352nd Fighter Group, Eighth AF), were preparing to take off on a morning patrol. Early morning fog had kept the planes grounded, but by eight it had begun to burn off, clearing slowly from east to west. The twelve Mustangs, motors warming on the frozen airstrip, awaited word from Meyer to take off. All were unaware of the approaching Messerschmitts and Focke-Wulfs hugging the floor of the valleys of the mountainous Eifel district, leading to Asche. They swooped in behind the veil of fog. It was approaching ten before Meyer could gun his engine and begin the takeoff. As he thundered down the runway he was surprised to see antiaircraft puffs bursting at the far end of the field. He called the control tower, asking if its radar had picked up "bogies" on its screen.

fighters were guided toward their targets by Junkers 88s. At a point near the target areas, the inexperienced pilots would have to rely upon special maps to find their targets; the Ju-88s turned back at the Rhine. The approach was made at very low level to avoid enemy radar; strict radio silence was observed.

Pilots, aircraft, and fuel had been hoarded for this great blow. For the second time within two weeks the Allies were dealt a shock by the Germans. The most successful attack was made upon the British Second Tactical Air Force base at Eindhoven. About forty German fighters swept in low over the field at the moment Mitchell bombers were lining up to take off. Hawker Typhoons of No. 438 and No. 439 Squadrons, Royal Canadian Air Force, were also caught on the ground; those pilots who attempted to take off were shot down only a few feet off the ground, encumbered as they were by bomb loads and unretracted landing gears. Some pilots abandoned their planes and ran for cover. Soon Eindhoven was strewn with burning wrecks. A single Spitfire took off in the maelstrom of smoke and fire, shot down one of the attackers, and then crashed into the ground itself.

Other Spitfires, of the No. 131 Wing (Nos. 302, 308, and 317, Polish squadrons), returning from a fighter sweep, however, were air-borne and upon

During a break in the weather C-47s of the 9th Troop Carrier Command come over to drop supplies to Americans encircled in Bastogne, Belgium. (U. S. AIR FORCE)

John C. Meyer, who was caught up in "the Great Blow," the Luftwaffe's last wasteful gasp during the Battle of the Bulge. (U. S. AIR FORCE)

"Negative."

Petie, Meyer's Mustang, picked up speed and raced toward the eastern end of the field and the ever thickening bursts. As the Mustang's wheels left the strip Meyer saw, as if out of nowhere, an FW-190 coming his way. With wheels still lowered, his engine striving for altitude, Meyer knew he was a sitting duck. But the German pilot, briefed to strafe the field, turned aside and fired on a C-47 (Dakota) on the edge of the runway. Shaken but apparently reprieved, Meyer hauled up his undercarriage, quickly went through all the "drill" for battle, and fired at the German fighter, still intent upon destroying the transport on the ground. The FW, hit by six .50-calibers, slammed to the ground beside the Dakota.

Another pilot, William T. Whisher, following Meyer, began firing at another Focke-Wulf thirty seconds after he had left the ground. He was two hundred feet above the earth, an unlikely height for a dogfight, and within a hundred yards of the German aircraft. The "Butcher Bird" winged over, smashed into the ground, and burned. In the en-

suing half hour, most of it over the base, Whisher knocked down another FW-190 and two Messerschmitts.

"There were plenty of Jerries left to shoot at," Whisher commented. Meyer meanwhile managed to gain a little altitude and found this to be only too true. What with trying to ascertain the identity of the aircraft—for now Thunderbolts too had joined the battle—sorting out the Me-109s from the Mustangs and the FW-190s from the Thunderbolts, plus twisting his neck to clear his tail, Meyer was busy indeed. There was still another hitch: the antiaircraft gunners were firing up at him as well as the enemy, and his P-51 was taking hits. A large chunk flew off his wing.

In spite of this distraction, Meyer got onto the tail of another FW-190. American ground gunners (still shooting at him) proved to be less effective than the American airman: pieces of the cowling flew away from the German fighter, the propeller slowed up and windmilled, and the pilot pointed the nose down. As Meyer watched, the FW, with wheels up, skidded into a field. The plane struck on its belly, bounced, thumped again, and then tossed over onto its back, over and over, flared, and broke up in a great flash of fire.

Turning back to the congested sky, Meyer found he had flown away from the base. Low on fuel and practically out of ammunition, he realized he had to land. A call to base informed him that the field was still under attack; it would be pointless to attempt to land there. Meyer then found what appeared to be an airfield and just as he was about to put down, three Me-109s bounced upon the Mustang's tail.

The four aircraft darted and maneuvered in an aerial ballet; Meyer got one of the Messerschmitts in a good spot, there was only a short burst from his guns, and he realized he was now really out of the battle. Suddenly, as it so often was in air combat, a swarm of planes filled the air around him: Mustangs. Drifting through the sky, looking for landmarks and checking for "bandits," Meyer worked his way back to Asche, which by eleven o'clock was clear.

Nearly half of the enemy attackers, twenty-three in all, had fallen to the guns of the 352nd Group —with no losses to the group itself. A few planes had been lost, but no pilots. Except for a few

A Luftwaffe pilot leaves his stricken plane over the Bulge after being shot up by James Dalglish, 354th Fighter Group, Ninth Air Force, flying a Thunderbolt. (U. S. AIR FORCE)

immolation (and perhaps sensing it), had sacrificed the German Air Force to his own peculiar gods, just as he had the Wehrmacht and the German people. "If the war is to be lost," he believed, "the nation also will perish. This fate is inevitable. There is no need to consider the basis even of a most primitive existence any longer. On the contrary," he told Speer, "it is better to destroy even that, and to destroy it ourselves. The nation has proved itself weak, and the future belongs solely to the stronger eastern nation. Besides, those who remain after the battle are of little value; for the good have fallen."

He had seen to that personally. He established himself in the Reich Chancellery in Berlin, by early 1945 a city of rubble, which he declared he would "defend to the last" despite the fact, as he believed, that the German people were "unworthy of my genius." While his armies desperately fought the Russians in the east and the British and Americans in the west, Hitler awaited the inevitable. But when

holes in *Petie* (many of which could be credited to friendly antiaircraft fire), Meyer was untouched (but it had been his last fight—in which he scored his twenty-fourth aerial victory—for before he took to the air again he was injured in an automobile accident, hospitalized for three months, and then returned to the United States).

When Operation Hermann ended the question arose again, "Where is the Luftwaffe?" The Great Blow had been, as all had wished in Hitler's headquarters, a surprising one. But it was the last. The Allies had lost 156 aircraft (120 British and 36 U.S.); the Germans lost over 200; only sixty Luftwaffe pilots were taken prisoner. Over fifty irreplaceable air leaders were thrown away in *Der Grosse Schlag;* even the reserves were sacrificed. Many of the losses could be attributed to inexperienced German pilots who inadvertently collided over their targets or were readily shot down by Allied pilots or antiaircraft.

The Luftwaffe? Hitler, approaching his Wagnerian

Jug pilots of the 354th Fighter Group discuss a strafing of German supply columns and communications targets. Left to right: Omer W. Culberson (Minneapolis), Orrin D. Rawlings (Depue, Illinois), Glenn T. Eagleston (Alhambra, California), James B. Dalglish (Rome, New York), and Lloyd J. Overfield (Leavenworth, Kansas.) (U. S. AIR FORCE)

And what they did: when the weather cleared over Belgium Ninth Air Force fighter-bombers tore Hitler's Ardennes offensive to bits. Here is what remained of *a German convoy after the P-47s caught it on a highway in Belgium.* (U. S. AIR FORCE)

he went, he wished the whole world to go with him.

"He had a special picture of the world," observed General Heinz Guderian, "and every fact had to be fitted into that fancied picture. As he believed, so the world must be, but, in fact, it was a picture of another world." How true: much of Germany and its cities bore the aspect of *Mondlandschaft*.

v

Although Hitler's mad counteroffensive had failed, no one in the Allied camp was aware of the extent of that failure: its losses in men, machines, muni-

tions, and expenditure of a continually diminishing supply of fuel. The Ardennes battle had in fact upset the Allied ground battle timetable and interfered with the strategic aerial plan. Heavy bombers diverted to ground co-operation led to some recovery of the German synthetic oil industry, for example.

There was little optimism in the Allied camp in early 1945. There seemed little hope for an early end to the war in Europe. A realist, Spaatz visualized the possibility of the war's continuing on into autumn. If, as revealed by *Der Grosse Schlag,* the Germans could muster counteroffensives in the future, it would be a very hard summer.

Winter 1944. Flying Fortresses heading for Germany to bomb railroad targets that did not yield to the heavy bomber. Easily repaired by slave labor gangs, these targets did not loom very large in the opinion of General Spaatz of the Strategic Air Forces.

(U. S. AIR FORCE)

ously Bomber Command attacked important rail centers and the Ruhr waterways, and contributed to the vexing Battle of the Atlantic by placing "Tallboys" (a twelve-thousand-pound, extremely destructive bomb devised by B. N. Wallis, inventor of the "Dam Buster" bombs) into the battleship *Tirpitz,* which turned over and blew up.

Harris deployed his heavies mainly in the Ruhr; the Mosquitos harassed Berlin as did the Eighth Air Force's Fortresses and Liberators. Flak was more of a menace than the Luftwaffe, and great forces of bombers crossed German skies, night and day, with little opposition.

As the ground forces closed in upon Hitler in his bunker in Berlin, British and American air power was employed in assisting the Russian advance from the east. This was mainly in the form of heavy bombardments of major transportation centers: Chemnitz, Leipzig, Cottbus, Berlin, and Dresden. In conjunction with a new Russian offensive, which opened the second week of January, various strikes by British and American bombers were made. In some quarters it was believed that such co-ordination of plans should prove disheartening to the Germans. Chief of Air Staff Sir Charles Portal, while voting for oil targets as top priority, believed also that the Allies "should use available effort in one big attack on Berlin and attacks on Dresden, Leipzig, Chemnitz, or any other cities where a severe blitz will not only cause confusion in the evacuation from the east but will also hamper the movement of troops from the west."

The Germans, on the other hand, were in worse condition than the Allies realized. Despite the use of the strategic bombers in the European land battle, the Lancasters, Fortresses, Liberators, and Mosquitos continued to appear over Germany with devastating effect. The Fifteenth Air Force, for example, was not tied down to the Battle of the Bulge, and its heavy bombers contributed its share to the bombing of the oil centers during that critical time. To Spaatz, oil and jets were the major anxieties and as soon as possible he hoped to aim his strategic forces at these targets. Even Harris's Bomber Command began attacking the despised panacea targets, namely the oil plants. By November 1944 Bomber Command was carrying heavy loads of explosives to various oil targets both night and day. Simultane-

A twelve-thousand-pound "Tallboy" devised by Barnes Wallis of the Dam Buster bombs and which proved effective against German dams and canals.

(U. S. AIR FORCE)

What emerged from this hopeful attempt to co-operate with an ally—a touchy and not always co-operative ally—was a classic example of the terrifying impact of total air war. This was the devastation of the city of Dresden by RAF Bomber Command and the Eighth Air Force beginning on the night of February 13, 1945, and continuing into the next day. Eight hundred Bomber Command heavies initiated the attack in a night raid and 311 Eighth Air Force B-17s completed it the following day. And the day after an additional 200 American bombers returned to churn up what was already a catastrophe.

The horror and terror on the ground was incredible, destruction was extensive, and the loss of life was frightful. The beautiful little city, its population swollen by an influx of refugees from the east fleeing before the Russians bent upon revenge, pillage, and rape, and its predominantly wooden buildings, ideal for incendiaries, all but vanished in a howling whirlwind of incineration. Although it is unlikely that the true toll will ever be known, the number of people probably killed at Dresden was about 135,000 (as compared with the atomic bombing of Hiroshima, which killed 71,379). Harris had been correct, they had reaped the whirlwind.

By April of 1945 the great European air war was virtually over. The most important targets remained those associated with the oil industry. Berlin, the objective of the Russians (although Stalin assured Eisenhower, rather significantly on April Fools' Day, that the German capital was of no military importance), continued to take a tremendous pounding from the air. On March 18 the Eighth Air Force mounted its largest daylight raid on Berlin—1250 Fortresses and Liberators escorted by 14 groups of Mustangs. Bombing through the overcast by instrument (H2X), they did great damage to transportation and industrial targets in the city. But on this day the German jets came out in numbers for the first time—three dozen intercepted the heavy bombers in spite of the poor weather and claimed 15 "kills" (two probable) of the day's total American loss of 24 bombers and 5 fighters. Only two Me-262s were shot down in the encounter. German flak, too, was particularly telling, and at least 600 bombers were damaged, 16 so badly that they were forced to crash-land behind the Russian lines beyond Berlin.

The success of the jet fighters that day was a foreboding development, an indication of what might materialize if the Luftwaffe could muster pilots, aircraft, and fuel. On April 10 no less than 50 jets intercepted a large (1232) raid on the Berlin area. The objectives were airfields, marshaling yards, jet assembly plants around the capital at Oranienburg, Rechlin-Larz, Brandenburg-Briest, Burg, and Parchim.

Mustangs of the Eighth Air Force attacked the "blow jobs" and shot down twenty in the vicinity of Oranienburg and other targets near Berlin. Another ten jets were claimed by bomber gunners, particularly those of the 13th Combat Wing (95th, 100th, and 390th Bomb Groups) over Berlin. A loss of at least thirty jets was the most severe of the war, to which could be added hundreds destroyed on the ground. The Eighth lost ten bombers in the widespread fighting, but the jets were as good as finished. That the slower P-51s had been able to deal so devastatingly with the Me-262s was undoubtedly because of the inexperience of most of the German pilots.

What occurred over and within Germany could no longer be called "battles." Deep underground, in his ill-ventilated, artificially lighted bunker Hitler marshaled forces he no longer had for battles that could not be fought. He believed, almost to the end, that some miracle—if not a miracle weapon—would save him from the Russians slashing at the gates of Berlin. For a brief time his "miracle" was Generaloberst Gotthard Heinrici, who with minimal forces somehow managed to hold the Russians in check temporarily in the face of military madness and hopelessness. By mid-April the Russians opened their final drive into the heart of Berlin. Within days the lone remaining outpost in all of Germany was the bunker under the Reich Chancellery. The glorious battle had degenerated into street fighting like that out of which the Third Reich had sprung; there were no more strategic targets, only fear-driven, depleted scarecrows. Chaos had indeed come to those who had lit the torch of war.

On April 16, 1945, General Carl Spaatz dispatched a message to Major General James Doolittle (Eighth Air Force) and Lieutenant General Nathan Twining (Fifteenth Air Force): "The advances of our ground forces have brought to a close the strategic air war waged by the United

The 384th over Dresden (after the terrible February 13–14, 1945, attacks that burned the city). The target is the rail yards, over which escaping Germans were expected to travel. (U. S. AIR FORCE)

States Strategic Air Forces and the Royal Air Force Bomber Command. . . .

"From now onward our Strategic Air Forces must operate with our Tactical Air Forces in close co-operation with our Armies.

"All units of the U. S. Strategic Air Forces are commended for their part in winning the Strategic Air War and are enjoined to continue with undiminished effort and precision the final tactical phase of air action to secure the ultimate objective—complete defeat of Germany."

Four days later Hitler celebrated his last, that is, fifty-sixth, birthday in the grim, unreal setting of his bunker. When Hitler emerged around noon to receive the tributes of his few remaining faithful (among them Goebbels, Martin Bormann, Speer, Von Ribbentrop, Himmler, Jodl, and Keitel), plus some SS troops and a contingent of Hitler Youth (children would have been a more appropriate designation). Hitler had aged, and those who had not seen him for a while were shocked at his appearance. He was bent, he dragged one foot, his hands trembled, and his color was ghastly.

Göring arrived later in the day to pay his respects; his plans were made. He evacuated Karinhall, had the Luftwaffe pack his treasure into a great convoy of trucks, and after dynamiting Karinhall, paid his visit to Hitler and fled to the south. Luftwaffe chief of staff Koller bitterly noted that Göring, as usual, had left him to deal with Hitler's fury. Göring's plan also included bargaining with the Allies, assuming that he would be able to do better than Hitler; after all, wasn't Göring a figure of fun to the Allies? They hated Hitler but they laughed at the Fat One. When he offered his services as peacemaker, the Führer (who had suffered a physical collapse) revived long enough to accuse the Reichsmarschall of "high treason" and ordered his arrest. He refused, however, under the urging of Goebbels and Bormann, to have Göring executed.

Göring was stripped of his offices, and appointed in his place as *Oberbefehlshaber der Luftwaffe* (of a non-existent Luftwaffe) was the faithful Robert Ritter von Greim, formerly chief of Luftflotte 6. In addition to this empty command, Hitler also presented Greim with a potassium cyanide capsule. Hitler had already begun to discuss his own impending end and Greim begged to be permitted to remain in Berlin to die with his Führer. So did Hanna Reitsch, famed prewar woman glider pilot and a dedicated Nazi test pilot.

On the night of April 28 Hanna Reitsch, with Greim as a passenger, flew a small Arado trainer off the streets of Berlin. Hitler had ordered them out of the bunker so that Greim could order Luftwaffe support for the decimated army of General Walther Wenck, attempting to break through the Russian armies encircling Berlin. It was, of course, another pointless gesture, and the little Arado managed to get off the rubble-strewn street and into the air despite the Russian small arms and anti-aircraft fire. Flying over the ruins of Berlin, aflame it seemed from end to end, Hanna Reitsch headed north. She survived the war, but Greim could not face the future he saw for Germany. Nor could Hitler, betrayed on all sides, who committed suicide in his bunker and then was burned along with his bride of a few hours, Eva Braun.

With the Luftwaffe burning on the ground, Allied fighters, in air-ground co-operation, made a shambles of any German convoy that attempted to move.
(U. S. ARMY)

cerebral hemorrhage) to inform him of the "plight of the civil population in Occupied Holland," which the Prime Minister believed to be "desperate." Perhaps three million people faced starvation in an area still held by the German Twenty-fifth Army, isolated but still holding out in "Fortress Holland."

"We believe," Churchill told Roosevelt, "that large numbers are dying daily, and the situation must deteriorate rapidly now that communications between Germany and Holland are virtually cut. I fear we may soon be in presence of a tragedy."

General Eisenhower too was aware of this dire possibility. "I still refused to consider a major offensive into the country," he wrote in his *Crusade in Europe.* To stop the Allied advance the Germans had opened the dikes, which flooded the Dutch countryside with sea water. To forestall further such desolation, Eisenhower held his forces in check, knowing that the German Army in Holland was virtually helpless insofar as it mattered in the Battle of Germany. If he pressed his advantage Eisen-

Last-ditch weapon: pick-a-back bomber. The lower plane, the Ju-88, was loaded with explosives, and the upper FW-190, with pilot, was supposed to fly the Ju-88 to its selected target, release it, and guide it the rest of the way by radio. (U. S. AIR FORCE)

Greim, captured by the victorious Allies, said upon swallowing the capsule the Führer had so thoughtfully given him, "I am head of the Luftwaffe but I have no Luftwaffe."

There was no Luftwaffe, just as there were no remaining strategic targets. Even the fighters were forbidden to strafe because of the general shambles and the possibility of hitting released prisoners or Allied troops.

However, among the final "targets" of the Eighth Air Force's B-17s were a racetrack and a golf course. These unusual objectives were to be hit from an altitude of about four hundred feet. The mission was not carried out with any levity, for behind it lay a great national crisis. On April 10 Churchill had communicated with Roosevelt (only two days before the American President died of a

Caught in the guns of Mustang pilot Bernard H. Howes, this pick-a-back is abandoned by the pilot (just below the tail of the Ju-88). (U. S. AIR FORCE)

Göring at journey's end; dismissed by Hitler, pursued by the Gestapo, but undismayed, Göring hoped to negotiate a peace with Eisenhower. (U. S. ARMY)

Hanna Reitsch, Germany's leading woman aviator, glider pilot, and jet test pilot. She flew Greim into and out of Berlin while the Russians encircled it and Allied bombers bombed it into rubble. (U. S. AIR FORCE)

Robert von Greim, last chief of the Luftwaffe.
(H. J. NOWARRA)

hower realized that "Not only would great additional destruction and suffering have resulted but the enemy's opening of dikes would further have flooded the country and destroyed much of its fertility for years to come."

The early flooding contributed to the starvation then afflicting the Dutch. But there was even more. A general railway strike in September of 1944 called by the government in exile from London inspired a German retaliation. All food supplies to western Holland were cut off for two months, thus hindering the stock-piling of food supplies. Further, all

". . . but I have no Luftwaffe. . . ." *Robert Ritter von Greim,* Oberbefehlshaber der Luftwaffe, *Berlin, April 1945.* (U. S. AIR FORCE)

means of Dutch transport were seized by the Germans to doubly ensure the edict. By November the first deaths by starvation occurred; by the spring the estimate was that a thousand Dutch died every day.

To alleviate the situation the Allies proposed a plan to the *Reichskommissar* in the Netherlands, Dr. Artur von Seyss-Inquart. The Allies would halt their westward advance into Holland if the Germans ceased their ruin of the Dutch earth and permitted wholesale drops of food and other supplies to the Dutch by air. Attempts were made, meanwhile, to provide relief by limited means but to no great effect, and the Luftwaffe's flak continued to be as deadly as ever.

To work out a solution Eisenhower sent his chief of staff, Brigadier General Walter Bedell Smith, into Holland to discuss it with Seyss-Inquart. Although Generaloberst Johannes Blaskowitz refused to surrender his troops, it was agreed that the Allies could fly large formations of bombers over certain areas of Holland at very low level and drop the supplies. Aircraft were to be de-gunned, no ammunition could be carried, and no photographs could be taken.

The two drop points were the racetrack at The Hague (one of the Nazi's major rocket-launching

centers) and a golf course at Rotterdam. Eisenhower accepted the proposals although he honestly believed that the "continued occupation of Holland was senseless" and warned Blaskowitz and Seyss-Inquart that he would "tolerate no interference with the relief program and that if the Germans were guilty of any breach of faith I would later refuse to treat them as prisoners of war."

The mercy mission, as the Air Force called it, was prepared with great enthusiasm by the men in the bombers. RAF's Bomber Command flew one of its most gratifying daylight missions (Operation Manna) on April 29, 1945, when the Lancasters and Mosquitos of Nos. 1, 3, and 8 Groups initiated the operation with more than 250 aircraft participating. No. 8 Group was comprised of nineteen—mostly Mosquito, with the rest Lancaster—squadrons of the legendary Pathfinder Force, which had so skillfully marked the targets in the wasted Ruhr. For Manna it marked the several drop zones assigned to Bomber Command: the Valkenburg airfield at Leiden, the racetrack and Ypenburg airfield at The Hague, the Waalhaven airfield and Kralingsche-Plas in Rotterdam and Gouda.

On May 1, after three days of cancellations because of the weather, the Eighth Air Force dispatched three wings, the 13th, 45th, and 93rd, of the 3rd Air Division. Its Flying Fortresses were loaded with nearly eight tons of food. At the premission briefing Sergeant Cecil Cohen, who among other duties functioned as the photographer in his 34th Bomb Group, recalled that he was told to take along a small reflex camera and "to get everything you can, but under no circumstances show the camera from a window." Cohen decided that he would take shots through the open bomb bay before and after the drop. Although the day's mission had not been scrubbed as the previous three, it was not an ideal day for flying, especially at low level.

As recalled by First Lieutenant Jerome Kagel, "The weather was bad—rain and gusty winds threw our ships about like model airplanes in a wind tunnel."

Cecil Cohen prepared his camera for his part in the mission. He placed filters over the lens to cut some of the haze. But the plane apparently had strayed from the designated corridor as they approached the Dutch coast—"one of the meanest in the world for flak." As they came in lower, it

Cecil Cohen in the waist of a Flying Fortress en route to Holland. (34TH BOMB GROUP)

dren danced around when they saw our planes. I even spotted a few enemy soldiers intermingled with the civilians.

"The people seemed to get all out of bounds as our supplies rained down. They ran toward the tumbling boxes of rations apparently heedless of the danger of being hit by bundles which fell with terrific impetus. I wouldn't be surprised if in their eagerness and their anguish for food some of them were hurt by the boxes or from being jostled in that tremendous throng. The whole thing made an exciting, heart-wrenching picture that will remain with me for a long time.

"I was soon absorbed in the amazing spectacle below, as I saw—actually saw—thousands of people mobbing the streets, gazing skyward and waving frantically at us. Boulevards, street corners, everywhere, civilians clustered, looking up at these former dealers of destruction that were now playing the lead roles as angels of mercy."

Cohen, meanwhile, was recording the mercy mission (military installations were of no real interest). To get another angle he stood on several boxes

was possible for Cohen to pick out German gun emplacements; there were even German troops moving around beneath their Fortress with seeming unconcern. But not a wary flak unit, which began firing at the straying plane. The pilot all but stood the big Fortress on one wing—Cohen and the other aircrew in the plane's waist were piled in a heap against the side—and returned to the correct flight path. Inside Holland they came down very low and the air was bumpy. On his stomach in the bomb bay, Cohen for the first time in his Air Force career became airsick. The strange position, the rough air had done it—and the result was the spoilage of the filter on Cohen's camera. It would be impossible to clean, so he merely threw it overboard and took several photographs with a filterless lens.

"When we came over the racetrack," Kagel saw "a surging crowd of excited people, hundreds of them, of every age. They filled the grandstands and seemed to be everywhere—on the paddock, along the track, hugging the guard rail. Women and chil-

Passing over a windmill, the crew of a Flying Fortress is greeted by arm-waving Dutch. (U. S. AIR FORCE)

Operation Manna: supplies rain down upon a drop site in Holland as this 390th Group Fortress opens its bomb bay. (U. S. AIR FORCE)

No other words required. (U. S. AIR FORCE)

that he had stacked in the nose of the plane. With a couple of crewmen grasping his legs, about half of his body projected from the upper nose of the B-17 as he snapped pictures blowing in the wind. If any German saw him, there were no official complaints registered. Aircraft did return to England with flak holes in their wings, but no serious incident marred the mission. For ten days these missions continued, missions the crews found more gratifying than their missions to Berlin—or Dresden.

Flight Lieutenant R. E. Wannop, RAF, summed up the emotions of all men when he described one of the final missions. "We crossed the Dutch coast at two thousand feet and began to come down to five hundred. Below lay the once fertile land now covered by many feet of sea water. Houses that had been the proud possessions of a happy, carefree people now stood forlorn surrounded by the whirling, surging flood, some with only a roof visible.

A double line of poplar trees would show where once there had been a busy highway.

"Children ran out of school waving excitedly. One old man stopped at a cross-roads and shook his umbrella. The roads were crowded with hundreds of people waving. . . .

"Nobody spoke in the aircraft. . . .

"My vision was a little misty. . . .

"Perhaps it was the rain on the perspex. . . ."

The last Manna mission was flown on May 8, 1945; the Third Reich on that day lay in ruins and Hitler's wretched heirs surrendered to the Allies. Signing for Germany, Generaloberst Alfred Jodl, German Chief of Staff, said, "With this signature, the German people and Armed Forces are—for better or worse—delivered into the victor's hands."

Hitler's war was over; the most powerful air forces the world had ever known could turn to the shriveled Greater East Asia Co-Prosperity Sphere.

Greim's Luftwaffe: May 8, 1945. (U. S. AIR FORCE)

BOOK II
The Divine Wind

The purity of youth will usher in the Divine Wind.

—VICE-ADMIRAL TAKIJIRO OHNISHI

5

"TYGER! TYGER! BURNING BRIGHT"

THE Boeing B-29 ("Superfortress") was not—as the legend goes—designed specifically to bomb Tokyo, but it did to a devastating degree. Its inception, the idea of General Henry Arnold, dates from November 1939—more than two years before the Pearl Harbor attack. This conception was inspired by the Nazi blitzkrieg in Europe and the high probability of a German victory and the possibility of a Nazi foothold "somewhere in the Americas" from which aerial attacks could easily be mounted against the United States.

The B-29 was designed to fly over longer distances, at higher altitudes, and at greater speeds and to carry heavier bomb loads than the B-17 and the B-24. The advent of war put the project on an emergency basis and orders were placed for the B-29 off the drawing board, even before the aircraft had been tested. Consequently, the development of the B-29, called "the three-billion-dollar gamble," was fraught with hazard and potential tragedy. An innovational concept—a new engine, pressurized crew stations, and remote-control gun turrets, to name a few—the B-29 also carried a full load of bugs. One of the most critical was a tendency for engines to catch fire. The second test model, flown by the chief test pilot on the project,

Edmund T. Allen, caught fire on February 18, 1943, during a test flight from Boeing Field, Seattle, and crashed, killing Allen and ten experienced B-29 specialists aboard. In addition, the plane, which Allen was attempting to land even while a sheet of flame trailed from his right wing, rammed into the Frye Packing Plant, killing several workers inside.

Despite such tragedies—for even after the B-29 went into combat in-flight engine fires plagued it— the gamble proved worthwhile. The B-29 emerged as the most formidable air weapon of the war. Although originally intended for use against Germany, by the summer of 1943 Air Force planning proceeded along a course aimed at Japan. Early in November, General Oliver P. Echols, Assistant Chief of Air Staff for Matériel, Maintenance, and Distribution, could state with more authority than historical truth that "the B-29 airplane was thought out and planned as a high-altitude, long-range bomber to attack Japan, her cities and industrial keypoints." The employment of the aircraft made the general's slight exaggeration a portentous historical truth.

With practically all of the bugs ironed out of the B-29 there still remained the problem of its deployment and command. The Pacific remained a

The Boeing B-29 "Superfortress," an aircraft designed for a very special mission. (U. S. AIR FORCE)

pail of worms, with its arguments over definition of command boundaries, supply distribution, and personality clashes. Once the Marianas were taken and bases established it was possible to attack Japan more efficiently than was possible from Indian and Chinese bases. But this would mean that the B-29s would "violate" the air over MacArthur's territory as well as the air over Nimitz's territory. The solution devised by the Joint Chiefs of Staff was the establishment of the Twentieth Air Force, under its direct control and with General Arnold as executive agent for the Joint Chiefs. This solved the problem of the B-29 units but, in effect, compounded those of logistics and administration, which devolved upon the theater commanders. The strained interservice relations (Navy vs. Air Force) were stretched nearly to the limit by the advent of the B-29 in the Pacific.

Since it became reasonably evident by the "Trident" conference in Washington (May 12–27, 1943)

The advent of the B-29 initiated an internal tug of war. Chennault—and especially Chiang Kai-shek— hoped to have them for the Fourteenth Air Force. Here Chennault conducts members of the Chinese Aero- *nautical Affairs Commission around a Fourteenth Air Force base. At this time not only did Chennault command the Fourteenth, he was also chief of staff to Chiang Kai-shek of the Chinese Air Force.*

(U. S. AIR FORCE)

that Germany was checked and that, given time and some luck, the Allies might open a second front in Europe by May 1944, it was decided that the B-29 would not be employed in Europe. To assuage the feelings of Chiang Kai-shek, who believed he was being given short shrift by the Allies, the B-29s were earmarked for China. On their part, the Allied planners did not believe that the war in the East could be decided in China, preferring to move toward Japan from the east and south. But with Chiang Kai-shek's seemingly unlimited manpower, it did seem feasible to furnish supplies to the Chinese—provided the Generalissimo could get them to fight the Japanese and not each other.

The thought of pouring U.S. divisions into China did not sit well with the U. S. Chiefs of Staff; nor did another suggestion that Chennault's Fourteenth Air Force be equipped with B-29s, plus additional fighter groups to escort them, for the bombing of the Japanese homeland. The latter idea, however, had its points, the most important of which was that a bomber offensive out of Chinese bases, or at least so the Air Force hoped, might "tremendously stimulate Chinese morale and unify the Chinese people under the leadership of Chiang Kai-shek."

At the same time Kenney in the southwest Pacific wrote Arnold that he assumed "that I am still to get the first B-29 unit. . . . If you want the B-29 used efficiently and effectively where it will do the

Building a B-29 air base in China with manpower. Rocks are brought to field site from the nearby hills in horse-drawn carts. (U. S. AIR FORCE)

most good in the shortest time, the southwest Pacific area is the place and the Fifth Air Force can do the job." The generally deteriorating military situation in the China-Burma area, however, favored the CBI (China-Burma-India) as the recipient of the first B-29s.

Arnold's solution was to establish the Twentieth Air Force directly under the control of the Joint Chiefs of Staff; this very effectively denied the B-29

An American construction engineer called this a "ten-ton, five-hundred-coolie-powered, rice-burning roller."

Stones, mud, and gravel were ground into the strip by manpower also. (U. S. AIR FORCE)

to the various warring factions. He kept the super-bomber out of the hands of Stilwell, MacArthur, and Nimitz, none of whom were particularly impressed with the strategic potential of what was then being called the VLR (very long-range) aircraft for employment by VHB (very heavy bomber) groups.

These groups (the 40th, 444th, 462nd, 468th) had been in existence since November 1943 and were assigned to the Twentieth Air Force in June of 1944 as the 58th Bombardment Wing (VH) of the 20th Bomber Command. The first B-29 landed at Kharagpur, about seventy miles west of Calcutta, India, on April 2, 1944. Before this was possible two months of very hard labor had been put in by the 853rd Engineer Aviation Battalion and the 382nd Engineer Construction Battalion (which had been borrowed from Stilwell's Ledo Road project). The labor force eventually numbered six thousand U.S. troops and twenty-seven thousand Indians. The preparation of the Indian bases was an epic in itself, for the B-29 required longer runways, which, in addition, had to be thicker than normal to withstand the weight of the great plane.

At the same time, since the B-29s would be based in India, out of the reach of the Japanese, staging areas in the neighborhood of Chengtu, China, were also constructed. Again conditions were at once contemporary and primitive, with American engineers directing Chinese laborers, doing most of the work literally by hand, numbering into the thousands. By May 10 the Chengtu bases were also ready for the B-29. These bases were within range of the Japanese homeland.

But there remained, as always, the problem of logistics. Before a mission could be mounted from Chengtu, supplies—fuel, ammunition, bombs, parts: everything—had to be moved from the Calcutta area, across the Hump, to China. Roughly it required six B-29 flights over the Hump and back to make possible one B-29 bombing mission upon Japan.

This in itself was a formidable undertaking. The Himalayas were the highest, most treacherous mountains in the world and the B-29 was not yet the world's most efficient aircraft. Even on the flight from the United States to India several of the planes were left behind with engine problems along the way and two were completely destroyed at Karachi.

A B-29 resting on a handmade strip in China.
(U. S. AIR FORCE)

The capricious engines continued to plague crews—and the heat of India contributed to the problem of overheating. Merely starting an engine could cause a cylinder to blow and the aircraft to catch fire. Crews looked at the crossing of the Himalayas in their unproved "superbomber" with skepticism. That they should be put to such inglorious work as hauling supplies instead of bomb loads was expressed in their own description of themselves as "a goddamed trucking outfit."

Two days after the India-to-China supply run had been initiated, a B-29 was attacked for the first time by enemy aircraft. The encounter occurred on April 26, 1944, late in the afternoon, when a B-29 (piloted by Major Charles H. Hansen) carrying a cargo of fuel had reached the Indo-Burmese frontier. The B-29 was cruising at sixteen thousand feet when Major Hansen saw, two thousand feet below and about five miles distant to the starboard, a formation of twelve Nakajima Ki. 43 "Oscars" (the Ki. was an abbreviation for *Hikoki,* meaning "aircraft").

Alerting his crew to battle stations, Hansen observed the Oscars as six of them began spiraling up toward their lone plane and the remaining six continued on in formation toward the Hump. The six Oscars that approached the B-29 then broke up into two formations of three on each side of the big bomber. They remained out of range, obviously studying the B-29, a plane none had probably ever seen before. This went on for nearly fifteen minutes as the nervous gunners on the bomber tracked the

Oscars. Suddenly the lead Oscar whipped out of formation and twisted in toward the B-29 almost directly from the starboard side. The wings winked with fire as the Oscar closed and a burst of fire cut across the B-29's midsection. A scream on the intercom meant that someone had been hit (Sergeant Walter W. Gilonske, a waist gunner, was wounded in this attack). The remaining Oscars followed in upon the bomber, now crippled—the top gun turrets were out, the 20-mm. tail cannon failed, and the twin .50s jammed. The latter were quickly cleared, however.

One of the Oscars came within a hundred yards of Sergeant Harold Lanhan's tail guns and left the battle smoking. The remaining Oscars continued attacking, but without conviction, for about twenty-five minutes and then left the battle. The American bomber had taken eight hits and, once Sergeant Gilonske was attended to, continued on to Chengtu unchallenged by other enemy aircraft.

Meanwhile, the B-29 crews operated primarily as

Kenneth B. Wolfe, first commander of 20th Bomber Command—which was specially set up to keep the B-29s under control of the Air Force. (U. S. AIR FORCE)

"truck drivers," which did not contribute to their efficiency in high-altitude formation flying, bombing, gunnery—the essentials to their primary mission. It was two months (less two days) before the first shakedown mission was scheduled for the 58th Bombardment Wing. Brigadier General Kenneth B. Wolfe, commanding 20th Bomber Command, hoped to compensate for the training deficiencies by bombing the target at night, each plane going in individually rather than in formation. Arnold, in Washington, rejected this and insisted upon a "daylight precision" attack because "the entire bomber program is predicated upon the B-29's employment as a visual precision weapon."

Wolfe rescheduled his shakedown operation, crammed some training time into the already strained program (B-29s flew in bomber formation over the Hump even while on trucking missions), and believed the wing ready for a strike upon the Makasan railway shops in Bangkok, Siam (Thailand). This would not yet be a strike against the Japanese homeland, but might very well interfere with Japanese operations in northern Burma.

The mission was set for June 5, 1944—the first B-29 mission of the war. One hundred of the big bombers were in readiness in the Kharagpur base area; the takeoff was to begin at 5:45 A.M., before the heat of the morning could overheat the engines and to afford as much daylight as possible for the long flight of about a thousand miles to—and, most importantly, a thousand miles from—Bangkok.

One plane of the 462nd Group developed mechanical problems and simply never left the ground. The 40th Group also left one plane behind. During takeoff at Chakulia Major John B. Keller's aircraft began behaving peculiarly about halfway down the runway: the nose of the plane lifted off the runway and for thousands of feet the B-29 maintained this curious attitude—its nosewheel in the air and the tail skid bumping against the ground. Then it left the ground and appeared to be taking off normally. The left wing suddenly dropped and Keller brought it up with a quick turn of the control column. But the wing dropped again and the plane, seemingly out of control, plowed into the ground, exploded, and left a flaming trail across the earth. Bombs exploded inside the fuselage, tearing it to bits and immediately killing all inside the plane except the copilot, Lieutenant B. A. Elsner, who could be heard whispering something about an engine failure before he died.

The remaining ninety-eight B-29s, led by Colonel Leonard F. Harman (commanding officer of the 40th Group), proceeded with the mission. If the takeoff had been complicated by ground mist, formation was rendered all but impossible by cloud and haze. Confused, apprehensive, the pilots joined up with the wrong elements, and as weather thickened, even the rudimentary formations disintegrated. It seemed better to risk what little Japanese opposition was expected singly than to chance a collision in mid-air. As was also expected, one by one planes developed some mechanical trouble or other and began turning back—a total of fourteen before the target was reached. Of the remaining eighty-four aircraft, seventy-seven actually dropped their bombs in the target area (and of these, forty-eight were forced to depend upon radar because of the overcast; the radar teams were not well trained, it might be noted).

After about six hours of touchy flying, with no improvement in the weather, the planes began arriving over Bangkok at 10:52 A.M.—and continued to arrive in a long stream (instead of the intended diamond formations) for over an hour. Japanese antiaircraft began bursting around the big bombers, and what might be called the Battle of Bangkok began. No flaming bomber went down before these guns—nor to any of the nine fighters that rose gingerly to make a few passes (a dozen in all) without effect.

But neither was the scattered, rather haphazard bombing very effective. The mission was regarded as an "operational success"—for a first mission. Bombs had fallen into the target area, some directly upon assembly and boiler shops, although it was admitted that the damage could not be expected to bring about a noticeable "decrease in the flow of troops and military supplies into Burma."

No aircraft was lost through enemy action, although the return trip to Bengal was more perilous than the long bomb runs over the target had been. With the monsoon season fast approaching, the weather, as a result rough and threatening, took its toll; as did the still emerging bugs. Fuel ran low because of faulty systems, engines froze up, propellers were feathered, and pilots fought to keep on course in the high winds, black clouds, and rain.

New weapon of war with teething troubles; the B-29 with engines warming up. Ground crew under wing is ready with fire extinguishers. (U. S. AIR FORCE)

After ten to twelve hours in the air, the B-29s began coming to earth wherever possible in friendly territory. Some landed in the home base area but others were scattered, after emergency landings, in a dozen British bases. Two of the big bombers were lost when the pilots were forced to ditch in the Bay of Bengal; another—with two engines malfunctioning—was abandoned over Yu-Chi (about sixty miles from Kunming), and a fourth crash-landed at the British base at Dumdum without injury to crew, although the B-29 was a total wreck.

Thus the shakedown mission to Bangkok had cost five B-29s (counting the one which exploded on takeoff) and fifteen lives. There were those who question the "operational success" of that mission. Still, a mission had taken place, seventy-three B-29s had made the round trip, bombs had fallen upon enemy installations, and crews had proved themselves and so, with some reservations, had the aircraft. It had been demonstrated that heavy loads could be carried over great distances and that was what the B-29 had been designed to do.

The question of what was to come next was answered with sudden unexpectedness. Even before all the strays had been reassembled from the initial mission Wolfe received urgent word from Arnold. A B-29 attack upon the Japanese homeland (which

Warming up; the giant waiting for the word to take off on a mission. (U. S. AIR FORCE)

had not been bombed since the Doolittle raid of 1942 except for small strikes in 1943 by the Eleventh Air Force, based in the Aleutians, on Paramushiro in the Kurile Islands) must be carried out by mid-June—a "maximum effort" which Arnold explained would help to divert the Japanese from their east China offensive then threatening Chennault's forward fields and also would tie in with an "important operation" in the western Pacific.

Wolfe hoped for a force of fifty B-29s for June 15 and an additional five if the mission could be postponed five days. Even such not very impressive numbers would put a strain upon the stockpile of supplies in China. Arnold was not pleased and called for an effort of no less than seventy bombers for June 15; if the Hump flights must be increased to accomplish this, then that too must be done. Wolfe proceeded as ordered, pressuring his crews over the Hump and cutting down on fuel for the fighters. But he knew that as The Day came, no matter how impressive the number, the inevitable arithmetic would set in and the maximum effort would be less than that.

The flight from the Chinese bases around Chengtu to the selected primary target—the Imperial iron- and steelworks at Yawata—was about sixteen hundred miles, making the round trip thirty-two hundred miles. Wolfe had had bomb bay fuel tanks, necessary for so long a mission, for eighty-six B-29s. This was a little better than Arnold's minimum of seventy. With a good deal of hard work in blistering heat, no less than ninety-two "Dreamboats" (one of the code words for the B-29) began moving into China on June 13. Of the ninety-two, seventy-nine arrived in China; of the thirteen that had not, for various mechanical reasons, one B-29 and its crew was lost.

Four bombers already at Chengtu were added to the arrivals, so that eighty-three stood ready for the mission. More mathematics ensued what with mechanical failures and by the afternoon of June 15 a total of sixty-eight B-29s would be air-borne for Japan. The force was led by Brigadier General LaVerne G. Saunders, commanding officer of the 58th Wing, in a plane from the 468th Group and piloted by Group Commander Colonel Howard Engler. Fifteen B-29s followed their aircraft, *The Lady Hamilton,* but the sixteenth faltered, smashed back to earth, and burned—without a single injury to any of the crew.

Takeoff had been set for shortly after four o'clock in the afternoon, which would bring the B-29s over Yawata before midnight. It would be no daylight precision attack. Soon after the mission was airborne more of the not yet debugged bombers were forced back by mechanical failures. Four canceled out early in the flight. The first of forty-seven B-29s which dropped bombs on Yawata flashed the signal "Betty" to 20th Bomber Command headquarters at 11:38 P.M. For the first time since 1942 bombs rained down upon Japan. "Betty, Betty" tapped the radio operator—an echo of the *Tora, Tora* ("Tiger, Tiger") of the Pearl Harbor attack.

The sky was lashed with searchlights and a few fighters came up, as did the antiaircraft fire, but as at Bangok, no damage resulted from enemy action. A half-dozen planes jettisoned their bombs because of mechanical problems, two bombed the secondary target (Laoyao Harbor), and five others bombed various targets of opportunity.

Despite the lack of enemy opposition, there were losses nonetheless. Besides the aircraft which crashed and burned during takeoff, five others were lost during the mission and another—making the total loss of seven B-29s—on a postmission reconnaissance flight. One of the bombers that was lost

Help from a very small friend: the jeep guides the B-29 to its hardstand. Note copilot leaning out of his cockpit window. (U. S. AIR FORCE)

was destroyed by Japanese aircraft. Captain Robert Root's plane had developed engine trouble, so he set it down at the Chinese base at Neihsiang, near the Chinese-Japanese lines. As he settled into the airfield he radioed for American fighter protection while he and the crew worked on the B-29.

No American fighters arrived, but within a few minutes after the plane had landed two Japanese fighters swept down from across a low mountain range. Harry Zinder, *Time* correspondent, watched the approach of the fighters, shouted to the men inside the plane, and took refuge in a ditch about fifty yards from the bomber.

"The fighters roared across," Zinder reported later, "pulled up and then turned down on our ship. They spattered bullets across the fuselage and wings, then started a little fire on the left side. We hugged the ground closer as bullets kicked up dust and grass alongside the ditch. They made many passes. When the fire was fully blazing they left."

During the lull, Root and the others who had been

inside the plane jumped out (two of the crew were injured) and ran for the ditch to join Zinder and the others. They had barely settled into it when they heard the sound of engines again.

"There were fifteen this time—six bombers and nine fighters. The fighters peeled off first and did a strafing job, and then the bombers went to work and finished the job. We were in the ditch again, renewing our prayers. We felt sure they must have seen us because we could see their bomb bay doors open, see their bombs fall on the ship and around it. We decided to spend the rest of the morning in the ditch."

The B-29 was nothing but a wreck, and while the Americans lay in the ditch, covered with tree branches and grass, Japanese planes continued to come over intermittently to bomb and strafe the already long-destroyed bomber. Their vengeance fulfilled, the Japanese finally stopped coming. Their long, unreasoning attack was an indication of the fury the renewed attack upon the homeland had engendered. The men who had been aboard the B-29 were flown out of Neihsiang in a B-25 dispatched from the nearby base at Hsinching.

Although headlines in the United States proclaimed the news of the Yawata attack and such phrases as "glowing mass of ruins" and "reduced to huge rubbish heap" were used with poetic abandon, the report by Colonel Alan D. Clark, who flew the mission as an observer, contained the sentence "The results of the mission were poor." He noted that only a few bombs actually fell into the target area and that some bombs fell as far as twenty miles away. This he attributed to inefficient "blind bombing" (i.e., radar) because radar operators were yet inexperienced and untrained. Where the bombs had scattered through industrial and business districts, the Japanese declared that the buildings destroyed were "hospitals and schools."

Japanese propaganda also claimed the destruction of one B-29 and the capture of a crew, no member of which was less than a major in rank. Most of the men claimed by the Japanese, important squadron leaders most of them, had not even been on the mission. Japanese radio also claimed the destruction of B-24s that, like the high brass, had not participated in the mission. The general outcry revealed that, even if the official American evaluation of the mission was "poor," it had incensed the Japanese. It was time to apologize to the Emperor again.

Even more important to the future and its portents was the "important operation" with which the Yawata mission was co-ordinated. On the same day the Marianas campaign opened with the assault upon Saipan. With that island secured, on October 12, 1944, Brigadier General Haywood S. Hansell brought the first B-29, *Joltin' Josie,* into Saipan's Isley Field. Brilliant, young (forty-one), Hansell had recommended the taking of the Marianas as a base for the giant bombers. On the day that *Joltin' Josie* set down on Saipan the strategic air war took an ominous turn for Japan.

II

While the Twentieth Air Force underwent its growing pains, some of which proved tragically fatal, the two major Pacific forces were converging on the road back to the Philippines.

MacArthur's southwest Pacific forces leapfrogged out of New Guinea and onto Morotai Island (in the Halmahera group south of the Philippines) as Nimitz's Pacific Ocean areas forces struck in the Palaus, taking Peleliu and Angaur islands, east of the Philippines. With American forces in the Palaus (in the western Carolines), such strong Japanese bases in the central and eastern Carolines as Truk were neutralized; so were once and for all the bases in the Bismarck Archipelago, Kavieng and Rabaul. From bases on Angaur the 494th Bombardment Group of the Seventh Air Force was within bombing range of Japanese airfields in the Philippines, among them Clark Field, which had not been much in the news since the gloomy December days of 1941. The 494th, nicknamed "Kelly's Cobras" for the group commander Colonel Laurence B. Kelly and equipped with B-24s, arrived in the Palaus in October (1944) after a remarkable mass flight from Hawaii. Within twenty-four hours the group was off to bomb Yap and Koror, the latter

20th Bomber Command B-29, an aircraft of the 468th Bomb Group, returns from bombing Anshan, Manchuria. The city was an important steel-producing center; later it would house a school for training kamikaze pilots. (U. S. AIR FORCE)

of the Philippines—at Leyte—was advanced two months. The Joint Chiefs of Staff, then meeting with their British counterparts in Quebec, approved the idea, as did also Roosevelt and Churchill. Only MacArthur remained, and he was incommunicado on the Morotai invasion. However, Sutherland, certain of his chief's views, agreed to the advanced

A Navy Vought OS2U "Kingfisher" dips over Angaur Island in the Palau group of the Carolines as invasion forces head for the beaches. The central Pacific forces were on the move closer to Japan.

(NAVY DEPT., NATIONAL ARCHIVES)

Japanese ships burning in a Palau island harbor; a Yorktown Hellcat *noses into the picture at left.*

(NAVY DEPT., NATIONAL ARCHIVES)

a neighboring island of the Palaus, and returned without a loss. The group would soon be employed in the preparation for MacArthur's promised return to the Philippines. The Morotai operation placed units of Kenney's Far East Air Forces (which in June, had joined the Fifth and Thirteenth Air Forces under his command) within bombing range of Japanese targets in Java, the Celebes, and Borneo, as well as the Philippines. Setting up bases on Morotai, the Thirteenth Air Force (under the command of Major General St. Clair Streett), with its B-24s, began bombing Balikpapan, Borneo's Ploesti. Like the Seventh, the Fifth and Thirteenth Air Forces soon turned to softening up Leyte in the Philippines.

Meanwhile Halsey's carriers had also been striking at the Philippines during the Palau and Morotai operations. Halsey described Japanese aerial resistance as "amazing and fantastic" in its apparent impotence. He heard also from a Navy pilot shot down over Leyte and later rescued that guerrillas he had met told him that there were no Japanese on Leyte. Halsey immediately recommended a startling change in the Pacific timetable. Why not bypass the Palaus completely, he suggested to Nimitz, and strike at the middle of the Philippines instead of Mindanao (the southernmost island)? Nimitz, to a great extent, agreed. Although Peleliu and Angaur were taken (the former at great cost), the invasion of Yap was canceled and the invasion

Closing in: a Liberator examining destruction to bridges over a river in Burma. (U. S. AIR FORCE)

R R SIDING

WATER BUFFALO
(FEMALE)

SECTION HOUSE

BOX CARS

Reconnaissance photograph of a railroad in north Borneo, Netherlands East Indies. Patient study of the *photo reveals the careful attention to detail by Air Force intelligence men.* (U. S. AIR FORCE)

date and to Leyte over Mindanao (despite the fact that Leyte was out of the range of Allied fighter cover). Sutherland, however, could not quite agree with Halsey's view that the Japanese air force in the Philippines was "a hollow shell operating on a shoestring."

There was some truth in this view, but that was not quite the way it really was. True, the Marianas "Turkey Shoot" had taken an irreplaceable toll in men, aircraft, and ships from which the Imperial Fleet would never recover—and certainly not in the less than six months which had passed. But, as usual, the Japanese had formulated a desperate plan, which they, with even more optimism than Halsey, called the *Sho* Operation; *sho* is the Japanese word for "victory." Conceived after the Marianas debacle, Operation *Sho* was expected to bring about the "decisive battle" for which the Japanese Navy had yearned since Midway. *Sho* was actually four plans in one, depending upon where the enemy's next major invasion would come. If, as was expected, it came in the Philippines, *Sho*-1 would be placed in operation; if the blow came in Formosa, Nansei Shoto, or Kyushu (the southern-

most of the home islands), it would initiate *Sho*-2; *Sho*-3 was to activate if Kyushu, Shikoku, and Honshu were the obvious objectives; *Sho*-4 was the plan should Hokkaido be the enemy's target. Whichever plan was to be the final one, all were basically

A Corsair lands on Peleliu Island airstrip in the Carolines just two weeks after the island's invasion.
(NAVY DEPT., NATIONAL ARCHIVES)

the same: all possible forces would be rushed into action to defeat the enemy, and wherever that was, it was to be a "theater of decisive action."

It might have come at any of the expected points, but the most likely was in the Philippines (although for a time the Chiefs of Staff considered bypassing the Philippines and striking Formosa instead). Mac-Arthur would want to keep his word about returning to the Philippines. Also, the Allies' ostensible ally, the Soviet Union, let a little hint slip through its foreign office in Moscow, which informed the Japanese Ambassador that the China-based Fourteenth and Twentieth Air Forces had been ordered to plan missions which would isolate the Philippines.

It would then be *Sho*-1; the Philippines would be the scene of the all-out decisive battle. Moscow had not informed Tokyo just where it would come—which of the several islands that comprised the Philippines—but the plan called for the last-ditch battle to be fought on the main island of Luzon. By late September reinforcements, ground and air, were sent to the Philippines. More ominously, on October 6 General Tomoyuki Yamashita, who had achieved notoriety (not necessarily deserved) as the "Tiger of Malaya" and the conqueror of impregnable Singapore, arrived to take command of the Fourteenth Army. He replaced Lieutenant General Shigenori Kuroda, who had, during the two-year occupation of the Philippines, grown soft. The "Tiger" would—and did—put some stiffening into the neglected defenses of the Philippines. The ground fighting would not prove to be a "hollow shell operating on a shoestring."

As Yamashita dug in, the Imperial Navy formulated its *Sho*-1 plans, although the date of activation remained unknown. Admiral Soemu Toyoda, Commander in Chief, Combined Fleet, would gamble the entire fleet in the operation. Like all Navy men, he distrusted the Japanese Army and expected little assistance from that quarter; the outcome of the battle, he believed, would depend upon his fleet. The idea was to destroy the "barbarians" before they could establish themselves back in the Philippines.

Toyoda's plan was as complex as it was grandly impressive—and therein lay its ultimate flaw. But he knew that if the Philippines fell, the shipping lanes to the south would be cut. This would deny fuel to the Imperial Fleet if it was to operate in home waters; if it escaped to southern waters, then it would be cut off from ammunition and guns from the homeland. "There was no sense in saving the fleet," Toyoda admitted with resignation, "at the expense of the loss of the Philippines." The Japanese philosophy in the face of reality was turning suicidal. The old, almost arrogant confidence in victory was gone, despite the name of the operation; but the stubborn determination remained.

That something was in the wind became clear about the second week of October. Kenney's forces continued to harass the Japanese as before, with some attention in mid-September given to Philippine airfields by Liberators. Then Halsey unleashed the Third Fleet, particularly Mitscher's carriers, whose planes began raking over Marcus Island (east of Iwo Jima) and then, almost at Japan's doorstep, Okinawa in the Ryukyus. The next day, October 11, 1944, Mitscher's Task Force 38 Hellcats swept down upon an undeveloped air facility at Aparri on Luzon in the northern Philippines. The attacks were surprising and destructive, but on the twelfth, when the Navy aircraft turned to Formosa, the jittery Japanese activated both *Sho*-1 and -2.

Reinforcements from the Second Air Fleet of Vice-Admiral Jisaburo Ozawa's carrier forces rushed to Formosa. This all but stripped Ozawa of his planes and pilots—replacements for the Marianas losses. Vice-Admiral Shigeru Fukudome, once Yamamoto's chief of staff, commanding the Sixth Base Air Force, observed the early clash of the American and Japanese planes from his command post in Formosa. As he watched, the sky blossomed with flame and smoke; explosives flashed for a moment and then a trail of smoke marked the death fall of a plane.

"Well done! Well done!" Fukudome declared, certain that the falling aircraft were American; but they were not, as he later learned to his "sudden disappointment." Most of the burning aircraft were Japanese, which cleared the way for American dive bombers and strafing of Formosa's ground installations and parked planes by fighters. U. S. Navy pilots claimed 193 planes shot down and 123 destroyed on the ground the first day of the three days of the Formosa attacks. On the second day, the thirteenth, Japanese planes did break through the all but overwhelming numbers of Hellcats to place torpedoes into two cruisers, the *Canberra* and the *Houston,* both of which had to be towed out of the battle area.

Besides these damages Task Force 38 had lost seventy-nine planes and sixty-four men in the air battles, as well as a number of seamen aboard those ships which had suffered attack. But the cost to the Japanese was great: between five hundred and six hundred aircraft. The result was the near decimation of Ozawa's carrier strength, although a number of land-based aircraft remained in the Philippines. The aerial aspect of the *Sho* plan was truly a "hollow shell."

With perverse alacrity the Japanese High Command, only too eager to believe the exaggerated claims of the few pilots who had returned from the attack on the American fleet, turned the great defeat into an overwhelming victory. Somehow the two hits on American cruisers multiplied into sinking aircraft carriers, battleships, and, in fact, just about all of Halsey's Task Force 38. The Third Fleet, Tokyo announced, had "ceased to be an organized striking force." There was literally dancing in the streets in a three-day celebration in Japan.

Americans on recently taken Peleliu were showered with leaflets heralding the destruction of Task Force 38 (which the leaflet writer called the "58th Fleet") at Taiwan (Formosa):

For Reckless Yankee Doodle

Do you know about the naval battle done by the American 58th Fleet at the sea near Taiwan and Philippine? Japanese powerful air force had sunk their 19 aeroplane carriers, 4 battleships, 10 several cruisers and destroyers along with sending 1,261 ship aeroplanes into the sea. . . .

When he heard the claims emanating from Japan, Halsey wired Nimitz "the comforting assurance that he [Halsey] is now retiring toward the enemy following the salvage of all the Third Fleet ships recently reported sunk by Radio Tokyo."

This message was made public on October 19. Two days before, with initial landings made upon islands in the entrance to Leyte Gulf, Toyoda ordered *Sho*-1 under way. This, he was finally certain, was the big American invasion—which explained the heavy aerial assaults upon Formosa and other possible staging areas into the Philippines.

With the activation of *Sho*-1, the Combined Fleet began its complex movements toward the Philippines. While it was still en route, MacArthur three

days later splashed through fifty yards of water, stepped ashore, and announced: "People of the Philippines: I have returned." Within two days more than 130,000 American troops and 200,000 tons of supplies had been placed ashore at Leyte by "MacArthur's navy," the Seventh Fleet (Vice-Admiral Thomas C. Kinkaid). And still the Combined Fleet pressed toward the Philippines determined to interfere with the amphibious operations, which were all but over.

Toyoda's plan, roughly, was this: Vice-Admiral Jisaburo Ozawa, commanding what was called the main body, consisting of all of the then operational carriers (one large, three light, and two converted battleship-carriers) plus three cruisers and ten destroyers, would leave the Inland Sea of Japan and head for the Philippines. He would expose his carriers to the Americans in the Philippine Sea, east of the northern coast of Luzon. The objective was to lure the American carrier forces away from the beaches of Leyte.

While the American carrier planes were thus diverted from the landing beaches, three other forces would converge upon the unprotected Americans and destroy them. Two of the forces came from the south, starting out from Lingga Anchorage (at Singapore), and after a refueling stop at Brunei Bay (Borneo) split up for a co-ordinated attack upon Leyte. The largest of these forces, under Vice-Admiral Takeo Kurita, consisted of no less than five battleships (two of them being the superships *Musashi* and *Yamato*), ten heavy cruisers, two light cruisers, and fifteen destroyers. Kurita's mission was to slip up the South China Sea, veer southeastward around the island of Mindoro, and thread his way through the Sibuyan Sea, traversing across the north-south axis of the Philippines and through the San Bernardino Strait into the Philippine Sea, all of this hopefully with the American carriers lured away to the north. Once in the Philippine Sea, Kurita would lead his forces (what was left of them: and he was prepared to lose at least half) around the island of Samar to a position off Leyte, where he would raise havoc with the American landing operations.

Another force, under Vice-Admiral Shoji Nishimura, which had split with Kurita's at Brunei Bay and which consisted of two battleships, one heavy cruiser, and four destroyers, was to bear east just north of Borneo. It would then negotiate the Sulu

Sea, pass north of the island of Mindanao, and come through the Surigao Strait (south of Leyte), where, in conjunction with Kurita's forces, the Nishimura force would pound the Leyte American positions and ships to bits.

But this was not all. Another force, under Vice-Admiral Kiyohide Shima (two heavy cruisers, one light cruiser, and seven destroyers), which had sortied from the Inland Sea and refueled at Bako (in the Pescadores off the coast of Formosa), was to combine with Nishimura's force for the attack upon Leyte, which came from the south.

It was a grand plan, dear to the heart of any Navy man worth his salt: great armadas of magnificent ships cutting through the seas on a split-second timetable converging upon the hated foe for a battle to the death. There were, however, a number of factors that, in fact, stripped the grand plan of its grandeur.

The split-second timing, for one. With ships converging from both north and south, communications became critical and communications between the different forces were not good. And those which might have been good could be (and in some instances were) knocked out by American attackers. Another flaw was that Toyoda had, in fact, set *Sho*-1 into motion too late to interfere with the landings on Leyte, which began on October 20. By the time the Kurita and the Nishimura-Shima forces were due off Leyte (October 25) the most vulnerable phase of the amphibious landings would be over. Not that the Japanese armada could not have done serious damage to the American positions, but the main chance had already evaporated when *Sho*-1 began.

There was one other, more serious imperfection in the Grand Thinking, as if the High Command had refused to learn anything from such battles as those at Midway and the Marianas. The Combined Fleet, virtually all of it, was venturing forth with practically no air cover.

Ozawa's carriers were just what they were intended to be, a ruse. The total aircraft borne by his four carriers were 108 (a single American fleet carrier carried 80 or more). The Marianas losses, and the more recent Formosa strikes, had seriously depleted the number of aircraft and pilots. Two carriers, for example, the *Junyo* and *Ryuho,* re-

mained behind in the Inland Sea because there were no planes for them.

Since Ozawa held no illusions, the only hope for any substantial air cover must come from land-based planes. Most of it would come from Vice-Admiral Shigeru Fukudome's Second Air Fleet— the survivors of Halsey's carrier attacks—moved from Formosan bases into the Philippines; Fukudome could muster about 300–350 planes. The First Air Fleet, already in the Philippines, demoralized and depleted, was placed under the command of Vice-Admiral Takijiro Ohnishi, one of the original architects of the Pearl Harbor attack. When he assumed command of the First Air Fleet on October 17, 1944—the day that *Sho*-1 went into motion— Ohnishi had few aircraft with which to provide air cover for Kurita's advance toward the American landing beaches. He had about sixty—at most a hundred—operational aircraft and eager, young, and inexperienced pilots. Ohnishi also had a scheme —in the words of Rear Admiral Toshiyuki Yokoi "conceived in futility and prepared for in despair" —that, Ohnishi hoped would put these few earnest young men and their obsolescent planes to very effective use. He called his conception *kamikaze.*

Also based in the Philippines was the Fourth Air Army, commanded by Lieutenant General Kyoji Tominaga, which had aircraft spread throughout the Philippines. But the Imperial Navy planners had few illusions of aid from that quarter. Japanese Army pilots were not noted for their intrepidity; still, Tominaga had about 150 aircraft of all types, which could be hurled against the invaders. However, mere numbers—Fukudome's 350, Ohnishi's 100, Tominaga's 150, and Ozawa's carrier planes amounting to 108: a total, roughly, of about seven hundred—were not so impressive when it is remembered that the pilots generally were very young and the aircraft old.

Two American fleets poised to challenge Toyoda's elaborate *Sho*-1 plan. Assigned to carry out and cover the actual landings was Kinkaid's Seventh Fleet with its six battleships, four heavy and four light cruisers, thirty destroyers, a dozen destroyer escorts, thirty-nine PT boats, as well as numerous landing craft, transports, and troop ships (more than seven hundred ships). Kinkaid's forces included also eighteen "baby flattops," the CVE (small escort carriers), which carried about five hundred assorted aircraft.

The Third Fleet (Halsey), with six battleships, six heavy and nine light cruisers, and fifty-eight destroyers, was also a formidable force. Its main punch lay in Mitscher's Fast Carrier Force, eight fleet (heavy) carriers and eight escort carriers with over a thousand aircraft aboard—Hellcats, Helldivers, and Avengers.

Closing in: a Navy task group steams for the Philippines.
(U. S. NAVY)

The command arrangement, although not as complex as that of the Japanese, was a bit intricate. Kinkaid was under MacArthur's command, but Halsey was not. He was directly under the command of Nimitz. Both Kinkaid and MacArthur seemed to understand that the function of Halsey's forces was to cover the beachhead at Leyte. Kinkaid's ships were excellent for amphibious operations but could not be expected to deal with an all-out surface attack by the Japanese fleet. Halsey, a crusty independent thinker, understood the need for protecting the landing areas, but as an airman, he also had a bloodthirsty gleam in his eye for the Japanese carriers. His understanding was that his primary task

was the destruction of the Japanese fleet (with special emphasis on the carriers) and that "strategic support" of the Leyte landings was of secondary importance.

Since Halsey was his own boss in the operation, the confusion, plus a near success by the Japanese, brought about the most trying moments of the Leyte Gulf battles and a naval controversy which has never been resolved.

Troops of Lieutenant General Walter Krueger's Sixth Army had been ashore for three days before the first guns in the Battle for Leyte Gulf were fired. As Kurita led his massive armada through the Palawan Passage (west of the Philippines), he was picked up on the radar of the submarine *Darter* (Commander David McClintock), which had surfaced near the *Dace* (Commander Bladen D. Claggett) to enable the two sub commanders to discuss plans via megaphone. As soon as contact had been made the two U.S. submarines submerged and headed for Kurita's ships. When he was within range McClintock opened the attack with torpedoes, which pierced the side of the *Atago*, a cruiser that also happened to be Kurita's flagship. It sank in less than twenty minutes, taking more than three hundred men with it; the indomitable Kurita transferred to the destroyer *Kishinami*—and later to the battleship *Yamato*. The *Darter* had opened the battle in fine style; besides sinking the *Atago* the submarine had also crippled the *Takao*. The *Dace* too drew blood by sinking the heavy cruiser *Maya*, which was forced to limp back to Brunei Bay accompanied by two destroyers. The initial action thus subtracted five ships from Kurita's force. This skirmish did not bode well for *Sho-1*.

Halsey, alerted by Commander McClintock's contact report, ordered the Fast Carrier Force to prepare for action. It consisted of three carrier groups—all veterans of several weeks of action and in need of rest. A fourth group, under Vice-Admiral John S. McCain, had been ordered to Ulithi, in the Carolines, for rest and reprovisioning. This deprived Task Force 38 of three large and two escort carriers. When word came in that Kurita's ships were steaming along Palawan, Halsey did not feel it necessary for McCain to hasten back to the Philippines—there were still plenty of aircraft in the remaining three groups.

Halsey positioned them east of the Philippines

Heavy seas: Hellcats with wings folded and lashed to the flight deck in the Pacific.

(NAVY DEPT., NATIONAL ARCHIVES)

running from central Luzon (Rear Admiral Frederick C. Sherman's Task Group 38.3), north of the island of Samar (Rear Admiral Gerald F. Bogan's TG 38.2), and off the southern point of Samar (Rear Admiral Ralph E. Davison's TG 38.4). Just south of this lay the Leyte Gulf area, which was guarded also by the Seventh Fleet. Since a large Japanese ship concentration had been sighted to the west, Halsey's search planes, launched in the morning of October 24, did not venture to the north-northeast of Luzon, where they might have sighted Ozawa's carriers approaching from the north.

Kurita's ships, since their harassment by the *Darter* and *Dace,* had pushed onward and easterly, rounded the island of Mindoro (where they were sighted by a submarine), and continued—obviously for the San Bernardino Strait—through the Sibuyan Sea. It was about at this point that Kurita's ships were sighted by Helldiver pilot Lieutenant Max Adams of the *Intrepid.* Halsey ordered his forces to prepare for strikes upon the oncoming enemy force; he also ordered McCain's Task Group 38.1 to refuel and to return to Philippine waters instead of proceeding to the Carolines. They might be required after all.

Before the American planes found the Japanese ships, Japanese land-based aircraft had spotted Sherman's task group and nearly all of Fukudome's

available aircraft were dispatched to strike at the group. There were about sixty bomber and torpedo planes accompanied by more than a hundred Zeros and Zekes. Radar picked them up, coming in three nearly equal waves of about sixty mixed aircraft each.

Most of Sherman's planes (from the *Lexington, Essex, Princeton,* and *Langley,* the latter two escort carriers) had already been launched for the search to the west for Kurita's ships. On deck were the bombers and torpedo planes, plus some escort Hellcats, awaiting contact so that the strike could be launched immediately. A few fighters circled over the ships of Sherman's group on combat air patrol: a dozen Hellcats, plus four others assigned to submarine patrol with four bombers.

Two large raids of more than a hundred aircraft were discovered approaching from the west before Sherman could launch his strike. A third group of enemy planes were quickly spotted at a distance of sixty miles. Both the *Princeton* and the *Langley* scrambled twelve fighters; the *Essex* contributed seven (these were led by Commander David McCampbell), and the *Lexington* launched its

A Curtiss SOC-4 is catapulted from a cruiser on a search mission. The slow biplane was considered a sitting duck and replaced by the Kingfisher. But it served also as fire-direction craft for naval gunfire on invasion beaches—with proper escort by fighters.

(U. S. NAVY)

Navy Hellcat having its wings folded for storage.
(NAVY DEPT., NATIONAL ARCHIVES)

eleven remaining *Hellcats.* The strike on Kurita was canceled for the time being as far as Sherman was concerned. Defense, not offense, was the issue.

McCampbell, commander of Fighting 15 aboard the *Essex,* had been scheduled to accompany the strike on Kurita. His other aircraft, twenty-nine Hellcats, had already taken off to strafe airfields in the Manila area. His Hellcat was ready for takeoff on Number one catapult, but he had orders not to participate in defensive scrambles. As the situation became more acute, as it became obvious that the Japanese strike was a massive one, McCampbell felt justified in taking off when Admiral Sherman himself ordered "all available fighter pilots to man their planes immediately."

Despite the fact that the fueling of his Hellcat had not been completed and because of the general hubbub, such as the bellowing through bull horns: "If the Air Group Commander's plane is not ready to go, send it below!"—because of this urgency, McCampbell signaled for his launch with only a full belly tank but with each of his two main tanks half full. This was something to consider as, with head tight against his headrest, he felt his Hellcat hurled into the air. The six other Hellcats followed. McCampbell was joined by his wingman, Lieutenant Roy W. Rushing. With the five other Hellcats trail-

ing, the two others headed for the oncoming enemy aircraft.

After several minutes of climbing McCampbell looked around for a sign of enemy planes. He saw a large formation—about sixty aircraft—too distant to identify. The formation was so beautifully composed that he was all but certain it was American.

"Are there any friendlies in this area?" he radioed Combat Information Center on the *Essex.*

"Negative, negative."

"In that case, I have the enemy in sight."

About two thousand feet above him and Rushing were twenty bombers, Vals and Bettys. Three thousand feet higher flew perhaps forty fighters, Zekes, Oscars, and Tonys. A total of sixty against his seven. Upon radioing the *Essex* again—"Please send help" —he was informed that none was available.

As he and Rushing climbed to get above the fighters, the five other Hellcats dived on the bombers. The Japanese bombers dived away through the clouds and lost contact with their escort—which soon became busy with its own problems. Before, however, the Japanese fighters became aware of the presence of McCampbell and Rushing, several of

David McCampbell, Hellcat pilot, U.S.S. Essex.
(NAVY DEPT., NATIONAL ARCHIVES)

their number fell to the guns of the Hellcats. The two Americans began picking away at the large enemy gaggle by coming up behind a straggler and blasting him out of the sky, and then finding another.

The first Japanese to fall under McCampbell's six .50-calibers was a Zeke. Under the impact of the heavy slugging, the Zeke began breaking up and then, after flaring from a wing root, disintegrated in the air. Certain of this victory, McCampbell ticked off a little pencil mark on his instrument panel: one.

After his second flamer, the enemy fighters became aware of their attackers and formed into a defensive circle, the so-called Lufbery Circle, nose to tail for mutual support. It was then all but impossible to hook onto a Zeke's tail without being fired upon by one of the Japanese fighters in the circle.

McCampbell led Rushing up to twenty-three

thousand feet to keep an eye on the circling Japanese aircraft and to try to decide what to do next. Another call to the *Essex* did not result in any reinforcement, although one of the five Hellcats which had gone after the bombers responded and joined the two Hellcats above the circle.

Then to their surprise, the circle opened up and the Japanese fighters strung along, apparently hoping to return to their bases in Luzon. The problem of fuel supply had begun to take effect. The Japanese planes then formed into wide, straggling Vs for the journey home. The three Hellcats dived on the disorganized Japanese fighters. Within seconds McCampbell had added a third tick on his instrument panel. For some reason the Japanese did not attempt to fight back as the American Hellcats decimated the formation.

The American planes dived, fired; a Japanese

The Princeton *after being struck by a bomb during the Battle of Leyte Gulf. The elevator has fallen below decks; explosions of gassed-up aircraft in the hangar* deck *caused serious damage and casualties. The carrier was finally sunk by American guns.*

plane fell burning into the sea or the jungle below as the victorious Hellcat climbed for altitude and another dive. After an hour and thirty-five minutes of combat—after which his short fuel supply was dangerously low—McCampbell had nine ticks on the instrument panel. Rushing, who had depleted his ammunition, had accounted for six. The other five Hellcats had destroyed nine aircraft, most of them bombers. The seven *Essex* Hellcats, without losses, had shot down at least twenty-four Japanese aircraft. Other, and larger, forces had fared as effectively: planes from the *Princeton* claimed thirty-four, *Lexington* Hellcats splashed thirteen, and four Hellcats from the *Langley* claimed five Japanese aircraft destroyed. The big Japanese raid was thoroughly dispersed and Fukudome's Luzon-based air strength was all but finished as far as the Leyte Gulf battle was concerned.

However, one lone Judy appeared as if out of nowhere, ran the gauntlet of antiaircraft fire from various ships, and planted a 550-pound bomb on the *Princeton*'s flight deck before being shot down. Although not ordinarily a death blow, the bomb ignited the fuel in six Avengers in the hangar below decks; the planes were armed with torpedoes and the fire that resulted led to a series of explosions during the salvage and rescue attempts. One of the explosions tore off the *Princeton*'s stern, great chunks of which ripped over the decks of the cruiser *Birmingham,* which stood alongside assisting in the fire fighting. The stunning blast of metal and fire transformed the *Birmingham,* in the words of its captain, Thomas B. Inglis, into "a veritable charnel house of dead, dying, and wounded." Blood ran literally like water and made the decks unsafe and slippery for rescuers and medical men. The dead numbered 229 (more than had died on the bomb-struck *Princeton*) and 420 were wounded, more than half seriously.

Despite this single strike upon the *Princeton* (which was later ordered sunk by Halsey when the battle took a new turn) and the subsequent tragedy of the *Birmingham,* the Japanese air forces had not fared too well that day.

General Tominaga also hoped to contribute to *Sho*-1 and ordered his planes to attack the Seventh Fleet's shipping in Leyte Gulf. About 150 Japanese Army planes took off in the early morning attack and ran into the aircraft from Rear Admiral C. A. F.

Sprague's baby flattops. Those Japanese planes which succeeded in fighting through the Hellcat screen came under heavy fire from the hundreds of ships in and around the gulf. Although some hits were scored upon the shipping, no serious damage was done, and when the day's fighting ended Tominaga was minus at least half of his total air force.

Kurita, meanwhile, gingerly though courageously negotiating the Sibuyan Sea, had requested air cover from Fukudome. None was forthcoming, for Fukudome's planes had been expended in what had been a fruitless search for the American carriers. As for Tominaga's planes, "No request was made of the army; I [did] not know whether there were any Army planes there or not." Although his ships bristled with great numbers of antiaircraft guns—even the big guns on some ships could be raised to fire into the air—Kurita kept a wary eye on the sky.

Some three hundred miles to the south Nishimura's force, with its seven warships entering the eastern Sulu Sea, was having its sky problems also. Spotted early in the morning, Nishimura's ships came under attack from *Enterprise* and *Franklin* (of Davison's Task Group 38.4) planes. Although the aircraft were forced to break off their attack prematurely because of dwindling fuel, some damage had been done to the battleship *Fuso* and the destroyer *Shigure.* Further: the Americans were now alerted to two forces, Kurita's in the Sibuyan Sea and Nishimura's in the Sulu Sea, both obviously headed for Leyte Gulf. As Nishimura pressed on after the American planes had left him, he saw no Japanese air cover for his ships, nor did he see the ships of Shima, which were to join his for the attack upon the landing beaches. Nishimura proceeded unperturbed; he had a rendezvous. His son, Teiji, had died in the Philippines and, with his meager forces, Nishimura was resigned to joining him. Not that the Japanese seaman was suicide-bent—he took precautions with his lone reconnaissance plane, which showed him to be more cautious than some of the others thrusting toward Leyte. But he proceeded, promising to "storm the center of the eastern shore of Leyte Gulf at 0400 on the 25th" with a premonition of disastrous outcome. When the American planes were forced to break off their attack, Nishimura was granted a few hours' reprieve.

Kurita's main force, however, was not so—temporarily—fortunate. It was a formidable array of ships plying eastward in the Sibuyan Sea. Kurita, in his flagship *Yamato,* led the first of the two formations; the second was formed around the *Kongo*. Each of these formations consisted of more than a dozen ships, ranging from giant battleship to destroyer (but, of course, no carriers). One of the units in Kurita's formation was the battleship

aircraft fire—the *Yamato* alone carried 150 anti-aircraft machine guns and even each cruiser had a hundred of them mounted and pointing skyward. The planes swept in to the attack and despite the concentrated barrage ejected their torpedoes and dropped their bombs. A Hellcat which had taken a direct hit by the AA flared and blew up. Two Avengers went down, but they made ditchings in the

A Wildcat goes into action aboard an escort ca

Musashi, which was one of the two largest battle-ships on earth—the other being the *Yamato*.

Early in the morning the *Yamato*'s radar picked up signs of enemy aircraft approaching from the east: these were twenty-five bombers—Avengers and Helldivers—escorted by nineteen Hellcats from the *Intrepid* and *Cabot,* two of Bogan's escort carriers standing off San Bernardino Strait. Led by Air Group Commander William E. Ellis, the American planes flew westward in near-perfect weather. There was no opposition to their flight—a surprising absence of Japanese aircraft was especially puzzling —until they approached the Japanese fleet. There they were were met by an intense barrage of anti-

water and the crews paddled to safety in their dinghys.

Although the heavy antiaircraft fire made observation difficult, returning pilots were certain they had placed two "fish" into the side of a "*Yamato*-class battleship" and one into a heavy cruiser. Bombers too claimed hits with their thousand-pound bombs.

This opening round of the battle was scarcely over when another *Intrepid* strike appeared over Kurita's ships. This force, with near-miraculous determination, was with one exception thirty miles closer to the San Bernardino Strait than when the first American strike had come. The exception was the cruiser *Myoko,* which because of a serious torpedo hit could not keep pace with the other ships and was ordered to return, as best it could alone, to Singapore. The *"Yamato*-class battleship" which had been hit was the *Musashi,* but the huge battleship seemed scarcely touched as it continued on its way into the Sibuyan Sea.

By now Kurita realized he had prowed into a

mained to go to his aid. Supposedly some land-based aircraft did take off to help him, but these were either lost or shot down by the Hellcats or heavy Japanese antiaircraft fire.

If the attacks were "almost enough to discourage" the Japanese, they were most encouraging to the American airmen, to the point of exaggeration. A normal reaction this, but it would lead to nearly

by flattop" of Leyte Gulf. (U. S. NAVY)

hornet's nest. There seemed to be no end to the American bombers and fighters determined to destroy his fleet. His chief of staff, Rear Admiral Tomiji Koyanagi, said, "We had expected air attacks, but this day's were almost enough to discourage us."

Avengers, Helldivers, and Hellcats from six carriers, the *Intrepid, Cabot, Lexington, Essex, Enterprise,* and *Franklin,* converged on the Japanese First Diversion Attack Force. The great battleships were like magnets as bombs and torpedoes rained down upon the dodging ships. Kurita's call for help from Philippine-based planes went unheeded, and by the afternoon, even if heeded, no planes re-

fatal consequences. As these battles developed and Mitscher's pilots hammered at Kurita's ships, Halsey pondered an obsessively haunting question: Where were the Japanese carriers? Now that he knew where Kurita and Nishimura's ships were, he knew the Japanese had planned a big operation. It was unlikely that the carriers would be omitted from such an undertaking. This was troubling, especially when it was noted that carrier planes had taken part in the early attacks upon Sherman's northern carrier force.

Ozawa had, in fact, launched his hundred-odd planes in the hope of luring the Third Fleet to the north. Because his pilots were anything but expert

Curtiss SB2C "Helldiver," the standard Navy dive bomber during the last two years of the war, circles an escort carrier. The baby flattop and the Helldiver were introduced in the Gilbert Islands campaign late in 1943. (NAVY DEPT., NATIONAL ARCHIVES)

in carrier landings he had given permission to the pilots who survived the attack on the Americans to land on Japanese bases on Luzon. Most of these planes were lost in the aerial fighting over Sherman's group; a total of twenty-nine returned to Ozawa's carriers, which were now all but empty. This was unknown to Halsey, who fretted over empty shells.

A merciful night fell upon the Sibuyan Sea, after Kurita's force had suffered well over 250 American attacks. Five hours of desperate fighting had cost the Americans a mere eighteen aircraft, but it had cost the Japanese their superbattleship *Musashi.* The indestructible had been destroyed and the unsinkable had sunk to the bottom of the Sibuyan Sea—about half of the ship's twenty-two-thousand-man crew went with it. Captain Toshihira Inoguchi prepared his final report, conveyed his apologies to the Emperor, and went down with his ship. Other ships, the *Yamato* (sister to the *Musashi*) and the *Nagato* among them, had also suffered hits but were able to go on.

One of the last glimpses that the last of the returning American pilots had of Kurita's fleet was that it appeared to be a smoking shambles; also, Kurita had ordered the ships to turn around, which made it appear that he had decided to give up the thrust for Leyte. For an hour and a half he led his ships—four surviving battleships, six heavy cruisers, two light cruisers, and eleven destroyers: still an imposing array—westward. At nightfall he turned eastward again. He would make the San Bernardino Strait at all costs.

However, the entire timetable was upset; he would never be able to rendezvous with Nishimura's and Shima's forces coming from the south for the assault upon Leyte.

Nishimura had escaped the full fury of the carrier plane attacks and true to his mission continued on toward Leyte. By the morning of October 25 he would emerge from the Mindanao Sea through the Surigao Strait for the early morning rendezvous with Kurita (which meeting was by this time academic). Nishimura had no real idea where Shima, who was in full charge of his own small armada, was; nor did he know of Ozawa's carrier disposition. He did know, however, where the American ships were and that they were numerous. This report, radioed by a scout plane dispatched by Nishimura, was the single bit of intelligence which Kurita received during the entire Battle of Leyte Gulf.

Nishimura's fate was not sealed by aircraft, although it was one of the several (at times simultaneous) actions of the sea-air battles over Leyte Gulf—none of which, incidentally, actually took place in the gulf.

During the night of the twenty-fourth Nishimura, as he quite literally steamed "Into the jaws of Death, Into the mouth of Hell," was harassed by PT boats in the Mindanao Sea. The little boats did not stop the seven Japanese ships, but they tracked them through the night. Around three in the morning Nishimura ran into the great forces of the Seventh Fleet, which had been prepared by Rear Admiral Jesse B. Oldendorf. On the battle line were six old battleships, five of them resurrected from the mud of Pearl Harbor. Nishimura ran the gauntlet of guns to the right and to the left of him. As his ships stopped dead in the water, burning, he merely pressed on toward Leyte. "Their strategy and intelligence," a U. S. Navy officer commented, "seemed to be inversely proportional to their courage." One by one the ships were blasted from the water, and at around 4:19 A.M. Nishimura, in his flagship Yamashiro, joined his son in death. His tactics had provided Oldendorf with a sea warrior's dream: "capping the T." With his battle line representing the horizontal line of the "T" Oldendorf could train full broadsides upon the approaching Japanese ships, coming in a straight line up the vertical line of the "T." Thus only Nishimura's forward batteries were able to fire at the battle line, which rained massive fire down upon the Japanese ships. By the time the Yamashiro capsized and sank only two of the original seven ships remained afloat, the Shigure, which miraculously escaped serious damage, and the Mogami, which, burning, scuttered away from the terrible scene.

About this time Shima, with his seven ships (none heavier than a cruiser), rounded the point of Panaon Island and entered the strait. All apparently was not well, for he had barely begun to steam for Leyte when one of his cruisers was struck by a torpedo from PT-137. It gave him pause to see the burning hulks of those ships that had preceded him, but he continued onward. A couple of his ships released torpedoes at radar blips but hit nothing. Then he came upon the retreating Shigure and the blistering Mogami. The radar screen picked up many enemy ships awaiting him. Within a few minutes daylight would be upon him. Shima, who took orders only from Toyoda in Tokyo, and who operated independently of Nishimura, Kurita, and Ozawa, with unique discretion in a desperate situation, decided to get out.

He did not do this without some confusion: his flagship, in making the turn, collided with the already crippled Nishimura survivor, the Mogami. The decision to run did not end the battle for Shima, for as he fled the scene he was pursued and harassed, bombarded by ship and bombed from the air. With the coming of day the carrier planes from Sprague's baby flattops chivvied the fleeing Japanese. Just before 9 A.M. Avengers swept in with torpedoes to finish off the burning Mogami, which had managed to make seventeen knots through the night, although to one observer it appeared like an entire city block on fire. The agony was ended by the Avengers off the southern tip of Panaon Island. Only the Shigure of Nishimura's entire force returned to a friendly port.

Shima lost only one ship in this phase of the battle: the crippled Abukuma. On the twenty-sixth it was found by B-24s of the Fifth and Thirteenth Air Forces operating out of Noemfoor, Biak, and Owi. Shima and his surviving though bloodied ships faded into the Pacific.

"Someone had blundered," Tennyson had written nearly a century before. Nishimura had literally marched "Into the jaws of Death" in a neat but suicidal single file. Neither he nor Shima had coordinated their movements. Shima had managed to plow into the Mogami and had not succeeded in making himself felt (except in this one ironic incident) in Surigao Strait. The southern approach to Leyte Gulf as far as Sho-1 was concerned was an utter debacle.

Another blunder was yet to follow. Late in the afternoon of October 24 and during the time that Nishimura was being destroyed on the following day Halsey set off in pursuit of Ozawa's carriers. As soon as a search plane had located the Japanese carriers, Halsey had no doubts about what he would do: get the carriers and destroy the Japanese fleet. He felt justified in turning away from Kurita's force (seemingly in retreat in the Sibuyan Sea), believing that the enemy was in a "fatally weakened condition" and that even if Kurita did turn about and emerge from the San Bernardino Strait he could be thoroughly dealt with by the Seventh Fleet's baby flattops. The reports of excited pilots had, of course, exaggerated the damage to Kurita's still powerful fleet.

With the discovery of Ozawa's carriers, Halsey set off in pursuit to the north. In doing this he removed all of his ships from the vicinity of San Bernardino Strait. Upon leaving he informed Kinkaid of the Seventh Fleet that he was off on the chase taking "three groups to attack enemy carrier force at dawn." This was literally true, for the fourth group (which Kinkaid imagined was guarding San Bernardino), McCain's Task Group 38.1, was still on its

way back to Philippine waters. There was an additional element: Halsey had also promised to form what he called "Task Force 34" "if the enemy sorties," presumably through the San Bernardino Strait into the Philippine Sea. At least this is what Kinkaid assumed. But when Halsey took Ozawa's bait, he did not form TF 34. Instead he made full speed northward taking all of his ships, carriers (under Mitscher's command), battleships, cruisers, and destroyers—the entire Third Fleet, excepting McCain's group—with him. Halsey fully expected to meet Ozawa in a full-scale engagement and, of course, had no inkling that the six Japanese carriers were capable of putting up a mere twenty-nine aircraft. Besides the carriers, Ozawa's so-called "main force" (generally called the Northern Force by American historians) was screened by three cruisers and ten destroyers. It was little else but a lure, but its composition was impressive.

So was Kurita's an impressive force. To the con-

Thomas C. Kinkaid, who believed that some of Halsey's ships guarded San Bernardino Strait and the vulnerable baby flattops.

(NAVY DEPT., NATIONAL ARCHIVES)

William Frederick Halsey (whom no one—except newspaper writers—addressed as "Bull"); Japanese carriers were his special obsession at Leyte.

(NAVY DEPT., NATIONAL ARCHIVES)

sternation of all, a Seventh Fleet Antisubmarine search plane from the escort carrier *Kadashan Bay* reported sighting a large Japanese fleet emerging from San Bernardino Strait and off the northern coast of the island of Samar. It was 6:47 A.M., October 25, 1944. Just ten minutes before, a radioman on the *Fanshaw Bay* (another escort carrier) had intercepted Japanese talk that was assumed to be a jamming attempt. But then, just a few minutes later, antiaircraft bursts appeared in the northwest; the American search plane had come under fire from Kurita's ships.

There was no doubt about it, a tremendous force of Japanese ships were intent upon rounding Samar just twenty miles away. Nothing stood between Kurita and the landing beaches at Leyte but the three escort carrier groups of the Seventh Fleet, the thin-skinned CVEs. A new man reporting aboard one of the new carrier escorts was generally informed that the initials stood for "Combustible, Vulnerable, Expendable." Carrying a few planes (from eighteen to thirty-six), the "jeep carriers" or "wind wagons" were not intended for intense surface battles; they were designed for the close support of amphibious operations, providing for combat air patrol and for antisubmarine patrols.

The CVEs were accompanied by destroyers and destroyer escorts, but neither were these any match for Kurita's force, the largest Japanese force since Midway. The big guns (18.1 caliber) of the *Yamato* opened up on the northern group ("Taffy 3" under Rear Admiral Clifton A. F. Sprague) of escort carriers. Even as the first shellbursts started splashing around them, the CVEs launched their fighters and bombers. The great Japanese fleet bore down upon the "wind wagons." The situation appeared hopeless—the Japanese not only outnumbered the American ships, but had the advantage of greater speed (thirty knots against the CVE's seventeen) and greater firepower.

"The enemy was closing with disconcerting rapidity and the volume and accuracy of fire was increasing," Clifton Sprague later remembered. "At this point it did not appear that any of our ships could survive another five minutes of the heavy-caliber fire being received. . . ."

Sprague, immediately sizing up the desperation of his plight, broadcast an appeal for help in the clear. This was picked up by Kinkaid aboard his flagship

Wasatch in Leyte Gulf. It was Kinkaid's first inkling of the proximity of the Japanese force approaching Leyte and, according to plots, only three hours distant. Kinkaid was in a serious quandary. He knew that the CVEs were incapable of standing off the heavy ships of Kurita; he had the Leyte Gulf beachhead, transports to consider—and, because of the night battle in Surigao Strait and the mopping up in the strait in progress, he had ships short of fuel and ammunition. He nevertheless ordered Oldendorf to form a striking force of three old battleships, four American and an Australian cruiser, and two squadrons of destroyers and make for the battle area. All possible aircraft were converged off Samar.

Kinkaid then learned that Halsey had *not* left any forces behind to guard San Bernardino Strait. The air was charged with messages requesting help.

Kurita's ships closed upon the carriers and screening ships of Taffy 3. A vicious, if uneven, surface battle ensued in which the American destroyers *Johnston* and *Hoel* and the destroyer escort *Samuel B. Roberts* were torn to pieces by the heavy Japanese guns and sank into the Philippine Sea. Great volleys of gunfire bracketed the CVE *Gambier Bay* —merciless fire from Kurita's heavy cruisers, of which the *Chikuma* was most persistent. Even as the *Gambier Bay* capsized and sank the *Chikuma* continued to pour shells into the little carrier from short range.

With the Japanese cruisers in the van, Kurita's force bore down upon Taffy 3. It seemed only a matter of time before the entire group would be wiped out and the Japanese ships would then descend upon the middle group ("Taffy 2," commanded by Rear Admiral Felix B. Stump). The small guns of all the Taffy ships would just not do.

It was some time, too, before air attacks from the baby flattops could contribute to the battle, because of the confusion caused by the sudden appearance of Kurita. The bulk of the aircraft had already been launched to provide ground support on Leyte. This meant that most aircraft were not armed for bombing battleships. Despite heavy Japanese gunfire Taffy 3 put up forty-four Avengers and sixty-five Wildcats and Hellcats. Not that every plane was prepared for battle, however. Many Avengers were armed with mere hundred-pound bombs, which could not penetrate heavy decks; the *Gambier Bay*'s nine Avengers, for example, were more formidable

"Taffy 3" under attack by Kurita's force, which had come through the San Bernardino Strait. The escort carrier Gambier Bay *is bracketed by Japanese shell-fire during the Battle of Leyte Gulf (which some critics of Halsey called "The Battle of Bull's Run"), October 25, 1944.* (NAVY DEPT., NATIONAL ARCHIVES)

on paper than in the air: two of them were armed with depth bombs with wrong fuse settings, two carried no bombs at all, and two which carried torpedoes took off with practically no fuel at all. Within minutes after leaving the deck of the *Gambier Bay* these two Avengers were forced to ditch in the water.

These mishaps did not occur because of any lack of efficiency but because of the general desperation. Men of deck crews—handling the planes as well as rearming and reloading them—worked with remarkable dispatch, often under heavy fire. Aircrews took

off, bombed and strafed, landed again to take on more ammunition. Landings were made under impossible conditions, despite strong cross winds if the fleeing CVEs happened not to be facing into the wind.

The stricken *Gambier Bay* was avenged by torpedo bombers of sister ship *Kitkun Bay*. Led by Commander Richard L. Fowler, six Avengers loaded with five-hundred-pound bombs found a large cruiser, the second in line of the ships bearing down upon Taffy 3. By the time Fowler had found the Japanese ships, the weather being intermittently squally and rainy, plus their having run into heavy Japanese antiaircraft fire, he had lost two Avengers and had no fighter cover.

Waiting for a good moment, when the sun suddenly broke through the cloudy skies, Fowler led his four Avengers in a diving attack out of the sun upon the cruiser (the *Chokai,* which had assisted in the sinking of the *Gambier Bay*). Inexplicably, no antiaircraft fire interfered with the Avengers, and within seconds eleven five-hundred-pound bombs were hurtled at the *Chokai.* Five struck amidships around the stack, one hit the stern as two others splashed into the water, and three others smashed into the bow. The *Chokai* took a sudden turn to port, careened for some hundreds of yards as it shook with three tremendous explosions. Steam and black smoke shot hundreds of feet into the air, taking the aggressive *Chokai* out of the battle. (The cruiser, unsalvageable, was later sunk by Japanese destroyers.)

Almost simultaneously Wildcats and Avengers from Taffy 2, whose carrier escorts lay about thirty miles south of those of Taffy 3, came upon the scene. These were actually two strikes with an aggregate of twenty-eight fighters and thirty-one Avengers, the latter armed with torpedoes. These planes added to the confusion of the Japanese ships and added another victim to the credit of the carrier planes: the *Chikuma.*

Air attacks stopped another cruiser, the *Suzuya,* but, as Kinkaid well knew, could not stop Kurita's fatal rush upon Taffy 3's hard-pressed forces. But once again "Someone blundered." For no reason that the beleaguered Americans could understand, the advance ships in Kurita's force stopped firing, turned about, and retired to the north. The more powerful, faster—and actually more victorious— Japanese fleet had broken off the action on the threshold of victory.

There were, for Kurita, several good reasons to call off the chase. One was, he wished to assemble his dispersed forces for the run in on Leyte. Another was, he lived in fear of heavy aerial attacks; it seemed that the attacks by carrier planes had been increasing; they had stopped three of his cruisers (his only serious losses in the entire engagement). Sprague's Taffy 3 had lost one small carrier—and would lose another before the day was over—besides two destroyers and a destroyer escort.

Further food for blunder: Kurita's staff had

A Navy Wildcat takes off the airstrip at Tacloban, Leyte. This was a substitute "carrier deck" after the escort carriers were sunk or damaged off Leyte Gulf. *The truck hauls away the wreckage of another plane.*
(U. S. AIR FORCE)

magnified, somehow, Taffy 3's potential. The escort carriers were mistaken for full-sized fleet carriers, and all the other ships were amplified one size larger. Kurita, then, was worried about the carriers. For all he knew, the planes had come from the Halsey-Mitscher force. Nor had Ozawa, with characteristic lack of communication, informed Kurita that he had succeeded in his role of decoy. But Kurita did know that Nishimura had been wiped out, which meant that only his force was left for shooting up the beachhead. Of his original force of five battleships, he still had four; of the ten heavy cruisers, five had been sunk (or were sinking) and three had left for safer seas in damaged state; and there were still ten destroyers. He still had a little more than half of his original force left and he was about two hours' running away from his primary objective, Leyte Gulf.

The more he reflected upon that objective the less he thought of it. The planes worried him. He had intercepted radio instructions for American pilots to land on airstrips at Tacloban and Dulag. These instructions, unknown to Kurita, were emergency measures for aircraft whose carriers had been sunk. To Kurita, however, it appeared that land-based American aircraft would soon pound down upon him as he approached the objective. What would be the point of wasting his survivors upon empty landing craft? Certainly by now all the transports would have scurried to safety.

After much soul-searching, decisions and counterdecisions, Kurita steamed back for the San Bernardino Strait (still minus any sign of Task Force 34) and for Brunei. Even this passage was made under harrowing conditions. McCain's carrier group had come upon the scene to speed him on his way. The Thirteenth Air Force provided B-24s for additional harassment and, insult to tragic injury, Kurita's retiring ships were bombed by two Japanese bombers.

Kurita's retirement did not end the battle around Leyte. His will to survive was not common to all Japanese, for early in the morning a Zeke dived out of the sun at the *Santee,* an escort carrier in Rear Admiral Thomas Sprague's Taffy 1 (Thomas Sprague was not related to Taffy 3's Clifton Sprague). The Zeke came in strafing the deck of the *Santee* but instead of pulling away crashed into the flight deck on the port side. The plane crashed

through the deck and exploded on the hangar deck, killing sixteen men and wounding scores of others. Soon after, another Zeke plunged into the *Suwanee.*

It appeared to the American crews that these planes had deliberately crashed onto the carriers. The first kamikazes had struck.

To the north, Taffy 3 was hit after it had appeared that Kurita had spared it. Dedicated young Lieutenant Yukio Seki led a formation of five Zero fighters, each carrying a bomb, toward the American carriers (like Kurita, Seki was sure the CVEs were fleet carriers). Of the northern group, the *Kalinin Bay, Kitkin Bay,* and *White Plains* were damaged by the diving Zeros. Seki may have been the pilot of the plane that smashed into the *Saint Lo,* which was so badly hit that the escort carrier sank, the first loss to a kamikaze.

These were planes from Ohnishi's land-based force, not from Ozawa's alluring carriers. The absence of the Third Fleet from the scene of action had generated many a sulphurous query. Kinkaid's unheeded requests for help off Samar produced a message to Halsey from Nimitz himself which was touched with Tennysonian mischief.

Halsey had snatched at Ozawa's bait, honestly believing that he was in fact accepting a challenge. With his 64 ships, the carriers of which mounted more than 780 aircraft (401 fighters, 214 dive bombers, and 171 torpedo bombers), Halsey went off in pursuit of Ozawa's 17 ships and a total of 29 planes). It was to deal with these that Halsey ultimately formed Task Force 34 (under the command of Vice-Admiral Willis A. Lee). This powerful force was detached from the Third Fleet's battleships, cruisers, and destroyers and was to proceed ten miles in advance of the three carrier groups. At the same time Halsey turned over command of the carriers to Mitscher and ordered the arming of the aircraft for an early morning strike on the Japanese ships. After the carrier planes had finished with Ozawa's ships and planes, Lee's battle line—TF 34—would move in for the mopping up. It was not, as Kinkaid assumed, off the San Bernardino Strait; and, as events unfolded, TF 34 turned out to be neither here nor there.

During the night search planes, suffering mechanical difficulties, lost track of the Japanese ships. At daybreak, however, the carrier decks boomed with the engines of aircraft being readied for the first strike. Combat air patrol was stationed over the American ships and search planes fanned out to relocate the Japanese. At the same time the first strike group—about 180 planes, bombers, torpedo bombers, and fighter escort—was launched and dispatched in the general direction of the Japanese fleet. They would, on first sighting, be ready for the attack. These planes had been air-borne for about an hour and a half before a fighter plane spotted Ozawa's full force, the large carrier *Zuikaku,* three light carriers (the *Chitose, Chiyoda,* and *Zuiho*), two battleships that had been converted to carriers (the *Ise* and *Hyuga*), three light cruisers, and eight destroyers. Halsey's meat.

Target co-ordinator of the first strike was Commander David McCampbell of the *Essex*. What was surprising was the lack of enemy planes, which lack was attributed to "tactical surprise." A few, between fifteen and twenty, planes took off the four true carriers (the *Ise* and *Hyuga* carried no planes) to intercept the American planes. One Avenger fell into the sea, but most of the Zekes were either shot down or driven off by the swarms of Hellcats and for the rest of the battle were seen no more. As usual with the Japanese ships, intense antiaircraft fire—varicolored to identify the bursts of the several batteries—swept up to meet the American attackers.

The philosophy of battle was in keeping with Hal-

Halsey's bait: a Japanese carrier—the Zuiho, *its aft flight deck buckled, bomb-pocked, and burning from strikes by Navy dive bombers, attempts vainly to dodge further blows. This oiler converted into a carrier is* disguised as a cruiser; note fake guns painted forward of the buckled deck. Moments after this photo was taken the Zuiho sank.

(NAVY DEPT., NATIONAL ARCHIVES)

sey's battle plan: Get the Carriers. McCampbell, flying above the battle area, assigned the *Essex* planes to a light carrier (the *Chitose*), which took eight bombs and was clearly seriously damaged. Avengers also ran in with torpedoes and more bombers, from the *Lexington,* before they could be diverted to a more profitable target, dropped more bombs on the burning, exploding *Chitose.* Other aircraft, however, attacked the *Zuikaku,* claiming hits although McCampbell saw little to back the claims. Another carrier, the *Chiyoda,* was struck and lay dead in the water. A destroyer, hit in the side by an Avenger's torpedo, blew up and sank. So did the *Chitose* as McCampbell watched.

The *Zuikaku* had been hit and its communications so badly shot up that Ozawa was forced to leave it, the flagship, to direct his end of the strange battle from the light cruiser *Oyodo.* There was jubilation on Halsey's flag bridge aboard the *New Jersey,* when first word was flashed to him at 8:50 A.M. (more than two hours after the first planes had left his carriers). At the close of round one the American planes had sunk a carrier and a cruiser and had damaged other ships, two of which may have been carriers—and this was only the beginning. It was a great day for the carriers: Halsey's.

But it was not destined to be Halsey's day.

As strike after strike went out to mangle the Japanese ships and excited word came back to the *New Jersey*—co-ordinator of the third strike Commander Theodore Hugh Winters of the *Lexington* watched the *Zuikaku* slip under the water flying "a battle flag of tremendous size, perhaps fifty feet square"—as these reports of the destruction to Ozawa's fleet came in from the north, Halsey also received disturbing word from the south. These were the dispatches from Kinkaid appealing for aid to deal with Kurita steaming out of San Bernardino Strait.

Question [a part of the first message read] IS TF 34 GUARDING SAN BERNARDINO STRAIT
Negative [a somewhat bewildered Halsey replied, for Kinkaid should not have known of TF 34, which was to be formed only when Halsey ordered it and that when the Japanese fleet, i.e., the carriers, had been located] IT IS WITH OUR CARRIERS NOW ENGAGING ENEMY CARRIERS

And then came word from his carrier pilots. The *Zuiho,* the last of Ozawa's carriers, was stopped during the third strike by a small force of planes, led by Commander Malcolm T. Wordell, which with bombs and torpedoes put it under the sea also. What a day for sea dog Halsey! When the great *Zuikaku* went down all the carriers that had attacked Pearl Harbor nearly three years before had been destroyed, most of them by aircraft. As for the *Zuiho,* its sinking was vengeance for the sinking of the old *Hornet* in which the Japanese carrier had participated.

But the pleas kept coming from Kinkaid, whose Taffy 3 was under attack by Kurita's great force. Messages, at least nine, came in so rapidly that some canceled the others out. Communications were not good and messages were delayed or overlapped, so that Halsey found it difficult to assess the true situation: 0802, ENEMY VESSELS RETIRING SURIGAO STRAIT. Halsey breathed a sigh. Then at 0822, ENEMY BBS [battleships] AND CRUISER REPORTED FIRING ON TU 77.4.3 (Taffy 3). Then at nine o'clock: OUR CVES BEING ATTACKED BY 4 BBS 8 CRUISERS PLUS OTHERS REQUEST LEE COVER LEYTE AT TOP SPEED.

Halsey had already ordered McCain to stop refueling and to speed westward at once. He wanted Lee's ships to finish off Ozawa.

0922: CTU 77.4.3. UNDER ATTACK BY CRUISERS AND BBS . . . REQUEST IMMEDIATE AIR STRIKE . . . ALSO REQUEST SUPPORT BY HEAVY SHIPS . . . MY OBBS [old battleships] LOW IN AMMUNITION . . .

Then at ten—WHERE IS LEE . . . SEND LEE (this message had been sent in the clear with no attempt to hide from the Japanese the desperation of the plight of Sprague's Taffy 3 baby flattops). Halsey could not believe that the situation was really that critical. Surely the Seventh Fleet could stand off the Japanese, even if only with their aircraft, at least until McCain arrived with his large force.

And then the Tennysonian clincher, a message from Nimitz himself. (It should be mentioned at this point that messages sent in code were sent with padding of nonsense phrases—set off by repeated letters—to confuse Japanese cryptographers. Before the dispatch was handed to the recipient, the pad-

Superbattleship Yamato *is hit forward of the No. 1 gun turret by a Helldiver piloted by Arthur L. Downing*

as it fled the Philippines. Photograph was taken by Downing's radio operator, John L. Carver.
(NAVY DEPT., NATIONAL ARCHIVES)

ding was torn off and discarded. But it was not to be on this October 25, 1944. As for Tennyson, one of the lines he had used to rhyme with "Someone had blundered" was "All the world wondered," a line that evidently had stuck in the memory, even if not precisely, of a naval yeoman.).

The message was dispatched, in code, from Pearl Harbor thus:

TURKEY TROTS TO WATER GG FROM CINCPAC ACTION COM THIRD FLEET INFO CTF 77 X WHERE IS RPT WHERE IS TASK FORCE THIRTY-FOUR RR THE WORLD WONDERS

The padding preceding the double "G" was dropped, but that following the double "R" was not. The standing rule was that no padding used was to make any possible kind of sense. Despite the "RR," what followed *did* seem to make sense. In

that form, then, it was handed to Halsey—and also to Kinkaid (CTF 77), which made it appear like a public rebuke.

"I was stunned as if I had been struck in the face," Halsey later remembered. "The paper rattled in my hands. I snatched off my cap, threw it on the deck, and shouted something that I am ashamed to remember. Mick [Rear Admiral Robert B.] Carney rushed over and grabbed my arm: 'Stop it! What the hell's the matter with you? Pull yourself together!' . . . I gave him the dispatch and turned my back. I was so mad I couldn't talk."

For an hour Halsey brooded before he ordered the bulk of Task Force 34 about, in company with Rear Admiral Gerald F. Bogan's Task Group 38.2, to head for Leyte. The remaining carriers, under Mitscher, continued to harass Ozawa's diminishing forces until darkness intervened. When it turned

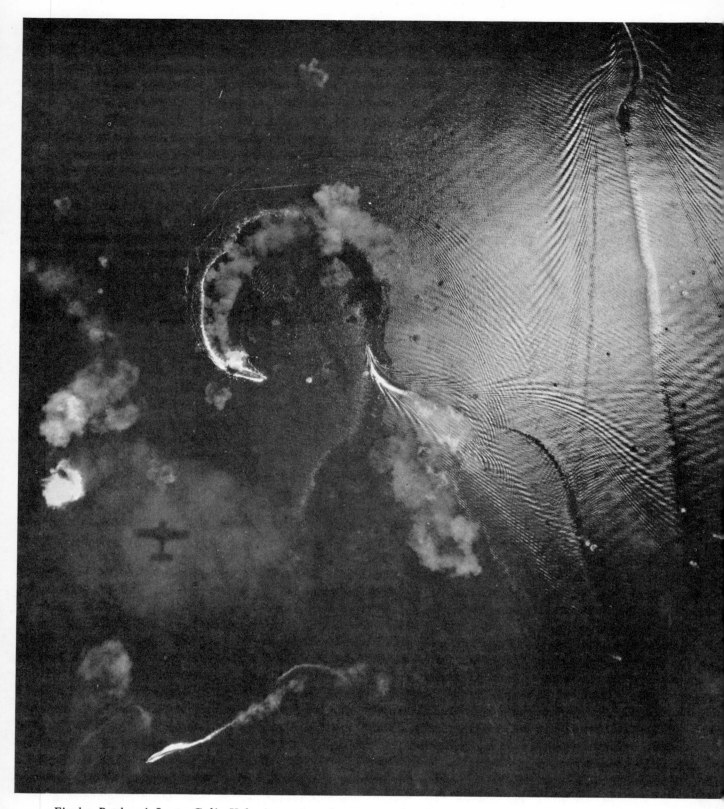

Finale: Battle of Leyte Gulf. Halsey's carrier planes catch the survivors of Kurita's fleet in Tablas Strait (southeast of Mindoro Island). The Japanese did not echo the query "Where is Task Force 34?" The wake of a dodging Japanese ship forms its own question mark: Had Sho-1 truly succeeded?

about, Task Force 34 was about forty miles from Ozawa's fleeing remnants. "I turned my back," Halsey bitterly commented, "on the opportunity I had dreamed of since my days as a cadet. For me, one of the biggest battles of the war was off." This turnabout, Halsey maintained, was his only blunder during the battle. He was off on another fruitless dash, this time to the south to intercept Kurita. By morning Kurita had slipped back into the San Bernardino Strait. Halsey missed that battle opportunity also.

But by October 26 the Battle of Leyte Gulf—and *Sho*-1—were finished. Of all the Japanese involved, only Ozawa had "succeeded" in his mission: he lost four carriers, a light cruiser, two destroyers, and all of his aircraft. He limped into port with many severely damaged ships. It was an expensive "success," for it virtually ended Japan's carrier force for the rest of the war.

Sho-1 had failed utterly. The Philippines would in time, and at great cost in lives, fall to the Americans because they had not been blasted out of Leyte Gulf. And the Pacific, in the phrase of the time, became "an American lake." Ozawa himself, after the war, summarized the ultimate result of the confusing, action-packed days of Leyte Gulf: "After this battle the surface forces became strictly auxiliary, so that we relied on land forces, special attack (kamikaze), and air power. There was no further use assigned to surface vessels, with exception of some special ships."

Sho-1 had cost the Japanese no less than twenty-six ships as against six lost by the Americans. The once great Imperial Japanese Navy was simply no longer of any consequence. There was much bitter land fighting and it was not until March of 1945 that Manila, on Luzon, was taken by MacArthur's forces. By this time the outcome of the war was imminent. Less than a week after Manila had fallen Tokyo had been set aflame by B-29s of the 21st Bomber Command operating out of Saipan. The great fires had finally come to Japan and the air war had assumed its ultimate twentieth-century form, a searing, fearful symmetry.

6

WHISTLING DEATH

On the same day (October 20, 1944) that Mac-Arthur stood upon the beach at Leyte and dramatically announced his return to the Philippines the first flight echelons of the 73rd Bombardment Wing arrived in Saipan. It was fervently hoped that from the Marianas the B-29s would prove more effective than they had in their initial operations from the bases in India and China.

The problems confronting Brigadier General Kenneth B. Wolfe in these far-flung parts were rather difficult to understand in Washington. The mechanical quirks, particularly of the engines, the transporting of supplies over the Hump, the weather—all of which conspired to put the big superbomber out of commission and inoperational when Washington ordered missions—were not easily solved under the primitive conditions at Chengtu and Kharagpur. But in Washington it seemed that if a hundred-plane mission was ordered, Wolf could at least manage to have half that number ready when the mission was run. There were many aborts and accidents—all, of course, the unfortunate growing pains of a new air force and a still not fully tested plane.

Wolfe returned to the United States and a promotion in "an important command assignment"—which could also be read "kicked upstairs"—at Wright Field as head of Matériel Command. Placed in temporary command of the 20th was Brigadier General LaVerne Saunders. Barely a month later

Major General Curtis E. LeMay arrived to assume command of the B-29s. "With all due respect to Wolfe," Arnold confided to General Spaatz later, "he did his best, and he did a grand job, but LeMay's operations make Wolfe's very amateurish."

LaVerne G. Saunders, who led some of the first B-29 raids against Japan and who replaced Wolfe as head of 20th Bomber Command. Saunders was injured in a B-25 crash after LeMay had come to succeed him as commander of the B-29s in the Pacific.

(U. S. AIR FORCE)

Wolfe, it might be pointed out, was an engineer, not a combat airman. The experience gleaned during the early B-29 missions was invaluable to Wolfe, who supervised the plane's future development and production.

LeMay was that rare man at the right time: a thoroughly contemporary warrior, hard-bitten, practical, an experienced tactician, and, so far as his men knew him, lacking in sentiment and emotion—they referred to him, among other epithets, as "Ironass." He was that; cool, determined, and in his way perhaps ruthless, but he, at the cost of endearment, saved their lives. He was the complete professional.

Before he accepted command of the 20th, LeMay insisted upon learning to fly the B-29 and learned to his dismay that the "engines overheated, cylinder heads often blew out the moment an engine started turning over, ignition was faulty, oil leaked excessively, fuel transfer systems gave endless trouble. There were scores of other defects readily apparent or—worse—appearing insidiously when an aircraft was at work and at altitude."

After he arrived in India, late in August 1944, LeMay began shaking up the command: he stepped up crew training (as he had in Europe); he realized that something must be done to improve the maintenance of the tricky aircraft, and he did not at all like the diamond formation flown by the big bombers; he believed in the concentrated combat box he had originated in Europe. There were performance improvements, but there was no getting around the problem of logistics.

By October, while the Philippines battle raged, it was decided to switch the concentration of attack from the steel industry (specifically the coke ovens, the heart of the industry) after nine B-29 missions to Japan's aircraft industry. Shipping too was regarded as an important target, since it was so essential to Japan's war industry, and the B-29s were employed in dropping mines into important harbor areas, such as Shanghai and Singapore, as well as areas in Indo-China and Sumatra. But what with the efforts of Kenney's ship busters and the Navy's submarines and carrier planes, shipping emerged as a lesser target.

Another idea was put forth also: the saturation bombing of a half-dozen urban industrial areas. The susceptibility of Japanese cities to fire was no legend.

But when LeMay took over the 20th Bomber

Preparation: construction crews digging coral for use in construction of B-29 runways on Saipan, Mariana Islands. (U. S. AIR FORCE)

Command the scattered operations were dispersed in three ways: support of operations in the China-Burma-India theater, support of the Pacific war, and —the 20th's major mission—operations as a separate strategic "global air force." The capability of the B-29 was demonstrated on November 5, 1944, with an attack upon Singapore, an important Japanese naval base. The round trip of nearly four thousand miles was in itself an obstacle, but of the seventy-six B-29s dispatched more than fifty bombed the primary target, the King George VI Graving Docks. Bombing was amazingly accurate and the docks were knocked out of commission for about three months. The cost of the mission was two B-29s and twelve men, including the leader of the 468th Group, Colonel Ted S. Faulkner. The losses were attributed to the hazards of the extremely long flight, not to the Japanese, whose opposition proved quite feeble.

And so it went on, missions of questionable consequence; and then with unexpected suddenness LeMay was transferred out of 20th Bomber Command. His job was taken over by Brigadier General Roger M. Ramey—one of Kenney's former "operators" and ex-chief of staff of 21st Bomber Command. Although he continued to mount missions,

Preparation: even as bulldozers made room for others, the first B-29s began arriving on Saipan for the opening of an aerial assault upon Japan.

(U. S. AIR FORCE)

Ramey was afforded no opportunity to operate in the classic Kenney style. His major concern was to get the 20th out of the CBI theater and into the Pacific proper. The forty-ninth and final mission of 20th Bomber Command (a night attack upon a tank farm on Bukum Island near Singapore) was flown on the night of March 29/30, 1945, after which the four combat groups (the 58th Bombardment Wing) left India for Tinian and Guam in the Marianas.

Twentieth Bomber Command in its roughly ten months of combat operations had fallen short of the goals projected for it in Washington. As James Lea Cate observes in *The Army Air Forces in World War II,* ". . . the strategic results of VHB operations from Chengtu were not a decisive factor in the Japanese surrender." The bold plan, code-named

Prepared: Isley Field, Saipan, two weeks before the first B-29 took off for Japan. Seventh Air Force

Liberators are parked on hardstands.

(U. S. AIR FORCE)

"Matterhorn" and entitled *Early Sustained Bombing of Japan,* Cate notes, rather sardonically, "was neither early nor sustained. It achieved no significant results of a tangible sort and the intangible effects were obtained at a dear price."

This is a rather stern appraisal and like all such can only be reached long after the fact. Not that the men of 20th Bomber Command were not aware of its deficiencies—they themselves were not deficient. It was only that they had so much to learn and learning invariably implies error. While there was a goodly amount of human error, the bulk could be laid to the machine and to nature. It would be, in a sense, an error to call the 20th a failure simply because it did not fulfill its officially defined mission: the failure may very well lay in the military pretentiousness, and prematurity, of that definition.

But what of the intangibles? If the 20th had not destroyed Japanese industry it had these intangibles to its credit, as enumerated by Cate: "To bolster Chinese morale; to take the war home to the Japanese people, badly misinformed by their officials, in raids which might tie down in the main islands fighter planes needed elsewhere; and to combat-test a new plane and a new type of bombardment organization." These were no small achievements, however intangible, though the price was dear.

II

LeMay arrived on January 19, 1945 at Guam to succeed Brigadier General Haywood S. Hansell as head of the 21st Bomber Command. It then consisted of three wings, the initial 73rd and the 313th and 314th. These were to be joined later by the 20th's 58th Bombardment Wing (March), the 315th (April), and the unique 509th Composite Group (May). Besides these "very heavy bomber" units, fighter groups were also stationed in the Marianas, notably those of the 7th Fighter Command and, later, the 301st Fighter Wing. And then there was the U. S. Navy, which LeMay often found to be his major opposition.

Twenty-first Bomber Command had begun operations about five months before LeMay's arrival. The first mission (October 28, 1944), actually a training mission to much bombed, bypassed Truk, was not very impressive. Because the schedule of ar-

rivals was somewhat off, Hansell could raise only about twenty B-29s for the strike (on the submarine pens at Truk), and after a delay owing to the possibility that the B-29s might be called upon to assist the Navy in the Battle of Leyte Gulf, eighteen planes finally took off. Four B-29s, including the lead plane carrying Hansell, were forced to return to Saipan. The remaining fourteen succeeded in dropping their bombs in and around the Dublon sub pens on Truk. To the men of the 497th and 498th Groups the sight of their bombs falling reasonably close to the target was a pleasing one (though as bombing goes, it was only partially effective). Japanese anti-aircraft fire proved even more ineffective at the high bombing altitude (twenty-five thousand feet), and one lone Zeke managed to get off the ground but chose to stay out of gun range.

Six shakedown missions were carried out between the first and last to Truk (on November 11). The former Japanese naval bastion (which served until war's end as an American practice bombing range) was hit four times, and Iwo Jima, about 730 miles

Curtis E. LeMay, commander of the 21st Bomber Command, Saipan, 1945. (U. S. AIR FORCE)

Isley Field, Saipan, after a Japanese strafing. More than a dozen Zekes swooped down and destroyed three B-29s and damaged others. The Japanese lost thirteen planes in the attack and three others were listed as "possibles." (U. S. AIR FORCE)

north of Saipan between the Marianas and the home islands, twice. Isley Field on Saipan had suffered strafing and bombing raids on November 2 (as the B-29s were bombing Truk for the third time) and November 27. The planes were believed to have come from Iwo Jima, a staging area for Japanese fighters. Bombing results of the initial missions were not very effective.

Even so, it was Japan itself that 21st Bomber Command aimed for, specifically the aircraft industries. So it was that on the first of November *Tokyo Rose* (an F-13, the reconnaissance version of the B-29), with Captain Ralph D. Steakley piloting, appeared over Tokyo. It was the first American aircraft to fly over the Japanese capital since April 1942. The day was bright and clear as the bomber lazily passed back and forth over the city taking photographs for thirty-five minutes. It was a shocking experience for the Japanese (to the degree that *two* B-29s were reported). With a minimum of fuel but a maximum of photographs, Steakley brought *Tokyo Rose* home. (The plane was named in honor of the English-speaking lady propagandist who broadcast the latest American popular music and military "secrets.") Among the prints were shots of the Musashino plant located in a suburb of Tokyo about ten miles from the Emperor's palace. In this plant Nakajima manufactured nearly 30 per cent of Japan's combat aircraft engines.

Twenty-four days later, after additional photo missions and weather delays, *Dauntless Dotty* took off from Saipan runway, skimmed the water, pulled up, and headed for Japan. At the controls of the B-29 was 73rd Wing commander Brigadier General Emmett O'Donnell; copilot was Major Robert K. Morgan, whose B-17, *Memphis Belle,* had been one of the most famed of the early Flying Fortresses. Behind *Dauntless Dotty* followed 110 Superfortresses loaded with bombs and fuel—and ammunition (for no less than 500 to 600 Japanese fighters were expected to meet them; actually there were only 375 in the entire home islands). But there were more formidable obstacles in the way; seventeen B-29s turned back en route with various mechanical troubles (six, which made it all the way, could not bomb because of similar failures).

Bugs, therefore, eliminated twenty-three bombers from the mission. Of the remaining eighty-eight a mere twenty-four bombed the primary objective, the Musashino engine plant; the rest (sixty-four) bombed various sections of Tokyo and the dock areas.

The anticipated heavy fighter counteraction did not materialize, although more than a hundred, a miscellany of Zekes, Tonys, Nicks, and Irvings, as well as others—no doubt scrapings of the defense barrel—came up to intercept the B-29s. American gunners claimed seven of the defenders destroyed, with another eighteen as probables and nine others damaged. The Japanese pilots varied as much as their aircraft, some being apparently timid (and likely half-trained), while others were highly com-

petent pilots and aggressive. Of the eleven damaged B-29s that returned to Saipan, eight had been hit by Japanese gunners (the other three bore the marks of hits from their own sister ships).

Of the ninety-four planes that made the full trip, two were lost, one in combat. A pilot of one of the defending Tonys, with either himself or his aircraft hit, deliberately dived into one of the Superfortresses. The impact slashed off part of the bomber's tail and the plane fell into the sea about twenty miles off the coast of the main island, Honshu. The other loss, a B-29 which had run out of fuel, ditched into the Pacific, but the crew was saved by the quite extensive, precautionary Air-Sea Rescue system that had been arranged in advance. Bombing Japan from the Marianas did not entail the risk of

Reconnaissance photo taken from Tokyo Rose, *the first American plane to fly over Japan since the Doo-* *little raid of 1942. This is the Musashino aircraft factory, near Tokyo, November 1, 1944.*

(U. S. AIR FORCE)

B-29s lining up for the first bombing mission to Tokyo.
(U. S. AIR FORCE)

amount of damage (besides killing fifty-seven and injuring seventy-five). High winds of near-gale velocity, plus obscuring cloud, which would be characteristic of practically every mission to Japan, made accuracy extremely difficult.

If anything, it was the high wind that swept through the bomber formations, generally above the thirty-thousand-foot level at which the B-29 was designed to operate, that might have been called "divine" by the Japanese. For nearly six months it would hamper the operations of the giant bombers, more certainly than the kamikazes.

The mission then was not militarily very significant, but it was the opening blow of the Battle of Tokyo. Once again American bombers had dared to appear over the Emperor's palace, despite the vows of the Imperial High Command and in the

Takeoff for Tokyo; the first mission, November 24, 1944. (U. S. AIR FORCE)

crossing the Hump (as had the China missions), but it did encompass a great deal of over-water flying.

Two losses—and only one in combat—was not too bad a toll. Nor, in fact, had the bombing been too bad—although strike photos picked up a mere sixteen hits in the target area. Actually three times that number fell into the factory and did a small

face of antiaircraft and fighter attack. And it would not be years before the silver giants would appear again. The renewal of the attack on Tokyo may not have opened very impressively, but it was the merest intimation of the devastation, the terror, and the horror to come within the next few months.

The missions during those months were generally executed according to the standard doctrine of day-

The major adversaries of the B-29 over Japan in the final months of the war: the Kawasaki Ki. 61 Hien *("Tony"), left, and the Mitsubishi J2M* Raiden *("Jack"), interceptor fighters. The Tony was generally used by the Army and the Jack by the Navy. The*

Jack replaced the Zeke, once its several bugs had been ironed out, as the Navy's chief fighter.
(U. S. AIR FORCE; NATIONAL AIR AND SPACE MUSEUM, SMITHSONIAN INSTITUTION)

light precision high-altitude bombings which had proved effective, if not decisive, in Europe. Hansell, one of the proponents of that doctrine, adhered to it in spite of Arnold's growing interest in the possibilities of area incendiary attacks. Hansell's term as head of 21st Bomber Command was characterized by what he himself termed a "deplorable" bombing record for accuracy; there was a high percentage of aborts; there were ditchings—and losses because of these ditchings—because of inferior maintenance. These were valid problems which Hansell sought to overcome, but there was little he could do about the weather, whose 180-mile-an-hour winds blew even the big B-29 across the skies of Japan, canceling out almost all the validity of Hansell's adherence to high-altitude precision bombardment.

The advent of LeMay, who took over, ironically, the day after Hansell's final and most effective mission, did not change all that immediately. That last mission, against the Kawasaki Aircraft Industries at Akashi on the Inland Sea about twelve miles from Kobe, just about blew the factory out of operation. Sixty-two of the seventy-seven B-29s dropped their bombs on target and succeeded in cutting aircraft engine and airframe production by 90 per cent. And all the B-29s returned safely. Not until after the war was it learned that Hansell had planned and executed so successful a mission. For some weeks

after, LeMay would continue to send out the B-29s with inconclusive results as before: no targets were wiped out.

As was customary, as soon as he arrived LeMay got a tough training program under way. It was obvious that the crews had much to learn about formation flying, among other essential operational tech-

The Musashino aircraft plant, which, before the B-29s began striking it, produced nearly three thousand aircraft engines a month for Japanese warplanes.
(U. S. AIR FORCE)

niques. Since he often confined his comments to monosyllables, or managed a sentence now and then in rebuke, LeMay soon did not qualify for any kind of popularity poll. But his crews were learning how to make it to the target and back and how to hit that target.

The U. S. Navy, which after all "owned" the Marianas, was a special problem. LeMay took the Navy on too. He managed somehow to get hold of a construction priority list and had to scan five pages before he found the Air Force mentioned. "They had built tennis courts for the Island Commander; they had built fleet recreation centers, Marine rehabilitation centers, dockage facilities for inter-island surface craft, and every damn thing in the world except subscribing to the original purpose in the occupation of those islands. The islands were attacked and taken and held because we needed them for air bases to strike against Japan."

LeMay sent the list to Arnold and started shaking and moving. In time the facilities were improved. However, when Brigadier General Thomas S. Powers, commander of the 314th Wing, arrived (also in January) at Guam with the first B-29s of his wing, the "only thing they'd built for him was a coral airstrip down through the jungle. He and his airmen slept on that, the first night they arrived. Next morning they had to tackle the jungle with pocketknives: no other equipment. This was the only manner in which they could clear away the brush and make space to set up their tents."

LeMay noted that Nimitz had "built himself a splendid house, way up on the very highest peak of the island. That was Living." After a round of socializing with the Navy, LeMay felt obligated to reciprocate. He invited the "Neptune" types to dine in his tent on flight rations out of cans. A far cry from Nimitz's "soup, fish course, then the roast and vegetables and salad, and a perfectly swell dessert, and demitasses, and brandy and cigars. . . ."

LeMay's table was not quite so grand. "I'll give the web-footed guests credit, and report they stood up like real men throughout it all. Didn't complain, told stories, were right good company. They ate the canned goods because they were pretty hungry, and had been working hard. I don't remember exactly what was being built that week. Maybe a roller-skating rink."

This near-tragic, not quite comic situation existed because of the command arrangement in the Pacific: Nimitz vs. MacArthur and now vs. LeMay (and eventually vs. the Japanese). The Navy, committed to the sea-air war, understandably looked after its own; it always had, it was tradition. If ships had refrigerator facilities it only followed that they must contain special goodies for the theater commander. Not that the web-footed types deliberately scuttled LeMay, he simply loomed less in their thinking. For all the success of the carriers, the Navy persisted in thinking in terms of ships at sea. Clearly, however, it was obvious that the Pacific war was primarily an air war.

But for some time even LeMay might have doubted that. He sent the B-29s out some sixteen times after he had taken over from Hansell and the results were hardly improved. It was something to think about and LeMay, in his way, did. He thought about those jet streams encountered at bombing altitude and how engines burned out so fast. He thought about bombing accuracy and how it rarely occurred. He thought about the subject, bandied about for so many months, of area bombing at night with incendiaries instead of (or coupled with) high explosives. He thought about clouds.

And he thought, especially, what it might cost in lives.

It was after a mission to Tokyo (February 25, 1945), in which General Power's 314th Wing (with only twenty-two planes at that date) made its first mission, that a new idea came to LeMay. Washington had ordered a "maximum effort" and, with the 314th's Superfortresses, LeMay was able to dispatch 231 of the big bombers. Each of these planes carried a single five-hundred-pound general-purpose bomb, the rest of the load consisting of E46 incendiaries.

Weather, as usual, interfered with the mission, but 172 Boeings dropped more than 450 tons of bombs on Tokyo depending on radar. The results were no better than before because of the scattered effect. But a reconnaissance photo taken after the raid showed an ominous black patch in one corner of Tokyo. A square mile of the city had been obliterated (27,970 buildings had been destroyed—although this was not known until after the war). Where the fire bombs had been concentrated, results had been impressive.

It had not been an unqualified success, but it had provided LeMay with concrete evidence to back

B-29s after a bombing mission to Japan; the Japanese coastline is at left. (U. S. AIR FORCE)

up a decision. When his plan was announced to the men who were to fly the mission, the revelation was a shock. The B-29s, designed to bomb from an average altitude of thirty thousand feet, would come in at low level (*Ploesti!*) at between five thousand to seven thousand feet. The mission would be made at night—the B-29 was designed for daytime operation; the previous nighttime missions even with radar had not accomplished much. They would not fly in LeMay's combat boxes, but singly—to avoid collision in the dark. They would carry only incendiary bombs. And finally, no guns and no ammunition.

Consider the final point. If gunners, guns, and ammunition remained behind, more bomb load could be carried. That made some sense, but what about Japanese night fighters? As far as was known, Japanese night fighters were all but non-existent and, according to Intelligence, Japanese radar was inferior to any other radar then in use. Of course, carrying no guns meant that the B-29s would not shoot at one another.

The low-level aspect was not too attractive either.

Way up at thirty thousand you felt quite secure from Japanese antiaircraft fire. What would happen at five thousand feet? Again, the Japanese had no radar to compare with that used with German flak guns, so that should not entail too great a risk. The Japanese would have to depend upon searchlights to find the B-29s, and that was hardly ideal—especially for a fast-flying aircraft.

The fire bombs—M47 (napalm) and M69s (oil)—would set difficult-to-contain fires which in turn would destroy the supposedly very combustible Japanese cities. A large proportion of Japanese military and industrial targets were concentrated in a few major metropolitan areas (unlike Germany), and these targets were surrounded by the flimsy dwellings of the workers. Also, hidden among the dwellings were small "shadow" factories devoted to turning out war materials. Work of this nature was done also in private homes. Defining the boundary between purely industrial and residential Japanese targets was all but impossible.

That was LeMay's decision: a medium-level,

nighttime maximum effort with incendiary bombs and without guns. After months of frustrating, inconclusive strikes, maybe this kind of tactic was the solution. Perhaps; if not, LeMay would have to be the goat. It was, ultimately, his idea, his responsibility, and—for all he knew—his funeral. And if it went wrong, if he was wrong, it would be the funeral flight of a lot of young airmen. If it went right, it also meant the funeral of a great number of Japanese—soldiers, civilians, women, and children. It was not an easy decision to make.

In the early morning of March 10, 1945, as he waited for the report of Bombs Away from Power, leading the mission, LeMay revealed, in what must have seemed an unusually long utterance for him, the real meaning of his decision. "If this raid works the way I think it will," he said, "we can shorten this war."

At 5:35 P.M., March 9, 1945, two groups of Power's 314th Wing—the 29th and the 19th—began lifting their seventy-ton, bomb-laden B-29s off the eighty-five-hundred-foot strip of North Field, Guam. A total of fifty-four took off after the green flare arched through the air, signaling that the mission to Tokyo was on. If tradition meant anything, the men of the 19th Group took off with resolution. Their predecessors had been bombed out of Clark Field in the Philippines the first day of the war; they had been pushed out of Java by the forces of the East Asia Co-Prosperity Sphere; they had participated in the Battle of the Coral Sea and as Kenney's war-weary kids had bombed Rabaul. That was as close as they had come to the Empire before the wrack of war had consumed their battered B-17s and dispirited them.

The Guam aircraft took off first because of their longer flight to Tokyo. The B-29s of O'Donnell's 73rd Wing followed from Isley Field (Saipan), and those of Brigadier General John H. Davies' 313th Wing (North Field, Tinian) left soon after. It took about two and three-quarter hours for the entire force, 334 Superfortresses carrying close to two thousand tons of fire bombs, to take off. There were a few aborts, but a total of 325 aircraft reached the target.

Shortly after midnight (it was now March 10) the pathfinders had arrived over Tokyo. Although turbulence and heavy cloud had been encountered on the flight, over Tokyo and particularly at the low altitude, visibility was very good. The pathfinders had no trouble finding the target area, a section of Tokyo about three by four miles, a densely populated, congested part of the city crowded with home industries and shadow factories. The dwellings were predominantly of wood, plaster, and bamboo construction.

It was simple to find the target because of the Sumida River, which ran through it, and the city's location to the north of Tokyo Bay. The pathfinders released their napalm bombs (M47s), timed to drop at intervals of a hundred feet. When the pathfinders had completed their work, a rough, blazing "X" lay in the heart of Tokyo. The fires ignited by the M47s would preoccupy Tokyo's courageous but not very efficient fire fighters. The remaining B-29s then followed—for about three hours—flinging their heavy loads of M69 clusters at the burning "X." These were timed to fall into the area at fifty-foot intervals; there were over eight thousand of these, which would place a density of about twenty-five tons per square mile. The fiendish aspect of the M69 was that it was devised as a cluster of bombs which would burst at two thousand feet altitude and spread the smaller blazing parts around the area into which it fell.

The bombers came in from altitudes varying from forty-nine hundred feet to ninety-two hundred feet and began dropping their bombs. To LeMay, anxiously waiting at Guam, the word came in: "Bombing the target visually. Large fires observed. Flak moderate. Fighter opposition nil."

That much of his plan had worked. Antiaircraft had been confused by the change in tactic as well as the large number of aircraft. As the fire spread, antiaircraft gunfire lessened, the gun positions being overrun by flame. Searchlights, too, poked up into the sky, but when the fire caught the searchlights were not needed: the sky was bright with flame. A number of Japanese fighters did come up and about forty closed in for attacks while a searchlight beam held one of the bombers. But no serious damage was attributed to Japanese fighters. Forty-two B-29s sustained damage from the antiaircraft fire and it was this which may have accounted for the fourteen B-29s that fell on the mission. Nine of the crews were lost; many may have fallen into their own fire in Tokyo, others may have crashed into the sea; however, five of the crews were saved by

Tokyo still smoldering after LeMay's first fire bombing, March 10, 1945. (U. S. AIR FORCE)

Air-Sea Rescue. Some may even have gone down, victims of the tremendous heat turbulence over which they flew. Returning crews reported being tossed thousands of feet upward as they came in to bomb. At least one B-29 was flipped over onto its back, out of control from an updraft of heated air, fell thousands of feet before the combined efforts of pilot and copilot brought it back under control, and headed back for the Marianas on strained, slightly bent wings.

Within thirty minutes of the first Bombs Away, the fire in Tokyo was completely out of hand. The fire department found it impossible to cope with the wide-ranging, rapidly spreading holocaust. Fire-fighting equipment, like the buildings in the target zone, went up in flames. Hoses shriveled up and burst into flame from the heat or flying debris, fire engines simply melted away (nearly a hundred were burned), and 125 firemen died in the fruitless attempts to contain the vicious conflagration. The mixture of the napalm and oil bombs was unquenchable, particularly when combined with the Japanese build-

ing construction and, nature's tragic contribution, a fairly strong wind.

Tokyo did not suffer a firestorm in the manner of Hamburg or Dresden; not the whirling, sucking inferno of those German cities, but a massive plunging fire—comparable to a moving prairie fire—sweeping all before it. The heat rose to more than 1800 degrees (F.) If this heat could fling about a 74,500-pound (empty) aircraft as if it were a leaf in the wind, only the imagination can conceive of what it did to the Japanese trapped in the immolation. No city on earth—not Warsaw, or Rotterdam or London, or Hamburg, or Berlin, not even Dresden (or to come: Hiroshima and Nagasaki)—suffered so great a disaster, so much agony, so much human despair and loss of life.

Radio Tokyo announced that about 130 Super-fortresses had "carried out indiscriminate bombings of the city area" but that the various fires had been put under control by eight o'clock in the morning. The fire, in fact, had burned itself out—there was little more destruction for it to do. The final statement was the nearest to the truth: "War results thus far verified include fifteen planes shot down [there were fourteen] and fifty others damaged." But the frightful truths soon spread throughout Tokyo and the official broadcasts became more shrill and more honest: ". . . the sea of flames which enclosed the residential and commercial sections of Tokyo was reminiscent of the holocaust of Rome, caused by the Emperor Nero." LeMay was quickly painted as a contemporary mad Nero and the mission was called by Radio Tokyo a "slaughter bombing." There are no other kinds of bombings, realist LeMay might have pointed out.

Nearly sixteen square miles of the main section of Tokyo had been wiped out, and along with it twenty-two industrial targets which had been marked for pin-point destruction by the Twentieth Air Force. One fourth of all the buildings in Tokyo had been destroyed; those few which remained standing—those made of concrete and brick—were nothing but burnt-out shells which had served as ovens for those hapless thousands who sought shelter in them. Sheer fright had led to panic, which contributed to the heavy toll in lives. An official of the Japanese Home Affairs Ministry summed up, succinctly, what had occurred: "People were unable to escape. They were found later piled upon the bridges, roads, and

Burned-out Tokyo; the result of the B-29 fire bombings. (U. S. AIR FORCE)

in the canals, eighty thousand dead and twice that many injured. We were instructed to report on actual conditions. Most of us were unable to do this because of the horrifying conditions beyond imagination."

The dead had succumbed first of all to the heat—some seemed to burst into flame as if by spontaneous combustion, some suffocated; others who sought refuge in the waters of the river drowned in the panic of the mobs rushing for the water. Those who hoped to save themselves in the smaller canals were broiled alive. Shelters were little more than death traps where the victims either burned, suffocated, or were literally torn limb from limb by one another.

Official figures listed 83,793 dead and 40,918 injured. It is likely that the death toll was much higher—and it is equally likely that its true figure will never be known. More than a million people were rendered homeless in the single bombing, placing a serious burden on Home Defense organizations in Japan. And there could be no questioning the terrible effect upon morale. The real war had come in full fury to Japan; the small flame ignited at Pearl Harbor had burgeoned into a pillar of fire.

LeMay's plan had worked and subsequent fire bombings, to a greater or lesser extent, proved that it had not been a fluke. When the results of the Tokyo bombing, and those which followed upon Nagoya, Osaka, and Kobe, were analyzed, the Joint Target Group in Washington voiced its full approval for the change in bombing techniques and compiled a target list designating thirty-three urban areas of Japan where its industries would suffer most from incendiary attacks. The assumption was that these attacks would pave the way for the projected Allied invasion of the home islands of Japan.

LeMay had another conception in the back of his mind; he believed that with proper support—supplies, crews, and B-29s—air power alone could force a Japanese surrender. In both, tactics and strategy, he was right. Japan was finished as a warmaking power, despite its still intact 2,500,000-man army awaiting the American invasion in the home islands (the Imperial Navy too could still muster 1.5 million men). The slaughter which might have ensued had the invasions, Operations Olympic and Coronet, planned, respectively, for the fall of 1945 and early spring of 1946, occurred would have made the fire

bombings of LeMay's B-29s seem like little pin pricks in casualties.

Despite the fact that militarily Japan was practically finished and to continue the war only meant growing casualty lists, the Japanese war lords insisted upon fighting on, however hopeless the war had become. They would not sacrifice "face" even at the cost of hundreds of thousands of lives. To have continued on in the face of certain defeat was no longer as much an aspect of Japanese military thinking as it was of Japanese culture and psychology.

III

A wide cultural gap separated the American and Japanese soldier. They killed each other but they did not understand one another; they shared neither the orthodox conventions of war nor certain values, emotions, and ways of thinking. The concept of surrender was alien to the Japanese; he fought until he died or, if he was not killed, charged screaming at his enemy in a suicidal, pointless evasion of surrender. When captured Allied soldiers asked that their families be notified of their imprisonment—and comparative safety—the Japanese were appalled. Why did these soldiers wish their families to know about their disgrace?

The Japanese did not surrender (especially in the early months of the war), because it was shameful and he could no longer, because of his shame, regard himself as Japanese. He also believed that the American enemy tortured and killed his prisoners—a powerful rumor was that at Guadalcanal all prisoners were disposed of by driving tanks over them. This explains why so few Japanese were taken prisoner (another was that they frequently made themselves walking booby traps and killed themselves and their captors) and why they treated prisoners so badly. Once "face" was lost, the prisoner was not fit for human treatment.

The Japanese were inculcated from birth with a number of basic beliefs: that things of the spirit were superior to material things, "to match our training against their numbers and our flesh against their steel." That Japan did not have the material resources of the United States meant nothing; Japanese spirit and discipline would win in the end.

Their training manuals invariably opened with the formula: "Read this and the war is won."

Another important concept was that of "place." At the top was the Emperor (just as Japan was at the top of the hierarchy of nations), who was above all material things. At the bottom was the lowly soldier, whose pleasure—whose duty—was to die for the Emperor. And war directives were issued by the High Command in the name of the Emperor whether he knew it or not. As the spiritual leader of Japan, the Emperor was above all that was mundane; if he was not a political nincompoop and a moral idiot he might just as well have been. His position was rarefied, detached from the life of Japan—although he symbolized Japan in the minds of his people, like the flag or an icon.

Dutiful Japanese believed what they were told. Radio Tokyo when it finally was permitted to announce certain defeats—the loss of Saipan, the fall of the Philippines—assured the Japanese that all was well because this had been predicted by the military leaders and therefore was perfectly all right.

When the B-29s began appearing over the home islands in greater profusion an official of the Aviation Manufacturers' Association spoke over Radio Tokyo saying, "Enemy planes finally have come over our very heads. However, we who are engaged in the aircraft production industry and who had always expected this to happen have made complete preparations to cope with this. Therefore, there is nothing to worry about."

The Japanese war hero was generally anonymous; it was taken for granted that he would conduct himself properly on the battlefield. If he died in combat for the Emperor he was sublimely fortunate and had gained spiritual immortality. Who needed medals and newspaper announcements to hail the common deeds of a true warrior?

Ruth Benedict in *The Chrysanthemum and the Sword* reproduced one of the broadcasts of Radio Tokyo, of which the moral is obvious. The hero is still anonymous, but he is an officer; individual accomplishments of mere enlisted men hardly ever attracted any attention. The broadcast told this story:

After the air battles were over, the Japanese planes returned to their base in small formations of three or four. A Captain was in one of the first planes to return. After alighting from his plane, he stood on the ground and gazed into the sky through his binoculars. As his men returned, he counted. He looked rather pale, but he was quite steady. After the last plane returned he made out a report and proceeded to Headquarters. At Headquarters he made his report to the Commanding Officer. As soon as he had finished his report, however, he suddenly dropped to the ground. The officers on the spot rushed to give assistance but alas! he was dead. On examining his body it was found that it was already cold, and he had a bullet wound in his chest, which had proved fatal. It is impossible for the body of a newly-dead person to be cold. Nevertheless the body of the dead Captain was as cold as ice. The Captain must have been dead long before, and it was his spirit that made the report. Such a miraculous fact must have been achieved by the strict sense of responsibility that the dead Captain possessed.

The Japanese listener was expected to believe this story—and probably did. There was a power much stronger than life itself. It was this belief in that power, plus a number of other beliefs, which made the Japanese soldier different from his occidental enemy. To the Japanese adding futility to futility was, within the patterns of his culture, not unnatural. Futility was, after all, a Western concept.

Those values which made up the Japanese national character and the Japanese warrior produced the war's most bizarre weapon, the kamikaze. The word, meaning "the divine wind," evoked the miraculous delivery of the Japanese from a Mongol invasion in the thirteenth century, when Kublai Khan's invasion fleet was dispersed and some of its ships capsized by a sudden typhoon. Obviously by the autumn of 1944 only a divine miracle could spare the Japanese another invasion.

Initially the Special Attack Corps, as the suicide units were called, were established on a limited basis: to participate in the *Sho*-1 defense of the Philippines. Time was running out on Japan and only unorthodox methods might save the Empire. The only offensive weapon remaining was the land-based aircraft of the Navy and Army. Ground troops must wait until the enemy attacked before they could participate; most of the carrier force—and the most experienced pilots—had been wiped out in the Marianas; the Navy's ships were depleted or crippled. Ordinary bombing rarely stopped the American ships because of antiaircraft fire and protective fighters which interfered with the bomb run. The invaders, and especially their carriers, must be stopped by deliberate crashing of a bombed-up aircraft onto a ship. And the only way of assuring that the aircraft would continue on its fatal trajectory was by having its pilot remain in the plane.

The idea was not new. A fatally stricken pilot or plane had crashed into ships, gun positions, or other planes before. But this resulted only after all other means had failed. And some crashes, however heroic they appeared to be, were not deliberate. The concept of a one-way mission had been introduced as early as Pearl Harbor with the midget submarines, which hardly had a chance, but the chance, however slim, was present. There was none of this in the kamikaze. The sacrifice of one's life for the Emperor was not therefore a new idea, but it had generally occurred in the heat of combat. But to devote a period of training to nothing else but sacrifice—this was regarded even by some Japanese commanders as a farfetched tactic.

One of the earliest suggestions for implementing this idea was submitted shortly after the Marianas Turkey Shoot by Captain Eiichiro Jyo, commander of the light carrier *Chiyoda,* who read the handwriting on the wall and himself wrote: "No longer can we hope to sink the numerically superior enemy aircraft carriers through ordinary attack methods. I urge the immediate organization of special attack units to carry out crash-dive tactics, and I ask to be placed in command of them."

Coincidentally, Jyo died on the same day that the first kamikaze Zero sank its first American ship. The *Chiyoda,* one of the units of Ozawa's decoys-for-Halsey force, was sunk by American carrier planes during the Battle of Leyte Gulf. Jyo went down with his ship.

Meanwhile, Vice-Admiral Takijiro Ohnishi, after serving in various high-level capacities, including the position of Chief of General Affairs, Bureau of the Aviation Department, in the Ministry of Munitions and as chief of staff of Navy land-based aviation during the early—victorious—battles in the Philippines and Malaya, arrived back in the Philippines to assume command of the First Air Fleet. The condition of the air fleet, depleted, its planes tattered and worn, its men dispirited, must have assured Ohnishi that the desperate plan he brought with him was the right one.

Before he had fully taken over his command Ohnishi personally traveled the fifty-odd miles from his post in Manila to Mabalacat Field (a part of Clark Field), where he placed his idea before Commander Asaichi Tamai, executive officer of the 201st Air Group (Sentai). American forces had already landed on Suluan Island at the entrance to Leyte Gulf; the *Sho*-1 operation would be put into force. The mission of the First Air Fleet—with its barely one hundred aircraft—was to provide cover for Kurita's advance into Leyte Gulf. To accomplish this, Ohnishi explained, the American carriers must be stopped—"we must hit the enemy's carriers and keep them neutralized for at least one week."

Ohnishi, his face impassive but obviously strained, went on, according to one of his officers, Captain Rikihei Inoguchi. "In my opinion," Ohnishi said, "there is only one way of assuring that our meager strength will be effective to a maximum degree. That is to organize suicide attack units composed of Zero fighters armed with two-hundred-and-fifty-kilogram [about five hundred pounds] bombs, with each plane to crash-dive into an enemy carrier. . . ."

When, after some discussion, the idea was placed before the twenty-three non-commissioned pilots of the 201st Air Group, Inoguchi described the reaction: "In a frenzy of emotion and joy, the arms of every pilot in the assembly went up in a gesture of complete accord." These volunteers were then placed under the command of Lieutenant Yukio Seki. Ohnishi had his first *Kamikaze Tokubetsu Kogekitai* (Divine Wind Special Attack Squad), twenty-four pilots and twenty-six Zeros. The unit, named *Shimpu* (another interpretation of the Japanese character for *kamikaze*), was divided into four sections, all poetically named: *Shikishima* (a poetic name for Japan), *Yamato* (an ancient name of Japan), *Asahi* (morning sun), and *Yamazakura* (mountain cherry blossoms).

It was not planned to send the full contingent upon suicide missions. Some pilots would escort the kamikaze planes, to protect them from enemy interference and also, if possible, to return and report on the success or failure of the mission. When the kamikaze idea was initiated and the secret became known among the young airmen of the First Air Fleet, it was seized upon as the one means of salvation for Japan. Emotions ran high and strong men literally sobbed when they were either accepted or denied membership in the unique unit. The two dozen men in Seki's *Shimpu* squadron were envied, for theirs would be an honor not all pilots would be privileged to share. That, at least, was the original intent: the kamikaze unit would help to turn the tide in the *Sho*-1 operation and Japan would win the war.

According to Inoguchi, when Ohnishi addressed Seki's men for the first time, the scene was charged with emotion.

"You are already gods," he told them, "without earthly desires. But one thing you want to know is that your crash-dive is not in vain. Regrettably, we will not be able to tell you the results. But I shall watch your efforts to the end and report your deeds to the Throne. You may all rest assured on this point. . . ." It would be the fulfillment of their lives, to be remembered to the Emperor. Their gratitude could barely be contained.

While Seki prepared his few men and planes for their first sortie, one of the units, the *Yamato,* was detached and flown four hundred miles to the south to Cebu, an island almost directly to the west of Leyte. Here Commander Tadashi Nakajima, flight operations officer of the 201st Air Group, organized yet another kamikaze unit. Volunteers leaped at the opportunity and Nakajima soon had an additional twenty pilots for the special attacks being planned for the American fleet. The only two pilots who did not volunteer had been hospitalized. Nakajima had led a flight of eight Zeros; besides his own aircraft and the four kamikaze planes, there had been escort planes. One of the pilots of the escorts (none of whom knew of the kamikaze plan), Lieutenant Yoshiyasu Kuno, when he learned of the plan, appeared before Nakajima in an excited but subdued state. He all but accused the commander of denying him the opportunity of participating in the special attacks, as if it were a kind of discrimination.

Nakajima assured him. "One of the Zeros we brought here from Mabalacat is reserved for *your* special attack mission." The Zero Nakajima had piloted was equipped to carry the five-hundred-pound bomb. Kuno left in a state of elation.

As the Battle of Leyte Gulf developed, the two kamikaze squadrons waited impatiently for an opportunity to strike at the hated enemy. This was an important factor too in their attitude. The Japanese had been indoctrinated since they were young that the United States had insulted the Empire, in its commercial dealings, in military demands—espe-

cially in the hated naval treaties and in diplomatic moves. Not until October 21 was the first sortie attempted. Lieutenant Seki, suffering from a debilitating attack of diarrhea, was to lead the *Shikishima* unit in the first attack. The takeoff was preceded by ceremony during which water was drunk from a container, a gift of Ohnishi, by the mission pilots. They then climbed into their Zeros to the sound of those pilots remaining behind singing an old song which closed with the words *Ogimi no he ni koso shiname/Nodo niwa shinaji* ("Thus for the Emperor I will not die peacefully at home").

Before he took off, the haggard Seki gave Commander Tamai an envelope containing a cutting of his hair. This was to be sent home to Seki's family, a recent wife and a widowed mother, as a memorial in traditional samurai manner. The four suicide planes took off accompanied by escort Zeros—and then all returned. They had not been able to find the American fleet. With tears in his eyes, Seki apologized for the failure of the mission.

The failure of the Cebu kamikazes was even more embarrassing. As three special attack planes and two escorts warmed up on the airstrip, American carrier planes swarmed down and shot them up, puncturing tanks, riddling the Zeros—all of which exploded and burned. This mission had not even gotten off the ground. After the carrier planes left, Nakajima prepared another three Zeros for a mission which would be led by Lieutenant Kuno—who had so feared he would be left out of the great events. The Zero pilots, hoping to find the source of their earlier ignominy, took off late in the afternoon. Poor weather intervened and two returned. They had not found the American ships. Kuno did not come back—nor was any American ship struck by a Japanese plane that day.

Weather and poor reconnaissance continued to add to the frustrations of the kamikaze pilots. Seki, for example, ventured out four times, four days running, only to return each time after a fruitless search for the enemy. The fifth time, leading his *Shikishima* unit (five kamikaze Zeroes with four escorts) on October 25, he came upon the beleaguered escort carriers off Samar. All five bomb-laden Zeros plunged upon the American fleet, and insofar as it is possible to know, Seki's Zero may have been the first kamikaze plane to score a hit upon an American carrier—the *Saint Lo*. Also hit were three other of the baby flattops, but the *Saint Lo*, struck by another kamikaze, ruptured and sank.

Thus on the climactic day of the Battle of Leyte Gulf, the Special Attack Corps had achieved its first victory. At the same time it also reported its first exaggerated account of that victory, and that would lead to the fatal decision of expanding the kamikaze. A witness, veteran pilot Hiroyoshi Nishizawa, one of Japan's leading aces, returned to describe Seki's efforts. (Nishizawa, incidentally, was killed a few days later in a transport after a flight to Cebu.) The news of the victory was quickly broadcast via Radio Tokyo: "The *Shikishima* unit of the Kamikaze Special Attack Corps made a successful surprise attack on an enemy task force containing four aircraft carriers at a point thirty miles northeast of Suluan Island at ten forty-five. Two planes hit one carrier, which was definitely sunk. A third plane hit another carrier, setting it aflame. A fourth hit a cruiser, which sank instantly."

A great thrill ran through the corps and Ohnishi could take some pride in the efficacy of his plan. Nishimura's, Shima's, and Kurita's ships had been all but devoured by the American carrier forces and had accomplished little—yet single men in a frail aircraft had actually sunk ships of the American fleet, carriers at that (the Japanese had not yet discerned the difference between a fleet carrier and an escort carrier).

The following day the Cebu-based *Yamato* unit had its chance. An early morning mission (two kamikazes with a single Zero escort) simply vanished off the face of the earth. But the second, airborne shortly after noon and consisting of three kamikazes with two escorts, struck to the east of Surigao, where Nishimura had fared so badly. One of the escort Zeros returned (the other having been destroyed by a wall of Hellcats) to claim another carrier definitely sunk and another seriously damaged. Here again exaggeration entered. On October 26 only the escort carrier *Suwanee* (of Taffy 1) was hit, and damaged, by a kamikaze plane; it did not sink, nor were any other ships damaged.

When the word of the kamikaze "triumphs" reached the Emperor he commented in a curious manner. The ambivalence of the Emperor's reaction, however, was ignored in the excitement of his special concern, and Ohnishi dispatched a message to the surviving pilots.

When told of the special attack, His Majesty said, "Was it necessary to go to this extreme? They certainly did a magnificent job." His Majesty's words suggest that His Majesty is greatly concerned. We must redouble our efforts to relieve His Majesty of this concern. I have pledged our every effort toward that end.

But Ohnishi had been perturbed by the Emperor's words, interpreting them as a form of criticism. Yet he had succeeded where the others had failed; he was determined that Japan must fight to the last man. He must extend the "life" of the kamikaze idea and expand the force with which to strike back at the enemy. And nothing so sustained his point of view as the dismal final outcome of the *Sho*-1 operation.

This was a major point in his argument with Vice-Admiral Shigeru Fukudome, whose Second Air Fleet had flown in from Formosa to make a small effort in the *Sho*-1 operation with its conventional air attacks. Since Ohnishi's smaller kamikaze units had wrought more harm to the American fleet than had Fukudome's large bomber formations, the junior officer (Ohnishi) won the argument and in the small hours of the morning of October 26, 1944, Fukudome reluctantly capitulated. The two air fleets were united as the Combined Land-based Air Force, under Fukudome's command and with Ohnishi as his chief of staff. Certain units were to be set up for kamikaze operations, for Fukudome wished to keep the greater proportions of his still operational air forces for orthodox attacks. But the spirit spread and within hours several new kamikaze squadrons had been formed—enough to establish a second Kamikaze Tokubetsu Kogekitai. The union of the two air fleets increased the supply of aircraft for the special attacks—until they were expended. Besides. the Zero, among the other early kamikaze planes were the single-engined, two-place "Judy" (Aichi D4Y, *Suisei*) and the "Frances" (Yokosuka P1Y, *Ginga*), a twin-engined bomber. The larger craft meant not only larger bomb loads, but also a crew of two rather than the single suicide pilot.

The kamikaze corps survived the failure of *Sho*-1. With the Imperial Navy cut in half, the Philippine battle devolved into a vicious land battle. Ohnishi's mission was changed accordingly and his kamikaze units were assigned sorties that would help the Japanese troops by striking at American transports bringing in reinforcements and supplies. But the very nature of his operation quickly depleted Ohnishi's limited supply of aircraft. In November he flew to Tokyo to present his case before the High Command, demanding that he be given three hundred planes for his Special Attack Corps. About half that number was finally granted, and these were scraped up from several training centers. If the aircraft were not in top condition, neither were the not fully trained young pilots. These youths were sent to Formosa for special training in how to experience a spectacular death.

The special indoctrination took only a week: two days on takeoff procedures, two days on formation flying, and the final three days on how to approach and attack a target. As quickly as this period was over the young pilots were rushed to the Philippines, where it was obvious that the Americans planned to move up the islands to Luzon. That the kamikaze volunteers were exceedingly young and ill trained meant little to their destruction-bent leaders. The poorly trained pilots were regarded as liabilities, even if only subconsciously. One of the critics of the kamikaze tactics, Rear Admiral Toshiyuki Yokoi, revealed this attitude when he observed of his own Fifth Air Fleet during the Okinawa campaign: "I knew that two of the eight units were practically untrained and *so were not fit for anything but suicide duty.*" (Italics added.) Obviously Yokoi did not venerate the kamikaze volunteers as Ohnishi did.

At the same time Japanese ground reinforcements were being slipped into the Philippines and the promise of an impending, even larger-scaled Guadalcanal loomed forbiddingly. The threat of another Tokyo Express, prolonging the fighting and intensifying the casualty toll, was ominously considered by the Americans. Nor did the Leyte airstrips provide Kenney with facilities from which he could operate very effectively. Tacloban, the principal airfield, was little more than a bog which defied Army engineers; the heavy-bomber strip at Tanauan was not operational until mid-December. Air cover, therefore, for the hard-fighting ground troops was provided mainly by the Navy.

During the air strikes upon Luzon to interfere

A Japanese suicide plane aimed at the Essex *near Luzon in the Philippines, November 25, 1944, when the first kamikaze planes began operations.*
(NAVY DEPT., NATIONAL ARCHIVES)

with Japanese reinforcement operations and in preparation for the proposed return to Luzon, Halsey's carriers came under powerful kamikaze attacks. On November 25 planes from the carrier *Ticonderoga* sank the heavy cruiser *Kumano* and smashed two coastal convoys, but a swarm of kamikaze planes came out—thirteen suicide planes with a nine-plane escort in two waves—and slashed into Halsey's carriers. The *Intrepid,* which had been hit so often it earned the nickname "Evil I," the *Cabot,* the *Hancock,* and the *Essex* were all hit, with severe damages and casualties. The *Intrepid,* crashed into by two planes, suffered a hundred dead. Once again, at the cost of men and machines, the Special Attack Corps "proved" itself to Ohnishi's satisfaction, but what he failed or preferred not to see was that it did not stop the Americans.

When American landings began (December 15, 1944) on Mindoro Island—a military steppingstone between unlovely Leyte and pivotal Luzon—about forty Japanese planes were still operational in the Philippines. And to these had been added the last thirteen suicide Zeros, which had been flown in from Formosa. The final phase of the Philippine kamikaze attacks was aimed at the Luzon landings in Lingayen Gulf. During these landings the U. S.

A kamikaze strikes the Intrepid, *Luzon, November 25.* (NAVY DEPT., NATIONAL ARCHIVES)

Crew fights the fire on the Intrepid *after being crashed by a kamikaze. Sixty men died in the crash and fire; the* Intrepid *was hit so often by kamikazes that it was nicknamed the "Evil I."*

(NAVY DEPT., NATIONAL ARCHIVES)

Navy was to realize for the first time the full implications of the kamikazes. This was brought home with force during the prelanding bombardment and minesweeping operations on January 6. A large force under Admiral J. B. Oldendorf (six battleships, six cruisers, nineteen destroyers, a dozen escort carriers which, in turn, were screened by twenty destroyers with escorts, minesweepers, transports, and gunboats) was headed for Luzon. A portent flew in on January 3 and smashed into the escort carrier *Ommaney Bay* (which sank the following day with a hundred dead). Curiously no Japanese claim was made for this sinking—the pilot

A burning "Frances, "a Nakajima land-based bomber, dispatched from Luzon, passes over the deck of escort carrier Ommaney Bay *during landings on Mindoro island, about three hundred miles northwest of Leyte.*

Taking Mindoro was essential to the planned campaign for Luzon to begin early in 1945. The Ommaney Bay *survived the air attacks at Mindoro, but was sunk by a kamikaze in Lingayen Gulf on January 4, 1945.* (NAVY DEPT., NATIONAL ARCHIVES)

who sank the carrier may not have been a kamikaze. The next day several attacks originating from Mabalacat, Luzon, spread flame, casualties, and foreboding through the American ships. No ships were sunk but two escort carriers, *Manila Bay* and *Savo,* an Australian ship, H.M.A.S. *Australia,* and six other ships were struck. The future appeared chilling to the Americans—who did shoot down some of the attackers. Still their determination carried some through the heavy antiaircraft fire and the fighter screen.

Vice-Admiral C. R. Brown expressed some of the emotions of the men aboard the targets of the kamikazes, to whom the very conception was inconceivable. "We watched each plunging kamikaze with the detached horror of one witnessing a terrible spectacle rather than as the intended victim. We forgot self for the moment as we groped hopelessly for the thoughts of that other man up there. And dominating it all was a strange admixture of respect and pity—respect for any person who offers the supreme sacrifice to the things he stands for, and pity for the utter frustration which was epitomized by the suicidal act. For whatever the gesture meant to that

central actor out there in space, and however painful might be the consequences to ourselves, no one of us questioned the outcome of the war now rushing to its conclusion."

The morning of the sixth brought a surprise to

Anxious carrier crewmen scan the horizon for kamikaze planes. (U. S. NAVY)

Commander Nakajima. He had fallen into an exhausted sleep certain that the last of the First Air Fleet's kamikazes had been expended the day before. But through the night ground crews had worked until they had patched together five Zeros, ready to fly and armed with the suicide bombs (three with the full five-hundred-pound bomb and two with lighter bombs). Thirty pilots remained, so it was a serious crisis in command, for all fought for the privilege of flying the barely airworthy Zeros. Nakajima silenced the squabbling with "Everyone wants to go. Don't be so selfish!"

The final choice was made by Nakajima in consultation with the commander of the group. Selected to lead the attack was a Lieutenant Nakano, only recently released from the hospital after an attack of tuberculosis. Nakano had begged to be given the chance to make a mission before a return of the illness deprived him of the honor of serving. "Remembering his plea," Nakajima wrote, "I kept him in mind for some short-range mission that would not tax his strength."

As the planes were preparing to take off, Nakano raised himself in his cockpit and shouted to Nakajima. "Fearing that something had gone wrong, I ran to the side of his plane to learn what troubled him. His face was wreathed in smiles as he called, 'Thank you, Commander. Thank you very much!'" As each of the remaining four planes poised in the takeoff position for a moment, the pilot waved and through the engine's roar Nakajima heard "his shrieked farewell: 'Thank you for choosing me!'"

A sudden fury descended upon the American fleet standing off Lingayen bombarding the invasion beaches. It began at noon when a flaming Zero (not one of Nakano's, which appeared later in the day) enveloped the navigating bridge of the battleship *New Mexico,* killing the commanding officer, Captain R. W. Fleming, Churchill's liaison officer to MacArthur, Lieutenant General Herbert Lumsden, a *Time* correspondent, William Chickering, and twenty-six other men; in addition eighty-seven were wounded. The destroyer *Walkde* nearby downed two approaching Zeros but a third broke through the curtain of fire and rammed into the bridge. Commander George F. Davis became a human torch until his men as quickly and as gently as possible smothered the flames. Meanwhile a fourth Zero had been destroyed by the *Walkde*'s gun crews. Com-

mander Davis, too terribly burned to survive, died later in the day.

About that time Nakano's Zeros swept in on Lingayen. An escort-observer claimed that the five patched-up Zeros struck a battleship, a cruiser, and three transports. The cruiser may well have been the *Louisville,* which received a Zero in the bridge. Flaming fuel drenched Rear Admiral Theodore E. Chandler, who nonetheless assisted in putting out the flames by manhandling a firehose with his men and only then took his place in line for treatment in sick bay. He died the next day because of severe damage to his lungs. More than thirty others died with him.

The day's toll was high: the minesweeper *Long* had been sunk, and besides the ships already mentioned, seven others plus the *Australia* (for the second time) were also damaged. And, if the ships did not sink, the injuries of the survivors were often frightful. Aboard the transport *Harris* Lieutenant G. R. Cassels-Smith observed in his diary (the date does not matter): "Two more burials at sea this evening—that makes four who have died so far and there are several more who may die. They are so badly burned or mangled that they are really better off dead."

But for all their appalling ferocity the kamikazes had not stopped the Luzon landings, which began on January 9, 1945. The following day Ohnishi and his staff flew out of the Philippines to Tainan, Formosa, where he would reorganize his Special Attack Corps for its final round of glory. Meanwhile, however, those Japanese Air Force men for whom no transportation could be found were left to serve as ground troops in the hills of the Philippines. Fukudome fled to Singapore by flying boat some days later. Tominaga, of the Army's ill-fated air forces, took to the hills as an infantryman.

Attacks from Formosa could still be mounted and were, but such missions were sporadic. One such mission on January 11—a Betty bomber with a dozen fighters as escorts—encountered the two P-51s of Captain William A. Shomo and Lieutenant Paul M. Lipscomb, themselves on an armed reconnaissance mission. The Americans' objectives were the Aparri and Laoag airdromes, which by that date presumably housed only wrecked Japanese aircraft and a few airmen destined for the infantry. The Betty, which they sighted when it was about

Mustangs of the 35th Fighter Group (Fifth Air Force) prepare for takeoff from Luzon airstrip to bomb and *strafe pockets of Japanese resistance in the northern section of the island.* (U. S. AIR FORCE)

2500 feet above them, may have actually been an evacuation plane carrying valuable aircrews out of the Philippines to Formosa. Thus the single twin-engined bomber and the rather large escort.

Neither Shomo, who commanded the 82nd Tactical Reconnaissance Squadron, nor Lipscomb had ever been in combat before. With the odds at thirteen to two, the green Kenney boys in their only recently arrived Mustangs climbed to the attack. Whatever the mission of the Japanese, they appeared to be more inexperienced than their attackers, for as the two Mustangs approached no attempt was made to challenge them. The formation flew blithely on its way. Kenney later suggested that the Japanese pilots mistook the new Mustang for the Tony and thought that reinforcements had arrived and did not expect an attack.

Shomo scored first: he came in under the third element and picked off the leading Zeke, which detonated in mid-air. Sweeping away from the debris and flame, Shomo ripped past the second element and shattered one of the fighters in that.

The Japanese realized then that they were under attack and formed into battle stations; even as they fluttered around to do this, Shomo careened around and subtracted one more from their number. This plane, his third victim, blew up also. This brought

Shomo's Mustang beneath the Betty; he raised the nose of the P-51, got the wing root of the Japanese bomber in his sight, and fired. The Betty dropped out of the formation, nosed down into the jungle of Luzon, and crashed. Orange flame and thick black

Ennis C. Whitehead, commander of the Fifth Air Force, with William A. Shomo, who became a fighter ace in his first air battle. (U. S. AIR FORCE)

smoke shot out of the thick, lush greenness of the jungle.

One of the escort Zekes came down with the bomber to challenge Shomo, but instead was dealt with: as he pulled up from watching the fall of the Betty, Shomo found himself looking into the nose of an oncoming Zeke. He pressed his gun button and the Zeke flipped out of his path and downward to join the blazing Betty. This had brought him up above the remaining Zekes. Shomo dived upon the lead fighter and with a short burst sent it down. Another Zeke slipped by diving and Shomo raced after it. When they were within three hundred feet of the jungle, Shomo caught the Zeke in his guns and it simply continued its dive into the treetops.

While Shomo was thus engaged, Lipscomb too had been busy. He accounted for three Zekes during the battle. With these three added to the seven Shomo had destroyed, the brief battle had eliminated ten aircraft from the already diminished Japanese Air Force. The surviving three Zekes found refuge in a cloud bank and managed to get away.

When they returned to the Fifth Air Force base on Mindoro Island (directly south of Luzon), the elated Shomo—who had become an ace on his very first mission—made the traditional "victory roll" over the field. He would roar over the field, twist and turn, then come back again and repeat the maneuver. The first couple of rolls were greeted with cheers, but then when the number reached five, then six, and finally seven, the cheering stopped. Obviously some hot-shot stick-jockey was making sport of the honored victory roll. This was a decided breach of etiquette and must be reprimanded officially. The brass jumped into jeeps and drove out to the strips.

Lipscomb had already landed and stood near his Mustang awaiting Shomo's landing. The loaded jeep pulled up alongside the lanky Texan. He being the nearest target, a colonel began reaming him for

Luzon from the air. Marine Dauntless in foreground is seeking a Japanese position on which to drop the five- *hundred-pound bomb it is carrying.*

(DEFENSE DEPT., MARINE CORPS)

Shomo's abuse of the symbol of victory. Lipscomb, in a lazy drawl, explained that Shomo was indeed legitimately exercising the honored privilege.

"Sir," Lipscomb said, "he got seven Japs." He then added, "And I got three."

It was a bit difficult to believe (but gun cameras proved it to be true). Then one of the brass suddenly realized another anomaly.

"Lieutenant," he asked, "if you got three planes, why didn't you make any victory rolls?"

"Well, sir," Lipscomb replied, taking his time with each southern-inflected syllable, "I just checked out on this airplane and I ain't sure I know how."

Kenney was of course delighted with the performance of his kids. Although they had had no previous combat experience, obviously their training had been greatly superior to that of the hapless Japanese pilots they had come upon that day. Jokingly he inquired, "Why'd you let the others get away?"

"To tell the truth, General," Shomo answered, "we ran out of bullets." Lipscomb, apparently having used up his syllables for the day, merely nodded. Kenney promoted both men on the spot and saw to it that Shomo received the Medal of Honor and Lipscomb the Distinguished Service Cross. With characteristic curiosity Kenney inquired about the prewar occupations of the two men. "Lipscomb was a Texas cowboy," Kenney learned, "Shomo—believe it or not—was a licensed embalmer. Poor Nips."

IV

On Formosa Ohnishi, a man now determined to establish an air force on a death wish, set to work on the reorganization of his First Air Fleet kamikazes for the predicted invasion of Okinawa.

The reorganization was completed by the first week in February and the new Special Attack Corps activated even earlier—on January 18—was named the Niitaka Unit (after the mountain on Formosa). Even this carried its special full-circle irony, alluding as it did to the Pearl Harbor attack message, "Climb Mount Niitaka." Within the month yet another Special Attack Unit was formed: the 601st Air Group of the Third Air Fleet (based in Japan in the Kanto Plain area around Tokyo). This unit consisted of thirty-two aircraft, a conglomeration of Zekes and Judys—fighters, bombers, and torpedo planes—organized into five elements ranging from

four to eight aircraft each. This unit first saw action during the invasion of what appeared to be the insignificant island of Iwo Jima.

Less than eight hundred miles from the Japanese homeland, Iwo Jima was a threat to LeMay's Twentieth Air Force B-29s because of a radar warning station on the island and the Japanese fighters stationed there. But there was an even more important function in mind for the roughly five-by-three-miles pork-chop-shaped dot in the Pacific, which lay halfway between the Marianas and Tokyo: in American hands Iwo could serve as an emergency landing field for distressed B-29s, navigational aids could be set up, fighters could be based there to provide escort for the Marianas-based Superfortresses, and it could be used as an Air-Sea Rescue base. Of especial interest were the three Japanese airfields, two of which were actually operational.

The battle for Iwo Jima in February of 1945 was primarily a land battle, one of the costliest in the history of the U. S. Marines in terms of land taken divided by lives lost.

Iwo, however, was but a portent of things to come. The island's commander, Lieutenant General

The first flag on Iwo Jima: Marines dug in around an antiaircraft gun with Mount Suribachi in the background. When the flag (in a famous staged ceremony) was put atop Suribachi the island would become a B-29 base from which to strike Japan. All this was done, but at great cost. (U. S. MARINE CORPS)

Iwo Jima as an American air base. More than a hundred Mustangs and a couple of B-29s parked on what had once been a Japanese airstrip.

(U. S. AIR FORCE)

My Girl *gets the go-sign for a B-29 escort mission. Iwo-based Mustangs rendezvoused with Marianas-based B-29s for bombing missions.* (U. S. AIR FORCE)

Tadamichi Kuribayashi, had developed the island's natural defense system by digging under the volcanic ash and into caves until he transformed it, as his orders had read, "into a fortress." Despite the heavy aerial bombardment by the Seventh Air Force's B-24s and the 313th Bombardment Wing's B-29s, plus a heavy naval bombardment followed by carrier plane attacks, the Japanese troops were generally unhurt. Nor did they come out to meet the invaders head on, as once they might have; instead, the Japanese waited in their caves and dugouts to render the taking of Iwo Jima a foot-by-foot nightmare. Instead of the planned-for two weeks, the securing of Iwo Jima required twice that time (and even after that, Marines and Army soldiers continued to flush out—and kill—the more recalcitrant of Kuribayashi's men). Nearly five thousand American lives were exchanged for that small island, and the wounded numbered well over twenty thousand. Japanese dead reached an estimated total of twenty-one thousand; about two hundred were taken prisoner. The savage fighting, deadly, resolute, and for the Japanese, to the death, was a devastating foreshadowing of what lay in the future.

As the casualties mounted the question was asked in stateside papers, "Is Iwo Jima worth the price?" —an insignificant little volcanic dot of no apparent strategic value. But even before the fighting had reached its full fury and the landing strips were fully readied by the Seabees and Air Force aviation engineers, the first B-29 landed on Iwo on March 4. Lieutenant Raymond Malo, whose plane had developed fuel problems, had to make a choice between ditching and violating orders: they were, not to land at Iwo Jima, which was not yet ready for them.

It was a relatively simple choice: Malo set course for Iwo. He first quizzed the crew, warning them that finding Iwo without radar (that too had malfunctioned) would be its own little problem; in addition, the war was still going on there, the runways were probably too short for the B-29 (the Tinian strip was eighty-five hundred feet, the Iwo strip four thousand feet), and there might be other problems. The crew voted for Iwo Jima.

Navigator Bernard Bennison, despite the poor weather and with no radar, found the island, and Malo, with copilot Edward Mochler, brought the big, sixty-ton aircraft onto the short runway with a squeal of brakes, the stench of burning rubber, and the information from the tower that the strip was under Japanese mortar fire. The landing was extremely delicate, for Malo and Mochler, in deference to the short and narrow runway, had to bring the plane in at near-stall air speed. With the crew at crash positions the pilots throttled back until the great plane all but dropped the few final feet to the runway. They were on land, but would they stay there? As they careened down the strip it seemed to contract with each fraction of a moment. With Mochler applying full brakes, with full flaps down, Malo attempted to keep the racing monster under control. Finally he kicked full left rudder, a telephone pole snapped as one wing flicked against it, and the plane came to a halt.

The Japanese immediately increased mortar fire on the strip, hoping to destroy the prize. But four hours later, after two thousand gallons of fuel had been poured into the B-29 by hand, Malo managed to take off from the strip using up only twenty-five hundred feet of runway. His plane and its eleven-man crew returned safely to Tinian (and no official reprimand, for he had already proved the value of taking Iwo Jima). Malo's B-29 was the first of twenty-four hundred Superfortresses that would land in distress upon Iwo Jima's two strips. Thus about twenty-five thousand men, a fraction at least of which might have been lost if they had been forced to ditch, landed safely on the ugly little island. Its importance to the final surrender of Japan is unquestionable. It would be impossible—and pointless—to attempt to compare the lives lost in taking the island with those saved after it was taken. Perhaps the best tribute was that of an anonymous B-29 pilot who said, "Whenever I land on this island, I thank God and the men who fought for it."

Certain Air Force commanders, among them Spaatz and LeMay, believed that Japan could be bombed into submission by the B-29s, but the Army commanders did not share that belief. The next step then was to take another island close to Japan, one large enough to serve as a staging area for the proposed invasion of the home islands. Formosa (Taiwan) had been bypassed in favor of the Philippine invasion; besides, it was heavily fortified and garrisoned. It was decided that next on the central Pacific schedule, therefore, should be one of the Ryukyu Islands, Okinawa, which lay about 350

miles south of Kyushu, the southernmost of the home islands of Japan.

And it was at Okinawa that the divine wind consummated its most lethal frenzy.

Following the abandonment of the Philippines the surviving naval air fleets were regrouped or combined with untried units into four air fleets—the First (at Formosa), the Third (in the Kanto Plain

Iwo as a hazardous haven: a damaged B-29, unable to make it all the way back to Saipan, made an emergency landing on Iwo. With brakes locked, the bomber turned into a line-up of Mustangs and crushed four before coming to a stop and bursting into flame. Only two members of the crew were injured seriously enough to require hospitalization. (U. S. AIR FORCE)

area), the Fifth (on Kyushu), and the Tenth, which was still, around the beginning of 1945, undergoing basic training and stationed on the main island of Honshu. Like the Tenth, the Fifth Air Fleet had not completed its training, so that the Imperial High Command saw nothing in the future for these two air fleets (of about a thousand planes) except special attacks. The more advanced Fifth would be expended upon enemy task forces and the unskilled Tenth on transports and lesser craft.

The Army air forces too were expected to participate in the special attacks, although never with quite

The invasion of Okinawa begins and the Franklin *is hit by bombs of a Japanese dive bomber.*
(NAVY DEPT., NATIONAL ARCHIVES)

the dedication as the Navy. In fact, only the Navy special attack pilots were called kamikaze pilots; the Army used the term *Tokko Tai,* an abbreviation of the official *Tokubetsu Kogekitai* (Special Attack Unit).

From the time Ohnishi had fled the Philippines in January until the invasion of Okinawa on Easter Sunday (April 1, 1945), the kamikaze concept spread and the organization solidified—as did the belief that suicide attacks would be the only means of stopping the enemy. The Imperial Navy was all but non-existent—only the great battleship *Yamato* remained of the superbattleships; the *Haruna,* the last remaining battleship of the *Kongo* class, was under repair. The decisive battle must take place in the air above and around Okinawa.

The opening action of the Okinawa campaign was carried out by carrier planes of Mitscher's Task Force 58, which during the period March 18–21 lashed out at airfields at Kyushu and shipping targets in the Inland Sea at Kure and Kobe. During these strikes, particularly those upon Kure Harbor, Japanese antiaircraft proved most effective and thirteen U. S. Navy planes were lost. Also the carrier *Franklin* became the victim of a lone single-engined Japanese plane, which placed two bombs upon the deck. The resulting fires, as well as the initial explosions, took a heavy toll in lives: more than 700 (and 265 wounded). The *Franklin,* although badly damaged, was towed out of the battle by the heavy cruiser *Pittsburgh.* Heavy air cover protected the

The Franklin, *burning and listing, and out of the battle for Okinawa.* (NAVY DEPT., NATIONAL ARCHIVES)

stricken carrier from further Japanese attack and the *Franklin* eventually arrived (after a twelve-thousand-mile voyage and only one stop between) in New York for repairs.

On the final day of the preliminary strikes, March 21, a large number of bogies were detected upon the radar screens and an equally large force of Hellcats (about 150) was scrambled to intercept. Two dozen Hellcats from the *Hornet, Bennington, Wasp,* and *Belleau Wood* were the first to meet the Japanese force of Betty bombers with Zeke escort. The first elements of Bettys and Zekes were disposed of in a brief, ferocious encounter, during which two of the Hellcats were lost.

The Navy pilots were especially surprised at how vulnerable some of the Bettys appeared to be—slower and less maneuverable than normally. Some even appeared to have a curious additional wing beneath the main wing. Unknown to the Hellcat pilots, they had broken up the first attempt at an *Ohka* bombing of the U.S. fleet.

The *Ohka* ("cherry blossom") bomb was a small glider, twenty feet long with a sixteen-foot wing span, with rocket boosters in the tail and a ton of explosives in the nose. It was literally a flying bomb with one exception: a pilot who guided it. The *Ohka* was carried under the fuselage of a Betty to the general target area, where the kamikaze pilot would transfer from the mother ship (through the bomb bay) into the tiny cockpit of the flying bomb. About twenty or thirty miles from the target, the *Ohka* was released and alternately gliding and rocketing would attain a speed of more than five hundred miles an hour by the time it was within striking distance of American ships. The *Ohka,* brain child of one Ensign Mitsuo Ohta, was a hard-luck design. An early shipment of fifty, for example, was lost when the battleship-turned-carrier carrying them, the *Shinano,* was sent to the bottom by a submarine early in November.

Likewise, the initial *Ohka* mission, which had consisted of eighteen Bettys (sixteen carrying the *Ohka*) and thirty fighters (of the fifty-five originally assigned), fared poorly. The Japanese formation got no closer than fifty or sixty miles to the American warships before it clashed with the Hellcats. Most of the Bettys managed to jettison their encumbering *Ohkas* (the suicide pilots, of course, remained in the bombers), but of the eighteen that had taken off

Japanese-manned flying torpedo, the Ohka *("cherry blossom") bomb, which was carried to its objectives by a bomber and released near the target. The small wooden craft carried more than a ton of explosives in its nose.* (NAVY DEPT., NATIONAL ARCHIVES)

A pre-kamikaze flight ceremony. Before taking off, the pilots went through a formal ceremony of a religious nature. It was a solemn rite, much like a funeral, which, in effect, it was. (U. S. AIR FORCE)

only three escaped destruction under the guns of the Hellcats. These three, one of them carrying the leader of the mission, Lieutenant Commander Goro Nonaka, slipped into a cloud bank. Even so, they were never heard from again. The fighter escort too was heavily decimated, and the first mission of the "cherry blossoms" was an abject failure.

When the *Ohka* appeared in the Okinawa area itself its name was quickly changed from the poetic cherry blossom by the U.S. sailors to a more blunt, precise *Baka* ("stupid"). It was not an inappropriate designation, considering the ultimate performance of the *Baka:* of the eight hundred manufactured fifty were used in suicide missions and three actually exploded on target. While the concept was *baka,* indeed, the devotion and courage of the *Ohka* pilots were exceptional.

V

When U. S. Army and Marine troops swarmed across the beaches on the East China Sea side of Okinawa on Easter Sunday morning, 1945, it appeared that the Japanese, unaccountably, had complied on this occasion with the treaty wrested from the Okinawans by Commodore Matthew C. Perry in 1854 (a quarter of a century before the Japanese annexed the Ryukyus).

"Hereafter," the treaty read, "whenever citizens of the United States come to Lew Chew [the original name of the Ryukyus], they shall be treated with great courtesy and friendship." And so it seemed to the citizens of the United States—about fifty thousand strong—who splashed ashore on "L-Day"—"L" for Landing. Resistance was so feeble that the Marines referred to it as "Love Day."

They had not expected this as they moved ashore taking two airfields and spread over a beachhead roughly eight miles wide and three to four miles deep. Okinawa, even those most ignorant of strategy realized, would be the prelude to the Last Battle—and it would have to be deadly and vicious. When an eager young Marine lieutenant attempted to explicate the taking of Okinawa into the Grand Strategy, he told his men, "From Okinawa we can bomb the Japs anywhere—Japan, China, Formosa . . ."

"Yeah," was the characteristic comment by the typical tough, realistic sergeant, "and vice versa."

It was food for thought and worry. Besides, as the ships stood off the beaches Tokyo Rose had promised them ill. "This is the Zero Hour, boys. It is broadcast for all you men in the Pacific, particularly those standing off the shores of Okinawa—because many of you will never hear another program. . . .

"Here's a good number," she purred, " 'Going

Home' . . . nice work if you can get it. . . . You boys off Okinawa listen and enjoy it while you can, because when you're dead you're a long time dead. . . ."

Later she would broadcast some of the latest hit records from the States—Miller, Dorsey, James. "Let's have a little jukebox music for the boys and make it hot. The boys are going to catch hell soon, and they might as well get used to the heat. . . ."

"Love Day" had not been hot at all and they went in "standing up," not as at Tarawa, Guadalcanal, or Iwo at all. Only skirmishes marred the calm. By the second day Major General Pedro del Valle, commanding the 1st Marine Division, called a press conference and said, "I don't know where the Japs are, and I can't offer you any good reason why they let us come ashore so easily. We're pushing on across the island as fast as we can move the men and equipment." The anticipated "most fanatical" resistance had simply not materialized.

Not yet and not for some days. ". . . Love Day turned into Honeymoon Week at Okinawa," Marine historian Robert Leckie observed. But then the honeymoon ended.

Okinawa was visualized by the Japanese High Command as a kind of massive sponge which would absorb American blood, ships, and aircraft, a tropical Stalingrad, perhaps. The island commander, capable, quiet Lieutenant General Mitsuru Ushijima, deployed his Thirty-second Army through the hills, cliffs, and caves of the southern third of the long (about sixty miles), narrow (ranging from two to eighteen miles) island. The bulk of Ushijima's roughly hundred thousand troops (about a fifth of whom were reluctant Okinawans) were concentrated in the southern third of the island; another, smaller, concentration was dug in to the north, on the Motobu Peninsula, off which lay the tiny Ie Shima (on which the beloved war correspondent Ernie Pyle was to be killed by a sniper on L plus 17).

The plan was to hold out as long as possible, killing the American invader, and to keep the American fleet within striking distance of the kamikazes. Okinawa would be the great proving ground for Ohnishi's Divine Wind. Ushijima's men would engage the ground troops while the kamikaze pilots—and suicide boats on the surface—eliminated the

American fleet. This accomplished, there would be no invasion—or else the Americans would be so badly torn up that their invasion attempt of Japan (finally set for November 1, 1945) would be weakened. Once again a kind of grim optimism emboldened the Japanese. Major General Isamu Cho, Ushijima's chief of staff, had traveled to the homeland from Okinawa to present Ushijima's plan for the defense of Okinawa to the High Command and returned not only with approval of the static defense plan but also with a high regard for the promise of the reorganized and augmented Special Attack Corps. Cho, hard-bitten, driving, and not very popular as Ushijima's tough right arm, returned to Okinawa in an expectant state, informing the commanders of the Thirty-second Army of the promise: "The brave ruddy-faced warriors with the white silken scarves tied about their heads, at peace in their favorite planes, dash out spiritedly to the attack. The skies are brightening."

In reality it was the glow of the setting sun; the brightness was the glare of sudden, violent, meaningless, and prodigal death. The major thrust of the kamikaze operations came from bases in southern Kyushu. The Formosa-based Special Attack Corps contributed little to the Okinawa campaign and Ohnishi himself was transferred to Japan to serve as vice-chief of the Naval General Staff. His forceful, outspoken devotion to an absolute Japanese-American Armageddon only added to his already tarnished popularity in Tokyo. So, with pervasive asperity, a sense of frustration and humiliation, Ohnishi—who had blueprinted Yamamoto's Hawaii Operation, which, despite his own doubts, had proved extravagantly successful—was forced to await the end in an office in Tokyo.

Yamamoto's chief of staff at the time of the Hawaii Operation, Vice-Admiral Matome Ugaki (who had escaped death when his chief was killed in the attack by the P-38s over Ballale) was given command of the Fifth Air Fleet, which, in turn, was placed under operational control of the Third and Tenth Air Fleets. Direction of the kamikaze attacks during the Okinawa campaign devolved upon Ugaki. When he had assumed his new post before the Pearl Harbor attack Ugaki had said in an impassioned speech to flag officers at naval headquarters in Tokyo that the "success of our surprise attack on Pearl Harbor will prove to be the Waterloo of the war to follow."

But whose Waterloo? Ugaki had falsified the results of the Midway war games, making it appear that Japan must be the victor in that battle—and the actual outcome was its own Waterloo. Ugaki, like Ohnishi, had been in on events from the glorious inception and was destined to play his role to the bitter end. His three air fleets could muster a combined strength of about 1815 aircraft, of which 540 were set aside for special attacks. The Sixth Army Air Force was ordered to co-operate with Ugaki's naval planes in annihilating the enemy in and around Okinawa. Besides the aircraft there remained also a fraction of the once proudly numerous Combined Fleet. Only one battleship, the superb *Yamato,* was operational at the time of the Okinawa invasion. There was, too, the light cruiser *Yahagi* and a handful (eight) of destroyers. This pitiable remnant was called the Second Fleet and placed under the command of Vice-Admiral Seiichi Ito; captain of the formidable *Yamato* was Kosaku Aruga. When this force sortied from the Inland Sea on April 6, 1945, the name had been changed to "Special Surface Attack Force."

The 10-ship fleet, without air cover, was intended to challenge Admiral Spruance's Fifth Fleet, which consisted of some 1500 ships. Among these, which included transports of the amphibious forces, minesweepers, salvage ships, and repair vessels, there were more than 40 carriers, 18 battleships, and 200 destroyers. Task Force 58, the Fast Carrier Force under Mitscher, itself was made up of over 100 ships, 10 of them heavy carriers and 6 escort carriers. Co-operating with the Americans was Task Force 57, 22 British ships under the command of Vice-Admiral H. B. Rawlings. Aboard the British carriers were 244 aircraft, while the American carriers could put up 919 planes, fighters, dive bombers, and torpedo planes. To augment the carrier air forces, the Okinawa invasion plan called for the establishment of a Tactical Air Force on the island itself as soon as possible. This would consist of Marine units as well as U. S. Army Air Force fighter, medium and heavy bomber groups; these forces would be under the command of a Marine, Major General Francis P. Mulcahy.

The invasion of Okinawa, code-named "Opera-

Navy 40-mm. guns firing at kamikaze planes.
(NAVY DEPT., NATIONAL ARCHIVES)

aiding the troops already ashore, where Ushijima's men would wipe them out.

In every aspect the *Kikusui* plan was suicidal; it was not even a gamble. It began with the early morning attack launched from Kanoya and Formosa, both kamikaze and conventional attackers taking part. Although the exact numbers that participated in this first, largest *Kikusui* attack cannot be determined with any accuracy, at least 198 suicide planes attacked the American fleet on April 6 (the attack, continued into the next day, is believed to have consisted of about 355 kamikaze planes alone, with perhaps an equal number of conventional planes participating).

The air filled with unreasoning death as hundreds of kamikazes swept in upon the concentration of American ships. This concentration was capable of ripping the very air to shreds with its antiaircraft guns, numbering literally in the thousands. Despera-

tion Iceberg," was the "most audacious and complex enterprise yet undertaken by the American amphibious forces," according to British observers. And, indeed, it was. It was also the bloodiest battle of the war; the spirit of "Love Day" had not persisted.

The Japanese name for the hellish reaction to the Okinawa invasion was beautiful, *Kikusui* ("floating chrysanthemum," obviously inspired by the banner of a fourteenth-century warrior patriot, Masashige Kusunoki, who led his men to certain death in the Battle of Minatogawa). The first *Kikusui* attack was scheduled to take place on April 6 and 7 and would be a mass, combined Navy and Army suicide plane attack in which the Second Fleet—the "Special Surface Attack Force" spearheaded by the *Yamato*—would participate. It was hoped that the *Yamato* and the nine other ships in the fleet would lure the American carrier planes away from Okinawa while the kamikaze planes, Navy and Army, dealt with the American fleet. Thus off balance, the Americans might not be capable of

A Judy falls to the guns of the Wasp *near Okinawa.*
(NAVY DEPT., NATIONAL ARCHIVES)

tion inspired the men aboard the ships to feats of remarkable endurance and firepower. Din and clatter, shouts and curses, the sound of a thousand rapid-firing guns, the cry of straining engines as a Zeke attempted to break through the myriad of black puffs: all these merged into a jungle of sound.

When word had come of large groups of bogies on the ship's radars, torpedo planes and bombers were struck below decks, their bombs removed and their fuel tanks emptied. Hellcats were quickly readied and the fighters of Task Force 58 were launched to meet the enemy. Combat Air Patrol planes met the first attackers midway between Kyushu and Okinawa and began shooting them out of the sky. But they came on like a swarm of hornets, singly and in large groups of thirty or more. The Japanese planes ranged from the most recent Zeke or Tony to ancient fabric-covered biplanes; few if any experienced pilots guided these planes, for the Task Force 58 airmen were amazed at the easy mark they made. By sheer weight of numbers, however, some of the suicide planes broke through the CAP, only to be met by the guns of the radar picket ships—destroyers which had been set out around the major ship concentration at Okinawa.

Antiaircraft fire stopped 39 of the kamikazes, which splashed and cartwheeled into the Pacific; escort carrier planes accounted for another 55 and the fighters of Task Force 58 destroyed 233 before they could do any damage. But 22 kamikaze planes dashed through the curtain of fire and spread havoc among the ships. As it would develop through the remaining nine major *Kikusui* attacks (from April 6 through June 22), the radar pickets suffered the worst of the attacks. The picket ships were not only bombed, but also took the brunt of the "floating chrysanthemums." On April 6 Radar Stations No. 1 (destroyer *Bush*) and No. 2 (destroyer *Calhoun*) were both sunk under the fury of the mass attacks. By the next day, when the attacks diminished, twenty-two other ships had taken kamikaze hits. Another destroyer, the *Emmons,* was sunk; 466 men were dead and 568 horribly wounded by fire. *Kikusui* No. 1, though heavily sacrificial, had hurt the American fleet. Reports, in fact, from the Thirty-second Army on Okinawa claimed that thirty American ships were seen sinking and an additional twenty or more burning. Because of the smoke-blackened skies, Japanese reconnaissance planes

A twin-engined suicide plane falls short of an escort carrier after being attacked by a Marine Corsair and finished off by a Navy gun crew.

(NAVY DEPT., NATIONAL ARCHIVES)

were unable to check the Army's extravagant report.

But *Kikusui* No. 1 had one more act to go: the drama of the Second Fleet. Before setting out Admiral Ito sent a message to the crews of the ten ships in his force in which he said that the "fate of the homeland rests on this operation. Our ships have been organized as a surface special attack corps. . . . Every unit participating in this operation, whether or not it has been assigned for a special attack, is expected to fight to the bitter end. Thereby the enemy will be annihilated and the eternal foundations of our motherland will be secured."

The *Yamato,* which had fuel enough to get to Okinawa only, was to shell the American positions with its giant 18.1 guns (which outranged any gun in the American or British fleets), while closer in the light cruiser *Yahagi* and the eight destroyers would do the same. The *Yamato* was the last survivor of the once great battleship array of the Japanese fleet (the *Haruna* was then under repair and was in fact the last surviving Japanese battleship; the *Yamato* was the last of the giants). American planes had contended with the big battleship on three other occasions: Midway, the Marianas, and Leyte Gulf, but the mammoth had escaped despite hits.

In the evening of April 6 the American submarines *Hackleback* and *Threadfin* reported the emergence of the Surface Special Attack Force from the Inland Sea through the Bungo Strait. There was literally no air cover, for the few planes which provided it were land-based and were forced to leave as soon as they had reached their maximum range. The one-way navy continued on through the night.

Word having reached Spruance and Mitscher of the approaching Japanese force, Mitscher immediately sent three of his task groups north to intercept. At dawn of April 7 forty Hellcats fanned out to the north and west searching for the *Yamato* and company. An *Essex* plane sighted the ships passing through Van Diemen Strait just south of Kyushu at eight twenty-three in the morning. The force seemed to be heading into the East China Sea away from Okinawa. Ito, however, was hoping to

elude the carrier planes by taking a course beyond their range. If lucky, he could approach Okinawa from the west and open up with his big guns—guns that hurled a projectile of more than a ton over a distance exceeding twenty miles. In the hold there were a thousand of these missiles.

The weather was not ideal: a low cloud ceiling (three thousand feet) with visibility from five to eight miles, hampered by rain squalls. As Ito watched from his bridge on the *Yamato*, the American planes gathered in the distance, first a few, then many. About half past twelve the first attack came. Although antiaircraft fire was intense it was not accurate and the Helldivers and Avengers swooped down upon the Japanese ships. Within ten minutes two bombs had struck the *Yamato* and an additional rent opened up its side as an Avenger placed a torpedo in its path. The *Yahagi* too had been hurt and for the next two hours scores of Avengers, Hellcats, and Helldivers slashed and ripped at the hapless ships. The *Yahagi* was the first to go, its deck a shambles and a slaughterhouse under the blows of a dozen bombs and seven torpedoes. The destroyers too suffered heavily, although they were not the major objectives: but the carrier planes sent four—the *Isokaze, Hamakaze,*

A kamikaze falls short of an escort carrier off Okinawa. (NAVY DEPT., NATIONAL ARCHIVES)

Kasumi, and *Asashimo*—to the bottom before the battle was over.

It was the *Yamato* that was the prize, however. After the first attack the big ship took a list to port but continued on course at a good speed and remained very active with antiaircraft fire. Desperately, Captain Aruga ordered the ship on a zigzag course, hoping to throw off the aim of the attackers. But there were too many of them. *Intrepid* planes swarmed around the ship with bombs and torpedoes, adding further to the battlewagon's distress. Then six *Yorktown* Avengers appeared on the scene. Because of the list to port, the starboard side had lifted from the water, exposing the thinner underplating of the "invincible" *Yamato.* The Avengers circled around to the starboard; torpedoes were set for a depth of from ten to twenty feet—and the Grummans dropped down for the run on the *Yamato.* The upper decks, as with the *Yahagi,* had been reduced to twisted wreckage, and the once formidable gun batteries were either silent or desultory, so that the Avengers made perfect runs; all six fish pierced the exposed underbelly.

A series of explosions shook the gigantic ship as if it were a child's toy in a bathtub. A thousand men below decks were trapped and had no chance to get out. On the bridge a typical argument ensued. Captain Aruga had ordered his executive officer to tie him to the remains of the bridge. He was afraid that if he once got into the water he would instinctively save himself. As the waves washed around him and the deck assumed an acute slant, Aruga spoke to Admiral Ito, commander of the no longer existing Second Fleet.

"You are indispensable," Aruga said. "Please leave the ship."

But Ito chose to remain; there would be no world for him in which Japan was vanquished and in which aircraft had written the final chapter in the history of the proud battleship.

The ship tipped and below decks the big shells rolled across the deck of the ammunition room. More explosions followed and the ship, 863 feet in length, turned over and churned to the bottom of the East China Sea, exploding and detonating as its compartments burst under air pressure and exploding ammunition. At two twenty-three in the afternoon of April 7, 1945, the world's greatest battleship no longer existed. And, for that matter,

neither did the Japanese Imperial Fleet (the last battleship, the *Haruna,* originally announced sunk by Captain Colin Kelly's B-17 attack early in the war, was sunk by carrier planes in its own dock at Kure Harbor on July 28, 1945). The death toll on the *Yamato* alone was 2488; the cost to the Navy attackers was four Helldivers, three Avengers, and three Hellcats (four pilots and eight aircrews were lost). During the battle the carrier *Hancock* was crashed by kamikaze planes twice with a toll of about seventy seamen killed.

Kikusui No. 1 had, like *Sho*-1, succeeded in its predicted Japanese losses, but it had decided nothing. Japan's military future now lay in the systematic, inconclusive pursuit of death.

This pursuit continued for the following several months, literally until the August surrender. In between the *Kikusui* mass raids, small groups or individual attacks also took place, so that from April through August it was impossible for the men in the

The Bunker Hill *shortly after being hit by a kamikaze during the sixth* Kikusui, *May 11, 1945.*

(NAVY DEPT., NATIONAL ARCHIVES)

Flight deck of the Bunker Hill, *with the fire nearly under control but with aircraft destroyed and men* dead and guns not manned.

ships in the Okinawa area to relax. The ten *Kikusui* assaults opened with the climax, during the April 6-7 raid, when six American ships were sunk and seventeen damaged (ten seriously enough to be out of the war for the duration). The other *Kikusui* attacks, with American losses from U. S. Navy sources, were:

2.	April 12-13	2 sunk; 9 damaged
3.	April 15-16	1 sunk; 6 damaged
4.	April 27-28	1 sunk; 4 damaged
5.	May 3-4	6 sunk; 6 damaged
6.	May 10-11	0 sunk; 4 damaged
7.	May 23-25	3 sunk; 6 damaged
8.	May 27-28	1 sunk; 7 damaged
9.	June 3-7	0 sunk; 3 damaged
10.	June 21-22	1 sunk; 4 damaged

These were but the major concerted Japanese Army and Navy attacks. Also there were rare lulls, while the Japanese scrounged more aircraft and impressed more young pilots into the Special Attack Corps. Weather too intervened. Even so, to the men on the American ships it was a rare day,

indeed, when they were not under the horror of the lunatic attacks.

During the second *Kikusui* another innovation fell upon them when Lieutenant Saburo Dohi piloted an *Ohka* bomb into the destroyer *Stanley;* Dohi had climbed into his flying bomb assuming that his target was a battleship. Of the eight *Ohka*-carrying bombers that were dispatched on April 12, only one—the one that had transported Dohi to the target area—returned. The others were destroyed before doing any damage. Dohi's *Ohka* did strike, but the *Stanley* was not seriously damaged. On the same day the destroyer *Mannert L. Abele* was crashed by a Zeke kamikaze; after being hit by what may have been an *Ohka,* the ship seemed to dissolve and sank within five minutes, with a loss of seventy-nine of the crew.

The special attacks did not, as the Japanese High Command so fervently believed, alter the course of the war. This must have been obvious even before all the chrysanthemums had fallen, but the mania grew more and more incurable as the situation grew worse. However, if the purpose of going out to battle is to kill, maim, and destroy (once accepting your own destruction as part of the price), then the kamikazes were a great success. The fiery charnel house each plane created when it struck was all but unspeakable.

"The deck near my [gun] mount was covered with blood, guts, brains, tongues, scalps, hearts, arms etc. from the Jap pilots," wrote Seaman First Class James J. Fahey in his *Pacific War Diary* aboard the *Montpelier* (in the Leyte Gulf area). "They had to put the hose on to wash the blood off the deck. The deck ran red with blood. The Japs were spattered all over the place. One of the fellows had a Jap scalp, it looked like you skinned an animal. The hair was black, but very short and the color of the skin was yellow, real Japanese. I do not think he was very old. I picked up a tin pie plate with a tongue on it. The pilots tooth mark was into it very deep. It was very big and long, it looked like part of his tonsils were attached to it. . . . This was the first time I ever saw a person's brains, what a mess. . . ."

Throughout the *Kikusui* attacks, the radar picket ships, stationed around Okinawa in all directions ranging in distances from eighteen to ninety-five miles out, bore the brunt of the devastation. If these ships were eliminated, the Japanese believed, it would be possible to get through to the more important larger ships closer to Okinawa. The pickets then became the most frequently struck victims. One enterprising seaman, after days of attack, put a sign out on his ship: THAT WAY TO THE CARRIERS.

But the only sure method of disrupting a suicide attacker who had slipped past the combat air patrol was to shoot him out of the air before he came in close enough to read the sardonic message. When a heavy raid developed there were simply too many targets to shoot at. During the fifth *Kikusui* (on May 3) the destroyer *Aaron Ward* rang with General Quarters at six twenty-two in the evening. In seven minutes a tiny speck materialized out of the sunset. Another minute, during which there had been a general intake of breath aboard the ship, and the speck became a Val. The guns of the *Aaron Ward* boomed and roared when the Japanese plane was still seven thousand yards dis-

tant. It would have been impossible, what with the massive cone of fire vectored on the lone plane, to have missed. The Val smoked but continued on its path toward the ship. It had already assumed the kamikaze approach dive before, at five hundred yards, a five-inch projectile from the *Aaron Ward*'s No. 53 Mount made a direct hit. The Val blew up, still coming on, and splashed into the water about a hundred yards from the ship. As the gunners watched spellbound, the Japanese pilot was hurled by the impact of the crash over the ship's deck and into the water on the other side. Parts of the wrecked Val smashed into the ship; the engine rammed into No. 53 Mount, putting it out of action for a while. Even when the engine was removed the mount would operate only on difficult manual control.

The Val's propeller whirled across the water and cut its way into the after deckhouse, where it jammed the door of the after passageway. The clean-up crew there found the pilot's boot near the deckhouse; his foot was still in it.

There was no time for speculation, for another Val appeared bearing down from the port bow, but that one splashed twelve hundred yards out, with no damage to the ship. Suddenly a Zeke came in from the port, undetected by radar but spotted by the gun captain of No. 42 Mount. Nothing seemed capable of stopping the Zeke, which magnified in size with alarming speed. When it was within a hundred yards the Zeke had begun to smoke and its bomb fell from underneath the belly—but struck the port side of the ship under No. 44 Gun. The Zeke continued on to wrap its flaming wreckage around the ship's superstructure.

The bomb struck the *Aaron Ward* below the water line, ripping open fifty feet of the hull upon exploding in the after engine room. The rudder jammed and the ship began circling to port as fuel from ruptured lines fed the flames topside. The deck was a shambles and a caldron. All men but two around No. 44 Gun were dead, burned to cinders, blown overboard, or just simply "missing," never to appear again. The wounded, burned and with broken limbs, writhed out of the way of the fire fighters. The horror of the kamikaze attack lay as much in its sensless persistence as in the gruesome details of the aftermath.

Was it the perverse human instinct for harassing

cripples? Despite the obvious fact that the *Aaron Ward* was listing, burning, and running in circles, this did not divert other kamikazes from hitting the ship again and again. The nearby *Little* was stricken too, so badly that it eventually sank (as did two other destroyers, the *Luce* and *Morrison*).

For an hour or more the Japanese aircraft sprinted in on Radar Picket 10—some splashed and others contributed to the misery aboard the mangled destroyers. The still operating gun mounts on the *Aaron Ward* spat out fire and succeeded in knocking down ten kamikazes before they reached the ship. Marine Corsairs from Okinawa strips some seventy miles away bore in to stop the ravaging planes. Even as they swept in to destroy the Zekes, Vals, and Bettys, the Corsairs suffered the hazards of "friendly fire," for the gunners on the beleaguered ships, overwrought, weary, and in pain, hated all things that flew; and there was no time to discriminate between friend and foe.

The fifth aircraft splashed in that flaming twilight was a twin-engined Betty, which burst into flame and went spinning into the water. The geyser of the impact had barely settled before two more Vals appeared; these had Marine Corsairs on their tails and in the near-surface battle one of the Vals erupted burning fragments and crashed into the water. But the other Val came on in a precipitous dive. All guns trained on the lone attacker, who appeared to ride in on the tracers. It capered through the serried air, its nose growing ever larger, its wings widening, reeling and yawing from hits— but coming on nonetheless. Suddenly it jinked, the nose snapped up, a wing dropped, and the Val cleared the bridge, its high wing ripping through the lines of the signal halyards, wrenched out most of the signal antennas, crunched the top of the forward stack, and, in a shower of debris, cartwheeled across the starboard rail into the sea.

The din that followed in the Val's wake was something out of a nightmare. The Val's slashing plunge across the deck had opened up steam lines to the ship's whistle and siren, which now hooted and shrieked in a crescendo of pandemonium. One sailor, a survivor of the sunken *Little* (not understanding the plight of the *Aaron Ward* nor noting the fires aboard), pondered in his own misery the sanity of a ship that, in mid-battle, would do nothing but go around in circles whistling and hooting.

This ludicrous situation was not appreciated by the men of the *Aaron Ward;* there were the wounded to care for, men whose burned flesh dripped from them as they moved, and the dead to identify, if possible. There were raging fires below decks and the word came round that the ship's sinking was imminent. No word to abandon ship came, however.

But another Val came in, the pilot strafing a path before him toward the bridge itself. No. 42 Gun's crew stood its ground in the face of the onslaught until a stream of fire chopped off a wing. But momentum carried the plane forward as the bomb fell short of the ship; the plane struck in a fiery mass onto the main deck and the bomb burst in the water adjacent to the ship. A hammer blow shook the *Aaron Ward,* a hole ripped into the forward fireroom, and the flood which followed drowned the last operating engine.

The *Aaron Ward* lay smoldering dead in the water as out of nowhere an unseen kamikaze added its bomb, fuel, and flame to the agony. Seconds later another unseen attacker smashed into the main deck. To the men aboard the *Aaron Ward* their world, confined to the single ship, had become a fiery bedlam and charnel house; flames lit up the sky, thick smoke choked them, and the decks grew slick with blood. It seemed that they had taken all anyone could be expected to endure.

But that was not to be—a Zeke slashed in and slammed into No. 43 Gun, the crew of which vanished in a ball of flame. Others in the area of impact were seared by the fire, others disappeared in the explosion over the side. There was barely time to attend to the dead and dying before the tenth attacker appeared.

"Here comes another one!" someone shouted.

"God, we can't take another one," the ship's executive officer, Karl Neuport, muttered.

Low on the water, difficult to see in the smoke and darkness, the Japanese plane came at them first from the starboard and then from aft. The remaining guns chopped away at the plane, which whipped down on the *Aaron Ward* and shattered against the base of the after stack. The bomb detonated as the stack, fragments of the plane, a searchlight tower, and guns lifted into the heavens and showered death and dreadful pain onto the decks.

Horror had accumulated upon horror, but it was

The Aaron Ward *after enduring a series of kamikaze attacks.* (NAVY DEPT., NATIONAL ARCHIVES)

the final attack of the day. "The once trim *Aaron Ward* resembled a floating junk pile from the bridge aft," wrote Lieutenant Commander Arnold Lott. "Stacks, guns, searchlight tower, boats, everything was smashed and battered beyond recognition. Fires raged on deck, in the officer's and chief's quarters, in both clipping rooms, and in the after engine room. The main deck was only inches above water, both firerooms flooded, after engine room flooded, after diesel engine room, machine shop, shaft alleys, crew's bunkrooms, all flooded. Dead and wounded littered the wardroom, mess hall, sick bay, fantail and passageways." But the *Aaron Ward* remained afloat.

As rescue ships pulled alongside, it was a relief to realize that the ordeal was over; but for the afflicted it was not over. Forty-five men were ultimately listed as dead (some were never found); forty-nine were wounded, some fatally, many horribly. None of the survivors would ever forget the testing of the *Aaron Ward* during *Kikusui* No. 5.

Not all Japanese operations during the *Kikusui* mass attacks were suicidal. Conventional bombing missions were attempted (generally with poor results, as the bombers were stopped by carrier air-

craft or the Marine and Army fighters based on Okinawa). A steady combat air patrol was maintained over Okinawa at all times. During one of these during the morning of May 10, 1945 (which opened *Kikusui* No. 6), a four-plane (Corsair) division of Marines took off from their base at Kadena, Okinawa. Led by Captain Kenneth L. Reusser, the four planes were flown by members of VMF-312; Reusser's wingman was a Navy and Marine veteran, twenty-eight-year-old Lieutenant Robert L. Klingman of Binger, Oklahoma.

The Corsairs had climbed to about ten thousand feet to patrol over Ie Jima, just west of northern Okinawa, when at an altitude fifteen thousand feet above them they detected the contrails of a twin-engined Japanese plane. Throttling up their engines the four Corsairs set off in pursuit of the lone intruder. As they climbed, so did the Nick (Kawasaki Ki. 45), apparently out on a photographic mission. At thirty-two thousand feet one of the Corsairs had gone as high as it could go—the engine simply refused to lift it higher. Four thousand feet higher and another Corsair left the chase for the same reason. Reusser and Klingman persisted, firing some of their ammunition to lighten the load. Fi-

Robert R. Klingman and the Corsair with which he chopped off the tail of a Japanese reconnaissance plane. (WILLIAM BEALL/U. S. MARINE CORPS)

ler started hacking away at the tail assembly, biting pieces out of the rudder and nearly into the rear cockpit, in which the Japanese gunner furiously pounded away at his own frozen guns. The Nick flew on—and so did Klingman's Corsair. He brought it around again and this time sheared away the rudder completely and chewed away a piece of the right stabilizer. Still flying, Klingman jammed rudder, turned, and came in for the third time. His buzz saw propeller went to work again on the Nick. The stabilizer fluttered away into the slipstream and the Nick bucked into a spin. By the time it had fallen to fifteen thousand feet the wings had snapped from the fuselage, and the Nick plunged into the water below.

But Klingman had overstayed his patrol. Before he could return to Kadena—with Reusser providing ammunition-less protection—his fuel supply ran out. Even so, he succeeded in bringing the Corsair into VMF-312's strip on Okinawa with a dead stick. Klingman jumped from the plane to inspect the damage and found that a generous portion of propeller tip was missing; wing, engine, and fuselage

nally, at thirty-eight thousand feet, they reached the Nick's level. The Marine Corsairs closed in. Reusser opened up first and with his remaining ammunition shot up the Nick's left wing and engine. But the Nick continued on its way, with the rear gunner menacing the Corsairs but not firing.

Klingman soon learned why as he moved in to take up where Reusser had been forced to leave off. Hoping to make certain his .50-calibers could finish off the Nick he throttled to within fifty feet of the Japanese plane. But when he pressed the gun switch he found that at the high altitude his guns had frozen. Incensed, Klingman moved ever closer upon the Nick, determined to get the plane one way or the other. The Corsair was equipped with a massive thirteen-foot propeller and a rugged, powerful Pratt and Whitney eighteen-cylinder engine; since his guns had gone dead, Klingman was determined to employ some of his plane's other assets.

He charged the fleeing Nick and with his propel-

The Enterprise *loses its No. 1 elevator, blown hundreds of feet into the air after a suicide Zeke crashed into the carrier.* (NAVY DEPT., NATIONAL ARCHIVES)

Carrier-based Corsairs leaving the Essex *for a strike upon Formosa. While the fighting continued on Oki-nawa, carrier strikes upon Formosa as well as the* Japanese homeland were made to throw Japanese fight-ers off balance. (NAVY DEPT., NATIONAL ARCHIVES)

were pocked and pieces of the Nick were found lodged in the Corsair's capacious cowling.

Klingman's adventure occurred during *Kikusui* No. 6; in the lull which followed sporadic kamikazes harried the invaders. During the early morning CAP on May 14, the *Enterprise,* 150 miles off the island of Kyushu, was alerted to individual or small attacks. One lone, determined Zeke broke through the Hellcats and the heavy 20-mm., 40-mm., and five-inch fire. As the Zeke came in close it appeared that he might overshoot, but at the last moment the pilot—whose name was Tomi Zai—flipped the Zeke onto its back and plunged inverted through the forward elevator. The flame shot out of the deck and the bomb continued through five decks before detonating. The explosion shot flames hundreds of feet into the air and No. 1 elevator ripped skyward four hundred feet above the flight deck of the *Enterprise.*

Tomi Zai had accomplished one of the few effective kamikaze attacks of the war. His crash had killed thirteen men and injured sixty-eight, but he also eliminated the *Enterprise* from battle for the rest of the war. There was, however, the other, eternal but: it did not alter the outcome.

After *Kikusui* No. 10, in late June, the kamikaze attacks waned except for rare, small flutters up to the moment of peace. Okinawa, eighty-two days after "Love Day," was declared secure by Marine Major General Roy S. Geiger, an airman who had led the fighting on Guadalcanal.

Except for skirmishes in isolated areas, or flushing still resisting remnants of the Japanese Thirty-second Army out of the hills and caves (often with napalm bombs lobbed into cave entrances), the fighting on Okinawa was ended. The technique of these mopping-up operations had been developed over more than eighty days of hard fighting. Close-support operations between ground and air men, called by Army Major General James L. Bradley (commander of the 96th Infantry Division) as "superior throughout," brought a scourge of napalm and rockets to the dug-in Japanese. Likewise, strafing runs upon Japanese positions directed by radio from the ground cleared the way for the advance of American ground troops. Especially effective in such operations was the Corsair, which earned the name from Marines of "Sweetheart of Okinawa." The Japanese name was not so affectionate. Because of

the aircraft's characteristic sound, the result of the rush of air through the vents on its bent wings, it was feared by the Japanese and called "Whistling Death."

It had been one of the bloodiest campaigns in the history of American arms; for the U. S. Navy it was the costliest battle of the war. Most of the Japanese fought to the death, many dying in the final days of the battle in senseless banzai charges upon Marine and Army positions with no other ammunition but dirt to throw into the faces of the Americans. Great numbers committed suicide in a frenzy of slaughter by throat gashing, holding hand grenades to heads, or leaping from cliffs.

The island's top commanders, Ushijima and Cho, went out in proper style. On the morning of June 22, ceremoniously dressed, the two men were disemboweled in a cave within a hundred feet of advancing Marines. Their deaths added but 2 to the 110,000 Japanese who died on Okinawa (about 10,000 were actually rounded up alive and taken prisoner). American losses too were high: about 12,000 killed; of these about 4000 were Navy men. At least 80 per cent of these deaths (there was an equal number of wounded) could be attributed to the kamikazes. The toll was high, but not determinative. Okinawa only meant that the fight for Japan in the home islands would have to be horrific.

But those who knew realized that the kamikazes failed in their defined mission; they succeeded only in killing, maiming, and destroying equipment. The Japanese people were not aware of this failure, although the general issue of sharpened bamboo stakes with which to meet the expected invader should have inspired at least a glimmer of misgiving. That and the effects of LeMay's B-29 fire raids on city after city.

Following the *Kikusui* No. 3 raid (April 16), Radio Tokyo informed the Japanese people that:

393 American warships have been sunk or damaged by the divine wind attackers since March 23. This includes 21 carriers, 19 battleships, 16 battleships or large cruisers, 26 large-type warships, 55 cruisers, and 53 destroyers. 217 ships, including 85 of cruiser size or larger, have definitely been sunk. 60 per cent of the Allied fleet in the Okinawa area have either been sunk or damaged.

Marines on Okinawa. As the fighting drew closer to Japan itself, it became more vicious than ever and required killing without mercy. This team—flame thrower and B.A.R. rifleman—stalks through the mist to clear caves of fanatical Japanese.

(DEFENSE DEPT., MARINE CORPS)

The truth was that at that time, 14, not 217, ships had been sunk. Throughout the entire Okinawa campaign a total of 17 American ships (including one baby flattop) were actually sunk; observers of the kamikaze flights (those that returned) claimed 44. Claims were put forth for 99 ships damaged; actually 198 American ships were damaged. (It might be noted that no British carrier was seriously damaged during the Okinawa campaign, because of the armored flight decks.) To sink those 17 and damage the 198 ships kamikazes were dispatched 1809 times; of these 879 returned and 930 planes were expended. Nearly an equal number of Army suicide planes were sortied, besides conventional aircraft. During the Okinawa fighting nearly 8000 Japanese aircraft—and pilots—were lost of all types. But Okinawa had fallen and the enemy was camped within 350 miles of Japan—the tactics of desperation had not worked. (All kamikaze operations beginning with Leyte Gulf and ending at Okinawa had actually sunk 34 American ships, although official claims were made for 81; 288 had been damaged, claims were made for 195. These "triumphs" had been gained at the cost of 1228 aircraft, a fraction of which carried two men.)

It was during the Okinawa *Kikusui* missions that

"Whistling Death" on Okinawa. A rocket-equipped Corsair provides close support for Marines clearing the hills of dug-in Japanese.

(DAVID DUNCAN/MARINE CORPS)

Marine airfield on Okinawa under a Japanese night attack; heavy American antiaircraft fire laces the sky.

(DEFENSE DEPT., MARINE CORPS)

The remains of what had once been a Japanese air-field on Okinawa. Bulldozed away, they made room for U. S. Marine and Navy aircraft.
(DEFENSE DEPT., U. S. MARINE CORPS)

American airmen of the Twentieth Air Force in-cinerated Japanese in the homeland in vaster num-bers than the falling chrysanthemums could ever achieve. For a time, from mid-April to May 11, LeMay's fire-spreading B-29s were diverted for the most part from their primary mission to attacks upon airfields on Kyushu and Shikoku. The objective of these diversions was to cripple the kamikaze effort

Signal to close bomb bay doors. A B-29 being readied for a mission to Japan on Guam. (U. S. AIR FORCE)

an obvious disenchantment with the kamikaze emerged. Rear Admiral Toshiyuki Yokoi, chief of staff of Fifth Air Fleet during the Okinawa cam-paign, noted that ". . . toward the last, the doomed pilots had good reason for doubting the validity of the cause in which they were told to die. The diffi-culties became especially apparent when men in aviation training were peremptorily ordered to the front and to death.

"When it came time for their takeoff, the pilots' attitude ranged from the despair of sheep headed for slaughter to open expressions of contempt for their superior officers. There were frequent and ob-vious cases of pilots returning from sorties claiming that they could not locate any enemy ships, and one pilot even strafed his commanding officer's quarters when he took off."

And to what purpose were they ordered to take off? Like Nicolai Rostov in *War and Peace,* the youthful Japanese pilots, sacrifices to the blindness and vanity of their elders, asked, "For what, then, those severed arms and legs, why those dead men?" When no reasonable answer was forthcoming, the shrieking horror of the divine wind became a whis-per.

VI

Even as the young Japanese kamikaze pilots in-cinerated young American seamen around Okinawa,

Long lines of Superforts rumble on the runway to take off in massed attacks upon Japan. (U. S. AIR FORCE)

B-29s of the 73rd Bomb Wing skirt Fujiyama over Japan. (U. S. AIR FORCE)

of Ukaki's units, besides destroying air installations and drawing off some of the aerial opposition from Okinawa.

Another diversion was the mining of Japanese waters, particularly in the Shimonoseki Strait between Kyushu and Honshu. Japanese shipping soon came to a practical standstill; in fact, the work of American submarines had nearly put it there even before the final blow was struck by Brigadier General John H. Davies' 313th Wing. It was because of this mining that the *Yamato* was forced to leave the Inland Sea via the Bungo Strait into the sights of U. S. Navy submarines and the bombs of carrier aircraft.

When he was released from the support of the Okinawa campaign, LeMay turned again to the desolation by fire of Japan's major industrial cities. Within a month—just before *Kikusui* No. 10—the campaign against the major cities—Tokyo, Nagoya, Kobe, Osaka, Yokohama, and Kawasaki—was over. One by one the cities were scratched off the target list. Not only had the industries of these cities been

destroyed, so had their people and vast areas of the cities. A third of Yokohama was burned in a single raid. On May 25 the second and last—and worst —fire raid was made upon Tokyo itself. Over five hundred B-29s appeared over the city at night and dropped their incendiaries, which burned sixteen

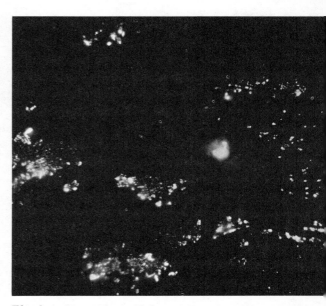

The last fire raid on Tokyo, May 26, 1945: the first fires begin to flicker (above) and then spread widely over the city in the most destructive raid of all.

(U. S. AIR FORCE)

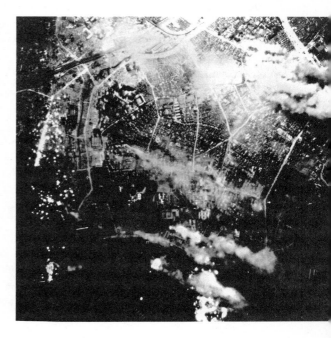

square miles out of the heart of the city. Antiaircraft fire that night was intense and twenty-six Superfortresses fell and a hundred returned to the Marianas with damages of varied seriousness. But when they had returned one half of Tokyo no longer existed. Even portions of the Emperor's sacred palace burned that night when the fires ran wild. The Emperor took this as a sign to his people that even he was not immune to attack and had no special dispensation from the gods.

The Emperor wrongly assumed that the palace had been deliberately bombed. But that was not the intent, for orders had long been in force to spare the Emperor. As Arnold had written to LeMay, "the Emperor of Japan is not at present a liability and may later become an asset." The fire in the palace raged for fourteen hours before it was brought under control. Twenty-eight members of the palace staff died in the fire, including twelve firemen who, because they had no orders to do otherwise, remained at their post in the path of the flames and burned.

The incendiary missions were supplemented by precision attacks, which included bombings of oil targets. These became the specialty of the 315th Wing, commanded by Brigadier General Frank A. Armstrong, a veteran of early Eighth Air Force strategic bombing over Europe.

LeMay turned his incendiary attacks upon the smaller cities after the middle of June. Between June 17 and August 14 some fifty of these secondary industrial-population centers were bombed with frequently devastating results. Several missions occurred simultaneously, which confused Japanese fighter defenses, but most of the secondary cities were practically defenseless, without antiaircraft guns or fighter protection.

At this time LeMay took yet another chance: he began dropping warning leaflets upon target cities in advance of B-29 raids. On the face of the leaflet the statement was simple and direct: "CIVILIANS! EVACUATE AT ONCE!" it warned. On the reverse face it read:

These leaflets are being dropped to notify you that your city has been listed for destruction by our powerful air force. The bombing will occur within 72 hours. This advance notice will give your military authorities ample time to take necessary defensive measures to protect you from our inevitable attack. Watch and see how powerless they are to protect you.

We give the military clique this notification of our plans because we know there is nothing they can do to stop our overwhelming power and our iron determination. We want you to see how powerless the military is to protect you. Systematic destruction of city after city will continue as long as you blindly follow your military leaders, whose blunders have placed you on the very brink of oblivion. It is your responsibility to overthrow the military government now and save what is left of your beautiful country.

"There wasn't any mass exodus until we knocked hell out of the first three towns," LeMay later learned. The Japanese took the warning as typical wartime propaganda; their only precaution was to fill the warned cities with fire engines, instead of massive concentrations of antiaircraft guns, as LeMay feared. As for the fire engines, which were lined up about a hundred feet apart along the streets, they "burned up with everything else."

The first three cities, Tsu, Aomori, and Ichinomiya (actually a total of six were struck on July 28), were, respectively, 57 per cent, 64 per cent, and 75 per cent destroyed. On August 1 the city of Toyama (population: 127,860) was all but totally eliminated out of existence; 99.5 per cent of it was nothing but a dark patch of earth.

The problem confronting the Emperor by this time was not how to win the war, not even how to lose it as gracefully as possible, but how to get out of it. Standing between him and this solution were his military leaders, chiefly his Minister of War, General Korechika Anami, and Army Chief of Staff General Yoshijiro Umezu; the Imperial Navy's chief advocates of a fight to the finish were Admiral Toyoda and Ohnishi. Nor was the newly appointed Premier, Admiral Kantaro Suzuki (the cabinet of Kuniaki Kioso had fallen a week after the invasion of Okinawa), of much help, although he was selected to find a means of an honorable peace. Old, nearly deaf, Suzuki rose up in a meeting of the Japanese Diet and cried out for a desperate last-ditch fight. If he were to die in the service of his Emperor, Suzuki said that he expected "the hundred million people of this glorious Empire to swell forward over my prostrate body and form themselves into a shield to protect the Emperor and this Imperial land from the invader!"

Soon there was an announcement of the formation

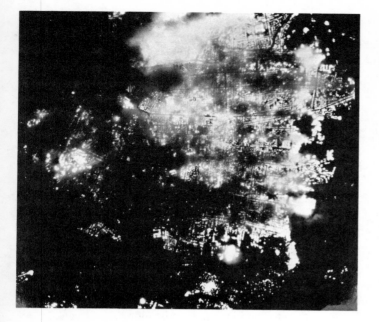

A fire bombing in full fury: Toyama, August 1, 1945. More than 95 per cent of the city was destroyed.
(U. S. AIR FORCE)

of a Japanese Peoples Vounteer Corps, whose "volunteers" were liable to defense duties, most undoubtedly with the sharpened bamboo poles. All men between the ages of fifteen and sixty and all women from seventeen to forty were expected to meet the invaders at the beaches. By July 21 Fifth Air Force Intelligence issued the statement: "There are no civilians in Japan. We are making War and making it in the all-out fashion which saves American lives, shortens the agony which War is and seeks to bring about an enduring Peace. We intend to seek out and destroy the enemy wherever he or she is, in the greatest possible numbers, in the shortest possible time."

At the same time plans were being drawn up for Operation Olympic, the invasion of southern Kyushu on November 1, 1945, to be followed by Coronet, the invasion of the main island, Honshu, on March 1, 1946. Predicted and expected losses ranged from 250,000 casualties to a million on each side.

There was every reason for Japan to surrender by July; in May Germany, Japan's only ally, was finished. The Soviet Union in April renounced its neutrality pact with Japan—and there had been

Leyte Gulf, Iwo Jima, and Okinawa. In June, with the Emperor's urging, attempts were made through the Russians to bring the war to a close. But the Russians were not very helpful; they were, in fact, often devious, apparently waiting for the moment to pounce. Stalin had promised that three months after Germany surrendered Russia would declare war upon Japan.

On July 26 the Allies, with Churchill, President Harry Truman, and Chiang Kai-shek as signatories, issued the Potsdam Declaration demanding the unconditional surrender of Japan. The alternative, the document warned, for Japan was "prompt and utter destruction." The offer was rejected in Tokyo, although the Emperor and the peace group, which now included the wavering Premier Suzuki, favored immediate acceptance. The war party—Anami, Umezu, and Toyoda—found the Declaration a threat to the entire Japanese way of life and to the Emperor—not to mention the fate of "war criminals." In the light of this argument, Suzuki decided it was best to postpone an immediate formal reply, although his statement to the press was interpreted by the Allies as an outright rejection.

In fact, the terms of the Potsdam Declaration were not regarded as particularly odious to many

Aftermath: the aspect of a burned-out city after a fire bombing. One propeller plant as well as 66 per cent of Shizuoka went up in smoke. (U. S. AIR FORCE)

The massive aerial concentration on Saipan creates a traffic problem. James B. Lazar acts as traffic director while Thunderbolts take off. Truck belongs to 805th Aviation Engineer Battalion. (U. S. AIR FORCE)

A conventional daylight B-29 mission, rather than a night fire bombing, struck at Tokuyama naval station by no less than 400 B-29s. (U. S. AIR FORCE)

of the Japanese cabinet. It was even considered as less severe than they expected: there was no direct threat to the Emperor, nor to the Japanese way of life. But as released to the press by the military leaders, the Potsdam Declaration was edited so that the people would not see the more attractive sections. Suzuki's blunder and the obtuse stupidity of the military faction sealed the fate of two Japanese cities, Hiroshima and Nagasaki.

VII

Of the 1767 men who made up the oddly structured 509th Composite Group, only one, its commander, Colonel Paul W. Tibbets, Jr., was aware of what the mission of the group was to be. Consisting of a single combat squadron, the 393rd Bom-

While the special B-29 squadron trained, the other Marianas-based B-29s continued bombing Japan with Mustang escort. The escorts frequently, as in the last days of the war in Germany, then went down on the deck to strafe. (U. S. AIR FORCE)

bardment Squadron (VH), the 509th was a self-sufficient unit with its own engineering and ordnance section, its own transports, and even its own Military Police Company. Fifteen modified B-29s were set aside for the 509th and its men; aircrews as well as ground crews were given special training for a very special mission. One of the maneuvers learned by the pilots was a steep diving turn of 158 degrees that enabled the plane to travel a distance of eight miles (presumably from the point it released its bomb) in forty-three seconds. For some strange reason formation flying, previously so critical in all bomber training, was not part of the program. High-altitude bombing and long over-water flights, on the other hand, were extremely important.

After several months of intensive training the 509th Composite Group began moving into North Field, Tinian, at the end of May 1945. By early July the complete group had settled into North Field as part of, yet separate from, the 313th Bombardment Wing. On July 20 the 393rd Squadron began flying its first combat missions, as part of preparation for its ultimate mission.

Still no one on the base knew what that mission was except Tibbets and a few scientists. The stand-offish demeanor of the men of the 509th, their seeming preferential treatment, their odd missions (small formations of three aircraft which, although the other men on Tinian did not know, dropped a single oddly shaped bomb which was called a "pumpkin"); and their planes were strange too: the bomb bay was different and there were no guns in the turrets excepting the twin .50s in the tails.

While the other units in the Marianas were burning up Japanese cities, destroying its aircraft industries, or mining the harbors, it appeared that the 509th was, in the folk idiom of the time, "goofing off." Men in the other units began composing satirical verses about the mysterious 509th:

> *Into the air the secret rose,*
> *Where they're going nobody knows;*
> *But we'll never know where they've been.*
> *Don't ask about results or such*
> *Unless you want to get in Dutch;*
> *But take it from one who is sure of the score,*
> *The 509th is winning the war.*

A second stanza repeated the taunting "The 509th is winning the war." It was true, of course, for the

"Little Boy," the bomb carried to Hiroshima in the single B-29 Enola Gay *on August 6, 1945.*
(U. S. AIR FORCE)

509th had been selected to drop a new bomb based upon the principal of atomic fission (and originally suggested to President Roosevelt by Dr. Albert Einstein in August 1939). Under the direction of Dr. J. R. Oppenheimer, such a bomb was actually perfected beginning in the spring of 1943, and the first so-called "atomic bomb" was detonated on July 16, 1945, during the Potsdam Conference. On the day of the Potsdam Declaration, July 26, the cruiser *Indianapolis* delivered materials, including uranium-235, for use in the atomic bomb. If the Japanese accepted the terms of the Potsdam Declaration the bomb would not be used (meanwhile a second and third were on the way, more powerful and efficient than the first). Ultimate decision lay with President Truman.

When it appeared that Suzuki had rejected the surrender ultimatum, using the word *mokusatsu* in his press release (the word implied that he would treat the ultimatum with "silent contempt," when he actually meant a simple "no comment"), Truman ordered the bomb to be used. He was at the time aboard ship in mid-Atlantic on the return trip from Potsdam.

The first bomb, called "Little Boy," was 120 inches in length and 28 inches in diameter and weighed nine thousand pounds. Its explosive yield was equal to about twenty thousand tons of conventional high explosives. Its assembly, in a well-guarded North Field bomb hut, where temperature and humidity were carefully controlled, was completed the first of August. On that same date General Carl A. Spaatz assumed command of the United States Army Strategic Air Forces, Pacific, on Guam. LeMay became his chief of staff, while Lieutenant General Nathan F. Twining took over the Twentieth Air Force; the Eighth Air Force, under Lieutenant General James H. Doolittle, had begun moving into the Pacific by the middle of July; it would be based on Okinawa. In effect, these preparations were directed toward the mounting Olympic, the invasion of Japan.

Spaatz, like LeMay, believed that Japan could be beaten into surrender without an invasion. This became a critical point in the light of the fighting on Iwo Jima and Okinawa. Once the President gave the word, Spaatz could use the atomic bombs; the word came that the bomb could be dropped after August 3 on the first possible day when weather made visual bombing feasible.

That day came on August 6, 1945. The city of Hiroshima was selected as the primary target. Other cities mentioned in the orders to Spaatz were Kokura, Niigata, and Nagasaki. Weather aircraft which had preceded the striking force (one bomb-laden plane plus two observation aircraft) radioed near-perfect weather over Hiroshima. Had it not been

favorable, Hiroshima might have been spared and one of the other cities bombed.

Hiroshima, from which, ironically, Yamamoto had directed the Hawaii Operation, was the home of the Second Army as well as several war industries, it was an important transport base, site of a shipbuilding yard, electrical works, and a railroad yard. Hiroshima had suffered very little bomb damage because it had been reserved as a target for the 509th Group. The populace had grown lax in their precautions. Even so, it is unlikely that, in view of the type of bombardment they suffered, it would have made any difference had the Hiroshimans sought shelter.

They had grown accustomed to seeing small formations of B-29s passing over harmlessly on reconnaissance flights. The three aircraft which passed over Hiroshima on that fateful day were the *Enola Gay,* carrying the single "Little Boy" and piloted by Colonel Tibbets; *Great Artiste* (pilot: Major Charles W. Sweeney); and aircraft number 44-27291, flown by Captain George W. Marquardt. The latter two planes carried scientific and military observers, cameras, and various measuring instruments.

At 8:15 A.M. (Hiroshima time) from an altitude of 31,600 feet, in perfect weather, the *Enola Gay* released the "Little Boy." Curious Japanese on their

The *Enola Gay, named for the mother of pilot Colonel Paul Tibbets, Jr., first aircraft to transport an atomic* weapon, to deliver the *"flame that burns to the bone." With this delivery war from the air took on a new, deadlier, meaning.* (U. S. AIR FORCE)

The Atomic Age is born with a blast of power and massive birth pains—and eighty thousand dead.
(U. S. AIR FORCE)

way to work or in their gardens watched the descent of the lone object as it fell into a heavily built-up residential, commercial, military, and industrial area just south of Second Army headquarters.

"Suddenly," an eyewitness Japanese newspaperman later told Marcel Junod of the International Red Cross, "a glaring whitish pinkish light appeared in the sky accompanied by an unnatural tremor which was followed almost immediately by a wave of suffocating heat and wind which swept everything in its path.

"Within a few seconds the thousands of people in the streets and the gardens in the center of the town were scorched by a wave of searing heat. Many were killed instantly, others lay writhing on the ground screaming in agony from the intolerable pain of their burns. Everything standing upright in the way of the blast—walls, houses, factories and other buildings—was annihilated and the debris spun round in a whirlwind and was carried up into the air. Trams were picked up and tossed aside as though they had neither weight nor solidity. Trains were flung off the rails as though they were toys. Horses, dogs and cattle suffered the same fate as

human beings. Every living thing was petrified in an attitude of indescribable suffering. Even the vegetation did not escape. Trees went up in flames, the rice plants lost their greenness, the grass burned on the ground like dry straw."

A violent fire was swept by powerful, unnatural winds. "By evening the fire began to die down and then went out. There was nothing left to burn. Hiroshima had ceased to exist."

As soon as bombardier Major Thomas W. Ferebee had toggled "Little Boy," Tibbets gripped the control column, turned the *Enola Gay* sharply around, and pushed the nose down to gain speed. In fifty seconds, when the plane and the two observation B-29s were about fifteen miles from Hiroshima, a great flash illuminated the interiors of the planes and powerful shocks convulsed the Superfortresses. After gazing with wonder and horror upon the disaster they had brought to Hiroshima, the men in the three planes returned to Tinian, twelve hours and thirteen minutes after they had taken off.

The war of the twenty-first century had arrived at Hiroshima. Eighty per cent of its buildings were totally destroyed. According to official figures 71,379 people were dead or missing, with an equal number injured. The death toll figure may be too

Hiroshima, 1945. A drainpipe on the Chugoku Power Company tells its own story of the profane wind.
(U. S. AIR FORCE)

the war according to the terms of the Potsdam Declaration.

Consequently, while conventional bombing missions continued, another bomb, this one using plutonium, was assembled at Tinian. Sixty inches in diameter and 128 inches long, the bulbous bomb was called "Fat Man." Three days after the destruction of Hiroshima, "Fat Man" was cranked into the bomb bay of the B-29 named *Bockscar* and with Major Sweeney as pilot set out for Kokura. (Sweeney's own plane, *Great Artiste* was flown by Captain Frederick C. Bock, with whom he had switched planes.) Bock accompanied the mission, along with another aircraft, Major James I. Hopkins, pilot, as observers.

Unlike the Hiroshima mission, the second atomic bombing mission did not proceed smoothly. Weather closed in and Sweeney lost contact in the heavy clouds with Hopkins' plane. Three bomb runs were made upon Kokura without any sighting of the target. This consumed fuel and appeared to be getting nowhere. *Bockscar* was then set for the secondary target, Nagasaki, with the decision that one run would be made and the bomb dropped by radar if necessary.

Cloud covered Nagaski also, but at 10:58 A.M. (Nagasaki time) bombardier Captain Kermit K. Beahan sighted the city in a cloud rent and in a flash

moderate—the number of dead may have reached about 80,000 (still less than the number of casualties of the Tokyo fire raids and the Dresden attacks). All this, however, by one single bomb.

Until President Truman announced that the destruction had been caused by history's first atomic bomb, the Japanese High Command had no idea of the nature of the force that had been unleashed at Hiroshima. Truman again appealed to the Japanese to surrender or "expect a rain of ruin from the air, the like of which has never been seen on this earth."

But no word, not even a *mokusatsu,* came from Tokyo. Nor did any mention of an atomic bomb appear in the Japanese press. The military conceded that some type of new "parachute bomb" had caused extensive devastation at Hiroshima and that it "should not be made light of." But there was no light shed on the situation by the High Command, despite the Emperor's obvious desires to end

General Carl A. Spaatz (second from right) and staff await the return of the Enola Gay *from Hiroshima.*
(U. S. AIR FORCE)

The bomb that fell on Nagasaki, "Fat Man," which subtracted forty thousand people from the population of Japan. (U. S. AIR FORCE)

—"a light brighter than a thousand suns"—thirty or forty thousand souls simply vanished from the face of the earth.

After taking the shock waves from the blast —"it was as if the B-29 were being beaten by a telephone pole"—Sweeney realized that the fuel expenditure had been high (plus the fact that six hundred gallons were wasted in a bomb bay tank because of malfunction). Instead of turning back for Tinian, he headed south for Okinawa, followed by Bock. After refueling, the B-29s were flown back to Tinian; all three had returned safely.

Even after the second atomic blast the Tokyo die-hard fanatics demanded that the war be continued to the very bitter end. They still had a large army in the home islands, there were perhaps 10,000 aircraft of assorted types (including wood and fabric trainers) and 500 pilots in kamikaze training. There was practically no Imperial Navy left, but there were hundreds of midget submarines, 120 *kaiten* (manned suicide torpedoes), about 2000 *shinyo* (motorboats loaded with explosives), and, of course, a fearful populace armed with their bamboo poles. There were broadcast threats to the "peace agitators" and "defeatists" over Radio Tokyo.

Immediately following the Nagasaki bombing an

Imperial Conference was called in which, at last, the Emperor intervened, announcing to the stunned assemblage that his decision was for an end to the war. Word of the decision was relayed to the Allies through Switzerland and was accepted. This acceptance was not gracefully taken in Tokyo. When the Imperial Conference met again on August 14, War Minister Anami, Army Chief of Staff Umezu, and Navy Chief of Staff Toyoda begged the Emperor that "one last battle" be fought in the home islands to preserve the national honor. But the Emperor was firm and had decided to record an Imperial rescript which would be broadcast to his people the following day, August 15, 1945.

There would be peace. Operation Olympic could be canceled; there would be no invasion. Nor would a third atomic bomb, then being readied, be dropped on the next selected target: Tokyo.

VIII

On "the 14th Day of the 8th month of the 20th year of Showa" an unprecedented event occurred:

While the world waited for word from Tokyo and the third atomic bomb was being prepared to be dropped on that city, a vigil was kept. A Wildcat takes off on a dawn patrol—Japan may have been beaten but its samurai and kamikazes were unwilling to accept that.
(U. S. NAVY)

for the first time in history the people of Japan heard the voice of their Emperor. At the sound of it many of the simple folk prostrated themselves before their radios, listening to the high-pitched, sometimes choked voice with foreheads pressed to the floor.

"To our good and loyal subjects," Hirohito began. He spoke in an archaic, royal dialect that was strange to most of his listeners.

"After pondering deeply the general trends of the world and the actual conditions obtaining in Our Empire today, We have decided to effect a settlement of the present situation by resorting to an extraordinary measure." The language was stilted, the delivery nervous, and the auditors had difficulty in grasping the point of the words.

"We, the Emperor, have ordered the Imperial Government to notify the Governments of the United States, Great Britain, China, and the Soviet Union that We accept their Joint Declaration."

He reminded them that the well-being of his subjects was the traditional rule left "Us by the Founder of the Empire of Our Illustrious Imperial Ancestors," who would wish to share "with all the countries of the world the joys of co-prosperity . . ." but that "the military situation can no longer take a favorable turn. . . .

"Moreover, the enemy has begun to employ a new and inhuman bomb, the power of which to do damage is indeed incalculable, taking a toll of many innocent lives. To continue the war under these conditions would not only lead to the annihilation of Our Nation, but to the destruction of human civilization as well."

The Emperor tendered his regrets to "our Allied nations in East Asia, who have consistently co-operated with the Empire toward the emancipation of East Asia." Thoughts of those who had died in the four long years of savagery "pains Our heart night and day. The welfare of the wounded and war-sufferers, and of those who have lost their homes and livelihood, are the objects of Our profound solicitude."

The broadcast drew to a close as Hirohito observed that "it is according to the dictate of time and fate that We have resolved to pave the way for a grand peace for all generations to come by enduring the unendurable and tolerating the intolerable." He was, of course, referring to the impending occupation.

The fanatics were still a problem—five of them

the previous night had tried to seize the recording of the rescript and prevent its broadcast—so Hirohito voiced a warning. "Beware most strictly of any outbursts of emotion which may engender needless complications, or any fraternal contention and strife which may create confusion, lead ye astray and cause ye to lose the confidence of the world."

The Emperor closed the rescript with a plea rather than a royal order. "We ask you, Our subjects," he said, "to be the incarnation of Our will."

A wave of national mourning followed in the wake of the speech, but so did rebelliousness, with cries of continuing the fight until the entire nation was destroyed and every last Japanese was dead. But only a small minority would have dared ignore

Night vigil: Northrop P-61s—"Black Widows"—the best of the American night fighters on the alert in the Pacific for Japanese surprise night attacks. Even after the Emperor had asked for peace, the possibility of last-ditch attacks by die-hard fanatical pilots was possible.
(U. S. AIR FORCE)

the Emperor's plea and his will. Such had been the group, led by Major Kenji Hatanaka, who had violated the Imperial palace grounds in search of the broadcast recording. When this failed, and when they could not enlist more men to their cause, four of the five plotters committed suicide.

A wave of high-level suicides followed the Emperor's broadcast, among them War Minister Anami, who had burst into tears when the Emperor had announced his decision for peace. General Hideki Tojo, who as Minister of War had planned the attack upon the United States, attempted suicide, bungled the job, and lived long enough to be hanged as a war criminal. Umezu and Toyoda, though they had urged for "one last battle," chose to live.

Admiral Ohnishi, the father of the kamikaze, dined with friends the evening of August 15, after which he retired to his study on the second floor of his official residence and disemboweled himself.

He had also attempted to cut his own throat but succeeded only in making a ragged wound. Thus he lingered in agony for several hours, refusing all aid and *coup de grâce,* until death came ten hours later. Before committing traditional hara-kari Ohnishi had written a note in which he said, "I wish to express my deep appreciation to the souls of the brave special attackers. They fought and died valiantly with faith in our ultimate victory. In death I wish to atone for my part in the failure to achieve that victory and I apologize to the souls of these dead fliers and their bereaved families. . . ."

The kamikaze spirit continued to burn in some breasts and there were loud boasts among pilots that when the *Missouri* steamed into Tokyo Bay for the surrender ceremonies they would crash into the American ship. This threat was squelched with the arrival of Prince Takamatsu, the Emperor's brother, at Atsugi airfield to put down an incipient re-

Vigil rewarded: American troops moving into Japan before the official surrender. Building in background *is part of an aircraft experimental grounds factory at Yokosuka.* (DEFENSE DEPT., MARINE CORPS)

bellion there. Leading it was Navy Captain Ammyo Kosono, who had showered leaflets upon Tokyo reading:

Government officials and senior statesmen who were caught in an enemy trap have enticed the Emperor to issue the message ending the war. It was a terrible thing to do. The Emperor is a God. There is no such thing as surrender in Japan. There is no surrender in the Imperial forces. We, as members of the Air Force, are sure of victory.

This threat expired when Kosono was removed from Atsugi to the Nobi Naval Hospital in a strait jacket.

There was, in fact, one final kamikaze attack after the broadcast of the Emperor's rescript. Vice-Admiral Matome Ugaki, who had commanded the devastating kamikaze attacks during the Okinawa campaign, had decided to lead one final attack upon the enemy at Okinawa despite the Emperor's plea. He ordered three aircraft of the Oita detachment of the 701st Air Group to attack the enemy fleet at Okinawa. "This attack," the order read, "will be led by the commanding admiral."

All attempts to dissuade Ugaki from the mission were fruitless and often tearful. And, in fact, when Ugaki came to the airstrip instead of three bombers he was surprised—and no doubt moved—to see eleven planes and twenty-two men. The unit commander, Lieutenant Tatsuo Nakatsuru, explained that when the commander himself was to lead an attack, a mere three aircraft would not suffice. "Every plane in my command will follow him!"

Deeply touched, Ugaki climbed into Nakatsuru's plane, taking the rear seat of Warrant Officer Akiyoshi Endo. Though Endo objected, Ugaki ordered him out of the plane. The young airmen jumped to the ground and then, determined, clambered back upon the wing to squeeze into the rear cockpit with his admiral. Ugaki, shaking his head in mock dismay at the show of zeal, made room for Endo. Then the eleven aircraft took off from the Oita base and headed for Okinawa.

Four of the dive bombers were forced to return with engine trouble, but Nakatsuru's lead plane continued on for Okinawa. Endo radioed Ugaki's final message to the base: "I alone am to blame for our failure to defend the homeland and to destroy the arrogant enemy," the message began. "I am going to make an attack at Okinawa where my men have

Clyde W. Cooksey, Jackson, Tennessee, cuts away the Japanese surrender flag in preparation for the raising of the Stars and Stripes on the crest of Tahyama, near Sasebo, Kyushu, Japan.

(DEFENSE DEPT., MARINE CORPS)

fallen like cherry blossoms. There I will crash into and destroy the conceited enemy in the true spirit of *Bushido,* with the firm conviction and faith in the eternity of Imperial Japan. . . ."

Why he did not realize that his attack might very well have led to a renewal of hostilities that could have doomed Imperial Japan into eternity is not known. The final words of the message were "Long live His Imperial Majesty the Emperor!"

Another message was flashed at 7:24 P.M. on that August 15, that the admiral's plane was making a plunge upon a target and the six others were following.

There was silence after that. Ironically, and fittingly perhaps, the last kamikaze attack of the Second World War was an utter failure. The fate of the

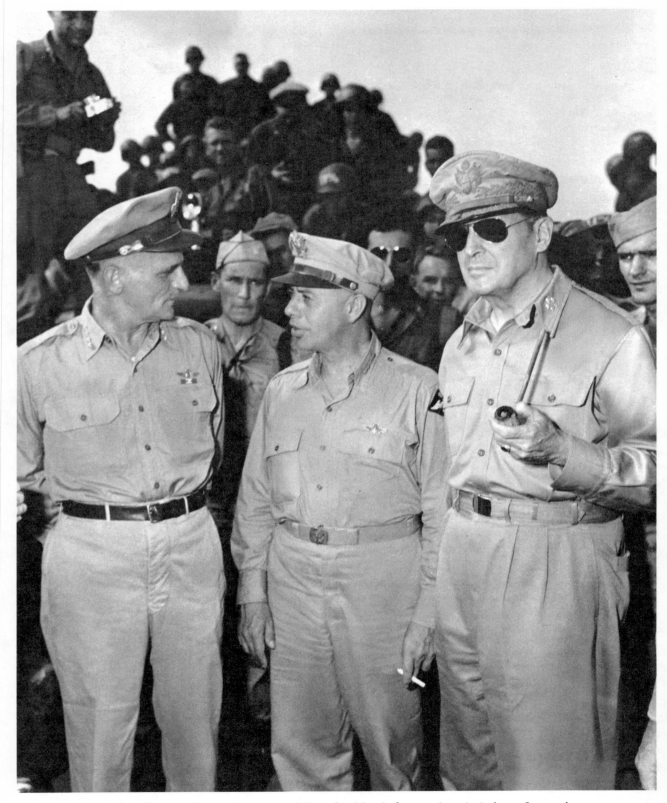

Carl A. Spaatz, George Kenney, and Douglas MacArthur at Atsugi air base, Japan, for the surrender ceremonies. (U. S. AIR FORCE)

U.S.S. Missouri, *Tokyo Bay, September 2, 1945, the close of the Second World War.*

seven dive bombers and the fifteen men remains one of the mysteries of the war. Not one of the aircraft hit any Allied ships, nor were they heard from again.

On Sunday, September 2, 1945, the formal surrender ceremonies took place aboard the *Missouri* in Tokyo Bay, without incident, and with General Douglas MacArthur presiding. After the formalities of affixing signatures to the documents were concluded at 9:25 A.M., the sun broke through the morning overcast and a deep rumble pervaded the air. It was as if Hollywood had set the scene: the blue sky, the broken clouds, the sun shafts, and the deep-throated rumble. After so many months of warring the very thought of peace was unreal.

Great armadas of B-29s swept over Tokyo Bay; to the sonority of their engines was added the roar of Air Force fighters, Mustangs and Thunderbolts and more than four hundred Navy Hellcats, Avengers, Helldivers, and the Marine's dreaded "Whistling Death" Corsair.

The war that had begun and closed with an aerial attack was over. In the recognition of the extreme and frightful disparity between those two attacks— a handful of Stukas and one lone B-29—lies the new definition of air war and the destiny of civilization. The Second World War closed, as had no previous major war in history, with all the weapons at hand for the Final World War.

Man, have pity on man.

Acknowledgments

My deepest debt I owe to my editor, Harold Kuebler, from this book's very inception through the long period of conception, and after. Harold is an extraordinary editor who not only knows his subject but has a genuine interest in it. He is blessed, too, with the gift of patience, gentle wit, and a total absence of affectation. Never over the years of our association has it congealed into the typical "editor-writer" relationship, which is roughly comparable to that of the Navy and the Marines.

For the bulk of the photographs I am indebted to Office of the Assistant Secretary of Defense's Magazine and Book Branch, Directorate for Information Services. Not only were these photographs freely supplied; so was certain specific information which I required along the line—from the correct spelling of names to the identification of Air Force units. This was an immense help, and a comforting one, for as the manuscript grew heavier the opportunity for error multiplied. The information I asked for was dug up out of the archives stored near Washington and it was indeed helpful that the digging was so graciously done for me, thus saving time that could be spent trying to conquer the typewriter. Individual names of those who assisted me in a time of need may be found listed after these opening paragraphs.

Another remarkable source of material, courteous service, and co-operation was the National Archives and Records Service of the General Services Administration in Washington, D.C. My impression is that every worthwhile photograph and document in existence is stored in our National Archives. Several of the beautiful carrier war photographs, many produced under the supervision of the great photographer Edward Steichen during the war, came from the Archives. Although I spent many hours in the National Archives (one easily might spend years there), much of the hard work was done by the U.S. mails, zip code and all. Thus was the often time-consuming and tiring work done for me by the superb staff of the National Archives.

In England I spent several days in the Imperial War Museum doing research through the vast files and picture collections. Here again the attention I received was thoughtful, courteous, and valuable. My guide through the great collections was an ex-RAF crewman, E. C. H. Hine, who could tell by simply looking at a photo of a Spitfire whether it had served during the Battle of Britain or not. Ed Hine is also a musical type—a Harold Arlen fan, in fact—so we did not spend all our time talking about the war. He was also delighted that the weather in England had been so "nice" during my stay. It was March—and true, the sun did shine, but frankly I froze.

Also in London I visited Mr. W. J. Taunton at

the Air Historical Branch, Ministry of Defence, Queen Anne's Chambers. Not only was I offered valuable suggestions (and later prompt replies to frantic queries), but also the best cup of tea I had in England. And I hate tea. Mr. Taunton also told me a fine joke, something to do with cricket balls, but I've only spoiled it ever since.

The Division of Information of the United States Marine Corps has also exceeded the call of duty in finding interesting photographs at the last minute.

Heinz J. Nowarra, the German aviation scholar and archivist, was most generous in making his great photo collection available to me; his own books on the Messerschmitt 109 and Focke-Wulf 190 were invaluable reference sources.

The "hapless designer" who so handsomely "put it all together" (the "all" adding up to more than a thousand pages of manuscript and nearly 800 illustrations) is Doubleday's own Jim Leach.

Nor can the following be overlooked or sufficiently thanked:

Sir Max Aitken, of *The Daily Express*, London, veteran of the Battle of Britain.

Robert R. Allen, Golden, Colorado, for a fund of technical information plus a treasury of tech manuals.

Anya and Harold Arlen for discussions while the work was in progress and refreshing friendship during the lulls between. Harold Arlen's regular line of work has nothing to do with aviation or war, but his several research suggestions were most perceptive.

Douglas R. S. Bader, of Shell Centre, London, and veteran of the Battle of Britain.

R. Baker, Chief Photographer, Home Counties Newspapers, Ltd., Luton Bedfordshire, England.

John F. Bartel, Bay City, Michigan—again.

J. Bax, Head, Press and Information Services, City of Rotterdam, the Netherlands.

John M. Bennett, Jr., Major General, USAF (Res.) and San Antonio, Texas—also again.

Jack Birdsall, Saginaw, Michigan, who is my sister Mary's husband, for helping so unselfishly during the final writing of this book in an especially trying time.

Sissel Bohman, secretary to Harold Kuebler, ever helpful, thoughtful, and understanding—pretty, too.

Robert S. Bolles, artist, an ex-ground crew man; possibly the only man in history who ever lost a DC-3—on the ground at that.

Lt. Col. C. W. Burtyk, Jr., U. S. Army, Office of the Assistant Secretary of Defense.

Col. F. C. Caldwell, Head, Historical Branch, U. S. Marine Corps, Department of the Navy, Washington, D.C.

John Camden, Republic Aviation Corporation, Farmingdale, N.Y.

Mrs. Sylvia Carson, P.S. 87 (Manhattan), for invaluable historical information on the development of the aircraft carrier.

Frank A. Celantano, ex-384th Bombardment Group (H) Eighth Air Force, now an attorney in New York City.

Robert C. Chapin, also ex-384th Bombardment Goup (H), now in public relations in Philadelphia and New York. Bob Chapin's collection of memorabilia, photographs, and technical material, carefully preserved since the war, was invaluable to me.

Alex Chervitz, flier and teacher, N.Y.

C. F. Clark, Librarian, Fox Photos, Ltd., London.

Claire and Peter Clay, Rickmansworth, Herts., England. Peter and I, musical pen pals from the beginning of the Second World War, never met until my research trip to England. Such meetings are always delicate, but I, for one, was thoroughly delighted. Claire and Peter provided me not only with a home for my entire stay but also with the atmosphere of a genuine English pub and meetings with ex-RAF types. Peter, incidentally, served in the RAF during the war; Claire was a nurse. Some of my affection for them is evident, I hope, in the dedication of this book

Cecil Cohen, ex-34th Bombardment Group, now Margaretville, N.Y.

Mrs. Jean Coleman, National Archives, Washington, D.C.

F. Czajkowski, Polish People's Republic Permanent Mission to the United Nations.

Grant Daly, Historian, Grumman Aviation Engineering Corp., Bethpage, N.Y.

Air Commodore Alan C. Deere, DSO, OBE, DFC— RAF.

Michael Farlam, Hawker Siddeley Group, Ltd., London.

Mrs. Virginia Fincik, Air Force Photo Center, Washington, D.C.

Royal D. Frey, Chief, Research Section, Air Force Museum, Wright-Patterson Air Force Base, Ohio. Again and again and again.

Col. Francis S. Gabreski, USAF (Ret.), with thanks for a pleasant visit to Suffolk County Air Force Base, lunch in the officers' mess (my first GI meal since 1945: no comment), and illuminating talks on the fighter pilot and an enlightened attitude toward war.

W. D. Gallavin, *Kent Messenger*, Maidstone, Kent, England, for a copy of *Hell's Corner* and photographs taken during the Battle of Britain.

M/Sgt. Beresford B. Gilkes, USAF (Ret.), Albuquerque, New Mexico, for excellent suggestions, lively letters, and photographs.

Col. C. V. Glines, USAF, from all parts: Washington, the Alaskan Command, and Virginia; he is the author of fine aviation books, from which I unashamedly cribbed.

Capt. J. M. Gratto, U. S. Marine Corps, Division of Information, Washington, D.C.

Lt/Col. Gene Guerny, USAF, author and friend.

Col. Grover Heiman, Jr., USAF, Office of the Assistant Secretary of Defense, Washington, D.C.

Raymond E. Houseman, Lt. Col. USAF (Ret.), "Pappy" —who kept the faith. Once one of Kenney's Kids, now with Lockheed Aircraft Corporation, N.Y.

Gordon M. Jackson, American Aviation Historical Society, General Dynamics, Convair Division, San Diego, California. As historian at Convair, Gordon Jackson is keeper of the files on the B-24 Liberator and permitted me to go through his collection on this bomber as well as the PBY Catalina.

Albert Jaynes, Bay City, Michigan, ex-Saipan resident, U. S. Army.

Jan Kinast, Press Secretary, Embassy of the Polish People's Republic, Washington, D.C.

Capt. F. Kent Loomis, USN (Ret.), Assistant Director of Naval History, Department of the Navy, Office of the Chief of Naval Operations, Washington, D.C.

William MacNamara, now of Brooklyn, but once one of Kenney's Kids.

Commander Joseph W. Marshall, USNR, Magazine and Book Division, Directorate for Defense Information, Office of the Assistant Secretary of Defense.

Crosby Maynard, Director of Public Relations, Douglas Aircraft Corporation, Santa Monica, California.

N. L. Mead, Curtiss-Wright Corp., Wood-Ridge, New Jersey

Bill Merklein, formerly of Polk's Hobby Shop, expert on aircraft and markings of the Second World War.

Elliot H. Miller, the Martin Company, Baltimore, Maryland.

Erik Miller, Lockheed-California Company, Burbank, California.

Col. W. Morris, U. S. Marine Corps, Washington, D.C.

Josephine Motylewski, National Archives, Washington, D.C.

Mark E. Nevils, The Boeing Company, New York, N.Y.

J. R. S. Nicholls, Hawker Siddeley Aviation, Ltd., Coventry, England.

Peter Northcote, RAF Association, N.Y.

Joseph Oravec, ex-Eighth Air Force, now of the Scranton Times, Scranton, Pa.: for a stream of ideas and suggestions plus the loan of old copies of Yank and Stars and Stripes.

Ramsay D. Potts, veteran of the Ploesti raid, now an attorney in Washington, D.C.

John F. J. Preston, American Aviation Historical Society, of Brooklyn, N.Y.

Helga Rippka, Lufthansa, New York.

Col. J. Rougevin-Baville, Conservateur du Musée de l'Air, Paris.

Arthur L. Schoeni, American Aviation Historical Society, Ling-Temco Vought, Inc., Dallas, Texas.

Robert H. Scholl, North American Aviation, El Segundo, California.

Ernest Shipman, formerly of the 31st Fighter Group, Fifteenth Air Force, and now with the 9215 Air Reserve Squadron, for assistance with many technical matters from this book's inception. I am especially grateful for the free use of his diary.

Major G. W. Smeltzer, Head, Service Branch, Division of Information, Marine Corps, Washington, D.C.

Winder D. Smith, ex-Fifteenth Air Force, now Hancock, New Hampshire.

Lt. Gerald Somers, USN, Public Relations Office, N.Y.

David Trollope, of Kent and Baker Street, London.

Lt. J. E. Tuthill, U. S. Naval Photographic Center, U. S. Naval Station, Washington, D.C.

Anna C. Urband, Office of the Assistant Secretary of Defense, Washington, D.C.

Stephen H. Vogel, National Archives, Washington, D.C.

John Owen Ward, Manager, Music Department, Oxford University Press, New York; once, however, of Biggin Hill and north Africa.

Lt/Col. Robert A. Webb, USAF, Magazine and Book Branch, Office of the Assistant Secretary of Defense, Washington, D.C.

Fred T. Wells, Pratt & Whitney Aircraft, East Hartford, Connecticut.

Paul White, National Archives, Washington, D.C.

Raymond C. Wier, Wellesley, Massachusetts, for unusual photographs taken by himself during the Ploesti raid.

Ursula Vaughan Williams, London, for permission to quote from her poem, an excerpt from "Noah's Ark" from Silence and Music (Essential Books, Fair Lawn, New Jersey, 1959). Thanks too for a wonderful musical afternoon in London, not to mention the fine lunch, the sherry, and the lively talk.

Margaret Yost, Lufthansa, New York.

Final personal note: Work on *Airwar* was begun at the home of my parents, William and Isabel Jablonski, in Beaverton, Michigan. It continued and grew in Washington, D.C., in Seattle, Washington, and in Luton and London, England. The final half was started in Santa Ana, California, and finally completed in New York in July 1968, almost three years after its inception. Throughout this extended period I was tendered (and I use the term advisedly, perhaps even in a Gertrude Stein-ish sense) every manner of loving support and understanding by my wife Edith (who, as an editor and columnist, had her own literary problems and deadlines). Without her, the spelling and punctuation, not to say semantics, would have been even stranger than they are. My son David (who is fifteen as this is being completed), was a constant source of enlightenment and information. One of the rare, true scholars, David has provided much instant information and research assistance. His knowledge of the aircraft and battles of the Second World War is impressive. My daughters Carla and Emily only dread war—they make no effort to understand it or to find some redeeming glorification or nostalgia in it. They impress me as being exceedingly wise. If we could all see war through their eyes, simply and realistically, we might yet have a chance of making it into the next century.

Bibliography

BESIDES personal interviews, contemporary newspapers and magazines, plus some checks into various official archives, the making of this book has depended a good deal upon the many postwar official histories published with the co-operation of various governments. Not only are these works of an imposing scholarship, they are often equally objective; they do not take sides, generally. The English are especially good at this sort of thing. To judge from what little is yet available, the Germans tend to lean the other way. Not so much to place the blame upon their enemies, as much as to attempt to explain away defeat in terms of the great betrayal by Hitler, or to scoff at the idea that Germany went into the war with the most powerful air force in the world.

Certain works, such as the multivolumned official histories or general histories of the war, were referred to throughout the writing of *Airwar*. Since footnotes have always annoyed me, I have refrained from using them. Having read through literally hundreds of works, ranging from those barely above the level of pulp magazines to those of impeccable scholarship, I am not convinced that a half page of footnotes really proves much. As a reader I have always expected an author to do his job to the best of his ability, to be honest, and to know what he's talking about. If he is dishonest, the footnotes make

no difference: I found this to be the case with one of the biographies of Göring.

Unless a book is little more than a listing of facts, it of course cannot be purely objective. We assume the author has a point of view and that the use he makes of facts (even to the point of twisting them: and the more skilled he is, the more subtle the twist) will conform to that point of view. Footnotes to back up the point of view won't undo the twist. The worst type of footnote is the one that compels the reader to turn to the back of the book. As a student, as a reader, and as a writer I have never quite been able to fathom this distracting practice.

Therefore no footnotes.

The facts that make up this book were drawn from the various sources already mentioned; that some of these were not facts I found upon checking several sources against each other. The interpretation of the facts and the "facts" are my own: I have, in other words, added my own of both varieties, no doubt. Needless to say, I have attempted to make the book as factual as humanly possible, and likewise my editor, Harold Kuebler, and Harold Grabau, copy editor at Doubleday (may his tribe increase!), have done all they could to assure the historical accuracy of the book.

The bibliography, for easier handling, has been

subdivided into three major sections. The first contains those books to which I referred throughout— of a synoptic nature, general histories of the war which may have had nothing to say about the aerial aspects, and reference books and anthologies.

The second section is devoted to memoir-histories, many of which are not quite either, but fascinating just the same. They present the views of the actors in the drama, generally after the fact, as if the actor himself is given the chance to revise the script. Curious memory slips, reinterpretation of events, axes to grind, self-justification: all these tend to make these works a bit suspect as pure history. Perhaps the major truth is that history is neither pure nor scientific. The views of the authors are always valuable, even if suspect.

Finally, a separate bibliography germane to each of the major units establishes the chief sources for the chapters within each unit. And for good measure a section entitled "Miscellaneous" is added for certain volumes, mainly pictorial, which were useful as reference and for the location of long-forgotten photographs.

David, my son, assisted in the compilation and arrangement of this bibliography. Many of the books listed, in fact, are from his personal library, which, I am happy to say, is not devoted exclusively to war. His science fiction collection is extensive and his section on paleontology is definitive.

SYNOPTIC AND GENERAL HISTORIES
ANTHOLOGIES AND REFERENCE WORKS

Baldwin, Hanson W.: *Battles Lost and Won,* New York: Harper & Row, 1966.

Bekker, Cajus: *The Luftwaffe War Diaries,* Garden City, N.Y.: Doubleday & Co., Inc., 1968.

Buchanan, A. R., editor: *The Navy's Air War,* New York: Harper & Brothers, 1946.

Carlisle, Norman: *The Air Force Reader,* Indianapolis: Bobbs-Merrill Co., 1944.

Craven, W. F. and Cate, J. L., editors: *The Army Air Forces in World War II* (7 vols.), Chicago: University of Chicago Press, 1948–58.

D'Albas, Andrieu: *Death of a Navy,* New York: Devin-Adair Co., 1957.

Davis, Kenneth S.: *Experience of War,* Garden City, N.Y.: Doubleday & Co., Inc., 1965.

Dupuy, Col. R. Ernest and Bregstein, Lt/Col. Herbert L.: *Soldier's Album,* Boston: Houghton Mifflin Co., 1946.

Emme, Eugene M.: *The Impact of Air Power,* Princeton, N.J.: D. Van Nostrand Co., Inc., 1959.

Esposito, Brig. Gen. Vincent J., editor: *A Concise History of World War II,* New York: Frederick A. Praeger, Publishers, 1964.

Flower, Desmond and Reeves, James, editors: *The Taste of Courage, The War 1939–1945,* New York: Harper & Brothers, 1960.

Goldberg, Alfred, editor: *A History of the United States Air Force,* Princeton, N.J.: D. Van Nostrand Co., Inc., 1957.

Green, William: *Famous Bombers of the Second World War* (2 vols.), Garden City, N.Y.: Doubleday & Co., Inc., 1959, 1960.

———: *Famous Fighters of the Second World War* (2 vols.), Garden City, N.Y.: Doubleday & Co., Inc., 1962.

Greenfield, Kent Roberts, editor: *Command Decisions,* Washington, D.C.: Office of the Chief of Military History, Department of the Army, 1960.

Gurney, Maj. Gene: *The War in the Air,* New York: Crown Publishers, Inc., 1962.

Hinton, Harold B.: *Air Victory,* New York: Harper & Brothers, 1948.

Jacobsen, H. A. and Rohwer, J., editors: *Decisive Battles of World War II: The German View,* New York: G. P. Putnam's Sons, 1964.

Killen, John: *The Luftwaffe: A History,* London: Frederick Muller, 1967.

King, Adm. Ernest J.: *U.S. Navy at War 1941–1945,* Washington, D.C.: United States Navy Dept., 1946.

Leckie, Robert: *Strong Men Armed,* New York: Random House, Inc., 1962.

Lee, Asher: *The German Air Force,* London: Duckworth, 1946.

Loosbrock, J. F. and Skinner, R. M., editors: *The Wild Blue,* New York: G. P. Putnam's Sons, 1961.

Marshall, Gen. George C., Arnold, Gen. H. H., and King, Adm. Ernest J.: *The War Reports,* Philadelphia, Pa.: J. B. Lippincott Co., 1947.

Martin, Ralph G.: *The G. I. War 1941–1945,* Boston: Little, Brown & Co., 1967.

Maurer, Maurer: *Air Force Combat Units of World War II,* New York: Franklin Watts, Inc., 1963.

Morison, Samuel Eliot: *The Two-Ocean War,* Boston: Little, Brown & Co., 1963.

Moyes, Philip: *Bomber Squadrons of the R.A.F.,* London: MacDonald, 1964.

Nowarra, Heinz J.: *The Messerschmitt 109—A Famous*

German Fighter, Letchworth, Herts., England: Harleyford Publications, 1963.

————: *The Focke-Wulf 190—A Famous German Fighter,* Letchworth, Herts., England: Harleyford Publications, 1965.

Richards, Denis and Saunders, Hilary St. George: *Royal Air Force* (3 vols.), London: Her Majesty's Stationery Office, 1953–54.

Robertson, Bruce: *Spitfire—The Story of a Famous Fighter,* Letchworth, Herts., England: Harleyford Publications, 1960.

————: *Lancaster—the Story of a Famous Bomber,* Letchworth, Herts., England: Harleyford Publications, 1963.

Sherrod, Robert: *History of Marine Corps Aviation in World War II,* Washington, D.C.: Combat Forces Press, 1952.

Shirer, William L.: *The Rise and Fall of the Third Reich,* New York: Simon & Schuster, 1960.

Smith, S. E., editor: *The United States Navy in World War II,* New York: Wm. Morrow & Co., Inc., 1966.

Snyder, Louis L.: *The War, A Concise History 1939–1945,* New York: Julian Messner, Inc., 1960.

Straubel, James H.: *Air Force Diary,* New York: Simon & Schuster, 1947.

Sulzberger, C. L. and the editors of *American Heritage: The American Heritage Picture History of World War II,* New York: American Heritage Publishing Co., Inc., 1966.

Tourtellot, Arthur B., editor: *Life's Picture History of World War II,* New York: Time, Inc., 1950.

Wagner, Ray: *American Combat Planes,* Garden City, N.Y.: Hanover House, 1968.

Watts, Anthony J.: *Japanese Warships of World War II,* London: Ian Allen, Ltd., 1966.

Webster, Sir Charles and Frankland, Noble: *The Strategic Air Offensive Against Germany* (4 vols.), London: Her Majesty's Stationery Office, 1961.

Weigley, Russell F.: *History of the United States Army,* New York: Macmillan Co., 1967.

MEMOIR-HISTORIES

Arnold, H. H.: *Global Mission,* New York: Harper & Brothers, 1949.

Baumbach, Werner: *The Life and the Death of the Luftwaffe,* New York: Coward-McCann, 1960.

Brereton, Lewis H.: *The Brereton Diaries,* New York: William Morrow & Co., 1946.

Churchill, Winston: *The Second World War* (6 vols.), Cambridge, Mass.: Houghton Mifflin Co., 1948–53.

Eisenhower, Dwight D.: *Crusade in Europe,* Garden City, N.Y.: Doubleday & Co., Inc., 1948.

Galland, Adolf: *The First and the Last,* New York: Henry Holt & Co., 1954.

Harris, Sir Arthur: *Bomber Offensive,* London: Collins, 1947.

Kenney, George C.: *General Kenney Reports,* New York: Duell, Sloan and Pearce, 1949.

LeMay, Gen. Curtis E. with Kantor, MacKinlay: *Mission with LeMay,* Garden City, N.Y.: Doubleday & Co., Inc., 1965.

Lochner, Louis P., editor: *The Goebbels Diaries,* Garden City, N.Y.: Doubleday & Co., Inc., 1948.

MacArthur, Douglas: *Reminiscences,* New York: McGraw-Hill Book Co., 1964.

Montgomery, Bernard Law: *The Memoirs of Field-Marshal the Viscount Montgomery of Alamein, K.G.,* Cleveland, Ohio: World Publishing Co., 1958.

Sherwood, Robert E.: *Roosevelt and Hopkins,* New York: Harper & Brothers, 1948.

White, Theodore H., editor: *The Stilwell Papers,* New York: William Sloane Associates, Inc., 1948.

UNIT BIBLIOGRAPHIES

PROLOGUE: *PAX GERMANICA*

Arps, Lt/Col. Leslie H. and Quigley, Frank V., "The Origin, Development and Organization of the Luftwaffe," paper, dated 1 October 1945; Special File of General Frederick H. Smith, Jr., U. S. Air Force.

Bewley, Charles: *Herman Göring and the Third Reich,* New York: Devin-Adair Co., 1962.

British Air Ministry: "Notes on the German Air Force," April 1943; U. S. Navy reprint.

Bullock, Alan: *Hitler, A Study in Tyranny,* New York: Harper & Brothers, 1960.

Carr, Edward Hallett: *German-Soviet Relations Between the Two World Wars,* Baltimore: Johns Hopkins Press, 1951.

Craig, Gordon A.: *The Politics of the Prussian Army,* New York: Oxford University Press, 1955.

Frischauer, Willi: *The Rise and Fall of Hermann Goering,* Boston: Houghton Mifflin Co., 1951.

Goerlitz, Walter: *History of the German General Staff,* New York: Frederick A. Praeger, 1953.

Hallgarten, George W. F.: "General Hans von Seeckt and Russia, 1920–1922," Chicago: *Journal of Modern History,* March 1949.

Hilger, Gustav and Meyer, Alfred G.: *The Incompatible Allies,* New York: Macmillan Co., 1953.

Manvell, Roger and Fraenkel, Heinrich: *Goering,* New York: Simon & Schuster, 1962.

Melville, Cecil F.: *The Russian Face of Germany,* London: Wishart & Co., 1932.

Wheeler-Bennett, John W.: *The Nemesis of Power,* New York: St. Martin's Press, 1954.

I. BLITZKRIEG

Benoist-Mechin, Jacques: *Sixty Days That Shook the West,* New York: G. P. Putnam's Sons, 1963.

Bolitho, Hector: *Combat Report,* London: B. T. Batsford, Ltd., 1943.

Divine, David: *The Nine Days of Dunkirk,* New York: W. W. Norton & Co., Inc., 1959.

Garnett, David: *War in the Air,* Garden City, N.Y.: Doubleday, Doran & Co., Inc., 1941.

Gourtard, A.: *The Battle for France,* New York: Ives Washburn, Inc., 1959.

Hagen, Louis, editor: *The Schellenberg Memoirs,* New York: Harper & Brothers, 1957.

Halstead, Ivor: *Wings of Victory,* New York: E. P. Dutton & Co., 1941.

Michaelis, Ralph: *From Bird Cage to Battle Plane,* New York: Thomas Y. Crowell Co., 1943.

Monks, Noel: *Squadrons Up!,* New York: Whittlesey House, McGraw-Hill Book Co., 1941.

Richey, Paul: *Fighter Pilot,* London: B. T. Batsford, Ltd., 1941.

Taylor, Telford: *The March of Conquest,* New York: Simon & Schuster, 1958.

Welles, Sumner: *The Time for Decision,* New York: Harper & Brothers, 1944.

II. THE BATTLE OF BRITAIN

Anon.: *Coastal Command,* New York: Macmillan Co., 1943.

————: *Front Line 1940–41,* London: His Majesty's Stationery Office, 1942.

————: *Ourselves in Wartime,* London: Odham's Press, Ltd., ca. 1941.

Boorman, H. P. P.: *Hell's Corner 1940,* Maidstone, Kent, England: Kent Messenger, 1941.

Brickhill, Paul: *Reach for the Sky,* New York: W. W. Norton & Co., 1954.

Childers, James Saxon: *War Eagles,* New York: D. Appleton-Century Co., 1943.

Collier, Basil: *The Defence of the United Kingdom,* London: Her Majesty's Stationery Office, 1957.

————: *Leader of the Few,* London: Jarrold's, 1966.

Collier, Richard: *Eagle Day,* New York: E. P. Dutton & Co., Inc., 1966.

Deere, Alan C.: *Nine Lives,* London: Hodder & Stoughton, 1959.

Fitzgibbon, Constantine: *The Winter of the Bombs,* New York: W. W. Norton & Co., Inc., 1957.

Forester, Larry: *Fly for Your Life,* London: Frederick Muller, Ltd., 1956.

Gribble, Leonard R.: *Epics of the Fighting R.A.F.,* London: George G. Harrap & Co., Ltd., 1943.

Kennerly, Byron: *The Eagles Roar!,* New York: Harper & Brothers, 1942.

Lane, B. J.: *Spitfire!,* London: John Murray, 1942.

Lasserre, Jean, editor: "The Battle of Britain," special issue, *Icare, revue des pilotes de ligne,* Orly, France: Automne-Hiver, 1965.

Mason, Francis K.: *Battle over Britain,* Garden City, N.Y.: Doubleday & Co., Inc., 1969.

Masters, David: *So Few,* London: Eyre & Spottiswoode, 1946.

McKee, Alexander: *Strike from the Sky,* London: Souvenir Press, 1960.

Middleton, Drew: *The Sky Suspended,* New York: Longmans, Green & Co., 1960.

Reynolds, James: *Paddy Finucane,* New York: Edmond Byrne Hackett, 1942.

Shores, Christopher and Williams, Clive: *Aces High,* London: Neville Spearman, 1966.

Spaight, J. M.: *The Battle of Britain 1940,* London: Geoffrey Bles, 1941.

Taylor, Telford: *The Breaking Wave,* New York: Simon & Schuster, 1967.

Thompson, Laurence: *1940,* New York: Wm. Morrow & Co., Inc., 1966.

Wood, Derek and Dempster, Derek: *The Narrow Margin,* New York: McGraw-Hill Book Co., Inc., 1961.

III. GREATER EAST ASIA CO-PROSPERITY SPHERE

Anders, Curt: *Fighting Airmen,* New York: G. P. Putnam's Sons, 1966.

Boyington, Gregory: *Baa Baa Black Sheep,* New York: G. P. Putnam's Sons, 1958.

Chennault, Claire Lee: *Way of a Fighter,* New York: G. P. Putnam's Sons, 1949.

Edmonds, Walter E.: *They Fought with What They Had,* Boston: Little, Brown & Co., 1951.

Fuchida, Mitsuo and Okumiya, Masatake: *Midway, the Battle That Doomed Japan,* Annapolis, Md.: U. S. Naval Institute, 1955.

Fukudome, Vice-Adm. Shigeru: "Hawaii Operation," Annapolis, Md.: *U. S. Naval Institute Proceedings,* December 1955.

Garfield, Brian: *The Thousand-Mile War,* Garden City, N.Y.: Doubleday & Co., Inc., 1969.

Glines, Carroll V.: *Doolittle's Tokyo Raiders,* Princeton, N.J.: D. Van Nostrand Co., Inc., 1964.

Gurney, Gene: *Five Down and Glory,* New York: G. P. Putnam's Sons, 1958.

Ito, Masanori with Pineau, Roger: *The End of the Imperial Japanese Navy,* New York: W. W. Norton & Co., 1962.

Lawson, Ted W. and Considine, Robert: *Thirty Seconds over Tokyo,* New York: Random House, 1943.

Lord, Walter: *Day of Infamy,* New York: Henry Holt & Co., 1957.

———: *Incredible Victory,* New York: Harper & Row, Inc., 1967.

MacDonald, Scot: *Evolution of Aircraft Carriers,* Washington, D.C.: Office of the Chief of Naval Operations, Department of the Navy, 1964.

Mears, Frederick: *Carrier Combat,* Garden City, N.Y.: Doubleday & Co., Inc., 1944.

Merrill, James M.: *Target Tokyo,* New York: Rand McNally & Co., 1964.

Miller, Lt. Max: *Daybreak for Our Carrier,* New York: Whittlesey House, McGraw-Hill Book Co., 1944.

Potter, John Deane: *Yamamoto, The Man Who Menaced America,* New York: Viking Press, 1965.

Reynolds, Quentin: *The Amazing Mr. Doolittle,* New York: Appleton-Century Crofts, Inc., 1953.

Scott, Robert L.: *God Is My Co-Pilot,* New York, Ballantine Books, 1956.

Stafford, Edward P.: *The Big E: The Story of the U.S.S. Enterprise,* New York: Random House, 1962.

Toland, John: *But Not in Shame,* New York: Random House, 1961.

Tuleja, Thaddeus V.: *Climax at Midway,* New York: W. W. Norton & Co., Inc., 1960.

Ulanoff, Stanley M.: *Fighter Pilot,* Garden City, N.Y.: Doubleday & Co., Inc., 1962.

Whelen, Russell: *The Flying Tigers,* New York: Viking Press, 1942.

Wohlstetter, Roberta: *Pearl Harbor: Warning and Decision,* Stanford, Cal.: Stanford University Press, 1962.

IV. THE BIG LEAGUE

Barker, Ralph: *The Thousand Plan,* London: Chatto & Windus, Ltd., 1965.

Brickhill, Paul: *The Dam Busters,* London: Evans Brothers, Ltd., 1951.

Burke, Edmund: *Guy Gibson, V.C.,* London: Arco Publications, 1961.

Caidin, Martin: *Black Thursday,* New York: E. P. Dutton & Co., 1960.

Dugan, James and Stewart, Carroll: *Ploesti,* New York: Random House, 1962.

Gibson, Guy: *Enemy Coast Ahead,* London: Michael Joseph, 1946.

Jostwick, Jerry J. and Keating, Lawrence A.: *Combat Camera Man,* New York: Chilton Co., 1961.

Morrison, Wilbur H.: *The Incredible 305th,* New York: Duell, Sloan & Pearce, 1962.

Owens, Walter E.: *As briefed, a family history of the 384th Bombardment Group,* copyright by Walter E. Owens, 1946.

Peaslee, Budd J.: *Heritage of Valor,* Philadelphia: J. B. Lippincott Co., 1964.

Rumpf, Hans: *The Bombing of Germany,* New York: Holt, Rinehart & Winston, 1963.

Saundby, Robert: *Air Bombardment,* New York: Harper & Brothers, 1961.

Wolff, Leon: *Low Level Mission,* Garden City, N.Y.: Doubleday & Co., Inc., 1951.

V. KENNEY'S KIDS, SOME SAILORS, AND A FEW MARINES

Johnston, Stanley: *The Grim Reapers,* Philadelphia: The Blakiston Co., 1943.

Simmons, Walter: *Joe Foss, Flying Marine,* New York: E. P. Dutton & Co., 1943.

VI. TARGET GERMANY

Collier, Basil: *The Battle of the V-Weapons 1944–45,* New York: Wm. Morrow & Co., 1965.

Devon, Francis: *Flak Bait,* New York: Duell, Sloan & Pearce, 1948.

Hall, Grover C.: *1000 Destroyed,* Dallas: Morgan Aviation Books, 1961.

Irving, David: *The Destruction of Dresden,* New York: Holt, Rinehart and Winston, 1964.

Johnson, Robert S. and Caidin, Martin: *Thunderbolt,* New York: Rinehart & Co., 1958.

Rust, Kenn C.: *The 9th Air Force in World War II,* Fallbrook, Cal.: Aero Publishers, Inc., 1967.

Ryan, Cornelius: *The Last Battle,* New York: Simon & Schuster, 1966.

Toland, John: *Battle, the Story of the Bulge,* New York: Random House, 1959.

———: *The Last 100 Days,* New York: Random House, 1966.

VII. THE DIVINE WIND

Benedict, Ruth: *The Chrysanthemum and the Sword,* Boston: Houghton Mifflin Co., 1946.

Caidin, Martin: *A Torch to the Enemy,* New York: Ballantine Books, 1960.

Craig, William: *The Fall of Japan,* New York: The Dial Press, 1967.

Fahey, James J.: *Pacific War Diary 1942–1945,* Boston: Houghton Mifflin Co., 1963.

Falk, Stanley L.: *Decision at Leyte,* New York: W. W. Norton & Co., 1966.

Gurney, Gene: *Journey of the Giants,* New York: Coward-McCann, Inc., 1961.

Inoguchi, Rikihei; Nakajima, Tadashi; and Pineau, Roger: *The Divine Wind,* Annapolis, Md.: U. S. Naval Institute, 1958.

Jablonski, David: "The Rise and Fall of the East Asia Co-Prosperity Sphere," New York: Bronx High School of Science, 1968.

Morrison, Wilbur H.: *Hellbirds: The Story of the B-29s in Combat,* New York: Duell, Sloan & Pearce, 1960.

Mosley, Leonard: *Hirohito, Emperor of Japan,* Englewood Cliffs, N.J.: Prentice-Hall, Inc., 1966.

Snyder, Earl: *General Leemy's Circus,* New York: Exposition Press, 1955.

Wehrmeister, R. L.: "Divine Wind over Okinawa," Annapolis, Md.: *U. S. Naval Institute Proceedings,* June 1957.

Woodward, Vann C.: *The Battle for Leyte Gulf,* New York: Macmillan Co., 1947.

Yokoi, Toshiyuki: "Kamikazes and the Okinawa Campaign," Annapolis, Md.: *U. S. Naval Institute Proceedings,* May 1954.

MISCELLANEOUS

Anon.: *Battle Stations! Your Navy in Action,* New York: Wm. H. Wise & Co., Inc., 1946.

Brandt, Lt. Robert, editor: *Into the Wind: U.S.S. Yorktown in World War II,* unit history of CV 10, undated.

Jensen, Lt. Oliver: *Carrier War,* New York: Simon & Schuster, 1945.

McCahill, Maj. William P., editor: *Hit the Beach! Your Marine Corps in Action,* New York: Wm. H. Wise & Co., Inc., 1948.

Silsbee, Col. Nathaniel F., editor: *Bombs Away! Your Air Force in Action,* New York: Wm. H. Wise & Co., Inc., 1949.

Steichen, Capt. Edward: *Power in the Pacific,* New York: U. S. Camera Publishing Corp., 1945.

Numerals in bold faced type refer to Volume number.
Note: References to illustrations are in *italics*.

A6M. *See* Zero
A-20 (Havoc), **II** 18, 19; **III** 12, *13,* 14, 20, 21, *45;*
    IV *94,* 95
A-24, **III** 5, 108
A-26 (Invader), **IV** 95, 99
Aaron Ward (U.S. naval vessel), **III** 90; **IV** 196–97,
    198
Abe, Hiroaki, **III** 83
Abukuma (Japanese naval vessel), **IV** 149
Acasta (British naval vessel), **I** 45
Adair, C. B., **II** 30
Adams, Max, **IV** 142
Adams, Samuel, **II** 98
Adler Tag, **I** 85–95
Admiral Scheer (German naval vessel), **I** 50, 51
Advanced Air Striking Force (AASF), **I** 53–55,
    61, 64–65, 73
Ady, Howard, **II** 84, 86
Africa. *See* North Africa; specific locations
Aichi D4Y. *See* Judy
Aikman, Alan, **I** 168
Airacobra (P-39), **III** 5, *9,* 15–17, 24, 36, *60,* 65, 68,
    90, 94, *104;* **IV** 84, 89
"Air Attack on Dams Committee," **II** 136
Air Component, **I** 54, 56, 73
Aircraft. *See* specific aircraft, nationalities
Air Forces. *See* specific nationalities
Aitken, John William "Max," **I** 87, *88*
Akagi (Japanese naval vessel), **II** 3, 12, 14, 15, 21, 23,
    24, 78, 86–88, 93–95, 97, 98, 104
Akamatsu, Temei, **III** 48
Akers, Frank, **II** 57
Akigumo (Japanese naval vessel), **III** 79

Albacore (U.S. naval vessel), **III** 127
Albania, **IV** 3
Aldworth, Richard T., **II** 30
Aleutian Islands, **II** 78, 80; **III** 104–7
Alexander, Sir Harold, **IV** 7
Alexander, John, **I** 166
Algar, Philip M., **I** 179, 181
Allen, Edmund T., **IV** 127
Allen, John I., **I** *129*
Allen, Luke, **I** *163*
Allied Air Forces, Pacific, **II** 112
Altmark (German naval vessel), **I** 37–38
American Volunteer Group. *See* Flying Tigers
Anami, Korechika, **IV** 205, 206, 212, 214
Anderson, Frederick L., **II** *175;* **IV** 53
Angaur Island, **IV** 135
Anglo-American air units, **IV** 33
    Mediterranean Allied Air Forces, **IV** 28, 32, 52, 53
    Northwest African Air Forces (NAAF), **IV** 12,
        23, 27, 28
Anson (British aircraft), **II** 116–17
Antonescu, Ion, **II** 155; **IV** 3, *4*
Antwerp, **IV** 108
Anzio, **IV** 28–31
Aoki, Taijiro, **II** 95–96
Appold, Norman C., **II** 161, 164, 166, *167,* 172
Arado (German aircraft), **IV** 117
Arashio (Japanese naval vessel), **II** 101; **III** 20
Arcadia conferences (1941–42), **II** 111
Ardennes, **IV** 108–13
Ardent (British naval vessel), **I** 45
Area bombing, **I** 150, 154–56; **II** 154, 155;
        IV 36–37, 168. *See also* Strategic bombing

Argument, Operation, **IV** 53
Arita, Hachiro, **II** 5
Arizona (U.S. naval vessel), **II** 17, 18, 21–23
Ark Royal (British naval vessel), **I** 41
Armed forces. *See* specific nationalities
Armée de l'Air, **I** 54. *See also* French aircraft
Armistead, Kirk, **II** 84
Armstrong, Frank A., **IV** 105
Armstrong, John D., **II** 31
Army Air Forces in World War II, The (Cate),
　　IV 162
Army Co-operation Command (British), **II** 115, 119
Arnim, Dietloff Jurgen von, **IV** 15
Arnold, Henry H., **I** xii; **II** *45, 46,* 51–55, 66, 67, 152,
　　189, 191; **III** 13, 32, 40, 42, 46, 47, 82
Aruga, Kosaku, **IV** 190, 193
Asahi Shimbun (newspaper), **II** 67–68
Asashimo (Japanese naval vessel), **IV** 194
Asche airfield (Belgium), **IV** 110–11
Aschersleben (Germany), **IV** 54
Ashmun, George M., **III** 98
Aslito Field. *See* Isley Field
Astell, William B., **II** 142, 143
Astoria (U.S. naval vessel), **II** 97
Astro Romana (Rumania), **II** 166, *168*
Atago (Japanese naval vessel), **III** 132; **IV** 141
Atkinson, Peter W., **II** 31
Atlantic, Battle of the, **I** 150–54; **II** 112, 115
Atomic bombs, **III** 50; **IV** 208–12, *208, 210, 212*
Attu, **II** 78, 80; **III** 104–7
Auchinleck, Sir Claude J. E., **IV** 7
Augsburg (Germany), **IV** 56
Australia, **II** 73. *See also* Australian aircraft; Australian
　　air units; Australian naval vessels
Australia (naval vessel), **II** 180, 181
Australian aircraft, **III** 33
　　Beaufighter, **III** 18, 21, 33
　　Beaufort, **III** 18
　　Boston, **III** 21
　　Catalina, **III** 18
Australian air units
　　groups:
　　　　9th Operational, **III** 18, 21
　　squadrons:
　　　　No. 3, **IV** 6–7
　　　　No. 30, **III** 33
　　　　No. 438, **IV** 110
　　　　No. 439, **IV** 110
Australian naval vessels
　　Australia, **IV** 180, 181
　　Moa, **III** 90
Austria. *See* specific locations
Avenger (aircraft), **II** 84, *86,* 87, 90; **III** 63, 68, 72, 75,
　　76, 77, *83,* 84, 85, 87, 88, 96, 97, *97, 112,*
　　113–14, *113,* 117, 121, 122, 132–35; **IV** 141
　　145–47, 149, 151–53, 155, 156, 193, 194,
　　218
AVG. *See* Flying Tigers
Awards. *See* specific awards
Azaña y Diaz, Manuel, **I** 4

B5N. *See* Kate
B6N. *See* Jill

B-17 (Flying Fortress), **I** xii, xiii, *150,* 151; **II** 15,
　　18, *20,* 78, 81, 82, 84, 87, 88, 98, 101, 151, 152,
　　153, 172, 173–74, *174, 176,* 177–78, *179,*
　　180, 181, 182, 185, *186, 187,* 188, 189; **III** 5, 7,
　　7, 8, 9, *10,* 11, 12, 14, 16, 18, 21, 22, 24, 26 32,
　　54, 65, 70, 72; **IV** 10, 11, 27, 29, 30, *32,* 38, 40,
　　48, *48, 50,* 51, *53,* 54, 55, 57, 58, *59, 68,*
　　92–94, *95,* 97, 99, *114,* 115, 118, 120, *121,*
　　122, 127, 164
B-18, **II** 18
B-23, **II** 51, 52
B-24 (Liberator), **I** 151–52; **III** 16, 18, 24, 26, 30,
　　34, 49, *105, 106,* 108, *109;* **IV** 8, 9, 10, 27, *28,*
　　30, *34,* 35, *42,* 48, 54, *55,* 58, 90, 91, *93,* 97, 98,
　　99, 100, *108,* 114, 115, 127, 135–36, *136,* 138,
　　149, 154, 185
B-25 (Mitchell), **II** 47, 50–56, *57,* 59, 60, *61, 62, 63,*
　　64–66, *67;* **III** 5, 9, 12, 18, 19–20, *20,* 21, 24,
　　25, 27, *28,* 29, 30, 32–34, *35,* 36–37, *38,*
　　99–100, *103;* **IV** 9, 10, *11,* 13, *14,* 27, *29,* 30,
　　31, 33, 110
B-26 (Marauder; Widow Maker), **II** *51,* 67, 78, 84,
　　86–87, 90, 108; **III** 5, 14; **IV** 27, 29, 30, *32,*
　　34, 78, 79, 95, 97, *98,* 99, 110
B-29 (Superfortress), **I** xii, xiii; **II** 174; **III** 114, 122,
　　133; **IV** 127–33, *128, 129, 130, 132, 133, 134,*
　　135, 159, 160, *161, 162,* 163, 164–65,
　　164, 166–68, *166, 169,* 170, *171, 172,* 173,
　　174, 185–86, 203–5, *203, 207,* 208, *209,* 218
Babington-Smith, Constance, **IV** 94
Bacon, Noel, **II** 37
Bader, Douglas, **I** 120, 127, 131, 132–34, *132, 161,*
　　162, 166, 168
Badoglio, Pietro, **IV** 26
Baggs, Joesph W., **II** 180–81
Bailey (pilot), **III** 61
Baka bombs. *See Ohka* bombs
Baker, Addison, **II** 159, 163, 164, 165, *165,* 166, 167,
　　169
Balch (U.S. naval vessel), **II** 103
Baldinus, Lawrence, **III** 64
Baldwin, J. E. A., **II** 117–18
Balikpapan, **IV** 136
Ball, Albert, **I** 55
Ball, George Eric, **I** 132
Ball-bearing industry, German, **IV** 37, 58, 61
Balloon bombs, **II** 70, *71,* 72
Balloon Command (British), **I** 88
Bangkok, **IV** 131, 132
Banks, William, **IV** 44
Barbarossa, Operation **II** 111; **IV** 19, 80, 82
Barber, Rex T., **II** 106–8
Barlow, R. N. G., **II** 141
Barnes, Richard, **II** 118, 125
Barr, George, **II** 70
Barratt, A. S., **I** 64, 75–76
Bartling, William, **II** 43
Barwell, George C., **II** 161, 167
Bataan (U.S. naval vessel), **III** 120
Bateman, Ed, **I** *163*
Bateson, R. N., **IV** 96–97
Bath (England), **II** 113

Battle (British aircraft), **I** 52–54, *54*, 61–63, *63*, *64*,
    65
Battleship Row (Pearl Harbor), **II** 18, 21, 22
Battleships. *See* by name
Bauer, Harold W., **III** *73*
Bauer, Joseph, **III** 86
Baumter, Albert J., **II** *48*
Baveystock, Leslie, **II** 118, 126
Bayerlein, Fritz, **IV** 99
Beach, John, **II** 128
Beahan, Kermit K., **IV** 211–12
Beakley, W. N., **III** *54*
Beaufighter, **I** 157–59, *157;* **III** 18, 21, 33; **IV** *19, 27,*
    35, *96*
Beaufort, **III** 18
Beaverbrook, William Maxwell Aitken, Lord, **I** 87, *88*
Beckett, Thomas P., **II** 179
Beeson, Duane W., **IV** 63, 64, 67, 73
Belgian aircraft, **I** 73–74
Belgian Army, **I** 36
Belgium, **I** 47, 61, 64, 66, 68; **II** 119. *See also* Belgian
    aircraft; Belgian Army; specific places
Belgrade, **IV** 15
Bell, Gordon A., **II** 69, 70
Belleau Wood (U.S. naval vessel), **III** 107, 108, 121,
    132; **IV** 188
Bellows Field (Hawaii), **II** 18
Benedict, St., **IV** 29
Benedict, Ruth, **IV** 174
Benghazi, **II** 156; **IV** 10
Benham (U.S. naval vessel), **II** 103
Benn, William, **III** 8, 11–12
Bennington (U.S. naval vessel), **IV** 187
Bennison, Bernard, **IV** 230
Benson, William W., **II** 85
Berlin, **I** xiv, 122, 149, 150; **II** 177, 178; **IV** *45*, 46,
    57–61, *62, 65,* 100, 114, 171
Bernburg (Germany), **IV** 54
Betty (Japanese aircraft), **II** 106–8; **III** 9, 55, *56*, 67,
    90, 92–93, 113; **IV** 143, 181–83, 188, 197
Big B. *See* Berlin
Biggin Hill (England), **I** 107, 110–12, 120
Big Week (February 1944), **IV** 54–57
"Big wing" tactic, **I** 162
Birch, John M., **II** 68
Birmingham (U.S. naval vessel), **IV** 145
Bishop, Billy, **I** 55
Bismarck (German naval vessel), **I** 150
Bismarck Sea, Battle of the, **III** 17–23, 90
Bissell, Clayton L., **II** 41, *45*, 46
"Black Day of August 17, The," **III** 27
Black Thursday. *See* Schweinfurt
Black Widow (P-61), **IV** 46, *213*
Blair, Samuel, **III** 44
Blakeslee, Donald, **IV** *57*, 58, 61, 62, 66, 68
Blamey, Sir Thomas, **III** *3*
Blanchard, J. W., **III** 127
Blaskowitz, Johannes, **IV** 120
Blechhammer (Poland), **IV** 100
Blenheim, **I** 50, *51*, 52, 54, *56*, 64, 65, 71, 86–88,
    99–100, 110, 156, 158, 160–61; **II** 42, 43,
    119; **IV** 7, 19,
Blind bombing. *See* Radar

Blitz. *See* London
Blitzkrieg, concept of, **I** 8
Bloody Ridge, Battle of, **III** 66, 67, 75
Blue Goose (U.S. aircraft), **III** *71*, 72
Bochum (Germany), **IV** 40
Bock, Frederick C., **IV** 211, 212
Bogan, Gerald F., **IV** 142, 146, 157
Bomber Command (British), **I** 47, 50–54, 98, 99,
    108, 116, 120, 122; **II** viii, 111, 112–17, 130,
    134, 154, 156, 173, 174, 91. *See also* British
    aircraft; British air units; Royal Air Force
Bomber Command (U.S.). *See* Specific units
Bombers, **I** xii, 3–15. *See also* specific aircraft,
    nationalities
Bond, Charles, **II** 43
Bong, Richard, **III** 40–50, 74; **IV** 63, 67
Booth, G. B., **I** *128*
Borah, William E., **I** 33
Boram airfield (New Guinea), **III** 24, 26
Bormann, Martin, **IV** 116, 117
Borneo, **IV** 136
Boston (aircraft), **II** 119; **III** 21
Bottomley, Sir Norman, **IV** 38, 53
Bouchier, Cecil, **I** 105
Bougainville, **III** 88, 96, 97
Box, A. J. R., **I** 154, 156
Boyington, Gregory, **II** 30–31, 38–41, 43, 45; **III**
    98, 99
Bradley, James L., **IV** 201
Braham, J. R. D., **I** 158
Brand, Christopher, **I** 88
Brandenburg, Ernst von, **I** 9, 10
Brandenburg-Briest, **IV** 115
Brannon, Dale, **III** 59
Brauchitsch, Walther von, **I** 32, 68, 77
Braun, Eva, **IV** 117
Brazi (Rumania), **II** 161, 167
Breamer, Fred A., **II** 66, 67
Bredow, Kurt von, **I** 12
Brereton, Lewis H., **II** *156*, 157–58, *161*, 162, 168,
    172, 175; **III** 6; **IV** 8, 9, 28, 93
Bright, John G., **II** 3, 47
Brighton Belle (British naval vessel), **I** 71
Britain, Battle of, **II** vii, 111, 132, 133; **IV** 21
British aircraft, **II** 34, 36, 113, 123, 130, 147; **IV** 6–7
    10, 18, 20–21, 38, 39, 40, 41, 44, 46, 53–56,
    74, 112, 115, 120
  A-20 (Havoc), **II** 119
  Anson, **II** 116–17
  B-17 (Flying Fortress), **I** *150*, 151
  B-24 (Liberator), **I** 151–52
  Beaufighter, **I** 157–58, *157;* **IV** *19, 27,* 35, *96*
  Blenheim, **I** 50, *51*, 52, 54, *56*, 64, 65, 71, 86–88,
      99–100, 110, 156, 158, 160–61; **II** 42, 43,
      119; **IV** 7, 19
  Buffalo, **II** 31, 32, 34–36, 38, 41
  C-47, **IV** *11*
  Catalina, **I** 151
  Dakota (C-47), **IV** *11*
  Defiant, **I** 87, 88, 99–100, *156*
  F2A (Buffalo), **II** 31, 32, 34–36, 38, 41
  Flying Fortress (B-17), **I** *150*, 151

Gladiator, **I** 42–45, *42, 56*, 87; **IV** 5, 7, 18
Halifax, **II** 116, 117, *122*, 123, 126; **IV** 40
Hampden, **I** 52, 122; **II** 116, 117, *120*, 133
Havoc, **II** 119
Hudson, **I** 37, *70, 123*, 124, 151, 152, *154;* **IV** 19
Hurricane, **I** 12, 42–45, 54–57, 59, 65, 71–73, *73*, 86–88, *87*, 91, 97, 99, 101–4, *101*, 107, 108, 110, 119, 120, 122, 130–34, 156–58, *163;* **II** 32, 41–43, 119, 152; **IV** 7, *8*, 10, *10*, 11, 18, 19, 21
Lancaster, **II** 116, 117, 119, *121, 123*, 126–28, *129*, 132, 135, 137, 140–43, *142, 144*, 145–47, 150; **IV** 37, 39, 40, *40*, 46, 55, *108*
Liberator (B-24), **I** 151–52
Lysander, **I** *54*, 72
Manchester, **II** 116–18, *119*, 125–26
Maryland, **IV** 19
Meteor, **IV** 103, 107
Mosquito, **I** 113, 158; **II** 128, *129*, 150; **IV** 39, 44, 95–97, 114, 120
Mustang (P-51), **IV** 54, 79, 95
Oxford, **I** 113
P-40, **I** 30, 45
P-51 (Mustang), **IV** 54, 79, 95
Proctor, **I** 113
Queen Bee, **IV** 5
Skua, **I** 42, 123; **IV** 19
Spitfire, **I** *159, 160;* **II** 152, 177; **IV** 12, 13, 20–21, 24, 25, 27, 63, 80, 95, *102, 103, 110*
Stirling, **I** 101–2; **II** 116, *117*, 118–23, *124*, 129
Sunderland, **I** *151, 153*
Swordfish, **II** 7; **IV** 5, 19
Tiger Moth, **I** 123; **II** 116–17; **IV** 5
Typhoon, **IV** *79*, 95, 110
Wellington, **I** 52, 53, 75, 76, 122, 152, 154, *155*, 156; **II** 115, *116*, 117, 119, *120*, 121–24, 135–37; **IV** 10, 19, 35, 40
Whitley, **I** 47–48, *48*, 49–50, 52, 75, 76, 122; **II** 116, 117, *125*
British air force. *See* British aircraft; British air units; Royal Air Force
British air units. *See also* Anglo-American air units; Bomber Command; Fighter Command; Fleet Air Arm
  air forces:
    Desert, **IV** 9, 32, 33
    Second Tactical, **IV** 74, 94, 95, 96, 110
    South African, **IV** 11
    Western Desert, **IV** 8, 10
    Women's Auxiliary (WAAF), **I** 93, 111–12, *111*
  groups:
    No. 1, **II** 124; **IV** 120
    No. 2, **II** 119
    No. 3, **I** 122; **II** 117, 119, 120; **IV** 120
    No. 4, **I** 99, 122; **II** 126
    No. 5, **I** 47, 122; **II** 126, 133, 140, 141, 148, 150
    No. 8, **IV** 120
    No. 10, **I** 88, 100, 103, 131, 134, 135
    No. 11, **I** 87–88, 94, 97, 100, 103, 109–12, 116–19, 122–24, 128–31, 134
    No. 12, **I** 88, 99, 112, 118–19, 128, 131

    No. 13, **I** 88, 98, 99
    No. 205, **IV** 33, 35
  squadrons:
    No. 1, **I** 54–56, 59, 62, 73, 75
    No. 3, **I** 73
    No. 6, **IV** 7, 11
    No. 7, **IV** 11
    No. 9, **I** 52, 53
    No. 10, **I** 75; **II** 125
    No. 11, **I** 71, 75
    No. 12 ("Dirty Dozen"), **I** 61, 65; **II** 120
    No. 15, **II** 121
    No. 17, **I** 75, 101
    No. 19, **I** 127, 131
    No. 21, **IV** 96
    No. 29, **I** 158; **II** 133
    No. 30, **IV** 5
    No. 35, **I** 94
    No. 37, **I** 53
    No. 43, **I** 71, 108
    No. 44, **I** 122
    No. 46, **I** 42, 44
    No. 49, **I** 122
    No. 50, **I** 122; **II** 123
    No. 51, **I** 47–50, 75
    No. 54, **I** 90, 104, 112, 129
    No. 55, **IV** 7
    No. 58, **I** 47, 75, 122
    No. 61, **I** 122; **II** 123, 127
    No. 65, **I** 93, 95
    No. 66, **II** 160
    No. 67, **II** 32, 35
    No. 71 ("Eagle"), **I** 162, *163*, 166; **IV** 63
    No. 72, **I** 98, 131
    No. 73, **I** 54, 57, 60, 73, 75, 76; **IV** 7, 10–11
    No. 74, **I** 71, 94, 129, 162
    No. 75 (New Zealand), **I** 154, *155*
    No. 79, **I** 73, 99
    No. 80, **IV** 5
    No. 83, **I** 122; **II** 133, 134
    No. 84, **IV** 5
    No. 87, **I** 54, 56, 58, 73
    No. 88, **I** 65
    No. 92, **I** 129, 131; **IV** 12
    No. 99, **I** 73, 122
    No. 101, **II** 120
    No. 102, **I** 75
    No. 103, **I** 64, 65; **II** 124
    No. 105, **I** 65; **II** 128
    No. 106, **I** 50, 52, 71
    No. 110, **I** 50–52
    No. 111, **I** 104
    No. 121 ("Eagle"), **I** 166
    No. 122, **I** *160*
    No. 133 ("Eagle"), **I** 166
    No. 139, **I** 50, *51*
    No. 142, **I** 65
    No. 145, **I** 71
    No. 149, **I** 52, 53
    No. 150, **I** 54, 64, 65
    No. 152, **I** 108
    No. 185, **II** 120
    No. 207, **II** 117, 119

No. 211, **IV** 5
No. 213, **I** 72
No. 218, **I** 54, 63, 65; **II** 118
No. 220, **II** 37
No. 224, **I** 133
No. 226, **I** 65
No. 242, **I** 75, 127, 132
No. 263, **I** 42, 43, 44
No. 302 (Polish), **I** 26, 133; **IV** 110
No. 303 (Polish), **I** 125, *127*
No. 308 (Polish), **IV** 110
No. 310 (Czech), **I** 127, 133
No. 315 ("Deblin"), **IV** 70
No. 317 (Polish), **IV** 110
No. 340 ("Ile de France"), **I** *164–65*
No. 464, **IV** 96
No. 487, **IV** 96
No. 601, **I** 87, 88
No. 602 ("City of Glasgow"), **I** 52; **IV** 80
No. 603 ("City of Edinburgh"), **I** 52, 53
No. 604, **I** 158
No. 607, **I** 52, 73
No. 609, **I** 95, 166
No. 611, **I** *82*, 131
No. 613, **IV** 96
No. 615, **I** 73
No. 616, **I** 100
No. 617 (X-Squadron), **II** 132–50
British Army (soldiers), **II** 112; **IV** 29. *See also* British
    army units; British Expeditionary Force
British army units
    armies:
        Second, **IV** 108
        Eighth (Western Desert Force), **IV** 5, 7, 15, 24,
            26, 27
    armored forces:
        7th, **IV** 5
    divisions:
        1st Airborne, **IV** 24, 27
British Expeditionary Force (BEF), **I** 54, 56,
    65–66, 68, 69–73, *69*, *73*
British naval units
    Mediterranean Fleet, **IV** 18
    Task Force 57, **IV** 190
British naval vessels
    Acasta, **I** 45
    Ardent, **I** 45
    Ark Royal, **I** 41
    Brighton Belle, **I** 71
    Clyde, **I** 45
    Cossack, **I** 37–38
    Eagle, **IV** 21
    Edinburgh, **I** 52
    Glorious, **I** 41, 42, 44, *45*
    Hood, **I** 52
    Illustrious, **II** 7; **IV** 5
    Mohawk, **I** 52
    Prince of Wales, **II** 73
    Repulse, **II** 73
    Southampton, **I** 52
British Navy. *See* British naval units; British naval
    vessels; Fleet Air Arm; Royal Navy
Broadley, J. A., **IV** 96

Brodie, C. A., **I** 160
Brooke, Sir Alan, **II** *152*
Brooks, G. W., **III** 62
Brooks, John A., **II** 169
Brooks, N. C., **II** 77
Brown (squadron leader), **IV** 88
Brown, C. R., **IV** 180
Brown, George B., **III** 133–35
Brown, George S., **II** 164
Brown, Harry M., **II** 21
Brown, K. W., **II** 147
Browning, Miles, **II** 89–90
Brunswick (Germany), **IV** 48, 54
Brüx (Czechoslovakia), **IV** 100
Bucharest, **II** 164
Buckmaster, Elliot, **II** 97, 103, 104
Buckner, Simon B., Jr., **III** 105
Budapest, **IV** 90
Buffalo (F2A), **II** 31, 32, 34–36, 38, 41, *84*, 108
Bulge, Battle of the, **IV** 108–13
Buna, **III** 10, 17–20
Bunker Hill (U.S. naval vessel), **III** 107, 120, 130, 131;
    IV *194*, *195*
Bunte, Allen, **IV** 61–62, 64
Burbridge, Bransome, **I** 158
Burcher, A. F., **II** 144
Burg (Germany), **IV** 115
Burke, Arleigh, **III** 135
Burma, **II** 5, 6, 29, 34–43. *See also* Flying Tigers
Burma Army, **II** 37, 42
Burma Road, **II** 29, *29*, 30, 37, 46
Burns, John A., **III** 119
Burpee, L. J., **II** 147, 150
Bush (U.S. naval vessel), **IV** 192
Buzzard Patrol, **III** 85, 86
Byers, V. A., **II** 141

C-46, **III** *4*
C-47 (Dakota), **III** *24*, 30, 49; **IV** *11*, 24, 33, *78*, 95,
    110, 111
C-202 (Italian aircraft), **IV** 12, 13, 26
Cabot (U.S. naval vessel), **III** 121, 131; **IV** 146, 147,
    148
Cactus Air Force, **III** 58–60, 61, 65, 66–68, 73
Caiden, Martin, **II** 191
Caldwell, Turner, **III** 59, 62
Calhoun (U.S. naval vessel), **II** 22–23
Callaghan, Daniel J., **III** 83
CAMCO, **II** 30
Campbell, R. J., **II** 117
Campina (Rumania), **II** 161, 163, 169
Canadian air units, Squadron No. 1, **I** 87
Canaris, Wilhelm, **I** 23
Canberra (U.S. naval vessel), **IV** 138
Canning, Douglas S., **II** 106
Caple, C. C. "Capable," **II** 140
Cardinal, Bud, **II** 117
Carl, Marion E., **III** 61, 66, 67, 69, 70
Carlson, Kendell E., **IV** 68
Carmichael, Richard N., **III** 8, 11
Carmody, Doan, **III** 84
Carney, Robert B., **IV** 157
Caroline Islands, **II** 4. *See also* specific islands

Carpet bombing, **IV** 35, 99, *100*
Carpets, radar-jamming, **II** 183, *184*
Carriers. *See* specific carriers, nationalities
Carton de Wiart, Sir Adrian, **I** 41
Carver, John L., **IV** 157
Casablanca Directive, **II** 154
Cassels-Smith, G. R., **IV** 181
Cassin (U.S. naval vessel), **II** 23
Castoldi, Mario, **IV** 26
Catalina (PBY) **I** 151; **II** 18, 80, 83, 84, 86, 92; **III** 16,
      18, *71*, 72, 75, 88
Cate, James Lea, **IV** 162–63
Cavalla (U.S. naval vessel), **III** 127
Celentano, Frank A., **II** 178, *179*, 181, 182, 186
Central Aircraft Manufacturing Corporation **II** 30
Ceylon, **II** 73
Chamberlain, Neville, **I** 33, 73
Chandler, Theodore E., **IV** 181
Chapin, Robert, **IV** 110, *105*
Chappell, C. J., Jr., **II** 12
Chase, William, **II** 84, 86
Cheli, Ralph, **III** 28–29
Chemnitz (Germany), **IV** 114
Chengtu (China), **IV** 130
Chennault, Claire Lee, **II** 27, *28*, 29–43, *45, 46, 47,
      48;* **III** 4; **IV** 128, 129, 133
Chennault, John, **III** 105
Cheshire, Leonard, **II** 126
Chewing, Walter, **III** 110
Chiang Kai-shek, **II** *27*, 30, 37, 41, 42, 45, 46, 57–58,
      60; **III** 4, 114; **IV** 128, 129, 206
Chiang Kai-shek, Madame, **II** 26, *27*, 30, 41, 45, 46, *69*
Chickering, William, **IV** 181
Chiengmai (Thailand), **II** 43
Chikuma (Japanese naval vessel), **II** 12, 98
Childress, Rollin D., **IV** 97
China, **II** 5, 49, 52, 57–58, 60, 66–69. *See also*
      Flying Tigers; specific branches of armed
      forces
Chinese aircraft,
   P-40, **II** 27, *29*, 30–35, *36*, 37, 38, *39*, 40–46, 48
Chinese Air Force, **II** 27, 29, 31; **IV** 128. *See also*
      Chinese aircraft, Flying Tigers
Chinese Army, **II** 6, 41, 42. *See also* Chinese army units
Chinese army units
      Fifth Army, **II** 41
      Sixth Army, **II** 41
Chitose (Japanese naval vessel), **III** 63, 120; **IV** 155,
      156
Chiyoda (Japanese naval vessel), **III** 120, 135; **IV** 155,
      156, 175
Cho, Isomu, **IV** 190, 201
Chokai (Japanese naval vessel), **IV** 153
Choltitz, Deitrich von, **I** 66
Christie, G. P., **I** 160
Christman, Allen, **II** 36, 38
Chrysanthemum and the Sword, The (Benedict), **IV**
      174
Chudoba, Edward, **III** 20–21
Churchill, Clementine, **I** 129
Churchill, Walter, **I** 166
Churchill, Sir Winston, **I** 37, 38, 70, 73, 75–76, 81,
      82, 84, 86, 91, *112,* 122, 123, 124, 129–31,

      134, 135–36, 140, 144, 149, 162; **II** 32, 37,
      111, 114, 130, 136, 150, 151, *152*, 154, 155; **III**
      5, 114; **IV** 9, 16, 64, 105, 118, 181, 206
"Churchill" tank, **I** *112*, 113
"Circus" (tactic), **I** 160–61
Claggett, Bladen D., **IV** 141
Claiborne, Harry C., **II** 30
Clark, Captain, **III** 21
Clark, Alan D., **IV** 135
Clark, James A., **IV** 68
Clark, Mark, **IV** 29
Clarke, "Nobby," **I** 123
Claude (Japanese aircraft) **II** 32, 39
Clemens, Martin, **III** 66
Clever, Robert, **II** 68
Clusters (target indicators), **IV** *41*
Clyde (British naval vessel), **I** 45
Coastal Command (British), **I** 37, 93, 101, 107–8,
      150, 151–52; **II** 113–15. *See also* British
      aircraft
Cobra, Operation, **IV** 97–100
Cochrane, Sir Ralph, **II** 133–34, 138, 140, 141, 145,
      148
Codes, breaking of Japanese, **II** 74, 78, 105
Coen, Oscar, **IV** 63
Coffin, Albert P., **III** 84, 85
Coffin Corner, **II** 178, *179*, 187
Cohen, Cecil, **IV** 120, *121,* 122
Cole, Richard E., **II** 66, 69
Collet, John A., **III** 77
Collins, James F., **II** 86, 87
Cologne, **II** 113–31
Columbia Aguila refinery (Rumania), **II** 169
Combined Bomber Offensive from the United
      Kingdom, **II** 154–55
Combined Chiefs of Staff (Allies), **II** 151, 154,
      155–56. *See also* Ploesti
Commando (C-46), **III** *4*
Compton, Keith K., **II** 159, 161–64, 166, 170, 172
Concordia Vega (Rumania), **II** 167, 172
Congressional Medal of Honor, **II** 21, 67, 165, 170, 172
Coningham, Sir Arthur, **IV** 10, 12
Connery, Augustus V., **III** 49
Cooksey, Clyde W., **IV** *215*
Coral Sea, Battle of the, **II** 74–75, *76,* 77; **III** 10
Corken, Ernest, **I** 152
Corkscrew, Operation, **IV** 21–24
Coronet, Operation, **IV** 206
Corregidor, **II** 73
Corry, Roy, **III** 61
Corsair (aircraft), **III** 88, *89,* 90, *101, 102, 117;* **IV**
      192, 197–99, *200,* 201, *202,* 218
Cossack (British naval vessel), **I** 37–38
Cottbus (Germany), **IV** 114
Coventry (England), **I** 141–43; **IV** 40
Cowpens (U.S. naval vessel), **III** 107, 108, 121, 130
Crace, Rear Admiral, **II** 75
Cram, Jack R., **III** 71, *72*
Creditul Minier refinery (Rumania), **II** 167
Crete, **IV** 16–19
Crews, Sidney W., **III** 33
Cripps, Sir Stafford, **II** 112
Cross, K. B., **I** 44, 45
Crown, Richard, **IV** 100, *105*

Cruisers. *See* specific ships
Culberson, Omer W., **IV** *112*
Cunningham, John, **I** *157*, 158
Curl, James M., **IV** 13
Curtiss (U.S. naval vessel), **II** 23
Curtiss Hawk II, **I** 13–14
Cushing, Wilson J., **IV** 97
Cyprus, **II** 171
Czechoslovakia, **IV** 3

D3A. *See* Val
D4Y. *See* Judy
Dace (U.S. naval vessel), **IV** 141, 142
Dagma airfield (New Guinea), **III** 24, 26–29
Dains, John L., **II** 21
Dakota (C-47), **III** *24*, 30, 49; **IV** *11*, 24, 33, *78*, 95,
    110, 111
Dalglish, James B., **IV** 112
"Dam Buster" bombs, **IV** 114. *See also* specific dams
Dann, C. L., **II** 138–39
Darter (U.S. naval vessel), **IV** 141, 142
Dauntless (SBD), **II** 24, 59, *82*, 84, 87, *92*, *93*, 94, 96,
    98, 100, 101, 108; **III** 12, *50*, 54–55, *54*, 59, 63,
    64, 68, *70*, 71, 72, 75–77, *79*, 83, 84–86, *84*,
    87, 88, 96, *109*, 121; **IV** *183*
Davenport, Dean, **II** 68, 69
Davenport, Merle, **III** 100, 101
Davies, J., **I** 112
Davies, John H., **IV** 170, 204
Davis, George F., **IV** 181
Davis, Leonard K., **III** 69
Davison, Ralph E., **IV** 142, 145
Davy, T. D. H., **I** 62
Daylight precision bombing, **II** 103, 151–56; **III**
    36–37, *47*, *50*, 131, 166–67. *See also* specific
    targets
Daymond, Gregory A., **I** *163*, 166
DC-3. *See* C-47
DeBlanc, Jefferson J., **III** *87*, 88
Decorations. *See* specific decorations
Deere, Alan C., **I** 90–92, 104–6, *104*, 112–13, *129*
Deering, G. A., **II** 142
Defiant (aircraft), **I** 87, 88, 99–100, *156*
Deflection shot, defined, **IV** 15
Deichmann, Paul, **I** 96, 106
Denmark, **I** 37–39
DePoix, Vincent, **III** 55
Derouin, R. J., **II** 80
DeShazer, Jacob, **II** 70
Destroyers. *See* specific destroyers
Devastator (TBD), **II** 24, *81*, 90–93
Dewoitine 520, **I** *74*
Diamare, Gregorio, **IV** 29
"Dicing," **IV** 75
Dickens, B. G., **II** 114
Diehl, John H., **II** 167
Dieter, William J., **II** 68
Dill, Sir John, **I** 76; **II** *45*
Dilley, Bruno, **I** 21
Disney, Walt, studios, **II** 32
Distinguished Flying Cross, **I** 61, 63, 102, 156, 166; **II**
    21, 132
Distinguished Flying Order, **II** 132

Distinguished Service Cross, **IV** 71, 184
Distinguished Service Order, **II** 150
Dohi, Saburo, **IV** 195
Dönitz, Karl, **I** 37
Doolittle, James H., **II** vii, *8*, 47, 49–72, *51*, *58*, *59*,
    61, *62*, *67*, 74; **III** 63, 78; **IV** 11, 12, 28, 53, 105,
    115, 133, 209
Doran, K. C., **I** 50–52
Dornier 17, **I** 11, 14, 16, 25, 55, 57, 71, 90, *94*, 101,
    104, 110–111, *120*, 124, 125, 131, 133, 136; **IV**
    44, 52
Dornier 9, **I** 13; **IV** 83–84
Dornier 217, **IV** 51, 52, 56
Dortmund (Germany), **II** 113; **IV** 40
Douglas, Sholto, **I** 119, 166
Douhet, Giulio, **I** xii, 12
Dowding, Hugh C. T. "Stuffy," **I** 75, *86*, 87–88, 92,
    108, 110, 113, 117, 119, 120, 122, 125,
    127–28, 135–36, 137
Down, Pilot Officer, **I** 152–53
Downing, Arthur L., **IV** 157
Downs (U.S. naval vessel), **III** 23
Dragoon, Operation, **IV** *33*
Dresden (Germany), **IV** 114, 115, *116*, 171, 211
Dugout Sunday, **III** 74, 75
Duisburg (Germany), **IV** *40*
Duke, Neville, **IV** 13
Duncan, Donald W., **II** *50*, 51–53
Dunham, William D., **III** 43, 44
Dunkirk, **I** 68, 69–73, *69*, 93
Dupouy, Parker, **II** 35, 42
Düsseldorf (Germany), **IV** 40
Dutch Harbor (Aleutians), **II** 78, 80

Eagle (British naval vessel), **IV** 21
"Eagle Day" (*Adler Tag*), **I** 85–95
Eagleston, Glenn T., **IV** *112*
Eaker, Ira C., **I** xii; **II** 152, 154–56, 174, 176, 183,
    192; **IV** 28–30, 53
Eaker Plan, **II** 154–55
Eason, Hoyt A., **III** 21
Eason, V. Van, **III** 135
Eastern Island (Midway atoll), **II** 77, 85
Eastern Solomons, Battle of the, **III** 59–63, 74
East Indies, **II** 36
Ebert Friedrich, **I** 4
Echols, Oliver P., **IV** 127
Eden, Anthony, **I** 76
Eder, Georg-Peter, **I** 122
Eder Dam (Germany), **II** 135, 138–40, 145–46
Edinburgh (British naval vessel), **I** 52
Edmonds, Walter D., **III** 12
Edsall, Eric, **I** 112–13
Eglin Field (Florida), **II** 53, 55
Egusa, Takashige, **II** 21
Egypt, **IV** 5, 19, 22
Eindhoven airfield (Belgium), **IV** 110
Einstein, Albert, **IV** 208
Eisenhower, Dwight D., **II** 151, 155; **IV** 11, *24*, *28*, 29,
    32, 74, 76, 92, 93, 95, 108, 115, 118–20
El Alamein, **II** 156; **IV** 7, 8, 10, 22
El Aouina air base (Tunisia), **IV** *12*
Elizabeth (wife of George VI), **II** *149*
Elliott, George, **II** 14–15

Elliott, George F. (U.S. naval vessel). *See George F. Elliott*
Ellis, William E., **IV** 146
Elsner, B. A., **IV** 131–32
Elton, Albert M., **IV** 58, 60
Emden (German naval vessel), **I** 50, 51
Emmons (U.S. naval vessel), **IV** 192
Enden (Germany), **II** 186
Endo, Akiyoshi, **IV** 215
Engines, **I** 48, 113, 130; **IV** 58. *See also* specific aircraft
England. *See* Great Britain
Engler, Howard, **IV** 133
Eniwetok, **III** 109, 117
Ennepe Dam (Germany), **II** 140
Ent, Uzal G., **II** 157, *158*, 159, 163, 164, 166, 172
Enterprise (U.S. naval vessel), **II** 12, 15, 24, 52, 53, 57, 58, 59, 74, 79, 80, *81*, *88*, 89, 90, 92, 94, 97, 98, 101; **III** *50*, 53, 55, 57, 59, 60–62, *63*, 66, 69, 74–75, *76*, 77, 79, *80*, 81, 83, 84, 85, 107, 108, *110*, 111, 113–14, 119, 121, 126; **IV** 145, 147, *199*, 201
Eroni, Corporal, **III** 66
Essen (Germany), **II** 113, 114, 130; **IV** 39–40
Essex (U.S. naval vessel), **III** 107, 111, 113, 121, 130, **IV** 142, 143, 144, 145, 147, 155, 156, 178, 193, *200*
Estes, Glen, **III** 85
Evers, W. H., **I** 41
Ewa air base (Hawaii), **II** 18

F2A (Buffalo), **II** 31, 32, 34–36, 38, 41, *84*, 108
F4F (Wildcat), **II** 12, 24–25, 59, *75*, *76*, 84, *88*, 90, 93, 96, 101, 108; **III** 54–56, *58*, 59, *60*, 61, 62, 66, 68, *69*, 70–73, 74, 75, 77, *80*, 83, 84, 86, 87, 88, 90, 91, 96, 111, 126, 130, 134; **IV** 146, 151, *153*
F4U-1 (Corsair), **III** 88, *89*, 90, 93–94, *95*, 96–97, 99, 100, *101*, *102*, *117*
F-5, **III** 35
F6F (Hellcat), **II** 81; **III** 99, 104, *110*, *111*, *112*, 113–14, 117, 119, 121, 122, *127*, 130–32, 125; *IV 136*, 138, 141, *142*, *143*, 144–47, 151, 155, 177, 188, 192–94, 201, 218
F-3, **IV** 164, 165
Fahey, James J., **IV** 196
Faktor, Leland, **II** 68
Falkson, Jack, **I** 43
Fanshaw Bay (U.S. naval vessel), **IV** 151
Farrow, William G., **II** 59, 61, 69–70
"Fat Man" (atomic bomb), **IV** 211, *212*
Faulkner, Ted S., **IV** 161
Faurot, Robert, **III** 16–17, 21
Fauth, John, **II** 42–43
Feliton, James A., **III** 88
Felmy, Helmuth, **I** 37
Ferebee, Thomas W., **IV** 210
Fergusson, Bernard, **I** 47
Fieberling, Langdon K., **II** 87
Field, R. M., **I** 75, 76
Fighter Command (British), **I** 72, 75, 86–88, 93, 97–116, 119, 120, 122–25, 127, 128–29, 130, 136; **II** 115, 119, 133. *See also* specific aircraft, units

Fighter Command (U.S.) *See* specific units
Fighters. *See* specific aircraft, nationalities
"Finger four" formation, **I** 162
Fink, Christian, **III** 64
Fink, Johannes, **I** 90, 93–95
Finland, **I** 35–37, 38
Finucane, Brenden "Paddy," **I** *167*, 168
Fire bombs, **III** 125; **IV** 169, 170. *See also* Napalm
Fire storms, **IV** 41
Fitzgerald, John E., **II** 52–53
Fitzmaurice, Donald, **II** 68
Fitzpatrick, A., **II** *80*
Fiume (Austria), **IV** 54
Flatney, James, **III** 80
Flavelle, Grian, **II** 161, 162, 172
Flax, Operation, **IV** 13
Fleet Air Arm (British), **I** 87, 107–8, 116; **II** 7
Fleet Problem xix, **II** 6–7
Fleming, R. W., **IV** 181
Fleming, Richard E., **II** 100, 101
Fletcher, Frank J., **II** 74, *77*, 79, 80, 82, 84, 90, 97, 98, 101; **III** 53, 54, 57, 60, 61, 63
Flying bombs. *See* V-weapons
Flying Fish (U.S. naval vessel), **III** 125
Flying Fortress (B-17), **I** xii, xiii, *150*, 151; **II** 15, 18, *20*, 78, 81, 82, 84, 87, 88, 98, 101, 151, 152, *153*, 172, 173–74, *174*, *176*, 177–78, *179*, *180*, 181, 182, 185, *186*, *187*, 188, 189; **III** 5, 7, 7, 8, 9, *10*, 11, 12, 14, 16, 18, 21, 22, 24, 26, 32, 54, 65, 70, 72; **IV** 10, 11, 27, 29, 30, *32*, 38, 40, 48, *48*, 50, 51, *53*, 54, 55, 57, 58, *59*, *68*, 92–94, *95*, 97, 99, *114*, 115, 118, 120, *121*, *122*, 127, 164
Flying Tigers, **II** vii, 26–48; **III** 98
Flying Training Command (British), **I** 119; **II** 114
Flynn, David, **II** 25
Focke-Wulf (FW) 190, **I** 25, 168; **II** 111, 154, *154*, 174–75, 179, 181, 186–87; **IV** 46, 48, 49, 51, 55, 56, 58, 59, 60, 63, 76, 77, 91, 96, 108–10, *118*
Focke-Wulf (FW) 200, **I** 40–41, *151*, 152–54
Foggia (Italy), **IV** 27, 28
Folgore (Italian aircraft) **IV** 26
Ford Island (Hawaii), **II** 15, 18, 22
Formosa, **IV** 138, 139
Fort, J., **II** 145
Foss, Joseph J., **III** 69, *74*, 75, 86, 90
Foster, Emma Jane, **II** 47
Fowler, Richard L., **IV** 152, 153
Fox, Harry, **II** 42
France, **I** 33, 64–66, 74–77; **II** 4–5, 29, 119; **IV** 32, *33*, 106, 107. *See also* specific branches of French armed forces, locations
Frances (Japanese aircraft), **IV** 177, *180*
Franco, Francisco, **I** 15
Frankfurt (Germany), **II** 183
Frankland, Noble, **II** 147
Franklin, C. E., **II** 147
Franklin (U.S. naval vessel), **IV** 145, 147, *187*, 188
Fraser, J. W., **II** 144
Frazier, Everette E., **III** 23
Frazier, Kenneth D., **III** 61
Freeman (wing commander), **III** 99

Freiburg (Germany), **IV** 40
French aircraft, **I** *74*
French Air Force, **I** 54
French Army, **I** 72. *See also* French army units
French army units
First Army, **I** 68
Ninth Army, **I**, 66, 68
Seventh Army, **I** 68
Freyberg, Bernard, **IV** 16, 18
Fridge, Benjamin, **III** 36
Frölich, Stephan, **IV** 7
Fuchido, Mitsuo, **II** 9, 12–15, 17, 21–24, 104
Fukudome, Shigeru, **II** 7; **IV** 138, 140, 142, 145, 177, 181
Fuso (Japanese naval vessel), **IV** 145
FW. *See* Focke-Wulf

Gabreski, Francis, **IV** 69, *70*, 71, 72–74, 80
Galer, Robert E., **III** 65, 66
Gallagher, O. D., **II** 42
Gallagher, Raymond K., **III** 43
Gallagher, T. A., **II** 62
Gallagher, Wilmer E., **II** 94, 98
Galland, Adolf, **I** 11, 15, 26, *65*, 73–74, 132, 166, 168; **IV** 51, 80, 101, 103, 104–5
Gambier Bay (U.S. naval vessel), **IV** 151, *152*, 153
Garden, Operation, **IV** 108
Gardner, Charles, **I** 57
Gardner, Matthias B., **III** 126
Garick, Steven, **IV** 71
Garland, Donald E., **I** 61–63
Gassner, Alfred, **I** 41
Gaulle, Charles de, **I** 76
Gay, George H., **II** *91*, 92–93
Gee (navigational device), **II** 112–14, 119, 120
Geiger, Roy S., **III** 66, 68–70, 72; **IV** 201
Geisler, Hans Ferdinand, **IV** 67
Genda, Miroru, **II** 7
Gentile, Don S., **IV** *57*, 61–63, *64*, 65, *66*, 67
Genyo Maru (Japanese naval vessel), **III** 133
George VI. King of England, **I** 56, 149; **II** *118, 149*
George F. Elliott (U.S. naval vessel), **III** 56
German aircraft, **II** 169–71, 173–74, 176–82, 185–89; **IV** 6, 7, 10, 12, 13, 15, 18, 19, 22, 28, 33, 48, 51, 55, 56, 57, 58, 61, 68, 69, 71, *72*, 74, 78–79, 82, 85, 86, 109, 110, 111, 112, 115
Arado, **IV** 117
Dornier 17, **I** 11, 14, 16, 25, 55, 57, 71, 90, *94*, 101, 104, 110–11, *120*, 124, 125, 131, 133, 136
Dornier 19, **I** 13; **IV** 83–84
Focke-Wulf (FW) 190, **I** 25, 168; **II** 111, 154, *154*, 174–75, 179, 181, 186–87; **IV** 46, 48, 49, 51, 55, 56, 58, 59, 60, 63, 76, 77, 91, 96, 108–10, *118*
Focke-Wulf (FW) 200, **I** 40–41, *151*, 152–54
Gotha, **I** 9
Heinkel 51, **I** 15, 16
Heinkel 52, **I** 15
Heinkel 59, **I** *91*
Heinkel 70, **I** 41
Heinkel 111, **I** 11, 13, 14, 16, 17, 25, 27, *28, 29*, 30–32, 41–43, 52, *56*, 66, 98, *99, 100*, 110,
124, 133, 135, 136, *139, 152*, 158; **IV** 40, *82*, 85, *86*
Heinkel 118, **I** 14
Heinkel 177, **IV** 56
Heinkel 280, **IV** 106
Henschel 123, **I** 25; **IV** *82*
Junkers (Ju), **I** 6
Junkers (Ju) 52, **I** *14*, 15, 17, 31–32, 40–43, 61, 64; **IV** 12, 13, *14, 17*, 18, 19, 85
Junkers (Ju) 87 (Stuka), **I** 13–16, *14*, 21, *22*, 25, 26, *27, 29*, 30, 41, 43, 44, 71, 72, 86, 90, 94–96 *97*, 100, 103, 107–8; **II** 32, 181; **IV** 7, 82, 83, 86, 87, *88*, 89, 218
Junkers (Ju) 88, **I** 13, 14, 25, *41*, 42, 52–53, 93, 94, 95, 99, *100*, 124, 133, 136, 152; **IV** 7, 27, 44, 48, 54, 56, 78, 110, *118*
Junkers (Ju) 89, **I** 13; **IV** 83–84
Messerschmitt (Me) 108, **I** 36
Messerschmitt (Me) 109, **I** 14, 15, 25, 26, *44*, 51–54, 60, 65, 71, 72, 73–74, 76, *85*, 87, 90, *91*, 92, 95, 100–1, 103–6, *106*, 107, 108, 110, 122, 124, *126*, 127, 131, 134, 136, 137, *145*, *159*, 160, 162; **II** 111, 154, *154*, 157, 169, 174, 186, 187; **IV** 7, 12, 13, 15, 19, 21, *37*, 48, 51, 54, 58, *59*, 62, 83, 87, 91, 92, 109–10
Messerschmitt (Me) 110, **I** 25, 27, 30, 40, 43, 53, 71, 72, 87, 90, 92–95, *92*, 98–100, 103–5, 107, 115–17, *117*, 124, 127, 134–36, 154; **II** 32, 124–25, 157, 181; **IV** 7, *9*, 12, 44, *44*, 48, 49, 51, 55, 56, 70–71
Messerchmitt (Me) 162, **IV** 103
Messerschmitt (Me) 262, **IV** 100–5, *106, 107*, 115
Messerschmitt (Me) 323, **IV** *14*
Messerschmitt (Me) 410, **IV** 56
Storch, **IV** 6
German Air Force, **I** 4, 6, 8, 11. *See also* German aircraft; German air units; Luftwaffe
German air units
"4th Squadron," **I** 6–7
Englandgeschwader, **I** 9
Erprobungsgruppe 210, **I** 92, 93, 100, 103–4
Fleigerdivision 7, **IV** 56
Fliegerkorps, **I** 85
2 (II) **I** 85; **IV** 10, 76, 77
8 (VIII) **I** 85, 86, 108
10 (X) **IV** 6, 10, 19
11 (XI) **IV** 18
Jagdgeschwader, **I** 25
1, **IV** 54
2 ("Richthofen"), **I** 65, 159–60
7, **IV** 103
11, **IV** 54
26, **I** 90, *102*, 132, 159–60; **II** 154; **IV** 76
27, **I** 51, 53, 65, 74, *102*, **IV** 7, 8, 15
51, **I** 85, 90, 126
77, **I** 44, 52, 53
104, **IV** 109
300, **IV** 46
301, **IV** 46
302, **IV** 46
Jagdverband 44, **IV** 103
Kampfgeschwader,
2, **I** 90, 93

3, **I** 101, 131
26, **I** 98
27, **I** 27
30, **I** 52
40, **I** 152
51, **IV** 107
54, **I** 30, 52, 66, 127
100, **I** 140, 144
Lehrgeschwader 1, **I** 85, 103
Luftflotte, **I** 24–25
    1, **I** 24–25, 37; **IV** 25
    2, **I** 37, 66, 85–86, 93, 94,
        96–97, 100, 105; **IV** 10, 25, 28
    3, **I** 85, 86, 93, 96–97, 100, 103,
        105, 146; **II** 111; **IV** 74, 80
    4, **I** 24–25; **IV** 15
    5, **I** 39, 40, 85, 93, 96–97, 99, 100, 105, 109
    6, **IV** 117
Nachtjagdfliegerkorps 12 (XII), **IV** 46
    1, **I** 21
    2, **IV** 86
    77, **I** 108
Zerstörergeschwader,
    26, **I** 94
    76, **I** 98
German Army (soldiers), **I** 4–9, 12; **IV** *16*, 18, 19, 85,
    109. *See also* Wehrmacht
German army units
    Afrika Korps, **II** vii
    armies:
        Eighteenth, **I** 66
        Eighth, **I** 24, 30, 32
        Fifth Panzer, **IV** 109
        Fourteenth, **I** 24; **IV** 35
        Fourth, **I** 21, 24, 64
        Sixth, **IV** 84, 85
        Sixth SS Panzer, **IV** 109
        Tenth, **I** 24, 30
        Third, **I** 21, 24
        Twenty-fifth, **IV** 118
    army groups:
        A, **I** 68
        C, **I** 34
        North, **I** 24, 25
        Panzer Group Kleist, **I** 64, 68
        South, **I** 24, 25, 30
    corps:
        XIV, **IV** 35
        XIX, **I** 68
        XXXIX, **I** 66
        Afrika Korps, **II** vii; **IV** 5, 7, 10, 11, 13, 15, 22
    divisions:
        1st Parachute, **IV** 25
        7th Panzer, **I** 64
        12th SS Panzer, **IV** 79
        17th Panzer, **IV** 97
        21st Panzer, **IV** 79
        "Hermann Göring," **IV** 25
        Panzer Lehr, **IV** 79, 99
    regiments:
        1st Parachute (Fallschirmjäger-Regiment), **I** 64;
            IV 17
        9th Infantry, **I** 8

    100th Mountain, **IV** 18
    902nd, **IV** 99
German General Staff, **I** 4–5, 9–10, 12
German High Command, **II** 175, 182
German Imperial Navy. *See* German Navy
German naval vessels, **I** 35, 150–54; **II** 151, 154; **IV** *14*,
    37–39
    Admiral Scheer, **I** 50, 51
    Altmark, **I** 37–38
    Bismarck, **I** 150
    Emden, **I** 50, 51
    Gneisenau, **I** 45, 52, 150, 168
    Graf Spee, **I** 35, 37
    Karlsruhe, **I** 45
    Königsberg, **I** 45
    Prinz Eugen, **I** 168
    Scharnhorst, **I** 45, 52, 150, 168
    Tirpitz, **II** 134, 137, 138, 150, 168
German Navy, **I** 45, 84, 85; **II** 155. *See also* German
    naval vessels
Germany, **I** xiii, 154; **II** viii, 5, 29, 111, 112,
    155–56, 172. *See also* specific branches of armed
    forces, cities
Gerow, Francis, **II** 179
Gerstenberg, Alfred, **II** 157
Geselbracht, Henry, **II** 44
Ghormley, Robert L., **III** 9, 16, 23, 53, 54, 60, 66, 73
Gibson, Guy Penrose, **I** 58; **II** viii, 132–50
Gibson, John, **I** 102
Gift, Ronald, **III** 133
Gilbert, Henry, **II** 34
Gilbert Islands, **II** 6; **III** 107–14
Gilmour, R. S., **II** 121
Gilonske, Walter W., **IV** 131
Gilpin, George, **II** 127–28
Ginga. See Frances
Gise, William, **III** 93
Gladiator, **I** 42–45, *42, 56,* 87; **IV** 5, 7, 18
Gliders, **IV** *17,* 18, 24, *77, 78*
Glorious (British naval vessel), **I** 41, 42, 44, *45*
Gloucester, Cape, **III** 102
Glover, Fred W., **IV** 67
Gneisenau (German naval vessel), **I** 45, 52, 150, 168
Gnys, W., **I** 26
Godfrey, John, **IV** *64, 65, 66*
Goebbels, Joseph, **III** 113, 130, 148;
        IV 24–25, 40, 41–42, 46, 58, 116, 117
Gonzales, Manuel, **II** 24
Goodson, James, **IV** 67
Goovers, J., **III** 80
Göring, Hermann, **I** 7, 9–12, *10,* 24, 27, 33, *34,* 36,
        38–40, 68, *77,* 84–85, 89, 92, 96, *97,* 106,
        107, 108–9, 110, 122, 124, 127, 137, 140, 143;
        II 121, 130–31; **IV** 8, 10, 16, 42, 43–44, 46,
        47, 57, 58, 64, 77, 80, 85, 101, 109, 116–17,
        119
Gotha (German aircraft), **I** 9
Gotha (Germany), **IV** 54, 55
Gothic Line, **IV** 32, 33
Goto, Inichi, **II** 17
Gould, Ernest D., **IV** *60*
Graf Spee (German naval vessel), **I** *35,* 37
Grafton-Underwood air base (England), **II** *181,* 182

Graham, R., II *112*
Grammell, I. F., II *80*
Gray, James F., II 90, 92
Gray, Robert M., II 68
Gray, Thomas, I 62–63
Graziani, Rodolfo, IV 5, 7
Great Britain (England), II 4–5, 6; IV 8, 41, 42, 56–57. *See also* British aircraft; British air units; British Army; British army units; British naval units; British naval vessels; British Navy; Royal Air Force
Greater East Asia Co-Prosperity Sphere, II 5
Greece, IV 3, 5, 15
Green, S., II 147
Greene, Paul, II 34
Greening, Charles Ross, II 53, 54, 56
Green Islands, III 102, *103*
Greenlaw, Harvey, II 27, 38–39
Greenlaw, Olga, II 39
Gregory, W. J., II 158
Greim, Robert Ritter von, IV 117, 118, *119, 120,* 123
Grice, Richard, I 111
Griffin, A., I 50
Groener, Wilhelm, I 4
Grohé, Joseph, II 130, 131
Grosse Schlag, Der, IV 109
Guadalcanal, II 105; III 17, 18, 52–103
Guam, II 4–5; III 114, 119, 122, 126, 131, 132, 136
Guderian, Heinz, I *26,* 65; IV 113
Guernica (Spain), I *16–17,* 142
Gunn, Paul I., III 12, 14, 18, 20, 23
Gunther, Siegfried, I 41
Gunther, Walter, I 41
Gustav Line, IV 27–29, 31, 33
Guterman, J., II 147
Guthrie, Anthony, I 137
Gutt, Fred, III 6

H2S (radar), IV 40, 48
H2X (radar), II 183; IV 48, *49, 68,* 115
Haberman, Roger, III 72, 80
Hackleback (U.S. naval vessel), IV 193
Hagie, Bradford, III 130
Haguro (Japanese naval vessel), III 127
Halberstadt (Germany), IV 48, 49
Halder, Franz, I 37
Halifax (British aircraft), II 116, 117, *122,* 123, 126; IV 40
Hall, Donald P., III 14, 24, 26
Hall, Grover C., Jr., IV 67
Hallmark, Dean, II 68, 70
Halsey, William Frederick, II *8,* 12, 24, *52,* 53, 57–61, 105; III 23, 38, 73, 90, 93, 96, 119; IV 136–42, 145, 147–49, *150,* 151, 152, 154, *155,* 156–59, 175
Halverson, Harry, IV 8
Halwiwa training field (Hawaii), II 18, 21
Hamakaze (Japanese naval vessel), IV 193
Hamburg (Germany), II 113–15, 176; IV 40–42, *43,* 44, 171
Hamilton, Duke of, I 146
Hamilton, Henry B., III 61
Hammann (U.S. naval vessel), II *103,* 104

Hammer, Maax, II 31
"Hamp" ("Hap"; Japanese aircraft), III *47,* 48
Hampden, (British aircraft), I 52, 122, II 116, 117, *120,* 133
Hancock (U.S. naval vessel), IV 178, 194
Hanoi, II 29, 33
Hansell, Haywood S., II *174;* IV 135, 163, 167, 168
Hansen, Charles H., IV 130
Hanson, Robert M., III 97, *98*
Hara, Chuichi, II 75; III 60
Hardeman (ensign), II 80
Hardison, Osborne B., III 79
Harmon, Millard F., II 54
Harris, Sir Arthur T., I 47–48, 148; II 111, 112–15, *112,* 118, 119, 130, 133, 135–36, 141, 145, 147, *148,* 154, 156, 173; III 39, 40, 44, 46, 52–53, 55, 92, 95, 96, 99, 115
Harris, George W., II 186
Harris, Leroy, III 80
Harris (U.S. naval vessel), IV 181
Haruna (Japanese naval vessel), II 87, 98; III 68–70, 77; IV 187, 193, 194
Hatanaka, Kenji, IV 214
Havoc (A-20), II 18, 119; III 12, *13, 45;* IV *94,* 95
Hawaii, II 9, 11–12, 73, 77. *See also* specific locations
Hedrick, Roger, III 100
Hein. See Tony
Heinkel 51, I 15, 16
Heinkel 52, I 15
Heinkel 59, I *91*
Heinkel 70, I 41
Heinkel 111; I 11, 13, 14, 16, 17, 25, 27, *28, 29,* 30–32, 41–43, 52, *56,* 66, 98, *99, 100,* 110, *124, 133, 135,* 136, *139,* 152, 158; IV 40, *82,* 85, *86*
Heinkel 118, I 14
Heinkel, 177, IV 56
Heinkel 280, IV 106
Heinrici, Gotthard, IV 115
Helbig, Jochen, I 103
Held, Alfred, I 52
He!en (Japanese aircraft), III *28*
Helena (U.S. naval vessel), II 23
Hellcat (F6F), II 81; III 99, 104, *110, 111, 112,* 113–14, 117, 119, 121, 122, *127,* 130–32, 135; IV *136,* 138, 141, *142, 143,* 144–47, 151, 155, 177, 188, 192–94, 201, 218
Helldiver (SB2-C), III 121, 135; IV 142, 146, 147, *148, 157,* 193, 194, 218
Helmick, Richard, IV 58, 60
Henderson, Elspeth, I 112
Henderson, Lofton B., II 84, 87, 88, 105
Henderson, Neville, I 33
Henderson Field (Guadalcanal), II 105; III 55, 58–59, *59–60,* 65, 66–75, 82, 84, 86
Henebry, John P., III 36, 37
Henschel (German aircraft), I 25; IV 82
Hermann, Hajo, IV 46
Hermann, Operation, IV 109
Herndon, Nolan, II 68
Hess, Rudolf, I 146
Hickam Field (Hawaii), II 15, 18, *20,* 22
Hiei (Japanese naval vessel), III 68, 83, 84, 86

Hilger, John A., **II** 53, 55, 56, 61, 63, 64, *69*
Hill, David L. "Tex," **II** *37,* 38, 47, 48
Hillary, Richard, **I** 112
Hilton, James, **II** 67
Himmelbetten, **IV** 44, *45,* 46
Himmler, Heinrich, **I** 23; **IV** 116
Hindenburg, Paul von, **I** 4, 8, 9, 12
Hine, Raymond, **II** 106–8
Hirano, Takeshi, **II** 24
Hirohito, Emperor, **III** 86, 136; **IV** 174, 176, 177, 205, 206, 207, 211, 212–13, 215
Hiroshima, **IV** 115, 171, 207, 209, 210, *211*
Hiryu (Japanese naval vessel), **II** 3, 78, 79, 87, 94, 96–99, 108
Hit and run principle, **II** 31, 35
Hite, Robert, **II** 70
Hitler, Adolf, **I** xiii, 3, 4, 7, 8, 9–12, *10,* 15, 21–22, 23, 33–39, *34,* 76, 77, 89, 104, 121–22, 146; **II** vii, 5, 30, 111, 113, 130–31, 148, 155, 172, 177, 191; **IV** 3, *4,* 7–11, 15, 16–19, 22, 25, 32, 42–43, 44, 46, 47, 51, 56, 57, 79, 80, 82–86, 94, 95–96, 101, 103, 105–9, 112, 113, 115–17
"Hitler first" strategy, **III** 6
Hively, Howard, **IV** 63, 67
Hiyo (Japanese naval vessel), **II** 84, 90, 120, 133–35
Hoel (U.S. naval vessel), **IV** 151
Hoenmanns, Erich, **I** 36
Hofer, Ralph K. "Kid," **IV** 67
Hoffman, Louis, **II** 39–41
Hohne, Otto, **I** 66
Holder, Paul, **II** 118
Holland, **I** 47, 61, 64, 66, *67;* **II** 119; **IV** 118–22
Holmberg, Paul, **II** 90, 94, 97
Holmes, Besby, **II** 106, *107,* 108
Holmes, Ray T., **I** 131–32
Honeychurch, Charles, **II** 117
Hong Kong, **II** 36, 73
Honolulu (U.S. naval vessel), **II** 23
Hood (British naval vessel), **I** 52
Hoover, Travis, **II** 56, 61
Hopgood, John V., **II** 141, 143, 144, 149
Hopkins, James I., **IV** 211
Hornet (U.S. naval vessel), **II** 12, 50, 52–53, 54, 55, 56, *57,* 59, 60, *61, 62,* 63, 66, 69, *79,* 80, 87, 89, 90, 97, 98, 101; **III** 63, 67, 74–80, 120; **IV** 156, 188
"Horse" gliders, **IV** *77, 78*
Horsley, Norman, **II** 118, 126
Hosho (Japanese naval vessel), **II** 78, 79
Hosogaya, Moshiiro, **II** 78
Houston (U.S. naval vessel), **IV** 139
Howard, James H., **II** *38,* 44–45; **IV** 49, 51, *52*
Howes, Bernard H., **IV** 118
Ho Yang Ling, **II** 66
Hubbard, Raymond B., **II** 168
Hudson (British aircraft), **I** 37, *70, 123,* 124, 151, 152, *154;* **IV** 19
Huff, Sargent, **III** 11
Hughes, Lloyd, **II** 169, *170,* 172
Hughes (U.S. naval vessel), **II** 101, *102*
Hump, the, **II** 46–48; **III** 4; **IV** 130, 131, 133
Humphries, H. R., **II** 141
Huntington, Robert, **II** 92

Hurricane (aircraft), **I** 12, 42–45, 54–57, 59, 65, 71–73, *73,* 86–88, *87,* 91, 97, 99, 101–4, *101,* 107, 108, 110, 119, 120, 122, 130–34, 156–58, *163;* **II** 32, 41–43, 119, 152; **IV** 7, 8, 10, *10,* 11, 18, 19, 21, 84
Hutchinson, David W., **III** 23
Hutchinson, R. G., **II** *142*
Huth (German Generalmajor), **IV** 56
Huth Joachim, **I** 94
Hyakutake, Harukichi, **III** 68–70, 73–75, 82–83
Hyuga (Japanese naval vessel), **IV** 155

I-15 (Russian aircraft), **IV** 84
I-16 (Russian aircraft), **I** 16; **IV** 83
I-21 (Japanese naval vessel), **III** 79
I-26 (Japanese naval vessel), **III** 66
I-53 (Russian aircraft), **IV** 83
I-175 (Japanese naval vessel), **III** 110
I-186 (Japanese naval vessel), **II** 102–4
Iceberg, Operation, **IV** 190–91
Ichiki, Kiyanao, **III** 58
Ichimaru, Toshinosuka, **III** 90
Ichinomiya (Japan), **IV** 205
I-go Sakusen operation, **III** 90–93
Illustrious (British naval vessel), **II** 7; **IV** 5
Ilyushin 2 (Sturmovik), **IV** 84
Imajuku, Jiichiro, **III** 78
Impact (publication), **II** 191
Independence (U.S. naval vessel), **III** 107
India, **II** 73. *See also* specific bases
Indianapolis (U.S. naval vessel), **IV** 208
Indo-China, **II** 29
Industrial sites, bombing of, **II** viii, 113, 154, 174–76. *See also* Strategic bombing; specific sites
Ise (Japanese naval vessel), **IV** 155
Ismay, Hastings, **I** 76
Isokaze (Japanese naval vessel), **IV** 155
Italian aircraft, **IV** 22
  C-202, **IV** 12, 13, 26
  Folgore 202, **IV** 26
Italian Air Force (Regia Aeronautica), **IV** 5, 10, 19, 24
Italian Army (soldiers), **IV** 5
Italian army units, Tenth Army, **IV** 5
Italian naval vessels, *Roma,* **IV** 27
Italian navy, **II** 7
Italy, **I** 75–76; **II** 5, 7; **IV** 3, 5, 19, 26–27. *See also* specific branches of armed forces, cities
Itaya, Shigeru, **II** 14
Ito, Seiichi, **IV** 190, 192–94
Iwo Jima, **IV** 163, 164, *184, 185, 186*

J2M. *See* Jack
Jack (Mitsubishi J2M), **IV** *167*
Jacobs, Randolph, **II** 182
Japan, **II** 4–5, 72, 74, 78, 105; **IV** 212–13, 214, *214. See also* specific battles, branches of armed forces, cities
Japanese aircraft, **II** 7, 14, 22, 33–36, 41–43, 48, 78, 83, 96–97, 105; **III** 11, 14, 19, 22, 24, 26–30, 34, 38, 42–46, 55, 59, 61, 62, 65, 69, 74–76, 79, 80, 92, 93, 96, 97, 117, 122, 123, 126, *128,* 130–32, 135; **IV** 138–39, 140, 142, 145, 148, 164, 165, 170, 178, 181–84, 188, 190

A6M. *See* Japanese aircraft: Zero
A6M2-N (Rufe), **III** 88, 100
A6M3 (Hamp), **III** *47, 48*
Aichi D4Y. *See* Japanese aircraft: Judy
B5N. *See* Japanese aircraft: Kate
Betty, **II** 106–8; **III** 9, *55, 56*, 67, 90, 92–93, 113
Claude, **II** 32, 39
D3A. *See* Japanese aircraft: Val
D4Y. *See* Japanese aircraft: Judy
Hamp (Hap; A6M3), **III** *47, 48*
Frances, **IV** 177, *180*
Helen, **III** *28*
Irving, **IV** 165
Jack, **IV** *167*
Jill, **III** *119*, 120, 127, 130, 132
Judy, **III** 120, 127, 130, 132; **IV** 145, 177, 184, *191*
Kate, **II** 9, 12, *13*, 14–18, 21, *23*, 32, 80, 83, *85;* **III** 61, 62, 76, *77*, 78–80, 90, 97, *114*, 120
Kawasaki Ki. 45 (Nick), **IV** 165, 198, 199
Kawasaki Ki. 61 (Tony), **III** *28*, 98, 100; **IV** 143, 165, *167*, 182, 192
Ki. 43, *See* Japanese aircraft: Oscar
Ki. 44. *See* Japanese aircraft: Tojo
Ki. 45. *See* Japanese aircraft: Nick
Ki. 61. *See* Japanese aircraft: Tony
L2D, **III** 49
Mitsubishi. *See* specific aircraft
Nakajima, **III** 35
Nakajima Ki. 43 (Oscar), **III** 27, 28; **IV** 130–31, 143
Nakajima Ki. 44 (Tojo), **III** 101, 102
Nakajima L2D, **III** 49
Nate, **II** 39
Nell, **III** 9, 90, 114
Nick, **IV** 165, 198, 199
Oscar, **III** 27, 28; **IV** 130–31, 143
Rufe (A6M2-N), **III** 88, 100
Sally, **II** 32–33; **III** *23, 24, 25,* 41
Tabby, **III** *49*
Tojo, **III** 101, 102
Tony, **III** *28*, 98, 100; **IV** 143, 165, *167*, 182, 192
Val, **II** 9, 12, *14,* 15, *16*, 17, *18*, 21, 22, 83, *85;* **III** 55, 62, 73, 76–80, 90–92, 93, 96, 120, 124, 134; **IV** 143, 196, 197
Zeke, **II** 105, 106; **III** 28, 33, 34, *61*, 89, 90–92, *90, 93*, 95, 96, 99–102, 111, 120, 127, 130, 132, 134, *135;* **IV** 142–44, 154, 155, 163, *164*, 165, 167, 182, 183, 184, 188, 192, 195, 196, 199
Zero (A6M), **II** vii, 9, *10*, 12, 13, 14, 15, 18, 20–22, *24*, 31, 32, 34–36, 42, 43, *79*, 80–81, 83–89, 91–93, 96, 97, 99, 101, 105, 106–8: **III** 9, 11, 16, 18, 21, 23, 34, 37, 41–42, 55, 56, *61*, 62, 67, 71, 72, 74, 76–78, 84, 86, 87, 88, 89, 104, 111; **IV** 142, 154, 175–77, 181. *See also* Japanese aircraft: Zeke; specific models
Japanese Air Force (airmen), **II** vii, 7, 9, 31, 40, 63–64, 75, 77, 94, 97–98, 104–5; **III** 9, 10, *17,* 22, 48–50, 60, 79, 82, 90, 100, 120, 135; **IV** 140, 154, 174–75, 175–81, *178, 179*, 184, 186–90, *191,* 192, *193,* 194–99, 201–2, 203, 212, 214, 215, 218. *See also* Japanese aircraft; Japanese air units

Japanese air units
air corps (Kokutai):
4th, **III** 9
601st, **III** 120
652nd, **III** 120
653rd, **III** 120
Tainan, **III** 9, 11
Yokohama, **III** 9
air fleets:
Fifth, **IV** 178, 186, 190, 203
First, **II** 9; **IV** 140, 175, 181, 184, 186
Fourth, **IV** 140
Second, **IV** 138, 140, 177, 190–94
Sixth Base, **IV** 138, 190
Tenth, **IV** 186, 190
Third, **IV** 184, 186, 190
Twenty-sixth (26th), **II** 58
air flotillas (Koku Sentai):
21st, **III** 90
25th, **III** 9, 55
26th, **III** 90, 100
air groups (Sentai):
201st, **IV** 175, 176
601st, **IV** 184
701st, **IV** 215
carrier divisions (Koku Sentai):
1st, **III** 37
2nd, **III** 100, 102
Combined Land-based Air Force, **IV** 177
Divine Wind Special Attack Squad, **IV** 175–76. *See also* Japanese Air Force
Special Attack Corps, **IV** 174, 177, 178, 181, 184, 190, 195
Japanese Army (soldiers), **II** 5, 7, 9, 73; **III** 22, 67, 82, 85, 107, 108, 114, 116, 136; **IV** 173–74, 185, 186–87, 201. *See also* Japanese army units
Japanese army units
armies:
Fifteenth, **II** 41
Fourteenth, **IV** 138
Second, **IV** 209, 210
Seventeenth, **II** 105; **III** 68
Thirty-second, **IV** 189, 190, 192, 201
divisions:
2nd, **III** 68
38th, **III** 68, 83, 84
51st Infantry, **III** 18
Ichiki detachment, **III** *57*, 58–59, 67, 68
Kawaguchi force, **III** 68
Japanese naval units
Carrier Striking Force, **II** 75
1st Carrier Force, **II** 78, 82
divisions:
1st Carrier, **III** 90, 120, 127, 130
2nd Carrier, **III** 90, 120, 131
3rd Carrier, **III** 120, 127, 130
First Attack Force, **IV** 147
fleets:
Combined, **II** 72, 73; **IV** 139
First, **II** 62
Fourth, **II** 74–75
Second (later Special Surface Attack Force), **II** 62, 99; **III** 75, 83

Third, **III** 75, 90
Special Surface Attack Force (formerly Second Fleet), **IV** 190, 191, 193
Japanese naval vessels, **II** 9, 11, 12, 22, 78–80, 94–96, 104–5; **III** 18, *19,* 20–22, 32, 34, 37, 38, 64, 65, 72, 75–76, 85, *86,* 117, 119, 127, 132, 133; **IV** *136,* 149, 153, *158,* 159, 193–94
Abukuma, **IV** 149
Akagi, **II** 3, 12, 14, 15, 21, 23, 24, 78, 86–88, 93–95, 97, 98, 104
Akigumo, **III** 79
Arashio, **II** 101; **III** 20
Asashimo, **IV** 194
Atago, **III** 132; **IV** 141
Chikuma, **II** 12, 98; **III** 77; **IV** 151, 153
Chitose, **III** 63, 120; **IV** 155, 156
Chiyoda, **III** 120, 135; **IV** 155, 156, 175
Chokai, **IV** 153
Fuso, **IV** 145
Genyo Maru, **III** 133
Haguro, **III** 127
Hamakaze, **IV** 193
Haruna, **II** 87, 98; **III** 68–70, 77; **IV** 187, 193, 194
Hiei, **III** 68, 83, 84, 86
Hiryu, **II** 3, 78, 87, 89, 94, 96–99, 108
Hiyo, **III** 84, 90, 120, 133–35
Hosho, **II** 78, 99
Hyuga, **IV** 155
I-21, **III** 79
I-26, **III** 66
I-168, **I** 102–4
I-175, **III** 110
Ise, **IV** 155
Isokaze, **IV** 155
Jintsu, **III** 64, 65
Junyo, **II** 78; **III** 67, 78–79, 81, 90; **IV** 140
Kaga **II** 3, 78, 87, 89, 92–96, 98, 100
Kagero, **III** 64
Kasumi, **IV** 194
Kembu Maru, **III** 18, 20
Kinyu Maru, **III** 64, 65
Kirishima, **II** 87; **III** 68, 83, 86
Kishinami, **IV** 141
Kongo, **III** 68–70, 71; **IV** 146, 187
Kumano, **II** 101; **IV** 178
Kyokusei Maru, **III** 18, 22
Makikumo, **III** 79
Maya, **IV** 141
Mikuma, **II** *100,* 101
Mogami, **II** 101; **IV** 149
Musashi, **III** 120; **IV** 139, 146, 148
Mutsuki, **III** 64, 65
Myoko, **IV** 147
Nagara, **II** 95, 105; **III** 83
Nagato, **II** 11, 12; **IV** 148
Nitto Maru (Patrol Boat No. 23), **II** 59, *60,* 61–63
Nojima, **III** 18, 20
Oyodo, **IV** 156
Ryuho, **III** 120, 135; **IV** 140
Ryujo, **II** 78, 80; **III** 60, 61, 65
Seiyo Maru, **II** 133
Shigure, **IV** 145, 149

Shinano, **IV** 188
Shoho, **II** 75, 77
Shokaku, **II** 3, 14, 75, 77, 78; **III** 37, 60, 61, 67, 75, 76, 78, 79, 120, 127
Soryu, **II** 3, 21, 78, 87, 89, 93–95, 97, 98, 100
Suzuya, **II** 101
Taiho, **III** 120, 127
Takao, **IV** 141
Tamei Maru, **III** 21
Tone, **II** 12, 84, 87, 98
Yahagi, **IV** 190, 192, 193
Yamashiro, **IV** 149
Yamato, **II** 78, 82, 89, 99, 105; **III** 120; **IV** 139, 141, 146, 148, 151, *157,* 187, 190–94, 204
Yayoi, **III** 64
Zuiho, **III** 37, 67, 75–76, 79, 90, 120; **IV** *155,* 156
Zuikaku, **II** 3, 21, 75, 77, 78; **III** 37, 60, 61, 63, 67, 75, 76, 78–79, 81, 90, 120, 127, 132, 135; **IV** 155, 156
Japanese Navy (seamen), **II** 3, 4, 5, 7, 9, 58, 72, 73, 74, 94, 96, 98, 99, 101, 104–5; **III** 85; **IV** 139–40, 141, 148, 151, 194. *See also* Japanese naval units; Japanese naval vessels
Jarvis (U.S. naval vessel), **III** 56
Java, **II** 5
Jedenastka (aircraft), **I** 25–26
Jernstedt, Kenneth, **II** 34, 42
Jerstad, John J., **II** 165, 172
Jeschonnek, Hans, **I** 7, *24,* 107; **II** 131; **IV** *43,* 44, 80, 85
Jets. *See* specific aircraft
Jill (Nakajima B6N; *Tenzen*), **III** *119,* 120, 127, 130, 132
Jinking (evasive action), **II** 123
Jintsu (Japanese naval vessel), **III** 64, 65
Jodl, Alfred, **II** 36–37, 46, 83, 84; **IV** 116, 122
Johnson, G. I., **II** 141
Johnson, Gerald R., **III** 47–48
Johnson, Gerald W., **IV** 69, 73
Johnson, Leon, **II** *159,* 162, 163, 167–69, 172
Johnson, Robert S., **IV** *60,* 61, 69
Johnson, Samuel, **I** 146
Johnson, W. E., **III** 84
Johnston (U.S. naval vessel), **IV** 151
Jojima, Takaji, **III** 100, 120
Jones, David M., **II** 56
Joubert, Sir Philip, **II** 114
Jouett, John H., **II** 27, 38
Judy (Yokosuka *Suisei*), **III** 120, 127, 130, 132
Junkers (Ju), **I** 6
52, **I** *14,* 15, 17, 31–32, 40–43, 61, *64;* **IV** 12, 13, *14, 17,* 18, 19, 85
87 (Stuka), **I** 13–16, *14,* 21, *22,* 25, 26, *27, 29,* 30, 41, 43, 44, 71, 72, 86, 90, 94–96, *97,* 100, 103, 107–8; **II** 32, 181; **IV** *7,* 82, 83, 86, 87, *88,* 89, 218
88, **I** 13, 14, 25, *41,* 42, 52–53, 93, 94, 95, 99, *100,* 124, 133, 136, 152; **IV** *7,* 27, 44, 48, 54, 56, 78, 110, *118*
89, **I** 13; **IV** 83–84
Junod, Marcel, **IV** 210
Junyo (Japanese naval vessel), **II** 78; **III** 67, 78–79, 81, 90; **IV** 140

Jurika, Stephen, **II** 57, 59
Jyo, Eiichiro, **IV** 175

Kadashan Bay (U.S. naval vessel), **IV** 151
Kaga (Japanese naval vessel), **II** 3, 78, 87, 89, 92–96, 98, 100
Kagel, Jerome, **IV** 120, 121
Kagero (Japanese naval vessel), **III** 64
Kain, Edgar J. "Cobber," **I** 55, 57–60, *60,* 61, 76; **IV** 7
Kaku, Tomeo, **II** 98, 99
Kakuda, Kakuji, **II** 78, **III** 78, 81, 120, 122, 126
Kalinin Bay (U.S. naval vessel), **IV** 154
Kamikaze, **IV** 175–76. *See also* Japanese Air Force
Kammhuber, Josef, **I** 37; **IV** 44, 46
"Kammhuber Line," **IV** 44
Kane, John R. "Killer," **II** 158–59, *158,* 162, 163, 166–69, 171, 172
Kaneohe Naval Air Station (Hawaii), **II** 22
Kanno, Naoshi, **III** 48
Karawha (U.S. naval vessel), **III** 90
Karinhall (Göring estate), **IV** 80
Karlsruhe (German naval vessel), **I** 45
Kassel (Germany), **IV** 46
Kasumi (Japanese naval vessel), **IV** 194
Kate (Japanese aircraft), **II** 9, 12, *13,* 14–18, 21, *23,* 32, 80, 83, *85;* **III** 61, 62, 76, *77,* 78–80, 90, 97, *114,* 120
Kaufman, Karl, **IV** 41–42
Kavieng (New Ireland), **III** 102; **IV** 135
Kawaguchi, Kiyotaki, **III** 67, 75
Kawasaki (Japan), **IV** 204
Kawasaki Ki. 45 (Nick), **IV** 165, 198, 199
Kawasaki Ki. 61 (Tony), **III** 28, 98, 100; **IV** 143, 165, *167,* 182, 192
Kearby, Neel E., **III** 24, 42, *43,* 44–45, 50
Keitel, Wilhelm, **I** *23,* 36–37, 77, 83; **IV** 17, 116
Keller, John B., **IV** 131
Kelly, Colin, **IV** 194
Kelly, Laurence B., **IV** 135
Kembu Maru (Japanese naval vessel), **III** 20
Kenney, George C., **II** 52; **III** 3, 6–9, *6,* 7, 10–14, 16–22, 23, 24, 30, 31–32, 34–36, 38, 40, 44, 45, 46–48, 50, 90, 100; **IV** 129, 136, 138, 161, 162, 178, 182, 184, *216*
Keogh, Vernon, **I** *162,* 166
Kenney cocktails, **III** 12, 36, *38*
Kepford, Ira C., **III** *100,* 101–2
Kepner, William, **IV** 63, 69
Kernan, A. B., **III** 113, 114
Kesselring, Albert, **I** 6, 10, *24,* 25, 77, 85, 94, 103, 119; **IV** 9–10, 20, 22, *25,* 26–27, 32, 35, 84
Kessler, Philip, **II** 191
Kharagpur air base (India), **IV** 130
Ki. 43. *See* Oscar
Ki. 44. *See* Tojo
Ki. 45. *See* Nick
Ki. 46. *See* Tony
Kidel, Isaac C., **II** 21
Kiel (Germany), **IV** 48
"Kill" scores, **IV** 63
Kimmel, Husband E., **II** 7, *8*

King, Ernest, J., **II** 49–52, 79, *152;* **III** 5, 53, 80, 83, 104–5, 114
Kingfisher (OS2U), **II** *19;* **III** *119;* **IV** *136*
Kinkaid, Thomas C., **II** 75, 81, 106; **IV** 139, 140, 141, *150,* 151, 154, 156–59
Kinryu Maru (Japanese naval vessel), **III** 64, 65
Kioso, Kuniaki, **IV** 205
Kirishima (Japanese naval vessel), **II** 87; **III** 68, 83, 86
Kisarazu Air Base (Japan), **II** 62, 63
Kishinami (Japanese naval vessel), **IV** 141
Kiska, **II** 78, 80; **III** 104–6
Kitkun Bay (U.S. naval vessel), **IV** 152, 154
Kittyhawk, **II** 30, 45
Kjell (Norwegian naval vessel), **I** 37
Kleist, Ewald von, **I** 64
Klingman, Robert L., **IV** 198, *199,* 201
Kluge, Günther von, **I** 64, 77
Klunkers (P-400), **III** 5, 59, *60,* 67, 68, 71
Knight, Clayton, **I** 166
Knight, L. G., **II** 142, 145–47
Knobloch, Richard A., **II** *64*
Knowling, Edward J., **II** 179–80
Knox, Brian, **I** 58, 60
Knox, Frank, **II** 7, *8,* 105
Kobayashi, Michio, **II** 80, 81, 96–97
Kobe (Japan), **II** 56; **IV** 173
Koga, Mineichi, **II** 108; **III** 93, 100, 108, 119–20
Koga, Tadayoshi, **II** 78–81
Kojedud, Ivan, **IV** 85
Kokoda trail, **III** 16
Kokura (Japan), **IV** 209, 211
Kolendorski, Stanley, **I** *163*
Koller, Karl, **IV** 80, 116
Komatsu, Sakio, **III** 127
Kon, Operation, **III** 122
Kondo, Nobutake, **II** 62, 99; **III** 61, 63, 75, 79, 81, 83, 84, 86
Kongo (Japanese naval vessel), **III** 68–70, 71; **IV** 146, 187
Konigsberg (German naval vessel), **I** 45
Konoye, Prince Fumimaro, **II** 5
Koper, Robert, **IV** 58
Koror (Japan), **IV** 135–36
Korten, Gunther, **IV** 44, 80
Kosomo, Ammyo, **IV** 215
Kossler, H. J., **III** 127
Koyanagi, Tomiji, **IV** 147
Kozaka, Kanae, **III** 90
Kreipe, Werner, **IV** 80
Krueger, Walter, **IV** 141
Krupp von Bohlen, Gustav, **IV** 40
Krupp works, **I** 6; **II** 113; **IV** 40
Kublai Khan, **IV** 174
Küchler, Georg von, **I** 66
Ku Cho-tung, **II** 66
Kumano (Japanese naval vessel), **II** 101; **IV** 178
Kunming (China), **II** 29, 32–33, 46
Kuno, Yoshiyasu, **IV** 176
Kure (Japan), **IV** 187
Kuribayashi, Tadamichi, **IV** 184–85
Kurile Islands, **IV** 133
Kurita, Takeo, **II** 101; **III** 120; **IV** 139–54, 175
Kuroda, Shigenori, **IV** 138

Kuroe, Yasuhiki, **III** 48
Kusaka, Ryunosuke, **II** 24, 95
Kusunoki, Masashige, **IV** 191
Kwajalein, **III** 109, 114, 116, 117
Kyokusei Maru (Japanese naval vessel), **III** 18, 22
Kyushu (Japan), **IV** 187

L2D, **III** 49
Lae (New Guinea), **III** 16–18, 23, 29–31, 43
Lancaster (British aircraft), **II** 116, 117, 119, *121, 123,*
        126–28, *129,* 132, 135, 137, 140–43, *142,*
        144, 145–47, 150; **IV** 37, 39, 40, *40,* 46, 55,
        108
Landry, Robert, **IV** 70
Langley (U.S. naval vessel), **III** 119, 121; **IV** 142, 145
Lanham, Harold, **IV** 131
Lanker, Albert, **IV** 75, 76
Lanphier, Thomas G., **II** 105–6, *107, 108*
Laoyao Harbor (Japan), **IV** 133
Larner, Edward, **III** 18–21
Larsen, Harold, **III** 63
Laurey, J. B., **II** 59
Lauro, F. G., **IV** 58
Lavochkin 5 (aircraft), **IV** 85
Lawlor, Frank, **II** 44
Lawson, Ted W., **II** 59, 69
Lawton, E. J., **III** 135
Lazar, James B., **IV** 207
Lea, Homer, **II** 6
Leathart, James A., **I** *129*
Leckie, Robert, **IV** 189
Leder, W. H., **III** 80
Lee, James R., **III** 85
Lee, Willis A., **IV** 154
Leeb, Wilhelm Ritter von, **I** 34, 77
Leigh, Vivien, **I** 137
Leigh-Mallory, Sir Trafford, **I** 88, 99, 118–19, *119;*
        IV 95, 97
Leipzig (Germany), **IV** 53, 54, 114
LeMay, Curtis E., **II** *174,* 175, 177, 180, 185; **IV** 54,
        160, 161, *163,* 167–71, 173, 184, 186, 203,
        204
Lend-Lease, **IV** 8
Lenin, V. I., **I** 6
Leonard, Paul J., **II** 66, 67
Leopold III, **I** 68
Leslie, Maxwell F., **II** 90, 93–94, 97
Lewis, Millard, **IV** 97
Lexington (U.S. naval vessel), **II** *12,* 74. 75, *76,* 77,
        103; **III** 53, 107, 108, 110–11, 121, *122,* 124,
        126, 130, 132; **IV** 142–43, 145, 147, 156
Ley, Robert, **I** 30
Leyte, **IV** 136–41
Leyte Gulf, Battle of, **IV** 139–59, 163, 175–77
Liberator (B-24), **I** 151–52; **III** 16, 18, 24, 26, 30,
        34, 49, *105, 106,* 108, *109;* **IV** 8, 9, 10, 27, *28,*
        30, *34.* 35, *42,* 48, 54, *55,* 58, 90, 91, *93,* 97, 98,
        99, 100, *108,* 114, 115, 127, 135–36, *136,* 138,
        149, 154, 185
Libya, **IV** 5–7, 19–20. *See also* specific locations
Liebolt, Edward J., **II** 42
Lightning (P-38), **II** 105, *106;* **III** *15,* 16, *17,* 21, 24,
        27, 30, 31, 32–37, 84, 89, 90, 93, 96, 106; **IV**

11, *13, 14,* 27, *34,* 35, 48, 54, 58, 69, *75, 81,* 87,
        91, 95
Lindley, John D., **III** 59
Lindsey, Eugene F., **II** 90, 92–93
Linz (Austria), **IV** 34
Lipscomb, Paul M., **IV** 181–84
Liscombe Bay (U.S. naval vessel), **III** 110, 114
Lister Dam (Germany), **II** 140, 147
Little (U.S. naval vessel), **IV** 97
"Little Boy" (atomic bomb), **IV** *208,* 209, 210
Lloyd, Sir Hugh P., **IV** 21
Lockard, Joseph, **II** 14–15
Lockspeiser, Sir Ben, **II** 139
Loehr (Löhr), Alexander, **I** 24, 25; **IV** 15, 16
Loerzer (Lörzer), Bruno, **I** 11, 85, 90, 96; **IV** 10, 20
London, **I** 104, 121–25, *125, 126,* 127–28,
        131–36, 137–48, *139, 142, 143, 147;* **IV**
        56–57, 171
Long (U.S. naval vessel), **IV** 181
Long, Worthy, **II** 166
Longmore, Sir Arthur M., **IV** 6, 9
Lorient (France), **IV** *36*
Los (aircraft), **I** 25
Lott, Arnold, **IV** 198
Louis the Louse, **III** 65, 69
Louisville (U.S. naval vessel), **IV** 181
Love, William F., **II** 165
Lovett, Robert M., **IV** 52
Low, Francis F., **II** 49–50, *50,* 51
Lübeck (Germany), **II** 113
Luce (U.S. naval vessel), **IV** 197
Ludendorf, Eric, **I** 7
Lufbery Circle, **IV** 144
Lufthansa, **I** 9
Luftwaffe (German airmen), **I** 3, 5, 7, 9–17, 23–25,
        33, 38–46, 50–55, 57, 61, 64–66, 68,
        69–73, *69,* 75, 84–85, 86, 89, 90, 92, 93,
        102, 103, 105, 106, 108–10, 113, *113–14,*
        115, 120, 121, 127, 128, 130, 136, *138,* 141,
        141, 158, 159–60; **II** 111, 119, 130–31, 148,
        151, 153, 155, 157, 160–66, 169–71,
        173–74, 176–82, 185–89; **IV** 11, *12,* 19, 24,
        27, 28, 32, 33, 35, *37, 38,* 42, 43, 47–58,
        76–79, 80, 82, 85, 105–6, 109, *112,* 117, 118,
        123. See also German aircraft; German air units
Lumsden, Herbert, **IV** 181
Luton (England), **I** *113–14.* 115, 141
Luzon (Philippines), **IV** 138, 178–81
Lydekker, Anthony, **I** 43
Lynch, Thomas J., **III** 42, *44,* 50
Lysander (aircraft), **I** *54,* 72

MI, Operation, **II** 73. *See also* Midway, Battle of
M47. *See* Napalm
M69. *See* Fire bombs
MacArthur, Douglas, **II** 111; **III** *3,* 4, 5, 6–8, 9–13,
        14, 16, 22, 23, 30, 32, 40, 42, 84, 102, 114, 119,
        122; **IV** 128, 130, 135, 138, 139, 141, 159, 160,
        168, 181, *216,* 218
"MacArthur's Navy." *See* United States naval units:
        fleets: Seventh
McCain, John S., **III** 65–66; **IV** 141, 142, 150, 154,
        156

McCampbell, David, **IV** 142, *143,* 144, 145, 155
McCarthy, James F., **II** 52–53
McCarthy, Joseph C., **II** *139,* 141, 147
McClellan Field (California), **II** 54–55
McClintock, David, **IV** 141
McClure, Charles L., **II** 68, 69
McClusky, Clarence W., **II** *89,* 90, 94, 98
McCormick, John B., **II** 170
McCrary, John "Tex," **II** 160
Macdonald, J. C., **II** 121
McDonald, William C., **II** 27
McElroy, Edgar E., **II** *64, 65*
McFarland (U.S. naval vessel), **III** 73
McGarry, William D., **II** 43
McGuire, Thomas B., Jr., **III** 45, *46,* 47–48, 50; **IV** 63
McIntosh, I. A., **I** 62
McKennon, Pierce W., **IV** 68
McKnight, William L., **I** 132
McLaughlin, James K., **II** 185, 186
McLean, D. A., **II** 141
MacMahon, Patrice, **I** 64
McMillan, George, **II** 34, 35
McMillan, S. L., **II** 176
McNair, Lesley J., **IV** 99
McPherson, A., **I** 50–52
McQueen, Donald, **III** 100
Magwe air base (Burma), **II** 42, 43
Mahurin, Walker, **IV** 69
Majuro (Marshalls), **III** 114, 116, 117, 121
Makikumo (Japanese naval vessel), **III** 79
Makin (Gilberts), **III** 107, 108, 114
Malan, Adolf G. "Sailor," **I** *129, 161,* 162, 168
Malaya, **II** 5, 9, 22, 36
Malo, Raymond, **IV** 185, 186
Malta, **II** 171; **IV** 5, 17, 19, *20,* 24, 25
Maltby, David, **II** 142, 145
Maltby, J. H., **II** 145, 147
Mamedoff, Andrew, **I** *162, 163,* 166
Manchester (British aircraft), **II** 116–18, *119,* 125–26
Mangrum, Richard C., **III** 59, 64, 69
Manila, **IV** 159
Manila Bay (U.S. naval vessel), **III** *124;* **IV** 180
Manna, Operation, **IV** 120–22
Mannert L. Abele (U.S. naval vessel), **IV** 195
Manser, Leslie, **II** 118, 125–26
Mao Tse-tung, **II** 27
Maranz, Nat, **I** 163
Marauder (B-26), **II** *51,* 67, 78, 84, 86–87, 90, 108; **III** 5, 14; **IV** 27, 29, 30, *32, 34, 78, 79,* 95, 97, *98,* 99, 110
Marcus Island, **III** 107–8; **IV** 138
Marianas Islands, **III** 120–36; **IV** 135, 137. *See also* specific islands
Marienburg (Germany), **II** 183, 185
Marilinan airfield (New Guinea), **III** 23, 24, 30
Market, Operation, **IV** 108
"Mark Twain" bombsight, **II** 53, 54
Marland, F., **I** 62
Marquardt, George W., **IV** 209
Marseille, Hans-Joachim, **IV** 15, *16*
Marshall, George C., **II** *152;* **III** 82

Marshall Islands, **II** 4, 6; **III** 114–20. *See also* specific islands
Martin, H. B. "Mickey," **II** 141, 144–45, 147
Martin, John, **I** 135
Martin, Neil, **II** 34
Martini, Wolfgang, **I** 93
Maruyama, Masao, **III** 73
Maryland (British aircraft), **IV** 19
Maryland (U.S. naval vessel), **II** 16, 21, 23
Mason, Paul, **III** 55
Massey, Lance E., **II** 93
Matsuya, Toleuzo, **III** 124
Matterhorn plan, **IV** 162–63
Maudslay, Henry E., **II** *139,* 142, 145–46
Maya (Japanese naval vessel), **IV** 141
Mayo, Charles, **III** 21
Me. *See* Messerschmitt
Meade (U.S. naval vessel), **III** 86
Medal of Honor, **III** 29, 37, 43–44, 59, 66, 69, 73, 74, *87,* 88, 91, 96, 110, 111; **IV** 49, 51, 184
Medals. *See* specific medals
Meder, Robert J., **II** 68, 70
Mediterranean Air Command (Allies), **II** 156
Mediterranean Allied Air Forces, **IV** 28, 32, 52, 53
Megura, Nicholas, **IV** 68
Menge, Herbert, **II** 25
Mercury, Operation, **IV** 17–18
Merrell, Robert W., **II** 165
Merritt, Kenneth, **II** 38
Merseburg (Germany), **IV** 100
Meshot air base (Burma), **II** 38
Messerschmitt (Me)
  108, **I** 36
  109, **I** 14, 15, 25, 26, *44,* 51–54, 60, 65, 71, 72, 73–74, 76, *85,* 87, 90, *91,* 92, 95, 100–1, 103–6, *106,* 107, 108, 110, 122, 124, *126,* 127, 131, 134, 136, 137, *145, 159,* 160, 162; **II** 111, 154, *154,* 157, 169, 174, 186, 187; **III** 62; **IV** 7, 12, 13, 15, 19, 21, *37,* 48, 51, 54, 58, *59,* 62, 83, 87, 91, 92, 109–10
  110, **I** 25, 27, 30, 40, 43, 53, 71, 72, 87, 90, 92–95, *92,* 98–100, 103–5, 107, 115–17, *117,* 124, 127, 134–36, 154; **II** 32, 124–25, 157, 181; **IV** 7, *9,* 12, 44, *44,* 48, 49, 51, 55, 56, 70–71
  163, **IV** 103
  262, **IV** 100–5, *106, 107,* 115
  363, **IV** *14*
  410, **IV** 56
Messina (Sicily), **IV** *23*
Meteor (British aircraft), **IV** 103, 107
Mever, John C., **IV** 110, *111,* 112
Midget submarines, **II** 11, 22
Midway, Battle of, **II** vii–viii, 73–108; **III** 3, 23, 87, 104. *See also* Coral Sea, Battle of the
Mikawa, Gunichi, **II** 3; **III** 56–57, 83
Mikuma (Japanese naval vessel), **II** *100,* 101
Milch, Edward, **I** 9–12, *39,* 40, 77, 85; **IV** 43, 47
Milk run, defined, **II** 185
Millennium, Operation, **II** 114–15. *See also* Cologne
Miller, Henry L., **II** 53, *54,* 56
Miller, Loring C., **II** 179, 181, 182
Millikan, Willard, **IV** 67–68
Mills, A. M., **II** 118, 126

Milton, Theodore Ross, **IV** 100, *105*
Mindoro Island, **IV** 178, 180
Mingaladon air base (China), **II** 34–37, 42
Missouri (U.S. naval vessel), **IV** 214, *217*, 218
Mitchell, John W., **II** 105, 106, 108
Mitchell, Ralph J., **III** 99
Mitchell, William, **I** xi–xii
Mitchell (B-25), **II** 47, 50–56, *57*, 59, 60, *61, 62, 63*,
        64–66, *67*; **III** 5, 9, 12, 18, 19–20, *20*, 21, 24,
        25, 27, *28*, 29, 30, 32–34, *35*, 36–37, *38*,
        99–100, *103*; **IV** 9, 10, *11*, 13, *14*, 27, *29*, 30,
        31, 33, 110
Mitscher, Marc A., **II** 52, 53, *55, 56, 58*, 60, 98, 101,
        105; **III** 117, 120, 121, 122, 126, *126*, 127,
        132–35; **IV** 138, 141, 147, 150, 154, 157, 187,
        190, 193
Mitsubishi. *See* specific aircraft
Moa (Australian naval vessel), **III** 90
Mochler, Edward, **IV** 185, 186
Mogami (Japanese naval vessel), **II** 101; **IV** 149
Mohawk (British naval vessel), **I** 52
Möhne Dam (Germany), **II** 135, 136, *137*, 138–41,
        143–45, *146*
Mölders, Werner, **I** 15, *65, 74*, 90; **IV** 44
Monte Cassino, **IV** 29, *30*
Monterey (U.S. naval vessel), **III** 107, 108, 121, 131
Montgomery, Bernard Law Montgomery, Viscount, **IV**
        7–11, 15, 19, 22, 24, 108
Montpelier (U.S. naval vessel), **IV** 196
Moore, Evelyn M. (Gibson), **II** 133, 150
Moore, John T., **III** 43
Moore, Malcolm A., **III** 23
Moore, Woodrow W., **III** 21
Morgan, Robert K., **IV** 164
Morgenthau, Henry, Jr., **II** 30
Morin, Raymond V., **IV** 97
Morison, Samuel Eliot, **II** 89; **III** 22, 38, 70; **IV** 27
Morner, A. P., **III** *123*
Morotai Island, **IV** 135, 136
Morris, Benjamin, **II** 84, 87, 88
Morrison (U.S. naval vessel), **IV** 197
Mosquito (aircraft), **I** 113, 158; **II** 128, *129*, 150
Mould, P. W. O., **I** 55–56
Mow, P. T., **II** 30
Mugford (U.S. naval vessel), **III** 55
Mulcahy, Francis P., **IV** 190
Mullinix, H. M., **III** 110
München Gladbach (Germany), **IV** 38
Munda, Battle of (New Georgia), **III** 93
Munro, K. L., **II** 141
Münster (Germany), **II** 185, 187
Murata, Shigeharu, **II** 14, 15, 17
Muriello, Samuel, **I** *163*
Murphy, John W., Jr., **II** 100
Murphy, Thomas, **II** 182
Murray, George D., **II** 58
Musashi (Japanese naval vessel), **III** 120; **IV** 139, 146,
        148
Musser, Francis, **II** 80
Mussolini, Benito, **I** 15, 33, 36, 75, 76; **IV** 3, *4*, 5, 7,
        15, 16, 19, 22, 24, 25–26, 32, 35
Mustang (P-51), **I** xiii; **II** 152; **IV** 26, 27, 35, 48, 49,
        50, 51, 54, 56, 57, 58, 60, 61, *63*, 66, 86, 87, *88*,

89, 90, 91, 95, 101, 102, 103, 104, 110, 115,
        118, 181–84, *182, 185, 207, 212*, 218
Muto, Kinsuke, **III** 48
Mutsuki (Japanese naval vessel), **III** 64, 65
Myoko (Japanese naval vessel), **IV** 47

Nadzab (New Guinea), **III** 29–31, 43
Nagano,Osami, **II** 73; **III** 86
Nagara (Japanese naval vessel), **II** 95, 105; **III** 83
Nagato (Japanese naval vessel), **II** 11, 12; **IV** 148
Nagoya (Japan), **II** 56; **IV** 173, 204
Nagumo, Chuichi, **II** 3–4, *4*, 11–13, 15, 23, 24, 62,
        78, 82–95, 99, 105; **III** 37, 60, 63, 75, 76, 78,
        90, 123
Nakajima, Chikataka, **III** 122
Nakajima, Tadashi, **IV** 176, 180–81
Nakajima (Japanese aircraft), **III** 35
    Ki. 43 (Oscar), **III** 27, 28; **IV** 130–31, 143
    Ki. 44 (Tojo), **III** 101, 102
    L2D, **III** 49
Nakamichi, Waturo, **III** 48
Nakano, Lieutenant, **IV** 181
Naketsuru, Tatsuo, **IV** 215
Napalm, **III** 125; **IV** 169, 170, 201
Naples, **IV** 27
Nashville (U.S. naval vessel), **II** 62, 69
Nate (Japanese aircraft), **II** 39
Natoma Bay (U.S. naval vessel), **II** 124
Naujocks, Alfred, **I** 23
Nautilus (U.S. naval vessel), **II** 94
Naval vessels. *See* specific nationalities, ships
Naylor, B. W., **II** 118, 126
Nazi-Soviet Pact (Treaty of Non-Aggression), **I** 33, 36
Neale, Robert, **II** 41–43
Neefus, James, **III** 94
Nell (Japanese aircraft), **III** 9, 90, 114
Nelson, R. S., **III** 132
Neosho (U.S. naval vessel), **II** 75
Nespor, Robert, **II** 162
Netherlands. *See* Holland
Nettuno landing (Italy), **IV** 28–29
Neuburg (Germany), **IV** 104
Neuport, Karl, **IV** 197
Nevada (U.S. naval vessel), **II** 16, 23
New Guinea, **II** 6, 74; **III** 22, 23, 38, 40. *See also*
        specific locations
New Jersey (U.S. naval vessel), **IV** 156
Newkirk, John, **II** 36–38, 43–44
New Mexico (U.S. naval vessel), **IV** 181
Newton, J. H., **II** 12
New Zealand aircraft, **III** 96
New Zealand air units
    squadrons:
        No. 14, **III** 99
        No. 16, **III** 99
        No. 18, **III** 96
New Zealand Royal Air Force, **III** 96
Nichol, Bromfield, **II** 24
Nichols, William, **I** 163
Nielsen, Chase J., **II** 68, 70
Niigata (Japan), **IV** 209
Nick (Japanese aircraft), **IV** 165, 198, 199
Nimitz, Chester A., **II** *8, 52*, 53, 74, 75, 77, 79, 80; **III**

5, 65–66, 72–73, 87; **IV** 128, 130, 135, 136, 139, 154, 156, 157, 168
Nishimura Shoji, **IV** 139, 140, 145, 145–49, 154, 177
Nishimura, Teji, **IV** 145
Nishizawa, Hiroyoshi, **III** 48, 49; **IV** 177
Nitto Maru (Patrol Boat No. 23; Japanese naval vessel), **II** 59, *60*, 61–63
Nojima (Japanese naval vessel), **III** 18, 20
Nomura, Kichisaburo, **II** 5
Non-Aggression, Treaty of (Nazi-Soviet Pact), **I** 33, 36
Nonaka, Goro, **IV** 188
Norden bombsight, **II** 53; **IV** 37
Normand, G. G. Y., **II** 186
Normandy, **IV** 28, 32, 48, 52, 53, 74–80, *75, 76,* 92–100
North Africa, **II** 151, 155; **IV** 3–15, 19, 22, 93. *See also* specific locations
North Carolina (U.S. naval vessel), **III** 62, 67, 110
North Field (Guam), **IV** 170
North Field (Tinian), **IV** 170
Northwest African Air Forces (NAAF), **IV** 12, 23, 27, 28
Norway, **I** 37–46
Norwegian naval vessel, **I** 37
Norwich (England), **II** 113
Nowotny, Walter, **IV** 103–4
Noyes, Leigh, **III** *54*
Nuclear weapons. *See* Atomic bombs
Nugent, L., **II** 147

Oahu (Hawaii), **II** 3, 11, 15, 18, 23, 24, 79
Obayashi, Sueo, **III** 76, 120
Oboe (electronic device), **IV** 39, 48
O'Brien (U.S. naval vessel), **III** 67
Observer Corps (British), **I** 88, 100, 110
O'Donnell, Emmett, **IV** 164, 170
Oglala (U.S. naval vessel), **II** 23
O'Hare, Edward H., **III** 43, 110, *111,* 113, 130
Ohka bombs, **IV** 188–89, *188,* 195
Ohmae, Toshikazu, **III** 83
Ohnishi, Takijuro, **II** 7; **IV** 140, 154, 175–78, 181, 184, 187, 189, 205, 214
Ohta, Mitsuo, **IV** 88
Oil industry, **IV** 37, 90, 92, 93, 100, 105–6, *108,* 113–14. *See also* specific locations
Okinawa, **IV** 138, 186, *187,* 188–201, *202, 203*
Oklahoma (U.S. naval vessel), **II** 6, 21, 22
Oldenburg (Germany), **IV** 70
Oldendorf, Jesse B., **IV** 149, 151, 179
Older, Charles, **II** 34
Olds, Archie J., Jr., **II** 186
Olivier, Sir Laurence, **I** 137
Olson, Arvid E., Jr., **II** 32, *34*
Olympic, Operation, **IV** 206
Omark, Warren, **III** 134, 135
Ommaney Bay (U.S. naval vessel), **IV** 179, *180*
Omori, Sentaro, **II** 3
Oncia, S., **II** 147
Ono, Lieutenant Commodore, **II** 88
Operational Training Units (British), **II** 114
Oppenheimer, J. R., **IV** 208
Oranienburg (Germany), **IV** 115
OS2U (Kingfisher), **II** *19;* **III** *119;* **IV** *136*

Osaka (Japan), **II** 45; **IV** 173, 204
Osborn, Edgar F., **II** 60
Oscar (Nakajima Ki. 43), **III** 27, 28; **IV** 130–31, 143
Oschersleben (Germany), **IV** 48, 49, 51, 54
Ota, Toshio, **III** 48
Ottley, W. H. T., **II** 147
Outfin, R. M., **I** 61
Overend, Edmund, **II** 35
Overfield, Lloyd J., **IV** *112*
Overlord, Operation, **IV** 52, 53, 95
Owen, Roderic, **IV** 33, 35
Owens, Walter E., **II** 182
Oxford (British aircraft), **I** 113
Oyodo (Japanese naval vessel), **IV** 156
Ozawa, Jisaburg, **III** 90, 120, 121, 122, 126, 127, 132, 133, 135; **IV** 138, 139, 147–50, 154–59, 175

P1Y. *See* Frances
P-36, **II** 21
P-38 (Lightning), **II** 105, *106;* **III** *15,* 16, *17,* 21, 24, 27, 30, 31, 32–37, 84, 89, 90, 93, 96, 106; **IV** 11, *13, 14,* 27, *34,* 35, 48, 54, 58, 69, *75, 81,* 91, 95
P-39 (Airacobra), **III** 5, *9,* 15–17, 24, 36, *60,* 65, 68, 90, 94, *104;* **IV** 84, 89
P-40 (Warhawk), **I** xiii; **II** 15, 21, 152; **III** 5–6, 15–17, 89, 94, 96, *105,* 106, 108; **IV** 10, 11, 12, 13, 15, 24
P-40B (Tomahawk), **II** 27, *29,* 30–35, *36,* 37, 38, *39,* 40–46; **IV** 48
P-40D (Kittyhawk), **II** 30
P-40E (Kittyhawk), **II** 45
P-40F, **IV** 9
P-47 (Thunderbolt), **II** 152, 177, 179, 183, 186, 187; **III** 24, 30, 42, 43, *124,* 125; **IV** *25,* 48, 54, 58, 60, 61, *62, 69,* 70, *70,* 71, *72,* 73, 95, 96, 98–100, *101,* 102, 103, 105, 111, 112, 113 *207,* 218
P-47B, **IV** 69
P-47D (Razorback), **IV** *62*
P-47N, **IV** *62*
P-51 (Mustang), **I** xiii; **II** 152; **IV** 26, 27, 35, 48, 49, *50,* 51, 54, 56, 57, 58, 60, 61, *63,* 66, 86, 87, *88,* 89, 90, 91, 95, 101, 102, 103, 104, 110, 115, 118, 181–84, *182, 185, 207, 212,* 218
P-61 (Black Widow), **IV** 46, *213*
P-80, **III** 50
P-400 (Klunkers), **III** 5, 59, *60,* 67, 68, 71
Pacific Fleet (U.S.), **II** 7, 9, 15, 22, 72, 73–74. *See also* specific battles
Palm, John, **II** 162, 163, 165
"Palm Sunday Massacre," **IV** 13
Pantelleria (Italy), **IV** *21, 22,* 23
Parafrags (parachute bombs), **III** 12, 14, 24, *26, 27,* 28, 29, *33, 34*
Paramushiro (Kurile Islands), **IV** 133
Parchim (Germany), **IV** 115
Paris, **II** 31
Park, Keith R., **I** 71, 87–88, 97, 103, 109, *109,* 110, 116–19, *120,* 122, 123, 124, 128, 129, 130 131 134, 135
Parks, Floyd B., **II** 84
Pathfinder bombing, **II** 113, 183

Patton, George, **IV** 24, 99, 107, 108
Paulus, Friedrich von, **IV** 84, 85
Pavesi, Gino, **IV** 24
Paxton, George, **II** 38
PB4Y, **III** 88, 89, 94, 95
PBY. *See* Catalina
Pearl Harbor, **II** vii, 3–25, *6, 10, 17,* 32; **III** 3–4,
        22; **IV** 5
Pease, Harl, **III** 11
Peaslee, Budd, **II** *185,* 186, 188
Peenemünde, (Germany), **IV** 44, *95*
Peirse, Sir Richard, **I** 154; **II** 111–12
Pelelin Island, **IV** 135, 137
Peltz, Dietrich, **IV** 42, 56
Pennsylvania (U.S. naval vessel), **II** 23
Perry, Matthew C., **IV** 189
Petacci, Clara, **IV** 35
Petach, John E., **II** 47, 48
Pétain, Henri Philippe, **I** 76
Peters, Walter, **II** 185
Peterson, Chesley, **I** *163,* 166; **IV** 57
Pflugbeil, Kurt, **IV** *4*
Phelps (U.S. naval vessel), **II** 76
Philippines, **II** 5, 9, 22, 32, 36, 73, 77, 111; **IV** 135,
        137, 138, 139, 140, 141, 159, 160, 174. *See also*
        Leyte Gulf, Battle of; specific locations
Philippine Sea, Battle of the, **III** 129–36
Phillips, John, **III** 113, 114
Phillipson, J. R., **I** 158
"Phony War," **II** 133
Picard, P. C., **IV** 96
Pierson, Rex K., **II** 135
Pissanos, Spiro, **IV** 64
Pistol Pete, **III** 69
Pitesti (Rumania), **II** 163
Pittsburgh (U.S. naval vessel), **IV** 187
"Plan for the Completion of the Combined Bomber
        Offensive" (Spaatz), **IV** 92
Playfair, P. H. L., **I** 61
Ploesti (Rumania), **II** viii, 155, 157–72, *160,* 175,
        187; **III** 3, 35, 61, 87, 100, *108*
Plutarch, **II** 172
Pohl, E. R. von, **IV** 32
Pohl, Helmut, **I** 52–53
Pointblank operations, **II** 155
Pokryshin, Alexander, **IV** 85
Poland, **I** xiv, 21–32, 153; **II** 148, 183. *See also*
        specific branches of Polish armed forces
Polikarpov. *See* I-16
Polish aircraft
  PZL-7, **I** 26
  PZL-11, **I** *25,* 30
  PZL-11c, **I** 25–26
  PZL-38, **I** 25
Polish Air Force, **I** 25–26, 30
Polish Posen Army, **I** *29, 30*
Pond, Zennith A., **III** 61
Ponks, Elmer, **IV** 28
Portal, Sir Charles, **I** 148; **II** 114, 136, *152*
Porter (U.S. naval vessel), **III** 79, 80
Port Moresby, **II** 74, 77; **III** 14, 16
Posey, James, **II** 167, 169
Potsdam Declaration, **IV** 206, 207

Potter, Henry A., **II** 66, 67
Potter, John Deane, **II** 108
Pöttgen, Rainer, **IV** 15
Potts, Ramsay D., Jr., **II** 159, *163,* 164, 166, 167, 172
Pound, Sir Dudley, **II** *152*
Powers, Thomas S., **III** 168, 170
Pownall, Charles A., **III** 108
Pranging, defined, **IV** 66
Priller, Josef, **IV** 76–78, 80
Prince of Wales (British naval vessel), **II** 73
Princeton (U.S. naval vessel), **III** 107, 108, 121, 130;
        IV 142, 144, 145
Prinz Eugen (German naval vessel), **I** 168
Proctor (British aircraft), **I** 113
Provenzano, Peter, **I** *163*
PT boats, **III** 84
        PT-137, **IV** *149*
Pulford, J., **II** *142,* 143
Putnam, Paul A., **II** 12
Pyle, Ernie, **IV** 189
Pyrrhus, **II** 172
PZL. *See* Polish aircraft

Queen Bee (British aircraft), **IV** 5
Quigley, D. J., **II** 59

Rabaul, **III** 10–11, 16, 31–38, *35, 36,* 99–100,
        102, *103;* **IV** 135
Radar, **I** xii, 1, 88–89, *89,* 92–93, 96, 103, 107, 108,
        110, 157, 158; **II** 86, 115, 136, 183, *184;* **IV** 40,
        44, 45, *45,* 46, 48, *49, 68,* 115, 132, 135, 169
Raeder, Erich, **I** *37,* 46, 84, 123
RAF. *See* Royal Air Force
Raiden. See Jack
Raleigh (U.S. naval vessel), **II** 23
Ramey, Roger M., **IV** 161, 162
Ramsay, Sir Bertram, **I** 70
Ramsey, Donald J., **II** 101
Rand, Hazen, **III** 113
Randall, G. D., **II** 62
Rangoon, **II** 29, 34–42
Rathenau, Walter, **I** 6
Rawlings, H. B., **IV** 190
Rawlings, Orrin, **IV** *112*
Rawnsley, C. F., **I** *157,* 158
Razorback (P-47D), **IV** 62
Read, Jack E., **III** 56
Read, Robert E., **III** 53
Rechlin-Lars (Germany), **IV** 115
Rector, Edward, **II** *33,* 34, 43, 47, 48
Red Army, **I** 30–32, 35–36. *See also* Soviet Union
Regensburg (Germany), **II** 174, 177–78, 182; **IV** 44,
        54–56
Regia Aeronautica (Italian Air Force), **IV** 5, 10, 19,
        24. *See also* Italian aircraft
Reichenau, Walther von, **I** 30, 77
Reichswehr. *See* German Army; Wehrmacht
Reid, Jewell H., **II** *80,* 81, 82
Reinberger, Helmut, **I** 36–37
Reitsch, Hanna, **IV** 117, *119*
Renault Works, **II** 112–13
Repulse (British naval vessel), **II** 73
Restemeyer, Werner, **I** 98

Reusser, Kenneth L., **IV** 198, 199
Reynaud, Paul, **I** 76
Reynolds, L. R., **I** 63
"Rhubarb," **I** 160
Ribbentrop, Joachim von, **I** 46; **IV** 116
Rice, G., **II** 141
Richard, Robert, **III** 85
Richards, Lewis, **II** 43
Richey, Paul, **I** 59–60
Richthofen, Manfred von, **I** 13, 32
Richthofen, Wolfram von, **I** 6, 14, 15, 30–32, *32*, 86, 108; **IV** 18, 28, 85
Rickenbacker, Eddie, **III** 42, 45; **IV** 64
Riley, Bruce R., **II** 188–89
Rimerman, Ben, **IV** 72
Ring, Stanhope C., **II** 90, 92
Rittmayer, Major, **III** 48
Rockets, **II** 181; **IV** 44, 48–49, 52, 94, 95, 100, *104, 105*
Röhm, Ernst, **I** 12
Roi (Marshalls), **III** 114, 116
Role of Defensive Pursuit, The (Chennault), **II** 27
Roma (Italian naval vessel), **IV** 27
Romana Americana refinery (Rumania), **II** 166, 172
Rome, **IV** 27, 28, 32
Rommel, Erwin, **I** 64; **II** vii, 156; **IV** 5–13, *6, 14, 15*, 19, 22, 74, 79, 80
Rooney, Andrew A., **IV** 49
Roosevelt, Franklin D., **I** 47; **II** 5, 8, 30, 37, 49, 67, 111, 151, *152, 154*, 155; **III** 114; **IV** 39, 118, 208
Roosevelt, Theodore, **II** 77
Root, John D., **IV** 97
Root, Robert, **IV** 134
Roper, Frank, **II** 117, 119
Rosenthal, Robert, **II** 185
Rostock (Germany), **II** 113
Rota (Marshalls), **III** 119, 132
Rotterdam, **I** *67;* **IV** 40, 171
Rouen-Sotteville (France), **II** 151, 173, 174
Rover Joes, **IV** 27
Rowell, Ross E., **III** 67–68
Royal Air Force (RAF; British airmen), **I** 3, 12, 47–49, 50–52, 53–55, 57, 58–61, 70–73, 75, 81, *82*, 85, 86, 89, 96, 107, 108, 109, 110, *111*, 116, 117–19, 129–31, 135, 156–59; **II** 30, 31, 34, 36, 114, 115, 117–18, 120, 123–26, 130, 134–35, 141, 144, 145, 147, 149–50, 191; **III** 4; **IV** 10–11, 37. *See also* British aircraft; British air units; specific branches
Royal Australian Air Force, **III** 6, 8–9, 16. *See also* Australian aircraft; Australian air units
Royal Canadian Air Force, **I** 87
Royal Flying Corps, **I** 54
Royal Navy (British), **I** 35, 45, 68, 69–73, *69*, 87, 107–8, 109, 116; **II** 7. *See also* British naval units; British naval vessels
Royce, Ralph, **III** 8
Rubber industry, synthetic (German), **IV** 37
Rubensdörfer, Walter, **I** 92, 103–4
Rudel, Hans-Ulrich, **IV** 86, *87*
Ruehlow, Stanley E., **III** 80

Rufe (A6M2-N), **III** 88, 100
Ruhland (Germany), **IV** 100
Ruhr, Battle of the, **IV** 38–40, 44
Rumania, **IV** 3, 86. *See also* Ploesti
Rundstedt, Gerd von, **I** 24, 68, 77; **IV** 106, 107, 108
Ruoff, Richard, **I** *32*
Russia. *See* Russian aircraft; Soviet Union
Russian aircraft, **IV** 82
  Airacobra (P-39), **IV** 84, 89
  Hurricane, **IV** 84
  I-15, **IV** 84
  I-16, **I** 16; **IV** *83*
  I-53, **IV** 83
  Ilyushin 2 (Sturmovik), **IV** 84
  Lavochkin 5, **IV** 85
  Mustang (P-51), **IV** 86, 87, *88,* 89
  P-39 (Airacobra) **IV** 84, 89
  P-40B (Tomahawk), **IV** 84
  P-51, **IV** 86, 87, *88,* 89
  Tomahawk, **IV** 84
  Yakovlev 9, **IV** *84*
Ryuho (Japanese naval vessel), **III** 120, 135; **IV** 140
Ryujo (Japanese naval vessel), **II** 78, 80; **III** 60, 61, 65

Sailer, Joseph, Jr., **III** 84–85
Saint-Exupéry, Antoine de, **I** 77
Saint-Lô (France), **IV** 100
Saint Lo (U.S. naval vessel), **IV** 154, 176–77
St. Paul's Cathedral (London), **I** *138*, 144–46, 148
"Saint Valentine's Day Massacre," **III** 89
Saipan, **III** 114, 119, 121, 122, *123*, 124, *133*, 136; **IV** 174. *See also* Isley Field
Saito, Yoshitsugo, **III** 23
Sakai, Saburo, **III** 11, 48, 55
Salerno, **IV** 27
Sally (Japanese aircraft), **II** 32–33; **III** 23, *24, 25*, 41
Samuel B. Roberts, **IV** 151
Sand Island (Midway atoll), **II** 77, 85
San Francisco (U.S. naval vessel), **III** 83
San Jacinto (U.S. naval vessel), **III** 121
San Juan (U.S. naval vessel), **III** 79
Sanjurjo Sacanell, José, **I** 14–15
Sano, Tadoyoshi, **III** 84
Santa Cruz, Battle of, **III** 73–77, *78,* 79–81
Santee (U.S. naval vessel), **IV** 154
Saratoga (U.S. naval vessel), **II** 6, 7, 12, 16; **III** *50,* 53–55, 57, 60–63, 66, 67, 74, 80, 107, 108
Saturation bombing, **II** 12; **IV** 161. *See also* Strategic bombing
Saul, Richard, **I** 88
Saundby, Robert H. M., **II** *112,* 113, 115, 133
Saunders, LaVerne, **III** 65; **IV** 133, *160*
Saur, Otto, **IV** 56
Savo (U.S. naval vessel), **IV** 180
Savo Island, Battle of, **III** 57, 60
Sawyer, Charles, **II** 47
Saxelby, Clive, **II** 124–25
SB2-C (Helldiver), **III** 121, 135; **IV** 142, 146, 147, *148, 157,* 193, 194, 218
SB2U (Vindicator), **II** 12, *83,* 84, 87, *100,* 101, 108
SBD (Dauntless), **II** 24, 59, *82,* 84, 87, *92, 93,* 94, 96, 98, 100, 101, 108; **III** 12, *50,* 54–55, *54,* 59,

63, 64, 68, *70,* 72, *75–77, 79,* 83, 84–86, *84,* 87, 88, 96, *109,* 121; **IV** *183*
Scharnhorst (German naval vessel), **I** 45, 52, 150, 168
Scharroo, P., **I** 66
Scheer. See Admiral Scheer
Schellenberg, Walter, **I** 32
Schick, William, **II** 20
Schiel, Frank, Jr., **II** 47
Schiffley, Fred D., **III** 21
Schilling, David, **IV** 69
Schimenek, John, **II** 179, 181
Schlegel, Heinz, **I** 94
Schleicher, Kurt von, **I** 12
Schmid, Josef "Beppo," **I** *97,* 107, 119–22, 132
Sealion, Operation (*Seelöwe*), **I** 82, 83–85, 106, 109, 119–20, 122, 123, 128, 136, 137, 149, 150
Sealion barges, **II** 133
Sedan (France), **I** 64–66
Seeckt, Hans von, **I** 4, 5–9; **IV** 82
Seipo, William, **II** 42–43
Seiyo Maru (Japanese naval vessel), **III** 133
Seki, Mamoru, **III** 61, 62, 76–78
Seki, Yukio, **IV** 154, 175–77
Senger und Etterlin, Fridolin von, **IV** 35
Sextant Conference (Cairo), **III** 114
Seymour, Thomas H., **IV** 97
Seyss-Inquart, Artur von, **IV** 120
Shafter, Fort, **II** 15
Shannon, David, **II** 142, 145–47
Shaw (U.S. naval vessel), **II** *22,* 23
Sherman, Forrest, **III** *54*
Sherman, Frederick C., **II** 77; **IV** 142, 143, 147, 148
Shibasaki Keiji, **III** 108
Shigure (Japanese naval vessel), **IV** 145, 149
Shilling, Erikson E., **II** 32
Shima, Kiyohide, **IV** 140, 148, 149, 177
Shimazaki, Shegekazu, **II** 21
Shinano (Japanese naval vessel), **IV** 188
Shingo, Hideki, **IV** 76–77
Shipman, Ernest, **IV** 87–91, *92*
Ships and shipping, **I** 73, 152; **IV** 10, 161. *See also* specific nationalities, ships
Shizuoka (Japan), **IV** *206*
Sho, Operation, **IV** 137–40
Shoestring, Operation, **III** 53. *See also* Guadalcanal
Shoho (Japanese naval vessel), **II** 75, 77
Shokaku (Japanese naval vessel), **II** 3, 14, 75, 77, 78; **III** 37, 60, 61, 67, 75, 76, 78, 79, 120, 127
Shoki. See Tojo
Shomo, William A., **IV** 181, *182,* 183, 184
Sicily, **II** 155, 171; **IV** 22–23, *24,* 25, 26
Sigourney (U.S. naval vessel), **III** 97
Sikorski, Wladislaw, **I** *127*
Silver Star, **II** 181; **III** 97
Simon, Sir John, **I** 12
Simpler, Leroy C., **III** 66
Sims (U.S. naval vessel), **II** 75
Sinclair, Archibald, **I** 119; **IV** 53
Singapore, **II** 41, 73; **IV** 161
Skelton, F. S., **I** 158
Skip-bombing, **III** 11–12, *13,* 20, 21, 35
Skon, Warren, **III** 113–14
Skua (aircraft), **I** 42, 123; **IV** 19

Slave labor, **II** 148, 172
Slessor, Sir John, **IV** 29
Smart, Jacob E., **II** *157,* 158
Smith, D. F., **III** *54*
Smith, Donald, **II** 61, 69
Smith, Holland M., **III** 124
Smith, John L., **III** *59,* 61, 64, 66, 69, 90
Smith, Leo R., **III** 65, 69
Smith, Robert, **II** 35
Smith, Walter Bedell, **IV** 120
Smith (U.S. naval vessel), **III** 79, 80
Snowden, Ernest M., **III** 130
Soapsuds, Operation, **II** 157. *See also* Ploesti
SOC-4 (aircraft), **IV** *142*
Solomon Islands, **II** 74, 105; **III** 9–11, 17–18. *See also* Guadalcanal
Sonnemann, Emmy, **IV** 80
Soong, Mei-ling. *See* Chiang Kai-shek, Madame
Soong, T. V., **II** 30, 31
Sorpe Dam (Germany), **II** 135, 138, 140, 141, 147, 149
Soryu (Japanese naval vessel), **II** 3, 21, 78, 87, 89, 93–95, 97, 98, 100
Soucek, Apollo, **II** 57
Southampton (British naval vessel), **I** 52
Southampton (England), **I** 95, 103, 135, 143
South Dakota (U.S. naval vessel), **III** 75, 79, 86, 130
Southwest Pacific area, **III** 4, 5
Soviet Union (Russia; U.S.S.R.), **I** 5, 6, 9, 24, 89, 152; **II** vii, 5, 29, 49, 52, 57, 68, 111, 130, 148, 151, 172; **IV** 19, 35, 80–86, 114–15, 206. *See also* Red Army; Russian aircraft
Spaatz, Carl A., **I** xii; **II** 52, 156; **IV** 12, 28, 53, 92, 93, 95, 100, 113, 114, 115–16, 160, 186, 209, *211, 216*
Spafford, F. M. "Spam," **II** *142,* 143, 144, *148*
Spain. *See* Guernica
Sparks, Kenneth C., **III** 42
Spatz, Harold, **II** 70
Special Aviation Project. *See* Tokyo
Speer, Albert, **II** 191; **IV** 42, 47, 51, 52, 55, 56, 106
Speidel, Hans, **IV** 79
Spence, Magnus, **II** 115, 118
Spencer, W. P., **III** 94
Sperrle, Hugo, **I** 6, 15, 77, 85, 103, 119, 146; **IV** 74, 78
Spitfire, **I** *159, 160;* **II** 152, 177; **IV** 11, 12, 13, 20–21, 24, 25, 27, 63, 80, 95, *102, 103,* 110
Sprague, Clifton A. F., **IV** 145, 149, 151, 153, 154
Sprague, Thomas, **IV** 154
Spruance, Raymond A., **II** 80, 84, 89, 90, 98, *98,* 99, 101, 105; **III** 107, 120, 126, 133; **IV** 190, 193
Staffel, defined, **I** 15
Stalin, Joseph, **I** 33; **IV** 22, 82, 115, 206
Stalingrad, **IV** 84, 85
Stanley (U.S. naval vessel), **IV** 195
Starks, Henry I., **II** 88
Steakley, Ralph D., **IV** 164
Steana Romana complex, **II** 169
Steichen, Edward, **III** 111
Stevens, E. E., **I** 53
Stevens, Richard Playne, **I** 158–59
Stewart, Everett W., **IV** 68

Stewart, Josephine, **II** 47
Stewart, Walter, **II** 166
Steyr (Austria), **IV** 54
Stilwell, Joseph W., **II** 41, 42, *45*, 46: **IV** 130
Stimson, Henry L., **II** 7, *8*
Stinzi, Vernon L., **II** 56
Stirling (aircraft), **I** 101–2; **II** 116, *117*, 118–23, *124*, 129
Storch, **IV** 6
Storm Troopers (*Sturmabteilungen*), **I** 7, 9, 12
Strafers. *See* B-25
Strafing, **IV** *67*, 71, *72*, 87, 100. *See also* specific aircraft, places
Strangle, Operation, **IV** 30–32
Strategic bombing, **II** 114, 135; **IV** 115–16. *See also* Area bombing; Dayling precision bombing; specific locations
Streett, St. Clair, **IV** 136
Strickland, H. E., **II** *48*
Strong, Stockton B., **III** 75, 76
Strother, Dean G., **II** *107*
Student, Kurt, **I** 11, 36, 66; **IV** 17–18
Stuka Pilot (Rudel), **IV** 86
Stukas. *See* Junkers (Ju): 87
Stumme, Georg von, **IV** 10
Stump, Felix B., **IV** 151
Stumpf, Hans-Jürgen, **I** 6, 10, *39*, 40
Stuttgart (Germany), **II** 183; **IV** 54, 56
Submarines, **II** 9, 11, 22, 58, 78–80, 94, 151, 154. *See also* specific submarines
Suffolk, Earl of, **I** 140
Sugita, Shoichi, **III** 48
Sugiyama, Hajime, **III** 86
Sumatra, **II** 5
Summera, Joseph "Mutt," **II** 136, 137
Sumpter, L. J., **II** 146
Sunderland (aircraft), **I** *151, 153*
Superfortress (B-29), **I** xii, xiii; **II** 174; **III** 114, 122, 133; **IV** 127–33, *128, 129, 130, 132, 133, 134*, 135, *135*, 159, 160, *161, 162*, 163, 164–65, *164*, 166–68, *166, 169*, 170, *171, 172*, 173, 174, 185–86, *203–4, 203, 207*, 208, *209*, 218
Supply lines, **IV** 12, 13, *14*, 15, 19, 30–33, 35, 107, 108, *113*. *See also* specific locations
Sutherland, Richard K., **III** *3, 5*–7; **IV** 137
Suwanee (U.S. naval vessel), **IV** 154, 177
Suzuki, Kantaro, **IV** 205–8
Suzuki, Mimori, **II** 23
Suzuya (Japanese naval vessel), **II** 101
Swan, R. A., **II** *80*
Swartout, Jack, **IV** 58, 60
Swartz, Frank N., **II** 42–43
Sweeney, Charles W., **IV** 209, 211, 212
Sweeney, Walter, **II** 81, 82, 87
Sweeny, Charles, **I** 166
Sweet, Malvern, **II** 177
Swenson, Raymond, **II** 20
Swett, James E., **III** 90, *91*, 92–93, 96
Swoose. See B-17
Swordfish (British aircraft), **II** 7; **IV** 5, 19

Tabby (Nakajima L2D), **III** *49*
Tackett, W., **III** 49

Taerum, H. T. "Terry," **II** *142*, 143, 144, 148
Taiho (Japanese naval vessel), **III** 120, 127
Takagi, Takeo, **II** 75
Takahashi, Kakuichi, **II** 14, 15
Tak air base (Thailand), **II** 37–38
Takamatsu, Prince, **IV** 214–15
Takao (Japanese naval vessel), **IV** 141
Takasu, Shiro, **II** 62
"Tallboy" bombs, **IV** 114
"Tally Ho!" procedure, **I** 110
Tamai, Asaichi, **IV** 175, 176
Tambor (U.S. naval vessel), **II** 101
Tamei Maru (Japanese naval vessel), **III** 21
Tanabe, Yahachi, **II** 104
Tanaka, Raizo, **II** 81; **III** 60, 63–65, 70, 83–86
Tank, Kurt, **IV** 59
Tankers. *See* specific ships
Tanks, **I** 5, 6, *112*, 113; **IV** 8, 10, 11, 82, 84, 87, 99, 100, *101*
Taranto (Italy), **IV** 5, 27
Tarawa, **III** 107, 108
Targoviste (Rumania), **II** 166
Taroa (Marshalls), **III** 114
Tarrant, Yancey, **IV** 87
Tate, Benjamin, **III** 134
Tate, Howard L., Jr., **II** 117
Taylor, K. S., **I** *163*
Taylor, Kenneth A., **II** 21
Taylor, W. E. G., **I** *163*
TBD (Devastator), **II** 24, *81*, 90–93
TBF (Avenger), **II** 84, *86*, 87, 90; **III** 63, 68, 72, 75, *76*, 77, *83*, 84, 85, 87, 88, 96, 97, *97, 112*, 113–14, *113*, 117, 121, 122, 132–35; **IV** 141, 145–47, 149, 151–53, 155, 156, 193, 194, 218
Tedder, Sir Arthur W., **II** 156, 158; **IV** 9, 20, 28, 92
Tell, Rudolf, **IV** 97
Temple of Heaven (Japanese Emperor's palace), **II** 45
Tenaru River, Battle of, **III** 58
Tennant, W. G., **I** 72
Tennessee (U.S. naval vessel), **II** 16, 23
Tennyson, Alfred Tennyson, Lord, **IV** 149, 156, 157
Tenzen. See Jill
Terror attacks (*Terrorangriffe*), **II** 113
Thailand, **II** 5. *See also* specific locations
Thatch, David J., **II** 68–69
Thatch, John S., **II** 90, 91
Theobald, Robert A., **II** 80; **III** 105
Thomas, Norman M., **I** 61, 62
Thompson, J. M., **I** 104
Thompson, Ralph, **II** 163
Thousand Plan, **II** 114–15. *See also* Cologne
Threadfin (U.S. naval vessel), **IV** 193
Thunderbolt (P-47), **II** 152, 177, 179, 183, 186, 187; **III** 24, 30, 42, 43, *124*, 125; **IV** *25*, 48, 54, 58, 60, 61, *62, 69*, 70, *70*, 71, *72*, 73, 95, 96, 98–100, *101*, 102, 103, 105, 111, 112, 113, *207*, 218
Thyssen steelworks (Germany), **II** 113
Tibbets, Paul W., Jr., **IV** 207–9
Ticonderoga (U.S. naval vessel), **IV** 178
Tidal Wave, Operation. *See* Ploesti
Tiger Moth (aircraft), **I** 123; **II** 116–17; **IV** 5

Timberlake, Edward J., **II** 159, *160,* 165, 172
Tinian (Marianas), **III** 114, 119, 122, *133,* 136
Tip and run raids, German, **II** 111
Tirpitz (German naval vessel), **II** 134, 137, 138, 150; **IV** 114
Tizard, Sir Henry, **II** 136
Tobin, Eugene **I** *162, 163,* 166
Tobruk (Libya), **II** vii, 156; **IV** 10, 22
Togo, Heihachiro, **II** 12
Tojo, Hideki, **II** *4, 5;* **III** 120, 136; **IV** 214
Tojo (Nakajima Ki. 44), **III** 101, 102
Tokuyama (Japan), **IV** 207
Tokyo, **II** vii, 47, 49–72, 74; **IV** 164, 168, 170, *171, 172,* 173, *204,* 205, 211, 212
Tokyo Express, **III** 58, 65, 82–103
Tokyo Rose, **II** 47; **IV** 189
Tomahawk (P-40B), **II** 27, *29,* 30–35, *36,* 37, 38, *39,* 40–46; **IV** 84
Tominaga, Kyoji, **IV** 140, 145, 181
Tomonaga, Joichi, **II** 83–85, 87–90, 96–98
Tone (Japanese naval vessel), **II** 12, 84, 87, 98
Tongue, R., **I** *163*
Tony (Kawasaki Ki. 61), **III** *28,* 98, 100; **IV** 143, 165, *167,* 182, 192
Torch, Operation, **II** 151, 155; **IV** 11, 19
Townsend, Peter, **I** *82*
Townsend, W. C., **II** 147
Toyama (Japan), **IV** *206*
Toyoda, Soemu, **III** 120–22, 132; **IV** 138–40, 149, 205, 206, 212, 214
Trautloft, Hannes, **I** 127
Trenchard, Hugh, **I** xi–xii
Trevor-Roper, R. D., **II** *142, 148*
Trident Conference, **IV** 128–29
Tripartite Pact, **II** 5
Tripoli, **IV** 10
True, Clinton U., **III** 32
Truk (Carolines), **III** 117; **IV** 135
Truman, Harry S, **IV** 206, 208, 209, 211
Tsu (Japan), **IV** 204
Tsushima Strait, Battle of, **II** 12
Tuck, Robert S., **I** 129
Tulagi (Solomons), **II** 74, 75; **III** 55
Tunisia, **IV** 11–15
Turkey, **II** 171
Turkey Shoot (Marianas), **II** 128–32
Turner, Helen, **I** 112
Turner, Richmond K., **III** 57, 121
Twining, Nathan F., **IV** 28, 53, 115, 209
Tyler, Kermit, **II** 15
Tyler, Marshall A., **II** 101
Typhoon (aircraft), **IV** *79,* 95, 110

Udet, Ernst, **I** *13,* 14, *65, 97;* **IV** *43,* 44
Ugaki, Matome, **II** 99–100, 105, 108; **IV** 190, 203–4, 215
Umezu, Yoshijira, **IV** 205, 206, 212, 214
United Kingdom. *See* Great Britain
United States, **II** 4–5, 29–30. *See also* specific branches of armed forces
United States aircraft, **II** 18, 19, 20, 23, 49, 53, 54, 68, 78, 90–93, 105, 155, 161–62, 164–67, 169–72, 174–76, 177, 178, 181, 182, 183, 185,

186, 187, 188, 189, 191; **III** 8, 9, 16, 21, 22, 24, 30, 33, 34, 35–36, 37, 41–42, 62, 69, 70, 80, 84, 86, 89, 92, 93, 117, 135; **IV** 13, 44, 46, 51, 54–56, 61, 74, 112, 115, 132, 133, 134, 139, 148, 161, 165, 170, 187, 188, 194, 205
A-20 (Havoc), **II** 18, 119; **III** 12, *13,* 14, 20, 21, *45;* **IV** *94,* 95
A-24, **III** 5, 108
A-26 (Invader), **IV** 95, 99
Airacobra (P-39), **III** 5, *9,* 15–17, 24, 36, *60,* 65, 68, 90, 94, *104;* **IV** 84, 89
Avenger (TBF), **II** 84, *86,* 87, 90; **III** 63, 68, 72, 75, *76,* 77, *83,* 84, 85, 87, 88, 96, 97, *97, 112,* 113–14, *113,* 117, 121, 122, 132–35; **IV** 141, 145–47, 149, 151–53, 155, 156, 193, 194, 218
B-17 (Flying Fortress), **I** xii, xiii, *150,* 151; **II** 15, 18, *20,* 78, 81, 82, 84, 87, 88, 98, 101, 151, 152, *153,* 172, 173–74, *174 176,* 177–78, *179, 180,* 181, 182, 185, *186, 187,* 188, 189; **III** 5, 7, *7,* 8, 9, *10,* 11, 12, 14, 16, 18, 21, 22, 24, 26, 32, 54, 65, 70, 72; **IV** 10, 11, 27, 29, 30, *32,* 38, 40, 48, *48, 50,* 51, *53,* 54, 55, 57, 58, *59, 68,* 92–94, *95,* 97, 99, *114,* 115, 118, 120, *121, 122,* 127, 164
B-17E, *7, 9*
B-18, **II** 18
B-23, **II** 51, 52
B-24 (Liberator), **I** 151–52; **III** 16, 18, 24, 26, 30, 34, 49, *105, 106,* 108, *109;* **IV** 8, 9, 10, 27, *28,* 30, *34,* 35, *42,* 48, 54, *55,* 58, 90, 91, *93,* 97, 98, *99,* 100, *108,* 114, 115, 127, 135–36, *136,* 138, 149, 154, 185
B-25 (Mitchell), **II** 47, 50–56, *57,* 59, 60, *61, 62, 63,* 64–66, *67;* **III** 5, 9, 12, 18, 19–20, *20,* 21, 24, 25, 27, *28,* 29, 30, 31, 32, 34, *35,* 36–37, *38,* 99–100, *103;* **IV** 9, 10, *11,* 13, *14,* 27, *29,* 30, *31,* 33, 110
B-25C1, **III** 18
B-26 (Marauder), **II** *51,* 67, 78, 84, 86–87, 90, 108; **III** 5, 14; **IV** 27, 29, 30, *32, 34, 78, 79,* 95, 97, *98,* 99, 110
B-29 (Superfortress), **I** xii, xiii; **II** 174; **III** 114, 122, 133; **IV** 127–33, *128, 129, 130, 132, 133, 134,* 135, *135,* 159, 160, *161, 162,* 163, 164–65, *164,* 166–68, *166, 169,* 170, *171, 172,* 173, 174, 185–86, 203–5, *203, 207,* 208, *209,* 218
Beaufighter, **IV** *27*
Black Widow (P-61), **IV** *213*
C-46 (Commando), **III** *4*
C-47 (Dakota), **III** *24,* 30, 49; **IV** 24, 33, *78,* 95, 110, 111
Catalina (PBY), **I** 151; **II** 18, 80, 81, 83, 84, 86, 92; **III** 16, 18, *71,* 72, 75, 88
Commando (C-46), **III** *4*
Corsair, **III** 88, *89,* 90, 93–94, *95,* 96–97, 99, 100, *101, 102, 117;* **IV** 192, 197–99, *200,* 201, *202,* 218
Dauntless (SBD), **II** 24, 59, *82,* 84, 87, *92, 93,* 94, 96, 98, 100, 101, 108; **III** 12, *50,* 54–55, *54,* 59, 63, 64, 68, *70,* 71, 72, 75–77, *79,* 83, 84–86, *84,* 87, 88, 96, *109,* 121; **IV** *183*
Devastator (TBD), **II** 24, *81,* 90–93
F4F (Wildcat), **II** 12, 24–25, 59, *75, 76,* 84, *88,*

90, 93, 96, 101, 108; **III** 54–56, *58*, 59, *60*, 61, 62, 66, 68, *69*, 70–73, 74, 75, 77, *80*, 83, 84, 86, 87, 88, 90, 91, 96, 111, 126, 130, *134*; **IV** *146*, 151, *153*

F-5 **III** 35

F6F (Hellcat), **II** 81; **III** 99, 104, *110*, *111*, *112*, 113–14, 117, 119, 121, 122, *127*, 130–32, 135; **IV** *136*, 138, 141, *142*, *143*, 144–47, 151, 155, 177, 188, 192–94, 201, 218

Flying Fortress (B-17), **I** xii, xiii, *150*, 151; **II** 15, 18, *20*, 78, 81, 82, 84, 87, 88, 98, 101, 151, 152, *153*, 172, 173–74, *174*, *176*, 177–78, *179*, *180*, 181, 182, 185, *186*, *187*, 188, 189; **III** 5, 7, *7*, 8, 9, *10*, 11, 12, 14, 16, 18, 21, 22, 24, 26, 32, 54, 65, 70, 72; **IV** 10, 11, 27, 29, 30, *32*, 38, 40, 48, *48*, *50*, 51, *53*, 54, 55, 57, 58, *59*, *68*, 92–94, *95*, 97, 99, *114*, 115, 118, 120, *121*, *122*, 127, 164

Havoc (A-20), **II** 18, 119; **III** 12, *13*, *45*; **IV** *94*, 95,

Hellcat (F6F), **II** 81; **III** 99, 104, *110*, *111*, *112*, 113–14, 117, 119, 121, 122, *127*, 130–32, 135; **IV** *136*, 138, 141, *142*, *143*, 144–47, 151, 155, 177, 188, 192–94, 201, 218

Helldiver (SB2-C), **III** 121, 135; **IV** 142, 146, 147, *148*, *157*, 193, 218

"Horsa" gliders, **IV** *77*, *78*

Kingfisher (OS2U), **II** *19*

Klunkers (P-400), **IV** 5, 59, *60*, 67, 68, 71

Liberator (B-24), **I** 151–52; **III** 16, 18, 24, 26, 30, 34, 49, *105*, *106*, 108, *109*; **IV** 8, 9, 10, 27, *28*, 30, *34*, 35, *42*, 48, 54, 55, 58, 90, 91, *93*, 97, 98, *99*, 100, *108*, 114, 115, 127, 135–36, *136*, 138, 149, 154, 185

Lightning (P-38), **II** 105, *106*; **III** *15*, 16, *17*, 21, 24, 27, 30, 31, 32–37, 84, 89, 90, 93, 96, 106; **IV** 11, *13*, *14*, 27, *34*, 35, 48, 54, 58, 69, *75*, *81*, 87, 91, 95

Marauder (B-26), **II** *51*, 67, 78, 84, 86–87, 90, 108; **III** 5, 14; **IV** 27, 29, 30, *32*, *34*, *78*, *79*, 95, 97, *98*, 99, 110

Mitchell (B-25), **II** 47, 50–56, *57*, 59, 60, *61*, *62*, *63*, 64–66, *67*; **III** 5, 9, 12, 18, 19–20, *20*, 21, 24, 25, 27, *28*, 29, 30, 31, 32, 34, *35*, 36–37, *38*, 99–100, *103*; **IV** 9, 10, *11*, 13, *14*, 27, *29*, 30, *31*, 33, 110

Mustang (P-51), **I** xiii; **II** 152; **IV** 26, 27, 35, 48, 49, *50*, 51, 54, 56, 57, 58, 60, 61, *63*, 66, 68, 87, *88*, 89, 90, 91, 95, 101, 102, 103, 104, 110, 115, 118, 181–84, *182*, *185*, *207*, *212*, 218

OS2U (Kingfisher), **II** *19*; **III** *119*; **IV** *136*

P-36, **II** 21

P-38 (Lightning), **II** 105, *106*; **III** *15*, 16, *17*, 21, 24, 27, 30, 31, 32–37, 84, 89, 90, 93, 96, 106; **IV** 11, *13*, *14*, 27, *34*, 35, 48, 54, 58, 69, *75*, *81*, 87, 91, 95

P-39 (Airacobra), **III** 5, *9*, 15–17, 24, 36, *60*, 65, 68, 90, 94, *104*; **IV** 84, 89

P-40 (Warhawk), **I** xiii; **II** 15, 21, 152; **III** 5–6, 15–17, 89, 94, 96, *105*, 106, 108; **IV** 10, 11, 12, 13, 15, 24

P-40F, **IV** 9

P-47 (Thunderbolt), **II** 152, 177, 179, 183, 186, 187;

III 24, 30, 42, 43, *124*, 125; **IV** *25*, 48, 54, 58, 60, 61, *62*, *69*, 70, *70*, 71, *72*, 73, 95, 96, 98–100, *101*, 102, 103, 105, 111, 112, 113, *207*, 218

P-47B, **IV** 69

P-47D (Razorback), **IV** *62*

P-47n, **IV** *62*

P-51 (Mustang), **I** xiii; **II** 152; **IV** 26, 27, 35, 48, 49, *50*, 51, 54, 56, 57, 58, 60, 61, *63*, 66, 68, 87, *88*, 89, 90, 91, 95, 101, 102, 103, 104, 110, 115, 118, 181–84, *182*, *185*, *207*, *212*, 218

P-61 (Black Widow), **IV** *213*

P-80, **III** 50

P-400 (Klunkers), **IV** 5, 59, *60*, 67, 68, 71

PBY (Catalina), **I** 151; **II** 18, 80, 81, 83, 84, 86, 92; **III** 16, 18, *71*, 72, 75, 88

Razorback (P-47D), **IV** *62*

SB2-C (Helldiver), **III** 121, 135; **IV** 142, 146, 147, *148*, *157*, 193, 194, 218

SB2U (Vindicator), **II** 12, *83*, 84, 87, *100*, 101, 108

SBD (Dauntless), **II** 24, 59, *82*, 84, 87, *92*, *93*, 94, 96, 98, 100, 101, 108; **III** 12, *50*, 54–55, *54*, 59, 63, 64, 68, *70*, 71, 72, 75–77, 79, 83, 84–86, *84*, 87, 88, 96, *109*, 121; **IV** *183*

SOC-4, **IV** *142*

Spitfire, **IV** 11

Superfortress (B-29), **I** xii, xiii; **II** 174; **III** 114, 122, 133; **IV** 127–33, *128*, *129*, *130*, *132*, *133*, *134*, 135, *135*, 159, 160, *161*, *162*, 163, 164, 166–68, *166*, *169*, 170, *171*, *172*, 173, 174, 185–86, 203–5, *203*, *207*, 208, *209*, 218

TBD (Devastator), **II** 24, *81*, 90–93

TBF (Avenger), **II** 84, *86*, 87, 90; **III** 63, 68, 72, 75, *76*, 77, *83*, 84, 85, 87, 88, 96, 97, *97*, *112*, 113–14, *113*, 117, 121, 122, 132–35; **IV** 141, 145–47, 149, 151–53, 155, 156, 193, 194, 218

Thunderbolt (P-47), **II** 152, 177, 179, 183, 186, 187; **III** 24, 30, 42, 43, *124*, 125; **IV** *25*, 48, 54, 58, 60, 61, *62*, *69*, 70, *70*, 71, *72*, 73, 95, 96, 98–100, *101*, 102, 103, 105, 111, 112, 113, 207, *218*

Vindicator (SB2U) **II** 12, *83*, 84, 87, *100*, 101, 108

Warhawk (P-40), **I** xiii; **II** 15, 21, 152; **III** 5–6, 15–17, 89, 94, 96, *105*, 106, 108; **IV** 10, 11, 12, 13, 15, 24

Wildcat (F4F), **II** 12, 24–25, 59, *75*, *76*, 84, *88*, 90, 93, 96, 101, 108; **III** 54–56, *58*, 59, *60*, 61, 62, 66, 68, *69*, 70–73, 74, 75, 77, *80*, 83, 84, 86, 87, 88, 90, 91, 96, 111, 126, 130, *134*; **IV** *146*, 151, *153*

United States Air Forces (airmen), **II** 21, 34, 35, 38, 40–43, 48, 53–57, 62, 68–70, 87–88, 91–93, 101, 105, 158, 162, 165–66, 170, 172, 181, 182, *183*, 187; **III** 5, 6, 7, 8, 17, 21, 22, 32, 37, 40–41, 46–48, 50, 61, 65, 69, 70, 90, 92; **IV** *13*, 65–66, 67–68, *112*, 131, 132, 133, 139, 161, 166, 170–71, 194. *See also* United States aircraft; specific branches of armed forces

United States Army (soldiers), **III** 116; **IV** 98, 99, 173, 185, 201. *See also* United States Army Air Corps; United States army air units; United States army units

United States Army Air Corps, **II** 51. *See also* United States aircraft; United States army air units

United States army air units, **IV** 8–11, 24, 48, 49, 51, 53–56, 57, 61, 74, 79–80, 97–99, 115, 131, 132, 133, 142–43, 163, 164, 168, 170, 204. *See also* Anglo-American air units

  air forces:

    Eighth, **II** 130, 151, 152, 154, 155, 156, 173, *174,* 175, 176, 177, 178, 182–83, 189, 191; **IV** 11, 28, 36–40, 42, 44, 46, 53–57, 63, 67, 68, 74, 92, 97, 98, 103, 110, 114, 115, 118, 120, 205, 209

    Eleventh, **III** 105, 106; **IV** 133

    Far East, **II** 156; **IV** 136

    Fifteenth, **II** 130, 172; **IV** 12, 28, 30, 32–36, 46, 52–54, 56, 90, 91, 114, 115

    Fifth, **III** 8, 11, 21, 32, 34, 35, 37, 38, 45, 65, 92; **IV** 129, 136, 149, 182, 183, 206

    Fourteenth (China Air Task Force), **I** 127; **II** 47, 48; **IV** 128, 129, 138

    Fourth, **III** 8, 40

    Middle East (later Ninth), **II** 156; **IV** 8

    Ninth (formerly Middle East), **II** 155–57, 172, 175; **IV** 8, 11, 12, 23, 28, 49, 54, 55, 57, 63, 67, 68, 74, 78, 79, 80, 93–95, 97, 98, 112, 113

    Northwest African, **II** 156

    Seventh, **II** 78, 83; **III** 108, 109, 114, 124–25, 136; **IV** 135, 136, 185

    Strategic, **IV** 53, 209

    Tactical, **IV** 27, 31

    Tenth, **II** 41, 45–47; **IV** 8

    Thirteenth, **II** 107; **III** 38, 48, 65, 99; **IV** 28, 136, 149, 154

    Twentieth, **IV** 128–30, 135, 138, 162, 163, 171, 184, 203, 209

  air divisions:

    1st (later 1st Bombardment Wing), **IV** 48, 54

    2nd, **IV** 48, 54

    3rd, **IV** 48, 54, 120

    4th. *See* United States army air units: wing: 4th

  groups:

    1st Fighter, **IV** 11

    3rd Bombardment (Light), **III** 12, 14, 18–20, 24, 27, 28, 33, 36

    4th Fighter (formerly Eagle Squadron), **I** 166; **IV** 57, 61–63, 66, 68, 73

    5th Bombardment, **II** 83

    7th Bombardment, **IV** 8

    8th Fighter, **II** 36

    11th Bombardment, **II** 83; **III** 54, 65, *136*

    12th Bombardment (M), **IV** 9

    14th Bombardment, **IV** 11

    15th Fighter, **IV** 70

    17th Bombardment, **II** 53; **IV** 104

    19th Bombardment (H), **III** 8, 11, 16, 31; **IV** 170

    22nd Bombardment(M), **II** 86

    23rd Fighter, **II** 41, 47–48

    29th Bombardment, **IV** 170

    31st Fighter, **IV** 11, 25, 87–92

    33rd Fighter, **IV** 11, 24, 25

    34th Bombardment, **IV** 120

    35th Fighter, **III** 8, 21, 24, 36; **IV** 182

    38th Bombardment (M), **II** 86; **III** 28, 33, 36

    40th Bombardment (VH), **IV** 130–32

    41st Bombardment **IV** 116

    43rd Bombardment, **III** 8, 12, 16, 18, 34

    44th Bombardment (Eight Balls), **II** 155, 159, 162, 163, 166–68, *169,* 171

    49th Fighter, **III** 5–6, 16, 36, 42, 45

    52nd Fighter, **IV** 11

    56th Fighter (Wolfpack), **II** 186; **IV** 60, 61, 63, 68, 69, 70, 73

    57th Fighter, **IV** 9, 12, 13

    90th Bombardment, **III** 16, 18, 34

    91st Bombardment, **II** *187,* 188

    92nd Bombardment, **II** 185, 186, 188; **IV** 109

    93rd Bombardment (Traveling Circus), **II** 155, 159, 160, *161,* 162, 163, *164,* 165–69, 171, 186

    94th Bombardment, **II** 186

    95th Bombardment, **II** 186; **IV** 57, 58, 60, 115

    96th Bombardment, **II** 177, 186

    97th Bombardment, **IV** 11, *34*

    98th Bombardment (H; Pyramiders), **II** 155, 158, 162, 163, 166, 167, *168,* 169; **IV** 9

    100th Bombardment, **II** 185, 186, 188; **IV** 57, 58, 60, 115

    301st Bombardment, **IV** 11

    303rd Bombardment, **II** 186

    306th Bombardment, **II** 185, 186, 188

    318th Fighter, **III** 124, 125

    324th Fighter, **IV** 12

    345th Bombardment (Air Apaches), **III** 32, 33, 36, 38

    348th Fighter, **III** 24, 42–43

    352nd Fighter, **IV** 110, 111

    353rd Fighter, **II** 187

    354th Fighter, **IV** 49, 57, 112

    363rd Fighter, **IV** 57

    365th Fighter, **IV** 101

    376th Bombardment (Liberandos), **II** 155, 159, *161,* 162–69, 171, 172

    379th Bombardment, **II** 186

    381st Bombardment, **II** 182

    384th Bombardment (H), **II** 175–79, *180* 182, 183, 185, 186, *191;* **IV** 50, 62, 100, 116

    385th Bombardment, **II** 186, 188

    386th Bombardment, **IV** 79

    387th Bombardment (M), **IV** 97

    388th Bombardment, **II** 186, 188

    389th Bombardment (Sky Scorpions), **II** 155, 159, 162, 163, 167, 169–71

    390th Bombardment, **II** 186, 188; **IV** 60, 115, 122

    392nd Bombardment, **II** 186

    401st Bombardment **IV** 95

    444th Bombardment (VH), **IV** 130

    453rd Bombardment, **IV** 55

    462nd Bombardment (VH), **IV** 130, 131

    464th Bombardment, **IV** 34

    468th Bombardment (VH), **IV** 130, 133, 135, 161

    475th Fighter, **III** 36, 45

    494th Bombardment, **IV** 135

    497th Bombardment, **IV** 163

    498th Bombardment, **IV** 163

    509th Composite, **IV** 163, 207–9

"Halverson Detachment," **II** 57
squadrons:
  6th Troop Carrier, **III** 24
  8th Photo, **III** 24, 26, 35–37
  9th, **IV** 8
  9th Fighter, **III** 36, 42
  11th Bombardment (M), **II** 47
  13th Bombardment, **III** 24, 26, 36
  15th, **IV** 9
  15th Bombardment (L), **IV** 11
  18th Fighter, **III** 106
  19th Fighter, **III** 124
  34th Bombardment, **IV** 104
  39th Fighter, **III** 36
  44th Pursuit, **II** 21
  45th Fighter, **IV** 70
  46th Pursuit, **II** 21
  47th Pursuit, **II** 18, 20
  54th Fighter, **III** 106
  61st Fighter, **IV** 70
  63rd Bombardment, **III** 8, 12
  64th, **IV** 9
  66th Fighter, **IV** 9, 12
  67th Bombardment, **III** 67
  67th Fighter, **IV** 9, 13
  70th Fighter, **II** 106; **III** 92
  71st Bombardment, **III** 36
  73rd Fighter, **III** 124
  80th Fighter, **III** 36
  89th Tactical Reconnaisance, **II** 53; **IV** 182
  307th, **IV** 87–92
  314th Fighter, **IV** 12
  334th Fighter, **IV** 62
  339th Fighter, **II** 105
  351st Bombardment, **IV** 58
  356th Fighter, **IV** 49
  393rd Bombardment (VH), **IV** 207–8
  405th Bombardment, **III** 28, 36
  431st Bombardment, **III** 108
  431st Fighter, **III** 36, 45, 46
  432nd Fighter, **III** 36
  433rd Fighter, **III** 36
  487th Fighter, **IV** 110
  498th Fighter, **III** 36
  499th Fighter, **III** 36
  500th Fighter, **III** 36
  501st Fighter, **III** 36
  531st Fighter Bomber, **III** 108
  546th Bombardment, **II** 178, 179
  779th Bombardment, **IV** 34
  820th Bombardment, **III** 116
  Eagle (later 4th Fighter Group), **IV** 57
wings:
  1st Bombardment (later 1st Air Division), **II** 174, 177, 187
  4th Bombardment (later 3rd Air Division), **II** 177
  13th Combat, **IV** 60, 115, 120
  40th Bombardment, **II** 185, 188
  41st Bombardment, **II** 186
  45th, **IV** 120
  45th Bombardment, **II** 186
  54th Troop Carrier, **III** 30

  58th Bombardment (VH), **IV** 130, 131, 133, 162, 163
  73rd Bombardment, **IV** 160, 161, 164, 170
  93rd **IV** 120
  98th Combat, **IV** 97
  301st Fighter, **IV** 163
  313th Bombardment, **IV** 161, 170, 185, 204, 208
  314th Bombardment, **IV** 161, 168, 170
  315th Bombardment, **IV** 163, 205
United States army units. *See also* United States army air units.
  armies:
    Fifth, **IV** 25, 27, 31, 32
    First, **IV** 99
    Seventh, **IV** 24
    Sixth, **IV** 141
    Third, **IV** 99, 107
  battalions:
    382nd Engineer Construction, **IV** 130
    805th Aviation Engineer, **IV** 207
    853rd Aviation Engineer, **IV** 130
  corps:
    VI, **IV** 28
  divisions:
    7th Infantry, **III** 106, 107 116
    27th Infantry, **III** 108, 122, 124
    30th Infantry, **IV** 98, 99
    32nd Infantry, **III** 14, 16
    82nd Airborne, **IV** 24
    96th Infantry, **IV** 201
  regiments:
    2nd Raider, **III** 96
    126th **III** 14, 16
    128th **III** 14, 16
    164th Infantry ("Americal Division"), **III** 69
    503rd Paratroop, **III** *29,* 30
United States marine air units
  Cactus Air Force, **III** 58–59. *See also* Cactus Air Force
  groups (Marine Aircraft Groups):
    MAG-4, **III** 69
    MAG-21, **II** 18
    MAG-22, **II** 101
    MAG-23 (Fighting 23), **III** 59, 61, 65–67, 69
    MAG-224, **III** 66
  squadrons (Marine Fighter Squadrons):
    VMF-112, **III** 87
    VMF-121, **III** 69, 72
    VMF-124, **III** 88, 89, 93
    VMF-212, **III** 73, 86
    VMF-214 (Black Sheep), **III** 98–99
    VMF-215, **III** 96
    VMF-221, 12, 84; **III** 90
    VMF-223, **III** 59, 61, 69
    VMF-224, **III** 65
    VMF-312, **IV** 198, 199
    VMSB-132 (Marine Scout Bomber Squadron), **III** 84–85
    VMSB-141, **III** 69
    VMSB-231, **II** 12; **III** 65, 69
    VMSB-241, **II** 88, 84
  wings (Marine Air Wing; MAW), 1st, **III** 66

United States Marines, **III** 60, *64,* 67, 82, 108, 114,
  116, *116;* **IV** 185, *202. See also* United States
  marine air units; United States marine units;
  specific battles
United States marine units. *See also* United States
  marine air units
 divisions:
  Ist, **III** 9–11, 55; **IV** 189
  2nd, **III** 108, 122
  3rd, **III** 96
  4th, **III** 122
  7th, **III** 67
United States naval air units,
 flights:
  58, **II** 84
  300, **III** 59, 62, 64, 69
 groups (Air Groups):
  6, **III** 83, 110
  10, **III** 76
  Hornet, **II** 90
 squadrons:
  Scouting Squadron 2, **II** 75
  Scouting Squadron 6, **II** 24
  VF-5, **III** 66, 111
  VF-9, **III** 111
  VF-10 (Grim Reapers), **III** 80
  VF-17, **III** 100
  VFN-76, **III** 127
  VS-10, **III** 85
  VT-3, **II** 93
  VT-6, **II** *81,* 90, 92
  VT-8, **II** 86–87, 89–92
  VT-10, **III** 77, 85
 task forces, 2nd Air, **III** 23
 wings, Patrol Wing 4, **III** 105
United States naval units. *See also* United States naval
  air units
 fleets:
  Fifth, **III** 107, *109;* **IV** 190
  Pacific, **II** 7, 9, 15, 22 72, 72–74. *See also* specific
   battles
  Seventh ("MacArthur's Navy"), **II** 75; **III** 21; **IV**
   139, 140, 142, 145, 149–51, 156
  Third, **IV** 138, 139, 141, 147, 150, 154
 task forces:
  16, **II** 58, 61, 63, 80, 98
  17, **II** 74, 75; **III** 75
  34, **IV** 150, 154, 156, 157, 159
  38, **IV** 138, 139, 141
  50, **III** 108
  57, **III** 108
  58 (Fast Carrier Force), **III** 120, *121,* 122,
   126, 135; **IV** 141, 187, 190, 192
 task groups:
  16.1, **II** 57
  16.2, **II** 56
  38.1, **IV** 142, 150
  38.2, **IV** 142, 157
  38.3, **IV** 142
  38.4, **IV** 142, 145
  50.1, **III** 108
  50.2 **III** 108

  50.4, **III** 108
  Taffy 1, **IV** 154
  Taffy 2, **IV** 151, 153
  Taffy 3, **IV** 151, *152,* 153, 154, 156
United States naval vessels, **II** 17, 18, 22–23, 75, *76,*
  77, 101, *102,* 103, 104; **III** 56, 57, 67, 78–80,
  90, 110; **IV** 144, 153, 154, 159, 176–77,
  179–81, 192, 194–96, 201–2
 Aaron Ward, **III** 90; **IV** 196–97, *198*
 Albacore, **III** 127
 Arizona, **II** 17, 18, 21–23
 Astoria, **II** 97
 Balch, **II** 103
 Bataan, **III** 120
 Belleau Wood, **III** 107, 108, 121, 132; **IV** 188
 Benham, **II** 103
 Bennington, **IV** 187
 Birmingham, **IV** 145
 Bunker Hill, **III** 107, 120, 130, 131; **IV** *194, 195*
 Bush, **IV** 192
 Cabot, **III** 121, 131; **IV** 146, 147, 148
 Calhoun, **IV** 192
 California, **II** 22–23
 Canberra, **IV** 138
 Cassin, **II** 23
 Cavalla, **III** 127
 Cowpens, **III** 107, 108, 121, 130
 Curtiss, **II** 23
 Dace, **IV** 141, 142
 Darter, **IV** 141, 142
 Downs, **II** 23
 Emmons, **IV** 192
 Enterprise, **II** 12, 15, 24, 52, 53, 57, 58, 59, 74, 79,
  80, *81, 88,* 89, 90, 92, 94, 97, 98, 101; **III** *50,*
  53, 55, 57, 59, 60–62, *63,* 66, 69, 74–75, *76,*
  77, 79, *80,* 81, 83, 84, 85, 107, 108, *110,* 111,
  113–14, 119, 121, 126; **IV** 145, 147, *199,* 201
 Essex, **III** 107, 111, 113, 121, 130, **IV** 142, 143, 144
  145, 147, 155, 156, 178, 193, *200*
 Fanshaw Bay, **IV** 151
 Flying Fish, **III** 125
 Franklin, **IV** 145, 147, *187,* 188
 Gambier Bay, **IV** 151, *152,* 153
 George F. Elliott, **III** 56
 Hackleback, **IV** 193
 Hammann, **II** *103,* 104
 Hancock, **IV** 178, 194
 Harris, **IV** 181
 Helena, **II** 23
 Hoel, **IV** 151
 Honolulu, **II** 23
 Hornet, **II** 12, 50, 52–53, 54, 55, 56, *57,* 59, 60, *61,*
  62, 63, 66, 69, *79,* 80, 87, 89, 90, 97, 98, 101;
  III 63, 67, 74–80, 120; **IV** 156, 188
 Houston, **IV** 139
 Independence, **III** 107
 Indianapolis, **IV** 208
 Intrepid (Evil I), **III** 107; **IV** 142, 146, 147, 178,
  179, 194
 Jarvis, **III** 56
 Johnston, **IV** 151

Kadashan Bay, **IV** 151
Kalinin Bay, **IV** 154
Karawha, **III** 90
Kitkun Bay, **IV** 152, 154
Langley, **III** 119, 121; **IV** 142, 145
Lexington, **II** 12, 74, 75, *76,* 77, *103;* **III** 53, 107,
    108, 110–11, 121, *122,* 124, 126, 130, 132; **IV**
    142–43, 145, 147, 156
Liscombe Bay, **III** 110, 114
Little, **IV** 197
Long, **IV** 181
Louisville, **IV** 181
Luce, **IV** 197
McFarland, **III** 73
Manila Bay, **III** *124;* **IV** 180
Mannert, L. Abele, **IV** 195
Maryland, **II** 16, 21, 23
Missouri, **IV** 214, *217,* 218
Monterey, **III** 107, 108, 121, 131
Montpelier, **IV** 196
Morrison, **IV** 197
Mugford, **III** 55
Nashville, **II** 62, 69
Natoma Bay, **III** 124
Nautilus, **II** 94
Neosho, **II** 75
Nevada, **II** 16, 23
New Jersey, **IV** 156
New Mexico, **IV** 181
North Carolina, **III** 62, 67, 110
O'Brien, **III** 67
Oglala, **II** 23
Oklahoma, **II** 12, 21, 22
Ommaney Bay, **IV** 179, *180*
Pennsylvania, **II** 23
Phelps, **II** 76
Pittsburgh, **IV** 187
Porter, **III** 79, 80
Princeton, **III** 107, 108, 121, 130; **IV** 142, 144, 145
PT boats, **III** 84
    PT-137, **IV** 149
Raleigh, **II** 23
Saint Lo, **IV** 154, 176–77
Samuel Roberts, **IV** 151
San Francisco, **III** 83
San Jacinto, **III** 121
San Juan, **III** 79
Santee, **IV** 154
Saratoga, **II** 6, 7, 12, 16; **III** *50,* 53–55, 57,
    60–63, 66, 67, 74, 80, 107, 108
Savo, **IV** 180
Seahorse, **III** 126
Shaw, **II** *22,* 23
Sigourney, **III** 97
Sims, **II** 75
Smith, **III** 79, 80
South Dakota, **III** 75, 79, 86, 130
Stanley, **IV** 195
Suwañee, **IV** 154, 177
Tambor, **II** 101
Tennessee, **II** 16, 23
Threadfin, **IV** 193
Ticonderoga, **IV** 178

Utah, **II** 16, 23
Vestal, **II** 16, 21, 23
Vireo, **II** 103
Walkde, **IV** 181
Wasatch, **IV** 151
Washington, **III** 75, 86
Wasp, **III** 53, *54,* 57, 60, 61, 67, *68,* 74, 121, 131; **IV**
    20–21, 188, *191*
West Virginia, **II** 16, *19,* 22–23
White Plains, **IV** 154
Yorktown, **II** 12, 74–75, 77, 78, 80, 84, 90, 93, *96,*
    97, 98, 101, *102,* 103, 104; **III** 53, *107,* 108,
    111, 114, 120, 132; **IV** 136, 194
United States Navy (seamen), **II** 12, 21, 22, 77, 78; **III**
    3–5, 9, *55,* 79, 83, 107, 110, 114; **IV** 140–41,
    145, 151, 154, 178–81, *180,* 187, 190, 192,
    195–98, 201. *See also* United States naval air
    units; United States naval units; United States
    naval vessels
Urbanowicz, Witold, **II** *127*
Ushijima, Mistsura, **IV** 189, 191, 201
Utah (U.S. naval vessel), **II** 16, 23
UBX Disposal Squads, **II** 140

V-1 bombs, **IV** 100, *102, 103,* 104
V-2 bombs, **I** 114; **IV** 94, 95, 100, *104, 105*
Val (Japanese aircraft), **II** 9, 12, *14,* 15, *16,* 17, *18,* 21,
    22, 83, *85;* **III** *55,* 62, 73, 76–80, 90–92, 93,
    96, 120, 124, 134; **IV** 143, 196, 197
Valetta (Malta), **IV** *20*
Valle, Pedro del, **IV** 189
Valor of Ignorance (Lea), **II** 6
Vandegrift, Alexander, A., **III** 55, 57–58, 69, 73, 75
Van Falkenburgh, Franklin, **II** 21
Vattendahl, Marjorie, **III** 50
Vegesack (Germany), **II** 183
Vejtasa, Stanley W., **III** 80
Vella Lavella, Battle of, **III** 93, 96
Versailles, Treaty of, **I** 4, 7, 12
Very High Frequency Radio Telephone, **II** 140
Vesta (U.S. naval vessel), **II** 16, 21, 23
Vian, Philip, **I** 37–38
Victor Emmanuel, King, **IV** 25–26
Victoria Cross, **I** 63, 156; **II** 126, 133, 150
Victory Disease (Japanese), **II** 73, 74, 77
Vietinghoff, Heinrich von, **IV** 35
Vincent, C. D., **II** 48
Vindicator (SB2U), **II** 12, *83,* 84, 87, *100,* 101, 108
Vireo (U.S. naval vessel), **II** 103
Vornstein, H., **II** 59
Vorse, A. O., **III** 62
Vose, James E., **III** 78
Vraicu, Alexander, **III** 130–31, *132*
Vunakanau airfield (New Britain), **IV** *31, 33*
V-weapons, **IV** 100, 108, *See also* V-1 bombs; V-2
    bombs

WAAF. *See* Women's Auxiliary Air Force
Wagner, Boyd D., **III** 42
Wake Island, **II** 73; **III** 107–9
Wake-Walker, William, **I** 72
Waldau, Hoffman von, **IV** 10
Waldron, J., **II** *89,* 90–93

Walkde (U.S. naval vessel), **IV** 181
Walker, Kenneth N., **III** 8, 32
Walker, Tommy, **I** 115
Wall, Robert W., **II** 57, 61, 70
Wallis, Barnes, **II** 135–41, *135,* 147, 149; **IV** 114
Wallis bombs, **II** 135–43, *144*
Walsh, Kenneth, **III** *93,* 94–96
Wang Poo-fang, **II** 70
Wannop, R. E., **IV** 122
Ward, James Allen, **I** 154, *155,* 156
Warhawk (P-40) **I** xiii; **II** 15, 21, 152; **III** 5–6, 15–17, 89, 94, 96, *105,* 106, 108; **IV** 10, 11, 12, 13, 15, 24
Warnemünde (Germany), **II** 174–75
Warning Control of Cologne, **II** 121
Warsaw, **I** xix, 27–32, 142; **IV** 171
Washing Machine Charlie, **III** 58, 65
Washington, D.C., **II** 3; **IV** 128–29
Washington (U.S. naval vessel), **III** 75, 86
Wasp (U.S. naval vessel), **III** 53, *54,* 57, 60, 61, 67, *68,* 74, 121, 123; **IV** 20–21, 188, *191*
Watanabe, Kusukichi, **III** 67
Watchtower, Operation, **III** 53. *See also* Guadalcanal
Watson, "Doc," **II** 140
Watson, Harold, **II** 70
Watson-Watt, Robert, **I** 88. *See also* Radar
Wavell, Sir Archibald, **II** 37, 41; **IV** 5, 7
Webster, Charles, **II** 147
Webster, John J., **II** 21
Wedgwood, Josiah, **I** 82
Wehrmacht, **I** 12, 23–24, 26–27, 30, 47, 61, 64, 68, 72–73; **II** vii, 155. *See also* German army units; specific sections
Welch, George S., **II** 21
Welles, Gideon, **II** 77
Welles, Sumner, **I** 33
Wellington, (British aircraft), **I** 52, 53, 75, 76, 122, 152, 154, *155,* 156; **II** 115, *116,* 117, 119, *120,* 121–24, 135–37; **IV** 10, 19, 35, 40
Wenck, Walther, **IV** 117
Wessman, Everett, **II** 81
West Virginia (U.S. naval vessel), **II** 16, *19,* 22–23
Wever, Walther, **I** 3, 4, 10–15, 24; **IV** 84
Wewak airfield (New Guinea), **III** 24, 26–29
Weygand, Maxine, **I** 76
Wheeler-Bennett, John, **I** 8, 17
Wheeler Field (Hawaii), **II** 15, 18
Whelan, Russell, **II** 32
White, Thomas R., **II** 69
Whitehead, Ennis C., **III** 8, 18, 21; **IV** *82*
White Plains (U.S. naval vessel), **IV** 154
Whitley (British aircraft), **I** 47–48, *48,* 49–50, 52, 75, 76, 122; **II** 116, 117, *125*
Whitman, Walt, **I** xiv
Whitworth, Charles, **II** 134
Widdowson, R. P., **I** 154–56
Widow Maker. *See* Marauder
Wiener Neustadt (Austria), **II** 158; **IV** *37*
Wight, R. D. G., **I** 72
Wildcat (F4F), **II** 12, 24–25, 59, *75, 76,* 84, *88,* 90, 93, 96, 101, 108; **III** 54–56, *58,* 59, *60,* 61, 62, 66, 68, *69,* 70–73, 74, 75, 77, *80,* 83, 84,

86, 87, 88, 90, 91, 96, 111, 126, 130, *134;* **IV** *146,* 151, *153*
Wilhelm, Prince, **I** 8
Wilhelmina, Queen, **I** 66
Wilhelmshaven (Germany), **IV** 39
Wilkins, Raymond H., **III** 37
Will, Robert E., **IV** 97
Williams, Robert, **III** 175, 179
Williams, Walden, **III** 92
Williamson, Herbert H., **III** 96–97
Williamson, John, **II** 27
Wilson, Sir Henry H., **IV** 29
Wilson, Robert, **II** 161, 162
Wiltsie, I. D., **III** 110
Windows (radar-jamming device), **II** 183, *184;* **IV** 40, 45
Wingman concept, **IV** 64
Winters, Theodore Hugh, **IV** 156
Wirth, Joseph, **I** 6
Wiseman, O. B., **II** 59
Witzleben, Erwin von, **I** 77
Wodarczyk, Heinz, **IV** 76–78
Wojtowicz, S., **I** 125, 127
Wolf, Fritz E., **II** 33
Wolfe, Kenneth B., **IV** *131,* 132-33, 160, 161
Wolfert, Ira, **IV** 64
Women's Auxiliary Air Force (WAAF), **I** 93, 111–12, *111*
Wood, Jack, **II** 159, 162, 163, 167, 169
Woodhouse, H. de C. A., **I** 166
Wordell, Malcolm, **IV** 156
Wotje (Marshalls), **III** 109
Wren, Christopher, **I** 144–46
Wright, Peter, **II** 36
Wright, William, **II** 162–65
Wuppertal (Germany), **IV** 40
Wurtsmith, Paul, **III** 44
"Wurzburgs" (German radar), **IV** 44, *45,* 46

XB-24. *See* Liberator
X-Day, **II** 9. *See also* Pearl Harbor
X-Gerät ("X-Device"), **I** 140–41, 144, 146

Yahagi (Japanese naval vessel), **IV** 190, 192, 193
Yakovlev (Russian aircraft), **IV** 84
Yamada, Sadayoshi, **III** 9
Yamagami, Masayuki, **III** 127
Yamaguchi, Tamon, **II** 88, 96, 98–99, 108
Yamamoto, Isoroku, **II** 4–7, 9, 11–13, 15, 22, 25, 72, 73–74, 75, 77, 78, 79, 80, 81, 82, 89, 97–101, 104, *104,* 105–8; **III** 60, 61, 70, 73–75, 82–84, 90, 92–93, 108, 120; **IV** 138, 190, 209
Yamashita, Tomoyuki, **IV** 138
Yamato (Japanese naval vessel), **II** 78, 82, 89, 99, 105; **III** 120; **IV** 139, 141, 146, 148, 151, *157, 187* 190–94, 204
Yanagimoto, Ryusaki, **II** 94
Yap (Carolines), **IV** 135–36
Yarnell, H. E., **II** 6–7
Yawata (Japan), **IV** 133–35
Yayoi (Japanese naval vessel), **IV** 204

Yokoi, Toshiyuki, **IV** 140, 178, 203
Yokosuka P1Y. *See* Frances
York, (England), **II** 113
York, Edward J. **II** 56, 68
Yorktown (U.S. naval vessel), **II** 12, 74–75, 77, 78, 80, 84, 90, 93, *96*, 97, 98, 101, *102*, 103, 104; **III** 53, *107*, 108, 111, 114, 120, 132; **IV** 136, 194
Yoshikawa, Takeo, **II** 12
Young, Howard L., **II** 24
Young, Melvyn "Dinghy," **II** 142, 145, 147
Yugoslavia, **IV** 15

Zai, Tomi, **IV** 201
Zaibatsu, **II** 5
Zeke (Japanese aircraft), **II** 105, 106; **III** 28, 33, 34, *61,* 89, 90–92, *90, 93,* 95, 96, 99–102, 111,
120, 127, 130, 132, 134, *135;* **IV** 142–44, 154, 155, 163, *164,* 165, 167, 182, 183, 184, 188, 192, 195, 196, 199
Zempke, Hubert A., **IV** 61, 63, 68, *69,* 73, 74
Zero (A6M,) **II** vii, 9, *10,* 12, 13, 14, 15, 18, 20–22, *24,* 31, 32, 34–36, 42, 43, *79,* 80–81, 83–89, 91–93, 96, 97, 99, 101, 105, 106–8; **III** 9, 11, 16, 18, 21, 23, 34, 37, 41–42, 55, 56, *61,* 62, 67, 71, 72, 74, 76–78, 84, 86, 87, 88, 89, 104, 111; **IV** 142, 154, 175–77, 181. *See also* Zeke; specific models
Zinder, Harry, **IV** 134
Zuiho (Japanese naval vessel) **III** 37, 67, 75–76, 79, 90, 120; **IV** *155,* 156
Zuikaku (Japanese naval vessel), **II** 3, 21, 75, 77, 78; **III** 37, 60, 61, 63, 67, 75, 76, 78–79, 81, 90, 120, 127, 132, 135; **IV** *155,* 156